W9-ASR-128

INVESTIGATION OF
THE ASSASSINATION OF PRESIDENT JOHN F. KENNEDY

HEARINGS
Before the President's Commission on the Assassination of President Kennedy

PURSUANT TO EXECUTIVE ORDER 11130, an Executive order creating a Commission to ascertain, evaluate, and report upon the facts relating to the assassination of the late President John F. Kennedy and the subsequent violent death of the man charged with the assassination and S.J. RES. 137, 88TH CONGRESS, a concurrent resolution conferring upon the Commission the power to administer oaths and affirmations, examine witnesses, receive evidence, and issue subpenas

EXHIBITS
1976 TO 2189

Volume
XXIV

UNITED STATES GOVERNMENT PRINTING OFFICE
WASHINGTON, D.C.

TEXAS SOUTHMOST COLLEGE LIBRARY
54442

U.S. GOVERNMENT PRINTING OFFICE, WASHINGTON : 1964

For sale in complete sets by the Superintendent of Documents, U.S. Government Printing Office
Washington, D.C., 20402

PRESIDENT'S COMMISSION ON THE ASSASSINATION OF PRESIDENT KENNEDY

CHIEF JUSTICE EARL WARREN, *Chairman*

SENATOR RICHARD B. RUSSELL
SENATOR JOHN SHERMAN COOPER
REPRESENTATIVE HALE BOGGS
REPRESENTATIVE GERALD R. FORD
MR. ALLEN W. DULLES
MR. JOHN J. MCCLOY

J. LEE RANKIN, *General Counsel*

Assistant Counsel

FRANCIS W. H. ADAMS
JOSEPH A. BALL
DAVID W. BELIN
WILLIAM T. COLEMAN, Jr.
MELVIN ARON EISENBERG
BURT W. GRIFFIN
LEON D. HUBERT, Jr.
ALBERT E. JENNER, Jr.
WESLEY J. LIEBELER
NORMAN REDLICH
W. DAVID SLAWSON
ARLEN SPECTER
SAMUEL A. STERN
HOWARD P. WILLENS*

Staff Members

PHILLIP BARSON
EDWARD A. CONROY
JOHN HART ELY
ALFRED GOLDBERG
MURRAY J. LAULICHT
ARTHUR MARMOR
RICHARD M. MOSK
JOHN J. O'BRIEN
STUART POLLAK
ALFREDDA SCOBEY
CHARLES N. SHAFFER, Jr.

Biographical information on the Commissioners and the staff can be found in the Commission's *Report*.

*Mr. Willens also acted as liaison between the Commission and the Department of Justice.

Contents

Re: ASSASSINATION OF PRESIDENT
JOHN FITZGERALD KENNEDY,
NOVEMBER 22, 1963, DALLAS, TEXAS

On May 15, 1964, Sergeant CALVIN B. OWENS, Dallas, Texas, Police Department, residence 1830 Melbourne, Dallas, Texas, furnished the following information concerning J. D. TIPPIT:

OWENS has been employed by the Dallas Police Department for twenty-three and one-half years and had known J. D. TIPPIT since about 1952, when TIPPIT came to work at the department. OWENS had been TIPPIT's immediate supervisor for about ten years.

On November 22, 1963, TIPPIT was assigned, alone, to patrol District 78, which is an area bordered by the Trinity River on the east and northeast, Southerland Avenue on the northwest, Sunnyvale and Keats Streets on the west, and Loop 12 or Ledbetter on the south. Sergeant OWENS explained that assignment of officers to an area does not restrict them to that area, in cases of emergency, and, due to the extreme emergency of November 22, 1963, numerous patrol units were assigned to different areas. Sergeant OWENS cited, for example, that units assigned to Districts 95 and 81 had been sent to the downtown area of Dallas immediately after the shooting of President KENNEDY. According to Sergeant OWENS, Officer TIPPIT had gone home to eat lunch, which was a normal and approved procedure, at about noontime. Sergeant OWENS advised he could not furnish any information as to when or how TIPPIT's assignment from District 78 had been changed as he, OWENS, had gone to lunch and had not returned during the time that TIPPIT's assignment had been changed.

TIPPIT had been assigned to District 78 for about six months to a year and had previously been assigned to patrol Districts 83 and 84 for three years. His assignment in each case was to patrol the area.

OWENS described TIPPIT as a morally upright person and a person about whom he had never heard anything derogatory. Sergeant OWENS rated TIPPIT as an average officer in work

- 8 -

COMMISSION EXHIBIT No. 1976

Re: ASSASSINATION OF PRESIDENT
JOHN FITZGERALD KENNEDY,
NOVEMBER 22, 1963, DALLAS, TEXAS

performance, who was well-liked, used good common sense and, as such, was a "good officer". According to OWENS, TIPPIT had off-duty, part-time jobs at Austin's Barbecue and Stevens Park Theatre and, because of this, "didn't have time to do any wrong." TIPPIT was a devoted family man, who spent what free time he had either at home or with relatives. TIPPIT was well-liked by all the other officers. OWENS did not know of any outside associates of TIPPIT and it appeared that the only associates he had were other police officers. TIPPIT appeared to be resigned to the fact that, because of his limited education, he would be unable to advance very far within the Police Department, and TIPPIT appeared satisfied with his work. OWENS stated he believes TIPPIT took promotional examinations, but had no information as to the results, but believes that the lack of promotion was due to a lack of education.

OWENS was of the opinion TIPPIT had always been assigned to the Oak Cliff and West Dallas areas.

OWENS described TIPPIT as a quiet, shy person and he never heard TIPPIT discuss politics or political personalities.

OWENS was unable to furnish any information concerning TIPPIT's outside activities or leisure activities. He did describe TIPPIT as the most honest, straightforward, morally upright, family-loving man he, OWENS, had ever known. He was a good officer who liked his job and tried to do a good job.

OWENS stated he never heard TIPPIT mention either JACK RUBY or LEE HARVEY OSWALD or ever mention having been in any of RUBY's night clubs. OWENS stated he has known RUBY for ten to twelve years and has had numerous conversations on an official basis with RUBY while RUBY was operating night clubs in the Dallas area. He stated RUBY was the type of person who would use another officer's name he had met when talking to officers, and RUBY never mentioned J. D. TIPPIT to OWENS. RUBY never mentioned LEE HARVEY OSWALD to OWENS. OWENS stated he had never heard of LEE HARVEY OSWALD prior to November 22, 1963.

- 9 -

COMMISSION EXHIBIT No. 1976—Continued

UNITED STATES DEPARTMENT OF JUSTICE
FEDERAL BUREAU OF INVESTIGATION

In Reply, Please Refer to
File No.

WASHINGTON 25, D. C.

March 17, 1964

LEE HARVEY OSWALD

The following information was furnished by a confidential source abroad on March 16, 1964:

1. Rifle C14 was manufactured by the Fabbrica Armi Esercito Terni - di Terni (the Army Arms Plant of Terni, Italy).

2. The number C2766 which appears on the barrel of the C14 rifle is the serial number of the rifle.

3. The C14 rifle is the only one of its type which bears serial number C2766.

4. It was not possible to definitely establish how many of this type of rifle were sold. It was established, however, that the Carlo Riva Machine Shop of Brescia, Italy, shipped rifles of the same type to Adam Consolidated Industries, Inc., 404 Fifth Avenue, New York 18, N. Y., telephone number WIsconsin 4-4490. Rifle C14 was one of the rifles in a lot of 5200 so shipped. This shipment, numbered 3376, was shipped from the Port of Genoa, Italy, on the ship "Elettra Fassio" on September 28, 1960.

Concerning the shipment of these rifles to Adam Consolidated Industries, Inc., there is presently a legal proceeding by the Carlo Riva Machine Shop to collect payment for the shipment of the rifles which Adam Consolidated Industries, Inc., claims were defective.

COMMISSION EXHIBIT No. 1977

The owner of the Carlo Riva Machine Shop, during a visit made to the United States in December of 1960, verified that about 7,000 of the rifles shipped to Adam Consolidated Industries, Inc., were in the possession of a company owned by Louis Feldsott of Yonkers, New York.

There follows a detailed description of the markings and numbers which appear in the photographs of the C14 rifle, serial number C2766.

Photograph 1. Depicts one of the weapons 91/38 modified by the Carlo Riva Machine Shop and sold to the Adam Consolidated Industries, Inc., of New York.

Photograph 2. The number C2766 is definitely the serial number of the rifle. The letters "SD" mean the inspector of the rifle.

Photograph 3. 1940 is the year of manufacture. The inscription "MADE ITALY" was placed on the rifle by Carlo Riva Machine Shop at the request of Adam Consolidated Industries, Inc. The crown emblem means the rifle was tested by the Army Arms Company.

Photograph 4. 1940 is the year of manufacture. "MADE ITALY" is the inscription Adam Consolidated Industries, Inc., wanted inscribed on the weapon prior to shipment. The crown R. E. Terni means the rifle was manufactured and tested by the Army Arms plant of Terni, Italy. "CAL.6.5" indicates the caliber of the rifle.

Photograph 5. The crown and TNI means the barrel of the rifle was inspected by an official of the Army Arms plant of Terni, Italy.

Photograph 6. It was not possible to establish what the letters "AG-47-2" mean; most probably they indicate the quality of steel used to manufacture the rifle and the letters remained after the rifle was completed.

Photograph 7. "Rocca" indicates the name of the designer or artisan of the rifle who manufactured and furnished the bolt cocking piece. Rocca, in fact, is named Giuseppe Rocca, who owned a machine shop in Lumezzane, Brescia, Italy. The shop is no longer in existence.

COMMISSION EXHIBIT No. 1977—Continued

Photograph 8. P.G indicate the in[illegible] of the designer who during the period of manufacture of the rifle furnished the bolt handle.

Photograph 9. The number 40 indicates the year of manufacture while the mark on the extreme right of the photograph is the inscription made by the person who inspected the breech.

- 3 -

COMMISSION EXHIBIT No. 1977—Continued

ELENCO MATRICOLE DI N. ______ MOD ____ CAL

SPEDITI DAL PORTO DI GENOVA CON LA M/N [illegible] IL [illegible]

Fo.210 8/35

CASSA N.	MATRICOLE	MATRICOLE	MATRICOLE	MATRICOLE	MATRICOLE
3362	D 2123 C 4542	[illegible] [illegible]	[illegible] [illegible]	[illegible] AS 6209	[illegible] [illegible]
3363	[illegible] BZ 1460	[illegible] [illegible]	[illegible] [illegible]	[illegible] [illegible] 3759	[illegible] XC [illegible]
3364	XA 7231 BO 6549	[illegible] [illegible]	BH 5497 S 7457	AX 4730 BT 3160	BD 678 [illegible]
3365	U 5006 S 6761	AF 146 [illegible]	[illegible] [illegible]	B[illegible] 1617 T 563	XC 84[illegible] BP [illegible]
3366	G 9135 AT 3989	AH 4593 [illegible]	[illegible] [illegible]	O [illegible] L [illegible]	B 7674 BO 71[illegible]
3367	AV 9722 BZ 4587	[illegible] AA [illegible]	[illegible] [illegible] 33	BY [illegible] AL 6381	B[illegible] 1991 BX 4[illegible]34
3368	BF 6171 UC 545	[illegible] BC [illegible]	[illegible] UC [illegible]	Q 8466 A[illegible] 4350	[illegible] [illegible]
3369	[illegible] D [illegible]	[illegible] C 2147	BY 4487 AY 4083	B[illegible] 6716 R 2[illegible]05	[illegible] [illegible]
3370	BF [illegible] XC 7514	[illegible] [illegible]	[illegible] B [illegible]	AG 1619 DA 4615	[illegible] [illegible]
3371	AT 2451 V 7[illegible]	[illegible] [illegible]	R [illegible] [illegible]	[illegible] U [illegible]	[illegible] [illegible]
3372	B[illegible] [illegible]	XC [illegible] UF 2129	[illegible] [illegible]	[illegible] [illegible] 9631	[illegible] [illegible]
3373	AY [illegible] BC 646	AL 7526 [illegible]	[illegible] [illegible]	[illegible] A [illegible]	AP [illegible] A[illegible]
3374	[illegible] BA 2147	[illegible] [illegible]	[illegible] [illegible]	BA [illegible] [illegible]	[illegible] [illegible]
3375	[illegible] [illegible] 4051	[illegible] K [illegible]	[illegible] AO 856	[illegible] K 3021	[illegible] [illegible]
[illegible]	[illegible] [illegible]	[illegible] [illegible]	[illegible] AI [illegible]	[illegible] [illegible]	[illegible] Y [illegible]
3377	[illegible] XD [illegible]	XG 5[illegible]7 V 7967	[illegible] [illegible]	[illegible] U[illegible] 6[illegible]10	[illegible] [illegible]
	[illegible] BY [illegible]	[illegible] [illegible]	[illegible] [illegible]	[illegible] DS 3[illegible]	[illegible] [illegible]
[illegible]	[illegible] [illegible]	[illegible] [illegible]	[illegible]	[illegible] I 9[illegible]79	[illegible] [illegible]
[illegible]	[illegible] [illegible]	[illegible] [illegible]	[illegible] [illegible]	[illegible] [illegible] 277	[illegible] 7771 [illegible]
3381	[illegible] 7157 A[illegible] 2140	[illegible] BS 3[illegible]	[illegible] [illegible]	[illegible] BI 9[illegible]	[illegible] [illegible]

COMMISSION EXHIBIT No. 1977—Continued

4

VOLUNTARY STATEMENT. Not Under Arrest. Form No. 86

SHERIFF'S DEPARTMENT
COUNTY OF DALLAS, TEXAS

Before me, the undersigned authority, on this the 22nd day of November A. D. 19 63

personally appeared Amos Lee Euins, Address 411 Avenue F Dallas, Texas

Age 15, Phone No. WH 3-9701

Deposes and says:- I am presently going to school at Franklin D. Roosevelt High School and am in the 9th grade. I got out of school this morning to see the President of the United States when he came to Dallas. I was standing on the corner of Elm and Houston street. From where I was standing I could look across the street and see a large red brick building. I saw the President turn the corner in front of me and I waived at him and he waived back. I watched the car on down the street and about the time the car got near the black and white sign I heard a shot. I started looking around and then I looked up in the red brick building. I saw a man in a window with a gun and I saw him shoot twice. He then stepped back behind some boxes. I could tell the gun was a rifle and it sounded like an automatic rifle the way he was shooting. I just saw a little bit of the barrel, and some of the trigger housing. This was a white man, he did not have on a hat. I just saw this man for a few seconds. As far as I know, I had never seen this man before.

Amos Lee Euins

Subscribed and sworn to before me on this the 22nd day of November A. D. 19 63

E. L. Jones
Notary Public, Dallas County, Texas

COMMISSION EXHIBIT NO. 1978

OPTIONAL FORM NO. 10
MAY 1962 EDITION
GSA GEN. REG. NO. 27
5010-106

UNITED STATES GOVERNMENT
Memorandum

CO-2-34,030

TO: Chief
ATTN: Inspector Kelley

DATE: June 17, 1964

FROM: SAIC Sorrels - Dallas

Bus Routes requested by Mr. David Belin of the President's Commission on the Assassination of President Kennedy

It is presumed that in the telephone conversation between Mr. David Belin and Special Agent Warner as referenced in SA Warner's M/R of 6-15-64 relative to various bus routes in the Oak Cliff area, that Mr. Belin was referring to a Dallas Transit Company route map.

Although the map is newly printed, it is out of date in re exact routing of buses. The map shows bus route No. 55 making a scheduled turn-around in the Ewing - Jefferson Streets area of Oak Cliff. This map is erroneous in that the bus on that route has not made that turn since February 1962.

A map is attached for your information. The questioned area is outlined in blue pencil.

RCW:wd
Enc: Dallas Transit Company bus schedule

COMMISSION EXHIBIT NO. 1979

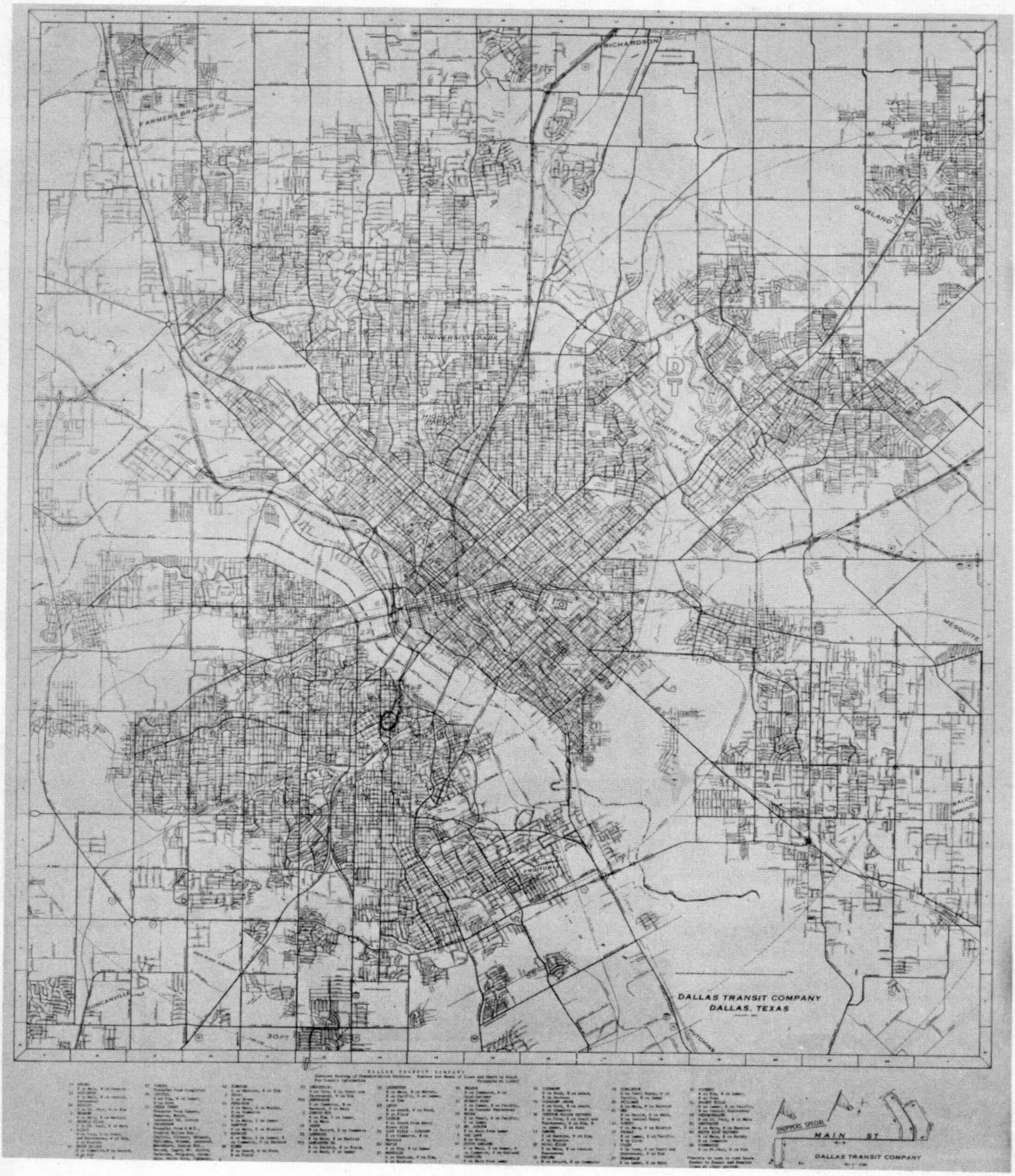

COMMISSION EXHIBIT No. 1979—Continued

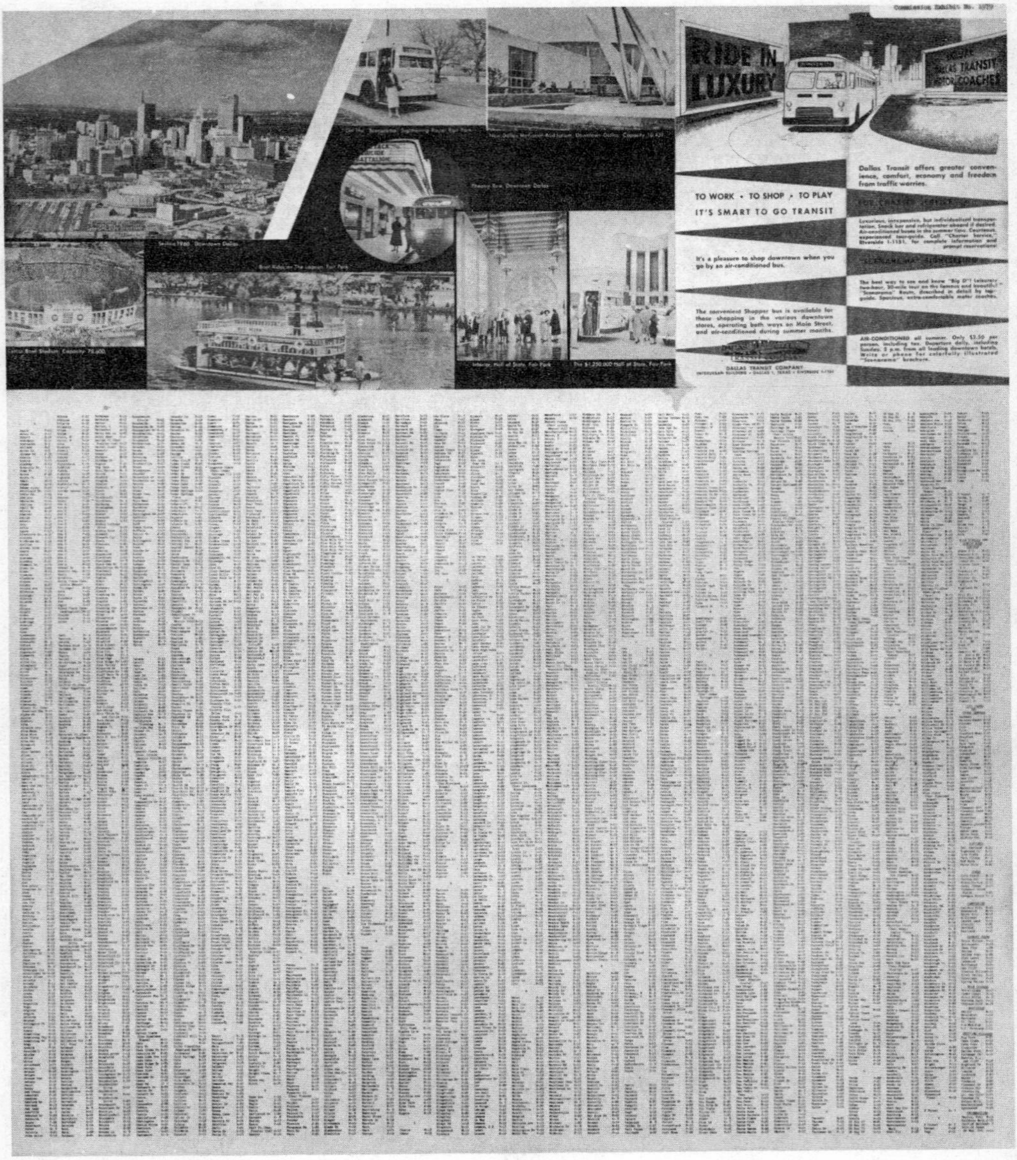

COMMISSION EXHIBIT No. 1979—Continued

UNITED STATES DEPARTMENT OF JUSTICE

FEDERAL BUREAU OF INVESTIGATION

In Reply, Please Refer to
File No.

Dallas, Texas
June 16, 1964

LEE HARVEY OSWALD

On June 15, 1964, fingerprints and palm prints were obtained from the following employees of the Texas School Book Depository Building, Dallas, Texas:

Daniel Garcia Arce
Jack Edwin Dougherty
Buell Wesley Frazier
Charles Douglas Givens
James Earl Jarman, Jr. / Piper + West Mrs reed
Frankie Kaiser
Roy Edward Lewis
Billy Nolan Lovelady
Eddie Piper
William Hoyt Shelley
Troy Eugene West
Bonnie Ray Williams.

On June 15, 1964, Mr. Roy S. Truly, Warehouse Superintendent, Texas School Book Depository Building, advised that employee Frankie Kaiser was not on duty on November 21 or 22, 1963.

On June 12, 1964, Mr. Roy S. Truly advised that the employees listed above are the only persons in this building who would ordinarily handle the cartons located near the sixth floor window. Mr. Truly therefore requested that other employees not be fingerprinted.

These fingerprints will be compared with the identifiable latent fingerprints and latent palm prints found on these cartons.

COMMISSION EXHIBIT No. 1980

OFFICE OF THE

COUNTY MEDICAL EXAMINER

5201 HARRY HINES BLVD.

DALLAS, TEXAS 75235

Autopsy Number: M63-356

Name: OSWALD, Lee Harvey Age: 24 Race: White Sex: Male

Autopsy date: 11-24-63, 2:45 P.M. Coroner: Judge Pierce McBride

Autopsy by: Earl F. Rose, M. D.
Assistant: Sidney C. Stewart, M. D.

EXTERNAL EXAMINATION:

External examination reveals a 5 foot, 9 inch white male, the estimated weight is 150 pounds. Rigor is not present, slight cooling of the body. There is faint posterior mottling lividity.

Identification bands on the left wrist, the right wrist, the left great toe. The head is examined. The hair is brown, slightly wavy. Small amount of dried blood in the hair which has run from the hairline to the right and backward. Slight frontal balding. To the right of the midline over the forehead is a 1/2 x 1/16 inch crusted superficial abrasion. The hairline, left temporal region, is a 1/16 inch very superficial abraded area. There is a left periorbital hematoma which is purple in the central portion, fading at the margins to a faint lemon-yellow. Total diameter of this is 1 3/4 x 1½ inch. The irides are grey-blue, the pupils are equal at 8 mm. The sclera and conjunctiva are not remarkable. Poorly defined scar on the dorsum of the nose which measures ¼ x ¼ inch. There is black material in the nares. Midline, upper lip, terminating at the vermillion margin is a ½ inch pale scar. To the left of the midline, the upper lip, is a 1/16 inch abrasion. The buccal cavity is otherwise not remarkable. Oral hygiene is fair with some fillings. The tongue is not remarkable. The beard measures between 1 to 2 mm. Examination of the neck is made. At the upper end of the right sternocleidomastoid over the skin is a transverse very superficial 3/4 inch scratch with some reddish antiseptic type of paint surrounding this. Hair distribution is normal. The pubic hair has been shaved. The penis is circumcised. The testes are descended. The abdomen is flat.

Over the left pectoral region, 14 inches from the top of the head and 2 3/4 inches to the left of the midline there is a 1½ inch wound. The edges of this are sharp. Over the left chest is an oblique wound which originates 17 inches from the top of the head and runs forward, downward toward the midline anteriorly measuring 7½ inches and closed by 12 running black sutures. This wound goes inferior to the left nipple. Over the lateral aspect of the left arm, 16 inches from the top of the head is a 3/4 x 3/8 inch wound. It goes into the subcutaneous tissue. 18 inches from the top of the head over the lateral aspect anteriorly of the right arm there is a 1 x ½ inch wound which goes into the subcutaneous tissue. 21½ inches from the top of the head originating slightly below the xiphoid running in the midline to above the pubis is a 10½ inch anterior midline wound closed by 5 wire sutures. Above

COMMISSION EXHIBIT No. 1981

the medial malleolus on the right side there is a 1 3/4 inch transverse cut-down incision. Cephalad to this is a transverse 1 3/4 inch superficial transverse incised wound. Above the left medial malleolus there is a 1½ inch cut-down type of incised wound. To the left of the midline region of the second thoracic vertebra there is a very faint 3/8 inch bluish discolored area. In the right antecubital fossa is a very tiny needle puncture type of wound surrounded by bluish discoloration. In the left antecubital fossa there are three small needle puncture type of wounds surrounded by bluish discoloration. The nails are examined. They are somewhat dirty although quite well cared for. No evidence of injury is noted. On the midportion dorsum of the left hand, there is a poorly defined pale white oblique ½ inch scar. Over the volar aspect of the right wrist there is a transverse superficial ¼ inch abrasion. Volar aspect of the left wrist there is a transverse 1 3/4 inch slightly raised white scar. Medial aspect of the right knee reddish very poorly defined 7/8 x 1/4 inch reddish discoloration. Over the left arm, below the deltoid there is a transverse 5/8 x 3/4 inch somewhat puckered and irregular scar. A few striae along the lateral aspect of the thighs. Some of the hair of the chest has been shaved. In addition, to the left of the midline there is a round poorly defined round impression on the skin, the diameter of which is 2 inches. Over the medial aspect mid-distal third of the left arm there is a 1½ inch vertical scar with cross hatching.

23 inches from the top of the head and 3 3/8 inches to the left of the midline anteriorly and 10 3/4 inches to the left of the midline posteriorly, over the lower aspect of the left chest there is an entrance type of wound which measures 1/4 x 5/16 inch in diameter. This is surrounded by a contusion ring, the total diameters of the contusion ring are 3/8 of an inch.

22 inches from the top of the head and 9 3/4 inches to the right of the midline anteriorly and 8½ inches to the right of the midline of the back there is a vertical 2 x 1 inch gaping wound. Posterior to this by ½ inch there is a 3/4 x 3/8 inch irregular contused area.

INCISIONS: The standard "Y" thoracoabdominal and intermastoid incisions are utilized. Reflecting the skin there is found to be a wound between the fourth and fifth rib which extends through the soft tissue and measures 6 inches in length. This conforms to the wound on the left chest. The incision is continued through the abdominal wound as well as the thoracotomy wound to the left of the midline of the chest.

SEROUS CAVITIES: Examination of the serous cavities is made. In the left pleural space approximately 175 cc. of blood. In the right pleural space there is in excess of 600 cc. of blood. In the peritoneal cavity there is in excess of 1000 cc. of blood with clot formation. In addition, there is massive retroperitoneal hemorrhage. The omentum adjacent to the transverse colon and stomach is hemorrhagic and irregularly torn.

The abdominal panniculus measures 1 3/4 inches.

THE COURSE OF THE WOUND IS FOLLOWED. It is found to notch the undersurface of the seventh rib at the costochondral junction, this is surrounded by hemorrhage. In its course it notches the diaphragmatic attachment in this region, however, the left lung is not penetrated. The course is found to go from left to right and backward. In its course it is found to strike the anterior edge of the spleen and there is a cruciate laceration of the spleen measuring approximately 1.5 x 2 cm.

The missile is found to penetrate the stomach along the greater curvature of the body of the stomach, the penetration measuring 9 cm. It exits from the stomach along the posterior wall, lesser curvature, 2 cm. distal to the cardioesophageal junction. The penetration measures 8 cm. It pursues a course backwards and to the right slightly caudal to the celiac axis and there is extensive hemorrhage in this area. The anterior and right anterio-lateral aspect of the aorta is torn with the superior mesenteric artery being severed. The right renal artery shows destruction and hemorrhage along the cephalad portion. The right renal vein is torn and the tear involves the inferior vena cava, the dorsal surface. It courses through the upper pole of the right kidney along the anterior surface causing a jagged and irregular laceration covering a distance of 5 x 2 cm. with penetration into the calyces. It becomes peritonealized in the hepatorenal pouch and there is a jagged and irregular laceration of the liver covering a distance of 9.5 x 2 x 2 cm. From the liver it penetrates the diaphragm posteriorly on the right side. It then passes adjacent to the lung in the pleural space and the right lung is not penetrated. The eleventh rib to the right of the midline is irregularly fractured and an exit type of wound in this region and in the soft tissue along the posterior axillary line right side there is an incised wound and fragmentation of the rib.

NECK ORGANS: The neck organs are examined. They are not remarkable. The hyoid is intact. No evidence of injury is noted. The thyroid gland is not remarkable grossly.

LUNGS: The trachea and bronchi are not remarkable. The right lung is quite well aerated. The left lung is atelectatic. The peribronchial tissue is not remarkable, however, there is hemorrhage in the posterior mediastinum.

HEART: Examination of the right atrium as well as the right ventricle and a pulmonary artery shows frothing bubbles. The epicardium is markedly congested with petechial hemorrhages, more marked over the left ventricular portion. The heart weighs 330 gm. There are a few subendocardial petechial hemorrhages. Along the anterior right ventricular surface there is a single suture. This is in the epicardial fat. The right ventricle measures 2 to 3 mm., the left 1.2 to 1.3 mm. The valvular circumferences are as follows: aortic valve - 7 cm., mitral valve - 10.5 cm., tricuspid valve - 11.5 cm., and pulmonic valve - 7 cm. The coronary ostia are in the normal location. The coronary arteries are examined in situ, found to be thin, delicate, of normal distribution and free of occlusions. There are left ventricular myocardial hemorrhages.

LIVER: The liver weighs 1260 gm. The penetration of the liver has previously been described.

GALLBLADDER & BILIARY TREE: Not remarkable.

PORTACAVAL SYSTEM: Examination of the portacaval system is made. There is frothing blood in the portacaval system. Extensive hemorrhage is noted to surround this, particularly in the region of the pancreas.

PANCREAS: The pancreas is surrounded by hemorrhage. The parenchyma of the pancreas is not penetrated and the ductal system is not remarkable.

SPLEEN: The spleen weighs 200 gm. The penetration of the spleen has previously been described.

DIAPHRAGMS: The penetrations of the diaphragms have previously been described.

M63-356

RETROPERITONEAL TISSUE: There is massive hemorrhage.

GREAT VESSELS: The penetration of the aorta has previously been described. The aorta is otherwise smooth and elastic. There is extensive periaortic hemorrhage which extends above the diaphragm in the posterior mediastinal tissue.

KIDNEYS: The kidneys weigh 490 gm. The destruction to the right kidney has previously been described. The capsule strips with slight difficulty. The cortical surfaces are smooth and pale. The corticomedullary junction is indistinct. The cortices measure 5 to 7 mm. There is hemorrhage into the parenchyma with destructio of the right kidney as previously described. The penetration of the calyces has also been described. About the pelvis of the right kidney there is extensive hemorrhage. The pelvis and ureters are otherwise not remarkable. The bladder contains bloody urine. The prostate is grossly not remarkable.

ADRENALS: The adrenals are both surrounded by hemorrhage, however, both are intact.

INTESTINAL TRACT: The small and large bowel are examined. They are free of penetrations. The appendix is identified. The large bowel contains some formed stool. The penetrations of the stomach have previously been described and there is blood in the stomach. The rugal pattern is not remarkable. The duodenum is not remarkabl

THYMUS: The thymus weighs approximately 15 gm., is quite fibrotic.

SCALP, SKULL, CRANIAL CAVITY & DURA: Not remarkable. No evidence of injury is noted.

BRAIN: The brain weighs 1450 gm. The brain is symmetrical. The external surface of the brain is not remarkable. Configuration is normal. Multiple sections through the brain are taken and fail to reveal any abnormalities. The ventricular system is symmetrical. No abnormalities are encountered. The vascular system is not remarkable and the vessels are thin and delicate. The calvarium is not remarkable. The cervical vertebra and odontoid are not remarkable.

COMMISSION EXHIBIT No. 1981—Continued

M63-356

MICROSCOPIC:

Aorta: There is disruption with fresh hemorrhage. No inflammation or organization.

Heart: There are hemorrhages in the epicardial fat, mild interstitial edema and focal fragmentation of the muscle fibers.

Lung: Areas of atelectasis and focal alveolar hemorrhagic extravasations.

Liver: Disruption with fresh hemorrhages, otherwise non-contributory.

Bowel: There are disruptions of the stomach with hemorrhages adjacent. The remainder of the bowel sections are non-contributory.

Spleen: There is disruption along one margin, otherwise non-contributory.

Thyroid: Non-contributory.

Pancreas: Non-contributory.

Gallbladder: Non-contributory.

Prostate: Non-contributory.

Lymph Nodes: Non-contributory.

Adrenals: There is extensive fresh hemorrhage adjacent, otherwise non-contributory.

Skin: Section through the entrance wound shows disruption with fresh hemorrhages. There is no organization or inflammation. Some amorphous debris and fibers in the depths of the wound.

Kidney: Sections show disruption of the right kidney with hemorrhages which are marked in the pelvic fat and perirenal tissue.

Central Nervous System: Multiple sections are examined and they are non-contributor

COMMISSION EXHIBIT No. 1981—Continued

ML63-356

FINDINGS:

Chest, left, gunshot wound.
Penetration of the spleen, stomach, aorta, kidney, liver and diaphragm.
Massive retroperitoneal hemorrhage.
Massive peritoneal hemorrhage.
Right and left hemothorax.
Heart, left ventricular epicardial and myocardial hemorrhages.
Atrium, right; ventricle, right; pulmonary artery, - air.
Lung, left, atelectasis.
Chest, left, thoracotomy.
Abdomen, laparotomy incision.
Arm, left; arm, right; ankle, right; ankle, left - cut-down incisions.
Chest, right, incised wound.
Eye, left, periorbital hematoma.
Forehead and lip, abrasion.
Left wrist and left arm, scars.

CAUSE OF DEATH:

Hemorrhage, secondary to gunshot wound of the chest.

____
Earl F. Rose, M. D.

COMMISSION EXHIBIT No. 1981—Continued

DALLAS COUNTY HOSPITAL DISTRICT
(Parkland Memorial Hospital)

Date 11/26/63

TOXICOLOGICAL REPORT

Case of Lee Harvey Oswald Autopsy No. ML63-356

Autopsy by Dr. Rose On 11/24/63

Examined for Alcohol and barbiturate.

Organs submitted Blood (see also report on skin, below).

RESULTS OF ANALYSIS:

Poisonous Gases	
Volatile Poisons	Negative.
Acid-Ether soluble poisons	Negative.
Alkaline-Ether soluble poisons	-
Ammonia-Ether or Amm.-Chloroform soluble poisons	-
Metallic Poisons	-
Mineral Acids and alkalies	-
Halogens and their salts	-
Salts of Oxy-acids	-
Poisons isolated by special methods	-

REMARKS: **Blood type = "A"**

No nitrates were detected around the bullet hole in the specimen of skin and specimen of ligament submitted.

Toxicologist, Dallas County Hospital District

COMMISSION EXHIBIT No. 1981—Continued

DALLAS CITY-COUNTY CRIMINAL INVESTIGATION LABORATORY
(Parkland Memorial Hospital
Dallas, Texas
BLOOD ALCOHOL REPORT

Case of ML63-356 Referred by Medical Staff

Blood drawn by ______ At Parkland Hospital

Date ______ Time ______ AM. PM. Antiseptic used ______

Officers, identification, etc.: ______

Specimen received from:

☐ Dallas P.D. Lock Box at ______ AM PM Date ______ By ______

☐ E.C.I. Lab. Lock Box at 1:15 AM PM Date 11/25/63 By W. Patterson

☒ Other (Describe): Morgue ice box.

Specimen transferred to H. R. Ray (Analyst).

Time 1:30 AM PM Date 11/25/63 By W. Patterson

Specimen container: One test tube stoppered with rubber stopper.

Information from: ______

Analytical

Specimen: Date and time of analysis 11/25/63 2:20 AM PM

☒ Whole Blood

☐ Plasma or serum Analyst: H. R. Ray

Data (Micro-Greenberg Method):

W_1 = 2.82	U_1 = 2.78	Calculation:
W_2 = 2.82	U_2 = 2.78	
W av. = 2.82	U av. = 2.78	Negative for alcohol.
B_1 = 2.86	S_1 = 0.19	
B_2 = 2.86	S_2 = 0.19	
B av. = 2.86		
Gas chromatogram	☐ Yes ☒ No	

Result: Alcohol content Negative %

[signature]
Dallas City-County Criminal
Investigation Laboratory

COMMISSION EXHIBIT No. 1981—Continued

Commission Exhibit No. 1982

FD-302 (Rev. 3-3-59)

FEDERAL BUREAU OF INVESTIGATION

1

Date 11/25/63

SA MANNING C. CLEMENTS was assigned, immediately upon receipt of information that President JOHN F. KENNEDY had been assassinated, to establish liaison with the office of Chief of Police JESSE E. CURRY.

Upon arrival at Chief CURRY's office at 1:00 PM, it was learned he was out of the office. SA CLEMENTS made his presence known to Captain GLEN D. KING, Administrative Assistant to the Chief; Deputy Chief R. H. LUNDAY, and to Sergeant ART HAMMETT, Public Relations Officer.

At instructions of SAC J. GORDON SHANKLIN, the above officers were informed of the extreme interest of Director HOOVER in the investigation and that the full facilities of the FBI Laboratory, Identification Division, and other services were available, that any requests would be immediately relayed. During the course of the period from 1:00 PM, November 22, 1963, to 2:00 PM, November 23, 1963, the above officers and other ranking personnel advised SA CLEMENTS of developments coming to their attention which were relayed to the FBI Office.

During the period described above and following the apprehension of LEE HARVEY OSWALD, it was observed large numbers of news reporters, cameramen, and perhaps others, congregated in the third floor corridors of the City Hall, housing administrative offices of the Police Department and various bureau offices, including Homicide & Robbery, where OSWALD was in custody.

Upon arrival of Chief CURRY at his office during the afternoon of November 22, 1963, SA CLEMENTS advised him of Agent's presence to relay any requests for FBI assistance, of Director HOOVER's extreme interest, and of the availability of FBI facilities. Upon instructions of SAC SHANKLIN, Chief CURRY was informed Director HOOVER had expressed his concern that OSWALD should be afforded the utmost security.

SA CLEMENTS did not observe any officers stationed at the third floor elevators to prevent the entrance of persons to the third floor at the outset. However, later in the afternoon, it was observed uniformed officers were stationed at the elevator and were looking at identification offered by persons who happened to be observed by SA CLEMENTS.

on 11/22-23/63 at Dallas, Texas File # DL 44-1639

by Special Agent MANNING C. CLEMENTS/eah Date dictated 11/25/63

29

This document contains neither recommendations nor conclusions of the FBI. It is the property of the FBI and is loaned to your agency; it and its contents are not to be distributed outside your agency.

COMMISSION EXHIBIT No. 1982

DL 44-1639

2

During the above-mentioned period, OSWALD was removed, to the certain knowledge of SA CLEMENTS, on two occasions, once to be shown in a line-up, and a second time at about midnight, for the purpose of a press conference in the assembly room in the basement. It was observed that during such times the corridors were extremely crowded. SA CLEMENTS observed OSWALD being brought through the corridor to the assembly room, that the corridor and room itself were crowded to overflowing. Numerous individuals recognized to be newsmen and others who had camera equipment were observed. The only individual observed by Agent who was known not to be an officer or connected with the press was one GEORGE SCHEPPS, member of a prominent Dallas family.

30

Commission Exhibit No. 1982—Continued

FD-204 (Rev. 3-3-59)

UNITED STATES DEPARTMENT OF JUSTICE
FEDERAL BUREAU OF INVESTIGATION

Copy to:

Report of: ROBERT JAMES NELSON   Office: Denver, Colorado
Date: March 14, 1964

Field Office File #: 105-1653   Bureau File #: 105-126128

Title: RUTH HYDE PAINE;
MICHAEL RALPH PAINE

Character: INTERNAL SECURITY - R

Synopsis:

DAVID and BARBARA HOUGHTON interviewed at Boulder, Colorado, 3/13/64. Both state acquaintanceship with RUTH PAINE resulted through mutual membership in Society of Friends religious movement. BARBARA HOUGHTON states had met MICHAEL PAINE and attended the PAINEs' wedding as a result of religious activities. Both HOUGHTONs state they do not know LEE HARVEY OSWALD, MARINA OSWALD, or GEORGE PAINE. HOUGHTONs state they have had no contact with RUTH PAINE since assassination.

-RUC-

DETAILS:

Commission Exhibit No. 1983

This document contains neither recommendations nor conclusions of the FBI. It is the property of the FBI and is loaned to your agency; it and its contents are not to be distributed outside your agency.

Commission Exhibit No. 1983

FD-302 (Rev. 1-25-60) FEDERAL BUREAU OF INVESTIGATION

Date March 13, 1964

DAVID D. HOUGHTON was contacted at the National Center for Atmospheric Research (NCAR), Boulder, Colorado. Mr. HOUGHTON volunteered that he had graduated from Pennsylvania State University in 1959 and had received a Ph. D. Degree in meteorology from the University of Washington in 1963. He stated he has been associated with NCAR for three months.

He stated he first met RUTH HYDE PAINE in December, 1957, at an East-West Contact Committee meeting of the Society of Friends religious movement. He stated this was a correspondence exchange program between the people of the United States of America and the USSR (Union of Soviet Socialist Republics). He advised at the time he was a student at Pennsylvania State University and had taken part in corresponding with individuals in Russia. He states he continues to correspond with individuals in Russia at this time. He stated this particular meeting in December, 1957, was a Young Friends Church group conference which was held in a small city on the north side of Philadelphia, Pennsylvania. He advised he could not recall the name of this city. RUTH HYDE at this time was the chairman of the Correspondence Committee. He advised that his contacts with her at this time were very limited and he could recall no specific information concerning this meeting.

In the summer of 1963, he and his wife, BARBARA COAN HOUGHTON, had come in contact with RUTH HYDE in Washington, D. C., where she was attending the Civil Rights March on Washington. He stated she had learned of the HOUGHTONs' address through a family acquaintance. She visited at the HOUGHTONs' apartment, 1842 Park Road, in Washington, and stayed for dinner. At this time she was accompanied by her two children who, Mr. HOUGHTON stated, were approximately three and five years old. The fact that she was married

On 3/13/64 at Boulder, Colorado File # Denver 105-1653

by SA KENNETH BRIDENSTINE; SA ROBERT JAMES NELSON:pmb Date dictated 3/13/64

2

This document contains neither recommendations nor conclusions of the FBI. It is the property of the FBI and is loaned to your agency; it and its contents are not to be distributed outside your agency.

COMMISSION EXHIBIT No. 1983—Continued

was brought up and when asked specifically about her husband by the HOUGHTONs, RUTH gave a very unclear answer. Mr. HOUGHTON stated that HYDE was returning to Texas and had stopped for the civil rights demonstration in Washington en route from a summer program in which she had been teaching Russian at an unknown area in up-State New York or New England. While at the HOUGHTONs' residence, she did not offer any information regarding her husband. HOUGHTON assumed that at this time HYDE was not living with her husband.

After leaving the HOUGHTON residence, HYDE indicated she would be in Washington for several days and was then returning to Texas.

Mr. HOUGHTON stated that he specifically recalls she mentioned that she had been helping a Russian woman in Dallas, Texas, to become acclimated to the United States way of life. Mr. HOUGHTON stated that if RUTH HYDE PAINE mentioned this woman's name, he did not recall it. He also gained the impression that PAINE had been tutoring in the Russian language in the Dallas area.

After Mrs. PAINE had departed Washington, no further contact was had with her. The next information brought to the HOUGHTONs attention was when they learned of RUTH HYDE PAINE's connection with individuals involved in the assassination of President JOHN F. KENNEDY. He stated that he and his wife did not associate PAINE with information of this act for approximately three or four days, and after reading "Time Magazine's" account, they identified this individual as the RUTH PAINE they knew.

To his knowledge, PAINE has never contacted BARBARA HOUGHTON since she departed Washington in the summer of 1963. HOUGHTON stated he had never met MICHAEL PAINE. He advised he did not know, nor had he ever met, LEE HARVEY OSWALD.

3

COMMISSION EXHIBIT No. 1983—Continued

He stated he does not know, nor has he ever met, MARINA OSWALD. He concluded that GEORGE PAINE is unknown to him. He does not know any relations of RUTH HYDE PAINE.

4

COMMISSION EXHIBIT No. 1983—Continued

FD-302 (Rev. 1-25-60) FEDERAL BUREAU OF INVESTIGATION

Date March 14, 1964

Mrs. BARBARA COAN HOUGHTON was contacted at her residence, 3131 - 7th Street, Boulder, Colorado, on March 13, 1964. She advised that she was the wife of DAVID HOUGHTON, and that she was a former resident of the State of Pennsylvania. She stated she was 31 years of age. She advised she graduated from the University of Pennsylvania and had received her Masters Degree from the University of Washington, at Seattle, Washington. She stated she has attended two summer sessions of study in the Chinese language and she is presently attending a class in the Chinese language and literature at the University of Colorado at Boulder.

Mrs. HOUGHTON stated she first met an individual she knew as RUTH HYDE and now knows as Mrs. MICHAEL PAINE at a Young Friends conference of the Society of Friends which was held at Quaker Haven, Indiana, in 1955. At this time she stated RUTH HYDE was the Program Chairman for this meeting. She stated at a later date in 1955, at a meditation group of the Young Friends, which was held at the Western Community House in Philadelphia, Pennsylvania, she met HYDE. At that time, RUTH HYDE was living in Philadelphia and was employed at the Jewish Community Center in that city. During this period, Mrs. HOUGHTON advised she had visited RUTH HYDE at her apartment in Philadelphia, which was located in the Powellton Village area. Later in the year Mrs. HOUGHTON traveled to Portland, Oregon, and while in Portland, where she was employed at the Portland Community Hospital, she corresponded regularly with RUTH HYDE.

Mrs. HOUGHTON returned to Philadelphia in the spring of 1956 and visited on one occasion with HYDE. Mrs. HOUGHTON, in late 1956, went on an American Friends project in El Salvador, and returned in the spring of 1957. She then sought employment in Boston, Massachusetts, and in late 1957 or 1958, she received an invitation to the wedding of RUTH

On 3/13/64 at Boulder, Colorado File # Denver 105-1653

by SA KENNETH BRIDENSTINE; SA ROBERT JAMES NELSON:pmb Date dictated 3/13/64

This document contains neither recommendations nor conclusions of the FBI. It is the property of the FBI and is loaned to your agency; it and its contents are not to be distributed outside your agency.

DN 105-1653
KB & RJN:pmb

HYDE and MICHAEL PAINE. She stated she returned to the Philadelphia area and attended a wedding-eve party which was held at the residence of MICHAEL PAINE's parents, Mr. and Mrs. ARTHUR YOUNG, who resided in a rural area near Paoli, Pennsylvania. The following day she attended the wedding which was held at the Providence Meeting of the Society of Friends.

Mrs. HOUGHTON stated she did not meet PAINE's parents but believed Mr. YOUNG was MICHAEL PAINE's stepfather and Mrs. YOUNG his mother.

During the period of 1958-1959, she visited on a number of occasions with RUTH PAINE in the Philadelphia area. At that time RUTH was taking a Berlitz Course in the Russian language in Philadelphia.

In late 1959, RUTH and MICHAEL PAINE left the Philadelphia area, stating they were going to Texas. Mrs. PAINE advised Mrs. HOUGHTON that MICHAEL intended to work in Texas with an organization in an industry or business. She stated she and RUTH PAINE wrote to each other sporadically and she did not see her again until September, 1960, when Mrs. PAINE came east to a Young Friends meeting of the East-West Contact Committee, which was held at Camp Cwnas, a Friends camp near the town of Newton, Pennsylvania. This committee was set up to encourage the contact between the United States and areas we have not previously been in contact with. At this time, Mrs. PAINE had one child with her and was pregnant. Mrs. HOUGHTON could recall no conversation concerning MICHAEL PAINE during this visit.

In the early part of 1963, Mrs. HOUGHTON received a congratulatory letter in reply to a wedding announcement that Mrs. HOUGHTON had sent to Mrs. PAINE. She stated the return address on Mrs. PAINE's letter was Irving, Texas.

DN 105-1653
KB & RJN:pmb

In August, 1963, Mrs. PAINE contacted the HOUGHTONs in Washington, D. C., where Mrs. HOUGHTON was employed. She believes that Mrs. PAINE learned of their address in Washington through the Providence Meeting group of the Young Friends. Then Mrs. HOUGHTON stated Mrs. PAINE had wanted to see the HOUGHTONs and to be present for the mass Civil Rights March which was made in Washington, D. C., on August 28, 1963. Mrs. PAINE joined the HOUGHTONs at dinner at their apartment in Washington. Mrs. HOUGHTON stated she was interested in knowing of MICHAEL PAINE's well-being and when she asked Mrs. PAINE this question, she received a very vague answer. She stated Mrs. PAINE volunteered nothing specific and only spoke in general and limited terms about her husband. At this time Mrs. PAINE had two children with her.

While in Washington, Mrs. PAINE had advised the HOUGHTONs that she had a Russian woman staying with her and that it worked very well for both herself and this woman, as Mrs. PAINE spoke Russian and the unknown woman spoke very little English. Mrs. PAINE was delighted as it gave both women a chance to assist the other in matters concerning their individual countries. Mrs. HOUGHTON stated she received the implication that for some reason, this woman was separated from her husband and that this worked very favorably for Mrs. PAINE as Mrs. HOUGHTON felt she also must be separated from her husband. At no time did the HOUGHTONs learn who the unknown woman from Russia was.

After this meeting, there were no letters or meetings between Mrs. PAINE and the HOUGHTONs. Approximately three or four days after the assassination of President JOHN F. KENNEDY on November 22, 1963, Mrs. HOUGHTON stated she was reading the "New York Times" and read of the notoriety given Mrs. PAINE as a result of the assassination. She

7

COMMISSION EXHIBIT No. 1983—Continued

DN 105-1653
KB & RJN:pmb

stated that this was the first information she had ever received concerning this matter. She advised she has received no letters from Mrs. PAINE since the assassination.

Concerning MICHAEL PAINE, she advised she met him on approximately two or three occasions, and that she could only describe him as a very tall, dark, shy young man. She did not know whether MICHAEL was a member of the Society of Friends or not.

She stated she had never met MARINA OSWALD and she only assumed that this was the Russian woman who was residing with RUTH PAINE during the summer of 1963. She stated she had never met, nor did she know, LEE HARVEY OSWALD, nor had she met GEORGE PAINE. She stated she had never heard RUTH PAINE speak of GEORGE PAINE. She stated she felt that Mrs. PAINE was very sincere in her beliefs of the Young Friends Society. She felt that she should not comment concerning those beliefs of MICHAEL PAINE.

8*

COMMISSION EXHIBIT No. 1983—Continued

2
DL 89-43

longer. He then told Mrs. BLEDSOE to clean up his room and make up his bed. Mrs. BLEDSOE stated she had been unable to do so since he had stayed in his room so much and she told him that when he left Monday she would clean his room up. OSWALD then told her that if she would give him $2.00 back on the rent he would leave then. Mrs. BLEDSOE told him she did not have $2.00 He finally left and she believes he caught the Marsalis bus going toward downtown Dallas.

On October 14, 1963, Monday, OSWALD came into the house about 9:00 or 10:00 in the morning, used the telephone, and left the house at about 10:00 a.m. without speaking to her although he walked by her while going out the front door.

Mrs. BLEDSOE stated that during the time OSWALD was living in the room she rented to him he did not have any visitors, never went out during the evenings except possibly to a nearby store for a very short period, and apparently was not working. He did not have a car and she did not see anyone pick him up at any time.

On November 22, 1963, Mrs. BLEDSOE watched the Presidential motorcade from a spot on the corner on the southeast corner of Main and St. Paul. She saw President JOHN KENNEDY pass this corner in a motorcade and she then walked to St. Paul and Elm Streets where she caught a Marsalis bus going west on Elm Street. This was approximately ten minutes after the motorcade had passed St. Paul and Main.

This bus proceeded west for several blocks and in the vicinity of Murphy Street she saw LEE OSWALD get on the bus. She does not believe that he saw her. He proceeded to the back of the bus. At this point no one on the bus had heard about the assassination but in a few minutes the driver of the bus heard from a driver of a car stalled in a traffic jam next to the bus that President KENNEDY had been shot. The driver turned around and told the passengers on the bus that the President had been shot. Everyone was talking about this and almost immediately LEE OSWALD got up from his seat in the rear of the bus and walked out the front door of the bus. He could have gotten off the side door but he did not do so. At this time the bus was about two blocks further west along Elm Street from the point where OSWALD had gotten on the bus but the bus had not yet reached Lamar Street.

343

COMMISSION EXHIBIT NO. 1984

FD-302 (Rev. 3-3-59) FEDERAL BUREAU OF INVESTIGATION

Date 11/24/63

1

Mrs. MARY E. BLEDSOE, 621 N. Marsalis, Dallas, was interviewed relative to any knowledge she had concerning LEE HARVEY OSWALD, and concerning this association she advised as follows.

LEE OSWALD had rented a room at her residence at 621 N. Marsalis, Dallas, on October 7 through October 14, 1963. During the course of his stay at her residence, she advised that she described him as a quiet roomer, very neat in appearance, stating he seldom left his room. On two occasions he alleged that he was attempting to obtain work at Texas Instruments and Collins Radio in Dallas and over the weekend of October 12-13, 1963, he was gone from the residence, allegedly spending the weekend with his wife in Irving. While at that residence she had heard OSWALD speaking over the telephone in a foreign language and had stated she had indicated a displeasure with him at remaining at her residence and on October 14, 1963, he returned from the weekend allegedly with his wife in Irving, Texas, collected his belongings and left.

Subsequently on the morning of November 22, 1963, she was in downtown Dallas and had occasion to view the motorcade in which President KENNEDY was riding at a vantage point on the street opposite from Titche's Department Store on Elm Street. After the motorcade went by her position she walked over to St. Paul and Elm Street across from the Dallas Athletic Club where she got on a bus, as she recalls, a Marsalis bus. She paid her fare and sat down in a seat directly opposite the driver facing the aisle and the bus proceeded down Elm Street. As she recalled, when the bus stopped on Murphy Street she saw LEE OSWALD get on the bus, pay his fare, and immediately walk to the rear of the bus where he sat down. She stated at this time the bus was not crowded and there were very few people on the bus. At that time she stated OSWALD appeared to be somewhat nervous and she noticed that he was wearing dirty clothes stating she felt this was strange inasmuch as when he resided with her he had been very neat in his personal appearance. After he got on the bus, traffic going west on Elm Street became extremely heavy and the bus made short, jerky moves in the congested traffic, and while stopped a passing motorist told the bus driver that the President had been shot.

340

on 11/23/63 at Dallas, Texas File # DL 89-43

by Special Agent RICHARD E. HARRISON and JAMES S. WEIR:jj Date dictated 11/24/63

This document contains neither recommendations nor conclusions of the FBI. It is the property of the FBI and is loaned to your agency; it and its contents are not to be distributed outside your agency.

Commission Exhibit 1985

COMMISSION EXHIBIT NO. 1985

FD-302 (Rev. 3-3-59)

FEDERAL BUREAU OF INVESTIGATION

Date 11/25/63

1

On November 24, 1963, Captain J. W. FRITZ, Homicide and Robbery Bureau, Dallas Police Department, furnished photographs of all of the articles contained in the wallet of LEE HARVEY OSWALD at the time of his arrest, November 22, 1963. Said photographs are listed as follows:

1. Membership card of the "Fair Play for Cuba Committee, New Orleans, Louisiana, in name of L. H. OSWALD, bearing the signature LEE H. OSWALD, issued June 15, 1963, signed A. J. HIDELL, chapter president.

2. Membership card for the "Fair Play for Cuba Committee", 799 Broadway, New York 3, New York, ORegon 4-8295, in name of LEE H. OSWALD, bearing signature LEE H. OSWALD, issued May 28, 1963, signed V. T. LEE, Executive Secretary.

3. Front and back of Certificate of Service, Armed Forces of the United States Marine Corps in name of LEE HARVEY OSWALD, 1653230

4. Front and back of Department of Defense identification card #N4,271,617 in the name of LEE H. O'WALD, reflecting service status as MCR/inact, service #1653230, bearing photograph of LEE HARVEY OSWALD and signed LEE H. OSWALD, expiration date being December 7, 1962.

5. Front and back of Dallas Public Library identification card in the name LEE HARVEY OSWALD, 602 Elsbeth, Dallas, bearing signature LEE H. OSWALD showing school or business as Jaggers - Chiles - Stovall which also reflects name of JACK L. BOWEN, 1916 Stevens Forest Dr., WH 8-8997, expiration date December 7, 1965.

6. Snapshot of LEE HARVEY OSWALD in Marine uniform.

7. Snapshot of small baby in white cap.

8. Social Security Card #433-54-3937 in name LEE HARVEY OSWALD. [redacted]

Commission Exhibit No. 1986

on 11/24/63 at Dallas, Texas File # DL 89-43

by Special Agent JAMES W. BOOKHOUT /wvm Date dictated 11/25/63

140

This document contains neither recommendations nor conclusions of the FBI. It is the property of the FBI and is loaned to your agency; it and its contents are not to be distributed outside your agency.

COMMISSION EXHIBIT No. 1986

2
DL 89-43

9. Front and back of U.S. Forces, Japan, identification card in name of LEE H. OSWALD, Private, SN 1653230, bearing signature of LEE H. OSWALD, issued May 8, 1958.

10. Photograph of MRS. LEE HARVEY OSWALD.

(4) 11. Front and back, street map, compliments of Ga-Jo-Enkanko Hotel, bearing telephone number ED 50755, and figure or telephone number 92463.

12. Front and back of Selective Service System notice of classification card in name ALEK JAMES HIDELL, which bears photograph of LEE HARVEY OSWALD and signature of ALEK J. HIDELL.

13. Front and back of Certificate of Service, U.S. Marine Corps, in name of ALEK JAMES HIDELL.

14. Front and back of Selective Service System Notice of Classification in name LEE HARVEY OSWALD, SSN 41-114-39-532, dated February 2, 1960.

15. Front and back of Selective Service System Registration Certificate in name LEE HARVEY OSWALD, SSN 41-114-39-532, bearing signature LEE H. OSWALD, dated October 18, 1939.

16. Slip of paper (Embassy USSR, 1609 Decatur St., N.W., Washington, D.C., Consular Pezhuyehko".

17. Slip of paper "The worke, 23 W. 26th St., New York 10, NY"; "The Worker, Box 28 Madison Sq. Station, New York 10, NY".

141

COMMISSION EXHIBIT No. 1986—Continued

54112
TEXAS SOUTHMOST COLLEGE LIBRARY

FD-302 (Rev. 3-3-59)

FEDERAL BUREAU OF INVESTIGATION

Date 11/29/63

1

The distance from the front door of 411 Elm Street (the Texas School Book Depository Building) to the bus stop at Murphy and Elm Streets in Dallas was walked three times by SA LEE, and the average time was 6½ minutes. This is a distance of approximately 7 blocks.

A bus in very heavy traffic was timed in its traveling the distance from the bus stop at Murphy and Elm Streets to the bus stop at Poydras and Elm Streets, a distance of two blocks, and it took this bus in this type traffic approximately four minutes.

The distance from the bus stop at Poydras and Elm Streets to the cab stand at the northwest corner of Lamar and Jackson Streets, four city blocks, was walked by SA LEE in three minutes.

SAS BARRETT and LEE drove the distance from the cab stand at Lamar and Jackson Streets to the 500 block of North Beckley with a maximum speed used of 35 miles per hour, a distance of 2.6 miles, in seven minutes. The same distance was driven with a maximum speed of 30 miles per hour in 8½ minutes. The same distance was driven with a maximum speed of 25 miles per hour in seven minutes. It was noted that at this speed of 25 miles per hour, a fewer number of stop lights were encountered than at the speed of 30 miles per hour.

The distance from the 500 block of North Beckley to 1026 North Beckley, 4/10 of a mile, was walked by SA BARRETT in six minutes.

The distance from 1026 North Beckley to the location in the 400 block of East 10th Street where Police Officer J. D. TIPPIT was shot and killed on November 22, 1963, 8/10 of a mile, was walked by SA BARRETT in 12 minutes.

The distance from the location in the 400 block of East 10th Street to the Texas Theater, 231 West Jefferson, a distance of 6/10 of a mile, was walked at a brisk pace by SA BARRETT in 10 minutes.

— Commission Exhibit No. 1987 —

on 11/28/63 at Dallas, Texas File # Dallas 89-43

by Special Agents IVAN D. LEE and ROBERT M. BARRETT/al Date dictated 11/29/63

123

This document contains neither recommendations nor conclusions of the FBI. It is the property of the FBI and is loaned to your agency; it and its contents are not to be distributed outside your agency.

COMMISSION EXHIBIT No. 1987

FD-302 (Rev. 3-3-59)

FEDERAL BUREAU OF INVESTIGATION

— Commission Exhibit No. 1988 —

Date 11/25/63

1

LEE HARVEY OSWALD was interviewed by Captain J. W. FRITZ, Homicide and Robbery Bureau, Dallas Police Department. OSWALD was advised of the identity of SA JAMES W. BOOKHOUT, and his capacity as a Special Agent of the Federal Bureau of Investigation. He was informed of his right to an attorney, that any statement he might make could be used against him in a court of law, and that any statement which he might make must be free and voluntary. He furnished the following information in the presence of T. J. ~~KELLY~~, U.S. Secret Service; DAVID B. GRANT, Secret Service; ROBERT I. NASH, United States Marshall; and Detectives BILLY L. SENKEL and FAY M. TURNER of the Homicide and Robbery Bureau, Dallas Police Department.

Following his departure from the Texas School Book Depository, he boarded a city bus to his residence and obtained transfer upon departure from the bus. He stated that officers at the time of arresting him took his transfer out of his pocket.

OSWALD advised that he had only one post offic box which was at Dallas, Texas. He denied bringing any package to work on the morning of November 22, 1963. He stated that he was not in the process of fixing up his apartment and he denied telling WESLEY FRAZIER that the purpose of his visit to Irving, Texas, on the night of November 21, 1963, was to obtain some curtain rods from MRS. RUTH PAINE.

OSWALD stated that it was not exactly true as recently stated by him that he rode a bus from his place of employment to his residence on November 22, 1963. He stated actually he did board a city bus at his place of employment but that after about a block or two, due to traffic congestion, he left the bus and rode a city cab to his apartment on North Beckley. He recalled that at the time of getting into the cab, some lady looked in and asked the driver to call her a cab. He stated that he might have made some remarks to the cab driver merely for the purpose of passing the time of day at that time. He recalled that

on 11/23/63 at Dallas, Texas File # DL 89-43

by Special Agent JAMES W. BOOKHOUT Date dictated 11/24/63

99

This document contains neither recommendations nor conclusions of the FBI. It is the property of the FBI and is loaned to your agency; it and its contents are not to be distributed outside your agency.

COMMISSION EXHIBIT No. 1988

his fare was approximately 85 cents. He stated that after arriving at his apartment, he changed his shirt and trousers because they were dirty. He described his dirty clothes as being a reddish colored, long sleeved, shirt with a button-down collar and gray colored trousers. He indicated that he had placed these articles of clothing in the lower drawer of his dresser.

OSWALD stated that on November 22, 1963, he had eaten lunch in the lunch room at the Texas School Book Depository, alone, but recalled possibly two Negro employees walking through the room during this period. He stated possibly one of these employees was called "Junior" and the other was a short individual whose name he could not recall but whom he would be able to recognize. He stated that his lunch had consisted of a cheese sandwich and an apple which he had obtained at MRS. RUTH PAINE's residence in Irving, Texas, upon his leaving for work that morning.

OSWALD stated that MRS. PAINE receives no pay for keeping his wife and children at her residence. He stated that their presence in MRS. PAINE's residence is a good arrangement for her because of her language interest, indicating that his wife speaks Russian and MRS. PAINE is interested in the Russian language.

OSWALD denied having kept a rifle in MRS. PAINE's garage at Irving, Texas, but stated that he did have certain articles stored in her garage, consisting of two sea bags, a couple of suitcases, and several boxes of kitchen articles and also kept his clothes at MRS. PAINE's residence. He stated that all of the articles in MRS. PAINE's garage had been brought there about September, 1963, from New Orleans, Louisiana.

OSWALD stated that he has had no visitors at his apartment on North Beckley.

OSWALD stated that he has no receipts for purchase of any guns and has never ordered any guns and does not own a rifle nor has he ever possessed a rifle.

OSWALD denied that he is a member of the Communist Party.

OSWALD stated that he purchased a pistol, which was taken off him by police officers November 22, 1963, about

100

six months ago. He declined to state where he had purchased it.

OSWALD stated that he arrived about July, 1962, from USSR and was interviewed by the FBI at Fort Worth, Texas. He stated that he felt they overstepped their bounds and had used various tactics in interviewing him.

He further complained that on interview of RUTH PAINE by the FBI regarding his wife, that he felt that his wife was intimidated.

OSWALD stated that he desired to contact Attorney ABT, New York City, indicating that ABT was the attorney who had defended the Smith Act case about 1949 - 1950. He stated that he does not know Attorney ABT personally. Captain FRITZ advised OSWALD that arrangements would be immediately made whereby he could call Attorney ABT.

OSWALD stated that prior to coming to Dallas from New Orleans he had resided at a furnished apartment at 4706 Magazine Street, New Orleans, Louisiana. While in New Orleans, he had been employed by WILLIAM B. RILEY Company, 640 Magazine Street, New Orleans.

4907

OSWALD stated that he has nothing against President JOHN F. KENNEDY personally; however in view of the present charges against him, he did not desire to discuss this phase further.

OSWALD stated that he would not agree to take a polygraph examination without the advice of counsel. He added that in the past he has refused to take polygraph examinations.

OSWALD stated that he is a member of the American Civil Liberties Union and added that MRS. RUTH PAINE was also a member of same.

With regard to Selective Service card in the possession of OSWALD bearing photograph of OSWALD and the name of ALEK JAMES HIDELL, OSWALD admitted that he carried this Selective Service card but declined to state that he wrote the signature of ALEK J. HIDELL appearing on same. He further declined to state the purpose of carrying same or any use he has made of same.

101

4
DL 89-43

OSWALD stated that an address book in his possession contains the names of various Russian immigrants residing in Dallas, Texas, whom he has visited with.

OSWALD denied shooting President JOHN F. KENNEDY on November 22, 1963, and added that he did not know that Governor JOHN CONNALLY had been shot and denied any knowledge concerning this incident.

102

COMMISSION EXHIBIT No. 1988—Continued

3

DL 89-43

Snapshot photo of woman, apparently wife

Snapshot photo of infant

White card with longhand, "Embassy USSR, 1609 Decatur, NW, Washington, D. C., Consular REZHUYEHKO" (indistinct)

Department of Defense Identification No. N4,271,617, issued to LEE H. OSWALD, expiration date December 7, 1962, Private First Class, E-2, MCR/INAC, Service No. 1653230. Card shows date of birth October 18, 1939, 5' 11", 145 lbs., brown hair, gray eyes.

Dallas Public Library card, undated, expiration date December 7, 1965, issued to LEE HARVEY OSWALD, 602 Elsbeth, Dallas, school or business - Jaggers - Chiles - Stovall, followed by the name JACK L. BOWEN, 1916 Stevens Forest Drive, WH 8-8997.

U. S. Forces, Japan Identification card issued to LEE H. OSWALD, Private, Service No. 1653230, organization - MACS-1 MAG-11 1st MAW. Identification card #00646, issued, May 8, 1958. Date of birth October 18, 1939, American.

Card, "Compliments GA - JO Enkanko Hotel, telephone number ED 5-0755 of reverse side.

Certificate of Service in Armed Forces of United States, issued to LEE HARVEY OSWALD, 1653230, reflected honorably served on active duty, U. S. Marine Corps, October 24, 1956 - September 11, 1959.

94

COMMISSION EXHIBIT No. 1989

Relatives (cont'd)

Father - ROBERT LEE OSWALD, deceased, August 31, 1939, New Orleans, Louisiana

Wife - MARINA; two infant children

Brothers - JOHN OSWALD, address unknown, last known at Fort Worth, Texas, five or six years ago, age about 30, works with pharmaceuticals, but not graduate pharmacist;

ROBERT OSWALD, 7313 Davenport, Fort Worth, Texas (wife - VADA, two small children), works for brick company (believed Acme)

Dress at Time of Interview

Black trousers, brown "salt and pepper", long sleeved shirt, bareheaded

Contents of Wallet

Had card in possession, LEE HARVEY OSWALD, Social Security No. 433-54-3937

Photo of Selective Service System card with photo of OSWALD, "Notice of Classification" and name "ALEK JAMES HIDELL, SSN 42-224-39-5321". Card shows classification IV___(?). Bears date February 5, 1962, reverse side shows card from Texas Local Board, 400 West Vickery, Fort Worth, Texas. Card shows erasures and retyping of the information indicated and bears longhand signature "ALEK J. HIDELL". Signature of member or clerk of local board (indistinct, may be GOOD____.

Local Board 114, Fort Worth, LEE HARVEY OSWALD, SSN 41-114-39-532, address 3124 West 5th Street, Fort Worth, Texas, registered September 14, 1959. Date of birth October 18, 1939, New Orleans, 5' 11", 150 lbs., blue eyes, brown hair. Mrs. ZOLA Z. BURGER, Clerk.

93

— Commission Exhibit No. 1990 —

COMMISSION EXHIBIT No. 1990

Snapshot photo of woman, apparently wife

Snapshot photo of infant

White card with longhand, "Embassy USSR, 1609 Decatur, NW, Washington, D. C., Consular REZHUYEHKO" (indistinct)

Department of Defense Identification No. N4,271,617, issued to LEE H. OSWALD, expiration date December 7, 1962, Private First Class, E-2, MCR/INAC, Service No. 1653230. Card shows date of birth October 18, 1939, 5' 11", 145 lbs., brown hair, gray eyes.

Dallas Public Library card, undated, expiration date December 7, 1965, issued to LEE HARVEY OSWALD, 602 Elsbeth, Dallas, school or business - Jaggers - Chiles - Stovall, followed by the name JACK L. BOWEN, 1916 Stevens Forest Drive, WH 8-8997.

U. S. Forces, Japan Identification card issued to LEE H. OSWALD, Private, Service No. 1653230, organization - MACS-1 MAG-11 1st MAW. Identification card #00646, issued, May 8, 1958. Date of birth October 18, 1939, American.

Card, "Compliments GA - JO Enkanko Hotel, telephone number ED 5-0755 of reverse side.

Certificate of Service in Armed Forces of United States, issued to LEE HARVEY OSWALD, 1653230, reflected honorably served on active duty, U. S. Marine Corps, October 24, 1956 - September 11, 1959.

94.

COMMISSION EXHIBIT No. 1990—Continued

4

DL 89-43

	Card of "Fair Play for Cuba Committee, 799 Broadway, New York 3, New York, telephone ORegon 4-8295", issued to LEE H. OSWALD, May 28, 1963, filed by V. T. LEE as Executive Secretary
	Card of "Fair Play for Cuba, New Orleans Chapter", issued to L. H. OSWALD, June 15, 1963, filed by A. T.(?) HIDELL, Chapter President (note name HIDELL on fictitious Selective Service card)
	Selective Service notice of classification card to LEE HARVEY OSWALD, Selective Service No. 41-114-39-532, IV-A, dated February 2, 1960, from Local Board 114, Fort Worth, Texas
	$13.00 in currency, consisting of one $5.00 bill and eight $1.00 bills
Residence	2515 West 5th Street, Irving, Texas, phone BL 3-1628 (residence of wife for past five weeks)
	Room in rooming house, 1026 North Beckley, for about five weeks. Phone number unknown.
Previous Residences	4706 Magazine Street, New Orleans, Louisiana, no phone (about three months)
	602 Elsbeth, no phone (about seven months), Dallas, Texas
	Unrecalled street in Fort Worth, Texas, (a few months), with brother in Fort Worth, Texas, for a few months.
	Previously in Soviet Union, until July, 1962.

95

COMMISSION EXHIBIT No. 1990—Continued

FD-302 (Rev. 3-3-59) FEDERAL BUREAU OF INVESTIGATION

Date 11/23/63

LEE HARVEY OSWALD, interviewed in offices of the Dallas Police Department, was advised that he did not have to make any statement, any statement he made could be used against him in court and of his right to an attorney. He was requested to furnish descriptive and biographical data concerning himself.

The following was obtained from his responses and examination of contents of his wallet:

OSWALD declined to explain his possession of a photograph of a Selective Service card in the name of "ALEK JAMES HIDELL".

When interview had been substantially completed and OSWALD was asked as to his present employment, he stated he thought perhaps interview to obtain descriptive information was too prolonged, that he had declined to be interviewed by any other officers previously, and did not desire to be interviewed by this agent. He remarked "I know your tactics - there is a similar agency in Russia. You are using the soft touch and, of course, the procedure in Russia would be quite different."

OSWALD was advised questions were intended to obtain his complete physical description and background. Upon repetition of the question as to his present employment, he furnished same without further discussion.

Race	White
Sex	Male
Date of Birth	October 18, 1939
Place of Birth	New Orleans, Louisiana
Height	5' 9"
Weight	140
Hair	Medium brown, worn medium length, needs haircut
Eyes	Blue-gray
Scars	No tattoos or permanent scars
Relatives	Mother - MARGUERITE OSWALD, unknown address, Arlington, Texas, practical nurse (has not seen for about one year)

on 11/22/63 at Dallas, Texas File # 89-43

by Special Agent MANNING C. CLEMENTS / mac Date dictated 11/23/63

92

This document contains neither recommendations nor conclusions of the FBI. It is the property of the FBI and is loaned to your agency; it and its contents are not to be distributed outside your agency.

COMMISSION EXHIBIT No. 1991

2

DL 89-43

Mr. CRAIG described the driver of the automobile as a white male, American, dark-complected, short hair, wearing a light colored jacket. Mr. CRAIG stated he had previously described this man as a Negro male, but has since decided that the driver was a white male.

Mr. CRAIG described the man whom he had seen running across the lawn in the following manner:

> White male, height 5'9", weight 140 pounds, build slender, hair sandy, dress - brown shirt, blue trousers.

Mr. CRAIG stated later the same afternoon he heard that Dallas Police Department had a suspect in the shooting of Officer TIPPITT in Oak Cliff. He stated at this time he called Captain W. FRITZ, Dallas Police Department, gave him the description of the man he had seen crossing the lawn and was advised to view the suspect at Dallas Police Department.

Mr. CRAIG stated he subsequently went to Dallas Police Department and there identified LEE HARVEY OSWALD as the person he had seen running from Texas School Book Depository. Mr. CRAIG further stated there is no doubt in his mind that the man he observed running from the Texas School Book Depository and the person he viewed at Dallas Police Department are identical.

72

COMMISSION EXHIBIT NO. 1992

FD-302 (Rev. 3-3-59)
1

FEDERAL BUREAU OF INVESTIGATION

Date November 25, 1963

ROGER CRAIG, 7711 Piedmont, Apartment B, employed as Deputy Sheriff, Dallas County Sheriff's Office, was reinterviewed. Mr. CRAIG stated that about 12:20 p.m., November 22, 1963, he was standing about 20 feet east of Houston Street on Main Street in downtown Dallas when he heard a noise which he presumed to be a gun shot. He states he immediately started west on Main Street toward Houston Street, and while en route, he heard two additional noises which he also presumed to be gun shots.

He stated he crossed Houston Street and there met a Dallas city police officer who advised him that the noises he had heard were in actuality gun shots. He stated he then proceeded to the Santa Fe railroad tracks which run alongside the Texas School Book Depository building, and while en route there noticed a car with a woman sitting in it. He stated he immediately took her to a Mr. LUMMY LEWIS, Dallas County Sheriff's Office, who took her name and address.

Mr. CRAIG stated he then went to the southwest corner of the Texas School Book Depository building and there talked with a young man and his wife who claimed they had observed a man through a window of the Texas School Book Depository holding a rifle about 15 minutes before the parade passed, but assumed he was a Secret Service man. CRAIG stated he also took these people to Mr. LEWIS, who took their names and addresses. CRAIG stated he then crossed to the south side of Elm Street in front of the Texas School Book Depository building to see if he could see marks on the pavement which would indicate that a bullet had ricocheted.

He stated that at that time he heard a shrill whistle, looked up, and saw a man running across the lawn toward Elm Street coming from direction of Texas School Book Depository building. He stated he also noticed an automobile traveling west on Elm, which he feels was a white Nash Rambler station wagon with a luggage rack on top. He stated he observed the driver look at the man running down the hill, then observed the driver stop at the curb. He stated the man on foot got in the Rambler and they left going west on Elm Street. Mr. CRAIG stated he did not have the license number, but feels that it was a 1963 Texas license.

on 11/25/63 at Dallas, Texas File # DL 89-43

by Special Agent BENJAMIN O. KEUTZER/pm Date dictated 11/25/63

71

This document contains neither recommendations nor conclusions of the FBI. It is the property of the FBI and is loaned to [redacted] your agency; it and its contents are not to be distributed outside your agency.

— Commission Exhibit No. 1993

COMMISSION EXHIBIT NO. 1993

FD-204 (Rev. 3-3-59)

UNITED STATES DEPARTMENT OF JUSTICE
FEDERAL BUREAU OF INVESTIGATION

Copy to:

Report of: SA MILTON L. NEWSOM   Office: DALLAS
Date: 3/21/64

Field Office File No.: 100-10461   Bureau File No.: 105-82555

Title: LEE HARVEY OSWALD

Character: INTERNAL SECURITY - RUSSIA - CUBA

Synopsis:

Special Agents of the FBI observed activities and contacts of MARINA OSWALD from 2/24/64, to 3/9/64, as set forth in the details of this report. On 2/24/64, MARINA OSWALD and her children were residing at the residence of KATHERINE and DECLAN FORD, 14057 Brookcrest, Dallas, Texas. MARINA OSWALD and children moved to a new residence located at 629 Belt Line Road, Richardson, Texas, on the afternoon of 2/29/64. MARINA OSWALD was in frequent contact with KATHERINE and DECLAN FORD during the above period, as well as with her attorney, WILLIAM A. MC KENZIE. Additional contacts and observations by Special Agents set forth.

\- P -

DETAILS:

Special Agents of the FBI observed the following activities of MARINA OSWALD from February 24, 1964, to March 9, 1964:

On February 24, 1964, MARINA OSWALD and her children were residing at the residence of KATHERINE and DECLAN FORD, 14057 Brookcrest, Dallas, Texas. On that date she was contacted at the FORD residence by her attorney, WILLIAM A. MC KENZIE, and his partner HENRY BAER.

This document contains neither recommendations nor conclusions of the FBI. It is the property of the FBI and is loaned to your agency; it and its contents are not to be distributed outside your agency.

COMMISSION EXHIBIT No. 1994

DL 100-10461

On February 25, 1964, MARINA OSWALD, accompanied by small child and DECLAN FORD, were observed shopping at a furniture store and appliance store in Richardson, Texas, a Dallas suburb. They then returned to the FORD residence and attorney HENRY BAER contacted MARINA there in the afternoon.

On the night of February 25, 1964, a white male, accompanied by a white female, driving a 1962 white Plymouth station wagon bearing Maryland license DX92-50, were observed visiting the residence of Mr. and Mrs. DECLAN FORD. The white male was later identified as ISAAC DON LEVINE, who has been previously identified as being from Baltimore, Maryland, and who has stated he was in Dallas for the purpose of interviews of MARINA OSWALD concerning possible contract to write a book concerning her.

The Baltimore Office advised on February 26, 1964, that the above license number is registered to ISAAC DON LEVINE, RFD # 1, Waldorf, Maryland.

On February 26, 1964, MARINA OSWALD, accompanied by Mrs. KATHERINE FORD and MARINA's small child, proceeded to the office of attorney WILLIAM A. MC KENZIE, Fidelity Union Life Building, Dallas, Texas.

They were observed leaving MC KENZIE's office with an individual answering MC KENZIE's description and they departed Dallas in a 1958 Thunderbird, registered to WILLIAM A. MC KENZIE, and proceeded to Fort Worth, Texas. At Fort Worth they entered the Medical Arts Building, located in the downtown section of Fort Worth, and went to Room 707, which is occupied by Dr. LOUIS A. SAUNDERS, Executive Secretary for the Fort Worth Area Council of Churches.

They then departed Fort Worth in MC KENZIE's automobile and drove to Grand Prairie, Texas, where the individual fitting description of WILLIAM A. MC KENZIE visited the office of attorney JOHN M. THORNE. They then returned to Dallas where Mrs. FORD, MARINA and her child returned to the FORD residence.

\- 2 -

COMMISSION EXHIBIT No. 1994—Continued

On February 27, 1964, MARINA OSWALD and Mrs. KATHERINE FORD were observed leaving the FORD residence and driving to Richardson, Texas, where they visited MARINA's new residence at 629 Belt Line Road. While they were at the residence, a Sears-Roebuck and Company truck delivered a few items of furniture.

On February 28, 1964, MARINA OSWALD and her small child, accompanied white male fitting description of DECLAN FORD from the FORD residence to the office of attorney WILLIAM A. MC KENZIE. The same individuals, accompanied by a white male fitting the description of WILLIAM A. MC KENZIE, departed MC KENZIE's office and went to the East Dallas Bank and Trust Company, Dallas, Texas. They then returned to MC KENZIE's office located in the Fidelity Union Life Building. MARINA, her child, and the white male fitting description of DECLAN FORD then drove to 6448 Dunston Lane where MARINA and the child remained in the car while the individual with them entered the residence at that address.

The 1963 Dallas City Directory reflects JOHN J. KNAPP, wife MARGARET, employed by the Xerox Corporation, Dallas, Texas, reside at 6448 Dunston Lane. There is no previous information identifiable with KNAPP in Dallas indices.

Following the above, the same individuals departed this residence and proceeded to 14057 Brookcrest. Thereafter MARINA and the individual fitting description of DECLAN FORD went to MARINA's future residence at 629 Belt Line Road, Richardson, Texas, where a moving van was observed unloading. MARINA and the above individuals returned to the FORD residence and no further activity was noted on the night of February 28, 1964.

On February 29, 1964, Mrs. KATHERINE FORD and MARINA OSWALD and children were observed leaving the FORD residence and traveling to Richardson Heights Shopping Center, Richardson, Texas, and to MARINA's new residence at 629 Belt Line Road. Thereafter Mrs. FORD left MARINA and her children at MARINA's new residence.

Commission Exhibit No. 1994—Continued

On March 1, 1964, a white female fitting description of KATHERINE FORD appeared at the residence of MARINA OSWALD in Richardson, Texas, and accompanied MARINA on a shopping trip at the Richardson Heights Shopping Center where they visited a drug store and grocery store. They then proceeded to the residence of KATHERINE FORD.

KATHERINE FORD and MARINA OSWALD returned to MARINA's residence, 629 Belt Line Road, Richardson, Texas, on March 1, 1964.

On March 2, 1964, Agents observed white female visiting MARINA OSWALD's residence who was driving 1962 Buick convertible bearing 1963 Texas License MU 9335 which was determined to be registered to Pollock-Ray, Post Office Box # 1, Dallas, Texas. Agents also observed white female visiting MARINA OSWALD's residence who was driving 1964 Chrysler with 1963 Texas License WM 7091 which is registered to M. D. WHITESIDE, 1217 Mohawk, Richardson, Texas.

On March 5, 1964, Mrs. BIRDIE SUE BELCHER, Merchants Retail Credit Association, advised SA ALFRED D. NEELEY her files reflect a record of FRANK HENRY RAY, born December 18, 1925, St. Louis, Missouri, and wife ANNA. She advised they reside at 4524 Alta Vista, Dallas, Texas, and employment in September 1963 was shown as Pollock-Ray Sales Company. ANNA RAY has been previously identified as an acquaintance of MARINA OSWALD.

On March 5, 1964, Miss MARON COOK, Retail Merchants Credit Association, Richardson, Texas, advised SA ALFRED D. NEELEY her files reflect MARION DEAN WHITESIDE, wife ALLIE, reside at 1217 Mohawk, Richardson, Texas. Records reflect Mr. WHITESIDE is employed as vice president, Professional Men's Association, Hartford Building, Dallas, Texas. Mrs. ALLIE WHITESIDE is employed as a newcomer hostess for the Retail Merchants Association, Richardson, Texas.

Miss JUDY HAHN and J. G. VICKERY, Dallas Police Department, and JAMES H. KITCHING, Dallas Sheriff's Office,

Commission Exhibit No. 1994—Continued

advised SA ALFRED D. NEELEY on March 5, 1964, their records contain no arrest record of MARION DEAN WHITESIDE or Mrs. MARION DEAN (ALLIE) WHITESIDE. Dallas indices contain no previous information identifiable with the above persons.

On the morning of March 3, 1964, Agents observed white male, white female and small child arrive at MARINA OSWALD's residence in automobile registered to Pollock-Ray.

On the evening of March 3, 1964, ROBERT OSWALD, accompanied by white female, and child, was observed by Agents visiting MARINA at her residence.

KATHERINE FORD was observed visiting MARINA OSWALD at her residence most of the day on March 4, 1964. Mrs. FORD took MARINA to the Richardson Heights Shopping Village where they were observed shopping in various stores.

On March 5, 1964, a white female driving 1964 Ford convertible with 1963 Texas License VM 4554, registered to BILLYE MEYER, 315 Phillips, Richardson, Texas, was observed visiting MARINA's residence for a short time. A white female driving a 1964 Ford, 1963 Texas License VM 4953, registered to J. E. SIMPSON, Box 578, McKinney, Texas, was observed visiting MARINA OSWALD's residence later on the same date. KATHERINE FORD appeared at MARINA's residence on March 5, 1964, and again accompanied MARINA on a shopping trip to the Richardson Heights Shopping Center. MARINA then accompanied Mrs. FORD to the FORD residence and later on the same date Mrs. FORD returned MARINA to her residence in Richardson, Texas.

On March 9, 1964, Mrs. COLLEEN LANGFORD, Retail Merchants Credit Association, Richardson, Texas, advised SA ALFRED D. NEELEY her files reflect a record of LESTER FLORENCE MEYER, wife BILLYE MEYER, who reside at 315 Phillips, Richardson, Texas. File reflects Mr. MEYER is part owner of Harben-Spotts Company (printing), Richardson, Texas, and Mrs. BILLYE MEYER is employed by the Citizens State Bank, Richardson, Texas, in the Public Relations Department, calling on new prospective customers.

On March 9, 1964, records of the Dallas Police Department and Sheriff's Office and the Richardson Police Department were checked by SA ALFRED D. NEELEY, but no record was found concerning the above individuals. Dallas indices contain no previous information identifiable with the above persons.

On March 6, 1964, DECLAN FORD arrived at MARINA's residence and shortly thereafter departed with MARINA OSWALD and her children and went directly to his residence.

Later on March 6, 1964, Mrs. KATHERINE FORD was observed returning MARINA OSWALD and children to her residence at 629 Belt Line Road, Richardson, Texas.

A 1955 Plymouth bearing 1963 Texas License PB 7607 was observed parked in the driveway of the FORD residence on March 6, 1964, while MARINA OSWALD was in contact with DECLAN and KATHERINE FORD. It was determined that the above car is registered to MADELINE DEENE MARTIN, 6523 Tulip Lane, Dallas, Texas. Dallas indices contain no previous information concerning this individual.

On March 9, 1964, Mrs. BIRDIE SUE BELCHER, Merchants Retail Credit Association, Dallas, Texas, advised SA ALFRED D. NEELEY her files reflect a record for MADELINE DEENE MARTIN, who resides at 6523 Tulip Lane, Dallas, Texas. Records reflect Miss MARTIN is retired and was previously employed by the Republic Bank, Braniff Airlines and Texas Utilities, all located in Dallas, Texas.

No arrest record could be located for MADELINE DEENE MARTIN at the Dallas Police Department or Sheriff's Office on March 9, 1964.

On March 7, 1964, MARINA OSWALD and her children were observed visiting residence located at 639 Belt Line Road.

On March 13, 1964, the records of the Richardson Utility Company were checked by SA ALFRED D. NEELEY and reflected JEFF D. SMITH resides at 639 Beltline Road, Richardson, Texas.

Miss MARON COOK, Retail Merchants Credit Association, Richardson, Texas, advised SA ALFRED D. NEELEY on March 13, 1964, that JEFF D. SMITH and wife CORA had been on record in her files since 1950 and record was last checked on June 6, 1962. His residence was shown as 639 Belt Line Road and he is self-employed as a truck driver, previously employed by McInerney Asphalt Company in 1957. Mrs. CORA SMITH was shown to be employed as a welder by Texas Instruments, Dallas, Texas. Credit record was reported satisfactory. Arrest records of Richardson Police Department were checked on March 13, 1964, by SA ALFRED D. NEELEY, but no record was found on JEFF D. SMITH or CORA SMITH. There is no previous information in Dallas indices concerning these individuals.

On March 8, 1964, ROBERT OSWALD was observed visiting MARINA OSWALD at 629 Belt Line Road, Richardson, Texas.

No further pertinent observations were made on March 8 and 9, 1964.

It should be noted that registrants of the above-mentioned license numbers were identified at the time of observation through a check of the records at the Dallas County Automobile Registration Bureau.

COMMISSION EXHIBIT No. 1994—Continued

INDEX

COMMISSION EXHIBIT No. 1994—Continued

DL 100-10461

COMMISSION EXHIBIT No. 1994—Continued

City of Dallas
OFFICE MEMORANDUM

To- Deputy Chief Smith

July 25, 1952

Subject:

Mr. J. D. Tippit is being employed as Apprentice Policeman effective July 28, 1952. He will report to Capt. Cameron for temporary assignment in the Records Bureau at 3 PM.

C. F. Hanssen
Chief of Police

cc: The Board
Ass't. Chief, Brogden
Night Chief Wright
Inspector Curry
Capt. Cameron
File

COMMISSION EXHIBIT No. 1995

UNITED STATES DEPARTMENT OF JUSTICE

FEDERAL BUREAU OF INVESTIGATION

In Reply, Please Refer to File No.

Dallas, Texas
July 24, 1964

JACK L. RUBY;
LEE HARVEY OSWALD

By letter dated July 10, 1964, the President's Commission on the Assassination of President Kennedy requested examination of records of telephone calls in connection with the obtaining of an armored truck by Dallas Police Department on November 24, 1963; and computation of driving time required from the terminal of Armored Motor Service, Incorporated, to the Dallas Police Department via the route previously described by Mr. Harold Fleming of the above-named company.

Attached are results of investigation in accordance with the requests. It will be noted only one long distance telephone call was made, a call from Mr. Fleming, Dallas, to Mr. Tom Mastin, Jr., Fort Worth, Texas. No written records are available as to local calls made.

Attachments

COMMISSION EXHIBIT No. 1996

FD-302 (Rev. 3-3-59)

FEDERAL BUREAU OF INVESTIGATION

1

Date 7/23/64

Assistant Chief CHARLES BATCHELOR, Dallas, Texas, Police Department, advised that on November 24, 1963, he made arrangements to have armored cars available to transport LEE HARVEY OSWALD from the Police Department to the Sheriff's Office.

On November 24, 1963, BATCHELOR advised that at about 9:30 AM he made a telephone call to HAROLD J. FLEMING at his residence, 10611 Lennox. He believes the conversation lasted two to three minutes and FLEMING inquired of BATCHELOR the dimensions of the entrance to the basement of the Dallas Police Department, at which time BATCHELOR stated he did not know the dimensions, but would check and furnish the information to FLEMING. BATCHELOR advised that FLEMING telephonically contacted him at police headquarters at about 10:00 AM and he believes the call lasted approximately three minutes, as he furnished FLEMING the dimensions to the entrance of the Dallas Police Department.

on 7/23/64 at Dallas, Texas File # DL 44-1639

by Special Agent WILL HAYDEN GRIFFIN/eah Date dictated 7/23/64

This document contains neither recommendations nor conclusions of the FBI. It is the property of the FBI and is loaned to your agency; it and its contents are not to be distributed outside your agency.

COMMISSION EXHIBIT No. 1996—Continued

FD-302 (Rev. 3-3-59)

FEDERAL BUREAU OF INVESTIGATION

Date 7/23/64

1

HAROLD J. FLEMING, 10611 Lennox, Dallas, Texas, of Armored Motor Service, Inc., 1800 Leonard Street, Dallas, advised that on November 24, 1963, he received a telephone call at about 9:35 AM at his residence from Assistant Chief CHARLES BATCHELOR, Dallas Police Department. BATCHELOR discussed borrowing an armored car to transport LEE HARVEY OSWALD from the Dallas Police Department to the Dallas County Sheriff's Office. FLEMING advised BATCHELOR that he would contact his drivers and requested that BATCHELOR determine the dimensions of the entrance to the basement of the Dallas Police Department.

Immediately upon the termination of the conversation, FLEMING attempted to reach two employees, but did not receive an answer and then he telephonically contacted TOM JAMES at his residence, and FLEMING believed the time to have been about 9:46 AM and the conversation lasted approximately two minutes, as FLEMING requested JAMES to immediately go to the headquarters of Armored Motor Service, Inc., 1800 Leonard Street, Dallas.

At about 9:55 AM, BERT HALL, 4112 Sun Valley Road, Dallas, contacted Mr. FLEMING at his residence telephonically and advised him he would report to the headquarters of the Armored Motor Service, Inc., and FLEMING advised this call lasted approximately two minutes. Immediately after completing the conversation with HALL, Mr. FLEMING telephonically contacted EDWARD C. DIETRICH, at 866 Harter Road, and he estimated the time at 9:59 AM and the call lasted approximately two minutes. Mr. FLEMING requested DIETRICH to report to the headquarters of the Armored Motor Service, Inc.

At 10:35 AM to 10:40 AM, Mr. FLEMING telephonically contacted Assistant Chief CHARLES BATCHELOR at police headquarters and this call was made from the Armored Motor Service, Inc., office and FLEMING informed BATCHELOR he would be leaving in a few minutes with the two armored cars for police headquarters. This call lasted approximately two minutes.

on 7/23/64 at Dallas, Texas File # DL 44-1639

by Special Agent WILL HAYDEN GRIFFIN/eah Date dictated 7/23/64

This document contains neither recommendations nor conclusions of the FBI. It is the property of the FBI and is loaned to your agency; it and its contents are not to be distributed outside your agency.

COMMISSION EXHIBIT No. 1996—Continued

FD-302 (Rev. 3-3-59)

FEDERAL BUREAU OF INVESTIGATION

Date 7/23/64

1

Mr. BERT HALL, residence, 4112 Sun Valley Road, Dallas, Texas, advised he is the local manager for Armored Motor Service, 1800 Leonard Street, Dallas.

On November 24, 1963, at about 9:50 AM, HALL telephonically contacted Mr. HAROLD J. FLEMING, Armored Motor Service, Inc., at his residence and advised Mr. FLEMING that he had been contacted by another employee and would report to the Armored Motor Service, Inc., headquarters. Mr. HALL advised the call lasted one and one-half to two minutes. Immediately upon completing the conversation, Mr. HALL, at Mr. FLEMING's request, contacted DONALD GOIN, at 6329 Denham Street, at approximately 9:53 AM, and instructed Mr. GOIN to meet him at the Armored Motor Service, Inc., to drive two armored cars to the Dallas Police Department. The call lasted approximately one and one-half minutes.

on 7/23/64 at Dallas, Texas File # DL 44-1639

by Special Agent WILL HAYDEN GRIFFIN/eah Date dictated 7/23/64

This document contains neither recommendations nor conclusions of the FBI. It is the property of the FBI and is loaned to your agency; it and its contents are not to be distributed outside your agency.

COMMISSION EXHIBIT No. 1996—Continued

FD-302 (Rev. 3-3-59)

FEDERAL BUREAU OF INVESTIGATION

Date 7/23/64

1

Records of Southwestern Bell Telephone Company disclosed that on November 24, 1963, at 9:41 a.m., a call was placed from EMerson 8-5013, listed to HAROLD FLEMING, 10611 Lennox, Dallas, Texas, person to person to TOM MASTIN, Jr., telephone PE 8-8010, Fort Worth, Texas. Conversation of two minutes and 31 seconds duration followed.

The above information can be produced upon issuance of a subpoena duces tecum directed to R. A. BURROW, Chief Special Agent, Southwestern Bell Telephone Company, Dallas, Texas.

on 7/22/64 at Dallas, Texas File # DL 44-1639

by Special Agent MANNING C. CLEMENTS:vm Date dictated 7/22/64

This document contains neither recommendations nor conclusions of the FBI. It is the property of the FBI and is loaned to your agency; it and its contents are not to be distributed outside your agency.

COMMISSION EXHIBIT No. 1996—Continued

FD-302 (Rev. 3-3-59)

FEDERAL BUREAU OF INVESTIGATION

1

Date 7/20/64

At 4:08 P.M., Friday, July 17, 1964, Special Agent RAYMOND P. YELCHAK drove a passenger automobile from just outside the Armored Motor Service, Inc. (1800 Leonard) parking lot, which is located next to the building, on Flora Street, proceeded west on Flora Street to Leonard, south on Leonard to Ross Avenue, west on Ross to Pearl, south on Pearl to Main Street, west on Main Street to Harwood, south on Harwood to Commerce, and then east on Commerce to the Commerce Street entrance to the Dallas City Hall Garage. All traffic signs and signals were obeyed and a legal and normal rate of speed was maintained. It was noted traffic was heavy due to the late afternoon rush. Travel time: 8 minutes.

At 10:00 A.M., Sunday, July 19, 1964, Special Agent YELCHAK traveled the same route. All traffic signs and signals were obeyed and a legal and normal rate of speed was maintained. It was noted traffic was light. Travel time: 5 minutes.

At 10:24 A.M., Sunday, July 19, 1964, Special Agent YELCHAK traveled the same route. All traffic signs and signals were obeyed and a legal and normal rate of speed was maintained. It was noted traffic was light. Travel time: 4 minutes.

on 7/17 and 19/64 at Dallas, Texas File # DL 44-1639

by Special Agent RAYMOND P. YELCHAK/ds Date dictated 7/20/64

This document contains neither recommendations nor conclusions of the FBI. It is the property of the FBI and is loaned to your agency; it and its contents are not to be distributed outside your agency.

COMMISSION EXHIBIT No. 1996—Continued

UNITED STATES DEPARTMENT OF JUSTICE

FEDERAL BUREAU OF INVESTIGATION

In Reply, Please Refer to
File No.

Oklahoma City, Oklahoma

July 31, 1964

ASSASSINATION OF PRESIDENT
JOHN FITZGERALD KENNEDY
NOVEMBER 22, 1963, DALLAS, TEXAS

The following supplements information furnished concerning WILLIAM MC EWAN DUFF, formerly employed as a batman by General EDWIN A. WALKER, and of whom allegations of association with LEE HARVEY OSWALD have been received, and an allegation by DUFF of possible association between General WALKER and JACK L. RUBY. The previous information furnished has been by memoranda dated June 26, 1964, July 16, 1964, and in report dated January 23, 1964, at Oklahoma City, Oklahoma.

The matter at hand concerns two of three rifle shells which CLYDE J. WATTS, Attorney and counsel for General EDWIN A. WALKER, produced on July 27, 1964, ascribing their source to WILLIAM MC ~~EWAN DUFF, as~~ obtained without his knowledge by WILLIAM KEESTER and CLIFF ROBERTS, private investigators retained by Mr. WATTS. The shells were reported to have been obtained in the spring of 1963, when KEESTER and ROBERTS had investigated DUFF as a suspect in the attempt to assassinate General WALKER. Mr. WATTS had been given the shells on conclusion of the investigation in the spring of 1963 and had retained them to this time, continuing to retain one of the three shells found.

The results of interviews concerning these shells with CLYDE J. WATTS, WILLIAM ROSS KEESTER, and CLIFF ROBERTS follow:

On July 27, 1964, Mr. CLYDE J. WATTS, Attorney, was contacted at his request at his office, 219 Couch Drive, Oklahoma City, Oklahoma. He furnished the following items:

Two (2) cartridges, approximately .30 caliber, three and one-fourth (3 1/4) inches in length, steel jacketed. Stamped on base of each cartridge is "L" "C" "53."

Mr. WATTS advised as follows:

COMMISSION EXHIBIT No. 1997

Assassination of President Kennedy

He obtained the above described cartridges (plus a third identical cartridge, which he, himself, is maintaining in his possession), from WILLIAM KEESTER. In the spring of 1963, he had hired WILLIAM KEESTER and CLIFF ROBERTS, Private Investigators of Oklahoma City, Oklahoma, to go to Dallas, Texas, to investigate the matter of somebody shooting at EDWIN A. WALKER, a former General of the United States Army. An individual named WILLIAM DUFF, a former employee of WALKER, was developed as a suspect in the shooting by KEESTER and ROBERTS. The three cartridges were obtained by KEESTER and ROBERTS from DUFF's residence without DUFF's knowledge. KEESTER delivered the three cartridges to him at his office in Oklahoma City, 219 Couch Drive, sometime during the summer of 1963. He placed the three cartridges in an envelope and put them in his desk at his office and they have been there ever since that time.

WATTS had completely forgotten about the three cartridges until a recent visit to Dallas, Texas, when he appeared before the Warren Commission. During this recent trip to Dallas, he talked with one Mr. LIEBLER (Phonetic), an attorney for the Warren Commission, at which time he recalled and mentioned to Mr. LIEBLER the incident concerning his obtaining the three cartridges.

Mr. LIEBLER told him to give the three cartridges to the FBI in Oklahoma City, Oklahoma, so that they could be forwarded to the Warren Commission in Washington, D. C.

WATTS desires to maintain possession of one of the cartridges. He believes KEESTER should be able to furnish specific details as to how he and ROBERTS came into possession of the three cartridges.

Mr. WATTS did not place any marks on the cartridges by which to identify them. He does not know if KEESTER or ROBERTS placed any identification marks on the cartridges. The two cartridges need not be returned to him.

Regarding WILLIAM DUFF, DUFF came to Oklahoma City about two months ago and told him he was being discharged from military service due to a fraudulent enlistment. He wanted to keep tabs on DUFF, so he prevailed upon a friend of his, H. W. THOMPSON, of the Oklahoma Paving Company, Oklahoma City, to give DUFF a job. As far as WATTS knows, DUFF is presently working for the Oklahoma Paving Company in Oklahoma City, Oklahoma.

- 2 -

COMMISSION EXHIBIT No. 1997—Continued

On July 28, 1964, WILLIAM ROSS KEESTER, 2224 Southwest 61st Terrace, telephone MUtual 5-2745, Oklahoma City, Oklahoma, operator of the K & R Investigation Service, 417 Leonhardt Building, telephone CEntral 2-0233, Oklahoma City, advised of the following relative to three rifle shells supplied on July 27, 1964, by Mr. CLYDE J. WATTS, Attorney, Oklahoma City, Oklahoma, who stated that he had obtained them from Mr. KEESTER in mid-1963 and that the shells related to the investigation of suspect WILLIAM MC EWAN DUFF in the attempted assassination of General EDWIN A. WALKER:

Mr. KEESTER advised that it is his recollection that the shells in question were obtained by CLIFF ROBERTS, with whom he had been associated in the investigation of DUFF at Dallas, Texas; that ROBERTS had delivered the shells to Mr. WATTS. Mr. KEESTER said he had no other recollection concerning the shells, suggesting contact with Mr. ROBERTS, now employed by the Oklahoma Bureau of Investigation, Oklahoma City, as an investigator.

On July 28, 1964, Mr. CLIFF ROBERTS, Investigator, Oklahoma State Crime Bureau, Oklahoma City, advised that in the spring of 1963 he had been associated with WILLIAM ROSS KEESTER in the operation of the K & R Investigation Service, 417 Leonhardt Building, Oklahoma City; that the partnership had been retained by Attorney CLYDE J. WATTS, counsel for General EDWIN A. WALKER, for purposes of conducting investigation relating to WILLIAM MC EWAN DUFF as a suspect in the attempted assassination of General WALKER.

In connection with the investigation concerning DUFF, as previously reported, ROBERTS said he and KEESTER had moved into the same apartment building with DUFF and, on an undercover basis, had established an acquaintanceship and then his confidence in a proposal that DUFF kill General WALKER for them. This was done in an effort to establish what knowledge DUFF might have had concerning the earlier attempt to assassinate General WALKER.

In the development of this proposal to DUFF, ROBERTS said he had obtained some rifle shells from DUFF's apartment without DUFF's knowledge. He did not recall how many he had obtained or how many he had found. As he recalled, he had found these shells in a shoe box in a closet located in DUFF's apartment. There were two other men, names not recalled, who were living at that time in the same apartment with DUFF. ROBERTS stated he cannot now recall how

he had identified the shells with DUFF, as opposed to the two others. There were two closets in the apartment and the effects of these individuals were commingled. It was ROBERTS' recollection that he had found something else in the shoe box which had identified the shoe box, containing the shells, with DUFF.

ROBERTS stated that he had not marked the shells with anything which he could identify when the shells were found, nor does he believe he now could identify the shells, except through a chain of evidence by testimony that he had given the shells to Mr. CLYDE J. WATTS, counsel for WALKER.

ROBERTS stated that he had found no evidence in his contacts with DUFF, nor when he had located the shells, that DUFF had a rifle, a firearm of any other type, or had any particular knowledge of the use of firearms.

Never, ROBERTS said, had he or KEESTER confronted DUFF with their knowledge of his possession of rifle ammunition, nor had they intimated this to DUFF. Not having discussed the ammunition with DUFF, ROBERTS said neither he nor KEESTER has any information as to its origin, or why DUFF might have retained it, unless as a souvenir of his military experience.

1
DL 100-10461
AEC:mvs

On January 9, 1964, ARTHUR STEVENS, Deputy District Court Clerk, Dallas County District Court, 505 Main Street, advised SA GEORGE T. BINNEY that he had received information that the Assistant District Attorney of Dallas, Texas, SAM PATERNOSTRO, had seen a rifle protruding from a window in the Texas School Book Depository building on November 22, 1963 at the time President KENNEDY was assasinated.

10

Commission Exhibit No. 1998

COMMISSION EXHIBIT NO. 1998

AFFIDAVIT IN ANY FACT

THE STATE OF TEXAS
COUNTY OF DALLAS

BEFORE ME, FRANCES BOCK

a Notary Public in and for said County, State of Texas, on this day personally appeared

ARTHUR E. EAVES

Who, after being by me duly sworn, on oath deposes and says:

My name is Arthur E. Eaves. I have been a member of the Dallas Police Department for 18½ years. I am assigned as Assistant Jailer. I was working in this capacity on November 23, 1963. Between the hours of 1:30 p.m. and 2:00 p.m., on November 23, 1963, I placed Lee Harvey Oswald on the telephone with the assistance of Patrolman B. T. Beddingfield, to make a long distance call to New York City, collect. The Homicide office had advised that it was all right for him to make any call he wished to make. I notified the City Hall operator that a prisoner wanted to call New York City, collect. I heard Oswald talking to someone after the call was placed. I have looked at a copy of the jail card used to record prisoner's phone calls. It shows that I placed Oswald on the telephone at 1:40 p.m., and the signature as shown on the card is my signature.

* * * * * * * * * * * * * *

Arthur E. Eaves

SUBSCRIBED AND SWORN TO BEFORE ME THIS 4th DAY OF August A.D. 1964

Frances Bock
FRANCES BOCK Notary Public, Dallas County, Texas

CPS-GF-413

18

Commission Exhibit No. 1999

COMMISSION EXHIBIT NO. 1999

AFFIDAVIT IN ANY FACT

THE STATE OF TEXAS
COUNTY OF DALLAS

BEFORE ME, FRANCES BOCK

a Notary Public in and for said County, State of Texas, on this day personally appeared BUEL T. BEDDINGFIELD

Who, after being by me duly sworn, on oath deposes and says: I have been a member of the Dallas Police Department for the past six (6) years. I am assigned to the City Jail as Assistant Jailer. I was working in that capacity November 23, 1963. I was assigned in front of the cell occupied by Lee Harvey Oswald to keep a close watch on him. At approximately 1:30 p.m., I was advised by Officer Eaves that Oswald wished to use the telephone to make a long distance call. Officer Eaves and I removed Oswald from his cell and placed him in the telephone booth. Officer Eaves advised the City Hall Operator that a prisoner wished to make a long distance call collect. While he was notifying the operator, I wrote Lee Harvey Oswald's name on the telephone log sheet where all prisoners' names are kept when they are permitted to use the telephone. I heard Oswald place a call to New York. After this call, he made a local call. Upon taking Oswald out of the telephone booth, I signed my last name on the telephone log sheet as to removing the prisoner from the booth, and Officer Eaves and I placed him back in his cell. The telephone log sheet on which I entered Oswald's name and which I signed myself has been turned over to Assistant Chief Batchelor.
xxxxxxxxxxxxxxxxxxxxxxxxxxxxxxxxxxxxxxxxxxxxxxxxxxxxxxxxxxxxxxxxxxxxxxxxxxxxxx

Buel T. Beddingfield

SUBSCRIBED AND SWORN TO BEFORE ME THIS 17th DAY OF August A.D. 1964

Frances Bock
FRANCES BOCK Notary Public, Dallas County, Texas

CPS-GF-413

19

COMMISSION EXHIBIT No. 1999—Continued

P. HENRY LANAUX
DEPUTY RECORDER OF
BIRTHS, MARRIAGES AND D[illegible]
PARISH OF ORLEANS

OFFICE OF
RECORDER OF [illegible], MARRIAGES AND DEATHS
PARISH OF ORLEANS
MUNICIPAL OFFICE BUILDING, CARONDELET AND LAFAYETTE STS.

New Orleans, La., July 22 193[illegible]

This is to certify, that it appears from the Records of this office that

Mr. Robert [illegible] Lee Oswald

and Mrs. Marguerite Frances [illegible]

were married on the 20 day of July 1933

by Rev. [illegible]

same being duly recorded in Book No. [illegible] Folio [illegible]

RECORDING FEE $1.00

P. Henry [illegible]
DEPUTY RECORDER.

COMMISSION EXHIBIT No. 2000

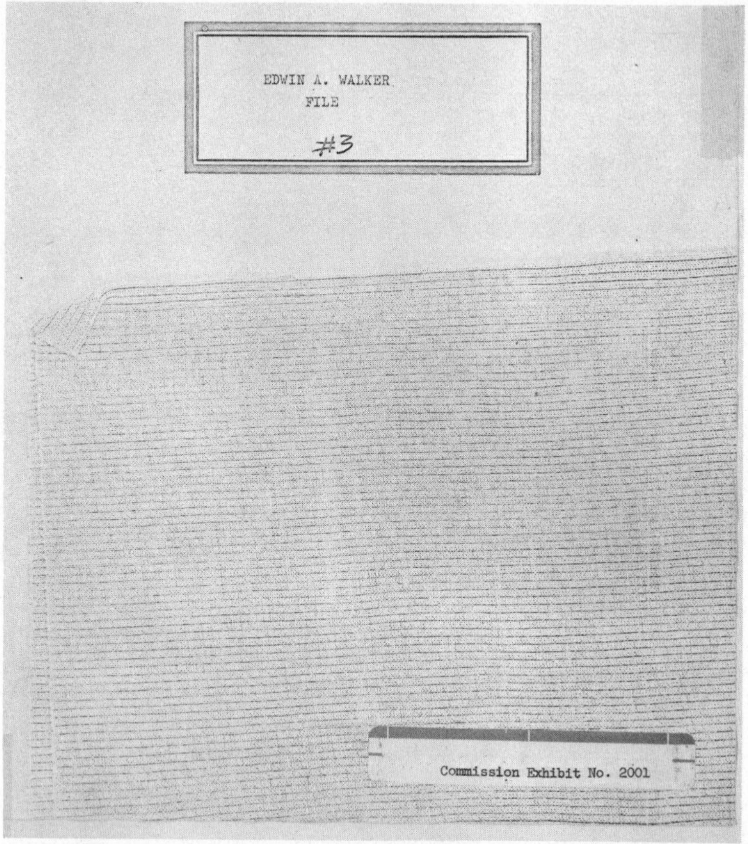

COMMISSION EXHIBIT No. 2001

January 3, 1964

The Honorable Waggoner Carr
Attorney General, State of Texas
Austin, Texas

Sir:

Attached is our complete file on the General Edwin A. Walker Case. I think the reports are self-explanatory.

I assure you this case will remain active in our files and you will be informed of any further developments in the case.

Sincerely yours,

J. E. Curry
J. E. Curry
Chief of Police

es
Att.

COMMISSION EXHIBIT No. 2001—Continued

January 3, 1964

Mr. J. E. Curry
Chief of Police

Subject: General Edwin A. Walker
Burglary by Firearms
Offense #F 48156

Sir:

On April 11, 1963, I was instructed by Captain O. A. Jones to make an investigation on the above offense.

This officer contacted General Walker at his home at 4011 Turtle Creek Blvd on April 12, 1963. In the course of this investigation I have personally interviewed General Walker at his home at least five times. I have had numerous telephone conversations with General Walker regarding this investigation. The last time I had telephone contact with General Walker was on the evening of December 20, 1963, at which time he had received a long distance call threatening his life.

At the present time this offense is still being investigated. I have received no instructions to close this case. This case will remain active until it can be shown who was responsible for this offense.

Respectfully,

E. L. Cunningham
E. L. Cunningham
Lt. of Police
Forgery Bureau

LT.ELC:ms

Commission Exhibit No. 2001—Continued

December 31, 1963

Mr. J. E. Curry
Chief of Police

Subject: General Edwin A. Walker
Burglary by Firearms
Offense # F 48156

Sir:

Pursuant to your instructions of December 24, 1963, a complete file of the investigation of Offense # F 48156 has been compiled. You will find 5 copies of this report attached.

It should be noted Exhibit H is included only in the #1 file as this is a tape of a conversation explained in attachment #9.

Respectfully,

O A Jones
O. A. Jones
Captain of Police
Forgery Bureau

OAJ:nw

Commission Exhibit No. 2001—Continued

December 31, 1963

Mr. J. E. Curry
Chief of Police

Subject: General Edwin A. Walker
Burglary by Firearms
Offense # F 48156

Sir:

General Walker was seated at his desk at approximately 9:00 p.m. on April 10, 1963, when a bullet was fired through the window of the room and continued on through the wall to the left of General Walker.

The bullet was recovered and released to Detective G. B. Brown of the Crime Scene Search Section of the Dallas Police Department.

Kirk Coleman W/M/14, 4338 Newton heard the shot from his room and was listed as a witness. (See attachment I)

Detectives D. E. McElroy and I. F. VanCleave made a follow-up investigation a few minutes after the original report was received. They also interviewed a business associate of General Walker by the name of Robert Surrey W/M/35, 3506 Lindenwood, LA6-7741. (See attachment 2)

Detectives C. R. Dellinger and F. M. Rose continued the investigation on April 11, 1963, and came to the conclusion that the unknown assailant fired the shot from the alley directly north of the rear of General Walker's house. Mr. Surrey was re-interviewed. (See attachment 3)

Detective W. C. Chambers contacted Kirk Coleman, W/M/14, 4338 Newton on April 11, 1963, and obtained information regarding the suspects being in one of several cars that were on the church parking lot that is adjacent to General Walker's house. No definite information was obtained. (See attachment 4)

Detective J. B. Toney contacted Mrs. Knecht, 5332 DeLoache, EM3-3389 on April 12, 1963. Mrs. Knecht who was employed by General Walker listed a "Bill Duff" as a possible suspect. She

COMMISSION EXHIBIT No. 2001—Continued

Page 2 - General Edwin A. Walker

stated that Duff was a voluntary worker for General Walker. Mr. Duff had been engaged to a Miss Whitley who was employed at 4228 Oak Lawn Avenue. Miss Whitley found that Mr. Duff had been borrowing money from Mrs. Whitley's mother. After this was known Mrs. Whitley checked with the British Embassy in Houston regarding Mr. Duff being an emigrant from Great Britain. Mrs. Whitley could obtain no confirmation and the engagement was broken. (See attachment 5)

Lieutenant E. L. Cunningham and Detective J. B. Toney contacted Mr. Robert Surrey, 3506 Lindenwood, LA6-7741 on April 12, 1963. Mr. Surrey was re-interviewed. Mr. Surrey gave additional information regarding "Bill Duff". (See attachment #6)

Lieutenant E. L. Cunningham contacted Mrs. Whitley at 4228 Oak Lawn who gave additional information on William MacEwan Duff, W/M/32, 4919 San Jacinto, Apartment 214, TA4-6134. Mr. Duff is an emigrant from Scotland who came to America on November 4, 1957. He joined the Air Force in December, 1957 and was discharged in December, 1960. He came to Dallas from Los Angeles, California in October, 1962 and married Frances Barnard, 5201 Willis, TA7-2583. The marriage was annulled after three weeks. Mr. Duff had not held a regular job since arriving in Dallas.

Mr. Duff was arrested, questioned, photographed and fingerprinted and then released pending further investigation. (See attachments 7, 8 and 8-A.)

In June, 1963, two private investigators, Mr. Bill Keester, MU5-2745, Oklahoma City, Oklahoma and Mr. Cliff Roberts, MU5-1587 contacted Lieutenant E. L. Cunningham saying they were employed by General Walker's attorneys, Looney, Watts and Looney of Oklahoma City, Oklahoma. They were investigating a "Bill Duff". They had contacted Mr. Duff and brought up the subject of killing General Walker. Apparently both Mr. Duff and the investigators considered the others serious as the investigators contacted this Department and Mr. Duff reported their actions to Special Agent Hostie of the local F.B.I. Office. The investigators furnished a tape of part of their conversation with Mr. Duff. (See attachment 9 and separate exhibit H.)

William McEwan Duff was given a polygraph examination by Detective R. D. Lewis on June 12, 1963 and the operator does not believe that Mr. Duff had any knowledge of the identity of assailant who fired at General Walker. (See attachment 10 and 11).

COMMISSION EXHIBIT No. 2001—Continued

Page 3 - General Edwin A. Walker

General Walker received a threat by a long distance telephone prior to 8:55 p.m. on December 20, 1963. The call was from Kaplan, Louisiana. This information was given to Special Agent Carl Underhill of the local FBI Office.

Special Agent Bob Barrett of the local FBI Office notified this Department on December 30, 1963, that the long distance call on December 20, 1963 was made by Gerald Crawford Vincent, White male of Kaplan, Louisiana. The Federal District Attorney at New Orleans declined to authorize a complaint being filed on Vincent. (See attachments 12 and 13).

The bullet recovered in General Walker's home on April 10, 1963, was released to Special Agent Bardwell Odom of the local F.B.I. on December 2, 1963 to be forwarded to the F.B.I. Laboratory in Washington. The laboratory made comparison tests with this bullet and the bullet and fragments recovered in connection with the assassination of President Kennedy. It was also compared with test bullets fired from the rifle recovered in the assassination investigation.

There were not sufficient markings to reach a positive conclusion although several similarities were present. (See attachment 14)

Mr. Forrest Sorrells, Special Agent in charge of the local Secret Service Field Office, forwarded to this Department of December 26, 1963 an excerpt of an interview with Mrs. Marina Oswald in which she stated her husband, Lee Harvey Oswald, returned home on the night of April 10, 1963 very late and was extremely nervous. He finally told her that he had shot General Walker with his rifle.

The excerpt also mentions a note that was left on a dresser with a post office key for her to use in case of his arrest. This note was written during the Walker episode and had nothing to do with President Kennedy's assassination. (This note is in hands of a federal agency) (See attachment 15.)

Although definite and absolute proof has not been obtained, there is a strong probability that the shot fired at General Walker at 9:00 p.m. on April 10, 1963 was fired by Lee Harvey Oswald.

Respectfully,

O. A. Jones
O. A. Jones
Captain of Police

OAJ:nw

Commission Exhibit No. 2001—Continued

POLICE DEPARTMENT — GENERAL OFFENSE REPORT — CITY OF DALLAS (3)

Complainant: Walker, General Edwin A. — w/m — 4011 Turtle Creek — Offense Serial No. F-49156
Reported By: Same — Address of Person Reporting: Same
Offense as Reported (Crime): Burglary by Fire Arm — Complainant's Phone: LA1 4115
Place of Occurrence: 4011 Turtle Creek — Division: R — Platoon: 3 — Beat: 27 — Officers Making Report: D. F. Tucker 1189, B. G. Norvell 1026
Day of Week: Wed — Date of Occurrence: 4/10/63 — Time of Day: approx 9pm — Date Reported: 4/10/63 — Time Reported: 9:10pm — Report Received By: D. Currie — Received: 10:45pm
Person Attacked: complainant — Injuries Received: M-Elroy-Van Cleave
Property Attacked: residence
How Attacked: indicated below

Details of Offense

Compl states about 9pm he was sitting at his desk doing some paper work, and the NW room in the house, lower floor, when he heared what sounded like a fire cracker explode above his head. He then looked and saw a hole in the wall to the left of where he was sitting. Officer Norvell found the bullet in the next room lying on stack of packages of paper. The bullet entered the window on the west side of the room after passing thru the wooden frame of the window, and passed by compl's head and went completely thru the wall and stopped on top the stacks of paper. Compl was hit in the right arm between elbow and wrist by either 2 [illegible] from the bullet, or wood, or pieces of glass. Compl states after he looked up and saw the hole and realized what had happened, he ran upstairs and got his pistol, and called police. He states immediately after he heard the bullet hit, he heard a car leave the parking lot of the [illegible] on the north side of the [illegible]. Compl does not think medical attention was necessary for his arm. A witness by car, Kirk Coleman, w/m/14, 4338 Newton, [illegible], states he was sitting in the back room of his home, and heard what sounded like a shot [illegible] over the fence in [illegible] yard, and he looked onto the church parking lot he saw some unk/w/m/ speed down the drive by [illegible] Turtle Creek, in either 49 or 50 Ford, light green. He then noticed what appeared to be [illegible] with the door open on a 58 Chev., blk with white stripe down side, states this person [illegible] had the [illegible] pushed up and was leaning over as if he was putting something into the floorboards. This person got inside the Chev. and sped away from the lot. (There was a meeting of some sort in the church, and the lot was full of car, but at the time the time the witness looked out there [illegible] only people on the lot). The bullet which was recovered appeared to be that of a high powered rifle, and was a steel jacket bullet. This was given to Det. G. B. Brown, Crime Lab Division. [illegible] of compl [illegible] Surrey, w/m, states Mon. he saw 2 men sitting in a [illegible] 63 Ford in alley behind compl's house for about 30 min. States after Compl went inside he saw these [illegible] compl's house. [illegible] got into car and drove down [illegible] to [illegible], then went left on Pacific where witness stopped following them. [illegible] states [illegible] were both dressed in suits, and the car had no license plates on it. D. E. McElroy & [illegible] were at scene. They still will supplement.

INVESTIGATING BUREAU

Commission Exhibit No. 2001—Continued

(5)

Form CPS-GF-355A—12
POLICE DEPARTMENT

SUPPLEMENTARY OFFENSE REPORT

CITY OF DALLAS

LAST NAME OF COMPLAINANT (FIRM NAME)—FIRST NAME	INITIAL	OFFENSE AS REPORTED AND DATE	THIS DATE	OFFENSE SERIAL NO.
WALKER, EDWIN A		BURG BY FIREARMS 4-10-63	4-10-63	

ADDITIONAL DETAILS, PROGRESS OF INVESTIGATION, ETC.

Detectives Van Cleave & McElroy arrived at 4011 Turtle Creek shortly after the incident was reported. The compl. stated that he was sitting at his desk in the den doing his income tax return when the incident occurred. Officers observed that a bullet of unknown caliber, steel jacket, had been shot through the window, piercing the frame of the window and going into the wall above comp's head. The bullet lodged in some paper in the next room. Comp. stated that when he heard the noise, he thought it was some sort of fireworks. Upon observing the evidence Comp. ran upstairs to his bedroom to get a pistol. He said that he has no idea of who could have committed this offense. The spent bullet was given to Det. B.G. Brown of the CSSS at the scene. We searched the grounds at the rear of the house and also the alley, with negative results. We also interviewed Robert Surrey W/M/35 of 3506 Lindo Wood LA 6-7741 who was at the scene upon our arrival. This subject is a business associate and aide to the complainant. Mr. Surrey stated that last Saturday, April 6th about 9:00 PM he drove up the alley behind the comp's house and noticed two W/M/-NOD sitting in a 1963 Ford dark purple or brown, parked at rear of the complainant's house. Mr. Surrey also stated that he observed these 2 men get out of the car and walk around the comp's house. The comp. did not seem to be disturbed about the incident. Mr. Surrey it was obvious that there were no license plates on the 1963 Ford. Patrol squad 26, Sgt. Hansen and 508 were also at the scene.

IF OFFENSE UNFOUNDED, GIVE REASON

LIST ADDITIONAL LOSS AND RECOVERED PROPERTY BELOW (Make Entry in Column (4) for Additional Loss Only)

(1) QTY.	(2) UNIT	(3) DESCRIPTION OF PROPERTY (USE STANDARD TERMS) SERIAL NOS.	(4) ESTIMATED VALUE	(5) DATE—RECOVERED—(6) VALUE

RECOVERED BY	RECOVERED AT	TOTAL VALUE	A	B	C	D	E	F	TOTAL
		Leave Blank → STOLEN							
		Leave Blank → RECOVERED							

INVESTIGATING OFFICERS	I. D. NO.	Bureau
DE. MCELROY	769	
?? VAN CLEAVE	1071	BT

PERSONS ARRESTED—NAME, ADDRESS	Race-Sex-Age	ARRESTING OFFICERS	I. D. NO.	DIV.	CHARGE

I RECOMM... THIS OFFENSE BE DECLARED
Unfounded ☐ Pending ☐ Cleared by Arrest ☐

REPORTING OFFICERS (I. D. NO.) (I. D. NO.) DATE 4-10-63 INVESTIGATING OFFICERS [signature: W. J. Van Cleave ~ D. E. McElroy]

DATE COMMANDING OFFICER

Approved:

...GATING BUREAU

COMMISSION EXHIBIT No. 2001—Continued

(6)

Form CPS-GF-355
POLICE DEPARTMENT

SUPPLEMENTARY OFFENSE REPORT

CITY OF DALLAS

LAST NAME OF COMPLAINANT (FIRM NAME) - FIRST NAME INITIAL	OFFENSE AS REPORTED AND DATE	THIS DATE	OFFENSE SERIAL NO.
Walker, General Edwin A.	Burg. by firearms 4/10/63	4/11/63	P-48156

ADDITIONAL DETAILS, PROGRESS OF INVESTIGATION, ETC.

Contacted the complainant on this date, Through interviews with the employees, who are all voluntary workers at this location. General Walker stays in the house at night alone. Investigation reveals that an unknown assailant in all likelihood fired the shot from the alley directly north of the rear part of the house. Investigating officers found a very small chipped edge of the top portion of the rear fence. This small chipped portion indicated that something had been laid on this board very recently, as this was a fresh chip. In lining up the path of the bullet, it would indicate that the shot was fired from just below the chipped portion of the fence. The bullet struck the window frame near the center locking device. From the point where the bullet hit the window frame to the point where it struck the wall is a downward trajectory. The back yard is an up-grade to the alley. The fence in the rear of the house at the alley is a lattice type fence made out of wood approximately 1x6, with approximately 8" open spots. It is the investigating officers opinion that the shot was fired from just below the top edge of the fence. The Walker home is adjoined by a parking lot of a church to the east. The alley runs into the rear part of the parking lot. The alley then takes up in a northerly direction into Newman street. The witness, Kirk Coleman, lives at the north east corner of the Walker property just across the alley and directly across north from the church parking lot. This person has not been contacted by us as he is a school boy, but will be contacted at a later time as he could furnish valuable information from which he observed the incident. An interview with the volunteer workers revealed that they had not received no crank calls or letters preceeding the incident. An interview with Mr. Surrey reveals that two white men in a 1963 Ford, dark purple or dark brown parked in the alley directly behind the complainant's house just off of Avondale street. These persons were witnessed getting out of the car and walking up to the property line and smoking the place over. Mr. Surrey became suspicious of these subjects and followed the car away from the location in an attempt to get a license number. Mr. Surrey states that there was no license plate on this car either front or rear, possibly this was a new car. A thorough search of the promises revealed no spent cartridges, no tracks or other evidence of value. The neighbor's dog to the west of the Walker property is a fanatical barker but on this incidence did not make a sound. Gen. Walker recently accepted the position of Military Editor for a monthly magazine the American Mercury and has traveled extensively since. It is assumed the suspects had a minimum of knowledge concerning the complainant's activities. From where the complainant was and from where the shot was fired from the distance is approximately thirty five to forty yards with a clear view as there are no window shades.

McAllen, Texas

3

REPORTING OFFICERS (I. D. NO.) [signature: C. K. Dellinger 756] (I. D. NO.) INVESTIGATING OFFICERS (I. D. NO.) [signature] (I. D. NO.)

COMMISSION EXHIBIT No. 2001—Continued

Form OPS-GF-355A—13
POLICE DEPARTMENT

SUPPLEMENTARY OFFENSE REPORT (7)

CITY OF DALLAS

LAST NAME OF COMPLAINANT (FIRM NAME)—FIRST NAME	INITIAL	OFFENSE AS REPORTED AND DATE	THIS DATE	OFFENSE SERIAL NO.
Walker, Edward A.		Assault to Murder 4/10/63	4/11/63	F-48156

ADDITIONAL DETAILS, PROGRESS OF INVESTIGATION, ETC.

This officer contacted Kirk Coleman W/M/14 of 4338 Newton. He stated that he was in the back room and heard a noise. He thought it was a blowout. The boy who was with him, Ronald Andries W/M/19 also of 4338 Newton said it was a gun shot. Kirk stated that he then ran out back and climbed the back fence and saw a man getting into a 1949 or 1950 Ford, Lt. Green or Lt. blue and take off. This was on the parking lot of the Church next to General Walker's home. Also on further down the parking lot was another car, unknown make or model and a man was in it. He had the dome light on and Kirk could see him bend over the front seat as if he was putting something in the back floorboard. The only description Kirk could give on this car was the fact that it was black with a white stripe. The other boy, Ronald, did not climb the fence so he did not see this. The only description the boy could give on the person who got into the Ford was that he was middle size and had long black hair. There were several other cars on the parking lot because some function was in prosess at the Church. The Church has lights for the parking lot but Kirk stated that the lights were not on. -- The person that was in the Ford took off in a hurry but the person in the other car did not seem to be in a hurry.

This boy made me promise him that this would not get out in the newspapers. His name is already in the newspaper and he is scared to death that the assasin will attempt to do away with him. He also stated that the part in the newspaper article about him saying that several people were in the Ford was wrong. This officer had a squad to come out to assure the boy and his family that they would check the house for them. We observed a plain car with an uniform officer as he kept circling the parking lot and General Walker's home with his lights out. This made Kirk feel a little better. This offense remains pending.

IF OFFENSE UNFOUNDED, GIVE REASON

LIST ADDITIONAL LOSS AND RECOVERED PROPERTY BELOW (Make Entry in Column (4) for Additional Loss Only)

(1) QTY.	(2) UNIT	(3) DESCRIPTION OF PROPERTY (USE STANDARD TERMS) SERIAL NOS.	(4) ESTIMATED VALUE	(5) DATE—RECOVERED	(6) VALUE

RECOVERED BY	RECOVERED AT	TOTAL VALUE	A	B	C	D	E	F	TOTAL
		Leave Blank → STOLEN							
INVESTIGATING OFFICERS: W.E. Chambers	I. D. NO.: 1087, Bureau: F	Leave Blank → RECOVERED							

PERSONS ARRESTED—NAME, ADDRESS	Race-Sex-Age	ARRESTING OFFICERS	I. D. NO.	DIV.	CHARGE

I RECOMMEND THIS OFFENSE BE DECLARED Unfounded ☐ Pending ☒ Cleared by Arrest ☐ DATE 4/11/63 INVESTIGATING OFFICERS W.E. C. 1087 4

REPORTING OFFICERS (I. D. NO.) (I. D. NO.) DATE COMMANDING OFFICER

D.P. Tucker 1189 B.G. Norvell 1826 Approved:

RECORDS BUREAU

Form OPS-GF-355A—13
POLICE DEPARTMENT

SUPPLEMENTARY OFFENSE REPORT (11)

CITY OF DALLAS

LAST NAME OF COMPLAINANT (FIRM NAME)—FIRST NAME	INITIAL	OFFENSE AS REPORTED AND DATE	THIS DATE	OFFENSE SERIAL NO.
WALKER, Edward A.		Assault to Murder 4-10-63	4-12-63	F 48156

ADDITIONAL DETAILS, PROGRESS OF INVESTIGATION, ETC.

Investigating Officers interviewed Mrs Knecht, home address 5332 De Loache, EM 3 3389, this date. Mrs Knecht stated that the SUBJECT Bill Duff first came to the General's home, he was driving a tan and brown Ford and had all his belongings in this car. After about a month people began to offer Duff jobs and he refused them and continued to stay at the General's house. Mrs Knecht gave Investigating Officers information that Duff had become engaged to Miss Whitley, employeed at 4228 Oak Lawn Avenue. Mrs Knecht stated that Miss Whitley stated to her that their engagement had been broken when she found out that Duff had been borrowing money from her mother. Mrs Knecht further stated that Miss Whitley had contacted the British Embassy in Houston and they had no knowledge of any such person on their records. Duff gave his full name to Miss Whitley as William Mac Cuin or Cuine Mc Duff. Mrs Knecht stated that Dr. Ruth Jackson, who lives next door to The General has a dog that barks at everybody and everything. The night that this offense occurred Dr. Jackson's dog did not bark at Suspects. Investigating Officers received further information from Mrs Knecht that Dr. Jackson's dog was very sick yesterday and is also sick today. Reason for this illness is unknown at this time.

Investigating Officers will interview Dr. Jackson and Miss Whitley 4-13-63.

IF OFFENSE UNFOUNDED, GIVE REASON

LIST ADDITIONAL LOSS AND RECOVERED PROPERTY BELOW (Make Entry in Column (4) for Additional Loss Only)

(1) QTY.	(2) UNIT	(3) DESCRIPTION OF PROPERTY (USE STANDARD TERMS) SERIAL NOS.	(4) ESTIMATED VALUE	(5) DATE—RECOVERED	(6) VALUE

RECOVERED BY	RECOVERED AT	TOTAL VALUE	A	B	C	D	E	F	TOTAL
		Leave Blank → STOLEN							
INVESTIGATING OFFICERS: J. B. Toney	I. D. NO.: 778, Bureau: F & S	Leave Blank → RECOVERED							

PERSONS ARRESTED—NAME, ADDRESS	Race-Sex-Age	ARRESTING OFFICERS	I. D. NO.	DIV.	CHARGE

I RECOMMEND THIS OFFENSE BE DECLARED Unfounded ☐ Pending ☒ Cleared by Arrest ☐ 4-12-63 DATE INVESTIGATING OFFICERS JB Toney 778 5

REPORTING OFFICERS (I. D. NO.) (I. D. NO.) DATE COMMANDING OFFICER

D. P. Tucker 1189 B.G. Norvell 1826 Approved:

RECORDS BUREAU

COMMISSION EXHIBIT No. 2001—Continued

COMMISSION EXHIBIT No. 2001—Continued

Form OPS-GF-355A—13
POLICE DEPARTMENT

SUPPLEMENTARY OFFENSE REPORT

(12)

CITY OF DALLAS

LAST NAME OF COMPLAINANT (FIRM NAME)—FIRST NAME	INITIAL	OFFENSE AS REPORTED AND DATE	THIS DATE	OFFENSE SERIAL NO.
WALKER, Edward A.		Assault to Murder 4-10-63	4-12-63	F 48156

ADDITIONAL DETAILS, PROGRESS OF INVESTIGATION, ETC.

This date Lieutenant Cunningham and Detective J. B. Toney contacted Robert Surrey, of 3506 Lindonwood LA 6 7741, business address Johnson Printing Company, 2700 North Haskell, TA 3 6191. This person is in the printing business however does administrative work for General Walker. Surrey was re-interviewed regarding incidents he observed the evening before this offense occurred at which then he could not give any additional information with the exception of the below listed. Surrey stated that a large flood light in the rear area of the General's home was burned out on the night the offense occurred. Surrey stated that the suspects he observed lurking around the General's house were driving a 1963 Ford Four door sedan, either purple or brown, was hard to tell due to the lighting situtation. Surrey gave Investigating Officers the name of a Subject, Bill Duff, white male approximately 32. Duff came to the General's home in early December 1962, and pretended to be an immigrant from Scotland. Duff stated he was interested in the type work the General was following and wanted to help him just for a place to stay Duff stated that he had only been in the Dallas area at that time two weeks and kept mentioning he had to study all the time to obtain his american citizenship papers. Duff became very lazy about the house after a while and would not work and about the 10th day of March 1963, Duff's luggage was moved into the hall and Duff was asked to leave the house. Surrey stated further that in packing Duff's luggage he found a receipt for an airline ticket made out to William Duff dated sometime in the spring of 1962 showing passage from San Francisco, California, to Seattle, Washington, indicating that Duff was not telling the truth about his arrival in this country. Surrey received information about Duff from other sources proved that Duff was not telling the truth about himself. Surrey advised Investigating Officers to contact the General's Secretary Mrs Knecht.

IF OFFENSE UNFOUNDED, GIVE REASON

LIST ADDITIONAL LOSS AND RECOVERED PROPERTY BELOW (Make Entry in Column (4) for Additional Loss Only)

(1) QTY.	(2) UNIT	(3) DESCRIPTION OF PROPERTY (USE STANDARD TERMS) SERIAL NOS.	(4) ESTIMATED VALUE	(5) DATE—RECOVERED—(6) VALUE

RECOVERED BY	RECOVERED AT		TOTAL VALUE	A	B	C	D	E	F	TOTAL
INVESTIGATING OFFICERS	I. D. NO.	Bureau	Leave Blank → STOLEN							
J. B. Toney	778	F&S	Leave Blank → RECOVERED							

PERSONS ARRESTED—NAME, ADDRESS	Race-Sex-Age	ARRESTING OFFICERS	I. D. NO.	DIV.	CHARGE

I RECOMMEND THIS OFFENSE BE DECLARED
Unfounded ☐ Pending ☒ Cleared by Arrest ☐ 4-12-63 DATE INVESTIGATING OFFICERS J B Toney 778

REPORTING OFFICERS (I. D. NO.) (I. D. NO.) DATE COMMANDING OFFICER
D. P. Tucker 1189 B. G. Norvell 1826 Approved:

RECORDS BUREAU

6

Form OPS-GF-355A—13
POLICE DEPARTMENT

SUPPLEMENTARY OFFENSE REPORT

(10)

CITY OF DALLAS

LAST NAME OF COMPLAINANT (FIRM NAME)—FIRST NAME	INITIAL	OFFENSE AS REPORTED AND DATE	THIS DATE	OFFENSE SERIAL NO.
Walker, Edwin A.		A to M 4/10/63	4/16/63	F-48156

ADDITIONAL DETAILS, PROGRESS OF INVESTIGATION, ETC.

Investigating officers interviewed a Mrs Whitley, 4228 Oak Lawn, La 1 2320. She stated that she had been engaged to William McDuff, w/m/33, 5-7, 165, described as having blue eyes, light colored hair, receding hair line. Mrs Whitley broke the engagement some three weeks ago. States that the last contact that she had had with McDuff was on April 6, 1963 about 2:30pm. Mrs Whitley stated tht she was of the opinion that McDuff to be an alien and that she had contacted the British Embassy in Houston, Tex. Who stated that they had no record in their office of this person being alien. She stated that she did not know what McDuff's occupation was. He told some friends of hers that he was in the auto sales business. She further stated that he had come by her place driving a 1957 model brown ford, 1962 model Oldsmobile, Ford Station Wagon, 1963 model ford, 1963 model chevrolet, and a 1958 model maroon T-bird. She did not know the address at which McDuff was staying, but gave the telephone number of TA7 1869. This number is listed at 4805 Coles Manor, to a R.B. Ruwalt. Officers contacted the mgr of these apts and was informed th t Mr. Ruwalt did not live there, but that his wife was living there. Wife owns a 1958 Maroon T-bird, and is reported to be a free lance model.

Contacted complainant who stated th t McDuff came back by his office Saturday Aft. 4/13/63 about 2 pm and told him that he was in Phoenix, Ariz. when he had heard of the assualt on complainant. Told Mr. Walker that he was driving for Denver, ~~Chicgx~~, Chicago Truck Lines. This time McDuff was driving a Volkswagen, 1963 Tex. MU 8239. Mr. Walker gave the name of two other Dallas citizend who were reported to be friends of McDuff. John Wilson, EM8 6669 and H.R. VonSchilling, EM3 4516. These people reported to be interested in money raising campaign for General Walkers cause. A mar by the name of Jess Arnold, of Wolf City called McDuff and made a diner engagement on the eve of his departure for his speaking tour. This was the middle of last month.

IF OFFENSE UNFOUNDED, GIVE REASON

An attempt was made to locate the Denver Chicago Truck Lines, but this business is unknown by the trucking industry in Dallas.

LIST ADDITIONAL LOSS AND RECOVERED PROPERTY BELOW (Make Entry in Column (4) for Additional Loss Only)

(1) QTY.	(2) UNIT	(3) DESCRIPTION OF PROPERTY (USE STANDARD TERMS) SERIAL NOS.	(4) ESTIMATED VALUE	(5) DATE—RECOVERED—(6) VALUE

General Walker thinks there may be a tie in between this offense and the recent offenses of the swastikas being painted on business and residents of promwniah Jewish business-men and citizens of this sity.

RECOVERED BY	RECOVERED AT		TOTAL VALUE	A	B	C	D	E	F	TOTAL
INVESTIGATING OFFICERS	I. D. NO.	Bureau	Leave Blank → STOLEN							
E.L. Cunningham Lt. of Police	464	FB	Leave Blank → RECOVERED							

PERSONS ARRESTED—NAME, ADDRESS	Race-Sex-Age	ARRESTING OFFICERS	I. D. NO.	DIV.	CHARGE

I RECOMMEND THIS OFFENSE BE DECLARED
Unfounded ☐ Pending XXX Cleared by Arrest ☐ 4/16/63 DATE INVESTIGATING OFFICERS E.L. CUNNINGHAM 464

REPORTING OFFICERS (I. D. NO.) (I. D. NO.) DATE COMMANDING OFFICER
D.P. Tucker 1189 and B.G. Norvell 1826 Approved:

RECORDS BUREAU

7

COMMISSION EXHIBIT No. 2001—Continued COMMISSION EXHIBIT No. 2001—Continued

Form CPS-GF-355
POLICE DEPARTMENT

SUPPLEMENTARY OFFENSE REPORT

(8)

CITY OF DALLAS

LAST NAME OF COMPLAINANT (FIRM NAME) – FIRST NAME INITIAL	OFFENSE AS REPORTED AND DATE	THIS DATE	OFFENSE SERIAL NO.
WALKER, EDWIN E.	Assault to murder 4-10-63	4-18-63	F 48156

ADDITIONAL DETAILS, PROGRESS OF INVESTIGATION, ETC.

Investigating officers arrested William MacEwan Duff, white male, 32, 4919 San Jacinto, Apt 214, TA4 6134, on April 18, 1963. This man worked for General Walker from December, 1962, until March 10, 1963. He lived in the house with General Walker. He was not paid a salary, just room and board. He was asked to leave because he was not dependable and told so many lies. Duff is an immigrant from Scotland, he came to America on November 4, 1957. Joined the Air Force in December, 1957, and was discharged December, 1960. Duff came to Dallas from Los Angeles, in October, 1962, and married Frances Barnard, who now lives at 5201 Willis, TA7 2583. He talked Frances into giving him $800.00 with which he bought a car. Three weeks after marriage they got an annulment. Duff has not been employed since coming to Dallas, making his living by sponging and mooching money from friends. Duff was placed in jail and printed and mugged and released.

5-4-63

Mrs Maxine Byrd Whaley, 409 No. West 11th St, Okla. City, Okla. P.O. Box 708, Came by office. She stated she would like to donate $100 toward a reward for capture of person who shot at Gen. Walker. Stated she thought the motive was jealousy.

I talked to her for sometime, she had no real reason for thinking this - just a hunch. She stated that she is a friend of Gen. Watts in Okla. City and knew Gen. Walker and that she knew that many women flocked around the Gen. and that he did not seem to notice them. Therefore she thinks one of them took a shot at him.

8

REPORTING OFFICERS (I. D. NO.)	(I. D. NO.)	INVESTIGATING OFFICERS (I. D. NO.)	(I. D. NO.)
E L Cunningham	464		

COMMISSION EXHIBIT NO. 2001—Continued

POLICE DEPARTMENT
CITY OF DALLAS
CPS-JS-356

ARREST REPORT
ON
INVESTIGATIVE PRISONER

ARREST NUMBER 63-45551
I. D. NUMBER 52495

FIRST NAME	MIDDLE NAME	LAST NAME	DATE	TIME
William	McEwan	Duff	4-18-63	11A M

RACE: WHITE ☒ COLORED ☐ — SEX: MALE ☒ FEMALE ☐ — AGE: 32 — DATE OF BIRTH: 11-4- — HOME ADDRESS: 4919 San Jacinto apt 214

ADDRESS WHERE ARREST MADE: 4919 San Jacinto apt 214 — TYPE PREMISES (IF BUSINESS, GIVE TRADE NAME ALSO): Apt.

CHARGE: Inv. Swindle

BUSINESS WHERE ARREST MADE HAS: BEER LICENSE ☐ LIQUOR LICENSE ☐ STATE LIC. NO.

HOW ARREST MADE: ON VIEW ☒ CALL ☐ WARRANT ☐ — LOCATION OF OFFENSE (IF OTHER THAN PLACE OF ARREST)

COMPLAINANT (NAME—RACE—SEX—AGE) — HOME ADDRESS—PHONE NO. — BUSINESS ADDRESS—PHONE NO.

WITNESS — HOME ADDRESS—PHONE NO. — BUSINESS ADDRESS—PHONE NO.

WITNESS — HOME ADDRESS—PHONE NO. — BUSINESS ADDRESS—PHONE NO.

PROPERTY PLACED IN POUND (MAKE, MODEL, LICENSE NO. OF AUTO) — PROPERTY PLACED IN PROPERTY ROOM

NAMES OF OTHERS ARRESTED AT SAME TIME IN CONNECTION WITH THE SAME OR SIMILAR OFFENSE

NAME OF AND/OR INFORMATION CONCERNING OTHER SUSPECTS NOT APPREHENDED

OTHER DETAILS OF THE ARREST

This subject is an immigrant from Scotland. He has lived in Dallas since Oct. 1962. Has not worked since coming to this city. Has been bumming off so called friends obtaining money under false pretenses. Please mug.

CHECK ALL ITEMS WHICH APPLY: DRUNK ☐ DRINKING ☐ CURSED ☐ RESISTED ☐ FOUGHT ☐ INJURED BEFORE ARREST ☐ INJURED DURING OR AFTER ARREST ☐ OFFICER(S) INJURED ☐ SPECIAL REPORT ☐

ARRESTING OFFICER	I. D. NO.	ARRESTING OFFICER	I. D. NO.
[illegible] Toney	778	E.L. Cunningham	464
OTHER OFFICER	I. D. NO.	OTHER OFFICER	I. D. NO.

INVESTIGATION ASSIGNED TO	CHARGE FILED	FILED BY	DATE	DATE - TIME TO CO. JAIL

RELEASED BY	DATE - TIME	H.C. BOND BY	DATE - TIME	COURT	DATE	TIME
[illegible]	4-18-63					

DISTRIBUTION: (REMOVE CARBON—CHECK ORIGINAL FOR RECORDS BU.—CHECK COPY FOR EACH BUREAU CONCERNED)
RECORDS BUREAU ☐ SPEC. SER. BUREAU ☐ HOMICIDE ROBBERY ☐ AUTO THEFT ☐ BURGLARY THEFT ☐ FORGERY ☐ JUVENILE ☐ TRAFFIC ☐
USE REVERSE SIDE IF MORE SPACE NEEDED

8-A

COMMISSION EXHIBIT NO. 2001—Continued

Form OPS-GF-355A-12
POLICE DEPARTMENT

SUPPLEMENTARY OFFENSE REPORT (9)

CITY OF DALLAS

(1) LAST NAME OF COMPLAINANT (FIRM NAME)—FIRST NAME INITIAL	(2) OFFENSE AS REPORTED AND DATE	(3) THIS DATE	(4) OFFENSE SERIAL NO.
Walker, Edwin E.	Assault to Murder	6-6-63	F-48156

(5) ADDITIONAL DETAILS, PROGRESS OF INVESTIGATION, ETC.

Mr. Bill Keester, MU5-2745, Oklahoma City, Okla. and Mr. Cliff Roberts, MU5-1587, Okla. City, contacted this officer and stated that they were employed by General Watts of Okla. City , Looney, Watts and Looney Law Firm, as special investigators. Gen. Watts sent them to Dallas to investigate a Mr Bill Duff. Roberts came to dallas the later part of May and rented an Apt. in the same building that Duff was living in. He made contact with Duff and they became rather close and did quite a bit of drinking together. After making casual conversation with Duff about Gen. Walker and Duff did not seem to be interested in him, Roberts made the statement that some-one should kill Walker. Duff ststed that he would kill him if the price was right. Roberts told Duff that he knew a party who would pay to have the job done. At this time Roberts called Keester who came to Dallas and met Duff. Keester told Duff that he had the money to pay for killing Walker. Duff,Roberts and Keester planed how the job was to be done. Roberts made a tape recording of the plans.(This officer has the tape). Killing was sit up for the night of June 10,1963, On this date, June 6,1963, Bill Duff called FBI Agent Hostie and told him of the arangement with the two men to kill Gen. Walker.This officer interviewed Duff again and ran him on Lie Detector. it is the ppenion of investigating officer that Duff never had any intention of shooting Walker, however I think he would have taken any money offered in advance. Duff stated

(6) IF OFFENSE UNFOUNDED, GIVE REASON

that he was just trying to get any information that these pepple may have as to who tried to kill Gen. Walker.

(7) LIST ADDITIONAL LOSS AND RECOVERED PROPERTY BELOW (Make Entry in Column (4) for Additional Loss Only)

(8) QTY.	(9) UNIT	(10) DESCRIPTION OF PROPERTY (USE STANDARD TERMS) SERIAL NOS.	(11) ESTIMATED VALUE	(12) DATE — RECOVERED — (13) VALUE

(14) RECOVERED BY | (15) RECOVERED AT | TOTAL VALUE

	A	B	C	D	E	F	TOTAL
Leave Blank → STOLEN							
Leave Blank → RECOVERED							

(16) INVESTIGATING OFFICERS | I. D. NO. | (17) Bureau

(18) PERSONS ARRESTED—NAME, ADDRESS | (19) Race-Sex-Age | (20) ARRESTING OFFICERS I. D. NO. | (21) Div. | (22) CHARGE

I RECOMMEND THIS OFFENSE BE DECLARED | (26) DATE | (27) INVESTIGATING OFFICERS

(23) Unfounded ☐ (24) Pending ☐ (25) Cleared by Arrest ☐

(28) REPORTING OFFICERS (I. D. NO.) | (I. D. NO.) | (29) DATE | (30) COMMANDING OFFICER

Lt. E.L. Cunningham | 464 | APPROVED:

RECORDS BUREAU

December 31, 1963

Mr. O. A. Jones
Captain of Police
Forgery Bureau

Subject: William McEwan Duff
Polygraph Examination

Sir:

A polygraph examination was given to William McEwan Duff upon the request of Lieutenant Cunningham to determine if he had any guilty knowledge about the shooting at General Edwin Walker. This test was conducted at 8:00 P.M. on June 12, 1963. Below is a list of pertinent questions asked.

1. Do you have a grudge with General Walker? Answer: No
2. Did you shoot at General Walker? Answer: No
3. Do you remember who you were with the night General Walker was shot at? Answer: No
4. Have you given information to anyone about the activity of General Walker or the layout of the house except the two men from Oklahoma? Answer: No
5. Have you owned or had in your possession a high powered rifle since you have been in Dallas? Answer: No
6. Do you know who shot at General Walker? Answer: No

Lieutenant Cunningham set this appointment up and was the investigating officer. This officer had left a set of questions for Lieutenant Potts to bring with Mr. Duff to be examined. Lieutenant Potts was not familar with this case. Lieutenant Potts was advised there was a definite language barrier between Mr. Duff and the examiner because Mr. Duff was an immigrant.

Taking everything in consideration, it was the opinion of this examiner, that Mr. Duff was truthful on all the above questions except question number three. Due to a lasp of time between the offense and examination, this person seemed puzzled over this question which could have caused the indication of deception. Due to the fact this person answered the other questions with the truth, it is believed Mr. Duff was confused rather than lying.

Respectfully submitted,

R. D. Lewis
R. D. Lewis
Detective of Police
Identification Bureau

RDL/mel

Form OPS-GF-355A-12
POLICE DEPARTMENT

SUPPLEMENTARY OFFENSE REPORT (13) CITY OF DALLAS

(1) LAST NAME OF COMPLAINANT (FIRM NAME)—FIRST NAME INITIAL	(2) OFFENSE AS REPORTED AND DATE	(3) THIS DATE	(4) OFFENSE SERIAL NO.
Walker, Edwin E.	Assault to Murder	6-27-63	F-48156

(5) ADDITIONAL DETAILS, PROGRESS OF INVESTIGATION, ETC.

Gen Walker called this officer on June 6,1963 and stated that two private investigators had been checking on Bill Duff. He stated that sometime during the latter part of May an unknown lady called his Secetary and told her that she knew that Bill Duff had told a Mr Charles Holloway, Apt. 123, 5420 Lewis, TA1-9091, That he Bill Duff, was the one who had shot at the General.I interviewed Mr. Holloway and he stated that Duff had never made such a statement. that Duff had moved into the Apt, with him several weeks prior to this time and that he had never talked of Gen. Walker. Holloway stated that there was a number of people who did not like Duff and that he owed several people money. One of these people was a Mrs Juanita Buchanon who runs the Eldorado Bar on No. Haskell. Mrs Buchanon stated she did not make the call to the Walker home. But she did think that Duff was capable of doing such a thing as shooting at someone. She stated that she had cashed several checks for Duff that were signed by Herman Garrard, 6218 Lavesta. TA 7-3182. I interviewed Garrard and his Mother, Mrs Garrard. They stated that Duff had spent a night or so at their house and ahd borrowed money from them. Mrs Garrard denied making the phone call to the Genrals home. At this time it is unknown who the lady is that made call to Compl. It is the openion of this officer that Bill Duff did not have anything to do with the assault on General Walker.

(6) IF OFFENSE UNFOUNDED, GIVE REASON

(7) LIST ADDITIONAL LOSS AND RECOVERED PROPERTY BELOW (Make Entry in Column (4) for Additional Loss Only)

(8) QTY.	(9) UNIT	(10) DESCRIPTION OF PROPERTY (USE STANDARD TERMS) SERIAL NOS.	(11) ESTIMATED VALUE	(12) DATE – RECOVERED – (13) VALUE

(14) RECOVERED BY	(15) RECOVERED AT	TOTAL VALUE	A	B	C	D	E	F	TOTAL
(16) INVESTIGATING OFFICERS	I. D. NO. (17) Bureau	Leave Blank → STOLEN							
Lt. E.L. Cunningham	464	Leave Blank → RECOVERED							

(18) PERSONS ARRESTED—NAME, ADDRESS | (19) Race-Sex-Age | (20) ARRESTING OFFICERS I. D. NO. | (21) Div. | (22) CHARGE

I RECOMMEND THIS OFFENSE BE DECLARED
(23) Unfounded ☐ (24) Pending ☐ (25) Cleared by Arrest ☐ | (26) DATE | (27) INVESTIGATING OFFICERS

(28) REPORTING OFFICERS (I. D. NO.) (I. D. NO.) | (29) DATE | (30) COMMANDING OFFICER 11

APPROVED:

RECORDS BUREAU

Commission Exhibit No. 2001—Continued

December 20, 1963

Mr. M. W. Stevenson
Deputy Chief of Police Commanding
Criminal Investigation Division

Subject: Threat on Life of General Edwin A. Walker

Sir:

At 8:55 PM this date Mr. Carroll Collier, Aide to General Walker, called Sergeant Passons and told him that the General was receiving a telephone call threatening his life. Sergeant Passons called Mrs. Allen, Chief Operator and asked her to trace call going to LA1-4115. Mrs. Allen checked and stated that it was a long distance call and that she could go no further than that.

I checked with Mr. Collier who stated that he had checked on call and that it came from Kempland, Louisiana. He contacted Unit 2 at Lafayette, Louisiana, Phone No. 2327011. She told him that call was made on credit card and that she would give further information only to police.

Party calling told the General that his name was Carpenter then later said that was not his name. Party told Walker that he was going to kill him, and called him vile names.

Information was given to Mr. Carl Underhill of FBI Office. Mr. Underhill alerted his offices in Lafayette and New Orleans. He asked that we leave the Lafayette Police Department out of it at present time.

Captain Frazier of Radio Patrol was notified.

Respectfully,

E. L. Cunningham
E. L. Cunningham
Lieutenant of Police
Forgery Bureau

OAJ:nw

Commission Exhibit No. 2001—Continued

December 30, 1963

Mr. J. E. Curry
Chief of Police

Subject: Threat on Life of
General Edwin A. Walker

Sir:

On this day Mr. Bob Barrett of the Federal Bureau of Investigation's Office called and stated that their agent's investigation revealed that the person who called General Walker on December 20, 1963, was a Gerald Crawford Vincent - White/Male of Kaplan, Louisiana. This person and his brother were intoxicated when this call was made.

The Federal District Attorney at New Orleans refused to take a complaint on this person.

Respectfully submitted,

E. L. Cunningham
Lieutenant, Forgery Bureau

ELC:mw

13

4-7-1a (Rev. 9-7-6

U

REPORT
of the
FBI
LABORATORY

FEDERAL BUREAU OF INVESTIGATION
WASHINGTON, D. C.

To: Mr. Jesse E. Curry
Chief of Police
Dallas, Texas

December 9, 1963

Airmail

This examination has been made with the understanding that the evidence is connected with an official investigation of a criminal matter and that the Laboratory report will be used for official purposes only, related to the investigation or a subsequent criminal prosecution. Authorization cannot be granted for the use of the Laboratory report in connection with a civil proceeding.

Re: UNKNOWN SUBJECT;
SHOOTING INTO HOME OF
EDWIN A. WALKER, APRIL 10, 1963

J. Edgar Hoover
John Edgar Hoover, Director

YOUR NO.
FBI FILE NO. 62-109060
LAB. NO. PC-78378 BX HB

Examination requested by: FBI, Dallas

Reference: Letter 12/2/63

Examination requested: Firearms - Spectrographic

Specimens:

Q188 Bullet from Edwin A. Walker's residence

Results of examination

The remaining physical characteristics of the bullet, Q188, are the same as those of the bullet and bullet fragments recovered in connection with the assassination of President John F. Kennedy and the same as those of 6.5 millimeter Mannlicher-Carcano bullets manufactured by the Western Cartridge Company. The mutilation of Q188 prevents stating that it is of Western manufacture to the exclusion of all other sources.

2 - FBI, Dallas

Page 1

(continued on next page)

14

(2)

Specimen Q188 was fired from a barrel rifled with four lands and grooves, right twist. Mannlicher-Carcano rifles of the type used in the assassination of President Kennedy (described as specimen K1 in Laboratory report PC-78243 BX) are among those which produce general rifling impressions such as were found on specimen Q188.

Because of the extreme mutilation and distortion of Q188 and because the individual microscopic marks left on bullets by the barrel of the K1 rifle could have changed subsequent to the time Q188 was fired, it was not possible to determine whether or not Q188 was fired from K1.

There are no specimens presently being maintained in the National Unidentified Ammunition File which could have been fired from the K1 rifle or which logically should be compared with Q188. Further, no bullets or rifles which logically should be compared with specimen Q188 have come to the attention of the FBI Laboratory since March, 1963.

The copper jacket and the lead core of the Q188 bullet were determined to be slightly different in compositions from the copper jackets and lead cores of the Q1 and Q2 bullets.

Although the differences in composition between the Q188 and the Q1 and Q2 bullets were small and do not indicate that these bullets represent two different types of bullets, it was not possible to determine if these bullets came from the same box. It is to be noted that there is no assurance in the fabrication of ammunition that all the ammunition ending up in one box possesses bullets from the same batch of metal, that is, with the same composition.

The bullet, Q188, is being temporarily retained in the Laboratory for comparison with any additional bullets which may be received.

Page 2
PC-78378 BX

14

REFER TO FILE CO-2-34,030

TREASURY DEPARTMENT
UNITED STATES SECRET SERVICE
FIELD FORCE

OFFICE Dallas
ADDRESS: P. O. LOCK BOX NO. 2089

Dallas, Texas, 75221
December 26, 1963

Mr. Jesse Curry,
Chief of Police,
Dallas, Texas.

Re: Attempted assassination of
General Edwin A. Walker, Dallas, Texas.

Dear Chief Curry:

The following information was developed by this Service relative to the attempted assassination of Retired General Edwin A. Walker, in Dallas, Texas, on April 10, 1963.

On December 2, 1963, there was received from the Irving Police Department, Irving, Texas, some belongings of Mrs. Marina Oswald which had been brought to the Police Station by Mrs. Ruth Paine with whom Mrs. Marina Oswald had been living. When these articles were examined in the Secret Service Office there was found in a book a note written in very poor Russian which was in the handwriting of Lee Harvey Oswald and which apparently was instructions to his wife what she should do in the event that he should be alive and taken as a prisoner.

On December 3, 1963 Mrs. Marina Oswald was questioned about this note by one of our special agents who speaks Russian and she stated that this note had nothing to do with the assassination of President Kennedy and that the note was written by her husband prior to his attempted assassination of former General Walker, whom she classified as the head of the Fascist Organization in the United States and who lived in Dallas, Texas, when they, the Oswalds, lived on Neely Street in Dallas; that the note, together with a Post Office key was left on a dresser of their bedroom and after reading the note she was afraid that her husband was planning on doing something dreadful due to his hate for the Fascist Organizations and their beliefs. She also stated that when her husband returned home late that night he was very nervous and finally told her that he shot Walker with his rifle and that it was best for everybody that he got rid of him.

Mrs. Oswald further stated that when it was learned the next day from radios and newspapers that the rifle shot fired by an unknown person had missed Walker that she decided to keep the note as a threat against her husband so that he would not mistreat her again (it was determined that when the Oswalds lived on Neely Street that people living downstairs beneath the Oswalds had complained to the landlord about Oswald beating his wife) which he had promised not to do. She further commented that she did not report this matter to the Police as she loved her husband and particularly that she did not report it to the Police on account of their child. She stated,

15

2.
CO-2-34,030

however, that had the shot hit General Walker, that she would have reported the matter to the Police. She was apprehensive about this matter being reported to the Police because she had a fear of being taken in custody by the Police because the information contained in this letter regarding the General Walker incident and the rifle would show that she had not told the Police all she knew when she was shown and questioned about the rifle that was used to assassinate President Kennedy.

On Dec. 10, 1963, our Special Agent had an opportunity to question Mrs. Marina Oswald more in detail regarding the General Walker incident and she stated that Lee Harvey Oswald told her that once before taking the shot at General Walker on April 10, 1963, he had gone to the Walker residence for the same purpose but he had changed his mind as the place had not looked just right for him and that 3 days prior to April 10, 1963, he took his rifle out of the house and buried it in a field near Walker's house. Mrs. Oswald further stated that upon her husband's return to the house after he had tried to kill General Walker and telling her about it that 3 days later she saw him taking his military green raincoat for the purpose of wrapping the rifle and bringing it home. However, she stated that when he returned home she did not see the rifle but several days later she saw the rifle on a shelf in the apartment where he always kept it. She also stated that the evening her husband shot at Walker he told her that the church which is located near the Walker house had some gathering; that there was plenty of noise and that after the shooting of Walker he buried the rifle in the same place.

Mrs. Marina Oswald further stated that Lee Harvey Oswald told her after reading in newspapers that some young man saw an automobile containing three men pulling away from the scene of the shooting, that the Americans always think they should have a car to get away from the scene of the crime but that he had rather use his feet to do so rather than a car, and he stated that he had taken a bus to go to the Walker residence and that he took a different bus to return home after the shooting.

Mrs. Marina Oswald was questioned as to how she was able to explain to her mother-in-law, Mrs. Marguerite Oswald, concerning the attempted assassination of General Walker by her husband, and she replied that she did to the best of her knowledge of the English language, and that no one else knew about the shooting at General Walker by her husband excepting her and her mother-in-law.

Very truly yours,

F. V. Sorrels

Forrest V. Sorrels,
Special Agent in Charge.

FVS:VS

15

COMMISSION EXHIBIT No. 2001—Continued

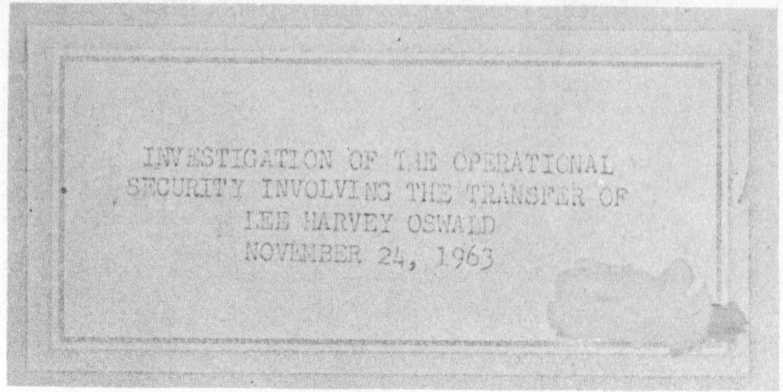

COMMISSION EXHIBIT No. 2002

December 19, 1963

Mr. J. E. Curry
Chief of Police

Sir:

Pursuant to your instructions of November 29, 1963, the unit assigned has completed an investigation of the Operational Security involving the transfer of Lee Harvey Oswald on November 24, 1963.

A summary of the investigation, along with an indexed complete investigative report, plus exhibits is forwarded under separate cover.

Respectfully submitted,

O. A. Jones

O. A. Jones
Captain of Police

OAJ:mw

COMMISSION EXHIBIT No. 2002—Continued

December 16, 1963

Mr. J. E. Curry
Chief of Police

Subject: Investigation of the Operational Security Involving the Transfer of Lee Harvey Oswald on November 24, 1963.

Sir:

The investigative team which you appointed on November 29, 1963, to make this investigation wishes to submit the following report:

Security was set up in the basement parking area of the City Hall at approximately 9 a.m. on Sunday, November 24, 1963. (See attachments)

The basement was searched and guards placed at all entrances. All unauthorized personnel were removed from the area. Security personnel and news media were then allowed to enter the basement.

An armored truck was ordered and arrived at the Commerce Street ramp at approximately 11:00 a.m. It was backed onto the ramp. The truck did not have sufficient clearance to be taken to the bottom of the ramp. The driver believed the truck might stall due to the weight if it was placed on the incline. It was then decided to leave the truck at the top of the Commerce Street ramp with the rear wheels on the incline and the front wheels on the sidewalk of the Commerce Street side of the City Hall.

The Jail Office corridor outside the Jail Office and the ramp area South of the Southeast corner of the Jail Office was cleared of everyone except security officers.

Plans were changed and Lieutenant R. S. Pierce drove a squad car out of the basement area and out the Main Street ramp. He was accompanied by Sergeants J. A. Putnam and B. J. Maxey. They made a left turn on Main Street, a left turn on Harwood Street and a left turn on Commerce Street. They were intending to lead the armored truck to the County Jail. The armored truck was to be a decoy and the prisoner was to be transferred in a plain car.

Detective Charles Brown drove a plain car on the Commerce Street ramp toward the armored truck. Detective C. N. Dhority then drove another plain car on the ramp behind Detective Charles Brown's car.

COMMISSION EXHIBIT No. 2002—Continued

Page 2

Detective C. N. Dhority was in the process of backing the car he was driving into position adjacent to the Jail Office entrance, when the prisoner was brought out of the Jail Office by Detectives J. R. Leavelle and L. C. Graves, preceded by Captain J. W. Fritz and Lieutenant R. E. Swain. They were followed by Detective L. D. Montgomery. The prisoner had taken a few steps toward the car.

Jack Ruby apparently was standing about 10 or 12 feet from the Southeast corner of the Jail Office, at the bottom of the Main Street Ramp near the pipe railing. Ruby lunged forward from a position between acting Detective W. J. Harrison and Robert S. Huffaker, Jr., a newsman for KRLD-TV. Ruby approached Lee Harvey Oswald with a revolver extended and fired one shot into Oswald below the rib cage on the left side.

The shot was fired at approximately 11:20 a.m. Ruby was immediately arrested. Lee Harvey Oswald expired at Parkland Hospital at 1:07 p.m.

This group interrogated 123 persons during the course of this investigation. This included 20 patrolmen, 21 reserves, 30 detectives, 19 supervisors, 13 reporters, 11 cameramen and 9 civilians. Most of the officers were assigned to provide security and the reporters and cameramen were in the basement at the time of the transfer. Only one of the civilians interrogated was in the basement at the time and this was Jack Ruby.

We have obtained the names of 10 newsmen that were in the basement that we have not been able to interview. We were able to determine there were approximately 10 members of the news media in the basement whose identity we have not been able to determine. It is believed these are newspaper correspondents representing publications from other areas of the country and even other countries. Time and money made the running down of these people inadvisable at this time, particularly since it is not believed that any of them could throw additional light on this matter.

Numerous side investigations which grew out of this investigation were also made. A separate report covering these incidents will be submitted.

We are convinced that our investigation has established to a reasonable certainty that Jack Leon Ruby entered the basement from the Main Street ramp and that no collusion existed between

COMMISSION EXHIBIT No. 2002—Continued

Page 3

him and any police officer or member of the press; that his entrance into the basement at this particular time was the result of a series of unfortunate coincidences which caused a momentary breakdown in the security measures adopted. We are also convinced that Ruby was in the basement for a maximum of 2 minutes.

The following evidence led us to the above conclusion:

I. Exhibit BB

A. Lieutenants Jack Revill and P. G. McCaghren interviewed Mr. Doyal Lane of 6549 Lake Circle, TA1-0560 at the Western Union Telegraph Company located at Main and Pearl Expressway in Dallas, Texas.

1. Mr. Lane is a supervisor for the Western Union Telegraph Company and was on duty at this location on November 24, 1963. At 11:16 a.m. Jack Ruby sent a $25.00 Money Order to an employee, Karen Bennett, Ft. Worth, Texas and was given a receipt which was stamped with the time (11:16 a.m.)

2. Mr. Lane was shown several photographs and he readily picked the photograph of Jack Ruby from these and stated that he knew Jack Ruby inasmuch as Ruby had sent several telegrams in the past.

II. Exhibit DD

A. Shows a distance of 339'6" from the Westernmost doorway at the Western Union Office to the center of the ramp leading into the basement of the City Hall from Main Street.

B. Shows a distance of 99' from the center of the sidewalk down the Main Street Ramp to a line running East from the Southeast corner of the Jail Office.

Page 4

C. Shows a distance of 16' from the Easternmost point of line mentioned in B above to point where Lee Oswald was shot.

D. Total minimum distance Ruby would have to travel to arrive at spot of shooting from doorway of Western Union equals 454'6".

III. Exhibit BB

A. Lieutenants Jack Revill and P. G. McCaghren on November 29, 1963, checked the time required to walk from inside the Western Union Office to the spot of the shooting in the basement of the City Hall.

1. It takes 1 minute and 13 seconds to walk this distance to the entrance of the Main Street ramp.

2. It requires another 22 seconds to walk down the ramp from Main Street to the location where Oswald was shot.

3. Total time required was 1 minute and 35 seconds.

IV. Exhibit CC

A. Lieutenants C. C. Wallace and P. G. McCaghren used a stop watch checking time required to walk from entrance of Western Union to location of Lee Oswald at time of shooting. Time required was 1 minute and 16 seconds.

B. It requires 10 seconds or more to go from the desk in the Western Union Office to the sidewalk outside the office.

C. Total time required was 1 minute and twenty-six seconds.

V. Time of Shooting

A. Patrolman Willie B. Slack (Attachment 91) called dispatcher for doctor and ambulance.

1. Dispatcher called O'Neal Funeral Home on "Hot Line" for ambulance.

(a) Funeral home logged call at 11:21 a.m., November 24, 1963.

(b) Funeral Home advised dispatcher to radio Ambulance 605 who was on the air.

2. Dispatcher notified Ambulance 605 at 11:22 a.m. November 24, 1963. (Exhibit BB) (Exhibit EE)

B. Statements by Ruby - Attachment 90.

1. To Lieutenants Jack Revill and F. I. Cornwall that he sent a telegram at 11:16 and did not speak to anyone in the basement prior to the shooting.

2. To Detective D. R. Archer (Attachment 2). "At this time P. T. Dean asked the suspect, Ruby, 'Jack, how did you get in the basement?' Ruby replied, 'You guys'll never believe this, but a little girl who works for me had called and asked that I send her some money to Ft. Worth. I had left my apartment, gone to Western Union at Main and the Expressway, and wired her $25.00. I left there and noticed the crowd around the City Hall. I walked up that way, thinking I might get a chance to see Oswald. As I reached the ramp that leads to the basement, I noticed Sam Pierce pull up from the ramp in a black car. The officer standing there turned to either answer a question or say something to Sam. - I don't know. As he did this, I walked down the ramp'."

Mr. Forrest Sorrells of the U. S. Secret Service was believed to be present at the time this statement was made to Sergeant Dean.

COMMISSION EXHIBIT No. 2002—Continued

3. To Detective B. S. Clardy (Attachment 17). "When asked why he shot Lee Oswald, Ruby replied, 'Somebody had to do it, Ya'll couldn't'. He said it was a spur of the moment thing and it was a million to one chance that he got down there at the actual time Oswald was brought down."

4. To Sergeant P. T. Dean (Attachment 27). "After Mr. Sorrells interrogated the subject I questioned Ruby as to how he had entered the basement and the length of time he had been there. Ruby then stated to me in the presence of Mr. Sorrells that he had entered the basement through the ramp entering on Main Street. He further stated that he would estimate his total time as about 3 minutes before the detectives brought Oswald into his view, then he immediately shot him (Oswald)."

5. To Detective T. D. McMillon(Attachment 74).

"We talked to him when we got to the fifth floor. On the fifth floor Ruby was asked how he got to the basement. He replied that he came from the Western Union Office where he wired a girl in Ft. Worth some money. He said he saw Rio Pierce drive out of the basement. He walked past the policeman standing there. He said a policeman hollered at him, but he ducked his head and kept going. He said that he knew he could always act like a reporter. He also said, 'Ya'll wont believe this, but I didn't have this planned. I couldn't have timed it so perfect.' He said just as he got there, Oswald was coming out."

6. To Patrolman W. J. Harrison (Attachment 45)

"'You all know me, I'm Jack Ruby'. One officer asked him why he did it, and he answered 'I hope I killed the S.O.B.'"

COMMISSION EXHIBIT No. 2002—Continued

VI. Car driven wrong way up Main Street Ramp.

A. Lieutenant R. S. Pierce, Sergeant Putnam and Sergeant Maxey were in car. (Attachments 85, 86 and 69.)

1. All statements state shooting occurred between time car left Main Street Ramp and arrival at Commerce Street Ramp.

B. Lieutenants C. C. Wallace and P. G. McCaghren interviewed Mr. Fritz Kuler of KRLD-TV. (Attachment 62) Mr. Kuler stated the video tape was continuous. The time recorded on the video machine of elapsed time from passage of Lieutenant Pierce's car in front of the TV camera until the sound of the shot was 56 seconds. This was checked twice.

VII. Officer R. E. Vaughn - Attachment 102.

A. Assigned to Main Street Ramp of City Hall.

B. Instructed by Sergeant P. T. Dean to guard the North Ramp.

C. Officer Vaughn questioned several people and admitted a city mechanic and 1 reporter.

D. Stepped out into Main Street to stop traffic and allow Lieutenant Pierce to make left turn onto Main Street.

E. Saw former Officer N. J. Daniels at Main Street Ramp.

F. Saw former shine-boy from locker room, Wilbert Ray Jones at Main Street Ramp.

G. Polygraph test showed truthful answers on all pertinent questions.

VIII. Statement of N. J. Daniels - Attachment 23.

A. Saw man enter Main Street Ramp.

B. Gave description of man.

C. Said man entered between himself and Officer Vaughn and the officer looked at him but did not stop him.

D. Polygraph test showed untruthfulness on all pertinent questions that were answered.

IX. Statement of Wilbert Ray Jones - Attachment 57

Had gone to parking lot at Commerce and Harwood at time of shot.

X. Statement of Reserve Officer W. J. Newman - Attachment 79.

Reserve Officer Newman saw someone running down the Main Street Ramp but could not definitely say the time. He believes it was about 1 minute before the shooting.

XI. Statement of Reserve Officer Sergeant Kenneth Croy - Attachment 21.

This officer gives description of man he believes to have been Jack Ruby, that was at foot of Main Street Ramp a while before the shooting. (Investigating Officers have determined that Robert Huffaker, KRLD-TV newsman was in this area at the time, and his clothes were identical to the clothing described by this officer.)

XII. Statements of Detectives B. L. Beaty and J. D. Hutchinson - Attachments 4 and 52.

These two detectives were stationed at the double doors leading into the City Hall from the basement parking area for more than 10 minutes before the shooting. They both knew Jack Ruby and neither saw him in the basement prior to the shooting. They say Ruby did not enter the basement area from the double doors from the Jail Office of the Police and Courts Building.

XIII. Statements of Sergeant Putnam, Reserve Captain Arnett and Reserve Lieutenant McCoy. - Attachments 86, 3 and 72.

These officers statements are regarding the search of the basement parking area and ramps and screening of personnel in area.

XIV. Newspaper article in Dallas Times Herald, Sunday, December 8, 1963. Statements of Darwin Payne, David Hughes and Sergeant P. T. Dean. - Attachments 82A, 50A and 27.

The article alleged that a Dallas Police Officer saw Jack Ruby as he came down the Main Street Ramp.

Sergeant Dean denied the allegation and the statements of the reporters and their notes show a presumption of the fact not confirmed by the evidence.

XV. Statement of Officer W. J. Harrison - Attachments 45 and 84-B.

Jack Ruby came from this officer's left side when he plunged forward to shoot Oswald.

Polygraph test by Detective P. L. Bentley shows that Officer Harrison did not see Ruby prior to the exit of Oswald from the Jail Office and did not recognize Ruby until instant shot was fired.

XVI. Security check of newsmen who entered the basement.

All members of the press who were interviewed stated their credentials were checked upon entering the basement, or that they knew the officers personally that admitted them to the basement.

COMMISSION EXHIBIT No. 2002—Continued

XVII. Use of Press Pass by Jack Ruby.

A. Statement by Eva Grant that she believed her brother had a Press Pass. See Exhibit 39-A.

B. Statement by Mr. Thad Ricks (Attachment 90) that no State Fair Pass was issued to Ruby.

C. Negative report from all officers and news media regarding seeing Ruby with a Press Pass.

D. An introductory card was found in Ruby's automobile glove compartment from former Judge Glen Byrd introducing the bearer as Jack Ruby and expressing appreciation for any help given bearer. (In Property Room)

XVIII. Conclusion:

A. This investigative team believes that Jack Ruby entered the Main Street ramp as the car driven by Lieutenant Rio Pierce was leaving the basement. Patrolman R. E. Vaughn was the only officer guarding the Main Street ramp at this time, and he had stepped into Main Street to halt traffic in order that Lieutenant Pierce could make a left turn onto Main Street.

B. We also feel it should be noted that no officer interviewed knew the time that Oswald was to be brought to the basement. The car that was to be used for the transfer was still in process of backing into position when Oswald was led from the Jail Office (Attachments 37 and 77)

C. The still pictures (Attachments 6-A and 53-A) show many of the detectives with their eyes on Oswald at the moment of the shooting, and not watching the viewers who were across the North Ramp and on the East side of the ramp

COMMISSION EXHIBIT No. 2002—Continued

Page 11

The bright lights illuminating area for the TV cameras were centered on the area adjacent to the Jail Office, making it difficult for the officers who were facing the lights and cameras to observe any movements originating from the Northeast side of the ramp.

D. These officers had been instructed to form two lines from the Jail Office door to the vehicle to be used for the transfer and to close in behind the prisoner. (See Attachments 4, 16, 18, 41, 52, 66, 87 and 104)

E. Exhibits 24-A, 43-A, GG & HH are sound films taken from video tape of the shooting.

F. Exhibit 84 is a silent film of the shooting.

The other members of this Unit, Lieutenants C. C. Wallace, Jack Revill, F. I. Cornwall, P. G. McCaghren and Detective H. M. Hart concur with the statements in this report.

Respectfully,

J. H. Sawyer
Inspector of Police

W. R. Westbrook
Captain of Police

O. A. Jones
Captain of Police

JHS:nw

COMMISSION EXHIBIT No. 2002—Continued

INDEX

1.	K. K. Anderson	Patrolman	Elm & Field
2.	D. R. Archer	Detective	Basement
3.	C. O. Arnett	Reserve	Basement
3-A	Charles Batchelor	Supervisor	Basement
4.	B. L. Beaty	Detective	Basement
5.	E. R. Beck	Detective	Basement
6.	Jack Beers	Photographer	Basement
6-A	Beers Photographs		Separate Exhibit
7.	D. G. Brantley	Detective	Basement
8.	B. R. Brock	Reserve	Basement
9.	J. D. Brockaway	Reserve	Basement
10.	C. W. Brown	Detective	Basement
11.	D. L. Burgess	Detective	Basement
12.	T. R. Burton	Patrolman	Commerce & Central
13.	George Butler	Supervisor	Basement
14.	V. C. Campbell	Detective	Basement
15.	A. W. Capps	Reserve	Commerce Street Sidewalk
16.	W. E. Chambers	Detective	Basement
17.	B. S. Clardy	Detective	Basement
18.	B. H. Combest	Detective	Basement
19.	R. A. Cox	Reserve	Commerce Street Ramp
20.	A. B. Craig	Reserve	Basement
21.	K. Croy	Reserve	Basement
22.	W. J. Cutchshaw	Detective	Basement
23.	N. J. Daniels	Civilian	Outside Main Street Ramp
24.	J. R. Davidson	Reporter	Basement
24-A	ABC-TV Sound Film		Separate Exhibit
25.	R. T. Davis	Reserve	Commerce & Harwood
26.	H. Dawson	Detective	Basement
27.	P. T. Dean	Supervisor	Basement
28.	Nolan Dement	Civilian	Commerce St.-Outside City Hall
29.	C. N. Dhority	Detective	Basement
30.	J. B. English	Cameraman	Basement
31.	D. K. Erwin	Patrolman	Commerce & Pearl Expressway
32.	N. E. Farris	Patrolman	Elm & Lamar
33.	Warren Furgeson	Reporter	Basement
34.	Bob Fenley	Reporter	Basement
35.	L. L. Fox	Patrolman	Harwood & Elm
36.	W. B. Frazier	Supervisor	Not at City Hall
37.	J. W. Fritz	Supervisor	Basement
38.	C. Goolsby	Detective	Basement
39.	Eva Grant	Civilian	Not present
39-A	Sound Tape of Eva Grant Interview		Separate Exhibit
40.	L. C. Graves	Detective	Basement
41.	C. A. Greeson	Detective	Basement
42.	T. R. Gregory	Patrolman	Central & Elm
43.	R. Hankal	Cameraman	Basement
43-A	KRLD-TV Sound Film		Separate Exhibit
43-B	KRLD-TV Still Pictures		Separate Exhibit
44.	O. W. Harrison	Reserve	Commerce Street Ramp

COMMISSION EXHIBIT No. 2002—Continued

45.	W. J. Harrison	Acting Detective	Basement
46.	H. H. Hatley	Reserve	Houston & Elm
47.	W. E. Hibbs	Patrolman	Akard & Elm
48.	H. B. Holly	Reserve	Main & Harwood-after shooting
49.	J. R. Hopkins	Reserve	Commerce Street Ramp
50.	R. S. Huffaker	Reporter	Basement
50-A	David Hughes	Reporter	Not Present
51.	J. C. Hunt	Reserve	Elm & Houston
52.	J. D. Hutchinson	Detective	Basement
53.	Robert Jackson	Photographer	Basement
53-A	Still Pictures by Robert Jackson		Separate Exhibit
54.	L. E. Jez	Patrolman	Basement
55.	F. B. Johnston	Cameraman	Basement
55-A	Still Pictures by Johnston		Separate Exhibit
56.	O. A. Jones	Supervisor	Basement
57.	W. R. Jones	Civilian	Main St. Ramp & Parking Lot of Commerce
58.	Seth Kantor	Reporter	Basement
59.	J. Kasten	Reserve	Sidewalk-Commerce St.
60.	G. D. King	Supervisor	Basement
61.	H. M. Kriss	Reserve	Basement
62.	F. Kuler	Reporter	Not present
63.	J. R. Leaville	Detective	Basement
64.	C. G. Lewis	Patrolman	Jail Elevator
65.	Joe Long	Newsman	Not present
66.	R. L. Lowery	Detective	Basement
66-A	G. L. Lumpkin	Supervisor	Basement
67.	R. H. Lunday	Supervisor	Not Present
68.	F. M. Martin	Supervisor	Basement
69.	B. J. Maxey	Sergeant	Car on Main & Harwood
70.	R. L. Mayo	Reserve	Commerce St. (South Side)
71.	J. C. McCain	Reserve	Commerce St. (North Side)
72.	B. C. McCoy	Reserve	Basement
73.	H. M. McGee	Detective	Basement
74.	T. D. McMillon	Detective	Basement
75.	B. Morrell	Reserve	Assembly Room
76.	L. D. Miller	Detective	Basement
77.	L. D. Montgomery	Detective	Basement
78.	R. C. Nelson	Patrolman	Outside Jail Office window
79.	W. J. Newman	Reserve	Basement
80.	J. F. Newton	Civilian	Jail Office
80-A	Ike Pappas	Reporter (Not interviewed)	Basement
81.	D. L. Pate	Patrolman	Basement
82.	B. G. Patterson	Patrolman	Basement
82-A	Darwin Payne	Reporter	Not Present
83.	Francois Pelou	Reporter	Basement
83-A	Tom Petit	Reporter (Not interviewed)	Basement
84	George Phenix	Cameraman	Basement
84-A	Silent Film by Phenix		Separate Exhibit
84-B	Still Shots from Phenix Film		Separate Exhibit
85.	R. S. Pierce	Supervisor	Car - Main & Harwood
86.	J. A. [illegible]tnam	Supervisor	Car - Main & Harwood
87.	J. K. Ramsey	Detective	Basement

COMMISSION EXHIBIT No. 2002—Continued

88.	J. Raz	Patrolman	Elm & Stone
89.	N. B. Neynolds	Detective	Basement
89-A	Warren Richey	Newsman	Truck on Commerce Street
90.	Jack Ruby	Civilian	Basement
91.	W. B. Slack	Patrolman	Jail Office
92.	J. D. Slocum	Civilian	Jail Office
93.	V. S. Smart	Supervisor	Basement
93-A	Mike Smith	Reporter (Not interviewed)	Basement
93-B	Johnny Smith	Newsman	Truck on Commerce
94.	D. F. Steele	Supervisor	Elm & Houston
95.	I. R. Stephens	Detective	Basement
95-A	M. W. Stevenson	Supervisor	Basement
96.	R. E. Swain	Supervisor	Basement
97	C. E. Talbert	Supervisor	Basement
97-A	John Tankersly	Cameraman	Basement
98.	L. C. Taylor	Patrolman	Basement
99	Robert Thornton	Reporter	Basement
99-A	Sound Tape by R. Thornton		Separate Exhibit
99-B	Transcription of Sound Tape		
99-C	David Timmons	Cameraman	Basement
100	G. L. Tolbert	Patrolman	Elm & Pearl
100-A	Unknown Japanese	Reporter (Not interviewed)	Basement
100-B	Unknown	Reporter (Not interviewed)	Basement
100-C	Jimmy Turner	Cameraman	Basement
101	I. F. VanCleave	Detective	Basement
102	R. E. Vaughn	Patrolman	Main Street Ramp
102-A	Homer Venso	Cameraman	Basement
103.	H. J. Wages	Patrolman	Main & Central
104.	R. C. Wagner	Detective	Basement
105.	R. A. Watkins	Patrolman	Basement
106.	J. C. Watson	Detective	Basement
107.	W. Wiggins	Supervisor	Basement
108.	M. L. Wise	Patrolman	Elm & St. Paul
109.	G. E. Worley	Reserve	Basement
110.	Tony Zoppi	Reporter	Not Present
111.	Exhibit AA-1	Transcript of Chief Curry's Time of Transfer	Statement
	Exhibit AA	Tape of Chief Curry's Statement	Separate Exhibit
112.	Exhibit BB	Mr. Doyal Lane (Western Union) Time Telegram Sent	
113.	Timing of walk from Western Union and of Lt. Pierce's Squad Car.		
	Exhibit DD	Map of Basement	Separate Exhibit
114.	Radio Call sheet for Ambulance		
115.	News Media present in basement but not interviewed		
	Exhibit GG	Sound Film from WBAP-TV	Separate Exhibit
	Exhibit HH	Sound Film from WBAP-TV	Separate Exhibit

COMMISSION EXHIBIT No. 2002—Continued

November 26, 1963

Mr. J. E. Curry
Chief of Police

Subject: Assignment of Officer
K. K. Anderson, #1336
Sunday, November 24, 1963

Sir:

At approximately 9:00 A.M., November 24, 1963, I received a Radio call to report to Patrol office. I arrived at about 9:15 A.M. I was instructed to remain there until I received other instructions. At about 9:45 A.M. I was instructed to report to Sgt. Dean in the basement.

I was then assigned to Elm Street and Field Street by Sgt. P. T. Dean for traffic assignment. I went immediately to my assignment.

At approximately 11:35 A.M., I received a Radio call to report to Parkland Hospital. I arrived at 5200 block of Harry Hines Blvd. and worked traffic at this location.

Respectfully submitted,

Kenneth K. Anderson
Kenneth K. Anderson
Patrolman #1336
Patrol Division

KKA/ch

COMMISSION EXHIBIT No. 2002—Continued

December 2, 1963

STATEMENT OF K. K. ANDERSON:

I left the basement of the City Hall about 10:15 A. M. for my traffic assignment, and did not return prior to the shooting.

I do not know Jack Ruby.

COMMISSION EXHIBIT No. 2002—Continued

December 1, 1963

J. E. Curry
Chief of Police

Re: Shooting of Lee Harvey Oswald
Interview of D. R. Archer

Sir:

D. R. Archer was interviewed by Lieutenants C. C. Wallace and F. G. McCaghren at 3:00 pm November 30, 1963. The interview was essentially the same as his original report dated November 27, 1963. The following was added by D. R. Archer:

I have been asked if I know Jack Ruby, and I do not. He was pointed out to me by another officer. This was several years ago.

After assisting in apprehending this subject and carrying him directly to the 5th floor along with Captain King, Detectives Clardy and Mc Millan, where we immediately took him back to an investigative section of the jail, we very carefully searched the subject for any weapons, not necessarily personal property, turning it over to the jailer which was Hanky, as we went. Then we removed all the clothing, leaving the subject only in his shorts with the thought of keeping him from harming himself or concealing another weapon. Shortly after we had completed this procedure, Sgt. P. T. Dean brought Mr. Sorrels, who I believe is in charge of Secret Service, into the room to interview this subject. At this time P. T. Dean asked the suspect Ruby, "Jack how did you get into the basement." Ruby replied, "You guys'll never believe this, but a little girl who works for me had called me and asked that I send her some money to Ft. Worth. I had left my apartment, gone to Western Union at Main and the Expressway, and wired her $25.00. I left there, and noticed the crowd around City Hall. I walked up that way, thinking I might get a chance to see Oswald. As I reached the ramp that leads to the basement, I noticed Sam Pierce pull up from the ramp in a black car. The officer standing there turned to either answer a question or say something to Sam, I don't know. As he did this, I walked down the ramp." This is to the best of my knowledge and memory of the exact conversation that took place at that time.

After seeing this suspect up in the jail after his initial arrest, I do know that I did not see this suspect in the area prior to this shooting or any other time in the City Hall.

Respectfully submitted,

C C Wallace
C. C. Wallace, Lieutenant
Juvenile Bureau

F G McCaghren
F. G. McCaghren, Lieutenant
Burglary & Theft Bureau

lh

2

COMMISSION EXHIBIT No. 2002—Continued

1

AFFIDAVIT IN ANY FACT

THE STATE OF TEXAS
COUNTY OF DALLAS

BEFORE ME, ______

a Notary Public in and for said County, State of Texas, on this day personally appeared ______

Who, after being by me duly sworn, on oath deposes and says: I was stationed on the North side door that exits into the basement from in front of the jail office and just South of the jail door in the basement garage corridor. As Oswald was brought past me he was being led by Captain Fritz and was between two Detectives. As they reached the edge of the ramp I saw a man dressed in a suit wearing a gray hat dart in front of Oswald and just behind "Captain Fritz." I distinctive heard the suspect shout a phrase, the only word I could make out was "Son of a bitch."

SUBSCRIBED AND SWORN TO BEFORE ME THIS ____ DAY OF ______ A.D. 196

Notary Public, Dallas County, Texas

CPS-GF-413

2

COMMISSION EXHIBIT No. 2002—Continued

2

AFFIDAVIT IN ANY FACT

THE STATE OF TEXAS
COUNTY OF DALLAS

BEFORE ME, ______

a Notary Public in and for said County, State of Texas, on this day personally appeared ______

Who, after being by me duly sworn, on oath deposes and says: Before I could move I saw someone grab his arm and at this time I caught a glimpse of a pistol and heard the report of the shot. Oswald shouted "Oh No!" and collapsed. As I started forward ~~&~~ I was cut off by the officers that had dove on the suspect and was pushed back. I then assisted in draging the prisoner to the jail office where he was held on the floor until Detective McMillon could get the hand

SUBSCRIBED AND SWORN TO BEFORE ME THIS ____ DAY OF ______ A.D. 196

Notary Public, Dallas County, Texas

CPS-GF-413

2

COMMISSION EXHIBIT No. 2002—Continued

3

AFFIDAVIT IN ANY FACT

THE STATE OF TEXAS
COUNTY OF DALLAS

BEFORE ME, ______

a Notary Public in and for said County, State of Texas, on this day personally appeared ______

Who, after being by me duly sworn, on oath deposes and says: cuffs on the prisoner. I asked "who is it?" and ~~the~~ the suspect turned his head my way and shouted "you know me, I'm Jack Ruby!" We then picked him up, and along with Captain King, Detective Clardy, Detective McMillon ~~escorted~~ and myself, we took him to the jail elevator and went directly to the fifth floor. We then removed his personal property, took off his clothes, and stayed with him until 3:30 Pm when Homicide officers came

SUBSCRIBED AND SWORN TO BEFORE ME THIS ____ DAY OF ______ A.D. 196__.

______
Notary Public, Dallas County, Texas

CPS-GF-413

2

3

4

AFFIDAVIT IN ANY FACT

THE STATE OF TEXAS
COUNTY OF DALLAS

BEFORE ME, ______

a Notary Public in and for said County, State of Texas, on this day personally appeared ______

Who, after being by me duly sworn, on oath deposes and says: to the jail and asked us to assist in escorting him to the Homicide Bureau, which we did and then returned to our office: the Auto Theft Bureau.

D. R. Archer 1028
11/24/63 4:15 Pm

SUBSCRIBED AND SWORN TO BEFORE ME THIS ____ DAY OF ______ A.D. 196__.

______
Notary Public, Dallas County, Texas

CPS-GF-413

4

2

November 27, 1963

Mr. J. E. Curry
Chief of Police

Sir:

This is a statement of facts relating to my activity as a Reserve Officer Sunday, November 24, 1963, to the best of my knowledge and recollection.

1. Approximate time I reported to duty. 9:00 A. M.

2. I reported to Lt. Merrell in Assembly Room.

3. I was assigned to - My first act was to request transportation for five Reserves to the Elm-Houston Area. Request was through Chief Lunday and Lt. Wiggins. A squad transferred these men. Sgt. Dean requested some men to assist in searching the basement. I summoned all the men we had on call in the assembly room at this time (approximately 10 men) and went with Sgt. Dean to the basement. Sgt. Dean and Sgt. Putnam directed the Reserves to other regular officers that were in process of searching the basement. When the search was completed and men assigned to a post, I took a position where the cars would enter the parking area from the ramp.

   I remained in this position until Reserve J. C. Hunt took this position. I then took a position at the base of the North ramp where it levels off. I remained at this position until after the shooting. Persons who were at this same position just prior to and at the time of the shooting were: A newsman with a microphone next to the west wall, then myself, then another newsman with a pencil and paper, then Capt. King, then another person to the east of Capt. King. Officer Blackie Harrison along with others I did not know the names of were directly ahead of the group I was with.

   After men had been assigned, Police Supervisors were requesting men, if we could spare them, and several were taken to other postions outside the basement. Some Reserve Supervisors who had no particular assignment took these positions that were being vacated.

   I saw Capt. Fritz entering the basement from the jail office, approximately four or five feet behind were the detectives with Oswald. Just as they entered the driveway I saw a man lunge (from beside the TV Camera that was on the east side of the drive where you enter the parking area) toward Oswald. I did not see the gun until after the shooting.

4. Names of other officers in the same area that I can recollect are: Capt. King, Sgt. Dean & Putnam, Capt. Talbert, Det. Beaty, Harrison, Lt. Wiggins, Officer Slack, Chief Batchelor.
   Reserves - Lts. McCoy, Kriss, Suits, Sgt. Croy, J. C. Hunt, H. H. Hatley, R. A. Cox, J. R. Hopkins, G. E. Worley, Kasten.

3

COMMISSION EXHIBIT No. 2002—Continued

5. Did you know Ruby? Not my name - but by sight as a night club operator.

6. When and under what circumstances did you see Ruby?

   See statement in body of report.

Signed: C O Arnett
C. O. Arnett, Reserve Captain

2

COMMISSION EXHIBIT No. 2002—Continued

December 9, 1963

Mr. J. E. Curry
Chief of Police

Re: Interview of Reserve Officer
Captain C. O. Arnett - #955

Sir:

On December 9, 1963, Reserve Officer, Captain C. O. Arnett was interviewed by the undersigned officers as to any information he might have concerning the shooting of Lee Harvey Oswald not covered in his original report dated November 24, 1963. After having read his original report Arnett stated that he recalls observing Lieutenant Pierce's driving a police squad car out of the basement of the City Hall via the Main Street ramp. This occurred just prior to the shooting of Oswald. He recalls assisting in moving members of the news media out of the path of the vehicle so it could exit from the City Hall. After the police vehicle drove off, a group of the news media and police officers regrouped at the foot of the Main Street ramp. Captain Arnett also recalls the white police vehicle being moved into line at the base of the ramp of the City Hall. This was also prior to the shooting.

In his original report, Captain Arnett stated that he knew of Ruby as a night club operator but that he did not know him by sight.

Captain Arnett stated that he has been interviewed by the Federal Bureau of Investigation.

Respectfully submitted,

F. I. Cornwall
F. I. Cornwall
Lieutenant, Special Service Bureau

Jack Revill
Jack Revill
Lieutenant, Special Service Bureau

JR:nw

2

December 12, 1963

Inspector J. H. Sawyer talked to Assistant Chief of Police, Mr. Chas. Batchelor and received the following statement:

"I went to the basement area of the City Hall at about 11:00 a.m. on the morning of November 24, 1963, to help in the transfer of Lee Harvey Oswald to the County Jail.

At the time of the shooting, I was standing about half way between the 2 detective's cars that were parked on the ramp. I was East of these 2 cars. I did not see the shooting. I heard someone call out "Here he comes", and I started up the ramp towards Commerce Street to close a door on the armored truck when I heard a shot.

I turned and went back and saw several officers struggling with someone on the floor. I didn't see who it was that had done the shooting until I went into the Jail Office where they had taken Jack Ruby. While in the Jail Office I watched the detectives struggling with Jack Ruby on the floor putting handcuffs on him.

I did not know Jack Ruby prior to his shooting of Lee Harvey Oswald."

J. H. Sawyer
Inspector of Police

JHS:nw

3A

November 27, 1963

Mr. J. E. Curry
Chief of Police

SUBJECT: Shooting of Lee Harvey Oswald

Sir:

On Sunday, November 24, 1963, about 11:00 A.M., I was in the basement of the City Hall, Police Courts Building. Captain O. A. Jones walked by and told me that some detectives from the third floor would be down shortly and for me to remain there and tell them to wait for him in front of the jail office window.

We were assigned to the basement hallway of the jail office by Captain O. A. Jones, evenly divided on each side of the hallway. Our instructions were to keep the hallway clear all the way to the armored car.

R. L. Lowery, B. H. Combest, Jerry Hutchinson, and myself and possibly some more, were assigned to the South side of the hallway directly across from the outside entrance to the jail office. On the other side of the hall were Charles Goolsby, James Watson, W. E. Chambers, W. J. Harrison and W. J. Cutshaw. I am not sure of the order of their stations.

About ten minutes passed when Captain Jones came over with Sergeant Putnam and they both told the people of the press to clear the hallway completely and to move out into the drive North of the hallway and to the East of the ramp drive where the armored car was parked. They then told them not to ask Oswald any questions as he was leaving the building.

About 11:30 A.M. Lieutenant R. E. Swain came out of the door of the jail office followed by Captain Fritz. The lights from the many cameras came on immediately. Following Captain Fritz was J. R. Leavelle, Lee Harvey Oswald and L. C. Graves. Following these was L. D. Montgomery.

- 1 -

wPG

2

4

About half way out of the hallway the press began to reach at Oswald with microphones asking him to make a statement.

I took one step into the hall anticipating following Oswald, Graves and Leavelle to the armored car. I heard a shot and looked over to see many police officers subduing Jack Ruby. I saw L. C. Graves take a snub-nose pistol from Ruby's hand as he was forced to the floor.

From where I was stationed, just inside the jail office hallway, I could see one police office and a reserve officer. They were stationed at the windows of the jail office and were checking everyone that came in and out of this entrance. I recall that either one or both had been there since 9:30 A.M., this date, and that on one occasion Melba Espinosa, an employee at the Information Desk, was refused admittance to the basement.

Never during the entire operation did I see anyone enter or leave the basement without being properly identified and in many instances searched. I never did see Ruby until after I heard the shot.

The following is a list of the officers I remember seeing close by:

B. H. Combest	Charles Goolsby
J. H. Hutchinson	W. E. Chambers
W. J. Harrison	Captain Frank Martin
Wilbur Cutshaw	Lieutenant W. Wiggins
James Watson	L. D. Miller
R. L. Lowery	R. U. Waggner

Respectfully submitted,

B. L. Beaty

B. L. Beaty, Detective
Special Service Bureau
Narcotic Section

BLB:mjr

4

November 29, 1963

Mr. J. E. Curry
Chief of Police

Sir:

Re: Interview of Detective B. L. Beaty, 637

On November 29, 1963 Detective B. L. Beaty was interviewed by the undersigned officers as to any information he might have concerning the shooting of Lee Harvey Oswald which was not covered in Beaty's original report dated November 27, 1963.

Detective Beaty stated, after reading his original report, that he had nothing of significance to add. He stated that he had known Jack Ruby for several years, but that on the date of Oswald's shooting he had not observed Ruby in the basement of City Hall.

Detective Beaty stated the he has not been interviewed by any federal agency at this time.

Respectfully submitted,

Jack Revill

Jack Revill, Lieutenant
Special Service Bureau

F. I. Cornwall

F. I. Cornwall, Lieutenant
Special Service Bureau

4

REPORT ON OFFICER'S DUTIES IN REGARDS TO OSWALD'S MURDER

E. R. BECK - #45

On Sunday, November 24, 1963, I got to the office at 6:30 AM.

At about 9:30 AM, Det. Leavelle, Graves, and Dhority went to the Jail to bring Oswald to Capt. Fritz's office. Det. Brown, Montgomery and myself waited at the third floor Jail elevator door and helped get Oswald to our office.

At about 11:10 AM, Capt. Fritz told Dets. Dhority, Brown, and myself to go to the basement and get the cars set up for Oswald's transfer. He told Det. Dhority to put his car by the Jail door, and for me to drive the lead car. Capt. Fritz told me that we would go to Commerce, East on Commerce to Preston, North to Main, then West on Main, and when we got to the entrance of the Jail on Main, I was to drive past the entrance, so that they could drive into the Jail entrance.

When we got to the basement, we had some trouble lining up the cars because of the TV cameras and the press. Detective Dhority was backing Capt. Fritz's car into position. I was standing just to the rear of the lead car telling Det. Brown to back up just a little more, when a shot was fired, and I ran back and helped Lt. Swain get the crowd back. I went into the Jail office, and Oswald was lying on the floor on the North side of the office and several officers had a man on the floor that I later found out was Jack Ruby.

An ambulance arrived and Oswald was placed in the ambulance, and Det. Graves, Dhority, and Leavelle went in the ambulance to Parkland. I got my

5

COMMISSION EXHIBIT No. 2002—Continued

E. R. BECK - Page 2 - (Oswald Murder)

car and Capt. Fritz got in the front seat, and Det. Montgomery and Brown in the back, and we went to Parkland Hospital. We went to Emergency Room, and the doctors and nurses were working on Oswald. Shortly after we arrived, Oswald was taken from the Emergency Room to the Operating Room on the Second floor. Capt. Fritz and I left the second floor and returned to our office, along with Det. Montgomery.

After we had gotten back to the office, Jack Ruby was brought to Capt. Fritz's office at 3:25 PM, and I helped other officers get him from the Jail Elevator door to our office. After Capt. Fritz talked to Jack Ruby, I helped other officers get him back to the elevator door.

5

COMMISSION EXHIBIT No. 2002—Continued

Mr. J. E. Curry
Chief of Police

December 5, 1963

Re: Interview with Jack Beers
Photographer - Dallas Morning News

Sir:

Mr. Beers was interviewed at approximately 3:00 p.m. on December 4, 1963. He had taken the position on the railing to the left of the 2 mounted cameras. Mr. Beers first picture shows Ruby as he lunged towards Oswald and fired the shot. He immediately took 7 other pictures in quick succession that recounts most of the activity following the shooting. These pictures will also enable us to establish the positions of many detectives as the prisoner was being brought from the jail office.

Mr. Beers is well acquainted with Jack Ruby but does not recall seeing him in the crowd prior to the shooting.

We are in possession of all of Beer's photographs.

Respectfully submitted,

P. J. McCaghren
Lieutenant, Burglary & Theft Bureau

C. C. Wallace
Lieutenant, Juvenile Bureau

nw

6

November 30, 1963

J. E. Curry
Chief of Police

Re: Shooting of Lee Harvey Oswald
D. G. Brantley

Sir:

D. G. Brantley was interviewed by Lieutenants C. C. Wallace and P. G. McCaghren at 9:35 am on November 30, 1963. The interview was essentially the same as his original report dated November 27, 1963. The following was added by D. G. Brantley:

I have been asked if I know Jack Ruby, and I do. I did not see him in the basement of the City Hall prior to the shooting. I never have seen him in the City Hall. The first time I saw him after the shooting was when they were taking him to the jail office.

I have no idea how this person Jack Ruby got into the basement of the City Hall.

On my original report dated November 27, 1963, I stated that I was accompanied on the elevator by Detective McGee. I also recall that Detectives Burgess and Van Cleave were on the elevator. Detective McGee and I helped two WBAP television cameramen push their camera off the elevator.

I have not been interviewed by the Federal Bureau of Investigation or anyone else regarding this incident.

Respectfully submitted,

C. C. Wallace, Lieutenant
Juvenile Bureau

P. G. McCaghren, Lieutenant
Burglary & Theft Bureau

lh

7

Copy—

November 27, 1963

J. E. Curry
Chief of Police

SUBJECT: Information regarding the murder of Lee Oswald

Sir:

On November 24, 1963 at about 11:15am, I was told by Lt. Swain to report to the lobby of the basement of the City Hall, and station myself somewhere in the basement lobby and stand by, as Oswald was being transferred to the County Jail.

I rode down on the elevator with Detective McGee. We were accompanied by two cameramen and their camera from WBAP TV. At that time Jack Ruby was not with them. I saw them as they pushed the camera through the lobby into the crowd of newsmen.

I went immediately to the lobby and stationed myself in front of the first window of the jail office and proceeded to watch for anything out of the ordinary in my area. At that time the lobby was crowded with cameramen and reporters. I saw Oswald as he was escorted from the elevator by several officers across the jail office to the ramp door at which point I lost sight of him.

Moments later I heard a shot and looked out the ramp area and saw several officers struggling with a white male. I immediately ran out into the ramp area and observed several officers carrying someone back into the jail office.

I was told at that time by Captain Jones to guard the door to the jail office. I remained at the door until later I was told by Captain Jones to go with Lt. McKinney to Parkland. I was stationed at the door of the Intensive Care Ward by Lt. McKinney, and remained at that location until told to return to the City Hall.

Respectfully submitted.

D G Brantley

D. G. Brantley 1012
Detective
Burglary & Theft Bureau

DGB/lh

7

COMMISSION EXHIBIT No. 2002—Continued

November 29, 1963

Statement of A. R. Brock:

At approximately 10:45 A. M., I left the City Hall Basement and was assigned to traffic at Elm and Ervay.

I know Jack Ruby by sight, but I did not see him at the City Hall on this date.

8

COMMISSION EXHIBIT No. 2002—Continued

November 26, 1963

Mr. J. E. Curry
Chief of Police

Subject: Assignment of Officer
Alvis R. Brock.#1661
Sunday, November 24, 1963

Sir:

On November 24, 1963 at about 9 A.M. I was advised to report to 511. At approximately 9:25 A.M. Lt. Pierce told me to report to Sgt. Dean in the Basement.

Sgt. Putnam assigned me to the elevators on the East side of the Basemen My instructions were to let no one but Police Officers and Newsmen into the basement and to check I.D. on everyone. There were several city employees standing in this area looking. I told these people to leave and advised the elevator operator to keep the elevator on the first floor. The only person using the elevator after this was a T.V. man who went to the fifth floor and returned. The elevator operator was told not to answer the buzzer to the Basement again. I remained at this assignment until about 10:45 when Sgt. Dean and Sgt. Putnam called several of us together for traffic assignments.

I was assigned to Elm and Ervay to stop traffic and reported immediately to this location. I remained there until about 11:30 A.M., when my partner picked me up and we reported to Parkland Hospital for assignment.

Respectfully submitted,

Alvis R. Brock
Patrolman, #1661
Patrol Division

ARB/eh

8

COMMISSION EXHIBIT No. 2002—Continued

November 27, 1963

Mr. J. E. Curry
Chief of Police

Sir:

This is a statement of facts relating to my activity as a Reserve Officer Sunday, November 24, 1963, to the best of my knowledge and recollection.

1. Approximate time I reported to duty. 11:25 A. M.

2. I reported to Assembly Room - Lt. Merrell.

3. Assignment - Lt. Merrell told me every one was busy searching and guarding the basement, that Oswald was about to be brought down. I went from the Assembly Room to the area and just as I was about to open the doors that lead into the parking area, it happened. I heard the shot. I had caught a glimpse of them bringing Oswald from the elevator. Then, I joined a group of Reserves in sealing off the area leading into the jail office where they took Oswald and Ruby. I don't believe any regular officer was there with us, but we sensed that the reporters and cameras should not be allowed to push their way into the jail office.

4. Names of other officers in the same area that I can recollect are:

   Lt. Merrell, A. B. Craig, and others I do not know their names.

5. Did you know Ruby? No.

6. When and under what circumstance did you see Ruby?

   Never could see him.

Signed: J. D. Brockway
J. D. Brockway

9

COMMISSION EXHIBIT No. 2002—Continued

November 30, 1963

Mr. J. E. Curry
Chief of Police

Sir:

Re: Interview of Reserve Officer,
Patrolman Jimmy D. Brockway, 398

On November 30, 1963 Reserve Officer, Patrolman Jimmy D. Brockway was interviewed by the undersigned officers as to any information he might have concerning the shooting of Lee Harvey Oswald which was not covered in his original report dated November 27, 1963.

The only discrepancy found in his original report is that he reported on duty at approximately 11:10 a.m. instead of 11:25 a.m. as originally reported. He further stated that he entered the Police and Courts Building via the basement doors on the Commerce Street side and that there was no one on duty at these doors. However, he stated that there was a reserve officer on duty on the sidewalk just outside these doors. Brockway does not remember who this reserve officer was.

Brockway further states that he has not been contacted by any federal agency at this time.

Respectfully submitted,

F. I. Cornwall
F. I.Cornwall, Lieutenant
Special Service Bureau

Jack Revill
Jack Revill, Lieutenant
Special Service Bureau

jh

9

COMMISSION EXHIBIT No. 2002—Continued

REPORT ON OFFICER'S DUTIES IN REGARDS TO OSWALD'S DEATH

C. W. BROWN - #759

On the 24th of November, 1963, I reported to work at 7:00 am driving Squad Car #376. After an interview of the suspect, Lee Harvey Oswald, by Captain Fritz, I was told to get my car and get in position in front of the other squad that was to carry Oswald to the County Jail. At approximately 11:40 am, I went to the City Hall basement and drove my car about half way up the south ramp, which leads out to Commerce Street, and my partner, Dhority, moved the other squad car up behind me. We both started attempting to back up to the jail office door when I heard a shot. I immediately put the emergency brake on and ran back to the other car. By this time, other officers had removed Lee Harvey Oswald and Jack Ruby into the jail office. I went back to my car and moved it back into the parking area so the ambulance could get through. When the ambulance arrived, Captain Fritz, Dets. F. R. Beck, L. D. Montgomery and I proceeded behind the ambulance to Parkland Hospital and set up security, first in the Emergency Room, then to the fourth floor, where Oswald underwent surgery. After Oswald died at 1:07 pm, the body was removed to the X-ray room on the ground floor. Judge Pierce McBride was contacted via telephone, and he reported to the morgue desk and gave authorization for a post mortem to be performed by Dr. Rose of the Parkland Staff. Dr. Rose took charge of the body, and I went with him and got the wife and mother of Oswald from the waiting room and let them view the body in the X-ray room. After the relatives viewed the body, I accompanied it along with my partner, C. N. Dhority, and Dr. Rose to the Morgue. At the Morgue, Dhority and I witnessed the preliminary photos taken of the body by Dr. Rose and his staff. After this, I returned to the office and continued our investigative work there.

10

November 27, 1963

J.E. Curry
Chief of Police

SUBJECT: Information Concerning the Murder of Lee Harvey Oswald

Sir:

At approximately 11:00 or 11:15a.m., I was instructed by Lieutenant Swain to leave the Burglary and Theft Bureau and report to the area near the information desk to assist in any manner needed in the transfer of Lee Harvey Oswald and await further instruction.

I rode down the elevator with several other detectives and a WBAP-TV camera and two newsmen with this camera.

I walked off the elevator and took a post near the jail office window to observe the crowd of photographers and newsmen who were in this area.

I was standing near the jail office window when the prisoner was escorted through the jail office. When he walked out of my view and out of the jail, office, I walked toward the basement doors. I heard a shot and ran into the basement.

Several officers were pulling the prisoner and another man toward the jail office door, and I heard one of them call to get a doctor.

I heard a Supervisory officer state, "Secure the basement." I ran around the officers and prisoners and up the ramp entrance on the north side to prevent any one from entering or leaving the basement.

Respectfully submitted,

D. L. Burgess

D.L. Burgess 1412, Detective
Burglary and Theft Bureau

11

November 30, 1963

J. E. Curry
Chief of Police

Re: Shooting of Lee Harvey Oswald
Interview of D. L. Burgess

Sir:

D. L. Burgess was interviewed by Lieutenants C. C. Wallace and P. G. McCaghren at 3:35pm on November 29, 1963. The interview was essentially the same as his original report dated November 27, 1963. The following was added by D. L. Burgess:

I have been asked if I know Jack Ruby. I do not know this man. I did not see this subject in the basement prior to the shooting, and have not seen him around City Hall.

I do not know how the subject got into the basement of the City Hall.

I have not been interviewed by anyone regarding this incident prior to this date.

Respectfully submitted,

C. C. Wallace
C. C. Wallace
Lieutenant of Juvenile Bureau
Dallas Police Department

P. G. McCaghren
P. G. McCaghren
Lieutenant of Burglary & Theft Bureau
Dallas Police Department

lh

11

COMMISSION EXHIBIT No. 2002—Continued

November 30, 1963

STATEMENT OF PATROLMAN T. R. BURTON:

I left the City Hall basement for my traffic assignment, Commerce and Central Expressway, at approximately 11:00 A. M., and did not return prior to the shooting.

I met Jack Ruby about 1956, when he was operating the Vegas Club, and I was working that district.

I did not see Ruby in or about the City Hall. I have not seen Ruby in two or three years.

12

COMMISSION EXHIBIT No. 2002—Continued

November 26, 1963

Mr. J. E. Curry
Chief of Police

Subject: Assignment of Officer
T. R. Burton, #1308
Sunday, November 24, 1963

Sir:

On Sunday, November 24, 1963 at approximately 9:20 A.M. I was instructed to report to Station 511, along with my partner D.K. Erwin. I arrived at Station 511 about 9:40 A.M.

I stayed on Station 511 until approximately 10:15 A.M., when I was advised to report to the basement.

Sgt. P. T.Dean assigned me to Commerce and Central Expressway as my traffic assignment. I left immediately and stayed on my traffic assignment until Captain Talbert stopped, with my partner, and advised us to report to Parkland Memorial Hospital, Code 2.

Respectfully submitted,

T. R. Burton
T. R. Burton
Patrolman #1308
Patrol Division

TRB/eh

12

COMMISSION EXHIBIT No. 2002—Continued

December 1, 1963

STATEMENT OF LT. GEORGE BUTLER:

I did see Jack Ruby in the City Hall, Friday; but, I did not see him in or near the City Hall on Sunday prior to the shooting.

13

COMMISSION EXHIBIT No. 2002—Continued

November 30, 1963

Mr. J. E. Curry
Chief of Police

Sir:

Sometime around 11:00 A. M. on November 24, 1963 Captain Frank Martin came into the Juvenile Bureau and asked that Detectives Lowery, Goolsby, Miller, Cutchshaw, Harrison and myself follow him to the City Hall basement. We did so. The basement was crowded with officers, newspaper, radio and television people. We proceeded to the area just outside the basement door that adjoins the parking area. We reported to Captain O. A. Jones who assigned the Detectives where he wanted them.

Shortly after our arrival an armored car backed partially on to the basement ramp on the Commerce Street side. Chief Batchelor, Sergeant P. T. Dean and myself proceeded to search the armored car. Nothing was found. I instructed officers on the Commerce Street exit not to let anyone in or out of the basement until we advised them otherwise.

Sergeant Dean and Chief Batchelor then left me with the armored car. Sergeant Dean returned and said his boss told him to ride inside the truck with the prisoner.

Shortly afterwards an unmarked police car drove on to the ramp from the basement area. This car parked near the jail door entrance on the ramp. I was aware from the excitement of the crowd that Lee Oswald was in sight but could not see anything for the police car between us. Next a shot was heard. I ran down, yelling to the officers not to let anyone out of the basement

I was advised by someone that Jack Ruby had shot Oswald. In a very short time an ambulance came and removed Oswald.

Just prior to my taking my position on the armored car, I had looked over the crowd carefully that was gathered near the door. I have known Jack Ruby for years but did not see him at that time. This observation made approximately ten minutes before the shooting.

Respectfully,

George Butler

George Butler
Lieutenant
Juvenile Bureau

13

COMMISSION EXHIBIT No. 2002—Continued

December 23, 1963

Mr. J. E. Curry
Chief of Police

Subject: Supplement Report regarding the Shooting of Lee Harvey Oswald.

Sir:

I hereby wish to supplement my report of November 24, 1963 concerning my activities at the time Lee Harvey Oswald was shot in the basement of the City Hall.

In searching the armored car that day, November 24, 1963, which was parked on the Commerce Street basement ramp, with Assistant Chief Charles Batchelor, we found an empty soda water bottle which fell out of the truck and broke.

This supplement made at the suggestion of Captain O. A. Jones.

Respectfully submitted,

George Butler
George E. Butler
Lieutenant of Police
Juvenile Bureau

GEB:mav

13

COMMISSION EXHIBIT No. 2002—Continued

November 27, 1963

J. E. Curry
Chief of Police

SUBJECT: Information regarding the murder of Lee Oswald

Sir:

On November 24, 1963 at approximately 11:00am, I was assigned by Lt. Swain to the basement hallways around the Records Bureau.

I was standing by the last window on the left of the jail office observing the people gathered there, when Oswald was brought down.

Just seconds after he was taken out the jail office door leading to the drive, I heard what sounded like a shot.

I then saw Detectives Combest, Graves, and Lavelle attempting to get Oswald, who was down, back into the jail office.

As I attempted to assist with Oswald the rush of the others bringing in the suspect carried me into the jail office.

I then attempted to assist with Oswald until we placed him on the ambulance stretcher.

After the ambulance left Lt. McKinney ordered me to Parkland Hospital. I stood guard at the East end of the second floor operating room the remainder of the day.

Respectfully submitted,

V. C. Campbell
V. C. Campbell
Detective
Burglary & Theft Bureau

VCC/lh

14

COMMISSION EXHIBIT No. 2002—Continued

November 30, 1963

J. E. Curry
Chief of Police

Re: Shooting of Lee Harvey Oswald
V. C. Campbell

Sir:

V. C. Campboll was interviewed by Lieutenants C. C. Wallace and P. G. McCaghren at 11:30 am on November 30, 1963. The interview was essentially the same as his original report dated November 27, 1963. The following was added by V. C. Campbell:

I have known Jack Ruby for about 5 years. I did not see him in the basement of the City Hall prior to the shooting, and do not recall seeing him in the City Hall before.

I have no idea how he got into the basement of the City Hall.

I have not been interviewed by the Federal Bureau of Investigation.

Respectfully submitted,

C C Wallace
C. C. Wallace, Lieutenant
Juvenile Bureau

P G McCaghren
P. G. McCaghron, Lieutenant
Burglary & Theft Bureau

lh

14

November 30, 1963

Mr. J. E. Curry
Chief of Police

Sir:

Re: Interview of Reserve Officer,
Patrolman Arthur W. Capps, 258

On November 30, 1963 Reserve Officer, Patrolman Arthur W. Capps was interviewed by the undersigned officers as to any information he might have concerning the shooting of Lee Harvey Oswald not covered in his original report dated November 26, 1963.

Patrolman Capps stated that at his place of assignment no one was allowed to pass except police officers. Two men in civilian dress were stopped by him as they were walking toward the City Hall. One of these men was identified as a Police Sergeant and the other as a Patrolman assigned to the Accident Prevention Bureau, but he could not identify himself as he had left his identification at home. Before this officer was allowed to pass he was identified as being a Policeman by Officer Patterson. These were the only two people dressed in civilian clothes who were allowed to pass through Police lines at his location.

Capps further states that he has not been contacted by any federal agency at this time.

Respectfully submitted,

F. I. Cornwall
F. I. Cornwall, Lieutenant
Special Service Bureau

Jack Revill
Jack Revill, Lieutenant
Special Service Bureau

jh

November 26, 1963

Mr. J. E. Curry
Chief of Police

Sir:

This is a statement of facts relating to my activity as a Reserve Officer Sunday, November 24, 1963, to the best of my knowledge and recollection.

1. Approximate time I reported to duty. 9:45 A. M.

2. I reported to Assembly Room.

3. I was assigned to North side of Commerce Street in front of City Hall and Credit Union to keep side walk clear. I was at this location at the time of the shooting.

4. Names of other officers in the same area that I can recollect are:

   Reserve Officer Wayne Harrison.

5. Did you know Ruby? No.

6. When and under what circumstance did you see Ruby?

   Did not see Ruby at all.

Signed: Arthur Capps
Arthur Capps

15

COMMISSION EXHIBIT No. 2002—Continued

November 27, 1963

Mr. J. E. Curry
Chief of Police

Subject: Incident involving Lee Harvey Oswald

Sir:

On November 24, 1963, at approximately 11:15 A. M., I was standing in the basement of the Police building as part of a security guard. I was standing about five feet from the door of the jail. Mr. Oswald was led by me and I was attempting to keep people away from him. I was standing just behind Mr. Oswald and saw a flash and heard a shot. I saw Mr. Oswald fall and this man was then facing me but he was crouched over. I caught a glimpse of a pistol he had in his right hand. I attempted to get the pistol and grabbed his arm. At that instant someone else grabbed the pistol and several other officers were helping to subdue him.

We then took the suspect into the jail office and searched him. Some other officers placed him on the jail elevator and I was ordered to go to Parkland Hospital to help the officers there.

Respectfully,

W. E. Chambers
W. E. Chambers
Detective 1087
Forgery Bureau

WEC:ms

16

COMMISSION EXHIBIT No. 2002—Continued

December 1, 1963

J. E. Curry
Chief of Police

Re: Shooting of Lee Harvey Oswald
Interview of W. E. Chambers

Sir:

W. E. Chambers was interviewed by Lieutenants C. C. Wallace and P. G. McCaghren at 4:05 pm on November 29, 1963. The interview was essentially the same as his original report dated November 27, 1963. The following was added by W. E. Chambers:

I have been asked if I know Jack Ruby. I do not know him. I was standing beside the jail office door and was guarding it. There was a large group of people coming and going. I was told by Captain Jones to keep the press personnel away from the prisoner. I was there approximately 15 minutes before Oswald was brought down.

After the shot was fired, I helped subdue the suspect, who I later found out to be Jack Ruby. I assisted in removing Ruby to the jail office. Later I helped carry and oad Oswald in the ambulance.

I over heard Detective Cutchshaw talking to two TV cameramen. Cutchshaw was saying that three of the cameramen came in with the camera and there were only two at the present time. The question was, where was the other man. I related this information to Captain King.

I have not been interviewed by the Federal Bureau of Investigation.

Respectfully submitted,

C. C. Wallace
C. C. Wallace, Lieutenant
Juvenile Bureau

P. G. McCaghren
P. G. McCaghren, Lieutenant
Burglary & Theft Bureau

lh

16

COMMISSION EXHIBIT No. 2002—Continued

December 1, 1963

J. E. Curry
Chief of Police

Re: Shooting of Lee Harvey Oswald
Interview of B. S. Clardy

Sir:

B. S. Clardy was interviewed by Lieutenants C. C. Wallace and P. G. McCaghren at 9:20 am on November 30, 1963. The interview was essentially the same as his original report dated November 27, 1963. The following was added by B. S. Clardy:

After the shot was fired, I went to the 5th floor with the prisoner. He was being questioned by several officers, and as I recall, the officers were Glenn King, Sgt. P. T. Dean, and Mr. Sorrels of the Secret Service. When asked why he did it, he replied, "Somebody had to do it, ya'll couldn't."

When asked how he got in, he said that he walked by the officer on the ramp when he turned to talk to Rio Pierce, who drove out the entrance. He said he heard somebody yell, "Hey you." He didn't know where it came from, so he ducked his head and kept walking.

He also told us that he sent $25.00 by wire to a girl in Ft. Worth.

He said also that it was a spur of the moment thing and it was a million to one chance that he got down there at the actual time Oswald was brought down.

I have been interviewed by the Federal Bureau of Investigation. They talked to me Monday around 2:30. I gave them the same information I have given here.

Respectfully submitted,

C. C. Wallace
C. C. Wallace, Lieutenant
Juvenile Bureau

P. G. McCaghren
P. G. McCaghren, Lieutenant
Burglary & Theft Bureau

lh

17

COMMISSION EXHIBIT No. 2002—Continued

November 27, 1963

Mr. J. E. Curry
Chief of Police

Sir:

I would like to submit the following report regarding the incident occurring in the basement on November 24, 1963.

On the morning of November 24, 1963 while on duty in the Auto Theft Bureau, Lieutenant Smart advised me not to leave the City Hall as I was to be available when the prisoner was escorted from the City Jail. About 10:00 a.m. Lieutenant Smart advised me and the other officers in the bureau to report to the jail office. Upon arrival I took a position near the southwest corner near the driveway. A couple of minutes before the prisoner was brought down, I had looked over the crowd, and, at this time, I did not see Jack Ruby in the crowd. I have known Jack Ruby for eight to ten years, and if I had seen him I would have recognized him.

As word was heard that the subject was being brought down, I was watching the driveway to the basement and to the driveway to Commerce Street where the armored truck was. I saw a fast blur of movement out of the corner of my left eye, and, before I could turn, I heard a shot. As I turned I partly lost my footing and was bumped by people from both sides at the same time. Before I could get balanced, the subject, Jack Ruby, was under a pile of officers.

I helped others try to keep the press back until both the prisoner and Jack Ruby were taken inside the jail office. I then went to the jail office, and at that time Detective J.C. Watson was at the door keeping other people from entering. Detective McMillon, Detective Archer, Detective Blackie Harrison, and Lieutenant Smart, and another officer were holding Jack Ruby on the floor. I took Detective McMillon's gun and placed his gun and my gun in the locker. Then Detective McMillon, Detective Archer, Detective Blackie Harrison, and myself took Jack Ruby directly to the fifth floor where we searched him. Then I took the handcuffs off and gave them to Detective McMillon as they were his cuffs. We then stripped Jack Ruby to his skin and searched his clothing completely.

Lieutenant Baker of homicide had been contacted and requested that we stay with the prisoner until the arrival of officers from the Homicide Bureau. Detective Harrison had left after helping take the prisoner up. Detective McMillon, Detective Archer, and myself were with the prisoner. Mr. Sorells of the Secret Service came to the jail office and talked to him briefly and left. Then F.B.I. Agent Hall came up and talked to Jack Ruby for some time, probably two hours or better.

A jailer came back and told us that a lawyer was to see Jack Ruby and it had been okayed by the Homicide Bureau. I am not sure which jailer this was. We took the prisoner to the fourth floor, Detective Archer, Detective McMillon, F.B.I. Agent Hall, one of the jailers,

17

Mr. J. E. Curry 2 November 27, 1963

and myself. He talked to a lawyer for about two minutes. Before he was returned to the fifth floor, he was checked by a city doctor who was on duty at this time. We returned to the fifth floor and F. B. I. Agent Hall continued to question Ruby until Homicide Detective K. L. Boyd, Detective M. G. Hall, and Detective Montgomery arrived on the fifth floor at about 2:30 p.m. Along with the three Homicide officers and Agent Hall we escorted the prisoner to the Homicide Bureau.

Respectfully submitted,

B. S. Clardy

B. S. Clardy
Detective
Criminal Investigation Division

17

November 29, 1963

Mr.J. E. Curry
Chief of Police

Sir:

Re: Interview of Detective B. H.Combest, 1148

On November 29, 1963 Detective B. H. Combest was interviewed by the undersigned officers as to any information he might have concerning the shooting of Lee Harvey Oswald which was not covered in Combest's original report dated November 26, 1963.

Detective Combest stated, after reading his original report, that he had nothing of significance to add. He stated that he had known Ruby for several years, but that he did not see him in the basement prior to the shooting.

Detective Combest states that he has not been interviewed by any federal agency at this time.

Respectfully submitted,

Jack Revill

Jack Revill, Lieutenant
Special Service Bureau

F. I. Cornwall

F. I. Cornwall, Lieutenant
Special Service Bureau

18

COMMISSION EXHIBIT No. 2002—Continued

November 26, 1963

Mr. J. E. Curry
Chief of Police

Subject: Shooting of Lee Harvey Oswald

Sir:

On Sunday, November 24, 1963, I was working regular hours of 8:00 A.M. until 4:00 P.M. in the Special Service Bureau, Vice Section.

At approximately 10:50 A.M., I was in the basement of City Hall near the jail office. I was engaged in conversation with Detective B. L. Beaty and Officer J. D. Hutchinson. We were approached by Captain O. A. Jones. Captain Jones told us to remain in the basement near the jail office. He further stated that all the other available officers in City Hall would be down into the basement soon.

I overheard Sergeant J. A. Putnam reiterate his orders to the officer and the reserve officer working the passageway leading out of the basement into the parking basement. He stated very emphatically to the officer that no one but police and press members with press passes were to be admitted to the parking basement.

A short time later several officers and detectives came down from upstairs. Captain Jones took all officers out into the passageway just outside the jail office. He told all of us that we were to form a line on each side of the passageway in order to make a lane for the prisoner Oswald to be escorted. He told some officers to get all the newsmen out of the jail office booking room. He then cleared the passageway immediately outside the jail office. At this time Sergeant J. A. Putnam asked all the newsmen to move to the far side of the driveway, this being the side across from the jail office. Captain Jones then told officers to keep the lines that we had and for officers to fall in behind and to keep newsmen from rushing in.

Besides the above listed officers, other officers that I remember to be in the basement were:

R. L. Lowery #1081, Chief M. W. Stevenson #16, T. D. McMillon #1349, W. E. Chambers #1087, Sgt. P. T. Dean #882, L. D. Montgomery #1047, J. R. Leavelle #736, L. C. Graves #702, C. N. Dhority #476, Charles Goolsby #1141, W. J. Harrison #579, L. D. Miller #1236, Capt. F. M. Martin #397,

COMMISSION EXHIBIT No. 2002—Continued

-2-

W. J. Cutchshaw #1111, Capt. C. E. Talbert #463, Lt. W. L. Wiggins #434, Chief Chas. Batchelor #11, Lt. G. E. Butler #51, Lt. R. E. Swain #531, C. W. Brown #759, Capt. J. W. Fritz #9.

I did not observe anyone that I knew who did not belong in the basement. Everyone that I saw were either police or people I thought to be newsmen. I did not observe Jack Ruby until just seconds before the shooting.

Respectfully submitted,

B H Combest
B. H. Combest #1148
Detective, Vice Section
Special Service Bureau

18

November 30, 1963

Mr. J. E. Curry
Chief of Police

Sir:

Re: Interview of Reserve Officer, Sergeant Roland A.Cox, 803

On November 30, 1963 Reserve Officer, Sergeant Roland A. Cox was interviewed by the undersigned officers as to any information he might have concerning the shooting of Lee Harvey Oswald not covered in his original report dated November 26, 1963.

After having read his original report, Cox stated that he could not add anything of significance to this first report.

Cox further states that he has not been contacted by any federal agency at this time.

Respectfully submitted,

F. I. Cornwall
F. I. Cornwall, Lieutenant
Special Service Bureau

Jack Revill
Jack Revill, Lieutenant
Special Service Bureau

jh

19

November 26, 1963

Mr. J. E. Curry
Chief of Police

Sir:

This is a statement of facts relating to my activity as a Reserve Officer Sunday, November 24, 1963, to the best of my knowledge and recollection.

1. Approximate time I reported to duty. 10:00 A. M.

2. I reported to Lt. Ben McCoy

3. I was assigned to Commerce Street on South side to keep crowd under control, and on the South sidewalk.

4. Names of other officers in the same area that I can recollect are:

   Reserve Sergeants J. R. Hopkins and Mayo.

5. Did you know Ruby?

   Yes, I worked at Vegas Club for Special Service about nine years ago.

6. When and under what circumstance did you see Ruby?

   Did not see Ruby at anytime on Sunday, November 24, 1963.

Signed Roland A Cox
Roland A. Cox

19

COMMISSION EXHIBIT No. 2002—Continued

November 27, 1963

Mr. J. E. Curry
Chief of Police

Sir:

This is a statement of facts relating to my activity as a Reserve Officer Sunday, November 24, 1963, to the best of my knowledge and recollection.

1. Approximate time I reported to duty. 9:30 A. M.

2. I reported to Lt. Merrell in Assembly Room.

3. I was assigned to the portion of the driveway that leads from the ramps to the parking area. I was at this post as guard from about 9:45 to 10:00 A. M. I was then assigned to assist Officer Nelson in the corridor where the barred windows open into the jail office. I was at this place till about 30 minutes after the shooting.

4. Names of other officers in the same area that I can recollect are:

   Capt. Talbert, two detectives (names unknown), and Reserve Lt. Merrell.

5. Did you know Ruby? No.

6. When and under what circumstance did you see Ruby?

   I got a glimpse of him in the jail office, but kept my eyes on the people in the basement.

Signed: A. B. Craig
A. B. Craig

20

COMMISSION EXHIBIT No. 2002—Continued

November 30, 1963

Mr. J. E. Curry
Chief of Police

Sir:

Re: Interview of Reserve Officer,
Patrolman Alvin B. Craig, 285

On November 30, 1963 Reserve Officer, Patrolman Alvin B. Craig was interviewed by the undersigned officers as to any information he might have concerning the shooting of Lee Harvey Oswald which was not covered in his original report dated November 27, 1963.

After having read his original report, Craig states that there is nothing of significance which he could add to this first report.

Craig further states that at this time he has not been contacted by and federal agency.

Respectfully submitted,

F. I. Cornwall
F. I. Cornwall, Lieutenant
Special Service Bureau

Jack Revill
Jack Revill, Lieutenant
Special Service Bureau

jh

20

November 26, 1963

Mr. J. E. Curry
Chief of Police

Sir:

This is a statement of facts relating to my activity as a Reserve Officer Sunday, November 24, 1963, to the best of my knowledge and recollection.

1. Approximate time I reported to duty. 8:35 A. M.

2. I reported to Lt. Merrell (Assembly Room)

3. I was assigned to the basement and Jail Office entrance, and my assignment was that of a guard.

4. Names of other officers in the same area that I can recollect are:

   Res. Capt. C. O. Arnett, Res. Lt. B. C. McCoy, Res. Lt. D. T. Suits,

   Res. Lt. H. M. Kriss, Res. Officer Gano Worley.

5. Did you know Ruby? Yes and no (see next statement)

6. When and under what circumstance did you see Ruby?

   Approximately three years ago, Jack Ruby bought myself and two other officers breakfast at Lucas B&B Cafe on Oak Lawn at 3:00 A. M. I have not seen this man since, however I have been in his club on several occasions when riding observation.

Signed Kenneth Hudson Croy
Kenneth Hudson Croy, Reserve Sergeant.

21

December 3, 1963

Mr. J. E. Curry
Chief of Police

Re: Interview of Reserve Police Officer Sergeant Kenneth Croy

Sir:

On December 1, 1963, Reserve Sergeant Croy was interviewed by the undersigned officers as to any information he might have concerning the shooting of Lee Harvey Oswald which was not covered in his original report dated November 26, 1963.

During this interview pertinent facts were uncovered and an affidavit was given by Mr. Croy concerning this. This affidavit is attached to this report.

Reserve Officer Sergeant Croy stated that he had not been interviewed by any Federal agency at this time.

Respectfully submitted,

F. I. Cornwall
F. I. Cornwall
Lieutenant, Special Service Bureau

Jack Revill
Jack Revill
Lieutenant, Special Service Bureau

Enclosure: Affidavit

21

AFFIDAVIT IN ANY FACT

THE STATE OF TEXAS
COUNTY OF DALLAS

BEFORE ME, A. L. CURTIS

a Notary Public in and for said County, State of Texas, on this day personally appeared Kenneth Hudson Croy,

Address: 2634 West Illinois, Telephone No.: FE 7-0621.

Who, after being by me duly sworn, on oath deposes and says: I am a Reserve Police Sergeant with the Dallas Police Reserve. On November 24, 1963 I reported to the Police Assembly Room at approximately 8:35 a.m. to Lieutenant Merrell who was making assignments. I then took over making assignments from him. I wrote the men up on the roster at the time they arrived and made assignments to them until approximately 10:00 a.m. At that time I went to the basement and worked from the basement of the City Hall, assigning reserve officers who were late arriving, and also checking on where my men had been assigned. Prior to Oswald's appearance into the basement of the City Hall I stationed myself at the foot of the north end of the ramp in the basement. I was there for quite some time watching the reporters. Someone had made the remark to watch the reporters, and to move them back against the rail. There were several reporters in front of me. Captain Arnett was standing to the right of me. I was approximately in the middle of the ramp between the wall and the rail. Someone in authority gave instructions to move the press back against the rail. At that time I turned and told two men standing to my left to move back against the rail. One of these men had a motion picture camera, the other was wearing a dark maroon coat with black thread woven into it. He was wearing a brown hat. (My father has a coat something similar to the one the man was wearing that I spoke to) I then turned my attention back to the reporters which were standing in front of me. I believe this man that I spoke to to have been Jack Ruby. The man with the motion picture camera got up on the rail. The man with the dark maroon coat stepped back a little. I turned back around and one or two officers came out of the jail office and then Captain Fritz, and then they brought Oswald out. He was handcuffed to one of the officers and there was a man on each side of him holding his arm. There was a reporter standing there with a microphone in his hand. The reporters then converged on Oswald. The reporter with the microphone stuck it up in Oswald's face and asked him, "Do you have any comment?" At this time I observed a blur come from my left side. I was off balance.
XXXXXXXXXXXXXXXXXXXXXXXXXXXXXXXXXXXXXXXXXXXXXXXXXXXXXXXXXXXXXXXXXX
PAGE 1 OF TWO PAGES

Kenneth Hudson Croy

SUBSCRIBED AND SWORN TO BEFORE ME THIS 1 DAY OF December A.D. 1963

A. L. Curtis
Notary Public, Dallas County, Texas

CPS-GF-413

21

AFFIDAVIT IN ANY FACT

THE STATE OF TEXAS
COUNTY OF DALLAS

BEFORE ME, A. L. CURTIS

a Notary Public in and for said County, State of Texas, on this day personally appeared Kenneth Hudson Croy,

Address: 2634 West Illinois, Telephone No.: FE 7-0621.

PAGE 2 of TWO PAGES

Who, after being by me duly sworn, on oath deposes and says: I saw a man running into the crowd in a crouch. At that moment I reached for this individual and touched his coat tail attempting to stop him. I saw him run right up to Oswald and I heard a shot. At the time I heard the shot, there were several officers who swarmed the him and wrestled him to the pavement. I also tried to grab hold of his gun, but there were too many men there for me to be effective. At that point an officer did disarm him and took him out. I didn't get to see the man they were wrestling to the floor because too many officers swarmed him. At this point orders were given to seal the basement. I ran approximately half way up the north ramp and stopped reporters trying to leave the basement. During the interview with Lieutenant Jack Revill and Lieutenant F. I. Cornwall something was mentioned about an automobile leaving the basement via the north ramp to the Main Street. I recall an automobile driving out, but I can't recall the time nor can I recall how many men were in this automobile. I seem to recall this automobile as being a light blue squad car.XXXXXXXXXXX
XXXXXXXXXXXXXXXXXXXXXXXXXXXXXXXXXXXXXXXXXXXXXXXXXXXXXXXXXXXXXXXXXXXXXXXXXX
XXXXXX XX X X X X X X X X X X XX X X XXXXXXXXXXXX

[signature]

SUBSCRIBED AND SWORN TO BEFORE ME THIS 1 DAY OF December A.D. 196

[signature: A. L. Curtis]
Notary Public, Dallas County, Texas

CPS-GF-413

21

November 30, 1963

J. E. Curry
Chief of Police

Re: Shooting of Lee Harvey Oswald
Interview of W. J. Cutchshaw

Sir:

W. J. Cutchshaw was interviewed at 2:00 pm this date by Lieutenants C. C. Wallace and F. G. McCaghren. This interview was essentially the same as his original report dated November 27, 1963. W. J. Cutchshaw added the following:

I have been asked if I know Jack Ruby. I have met Ruby, but I do not recognize him by sight. After assisting in the arrest, I was told that this man was Jack Ruby and that he owned the Carosel Club.

I have not seen the person who shot Oswald in the City Hall before or prior to the shooting.

I was interviewed in Juvenile Bureau at approximately 7:00 by The Federal Bureau of Investigation Agent Bookout.

Respectfully submitted,

[signature: C. C. Wallace]
C. C. Wallace, Lieutenant
Juvenile Bureau

[signature: F. G. McCaghren]
F. G. McCaghren, Lieutenant
Burglary & Theft Bureau

lh

22

November 24, 1963

Mr. J. E. Curry
Chief of Police

Subject: Shooting of Lee Harvey Oswald.

Sir:

At the time that Oswald was being brought down from the jail, I was stationed next to the door leading to the jail office. Prior to Oswald coming out, a T. V. Camera was pushed out of the basement lobby into the basement. There were three men pushing the camera. The man with the green shirt was on the right and the man with the black rain coat was on the left. The third person was in the center and had on a dark suit. He was bent over low behind the camera pushing on the base. The camera was pushed down the ramp into the parking area but was not hooked up. After the shooting the camera was being pushed up the ramp by two men. The man in the dark suit was not one of them. I stopped the two men and asked them where the other man was that helped them push the camera out. They stated that no one was with them.

After the shot, I jumped on the man and had him by the left arm. I held this position till we reached the jail office door where I had to release my hold so they could get inside the jail office. After they got inside I stood guard on the door.

Respectfully submitted,

W. J. Cutchshaw (signature)
W. J. Cutchshaw
Detective, ID#1111
Juvenile Bureau
Criminal Investigation Division
W. J. Cutchshaw (signature)

22

COMMISSION EXHIBIT No. 2002—Continued

Mr. J. E. Curry
Chief of Police

December 3, 1963

Re: Interview with Mr. N. J. Daniels,
2229 Sutter

Sir:

On November 29, 1963, Mr. N. J. Daniels was interviewed by the undersigned officers as to any information he might have concerning the shooting of Lee Harvey Oswald and if he could give any information as to how Jack Ruby gained entrance to the basement of the City Hall.

A lengthy interview was held with Mr. Daniels and an affidavit-in-fact taken - copy attached.

Mr. N. J. Daniels stated at the time of this interview that he had not been contacted by any Federal agency.

Respectfully submitted,

F. I. Cornwall (signature)
F. I. Cornwall
Lieutenant, Special Service Bureau

Jack Revill (signature)
Jack Revill
Lieutenant, Special Service Bureau

Enclosure: Affidavit

23

COMMISSION EXHIBIT No. 2002—Continued

AFFIDAVIT IN ANY FACT

THE STATE OF TEXAS
COUNTY OF DALLAS

BEFORE ME, Ann Schreiber

a Notary Public in and for said County, State of Texas, on this day personally appeared N. J. Daniels, 2229 Sutter, Dallas, Texas, FR 4-6179.

Who, after being by me duly sworn, on oath deposes and says: On Sunday, November 24, at approximately 11:00 A.M., I came up to the Main Street ramp to the basement of the city hall. I was standing on the Western Union side of the ramp and I spoke to Officer Vaughn, he was on duty at that location. Officer Vaughn was standing in the center of the ramp keeping people from entering the basement of the city hall. I had been standing there several minutes when a squad car drove up the ramp with three officers inside, they drove on to Main Street and turned west on Main. At this time Officer Vaughn stepped out into the middle of Main Street and stopped the west bound traffic on Main so this squad car could make its turn on Main Street. For a brief moment while Officer Vaughn was blocking traffic, the ramp entrance at this location was left unguarded. I was standing at the east corner of the ramp and turned to watch Officer Vaughn stop the traffic. From the position where I was standing it was impossible for anyone to walk behind me and gain entrance into the basement. I did not notice anyone walk in front of me and go into the basement. At this time I was thinking to myself that if I saw anyone go in I would so advise Officer Vaughn. After stopping traffic for this squad car Officer Vaughn took up his duties in the middle of the ramp. Several minutes later I stepped out towards the street so that I could have a better view down the ramp. As I did so I noticed a white male, approximately 50 years of age, 5'10", weighing about 155-160#, wearing a dark(blue or brown) single breasted suit, white shirt, and dark colored tie, this man was not wearing a hat, he had light colored hir thinning on top, round face, kind of small head, fair complexion, he was not wearing an overcoat nor was he carrying one but he did have his right hand inside of his right suit coat pocket, approaching the ramp from the direction of the Western Union. This person walked in the ramp and into the basement going between Officer Vaughn and the east side of the building. Officer Vaughn at this time ~~was standing at the top of the ramp~~ in the middle of it facing towards Main. I did not see Officer Vaughn challenge this person nor did he ~~show any signs of recognizing him,~~

SUBSCRIBED AND SWORN TO BEFORE ME THIS____ DAY OF____ A.D. 196

Notary Public, Dallas County, Texas

CPS-GF-413

NJD

23

COMMISSION EXHIBIT No. 2002—Continued

AFFIDAVIT IN ANY FACT

THE STATE OF TEXAS
COUNTY OF DALLAS

(page two)

BEFORE ME, Ann Schreiber

a Notary Public in and for said County, State of Texas, on this day personally appeared N. J. Daniels

(continued frompage one)

Who, after being by me duly sworn, on oath deposes and says: nor even being aware that he was passing, but I know that he saw him. It struck me odd at the time that Officer Vaughn did not say something to this man. Approximately two minutes after this man had walked down the ramp I saw quite a bit of movement in the basement outside the jail office and then I heard a shot. From the time that I first spoke to Officer Vaughn until I heard the shot, which was approximately a period of twenty-five minutes, at no time did I see anyone leave or enter the basement of the city hall from the ramp entrance on Main Street except one squad car which contained three officers and this one unknown white man who entered. On Monday, November 25, 1963, at approximately 9:00 A.M., Officer Vaughn called me on the telephone at home and asked me if I had noticed anyone going into the basement while Lieutenant Pierce was coming out, I told him "no" I did not. He told me he was bothered about the possibility that someone could have gone in there while Lieutenant Pierce and the other two officerms were coming out in the squad car. I told him "no, I did not." But I did not mention the other fellow I saw go in because I was sure he had seen him.

N. J. Daniels

SUBSCRIBED AND SWORN TO BEFORE ME THIS 29 DAY OF November A.D. 1963

Ann Schreiber
Notary Public, Dallas County, Texas
ANN SCHREIBER

CPS-GF-413

23

COMMISSION EXHIBIT No. 2002—Continued

December 12, 1963

Mr. J. E. Curry
Chief of Police

Subject: Polygraph examination given to
N. J. Daniels C/M/32

Sir:

At 3:10 P.M., December 11, 1963, a polygraph examination was given to N. J. Daniels.

This examination was given to determine if Mr. Daniels was telling the truth in the statement he had given.

During the pre-test interview with Mr. Daniels, he stated that he was sure the person he stated he had seen enter the city hall basement was not Jack Ruby. He stated that he was shown a picture of Jack Ruby and that Ruby did not look like the person he stated that he had seen. He was very confused during this interview and stated he was not sure of anything in his statement. He also stated that he felt like the squad he saw come out of the basement had enough time to get to the county jail before this person entered the basement of the city hall.

He was then placed on the polygraph and the following pertinent questions were asked and answers given.

1. Have you told the complete truth in the statement you gave?
Answer: Yes Indication: False

2. Have you deliberatly made up any of this story?
Answer: No Indication: False

3. Do you think the person you stated you saw enter the basement at that time was Jack Ruby?
Answer: No Indication: True

4. Did you actually see the person you described come from the direction of the Western Union?
Answer: Yes Indication: False

5. Do you think this person entered the basement of the city hall after the squad drove out? Did not answer this question.

-1-

23

COMMISSION EXHIBIT No. 2002—Continued

December 12, 1963

Page 2

6. Have you seen the person you described in your statement around the city hall before? Did not answer this question.

7. Have you given a true description of the person you stated you saw enter the basement of the city hall?
Answer: Yes Indication: False

8. Did you actually see the person you described enter the basement of the city hall?
Answer: Yes Indication: False

9. Did you get a good look at this person?
Answer: Yes Indication: False

Most of the above questions were repeated on other charts with the same answers given and same indictions noted.

Respectfully submitted,

P. L. Bentley
P. L. Bentley
Detective of Police
Identification Bureau

PLB/mel

23

COMMISSION EXHIBIT No. 2002—Continued

AFFIDAVIT IN ANY FACT

THE STATE OF TEXAS

COUNTY OF DALLAS

BEFORE ME, Ruby Smith RUBY SMITH

a Notary Public in and for said County, State of Texas, on this day personally appeared James R. Davidson - 4708 Wedgewood, Belaire, Texas - MO 4-3206

Who, after being by me duly sworn, on oath deposes and says:

I was in Dallas to cover the assassination of President Kennedy. I was called by ABC of New York on Friday afternoon, November 22 to represent them. I arrived in Dallas about 7:15 p.m. Friday, November 22, 1963. My crew and I were set up on the third floor of the Police and Courts Building most the time. Warren Ferguson - free lance - sound man - 5406 Windswept, Houston, MO 5-6461, was the sound man and Bill Lord, Staff Reporter for ABC - New York, 7 West 66th Street, New York, 36, was in control. We worked from the third floor of the Police and Courts Building Friday night, all day Saturday and most of Saturday night. Since the shooting of Oswald Sunday morning, November 24, 1963, I have seen Ruby personally while photographing him and have also seen pictures of him. To the best of my knowledge, I never saw Jack Ruby prior to the shooting of Oswald on Sunday, November 24, 1963.

On Sunday morning, Bill Lord moved us to the jail office to cover the transfer of Oswald to the County Jail. This was about 8:30 a.m. From 8:30 a.m. until about 10:00 a.m. I spent most of the time standing on a shelf with a camera waiting for Oswald to come out of the elevator. This shelf is on the last wall of the jail office.

Warren Ferguson was with me as the sound man. Bill Lord had been called to one of the pay phones just outside the jail office and he remained on this phone to New York to keep the line open before and during the shooting of Oswald.

At about 10:00 a.m. an officer came into the jail office and stated we would have to clear the room. Everyone but the police personnel were removed.

24

Page 2 AFFIDAVIT IN ANY FACT

James R. Davidson - 4708 Wedgewood, Belaire, Texas - MO 4-3206

Warren Ferguson and I then set up in the hall just outside the jail office where I could get a picture of Oswald through the jail office window as he left the elevator. We stayed here until the officers brought Oswald off the elevator and through the jail office door into the entrance to the parking area. I got some movie film of Oswald and the officers leaving the elevator and going through the jail office. I then followed through the double doors into the entry area to the parking area. I was outside the double doors taking sound movie at the time the shot was fired. There were a number of people between me and Oswald and these people blocked my line of vision so I did not get a good shot of Oswald. Warren Ferguson was with me during this time. A cluster of officers re-entered the jail office and I backed into the hallway just outside the jail office and took shots of the activity in the jail office through the jail office window. After the jail office was cleared, I went inside and received permission from a lieutenant to photograph the inside of the jail office.

Either a UPI or a CBS cameraman was in the jail office prior to 10:00 a.m. on Sunday morning, November 24, 1963. His sound crew was with him, but at about 10:30 a.m. the sound crew was sent to cover an interview with Mrs. Connally at Parkland. The UPI or CBS cameraman had a Bolex hand camera and until we were cleared from the jail office, he stood at the East counter inside the jail office. A two man NBC crew was also in the jail office standing at the same counter with the UPI or CBS man. When the jail office was cleared the NBC crew and the UPI or CBS man moved to the corridor outside the jail office with me and all of us were taking pictures through the same window.

As soon as the NBC crew had photographed Oswald leaving the elevator, they took their equipment and ran down the corridor inside the Police and Courts Building toward Commerce Street to attempt to obtain a picture of Oswald being driven to the County Jail.

The UPI or CBS man after photographing Oswald coming off the elevator ran out the double doors entering the basement parking area ahead of Oswald. I understand he got pictures of the shooting and that he got knocked down during the melee.

24

James R. Davidson - 4708 Wedgewood, Belaire, Texas - MO 4-3206

I don't recall any of the other press representatives that were present in or around the area where Oswald was shot.

When I entered the basement on Sunday morning, November 24, 1963, my credentials were checked by a police officer as we left the elevator. I did not have any identification pinned on my clothes. I was in and out of the basement 2 or 3 times during the morning of November 24, 1963. My credentials were checked each time I returned to the jail office area.

I have been interviewed by an agent of the Federal Bureau of Investigation.

James R. Davidson

SUBSCRIBED AND SWORN TO BEFORE ME THIS 7th DAY OF December A.D.1963

Ruby Smith
Notary Public, Dallas County, Texas

RUBY SMITH

24

COMMISSION EXHIBIT No. 2002—Continued

November 26, 1963

Captain J. M. Solomon
Dallas Police Reserve Coordinator
Dallas Police Department
2828 Shorecrest Drive
Dallas 35, Texas

Dear Captain Solomon:

I reported for duty in the Assembly Room, Sunday, November 24, 1963, at approximately 8:30 AM. I waited in the Assembly Room until I was assigned to help search the basement garage. I searched cars in spaces one through 16 and the two cars beside the outbound ramp. I also crawled behind the air conditioning machinery beside the outbound ramp to make sure no one was there. I was then assigned to the corner of Commerce and Harwood with Reserve Officer Harold Jacobs and was instructed to allow no one to pass down the north sidewalk of Commerce unless they were police officers or had a "press card."

I stopped traffic at this intersection to allow the armored car turn from Harwood on to Commerce. I was standing on the northeast corner of Commerce and Harwood when the shooting took place.

A few seconds after the shot was fired, a detective ran out and instructed us to seal off all exits. I proceeded to the Harwood exit and there Sgt. Putman and I apprehended a suspect who was running down the hall on the Court's floor of City Hall. I put my handcuffs on him, took him to the Homicide Bureau and stayed with him for about 30 minutes. Detectives then released the suspect and me and I returned to the Assembly Room.

I did not see Ruby until about 6:00 PM when I reported to the 5th Floor Jail to guard him with Reserve Officer D. J. McDonald. Until that time I had never met Mr. Ruby.

Yours truly,

Robert T. Davis
Robert T. Davis
Reserve Officer #957

25

COMMISSION EXHIBIT No. 2002—Continued

November 30, 1963

Mr. J. E. Curry
Chief of Police

Sir:

Re: Interview of Reserve Officer,
Patrolman Robert T. Davis, 957

On November 30, 1963 Reserve Officer, Patrolman Robert T. Davis was interviewed by the undersigned officers as to any information he might have concerning the shooting of Lee Harvey Oswald which was not covered in his original report dated November 26, 1963.

After having read his original report, Davis stated that there is nothing of significance which he could add to this first report.

Davis further states that at this time he has not been contacted by any federal agency.

Respectfully submitted,

F. I. Cornwall
F. I. Cornwall, Lieutenant
Special Service Bureau

Jack Revill
Jack Revill, Lieutenant
Special Service Bureau

jh

25

November 27, 1963

Mr. J. E. Curry
Chief of Police

Sir:

I should like to submit the following report of the events occurring in the basement on November 24, 1963.

I was on duty in the Auto Theft Bureau beginning at 8:00 a.m. I was told to stand by in the office until further notice. At approximately 11:45 a.m. all members of our bureau on duty, except the desk man, went to the basement of the City Hall and waited in the corridor just outside the jail office.

About fifteen minutes later the prisoner was brought down to the jail office and we heard he was being brought through the office. At this time I closed the double doors and held them, not allowing anyone through these doors as he was escorted out the door of the booking office.

I could see the prisoner for a few seconds through the doors glass partition. At this time I heard a shot, but could not see the prisoner or the person who fired the shot. The photographers in the corridor behind me had to make their pictures through the glass. Then the prisoner was taken back into the booking office until the ambulance arrived and he was placed in it with officers escorting him.

I did not see the man who fired the shot because he was hustled out of sight into the jail office and elevator. I did not see the man before or after the shot was fired, but heard the name Jack Ruby called out as the man who shot the prisoner.

I was told by Captain Jones to remain on this door until relieved and check everyone who entered or exited for their credentials, as Press Photographers, Press Reporters, and authorized Police and City of Dallas civilian personnel on duty. I was relieved about thirty minutes later by Lieutenant R. S. Pierce who said I could return to my office.

Respectfully submitted,

H. L. Dawson
H. L. Dawson
Detective
Criminal Investigation Division

26

November 30, 1963

J. E. Curry
Chief of Police

Re: Shooting of Lee Harvey Oswald
Interview of Harold Dawson

Sir:

Harold Dawson was interviewed at 1:40pm on November 29, 1963 by Lieutenants C. C. Wallace and P. G. McCaghren. Dawson added the following to his original report:

I have re-read the statement I made November 27, 1963. The only correction I would like to make is in the time element, which occured approximately 30 or 40 minutes earlier than I originally stated.

At approximately 11:15 I was dispatched to the basement of the City Hall by Lt. Smart to act as security for Lee Oswald. When we got to the basement, we waited in the jail corridor approximately 15 minutes. We then heard that Oswald was on his way down, and there were some photographers and reporters on the phones. I closed the doors and wouldn't let them come onto the corridor, so that no one could come in behind me. No one told me to close the doors.

When he was shot, I was at the same place. I heard the shot, but I couldn't see him or the man who shot him.

I would also like to add that I know Jack Ruby by sight and would recognize him if I saw him, but I have not seen him in the City Hall.

I have talked to Federal Bureau of Investigation Agent Carlson, and I explained to him that I had guessed at the time in my original report, and was probably in error.

Respectfully submitted,

C C Wallace
C. C. Wallace, Lieutenant
Juvenile Bureau

P. G. McCaghren
P. G. McCaghren, Lieutenant
Burglary & Theft Bureau

lh

26

November 26, 1963

Mr. J. E. Curry
Chief of Police

Subject: Assignment Of Sergeant
Patrick T. Dean On
Sunday, November 24, 1963

Sir:

On Sunday, November 24, 1963 at approximately 9:00 A.M., I was advised by Lieutenant R. S. Pierce to take a group of men and thoroughly search the garage portion of the basement. This assignment was in preparation and security purposes in the transfer of Harvey Lee Oswald, W/M/24, to the County Jail from the City Jail.

I then obtained thisteen (13) Reserve Officers from the Detail Room and with the aid of Sergeant J. A. Putnam, Officers L. E. Jez, and A. R. Brook we conducted a systematic search of the basement. The men were advised to check very carefully the cars, trucks, and the overhanging pipes, and air conditioning ducts. Before the search was started at the northern side of the basement, the following men were assigned at these locations:

B. G. Patterson	Top of ramp on Commerce
R. E. Vaughn	Top of ramp on Main
A. R. Brook	Basement Elevators
R. C. Nelson	Basement Entrance From City Hall
Reserve Officer	South Portion Of Basement At The Engine Room Entrance

These men were advised to permit no one in the basement other than properly identified pressmen or law enforcement officers, and not to leave these assignments for any reason until relieved, by either myself or Sergeant Putnam.

The above assignments were later supplemented by the officers as follows:

L. E. Jez	Top Commerce Street Ramp
L. C. Taylor	Top Commerce Street Ramp

In addition numerous reserve officers (names of which I did not retain) were assigned to these locations.

At approximately 11:00 A.M. an armored car was backed into the Commerce Street Exit to the basement.

27

COMMISSION EXHIBIT No. 2002—Continued

Page 2

Shortly after, approximately 11:15 A.M., Lieutenant Pierce approached me just outside the Jail Office and advised me to ride in the Armored Car and to give him two (2) officers to go with him in his car. I advised Sergeant Putnam to get an unassigned man (Sergeant Maxey) and go with Lieutenant Pierce.

I then went to the Armored Car and remained approximately five minutes until I heard the shot and saw the commotion at the bottom of the ramp which was approximately fifty (50) feet from me.

I immediately ran to the location to assist the officers with the crowd.

It was then, while the detectives had the suspect on the floor, that I recognized him (the suspect) as Jack Ruby.

I knew Jack Ruby as the manager of the Carousel Club located in the 1300 block of Commerce. I met him while I was assigned as a sergeant on Zone 100 which includes the location of the Carousel Club.

At no time during the day had I seen Jack Ruby either in nor around the City Hall. In fact I have not seen him for several months.

At approximately 12:00 Noon Chief Curry contacted me just outside his office and instructed me to escort Mr. Forrest V. Sorrells, Agent in charge of the local Secret Service, to the Fifth Floor Jail for Mr. Sorrells to interview Mr. Ruby.

After Mr. Sorrells interrogated the subject I questioned Ruby as to how he had entered the basement and the length of time he had been there. Ruby then stated to me in the presence of Sorrells that he had entered the basement through the ramp entering on Main Street. He further stated that he would estimate his total time as about three minutes before the detectives brought Oswald into his view, then he immediately shot him (Oswald).

Respectfully submitted,

[signature]
Patrick T. Dean
Sergeant of Police
Patrol Division

PTD/bb

27

COMMISSION EXHIBIT No. 2002—Continued

December 3, 1963

STATEMENT OF P. T. DEAN:

I know Jack Ruby and would recognize him on sight.

I did not see him in or about the City Hall prior to the shooting.

All other facts are covered in my report of November 26, 1963.

27

COMMISSION EXHIBIT No. 2002—Continued

December 8, 1963

Mr. J. E. Curry
Chief of Police

SUBJECT: Information concerning article published December 8, 1963, Dallas Times Herald.

P.T. Dean

Sir:

On December 7, 1963, at approximately 1:30 P.M., I received a telephone call at my home from a person identifying himself as Darwin Payne, representative of the Dallas Times Herald.

Mr. Payne stated his reason for calling was to verify statements made by me to the Radio and Television News Media on November 24, 1963 shortly after the assassination of Lee Harvey Oswald (accused assassinator of President John Fitzgerald Kennedy.)

Mr. Payne then asked several questions pertaining to that interview of November 24, 1963. Mr. Payne's questions seemed to be verbatim of the interview in question.

I will quote them as near as possible as they were asked, in their sequence and also my answers, which were nearly always in the affirmative or negative.

Mr. Payne: - "Were you at the Armored Car when the shot was fired?"

Answer: - "Yes."

Payne: - "Did you see the person that fired the shot at the time it was fired?"

Answer: - "No."

Payne: - "Did you see the person that fired the shot shortly after it was fired?"

Answer: - "Yes."

Payne: - "Where? Was he inside the jail office and on the floor at that time?"

Answer: - "Yes - he was on the floor and being restrained and handcuffed by several plainclothes officers."

Payne: - "Did you recognize the subject at that time as a person you knew by sight?"

Answer: - "Yes."

27

Payne: - "Did you or had you seen this person prior to this time in or around the City Hall?"

Answer: - "No."

Payne: - "And you didn't see this person enter from the Main Street ramp?"

Answer: - "Definetely not."

Payne: - "Did you see anything at the time of the shooting?"

I assumed by this question that he meant a flash from the gunfire and I asked him was this what he meant and he said yes. I then advised him that I saw smoke from the blast, and I ran immediately to the scene to control the crowd.

This terminated his questions and I asked Mr. Payne the reason for him calling as all this was old news. He then stated he was just verifying this interview and that he didn't really know what the Times Herald was going to do with this information.

I made myself very clear to Mr. Payne that I had not seen Ruby at anytime before the shooting in or around the City Hall.

On Sunday when I arrived at my home I noticed the subject article and read same with much interest and reached the conclusion that this article possibly had evolved from the telephone conversation on the previous day.

I immediately called an acquaintance and friend that is employed by the Times Herald to ascertain the identity of the reporter and this person stated that he did not know who had written the article. I then noticed the name of a reporter in the same edition, Mr. Bob Henley, and I called him, identified myself and asked him if he could advise me who had written the article. Mr. Henley stated that he didn't know for sure and related several names of persons that would have been on duty and mentioned the name of this Darwin Payne. I recognized this as the person that had called me.

I then called Mr. Payne at his home, telephone WH 6-5892, and asked him if he had written the article and he stated that he did.

The following are questions and answers I asked of Mr. Payne during this telephone conversation.

Question: - "Why did you print that I had seen Ruby enter the basement?"

Mr. Payne then answered: - "Well, I thought that you had seen him."

27

Page 3.

Question: - "What led you to believe this?"

Answer: - "This was stated in your previous interview." (Relating to the original interview of November 24, 1963.)

I then stated to Mr. Payne that I had never made such a statement to him or anyone to substantiate this conclusion. Mr. Payne then stated that he had read to me my original interview and I had confirmed all the statements in the article and that he could prove them. I advised him again that I had not, and then asked him where he had obtained a copy of my interview.

Mr. Payne then seemed to evade this question and asked me to let him call the person that had given him this assignment and that he would have him call me. I again asked him from whom he had received the assignment and he evaded again and then stated that he had not written the story, that he had only verified my previous interview. This was contradictory to his original statement, that he had written the story. He then asked me not to call the City Editor as he would contact him and advise him that I was protesting the article.

After asking him the third time Mr. Payne then stated Mr. Ken Smart (As I recollect, had assigned him the job.)

I then asked Mr. Payne if he didn't think such a statement on my part would jeopardize my job. He answered, "I imagine it would." I then thanked Mr. Payne and terminated the conversation.

At this time I contacted Captain C. E. Talbert and advised him that the article was relative to my conversation the previous day. Captain Talbert suggested I call Chief Fisher at home.

I tried to call Chief Fisher, also Chief Batchelor, and Chief Curry. I made no contact with anyone of these Chiefs. This was approximately 10:30 A.M.

I then called the Chief's offices downtown in an effort to locate one of them. Captain O. A. Jones answered and when I identified myself he (Captain Jones) advised me to come downtown, that he wanted to talk to me. I asked him was it regarding the article in the paper and he stated yes.

At no time during my conversations with Mr. Payne or anyone from the Times Herald was there any verbal abuse or altercation.

Respectfully submitted,

P. TREVORE DEAN
SERGEANT OF POLICE
PATROL DIVISION

PTD/pf

27

COMMISSION EXHIBIT No. 2002—Continued

Mr. J. E. Curry
Chief of Police

December 5, 1963

Re: Interview with Nolan Dement
White Male - 19 years old
3301 Worth St.
TA 6-1490

Sir:

Mr. Dement was interviewed at his place of employment, Colonial Western Insurance Company, at approximately 1:30 p.m., December 5, 1963, to determine if he had been in the basement of the City Hall on the morning of the Oswald shooting and to know and determine if he had taken any pictures while there.

Mr. Dement stated he had not entered the basement of the City Hall; that he was on the Commerce Street side of the City Hall on the morning of the shooting; did not take any pictures and could not add anything of value to the investigation.

Respectfully submitted,

P. J. McCaghren
P. J. McCaghren
Lieutenant, Burglary & Theft Bureau

C. C. Wallace
C. C. Wallace
Lieutenant, Juvenile Bureau

mw

28

COMMISSION EXHIBIT No. 2002—Continued

REPORT ON OFFICER'S DUTIES IN REGARDS TO OSWALD'S MURDER

C. N. DHORITY - #476

Sunday, November 24, 1963, about 9:30 AM, Capt. Fritz directed Dets. J. R. Leavelle, L. C. Graves and myself to go to the fifth floor jail and bring Lee Harvey Oswald to his office. We brought Oswald to Captain Fritz's office, where he was interrogated by Capt. Fritz, Mr. Kelly of the Secret Service, Mr. Sorrels of the Secret Service, and Mr. Holmes of the Postal Department. They talked to Oswald until about 11:10 AM. Chief Curry came into Capt. Fritz's office when the interrogation was going on. At the end of the interrogation, Capt. Fritz gave me the keys to his car, and told me to park it along the door from the jail office in the basement. I went to the basement and unlocked Capt. Fritz's car and proceeded to drive the car into the driveway. There was a plain black police car in front of me, and the officers who I could not recognize, drove this car up the ramp to Main Street exit. I was backing Capt. Fritz's car in front of the jail office, and was having trouble getting through the news reporters that had jammed the ramp driveway. While I was backing up, I was turned around in the seat looking back to keep from running over the reporters. Capt. Fritz came out of the jail door, followed by Det. J. R. Leavelle handcuffed to Oswald. Det. L. C. Graves was to Oswald's left. They were walking to the car while I was still moving the car back. Capt. Fritz opened the right rear door of the car I was driving, and I noticed a man move quickly across the right rear of the car. This man moved to Oswald and shot. I recognized this man as Jack Ruby, a man I had seen a few times before in previous years. When Ruby shot, Det. Graves grabbed the pistol Ruby had in his hand. The crowd of reporters closed in with the police officers, and I jumped out of the car, and went into the jail office.

29

COMMISSION EXHIBIT No. 2002—Continued

C. N. DHORITY - (Oswald Murder) - Page 2

The officers had Ruby, and Det. Leavelle was being unhandcuffed from Oswald. Capt. Fritz directed me to return to the basement and have the Supervisor Officer to obtain the names of everyone in the basement. I went to Capt. C. E. Talbert and gave him Capt. Fritz's message. I then moved Capt. Fritz's car out of the driveway where the ambulance could get to the jail office. When the ambulance came, I rode in the ambulance with Oswald to Parkland Hospital. I stayed at Parkland Hospital until Oswald was pronounced dead. Det. C. W. Brown and I went with Oswald's body to the morgue where we waited until Dr. Earl Rose made his preliminary pictures of the body prior to the autopsy. I turned over Oswald's clothing to Dr. Earl Rose, and returned to the Homicide Office in the City Hall approximately 5:30 PM. I stayed in the Homicide Office with Mr. Stewart and went through the property of Oswald. I made copies of letters and identification from Oswald's property for Mr. Stewart. I also made copies of all the affidavits that had been taken by the Homicide Office and Sheriff's Office for Mr. Sorrells of the Secret Service.

29

COMMISSION EXHIBIT No. 2002—Continued

December 9, 1963

Mr. J. E. Curry
Chief of Police

Subject: Telephone Interview with Mr. J. B. English, KRLD-TV Cameraman, 4509 Live Oak, TA1-5554.

Sir:

At approximately 3:30 p.m., December 9, 1963, I contacted Mr. J. B. English, by telephone, regarding his knowledge of the incident (Oswald shooting) which occurred Sunday morning, November 24, 1963.

Mr. English stated he was taking continuous pictures in the basement of the City Hall and started taking film at the time they backed the armored car into the Commerce Street ramp. He was working with Channel 4 Camera behind the railing, this would be the camera on the North side, and that he was "feeding all the time".

Mr. English stated he did not know Jack Ruby and did not see Jack Ruby prior to the shooting.

Mr. English also stated he did not take any shots toward the Main Street ramp. I asked him if he could tell me if this was one continuous film that we viewed on video tape at the KRLD-TV Station. He stated that he would have no way of knowing whether the control monitored all of his continuous pictures.

Mr. English stated he had been interviewed by Agents of the Federal Bureau of Investigation.

Respectfully submitted,

C C Wallace
C. C. Wallace
Lieutenant of Police
Juvenile Bureau

30

November 30, 1963

STATEMENT OF D. K. ERWIN:

I left theCity Hall at approximately 11:00 A. M. for my traffic assignment at Commerce and Pearl Expressway, and did not return prior to the shooting.

I do not know Jack Ruby.

31

November 26, 1963

Mr. J. E. Curry
Chief of Police

Subject: Assignment of Officer
D. K. Erwin, #1849
Sunday, November 24, 1963

Sir:

At approximately 9:20 A.M., November 24, 1963, my partner, T. R. Burton #1308 and myself, received a radio call to report to 511.

We arrived at 511 a few minutes later and were advised to report to the basement of city hall to Sgt. Dean.

Sgt. Dean assigned me to report to the corner of Commerce Street and Pearl Expressway to work traffic. I left immediately for this assignment. I worked this assignment for approximately 30 minutes, then Captain Talbert told me to report to command post at Parkland Hospital Code 2, which I did.

Respectfully submitted,

D. K. Erwin
D. K. Erwin
Patrolman, #1849
Patrol Division

DKE/ch

31

COMMISSION EXHIBIT No. 2002—Continued

November 26, 1963

Mr. J. E. Curry
Chief of Police

Subject: Assignment of Officer
M. E. Farris #1832
Sunday, November 24, 1963

Sir:

On November 24, 1963, at approximately 10:00 A.M., I reported to the Patrol Captain's office. At the direction of Captain Talbert I reported to the basement parking area to receive assignment.

At approximately 10:45 A.M. I was assigned to the intersection of Elm and Lamar, with instructions from Sgt. Dean to clear the intersection of all traffic upon the approach of the vehicle bearing the prisoner. I immediately left the basement and proceeded to my assignment.

At approximately 11:30 A.M., Officer G. L. Tolbert drove up in a squad car and advised that we were to report to Parkland Hospital. We immediately proceeded to Parkland and reported to Sgt. Steel for assignment.

Respectfully submitted,

M. E. Farris,
Patrolman #1832
Patrol Division

MEF/ch

32

COMMISSION EXHIBIT No. 2002—Continued

November 29, 1963

Statement of M. E. Farris:

I left the City Hall at 10:45 A. M., for a traffic assignment at Elm and Lamar, and did not return prior to the shooting.

I do not know Jack Ruby.

32

COMMISSION EXHIBIT No. 2002—Continued

December 9, 1963

Mr. J. E. Curry
Chief of Police

Re: Interview with Mr. Warren Ferguson
5406 Windswept
Houston, Texas
Home Phone: MO5-6461
Business Phone: SU1-1141

Sir:

On December 5, 1963, Lieutenant F. I. Cornwall and Lieutenant Jack Revill interviewed Warren Ferguson in Houston, Texas, at the Houston Police Department.

Mr. Ferguson states that on Sunday, November 24, 1963, that he was working for ABC Television as a soundman for Mr. James R. Davidson, who is a cameraman for ABC. His assignment was to cover the transfer of Oswald from the City Jail to the County Jail. At about 8:30 a.m. Mr. Ferguson, along with the rest of the crew, went to the basement of the Police and Courts Building and into the Jail Office. They stayed inside the Jail Office until approximately 10:00 a.m. At that time an officer came into the room and stated that all persons except police officers would have to clear the area. Mr. Ferguson and his cameraman then moved into the hallway directly in front of the Jail Office so that they might get pictures of Lee Harvey Oswald through the Jail Office window. This location is in front of where you pay your fines inside of the double doors. They stayed at this location until Oswald was brought down on the elevator for the transfer.

When Oswald was brought down on the elevators and walked through the Jail Office into the basement, they stayed at this same location taking pictures, and as Oswald entered the basement from the Jail Office, their view was blocked by Oswald's escort and the double doors, and they were unable to get any pictures of the shooting.

Mr. Ferguson further stated that from the time when he first arrived at the Police and Courts Building, which was Friday afternoon, November 22, 1963, and until the time of the shooting, November 24, 1963, at no time did he ever see Jack Ruby

The film that was shot during the incident of November 24, 1963, was sent to Mr. Jack Bush, News Director, American Broadcasting Company, 7 West 66th Street, New York 23, New York.

Mr. Ferguson further stated that he had been interviewed by an agent of the Federal Bureau of Investigation.

F. I. Cornwall
F. I. Cornwall
Lieutenant, Special Service Bureau

Jack Revill
Jack Revill
Lieutenant, Special Service Bureau

FIC:nw

33

COMMISSION EXHIBIT No. 2002—Continued

Mr. J. E. Curry
Chief of Police

December 5, 1963

Re: Interview with Bob Finley - Dallas Times Herald

Sir:

Mr. Finley was interviewed at approximately 4:45 p.m., December 4, 1963. Mr. Finley stated that he arrived at the City Hall November 24, 1963, at approximately 8:15 a.m. with his helper, Bob Jackson and that his identification was actually not checked but he personally knew those officers when he entered.

Mr. Finley actually didn't take any pictures but was standing in the area where the cars would turn to go into the basement parking with Bob Jackson standing to his left.

Mr. Finley stated he did not know Jack Ruby and would have had a chance to at least see most of the people present before the shooting, but does not remember seeing this man there.

Respectfully submitted,

P. J. McCaghren
Lieutenant, Burglary & Theft Bureau

C. C. Wallace
Lieutenant, Juvenile Bureau

nw

34

Commission Exhibit No. 2002—Continued

No ... er 29, 1963

Statement of L. L. ...

I left the City Hall at 10:45 A. M. to work tr... at Harwoo... and Elm, and did not return to the City Hall.

I do not know Jack Ruby.

35

Commission Exhibit No. 2002—Continued

November 26, 19

Mr. J. E. Curry
Chief of Police

Subject: Assignment of Officer
Leon L. Fox, #1562
Sunday, November 24, 1963

Sir:

On Sunday, November 24, 1963, shortly after 9:00 A.M. I received an order to report to station 511. On my arrival I was told to stand by at this location for further instructions. At approximately 10:15 A.M., I was told, along with other officers, to report to the City Hall basement. These instructions were relayed to us by Patrolman L. C. Taylor. After we reported to the basement we were advised to bring our shot guns from our cars for safe keeping. The cars were parked on the street.

I was given a corner assignment by Sergeant P. T. Dean at Harwood and Elm Street and left the City Hall about 10:45 A.M. to report to this location. I stayed at this location until I heard over another officer's radio, stopped near my corner, that all officers working corner assignments were to report to Parkland Hospital. I then left my corner and reported to the entrance of Parkland Hospital, where I was given the assignment of checking identification of each person entering the hospital.

Respectfully submitted,

Leon L. Fox

Leon L. Fox
Patrolman, #1562
Patrol Division

LLF/ch

35

Commission Exhibit No. 2002—Continued

December 6, 1963

Mr. J.E. Curry
Chief of Police

Subject: Threatening Call
Regarding Oswald

Sir:

At about 3:45 A.M. November 24, 1963 Mr. Newsome of the Federal Bureau of Investigation called this office and stated his office had received an anonymous call from a male individual indicating that a group was going to kill Oswald that day, that night or the following day. Caller stated that he did not want any officer hurt, that was the reason for the call, but they were going to kill Oswald and there was nothing anyone could do about it.

Subsequently about 5:00 A.M. or 5:30 A.M. I called Captain Fritz at home and related substance of the threatening call. Captain Fritz told me Chief Curry was handling the transfer of Oswald and suggested I call him.

Between 5:30 A.M. and 5:45 A.M. Deputy Cox or Coy, exact name unknown, of the Dallas Sheriff's Office called this office and stated that Sheriff Decker had instructed him to call the Dallas Police Department and request that Chief Curry call him about the transfer of Oswald. The Deputy Sheriff indicated Sheriff Decker wanted Oswald moved as soon as possible.

As I recall I had a second conversation with Captain Fritz regarding Decker wanting to move Oswald as soon as possible. Fritz stated that I should call Chief Curry.

About 6:00 A.M. I attempted to call Chief Curry at home. The telephone was busy, and after about fifteen minutes, I asked the operator to check the line for conversation. She reported trouble on the line.

By this time it was approximately 6:15 A.M., and Captain C.E. Talbert relieved me. I told Talbert of the threat, of the Deputy Sheriff's call, and my attempt to contact Chief Curry. Captain Talbert said he would send a squad by the residence of Chief Curry and have him call the office.

Respectfully submitted,

William B. Frazier
WILLIAM B. FRAZIER
CAPTAIN OF POLICE

WBF/jh

36

Commission Exhibit No. 2002—Continued

December 8, 1963

Mr. J. E. Curry
Chief of Police

Capt Fritz

Sir:

I wish to submit the following report relative to the transfer of Lee Oswald.

In the early afternoon of November 23, 1963 Chief Curry called me by telephone and asked me when we would be ready to transfer Oswald. Either this conversation or a later conversation I made some remark that I didn't know whether we were to transfer him or whether someone else was going to transfer him, and the Chief made some remark about talking to the Sheriff and that we were to transfer him. I told the Chief we were still talking to him, and he asked me if we could be ready to transfer him by 4:00 pm. I told him I didn't think we could finish our questioning by that time, and he asked me if we could be finished by 10:00 am the next morning. Chief Curry said, "I need to tell these people something definite." Who he was referring to I do not know. I told him I thought we could be ready by that time.

During the night or early morning hours of November 23, I received a telephone call from Captain W. B. Frazier, who told me that they were going to have to transfer Oswald as some threat had been received and that someone was going to try to kill him. I told Captain Frazier that no security had been set up for his transfer at that time and that he had better check with the Chief, as he was making some arrangements for the transfer. Later, Captain Frazier called me back and said that he was unable to reach the Chief and he was going to leave him where he was.

While interviewing Oswald on November 24 in conjunction with Harry D. Holmes, Post Office Inspector, Forrest Sorrels and Tom Kelly of the Secret Service, and in the presence of L. D. Montgomery, L. C. Graves, J. R. Leavelle and C. N. Dhority of the Homicide and Robbery Bureau, Chief Curry came to the office and

37

asked if I was ready to transfer the prisoner to the Dallas County Jail. James Bookhout, F. B. I. and possibly other officers, who were assisting in the investigation and questioning, were standing in or just outside my office door. I told him I was ready to start any time the security was completed. Chief Curry advised me that the large cameras had been moved away from the jail office and that everything was prepared and that the people had been moved back across Commerce and that some newsmen would be in the basement, but would be well back in the garage.

Someone had ordered an armored truck, and it was agreed that we let a police car lead the armored truck as if the prisoner was in it, and when he turned to the left off Commerce where he was to go to Elm and turn left, while we would actually have the prisoner in an unmarked police car and turn to the left on Main Street followed by another group of officers in another police car and take him to the County Jail.

Security had been set up, we were told, at the County Jail, and I instructed the officers in the car that did not have the prisoner to drive just past the back entrance to the County Jail, and we would drive in the passageway made for unloading prisoners where a steel door could be dropped down behind us.

Chief Curry then told me that he and Chief Stevenson, who was with him, would go on to the County Jail and meet us there.

I instructed James R. Leavelle to handcuff his left hand to the prisoner's right hand. The prisoner was already handcuffed. I instructed L. C. Graves to walk to his left and L. D. Montgomery directly behind him, and I told them that I would walk in front of the prisoner out of the door to the car. We decided that the best route would be through the jail and out of the left door

37

of the jail and then to the basement giving us but a few feet to the car.

As we were leaving to go to the jail elevator, I told Det. T. L. Baker to call downstairs and tell them we were on the way down and have the car ready. Det. Baker called and Lt. Wiggins said all was clear.

Before taking the man out of the jail office I asked one of the uniform officers who was standing to my right if everything was secure. I believe that two officers answered me that everything was all right. I then advised the officers following me to come on, and at this moment Officer Dhority, who was driving the police car for the prisoner, was backing into position with the police car we were to put the prisoner in. As I reached for the car door and told the officer to put him in the car, I heard a shot. On my left I saw Officer Graves and a number of officers grab this man and pull him to the pavement. Det. Graves twisted the gun from his hand and handed it to me. The prisoner was carried into the jail office and a doctor was summoned and arrived almost immediately and went to work with the prisoner until an ambulance arrived. Some of the other officers took the man that I found was Jack Ruby up into the jail.

I instructed Officers Dhority, Leavelle and Graves to ride with the prisoner in the ambulance. Dets. E. R. Beck, L. D. Montgomery, C. W. Brown and myself followed the ambulance to the hospital, where security was kept until he was released to an undertaker.

Immediately after the shooting, I asked Detective Dhority to contact the captain of the Uniform Division to secure the names of all of the people in the basement at the time of the shooting.

37

November 30, 1963

J. E. Curry
Chief of Police

Re: Shooting of Lee Harvey Oswald
C. Goolsby

Sir:

C. Goolsby was interviewed by Lieutenants C. C. Wallace and P. G. McCaghren at 10:25 am on November 30, 1963. The interview was essentially the same as his original report dated November 27, 1963. The following was added by C. Goolsby:

I have been asked if I know Jack Ruby, and have been shown a picture of him. I do not know this man. I have no idea how he got into the basement of the City Hall.

Immediately after the shooting, I heard someone say it was Jack Ruby who did the shooting.

I have not been interviewed by the Federal Bureau of Investigation.

Respectfully submitted,

C C Wallace
C. C. Wallace, Lieutenant
Juvenile Bureau

P G McCaghren
P. G. McCaghren, Lieutenant
Burglary & Theft Bureau

lh

38

November 24, 1963

Mr. J. E. Curry
Chief of Police

Subject: Shooting of Lee Harvey Oswald.

Sir:

At the time Lee Harvey Oswald was shot, I was stationed by the double doors leading from the jail lobby to our basement parking area, just opposite the door going into the jail booking office. I observed some members of the press standing opposite my position. They had been directed against the opposite wall, leaving a corridor between the group on my side and the group on that side.

As Captain Fritz, Detective Leavelle and Detective Graves emerged with the prisoner, a group of reporters fell in back of them as they walked. I overheard one of them ask, "What have you got to say now?". At this exact moment, I heard the shot. Due to the crowd having closed behind the men, I was unable to see anything. Immediately after the shot, so many officers grabbed the suspect and completely engulfed him that it was impossible to see who he was. Almost immediately, Lieutenant McKinney told me to go into the jail lobby and stop incoming people. I was assisted by Detective B. L. Beaty and two uniform officers, whose identity I cannot recall.

Respectfully submitted,

C Goolsby

C. Goolsby
Detective, ID#1141
Juvenile Bureau
Criminal Investigation Division

38

COMMISSION EXHIBIT No. 2002—Continued

December 4, 1963

Mr. J. E. Curry
Chief of Police

Re: Interview of Eva Grant by Mr. Joe Long of Radio Station KLIF

Sir:

The following is a taped interview with Eva Grant, sister of Jack Ruby. This interview was conducted by Mr. Joe Long of Radio Station KLIF on Sunday, November 24, 1963:

"I want it known by everyone that I do not blame the Dallas Police Department for what happened Sunday morning. Chief Curry and his men did not neglect their duty. I honestly believe my brother had got hold of a press pass which got him into the Police Department. This criticism of the Police Department is uncalled for and they must not be held in blame. My brother was grieving so, and I feel it got the best of him. I know; he was with me a great deal Friday and Saturday. He was very upset about the death of the President. When he came face to face with Oswald, he must have thought this man had done him some personal harm and I believe my brother become insane suddenly. Otherwise this never could have been done. Please, please, don't blame the Police Department."

Respectfully submitted,

J. H. Sawyer
Inspector
Dallas Police Department

lh

39

COMMISSION EXHIBIT No. 2002—Continued

REPORT ON OFFICER'S DUTIES IN REGARDS TO OSWALD'S MURDER

L. C. GRAVES - #702

Sunday, November 24, 1963, was the day set for the transfer of Lee Harvey Oswald to the County Jail. The time set for the transfer was 10:00 AM. Shortly before 9:30 AM, J. R. Leavelle, C. N. Dhority, and I brought Oswald down from the fifth floor jail for final questioning by Capt. Fritz, Agents Sorrel and Kelly from the Secret Service. Others present during the questioning were Mr. Holmes from the U. S. Post Office Department, Detectives L. D. Montgomery, C. N. Dhority, J. R. Leavelle, and I. Chief Curry was present only a few minutes at the beginning of the questioning and at the end just prior to Oswald's removal to the basement. Before leaving our office with Oswald, Capt. Fritz instructed J. R. Leavelle to handcuff his left arm to the right arm of Oswald. I was to walk by Oswald's left side, holding his left arm. Oswald's hands were handcuffed together in front of him. Det. Leavelle, Oswald, and I were escorted from this office via the jail elevator to the jail office by Capt. Fritz, Lt. Swain, and Det. L. D. Montgomery. At the jail office door that leads into the hall, we stopped for a few seconds until Capt. Fritz and Lt. Swain made sure the hall-way was clear. We got the all clear sign and made our way through the hall to the edge of the ramp where we had paused momentarily awaiting the arrival of our car, when suddenly out of the surging line of camera men and glaring camera lights, Jack Ruby sprang forward and fired one round from a pistol into the stomach of Lee Harvey Oswald before I could grab his pistol and disarm him.

Oswald was immediately placed in an O'Neal ambulance and rushed to Parkland Hospital, where he underwent surgery within 10 minutes after his

40

L. C. Graves - Page 2 (Oswald's Murder)

arrival. Oswald was pronounced dead at 1:07 PM, November 24, 1963, by Dr. Tom Shires, Parkland Staff. Detectives J. R. Leavelle, Burgess, and I, along with Dr. Bieberdorf, rode in the ambulance with Oswald to Parkland. At the hospital I changed into operating room clothing and accompanied Oswald to the Operating Room and stood guard until he was pronounced dead.

The pistol I took from Jack Ruby was turned over to Capt. Fritz at Parkland Hospital.

40

November 30, 1963

J. E. Curry
Chief of Police

Re: Shooting of Lee Harvey Oswald
Interview of C. A. Greeson

Sir:

C. A. Greeson was interviewed by Lieutenants C. C. Wallace and P. G. McCaghren at 2:50 pm on November 29, 1963. The interview was essentially the same as his original report dated November 27, 1963. The following was added by C. A. Greeson:

I have been asked if I know Jack Ruby. I believe I saw the person one time in 1957, I am not sure. I did not see this person in the City Hall prior to the shooting.

The first time I heard the man's name in the basement of the City Hall was when I overheard some detectives state that the person who shot Oswald was Jack Ruby. I have no idea how he got into the basement of City Hall.

I have been interviewed by Federal Bureau Investigation agent Scott.

Respectfully submitted,

C C Wallace
C. C. Wallace, Lieutenant
Juvenile Bureau

P G McCaghren
P. G. McCaghren, Lieutenant
Burglary & Theft Bureau

lh

41

COMMISSION EXHIBIT No. 2002—Continued

AFFIDAVIT IN ANY FACT

THE STATE OF TEXAS
COUNTY OF DALLAS

11/24/63
4:15 pm

BEFORE ME, ______________________

a Notary Public in and for said County, State of Texas, on this day personally appeared ______________________

Who, after being by me duly sworn, on oath deposes and says:

I was assigned at about 10:30 this morning to go downstairs to help guard the departure of Oswald. I was following a group of fifteen or twenty detectives. I was standing in the doorway by the telephone booths directly across from the jail office windows. Capt. Jones was giving instructions to keep an aisle open from the jail office to the ramp. There was a lot of newsmen and cameramen moving in and out. I was flanked by Det. Chambers on my right and Detectives Dawson and Archer on my left. At about 11:25 AM when Capt. Fritz came out of the jail office followed by his detectives from his bureau who had Oswald between them. We started closing up the rear and there was the sound of a gunshot. I had momentarily lost sight of Oswald and the officers escorting him because other detectives were closing in behind them. I did see a man holding a gun and detectives diving at him attempting to wrest the gun from him and subdue him. I jumped toward the man trying to grab the gun but was blocked out by other detectives. I didn't see where the man with the gun came from or see the shot fired.

SUBSCRIBED AND SWORN TO BEFORE ME THIS ______ DAY OF ______________ A.D. 196__

____
Notary Public, Dallas County, Texas

CPS-GF-413

COMMISSION EXHIBIT No. 2002—Continued

AFFIDAVIT IN ANY FACT

THE STATE OF TEXAS
COUNTY OF DALLAS

BEFORE ME, ______________________________

a Notary Public in and for said County, State of Texas, on this day personally appeared ______________________________

Who, after being by me duly sworn, on oath deposes and says: Eight or ten detectives wrestled the man to the floor and I heard Capt. Talbert yell to block off all exits and entrances to the basement. I went to the doors leading out of the basement by the information desk and wouldn't let anyone in or out. I remained here until Capt. Jones sent me to Parkland Hospt. with a group of eight other detectives and Lt. McKinley to guard exits and entrances to the third floor where Oswald had been taken. I remained on this assignment until relieved at about 3[10] pm

C A Greeson 1250
____

SUBSCRIBED AND SWORN TO BEFORE ME THIS ____ DAY OF ______________ A.D. 196

____
Notary Public, Dallas County, Texas

CPS-GF-413

41

COMMISSION EXHIBIT NO. 2002—Continued

November 27, 1963

Mr. J. E. Curry
Chief of Police

Sir:

I should like to submit the following report concerning the events occurring on November 24, 1963.

About 10:30 a.m. on November 24, 1963, I was assigned to go downstairs to help guard the departure of Oswald. I was following a group of fifteen or twenty detectives. I was standing in the doorway by the telephone booths directly across from the jail office windows. Captain Jones was giving instructions to keep an aisle open from the jail office to the ramp. There were a lot of newsmen and cameramen moving in and out. I was flanked by Detective Chambers on my right and Detectives Dawson and Archer on my left.

About 11:25 a.m. when Captain Fritz came out of the jail office, he was followed by two detectives from his bureau who had Oswald between them. We started closing up the rear and there was the sound of a gunshot. I had momentarily lost sight of Oswald and the officers escorting him because other detectives were closing in behind them. I did see a man holding a gun and detectives diving at him attempting to wrest the gun from him and subdue him.

I jumped toward the man trying to grab the gun but was blocked out by other detectives. I didn't see where the man with the gun came from or see the shot fired.

Eight or ten detectives wrestled the man to the floor and I heard Captain Talbert yell to block off all exits and entrances to the basement. I went to the doors leading out of the basement by the information desk and wouldn't let anyone in or out.

I remained here until Captain Jones sent me to Parkland Hospital with a group of eight other detectives and Lieutenant McKinley to guard exits and entrances to the third floor where Oswald had been taken. I remained on this assignment until relieved at about 3:10 p.m.

Respectfully submitted,

C. A. Greeson

C. A. Greeson
Detective
Criminal Investigation Division

41

November 29, 1963

STATEMENT OF T. R. GREGORY.

I left the City Hall at approximately 10:50 a.m. for my traffic assignment at Central and Elm Streets.

I do not know Jack Ruby and never heard of him until this incident.

42

COMMISSION EXHIBIT No. 2002—Continued

November 27, 1963

Mr. J. E. Curry
Chief of Police

Subject: Special Assignment Of Officer T. R. Gregory #1848 On Sunday, November 24, 1963

Sir:

At 9:00 A.M., Sunday, November 24, 1963 I was working Squad 93 with Officer H. J. Wages. We received a call to report to Station 511. We arrived at Station 511 at 9:25 A.M. and remained there until 9:50 A.M.

At that time we were told to go to the basement of the City Hall. There I was assigned to the corner of Central and Elm Streets. I was to stop all traffic at that corner when the Special Detail flashed its lights at me, and then follow behind to the County Jail to help with the crowd control.

At approximately 11:50 A.M. we were told to report to Parkland Hospital for an assignment there.

Respectfully submitted,

Thomas R. Gregory
Thomas R. Gregory
Patrolman #1848
Patrol Division

TRG/bb

42

COMMISSION EXHIBIT No. 2002—Continued

Mr. J. E. Curry
Chief of Police

December 5, 1963

Re: Interview with Robert Hankal
4233 Travis, Apartment 214
KRLD-TV

Sir:

Mr. Hankal was interviewed at approximately 4:20 p.m., December 4, 1963. He was operating with CBS-Live Camera on the East side of the driveway. Mr. Hankal stated he did not know Jack Ruby and being busy with the camera, he had no opportunity to see him until the time the shot was being fired. Mr. Hankal stated his identification had been checked when he entered the basement.

We contacted Mr. Fritz Kuler of KRLD-TV and made arrangements to obtain the pictures taken by Robert Hankal. They should be ready sometime today.

Respectfully submitted,

F. J. McCaghren
Lieutenant, Burglary & Theft Bureau

C. C. Wallace
Lieutenant, Juvenile Bureau

nw

43

COMMISSION EXHIBIT No. 2002—Continued

November 30, 1963

Mr. J. E. Curry
Chief of Police

Sir:

Re: Interview of Reserve Officer,
Patrolman Oliver W. Harrison, 423

On November 30, 1963 Reserve Officer, Patrolman Oliver W. Harrison was interviewed by the undersigned officers as to any information he might have concerning the shooting of Lee Harvey Oswald which was not covered in his original report dated November 27, 1963.

Patrolman Harrison stated that the only discrepancy in his original report is that he was assigned to the Municipal Building and not to the Police and Records Building as his original report stated. As this first report was given by telephone, Harrison feels that he was probably misunderstood by the person taking the report.

Harrison further states that he has not been contacted by any federal agency at this time.

Respectfully submitted,

F.I. Cornwall, Lieutenant
Special Service Bureau

Jack Revill, Lieutenant
Special Service Bureau

jh

44

COMMISSION EXHIBIT No. 2002—Continued

November 27, 1963

Mr. J. E. Curry
Chief of Police

Sir:

This is a statement of facts relating to my activity as a Reserve Officer Sunday, November 24, 1963, to the best of my knowledge and recollection.

1. Approximate time I reported to duty. 10:00 A. M.

2. I reported to Lt. Merrell in Assembly Room.

3. I was assigned ----

   Shortly after I arrived I was assigned to the sidewalk on the south side of the City Hall near the ramp exit. Some regular officers were guarding the ramp exit. After a few minutes a man who I recognized to be a detective asked me to see that the glass doors at the top of the steps of the police and courts building were kept closed, and no one to leave or enter. I remained in this position for about 30 minutes after the shooting.

4. Names of other officers in the same area that I can recollect are:

   Res. Lt. Suits, Montgomery, A. W. Capps, and several I do not know names of.

5. Did you know Ruby? No.

6. When and under what circumstance did you see Ruby?

   Never did see him.

Signed: Oliver Wayne Harrison
O. W. Harrison

44

November 30, 1963

J. E. Curry
Chief of Police

Re: Shooting of Lee Harvey Oswald
Interview of W. J. Harrison

Sir:

W. J. Harrison was interviewed by Lieutenants C. C. Wallace and P. G. McCaghren at 12 noon on November 29, 1963. The interview was essentially the same as his original report dated November 27, 1963. The following was added by W. J. Harrison:

I was assigned to the basement of the City Hall by Captain Martin. I was there approximately 10 minutes before the prisioner Oswald was brought out onto the ramp. Prior to that I took up a post between the west wall of the drive way and the ramp. As I recall, the television lights were to my left and there was a reporter with a mike, who is shown in the picture of the shooting, standing to my right. As Oswald and the escorts came out on the ramp, Jack Ruby, who I have known for several years lunged past me on my left side and was pulling his gun at the time. I immediately recognized him and shouted, "Jack." I tried to grab him as he passed me.

Ruby was not in the crowd prior to this time.

As the shooting was over, I held Ruby down while another officer searched him. I believe this man was Captain King. I recall Ruby saying, "You all know me, I'm Jack Ruby." One officer asked him why he did it, and he answered, "I hope I killed the S. O. B."

Ruby was taken to the jail office and then placed on the jail elevator which was run by Officer Lewis. Captain King, Myself, and another officer, I do not recall who, took the prisioner to the 5th floor. I recall Ruby stating on the elevator, "Do you think I'm going to let the man who shot our President get away with it?"

I have previously talked to the Federal Bureau of Investigation regarding this matter.

Respectfully submitted,

C. C. Wallace
C. C. Wallace, Lieutenant
Juvenile Bureau

P. G. McCaghren
P. G. McCaghren, Lieutenant
Burglary & Theft Bureau

lh

45

December 7, 1963

Mr. J. E. Curry
Chief of Police

Re: Second Interview of
Officer W. J. Harrison

This interview was on December 1, 1963, Further information obtained from Officer Harrison during this interview brought out other information that we considered to be important.

He stated he could not remember exactly where any of the officers were that were standing near him. He remembers 2 automobiles going out the Main Street ramp and believes that the last automobile to leave the basement was occupied by Lieutenant Pierce and other officers. He said the auto stopped at the Main Street entrance and stayed there a very short time. He said he glanced up the ramp several times and was looking toward the Main Street ramp when Lieutenant Pierce's auto made a left turn into Main Street. He also said he did not observe anyone coming down the ramp on Main Street.

Respectfully submitted,

C C Wallace
C. C. Wallace
Lieutenant, Juvenile Bureau

CCW:mw

45

COMMISSION EXHIBIT No. 2002—Continued

STATEMENT OF PATROLMAN W. J. HARRISON:

About seven or eight minutes before the shooting, I assisted a patrolman driving a squad car to go out the Main Street Ramp because the Commerce Street Ramp was blocked.

About four or five minutes after this, Lt. Pierce drove a squad car out the Main Street Ramp. I assisted him in getting through the crowd. This was about two or four minutes before the shooting.

45

COMMISSION EXHIBIT No. 2002—Continued

November 24, 1963

Mr. J. E. Curry
Chief of Police

Subject: Shooting of Lee Harvey Oswald.

Sir:

I was standing about half-way between the West wall of the driveway and the rail. As the detectives brought the prisoner out, Jack Ruby came by me from my left side with the gun in his hand. As he came by me the gun was about a foot from me in Jack's right hand. As he shot I made a move to get him and went to the floor with him as there were about six (6) of us on him at one time. I tried to grab the hand that held the pistol and the pistol was knocked out of Jack's hand after we were on the floor. I remember Detectives Cutchshaw and Lowery being on him as well as other officers. I could not say where he (Jack) came from. All I know is that he came from the rear and left of us.

After we took him in the Jail Office and was putting the handcuffs on him, he (Jack) said, "I hope I killed the S. O. B.". That is all he said until I left him on the fifth floor jail with some of the detectives.

Respectfully submitted,

W. J. Harrison

W. J. Harrison
Patrolman, ID#579
Juvenile Bureau
Criminal Investigation Division

45

COMMISSION EXHIBIT No. 2002—Continued

December 16, 1963

Mr. J. E. Curry
Chief of Police

Subject: Polygraph examination given to William J. Harrison.

Sir:

At 4:25 P.M., December 13, 1963, a polygraph examination was given to Mr. William J. Harrison.

This examination was given to determine if Mr. Harrison was telling the truth in the statement he had given. Also to determine if he saw Jack Ruby come into the basement of the City Hall prior to the shooting of Lee Harvey Oswald.

During the pre-test interview with Mr. Harrison, he stated that he was not sure that he saw the Police squad actually make a left turn on Main Street. He also stated that he did not recognize Jack Ruby until about the time the shot was fired.

The examination indicated that Mr. Harrison did not see Jack Ruby until about the time the shot was fired.

The following is a list of the pertinent questions asked and answers given.

1. Did you actually see Jack Ruby enter the basement of the City Hall?
   Answer: No Indication: True

2. Did you recognize this man to be Jack Ruby at the time of the shooting?
   Answer: Yes Indication: True

3. Did you see Jack Ruby that day before he brushed beside you?
   Answer: No Indication: True

4. Did you see Jack Ruby come down the Main Street ramp just before the shooting?
   Answer: No Indication: True

5. Did you see Jack Ruby anywhere in the basement of the City Hall before the shooting?
   Answer: No Indication: True

-1-

45

COMMISSION EXHIBIT No. 2002—Continued

December 16, 1963

Page 2

6. Did you grab at Jack Ruby about the time of the shooting?
Answer: Yes Indication: True

7. Did you speak to Jack Ruby that day before the shooting?
Answer: No Indication: True

All of the above questions were repeated during this examination with the same answers given and same indications noted.

Respectfully submitted,

Paul L. Bentley
Paul L. Bentley
Detective of Police
Identification Bureau

PLB/mol

45

COMMISSION EXHIBIT No. 2002—Continued

Mr. J. E. Curry
Chief of Police

November 27, 1963

Sir:

This is a statement of facts relating to my activity as a Reserve Officer Sunday, November 24, 1963, to the best of my knowledge and recollection.

1. Approximate time I reported to duty. 9:00 A. M.

2. I reported to Lt. Merrell in Assembly room.

3. I was in a group of five Reserves assigned to assist in the Houston-Elm area. While we were waiting for transportation (30 or 40 minutes) in the basement parking area, I assisted in holding and placing the TV Camera cables that were being set up. We were taken to the Houston-Elm area by a police squad.

4. Names of other officers in the same area that I can recollect are:

L. R. Bridges, T. D. Clinkscales.

5. Did you know Ruby? No.

6. When and under what circumstance did you see Ruby?

Never did see him.

Signed: H. H. Hatley
H. H. Hatley

46

COMMISSION EXHIBIT No. 2002—Continued

Mr. J. E. Curry
Chief of Police

Date: Nov 27, 1963

Sir:

This is a statement of facts relating to my activity as a Reserve Officr Sunday, November 24, 1963, to the best of my knowledge and recollection.

1. Approximate time I reported to duty. 9:00 a.m.

2. I reported to (person and place). LT. MERRELL in Assembly Room

3. I was assigned to (state place or area and who you assisted and what assignment consisted of such as crowd control, search, guard, etc.).
I was in a group of five Reserves assigned to assist in the Houston-Elm area. While we were waiting for transportation (30 or 40 minutes) in the basement parking area I assisted in holding a placing the TV camera Cables that were being set up. We were taken to the Houston-Elm area by a police squad.

4. Names of other officers in the same area that I can recollect are:
L.R. BRIDGES, T.D. CLINKSCALES.

5. Did you know Ruby? NO

6. When and under what circumstance did you see Ruby?
NEVER DID SEE HIM.

Print name H. H. HATLEY

Information taken by phone JMS

46

COMMISSION EXHIBIT No. 2002—Continued

November 29, 1963

STATEMENT OF OFFICER W. E. HIBBS

I left the City Hall at 11:00 a.m. to work traffic at Akard and Elm Streets and did not return to the City Hall prior to the shooting.

I do not know Jack Ruby.

47

November 26, 1963

Mr. J. E. Curry
Chief of Police

Subject: Assignment of Officer
W. E. Hibbs #825
Sunday, November 24, 1963

Sir:

On November 24, 1963 at approximately 9 A.M., I was given a call to report to 511. I arrived at the Patrol office and remained in the Sergeant's room. About 10:15 A.M. we were instructed to report to the basement. After arriving in the basement Sgt. Dean told me to get my shot gun from my car and return to the basement. When I returned, I was told to place the shot gun in a squad car.

While I was waiting for further instructions I observed Sgt. Putnam looking in a Detective's car and then stop the Police Pattie Wagon as it came into the basement. He looked in the front and then opened the rear doors and looked in.

Sgt. Putnam then directed Officer Tolbert and myself to take a position at the bottom of the North ramp, and check all cars or trucks entering the basement. While we were there, approximately 20 or 30 minutes, no vehicles or persons came down the ramp.

Sgt. Putnam then directed us to come to a spot in the parking area of the basement. We were assigned traffic corners. I reported to my corner, Akard and Elm, and there remained about 20 minutes when a passer-by informed me that Oswold had been shot. About this time I heard several sirens. I went to my squad car and asked the dispatcher if there were any instructions for the men working Elm Street. I was directed to remain on my corner till otherwise informed.

In a very short time squads from the other corners began to come South on Elm Street, Code 3. One of them stopped and told me we were to report to Parkland Code 3.

Respectfully submitted,

W. E. Hibbs

W. E. Hibbs
Patrolman #825
Patrol Division

WEH/ch

47

December 1, 1963

Mr. J. E. Curry
Chief of Police

Sir:

Re: Interview of Reserve Officer,
Patrolman Harold B. Holly Jr., 325

On December 1, 1963 Reserve Officer, Patrolman Harold B. Holly Jr. was interviewed by the undersigned officers as to any information he might have concerning the shooting of Lee Harvey Oswald. Holly had not submitted a report prior to the interview with these officers.

Patrolman Holly stated that he reported to the City Hall at approximately 11:30 a.m. on November 24, 1963. He was assigned to work traffic at the intersection of Main and Harwood Streets. At approximately 11:45 a.m. he was assigned to Parkland Hospital to assist in the handling of traffic at that location.

While there, Holly stated that an unknown reserve police officer related to him that he, the unknown reserve officer, had passed Jack Ruby into the basement of the City Hall after Ruby had presented press credentials.

Holly was shown photographs of several reserve officers by Captain J. M. Solomon and was unable to identify this unknown reserve officer.

Captain Solomon advised the undersigned officers to be skeptical of this information and not to place too much credence in it.

Holly stated that he was not familiar with Jack Ruby and had not seen him on the date of Oswald's shooting. At this time Holly has not been contacted by any federal agency.

Respectfully submitted,

Jack Revill

Jack Revill, Lieutenant
Special Service Bureau

C C Wallace

C. C. Wallace, Lieutenant
Criminal Investigation Division

jh

48

COMMISSION EXHIBIT No. 2002—Continued

November 29, 1963

Mr. J. E. Curry
Chief of Police

SUBJECT: Security Transfer of Prisoner

Sir:

Our Reserve Officer, H. B. Holly, Jr. No. 710 C I, 3429 Antilles, Mesquite, informed me this date that he was working Sunday, November 24, at City Hall approximately ten minutes after the shooting of Oswald, and then he was sent to Parkland. While at Parkland, he engaged in conversation with another Reserve Officer whose name is unknown to him.

This Reserve Officer told Mr. Holly that prior to the shooting, he either observed, or himself admitted Jack Ruby to the basement. That Mr. Ruby was wearing a press identification card on his jacket.

Mr. Holly states he could recognize this Reserve Officer if he could see him again. He also states that there was a roster that he himself was on this work roster.

Respectfully submitted,

A M Eberhardt

A. M. Eberhardt, 1267
Detective
Burglary and Theft Bureau

AME/pst

48

COMMISSION EXHIBIT No. 2002—Continued

November 30, 1963

Mr. J. E. Curry
Chief of Police

Sir:

Re: Interview of Reserve Officer,
Sergeant Jimmy R. Hopkins, 855

On November 30, 1963 Reserve Officer, Sergeant Jimmy R. Hopkins was interviewed by the undersigned officers as to any information he might have concerning the shooting of Lee Harvey Oswald not covered in his original report dated November 26, 1963.

After having read his original report, Hopkins stated that he could not add anything of significance to this first report.

Hopkins further stated that he has not been contacted by any federal agency.

Respectfully submitted,

F. I. Cornwall
F. I. Cornwall, Lieutenant
Special Service Bureau

Jack Revill
Jack Revill, Lieutenant
Special Service Bureau

jh

49

COMMISSION EXHIBIT No. 2002—Continued

November 26, 1963

Mr. J. E. Curry
Chief of Police

Sir:

This is a statement of facts relating to my activity as a Reserve Officer Sunday, November 24, 1963, to the best of my knowledge and recollection.

1. Approximate time I reported to duty. 9:30 A. M.

2. I reported to Capt. Arnett.

3. I arrived at the City Hall about 9:30 A. M., Sunday morning. I arrived in the Assembly Room about 9:40 A. M. and reported to Capt. Arnett. I had just checked in when Sgt. Dean, Dallas Police Department, came in and asked all Reserve Officers to help search the parking area in the basement of the City Hall. I personally searched all air conditioning ducts and heating ducts, above all pipes that run just under the ceiling in the basement. I also checked the open space under north ramp. I searched several cars. They all belonged to the City of Dallas.

I reported to Capt. Arnett, Police Reserve, and Sgt. Dean, Dallas Police Department, where I had searched and found clear. I was ordered to stand by for further assignment. At approximately 10:40 A. M., I was ordered by Lt. Ben McCoy to check the condition on Commerce Street in regard to number of Police Reserves to handle sightseers and traffic. I remained on Commerce Street as the Reserve Supervisor in charge of the Reserve Officers on Commerce Street, 2000 block.

At approximately 11:00, Police Chief Batchelor's car was brought out of the basement to the officer double parked just east of ramp exit. I was told by the officer that this was the Chief's car, that he left the keys in it and wanted me to keep an eye on it! I placed a Reserve by it to work traffic around it. I was told a few minutes later by Chief Batchelor that an armored truck was on the way to the City Hall. He said the truck would have to back down the exit ramp. I was asked to assist the armored truck to back down ramp. The truck arrived, two other Reserve Officers and myself worked traffic to help truck driver back down ramp. A second armored truck was parked just ahead of the Chief's car. I was working Commerce Street when the shot was fired in the basement. A detective came running out of the basement and said to seal the doors leading into City Hall. I had one man on Commerce Street door, two men on Harwood Street door, one man on Main Street door.

These were my movements from 9:35 A. M. to 11:45 A. M., Sunday morning, November 24, 1963.

Signed: J. R. Hopkins
J. R. Hopkins

49

COMMISSION EXHIBIT No. 2002—Continued

Statement of Reserve Officer J. R. Hopkins   Page 2

4. Names of other officers in the same area that I can recollect are:

Sgt. Mayo, L. W., Patrolman Chennault, J. R., and Patrolman Craig, A. B.

5. Did you know Ruby? No.

6. When and under what circumstance did you see Ruby?

Signed: J. R. Hopkins
J. R. Hopkins

49

Mr. J. E. Curry
Chief of Police

December 9, 1963

Re: Interview of Robert S. Huffaker, Jr.
4700 East Side Avenue - Apartment 115
TA 3-7269

Sir:

On December 4, 1963, Lieutenant Jack Revill and Lieutenant F. I. Cornwall interviewed Robert S. Huffaker, Jr. at Ft. Hood, Texas. Mr. Huffaker is presently serving 2 weeks active duty with the U. S. Army.

Mr. Huffaker stated that he is employed by Radio Station KRLD-TV and was on duty as a newsman in the basement of the City Hall on November 24, 1963. He stated he was operating a live microphone for both radio and TV and was stationed at the foot of the Main Street ramp of the City Hall basement. He stated to the best of his knowledge he was standing next to the railing and was to the immediate left of Police Officer W. J. Harrison.

Huffaker stated that he did not see the actual shooting of Lee Harvey Oswald as he was watching the police vehicle being backed toward his location. He stated that he was conscious of a movement to his immediate right and then heard a pistol shot. He further stated that he could not tell who shot Oswald. He first observed Jack Ruby after he had been apprehended by police officers.

Mr. Huffaker stated that he was working with the following named personnel from Station KRLD, James English, Bob Kinkle and George Phenix. These 3 individuals were also in the basement of the City Hall at the time of the Oswald shooting.

Mr. Huffaker stated that he was compelled to present his press credentials prior to gaining access to the basement and that he observed numerous members of the news media showing their press credentials before entering the basement.

Mr. Huffaker stated that he did not know Jack Ruby and that he has been interviewed by the Federal Bureau of Investigation.

Respectfully submitted,

Jack Revill
Jack Revill
Lieutenant, Special Service Bureau

F. I. Cornwall
F. I. Cornwall
Lieutenant, Special Service Bureau

JR:mw

50

December 11, 1963

Mr. J. E. Curry
Chief of Police

Subject: Interview of Mr. David Hughes

Sir:

On December 11, 1963, Lieutenant Jack Revill and Lieutenant F. I. Cornwall interviewed Mr. David Hughes of 2948 Binkley, Apartment 3, EM3-2851. Mr. Hughes is employed as a reporter by the Dallas Times Herald.

Mr. Hughes stated that he was at home on November 24, 1963, when Lee Harvey Oswald was shot by Jack Ruby; that he was viewing television and saw the shooting on television; that he immediately dressed and reported to the Times Herald City Desk for assignment. He was subsequently assigned to the City Hall and arrived there at approximately 12:15 p.m.

Mr. Hughes stated that he was instructed to interview both police officers and other persons to get their reactions to the shooting of Oswald.

Mr. Hughes stated that he interviewed Sergeant P. T. Dean and Patrolman R. E. Vaughn shortly after arriving at the City Hall. Mr. Hughes stated that Sergeant Dean was explicitly precise in what he said; that Sergeant Dean related that Jack Ruby came from the Main Street entrance ramp. Sgt. Dean did not state that he had observed Ruby come down the ramp.

A copy of Mr. Hughes original notes pertaining to the interview with Sergeant Dean are attached to this report.

Mr. Hughes stated that Patrolman Vaughn related that Ruby apparently gained access to the City Hall basement via the Main Street ramp. Mr. Vaughn stated that he did not see Ruby pass by his duty assignment.

A copy of Mr. Hughes original notes pertaining to the interview with Patrolman Vaughn are attached to this report.

Respectfully submitted,

Jack Revill

Jack Revill, Lieutenant
Special Service Bureau

F. I. Cornwall

F. I. Cornwall, Lieutenant
Special Service Bureau

JR:nw

50-A

Commission Exhibit No. 2002—Continued

hughes. ruby notes.

Dallas police sergeant P. T. Dean was standing by the armored car which was to have taken Harvey Oswald to the county jail when he was shoot. Dean said he heard someone shout"ther are bringing him out." "I focused my attention on the door where they were bringing him out. I didn't see the gun, but I heard the shot and saw the smoke from the gun. Police officers surrounding Oswald prevented me from seeing much else. Jack Ruby, Oswald's assassin, came from the north entrance(Main St. auto entrance) down the ramp. There were many ~~pik~~ police officers and press representatives in the area. Ruby jumped out from the crowd as Oswald passed and fired one shot point blank at Oswald.Following the shot I ran from the armored car to the spot of the shboting to assist in the arrest. When I got there officers had Ruby on the ground and were handcuffing him.

I went then to Oswald. He was lying on the ground, unconcious and gasping for breath - a bullet hole in his lower left side.Officers removed Ruby and Oswald was put in an ambulance, still unconcious, and taken to Parkland hospital.(Oswald was taken to emergencey room 2, next to the one Kennedy was in)

Commission Exhibit No. 2002—Continued

P.T. DEAN

Dallas police sergeant at the scene of shhoting said,"When we arrested Ruby immediately after the shooting he related that he had been to Weste n Unionwhere he sent a money order to Ft. Worth. Dean said Ruby told police that the main reason he did it was out of sympathy for Jackie Kennedy and the dead police officer. Ruby said he din't want Mrs. Kennedy to have to come back to Dallas to go through the ordeal of a trial.Ruby told police he had a gun because he often carried large sums of money with him at times. Ruby said,"I just didn't want Jackie to be subjected to the trial. I don't want to be a dead hero., but I didn't want her to have to go through the long due process of law, although I believe in it.

Dean said that he knew Ruby, but had no other comment on the acquaintence. "~~XXXXXXXX~~ Ruby ~~xxxxxxxxxxxxx~~ said of himself after his arrest that he was very sentimental. He had closed his buness for the last three days, He also said he was not a political fanatic.

50-A

Hughes.. shoot g notes

Patrolmen R. E. Vaughn of the Dallas police department was ~~xxxxx~~ standing the the doorway of the north auto entrance to police headquaters. Jack Ruby, Harvey Oswalds assailant, apparently entere d through this entrahce and down the auto ramp acco dng to police. Vaughn said he had been on duty at the entrahce for two and a half hours prior to the shooting. He said no one was admitted but police officers and press representatives. Everyone who was admitted was required to show identification. Vaughn said that police paddy wagons were searched before they were allowed to enter the building."I heard someone say here he comes and then the shot. I saw three police officers wrestling for the gun. ~~Ex~~ Everyone in the building had been screened closely. There were officers on the elevators and at all entrances. Everyone, including police and press had to show identification. A man would have to be very foolish to do something like this," Vaughn said.

50-A

November 30, 1963

Mr. J. E. Curry
Chief of Police

Sir:

Re: Interview of Reserve Officer,
Patrolman Jessie C. Hunt, 229

On November 30, 1963 Reserve Officer, Patrolman Jessie C. Hunt was interviewed by the undersigned officers as to any information he might have concerning the shooting of Lee Harvey Oswald which was not covered in his original report dated November 27, 1963.

Hunt stated, after reading his original report, that there was nothing of significance which he could add.

Hunt further stated that he has not been contacted by any federal agency at this time.

Respectfully submitted,

F. I. Cornwall
F. I. Cornwall, Lieutenant
Special Service Bureau

Jack Revill
Jack Revill, Lieutenant
Special Service Bureau

jh

51

COMMISSION EXHIBIT No. 2002—Continued

November 27, 1963

Mr. J. E. Curry
Chief of Police

Sir:

This is a statement of facts relating to my activity as a Reserve Officer Sunday, November 24, 1963, to the best of my knowledge and recollection.

1. Approximate time I reported to duty. 7:50 A. M.

2. I reported to Assembly Room.

3. I was assigned to ——— I was in a group of approximately ten reserves that was taken to the basement parking area to assist in searching the place.

   About 10:00 or 10:30 A. M., I was taken along with another group of reserves to the Elm-Houston area to assist in the handling the crowd there.

4. Names of other officers in the same area that I can recollect are:

   Capt. Arnett, Lt. Merrell and several others that I do not know by name.

5. Did you know Ruby? No.

6. When and under what circumstance did you see Ruby?

   Never did see him.

Signed: J. C. Hunt
J. C. Hunt

RW

51

COMMISSION EXHIBIT No. 2002—Continued

November 29, 1963

Mr. J. E. Curry
Chief of Police

Dear Sir:

Re: Interview of Patrolman
Jerry D. Hutchinson, 1778

On November 29, 1963 Patrolman J.D. Hutchinson was interviewed by the undersigned officers as to any information he might have concerning the shooting of Lee Harvey Oswald which was not covered in his original report dated November 27, 1963.

Patrolman Hutchinson stated, after reading his original report, that the only addition he could make is that from approximately 11:00 a.m. when he was assigned his duty just outside the jail office door until the time Lee Harvey Oswald was shot no one entered the basement from the Police and Records Building who was not authorized.

Hutchinson further stated that he knows Jack Ruby and that he did not gain entrance to the basement through these double doors from 11:00 a.m. until the time of the shooting.

Patrolman Hutchinson states that he has not been contacted by any federal agency at this time.

Respectfully submitted,

Jack Revill

Jack Revill, Lieutenant
Special Service Bureau

F. I. Cornwall

F. I. Cornwall, Lieutenant
Special Service Bureau

jh

52

COMMISSION EXHIBIT No. 2002—Continued

November 27, 1963

Mr. J. E. Curry
Chief of Police

Subject: Shooting of Lee Harvey Oswald

Sir:

At approximately 11:00 A.M. on Sunday, November 24, 1963, I was standing in the basement of the City Hall with Detective B. H. Combest #1148 and Detective B. L. Beaty #637. We were standing next to a regular Police Officer and a reserve Police Officer who were checking the press for their press cards as they came through. Captain O. A. Jones came up and said he wanted all detectives and plain-clothes officers to go to the outside jail entrance, and to form a line on each side of the hallway leading from the jail office. Our instructions were to keep the hallway clear all the way to the armored car, which was half way down the ramp of the Commerce Street exit.

My position was directly across from the jail office entrance door. As Lee Harvey Oswald was brought from the jail office by Homicide Detectives he passed by in front of me. When he turned the corner at the end of the hallway he was shot. I did not see the actual shooting, but when I heard the shot I rushed forward as Officers were subduing Jack Ruby.

Other Officers I saw at the scene were:

Chief Chas. Batchelor	Sgt. P.T. Dean #882
Chief M.W. Stevenson	Det. R.C. Wagner #1480
Captain C.E. Talbert #463	Det. J.K. Ramsey #1627
Lt. W.L. Wiggins #434	Det. L.D. Miller #1236
Sgt. J.A. Putnam, #904	

I did not see any unauthorized persons in the basement area. The only persons I saw were Police Officers and people who I believed to be of the News media.

Respectfully submitted,

Jerry D. Hutchinson

Jerry D. Hutchinson #1778
Patrolman
Special Service Bureau
Vice Section

JDH:crl

52.

COMMISSION EXHIBIT No. 2002—Continued

Mr. J. E. Curry
Chief of Police

December 5, 1963

Re: Interview with Robert Jackson
Dallas Times Herald
4030 Sperry
TA 4-7840

Sir:

Mr. Jackson was interviewed at approximately 5:00 p.m. on December 4, 1963. Mr. Jackson arrived at the City Hall with Bob Finley. He took no pictures before the shooting; he took 1 picture about the instant of the shooting and 2 pictures later - one showing Oswald being placed in the ambulance. These pictures are not available at this time and are in New York and will probably be available sometime tomorrow.

Robert Jackson stated he had seen Jack Ruby at one occasion at the photo-laboratory, Times Herald, and thinks he would have recognized him if he had seen him in the basement of the City Hall. Mr. Jackson was standing near the automobile that was headed out the Commerce Street exit.

Respectfully submitted,

P. J. McCaghren
Lieutenant, Burglary & Theft Bureau

C. C. Wallace
Lieutenant, Juvenile Bureau

mw

53

COMMISSION EXHIBIT No. 2002—Continued

November 30, 1963

STATEMENT OF PATROLMAN L. E. JEZ:

I left the Commerce Street ramp entrance of the City Hall to work traffic at Commerce and Harwood at approximately 11:00 A.M., and did not return to the basement prior to the shooting.

I met Jack Ruby about three years ago, and know him when I see him. I did not see Ruby in or near the City Hall prior to the shooting. The last time I saw him was at the Carousel Club about a month ago.

54

COMMISSION EXHIBIT No. 2002—Continued

November 26, 1963

Mr. J. E. Curry
Chief of Police

Subject: Assignment Of Officer
L. E. Jez #1479 On
Sunday, November 24, 1963

Sir:

At approximately 9:00 A.M., Sunday, November 24, 1963 I was relieved of my post on the Third Floor of the City Hall by Sergeant Putnam. I went to the basement of the City Hall where I reported to Sergeant Dean. I was assigned to the City Hall Doctor's Office and the two adjacent doors, one of which was the annex stairway door. I then stood by the stairway door until Sergeant Putnam and Sergeant Dean arrived in the basement with several Reserve Police Officers at which time another officer was assigned to this position and I helped search the basement for unauthorized personnel. This assignment was completed at approximately 9:25 A.M.

I was then assigned to Sergeant Steele and we went across Commerce Street to search the buildings lining the south side of the street. This assignment was completed at approximately 9:55 A.M. After this, I was posted at the Commerce Street exit ramp of the City Hall Basement. I remained at this post and allowed only properly identified press and police personnel to enter. At approximately 11:00 A.M. two armored cars arrived at the ramp exit and my assignment was to assist these trucks backing into the ramp.

I then went to the intersection of Commerce and Harwood to stop the flow of traffic until the armored trucks and escort cars could leave.the City Hall. I worked traffic until approximately 12:30 P.M. when I returned to the exit ramp.

I was relieved by Sergeant Dean at approximately 1:00 P.M. at which time I went to the Patrol Office (Station 511).

Respectfully submitted,

L. E. Jez
Patrolman #1479
Patrol Division

LEZ/bb

54

COMMISSION EXHIBIT NO. 2002—Continued

December 9, 1963

Mr. J. E. Curry
Chief of Police

Re: Interview with Mr. Frank B. Johnston
3011 Whitis Avenue
Apartment 205
Austin, Texas
Cameraman for U.P.I.

Sir:

On December 5, 1963, Lieutenant F. I. Cornwall and Lieutenant Jack Revill interviewed Mr. Frank B. Johnston at his residence in Austin, Texas regarding his assignment in the basement of the City Hall on November 24, 1963. Mr. Johnston stated that he is employed by U.P.I. as a still cameraman and is assigned to the Austin, Texas, office. He was called to Dallas to cover the assassination of President Kennedy.

He states that on November 24, 1963, he arrived in the basement of the Police and Courts Building at approximately 4:30 a.m. He stated that he had moved around in the basement and in the Police and Courts Building awaiting the transfer of Oswald and that he was checked numerous times for his press identification. At approximately 11:00 a.m. he was standing by the concrete post in the basement just south of the television camera operated by WBAP-Channel 5. He further stated just as they were bringing Oswald out of the Jail Office that an automobile started backing in the basement area and that he looked to observe where this automobile was going and just at that time Ruby rushed forward and shot Oswald. Due to this distraction of the moving automobile, he did not get a picture of the incident nor did he observe Ruby shoot Oswald. He did state further, however, that he had taken pictures during his assignment in the basement and they were all sent to Mr. Harold Blumenfeld, Picture editor U.P.I., New York City.

At the time of this interview, Mr. Johnston had been interviewed by the Federal Bureau of Investigation.

Respectfully submitted,

F. I. Cornwall
Lieutenant, Special Service Bureau

Jack Revill
Lieutenant, Special Service Bureau

55

FIC:nw

COMMISSION EXHIBIT NO. 2002—Continued

December 9, 1963

Mr. J. E. Curry
Chief of Police

Subject: Telephone Interview with UPI Office, New York City, New York.

Sir:

At approximately 3:50 p.m., December 5, 1963, I contacted Mr. Harold Blumenfeld, Picture Editor, United Press International, New York City, New York, Telephone NU2-0400, by long distance telephone and asked that he send us all of the still shots that their UPI Office had of the Oswald shooting. He told me that they would probably have approximately six (6) still shots and that he would send them to the Dallas Police Department as soon as possible via Air Mail.

Respectfully submitted,

C. C. Wallace
C. C. Wallace
Lieutenant of Police
Juvenile Bureau

CCW:mav

55

COMMISSION EXHIBIT No. 2002—Continued

December 1, 1963

STATEMENT OF CAPTAIN O. A. JONES:

I can add nothing of any value that is not covered in the report.

56

COMMISSION EXHIBIT No. 2002—Continued

November 26, 1963

Mr. J.E. Curry,
Chief of Police

Subject: Shooting of Lee Oswald

Sir:

On Sunday, November 24, 1963, at around 11AM, Deputy Chief Stevenson approached me in the administration offices and directed me to place two officers at the Commerce Street entrance to the ramp leading into the basement of the City Hall. He said to instruct these two officers that an armored truck was enroute and for them to assist the truck back as far as possible down the ramp into the City Hall. He also told me to take any remaining detectives that were available on the third floor to the basement and place them any place they were needed in the basement to supplement the officers already stationed. Most of the detectives had previously been sent to the basement. I entered each of the bureaus except Homicide and Robbery and told the duty officer to have any available officers to report outside the jail office and went to the basement. Two or three detectives accompanied me and remained near the jail office. I went to the head of the ramp on Commerce Street and informed Patrolman Jez and one other patrolman to remain there and keep the way clear and to assist the armored truck in backing into the City Hall. I informed Captain Talbert of these instructions.

I then returned to near the jail office and stationed some of the detectives at the doors leading into the building proper, and noticed the Press Media was inside the jail office, but outside the admitting desk. I saw Assistant Chief Batchelor and Deputy Chief Stevenson and called Chief Batchelor's attention to the people in the jail office. I accompanied him inside and upon his instructions this area was cleared. Upon leaving the jail office we also had all persons except security personnel moved north of a line running east from the brick corner of the jail office to the railing on the opposite side and on a line from this point running east to the exit lanes for cars from the basement to the ramp itself.

Deputy Chief Stevenson then approached and said there had been a change in plans and, as the truck could not get into the City Hall, they were going to use two cars. At this time two police cars were started and brought up onto the ramp. Several officers had to move to allow the cars to get onto the ramp. I had given instructions to (cont'd)

54

COMMISSION EXHIBIT No. 2002—Continued

all officers near the jail officeand at the doors to allow no one in the area from the jail to the cars and on down the route the prisoner would take, and that the press would not be allowed to approach or even to attempt to converse with the prisoner, and that no one was to follow until after the cars left the basement.

I was about midway between the corner of the jail office and the back of the car on the ramp, when someone shouted "here he comes!". I was on the east side of the ramp at at this time. I turned to walk to the car on the ramp to make sure the way was clear and that officers were stationed on each side of the cars and all the way down the east side of the ramp to the cars. I saw officers along the route and officers on each side of the ramp near the cars and at the top of the ramp. I also saw Chief Stevenson on the ramp, so I turned to watch the parking area in the basement of the City Hall, when I heard a shot. This was sometime shortly before noon, but I don't remember the exact time. I turned toward the sound of the shot which had come from my left and to my rear. I shouted to the officers to bar all exits and all ramps. I saw the officers closing the exits and went toward the scuffle where apparently officers had a man in custody. As I approached the center of the scuffle several voices said "It was Jack Ruby". I do not know who said this, but as the prisoner was on his feet by this time I could see he was Jack Ruby, whom I had known 10 or 12 years before as the owner of the Silver Spur, a nightclub on South Ervay. I told the officers to take him to the jail and then had other officers assist Lt. Swain in keeping the crowd in the designated area. I assisted in this measure until after the ambulance left with Oswald and I then returned to the third floor after instructing the officers on the doors to let only persons with identification come to the third floor. After returning to the third floor, I assisted in the administration offices.

I had not seen a man that I recognized as Jack Ruby in the City Hall during the period of the investigation, until after the shooting in the basement.

Respectfully,

O.A. Jones

O.A. JONES,
Captain of Police
Forgery Bureau

56

December 1, 1963

Mr. J. E. Curry
Chief of Police

Re: Interview with Wilford Ray Jones c/m
Concerning Slaying of Lee Harvey Oswald

Sir:

This subject was interviewed at the V. A. Hospital this date by Lts. P. G. McCaghren and F. I. Cornwall. Subject's home address is 4311 Willow Springs, telephone HA 8 3374.

Jones stated on the date of the slaying, he had approached the City Hall on Main Street and walked to the Main Street ramp and borrowed a cigarette from Officer Vaughn. He related he saw no other subject that he was aquainted with near the ramp entrance at that time. Jones then walked to the Commerce Street side of the City Hall, across the street from where the armored car was parked. He remained at this location approximately 15 minutes. After the shot was fired, Jones then ran from the location to a near by parking lot. He stayed in this position approximately 15 minutes and returned to the Main Street basement entrance. It was then that Jones saw N. J. Daniels. At this time there were several reporters on the scene interviewing Attorney Tom Howard. Jones recalled Howard stating that he was enroute to his home when he heard on the radio that Ruby shot Oswald.

We were not able to ascertain that Jones saw anyone entering the basement of the City Hall at the time he had approached Vaughn for a cigarette.

Respectfully submitted,

P. G. McCaghren

P. G. McCaghren, Lieutenant
Burglary & Theft Bureau

F. I. Cornwall

F. I. Cornwall, Lieutenant
Special Service Bureau

lh

57

AFFIDAVIT IN ANY FACT

THE STATE OF TEXAS
COUNTY OF DALLAS

BEFORE ME, *Frances Bock*

a Notary Public in and for said County, State of Texas, on this day personally appeared **Seth Kantor,**

1013 13th Street N.W., Washington, D.C., DI7-7750

Who, after being by me duly sworn, on oath deposes and says:

I work for the Scripps Howard Company in Washington, D.C.

On Sunday, November 24, 1963, I came down the elevator to the basement of the Police and Courts Building. I was double checked when I got out of the elevator in the basement. I was still wearing a paper badge on my lapel and I showed my Washington press I.D. to a uniformed officer and he still would not allow me to pass until he called another officer, whom I believe was a plain clothes officer, and he allowed me to go on into the basement area past the corridor that is in front of the windows to the jail office.

I went on into the jail office outside of the admitting desks and remained there by the east wall until approximately four minutes prior to the shooting when officers came in the jail office and had us move out across to the east side of the ramp. Bob Fenley and I remained beside the post at the north end of the exit that is between the ramp and the basement parking area.

I do know Jack Ruby. I did not see Jack Ruby in the basement of the City Hall until Oswald came out of the jail office. I heard someone say, "Here he comes," then, while looking intently at Oswald, I did see an arm with a hand holding a gun come into view. I heard an officer shout, "Jack, you S.O.B.", just immediately before the shot. I did not see Ruby well enough to know whom the officers had arrested until I was told it was Jack Ruby. This information was given to Bob Fenley by some detective who appeared to be weeping. I saw Ruby's hat on the floor of the basement. I knew Ruby fairly well when I worked with the Times Herald and I remember at Parkland Hospital on Friday he came up behind me and pulled the back of my coattail. I turned around and he called me by my name and we shook hands. This was just before 1:30 p.m. Ruby said, "This

Seth Kantor

SUBSCRIBED AND SWORN TO BEFORE ME THIS *4th* DAY OF *December* A.D. 1963

Frances Bock
Notary Public, Dallas County, Texas
FRANCES BOCK

CPS-GF-413

58

COMMISSION EXHIBIT NO. 2002—Continued

Statement of Seth Kantor, con't.

AFFIDAVIT IN ANY FACT

THE STATE OF TEXAS
COUNTY OF DALLAS

BEFORE ME, *Frances Bock*

a Notary Public in and for said County, State of Texas, on this day personally appeared

Who, after being by me duly sworn, on oath deposes and says:

"is terrible. Should I close my places for three days." He appeared to be very upset. I told him I thought he should, but did not continue the conversation.

That was the only time I saw Jack Ruby during the period of Friday, November 22, 1963, until the moment of the shot in the basement on Sunday, November 24, 1963. xxxxxxxxxxxxxxxxxxxxxxxxxxxxxxxxxxxxxxxxxxxxxxxxxxxxxxxxxxxxx

Seth Kantor

SUBSCRIBED AND SWORN TO BEFORE ME THIS *4th* DAY OF *December* A.D. 1963

Frances Bock
Notary Public, Dallas County, Texas
FRANCES BOCK

CPS-GF-413

58

COMMISSION EXHIBIT NO. 2002—Continued

November 30, 1963

Mr. J. E. Curry
Chief of Police

Sir:

Re; Interview of Reserve Officer, Patrolman Jerome Kasten, 333

On November 30, 1963 Reserve Officer, Patrolman Jerome Kasten was interviewed by the undersigned officers as to any information he might have concerning the shooting of Lee Harvey Oswald which was not covered in his original report, dated November 27, 1963.

Kasten stated, after reading his original report, that there was nothing of significance which he could add.

Kasten further stated that he has not been contacted by any federal agency at this time.

Respectfully submitted,

F. I. Cornwall (signature)
F. I. Cornwall, Lieutenant
Special Service Bureau

Jack Revill (signature)
Jack Revill, Lieutenant
Special Service Bureau

jh

59

November 27, 1963

Mr. J. E. Curry
Chief of Police

Sir:

This is a statement of facts relating to my activity as a Reserve Officer Sunday, November 24, 1963, to the best of my knowledge and recollection.

1. Approximate time I reported to duty. 8:30 A. M.

2. I reported to Lt. Merrell in Assembly Room.

3. I was assigned to the basement parking area about 9:00 A. M. to assist Sgt. Putnam search the area. I saw a rifle taken from a car I guess was a detective's car. About 10:00 A. M., an officer requested Sgt. Putnam to send me to Commerce and Pearl to control traffic because of a stuck signal light. About 10:30 I movedback in front of City Hall on Commerce and assisted with crowds and traffic after the shooting. Then back to assembly room.

4. Names of other officers in the same area that I can recollect are:

A. W. Capps, O. W. Harrison, Sgt. Putnam.

5. Did you know Ruby? Yes. I was with a squad seferal weeks ago that answered a call to a night club (don't recall location) regarding a drunk. We were unable to locate the subject and just as we were leaving the driveway a man was getting in a car and the officers paused long enough to say, "Hello, Jack", and told him they were loc'ing for a drunk. The man called Jack said, "OH", "I took care of him." The officers said this was Jack Ruby.

6. When and under what circumstance did you see Ruby?

Never did see him, Sunday morning.

Signed: Jerome Kasten (signature)
J. Kasten

59

December 2, 1963

Mr. J. E. Curry
Chief of Police

Subject: Murder of Lee Harvey Oswald

Sir:

The following information is submitted relevant to my activities in the basement of the Police and Courts Building immediately prior to, at the time of, and immediately following the murder of Lee Harvey Oswald by Jack Ruby, Alias Jack Leon Rubenstein.

At approximately 10:45 a.m. on November 24, I went to the basement of the Police and Courts Building because of the number of newsmen who were assembled at that location. The newsmen were there because of the impending transfer of Oswald from the City to the County Jail.

When I went into the parking area and driveway, a large number of newsmen were already there. I spoke briefly with Jack Beers, photographer for the Dallas Morning News who was, at that time, standing on the rail on the eastern side of the driveway. I stayed in the basement talking with newsmen and preventing them from going up the south ramp toward the location where the armored car was parked.

I talked briefly with Captain O. A. Jones, Captain C. E. Talbert and Captain Arnett of the Police Reserves.

When the vehicle, driven by Lieutenant R. S. Pierce, was driven from the basement to Main Street, I was on the west side of the driveway near where the ramp to Commerce Street starts up. I was at this location when the vehicle, driven by Detective C. N. Dhority, was backed toward Main Street and I was watching this vehicle when I heard the shot. I yelled for the officers on the Commerce Street side to keep people from coming in or leaving and then went over to where Ruby was being held. The persons I remember seeing with Ruby were Officer W. J. Harrison of the Juvenile Bureau and Detective D. R. Archer of the Auto Theft Bureau. I went with these officers inside the Jail Office with Ruby and then up the elevator to the 5th Floor where I left them and returned to the basement. When I returned to the basement, Oswald had already been picked up by the ambulance. I then returned to my office and talked with newsmen who continued to come into the Administrative Office inquiring about the incident which had occurred in the basement.

Respectfully submitted,

Glen D. King
Captain of Police

GDK:PA

60

COMMISSION EXHIBIT No. 2002—Continued

November 30, 1963

Mr. J. E. Curry
Chief of Police

Sir:

Re: Interview of Reserve Officer,
Lieutenant Harry M. Kriss, 905

On November 30, 1963 Reserve Officer, Lieutenant Harry M. Kriss was interviewed by the undersigned officers as to any information he might have concerning the shooting of Lee Harvey Oswald which was not covered in his original report dated November 26, 1963.

Kriss, stated, after reading his original report, that there was nothing of significance which he could add.

Lieutenant Kriss further states that at this time he has not been contacted by any federal agency.

Respectfully submitted,

F. I. Cornwall, Lieutenant
Special Service Bureau

Jack Revill, Lieutenant
Special Service Bureau

jh

61

COMMISSION EXHIBIT No. 2002—Continued

November 26, 1963

Mr. J. E. Curry
Chief of Police
Dallas Police Department
Dallas, Texas

Sir:

On Sunday, November 24, at approximately 9:45 A.M., I arrived at the basement of the City Hall and reported to Captain Arnett. They had just completed searching the basement, I had no specific assignment. I was told to stand around and keep my eyes open, to let no-one in the part of the basement where the cars come and leave unless they had a Press Card.

I noted every car that came into the basement was thoroughly searched by the regular officers.

At different times I walked up both ramps to observe the crowds that were gathering, and talked to the officers standing at both entrances to the basement.

I was constantly bothered by reporters, asking questions and wanting information which I did not know.

I was told rumors were that there were several threats going around, and that was the reason for all the security.

Prior to Oswald's arrival from the Jail Office we were told to keep the Press against the railing and to keep one side clear, which we did. In a few minutes Oswald came out of the door and had just rounded the corner. I was looking at his face, and in just a fraction of a second later I saw a blur, my thoughts were that some reporter was attacking him (Oswald). I then heard a muffled shot, and heard someone say "get the Doctor". I saw Captain Arnett grappling in the crowd and ran to his aid, but saw he was o.k. Then, heard someone holler not to let anyone out, so I ran halfway up the North ramp and stood there. No-one passed.

I did not know the subject Ruby and had never seen him to the best of my knowledge.

Respectfully,

Harry M. Kriss
Harry M. Kriss
Lieutenant
Dallas Police Reserve

61

December 9, 1963

Mr. J. E. Curry
Chief of Police

Subject: Interview with Mr. Fritz Kuler, of KRLD-TV Station, and Viewing of Video Tape (Oswald Shooting).

Sir:

Mr. Kuler, an official of KRLD-TV Station, was contacted by the Investigating Officers and stated that on Sunday morning, November 24, 1963, he was in the Control Room at KRLD-TV Station, and was watching everything that was being monitored at that time. He stated that the Video tape viewed by the Investigating Officers was a continuous tape. He also stated that the live portion started about the time that the Cameraman came from in front of the Jail Office windows into the basement ramp area just prior to Lieutenant R. E. Swain and Captain J. W. Fritz coming out of the Jail Office.

The Investigating Officers timed the video tape from the time Lieutenant R. S. Pierce's car left the basement and started out Main Street until the time the shot was fired. The time recorded on the video machine and checked twice was fifty-six (56) seconds.

Respectfully submitted,

C C Wallace
C. C. Wallace
Lieutenant of Police
(Investigating Officer)
Juvenile Bureau

P G McCaghren
P. G. McCaghren
Lieutenant of Police
(Investigating Officer)
Burglary & Theft Bureau

CCW/PGM/mav

[illegible]

62

REPORT ON OFFICER'S DUTIES IN REGARDS TO OSWALD'S DEATH

J. R. LEAVELLE - #736

I arrived Sunday morning, November 24, 1963 about 8:00 am. We received word from Mr. Perry, Security Officer of the Statler-Hilton that they had a man check in who said he represented a munition company out of California. I went to the hotel in company with Det. C. N. Dhority and Mr. C. W. Brown. We talked with Robert W. Parker, 544 North Cypress, Orange, California. We satisfied ourselves he was O. K. and returned to the office.

At 9:30 am I was instructed, along with Det. L. C. Graves and Det. C. N. Dhority to go up in the jail and get Lee Oswald. I went to his cell and put the handcuff on him with his hands in front of him.

We returned to Captain Fritz's office where Captain Fritz, Mr. Sorrolls and Mr. Thomas Kelly of the Secret Service questioned Oswald. Also in the room were Detectives L. D. Montgomery, L. C. Graves, C. N. Dhority and Inspector Holmes of the Post Office Department and myself.

Shortly after 11:00 am we began the transfer. Chief Curry had come to Captain Fritz's office. I had made a suggestion earlier to double cross the press and take Oswald out on the first floor via the Main Street door, leaving the press waiting in the basement and on Commerce Street.

Also it was suggested to go out the Main Street ramp and west on Main Street. These suggestions were turned down by Chief Curry who stated that we had better go ahead with the transfer as planned, since he had given his word on it.

Approximately 11:15 am we left the third floor office with Oswald handcuffed to my left arm with Det. L. C. Graves holding to Oswald's left arm, preceded to the jail elevator by Captain Fritz, Lt. Swain, Detective L. D. Montgomery. We reached the basement jail office with officers in front we headed to the automobile ramp just outside the jail office door. We hesitated just inside the jail door,

J.R. Leavelle

63

COMMISSION EXHIBIT No. 2002—Continued

J. R. Leavelle-Page 2

then was given the all clear sign. We walked out and had just reached the ramp where the car we were to ride in was being backed into position by Detective Dhority when out of the mass of humanity composed of all the news media, which had surged forward to within six or seven feet of us, came the figure of a man with a gun in hand. He took two quick steps and double actioned a .38 revolver point blank at Oswald. I jerked back on Oswald, at the same time reaching out and catching Jack Ruby on the left shoulder, shoving back and down on him, bringing myself between Ruby and Oswald. I could see Det. Graves had Ruby's gun hand and gun in his hands. I turned my attention to Oswald and with the help of Det. Combest we took Oswald back into the jail office and laid him down. Handcuffs were removed and the city hall doctor, Dr. Bieberdorf was summoned. We also called O'Neal ambulance. Oswald was placed in the ambulance and rushed to Parkland Hospital. In the ambulance besides the crew was Dr. Bieberdorf, Det. L. C. Graves, Det. C. N. Dhority and myself.

He was rushed to surgery where he expired at 1:07 pm, November 24, 1963, pronounced by Dr. Tom Shires. Judge Pierce McBride was summoned. I gave him all the information needed to request an autopsy. When all necessary reports were made, I returned to the city hall where I made the offense report on Lee Harvey Oswald.

63

COMMISSION EXHIBIT No. 2002—Continued

December 1, 1963

STATEMENT OF C. G. LEWIS:

I was on the Jail Elevator and did not see the shooting.

I met Jack Ruby several years ago, and would not recognize him if I saw him.

64

COMMISSION EXHIBIT No. 2002—Continued

Mr. J. E. Curry
Chief of Police

November 27, 1963

Subject: Jack Ruby

Sir:

On October 24, 1963, I was stationed on the Jail Elevator, and was to operate it. I was assigned by Sgt. M. O. Rogers, as it was felt this would enhance security.

I had seen Jack Ruby around nine years ago, but I had never talked to him nor met him personally, while as a apprentice policeman, working the district that the Vegas Club was on.

I did not see Jack Ruby in the basement, and I probably would not have recognized him had I saw him.

I did not witness the shooting of Oswald, but I was standing by with the elevator in the Jail Office.

Respectfully submitted

C. G. Lewis

C. G. Lewis #1026
Patrolman
Dallas Police Department

64

December 4, 1963

Mr. J. E. Curry
Chief of Police

Re: Telephonic Interview of Joe Long
Radio Station KLIF on December 1, 1963

I contacted the subject on this date and he made arrangements to furnish this Department with a copy of the taped interview with Mrs. Eva Grant that was broadcast on Radio Station KLIF, Tuesday evening, November 26 and Wednesday, November 27. Mr. Long stated that the entire interview which took place in Mrs. Grant's apartment lasted for approximately 3½ hours. He said she would not allow a record of the entire interview but would allow a recording of a prepared speech which she read.

I questioned Mr. Long regarding the reason Mrs. Grant gave for believing her brother Jack Ruby had a press pass or identification card when he was in the City Hall prior to the shooting of Lee Oswald on Sunday, November 24, 1963. Mr. Long stated Mrs. Grant told him that she had attended the State Fair of Texas with her brother in October, 1963, and as they went in the gate Jack Ruby told her to purchase a ticket for her own admission and pointed out an "Operations" press pass on his windshield and said this pass would admit the car and he had his own individual pass to procure his own admission.

Mr. Long also stated that sometime after midnight Friday night, November 22, 1963, which would be in the early hours of Saturday morning, that Jack Ruby came to the KLIF Studios, Pearl Expressway and Jackson Street with sandwiches for some of the KLIF personnel.

Mr. Long was questioned further without obtaining more information that was considered pertinent but volunteered to be available at any future time that we might want to contact him.

Respectfully submitted,

O. A. Jones

O. A. Jones
Captain of Police

OAJ:nw

65

December 1, 1963

Mr. J. E. Curry
Chief of Police

Re: Interview of R. L. Lowery
Concerning Shooting of Lee Harvey Oswald

Sir:

R. L. Lowery was interviewed by Lieutenants C. C. Wallace and P. G. McCaghren at 9:00 am on November 29, 1963. The interview was essentially the same as his original report dated November 27, 1963. R. L. Lowery had this to add:

I would like to give in more detail a report of the shooting of Lee Harvey Oswald.

On Sunday, November 24, 1963, approximately 9:00 am, Chief Stevenson came to the Juvenile Bureau and told all bureau personnel to stand by.

Approximately 11:05 am, November 24, Captain Martin told us to come with him. At that time, those present were: C. Goolsby, W. J. Cutchshaw, W. J. Harrison, L. D. Miller, and myself. We went with Captain Martin to the elevator and went to the basement.

As we approached the information or pay office windows of the jail, I noticed Patrolman Nelson and he asked for identification from someone. There were other officers there in uniform, possibly reserves and I can't recall the names of any other officers there at the area of the jail office. Captain Jones met us at this point and told us to stand by for further instructions. Captain Jones went out through the double doors into ramp entrance and Captain Martin followed him.

A few minutes later Captain Jones returned and called for everyones attention. He then told officers to take positions in the ramp area of the corridor. Also advised both officers and newsmen to take their position in the ramp area. We eased into ramp area and I took up a position at the SW corner of the corridor and ramp drive way.

At this time several other officers took their positions on both sides of corridor from jail office door to ramp area.

I believe Captain Jones repeated his instructions to everyone, that he would like officers to form line on both sides of corridor, and also instructing news personell where they should be. He told news people to get on east of ramp drive. From my position, because of the strong lights set up for the TV camera, I could not clearly see the position of all the other officers. Detective Combest was on my immediate left.

66

COMMISSION EXHIBIT No. 2002—Continued

After taking my position, I looked to my left and saw NBC Channel 5 TV camera, mounted on tripod with rollers, it appeared that there were three men pushing the camera. One was later identified as John Alexander, w/m/39. I could not see the faces of these three men because they were stooped over with heads down; as they rolled past me, down a slight decline, the camera acted as if it wanted to tip over, and I steadied the camera with my left hand. They stopped at the bottom of the south ramp and I heard one of the men say "We can't get up here." They then moved through the line of newsmen on the east side of the ramp.

Two or three minutes later, I heard someone inside jail office say, "Here he comes." I looked to my left, toward the jail office door, and observed Lt. Swain appear through jail office door. Then approximately 10 to 12 feet behind Lt. Swain, Captain Fritz appeared. Then approximately 5 ft. behind Captain Fritz, I observed Detective Leavelle, with Oswald handcuffed to Leavelle's left arm, I also noticed a detective on Oswald's left holding Oswald's arm, but didn't notice who the detective was at that time.

As Leavelle and his partner along with Oswald, appeared through the jail office door, the press personnel began to crowd forward, taking pictures and asking questions. "Did you shoot the President." etc.

As captain Fritz past me, and as Leavelle, his partner, and Oswald approached my position, I saw a man lunge from the crowd of newsmen, opposite my position. As this lunged forward extending his right arm, and firing almost simultaneously.

Oswald fell back a step and Leavelle, laid Oswald down on the floor. At the same instant the shot was fired, serveral officers, I know Cutchshaw and Harrison, subdued the man who fired the shot, and took the gun from him.

I recognized the man that fired the shot as Jack Ruby. I had not noticed Jack Ruby before he fired the shot. I do know Jack Ruby by sight and have never seen him in the City Hall.

I assisted several other officers take Jack Ruby into jail office, where he was searched. I did not help take him upstairs, but remained as security at the jail office door.

I have talked to Federal Bureau of Investigation Agent Bookout in regards to this incident.

Respectfully submitted,

P. G. McCaghren, Lieutenant
Burglary & Theft Bureau

C. C. Wallace, Lieutenant
Juvenile Bureau

11

66

COMMISSION EXHIBIT No. 2002—Continued

November 24, 1963

Mr. J. E. Curry
Chief of Police

Subject: Shooting of Lee Harvey Oswald.

Sir:

Approximately three to five minutes before the prisoner was brought out, I observed a Channel 5 Camera mounted on tripod rollers come through the doors in front of the jail office to the ramp. I observed three men pushing the camera, one on each side and one man crouched down in rear head down as if pushing the camera. As the camera came down the slope from entrance to ramp, I grabbed one of the tripods to steady the camera. As the camera men pushed the camera into the ramp they turned slightly to the right, one attendant stated "We can't get out this way", they then pushed the camera into the crowd of newsmen on the East side of the ramp area and disappeared into the rear of the crowd. At this time I heard someone in the jail office door state, "Here he comes". As I looked towards the jail office door, I saw Lieutenant Swain come out. Approximately ten to fifteen feet behind Lieutenant Swain, Captain Fritz came out, only six to eight feet behind Captain Fritz, Detective J. R. Leavelle leading Oswald (handcuffed) by the right arm. I could not identify the detective on Oswald's right. As both Leavelle, Oswald and unknown detective approached entrance to the basement ramp, I saw Jack Ruby lunge from the Northeast corner of the ramp area. I saw what looked like a blue steel snub nose revolver, almost simultaneously Ruby fired. Oswald let out a long "O-o-o-h". Several officers including myself attempted to grab the suspect. The suspect was then wrestled to the floor by several officers.

I know Jack Ruby and had not seen him in the crowd or building until I saw him lunge and fire at Oswald.

Respectfully submitted,

R. L. Lowery
R. L. Lowery
Detective, ID#1081
Juvenile Bureau
Criminal Investigation Division

66

COMMISSION EXHIBIT No. 2002—Continued

December 12, 1963

Inspector J. H. Sawyer talked to Deputy Chief George L. Lumpkin and received the following statement:

"I went to the basement of the City Hall on November 24, 1963, to observe the transfer of Lee Harvey Oswald to the County Jail. I arrived about 3 minutes before they brought Lee Harvey Oswald out of the Jail Office.

I was standing on the flat part of the ramp near the right front fender of the car driven by Detective C. N. Dhority. This was on the West side of the car.

I did not know Jack Ruby and I did not see him in the basement. I did not see the shooting although I did hear the shot."

J. H. Sawyer
Inspector of Police

JHS:nw

66A

COMMISSION EXHIBIT No. 2002—Continued

November 27, 1963

Mr. J. E. Curry
Chief of Police

Subject: Traffic and Security Assignments on Jail Transfer of Lee Oswald

Sir:

On November 24, 1963, the Solo Motorcycle Section detail, consisting of 10 officers, reported to Elm and Houston Streets at 8:30 A.M. By 9:00 A.M. this detail had been augmented by eleven Police Reserve officers. Supervisors present, were Captain P. W. Lawrence, Captain J. M. Solomon, Lieutenant W. F. Southard, Sergeant S. Q. Bellah and myself. Shortly before the prisoner was to be transferred, Sergeant D. F. Steele reported to the location.

The west side of Houston was roped off between Elm and Main Streets. A large number of persons were congregated behind the ropes along Houston and on both sides of Elm Street between Houston and the Triple Underpass. I would estimate the total crowd to be between 500 and 600 persons.

Two officers were assigned at Elm and Houston and two at Main and Houston. One officer was assigned at Elm and Record and one at Main and Record. Four patrolmen, seven Reserve officers and five supervisors, including myself, were stationed at intervals along the west side of Houston between Elm and Main. Four Reserve officers were assigned along Elm Street between Houston and the Triple Underpass. All officers were instructed to keep a close watch on the crowd and to be particularly alert for any signs of violence.

When radio stations announced that the prisoner had been shot, most of the crowd dispersed and approximately one-half of the officers were reassigned to other locations.

Respectfully,

R. H. Lunday

R. H. Lunday
Deputy Chief of Police
Traffic Division

RHL:mfm

67

COMMISSION EXHIBIT No. 2002—Continued

December 1, 1963

STATEMENT OF CAPTAIN F. M. MARTIN:

I have covered everything of importance in my report.

68

COMMISSION EXHIBIT No. 2002—Continued

November 26, 1963

Mr. J. E. Curry
Chief of Police

Subject: Shooting of Lee Harvey Oswald.

Sir:

On Sunday, November 24, 1963, I was stationed in the City Hall basement as security for the transfer of Oswald.

When he came out of the jail office I was standing about mid-way of the driveway going into the parking area. There was a police car between me and the jail office. I did not see anything but heard the shot that was fired. By the time I could get around to the jail, Oswald and Ruby had been pulled back into the jail office. Ruby was down with three or four officers holding him. Oswald was lying on the North side of the jail office on the floor. The doctor and ambulance arrived shortly after I got into the jail office.

I did know Jack Ruby but did not see him prior to this incident.

Respectfully submitted,

F. M. Martin

F. M. Martin
Captain of Police
Juvenile Bureau

FMM:mav

68

COMMISSION EXHIBIT No. 2002—Continued

December 2, 1963

STATEMENT OF BILLY J. MAXEY:

I know Jack Ruby, but I did not see him in or near the City Hall prior to the shooting of Lee Harvey Oswald.

69

-0 'H DA78143

November 26, 1963

Mr. J. E. Curry
Chief of Police

Subject: Assignment Of Sergeant Billy J. Maxey On Sunday, November 24, 1963

Sir:

At approximately 11:00 A.M., Sunday, November 24, 1963, I arrived at Central Station. I was working "16", Acting Lieutenant), Northeast Substation. The Patrol Officers were leaving for their traffic assignments, and there was a large group of reporters standing in the hall leading to the Jail Office.

I did not have an assignment at the time of my arrival and when Lieutenant Pierce came down and got into his car I asked him if I could help. Lieutenant Pierce advised me to ride with him and Sergeant Putnam to escort the Armored Car which had been backed partially onto the south ramp.

Lieutenant Pierce drove the car, I was sitting in the back seat, on the left side and Sergeant Putnam, after moving the crowd of reporters out of our path, got into the front seat on the right side. We traveled up the north ramp and made a left turn onto Main Street. Officer R. E. Vaughn was standing on our right side at the top of the ramp as we went out onto Main Street.

I did not see Jack Ruby or anyone else go down the ramp as we drove out. I know Jack Ruby by sight and I also did not see him in the basement while I was at that location.

We proceeded to the top of the south ramp via Main Street to Harwood Street to Commerce Street and took a position in front of the Armored Car.

Apparently the shooting of Lee Harvey Oswald had just happened because I did not hear the shot and officers were rushing to cover the exits of the Police and Courts Building and the City Hall as we pulled into position.

After the shooting, Lieutenant Pierce, Sergeant Putnam, and I went to Parkland Hospital and set up security in the building and the Emergency Entrance Parking Lot.

Respectfully submitted,
Billy J. Maxey
Billy J. Maxey
Sergeant Of Police
Patrol Division

69

BJM/bb

December 3, 1963

Mr. J. E. Curry
Chief of Police

Re: Interview of Reserve Officer
Sergeant R. L. Mayo - 862

Sir:

On December 1, 1963, Reserve Officer Sergeant R. L. Mayo was interviewed by the undersigned officers as to any information he might have concerning the shooting of Lee Harvey Oswald not covered in his original report dated November 26, 1963.

Sergeant Mayo stated that his duty assignment was on Commerce Street across from the City Hall. He stated that an unknown white male approximately 25 years of age attempted to enter the basement of the City Hall. This unknown male was wearing a white streamer on his lapel. This streamer had the words "White House Press". Sergeant Mayo stated that he attempted to refer this unknown to a regular police officer but this individual declined stating that he did not want to be a bother.

Sergeant Mayo further stated that this unknown individual disappeared shortly after the shooting of Oswald.

Sergeant Mayo does not know Jack Ruby nor has he been contacted by any Federal agency at this time.

Respectfully submitted,

Jack Revill
Jack Revill
Lieutenant, Special Service Bureau

F. I. Cornwall
F. I. Cornwall
Lieutenant, Special Service Bureau

70

COMMISSION EXHIBIT No. 2002—Continued

November 26, 1963

Mr. J. E. Curry
Chief of Police

Sir:

I am a Sergeant in the Dallas Police Reserve.

I reported in uniform to the City Hall on Sunday, November 24, at about 9:15 A. M. for duty. I was assigned by Lt. Ben McCoy to a station on Commerce Street across from the City Hall. This was to keep the crowds back from the entrance of the City Jail when Lee Harvey Oswald was transferred to the County Jail.

About 11:25, I saw several officers running down Commerce Street to the entrance of the building. One of the crowd (a man) had a small radio, and I heard the announcer say that Lee Harvey Oswald had been shot. He did not say who. Just a few minutes later an ambulance came out of the basement and I saw a man on the cot inside.

1. I did not see the shooting or hear a shot due to being outside.
2. I do not know the suspect Jack Ruby.
3. I do not know Lee Harvey Oswald.
4. I did not hear any noise in the basement.

Signed: L W Mayo
Sgt . L. W. Mayo
C-1-1

70

COMMISSION EXHIBIT No. 2002—Continued

December 1, 1963

Mr. J. E. Curry
Chief of Police

Sir:

Re: Interview of Reserve Officer,
Sergeant James C. McCain, 859

On December 1, 1963 Reserve Officer, Sergeant James C. McCain was interviewed by the undersigned officers as to any information he might have concerning the shooting of Lee Harvey Oswald which was not covered in his original report dated November 26, 1963.

McCain stated, after reading his original report, that there was nothing of significance which he could add.

Sergeant McCain further stated that at this time he has not been contacted by any federal agency.

Respectfully submitted,

F. I. Cornwall
F. I. Cornwall, Lieutenant
Special Service Bureau

Jack Revill
Jack Revill, Lieutenant
Special Service Bureau

jh

71

COMMISSION EXHIBIT No. 2002—Continued

November 26, 1963

Mr. J. E. Curry
Chief of Police

Sir:

This is statement of facts relating to my activity as a Reserve Officer Sunday, November 24, 1963, to the best of my knowledge and recollection.

1. Approximate time I reported to duty. 9:15 A. M.

2. I reported to Assembly Room.

3. I was assigned to the north side of Commerce Street at exit of ramp (South).

4. Names of other officers in the same area that I can recollect are:

   Reserves Wayne Harrison and Arthur Capps.

5. Did you know Ruby? No.

6. When and under what circumstances did you see Ruby?

   Did not see him at all.

Signed: J. C. McCain
J. C. McCain

71

COMMISSION EXHIBIT No. 2002—Continued

November 30, 1963

Mr. J. E. Curry
Chief of Police

Dear Sir:

Re: Interview of Reserve Officer,
Lieutenant Ben C. McCoy, 907

On November 30, 1963 Reserve Officer, Lieutenant Ben C. McCoy, was interviewed by the undersigned officers as to any information he might have concerning the shooting of Lee Harvey Oswald which was not covered in his original report dated November 26, 1963.

McCoy stated, after reading his original report, that there was nothing of significance which he could add.

Lieutenant McCoy further states that he has not been contacted by any federal agency at this time.

Respectfully submitted,

F. I. Cornwall
F. I. Cornwall, Lieutenant
Special Service Bureau

Jack Revill
Jack Revill, Lieutenant
Special Service Bureau

jh

72

Commission Exhibit No. 2002—Continued

November 26, 1963

Mr. J. E. Curry
Chief of Police

Sir:

I arrived at the City Hall, Sunday morning, November 24, 1963, at approximately 9:25 A. M. I went to the Police Assembly Room in the basement and reported in to Lt. B. C. Morrell, and asked him where Captain Arnett was. Lt. Morrell informed me that Captain Arnett and all of the Reserves who had been there were taken into the basement parking area by Sgt. P. T. Deen to search it.

I then went to the basement parking area and reported to Captain Arnett who was standing about 15 feet behind two television cameras that were set up in the first two parking stalls, facing the entranceway into the jail hallway. Reserve Officer G. E. Worley was standing beside Captain Arnett. I observed Reserve Lt. D. T. Suits standing at the bottom of the ramp, leading into the parking area. I also noticed Reserve Patrolman W. J. Newman standing at the extreme south end of the parking area. A radio patrol officer was standing in front of the elevators that are on the center east side of the parking area. I asked Captain Arnett what the situation was, and he told me that they had just finished searching the basement under the direction of Sgt. P. T. Deen, and they had been instructed to stay in the basement area and keep people out of the parking area.

Captain Talbot came by and asked if the air conditioning vents had been checked and Sgt. J. R. Hopkins (Reserve) walked up at this time and said that he had just finished checking them. I stayed with Captain Arnett to help in coordinating the assignments requested of the Reserves.

Two conferences were held by the regular officers in the parking area, but we were not asked to listen in or not told what was going on. After these conferences, the regular officers left the basement area with shotguns.

Sgt. Deen requested that we send a man to Commerce and Pearl to work the traffic as a signal light was stuck at this location. I sent Patrolman G. E. Worley to work this.

A request was made that we send men to the south ramp entrance to move the crowd that had gathered there across the street to the south sidewalk and hold them there. I made several trips to and from the assembly room to get reserves as they reported in to Lt. Morrell to help handle this crowd. I sent Reserve Sgt. Hopkins up to the Commerce Street side to supervise the operation and to keep me informed of the situation there. A request was made that a Reserve Officer be placed in the hall in front of the jail office window to help the regular officer there check people out. Reserve Officer A. B. Craig was assigned to this location.

72

Commission Exhibit No. 2002—Continued

On several occasions, and from time to time, I observed men in plain clothes coming down the ramps and going into the hall in front of the jail. I assumed that these were press personnel and I did not take any special note, because of the regular officers that were supposed to check everyone out at the top of the ramps.

Much shuffling of cars took place in the parking area. I observed the paddy wagon come down the north ramp with Patrolman Lewis driving. I saw Sgt. Deen stop him and search the back of the wagon and then permit Lewis to go on into the parking area.

I observed squad cars being lined up in the north and south sides of the basement parking area. I observed Sgt. Steele and Reserve Patrolman J. H. Harrison leave the basement area in a squad car and drive out the South Ramp.

I then observed Chief Batchelor get into his car and leave by the South Ramp. I then observed the Armored car being backed into the South Ramp. Some men in plain clothes got into the back, a bottle fell out, and I saw one of the men in plain clothes picking up the glass from the ramp. I observed Sgt. Deen get into the Armored car and then come out. About this time, two men came into the outer jail hall and told the press personnel that they should stand along the north wall of the jail hall and along the east railing of the ramp, so they would all be able to get pictures without bunching up.

Two plain cars were brought out of the parking area and parked on the ramp headed south. I assisted in getting the cars through the crowd that was blocking the entrance to the parking area. I then moved several people who I assumed were press people away from the west wall of the south ramp over to the east side, and then stood by the west wall approximately one foot south of the jail hall. I heard a commotion and glanced to my left; I saw two plainclothesmen with a man between them coming toward the ramp; I looked back to my front and right to see what the press people were doing, and I heard what I thought was a flashbulb exploding. I looked back to my left and saw a man with a gun pointed at the midsection of the man the two plainclothesmen had between them.

I immediately jumped on the man, along with Reserve Captain Arnett and Reserve Sgt. K. H. Croy, and several other men. When the man was subdued, I heard some shout, "No One Out! No One Out!" I joined hands with Reserve Patrolman J. D. Brockway and kept the people from going into the jail hall. Captain Arnett and Reserve Sgt. Croy joined us.

We stayed in this position until the O'Neal ambulance came and they took Oswald off to the hospital. A man in plain clothes then came out and told the press people that they would be admitted to the building proper by press car. We then went inside the building to the assembly room to be assigned where needed.

Several men were sent to various locations to seal off the building entrances and several were sent to work traffic around the city hall. We were moved from the assembly room so the press could use it and set up our C. P. on the second floor in the Planning Commission room.

72

To my knowledge, I had never seen nor met the subject Ruby before I saw him with the gun in his hand at the time of the shooting of Oswald.

Respectfully,
Ben McCoy
Ben C. McCoy
Lieutenant
Dallas Police Reserve

RW

72

November 24, 1963

Mr. J.E. Curry
Chief of Police

Subject: Location of Detective H.L. McGee at the time of the Lee Oswald shooting

Sir:

Prior to the transfer of Lee Oswald, Lieutenant Swain instructed me to go to the basement near the information desk to assist in the transfer of Lee Oswald in any manner that I might be needed.

I rode the main elevator from the third floor with two WBAP-TV camramen and Detectives D.C. Brantley and D.L. Burgess. When I got off the elevator in the basement I saw a large group of camramen and newsmen congregated in the area in front of the jail office windows. I know that Jack Ruby was not with the two WBAP-TV camramen when they pushed their camra up to the crowd of other newsmen.

I stationed myself in the general area in front of the information desk to await the transfer.

While I was in this area, the only person I noticed come into the building from either the Commerce Street or Harwood Street doors was Attorney Tom Howard. He came in through the Harwood Street entrance and walked up to the jail office window.

At this time Oswald was brought off the jail elevator and Tom Howard turned away from the window and went back toward the Harwood Street door. He waved at me as he went by and said, "That's all I wanted to see."

Shortly after that I heard a shot and someone said, "Oh". I did not see the shooting.

At that time I went to the vehicle ramp and helped Lieutenant Swain hold back the crowd.

Respectfully submitted,

H. L. McGee

H. L. McGee
Detective
Burglary and Theft Bureau

73

November 30, 1963

J. E. Curry
Chief of Police

Re: Shooting of Lee Harvey Oswald
H. L. McGee

Sir:

H. L. McGee was interviewed by Lieutenants C. C. Wallace and P. G. McCaghren at 9:00am on November 30, 1963. The interview was essentially the same as his original report dated November 27, 1963. The following was added by H. L. McGee:

I have been asked if I know Jack Ruby. I do know Jack Ruby. I did not see him in the basement and I do not recall ever seeing him in the City Hall. I did not know it was Jack Ruby who shot Oswald until I over heard someone in the crowd say it was Jack Ruby.

I have no idea how he got into the City Hall or into the basement.

I have not been interviewed by the Federal Bureau of Investigation.

Respectfully submitted,

C C Wallace
C. C. Wallace, Lieutenant
Juvenile Bureau

P G McCaghren
P. G. McCaghren, Lieutenant
Burglary & Theft Bureau

lh

73

COMMISSION EXHIBIT No. 2002—Continued

November 30, 1963

J. E. Curry
Chief of Police

Re: Shooting of Lee Harvey Oswald
T. D. McMillon

Sir:

T. D. McMillon was interviewed by Lieutenants C. C. Wallace and P. G. McCaghren at 9:45 am on November 30, 1963. He had this to add to his original report:

I would like to make one correction that I now know to be true; that Detective Leavelle was on the prisioner's right rather than on the prisioner's left as I stated on my original report. Also I would like to correct that the person, Jack Ruby, came from my left instead of my right as I stated in my original report.

I have been asked if I know Jack Ruby, and I do know him by sight. I did not see him in the basement before the shooting, and can never recall seeing him around the City Hall.

We talked to him when we got to the 5th floor. On the 5th floor Rub was asked how he got to the basement. He replied that he came from the Western Union office where he wired a girl in Fort Worth some money. He said he saw Rio Pierce drive out of the basement. He walked past the policeman standing there. He said a policeman hollored at him, but he ducked his head and kept going. He said that he knew he could always act like a reporter.

He also said, "Ya'll won't believe this, but I didn't have this planned. I couldn't have timed it so perfect." He said just as he got there, Oswald was coming out.

He stated he always carried a gun in the car because he always had some money.

I overheard Ruby say that after coming out of the Western Union office, he saw the armored car there and came to see what was going on.

Ruby said he figured he could get off at least three shots before he would be caught. Ruby related that he knew he was shooting the right person, as he had attended the show-up Friday night at City Hall. He related how Henry Wade had made numerous references to the organization that Oswald belonged to, and that Ruby himself had corrected Henry Wade because he didn't want him to be embarrassed in public.

I have been interviewed by the Federal Bureau of Investigation.

Respectfully submitted,
C C Wallace
C. C. Wallace, Lieutenant Juvenile Bureau
P G McCaghren
P. G. McCaghren, Lieutenant Burglary & Theft Bureau

lh

74

Commission Exhibit No. 2002—Continued

Mc Millon

November 27, 1963

Mr. J. E. Curry
Chief of Police

Sir:

I should like to submit the following report regarding the incident occurring in the basement on November 24, 1963.

On November 24, 1963, I was assigned to the basement of the City Hall at approximately 11:10 a.m. for the purpose of security in the transferring of Lee Harvey Oswald from the City Jail to the County Jail. I was stationed near the jail office door which exits onto the ramp leading in a northerly direction toward Main Street. Detective L. D. Miller was stationed to my immediate right and I was the second person from the door on the north side of the hallway which leads to the jail office door. I do not know who was on my left.

At approximately 11:25 a.m. Captain Fritz came out of the jail office door and asked if everything was all right, and I answered, "Yes sir." I do not know if he was speaking directly to me. Two Homicide detectives were holding onto the prisoner escorting him, and I recognized Detective Leavelle on the prisoner's left. Captain Fritz had proceeded past me and the two Homicide detectives with the prisoner had proceeded slightly past me. As the prisoner was even with me, I made a left face which caused me to be walking in a southeasterly direction. Just as I had taken about one or two steps in forming the barrier on the north side of the prisoner, a man jumped from somewhere slightly to my right and in front of me. I heard this man yell, "You rat son-of-a-bitch, you shot the President." I saw the man as he appeared to jump or lunge toward the prisoner. I saw a short barrel revolver and heard one shot. I attempted to grab this man by the right arm and could still see the revolver. But after I had gotten hold of this man's right arm, several more officers were also trying to subdue him. At this point, I was on the floor just outside the jail office and the man said, "I hope I killed the rat son-of-a-bitch." I do not know who took the gun from this man, but Detectives Archer, Chambers, Clardy, Waggoner, and some more officers took this man into the jail office and at the time he was on the floor and I recognized him as Jack Ruby. We placed my handcuffs on this man and Detectives Clardy, Archer, and Captain King, and I took this man directly to the fifth floor men's jail, after a preliminary search in the jail office.

On the fifth floor men's jail we instructed jailers to search this man and strip him leaving him clad in only his shorts. We also instructed the jailers to notify the jail doctor to come and examine this man.

Detectives Clardy, Archer, and I stayed with this prisoner from 11:25 a.m. until relieved by Homicide detectives at approximately 3:25 p.m. During the time we were with this man, he was interrogated by Mr. Sorrells of Secret Service and Mr. Hall of the F.B.I. He was contacted by an attorney, Mr. Tom Howard, and he was examined by Dr. Bieberdorf when we were relieved by Homicide officers.

74

Commission Exhibit No. 2002—Continued

Mr. J. E. Curry 2 November 27, 1963

Detectives Clardy, Archer, and I assisted in getting this man from the fifth floor jail to the Homicide and Robbery Bureau.

Respectfully submitted,

T. D. McMillon
T. D. McMillon
Detective
Criminal Investigation Divisio

74

COMMISSION EXHIBIT No. 2002—Continued

24 NOV 1963

MR J. E. CURRY
CHIEF OF POLICE

SUBJECT: ASSIGNMENT FOR SECURITY OF LEE HARVEY OSWALD

SIR:

ON 24 NOV 1963 I WAS ASSIGNED TO THE BASEME OF THE CITY HALL AT APPROXIMATELY 11:10 AM FOR THE PURPOSE OF SECURITY IN THE TRANSFERRI OF LEE HARVEY OSWALD FROM THE CITY JAI TO THE DALLAS COUNTY JAIL.

I WAS STATIONED NEAR THE JAIL OFFICE DOOR WHICH EXITS ONTO THE RAMP LEADING IN A NORTHERLY DIRECTION TOWARD MAIN STREET.

DETECTIVE L. D. MILLER WAS STATIONED TO

74

COMMISSION EXHIBIT No. 2002—Continued

2

MY IMMEDIATE RIGHT AND I WAS THE SECOND
PERSON FROM THE DOOR ON THE NORTH SIDE OF
THE HALLWAY WHICH LEADS TO THE JAIL OFFICE
DOOR. I DO NOT KNOW WHO WAS ON MY LEFT.
AT APPROXIMATELY 11:25AM
CAPTAIN FRITZ CAME OUT THE JAIL OFFICE
DOOR AND ASKED WAS EVERYTHING ALL RIGHT
AND I ANSWERED "YES SIR". I DO NOT KNOW IF
HE WAS SPEAKING DIRECTLY TO ME. TWO
HOMOCIDE DETECTIVES WERE HOLDING ONTO THE
PRISONER ESCORTING HIM AND I RECOGNIZED
DETECTIVE LAVELLE ON THE PRISONER'S LEFT.
CAPTAIN FRITZ HAD PROCEEDED PAST ME AND
THE 2 HOMOCIDE DETECTIVES WITH
THE PRISONER HAD PROCEEDED SLIGHTLY

2 LY

3

PAST ME AS THE PRISONER
WAS EVEN WITH ME I MADE
A LEFT FACE WHICH CAUSED ME TO
BE WALKING IN A SOUTHEASTERLY DIRECTION
JUST AS I HAD TAKEN ABOUT 1 OR 2
STEPS IN FORMING THE BARRIER ON THE NORTH
SIDE OF THE PRISONER A MAN JUMPED FROM
SOMEWHERE SLIGHTLY TO MY RIGHT AND IN FRONT
OF ME. I HEARD THIS MAN YELL "YOU RAT
SON-OF-A-BITCH YOU SHOT THE PRESIDENT." I SAW
THE MAN AS HE APPEARED TO JUMP OR LUNGE
TOWARD THE PRISONER. I SAW A SHORT
BARREL REVOLVER AND HEARD ONE SHOT.
I ATTEMPTED TO GRAB THIS MAN BY THE
RIGHT ARM AND COULD STILL SEE THE REVOLVER

LY

4

BUT AFTER I HAD GOTTEN HOLD OF THIS MAN'S RIGHT ARM SEVERAL MORE OFFICERS WERE ALSO TRYING TO SUBDUE HIM. AT THIS POINT I WAS ON THE FLOOR JUST OUTSIDE THE JAILED OFFICE AND THE MAN SAID "I HOPE I KILLED THE RAT-SON-OF-A-BITCH." I DO NOT KNOW WHO TOOK THE GUN FROM THIS MAN BUT DETECTIVES ARCHER, CHAMBERS, CLARDY, WAGGONER AND SOME MORE OFFICER TOOK THIS MAN INTO THE JAIL OFFICE AND AT THIS TIME HE WAS ON THE FLOOR AND I RECOGNIZED HIM A JACK RUBY. WE PLACE MY HANDCUFFS ON THIS MAN AND DETECTIVES CLARDY, ARCHER, CAPT. KING AND I TOOK THIS MAN TO DIRECTLY TO THE 5TH FLOOR MEN'S JAIL

4 44

5

AFTER A PRELIMARY SEARCH IN THE JAIL OFFICE. ON THE 5TH FLOOR MEN'S JAIL WE INSTRUCTED JAILERS TO SEARCH THIS MAN AND STRIP HIM LEAVING HIM CLAD IN ONLY HIS SHORTS. WE ALSO INSTRUCTED THE JAILERS TO NOTIFY THE JAIL DOCTOR TO COME AND EXAMINE THIS MAN. DETECTIVES CLARDY, ARCHER AND I STAYED WITH THIS PRISONER FROM 11:25 AM UNTIL RELIEVED BY HOMOCIDE DETECTIVES AT APPROXIMATELY 3:25 PM. DURING THE TIME WE WERE WITH THIS MAN HE WAS INTERROGATED BY MR. SORRELLS OF SECRET SERVICE AND MR. HALL OF F.B.I. HE WAS CONTACTED BY AN ATTORNEY, MR. TOM HOWARD AND HE WAS EXAMINED BY DR. BIEBERDORF. WHEN WE WERE RELIEVED BY HOMOCIDE OFFICERS, DETECTIVES CLARDY, ARCHER AND I ASSISTED IN GETTING THIS MAN FROM

5 44

COMMISSION EXHIBIT No. 2002—Continued

6

THE 5TH FLOOR JAIL TO THE HOMOCIDE ~~[illegible]~~ AND ROBBERY BUREAU OFFICE.

RESPECTFULLY SUBMITTED,

T. D. McMillon #1349
DETECTIVE, C.I.D. AUTO THEFT
BUREAU.

6 74

November 30, 1963

Mr. J. E. Curry
Chief of Police

Sir:

Re: Interview of Reserve Officer,
Lieutenant Barnie Merrell, 901

On November 30, 1963 Reserve Officer, Lieutenant Barnie Merrell was interviewed by the undersigned officers as to any information he might have concerning the shooting of Lee Harvey Oswald which was not covered in his original report dated November 26, 1963.

After reading his original report, Merrell stated that there was nothing of significance which he could add.

Merrell further states that he has not been contacted by any federal agency at this time.

Respectfully submitted,

F. I. Cornwall
F. I. Cornwall, Lieutenant
Special Service Bureau

Jack Revill
Jack Revill, Lieutenant
Special Service Bureau

jh

75

Mr. J. E. Curry
Chief of Police

Date: 11-26-63

Sir:

This is a statement of facts relating to my activity as a Reserve Officr Sunday, November 24, 1963, to the best of my knowledge and recollection.

1. Approximate time I reported to duty. 7 45 a.m.

2. I reported to (person and place). Assembly Room

3. I was assigned to (state place or area and who you assisted and what assignment consisted of such as crowd control, search, guard, etc.).

I was answering the telephone and making assignments from the assembly room. I assumed charge of men reporting and set up a man power pool to be used as needed.

4. Names of other officers in the same area that I can recollect are: Reserve officer A.B. Craig was guarding the double doors between the main building and the basement parking area.

5. Did you know Ruby? No

6. When and under what circumstance did you see Ruby? after the shooting when Ruby was placed on the jail elevator

Print name Lt. Barnie Merrell

75

November 26, 1963

Mr. J. E. Curry
Chief of Police

Sir:

This is a statement of facts relating to my activity as a Reserve Officer Sunday, November 24, 1963, to the best of my knowledge and recollection.

1. Approximate time I reported to duty. 7:45 A. M.

2. I reported to Assembly Room.

3. I was assigned to ----

I was answering the telephone and making assignments from the Assembly Room. I assumed charge of men reporting and set up a man power pool to be used as needed.

4. Names of other officers in the same ar ea that I can recollect are:

Reserve Officer A. B. Craig was guarding the double doors between the main building and the basement parking area.

5. Did you know Ruby? No.

6. When and under what circumstance did you see Ruby?

After the shooting when Ruby was placed on the jail elevator.

Signed: Barnie Merrell
Lt. Barnie Merrell

75

November 30, 1963

J. E. Curry
Chief of Police

Re: Shooting of Lee Harvey Oswald
L. D. Miller

Sir:

L. D. Miller was interviewed by Lieutenants C. C. Wallace and P. G. McCaghren at 9:15 am on November 30, 1963. The interview was essentially the same as his original report dated November 27, 1963. The following was added by L. D. Miller:

I have not been interviewed by the Federal Bureau of Investigation regarding this incident, and have no knowledge how this person got into the City Hall.

Respectfully submitted,

C C Wallace
C. C. Wallace, Lieutenant
Juvenile Bureau

P G McCaghren
P. C. McCaghren, Lieutenant
Burglary & Theft Bureau

lh

76

November 26, 1963

Mr. J.E. Curry
Chief of Police

Subject: Shooting of Harvey Oswald

Sir:

On Sunday November 24, 1963 when prisoner Harvey Oswald was being brought from the jail into the asement I was standing on the east side of the door to the jail office. Detective Cutchshaw was on the west side of the door and Detective McMillan was standing next to me.

I saw the movement of a person coming across the ramp from the east of me and heard a shot at about the same time. This person was hit from behind and propelled in my direction. I grabbed him around the neck and helped to take him into the jail office. When I first made contact with this person he still had a pistol in his hand.

I did not know this person and to my knowledge had never seen him before.

Respectfully Submitted

Louis D. Miller
Louis D. Miller 1236
Detective
Criminal Investigation Division

76

REPORT OF OFFICER'S DUTIES IN REGARDS TO OSWALD'S DEATH

LESLIE D. MONTGOMERY - #1047

On Sunday November 24, 1963 at 11:15 am Captain Fritz, Lt. R. E. Swain, Det. J. R. Leavelle, Det. L. C. Graves and myself escorted Oswald from Captain Fritz's office to the jail elevator. Det. Leavelle had been handcuffed to Oswald. Patrolman C. G. Lewis, Jr., was the elevator operator as we carried Oswald down from the 3rd floor of the city hall to the basement. When we got off of the elevator in the basement, Lt. R. E. Swain walked out in front of Captain Fritz. Det. Leavelle was to Oswald's right and Det. Graves was to Oswald's left, and I was in back of Oswald about three feet as we approached the door leading from the basement and jail office. Captain Fritz told us to stop, that he was going to check one more time. The captain said, "All right, come on." We walked out of the door leading from the basement jail office to the ramp where the cars come down into the basement. We had to stop approximately five feet from the driveway of the ramp because the car was not in position. When we stopped I saw a blur of something and heard a shot. I went around Det. Graves and grabbed Jack Ruby by the head. At the time I grabbed Ruby by the head he was being held by W. J. Harrison, T. D. McMillon, R. L. Lowery and W. J. Cutshaw. We forced Ruby to the ground and a check was made for the weapon. We then moved Ruby into the basement jail office and put him back on the floor being held down by the same officers. While being held down on the floor of the basement jail office, Ruby said, "I hope I killed the son-of-a-bitch." I asked Chief Batchelor if we had better get Ruby on the elevator and get him up into the jail. Chief Batchelor said yes, and Ruby was taken to the elevator. I then went to where Oswald was lying on the jail office floor. A doctor was applying artificial respiration. The ambulance people arrived and loaded Oswald on the cot, and I went with the cot to the ambulance.

77

COMMISSION EXHIBIT No. 2002—Continued

Leslie D. Montgomery-Page 2

I then joined Captain Fritz, Detective E. R. Beck and C. W. Brown in their car and went with them to Parkland Memorial Hospital, 5201 Harry Hines Blvd. Upon our arrival at the hospital I was told by Captain Fritz to guard the east end of the hall of the Emergency Room. Oswald was taken to the operating room and I then moved up to the first floor main entrance to help maintain security. I was then relieved and returned to the outside entrance of the Emergency Room where I joined Captain Fritz and Det. E. R. Beck, and we all three returned to the city hall to our office. I answered the telephone and stood by for further orders. At 3:25 pm on Sunday November 24, 1963 Dets. E. L. Boyd, M. G. Hall and myself were told by Captain Fritz to get Ruby out of jail and bring Ruby to Captain Fritz's office. We checked Ruby out of the jail and brought him to Captain Fritz's office.

I then answered the telephone and stood by for further orders. I was told by Lt. Wells to interview a Bill DeMar (stage name)true name, William Delano Crowe, Jr. I interviewed this person and found him to be the master of ceremonies at the Carousel Club. The over-all content of the interview was the fact that this person was broke and that Ruby was supposed to pay him. He did also state that he thought Oswald was in the Carousel Club on November 20, 1963-Wednesday. DeMar said he could not be definite about this but he felt it was Oswald. This person was released without an affidavit taken. I then stood by for further orders and answered the telephone.

At 10:30 pm Sunday, November 24, 1963 I was told by Captain Fritz to go home and return at 8:00 am November 25, 1963.

77

COMMISSION EXHIBIT No. 2002—Continued

STATEMENT OF R. C. NELSON:

I do not know Jack Ruby.

I saw him after the shooting and I had not seen this man in the basement of the City Hall prior to the shooting.

78

November 26, 1963

Mr. J. E. Curry
Chief of Police

Subject: Assignment of Officer
R. C. Nelson, #1652
Sunday, November 24, 1963

Sir:

On Sunday, November 24, 1963 at approximately 9:00 A.M., I was told to report to 511.

On arrival Lt. Pierce told me and 3 other men to report to Sgt. Dean in the basement of the City Hall. Upon reaching the basement, Sgt. Dean and Sgt. Putnam advised me to check people in both sections of the basement.

I stationed myself inside the building just West of the exit door from the jail office. I had been at this position approximately 3 minutes when a man asked if he could go to the window of the jail office to get someone out of jail. Sgt. Putnam came up and I asked him about letting people go to the jail office window. He told me to station myself by the first window of the jail office and let people use this window to contact jail office personnel.

At approximately 9:45 A. ., a reserve policeman stationed himself in the hall way on my left side. I do not know this officer's name. The reserve and I checked everyone who came by us for identification.

At approximately 10:45 A.M. I noticed a television camera on the elevator in the basement, two men were with this camera. One of these men approached me and asked if they could move the camera through my position into the parking area of the basement. I told Lt. Pierce, who was standing close by what the man wanted. Lt. Pierce talked with this man and then told me it would be all right to let them pass. The two men who were iginally with the camera, pushed it by me and the reserve officer.

At approximately 11:20 A.M., I heard a shot come from the area outside the basement doors. Several reporters who were standing in front of the jail office windows started toward the double doors of the basement. I ran to the door in an effort to keep persons from coming through the doors at this time. Several officers were subduing the suspect (Ruby) in front of me, someone yelled to watch for the gun. I reached for the suspect's left hand and felt for a gun. After this I returned to the area outside the jail office windows and remained there until relieved by Lt. Pierce.

Respectfully submitted,

Ronald C. Nelson

Ronald C. Nelson
Patrolman, #1652
Patrol Division

RCN/ch

78

Mr. J. E. Curry
Chief of Police

Date: 11-26-63

Sir:

This is a statement of facts relating to my activity as a Reserve Officr Sunday, November 24, 1963, to the best of my knowledge and recollection.

1. Approximate time I reported to duty. 9:30 AM

2. I reported to (person and place). LT. MERREL, ASSEMBLY ROOM

3. I was assigned to (state place or area and who you assisted and what assignment consisted of such as crowd control, search, guard, etc.).

THE GARAGE AREA OF THE BASEMENT IMMEDIATELY BELOW THE COMMERCE STREET EXIT. MY ASSIGNMENT WAS TO COVER THE DOOR OPENING INTO THE SUB-BASEMENT MACHINERY AREA. I WAS ON THIS ASSIGNMENT UNTIL APPROXIMATELY 15 MINUTES AFTER THE SHOOTING.

4. Names of other officers in the same area that I can recollect are:

LT. SUITS, SGT CROY (RESERVES)

5. Did you know Ruby? NO

6. When and under what circumstance did you see Ruby? DID NOT SEE HIM

Print name W. J. NEWMAN

79

Commission Exhibit No. 2002—Continued

November 26, 1963

Mr. J. E. Curry
Chief of Police

Sir:

This is a statementof facts relating to my activity as a Reserve Officer Sunday, November 24, 1963, to the best of my knowledge and recollection.

1. Approximate time I reported to duty. 9:30 A. M.

2. I reported to Lt. Merrell, Assembly Room.

3. I was assigned to the garage area of the basement immediately below the Commerce Street exit. My assignment was to cover the door opening into the sub-basement machinery area. I was on this assignment until approximately 15 minutes after the shooting.

4. Names of other officers in the same area that I can recollect are:

Lt. Suits, Sgt. Croy (Reserves)

5. Did you know Ruby? No.

6. When and under what circumstance did you see Ruby?

Did not see him.

Signed: W. J. Newman
W. J. Newman

79

Commission Exhibit No. 2002—Continued

City of Dallas

OFFICE MEMORANDUM

Riedel for information

To Lt. Revill

December 6, 1963

Subject: Reserve Police Officer W.J. Newman
Res: 10923 Cotillion, BR-9-5923
Bus: 4112 S. Buckner, EV-1-7161

Sir:

SUBJECT called this date and stated that he remembered someone going over the railing at the ramp leading into the parking area of the basement the morning OSWALD was shot. He further stated that he could not remember whether it was before or after the shooting. Also that he saw the person was wearing a suit, and he saw only his back, and could not identify him.

Respectfully submitted,

R.W. Westphal
R.W. Westphal, Detective
Criminal Intelligence Section

The only reason you and I are here is to assist the people of Dallas

Dallas Texas March 26, 1964 Ex 5038 B deposition of W.J. Newman Leon D. Hubert
W.J. Newman

79

STATEMENT OF POLICE RESERVE OFFICER W. J. NEWMAN:

I recall someone going over the railing at the bottom of the Main Street ramp, but I have racked my brain and cannot recall whether it was before or after the shooting.

I do remember that the person had on a suit, but I do not know the color. I don't remember seeing a hat, but I can't say whether he was wearing one or not. This could have been about the time the ambulance pulled in.

Dallas Texas March 26, 1964 Ex 5038 A deposition of W J Newman Leon D Hubert
W.J. Newman

79

December 1, 1963

Mr. J. E. Curry
Chief of Police

Sir:

Re: Interview of Reserve Officer,
Patrolman William J. Newman, 317

On December 1, 1963 Reserve Officer, Patrolman William J. Newman was interviewed by the undersigned officers as to any information he might have concerning the shooting of Lee Harvey Oswald which was not covered in his original report dated November 26, 1963.

Newman stated, after reading his original report, that he recalled observing an unknown white male run down the Main Street ramp into the basement of the City Hall, approximately one minute prior to the shooting of Oswald. This unknown male disappeared into the group of newsmen and police officers and was not observed by Newman again.

Patrolman Newman states that he observed this individual just prior to someone in the crowd announcing, "Here he comes!" Less than a minute lapsed from this time until the shooting of Oswald. Newman states that he did not know Jack Ruby.

At this time Patrolman Newman has not been contacted by any federal agency.

Respectfully submitted,

Jack Revill
Jack Revill, Lieutenant
Special Service Bureau

C. C. Wallace
C. C. Wallace, Lieutenant
Special Service Bureau

jh

Dallas Tex Mar 26 1964
Ex. 5038
W. J. Newman
79

Commission Exhibit No. 2002—Continued

Day off

November 27, 1963

Mr. J. E. Curry
Chief of Police

Subject: Jack Ruby

Sir:

On Sunday, November 24, 1963, I was assigned by Lieutenant Wiggins to the Downstairs Jail Office. I am a Police Clerk and was following normal duties assigned to me.

I did not know Jack Ruby and had never seen him before the shooting of Lee Harvey Oswald. I did not see Ruby until he was brought in by the arresting officers. I did not see the shooting.

Respectfully submitted,

Johnnie F. Newton

Johnnie F. Newton
Police Clerk 6
Service Division

Commission Exhibit No. 2002—Continued

November 30, 1963

STATEMENT OF POLICE CLERK JOHNNIE F. NEWTON:

I did not see the actual shooting because my view was blocked by several officers. I did not know Jack Ruby and do not recall ever having seen him before.

80

December 11, 1963

Mr. J. E. Curry
Chief of Police

Subject: Telephone Interview with Ike Pappas -
301 East 48th Street
New York City, New York
Plaza 2-5463
Radio Station WNEW

Sir:

On December 11, 1963 at 3:30 p.m. Mr. Pappas called and I talked to him regarding the Oswald shooting, November 24, 1963. Mr. Pappas stated that he was on the third floor of the City Hall and that he observed Captain Fritz and the Detectives as Oswald left their office and went downstairs on the jail elevator. He took the City Hall elevator to the basement and hurried into the basement ramp area and got there about one minute before Oswald was brought out. He took a position about the middle of the driveway on the North side. Jack Ruby came from a position to Pappas's left side.

Mr. Pappas stated that he had seen Jack Ruby at the press conference late Friday night and that at that time Jack Ruby gave him a guest pass to the Carousel Club. He stated he had not seen Jack Ruby on Saturday at the City Hall.

Mr. Pappas stated he knew 2 other men that were present at the time of the shooting - one man was Hank Machriella of the Daily Tribune, New York City, New York (a writer) and the other man was Tom Petit, also of New York.

Respectfully submitted,

C C Wallace
C. C. Wallace, Lieutenant
Juvenile Bureau

CCW:mw

80-A

Lay: a TP -

November 26, 1963

Mr. J. E. Curry
Chief of Police

Subject: Assignment of Officer
Officer D. L. Pate #1183
Sunday, November 24, 1963

Sir:

On Sunday, November 24, 1963 at approximately 9:00 A.M. I was told to report to the Patrol Captain's office along with several other officers.

We stayed in the Captain's office until approximately 9:45 A.M. when Captain Talbert advised us to report to the basement. When we got to the basement, Captain Talbert gave me the keys to his car and told me to pull the car out of the parking space and put it in a position to drive out.

I stayed with the Captain's car until approximately 10:45 A.M. when Captain Talbert came and told me to park the car back in a parking space and take a position at the base of the ramp leading out to Commerce Street.

He ordered me to watch the armored car when it backed down the ramp and not let it hit the over head.

After the armored car arrived and backed into the Commerce entrance, Captain Talbert ordered me to take a post at the front of the ramp leading out to Commerce Street and not let anyone onto the ramp when they carried the prisoner to the armored car.

I called Officer L. C. Taylor, #1430 and asked him to stand on the side next to the building and help me keep everyone off the ramp.

I was at this post when the prisoner was shot.

When I heard the shot I started toward the scene and then someone hollered not to let anyone out of the basement. I then went to the back of the basement where I could cover the elevators leading to the new city hall.

Respectfully submitted,

D. L. Pate

D. L. Pate
Patrolman #1183
Patrol Division

DLP/ch

81

COMMISSION EXHIBIT No. 2002—Continued

November 29, 1963

STATEMENT OF D. L. PATE

I was assigned to a post at the bottom of the Commerce Street ramp. I took this position at about 11:05 a.m. My duty was to keep everyone off the ramp when they came up with the prisoner. I left for about 3 minutes to take my shotgun on the inside of the jail and then returned directly to the post.

I know Jack Ruby but I did not see him in or about the City Hall. I have known Ruby about 6 or 7 years. The last time I saw Ruby was about 3 months ago.

81

COMMISSION EXHIBIT No. 2002—Continued

3K9-0391

November 26, 1963

Mr. J. E. Curry,
Chief of Police.

Subject: Assignment of Officer
B. G. Patterson #1553,
on Sunday, November 24, 1963.

Sir:

Approximately 9:00 A.M., November 24, 1963, I received instructions to report to Station 511 for assignment. I arrived at 511 at approximately 9:10 A.M., and was told by Lieutenant Pierce to report to Sergeant Dean in the basement. Sergeant Dean gave me my assignment which was the south ramp exit on Commerce Street. My orders were not to let anyone in the basement except members of Press and Police with proper identification. Sergeant Dean said I would have another officer to assist me as soon as they completed a search of the basement.

Officer L. E. Jez came up the ramp to Commerce Street Exit to assist me at approximately 9:45 A.M.. There were also about threeor four reserve officers at my location. Officer Jez went across Commerce Street with several other officers to search a building, then returned to his assignment. At 11:00 am, Lieutenant Pierce said the subject would be moved in an armored car and for me to guard the right side as it was backed down the Ramp. The car arrived at about 11:10 A.M., and was backed into the opening of the Ramp. No unauthorized person entered the basement during this time. I remained at my assignment on the right side of the car.

A few minutes later I heard noise in the basement. I saw someone walking across the top of a car. A little later I heard a siren and saw the ambulance pull into the Main Street Ramp enterance. Someone said to move the Armored car out of the way of the ambulance, so I got in and told the driver to move it to the south side of Commerce Street. The ambulance came out of the basement and I returned to my assignment on the ramp until relieved by Sergeant Dean.

Respectfully submitted,

B. G. Patterson (signature)

B. G. Patterson
Patrolman, #1553
Patrol Division

OK

BGP/mb

82

COMMISSION EXHIBIT No. 2002—Continued

December 1, 1963

STATEMENT OF B. G. PATTERSON:

I was stationed on the West side of the armored car when it backed into the Commerce Street ramp. It was so close to the wall that no one could have walked through.

I met Jack Ruby about two years ago, but I don't think I would know him if I saw him. I did not see him in the basement or around the City Hall to recognize him.

82

COMMISSION EXHIBIT No. 2002—Continued

December 11, 1963

Mr. J. E. Curry
Chief of Police

Subject: Interview with Mr. Darwin Payne, Reporter for Dallas Times Herald

Sir:

On December 10, 1963, Lieutenant F. I. Cornwall and Lieutenant Jack Revill interviewed Mr. Darwin Payne in regards to an article that was written by him and printed in the Dallas Times Herald, December 8, 1963. Mr. Payne stated that on Saturday, December 7, 1963, at about 1:30 p.m. he called Sergeant P. T. Dean at home and told him that he was assigned to verify an article written by Mr. David Hughes and published in the Times Herald shortly after the shooting of Lee Harvey Oswald.

Mr. Payne said that he then read the article written by Mr. David Hughes to Sergeant Dean (copy of these notes are attached to the interview of David Hughes) and asked him if this was about the way it was or if there were any changes he would like to make. Sergeant Dean advised him that he did not have any changes to make from the original interview given Mr. Hughes. The article written by Mr. Payne which appeared in the Dallas Times Herald on December 8, 1963, states "Officer says he saw Ruby". In regard to this statement I asked Mr. Payne if Sergeant Dean had made this statement, that he had seen Jack Ruby come down the North ramp and Mr. Payne replied that Sergeant Dean did not say this but that he merely verified what had been written in the first article.

When asked how this mistake was made, Mr. Payne stated that it was probably done by the rewrite man.

At the time of this interview, Mr. Payne said he had been questioned by the Federal Bureau of Investigation.

Respectfully submitted,

F. I. Cornwall
F. I. Cornwall, Lieutenant
Special Service Bureau

Jack Revill
Jack Revill, Lieutenant
Special Service Bureau

FIC:nw
Enclosure - Copy of article in Dallas Times Herald

82-A

Commission Exhibit No. 2002—Continued

DALLAS TIMES HERALD
DECEMBER 8, 1963

TIMES RI-1-4355 HERALD
DECEMBER 8, 1963

OFFICER SAYS HE SAW RUBY

DARWIN PAYNE - WH6-5892

A Dallas police officer said Saturday that he saw self-appointed executioner Jack Ruby come through the Main Street entrance of the City Hall basement minutes before he fired a fatal, point-blank shot into the body of Lee Harvey Oswald.

The officer, stationed near the armored car at the Commerce Street exit from the basement, told The Times Herald:

"Jack Ruby, Oswald's assassin, came from the north (Main Street) entrance down the ramp. There were many police officers and press representatives in the area.

"Ruby jumped out of the crowd as Oswald passed and fired one shot point-blank at Oswald."

How Ruby entered the City Hall basement has been subject of an extensive investigation within the police department. No official explanation has been made, and police officials have declined comment on reports that several officers have been asked to take lie-detector tests in connection with the probe.

STORIES MATCH

The officer's story matches that of Ruby as told through his attorney Tom Howard. There has been speculation that Ruby had waited in the basement, mingling with members of the press until Oswald stepped into the basement parking area.

An officer on duty at the Main Street exit said he had not seen Ruby enter the basement.

The officer said he had been on guard at the Main Street exit for two and one half hours prior to the shooting and had admitted no one but police officers and press representatives. Everyone, he said, was required to show identification.

In another development, the owner of a public gun range said Saturday the FBI had taken pounds of empty shells in an attempt to confirm that Oswald had

See RUBY on Page 8

★ RUBY

Continued From Page 1

practiced shooting there as recently as five days before the assassination of President Kennedy.

Floyd Davis, owner of the Sportsdrome Gun Range near Grand Prairie, said neither he nor his wife, Virginia, had ever seen Oswald at the range.

"But there were three different people here at three different times who told us about seeing Oswald," Davis said.

Meanwhile, an 18-year-old self-styled Nazi from Arlington, Va., was marched into the Dallas police department, accompanied by a detective carrying a near-lifesized "dummy" of Cuban strongman Fidel Castro.

The youth wore a brown shirt and a Swastika arm band. He said he was "just trying to inform the American people."

CASTRO BLAMED

A sign affixed to the Castro effigy blamed the Cuban dictator for President John F. Kennedy's assassination and urged an invasion of the Communist-controlled island.

The Secret Service arrived minutes later and clamped a security lid on the Dallas Police Department's special services bureau.

It was also learned Saturday that an early suspect in the assassination of President Kennedy was still in jail—but no longer as a suspect in the killing.

The man, a 31-year-old man who gave a Knight Street address, was arrested minutes after the assassination when officers swarmed railroad yards near the assassination scene.

A man was reported seen in that area carrying a rifle.

STILL IN JAIL

The suspect was unarmed when arrested but booked, along with others arrested in the hectic hours following the assassination, on charges of "investigation of conspiracy to commit murder."

The investigative charges were dropped Monday morning but the man was held in jail on "city charges."

And in another phase of the investigation, authorities still declined to comment on a possible link between the President's assassination and a sniper's shot at former Maj. Gen. Edwin A. Walker last spring.

Oswald's widow is reported to have told authorities her husband boasted of firing a shot at Mr. Walker last April 10, and there were reports that the ex-general's name and telephone number were found in a book recovered among Oswald's possessions.

The shot barely missed the general as he sat in the study of his home on Turtle Creek Boulevard.

82-A

Commission Exhibit No. 2002—Continued

Francious Pelou

I am a reporter with AFP - 50 Rockefeller Plaza, New York - PL 7-6712. This is a group of French and National Press. I arrived in Dallas Friday night, November 22, 1963, following the assassination of President Kennedy. I arrived at the City Hall and attended the interview of Oswald in the basement late that night. I have been asked if I know Jack Ruby. I recall Ike Pappas, another reporter from New York, referring to a person that had brought sandwiches to the press as Jack. I later understood this to be Jack Ruby. To my knowledge I did not see this person Saturday. Sunday morning, November 24, 1963, I entered the basement of the City Hall and was thoroughly checked for my press credentials.

At the time of the shooting I was standing on the East side of the ramp with the two live-TV cameras to my right. I observed Oswald as he was being taken from the Jail Office. I took notice when he turned his head to the left. I also turned and looked in the same direction as Oswald looked and found the person who I now know to be Jack Ruby as he lunged from the crowd and shot Oswald. I carried this story as a lead in my paper that Oswald saw his killer before anyone else.

François Pelou

Subscribed + Sworn to Before me, this 7th day of December 1963

Ruby Smith
RUBY SMITH
Notary Public, Dallas County Texas

83

Mr. J. E. Curry
Chief of Police

December 5, 1963

Re: Interview with George Phenix
KRLD-TV - 2550 Klondike
DA 7-8070

Sir:

We went to the home of George Phenix at approximately 1:30 p.m. on December 4, 1963. He stated that he arrived at the basement of the City Hall, Sunday morning, November 24, 1963 with Wes Wise in a mobil unit. They drove into the basement of the City Hall and shortly thereafter Wes Wise left in the mobile unit. Mr. Phenix stated he took film of someone measuring the height of the Commerce Street ramp to determine if the armored car could be brought in from that exit.

Mr. Phenix was vague about other newsmen in the vicinity as he has only held his present position for about 6 months and is not familiar with other newsmen.

The pictures Mr. Phenix took in the basement showed the top of Jack Ruby's hat and also showed Ruby as he lunged past Officer Harrison on his left side. Phenix was not aware of Ruby's presence before the shooting and actually was not aware he was in the picture until the shot was fired. Mr. Phenix was standing on the East curb of the ramp and leaning against the railing taking his pictures when Ruby apparently entered the scene between Mr. Phenix and Officer Harrison. We have Mr. Phenix's pictures in our possession.

Respectfully submitted,

P. J. McCaghren
P. J. McCaghren
Lieutenant, Burglary & Theft Bureau

C. C. Wallace
C. C. Wallace
Lieutenant, Juvenile Bureau

mw

84

November 26, 1963

Mr. J. E. Curry
Chief of Police

Subject: Security Of Parking Area
Of City Hall During Transfer
Of Lee Harvey Oswald

Sir:

At approximately 9:00 A.M., Sunday, November 24, 1963, I was instructed by Captain Talbert to call enough squads to the City Hall to assist in the transfer of Lee Harvey Oswald. I called thirteen (13) squads to report to Station 511. This was a total of nineteen (19) men.

When the officers started arriving I instructed Sergeant P. T. Dean to report to the parking area and remove all unauthorized persons from this area and keep this area free from such persons until after the transfer had been made.

At approximately 9:40 A.M. I instructed four (4) officers to report to Sergeant Dean for the purpose of securing this area and instructed the remainder of the officers who had been called to the station to remain in the Sergeant's Room of the Patrol Office to be used as a pool as needed.

I later checked the parking area at approximately 10:15 A.M. and found it to be free of unauthorized personnel.

I then went to the Homicide Bureau for additional information. I remained at this location until the interrogation had been completed. At this time Chief Curry and Chief Stevenson instructed me to secure a car and some uniform officers and escort the armored trucks via Elm Street to the Court House.

I rode the elevator to the basement and got equipment number 205. The exit ramp was blocked leading to Commerce Street by one of the armored trucks and it was necessary for me to exit on Main Street. Sergeants B. J. Maxey and J. A. Putnam were in the car with me. Sergeant Putnam was seated on the right front and Sergeant Maxey on left rear.

At this time a large number of members of the press were located at the bottom of the ramp. Sergeant Putnam got out of the car and assisted me while getting through the crowd. He then returned to the right front of the car.

I continued up the ramp where I observed Officer R. E. Vaughn at the top of the ramp. He was standing just outside the ramp on my right.

85

COMMISSION EXHIBIT No. 2002—Continued

Page 2

No one entered the basement by the north ramp while we were leaving.

We made a left turn from the basement on Main Street and stopped for a short time for the red light on Main and Harwood, then continued to the top of the ramp on Commerce Street.

By the time we were in position in front of the armored car the shooting must have already occurred as officers were running to cover all exits of the City Hall.

Respectfully submitted,

Rio S. Pierce
Lieutenant of Police
Patrol Division

RSP/bb

85

COMMISSION EXHIBIT No. 2002—Continued

November 30, 1963

STATEMENT OF LT. RIO S. PIERCE

I know Jack Ruby and have known him since 1949. I did not see him at or near the City Hall prior to the shooting.

I was driving the squad car; Putnam was sitting in the front seat; and, Maxey in the back on the lefthand side.

When we drove out the Main Street ramp, there were some people on the sidewalk, but vehicular traffic was very light. I did see Vaughn after I passed him and this was about six feet from the building.

I pulled on to Main Street and stopped for the traffic light. When it changed, I pulled into the intersection and did let two cars pass, and made a left turn onto Harwood and a left at Commerce.

When we arrived at the Commerce Street ramp entrance, Maxey and Putnam got out of the car and I backed up in front of the armored car. I got out of the car and I could tell something had happened, and we sealed off the Commerce Street entrance.

85

COMMISSION EXHIBIT No. 2002—Continued

City of Dallas

OFFICE MEMORANDUM

To- Mr. J. E. Curry
Chief of Police

November 23, 1963

Subject: City Hall Security

Sir:

The following men from the Second Platoon were releived from their regular assignment for Security of the City Hall. Officers who were assigned a traffic corner location, remained on Station 511 till reporting to their Special Assignment.

Wise, M. L.	St. Paul & Elm
Brock, A. R.	Basement Elevator
Patterson, B. G.	Ramp on Commerce
Jez, L. E.	Ramp on Commerce
Vaughn, R. E.	Ramp on Main
Raz, J.	Stone & Elm
Anderson, K. K.	Field & Elm
Pate, D. L.	Ramp on Commerce
Nelson, R. C.	In hall at Jail Entrance
Wages, H. J.	Central & Main
Gregory , T. E.	Central & Elm
Fox, L. L.	Harwood & Elm
Taylor, L. C.	Bottom of Ramp, Commerce Street Side
Burton, T. R.	Commerce & Central
Erwin, T. K.	Commerce & Pearl
Hibbs, W. E.	Akard & Elm
Tolbert, G. L.	Pearl & Elm
Farris, M. E.	Lamar & Elm
Watkins, R. A.	Commerce Street Ramp, With Truck

Respectfully submitted,

Rio S. Pierce
Rio S. Pierce
Lieutenant of Police
Patrol Division

RSP/lot

85

The only reason you and I are here is to assist the people of Dallas

COMMISSION EXHIBIT No. 2002—Continued

November 29, 1963

STATEMENT OF SERGEANT J. A. PUTNAM

Sergeant J. A. Putnam stated that he was sitting in the front seat (passenger side) of the squad car driven by Lieutenant R. S. Pierce with Sergeant Maxey riding in the back seat behind the driver. Lieutenant Pierce hesitated as the front end of the squad arrived at the sidewalk. At this time Vaughn was standing on the sidewalk in front of the car. He moved to my right and about two feet off the sidewalk into the street and glanced to the east on Main Street and motioned us on. I am not sure he held up his hand to stop traffic or not. Pierce hesitated slightly and drove into the street. I do not remember whether we had to stop at a traffic light on Main and Harwood, but I know we did not stop at Harwood and Commerce. As we stopped at the Commerce Street Ramp a detective was running up the ramp yelling "Cover off the building."

I do not recall seeing anyone to the right of the squad car as we drove out by the Main Street entrance, but a few people were to the left. Captain Talbert and I ran several City employees from the basement. I talked to three porters and had them leave the building.

86

COMMISSION EXHIBIT No. 2002—Continued

November 26, 1963

Mr. J. E. Curry
Chief of Police

Subject: Assignment Of Sergeant
James A. Putnam On
Sunday, November 24, 1963

Sir:

On Sunday, November 24, 1963, at approximately 9:00 A.M., Sergeant Dean advised me he had instructions to search the basement parking area and instructed me to assist him. I was with Sergeant Dean when he assigned the officers at each entrance to the area to be searched. The assignments were as follows:

R. C. Nelson	Basement Entrance From Police & Courts Building
R. E. Vaughn	North Ramp Entrance on Main Street
B. G. Patterson	South Ramp Exit On Commerce Street
A. R. Brock	Elevators In Basement

Reserve Officer Assigned by Reserve Captain Arnett. Entrance On South Side From Engine Room

Sergeant Dean instructed the men on these posts to refuse entrance to anyone except properly identified Police Officers and members of the Press.

After securing the area, Sergeant Dean contacted Reserve Captain Arnett, who provided approximately twelve (12) Reserve Policemen to assist us with the search. Officer L. E. Jez, Sergeant Dean, Reserve Captain Arnett, approximately twelve (12) other Reserve Policemen and I conducted a search of all vehicles and all of the possible hiding places in the basement parking area.

I assisted Sergeant Dean by remaining in the basement and checking the posts as often as possible and also asking for identification of anyone in the basement that I did not recognize, as Police or Press Personnel.

Shortly after the search was completed an unmarked police car occupied by two detectives drove into the basement. I checked the

86

COMMISSION EXHIBIT No. 2002—Continued

Page 2

inside of their car. Following this car was a police patrol wagon, driven by C. G. Lewis. He stopped the vehicle and I checked the cab and opened the rear doors of the passenger compartment. I then assigned Officer W. E. Hibbs, and Officer G. L. Tolbert to take a position at the bottom of the north ramp and instructed them to look into all vehicles that came into the basement.

At approximately 10:45 A.M. Sergeant Dean called approximately twelve (12) officers together that had been standing by in the basement and gave them traffic assignments at each intersection that the prisoner was supposed to travel enroute to the County Jail.

At approximately 11:18 A.M. Sergeant Dean advised me to go with Lieutenant Pierce in his car and to get one man to go with us.

I asked Sergeant Maxey to come with us and the three of us left the basement by the Main Street ramp, at approximately 11:20 A.M. When we arrived at the top of the ramp I observed Officer R. E. Vaughn standing to my right. I did not see anyone come into the basement as we left.

We went to the Commerce Street side of the ramp and as we stopped the car, Detective Reynolds ran from the basement beside the armored car and yelled to cover off the Police and Courts Building, Oswald had been shot. I assisted him temporarily and then returned to Lieutenant Pierce's car.

Respectfully submitted,

James A. Putnam
James A. Putnam
Sergeant Of Police
Patrol Division

JAP/bb

86

COMMISSION EXHIBIT NO. 2002—Continued

November 27, 1963

Mr. J. E. Curry
Chief of Police

Subject: Incident Involving Lee Harvey Oswald

Sir:

At approximately 10:30 A. M. on November 24, 1963, I, Detective James K. Ramsey 1527, went into the basement of the city hall and stationed myself by the cement pillars next to the three parking stalls reserved for the Chief Officers.

I received instructions along with other detectives from Captain O. A. Jones to place myself approximately at the start of the exit ramp for the security of Lee Harvey Oswald.

I saw Mr. Oswald being led on to the ramp in the basement when I heard a shot, and I immediately started running toward a white male detective W. E. Chambers and a few other officers had seized the suspect. When I reached the suspect, approximately five to six officers and I assisted in subducing the suspect and taking him to the jail office. I assisted in the search of the suspect's person. He was handcuffed and as he was being picked up from the floor, the suspect stated, "I wanted to save the State some money". He was then taken by other police officers into the jail office elevator. I then went to Lee Harvey Oswald who was lying on the floor inside the jail office and observed the City Doctor administer aid to him. There was a bullet wound in Oswald's left side, and there was powder burns around the wound.

I then helped other officers and ambulance attendants place Oswald on the stretcher and place him into the ambulance, which was waiting on the ramp in the basement.

I then accompanied Lt. McKinney and four other detectives to Parkland Hospital to establish security measures at the Hospital.

Respectfully,
James K. Ramsey
James K. Ramsey
Detective 1627
Forgery Bureau

JKR:ms

87

COMMISSION EXHIBIT NO. 2002—Continued

November 30, 1963

J. E. Curry
Chief of Police

RE: Shooting of Lee Harvey Oswald
J. K. Ramsey

Sir:

J. K. Ramsey was interviewed by Lieutenants C. C. Wallace and P. G. McCaghren at 4:20pm on November 29, 1963. The interview was essentially the same as his original report dated November 27, 1963. The following was added by J. K. Ramsey:

I was stationed in the basement on the Commerce Street ramp near Detective Wagnor. I have been shown a picture of Jack Ruby and to my knowledge I did not see him come down this Commerce Street ramp. I do not know this person and have never seen him in the basement of the City Hall. I saw him after Oswald was shot when I helped subdue him.

I assisted other officers in taking him to the jail office. I remained in the jail office and assisted loading Oswald into the ambulance.

I do not have any ida how Jack Ruby got into the City Hall.

I have not been interviewed previously regarding this incident.

Respectfully submitted,

C C Wallace
C. C. Wallace, Lieutenant
Juvenile Bureau

P G McCaghren
P. G. McCaghren, Lieutenant
Burglary & Theft Bureau

lh

COMMISSION EXHIBIT No. 2002—Continued

November 26, 1963

Mr. J. E. Curry
Chief of Police

Subject: Assignment of Officer
Jerry Raz, #1551
Sunday, November 24, 1963

Sir:

On Sunday, November 24, 1963 at approximately 9:30 A.M., I reported to Station 511. I waited in the Radio Patrol office until about 10:15 A.M. At this time Captain Talbert took me along with about 10 other officers to the basement of City Hall and into the parking area. I waited in a group with the other officers until about 11:00 A.M. At this time Sergeants Dean and Putnam assigned me to work traffic at Elm and Stone Street.

While waiting for my assignment I did not have to confront anyone for entry or exit to the city hall basement. I did observe two TV cameras and about twenty reporters.

I departed the City Hall basement approximately 11:05 A.M. and reported to my traffic assignment. About 11:30 A.M., I was informed by Police Radio to report to Parkland Hospital. I arrived at Parkland Hospital and worked traffic on Harry Hines Blvd. at the hospital entrance. I was relieved from this post at 1:00 P.M. by a Police Reserve Officer. I then went back to my patrol duties.

Respectfully submitted,

Jerry Raz
Patrolman #1551
Patrol Division

JR/ch

88

COMMISSION EXHIBIT No. 2002—Continued

November 29, 1963

Statement of Jerry Raz:

I left the basement of the City Hall about 11:00 A. M. for a traffic assignment at Elm and Stone Streets, and did not return prior to the shooting.

I do not know Jack Ruby.

88

November 26, 1963

Mr. J. E. Curry
Chief of Police

SUBJECT: Location of Detective H. B. Reynolds at the time of the shooting of Oswald, November 24, 1963

Sir:

Below is submitted report supplied by Detective H. B. Reynolds as regarding his activities on November 24, 1963.

At 11:00 Lieutenant Swain came into the office and told us, one by one, to start toward Jail office. Stephens and I, the last two left, and I went to the double doors leading outside into the ramp area. I was there when Oswald was brought out of the elevator. At this time, I noticed that an attorney Tom Howard was standing in the lobby outside of the Jail office behind the uniformed officer stationed there. As officers escorting Oswald started out into the ramp area, I heard a shot.

I ran back into the lobby and down the lobby to the Commerce Street exit, and up on the street and ordered an uniformed officer to block the Commerce Street exit to the old City Hall and to not let any one out. I ran to the Harwood Street exit and ordered an uniformed officer to not let any one out of that exit. I came back to the Commerce Street exit and entered on the first floor of the City Hall to see a Negro running toward the exit on the Main Street. I immediately went after him along with Sgt. Everett and a reserved officer who were catching up with him at that time. This colored male was handcuffed, and I took possession of him and took him to the Homicide office where I released him to Detective Baker, and then I took position in front of the Chief's office to stop pressmen from entering into this office.

Respectfully submitted,

R. E. Swain, Lieutenant
Burglary and Theft Bureau

RES/pst

89

December 1, 1963

J. E. Curry
Chief of Police

Re: Shooting of Lee Harvey Oswald
Interview of H. B. Reynolds

Sir:

H. B. Reynolds was interviewed by Lieutenants C. C. Wallace and P. G. McCaghren at 2:30 pm on November 29, 1963. The interview was essentially the same as his original report dated November 27, 1963. The following was added by H. B. Reynolds:

I have been asked if I know Jack Ruby, and I do not. I did not see him prior to the shooting and was unable to see him after the shooting.

On the morning of November 29, 1963, in the sub basement of the City Hall, I over heard a conversation between Officer Vaughn and an officer unknown to me regarding Jack Ruby. The officer not known to me stated to Vaughn that he had seen a picture of Jack Ruby where there was a press card stuck in his hat.

I have not been interviewed by anyone regarding this incident prior to this date.

Respectfully submitted,

C C Wallace
C. C. Wallace, Lieutenant
Juvenile Bureau

P G McCaghren
P. G. McCaghren, Lieutenant
Burglary & Theft Bureau

lh

89

COMMISSION EXHIBIT No. 2002—Continued

December 18, 1963

Mr. J. E. Curry
Chief of Police

Subject: Interview of Warren Rickey - WBAP
1600 Grantland Circle
Ft. Worth, Texas
GL1-5963 - AN4-2484
December 17, 1963

Sir:

Mr. Rickey came to Dallas early Sunday morning, November 24, 1963, with WBAP-TV crew. He is an engineer and was assigned to top of Mobile Unit parked on Commerce Street beside City Hall. He had a T.V. camera on top of the truck and could not hear too much of what was said by anyone on the street. He stated he saw some man walking back and forth on sidewalk on Commerce Street side of the City Hall. This was before the armored car was brought to City Hall. Last time he saw this same man was approximately 10:00 a.m. or shortly before 10:00 a.m., and the man was standing in a group of people just East of the Commerce Street Ramp exit.

Mr. Rickey did not know Jack Ruby and later recognized the man from a picture in a Dallas paper, where Ruby was wearing a hat. Mr. Rickey stated he did not see a press pass on this man.

Respectfully submitted,

C C Wallace
C. C. Wallace, Lieutenant
Juvenile Bureau

CCW:nw

89-A

COMMISSION EXHIBIT No. 2002—Continued

November 25, 1963

Mr. J.E. Curry
Chief of Police

Subject: Jack Leon Ruby

Sir:

On November 21, 1963 at approximately 12 Noon I, along with Officers V.D. Monaghen, T.O. Trotman, D.E. Geer, and H.R. Arnold, was in assistant District Attorney Ben Ellis' office, which is on the sixth floor of the Records Building. The window in this office faces Record Street, with a view of both Elm and Main Streets.

The above captioned Subject came into the office while we were there and passed out some advertisement cards concerning a stripper known as "Jada." To my knowledge Subject did not stand at the window, nor did he pause any length of time at the window.

As Subject was leaving the office, assistant District Attorneys Ben Ellis and Don Stodghill entered. Subject introduced himself to Ben Ellis and told Mr. Ellis, "You probably don't know me now, but you will."

Respectfully submitted,

W.F. Dyson
Lieutenant of Police

90

3 December 1963

Captain W.P. Gannaway
Special Service Bureau
Dallas Police Department

Thru:
Lieutenant Jack Revill
Criminal Intelligence Section
Special Service Bureau
Dallas Police Department

Subject: Criminal Intelligence (1)
JACK RUBY [illegible]

Sir:

Pursuant to your instructions, the following is submitted.

The indices of the [illegible] NATIONAL BANK failed to reveal any information regarding SUBJECT being the co-maker of any loans for any Police Officers of this Department. This search of indices was made through Mr. [illegible], Vice-President of [illegible] NATIONAL BANK.

The indices of the FIRST NATIONAL BANK failed to reveal SUBJECT as being the co-maker for any loans to Police Officers of this Department. It was further determined that SUBJECT has never been involved in any business transactions at this bank. The search of indices was made through Mr. [illegible], Chairman of the Executive Committee of the FIRST NATIONAL BANK.

The indices of the OAK CLIFF BANK & TRUST COMPANY failed to reveal any information regarding SUBJECT. It has also been determined that SUBJECT has not been the co-maker on any notes or loans to any Police Officers of this Department. SUBJECT has never conducted any business transactions at this bank. The search of indices was made through Mr. J.C. [illegible], President, and Mr. [illegible], bank auditor.

90

Page 2- JACK RUBY DPD#54018- 3 December 1963-

The indices of the AMERICAN BANK & TRUST were searched with negative results on SUBJECT. It has been determined that SUBJECT has never conducted any business through this bank and further that SUBJECT has never been the co-maker on any loans involving Police Officers of this Department. The search of indices was made through MR. A.R. WRIGHT, SR., Chairman of the Board and MR. TERRY DICKENS, Vice President.

Respectfully submitted,

H. M. Hart

H.M. Hart, Detective
Criminal Intelligence Section

90

COMMISSION EXHIBIT No. 2002—Continued

December 4, 1963

Mr. J. E. Curry
Chief of Police

Re: Interview with Jack Ruby

Sir:

On December 1, 1963, Lieutenant Jack Revill and Lieutenant F. E. Cornwall interviewed Jack Ruby, presently confined in the Dallas County Jail for the murder of L. H. Oswald. The purpose of this interview was to determine how Ruby gained access to the basement of the City Hall.

During the interview with Ruby it became apparent that he was not going to cooperate in any way as he stated that he did not want to get any police officers in trouble and also anything that he might tell us might be used against him in his forthcoming trial for murder. He did state that he had sent a $25.00 money order to a friend of his in Ft. Worth from the Western Union Telegraph Company, 2034 Main, at 11:16 a.m. on November 24, 1963. Upon questioning him as to how he gained access to the basement of the City Hall, he became evasive and refused to furnish that information. However, in answer to a direct question as to whether he spoke to anyone in the basement prior to the shooting he definitely stated, "No", that he did not speak to anyone.

He did state that he would cooperate with the Police Department if his attorney, Mr. Tom Howard would give him permission to do so. Mr. Howard telephonically was contacted by Lieutenant Cornwall and requested to come to the County Jail to sit in on the interview with his client, Ruby. Mr. Howard did so and after discussing the matter with Ruby in privacy, they both decided that Ruby would not give us the requested information.

Prior to the termination of this interview, both Attorney Howard and Ruby stated that Ruby would be willing to submit to a polygraph examination; that they had made an attempt to get said polygraph examination but that District Attorney Henry Wade had refused.

90

COMMISSION EXHIBIT No. 2002—Continued

Page 2

The interview was terminated at this point and Mr. Howard stated that he would contact his other law partners and if they agreed he would give us information which might be significant to the Dallas Police Department investigation. He advised the undersigned officers that he would contact them Monday or Tuesday as to what decision they had reached.

On the morning of December 3, 1963, Inspector Sawyer contacted Mr. Howard, attorney for Jack Ruby and asked him if he had reached any decision regarding the polygraph examination for his client and supplying the Police Department with the information as to how he gained access to the basement of the City Hall. Mr. Howard became evasive and stated that he was going to call in some more lawyers on Friday, December 6, 1963, and that after he had a discussion with them, he would let us know his decision - until this conference would be held, his answer would be negative as far as the polygraph examination was concerned.

On December 3, 1963, Lieutenant Jack Revill and F. E. Cornwall again interviewed Jack Ruby in the County Jail. He was personally given the opportunity to submit to a polygraph examination. He refused, saying he would have to get permission from his legal advisor, Mr. Tom Howard. An attempt was made to gain information from Ruby as to his activities on the morning of November 24, 1963. He refused to furnish any information. He said that it would all come out during his trial and that he wants to tell the world what a great Police Department Dallas has and how much he loves Dallas. During the interview, Ruby became very emotional and was almost to the point of hysteria in his effort to protect any police officer from being implicated into his entrance into the basement of the City Hall.

He related in detail his activities for November 22, 1963, such as upon hearing that the President had been assassinated, he immediately stopped some ads which he had placed earlier that morning in the Dallas Morning News pertaining to his night club, the Carousel Night Club. He related that he became emotionally upset and was in a trance. He went to the Ritz Delicatessen and purchased $10.00 worth of Kosher type food. He was very specific in getting this information over to us. He then stated that he went to his sister's home and spent the remainder of the afternoon with her. In the late afternoon still feeling disturbed, he drove through the City of Dallas checking to see what business establishments were closed. He felt that inasmuch as he had closed his

90

Page 3

nightclub that the other business establishments should have also been closed out of sympathy for the death of the President. He went to a delicatessen and purchased sandwiches with the intention of bringing said sandwiches to his friends at the Police Department. He called the Homicide and Robbery Bureau and told them that he had these sandwiches and was going to bring them to the Police Department. He was advised by Detective R. M. Sims that they had already eaten but he thanked him for the gesture. Ruby then stated that he drove to the City Hall and went to the basement and mingled with the crowd. He was present in the Police Assembly Room when Lee Harvey Oswald was interviewed by the press. After this interview Ruby stated that he called Radio Station KLIF and got an exclusive interview with District Attorney H. Wade with KLIF. He left the City Hall and drove to Radio Station KLIF with the idea of giving the sandwiches to personnel at that location. The door was locked and he had to wait approximately 15 minutes before Joe Long of Radio Station KLIF drove up and opened the door. He stated that he remained there for sometime and then went home. At this point he became irrational and advised us that he was not going to discuss it any further. At this point the interview was terminated.

Due to Ruby's emotional state, the undersigned officers made no attempt to take notes during either interview. The forgoing information is to the best of our recollection.

Respectfully submitted,

Jack Revill
Lieutenant, Special Service Bureau

F. E. Cornwall
Lieutenant, Special Service Bureau

J. H. Sawyer
Inspector of Police

FEC:nw

90

December 6, 1963

Mr. J. E. Curry
Chief of Police

Re: Jack Ruby's Automobile

Lieutenant Vernon Smart obtained the following information:

Theodore Jackson c-m, 1710 Pine, usually can be found at RI 8-4645, 2001 Pacific; employed by Mr. B. D. Waters who owns and operates the parking lot at 2035 Main Street. Jackson was on duty at 2035 Main Street last Sunday, November 24, 1963. He stated that the 1960 Oldsmobile in question was parked on his lot when he opened the lot. He did not know the exact time but stated that it was about noon.

Johnnie L. Daniel c-m employed by Norton parking system next door to this lot stated that he opened his lot about the same time and that he saw this Oldsmobile parked there at the time. He stated that he arrived just a few minutes ahead of Jackson. Daniels address is Pacific Hotel.

Mr. Waters, owner of the lot, has an office at 2001 Pacific, Phone RI8-4645, listed as Allstate Parking.

Respectfully submitted,

O. A. Jones
O. A. Jones
Captain of Police

OAJ:nw

90

COMMISSION EXHIBIT No. 2002—Continued

Re: Ruby

December 9, 1963

Mr. J. E. Curry
Chief of Police

Sir:

On December 9, 1963, Mr. Thad Ricks was telephonically contacted regarding Jack Ruby having been issued a press pass during the 1963 State Fair of Texas. Mr. Ricks is with the Public Relations Department, State Fair of Texas, and stated that his office does not reflect any issuance of press credentials being issued to Ruby.

Respectfully submitted,

Jack Revill
Jack Revill
Lieutenant, Special Service Bureau

JR:nw

90

COMMISSION EXHIBIT No. 2002—Continued

December 16, 1963

Mr. J. E. Curry
Chief of Police

Subject: Jack Ruby

Mr. H. E. Crabbe, Assistant Vice-President, Merchant's State Bank was interviewed Friday, December 13, 1963, regarding Jack Ruby and any loan transactions involving Jack Ruby and any Dallas Police Officers.

A list of officers assigned to the security of the transfer of Lee Harvey Oswald on November 24, 1963, was furnished to the bank. The loan records of the Merchant's State Bank failed to reveal Jack Ruby being a co-maker of any loans to Dallas Police Officers.

Mr. Crabbe was assisted by Mr. Vince Torres, an employee of the bank Loan Department. This search revealed that Jack Ruby is not now nor has he ever been a co-maker of any loan.

Respectfully submitted,

H M Hart

H. M. Hart, Detective
Special Service Bureau

HMH:nw

90

COMMISSION EXHIBIT No. 2002—Continued

December 13, 1963

Mr. J. E. Curry
Chief of Police

Subject: Explanation of News Coverage on Date of Oswald shooting.

This information obtained from Bert Shipp, WFFA-TV.

WBAP - is an NBC Station and it was WBAP that had a live camera in the City Hall basement. The WBAP crew did the live pick-up and fed it to both NBC & CBS.

KRLD was at the courthouse to do a live pick-up for both NBC AND CBS.

KRLD is a CBS Station doing the pick-up live which was fed to both networks on a pool basis.

Neither CBS nor NBC actually had live cameras there. KRLD and WBAP did the live pick-up for the network.

Jim Davidson and Warren Ferguson both shot film for ABC, the network which had no live cameras there. WFAA-TV had no one in the basement. WFAA Radio had one man with a tape recorder. He was Bob Thornton.

Respectfully submitted,

P. G. McCaghren

P. G. McCaghren, Lieutenant
Burglary & Theft Bureau

PGM:nw

90-A

COMMISSION EXHIBIT No. 2002—Continued

Mr. J. E. Curry
Chief of Police

November 27, 1963

Subject: Jack Ruby

Sir:

On Sunday November 24, 1963, I was assigned to down stairs Jail Office by Lt. Wiggins. I had instructions to stay by the phone and to advise the dispatcher when Oswald had been loaded into armor car and was in route to County Jail.

I did not know Jack Ruby personally nor would I have known him if I had seen him, but I have heard his name before as owning a night club.

I did not see the shooting, but I was looking out glass in door to see when he was loaded into armored car. There was a shot and a scuffle and Lt. Wiggins said Oswald was shot and to call a doctor. I then called dispatcher for a doctor.

I did not see Jack Ruby in the basement until after the shooting when dectives brought him into Jail Office under arrest.

Respectfully submitted

Willie B. Slack

Willie B. Slack #992
Patrolman
Dallas Police Department

FR 5-5729

91

COMMISSION EXHIBIT No. 2002—Continued

December 1, 1963

STATEMENT OF WILLIE B. SLACK:

I think everything of importance was covered in my report.

91

COMMISSION EXHIBIT No. 2002—Continued

Mr. J. E. Curry
Chief of Police

November 27, 1963

Subject: Jack Ruby

Sir:

On Sunday, November 24, 1963, I was assigned by Lt. Wiggins to the down stairs Jail Office. I am a police clerk and was following normal duties assigned to me.

I did not know Jack Ruby personally and would not have known him had I seen him. I did not see him in the basement until after the shooting, when he was brought in by the arresting officers.

I did not see the shooting of Lee Harvey Oswald.

Respectfully submitted

Jerry D. Slocum

Jerry D. Slocum
Police Clerk 6
Dallas Police Department

92

COMMISSION EXHIBIT No. 2002—Continued

December 1, 1963

STATEMENT OF JERRY D. SLOCUM:

I was on duty in the Jail Office when Oswald was shot.

I did not see the shooting because my view was blocked by officers and camera men.

I do not know Ruby, but I saw him after the shooting. I do not recall having seen this man around the City Hall before.

92

COMMISSION EXHIBIT No. 2002—Continued

AFFIDAVIT IN ANY FACT

11-24-63

THE STATE OF TEXAS
COUNTY OF DALLAS

BEFORE ME, ______________________________

a Notary Public in and for said County, State of Texas, on this day personally appeared ______________________________

Who, after being by me duly sworn, on oath deposes and says:

I was on the ramp when the truck was backed in to take the prisoner to the Co Jail. I was accompanied by Ch. Batchelor. The Dep Sheriff opened the rear doors of truck and a nehi bottle fell out & broke. Chief Batchelor & I searched the truck completely, found one coke bottle & planned seating arrangements in truck. We had just finished and I was still facing truck & outside to see if all officers were in their place when I heard one shot. I immediately looked around & saw a scuffle. I was not aware that the prisoner was being brought out at that time. I immediately ran down to try to be of assistance. Several officers had Ruby down & were handcuffing him.

SUBSCRIBED AND SWORN TO BEFORE ME THIS ______ DAY OF ______ A.D. 196__

Lt V. S. Smart

____
Notary Public, Dallas County, Texas

CPS-GF-413

93

COMMISSION EXHIBIT No. 2002—Continued

November 27, 1963

Mr. J. E. Curry
Chief of Police

Sir:

I should like to submit the following report regarding the incident occurring in the basement on November 24, 1963.

I was on the ramp when the truck was backed in to take the prisoner to the County Jail. I was accompanied by Chief Batchelor. The Deputy Sheriff opened the rear doors of the truck and a Nehi bottle fell out and broke. Chief Batchelor and I searched the truck completely, found one coke bottle, and planned seating arrangement in the truck.

We had just finished and I was still facing the truck and outside to see if all officers were in their place when I heard one shot. Immediately I looked around and saw a scuffle. I was not aware that the prisoner was being brought out at that time.

I immediately ran down to try to be of assistance. Several officers had Ruby down and were handcuffing him.

Respectfully submitted,

V. S. Smart
V. S. Smart
Lieutenant
Criminal Investigation Division

93

COMMISSION EXHIBIT No. 2002—Continued

December 1, 1963

STATEMENT OF LT. V. S. SMART:

I do not know Jack Ruby.

After the shooting, I saw him at the elevator. I do not recall ever having seen him before.

93

COMMISSION EXHIBIT No. 2002—Continued

December 18, 1963

Mr. J. E. Curry
Chief of Police

Subject: Interview of Johnnie Smith - WBAP-TV
22 Shadowbrook
Hurst, Texas
BU2-2726 - AN4-2484
December 17, 1963

Sir:

Mr. Smith is a video engineer for WBAP-TV and came to Dallas early Sunday morning, November 24, 1963, with other personnel from WBAP-TV. He was in the mobile truck parked on Commerce Street, approximately one car length, West of Commerce Street exit.

About 8:00 a.m. Mr. Smith got out of the mobile unit truck and walked around on Harwood Street to the Telephone Company truck that was parked there. He saw a man standing on Harwood looking up at cables running to third floor of City Hall, where Chief Curry's Office is located. Mr. Smith went back to the mobile truck and about 8:30 a.m. this same man walked up to truck window and asked "Have they brought Oswald down yet?" and Smith said "No". Mr. Smith said he believes he saw this same man again at approximately 10:00 a.m. to 10:15 a.m. standing with a group of people approximately 10 feet East of Commerce Street ramp on the sidewalk.

Mr. Smith says he recognized this man later as Jack Ruby from a picture that he saw in a Dallas paper, where Ruby was wearing a hat. He thinks this was a Monday paper. Mr. Smith said he could not recognize Ruby from the mug shot showed him by F.B.I. agent.

Respectfully submitted,

C C Wallace

C. C. Wallace, Lieutenant
Juvenile Bureau

CCW:nw

93-B

COMMISSION EXHIBIT No. 2002—Continued

Clay off

November 26, 1963

Mr. J. E. Curry
Chief of Police

Subject: Assignment of Sergeant
D. F. Steele
Sunday, November 24, 1963

Sir:

On Sunday, November 24, 1963 I was acting area commander of the Oak Cliff Sub-station. At 9:15 A.M., accompanied by Reserve Officer J. F. Harrison, I reported to Lt. R. S. Pierce at the Central Station. I was instructed by Lt. Pierce to stand by in the Patrol office for assignment.

At 9:30 A.M., I accompanied Captain C.E. Talbert to the first floor exit onto Commerce Street. Captain Talbert instructed me to get a man and check the roof of the building across Commerce Street from the vehicular exit of City Hall. This area was checked and was secure. Upon completion of this assignment I secured five reserve officers and assigned them to move all by-standers from the North side of the 2000 block of Commerce. After this assignment I placed 2 reserve officers at Commerce and Pearl and 2 at Commerce and Harwood to stop all pedestrian traffic on the North side of Commerce Street. In addition I placed a reserve officer at the Commerce Street entrance to City Hall to restrict exits onto Commerce St.

Upon completion of these assignments I assisted Sgt. J. A. Putnam and P.T. Dean in assigning officers to traffic corners on Elm Street.

At 11:00 A.M., Captain C.E. Talbert instructed me to report to the traffic command post at Elm and Houston to secure 3 traffic men to complete the coverage of all intersections on Elm Street.

Respectfully submitted,

D. F. Steele

D. F. Steele
Sergeant of Police
Patrol Division

DFS/ch

94

COMMISSION EXHIBIT No. 2002—Continued

November 29, 1963

STATEMENT OF D. F. STEELE:

I left the City Hall at 11:00 a.m. for an assignment at Elm and Houston and did not return to the City Hall prior to the shooting.

I know Jack Ruby but I did not see him in or near the City Hall at this time.

94

December 3, 1963

Mr. J. E. Curry
Chief of Police

Re: Shooting of Lee Harvey Oswald
Interview of I. R. Stephens

Sir:

I. R. Stephens was interviewed by Lieutenants C. C. Wallace and P. G. McCaghren at 3:30 pm on December 2, 1963. This interview was essentially the same as his original report dated November 27, 1963. I. R. Stephens had this to add:

I have been asked if I know Jack Ruby and I have seen him before, but I doubt if I would recognize him. I didn't see him in the crowd in the basement of the City Hall. I have no idea how he got into the basement. I was down stairs approximately 5 or 10 minutes before Oswald was brought down, and nobody came by my post while I was there.

I have not been interviewed by the Federal Bureau of Investigation.

Respectfully submitted,

C C Wallace
C. C. Wallace, Lieutenant
Juvenile Bureau

P G McCaghren
P. G. McCaghren, Lieutenant
Burglary & Theft Bureau

lh

95.

November 26, 1963

Mr. J. E. Curry
Chief of Police

SUBJECT: Location of Detective Ivan R. Stephens at the time of the shooting of Oswald, November 24, 1963.

Sir:

The following is a report submitted by Detective Ivan R. Stephens regarding his activities on November 24, 1963 at the time of the incident at the basement.

At about 11:15 a.m., November 24, 1963, Lieutenant Swain ordered me to the basement of the City Hall to aid in the transfer of the prisoner, Lee Harvey Oswald to the County Jail. I went to the basement and remained in the lobby in front of the jail office when the Homicide men brought Oswald down on the inside jail elevator and started to the East Jail Door that leads to the parking area. These door were open at the time. I was behind the pressmen that were taking pictures through the Cashier's Doors of the jail, and I remained behind these pressmen and photographers in order to keep out any unauthorized persons that might attempt to come in behind the prisoner through the lobby.

I heard the shot and heard someone cry that the prisoner had been shot. I did not see the scene and was about forty feet from where the prisoner was shot. I saw the detectives carry Oswald inside the jail office and also saw some detectives attempting to carry a man inside of the jail office that was the one someone had said had shot the prisoner. I attempted to help these men get the prisoner inside the office. As soon as the prisoner was secured, I walked over where Oswald was lying on the floor, and saw a bullet hole in his left side as he was lying on the floor. He appeared to be conscience at the time and city doctor was called and was working on him when the ambulance came for him. I returned to the third floor for further assignment.

Respectfully submitted,

R. E. Swain, Lieutenant
Burglary and Theft Bureau

REC/pat

95

December 12, 1963

Inspector J. H. Sawyer talked to Deputy Chief M. W. Stevenson and received the following statement:

"I arrived in the basement of the City Hall on November 24, 1963, about 3 to 5 minutes prior to the shooting of Lee Harvey Oswald. I was standing on the West side of the middle ramp near the West wall and at the front door on the righthand side of Dhority's car.

I did not know Jack Ruby prior to the shooting of Lee Harvey Oswald and I did not see him in the basement until after he was arrested.

I saw Captain Fritz emerging from the jail corridor at which time I directed my attention to watching the crowd in the basement area.

I heard a shot but I did not see the shooting."

J. H. Sawyer
Inspector of Police

JHS:nw

Dallas Texas March 23, 1964 Ex. 5051 Deposition of M.W. Stevenson ... [illegible]

M W Stevenson

95A

December 12, 1963

Mr. J. E. Curry
Chief of Police

Subject: Interview of Reserve Officer Patrolman Donald Suits

Sir:

On November 30, 1963, Reserve Officer Patrolman Donald Suits was interviewed by the undersigned officers as to any information he might have concerning the shooting of Lee Harvey Oswald which was not covered in his original report dated November 26, 1963.

After having read his original report, Mr. Suits stated that there is nothing of significance which he could add to this first report.

Mr. Suits further states that at the time of this interview he had not been contacted by any federal agency.

Respectfully submitted,

F. I. Cornwall, Lieutenant
Special Service Bureau

Jack Revill, Lieutenant
Special Service Bureau

FIC:nw

95-B

November 26, 1963

Mr. J. E. Curry
Chief of Police

Sir:

This is a statement of facts relating to my activity as a Reserve Officer Sunday, November 24, 1963, to the best of my knowledge and recollection.

1. Approximate time I reported to duty. 9:00 A. M.

2. I reported to Assembly Room.

3. I was assigned to the Assembly Room and I remained in the Assembly Room until Sgt. P. T. Dean and another Sergeant came in and requested that all Reserve Officers that were not assigned to report to the basement and help shake it down.

   We started at the north wall and searched the air conditioning ducts, cars and all places where a weapon could be concealed. After the search, several of the officers were given traffic assignments, and the rest of us remained in the basement for further assignments. As we were waiting I noticed that each person that came in through the ramps were being checked for "Press Pass" or Police I.D.

   Dallas Police Reserve Patrolman W. J. Newman was assigned to the lower south end of the ramp, and Sgt. Dean requested that a man guard the south basement employee entrance, and I assigned Patrolman Newman to this door and took his place at the ramp. I noticed the regular officers were checking each person as they came in.

4. Names of other officers in the same area that I can recollect are:

   Reserve Lt. Ben McCoy, Lt. H. M. Kriss, Sgt. K. H. Croy, Reserve Captain C. O. Arnett.

5. Did you know Ruby? No.

6. When and under what circumstances did you see Ruby?

   I did not see Ruby at all except for a momentary glance. The other officer in the immediate area was standing there trying to seal off the south area after the shot.

Signed: Donald T. Suits
Donald Suits

95-B

December 4, 1963

Mr. J. E. Curry
Chief of Police

Re: Shooting of Lee Harvey Oswald

Sir:

I had been available to Captain Fritz's office most of the morning of November 24, 1963. I was in this office shortly before 11:00am. Seeing that preparations were under way to move Oswald out of the building, I stepped across the hall to the Burglary and Theft Office and instructed the men who were standing by to report to the jail office two at a time. These men were instructed to assist in any manner needed.

About 11:00am, the party in Captain Fritz's office started moving out. I was the first out of the office; walking to the hall door leading to the jail elevator. I unlocked this door and admitted Captain Fritz, Detective Leavelle, Graves, and Montogomery, and the prisoner Oswald. Oswald was hancuffed to Detective Leavelle.

When the elevator was loaded, I was the last person to enter the elevator. When we reached the basement, I was the first person off. About the time we got off the elevator, Captain Fritz was behind me, and he told me I would have to ride in the second car because we could only get five in the first car which contained the prisoner. He motioned for me to lead out. We went out the door on the East side of the jail desk.

When I walked out into the driveway, I found that press photographers and news media were surrounding the area. Strong flood lights were focused in the direction of the jail office. They were blinding. These lights were located at the Northeast corner of the area of the opening leading from the jail office.

The vehicle in which the prisoner was to be loaded was attempting to back into the opening in front of the jail office where unruley prisoners are generally unloaded. I immediately moved forward toward the east side and on the south edge of this crowd, moving the crowd of photographers and newsmen backward. These people were blocking the vehicle's movement, being in between the vehicle and the prisoner. I had both arms out stretched and was able to contain these people in a fairly wide area. I was facing east with my back to the prisoner. To my left I could see that everything was clear nearly to the flood lights. There was about two officers to my left along the drive way. However, the news media were standing about three deep.

96

I glanced quickly to my right from my left motioning some of these people to move backward as the vehicle was also moving backward. At this time I heard a gun discharge. With my arms out stretched, I wheeled to my left over my shoulder. I saw officers struggling with the person who had apparantly shot Oswald, and other officers were moving Oswald back into the jail office.

Almost at the time the shot was fired, the news media and photographers plunged forward upon the scene. I immediately forced them backwards while the other officers were subduing the person who fired the shot. I was able to contain these people until additional help arrived. Some of the officers that I know came to my assistance very quick were Sgt. P. T. Dean, Detectives H. L. McGee, and I. F. Van Cleave. At the time the prisoner Oswald emerged from the jail office, the central area of the ramp was clear except for photographers and news media who were blocking the vehicle.

While I was moving those persons blocking the ramp on my right and to the south, I glanced toward the prisoner Oswald and saw two or possibly three news media to the left of Detective Graves, and slightly in front of him, they had microphones to portable recorders stuck up in front of Oswald and Graves. I know that Officer W. J. Harrison was several feet to my left in front of the TV lights, and to the best of my knowledge he was facing the lights just prior to the time the shot was fired. Along with several officers I continued to restrain the photographers and news media while the ambulance arrived and took the prisoner Oswald from the basement.

I remained in the basement area until it was cleared. During this time, Officer Harrison told me that the person who fired the shot was Jack Ruby. I have known Jack Ruby since about 1948. I have not seen him since about 1948 or 1949.

I am sure the man Ruby did not pass between Officer Harrison and Myself.

Respectfully submitted,

[signature]
R. E. Swain, Lieutenant
Burglary & Theft Bureau

RES/lh

96

November 26, 1963

Mr. J. E. Curry
Chief of Police

Subject: Security Of Police Parking
And Prisoner Loading Area
Sunday, November 24, 1963

Sir:

At approximately 9:00 A.M., Sunday, November 24, 1963 I discussed the need for coverage against possible violence around the City Hall with Lieutenant R. S. Pierce. I instructed him to call three squads from their district assignments from the three stations and pull four from Headquarters Station, getting two man squads where possible. The officers were to be in Central Station with their squad cars parked on the street, available for immediate use but dispersed in parking, not later than 9:30 A.M. Out of thirteen squads we obtained a total of nineteen (19) patrolmen. Supervisors at the station for the security were Lieutenant Pierce, Sergeant P. T. Dean, Sergeant Putnam, Sergeant Steele, and I. Lieutenant Wiggins was in the Jail Office.

Lieutenant Pierce instructed Sergeant Dean to secure all entrances and exits to the parking and prisoner loading area, then clear the basement of all personnel other than police, and reserves. Sergeant Putnam was instructed to assist in the assignment.

The area in which the prisoner Oswald would be escorted was to be thoroughly searched. Areas searched were the cars parked in the basement, including their trunks, and engine compartments, the tops of all pipes, and air conditioning ducts, the service rooms opening into the basement were to be locked after clearing them of personnel. The building elevators were cut off on the first floor so they could not be used to reach the basement and the parking attendents were sent from the basement to the first floor of the City Hall with instructions to remain with the elevators to prevent tampering. The City Hall service elevator is a self-service type but had an operator. This man was instructed that he was not to go below the first floor until notified. The service elevator from the sub basement of the Police and Courts Building exit, into the basement parking area and has no doors to lock so a reserve officer was stationed there.

The sergeants used a total of seventeen (17) regular and reserve officers to execute the search. The extra officers were held in the sergeant's room at my office and the reserves were retained in the assembly room. These officers were not permitted in the basement to insure no confusion in the systematic search.

97

Commission Exhibit No. 2002—Continued

Page 2

After the area was secured and cleared only officers, reserves, and accredited news press were permitted to re-enter. Identification of the news personnel was made by their press credentials. All civilian employees of the Department were cleared from the basement lobby and instructed to remain at their desk.

Officer R. C. Nelson and a reserve officer were stationed in the hall leading to the jail service windows. The door from the jail to the lobby remained locked and the public used the first window, set at an angle, to conduct jail business.

Detective Beaty and Lowery remained with the officers during most of the period the parking and prisoner area was closed off. Everyone conducting business at the jail was scrutinized and if they did not appear to have legitimate business, they were conducted from the basement.

There was little traffic on Main and no one loitering. A large crowd was gathering on Commerce. I had everyone removed from the City Hall side (north) of Commerce to the south side. Sergeant Steele and Reserve Harrison checked the buildings opposite the basement drive for possible snipers.

The information received from the FBI by Captain Frazier was: two calls from males stated "one hundred of us will kill Oswald before he gets to the County Jail". Due to this and the crowds formation I built up my personnel on the Commerce Street side.

I called Homicide and told Detective Beck of the parking area check and asked if Captain Fritz wanted uniformed officers to proceed and follow the transfer vehicle. He said Captain Fritz was with the prisoner and they would let me know. I prepared three plain and three marked cars to use either type Homicide desired.

I was contacted by Chief Stevenson and Chief Lumpkin regarding an armored car. It was to back into the drive as far as possible from Commerce. When it arrived two more officers were stationed at the bottom of the Commerce Street ramp with instructions that no one was to pass up or down the ramp after the prisoner passed them. Due to its height, the armored car could only be backed in a short distance.

Before the arrival of the Armored Car, Chief Lumpkin, Chief Stevenson, and I discussed the route and traffic obstructions. They were reportedly six hundred (600) people around the County Jail. I instructed Sergeant Steele to place a regular officer at each traffic light with his squad car close by. The lead car would flash its lights as they approached and the officer would cut all opposing traffic. After the vehicle passed they were to enter their cars and follow to the County Jail to assist with any trouble. The entire traffic detail was in the County Jail Area.

97

Commission Exhibit No. 2002—Continued

Page 3

Sergeant Steele contacted Captain Lawrence for additional officers for intersection coverage. As the vehicle cleared the city hall all officers and reserves at the City Hallwere to report by a parallel route to the County Jail. I would use Channel Two and tell Sergeant Steele to out it. He had a motorcycle officer to send to Elm and Field to instfuct the officers on the corners to divert all traffic from Elm between Field and Houston. Regular traffic was heavy.

After the Armored Car arrived we sent a plain car out the Main Street side. This was the lead car and contained Lieutenant Pierce driving, Sergeant Putnam on the right front, and Sergeant B. J. Maxey in the rear.

A Homicide Detective pulled a plain car on the ramp behind the armored car then another Homicide Detective pulled in behind him and attempted to straighten his car and back up. Several reserve officers and I were attempting to push the news people back to give the vehicle room to manuever. I was pushing several people back at the left front fender when the shot was fired. I assisted the officers in clearing news personnel from the prisoner and officers who were down then ordered that no one was to be permitted out of the basement.

I checked the parking area several times and saw no unauthorized personnel. I removed a number of people from the first floor and basement lobby, this was a continious check prior to the transfer.

After the prisoner entered the ambulance and I gathered my personnel from Elm and reported to Parkland Hospital, we secured the hospital.

Respectfully submitted,

C. E. Talbert

Cecil E. Talbert
Captain of Police.
Patrol Division

CET/bb

97

COMMISSION EXHIBIT No. 2002—Continued

November 29, 1963

Statement of Captain C. E. Talbert: ✓

I was in charge of the Radio Patrol personnel and we had secured the basement from all unauthorized personnel, including all civilian employees, Records Bureau personnel, porters, parking attendants and elevator operators.

I met Jack Ruby about two years ago for only a minute, and after his arrest I recognized his face, but did not connect him with the name of Jack Ruby.

I did not see this man in the basement prior to the shooting.

97

COMMISSION EXHIBIT No. 2002—Continued

December 18, 1963

Mr. J. E. Curry
Chief of Police

Subject: Interview of John Tankersley
WBAP-TV
1967 Nilam
Ft. Worth, Texas
GL1-1933 - AN4-2484
December 17, 1963

Sir:

Mr. Tankersley stated he came to Dallas early Sunday morning, November 24, 1963, with crew from WBAP-TV. He was working with David Timmons. They went to the third floor of the City Hall and was at Chief Curry's Office until 10 to 15 minutes before the shooting. They went down on the elevator to the basement and pushed their camera out through the double doors into the basement driveway area. He says their camera was mounted on tripod as high as possible to see over the crowd, making the camera top-heavy, and at one time it nearly tipped over, and one of the detectives helped steady the camera. He also remembered that Jimmie Turner came across the rail and helped them push the camera out into the basement parking area. They did not have time to get the camera into operation, and tied it to the railing.

Mr. Tankersley said that when Oswald was brought out, he was standing in the area that leads to basement parking. He remembers the movement of some autos about the time of the shooting. He did not know Jack Ruby or see him prior to shooting.

Mr. Tankersley gave me a short 16mm film of the shooting. This film is one that he had for himself and said we could have it, and he would make another later.

Respectfully submitted,

C C Wallace
C. C. Wallace, Lieutenant
Juvenile Bureau

CCW:nw

97A

COMMISSION EXHIBIT NO. 2002—Continued

November 26, 1963

Mr. J. E. Curry
Chief of Police

Subject: Assignment Of Officer
Lester C. Taylor On
Sunday, November 24, 1963

Sir:

On Sunday, November 24, 1963 I was assigned to the Patrol Captain's Office. At approximately 11:00 A.M., Officer Taylor went to the basement of the Police and Courts Building to Station 505. I was contacted by Captain C. E. Talbert. He asked if we were busy upstairs and I told him "no". Captain Talbert advised me to go out on the ramp and see if I could be of any assistance. I contacted Sergeant Patrick T. Dean who assigned me beside the Armored Car on the Commerce Street ramp on the east side of the vehicle. Later Officer R. A. Watkins came up on the ramp and took a position at my location.

Just before Oswald was brought out, Officer D. L. Pate asked me to come on down to the bottom of the ramp and help him keep the reporters from coming up the ramp to the armored car. This was my location when Oswald was shot.

To the best of my knowledge I let one (1) person into the building from my location. He was a white male approximately 6'2", 190 pounds, with grey hair, no hat. This man had a press card, color green.

Officer Watkins was at my location when this man was admitted.

Respectfully submitted,

Lester C. Taylor
Lester C. Taylor
Patrolman #1430
Patrol Division

LCT/bb

98

COMMISSION EXHIBIT NO. 2002—Continued

November 29, 1963

STATEMENT OF L. C. TAYLOR

At 11:00 a.m. I was assigned to guard the Commerce Street Ramp. An armored car was parked, headed toward Commerce at the ramp entrance. The car was parked so close against the West wall that no one could possibly squeeze through. After I took my position on the East side of the armored car, R. A. Watkins arrived and assisted me in guarding the entrance. No one came through this entrance prior to the shooting.

I met Jack Ruby about 1959 when he owned the Vegas Club and I was working that district. I have not seen Ruby in the last two or three years. I did not see him in or near the City Hall prior to the shooting.

98

COMMISSION EXHIBIT No. 2002—Continued

Mr. J. E. Curry
Chief of Police

December 5, 1963

Re: Interview with Robert Thornton
WFAA News - 7819 Hillstone

Sir:

Mr. Thornton arrived at the basement of the City Hall at approximately 10:00 a.m. Sunday, November 24, 1963. He left the City Hall and called his office and was instructed to return to the basement of the City Hall and was only gone approximately 10 minutes. He was required to show his identification as he re-entered the ramp of the City Hall. He was standing near the Northwest corner of the basement corridor ramp area and recorded the events of the shooting.

Mr. Thornton's tape consists of his recounting Oswald's appearance on the ramp, the sound of a shot preceded by a horn blast and a description of the melee as followed. We obtained 7½ speed tape from Mr. Thornton.

Mr. Thornton stated he does not know Jack Ruby and did not see this man before the shot was fired.

Respectfully submitted

P. J. McCaghren
Lieutenant, Burglary & Theft Bureau

C. C. Wallace
Lieutenant, Juvenile Bureau

nw

99

COMMISSION EXHIBIT No. 2002—Continued

Excerpt from recording made by Robert Thornton - WFAA immediately before and during shooting of Lee Harvey Oswald on November 24, 1963:

"- - - - automobile horn sound (in the background) Get out of the way (in the background) Here comes - - shot - - Harvey - Oh, no. Oh my God. Somebody just shot Lee Harvey Oswald - - - - -"

Exhibit 99-B

COMMISSION EXHIBIT No. 2002—Continued

December 18, 1963

Mr. J. E. Curry
Chief of Police

Subject: Interview of
David Timmons, WBAP-TV
1900 Marigold
Ft. Worth, Texas
TE4-3940 - AN4-2484

Sir:

Mr. Timmons stated he was with John Tankerley, also of WBAP-TV and that they came to Dallas, early Sunday morning, November 24, 1963. They took their camera to the third floor of City Hall and spent some time there.

They also had a short interview with Chief Curry and came down elevator and into basement some 5 to 10 minutes before the shooting.

They were assisted by Mr. Turner in the basement, but still did not have time to get their camera hooked up. They pushed their camera down the driveway to the basement parking area and tied it up to railing to keep someone from knocking it over.

Mr. Timmons said he remembered two cars going out the Main Street ramp but does not have any idea what kind of autos or who was in the cars. Mr. Timmons said that just before the shooting he moved up to their other camera with Venso and Turner and was behind the camera assisting them at the time of the shooting.

Mr. Timmons stated he did not know Ruby prior to the shooting, and did not see this man in basement prior to shooting.

He stated that since he came in with the WBAP-TV camera, that his press card was not checked.

Respectfully submitted,

C C Wallace
C. C. Wallace, Lieutenant
Juvenile Bureau

CCW:nw

99C

COMMISSION EXHIBIT No. 2002—Continued

November 29, 1963

Statement of Officer Gerald L. Tolbert:

I was assigned to drive car #122 as an escort for the transfer of the prisoner.

This assignment was changed at 10:55 A. M., and I was assigned to work traffic at Elm and Pearl Streets. I left the City Hall at this time and did not return prior to the shooting.

I do not know Jack Ruby.

100

COMMISSION EXHIBIT No. 2002—Continued

November 26, 1963

Mr. J. E. Curry
Chief of Police

Subject: Assignment Of Officer
Gerald L. Tolbert #1473
On Sunday, November 24, 1963

Sir:

At approximately 9:25 A.M. on Sunday, November 24, 1963, while working Squad 53, with M. E. Farris #1852, we received a call on the Radio to contact Station 511 by telephone. M. E. Farris at this time made contact with Station 511 on the telephone and Squad 53 was advised to report to Station 511 on markout.

On arrival at Station 511 we were advised by other officers present to stand by at Station 511 until approximately 10 A.M. when we would be needed to transfer Lee H. Oswald to County Jail. At approximately 10:15 A.M. I was ordered to report to the basement of City Hall. On arrival I was instructed by Sergeant J. A. Putnam to back Squad Car #122 out of marked off basement parking area and line it up behind the station wagon at the north end of the basement, then stand by to drive squad car number 122 to the County in escort for the transfer of Lee Harvey Oswald.

I was then advised by Sergeant Putnam to back squad car #122 into the parking area again and get three other officers to accompany me in the car. They were M. E. Farris, D. K. Erwin, and W. E. Hibbs. After I did this, I was advised by Sergeant Putnam to stand by the botton of north ramp to City Hall Basement and check any vehicle that came down the ramp. No cars came down the ramp while I was standing at this position.

At approximately 10:55 A.M. I was taken off of this position by Sergeant Putnam and was assigned to the Elm Street and Pearl Expressway to work traffic. I was told Lee Harvey Oswald was to be transferred by armored car. A squad car would proceed the armored car and I was to halt traffic at my intersection until escort had cleared the intersection and then I was to proceed to the County Jail to assist with crowds at this location. I got in my squad and proceeded to my assignment. I arrived on my traffic corner at approximately 11:15 A.M. While standing at the intersection of Elm and Pearl, I observed two armored cars turn west on Elm Street from Pearl Expressway and proceed down Elm to Harwood. At approximately 11:25 A.M. a citizen stopped at the intersection and informed me that Lee Harvey Oswald had been shot in the basement of the City Hall. At this time I heard sirens and a squad car came down Pearl Expressway, and turned west on Elm to Harwood, running Code Three. A short time later I stopped traffic

100

COMMISSION EXHIBIT No. 2002—Continued

Page 2

at this intersection to let an ambulance and squad car proceed west on Elm Street, Code 3. At this time I checked by Radio to see if any other emergency vehicles were in this vicinity and to see if we would be needed elsewhere. I was advised to stand by my present position. At this time Sergeant Flusche working Squad 40 stopped at my location. I heard on his radio the Dispatcher ask for a two man squad and someone told the Dispatcher Squad 53 was a two man squad. The Dispatcher called me and I was advised to pick up my partner, Max E. Farris, at Elm and Lamar, then proceed Code #3 to Parkland Hospital.

Respectfully submitted,

Gerald L. Tolbert
Patrolman #1473
Patrol Division

GLT/bb

100

COMMISSION EXHIBIT No. 2002—Continued

December 18, 1963

Mr. J. E. Curry
Chief of Police

Subject: Jimmie L. Turner
6337 Norma
Ft. Worth, Texas
GL1-2355 - AN4-2484
WBAP-TV

Sir:

Mr. Turner stated that he was sent to Dallas early Sunday morning, November 24, 1963, and that he was with Homer Venso, and that they had their WBAP-TV camera set up in the City Hall basement by 9:15 a.m.

Their TV camera was located behind the railing on the east side of the ramp driveway. Turner stated he was behind the camera and near Jack Beers. Turner stated he had a press card or press pass, and was not questioned. He said he saw officers searching basement area and checking security early Sunday morning.

Mr. Turner said that he knew there was some question about a third man on the last TV camera to be brought into the basement, shortly before the shooting, and that he could clear up this question.

Turner stated that as the camera was brought into the basement, he climbed over the rail, and joined the other two men (Tankerley and Timmons - WBAP-TV) and assisted them get the camera through driveway.

Mr. Turner stated he saw Jack Ruby just a split second before the shot was fired. He did not know Ruby prior to shooting and does not recall seeing this man in basement.

Mr. Turner stated that after the shooting, their camera view was blocked and they moved their camera to the right of Channel 4 camera, and shot scenes of basement from that position.

100C

COMMISSION EXHIBIT No. 2002—Continued

Page 2

Mr. Turner arranged for me to view the video tape of the Oswald shooting, and introduced me to Mr. Jett Jamison, who is going to make us a film of the video tape. This film will be available soon.

Respectfully submitted,

C. C. Wallace
C. C. Wallace, Lieutenant
Juvenile Bureau

CCW:nw

100C

COMMISSION EXHIBIT No. 2002—Continued

December 2, 1963

Mr. J. E. Curry
Chief of Police

Re: Shooting of Lee Harvey Oswald
Interview of I. F. Van Cleave

Sir:

I. F. Van Cleave was interviewed by Lieutenants P. G. McCaghren and C. C. Wallace at 8:30 am on December 2, 1963. The interview was essentially the same as his original report dated November 27, 1963. I. F. Van Cleave had this to add:

I do know Jack Ruby vaguely. He was a complainant several years ago on one of my beefs. If Ruby was in the crowd, I did not recognize him.

My position was inside the double doors leading onto the ramp. I came down the elevator with several other detectives and two TV cameramen.

I was not in a position to see the shooting.

I have not been interviewed by the Federal Bureau of Investigation.

Respectfully submitted,

P. G. McCaghren
P. G. McCaghren, Lieutenant
Burglary & Theft Bureau

C. C. Wallace
C. C. Wallace, Lieutenant
Juvenile Bureau

lh

101

COMMISSION EXHIBIT No. 2002—Continued

November 29, 1963

STATEMENT BY ROY E. VAUGHN

During the time I was guarding the Main Street Ramp several squad cars with prisoners came into the basement. I checked each car and occupant to make sure.

About 30 minutes prior to the shooting Tommy, a City mechanic, attempted to drive a police car into the basement and I stopped him. He parked the squad a short distance away and came back to where I was standing and told me that he had to go into the basement to check the automobile or parking situation and I let him through. He explained that he had worked late the two previous days.

I noticed that Sergeant Dean was talking to Tommy at the bottom of the ramp and Tommy came back up the ramp and stayed around a few minutes and left.

A United or Associated Press reporter in his middle twenties identified himself by an official press card and I let him through. This to the best of my knowledge was about twenty minutes prior to the shooting.

At approximately 2 or 3 minutes prior to the shooting Lieutenant Pierce, Sergeant Maxey and Sergeant Putnam drove a squad car up the ramp onto Main Street. This was the only car that drove out the Main Street Ramp while I was on duty. As this car came up the ramp I was standing in the middle between the raised sides and I stepped to the right by the car and walked to the edge of the street to assist them onto Main. Traffic was not heavy but was steady. I do not recall whether or not it was necessary to stop any cars for them. As soon as they drove out I assumed my previous position between the raised portions of the ramp.

There were about 6 people standing on the sidewalk on the west side of the ramp. Ex-officer N. J. Daniels was standing on the east side of the ramp. One of the group on the west side was one of our ex-shine boys. He had a pair of binoculars. Pedestrian traffic was very light. The ones that came by would generally look down the ramp but be on their way.

I met Jack Ruby in 1959 and I have seen him once since that time. I do not believe that I would recognize Ruby if I passed him on the street but probably would if I had a conversation with him. I have not seen him to know him since December of 1961.

102

COMMISSION EXHIBIT No. 2002—Continued

Page 2 - Statement by Roy E. Vaughn

I called N. J. Daniels the next day about 9:00 a.m. I told him who I was and that I remembered seeing him. I asked if he remembered seeing the squad car come out. He said that he did. I asked him if he saw anybody go into the basement while I was assisting the car to get out, and he said he definitely did not see anyone.

102

COMMISSION EXHIBIT No. 2002—Continued

City of Dallas

OFFICE MEMORANDUM

To- Mr. J. E. Curry
Chief of Police

December 6, 1963

Subject: Polygraph Examination
Roy E. Vaughn

A polygraph examination was given Roy E. Vaughn (W/M/28) at the request of Deputy Chief N. T. Fisher. This examination was given on November 28, 1963. Below is a list of pertinent questions that were asked during this examination.

1. Did you see Jack Ruby near the Main Street entrance of the City Hall between 9:30 a.m. and 11:30 a.m. last Sunday morning? Answer—No
2. Did you allow Jack Ruby to enter the basement of the City Hall last Sunday morning? Answer —No
3. Did you talk with Jack Ruby last Sunday morning? Answer —No
4. Did you allow anybody to enter the basement of the City Hall last Sunday morning that did not show you proper identification other than the two men you told Chief Fisher about? Answer —No

No Number: Did you lie to Chief Fisher regarding this incident? Answer—No

Have you told Chief Fisher the complete truth regarding this incident? Answer —Yes

It is the opinion of this Examiner this person answered each of the questions with the truth.

P. L. Bentley
P. L. Bentley
Detective of Police
Identification Bureau

nw

The only reason you and I are here is to assist the people of Dallas

102

COMMISSION EXHIBIT No. 2002—Continued

November 26, 1963

Mr. J. E. Curry
Chief of Police

Subject: Assignment Of Officer
Roy E. Vaughn #1539
Sunday, November 24, 1963

Sir:

At approximately 9:00 A.M. while working Squad 105, Officer Roy E. Vaughn received a call to call Extension 511. Officer L. C. Taylor advised me to report to the City Hall and to park the squad car on the street and report to Station 511.

At approximately 9:15 A.M. or 9:30 A.M., Lieutenant R. S. Pierce told Officers A. R. Brock and B. G. Patterson; R. C. Nelson, and I to report to Sergeant Patrick T. Dean in the basement of the City Hall.

Officer B. G. Patterson and I were instructed by Sergeant Dean to guard the north and south ramps of the City Hall. I was assigned to the Main Street Ramp.

During this time there were several police vehicles which contained police officers that entered the basement by this ramp.

At approximately 10:15 A.M. Ex-Police Officer N. J. Daniels came by this location and remained until after the shooting occurred.

At approximately 11;18 A.M. a city squad car which contained Lieutenant Pierce, Sergeant Maxey and Sergeant Putnam exited by this ramp.

At approximately 11:21 A.M. I heard what sounded to be a shot, I stayed by the post and allowed no one to enter or leave the basement area. After the shooting, about five (5) police reserves were sent to this ramp to assist with the crowd and traffic.

At approximately 12:45 P.M. a white male approached me at this entrance and stated that he was an employee of Jack Ruby and would like to talk to someone about this. I escorted this person to the basement of the City Hall after being relieved on my post by a police reserve and called Captain Fritz's office and Detective Boyd came to the basement and took custody of this person.

I contacted Lieutenant Pierce in the Patrol Office and he advised me to secure the post and return to service with the Dispatcher.

Respectfully submitted,

Roy E. Vaughn
Patrolman #1539
Patrol Division

REV/hb

102

COMMISSION EXHIBIT No. 2002—Continued

December 18, 1963

Mr. J. E. Curry
Chief of Police

Subject: Interview of Homer Venso - WBAP-TV.
1812 Junius
Ft. Worth, Texas
JE5-0530 - AN4-2484
December 17, 1963

Sir:

Mr. Venso stated he came to Dallas early Sunday morning, November 24, 1963, with WBAP-TV camera crew, and went to the basement of the City Hall with Jimmie L. Turner, WBAP-TV about 8:00 a.m. They wanted to set up their camera just outside the double doors near Jail Office, but Chief Curry came down and told them they would have to move from there. They were advised to set up behind the rail, and two cars were moved so they could set-up just east of the rail.

Mr. Venso said he was working with camera and was not checked for identification. He said he could not remember any cars going out the Main Street ramp. He said that he does not know Jack Ruby, and did not remember seeing the person there prior to shooting.

Respectfully submitted,

C C Wallace
C. C. Wallace, Lieutenant
Juvenile Bureau

CCW:rw

COMMISSION EXHIBIT No. 2002—Continued

November 26, 1963

Mr. J. E. Curry
Chief of Police

Subject: Assignment Of Officer
Homer J. Wages #1305
On Sunday, November 24, 1963

Sir:

At approximately 9:00 A.M., Sunday, November 24, 1963, I was working Squad #93 with Officer T. R. Gregory and was advised to report to Station 511 on Special Assignment. We arrived at Station 511 at about 9:20 A.M. and remained there until approximately 9:45 A.M. when we were told to go to the basement to get our assignments. I remained in the basement until given my assignment by the supervisors in charge. My assignment was to stop traffic at Main Street and Central Expressway. After I received my assignment, I immediately went to my corner and remained there until about 11:50 A.M. when I was advised to report to Parkland Hospital.

Respectfully submitted,

Homer Wages
Homer J. Wages
Patrolman #1305
Patrol Division

103

HJW/bb

COMMISSION EXHIBIT No. 2002—Continued

November 30, 1963

STATEMENT OF H. J. WAGES:

I left the basement of the City Hall about 10:45 A. M., to go to my traffic corner at Main and Central Expressway.

I do not know Jack Ruby.

103

COMMISSION EXHIBIT No. 2002—Continued

November 27, 1963

Mr. J. E. Curry
Chief of Police

Subject: Incident involving Lee Harvey Oswald

Sir:

At approximately 10:30 A. M., November 24, 1963, I was working as a detective assigned to the Forgery Bureau detail and was on duty stationed in the basement of the city hall directly in front of the pay telephone booths at the exit to the basement into the driveway parking area in the basement to await further security instructions from Captain O. A. Jones.

I stayed in this general area until Captain Jones arrived and gave instructions to about twenty-five detectives including myself. We were placed in two lines to give maximum security to the prisoner.

A blue detective's car was backed into position which blocked my view when the deceased was brought from the hallway. I saw a sudden movement from the suspect and heard a gun blast. There were so many reporters that pushed their way forward that I was unable to get to the suspect. I jumped across the trunk of the car and grabbed the suspect, and there were two other officers attempting to wrestle the gun away from him. We all fell to the floor where the suspect was subdued and disarmed.

Respectfully,

R. C. Wagner
R. C. Wagner
Detective 1480
Forgery Bureau

RCW:ms

104

Commission Exhibit No. 2002—Continued

November 30, 1963

J. E. Curry
Chief of Police

Re: Shooting of Lee Harvey Oswald
Interviewing of R. C. Wagner

Sir:

R. C. Wagner was interviewed by Lieutenants C. C. Wallace and P. G. McCaghren at 3:50pm on November 29, 1963. The interview was essentially the same as his original report dated November 27, 1963. The following was added by R. C. Wagner:

I have been asked if I know Jack Ruby and have been shown a picture of him. I do not know him. To my knowledge I have never seen this person before. I do not recall seeing this person in the basement prior to the shooting. I do not have any idea how Jack Ruby got into the City Hall.

I was standing by the foot of the Commerce Street ramp 10 minutes before the shot was fired. I know that Jack Ruby did not come down this ramp because no unidentified persons came by me.

After the shooting, I assisted in taking Ruby to the jail office. I stayed with the Doctor and helped him with Oswald. I helped lift the stretcher and put it in the ambulance.

I have not been interviewed by the Federal Bureau of Investigation regarding this incident.

Respectfully submitted,

C C Wallace
C. C. Wallace
Lieutenant of Juvenile Bureau
Dallas Police Department

P G McCaghren
P. G. McCaghren
Lieutenant of Burglary & Theft Bureau
Dallas Police Department

lh

104

Commission Exhibit No. 2002—Continued

December 18, 1963

Mr. J. E. Curry
Chief of Police

Subject: Interview of I. N. Walker, WBAP-TV.
6913 Hightower
Ft. Worth, Texas
GL1-5549 - AN4-2484
December 17, 1963

Sir:

Mr. Walker stated he was in the WBAP-TV Mobile Unit truck parked outside the Dallas City Hall on Commerce Street, approximately one cars length west of Commerce Street exit.

Walker stated that on two occasions the same man came over to the truck and asked him through the truck window, "Have they brought Oswald down yet?" Mr. Walker said he was very busy and does not know exactly what he answered the man. Walker does not know what time the man came by or how long before the shooting. He said there was no way he could establish the time.

Mr. Walker stated he had been talked to by FBI agents and could not identify the mug shots of Jack Ruby but recognized the man that asked him the question "Have they brought Oswald down yet?" as Jack Ruby from a picture in a Dallas paper on Monday morning following the shooting. This picture showed Ruby with a hat on.

Mr. Walker seems positive in his identification of Jack Ruby and said this person came up to his truck window (open) twice, and he saw him from a very close distance.

Respectfully submitted,

C C Wallace
C. C. Wallace, Lieutenant
Juvenile Bureau

CCW:mw

104A

November 30, 1963

STATEMENT OF RICHARD A. WATKINS:

I reported to the City Hall at 10:20 A. M., and was given an assignment on garage side of the double doors leading into the jail.

I stayed at this location for ten or fifteen minutes and then Sergeant Dean assigned me to the head of the ramp by the armored car. The armored car was parked so close to the West Wall, it would have been impossible for anyone to have passed through on the West Side.

No one entered the basement through the Commerce Street ramp before the shooting, after I was assigned there.

I do not know Jack Ruby.

105

November 26, 1963

Mr. J. E. Curry,
Chief of Police.

Subject: Assignment of Officer
R. A. Watkins on
Sunday, November 24, 1963.

Sir:

On November 24, 1963, at 10:20 A.M., I was told to report to the basement. Captain Jones advised me, along with several detgtives, to stand by near the Jail Office entrance in the garage part of the basement.

Officer D. L. Pate came down the ramp and said he needed some assistance at the ramp entrance to the basement on the Commerce Street side. The armored truck was already in position at the entrance. Sergeant Dean told me to report to the top of the Commerce Street ramp on the East side of the armored car with instructions to keep unauthorized persons out.

I remained at this location until I was relieved by Officer W. J. HArrison at approximately 12:15 P.M..

Respectfully submitted,

Richard A. Watkins

Richard A. Watkins
Patrolman, #1419
Patrol Division

RAW/mb

105

Commission Exhibit No. 2002—Continued

November 27, 1963

Mr. J. E. Curry
Chief of Police

Sir:

I should like to submit the following report of the events occurring in the basement on November 24, 1963.

I was in a group of detectives under Captain Jones and Lieutenant Smart on November 24, 1963, at about 11:30 a.m. or a little later. The group was to assist in keeping press men and photographers back while Captain Fritz and his men brought Lee Harvey Oswald down from the City Jail to an armored truck waiting at the top of the basement ramp. The Dallas Sheriff's Office was waiting with the armored truck to transfer Oswald to the County Sheriff's office for confinement.

I was standing at the northwest corner of the driveway opening in the basement approximately 26 feet east of the jail office door.

As Captain Fritz came out of the jail door and came east toward the parking area in the basement, he was followed closely by Lee Harvey Oswald with detectives holding both arms and other detectives immediately behind Oswald. As I saw Captain Fritz and then looked at Oswald and the detectives holding and following him, they reached a point just past the corner where they would turn right to go up the ramp approximately 75 feet to the waiting armored car.

I was looking to the right back toward the jail office and hall in front of the jail office. At this time I heard a loud noise like a gun firing or a firecracker. I never saw anyone as I was looking right and the sound was muffled as if it were a gun jammed close to someone and fired. As I looked back left, six or eight detectives or more grabbed a man and wrestled him to the floor. I did not touch him as there were too many officers on him already.

The officers carried the suspect back to the jail office. During this time I was watching press men and photographers to keep down any interference. I just stayed in the immediate area and tried to keep anyone from leaving. I then went to the jail office door and kept unauthorized persons out and, as I looked in, I saw the suspect clearly lying on the floor, being held by Police.

I guarded the jail door until they took Oswald out to a waiting ambulance in this same basement driveway. I saw

Dallas Texas March 26 1964
4:15 P.M. Reported by J C Walsh
for [illegible]
James E. Watson

106

Commission Exhibit No. 2002—Continued

Mr. J. E. Curry   2   November 27, 1963

Oswald on the stretcher carried from the jail office to the waiting ambulance. I remained in the basement, and on orders from Captain Jones and Lieutenant Smart, checked everyone coming or going for the next one to two hours.

I never saw the suspect or the gun before the shot was fired, then the officers covered the suspect and took him to the jail office. I never saw the gun after it was fired, but tried to keep press and all back so the officers could handle the suspect and Oswald. This is all I know or saw.

Respectfully submitted,

J.C. Watson

J. C. Watson
Detective
Criminal Investigation Division

J.C.W.

106

COMMISSION EXHIBIT No. 2002—Continued

November 30, 1963

J. E. Curry
Chief of Police

Re: Shooting of Lee Harvey Oswald
Interview of J. C. Watson

Sir:

J. C. Watson was interviewed by Lieutenants C. C. Wallace and P. G. McCaghren at 3:30pm on November 29, 1963. The interview was essentially the same as his original report dated November 24, 1963. The following was added by J. C. Watson:

I have been asked if I know Jack Ruby. I have seen this person on one occasion at a club on Oak Lawn approximatly 3 or 4 years ago. I do not know this man. I did not see him in the basement of the City Hall prior to the shooting. I only saw him after the shooting when there were detectives all around him.

I never saw the man Jack Ruby around the City Hall before.

I have no idea how Jack Ruby got into the City Hall basement.

I was interviewed by Federal Bureau of Investigation agent Scott at 7:30pm Wednesday night.

Respectfully submitted,

C C Wallace

C. C. Wallace
Lieutenant of Juvenile Bureau
Dallas Police Department

P. G. McCaghren
Lieutenant of Burglary & Theft Bureau
Dallas Police Department

lh

106

COMMISSION EXHIBIT No. 2002—Continued

December 1, 1963

STATEMENT OF LT. WOODROW WIGGINS:

I cannot recall anything that is not included in my report.

107

COMMISSION EXHIBIT No. 2002—Continued

November 27, 1963

Mr. J. E. Curry
Chief of Police

Subject: Murder of Lee H. Oswald

Sir:

On Sunday, November 24, 1963, my tour of duty was from 6:30 a.m. to 2:30 p.m. My assignment was the Jail Office and the Jail. I had no instructions to provide security outside the Jail and Jail Office.

I received a call, and I do not remember who called me, which told me they were bringing Oswald down from the third floor. I had hung up the phone when I noticed the elevator was enroute to the basement, and as the elevator opened at approximately 11:20 a.m., Captain Fritz and four detectives brought Lee H. Oswald from the jail elevator taking him into the basement to transfer him to the County.

Captain Fritz asked if everything was in readiness, and I stepped outside the Jail Office into the hallway leading to the basement where I stopped. Captain Fritz came out of the Jail Office, followed by the detectives and Oswald.

They had passed where I was standing approximately six or seven feet when I saw a man lunge toward Oswald and heard a shot. I saw several officers grab the man with the pistol and wrestle him to the floor. Immediately, they picked him up and brought him into the Jail Office and disarmed him. They then brought Oswald into the Jail Office and laid him on the floor. I called for a doctor and an ambulance, Code 3.

As they were taking the man who did the shooting from the floor, I recognized him as Jack Ruby, who is a night club operator and well known in police circles. Ruby was placed on the Jail elevator and taken upstairs.

The Jail Intern came into the Jail Office and tried to give Oswald some attention, but the ambulance arrived, he was placed in it and taken to Parkland Hospital.

I have known Ruby for several years. I have been in his businesses, The Silver Spur, 1717 S. Ervay, and The Vegas Club, 3508 Oak Lawn, both on and off duty. My visits to his places of business while on duty were for police business. My visits to his places of business while off duty were for personal recreation for my wife, myself and friends.

I have not been in his places of business, nor have I seen him, in the last three or four years. I did not see him in the basement prior to the shooting of Oswald.

Respectfully submitted,

FR6-9687

W. Wiggins

WW:fb

W. Wiggins
Lieutenant of Police
Service Division

107

COMMISSION EXHIBIT No. 2002—Continued

November 26, 1963

Mr. J. E. Curry
Chief of Police

Subject: Assignment Of Officer
Marvin L. Wise #1572
On Sunday, November 24, 1963

Sir:

On Sunday, November 24, 1963, working Squad 71, I was advised to report to Station 511. This was at approximately 9:00 A.M. I remained at Station 511 until told by Lieutenant Pierce to report to the basement and stand by for assignment. This was at about 10:15 A.M. I reported to Sergeant Dean and was assigned traffic assignment at Elm and St. Paul by Sergeant Dean. I remained at St. Paul and Elm until approximately 11:35 A.M.

I was then advised by radio to report to Parkland Hospital Command Post. I remained at Parkland Hospital until 1:45 P.M. I then cleared with the Dispatcher.

Respectfully submitted,

Marvin L. Wise

Marvin L. Wise
Patrolman #1572
Patrol Division

MLW/bb

108

COMMISSION EXHIBIT No. 2002—Continued

November 29, 1963

Statement of Marvin L. Wise:

I was assigned to traffic at Elm and St. Paul, and I left the City Hall at approximately 11:00 A. M., and did not return prior to the shooting.

I know Jack Ruby and was in the basement to the City Hall from about 10:15 A. M. to 11:00 A. M., and I did not see him in or near the City Hall.

108

COMMISSION EXHIBIT No. 2002—Continued

Nove ber 30, 1963

Mr. J. E. Curry
Chief of Police

Dear Sir:

Re: Interview of Reserve Officer,
Patrolman Gano E. Worley, 516

On November 30, 1963 Reserve Officer, Patrolman Gano E. Worley was interviewed by the undersigned officers as to any information he might have concerning the shooting of Lee Harvey Oswald which was not covered in his original report dated November 26, 1963.

Worley stated that he would like to add that at approximately 1[illegible]:30 a.m. from his position in the first two parking places on the north side of the parking area in the basement he saw a man come down the north ramp and jump over the rail into the the parking area. He described this man as being a white male, 35, 5 feet, 8 inches, 175 pounds, wearing tan khaki trousers, tan kha[illegible] shirt, and hip length zip-up light brown jacket. This man was stopped and was identified by one of the officers in the basement as being a maintenance man for the city of Dallas.

Patrolman Worley further states that he has not been contacted by any federal agency at this time.

Respectfully submitted,

F. I. Cornwall
F. I. Cornwall, Lieutenant
Special Service Bureau

Jack Revill
Jack Revill, Lieutenant
Special Service Bureau

109

November 26, 1963

Mr. J. E. Curry
Chief of Police

Sir:

I arrived at the City Hall at 8:30 A. M. and went to the 3rd floor as directed. I was then told to report to the Assembly Room for assignment. Upon arriving at the Assembly Room, I was assigned by Reserve Sgt. Croy to stand by the Basement Information Desk and direct all reserve officers to report to the Assembly Room for assignment. At approximately 9:15 A. M. Reserve Capt. Arnett moved me to theparking area in the basement. I was to keep any cars from parking in the first two parking places on the North side of parking area. I stood at this post till about ten or fifteen minutes before Lee Harvey Oswald was shot. I was moved from the post by Lt. McCoy and assigned to the corner of Commerce and Central Expressway (Northbound) to help the regular patrolman (Burton) direct traffic and was at this location when the prisoner, Lee Harvey Oswald, was shot. The regular officer (Burton) was sent to Parkland Hospital and I returned to the basement of City Hall. Reserve Lt. McCoy assigned me to the basement entrance (North) to keep the people from blocking the drive to the basement. I stayed at this assignment till 12:00 Noon, at which time I was relieved and went home.

I had met Jack Rubenstein when working with Squad 105, five or six months ago. I did not see him in any part of the City Hall on November 24, 1963. I probably would not have recognized him if I had seen him, since I had only seen him one time.

Signed G. E. Worley Jr.
G. E. Worley, Jr., Reserve Patrolman
Badge 516

109

November 26, 1963

Dear Chief Curry:

I arrived at the City Hall at 8:30 A.M. and went to the 3rd floor as directed. I was then told to report to the Assembly Room for assignment. Upon arriving at the Assembly Room, I was assigned by Reserve Sgt. Croy to stand by the Basement Information Desk and direct all reserve officers to report to the Assembly Room for assignment. At approximately 9:15 A.M. Reserve Capt. Arnett moved me to the parking area in the basement. I was to keep any cars from parking in the first two parking places on the North side of parking area. I stood at this post till about ten or fifteen minutes before Lee Harvey Oswald was shot. I was moved from this post by Lt. McCoy and assigned to the corner of Commerce and Central Expressway (North Bound) to help the regular patrolman (Burton) direct traffic and was at this location when the prisoner, Lee Harvey Oswald, was shot. The regular officer (Burton) was sent to Parkland Hospital and I returned to the basement of City Hall. Reserve Lt. McCoy assigned me to the basement entrance (North) to keep the people from blocking the drive to the basement. I stayed at this assignment till 12:00 noon at which time I was relieved and went home.

I had met Jack Rubenstein when working with Squad 105, five or six months ago. I did not see him in any part of the City Hall on November 24, 1963. I probably would not have recognized him if I had seen him, since I had only seen him one time.

G. E. Worley, Jr.
G. E. WORLEY, JR. RESERVE PATROLMAN
Badge 516

109

COMMISSION EXHIBIT No. 2002—Continued

December 2, 1963

Mr. J. E. Curry
Chief of Police

Re: Interview with Tony Zoppi

Sir:

At approximately 3:30 pm, December 1, 1963, we interviewed Tony Zoppi at his office at the Dallas Morning News. He said he did not see Jack Ruby in the City Hall, but he had heard that Jack Ruby had been down at the City Hall passing out sandwiches and coffee to newsmen, especially those newsmen from KLIF, and he understood that possibly some of the drinks were furnished to officers as well. That he heard that Jack Ruby was passing out guest passes to newsmen from all parts of the country inviting them to visit the Carosel Club.

He stated that he had visited Jack Ruby's Carosel Club on several occasions and at that time he had noticed that Detectives would come in and check the place in a business like manner and leave. That he had also visited other night spots, and detectives also checked those places in what he would consider business like manner.

He also stated he does not know how Jack Ruby could have gotten into the basement of City Hall. That he does not know whether or not he had a press pass, and that he does not believe of his own knowledge that Jack Ruby knows Oswald.

Respectfully submitted,

C C Wallace
C. C. Wallace, Lieutenant
Juvenile Bureau

P. G. McCaghren
P. G. McCaghren, Lieutenant
Burglary & Theft Bureau

lh

110

COMMISSION EXHIBIT No. 2002—Continued

Excerpt from recording made by KRLD-TV during press interview with Chief Curry on afternoon of November 23, 1963:

"- - - - we plan to transfer this man, not tonight. If you men will be here, no later than 10:00 o'clock in the morning, why it will be soon enough - - - -"

111
Exhibit
AA-1

COMMISSION EXHIBIT No. 2002—Continued

November 29, 1963

Mr. J. E. Curry
Chief of Police

Sir:

On November 29, 1963, Lieutenant Jack Revill and Lieutenant P. G. McCaghren went to the Western Union Telegraph Company offices located at 2034 Main Street and interviewed Mr. Doyal Lane of 6549 Lake Circle, TA 1 0560.

Mr. Lane is a supervicor for the Western Union Telegraph Company and was on duty at this location on November 24, 1963. At 11:16 A.M., Jack Ruby sent a $25.00 Money Order to an employee and was given a receipt which was stamped with the time (11:16 A.M.).

Mr. Lane was shown several photographs, and he readily picked the photograph of Jack Ruby from these and stated that he knew Jack Ruby inasmuch as he had sent several telegrams in the past.

Lieutenants Revill and McCaghren timed, by watch, the amount of time needed to walk from the Western Union offices to the Main Street ramp into the City Hall basement. It takes 1 (one) minute and 13 (thirteen) seconds to walk this distance. It requires another 22 (twenty-two) seconds to walk down the ramp from Main Street to the location where Oswald was shot.

A check of the dispatcher's records reveals that a call was placed for an ambulance at 11:21 A.M.

Respectfully submitted,

Jack Revill
JACK REVILL, Lieutenant
Criminal Intelligence Section
Special Service Bureau

P. G. McCaghren
P. G. McCAGHREN, Lieutenant
Criminal Investigative Division

112
Exhibit
BB

COMMISSION EXHIBIT No. 2002—Continued

December 1, 1963

J. E. Curry
Chief of Police

Sir:

We used a stop watch to determine time necessary for a man to walk briskly from the entrance of the Main Street Western Union Office to the location where Oswald was shot. The time needed was 1 minute and 16 seconds.

We also used a stop watch to determine time needed for an automobile to leave the Main Street entrance to the basement, turn left onto Main Street, turn left onto Harwood, and turn left onto Commerce and approach the Commerce Street exit to the City Hall. The time needed was 1 minute and 10 seconds, starting the watch at the time we left the Main Street entrance and stopping at the Commerce Street exit.

Respectfully submitted,

C. C. Wallace
C. C. Wallace, Lieutenant
Juvenile Bureau

P. G. McCaghren
P. G. McCaghren, Lieutenant
Burglary & Theft Bureau

lh

113
Exhibit
CC

COMMISSION EXHIBIT No. 2002—Continued

CPS CS 21

RADIO CALL SHEET 5-45-13-18

ADDRESS FOR SQUAD

DISTRICT

INFORMATION - APARTMENT NUMBER - BUSINESS

DO DO NOT
CONTACT COMP.

COMPLAINANT - NAME - ADDRESS - TELEPHONE			
6	DISTURBANCE	20	ROBBERY
7	ACCIDENT	20A	ROBBERY IN PROG.
8	DRUNK	21	DOG BITE VICT.
9	THEFT	22	ANIMAL COMP.
9A	THEFT AUTO	23	PARKING VIO.
11	BURGLARY	24	ABANDONED PROP.
11A	BURG. IN BLDG.	24A	ABANDONED CAR
12	SILENT ALARM	25	AGG. ASSAULT
12A	AUDIBLE ALARM	26	MISSING PERS.
13	PROWLER	27	DEAD PERSON
14	CUTTING	28	SICK PERSON
15	MEET OFFICER	29	LOOSE STOCK
16	INJ. PERSON	30	PRISONER PICK UP
17	GANG FIGHT	31	MALICIOUS MISCH.
18	FIRE CALL	32	SUSPICIOUS PERS.
19	SHOOTING	32A	SUSPICIOUS IN CAR

NOTES	BY	
		WRECKER ORDERED
615		AMBULANCE ORDERED C 11 21 Nov 24
		TIME RECEIVED C 11 21 Nov 24
118	M.	TIME DISPATCHED 22 Nov 24
SQUADS ASSIGNED		TIME CLEAR

Dallas Texas
April 1, 1964
Ext. 5135, Examined
Francis Cason, C E Hulse
[illegible]

C E Hulse
Francis M. Cason

2

114

Exhibit
EF

COMMISSION EXHIBIT No. 2002—Continued

DA. / REPORT OF RADIO C LL!

POLICE DEPARTMENT CITY OF DALLAS

DATE MO.	DAY	YR.	TIME OF CALL	STREET	D	STREET NUMBER	TYPE CALL	TIME CLEARED	FIRST SQUAD	SECOND SQUAD	DISTRICT
11	24	3	0442	LANCASTER	N	612	5016		81		109
11	24	3	1651	LANCASTER	S	829	4448	1657	85		81
11	24	3	2211	LANCASTER	S	4435	4428	2242	78		77
11	24	3	1723	LAWTHER	W	4829	4459	1953	45		45
11	24	3	1555	LEMMON OAK LAWN			4411	1616	35		27
11	24	3	2132	LEMMON MANOR			4447	2248	212	32	32
11	24	3	2254	LEMMON REAGAN			5003	2316	33		27
11	24	3	0152	LEMMON		5000	4428	200	31		31
11	24	3	0022	LEMMON		5018	4416	206	32		31
11	24	3	2328	LEONARD		2102	4472	14	113		115
11	24	3	0150	LIBERTY		.813	4448	209	102		113
11	24	3	0841	LINDEN LANE		6423	4459	921	48		49
11	24	3	1543	LINDSLEY		5222	4485	1553	118		52
11	24	3	1543	LINDSLEY		5222	4448	1652	111		52
11	24	3	1348	LIPPITT		10438	5003	1420	57		57
11	24	3	2209	LIVE OAK		1719	4411	2325	111		104
11	24	3	0002	LIVE OAK		2000	5004	34	211	118	102
11	24	3	1508	LIVE OAK		5109	4459	1543	119		51
11	24	3	1137	LIVENSHIRE		9034	4459	1217	68		59
11	24	3	1805	LLEWELLYN	N	313	5003	1823	93		91
11	24	3	2251	LOGAN OAKLAND			4447	12	242		61
11	24	3	1153	LOGAN		2410	4462	1331	72		71
11	24	3	1945	LOVE FIELD			4417	1949	39		32
11	24	3	2143	LOVE FIELD			4417	2146	39		32
11	24	3	1747	LOVEFIELD			4417	1748	39		32
11	24	3	1548	LOVERS LN	W	5656	4448	1603	26		33
11	24	3	1522	LOVETT		6622	4495	1631	65		65
11	24	3	2010	LOWERY		2503	4448	2019	75		75
11	24	3	1144	LUCKEY LN		2719	4448	1202	85	76	79
11	24	3	1924	LUTHER LN		5941	4459	2027	48		48
11	24	3	1010	MADDOX		8131	4459	1112	68	66	69
11	24	3	0314	MAIN		1404	4459	418	102		105
11	24	3	1121	MAIN		2000	4485	1349	118	95	102
11	24	3	1811	MAIN		2000	4472	1957	108		102
11	24	3	0924	MAIN		2026	4428	936	101		102
11	24	3	1352	MALDEN LANE		4631	4429	1431	85		86
11	24	3	2030	MANANA		2351	4417	2129	35		35
11	24	3	0005	MANOR WAY		3304	4462	39	23		32
11	24	3	0752	MANUS	S	607	5003	839	85		83
11	24	3	0045	MARQUITA		6172	4422	128	45		44
11	24	3	0902	MARSALIS	N	715	4459	907	91		109
11	24	3	2108	MARSALIS	N	929	4459	2150	91		91
11	24	3	1500	MARSH N WEST HWY			4481	1549	32		32
11	24	3	2005	MARTINIQUE		802	4443	2019	51		54
11	24	3	0253	MARY DAN		7636	4459	436	69		69
11	24	3	0920	MATEUR		2718	4417	943	83		85
11	24	3	0119	MCKINNEY		1001	4459	150	101		101
11	24	3	0239	MCKINNEY		1001	4411	331	116		101
11	24	3	1623	MCKINNEY		2403	4448	1638	101		115
11	24	3	0052	MCKINNEY		3030	4448	200	118		115
11	24	3	0000	MCKINNEY		4225	4448	16	41		41
11	24	3	1935	MCNEAL		3519	4459	1957	68		35
11	24	3	1732	MEADOW METROPOLITAN			4459	1757	63		62
11	24	3	0921	MERLIN		2634	4459	933	61		61

114

Exhibit E-2

COMMISSION EXHIBIT No. 2002—Continued

December 16, 1963

Mr. J. E. Curry
Chief of Police

Subject: New Media Present at Oswald Shooting

Sir:

The following list of names have been mentioned as being present in the basement of City Hall, when Lee Harvey Oswald was shot. These people have not been contacted.

1. Milt Sosin, Miami Florida Reporter
2. Paul Cisco, Unknown - Not local
3. Oliver Oakes, Unknown - Not Local
4. John Alexander, Unknown - Not local
5. Tom Petit, N.B.C. (Commentator) Los Angeles, Calif.
6. Jim Standard, Oklahoma City, Okla. - Newspaper
7. Mike Smith, A. P. - Los Angeles, California
8. Bert Rhinehart, U.P.I. New York City, N. Y.
9. Hank Machariella, Daily Tribune, New York City, N. Y.

Respectfully submitted,

C C Wallace
C. C. Wallace, Lieutenant
Juvenile Bureau

CCW:nw

115

Exhibit FF

COMMISSION EXHIBIT No. 2002—Continued

THE KEY TO PERSONNEL SHOWN ON THE SCHEMATIC DIAGRAM OF THE BASEMENT PARKING [illegible], CITY HALL, INVOLVED IN THE SHOOTING OF LEE HARVEY OSWALD BY JACK RUBY. NUMBERS INDICATE POSITION OF PERSONNEL AT THE TIME OF THE SHOOTING ON NOVEMBER 24, 1963.

2	D. R. Archer
3	C. O. Arnett
3-A	Asst. Ch. Charles Batchelor
4	B. L. Beaty
5	E. R. Beck
6	Jack Beers
7	D. G. Brantley
8	A. R. Brock
9	J. D. Brockaway
10	C. W. Brown
11	D. L. Burgess
13	Lt. George Butler
14	V. C. Campbell
15	A. W. Capps
16	W. E. Chambers
17	B. S. Clardy
18	B. H. Combest
19	R. A. Cox
20	A. B. Craig
21	K. Croy
22	W. J. Cutchshaw
23	N. J. Daniels
24	J. R. Davidson
26	Harold Dawson
27	Sgt. P. T. Dean
29	C. N. Dhority
30	J. B. English
33	Warren Ferguson
34	Bob Fenley
37	Capt. J. W. Fritz
38	C. Goolsby
40	L. C. Graves
41	C. A. Greeson
43	R. Hankal
44	O. W. Harrison
45	W. J. Harrison
49	J. R. Hopkins
50	R. S. Huffaker
52	J. D. Hutchinson
53	Robert Jackson
54	L. E. Jez
55	F. B. Johnson
56	Capt. O. A. Jones
58	Seth Kantor
59	J. Kasten
60	Capt. G. D. King
61	H. M. Kriss
63	J. R. Leavell
64	C. G. Lewis
66	R. L. Lowery
66-A	Dep. Ch. G. L. Lumpkin
68	Capt. F. M. Martin
69	B. J. Maxey
71	J. C. McCain
72	B. C. McCoy
73	H. M. McGee
74	T. D. McMillon
75	B. Merrell
76	L. D. Miller
77	L. D. Montgomery
78	R. C. Nelson
79	W. J. Newman
80	J. F. Newton
80-A	Ike Pappas
81	D. L. Pate
82	B. G. Patterson
83	Francois Pelou
83-A	Tom Pettit
84	George Phenix
85	Lt. R. S. Pierce
86	Sgt. J. A. Putnam
87	J. K. Ramsey
89	H. B. Reynolds
89-A	Warren Richey
90	Jack Ruby
91	W. B. Slack
92	J. D. Slocum
93	Lt. V. S. Smart
93-A	Mike Smith
93-B	Johnny Smith
95	I. R. Stephens
95-A	Dep. Ch. M. W. Stevenson
95-B	Donald Suits
96	Lt. R. E. Swain
97	Capt. C. E. Talbert
97-A	John Tankersly
98	L. C. Taylor
99	Robert Thornton

- 2 -

99-A	David Timmons
100-A	Unknown Jap. Reporter
100-B	Unknown Reporter
100-C	Jimmy Turner
101	I. F. VanCleave
102	R. E. Vaughn
102-A	Homer Venso
104	R. C. Wagner
104-A	I. N. Walker
105	R. A. Watkins
106	J. C. Watson
107	Lt. W. Wiggins
109	G. E. Worley

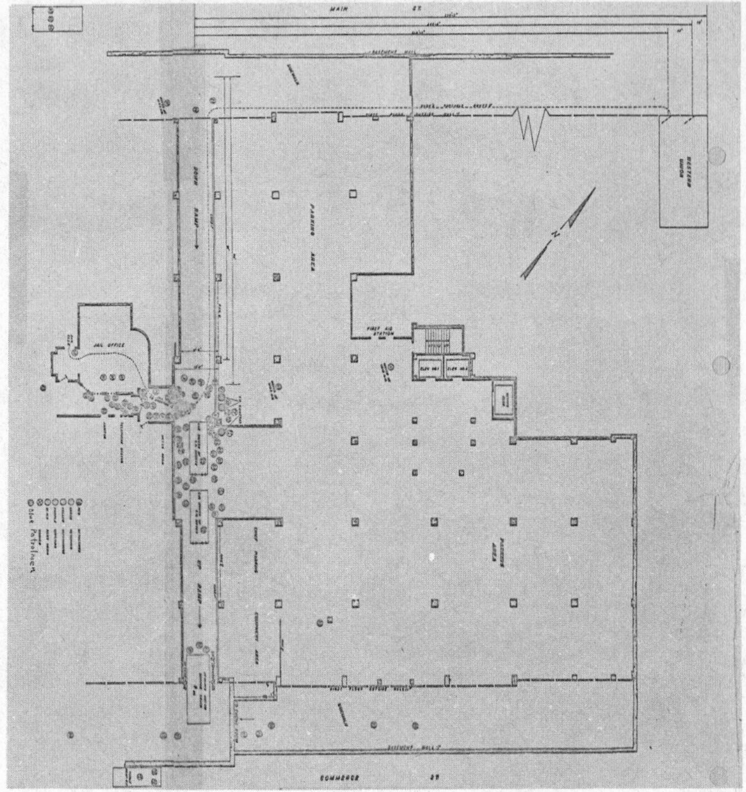

COMMISSION EXHIBIT No. 2002—Continued

- 3 -

COMMISSION EXHIBIT No. 2002—Continued

INVESTIGATION

OF THE ASSASSINATION OF THE PRESIDENT

COMMISSION EXHIBIT No. 2003

AFFIDAVITS ... IN CONNECTION WITH THE PRESIDENT'S ASSASSINAT.

AFFIDAVITS TAKEN IN CONNECTION WITH THE PRESIDENT'S ASSASSINATION

	PAGE NO.	Taken by:
Applin, George Jefferson, Jr. w/m/21	4	
Arce, Danny Garcia w/m/18	5	W. E. Potts
Baker, M. L. (patrolman)	6	M. Johnson
√ Botzner, Hugh Williams, Jr. age 22	7-8	Sheriff's Office
Bledsoe, Mrs. Mary E. w/f/67	9	L. C. Graves
√ Bowers, Lee E., Jr. w/m/38	10	
√ Bowley, T. F. w/m/35	11	J. P. Adamcik
√ Braden, Jim age 49	12	Sheriff's Office
Brennan, Howard Leslie age 44	13	Sheriff's Office
√ Brewer, Johnny Calvin	14	M. Johnson
Callaway, Ted w/m/40	15	J. R. Leavelle
√ Chism, John Arthur age 23	16	Sheriff's Office
√ Chism, Marvin Faye age 19	17	Sheriff's Office
Davis, Barbara Jeanette w/f/22	18	C. W. Brown
Davis, Mrs. Virginia w/f/16	19	C. N. Dhority
Dougherty, Jack E. w/m/40	20	W. E. Potts
Edwards, Robert E. (Bob) age 22	21	Sheriff's Office
Euins, Amos Lee age 15	22	Sheriff's Office
Fischer, Ronald B. age 24	23	Sheriff's Office
√ Florer, Larry age 23	24	Sheriff's Office
Frazier, Buell Wesley age 19	25-26	G. F. Rose
Givens, Charles Douglas c/m/37	27	J. R. Leavelle
√ Guinyard, Sam	28	J. R. Leavelle
√ Hathaway, Philip Ben age 28	29	Sheriff's Office
√ Hest Charles age 28	30	Sheriff's Office
√ Hill, Jean age 32	31	Sheriff's Office
√ Holland, S. M. age 57	32	Sheriff's Office
√ Hudson, Emmett Joseph	33	Sheriff's Office
Jarman, James Earl, Jr. c/m/33	34	

1

COMMISSION EXHIBIT No. 2003—Continued

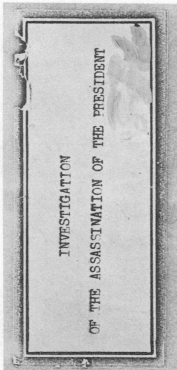

Affidavits-Page 2

	PAGE NO.	Taken by :
✓ Lawrence, John Stevens Ruttor age 23	35	Sheriff's Office
Lovelady, Billy Nolan w/m/26	36	J. R. Leavelle
McWatters, Cecil J.	38	C. N. Dhority
Markham, Helen Louise	37	L. C. Graves
Mercer, Julia Ann age 23	39-40	Sheriff's Office
Miller, Austin Lawrence	41	Sheriff's Office
Moorman, Mary Ann age 31	42	Sheriff's Office
Newman, Gayle age 22	43	Sheriff's Office
Newman, Jean age 21	44	Sheriff's Office
Newman, William Eugene age 22	45	Sheriff's Office
Oswald, Marina w/f/22	46	B.L. Senkel
Owens, Ernost Jan age 36	47	Sheriff's Office
Paine, Michael Ralph w/m/35	48	H. M. Moore
Paine, Ruth Hyde w/f/31	49	J. P. Adamcik
Postal, Julia w/f/39	50-51	E. L. Boyd
Price, J. C. age 62	52	Sheriff's Office
Randle, Linnie Mae w/f/30	53	G. F. Rose & R. S. Stovall
Reid, Mrs. R.A.	54	J.R. Leavelle
Rowland, Arnold Louis age 18	55	Sheriff's Office
Rowland, Barbara Walker age 17	56	Sheriff's Office
Scoggins, W.W.	57	J. R. Leavelle
Senator, George w/m/50	58	William F. (Bill) Alexander
Shelley, William H. w/m/37 (made 2)	59-60	C. W. Brown took both
Skelton, Royce Glenn age 23	61	Sheriff's Office
Truly, Roy S. w/m	62	J. R. Leavelle
Weitzman, Seymour w/m	63	C. W. Brown
Whaley, William Wayne	64	C. N. Dhority
Williams, Bonnie Ray	65	B. L. Senkel

2

COMMISSION EXHIBIT No. 2003—Continued

Affidavits-Page 3

	PAGE NO.	Taken By:
Williams, Jesse James age 40	66-67	Sheriff's Office
Willis, Billy Joe w/m/34	68	
Worrell, James Richard, Jr. w/m/20	69	

3

COMMISSION EXHIBIT No. 2003—Continued

The information contained in this report was compiled by the Homicide and Robbery Bureau of the Dallas Police Department, Dallas, Texas. Further information obtained regarding these offenses will be added as suppliments to this report.

Capt J W Fritz

CAPTAIN J.W. FRITZ
HOMICIDE AND ROBBERY BUREAU

COMMISSION EXHIBIT No. 2003—Continued

INDEX

COMMISSION EXHIBIT No. 2003—Continued

COMMISSION EXHIBIT No. 2003—Continued

- P -

Pictorial Record, not complete	P 255
Positions Assigned Homicide Men for Security of President	P 258
Post Office Box Records	E 130a
Principals Involved in Offenses (names and addresses)	P 257

- Q -

- R -

Receipt To Captain Fritz from James P. Hosty, Jr., F.B.I.	R 292

- S -

Searches and Seizures	S 294-300
Showups (Oswald)	S 293
Size of Captain Fritz's office	D 125

- T -

Telegrams Re: Ruby	
After Oswald's Murder	T 332-392
Money Orders to Ruby	T 355, 356, 384

- U -

- V -

Visitors	
Oswald	V 393
Ruby	V 394

- W -

Warrants	
Oswald - Tippit	W 405
Oswald - Kennedy	W 403
Ruby - Oswald	W 406

- X -

- Y -

- Z -

COMMISSION EXHIBIT No. 2003—Continued

AFFIDAVIT IN ANY FACT

THE STATE OF TEXAS
COUNTY OF DALLAS

BEFORE ME, EUNICE SORRELLS

a Notary Public in and for said County, State of Texas, on this day personally appeared George Jefferson Applin, Jr., w/m 21, of 3423 Weisenberger Drive, Dallas, Dallas County, Texas

Who, after being by me duly sworn, on oath deposes and says: On Friday evening, November 22, 1963 at about 1:45 p.m., I was seated on the main floor of the Texas Theater on West Jefferson in Dallas, Texas. As I watched the movie I saw an officer walking down the isle with a riot gun and about that time the light came on in the theater. One of the patrolmen walked down to the front of the theater and walked back up the isle and I got up and started walking toward the front of the theater. I saw the officer shake two men down and then asked a man sitting by himself to stand up. As the officer started to shake him down, and when he did, this boy took a swing at the officer and then the next thing I could see was this boy had his arm around the officer's left shoulder and had a pistol in his hand. I heard the pistol snap at least once. Then I saw a large group of officers subdue this boy and arrest him.xxxxxxxxxxxxxxxxxxxxxxxxxxxx
xxxxxxxxxxxxxxxxxxxxxxxxxxxxxxxxxxxxxxxxxxxxxxxxxxxxxxxxxxxxxxxx
xxxx xxxx xxxx xxxxx xxxxxxxx xxxxxx xxxxx George Jefferson Applin Jr.

3423 Weisenberger Drive
Dallas 12, Texas
FE7-3491

SIGNATURE WITNESSED BY:
Catherine Teague
806 Clearwood
Dallas Texas

SUBSCRIBED AND SWORN TO BEFORE ME THIS 22nd DAY OF November A.D. 1963

EUNICE SORRELLS
Eunice Sorrells
Notary Public, Dallas County, Texas

CPS-GF-413

4

COMMISSION EXHIBIT No. 2003—Continued

AFFIDAVIT IN ANY FACT

THE STATE OF TEXAS
COUNTY OF DALLAS

BEFORE ME, Mary Rattan

a Notary Public in and for said County, State of Texas, on this day personally appeared Danny Garcia Arce w/m/18 of 1502 Bennett, TA1 3289

Who, after being by me duly sworn, on oath deposes and says: I am employed at Texas School Book Depository at 411 Elm. I work all over the building. I was working on the sixth floor all morning. At lunch time at 12:00 noon I went down on the street to see the parade, and get a look at the President. I was standing on the corner of Elm and Houston, and I heard three shots ring out. I didn't know what had happened until I heard a woman scream that the President had been shot. While working on the sixth floor of the Texas School Book Depository the only people I saw all morning was Bill Shelly, Bonnie Ray Williams, Charles Douglas Givens, Billy Lovelady and Jack E. Dougherty. The only person I saw was a real old man, and he had on an old brown suit and a western type hat. I saw this man leave the building and drive off in an old black Buick. This man was not carrying anything in his hands when I saw him. This man was in the building after lunch. This man left in the car before the President was shot. I didn't see any other people in the building but this old man, other than the people that I named that worked there. There was another employee that I saw named Lee Oswald. He was on the first floor of the building when I saw him at 8:00 am. He is the same man I saw the police bring into the Homicide Bureau about 2:00 pm. I also saw him on the 5th floor as we were leaving for lunch at 11:50 am.

Danny Garcia Arce

SUBSCRIBED AND SWORN TO BEFORE ME THIS 22 DAY OF November A.D. 1963

Mary Rattan Mary Rattan
Notary Public, Dallas County, Texas

CPS-GF-413

5

COMMISSION EXHIBIT No. 2003—Continued

AFFIDAVIT IN ANY FACT

THE STATE OF TEXAS
COUNTY OF DALLAS

BEFORE ME, Mary Rattan

a Notary Public in and for said County, State of Texas, on this day personally appeared M. L. Baker, Patrolman Dallas Police Department

Who, after being by me duly sworn, on oath deposes and says: Friday November 22, 1963 I was riding motorcycle escort for the President of the United States. At approximately 12:30 pm I was on Houston Street and the President's car had made a left turn from Houston onto Elm Street. Just as I approached Elm and Houston I heard three shots. I realized these shots were rifle shots and I began to try to figure out where they came from. I decided the shots had come from the building on the northwest corner of Elm and Houston. This building is used by the Board of Education for book storage. I jumped off my motor and ran inside the building. As I entered the door I saw several people standing around. I asked these people where the stairs were. A man stepped forward and stated he was the building manager and that he would show me where the stairs were. I followed the man to the rear of the building and he said, "Let's take the elevator." The elevator was hung several floors up so we used the stairs instead. As we reached the third or fourth floor I saw a man walking away from the stairway. I called to the man and he turned around and came back toward me. The manager said, "I know that man, he works here." I then turned the man loose and went up to the top floor. The man I saw was a white man approximately 30 years old, 5'9", 165 pounds, dark hair and wearing a light brown jacket.

M. L. Baker

SUBSCRIBED AND SWORN TO BEFORE ME THIS 22 DAY OF November A.D. 1963

Mary Rattan Mary Rattan
Notary Public, Dallas County, Texas

CPS-GF-413

6

COMMISSION EXHIBIT No. 2003—Continued

VOLUNTARY STATEMENT. Not Under Arrest. Form No. 86 (35)

SHERIFF'S DEPARTMENT
COUNTY OF DALLAS, TEXAS

Before me, the undersigned authority, on this the 22nd day of November A. D. 19 63 personally appeared Hugh William Betzner, Jr., Address 5922 Velasco, Dallas

Age 22, Phone No. TA 7-9761

Deposes and says:- I was standing on Houston Street near the intersection of Elm Street. I took a picture of President Kennedy's car as it passed along Houston Street. I have an old camera. I looked down real quick and rolled the film to take the next picture. I then ran down to the corner of Elm andHouston Streets, this being the southwest corner. I took another picture just as President Kennedy's car rounded the corner. He was just about all the way around the corner. I was standing back from the corner and had to take the pictures through some of the crowd. I ran on down Elm a little more and President Kennedy's car was starting to go down the hill to the triple underpass. I was running trying to keep the President's car in my view and was winding my film as I ran. I was looking doOn at my camera to see the number of the film as I ran. I took another picture as the President's car was going down the hill on Elm Street. I started to wind my film again and I heard a loud noise. I thought that this noise was either a firecracker on a car had backfired. I looked up and it seemed like there was another loud noise in the matter of a few seconds. I looked down the street and I could see the President's car and another one and they looked like the cars were stopped. Then I saw a a flash of pink like someone standing up and then sitting back down in the car. Then I ran around so I could look over the back of a monument and I either saw the following then or when I was standing back down on the corner of Elm Street. I cannot remember exactly where I was when I saw the following: I heard at least two shots fired and I saw what looked like a firecracker going off in the president's car. My assumption for this was because I saw fragments going up in the air. I alsosaw a man in either the President's car or the car behind his and someone down in one of those cars pulled out what looked like a rifle. I also remember seeing what looked like a nickel revolver in someone's hand in the President's car or somewhere immediately around his car. Then the President's car sped on under the underpass. Police and a lot of spectators started running up the hill on the opposite side of the street from me to a fence of wood. I assumed that that was where the shot was fired from at that time. I kept watching the crowd. Then I came around the monument over to Main Street. I walked down toward where the President's car had stopped. I saw a Police Officer and some men in plain clothes. I don't know who they were. These Police Officers and the men in plain clothes were digging around in the dirt as if they were looking for a bullet. I walked back around the monument over to Elm Street where they were digging in the dirt. I went on across the street and up the embankment to where the fence is located. By this time almost all of the people had left. There were quite a few people down on the street crowded around a motorcycle. I was looking around the fence as the rumor had spread that that was where the shot had

Subscribed and sworn to before me on this the 22nd day of November A. D. 1963
Hugh William Betzner, Jr.

Aleen Davis
Notary Public, Dallas County, Texas

7

COMMISSION EXHIBIT No. 2003—Continued

PAGE -2 -

VOLUNTARY STATEMENT. Not Under Arrest. Form No. 86 (36)

SHERIFF'S DEPARTMENT
COUNTY OF DALLAS, TEXAS

Before me, the undersigned authority, on this the 22nd day of November A. D. 19 63 personally appeared Hugh William Betzner, Jr., Address 5922 Velasco, Dallas

Age 22, Phone No. TA 7-9761

Deposes and says:- come from. I started figuring where I was when I had taken the third picture and it seemed to me that the fence row would have been in the picture. I saw a group of men who looked like they might be officers and one of them turned out to be Deputy Sheriff Boone. I told him about the picture I had taken. Deputy Sheriff Boone contacted superiors and was told to bring me over to the Sheriff's Office. Deputy Sheriff Boone took my camera and asked me to wait. I waited in the Sheriff's Office and some time later, an hour or two, he brought my camera back and told me that as soon as they got through with the film and they were dry that they would give me the film. A little later he came in and gave me the negatives and told me that they were intersted in a couple of pictures and implied that the negatives was all I was going to get back. To the best of my knowledge, this is all I know about this incident.

X
X
X
X
X
X
X
X
X

Hugh William Betzner, Jr.

Subscribed and sworn to before me on this the 22nd day of November A. D. 19 63

Aleen Davis
Notary Public, Dallas County, Texas

8

COMMISSION EXHIBIT No. 2003—Continued

AFFIDAVIT IN ANY FACT

THE STATE OF TEXAS
COUNTY OF DALLAS

BEFORE ME, PATSY COLLINS

a Notary Public in and for said County, State of Texas, on this day personally appeared Mrs. Mary E. Bledsoe, w/f 67, 621 N. Marsalis, Dallas, Texas, Telephone WH2-1985

Who, after being by me duly sworn, on oath deposes and says: Last Friday, November 22, 1963, I went downtown to see the President. I stood on Main Street just across the street from Titche's until the parade passed by. Then I walked over to Elm Street and caught a bus to go home. The bus traveled West on Elm Street to about Murphy Street and made a stop and that is when I saw Lee Oswald get on the bus. The traffic was heavy and took it quite sometime to travel two or three blocks. During that time someone made the statement that the President had been shot and while the bus was stopped due to the heavy traffic, Oswald got off the bus and I didn't see him again. I know this man wa s Lee Oswald because he lived in my home from October 7, 1963 to October 14, 1963.XXXXXXX XXXXXXXXXXXXXXXXXXXXXXXXXXXXXXXXXXXXXXXXXXXXXXXXXXXXXXXXXXXXXXXX

Mrs Mary E. Bledsoe

SUBSCRIBED AND SWORN TO BEFORE ME THIS 23RD DAY OF NOVEMBER A.D. 1963

Patsy Collins
Notary Public, Dallas County, Texas

CPS-GF-413

9

COMMISSION EXHIBIT NO. 2003—Continued

AFFIDAVIT IN ANY FACT

THE STATE OF TEXAS
COUNTY OF DALLAS

BEFORE ME, Patsy Collins

a Notary Public in and for said County, State of Texas, on this day personally appeared Lee E. Bowers Jr., w/m/38 of 10508 Maplegrove Lane, Dallas, Texas DA-1-1909

Who, after being by me duly sworn, on oath deposes and says: I work at North Tower Union Terminal Co. RI-8-4698, 7 am to 3 pm Monday thur Friday. The tower where I work is West and a little north of the Texas Book Depository Building. I was on duty today and about 11:55 am I saw a dirty 1959 Oldsmobile Station Wagon come down the street toward my building. This street dead ends in the railroad yard. This car had out of state license plates with white background and black numbers, no letters. It also had a Goldwater for "64" sticker in the rear window. This car just drove around slowly and left the area. It was occupied by a middle aged white man partly grey hair. At about 12:15 pm another car came in the area with a white man about 25 to 35 years old driving. This car was a 1957 Ford, Black, 2 door with Texas license. This man appeared to have a mike or telephone in the car. Just a few minutes after this car left at 12:20 pm another car pulled in. This car was a 1961 Chevrolet, Impalla, 4 door, am not sure that this was a 4 door, color white and dirty up to the windows. This car also had a Goldwater for "64" sticker. This car was driven by a white male about 25 to 35 years old with long blond hair. He stayed in the area longer than the others. This car also had the XXX same type license plates as the 1959 Oldsmobile. He left this area about 12:25 pm. About 8 or 10 minutes after he left I heard at least 3 shots very close together. Just after the shots the area became crowded with people coming from Elm Street and the slope just North of Elm.XXXXXXXXXXXXXXXXXXXXXXXXX

Lee E. Bowers Jr.

SUBSCRIBED AND SWORN TO BEFORE ME THIS 22 DAY OF November A.D. 1963

Patsy Collins — Patsy Collins
Notary Public, Dallas County, Texas

CPS-GF-413

10

COMMISSION EXHIBIT NO. 2003—Continued

AFFIDAVIT IN ANY FACT

THE STATE OF TEXAS
COUNTY OF DALLAS

BEFORE ME, Mary Rattan

a Notary Public in and for said County, State of Texas, on this day personally appeared

T. F. Bowley w/m/35 of 1454 Summertime Lane, IR6 5965

Who, after being by me duly sworn, on oath deposes and says: On Friday November 22, 1963 I picked up my daughter at the R. L. Thornton School in Singing Hills at about 12:55 pm. I then lft the school to pick up my wife who was at work at the Telephone Company at Ninth Street and Zangs Street. I was headed north on Marsalis and turned west on 10th Street. I traveled about a block and noticed a Dallas police squad car stopped in the traffic lane headed east on 10th Street. I saw a police officer lying next to the left front wheel. I stopped my car and got out to go to the scene. I looked at my watch and it said 1:10 pm. Several people were at the scene. When I got there the first thing I did was try to help the officer. He appeared beyond help to me. A man was trying to use the radio in the squad car but stated he didn't know how to operate it. I knew how and took the radio from him. I said, "Hello, operator. A police officer has been shot here." The dispatcher asked for the location. I found out the location and told the dispatcher what it was. A few minutes later an ambulance came to the scene. I helped load the officer onto the stretcher and into the ambulance. As we picked the officer up, I noticed his pistol laying on the ground under him. Someone picked the pistol up and laid it on the hood of the squad car. When the ambulance left, I took the gun and put it inside the squad car. A man took the pistol out and said, "Let's catch him." He opened the cylinder, and I saw that no rounds in it had been fired. This man then took the pistol with him and got into a cab and drove off. The police arrived and I talked to a police sergeant at the scene. I told him I did not witness the shooting and after questioning me, he said it was all right for me to leave. I then went on to the Telephone Company office at Ninth and Zangs. T. F. Bowley

SUBSCRIBED AND SWORN TO BEFORE ME THIS 2 DAY OF December A.D. 1963

Mary Rattan Mary Rattan
Notary Public, Dallas County, Texas

CPS-GF-413

11

COMMISSION EXHIBIT No. 2003—Continued

VOLUNTARY STATEMENT. Not Under Arrest. Form No. 86

SHERIFF'S DEPARTMENT
COUNTY OF DALLAS, TEXAS

Before me, the undersigned authority, on this the 22 day of November A. D. 19 63

personally appeared Jim Bradon, Address 621 S. Barington Dr. Apt. 6 Los Angeles, Calf.

Age 49, Phone No. 4725301 Home Office 215 S. La Cienega Blvd. Beverly Hills, California

Deposes and says:-

I am here on business (oil business) and was walking down Elm Street trying to get a cab and there wasn't any. I heard people talking saying "My God the President has been shot." Police cars were passing me coming down toward the triple underpass and I walked up among many other people and this building was surrounded by police officers with guns and we were all watching them. I moved on up to the building across the street from the building that was surrounded and I ask one of the girls if there was a telephone that I could use and she said "Yes, there is one on the third floor of the building where I work". I walked through a passage to the elevator they were all getting on (freight elevator) and I got off on the third floor with all the other people and there was a lady using the pay telephone and I ask her if I could use it when she hung up and she said it was out of order and I tried to use it but with no success. I ask her how I can get out of this building and she said that there is an exit right there and then she said wait a minute here is the elevator now. I got on the elevator and returned to the ground floor and the colored man who ran the elevator said you are a stranger in this building and I am was notsuppose to let you up and he ran outside to an officer and said to the officerthathe had just taken me up and down in the elevator and the officer said for me to identify myself and I presented him with a credit card and he said well we have to check out everything and took me to his superior and said for me to wait and we will check it out. I was then taken to the Sheriffs office and interrogated.

Jim Braden

Subscribed and sworn to before me on this the 22nd day of Nov A. D. 19 63

Evelyn Cox
Notary Public, Dallas County, Texas

12

COMMISSION EXHIBIT No. 2003—Continued

VOLUNTARY STATE . N. Under Arrest. Form No. 86

(25)

SHERIFF'S DEPARTMENT
COUNTY OF DALLAS, TEXAS

Before me, the undersigned authority, on this the 22nd day of November A. D. 1963

personally appeared Howard Leslie Brennan, Address 6814 Woodard Dallas, Texas

Age 44, Phone No. EV 1-2713

Deposes and says: I am presently employed by the Wallace and Beard Construction Company as a Steam fitter and have been so employed for about the past 7 weeks. I am working ~~on a pipe line~~ in the Katy Railroad yards at the West end of Pacific Street near the railroad tracks. We had k nocked off for lunch and I had dinner at the cafeteria at Record and Main Street and had come back to see the President of the United States. I was sitting on a ledge or wall near the intersection of Houston Street and Elm Street near the red light pole. I was facing in a northerly direction looking not only at Elm street but I could see the large red brick building across the street from where I was sitting. I take this building across the street to be about 7 stories anyway in the east endof the building and the second row of windows from the top I saw a man in this window. I had seen him before the President's car arrived. He was just sitting up there looking down apparantly waiting for the same thing I was to see the President. I did not notice anything unusual about this man. He was a white man in his early 30's, slender, nice looking, slender and would weigh about 165 to 175 pounds. He had on light colored clothing but definately not a suit. I proceeded to watch the President's car as it turned left at the corner where I was and about 50 yards from the intersection of Elm and Houston and to a point I would say the President's back was in line with the last window I have previously described I heard what I thought was a back fire. It run in my mind that it might be someone throwing firecrackers out the window of the red brick building and I looked up at the building. I then saw this man I have described in the window and he was taking aim with a high powered rifle. I could see all of the barrel of the gun. I do not know if it had a scope on it or not. I was looking at the man in this window at the time of the last explosion. Then this man let the gun down to his side and stepped down out of sight. He did not seem to be in any hurry. I could see this man from about his belt up. There was nothing unusual about him at all in appearance. I believe that I could identify this man if I ever saw him again.

H. L. Brennan

Subscribed and sworn to before me on this the 22nd day of November A. D. 19 63

Ed Jones
Notary Public, Dallas County, Texas

13

COMMISSION EXHIBIT No. 2003—Continued

AFFIDAVIT IN ANY FACT

THE STATE OF TEXAS
COUNTY OF DALLAS

BEFORE ME, Mary Rattan

a Notary Public in and for said County, State of Texas, on this day personally appeared

Johnny Calvin Brewer w/m/22 of 512 N. Lancaster, Apt. 102, WH1 4793. Bus: 213 W. Jefferson, Hardy Shoe Store

Who, after being by me duly sworn, on oath deposes and says: Friday November 22, 1963 I was at work at Hardy's Shoe Store, 213 W. Jefferson. I had heard on the radio that the President had been shot, also that a policeman had been shot in Oak Cliff. About 1:30 pm I saw a man standing in the lobby of the shoe store. This man was wearing a brown sport shirt. He also acted as if he was scared. About this time a police car came up the street going west on Jefferson. When the police car reached Zangs it made a turn and went back east on Jefferson. After the police car passed, the man in the lobby walked on up Jefferson toward the Texas Theater. I followed the man up the street and he went into the theater. I asked the girl in the box office if she sold the man a ticket and she replied that she did not think so, that she had been listening to the radio and did not remember. I went into the show and asked Butch, the concession man, if he had seen the man come in. Butch said that he had been busy and did not notice. Butch and I then checked the exits to see if any of them had been opened. The exits were all closed and did not appear to have been opened. I then went back to the box office and told Julie to call the police. When the police arrived the show was stopped and the lights were turned on. A man in the middle section and about five or six rows of seats from the back stood up when the lights were turned on. An officer approached him and he hit the officer and knocked him back. Several other officers then joined the fight and the man was taken out of the theater. This was the same man I had seen in front of the shoe store where I work. The reason I noticed the man in front of the store was because he acted so nervous, and I thought at the time he might be the man that had shot the policeman.

Johnny C. Brewer

SUBSCRIBED AND SWORN TO BEFORE ME THIS 6 DAY OF December A.D. 1963

Mary Rattan Mary Rattan
Notary Public, Dallas County, Texas

CPS-GF-413

14

COMMISSION EXHIBIT No. 2003—Continued

AFFIDAVIT IN ANY FACT

THE STATE OF TEXAS
COUNTY OF DALLAS

BEFORE ME, Patsy Collins

a Notary Public in and for said County, State of Texas, on this day personally appeared

Ted Callaway w/m/40 of 805 West 8th Street, WH-6-8045

Who, after being by me duly sworn, on oath deposes and says: I am the manager of the Used Car lot at 501 E. Jefferson. I was working today when I heard some shots. This was about 1 pm. I ran out into Patton Street and looked to see what the shooting was about. I saw a white man running South on Patton with a pistol in hand. I hollered at him and he looked around at me, then kept on going. I ran around on 10th Street and saw a Police officer laying in the street. He looked dead to me. I got the officer's gun and hollered at a cab driver to come on, We might catch the man. We got into his cab, number 213 and drove up Patton to Jefferson and looked all around, but did not see him. The number 2 man in the line up that I saw at City Hall is the man I saw with the gun in his hand.XXXXXX XXXXXXXXXXXXXXXXX

Ted Callaway

SUBSCRIBED AND SWORN TO BEFORE ME THIS 22 DAY OF November A.D. 1963

Patsy Collins Patsy Collins
Notary Public, Dallas County, Texas

CPS-GF-413

jrl

15

VOLUNTARY STATEMENT No. Under Arrest. Form No. 86

C. L. Lewis
(46)

SHERIFF'S DEPARTMENT
COUNTY OF DALLAS, TEXAS

Before me, the undersigned authority, on this the 22nd day of November A.D. 19 63

personally appeared John Arthur Chism, Address 4502 Underwood Drive Lisbon, Oak Cliff.

Age 23, Phone No.

Deposes and says:-

I am married and have three children. I was standing with my wife and three year old boy, we were directly in front of the Stemmons Freeway sign, as the motorcade rounded the corner from Houston onto Elm.

When I saw the motorcade round the corner, the President was standing and waving to the crowd. And just as he got just about in front of me, he turned and waved at the crowd on this side of the street, the right side; at this point I heard what sounded like one shot, and I saw him, "The President," sit back in his seat and lean his head to his left side. At this point, I saw Mrs. Kennedy stand up and pull his head over in her lap, and then lay down over him as if to shield him.

And the two men in the front seat, I don't know who they were, looked back, and just about the time they looked back, the second shot was fired.

At this point, I looked behind me, to see whether it was a fireworks display or something. And then I saw a lot of people running for cover, behind the embankment there back up on the grass.

And at this point, I turned back around and saw the motorcade beginning to speed up, and everybody was laying down but the driver, of course. I didn't notice where it went.

My wife and I began seeking cover, and we went to our car, and then we told the policeman about what we knew.

John Arthur Chism

Subscribed and sworn to before me on this the 22nd day of November A.D. 19 63

James J. Mulcahy
Notary Public, Dallas County, Texas

16

VOLUNTARY STATEMENT Not Under Arrest. Form No. 86

C. L. Lewis
SO

(47)

SHERIFF'S DEPARTMENT
COUNTY OF DALLAS, TEXAS

Before me, the undersigned authority, on this the 22nd day of November A. D. 19 63

personally appeared Marvin Faye Chism, Address 4502 Underwood Lisbon, Oak Cliff

Age 19, Phone No. ______

Deposes and says:-

I was with my husband and three year old child, we were standing at the corner where the sign says "Stemmons Freeway" to the right.

As the President was coming through, I heard this first shot, and the President fell to his left. The President's wife immediately stood over him, and she pulled him up, and lay him down in the seat, and she stood up over him in the car. The President was standing and waving and smiling at the people when the shot happened.

And then there was a second shot that I heard, after the President's wife had pulled him down in the seat. It came from what I thought was behind us and I looked but I couldn't see anything.

The two men in the front of the car stood up, and then when the second shot was fired, they all fell down and the car took off just like that. After the motorcade went by, after that, I jumped up and headed for my car, we were parked up on the freeway. A police patrolman came up where we were, and we told him what we saw.

Marvin Faye Chism

Subscribed and sworn to before me on this the 22nd day of November A. D. 19 63

James J. Mulcady
Notary Public, Dallas County, Texas

17

COMMISSION EXHIBIT No. 2003—Continued

AFFIDAVIT IN ANY FACT

F 85827

THE STATE OF TEXAS
COUNTY OF DALLAS

BEFORE ME, Mary Rattan

a Notary Public in and for said County, State of Texas, on this day personally appeared Barbara Jeanette Davis w/f/22, 400 E. 10th, WH3 8120. Bus: same

Who, after being by me duly sworn, on oath deposes and says: Today November 22, 1963 shortly after 1:00 pm, my sister-in-law, Virginia Davis, and I were lying on the bed with the kids. I heard a shot and jumped up and heard another shot. I put on my shoes and went to the door and I saw this man walking across my front yard unloading a gun. A woman was standing across the street screaming that "he shot him, he killed him" and pointed towards a police car. That is the first time I noticed a police car there. I ran back in the house and called the operator and reported this to the police. When the police arrived I showed one of them where I saw this man emptying his gun and we found a shell. After the police had left I went back into the yard and Virginia found another shell which I turned over to the police. About 8:00 pm the same day, the police came after me and took me downtown to the city hall where I saw this man in a lineup. The #2 man in a 4-man lineup was the same man I saw in my yard, also the one that was unloading the gun.

Barbara Jeanette Davis

SUBSCRIBED AND SWORN TO BEFORE ME THIS 22 DAY OF November A.D. 1963

Mary Rattan Mary Rattan
Notary Public, Dallas County, Texas

CPS-GF-413

18

COMMISSION EXHIBIT No. 2003—Continued

AFFIDAVIT IN ANY FACT

THE STATE OF TEXAS
COUNTY OF DALLAS

BEFORE ME, Patsy Collins

a Notary Public in and for said County, State of Texas, on this day personally appeared

Mrs. Virginia Davis, w/m/16, of 400 E. 10th WH-3-8120

Who, after being by me duly sworn, on oath deposes and says: Today November 22, 1963 about 1:30 pm my sister-in-law and myself were lying down in our apartment. My sister-in-law is Jeanette Davis, we live in the same house in different apartments. We heard a shot and then another shot and ran to side door at Patton Street. I saw the boy cutting across our yard and he was unloading his gun. We walked outside and a woman was hollering "he's dead, he's dead, he's shot". This woman told Jeanette to call the Police andshe did. I saw the officer that had been shot lying on Tenth street after Jeanette had called the Police. Jeanette found a empty shell that the man had unloaded and gave it to the police. After the Police had left I found a empty shell in our yard. This is the same shell I gave to Detective Dhority. The man that was unloading the gun was the same man that I saw tonight as number 2 man in a line up.XXXXXXXXXXXXXXXXXXXXXXXXXXXX

Mrs. Virginia Davis

SUBSCRIBED AND SWORN TO BEFORE ME THIS 22 DAY OF November A.D. 1963

Patsy Collins Patsy Collins
Notary Public, Dallas County, Texas

CPS-GF-413

19

cd

COMMISSION EXHIBIT No. 2003—Continued

AFFIDAVIT IN ANY FACT

THE STATE OF TEXAS
COUNTY OF DALLAS

BEFORE ME, Patsy Collins

a Notary Public in and for said County, State of Texas, on this day personally appeared Jack E. Dougherty

w/m/40, 1827 So. Marsalis WH-6-7170

Who, after being by me duly sworn, on oath deposes and says: I am employed at the Texas School Book Depository at 411 Elm and have been since 1952. I was working on the sixth floor today. There was six of us working on the floor. The others were Bill Lovelady, William Shelby, Danny Arce, Bonnie Williams, and Charles Givens. I worked until 12:00 noon, and went down on the first floor and ate my lunch and went back to work at 12:45 p.m. I had already gone back to work and I gone down on the fifth to get some stock when I heard a shot. It sounded like it was coming from inside the building, but I couldn't tell from where. I went down on the first floor, and asked a man named Eddie Piper if he had heard anything and he said yes, that he had heard three shots. I then went back on the sixth floor. I didn't see anyone on the floor except the people I named. There was another employee that is named Lee Oswald that I saw on the sixth floor. He works all over the building, but I saw him on the sixth floor shortly before noon. I didn't see Oswald in the building after lunch.XXXXXXXXXXXXXXXXXXXXXXXX

Jack E. Dougherty

SUBSCRIBED AND SWORN TO BEFORE ME THIS 22 DAY OF November A.D. 1963

Patsy Collins
Notary Public, Dallas County, Texas

CPS-GF-413

20

COMMISSION EXHIBIT No. 2003—Continued

VOLUNTARY STATE. .T. N. Under Arrest. Form No. 86

C. L. Lewis
5
(31)

SHERIFF'S DEPARTMENT
COUNTY OF DALLAS, TEXAS

Before me, the undersigned authority, on this the 22nd day of November A. D. 19 63

personally appeared Robert E. (Bob) Edwards, Address 821 South Nursery Irving, Texas

Age 22, Phone No. None

Deposes and says:- (Employed by the Dallas County Auditor's Office.)

Today, November 22nd, 1963, I was with Ronald Fischer, and we were on the corner at Elm and Houston, and I happened to look up there at the building, the Texas School Book Depository Building, and I saw a man at the window on the fifth floor, the window was wide open all the way; there was a stack of boxes around him, I could see. Bob remarked that he must be hiding from somebody. I noticed that he had on a sport shirt, it was light colored, it was yellow or white, something to that effect, and his hair was rather short; I thought he might be something around twenty-six, as near as I could tell.

The motorcade rounded the corner about this time, and then I thought I heard four shots, but it never occurred to us what it was. The shots seemed to come from that building there.

Robert E. Edwards

Subscribed and sworn to before me on this the 22nd day of November A. D. 19 63

James J. Mulcahy
Notary Public, Dallas County, Texas

21

COMMISSION EXHIBIT No. 2003—Continued

VOLUNTARY STATE. .T. N. Under Arrest. Form No. 86

SHERIFF'S DEPARTMENT
COUNTY OF DALLAS, TEXAS

Before me, the undersigned authority, on this the 22nd day of November A. D. 19 63

personally appeared Amos Lee Euins, Address 411 Avenue F Dallas, Texas

Age 15, Phone No. WH 3-9701

Deposes and says:- I am presently going to school at Franklin D. Roosevelt High School and am in the 9th grade. I got out of school this morning to see the President of the United States when he came to Dallas. I was standing on the corner of Elm and Houston street. From where I was standing I could look across the street and see a large red brick building. I saw the President turn the corner in front of me and I waived at him and he waived back. I watched the car on down the street and about the time the car got near the black and white sign I heard a shot. I started looking around and then I looked up in the red brick building. I saw a man in a window with a gun and I saw him shoot twice. He then stepped back behind some boxes. I could tell the gun was a rifle and it sounded like an automatic rifle the way he was shooting. I just saw a little bit of the barrel, and some of the trigger housing. This was a white man, he did not have on a hat. I just saw this man for a few seconds. As far as I know, I had never seen this man before.

Amos Lee Euins

Subscribed and sworn to before me on this the 22nd day of November A. D. 19 63

C. L. Jones
Notary Public, Dallas County, Texas

22

COMMISSION EXHIBIT No. 2003—Continued

VOLUNTARY STATEMENT Not Under Arrest. Form No. 86

(30)

SHERIFF'S DEPARTMENT
COUNTY OF DALLAS, TEXAS

Before me, the undersigned authority, on this the 22nd day of November A. D. 19 63 personally appeared Ronald B. Fischer, Address 4007 Flamingo Drive, Mesquite, Texas

Age 24, Phone No. ER 9-0950 (Employed by the Dallas County Auditor's Office.)

Deposes and says:-

Today, November 22nd, 1963, I was with Robert E. (Bob) Edwards, we were standing on the corner of Elm and Houston, on the southwest corner; about thirty seconds before the motorcade came by, Bob turned to me and said that there was a man on the fifth floor of the Texas School Book Depository Building, at the window there, and I looked up and saw the man. I looked up at the window and I noticed that he seemed to be laying down there or in a funny position anyway, because all I could see was his head. I noticed that he was light-headed and that he had on an open-neck shirt, and that was before the motorcade rounded the corner. I noticed his complexion seemed to be clear, and that he was in his twenty's, appeared to be in his twenty's.

I turned away and by that time the motorcade rounded the corner. And then I heard what I thought was three shots, and the motorcade was about where that Stemmons Freeway sign is there.

I do remember one peculair thing happened just at the time I saw the man up there. There was a girl walked in the Texas School Book Depository Building, a rather tall girl, and looked to me like she might be an employee in that building. She was walking in while, everyone else had been coming out.

Ronald B. Fischer

Subscribed and sworn to before me on this the 22nd day of November A. D. 19 63

James J. Mulcahy
Notary Public, Dallas County, Texas

23

COMMISSION EXHIBIT No. 2003—Continued

VOLUNTARY STATEMENT Not Under Arrest. Form No. 86

(53)

SHERIFF'S DEPARTMENT
COUNTY OF DALLAS, TEXAS

Before me, the undersigned authority, on this the 22nd day of November A. D. 19 1963 personally appeared Larry Floror, Address 3609 Potomic Dallas, Texas

Age 23, Phone No. [illegible] LA 1-7150

Deposes and says:- This afternoon about 10 minutes after the parade passed Poydras and Main Streets I went to a little Bar-B-Que place on Pacific. I do not know the name of this place and I went in and had a grilled cheese sandwich with a friend of mine, Richard Bartholow, who works at the National Bank of Commerce. They had a radio going on in the cafe, two gentlemen that were seated at the table next to us had the radio on . And something came on the radio about the President being shot at, so I walked out with this othe r boy and he went on the bank and I walked down to the railroad tracks at Pacific and Houston Street. I was walking parallel to some of the tracks and there were quite a few other people walking in the same direction I was going. I stopped on east side of Houston street across the street from the Texas School Book Depository. I stood there for a few minutes and then a lady that was standing next tome, I asked her where there was a telephone, and she said that the only pay phone that she knew of was in the County Records building. She said that there were a lot of phones on the third floor of this building that I was standing in front of. She said that she worked on the third ~~fl~~ floor and there was probably a phone up there that I could use. So I rode up the elevator with this lady and got off onthe third floor with this lady and we walked to the information desk and this lady went on back to her department, to her spot. So then I, there was a lady at the information desk and I asked her if I could borrow her telephone and she said that all the lines were busy, or something to that effect. So I stood there for a minute and a fellow walked up to me. He asked me what I want ed and he told me that I couldn't use the phone. So I walked back down ~~him~~ to the elevator and rode it back down to the lobby. As soon as I got to the lobby I walked back outside and the fellow that I had talked to about using the phone was pointing out the window, pointing toward me and said that I was the man that was on the third floor. At this time two officer walked up and said for me to come with them. These officers brought me to the County Sheriff's Office. At no time did I see anyone leaving the building, the Texas School Book Depository, while I was across the street from it.

Larry Florer

Subscribed and sworn to before me on this the 22nd day of November A. D. 19 63

C. C. Gentry
C. C. GENTRY
Notary Public, Dallas County, Texas

24

COMMISSION EXHIBIT No. 2003—Continued

AFFIDAVIT IN ANY FACT

THE STATE OF TEXAS
COUNTY OF DALLAS

BEFORE ME, Mary Rattan

a Notary Public in and for said County, State of Texas, on this day personally appeared Buell Wesley Frazier, Age 19, 2439 West 5th Street, Irving, Texas BL 3-8965

Who, after being by me duly sworn, on oath deposes and says: I work at Texas School Book Depository, Corner Elm and Houston. I have worked there since September 13, 1963. I fill orders. About a month ago, I met Lee Harvey Oswald at work. I saw that he was a new man, and I walked up to him and asked him if he was Lee. I figured he must be Lee as my sister had told me about him. I asked him if he would like to ride back and forth with me as I knew his wife lived with Ruth Paine near my house, and he said he would, But only on week ends as he had an apartment of his own in Oak Cliff. After that every Friday evening Lee would ride home with me and then ride back to work with me on Monday morning. He has only rode home from work with me on Fridays, but yesterday morning, Thursday, November 21, 1963, Lee told me that he wanted to ride home with me that evening. I was surprised, and I asked him if he was going home with me Friday also, and he said, "No". He told me that he was going home to get some curtain rods. Thursday afternoon Lee rode to Irving with me to Ruth Paine's house, where his wife is staying. I let him out of my car in front of Ruth's house, then I went on. This morning, Friday, November 22, 1963, I got up between 6:00 - 6:30 AM, and got ready to go to work, and then sit down to eat breakfast, about 7:15 AM, me, my mother, and my two little neices were at the table, and my sister was at the sink. My mother looked up and said, "Who is that looking in the window?" I looked up and said, "That's Lee." I got up and finished getting ready and got my lunch and went to the door and met Lee on the car port. We then walked to my car, it was parked backed up at the side of the car port. Before I got in the car, I glanced in the back seat, and saw a big sack. It must have been about 2' long, and the top of the sack was sort of folded up, and the rest of the sack had been kind of folded under. I asked Lee what was in the sack, and he said "curtain rods", and I remembered that he had told me the day before that he was going to bring some curtain rods. We drove to work the same way that I usually go. We came into town on Stemmons Freeway to Main and Main to Record, and then on across to Mc Kinney and by the warehouse to the parking lot. I parked the car and sit there awhile and run the motor to charge the battery, and while I was doing that, Lee got out and opened the back door and got the package out of the back seat and walked behind the car, When I got out of the car and started ~~walking toward the building where I work.~~
(Continued next page)

Wesley Frazier

SUBSCRIBED AND SWORN TO BEFORE ME THIS 22 DAY OF November A.D. 1963

Mary Rattan
MARY RATTAN
Notary Public, Dallas County, Texas

CPS-GF-413

GFR

25

COMMISSION EXHIBIT No. 2003—Continued

AFFIDAVIT IN ANY FACT

THE STATE OF TEXAS
COUNTY OF DALLAS

BEFORE ME, Mary Rattan

a Notary Public in and for said County, State of Texas, on this day personally appeared Buell Wesley Frazier, age 19, 2439 West 5th Street, Irving, Texas - BL 3-8965

Who, after being by me duly sworn, on oath deposes and says:
(Continued from page 2)
I noticed that Lee had the package in his right hand under his arm, and the package was straight up and down, and he had his arm down, and you could not see much of the package. When we started walking, Lee was just a few feet ahead of me, but he kept walking faster than me, and finally got way ahead of me. I saw him go in the back door at the Loading Dock of the building that we work in, and he still had the package under his arm. I did not see him anymore for about 30 minutes, and then we were both working. Lee did not carry his lunch today. He told me this morning he was going to buy his lunch today. I was standing on the front steps of the building when the Parade came by, and I watched the Parade go by. After President Kennedy had got out of my sight, I heard three shots. I stood there, then people started running by, and I turned, and went back in the building and got my lunch and eat it. I did not see Lee anymore after about 11:00 AM today, and at that time, we were both working, and we were on the first floor.XXXXXXXXXXXXXXXXXXXXXXXX XXXXXXXXX

Wesley Frazier

SUBSCRIBED AND SWORN TO BEFORE ME THIS 22 DAY OF November A.D. 1963

Mary Rattan
MARY RATTAN
Notary Public, Dallas County, Texas

CPS-GF-413

GFR

26

COMMISSION EXHIBIT No. 2003—Continued

AFFIDAVIT IN ANY FACT

THE STATE OF TEXAS
COUNTY OF DALLAS

BEFORE ME, Mary Rattan

a Notary Public in and for said County, State of Texas, on this day personally appeared

Charles Douglas Givens c/m/37, 2511 Carpenter, RI2 4670

Who, after being by me duly sworn, on oath deposes and says: I work for the Texas School Book Depository, 411 Elm Street. I worked up on the 6th floor today until about 11:30 am. Then I went downstairs and into the bathroom. At twelve o'clock I took my lunch period. I went to the parking lot at Record and Elm street. I have a friend who works at the parking lot. We walked up to Main and Record when the President passed by. We then walked back to the parking lot after the President had passed by. We had just got back to the lot when we heard the shooting. I think I heard three shots. I did not see anyone in the building that was not supposed to be there this morning.

Charles Douglas Givens

SUBSCRIBED AND SWORN TO BEFORE ME THIS 22 DAY OF November A.D. 1963

Mary Rattan Mary Rattan
Notary Public, Dallas County, Texas

CPS-GF-413

JRL 27

COMMISSION EXHIBIT No. 2003—Continued

AFFIDAVIT IN ANY FACT

THE STATE OF TEXAS
COUNTY OF DALLAS

BEFORE ME, Mary Rattan

a Notary Public in and for said County, State of Texas, on this day personally appeared

Sam Guinyard c/m/38 of 605 East Park St, Waxahachie, Texas

Who, after being by me duly sworn, on oath deposes and says: I work as a porter at the used car lot at 501 E. Jefferson. Today about 1:00 pm I heard some shooting near Patton and 10th Street. I ran out and looked. I saw a white man running south on Patton Street with a pistol in his hand. The last I saw of this man he was running west on Jefferson. I went around on 10th Street and saw a policeman laying in the street. He was bloody and looked dead to me. The #2 man in the lineup I saw at the city hall is the same man I saw running with the pistol in his hand.

Sam Guinyard

SUBSCRIBED AND SWORN TO BEFORE ME THIS 22 DAY OF November A.D. 1963

Mary Rattan Mary Rattan
Notary Public, Dallas County, Texas

CPS-GF-413

JRL 28

COMMISSION EXHIBIT No. 2003—Continued

VOLUNTARY STATE[illegible]. No[illegible] Under Arrest. Form No. 86

(42)

SHERIFF'S DEPARTMENT
COUNTY OF DALLAS, TEXAS

Before me, the undersigned authority, on this the 22nd day of November A. D. 19 63

personally appeared Philip Ben Hathaway, Address 11021 Quail Run, Dallas

Age 28, Phone No. DI 8 6532
Deposes and says:- DOB: July 9, 1935 DOB: Chicago, Ill. Wks: Lone Star Gas Co, Research & Developement Dept. RI 1 3711 Ext 776

Just before Noon today, my friend John Stevens Rutter Lawrence, who works with me, and I and two other friends left the Texaco Building where we work going to the parade. We were walking down Commerce up to Main and Main to Akard andwhile we were walking up Akard towards Main Street we passed a man who was carrying a rifle in a gun case. I saw this man walking towards me, walking towards Commerce, and took particular attention to him because ofhis size. I am 6'5" and weigh 200 pounds. This man was very tall, approx 6'6" or 6'7" over 250 pounds, very thick and big through the chest, in his 30's, dirty blonde hair worn in a crew cut. Was wearing a grey colored business suit with white dress shirt, fair complexion. I remarked to my friend that there was a guy carrying a gun in all this crowd and made the remark that he was probably a secret service man. I could very easily identify this man if I ever saw him again. The gun case was holding a rifle because I could tell there was a gun in it as it was a combination leather and cloth gun case and without a gun, it would have been limp, but it was heavy and he was carrying it by the handle and the barrell of the gun was up at a 45 degree angle. It was beigh or tan leather and olive drab material.

We can place the time that we saw this man walking with the gun as I recall someone in the crowd asking for the time and they said it was 11:50A.M.

Philip Ben Hathaway

Subscribed and sworn to before me on this the 22nd day of November A. D. 1963

Rosemary Allen
Notary Public, Dallas County, Texas

29

COMMISSION EXHIBIT No. 2003—Continued

VOLUNTARY STATEMENT. Not Under Arrest. Form No. 86

(56)

SHERIFF'S DEPARTMENT
COUNTY OF DALLAS, TEXAS

Before me, the undersigned authority, on this the 22nd day of November A. D. 1963

personally appeared Charles Hester, Address 2616 Keyhole, Irving

Age 28, Phone No. None

Deposes and says:- My wife, Beatrice and I were sitting on the grass on the slope on Elm Street where the park is located. When President Kennedy's car got almost down to the underpass, I heard two shots ring out. Thye sounded like they came from immediately behind us and over our heads. We did see the shooting. I immediately turned and looked at the Texas Book Depository building and did not see anyone. The shots sounded like the definitely came from in or around the building. I grabbed my wife because I didn't know where the next shot was coming from and dragged her up next to the concrete imbankment and threw her down on the ground and got on the ground with her. Then there was utter confusion. The Police rushed toward the railroad tracks and I finally found an officer to go to the Texas Book Depository Building. The officer I contacted was Officer Wiseman of the Dallas Sheriff's Department.

X
X
X
X
X
X
X
X
X

Charles Hester

Subscribed and sworn to before me on this the 22nd day of November A. D. 19 63

Aleen Davis
Notary Public, Dallas County, Texas

30

COMMISSION EXHIBIT No. 2003—Continued

VOLUNTARY STATEMENT. Not Under Arrest. Form No. 86 (75)

SHERIFF'S DEPARTMENT
COUNTY OF DALLAS, TEXAS

Before me, the undersigned authority, on this the 22nd day of November A. D. 19 63
personally appeared Jean Hill, Address 9402 Bluffcreek Dallas 27, Texas
Age 32, Phone No. EV1-7419
Deposes and says:-

Mary and I were wanting to take some pictures of the President so we purposely tried to find a place that was open where no people was around and we had been standing half way down toward the underpass on Elm Street on the south side. We were the only people in that area and we were standing right at the curb. The Presidents car came around the corner and it was over on our side of the street. Just as Mary Moorman started to take a picture we were looking at the president and Jackie in the back seat and they looking at a little dog between them. Just as the president looked up toward us two shots rang out and I saw the President grab his chest and fall forward across Jackies lap and she fell across his back and said "My God he has been shot". There was an instant pause between the first two shots and the motor cade seemingly halted for an instant and three or four more shots rang out and the motor cade sped away. I thought I saw some men in plain clothes shooting back but everything was such a blur and Mary was pulling on my leg saying "Get down thery are shooting". I looked across the street and up the hill and saw a man running toward the monument and I started running over there. By the time I got up to the rail road tracks some policeman that I suppose were in the motor cade or near by had also arrived and was turning us back and as I came back down the hill Mr. Featherstone of the Times Herald had gotten to Mary and ask her for her picture she had taken of the President, and he brought us to the press room down at the Sheriffs office and ask to stay.

Jean Hill

Subscribed and sworn to before me on this the 22nd day of November A. D. 19 63
Albert Davis
Notary Public, Dallas County, Texas

31

VOLUNTARY STATEMENT. Not Under Arrest. Form No. 86 (50)

SHERIFF'S DEPARTMENT
COUNTY OF DALLAS, TEXAS

Before me, the undersigned authority, on this the 22 day of November A. D. 19 63
personally appeared S. M. Holland, Address 1119 Lucillo, Irving, Texas
Age 57, Phone No. BL3-2185
Deposes and says:- I am signal supervisor for the Union Terminal and I was inspecting signal and switches and stopped to watch the parade. I was standing on top of the triple underpass and the President's Car was coming down Elm Street and when they got just about to the Arcade I heard what I thought for the moment was a fire cracker and he slumped over and I looked over toward the arcade and trees and saw a puff of smoke come from the trees and I heard three more shots after the first shot but that was the only puff of smoke I saw. I immediately ran around to where I could see behind the arcade and did not see anyone running from there. But the puff of smoke I saw definitely came from behind the arcade through the trees. After the first shot the President slumped over and Mrs. Kennedy jumped up and tried to get over in the back seat to him and then the second shot rang out. After the first shot the secret service man raised up in the seat with a machine gun and then dropped back down in the seat. And they immediately sped off. Everything is spinning in my head and if I remember anything else later I will come back and tell Bill.

S M Holland

Subscribed and sworn to before me on this the 22nd day of November A. D. 19 63
Albert Davis
Notary Public, Dallas County, Texas

32

COMMISSION EXHIBIT No. 2003—Continued

VOLUNTARY STATEM . . ot Under Arrest. Form No. 83

(57)

SHERIFF'S DEPARTMENT
COUNTY OF DALLAS, TEXAS

Before me, the undersigned authority, on this the 22nd day of November A. D. 1963

personally appeared Emmett Joseph Hudson, Address 707 South Bishop Dallas, Texas

Age 56, Phone No. WH 2-2008

Deposes and says:- I am presently employed by the City of Dallas, Texas in the Park Department. I have been so employed for the past 6 years. My position is to take care of the property located on the West side of Houston Street between Houston Street and the Tripple Underpass. I also take care of the fountain in front of the Union Terminal. This day I was sitting on the front steps of the slopping area and about half way down the steps. There was another man sitting there with me. He was sitting on my left and we were both facing the street with our backs to the railroad yards and the brick building. At the same time the President's car was directly in front of us, I heard a shot and I saw the President fall over in the seat. I do not know who this other man was that was sitting beside me. In our conversation he talked about having a hard time finding a place to park. He also talked about working somewhere over on Industrial Blvd. This man said lay down and we did. I definately heard 3 shots. The shots that I heard definately came from behind and above me. When I laid down on the ground, I laid on my right side and my view was still toward the street where the President's car had passed. I did look around but I did not see anything unusual, either anyone running and I did not see any firearms at all. This shot sounded to me like a high powered rifle.

Emmett J. Hudson

Witness; F. V. Gonda, DSS

Subscribed and sworn to before me on this the 22nd day of November A. D. 1963

Ed Jones
Notary Public, Dallas County, Texas

33

COMMISSION EXHIBIT NO. 2003—Continued

AFFIDAVIT IN ANY FACT

THE STATE OF TEXAS
COUNTY OF DALLAS

BEFORE ME, PATSY COLLINS

a Notary Public in and for said County, State of Texas, on this day personally appeared

James Earl Jarman, Jr., c/m 33, 3942 Atlanta Street, Dallas, Texas HA8-1837

Who, after being by me duly sworn, on oath deposes and says: I work for the Texas School Book Depository, 411 Elm Street, as a Checker on the first floor for Mr. Roy S. Truly. On Friday, November 22, 1963, I got to work at 8:05 a.m. The first time I saw Lee Oswald on Friday, November 22, 1963 was about 8:15 a.m. He was filling orders on the first floor. A little after 9:00 a.m. Lee Oswald asked me what all the people were doing standing on the street. I told him that the President was supposed to come this way sometime this morning. He asked me, "Which way do you think he is coming?". I told him that the President would probably come down Main Street and turn on Houston and then go down Elm Street. He said, "Yes, I see". I only talked with him for about three or four minutes. The last time I saw Lee Oswald on Friday, November 22, 1963 was between 11:30 a.m. and 12:00 noon when he was taking the elevator upstairs to go get some boxes. At about 11:45 a.m. all of the employees who were working on the 6th floor came downstairs and we were all out on the street at about 12:00 o'clock noon. These employees were: Bill Shelley, Charles Givens, Billy Lovelady, Bonnie Ray (last name not known) and a Spanish boy (his name I cannot remember). To my knowledge Lee Oswald was not with us while we were watching the parade. XXXXXXXXXXXXXXXXXXXXXXXXXXXXXXXXXXXXXXXXXXXXXXXXXXXXXXXXXXXXXXX XXXXXXXXXXX

XXXXXXXXX

XXXXXXXXX

XXXXXXXXX James Earl Jarman, Jr.

SUBSCRIBED AND SWORN TO BEFORE ME THIS 23RD' DAY OF NOVEMBER A.D. 1963

Patsy Collins
Notary Public, Dallas County, Texas

CPS-GF-413

34

COMMISSION EXHIBIT NO. 2003—Continued

VOLUNTARY STATEMENT Not Under Arrest. Form No. 86

(43)

SHERIFF'S DEPARTMENT
COUNTY OF DALLAS, TEXAS

Before me, the undersigned authority, on this the 22nd day of November A. D. 19 63

personally appeared John Stevens Rutter Lawrence Address 709 Devonshire

DOB: 5-21-40 POB: Oak Park, Ill. Richardson, Texas

Age 23, Phone No. ____

Deposes and says:-

Today at about 11:45AM, me and Phil Hathaway and two other fellows left the Texaco Building, where we all work together, to go see the parade and President Kennedy. In just a few minutes after we got out on the street and walking down Akard, Phil called to my attention a big man and said he was carrying a rifle. I looked and saw the man but due to a big rush of noontime people, I did not see the rifle. I took particular attention to him because of his size. I was walking with my friend Phil Hathaway who is 6'5" and this man was fairly close to his size, maybe a little taller, he was very thick chested and big through the shoulders, maybe 250 pounds or more, but no fat, he gave me the impression of perhaps a professional football player. He had dirty blonde hair and was a short crew cut. He was approximately in his 30's. He was wearing a business suit and I believe it was light in color, perhaps tan, a white business shirt. I could identify this man if I ever saw him again.

John Stevens Rutter Lawrence

Subscribed and sworn to before me on this the 22nd day of November A.D. 19 63

Rosemary Allen
Notary Public, Dallas County, Texas

35

COMMISSION EXHIBIT No. 2003—Continued

AFFIDAVIT IN ANY FACT

THE STATE OF TEXAS
COUNTY OF DALLAS

BEFORE ME, Mary Rattan

a Notary Public in and for said County, State of Texas, on this day personally appeared

Billy Nolan Lovelady w/m/26 of 7722 Hume Drive, Dallas, Texas

Who, after being by me duly sworn, on oath deposes and says: I work at Texas School Book Depository 411 Elm. On Friday November 22, 1963 I worked on the 6th floor along with Danny Arce, Jack Dougherty, Bill Shelley and Charles Givens. When the President came by Bill Shelley and I was standing on the steps in front of the building where I work. After he had passed and was about 50 yards past us I heard three shots. There was a slight pause after the first shot then the next two was right close together. I could not tell where the shots come from but sounded like they were across the street from us. However, that could have been caused by the echo. After it was over we went back into the building and I took some police officers up to search the building. I did not see anyone around the building that was not supposed to be there. Our lunch period is from 12 to 12:45 pm. All of us had left the 6th floor to see the President.

Billy Nolan Lovelady

SUBSCRIBED AND SWORN TO BEFORE ME THIS 22 DAY OF November A.D. 1963

Mary Rattan Mary Rattan
Notary Public, Dallas County, Texas

CPS-GF-413

JRL

36

COMMISSION EXHIBIT No. 2003—Continued

AFFIDAVIT IN ANY FACT

THE STATE OF TEXAS
COUNTY OF DALLAS

BEFORE ME, ROBERT WISDOM

a Notary Public in and for said County, State of Texas, on this day personally appeared

Helen Louise Markham 328½ East 9th
Bus: Eat Well Cafe RI-8-2475

Who, after being by me duly sworn, on oath deposes and says:

At approximately 1:06 PM, November 22, 1963--I was standing on the corner of E. 10th and Patton Street waiting for traffic to go by when I saw a squad car stop in front of 404 E. 10th about 50 feet from where I was standing. I saw a young white man walk up to the squad car opposite the driver's side, lean over & put his arms on the door of the car for a few seconds, then straighten up and step back from the car two or three feet. At this point the officer got out of the squad car and started around in front of the car and just as he got even with the left front wheel this young white man shot the officer and the officer fell to the pavement. I screamed and the man ran west on E. 10th across Patton Street and went out of sight.

Helen L Markham

SUBSCRIBED AND SWORN TO BEFORE ME THIS 22nd DAY OF November A.D. 1963

ROBERT WISDOM Robert Wisdom
Notary Public, Dallas County, Texas

CPS-GF-413

37

COMMISSION EXHIBIT No. 2003—Continued

AFFIDAVIT IN ANY FACT

THE STATE OF TEXAS
COUNTY OF DALLAS

BEFORE ME, PATSY COLLINS

a Notary Public in and for said County, State of Texas, on this day personally appeared

Cecil J. McWatters, 2523 Blyth, DA1-2909, Dallas, Texas
Business Address: Dallas Transit Company

Who, after being by me duly sworn, on oath deposes and says: Today, November 22, 1963 about 12:40 p.m. I was driving Marsalis Bus No. 1213. I picked up a man on the lower end of town on Elm around Houston. I went on out Marsalis and picked up a woman. I asked her if she knew the President had been shot and she thought I was kidding. I told her if she did not believe me to ask the man behind her that he had told me the President was shot in the temple. This man was grinning and never did say anything. The woman said that it was not a grinning matter. I don't remember where I let this man off. This man looks like the #2 man I saw in a line-up tonight. The transfer #004459 is a transfer from my bus with my punch mark. XXXXXXXXXXXXXXXXXXXXXXXXXXXXXXXXXXXXXXXXXXXXXXXXXXXXXXXXXXXXXXX
XXXXXXXXXXXXXXXXXXXXXXXXXXXXXXXXXXXXXXXXXXXXXXXXXXXXXXXXXXXXXXXXXXXX

Cecil J. McWatters

SUBSCRIBED AND SWORN TO BEFORE ME THIS 22nd DAY OF November A.D. 1963

Patsy Collins
Notary Public, Dallas County, Texas

CPS-GF-413

38

COMMISSION EXHIBIT No. 2003—Continued

VOLUNTARY STATEMENT. Not Under Arrest. Form No. 86

(40)

SHERIFF'S DEPARTMENT
COUNTY OF DALLAS, TEXAS

Before me, the undersigned authority, on this the 22nd day of November A. D. 19 63

personally appeared Julia Ann Mercer, Address 5200 Belmont, No. 208 Dallas

Born 2-10-40 Chattanooga, Tenn.

Age 23, Phone No.

Employed: Automat Distributors, 1720 Canton, Dallas.

Deposes and says:-

On November 22, 1963, I was driving a rented White Valiant automobile west on Elm Street and was proceeding to the overpass in a westerly direction and at a point about 45 or 50 feet east of the overhead signs of the right entrance road to the overpass, there was a truck parked on the right hand side of the road. The truck looked like it had 1 or 2 wheels up on the curb. The hood of the truck was open. On the drivers side of the truck, there were printed letters in black, oval shaped, which said, "Air Conditioning". This was a pickup truck and along the back side of the truck were what appeared to be tool boxes. The truck was a green Ford with a Texas license. I remember seeing the word "Ford" at the back of the truck.

A man was sitting under the wheel of the car and slouched over the wheel. This man had on a green jacket, was a white male and about his 40's and was heavy set. I did not see him too clearly. Another man was at the back of the truck and reached over the tailgate and took out from the truck what appeared to be a gun case. This case was about 8" wide at it's widest spot and tapered down to a width of about 4" or 5". It was brown in color. It had a handle and was about 3½ to 4 feet long. The man who took this out of the truck then proceeded to walk away from the truck and as he did, the small end of the case caught in the grass or sidewalk and he reached down to free it. He then proceeded to walk across the grass and up the grassy hill which forms part of the overpass. This is the last I saw of this man.

I had been delayed because the truck which I described above was blocking my passage and I had to await until the lane to myleft cleared so I could go by the truck.

During the time that I was at this point and observed the above incident there were 3 policeman standing talking near a motorcycle on the bridge just west of me.

The man who took what appeared to be the gun case out of the truck was a white male, who appeared to be in his late 20's or early 30's and he was

Julia Ann Mercer

Subscribed and sworn to before me on this the 22nd day of November A. D. 19 63

Rosemary Allen

Notary Public, Dallas County, Texas

39

VOLUNTARY STATEMENT. Not Under Arrest. Form No. 86

(41)

SHERIFF'S DEPARTMENT
COUNTY OF DALLAS, TEXAS

Before me, the undersigned authority, on this the 22nd day of November A. D. 19 63

personally appeared Julia Ann Mercer, Address 5200 Belmont, No. 208 Dallas

Age 23, Phone No.

Deposes and says:-

wearing a grey jacket, brown pants andplaid shirt as best as I can remember. I remember he had on some kind of a hat that looked like a wool stocking hat with a tassell in the middle of it. I believe that I can identify this man if I see him again. [illegible].

The man who remained in the truck had light brown hair and I believe I could identify him also if I were to see him again.

Julia Ann Mercer

Subscribed and sworn to before me on this the 22nd day of November A. D. 19 63

Rosemary Allen

Notary Public, Dallas County, Texas

40

VOLUNTARY STATEMENT. Not Under Arrest. Form No. 86

(47)

SHERIFF'S DEPARTMENT
COUNTY OF DALLAS, TEXAS

Before me, the undersigned authority, on this the 22nd day of November A. D. 19 63

personally appeared Austin Lawrence Miller W/M 26 Address 1006 Powhal Circle, Mesquite

Age ____, Phone No. AT 5-2998

Deposes and says:- My Business Address is Texas and Louisana Freight Bureau, 215 Union Terminal Bldg. and the phone number is RI 1-1396. I and Roy Shelton who works with me was standing on the Tripple Underpass bridge with a large group of people watching for the Presidential Motorcade. I saw a Convertable automobile turn West on Elm off Houston Street. It had preceeded about halfway from Houston Street to the underpass when I heard what sounded like a shot a short second two more sharp reports. A man in the back seat slumped over and a woman in bright colored dress (Orange or Yellow) grabbed the man and yelled. One shot apparently hit the street past the car. I saw something which I thought was smoke or steam coming from a group of trees north of Elm off the Railroad tracks. I did not see anyone on the tracks or in the trees. A large group of people concreated and a motorcycle officer dropped his motor and took off on foot to the car.XXXXXXXXXX

Austin L Miller

Subscribed and sworn to before me on this the 22nd day of November A. D. 19 63

Lena Price Turner
Notary Public, Dallas County, Texas

41

COMMISSION EXHIBIT No. 2003—Continued

VOLUNTARY STATEMENT. Not Under Arrest. Form No. 86

(48)

SHERIFF'S DEPARTMENT
COUNTY OF DALLAS, TEXAS

Before me, the undersigned authority, on this the 22nd day of November A. D. 19 63

personally appeared Mary Ann Moorman, Address 2832 Ripplewood, Dallas

Age 31, Phone No. DA 1-9390

Deposes and says:- Mrs. Jean Hill and I were standing on the grass by the park on Elm Street between the underpass and the corner of Elm & Houston. I had a Polariod Camera with me and was intending to take pictures of President Kennedy and the motorcade. As the motorcade started toward me I took two pictures. As President Kennedy was opposite me, I took a picture of him. As I snapped the picture of President Kennedy, I heard a shot ring out. President Kennedy kind of slumped over. Then I heard another shot ring out and Mrs. Kennedy jumped up in the car and said, "My God, he has been shot." When I heard these shots ring out, I fell to the ground to keep from being hit myself. I heard three or four shots in all. After the pictures I took were developed, the Picture of President Kennedy showed him slumped over. When the pictures were developed, they came out real light. These pictures have been turned over to Officers investigating this incident.

XXXXXXXXX

Mary Ann Moorman

Subscribed and sworn to before me on this the 22nd day of November A. D. 19 63

Aleen Davis
Aleen Davis
Notary Public, Dallas County, Texas

42

COMMISSION EXHIBIT No. 2003—Continued

VOLUNTARY STATEMENT. Not Under Arrest. Form No. 86 (51)

SHERIFF'S DEPARTMENT
COUNTY OF DALLAS, TEXAS

Before me, the undersigned authority, on this the 22nd day of November A. D. 1963

personally appeared Gayle Newman, Address 713 W. Clarendon, Dallas

Age 22, Phone No. WH 8-6082

Deposes and says:- My husband, Billy, myself and our children were standing about halfway betöeen the corner of Elm and Houston and the underpass. We were the last people in line going toward the underpass. When President Kennedy's car was about ten feet from us, I heard a noise that sounded like a firecracker going off. President Kennedy kind of jumped like he was startled and covered his head with his hands and then raised up. After I heard the first shot, another shot sounded and Governor Connally kind of grabbed his chest and lay back on the seat of the car. When I first saw and heard all of this, I thought it was all of a joke. Just about the time President Kennedy was right in front of us, I heard another shot ring out and the President put his hands up to his head. I saw blood all over the side of his head. About this time Mrs. Kennedy grabbed the President and he kind of lay over to the side kind of in her arms. Then my husband, Billy, said it is a shot. We grabbed our two children and my husband lay on one child and I lay on the other one on the grass. We started to get up and then all of a sudden we lay back down. I don't know what it was but another shot may have been fired that caused us to lay back down. Everyone started running back toward the brick structure. We got up and went back there. Everyone was saying, "What happened? What happened.?" Some man from Channel 8 here in Dallas took us over to thó studio where we gave statements of what we had seen. This is all I saw of know of the incident.

X
X
XX
X
X
X Gayle Newman.

Subscribed and sworn to before me on this the 22nd day of November A. D. 19 63

Aleen Davis
Notary Public, Dallas County, Texas

43

VOLUNTARY STATEMENT. Not Under Arrest. Form No. 86 (39)

SHERIFF'S DEPARTMENT
COUNTY OF DALLAS, TEXAS

Before me, the undersigned authority, on this the 22nd day of November A. D. 19 63

personally appeared Jean Newman, Address 3893 Clover Lane Dallas, Texas

Age 21, Phone No. FL 2-4222

Deposes and says:-

My name is Jean Newman, I live with my parents, my father's name is G. C. Kimbriel. I work at the Rheem Manufacturing Company.

I was standing right on this side of the Stemmons Freeway sign, about half-way between the sign and the edge of the building on the corner. I was by myself, there were other people around watching the motorcade. The motorcade had just passed me when I heard something that I thought was a firecracker at first, and the President had just passed me, because after he had just passed, there was a loud report, it just scared me, and I noticed that the President jumped, he sort of ducked his head down and I thought at the time that it probably scared him, too, just like it did me, because he flinched, like he jumped. I saw him put his elbows like this, with his hands on his chest.

By this time, the motorcade never did stop, and the President fell to his left and his wife jumped up on her knees, I believe it was, in the back of the car on her knees, I couldn't say that for sure. And I realized then it had been a shot. I looked in the car and she was on her knees, and he wasn't even visible in the car. I looked around then and everybody was running every which way, I don't know why I didn't run, I just stood there and backed up and looked around to see if I could see anything, but I saw no one whatever with anything that resembled a gun or anything of that kind.

I just heard two shots. When it happened, I was just looking at the President and his wife, and when she jumped up in the car, I had my vision focused on her, and I didn't see anything else, about the others in the front of the car.

The first impression I had was that the shots came from my right.

Jean Newman

Subscribed and sworn to before me on this the 22nd day of November A. D. 19 63

rb

James J. Mulcahy
Notary Public, Dallas County, Texas

44

VOLUNTARY STATE . N Under Arrest. Form No. 86

(52)

SHERIFF'S DEPARTMENT
COUNTY OF DALLAS, TEXAS

Before me, the undersigned authority, on this the 22nd day of November A. D. 19 63

personally appeared William Eugene Newman, Address 718 W. Clarendon, Dallas, Texas

Age 22, Phone No. WH 8-6082

Deposes and says:- Today at about 12:45 pm I was standing in a group of people on Elm Street near the west end of the concrete standard when the President's car turned left off Houston Street onto Elm Street. We were standing at the edge of the curb looking at the car as it was coming toward us and all of a sudden there was a noise, apparently gunshot. The President jumped up in his seat, and it looked like what I thought was a firecracker had went off and I thought he had realized it. It was just like an explosión and he was standing up. By this time he was directly in front of us and I was looking directly at him when he was hit in the side of the head. Then he fell back and Governor Connally was holding his middle section. Then we fell down on the grass as it seemed that we were in direct path of fire. It looked like Mrs. Kennedy jumped on top of the President. He kinda fell back and it looked like she was holding him. Then the car sped away and everybody in that area had run upon top of that little mound. I thought the shot had come from the garden directly behind me, that was on an elevation from where I was as I was right on the curb. I do not recall looking toward the Texas School Book Depository. I looked back in the vacinity of the garden.

William E. Newman Jr.

Subscribed and sworn to before me on this the 22nd day of November A. D. 19 63

C. C. Gentry
C. C. GENTRY
Notary Public, Dallas County, Texas

45

COMMISSION EXHIBIT No. 2003—Continued

AFFIDAVIT IN ANY FACT

THE STATE OF TEXAS
COUNTY OF DALLAS

BEFORE ME, Mary Rattan

a Notary Public in and for said County, State of Texas, on this day personally appeared

Marina Oswald w/f/22 2515 W. 5th Irving, Texas

Who, after being by me duly sworn, on oath deposes and says: I am the wife of Lee Harvey Oswald. I will be married to him 3 years in April. We got married in Minsk, Russia. We came to America in June 13, 1962. One day in New York then we took a plane to Fort Worth. We stayed with Lee's brother Robert Oswald in Fort Worth. Robert now is in Denton with his company. We stayed one month with his brother and then rented a apartment. ~~xxxxxxxx~~ We left Fort Worth. In October 1962 we rented an apartment in Dallas. This was on Elsbeth and then on Neeley. Lee then went to New Orleans in May to look for work. In the last part of May of this year I went to New Orleans. At the end of September about the 24th I came back to Irving. Lee came back to Dallas about 2 weeks later. Lee rented a room in Dallas and would come to Irving and spend the weekends. Lee went to work for a book company. Mrs. Paine pointed out the place on HINES ~~him~~ that Lee worked for. Lee started working there on October 15, 1963. Lee spent the night ~~there~~ ~~xx~~ in Irving last night. This morning Lee was gone before I got up. When the Officers came to my house they asked me if Leo had a ~~xifxx~~ rifle. I told them he used to have a rifle to hunt with in Russia. I knew there was a rifle in Mrs. Paine's garage. Two weeks ago I was in the garage and saw the same blanket that the Police got. I opened the blanket and saw a rifle in it. This blanket is the same one that I saw today in the same place. Today is the first time I saw the blanket empty. Today at Police station they showed me a rifle. This was like the rifle my husband had. It was a dark gun. But I don't ~~xxx~~ remember the sight on it. It could be the same rifle but I'm not sure. Lee packed our things in Mrs. Paine's car in New Orleans. Mrs. Paine and me drove to Dallas.

Mrs. Marina Oswald

SUBSCRIBED AND SWORN TO BEFORE ME THIS 22 DAY OF November A.D. 1963

Mary Rattan
MARY RATTAN
Notary Public, Dallas County, Texas

CPS-GF-413

Witness: [signature]

46

COMMISSION EXHIBIT No. 2003—Continued

VOLUNTARY STATEMENT Not Under Arrest. Form No. 88 (37)

SHERIFF'S DEPARTMENT
COUNTY OF DALLAS, TEXAS

Before me, the undersigned authority, on this the 22nd day of November A. D. 19 63

personally appeared Ernest Jay Owens, Address 3005 Peachtree, Mesquite, Texas

Age 36, Phone No. None

Deposes and says:- Yesterday afternoon, Thursday, and while on my way home from work, I passed a man walking in a westerly direction on Wood Street as well as I can remember about Good-Lattimer Expressway. I was headed in an Easterly direction in my car and this was sometime between 4:55pm and 5:15pm. This man I saw was a White Male, about 5 foot 4 to 5 foot 6 inches tall and heavy build, not fat but large shoulders. This man was carrying a foreign made rifle, long blue steel barrel and a long yellow stock. This man was wearing a dark colored suit and was bareheaded. He was carrying the gun on his right side in his right hand. As far as I know I have never seen this man before and I could not be sure that I could identify him if I ever saw him again. This man came out of a parking lot with the gun in his hand. I can not be sure if this weapon had a scope on it or not. I would say this man's age was between 35 and 45 years and he did not have glasses on.

Ernest J. Owens

Subscribed and sworn to before me on this the 22nd day of November A. D. 19 63

C. M. Jones
Notary Public, Dallas County, Texas

47

COMMISSION EXHIBIT NO. 2003—Continued

AFFIDAVIT IN ANY FACT

THE STATE OF TEXAS
COUNTY OF DALLAS

BEFORE ME, ANGELA M. FLOWERS

a Notary Public in and for said County, State of Texas, on this day personally appeared Michael Ralph Paine, w/m/35, 2377 Walworth, Apartment 217, Grand Prairie, Texas

Who, after being by me duly sworn, on oath deposes and says: My wife, Ruth, and I are separated. Sometime in May or June this year, I met Lee Oswald. I met him through my wife who knew him a little longer. Once, while I was at my wife's house, I saw a heavy pipe-like object wrapped in a rough blanket tied with string. This was in the garage. I picked this object up to get it out of the way of my power saw and thought it was tenting equipment. I don't recall exactly when this took place, but I think it was about the beginning of October. Since then I have moved this object a couple of times. The last time I saw Oswald was two weekends ago. I took Oswald to a meeting of American Civil Liberties Union once about the middle of October. On Friday, November 22, 1963, I was at work at Bell Helicopter, when I heard of the President's being shot. A short time later, I heard that the President was shot from the Texas School Book Depository Building. I knew that Lee Oswald worked there, and I immediately thought of him and wondered if he might have shot the President and wondered if I should call the F. B. I. I thought it unlikely that he shot the President, and that the F. B. I. was fully aware of his presence there, and I did not want to contribute to his harassment which would be likely to occur due to his known Marxist views.
XXXXXXXXXXXXXXXXXXXXXXXXXXXXXXXXXXXXXXXXXXXXXXXXXXXXXXXXXXXXXXXXXX

Michael R. Paine

SUBSCRIBED AND SWORN TO BEFORE ME THIS 23rd DAY OF November A.D. 1963

Angela M. Flowers
Notary Public, Dallas County, Texas ANGELA M. FLOWERS

CPS-GF-413

48

COMMISSION EXHIBIT NO. 2003—Continued

AFFIDAVIT IN ANY FACT

THE STATE OF TEXAS
COUNTY OF DALLAS

BEFORE ME, Patsy Collins

a Notary Public in and for said County, State of Texas, on this day personally appeared

Ruth Hyde Payne/ w/f/31, 2515 W. Fifth Street, Irving, Texas

Who, after being by me duly sworn, on oath deposes and says: I have lived at the above address for about 4 years. My husband, Michael and I had been separated for about a year. In the early winter of 1963, I went to a party in Dallas because I heard that some people would be there that spoke Russian. I was interested in the language. At that party I met Lee Oswald and his Russian wife Marina. About a month later I went to visit them on Neely Street. In May I asked her to stay with me because Lee went to New Orleans to look for work. About two weeks later I took Marina to New Orleans to join her husband. Around the end of September I stopped by to see them while I was on vacation. I brought Marina back with me to Irving. He came in 2 weeks,later, but did not stay with his wife and me. Marina's husband would come and spend most of the weekends with his wife. Through my neighbor, we heard there was an opening at the Texas School Book Depository. Lee Applied and was accepted. Lee did not spend last weekend there. He came in about 5 pm yesterday and spent the night. I was aslcep this morning when he left for work.XXXXXXXXXXXXXXXXXXXXXXXXXXXXXXXXXXXXXXXXXXXXXXXXXXXX

Ruth Hyde Paine

SUBSCRIBED AND SWORN TO BEFORE ME THIS 22 DAY OF November A.D. 1963

Patsy Collins
Notary Public, Dallas County, Texas

CPS-GF-413
jpa

49

COMMISSION EXHIBIT No. 2003—Continued

AFFIDAVIT IN ANY FACT

THE STATE OF TEXAS
COUNTY OF DALLAS

BEFORE ME, GEORGE F. SNYDER

a Notary Public in and for said County, State of Texas, on this day personally appeared Julia Postal,

w/f/39, 2728 Seevers, FR 6-5750.

Who, after being by me duly sworn, on oath deposes and says: I work at the Texas Theatre at 231 West Jefferson, WH 6-2161. I have worked there since November 24, 1952. On Friday, November 22, 1963, at approximately 1:30 PM or a little later I was working in the ticket office at the theater. I was listening to my transistor radio, and KLIF had just announced that President Kennedy was dead. I had just seen a police car go west on Jefferson. As the police went by, a man ducked inside the theater. My boss, Mr. John A. Callahan went outside, got in his car and left to see where the police were going. I stepped from the box office to the front and looked west. When I turned around, Johnny Brewer, Manager of Hardy's Shoes Store, was standing there. As I started back in the box office, Johnny asked me if I sold that man a ticket. I asked him what man. He said that man that just ducked in here. I told him no, I didn't, but I had noticed him as he ducked in here. I asked Johnny if he would go inside and see if he could see him. He went in and looked, then came out and said that he didn't see him. I told Johnny that he had to be in there, and that he was running from the Police for something. I then asked Johnny to prop the center door open so I could see the concession. Then I asked Johnny and Warren Burroughs, an usher, to go and look again real good and check the lounges as well. Then the two of them came back out, and Johnny said he just wasn't in there. Johnny said that he had heard a seat pop as if someone had gotten out of it, but didn't see anyone. I told him that I was going to call the Police and asked him and Warren to check the two exits to see if they had been opened and if not, to stand by them. I called the Police Department, and some woman answered, and I told her that I wanted to talk to an officer about a suspect. She referred me to a man, and I told him that this is the Texas Theatre at 231 West Jefferson. I told him that I knew that you men are very busy, but that I have a man in the theater that is running from you for some reason. The officer asked me what made me think he was running from us. I told him when the police drove by, that the man ducked in. The officer asked me if the man bought a ticket, and I told him no, he did not. Then he asked me what made

(Continued next page)

Julia Postal

SUBSCRIBED AND SWORN TO BEFORE ME THIS ____ DAY OF ____ A.D. 196
278

Notary Public, Dallas County, Texas

CPS-GF-413

50

COMMISSION EXHIBIT No. 2003—Continued

Affidavit Continued - Julia Postal - Page 2

me so sure that he was in the theatre. I told him that I knew he was in there, because he couldn't have gone by me. I told him to call it woman's intuition, or whatever he liked, but that man is in the theater, and he's running from you people, for something. I told the officer that I had just heard officially that the President had been assassinated. I told him that I didn't know if this man had anything to do with it or not, but that he was running from something. The officer asked me if the man fit the description of the suspect. I told him that I didn't know because I hadn't heard the description of the suspect. I told the officer that I would describe the man to him, and that he could take it from there. After I gave the officer the description of the man in the theater, he said, "Thank you, we'll be right there". I then called the projectionist on the intercom and asked him if he could see anyone, and told him that I had called the police. He told me that he couldn't and asked if I wanted him to stop the picture. I told him, "No", just to let it go until they got here. In a minute or two the police were there. There were some motorcycle officers, some uniformed officers in squad cars, and some plain clothes officers. They all rushed in the theater carrying guns. Some had pistols and some had shotguns. I didn't see anything that went on inside the theater. In a matter of about 10 minutes, the officers came out with the man that I had called about. When the officers brought him out, he was still struggling with them. There was a lot of people out in the street and on the sidewalk. Someone asked me what was going on, and I said that it's just a suspect. The crowd of people moved in, trying to get to the man. The officers got the man in the car and left. About this time, some officer said, "I'm sure we've got the man that shot officer Tippit. This was the first I knew of an officer being shot. I asked him where Officer Tippit had gotten shot, and he said down on Tenth. Later on I found out that the man's name, who the officers arrested at the Texas Theater, was Lee Harvey Oswald.

Julia Postal

SUBSCRIBED AND SWORN TO BEFORE ME THIS 4th DAY OF December A.D. 1963

7:45 pm

George F. Snyder
Notary Public, Dallas County, Texas
GEORGE F. SNYDER

ELB

COMMISSION EXHIBIT No. 2003—Continued

VOLUNTARY STATEMENT Not Under Arrest. Form No. 86

(55)

SHERIFF'S DEPARTMENT
COUNTY OF DALLAS, TEXAS

Before me, the undersigned authority, on this the 22nd day of November A. D. 19 63

personally appeared Mr J.C. Price, Address 2602 Astor, Dallas

Age 62, Phone No. WH 1 1940 Bus. Terminal Annex, Gen. Service RI 8 5611 Ext 3105

Deposes and says:-

This day at about 1235 PM I was on the roof of the Termaniel Annex Bldg on the NE Corner when the prosidential Motorcade came down Main to Houston, North on Houston and then West on Elm. The cars had proceeded West on Elm and was just a short distance from the Tripple underpass, when I saw Gov. Connelly slump over. I did not see the president as his car had gotten out of my view under the underpass. There was a volley of shots, I think five and then much later, maybe as much as five minutes later another one. I saw one man run towards the passenger cars on the railroad siding after the volley of shots. This man had a white dress shirt, no tie and kahki colored trousers. His hair appeared to be long and dark and his agility running could be about 25 yrs of ago. He had something in his hand. I couldn't be sure but it may have been a head piece.XXXXXXXXXXXXXXXXXXXX

J.C. Price

Subscribed and sworn to before me on this the 23 day of Nov A.D. 19 63

Notary Public, Dallas County, Texas

COMMISSION EXHIBIT No. 2003—Continued

AFFIDAVIT IN ANY FACT

THE STATE OF TEXAS
COUNTY OF DALLAS

BEFORE ME, Patsy Collins

a Notary Public in and for said County, State of Texas, on this day personally appeared

~~Linnie Mae Randle, w/f/30, of 2439 West 5th Irving, Texas BL-3-8965~~

Who, after being by me duly sworn, on oath deposes and says: My brother Wesley Frazier lives with me. Wesley works at the Texas XX School book Depository at Elm and Houston Streets. A boy named Lee Oswald works with Wesley. I have seen this boy Lee a few times. His wife and his children lives with one of my neighbors, Mrs. Michael Paine, 2515 West 5th. His wifes name is Marina. I have met her twice. Lee usually rides home with Wesley on Friday evenings and stays the weekend with his wife and rides back on Monday mornings. Yesterday, Thursday, November 21, 1963, I was going to the store about 5:30 p.m. I saw Wesley letting this boy, Lee, out down at Mrs. Paine's house. I didn't see Lee again until this morning, Friday, November 22, 1963 about 7:10 or 7:15 a.m. I saw Lee walk up my driveway carrying a long brown package. I saw him put it in Wesley's car, then he walked back to the side of the house and stood and waited until Wesley came out about 7:25 a.m. They both left for work. Lee was bareheaded, wearing a light brown or tan shirt. I don't remember what kind of trousers he had on. My brother has a 1954 black four-door Chevrolet car that they went to work in.XX XXXXXXXXXXXXXXXXXXXXXXXXXXXXXXXXXXXXXXXXXXXXXXXXXXXXXXXXXXXXXXXXXXXXXXXXX

Mrs. Linnie Mae Randle

SUBSCRIBED AND SWORN TO BEFORE ME THIS 22ND DAY OF NOVEMBER A.D. 1963

Patsy Collins
Notary Public, Dallas County, Texas

CPS-GF-413

53

COMMISSION EXHIBIT No. 2003—Continued

AFFIDAVIT IN ANY FACT

THE STATE OF TEXAS
COUNTY OF DALLAS

BEFORE ME, Patsy Collins

a Notary Public in and for said County, State of Texas, on this day personally appeared

Mrs. R. A. Reid, 1914 Elmwood, FE-1-6617

Who, after being by me duly sworn, on oath deposes and says: I work for the Texas School Book Depository I have worked for them seven years, at 411 Elm Street.
Yesterday November 22, 1963 I was working, we took our lunch period from 12 to 1pm I went out side to watch the parade go by. I was standing on the front steps of our Building, as the parade drew near I walked closer to the street. Just after the President passed by I heard three shots. The first thing I thought of was someone was shooting at the President. I remarked to Mr. Campbell who was standing near by that I thought the shots had come from our building. But I heard someone else say no, I think it was farther down the street. I went back into our building and up to the second floor to our office, just after I entered the office I saw one of the men who work in the warehouse come through the back office door. This door is located near the lunch room and the rear stairway. I did not know this man's name at the time for he had not worked there long. However I now know his name to be Lee Oswald. I said to Lee, Oh! someone has shot at the President. I hope they didn't hit him. Lee mumbled something and walked on out of the office. I did not understand what he said, he had a coke in his hand. When I saw him he was dressed in a white T-shirt and I don't recall what his trousers was like. I did not see him anymore after that.XXXXXXXX XXXXXXXXX

Mrs. R. A. Reid

SUBSCRIBED AND SWORN TO BEFORE ME THIS 23 DAY OF November A.D. 1963

Patsy Collins
Notary Public, Dallas County, Texas

jrl
CPS-GF-413

54

COMMISSION EXHIBIT No. 2003—Continued

VOLUNTARY STATEMENT. Not Under Arrest. Form No. 86 (32)

SHERIFF'S DEPARTMENT
COUNTY OF DALLAS, TEXAS

Before me, the undersigned authority, on this the 22nd day of November A. D. 19 63 personally appeared Arnold Louis Rowland, Address 3026 Hemmerly St., Dallas, Texas
DOB 4-29-45 POB: Corpus Christi, Texas
Age____, Phone No. FE 7 1861
Deposes and says:-

I am a student at Adamson High School in Dallas, Texas. I am employed on weekends at the Pizza Inn located on West Davis Avenue in Dallas. At approximately 12:10PM today, my wife Barbara and I arrived in downtown Dallas and took position to see the President's motorcade. We took position at the west entrance of the Sheriff's Office on Houston Street. We stood there for a time talking about various things and were talking about the security measures that were being made for the president's visit in view of the recent trouble when Mr. Adalai Stevenson had been a recent visitor to Dallas. It must have been 5 or 10 minutes later when we were just looking at the surrounding buildings when I looked up at the Texas Book Depository building and noticed that the second floor from the top had two adjoining windows which were wide open, and upon looking I saw what I thought was a man standing back about 15 feet from the windows and was holding in his arms what appeared to be a hi powered rifle because it looked as though it had a scope on it. He appeared to be holding this at a parade rest sort of position. I mentioned this to my wife and merely made the remark that it must be the secret service man. This man appeared to be a white man and appeared to have a light colored shirt on, open at the neck. He appeared to be of slender build and appeared to have dark hair. In about 15 minutes President Kennedy passed the spot where we were standing and the motorcade had just turned west on Elm heading down the hill when I heard a noise which I thought to be a back fire. In fact some of the people around laughed and then in about 8 seconds I heard another report and in about 3 seconds a third report. My wife, who had ahold, of my hand, started running and dragging me across the street and I never did look up again at this window.

This statement is true and correct to the best of my knowledge and belief.

Arnold L. Rowland

Subscribed and sworn to before me on this the 22nd day of November A. D. 19 63
Rosemary Allen
Notary Public, Dallas County, Texas

55

COMMISSION EXHIBIT No. 2003—Continued

VOLUNTARY STATEMENT. Not Under Arrest. Form No. 86 (49)

SHERIFF'S DEPARTMENT
COUNTY OF DALLAS, TEXAS

Before me, the undersigned authority, on this the 22nd day of November A. D. 19 63 personally appeared Barbara Walker Rowland, Address 3026 Hemmerly St., Dallas, Texas
DOB: 4-5-46
Age 17, Phone No. FE 7 1861
POB: Grand Prairie, Texas
Deposes and says:-

My husband, Arnold Rowland and I came to downtown Dallas today at approximately 12:10PM to see the President in the motorcade. We are both students at Adamson High School, but my husband has been ill and neither of us went to school today in order to see the President. We had taken a position at the side entrance of the Sheriff's Office on Houston Street and were standing there talking. We talked about security measures for the President and had talked about the recent affair with Mr. Stevenson. Arnold told me to look up at the building which was the Texas Book Depository at two adjoining open windows, that there was a man up there holding a rifle and he must be a secret service man. I looked up and Arnold told me he had moved back, but I didn't see anything because I am very nearsighted and I didn't have my glasses on. We didn't think anything more of this and in about 15 minutes the President passed where we were standing and turned left onto Elm Street and started down towards the unerpass when I heard a report and thought it was a backfire then in a few seconds another report sounded and in another few seconds the third report. We started running towards Elm Street and that is all I know.

Mrs. Barbara Rowland.

Subscribed and sworn to before me on this the 22nd day of November A. D. 19 63
Rosemary Allen
Notary Public, Dallas County, Texas

56

COMMISSION EXHIBIT No. 2003—Continued

AFFIDAVIT IN ANY FACT

THE STATE OF TEXAS
COUNTY OF DALLAS

BEFORE ME, PATSY COLLINS

a Notary Public in and for said County, State of Texas, on this day personally appeared W. W. Scoggins

3138 Alaska, FR 4-2955, Business: WH 2-6203

Who, after being by me duly sworn, on oath deposes and says: I am a driver for Oak Cliff Cab Company. Friday, November 22, 1963 at approximately 1:00 p.m., I discharged a passenger at 321 North Ewing. I then drove my cab to the Gentlemen's Club at 125 South Patton to get a cold drink to go with my lunch. I could not find a parking place in front of the club, so I drove to Tenth Street. I parked on Patton at Tenth headed north and walked back to the club to get thecold drink. I watched tv a little while then went back to my cab to eat my lunch. About the time I started to eat my lunch I saw a Police car going east on Tenth. The Police stopped on Tenth just east of Patton . The officer got out of his car and evidently said something to a manwho was walking west on Tenth. When the Policeman spoke to him, the man stopped. The next thing that attracted my attention was a gun firing. I heard three or four shots, and I saw smoke near the squad car. The officer fell beside the squad car on the driver's side and the man the officer was talking to started running. He ran west on Tenth to Patton then south on Patton to Jefferson. After the man passed my cab, I picked up my mike and reported the shooting to my dispatcher. He asked if I needed an ambulance and I said "yes." Very shortly an ambulance arrived. I do not know the man that shot the officer, but I would recognize him if I saw him again. When the man ran past my cab, he had a pistol in his left hand. I heard him mumble something like "pore dumb cop" or "pore damn cop" twice as he went past. Another man ran up to me. He had a gun in his hand, I thought he was a Policeman, and said let's see if we can find him. This man got into the cab with me and we circled around several blocks but did not see this man who shot the officer.XXXXX XXXXXXXXXXXXXXXXXXXXXXXXXXXXXXXXXXXXXXXXXXXXXXXXXXXXXXXXXXXXXX XXXXXXXXXX

XX
XXX
X
X XXXXXXXXXXXXXXXXXX W. W. Scoggins

SUBSCRIBED AND SWORN TO BEFORE ME THIS 23 DAY OF November A.D. 1963.

Patsy Collins
Notary Public, Dallas County, Texas

CPS-GF-413

57

COMMISSION EXHIBIT No. 2003—Continued

AFFIDAVIT IN ANY FACT

THE STATE OF TEXAS
COUNTY OF DALLAS

BEFORE ME, William F. Alexander

a Notary Public in and for said County, State of Texas, on this day personally appeared

George Senator, w/m/50, 223 So. Ewing, Apt. 207, WH 1 5601, 3616 Cedar Springs, no business phone.

Who, after being by me duly sworn, on oath deposes and says:
I have known Jack Ruby about 8 years. I first lived with Jack in 1962 for 5 or 6 months at the Marsalis Pl. or Arms apartments. I have lived with Jack this time since November of 1963. Early last saturday morning about 3:00 AM Jack woke me up. We discussed about President Kennedy being killed. Jack told me that he had been one of the first ones to run a ad in the paper stating his club would be closed Friday, Saturday and Sunday in memory of the President. Jack said it would hurt him money wise but he just could'nt open up with the President dead. I could tell Jack was taking the President's death hard and he kept repeating he felt sorry for the President's family. Jack was too sad to go to bed and he ask me to go out and have coffee with him. We went to the Southland hotel for coffee and I had some coffee and Jack had some grapefruit juice. He acted like he was stunned and shocked and we went on home. That was the first time I ever saw tears in his eyes. I got out of bed saturday morning and woke Jack up about 10:00 or 10:30 AM. We wat hed TV and had coffee. He was still sad and very sorry for the President's family. I had some things to do so I left the house around noon. I went back home about 7:30 PM and Jack was'nt there. I ate a bit and went back out. I got back home about 10:30 saturday evening and Jack was home. Jack told me he had to go to the club and check up on something. I went on to bed. When I got up this morning about 9:00 AM Jack was sleeping. Jack heard me walking around and he got up. I could tell Jack was brooding and still check up. We watched a church sermon on T. V. and Jack kept repeating about the President's family and how sorry he felt for Mrs Kennedy. Around 10:30 AM he told me he was going to take Sheba, his dog down to the club where the rest of his dogs were. Jack then left and I did'nt see him any more. I went down to the Eatwell on Main street and had some coffee. While I was at the Eatwell I heard Jack Ruby had shot Oswald. I have seen Jack's pistol and the last time I saw it was Thursday night. XXXXXXXXXXXXXXXXXXXXXXXXXXXXXXXXXXXXXXXXXXXXXXXXXXXXXXXXXXXXX XXXXXX

George Senator

SUBSCRIBED AND SWORN TO BEFORE ME THIS 24th DAY OF November A.D. 1963

William F. Alexander
Notary Public, Dallas County, Texas

CPS-GF-413

58

COMMISSION EXHIBIT No. 2003—Continued

AFFIDAVIT IN ANY FACT

THE STATE OF TEXAS
COUNTY OF DALLAS

BEFORE ME, Mary Rattan

a Notary Public in and for said County, State of Texas, on this day personally appeared

William H. Shelley w/m/37 of 126 S. Tatum, FE7 1969. Bus: 411 Elm, RI7 3521

Who, after being by me duly sworn, on oath deposes and says: Today approximately 12:30 pm November 22, 1963 I was standing on the front steps at 411 Elm watching the President in the parade. The President's car was about half way from Houston Street to the Triple Underpass when I heard what sounded like three shots. I couldn't tell where they were coming from. I ran across the street to the corner of the park and ran into a girl crying and she said the President had been shot. This girl's name is Gloria Calvery who is an employee of this same building. I went back to the building and went inside and called my wife and told her what happened. I was on the first floor then and I stayed at the elevator and was told not to let anyone out of the elevator. I left the elevator and went with the police on up to the other floors. I left Jack Dougherty in charge of the elevator.

William H. Shelley

SUBSCRIBED AND SWORN TO BEFORE ME THIS 22 DAY OF November A.D. 1963

Mary Rattan Mary Rattan
Notary Public, Dallas County, Texas

CPS-GF-413

59

Commission Exhibit No. 2003—Continued

AFFIDAVIT IN ANY FACT

THE STATE OF TEXAS
COUNTY OF DALLAS

BEFORE ME, Patsy Collins

a Notary Public in and for said County, State of Texas, on this day personally appeared

William H. Sholley, w/m/37 of 126 S. Tatum, FE-7-1969. Bus 411 Elm, RI-7-3521

Who, after being by me duly sworn, on oath deposes and says: Approximately October 10th or 12th, 1963 a man by the name of Lee Oswald w/m/21, came to work wher I do. I was put in charge of him by Mr. Truly to show him what to do. I have been working close with this man since he has been there. This man stayed by him-self most of the time, and would go for a walk at noon time. Lee would bring his lunch and usually eat with us in the lounge and read the paper. He would usually read about politics. Today I arrived for work about 8 am and went about my usual duties. Lee was already filling some orders just outside my office. I saw him periodically all morning with the exception of when we were on the sixth floor. At noon I started eating my lunch in my office and I went outside to see the President. W.S. ~~XX~~ After the Presidents accident, I started checking around and I ~~XX~~ missed Lee. I ask Mr. Truly about him and He told me he had not seen him. I didn't see Lee until the Police brought him in to the Police Homicide Bureau. XXXXXXXXXXXXXXXX

William H. Shelley

SUBSCRIBED AND SWORN TO BEFORE ME THIS 22 DAY OF November A.D. 1963

Patsy Collins
Notary Public, Dallas County, Texas

CPS-GF-413

60

Commission Exhibit No. 2003—Continued

VOLUNTARY STATEMENT Under Arrest. Form No. 86

(54)

SHERIFF'S DEPARTMENT
COUNTY OF DALLAS, TEXAS

Before me, the undersigned authority, on this the 22 day of November A. D. 19 63

personally appeared ~~Royce Glenn Rak Skelton~~, Address ~~2509 Reagan~~ La 1 2745

Age 23, Phone No. NA Bus. address 215 Union Terminal Ri 1 1396

Deposes and says:-

I was standing on top of the train trestle where it crosses Elm Street with Austin Miller. We saw the motorcade come around the corner and I heard something which I thought was fireworks. I saw something hit the pavement at the left rear of the car, then the car got in the right hand lane and I heard two more shots. I hedd a [hear] woman sa "Oh no" or something and grab a man inside the car. I then heard another shot and saw the bullet hit the pavement. The concrete was knocked to the South away from the car. ~~xxx~~ It hit the pavement in the left or middle lane. I then went down to my car radio to see if I could find out what happened. After I came back up, a policeman askedme if I had seen anything and brought me to the Sheriff's Office.

R L Skelton

Subscribed and sworn to before me on this the 22 day of November A. D. 19 63

[signature]

Notary Public, Dallas County, Texas

61

COMMISSION EXHIBIT No. 2003—Continued

AFFIDAVIT IN ANY FACT

THE STATE OF TEXAS
COUNTY OF DALLAS

BEFORE ME, Mary Rattan

a Notary Public in and for said County, State of Texas, on this day personally appeared

Roy S. Truly, 4932 Jade Dr., FR6 9893

Who, after being by me duly sworn, on oath deposes and says: I am superintendent of the Texas School Book Depository, 411 Elm Street in Dallas, Texas. I was working in that capacity yesterday Friday November 22, 1963. I have 19 employees in the plant. Lee Harvey Oswald was one of these employees. We considered him a temporary employee. We work a lot of extra employees during the summer and fall. RST Mr. O. V. Campbell, one of the owners, and I started to lunch a few minutes after twelve o'clock. We saw that the parade was nearly down to us, so we stopped and watched the President go by. After the President passed, we heard what sounded like an explosion. I heard three such explosions. Then I realized that they must have been shots. I saw an officer break t through the crowd and go into our building. I realized he did not know anything about the building, so I ran in with him. The officer and I went through the shipping department to the freight elevator. We then started up the stairway. We hit the second floor landing, the officer stuck his head into the lunch room area where there are coke and candy machines. Lee Oswald was in there. The officer had his gun on Oswald and asked me if he was an employee. I answered yes. We then went up the stairs to the 5th floor where we found the elevator open. We took the elevator to the 7th floor and out on the roof. We searched the roof and a small room, also checked the landings. We could look out over the tracks and street below. We did not find anything. We started down on the elevator. The officer took a hurried look on a couple floors on the way down. We then met some other officers on the 4th floor searching the building. I overheard someone say that the shot came from the window of our building. By that time there was several people in the building. Some fifteen minutes later I was checking our employees, and I did not find Lee. I asked Mr. Shelley if he had seen Lee. He said no. I then contacted Chief Lumpkin and ~~XX~~ told him Lee was missing. Then both of us went up on the sixth floor where Captain Fritz was and I told Captain Fritz about Lee being missing and where he lived. I did not see Lee Oswald any more. We don't run a thorough check on our temporary employees. They fill out an application form. In Lee Oswald's case, a lady from Irving called and said a neighbor had a brother working for me, and he had said we could use some more help. This woman said she knew a nice young boy

R S Truly

SUBSCRIBED AND SWORN TO BEFORE ME THIS 23 DAY OF November A.D. 1963

Mary Rattan Mary Rattan
Notary Public, Dallas County, Texas

CPS-GF-413
JRL

62

COMMISSION EXHIBIT No. 2003—Continued

AFFIDAVIT IN ANY FACT

THE STATE OF TEXAS
COUNTY OF DALLAS

BEFORE ME, Mary Rattan

a Notary Public in and for said County, State of Texas, on this day personally appeared

Seymour Weitzman w/m, 2802 Oates Drive, DA7 6624. Bus. Robie Love, RI1 1483

Who, after being by me duly sworn, on oath deposes and says: Yesterday November 22, 1963 I was standing on the corner of Main and Houston, and as the President passed and made his turn going west towards Stemmons, I walked casually around. At this time my partner was behind me and asked me something. I looked back at him and heard 3 shots. I ran in a northwest direction and scaled a fence towards where we thought the shots came from. Then someone said they thought the shots came from the old Texas Building. I immediately ran to the Texas Building and started looking inside. At this time Captain Fritz arrived and ordered all of the sixth floor sealed off and searched. I was working with Deputy S. Boone of the Sheriff's Department and helping in the search. We were in the northwest corner of the sixth floor when Deputy Boone and myself spotted the rifle about the same time. This rifle was a 7.65 Mauser bolt action equipped with a 4/18 scope, a thick leather brownish-black sling on it. The rifle was between some boxes near the stairway. The time the rifle was found was 1:22 pm. Captain Fritz took charge of the rifle and ejected one live round from the chamber. I then went back to the office after this.

Seymour Weitzman

SUBSCRIBED AND SWORN TO BEFORE ME THIS 23 DAY OF November A.D. 1963

Mary Rattan Mary Rattan
Notary Public, Dallas County, Texas

CPS-GF-413

63

COMMISSION EXHIBIT No. 2003—Continued

AFFIDAVIT IN ANY FACT

THE STATE OF TEXAS
COUNTY OF DALLAS

BEFORE ME, Patsy Collins

a Notary Public in and for said County, State of Texas, on this day personally appeared

William Wayne Whaley, 619 Pine Street, Lewisville 2, Texas, Bus 610 S. Akard
Bus phone RI-2-9191

Who, after being by me duly sworn, on oath deposes and says: Yesterday 11-22-63 I was sitting at Lamar and Jackson at the Greyhound Bus Station at 12:30 pm waiting for a fare. This boy walked up to the cab, he was walking South on Lamar from Commerce, he asked if he could get a cab, I told him, yes, and I opened the back door. He shut the back door and said he wanted to sit in the front. The boy said he wanted to go to the 500 Block of North Beckley. After we had gotten into the cab and I had turned my meter on, a lady came up to the cab and ask if she could get this cab. As i recall I said there will be one behind me very soon. I am not sure whether the man passenger repeated this to her or not, but I think he may have. I then drove away. I ask him what all of the sirens were about and he didn't say anything so I didn't say anymore to him. I turned right on Jackson and traveled to Austin Street where I turned left and traveled Austin to Wood Street where I turned right on Wood Street. I traveled Wood Street to Houston Stre t turned left went over the viaduct to Zangs Blvd. and traveled Zangs to Beckley and turned lef t and traveled on Beckley until I reached the 500 Block of North Beckley. When I got in the 500 Block of North Beckley he said this will do and I stopped The fare was 95 cents and he gave me a dollar and told me to keep the change. The boy got out of the cab and walked in front of the cab at an angle south on Beckley Street. This boy was small, five feet eight inches, slender had on a dark shirt with white spots of something on it. He had a braclet on his left wrist. He looked like he was 25 or 26 years old. At approximately 2:15 pm this afternoon I viewed a line up of 4 men in this City Hall. The number 3 man who I now know as Lee Harvey Oswald was the man who I carried from the Greyhound Bus Station to the 500 block of North Beckley.XXXXXXXXXX XXX

William Wayne Whaley

SUBSCRIBED AND SWORN TO BEFORE ME THIS 23 DAY OF November A.D. 1963

Patsy Collins Patsy Collins
Notary Public, Dallas County, Texas

CPS-GF-413

64

COMMISSION EXHIBIT No. 2003—Continued

AFFIDAVIT IN ANY FACT

THE STATE OF TEXAS
COUNTY OF DALLAS

BEFORE ME, Patsy Collins

a Notary Public in and for said County, State of Texas, on this day personally appeared Bonnie Ray Williams

1502 Avenue B. Apartment B, Bus. 411 Elm

Who, after being by me duly sworn, on oath deposes and says: I went to work at 8 am this morning. I worked on the 6th floor today with Mr. Bill Danny, Charles and a Billy Lovelady. Charles was outside and couldn't get back in, so I guess he went home. We worked up until about 10 minutes to 12. Then we went downstairs. We rode the elevator to the 1st floor and got our lunches. I went back on the 5th floor with a fellow called Hank and Junior, I don't know his last name. Just after we got on the 5th floor we saw the President coming around the corner on Houston from Main Street. I heard 2 shots it sounded like they came from just above us. We ran to the west side of the building. We didn't see anybody. We looked down and saw people running and hollering. We stayed there and in a little while some officers came up. They left and then we took the elevator to the 4th floor. We stayed there awhile and then went on out. Lee Oswald was there when I got to work this morning at 8 am. He fills orders and goes all over the building. I didn't see Oswald anymore, that I remember, after I saw him at 8 am. I recognized him just a few minutes ago when the officers brought him in the office. Oswald has been working at the Texas School Book Depository for about 6 weeks.XXXXXXXXXXX

Bonnie Ray Williams

SUBSCRIBED AND SWORN TO BEFORE ME THIS 22 DAY OF November A.D. 1963

Patsy Collins
Notary Public, Dallas County, Texas

CPS-GF-413

65

COMMISSION EXHIBIT No. 2003—Continued

VOLUNTARY STATEMENT Not Under Arrest. Form No. 86 (33)

SHERIFF'S DEPARTMENT
COUNTY OF DALLAS, TEXAS

Before me, the undersigned authority, on this the 22 day of ~~November~~ A. D. 1963

personally appeared ~~Jesse James Williams~~, Address ~~1211 Columbia Drive~~ Longview, Texas; or 1103 Allen St., Apt.114, Irving, Texas.

Age 40, Phone No. PL 3 7036 Longview

Deposes and says:

Last Tuesday evening at approximately 12:15 AM (Wednesday morning), a lady friend and myselfjxx we had made an acquaintance, of a man who invited us to his Motel for some after hours drinking (after 12 at night). I don't have his name but I have the license number of the car he was driving. I left my car at the parking lotx near the Baker Hotel, in Dallas, and we proceeded to his motel, a large kitchenette motel, as you go across the Houston street xxxxxxx viaduct it is the first motel on the right, it's a big white motel, not too modern, I don't know the name of it. After the three of us got to his motel, where he was previously registered, we had a few drinks in his room. He proceeded to entexxx tain us with a mandolin and seemed to be pretty good with it. We had been there about 30 minutes, as well as I remember. About this time this fellow began to make indecent remarks to the woman, to the effect that he wanted her to get in bed with him. We had all been drinking, I was fairly well polluted, more so than the others but still had my mental and reasoning powers. At this point I objected to his language and overtures and we became involved in an argument of words. Something came up to the effect that he mxx must be a queer or something. Then he tells me to get the hell out of there and if there's not going to be a party get the hell out of the place, I believe is the way he said it; and as I turned to walk toward the door and told the woman with me let's go, he pulled a rifle out of the closet, and put a round into the chamber, pointed it at me, and said: "Leave "... in so many words that's what it amounted to . As the woman and I got to the door he said, "I should make you strip and let me see your beautiful body." With that we walked out the door. He left the rifle inside the room and came outside and told us to get into the car and he would take us back to our car. Whenn we got back to the parking lot where we had previously left xxxxxxx my car, after some more conversation to the effect that I didn't appreciate what he had done and this and that, then he pulls a pistol -- I don't know where it came from, whether from his pocket or from the seat of the car on the left. He had the pistol in his lefthand. We were still in his car just as we were about to get out. And he said to sit still. And the woman put her hand on the barrel of the gun and told him to point it the other way, she was scared. I said to her, "Let's go." And opened the c ar door. We got out of the car and walked over to our car, which was about six feet away from his at the time. As he drove off in his car, the woman and I both got the xxxxxx license number on his car, and we each repeated it aloud to each other, I continued to repeat the number until we got in my car and the woman wrote the number down on the back of a check book that was laying on the dash of my car. (continued next page).

Subscribed and sworn to before me on this the ______ day of ______ A. D. 19 ___

J. J. W.

Notary Public, Dallas County, Texas

66

COMMISSION EXHIBIT No. 2003—Continued

VOLUNTARY STATEMENT. Not Under Arrest. Form No. 88 (34)

Page #2

SHERIFF'S DEPARTMENT
COUNTY OF DALLAS, TEXAS

Before me, the undersigned authority, on this the ______ day of ______ A. D. 19____

personally appeared Jesse James Williams, Address ______

Age______, Phone No. ______

Deposes and says:-

Page #2.

That was the last I saw of him. This man, to the best of my recollection, was approximately five foot eight inches tall, weighing approximately 175 pounds; with dark hair; normal complexion; approximately 30 years old. He didn't appear to be a learned person, that is too well educated, and did not appear to be ignorant by any means.

The woman friend says that he had real wavy black hair and was in her opinion about five foot ten, and would weigh about 165, and about 30 years old.

The best I can describe the rifle, it appeared to be well kept, a deer rifle or something, I don't know too much about guns; it I know it was not a .22; I know that it was a larger caliber gun, perhaps in my judgment a 303 caliber...that would be my guess what it would be. It had a chrome appearance about it somewhere.

I heard him cock the pistol as he told us to sit still, and I got a very dim look at the gun, it seemed a long barrel like a police officer normally carries.

We both agreed it was a light green car, a new model somewhat on the smaller side, about like the appearance of a Chevy II. She says it was an extremely light green. The License Number on the car was EX--- CD 1583 Texas.

After the tragic incidents that have occurred in Dallas this date, upon hearing about the killing of the police officer I thought about the incidents related above about the man with the rifle in the car, and for these reasons I decided to give the information contained herein to the proper authorities for whatever value it may have.

Jesse James Williams

Subscribed and sworn to before me on this the 22 day of November A. D. 19 63

James J. Mulcahy
Notary Public, Dallas County, Texas

67

AFFIDAVIT IN ANY FACT

THE STATE OF TEXAS
COUNTY OF DALLAS

BEFORE ME, GEORGE F. SNYDER

a Notary Public in and for said County, State of Texas, on this day personally appeared

Billy Joe Willis w/m/34 6922 Forney Road EV1 3965

Who, after being by me duly sworn, on oath deposes and says: I have known Jack Ruby for about 12 years. I believe his true name is Jack Rubinsky. I started to work for Jack in October of 1961 as a drummer in the Carousel Club. I last saw Jack about 2:00 AM, Friday morning. About 5:00 PM Friday I talked to Jack by phone and he told me that the club would be closed Friday night. I asked him when he would be open again and he said it may be as late as Monday. I told him what a terrible tragic thing that had happened to the President. He said that this was the most horrible thing that had ever happened and began crying. Jack said the man must have been a nut or a louse and said "How could any man do such a thing." Then he hung up. I was amazed at how hard he was taking the death of the President and I told my girl friend, Joan McCline, that I couldn't understand Jack being so torn up about it. I tried to call Jack again Saturday, but didn't get an answer. I haven't talked to him or saw him since. Today about 11:30 AM I was home in bed asleep and the phone rang and woke me up. My father R.L. Willis was in the next room. I got up and answered the phone and it was my girl friend Joan McClure at 6203 Bordeaux, FL2 7312. She told me that she had heard on the news that Jack Ruby had shot and killed this man Oswald. I tried to get in touch with Lt Gilmore as he knew I worked for Jack and might want to get in touch with me. He wasn't in so I talked to Lt Cornwall. He took my phone number so I told him I would just come on down. I drove my 1954 Pontiac to the police station. I came alone.

Billy Joe Willis

SUBSCRIBED AND SWORN TO BEFORE ME THIS 24th DAY OF November A.D. 1963
2:27 pm

George F. Snyder
Notary Public, Dallas County, Texas
GEORGE F. SNYDER

CPS-GF-413

68

COMMISSION EXHIBIT No. 2003—Continued

AFFIDAVIT IN ANY FACT

THE STATE OF TEXAS
COUNTY OF DALLAS

BEFORE ME, Mary Rattan

a Notary Public in and for said County, State of Texas, on this day personally appeared James Richard Worrell, Jr., w/m/20 of 13510 Winterhaven, CH7 2378. Thomas Jefferson High

Who, after being by me duly sworn, on oath deposes and says: Yesterday afternoon at approximately 12:30 pm I was standing on the sidewalk against a building on the corner of Elm and Houston Streets watching the motor cade of the President. I heard loud noise like a fire cracker or gun shots. I look around to see where the noise came from. I looked up and saw the barrel of a rifle sticking out of a window over my head about 5 or 6 stories up. While I was looking at the gun it was fired again. I looked back at Mr. Kennedy and he was slumping over. I got scared and ran from the location. While I was running I heard the gun fire two more times. I ran from Elm Street to Pacific Street on Houston. When I was about 100 yards from the building I stopped to get my breath and looked back at the building. I saw a w/m, 5'8" to 5'10", dark hair, average weight for height, dark shirt or jacket open down front, no hat, didn't have anything in hands, come out of the building and run in the opposite direction from me. I then caught a bus to my home. James Richard Worrell Jr.

SUBSCRIBED AND SWORN TO BEFORE ME THIS 23 DAY OF November A.D. 1963

Mary Rattan Mary Rattan
Notary Public, Dallas County, Texas

CPS-GF-413

69

COMMISSION EXHIBIT No. 2003—Continued

First: JACK; Middle: EBRX (struck); Last name: RUBY; R-S-Age: WM47; 59- 65906
Home address: 4727 Homer; Date of birth: 3 25 12; Occupation:
Address where arrested: 3508 Oak Lawn; Business address:
Arresting officers: P M PARKS 1215 V D MONAGHEN 801
Date: 6 59; Time (A.M.): 2:30a; Division: SSB
Desk officer: wisseman; Clerk: mc; Station: dt; View: x
Charged when booked: PERMITTING DANCING AFTER HOURS
Bailed: Dismissed 7-8-59
Released by (not charged) date – time: 6 21 59 3a; Amt.: $25; Bond No.: 83009; X X 8 X 8

FORM 12-39 — 54 No. 54814
First name: JACK; Middle name: LEON; Last name: RUBY; Age: 43; Sex: M; Race: W; Occ.: Tavern O
Address: 1719 1/2 S Ervay
Arresting officers: E EEarlson 774, D IBlankenship 633
Place of arrest: 1717 S Ervay
Date: 12-5-54; Time: 1:30A
C V P
Chg. when booked: Inv Vio St Liq Law
Court No.: CCC#3 1789C+1686C; Court disposition: Dismissed 2-8-55

First: JACK; Middle: RUBY; R-S-Age: WM41; 30069
Home address: 3929 Rawlins; Date of birth: 3-25-21
Address where arrested: City Hall
Arresting officers: J B Toney 773
Date: 2-12-63; Time (P.M.): 11:00 P; Division: R; Platoon: 3; District: 102
Desk officer: Warren; Clerk: re; Station: dt; View: x
Charged when booked: Simple Assault
Bailed: Ticket No. 5 22603 (Not Guilty) 2-27-63

First: JACK; Middle: L.; Last name: RUBY; R-S-Age: WM51; 63- 37112
Home address: 3929 Rawlins; Date of birth: 3-25-21
Address where arrested: 106 S. Harwood
Arresting officers: B.J. HOLLOWAY 224
Date: 3-14-63; Time (A.M.): 10:25; Division: W; Platoon: 2; District: 102
Desk officer: WWW; Clerk: mcf; Station: dt; View: x
Bailed: Alias-Ticket-240404
Released by (not charged): Relto appear 3-14-63; Cash: X; Amt.: $35.00; Bond No.: 21004

First: Jack; Middle: Leon; Last name: Ruby; R-S-Age: WM49; 60- 76407
Home address: 4727 Homer; Date of birth: 3-25-11; Occupation: Dance Hall
Address where arrested: 3508 Oak Lawn
Arresting officers: B J Gee 832 G R Johnston 1259
Date: 8-21-60; Time (A.M.): 2:20 A; Division: BSB; Platoon: 1; District: 26
Desk officer: Gassett; Clerk: re; Station: dt; View: X
Charged when booked: Vio. Dance Hall Ord. # 1156
Bailed: $25 Bond

73

COMMISSION EXHIBIT No. 2003—Continued

ARRAIGNMENT OF OSWALD
for J. D. Tippit's murder

11-22-63 at 7:10 pm

Judge Johnston-magistrate

Wm. Alexander of the District Attorney's office accepted signed complaint from

Captain Fritz. R. M. Sims, E. L. Boyd and M. G. Hall were present.

ARRAIGNMENT OF OSWALD
for John F. Kennedy's murder
11-23-63 at approx. 1:35 am
Judge Dave Johnston-magistrate

Henry Wade and William Alexander of District Attorney's office accepted complaint

from Captain Fritz. Jim Allen present.

ARRAIGNMENT OF JACK RUBY
for Oswald's murder

11-24-63 3:05 PM

Judge Pierce McBride-magistrate

William Alexander of the District Attorney's office accepted complaint from

Captain Fritz. Detective G.F. Rose and Inspector Kelly of Secret Service present.

ARRESTING OFFICERS AND TIMES OF ARREST

ON OSWALD

11-22-63, 231 W. Jefferson

Arrested by: M. N. McDonald # 1180
T. A. Hutson # 1116
B. K. Carroll # 923
Ray Hawkins # 887

ON RUBY

11-24-63, Basement, City Police and Courts Building

Arrested by: L. C. Graves # 702
W. J. Harrison # 579

TIME OF ARREST

Oswald's arrest 1:40 pm 11-22-63

Ruby's arrest 11:21 am 11-24-63

OFFICERS PRESENT AT OSWALD'S ARREST AT 231 W. JEFFERSON (TEXAS THEATER)

BAGGETT, E. R., PAT. TRAFFIC

BARRETT, BOB F. B. I.

BENTLEY, PAUL L., DET. I. D. BUR.

BUHK, M. A., DET. FORGERY

CARROLL, BOB K., DET. SP. SER.

CUNNINGHAM, E. L., LT. FORGERY

HAWKINS, RAY, PAT. TRAFFIC

HILL, GERALD L., SGT. PERSONNEL

HUTSON, T. A., PAT. TRAFFIC

LYONS, K. E., PAT.,SP. SER.

MC DONALD, M. N., PAT. PATROL

STRINGER, H. H., SGT.,PERSONNEL

TAYLOR, E. E., SGT., PERSONNEL

TONEY, JOHN B., DET., FORGERY

WALKER, CHARLES T., PAT., TRAFFIC

WESTBROOK, W. R., CAPT., PERSONNEL

December 2, 1963

Mr. J. E. Curry
Chief of Police

Subject: Arrest of Lee Harvey Oswald

Sir:

On November 22, 1963, I was working Squad #211 with Officer Ray Hawkins. We had received information that a Police Officer had been shot in the 400 block East Tenth Street. We reported to the area with several other officers, and began a search for the suspect in the shooting.

The Dispatcher gave information that a person fitting the description of the suspect had entered the Texas Theater in the 400 block West Jefferson. We drove into the alley at the rear of the theater and Officer T. A. Hutson, who was riding with us, and Officer Hawkins, went inside the theater. I was in the alley with several other officers when this suspect was arrested.

Respectfully submitted,

E. R. Baggett
Patrolman, #1384
Traffic Division

ERB/jh
Copied: MR-12-5-63

76

COMMISSION EXHIBIT No. 2003—Continued

December 3, 1963

Mr. J. E. Curry
Chief of Police

Sir:

The following is a report on my part in the arrest of Lee Harvey Oswald on Friday, November 22,1963.

At 1:40 pm on November 22, 1963, Captain C. M. Doughty and Sgt. W. E. Barnes received a call to Tenth and Patton Streets regarding the shooting of Officer J. D. Tippit.

As they were preparing to leave the City Hall, I asked Captain Doughty if I could go with them and I was told that I could. We proceeded to the location and after we had been there about five (5) minutes a call came out that the shooting suspect was in the Texas Theater.

Captain Talbert was answering this call and he was alone, so I asked if I might go with him. As we proceeded to the Texas Theater the Dispatcher asked that the rear of the theater be covered. Captain Talbert let me out in the front and told me that he would cover the rear.

As I entered the theater, I was told by Det. John Toney that the suspect was in the balcony. I went to the balcony and searched the men and women's restrooms on my way up there. A patrolman was with me, but I did not know his name.

As I went into the balcony I asked the projectionist to turn on the house lights. When the lights were turned on I noticed several people up there. By this time there were several other patrolmen in the balcony, one was C. F. Bentley, Jr., whom I told to search all of the people in the balcony and get their names.

After this, I went back to the lower floor. Just as I entered the lower floor I saw Patrolman McDonald fighting with this suspect. I saw this suspect pull a pistol from his shirt, so I went to Patrolman McDonald's aid immediately.

77

COMMISSION EXHIBIT No. 2003—Continued

Paul L. Bentley-page 2

I grabbed the suspect by the neck and attempted to get his right arm. By this time other officers came to our assistance.

We subdued the suspect and placed handcuffs on him. I took hold of his belt behind his back, Sgt. Jerry Hill was on one side of him, Det. Bob Carroll was on the other side, and Patrolman C. E. Walker took hold of his belt in front. Det. Lyons also helped us get him to the car parked in front of the theater.

I got in the back seat and the suspect was put in next to me, and Patrolman Walker got in on his right. Det. Carroll, Sgt. Hill, and Det. Lyons were in the front seat, as we proceeded to the City Hall.

On the way to the City Hall I removed the suspect's wallet and obtained his name. He made several remarks enroute to the City Hall about police brutality and denied shooting anybody.

Sgt. Jerry Hill had the S&W 38 cal. pistol with six (6) shells in his possession on the way to the City Hall. This pistol was initialed by me and turned over to Lt. Baker and Captain Fritz by Sgt. Hill.

I turned his identification over to Lt. Baker. I then went to Captain Westbrook's Office to make a report of this arrest.

I then was told by Inspector Kockos to go to Baylor Hospital to receive treatment for the injured foot I received in making the arrest.

My foot was X-rayed at Baylor Hospital and I was told that I had pulled several ligaments in both sides of my right foot.

A cast was placed on my foot and leg and I was given a pair of crutches to use. I was told to report to Dr. Boswell on Tuesday, November 26, 1963 at 4:00 pm.

After an examination by Dr. Boswell, I was told that the cast would have to remain on the foot and leg until about December 20, 1963.

Respectfully submitted,

Paul L. Bentley
Detective of Police
Identification Bureau

Copied: MR-12-5-63

78

COMMISSION EXHIBIT No. 2003—Continued

December 3, 1963

Mr. J. E. Curry
Chief of Police

Subject: Arrest of Lee Harvey Oswald

Sir:

On November 22, 1963, I was on duty on the 4th floor at the Trade Mart on Stemmons and we received the information that the President had been shot. Captain Jones told me to go with Lt. Cunningham to the scene of the shooting and see what we could do. E. E. Taylor and J. B. Toney were with us. Enroute to the scene we heard the report of the officer being shot on Jefferson Boulevard in Oak Cliff and Lt. Cunningham decided we could do more good by going to that location immediately rather than by way of the scene of the President's shooting. We next heard the call regarding the suspect being in the Branch Library on Jefferson. We converged on that location and there were Secret Service men and other patrol and CID officers present when all the people were ordered out of the building. One of the Secret Service men stated the person who came out of the basement with the others was not the suspect and that he had already talked to him a few minutes previously. We then went back to the car and a call saying the suspect was going down an alley reloading a gun. We couldn't go west on Jefferson so we went over a couple block north to Tenth Street then to Tyler - north on Tyler to Davis - Davis to Llewellyn. We then heard a call that suspect was in balcony of the Texas Theatre. We went north on Llewellyn to Jefferson and Jefferson to Madison at the Texas Theatre. We parked in front of Ward's Drug Store and Lt. Cunningham told me to keep radio contact while he and the other two went to the theatre. They later brought a witness along from the theatre and we brought him to City Hall and Detective Toney later took an affidavit.

79

Marvin A. Buhk - Page 2

Respectfully,

O/S Marvin A. Buhk

Marvin A. Buhk
Detective 724
Forgery Bureau

MAB:ms

Copied by MM - 12-5-63

80

COMMISSION EXHIBIT No. 2003—Continued

December 4, 1963

Mr. J. E. Curry
Chief of Police

Subject: Arrest of Lee Harvey Oswald, w/m/24

Sir:

On November 22, 1963 Officer K.E. Lyon and myself were in the 300 block of East Jefferson assisting in the search for the person who shot and killed Officer J. D. Tippit.

We heard the police radio report that a suspect had entered the Texas Theatre. We went to this location Code 3. When we entered the theatre, we were told by a white female that the suspect was in the balcony.

We went to the balcony and searched it. While in the balcony, I heard someone shout that he was on the lower floor. We started down. Lyon slipped and sprained his ankle; I continued on down. When I arrived at the lower floor, Lee Harvey Oswald was resisting vigorously. Sgt. Jerry Hill, Officer M. N. McDonald, C. T. Walker, and Ray Hawkins and myself converged on Oswald. At this time I observed a pistol with the muzzle pointed in my direction. I grabbed the pistol and stuck it in my belt and then continued to assist in the subduing of Oswald. After Oswald was handcuffed we were instructed by Captain W.R. Westbrook to take him directly to the City Hall.

We removed Oswald from the theatre. When we were removing Oswald from the theatre, he was hollering that he had not resisted arrest and that he wanted to complain of police brutality. There was a crowd in front of the theatre yelling, "Kill the dirty 'Sob'." We put Oswald into police equipment #226 and drove directly to the City Hall. While enroute to the

81

COMMISSION EXHIBIT No. 2003—Continued

Bob K. Carroll-page 2

City Hall, I released the pistol to Sgt. Jerry Hill. The officers who brought Oswald to the City Hall were myself, Sergeant Jerry Hill, Detective Paul Bentley, K. E. Lyon, M. N. McDonald and C. T. Waker. Enroute to the City Hall, Oswald was belligerent and said very little except that why was he being arrested other than for having a pistol.

Upon arrival at the City Hall, Oswald was taken to the Homicide and Robbery Bureau Office and there released to officers of that bureau.

Respectfully submitted,

Bob K. Carroll, #923
Detective - Administrative Section
Special Service Bureau

Copied-MR
12-5-63

December 3, 1963

Mr. J. E. Curry
Chief of Police

Subject: Arrest of Lee Harvey Oswald

Sir:

On November 22, 1963, I was assigned to work at the Trade Mart where the President was scheduled to speak. When it was announced that the President had been shot, Captain O. A. Jones told me to take three men and report to the vicinity of the Court House.

Detective J. B. Toney, M. A. Buhk, E. E. Taylor and myself left the Trade Mart going south on Industrial Blvd. When we reached Oak Lawn Avenue, the police dispatcher requested all available squads to report to vicinity of East Jefferson and Tenth Street. I checked out to this location. Prior to arrival at Jefferson and Tenth, we received informa- that suspect was seen going into the Public Library at Marsalis and Jefferson. We checked this out and found it to be a false report. We continued to cruise in the area and were at Davis and Llewellyn when we received information that the suspect was seen running into the Texas Theatre. We went to the Texas Theatre. I instructed Detective Buhk to remain with the radio and Toney, Taylor and I went into the theatre. We were told that the suspect was in the balcony. We were questioning a young man who was sitting on the stairs in the balcony when the manager told us the suspect was on the first floor. When I reached the seating area on main floor, several officers were in the process of disarming and handcuffing the suspect. The suspect yelled "I know my rights, this is police brutality". I did not see anything that indicated that any more force was used than was absolutely necessary to effect the arrest.

E. L. Cunningham - Page 2

I told the uniform officers to take the suspect to the City Hall. The front door of the theatre was locked and Toney, Taylor and I searched the first floor and interviewed the occupants that were seated near where the suspect was arrested.

One of the witnesses who was seated near the scene of the arrest was brought to the City Hall, Room 315, where Detective Toney took an affidavit from him.

Respectfully,

O/S E. L. Cunningham

E. L. Cunningham
Lt. of Police
Forgery Bureau

ELC:ms

Copied by MM - 12-5-63

84

COMMISSION EXHIBIT No. 2003—Continued

December 2, 1963

Mr. J. E. Curry
Chief of Police

Subject: Arrest of Lee Harvey Oswald

Sir:

On November 22, 1963, I was working Squad #211 with Officer E. R. Baggett. We have received information that an officer had been shot in the 400 Block East Tenth Street. We reported to the area, and began a search with several other officers for the suspect in the shooting.

The Dispatcher gave information that a person fitting the description of the suspect had entered the Texas Theater in the 400 block W. Jefferson. I drove up the alley to the rear of the theater and Officer T. A. Hutson, who had started riding with us during the search, went to the exit door of the theater. There was a white male at the door who said that he was the manager of the shoe store next door, and that he had seen the person inside the theater.

Offiers C. T. Walker, M. N. McDonald, and Officer Hutson had entered the theater and I walked in with the person who said he had seen the suspect. He pointed to a white male sitting in the rear of the center section, and at this time I jumped off the stage and started toward the person. I was walking up the north aisle when Officer McDonald, who had walked up the south aisle, approached the person in question. The subject stood up and as Officer McDonald started to search him, he struck Officer McDonald in the face. The subject and Officer McDonald began to fight and both fell down in the seats.

Officer Walker and I ran toward the subject and grabbed him by his left arm. The subject had reached in his belt for a gun, and Officer McDonald

85

COMMISSION EXHIBIT No. 2003—Continued

was holding his right hand with the gun in it. Officer Hutson had entered the row behind the suspect, and grabbed him around the neck and held him up. Sergeant G. L. Hill then took the gun.

I got my handcuffs out and placed the cuff on his left wrist first, and then the other officers pulled his right arm behind him, and I placed the right cuff on this wrist.

The suspect was then walked out the north end of the aisle. Officer Walker and Detective Bentley and Sergeant Hill, along with other officers, took the subject to a plain car in front of the theater and he was placed in this car and brought to the City Hall.

Respectfully,

O/S Ray Hawkins

Ray Hawkins
Patrolman, #887
Traffic Division

RH/jh

Copied by MM - 12-5-63

December 5, 1963

Mr. J. E. Curry
Chief of Police

Subject: Arrest of Lee Harvey Oswald

Sir:

At approximately 1:55 pm Friday, November 22, 1963, I was in the vicinity of the Texas Theater in the Oak Cliff section of Dallas, looking for the suspect in the slaying of Officer J. D. Tippit.

By police radio, I received information the suspect was at the Texas Theater and I reported to that location. On arrival, I was told that the building was covered off outside and to go inside the theater.

Once inside, I requested either an usher or the Assistant Manager to turn on as many lights as possible.

Detective Paul Bentley and I, along with some uniform officers, went to the balcony of the theater. We checked to see that all the fire exits were covered and that a check of the patrons was being made, and then we started back to the lower floor to see the situation at that location.

About the time I reached the bottom of the stairs, I heard an officer yell, "I've got him!" And, I also heard a struggle. I ran inside the lower floor of the theater and saw several officers attempting to restrain a person. Someone yelled that the man had a pistol and then as I joined the other officers in attempting to complete the arrest, I heard someone else say they had the gun.

Officers M. N. McDonald, T. A. Hutson, Ray Hawkins, C. T. Walker, Bob Carroll, K. E. Lyons, Paul Bentley, Bob Barrett from the FBI, and I succeeded in subduing the suspect, and while the other officers held the suspect, Officer Ray Hawkins and I handcuffed the suspect.

Captain W. R. Westbrook instructed us to get the prisoner away from the location as soon as possible. Officers Walker, Lyons, Carroll, Bentley, and I

Gerald L. Hill-page 2

flanked the man and also protected him from the front and rear. In this formation, we moved through the lobby of the theater and out to a car parked in front of the theater.

We placed the suspect in the rear seat of the car with Officer Bentley on his left and Officer Walker on his right. I sat in the center of the front seat with Officer Lyons on my right and Officer Carroll drove.

As Officer Carroll started to get into the car, he pulled a snub-nosed revolver from his belt and handed it to me. He stated this was the suspect's gun and that he had obtained it from Officer McDonald immediately after the suspect was subdued. When the pistol was given to me, it was fully loaded and one of the shells had a hammer mark on the primer.

I retained this gun in my possession until approximately 3:15 pm, Friday, November 22, 1963, when in the presence of Officers Carroll and McDonald, I turned the weapon over to Detective T. L. Baker of the Homicide and Robbery Bureau.

At the time the pistol was released to Detective Baker, McDonald, Carroll and I had all marked it for identification purposes, and in the presence of McDonald and Carroll, I marked the side of the casing on all the shells, which were also turned over to Detective Baker at the same time.

Respectfully submitted,

Gerald L. Hill
Sergeant of Police
Personnel Bureau

GLH:RW
Copied-MR-12-5-63

88

COMMISSION EXHIBIT No. 2003—Continued

December 3, 1963

Mr. J. E. Curry
Chief of Police

Subject: Arrest of Lee Harvey Oswald, w/m/24

Sir:

On November 22, 1963, at 1:45 pm, I was working Districk #284 and was in the Oak Cliff area searching for the suspect who shot Officer J. D. Tippit. I was riding in a squad with Officers Ray Hawkins and E. R. Baggett when we received a radio transmission that a suspect had entered the Texas Theater in the 200 Block West Jefferson Blvd. We proceeded to this location and approached from the alley at the rear of the theater.

An unknown white male opened the fire exit door near the stage and I searched his person as he identified himself as an employee at Hardy's Shoe Store. He said the suspect was in the theater. Officers C. T. Walker and Ray Hawkins entered the door with me while Officer Baggett cover d the exit. I walked down the steps and into the theater, walking up the aisle North of the center section of seats toward the back. I observed Officers M. N. McDonald and C. T. Walker searching two suspects who were sitting half way down in the center poction of seats. I continued on up the aisle and Officer McDonald as walking parallel to me up the opposite aisle.

I observed the suspect sitting in the center section of the third row from the back and the fifth seat North of the South aisle of the center section. As I entered the row of seats behind the suspect he jumped up and hit Officer McDonald in the face with his fist. Officer McDonald was in the seat next to the one in which the suspect was originally sitting, and the suspect was up out of his seat struggling with Officer McDonald. I reached over the back of the seats and placed my right arm around the suspect's neck and pulled him up on the back of the seat.

89

COMMISSION EXHIBIT No. 2003—Continued

T. A. Hutson-page 2

Officer C. T. Waker came up and was struggling with the suspect's left hand, and as Officer McDonald struggled with the suspect's right hand, he moved it to his waist and drew a pistol and as Officer McDonald tried to disarm the suspect, I heard the pistol snap. Officer Ray Hawkins came over and helped in the struggle as Officer McDonald took the pistol from the suspect's right hand. Several other Officers came over as we were handcuffing the suspect. They removed the suspect to the Central Police Station.

The only Officers I can recall in this group that brought the prisoner to the station were Sgt. Jerry Hill and Officer C. T. Waker. I remained in the theater and continued the search around and between seats.

Respectfully submitted.

T. A. Hutson
Patrolman # 1146
Traffic Division

TAH/kc
Copied: MR-12-5-63

90

COMMISSION EXHIBIT No. 2003—Continued

December 4, 1963

Mr. J. E. Curry
Chief of Police

Subject: Arrest of Lee Harvey Oswald

Sir:

On November 22, 1963 at approximately 2:00 pm, Detective B. K. Carroll and I were instructed by Lieutenant E. Kaminski to go to the Oak Cliff area where Officer J. D. Tippit had been shot.

While enroute to Oak Cliff, we received information on our police radio that the suspect had entered the Texas Theatre, 231 West Jefferson. When we arrived at the Texas Theatre, we were told that the suspect had gone to the balcony. While searching the balcony, I heard someone call from the lower floor that the suspect was down there. I ran down the steps, and as I neared the bottom, I sprained my left ankle.

I then proceeded to the location where Officers P. L. Bentley, M. N. McDonald C. T. Walker, and other officers were attempting to disarm Lee Harvey Oswald. During this time, Lee Harvey Oswald kept yelling, "I am not resisting arrest. I am not resisting arrest. I want to complain of police brutality."

Captain W. R. Westbrook then told several of the officers to take Oswald directly to the City Hall.

Officers B. K. Carroll, Sergeant Jerry Hill, P. L. Bentley, C. T. Walker, and myself transported Oswald to the City Hall.

Enroute to the City Hall, Oswald refused to answer all questions, and he kept repeating, "Why am I being arrested? I know I was carrying a gun, but why else am I being arrested?"

Lee Harvey Oswald was released to Captain Fritz at the Homicide and Robbery Bureau by the transporting officers.

Respectfully submitted,
K. E. Lyon, #1276
Patrolman - Vice Section
Special Service Bureau

Copied: MR-12-5-63

91

COMMISSION EXHIBIT No. 2003—Continued

December 3, 1963

Mr. J. E. Curry
Chief of Police

Subject: The Arrest of Lee Harvey Oswald.

Sir:

At approximately 2:00 PM, November 22, 1963, I entered the rear exit door of the Texas Theatre, 231 West Jefferson Boulevard, with three other uniformed police officers. We were met by a man dressed in Civilian clothes, who told us that the suspect, that had acted suspicious as he ran into the theatre, was sitting at the rear alone, wearing a brown shirt. I noticed that there were only 10 or 15 people sitting in the theatre. The house lights became dim and I walked into the row of seats directly behind two men seated in the center and made a quick search of their persons and found no weapon. I then walked out of the row and up the rear towards the suspect. When I got within one foot of him, I told the suspect to get on his feet. He stood up immediately, bringing his hands up about shoulder high and saying, "Well, it's all over now." I was reaching for his waist and he struck me on the nose with his left hand. With his right hand, he reached to his waist and both of our hands were on a pistol that was stuck in his belt under his shirt. We both fell into the seats struggling for the pistol. At this time I yelled, "I've got him." Three uniformed officers came to my aid immediately. One on the suspect's left, one to the rear in the row behind and one to the front in the row directly in front of the suspect and I. I managed to get my right hand on the pistol over the suspect's hand. I could feel his hand on the trigger. I then got a secure grip on the butt of the pistol. I jerked the pistol and as it was clearing the suspect's clothing and grip I heard the snap of the hammer and the pistol crossed over my left cheeck, causing a four inch scratch.

92

I brought the pistol away still holding the butt and pointing it to the floor at arms length away from anyone. By this time there were 7 or 8 officers aroun the scene including Detectives in plain clothes. I recognized Officer Bob Carroll and handed the pistol to him. I was holding the suspect with my left arm. The suspect was then taken out of the theatre by the assisting officers.

This was the last contact I had with the suspect. I marked the pistol and six rounds at Central Station. The primer of one round was dented on misfire at the time of the struggle with the suspect.

Respectfully Submitted,

O/S M. N. McDonald

M. N. McDonald
Patrolman # 1178
Patrol Division

MNM/bbd

Copied by MM - 12-5-63

93

December 3, 1963

Mr. J. E. Curry
Chief of Police

Subject: Arrest of Lee Harvey Oswald

Sir:

Shortly prior to the report this suspect was seen to enter the Texas Theater, a Radio Patrol officer, whose name I do not know, was questioning a young man in the 100 Block South Patton. The officer asked me what I thought about the boy. I was not of the opinion the boy he was questioning was the right one. As the report was broadcast about the suspect entering the theater, I asked the officer if he had this boy's name and address. When he said he did, I told the boy he could go.

Then, I rode in the squad car with the officer to the rear of the Texas Theater, where there were already several officers present. Captain Talbert and some more officers were questioning a boy in the alley. There was a pickup truck setting just north off the alley with the motor running. I checked the truck for a weapon and had just walked back to the alley, when I heard a voice, that appeared to come from inside the front part of the theater, say, "We got him!"

Just instantly following that, Sergeant Gerry Hill opened the door from inside the back part of the second floor level of the theater building, and walked out onto the fire escape. I asked him if they had the suspect arrested, telling him we had heard someone yell, "We got him!" He looked back into the building and said, "No, we haven't got him."

Then, as Sergeant Hill re-entered the door leading to the fire escape, we again heard the voice yell, "We got him!" The voice was convincing enough

that it could be sensed among all the officers at the rear of the building that the arrest was secured.

Immediately thereafter, Captain Westbrook and two or three other officers returned to the alley and reported the suspect was enroute to the station.

Respectfully submitted,

O/S H. H. Stringer

H. H. Stringer
Sergeant of Police
Personnel Bureau

HHS:RW

Copied by KM - 12-5-63

December 3, 1963

Mr. J. E. Curry
Chief of Police

Subject: Arrest of
Lee Harvey Oswald w/m/24

Sir:

On November 22, 1963 I was assigned to the Trade Mart as part of a security force under the supervision of Captain O. A. Jones. After hearing of the President's assassination I, along with Lt. J. L. Cunningham, J. B. Tony, and M. A. Buhk, was instructed by Captain Jones to proceed to the scene of the assassination.

Enroute we heard on the police radio that Officer J. D. Tippit had been shot in Oak Cliff and a suspect had been seen going into the library at E. Jefferson and Marsalis. We proceeded to this location and upon arriving found it to be false.

We left the library and heard a report that a suspect fitting the description was seen in the Texas Theatre, 231 W. Jefferson, and was hiding in the balcony. We proceeded to this location and I began searching the balcony. I started down the stairs and heard someone shout, "I've got him down here". I went downstairs and assisted in arresting Lee Harvey Oswald. At this time, Officer M. N. McDonald had this subject and was attempting to take a pistol out of his hand. I along with numerous other officers grabbed Oswald and someone took the pistol out of his hand. Handcuffs were then placed on the subject. At this time the prisoner began shouting "I'm not resisting and I'm proclaiming police brutality". We were instructed by Captain

Westbrook to get the prisoner in a car and take him to the City Hall. At this time Detective B. K. Carroll and other officers took the prisoner out the front door of the Theatre where there was a large crowd of people gathered outside. The people were shouting "kill him" and "let us kill him". The prisoner was placed in a squad car and immediately taken away.

I along with Lt. Cunningham and J. B. Tony remained at the Theatre and took the names and addresses of the occupants of the Theatre. We brought a witness to the City Hall who saw Oswald in the Theatre and also heard the pistol click when it misfired as Officer McDonald attempted to arrest Oswald.

Respectfully submitted,

O/S E. E. Taylor

E. E. Taylor #1225
Detective
Narcotic Section
Special Service Bureau

EET:crl

Copied by MM 12-5-63 for Capt. Fritz.

December 3, 1963

Mr. J. E. Curry
Chief of Police

Subject: Arrest of Lee Harvey Oswald

Sir:

At approximately 1:50 PM, November 22, 1963, while cruising the Oak Cliff area of Dallas, Texas, was Lt. E. L. Cunningham and Detective M. A. Buhk, we heard a radio dispatch informing all units of the shooting of a police officer, giving information that a suspect was in the balcony section of the Texas Theatre located in the 200 block of West Jefferson.

We proceeded to that location and went into the theatre. Detective Buhk remained in the car to maintain liaison with the dispatchers office.

Lt. Cunningham and I went into the theatre and up to the balcony section. There was a young man sitting near the top of the stairs and we ascertained from manager on duty that this subject had been in the theatre since about 12:05 PM. My watch indicated 1:55 P. M. at that time. At this time I heard someone from the main floor say in a loud voice, "He's down here". I ran downstairs and into the seating area of the main floor. I saw a uniformed officer whom I later recognized to be Officer M. N. McDonald, attempting to subdue a subject who had a gun. Later identified as Lee Harvey Oswald. The subject Oswald had the pistol in his right hand, his right arm pinioned across the left shoulder of Officer McDonald. At the time I was in the aisle approximately fifteen feet to the rear of Officer McDonald.

There were several officers nearer Officer McDonald than I at this time. We all immediately converged to that point. One of the officers stated "I have the gun". Oswald was then subdued, handcuffed and removed from the building for transporting to the city hall.

JOHN B. TONEY - Page 2

Lt. Cunningham was in charge at the scene and requested that uniformed officers to keep the theatre closed for the purpose of interviewing the witnesses inside the theatre.

Respectfully,

O/S John B. Toney
Detective 778
Forgery Bureau

JBT:ms

Copied by MM - 12-5-63

December 2, 1963

Mr. J. E. Curry
Chief of Police

Subject: Arrest of Lee Harvey Oswald

Sir:

At approximately 2:00 pm, November 22, 1963, I was working Squad #223 in Oak Cliff. I was cruising in the area of Tenth Street and Beckley Avenue looking for the killer of Officer J. D. Tippit. The Dispatcher put out a call stating that the suspect was in the Texas Theater on Jefferson Blvd. I proceeded to the rear of the Theater and parked my squad car in the alley. I entered the rear door with Officers M. N. McDonald and T. A. Hutson. Officer McDonald and I walked across the stage and jumped down to the main seating area. Officer Hutson walked down the stairs next to the door we had entered. I started walking up the north aisle toward two men who were observed sitting in the middle of the show.

Officer McDonald was walking up the South aisle also toward the two men. Officer McDonald and I waked up to these two men and searched them. While searching these two men the arrested person was observed sitting farther back in the show on the third seat from the rear of the show. I walked back to the North aisle and back to the row where the suspect was sitting. Officer McDonald had walked back to the row where the suspect was. Officer Hutson had entered the row behind the suspect, walking ahead of me, toward the suspect.

I observed Officer McDonald as he walked up to the suspect and said something to him. The suspect stood up and faced Officer McDonald. At that time I was approaching the suspect from his back. Officer McDonald reached down as if to search the suspect and as he did the suspect hit him

100

COMMISSION EXHIBIT No. 2003—Continued

Charles T. Walker-page 2

in the face. Officer McDonald started grappling with the suspect and Officer Hutson and I ran toward them. Officer Hutson reached over from the seat behind the suspect and grabbed him around the neck. I reached and grabbed the suspect's left arm. I do not know where Officer Ray Hawkins came from, but he was to my left in front of the suspect, also attempting to hold him. I could see Officer McDonald and the suspect grappling over the gun. The suspect had his right hand on it and so did Officer McDonald. The gun was being waved around approximately waist high. I heard a click of the revolver as it snapped, but I do not know what direction the revolver was pointing when it snapped. Officer Hawkins told me to bring the suspect's arm around a little so he could get the handcuffs on. I did this and started bringing the suspect out the aisle I had entered. I took hold of the suspect's right arm when we got to the North aisle. Detective Paul Bentley took his left arm and we took the suspect out the front door of the Theater. We put the suspect in the rear of a plain squad car and brought the suspect to the City Hall.

There were three plainclothes Officers in the front seat of the car that the suspect was brought down in. Sgt. Jerry Hill was one of the Officers and I do not know the names of the others.

Respectfully,

Charles T. Walker
Patrolman #1592
Traffic Division

CTW/kc
Copied-MR-12-5-63

101

COMMISSION EXHIBIT No. 2003—Continued

December 3, 1963

Mr. J. E. Curry
Chief of Police

Subject: Arrest of Lee Harvey Oswald

Sir:

This investigator was in the 400 block of West Tenth Street, interviewing a witness to the shooting of Officer J. D. Tippit.

Information was received over the police radio that a suspect was in the Texas Theater.

F. B. I. Agent Bob Barrett and this investigator rode in a squad car with a radio patrolman to the rear of the Texas Theater. The name of the patrolman cannot be recalled.

Barrett and this investigator stopped at one rear door and the patrolman proceeded to the next one. After entering this door, it was observed that the overhead lights were on and the picture was still being projected on the screen. This investigator was on the stage at one side of the screen.

A Male employee said, "The man in the fourth row from the back in the middle aisle is the man."

At this time, Officer M. N. McDonald approached the suspect and made contact, and he resisted.

This investigator then ran down three or four steps to the floor and up the aisle; as he reached the row of seats where the arrest was in progress, several officers were struggling with the suspect.

Detective Bob Carroll said that he had the suspect's gun. The suspect was overpowered and handcuffed. He said several words; the words cannot be

102

COMMISSION EXHIBIT No. 2003—Continued

W. R. Westbrook - Page 2

recalled with the exception of "Police Brutality" and "I haven't done nothing."

This investigator asked the suspect his name, but he did not reply.

This investigator then ordered the arresting officers to remove the suspect to the City Hall with all possible speed and this was done.

Respectfully,

O/S W. R. Westbrook

W. R. Westbrook
Captain of Police
Personnel Bureau

WRW:RW

Copied by MM - 12-5-63

103

COMMISSION EXHIBIT No. 2003—Continued

POLICE DEPARTMENT
CITY OF DALLAS
CPS-JS-566

ARREST REPORT ON INVESTIGATIVE PRISONER

FIRST NAME: LEE	MIDDLE NAME: HARVEY	LAST NAME: OSWALD	DATE: 11-22-63	TIME: 1:40 PM
RACE: WHITE ☐ COLORED ☐	SEX: MALE ☐ FEMALE ☐	AGE: 24	DATE OF BIRTH: OCT. 15-39	HOME ADDRESS: 1026 N. BECKLEY
ADDRESS WHERE ARREST MADE: 231 W JEFFERSON	TYPE PREMISES (IF BUSINESS, GIVE TRADE NAME ALSO): THEATRE			
CHARGE: INV. MURDER	BUSINESS WHERE ARREST MADE HAS: BEER LICENSE ☐ LIQUOR LICENSE ☐ STATE LIC. NO.			
HOW ARREST MADE: ON VIEW ☐ CALL ☐ WARRANT ☐	LOCATION OF OFFENSE (IF OTHER THAN PLACE OF ARREST)			

RT. THUMB PRINT — I. D. NUMBER — ARREST NUMBER

COMPLAINANT (NAME—RACE—SEX—AGE) — HOME ADDRESS—PHONE NO. — BUSINESS ADDRESS—PHONE NO.

WITNESS — HOME ADDRESS—PHONE NO. — BUSINESS ADDRESS—PHONE NO.

WITNESS — HOME ADDRESS—PHONE NO. — BUSINESS ADDRESS—PHONE NO.

PROPERTY PLACED IN POUND (MAKE, MODEL, LICENSE NO. OF AUTO) — PROPERTY PLACED IN PROPERTY ROOM

NAMES OF OTHERS ARRESTED AT SAME TIME IN CONNECTION WITH THE SAME OR SIMILAR OFFENSE

NAME OF AND/OR INFORMATION CONCERNING OTHER SUSPECTS NOT APPREHENDED

OTHER DETAILS OF THE ARREST

This man shot and Killed President John F. Kennedy and Police Officer J. D. Tippit. He also shot and wounded Govenor John Connally.

CHECK ALL ITEMS WHICH APPLY: DRUNK ☐ DRINKING ☐ CURSED ☐ RESISTED ☐ FOUGHT ☐ INJURED BEFORE ARREST ☐ INJURED DURING OR AFTER ARREST ☐ OFFICER(S) INJURED ☐ SPECIAL REPORT ☐

ARRESTING OFFICER: M. N. McDONALD	I. D. NO. 1175	ARRESTING OFFICER: K.E. LYONS	I. D. NO. 1276
OTHER OFFICER: LT. E.L. CUNNINGHAM	I. D. NO.	OTHER OFFICER: P.L. BENTLEY	I. D. NO. 526

INVESTIGATION ASSIGNED TO — CHARGE FILED — FILED BY — DATE — DATE - TIME TO CO. JAIL

RELEASED BY — DATE - TIME — H.C. BOND BY — DATE - TIME — COURT — DATE — TIME

DISTRIBUTION: (REMOVE CARBON—CHECK ORIGINAL FOR RECORDS BU.—CHECK COPY FOR EACH BUREAU CONCERNED) RECORDS BUREAU ☐ SPEC. SER. BUREAU ☐ HOMICIDE ROBBERY ☐ AUTO THEFT ☐ BURGLARY THEFT ☐ FORGERY ☐ JUVENILE ☐ TRAFFIC ☐

USE REVERSE SIDE IF MORE SPACE NEEDED

105

Commission Exhibit No. 2003—Continued

POLICE DEPARTMENT
CITY OF DALLAS
CPS-JS-566

ARREST REPORT ON INVESTIGATIVE PRISONER

FIRST NAME: JACK	MIDDLE NAME:	LAST NAME: Ruby	DATE: 11-24-62	TIME: M
RACE: WHITE ☒ COLORED ☐	SEX: MALE ☒ FEMALE ☐	AGE: 52	DATE OF BIRTH: 3-19-11	HOME ADDRESS: 223 So. Ewing
ADDRESS WHERE ARREST MADE: 106 So. Harwood Basement City Hall	TYPE PREMISES (IF BUSINESS, GIVE TRADE NAME ALSO): City HALL			
CHARGE: Inv. Murder	BUSINESS WHERE ARREST MADE HAS: BEER LICENSE ☐ LIQUOR LICENSE ☐ STATE LIC. NO.			
HOW ARREST MADE: ON VIEW ☒ CALL ☐ WARRANT ☐	LOCATION OF OFFENSE (IF OTHER THAN PLACE OF ARREST)			

RT. THUMB PRINT — I. D. NUMBER — ARREST NUMBER

COMPLAINANT (NAME—RACE—SEX—AGE) — HOME ADDRESS—PHONE NO. — BUSINESS ADDRESS—PHONE NO.

WITNESS — HOME ADDRESS—PHONE NO. — BUSINESS ADDRESS—PHONE NO.

WITNESS — HOME ADDRESS—PHONE NO. — BUSINESS ADDRESS—PHONE NO.

PROPERTY PLACED IN POUND (MAKE, MODEL, LICENSE NO. OF AUTO) — PROPERTY PLACED IN PROPERTY ROOM

NAMES OF OTHERS ARRESTED AT SAME TIME IN CONNECTION WITH THE SAME OR SIMILAR OFFENSE

NAME OF AND/OR INFORMATION CONCERNING OTHER SUSPECTS NOT APPREHENDED

OTHER DETAILS OF THE ARREST

This Subject Shot and Killed Lee Harvey Oswald.

CHECK ALL ITEMS WHICH APPLY: DRUNK ☐ DRINKING ☐ CURSED ☐ RESISTED ☐ FOUGHT ☐ INJURED BEFORE ARREST ☐ INJURED DURING OR AFTER ARREST ☐ OFFICER(S) INJURED ☐ SPECIAL REPORT ☐

ARRESTING OFFICER: L.C. Graves	I. D. NO. 702	ARRESTING OFFICER: W. J. Harrison	I. D. NO. 579
OTHER OFFICER: W. J. Cutshaw	I. D. NO. 1111	OTHER OFFICER: R.L. Lowery	I. D. NO. 1081

INVESTIGATION ASSIGNED TO — CHARGE FILED: Murder — FILED BY: Capt Fritz — DATE: 11-24-63 — DATE - TIME TO CO. JAIL

RELEASED BY — DATE - TIME — H.C. BOND BY — DATE - TIME — COURT — DATE — TIME

DISTRIBUTION: (REMOVE CARBON—CHECK ORIGINAL FOR RECORDS BU.—CHECK COPY FOR EACH BUREAU CONCERNED) RECORDS BUREAU ☐ SPEC. SER. BUREAU ☐ HOMICIDE ROBBERY ☐ AUTO THEFT ☐ BURGLARY THEFT ☐ FORGERY ☐ JUVENILE ☐ TRAFFIC ☐

USE REVERSE SIDE IF MORE SPACE NEEDED

Commission Exhibit No. 2003—Continued

FORM 12-39

54 No. 20984

FIRST NAME	MIDDLE NAME	LAST NAME	AGE	SEX	RACE
JACK		[illegible]BY	43	M	W

ADDRESS 1719 1/2 SErvay
BUSINESS ADDRESS
ARRESTING OFFICERS JF Holcomb 708, C M Barnhart 925
PLACE OF ARREST 3508 Oak Lawn
DATE 5-1-54 TIME 12:50P
C R. 2 B 33 DESK OFFICER Wissemon-pdg
PICK UP ☐ RADIO CALL ☐ WARRANT ☐ ON VIEW ☒ RESULT OF ACCIDENT ☐ SUMMONS—NOT PL
CHG. WHEN BOOKED Inv CCW (Pistol)
CHARGE CHANGED TO
REL. Released — no C.F. DATE TIME BAILED TO BY
COURT NO. DATE AND TIME SET FOR COURT COURT DISPOSITION

FORM 12-39

54 No. 21114

FIRST NAME	MIDDLE NAME	LAST NAME	AGE	SEX	RACE
JACK		RUBY	43	M	W

ADDRESS 1717 S.Ervay
BUSINESS ADDRESS
ARRESTING OFFICERS J.R.Stephens 918 & H.M.Collins 850
PLACE OF ARREST 3508 Oak Lawn
DATE 5-1-54 TIME A.M. ☒ 9:05 P.M.
C R. 3 B 33 DESK OFFICER Skains
PICK UP ☐ RADIO CALL ☒ WARRANT ☐ ON VIEW ☐ RESULT OF ACCIDENT ☐ SUMMONS—NOT PL
CHG. WHEN BOOKED Inv Peace Bond Vio (Hold for Chandler)
CHARGE CHANGED TO
Released — no C.F. DATE TIME BAILED TO BY
COURT NO. DATE AND TIME SET FOR COURT COURT DISPOSITION

FORM 12-39

No. 99090

FIRST NAME	MIDDLE NAME	LAST NAME	AGE	SEX	RACE	OCC
Jack	L.	Ruby	37	M	W	Cafe

ADDRESS 1717 S. Ervay
BUSINESS ADDRESS 1717 S. Ervay
ARRESTING OFFICERS D N Boyd 586 L P Passons 396
PLACE OF ARREST 1404 Main DATE 2-4-49 TIME 1
R 1 B 40 DESK OFFICER Wood
PICK UP ☐ RADIO CALL ☒ WARRANT ☐ ON VIEW ☐ RESULT OF ACCIDENT ☐ SUMMONS—NOT
CHARGE WHEN BOOKED Dist. Peace
CHARGE CHANGED TO
REL. BY Pl. 10.00 DATE 2-4-49 TIME BAILED TO BY
COURT NO. REMARKS:

FORM 12-39

53 No. 65478

FIRST NAME	MIDDLE NAME	LAST NAME	AGE	SEX	RACE
Jack		Ruby	42	M	W

ADDRESS 1717 S. Ervay
BUSINESS ADDRESS
ARRESTING OFFICERS W. M. Wall 857 & C. W. Daloney 751
PLACE OF ARREST 3520 Oaklawn DATE 7-26-53 TIME 3:
C R I 33 DESK OFFICER Skaine
PIC ☐ RADIO CALL ☐ WARRANT ☐ ON VIEW ☒ RESULT OF ACCIDENT ☐ SUMMONS—NOT
CHARGE WHEN BOOKED Inv. C. C. W.
CHARGE CHANGED TO
Released no C.F. DATE TIME BAILED TO BY
CO. NO. REMARKS:
FINE PAID ☐ DATE AMOUNT

FIRST	MIDDLE	LAST NAME	R-S-AGE	
JACK	(N)	RUBY	WM52	63- 98531

HOME ADDRESS 223 S. Ewing
DATE OF BIRTH 3 19 11 OCCUPATION bus. owner
ADDRESS WHERE ARRESTED 106 S. Harwood City Hall
BUSINESS ADDRESS
ARRESTING OFFICERS (INCLUDE I D NUMBERS) L C GRAVES 702 W J HARRISON 579

DATE	(A.M.)	TIME	(P.M.)	DIVISION	PLATOON	DISTRICT
11 24 63	1130			CID 2	102	

DESK OFFICER	CLERK	STATION	RADIO CALL	VIEW	WARRANT	SUM
LT. WIGGINS	J. NEWTON	DT		XX		

CHARGED WHEN BOOKED INV. MURDER CHANGED TO
BAILED TO BY DATE - TIME
H.C.B. ☐ CASH ☐ APP. ☐ AMT. BOND NO.
RELEASED BY (NOT CHARGED) DATE - TIME COUNTY JAIL AMT. FINE PAID RECEIPT NO. NO. DAYS SERVED

108

COMMISSION EXHIBIT No. 2003—Continued

Form No. CPS—GF—379

POLICE DEPARTMENT

CITY OF DALLAS

CASE REPORT

Disposition

Date

Court

Docket

Method

Disposition

Filed

Date November 22, 1963

With Alexander

By Capt. Fritz

C. N. Dhority - C. W. Brown

Investigating Officers

Lt. L. E. Cunningham
M. N. McDonald

Arresting Officers

Deceased

Location of Defendant

Defendant Lee Harvey OSWALD

Race White Age 24 Sex Male Residence 1026 North Beckley

Date of Arrest November 22, 1963 - 2:00 PM Identification No. 54018

Place of Arrest 231 West Jefferson Arrest No. 63-98155

Date and Time of Offense November 22, 1963, approximately 12:30PM Offense No. F-85950

Complainant John F. Kennedy, w/m/47, Deceased

Where and How Committed On Elm West of Houston - Shot with rifle

Charge Murder

Property Taken and Value

Evidence and Seizures Attached

Voluntary Statement No

Accomplices

List Witnesses and What Each Can Testify to on Reverse Side

Summary of Case Deceased was riding in motorcade with his wife and Governor Connally and his wife. Witnesses heard gun shot and saw deceased slump forward. More shots were fired and deceased fell forward. Governor Connally was also shot. Officers determined where shots came from and covered the building and went into the building. Capt. Fritz had name of Defendant, but Defendant was not in the building. Capt. Fritz received information that Defendant had killed Officer Tippit in Oak Cliff. Arresting officers brought Defendant to City Hall.

109

Any additional information may be placed on reverse side.

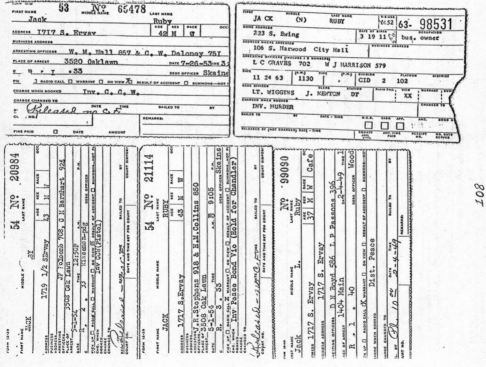

COMMISSION EXHIBIT No. 2003—Continued

OFFICER WITNESSES:

M. L. Baker Solo Motor Officer Traffic Division	Saw Oswald in building after shooting. Identified him in line up. See affidavit.
Deputy S. Boone Sheriff's Office	Found rifle used in offense, Northwest corner of sixth floor of Texas School Book Depository Building. Turned rifle over to Capt. Fritz.
Deputy Seymour Weitzman 2802 Oates Drive, DA 7-6624 Bus. Robie Love RI 1-1483	Same as above.
Capt. J. W. Fritz #9 CID	Made investigation of offense. Found empty and live shells used in offense.
Lt. J. C. Day Crime Lab	Made investigation at Texas School Book Depository. Took charge of rifle used. Lifted prints on building and from rifle and paper rifle was wrapped in.
Det. R. L. Studebaker Crime Lab	Made investigation where offense was committed.
Det. Johnny Hicks Crime Lab	Made paraffin case of Defendant's hands and face.
Det. Pete Barnes Crime Lab	Made paraffin cast of Defendant's hands and face.
Capt. G. M. Doughty ID Bureau	Had charge of evidence which he turned over to F. B. I.
G.L. Hill, Sgt. 1180 Radio Patrol, Sta. 511	Arrested defendant.
M. N. McDonald 1178 City P. D., Sta. 511	Arrested defendant.
C. T. Walker 1529 City P. D., Sta. 501	Arrested defendant.
Ray Hawkins 887 City P. D., APB, Sta. 515	Arrested defendant.
T. A. Hutson 1146 City P. D., Sta. 501	Arrested Defendant.
B. K. Carroll 923 City P. D., Spl. Ser. Sta. 566	Arrested defendant.
Deputy Sheriff Luke E. Mooney Dallas Co. Sheriff's Office	Found 3 empty 6.5 rifle shells on 6th floor Texas Book Depository Bldg. and notified Capt. Fritz.

COMMISSION EXHIBIT No. 2003—Continued

(1) witnesses continu Defer t: Lee Harvey Oswald Murder ffense 5950

O. P. Wright Security Officer, Parkland Hosp. 2502 Also, WH6 2736	Recovered 6.5 rifle slug, turned it over to Secret Service at Parkland.
Det. Marvin Johnson 879 City P. D., Sta. 551	Made investigation at Texas Book Depository. Recovered long brown paper rifle was wrapped in and Dr. Pepper bottle at scene. Took affidavit from cab driver Whaley and officer Baker.
Dt. L. D. Montgomery 1047 City P. D., Sta. 551	Same as Officer Johnson above.
Det. L. C. Graves 702 City P. D., Sta. 551	Took affidavit from Helen L. Markham and Mrs. Mary E. Bledsoe.
Det. B. L. Senkel 714	Was in motorcade about seven blocks ahead of President's car. Followed President's car to Parkland Hospital. Made investigation at Texas Book Depository. Made search of defendant's room at 1026 N. Beckley. Took affidavit from defendant's wife. Made search
Det. F. M. Turner 809 City P. D., Sta. 551	Same as Senkel above. Made identification of defendant's picture from witness Ronald B. Fischer who saw defendant before shooting. Not positive on identification. Made search 1026 N. Beckley.
Det. W. E. Potts 576 City P. D., Sta. 551	Made identification of defendant's picture from witness Ronald B. Fischer who saw defendant before shooting. Not positive on identification. Recovered map, 1026 N. Beckley.
Det. C. N. Dhority 476 City P. D., Sta. 551	Was present at lineup on defendant for William W. Whaley, cab driver who picked up defendant. Mr. Whaley made identification as #3 man in 4-man lineup, 2:15 pm, 11-23-63, city hall. Took affidavit and held lineup from Cecil J. McWatters bus driver who picked up defendant. Also made identification of bus transfer defendant had in his pocket. 11-23-63, 6:30 pm identified defendant as #2 man in 4-man lineup. Took 3 spent 6.5 rifle shells to crime lab. Made copies of defendant's identification papers for Mr. Stewart of Secret Service. Prepared case report.
C. W. Brown 759 City P. D., Sta. 551	Made investigation at Texas Book Depository Bldg. Took witnesses from Book Depository to room 317 City Hall, took affidavits from William H. Shelley and Seymour Weitzman. Was present at lineup when Mr. McWatters made identification of defendant and transfer, which defendant had in his possession at time of arrest.

110

COMMISSION EXHIBIT No. 2003—Continued

(2) supplementary esse.-continued-Defendant: Lee Harvey Oswald der Offense F 85950

G. F. Rose 1026 City P. D., Sta. 551	Made search of 2515 W. 5th St., Irving, Texas. Recovered blanket rifle was wrapped in, personal papers and pictures of defendant. Brought witness Wesley Frazier to city hall for affidavit and polygraph. Brought defendant's wife and Mrs. Ruth Paine to City Hall.
R. S. Stovall 1031 City P. D., Sta. 551	Same as above.
H. M. Moore 679 City P. D., Sta. 551	Made search of 2515 W. 5th St., Irving, Texas. Found picture of defendant holding a rifle similar to the one defendant used at time of offense.
J. P. Adamcik 1548 City P. D., Sta. 551	Made search of 2515 W. 5th, Irving, Texas. Was present when defendant's wife made identification of defendant's rifle. Took affidavits from defendant's mother and brother and Michael Paine.
K. L. Anderton 1506 V. D. Monaghen 801 City P. D., Sta. 551	Was present at Texas Book Depository when investigation was made.
J. R. Leavelle 736 City P. D., Sta. 551	Held lineup when Helen Markham made identification of defendant as the man who killed officer Tippit. Took affidavits from Ted Calloway, Sam Guinyard, R. S. Truly, Mrs. R. A. Reid and W. W. Scoggins.
E. R. Beck 45 City P. D., Sta. 551	Assisted officers in moving defendant from jail to Room 317. Took affidavit from Mrs. Geneva L. Hine.
R. M. Sims 629 City P. D., Sta. 551	Made investigation at Texas Book Depository. Recovered evidence from this building, took defendant from jail to Room 317, recovered bus transfer slip from defendant's shirt pocket.
E. L. Boyd 810 City P. D., Sta. 551	Same as above, also found 5 live .38 shells in left front pocket of defendant when searched in the showup room.
M. G. Hall 540 City P. D., Sta. 551	Took defendant from room 317 to showup room. Took affidavit from Lee E. Bowers. Was present when defendant's mother and brother talked with defendant in city jail.

(3) witnesses cont d--Defendant: Lee Harvey Oswald Murd Offense 85950

Marina Oswald w/f/22 2515 W. 5th St., Irving, Tex.	Wife of defendant. See affidavit #1.
Seymour Weitzman w/m 2802 Oates Dr., DA7 6624 Bus: Robie Love, RI1 1483	Was at place of offense. See affidavit #2.
James Richard Worrell, Jr. w/m/20 13510 Winterhaven, CH7 2378 bus: Thomas Jefferson High	Was at place of offense. See affidavit #3.
William Wayne Whaley w/m 619 Pine St., Lewisville, Tex. bus: 610 S. Akard, RI2 9191	Cab driver who picked up defendant. See affidavit # 4.
Mrs. Mary E. Bledsoe w/f 621 N. Marsalis, WH421985	Saw defendant get on city bus knows defendant. See affidavit #5.
Lee E. Bowers, Jr. w/m/38 10508 Maplegrove Lane, DA1 1909 bus: Union Terminal Co., RI8 4698	Was at place of offense. See affidavit #6.
Cecil J. McWatters w/m 2523 Blyth, DA1 2909 Bus: Dallas Transit Co., RI1 1151	Picked defendant up on his bus. See affidavit #7.
Helen Louise Markham w/f 328½ E. 9th bus: Eat Well Cafe, RI8 2475	Saw Officer Tippit killed by defendant. See affidavit #8.
Jeanette Davis w/f/22 400 E. Tenth, WH3 8120	Saw officer Tippit killed-recovered evidence. See affidavit #9.
Virginia Davis w/f/16 400 E. 10th, WH3 8120	Saw Officer Tippit killed-recovered evidence. See affidavit #10
W. W. Scoggins w/m 3138 Alaska, FR4 2955 Bus: Oak Cliff Cab, WH2 6203	Saw officer killed. See affidavit #11.
Ted Callaway w/m/40 805 W. 8th St., WH6 8045 bus: 501 S. Jefferson	Heard shots, saw defendant run with pistol when officer was killed. See affidavit # 12.
George Jefferson Applin, Jr. w/m/21 3423 Weisenberger, no pho. or bus.	Saw defendant come into picture show. See affidavit #13.
Ruth Hyde Paine w/f/31 2515 W. Fifth St., Irving, Tex.	Owns house where defendant and his wife lived, also lives there. See affidavit #14.
Michael Ralph Paine w/m/35 2515 W. Fifth St., Irving, Tex.	Owns house and lives where defendant and his wife lived. See affidavit #15.
Buel Wesley Frazier w/m/19 2439 W. 5th St., Irving, Texas BL3 8965	Works Texas School Book Depository. See affidavit #16. (All listed below were there when offense happened)

(4) Supplementary Witnesses continued Def: Lee Harvey Oswald Murder Offense F 85950

Roy S. Truly w/m 4932 Jade Dr., FR6 9893	Works Texas School Book Depository. See affidavit # 17.
William H. Shelley w/m/37 126 S. Tatum, FE7 1969	Works Texas School Book Depository. See affidavit #18
Mrs. P. A. Reid w/f 1914 Elmwood, FE1 6617	Works Texas School Book Depository See affi avit #19.
Bonnie Ray Williams c/m 1502 Avenue B., Apt. B	Works Texas School Book Depository See affidavit #20.
Linnie Mae Randle w/f/30 2439 W. 5th, Irving, Tex. BL3 8965	Works Texas School Book Depository. See affidavit #21.
Jack E. Dougherty w/m/40 1827 S. Marsalis, WH6 7170	Works Texas School Book Depository. See affidavit #22.
James Earl Jarman, Jr. c/m/33 3942 Atlanta St., HA 8 1837	Works Texas School Book Depository See affidavit #23.
William H. Shelley w/m/37 126 S. Tatum, FE7 1969	Works Texas School Book Depository. See affidavit #24.
Danny Garcia Arce w/m/18 1502 Bennett, TA1 3289	Works Texas School Book Depository See affidavit #25
Billy Nolan Lovelady w/m/26 7722 Hume Dr.	Works Texas School Book Depository. See affidavit #26.
Charles Douglas Givens c/m/37 2511 Carpenter, RI2 4670	Works Texas School Book Depository. See affidavit #27.
Howard Leslie Brennan w/m/44 6814 Woodard, EV1 2713	Saw shooting; was at place of offense of President Kennedy, See affidavit #28.
Amos Lee Euins c/m/15 411 Ave. F., WH3 9701	Was at place of offense, saw shooting. See affidavit #29.
Ronald B. Fischer w/m/24 4007 Flamingo Dr., Mesquite, Texas BR9 0950 Dallas County Auditor's Office	Was at place of offense; saw shooting. See affidavit #30.
Robert E. Edwards w/m/22 821 S. Nursery, Irving, Texas Bus: Dallas County Auditor's Office	Was at place of offense, saw shooting. See affidavit #31
Arnold Lewis Rowland w/m/17 3026 Hammerly St., FE7 1861 Student, Adamson High	Was at place of offense; saw shooting. See affidavit #32.
Jesse James Williams w/m/40 1108 Allen St., Apt. 114, Irving, Texas, or phone PL3 7086 Longview, Texas	Was at place of offense. See Affidavits #33 and #34.

113

COMMISSION EXHIBIT No. 2003—Continued

(5) Supplementary Witnesses continued. Def: Lee Harvey Oswald Murder Offense F 85950

Hugh William Betzner, Jr. 5922 Velasco, TA7 9761	Was at place of offense. See affidavits #35 & #36.
Ernest Jay Owens w/m/36 3005 Peachtree, Mesquite, Tex.	Was at place of offense. See affidavit #37.
Jim Braden w/m/49 621 S. Barrington Dr. Los Angeles, Calif. Pho. 4725301	Was at place of offense. See affidavit #38.
Jean Newman w/f 3893 Clover Lane, FL2 4222	Was at place of offense. See affidavit. #39.
Julia Ann Mercer w/f/23 5200 Belmont, Apt. 208 Bus: 1720 Canton	Was at place of offense. See affidavit # 41 & 40.
Philip Ben Hathaway w/m/28 11021 Quail Run, DI8 6532	Was at place of offense. See affidavit #42.
John Stevens Rutter Lawrence w/m/23 709 Devonshire, Richardson, Tex.	Was at place of offense. See affidavit, #43.
Barbara Walker Rowland w/f/17 3026 Hammerly St., FE7 1861	Was at place of offense. See affidavit #44.
Jean Hill w/f/32 9402 Bluffcreek, EV1 7419	Was at place of offense. See affidavit #45.
John Arthur Chism w/m/23 4502 Underwood Dr., no phone	Was at place of offense. See affidavit #46.
Marvin Faye Chism w/m/19 4502 Underwood Dr.	See affidavit #47.
Mary Ann Moorman w/f/31 2832 Ripplewood, DA1 9390	Was at place of offense. See affidavit #48.
Austin Lawrence Miller w/m 1006 Powell Circle, Mesquite, Tex. AT5 2998	Was at place of offense. See affidavit #49.
S. M. Holland w/m/57 1119 Lucille, Irving, Tex BL3 2185	Was at place of offense. See affidavit #50
Gayle Newman w/m/22 718 W. Clarendon, WH8 6082	Was at place of offense. See affidavit #51.
William Eugene Newman w/m/22 718 W. Clarendon, WH8 6082	Was at place of offense. See affidavit #52.
Larry Florer w/m/23 3609 Potomac	Was at place of offense. See affidavit #53.
Royce Glenn Skelton w/m/23 2509 Reagan, LA1 2745 Bus: 215 Union Terminal, RI1 1396	Was at place of offense. See affidavit #54.

114

COMMISSION EXHIBIT No. 2003—Continued

(6) Supplementary · .esses continued. Ref: Lee Harvey Oswald, Murder, ffense F 85950

J. C. Price w/m/62 2602 Astor, WI 1940 Bus: Terminal Annex, PI8 5611 Ext. 3105	Was at place of offense. See affidavit #55.
Charles Hester w/m/28 2616 Keyhole, Irving, Tex. No phone	Was at place of offense. See affidavit #56.
Emmett Joseph Hudson w/m/56 107 S. Bishop, WH2 2008 bus: City of Dallas Park Dept.	Was at place of offense. See affidavit #57.

115

Form CPS-PC-447

POLICE DEPARTMEN

CITY OF DALLAS

PROPERTY ...

This is a list of evidence released to the FBI from our crime lab 11-26-63

QUANTITY	ARTICLE	BIN NO.	DISPOSITION
1	Italian make 6.5 Rifle Ser. # C 2766 blue steel - wood stock - brn leather sling with 4 x 18 Coated Ordinance ~~Optics Inc Hollywood California~~ O 10 Japan tele scopic sight	Released	
1	Green and Brown Wool Striped Blanket	"	
1	Slug (believed to be 38 Cal)	"	
1	Button off of Policeman's Uniform	"	
1	Homemade paper bag resembling homemade gun case		
1	38 Cal S & W Revolver - Sandblast brn wd hndles - 2" bbl Ser #510210	"	
1	Bullet fragment taken from the body of Gov. John Connally	"	
1	Live round 6.5 mm shell	"	
2	Spent 6.5 hulls ("found under window")	"	
1	Mans brown sport shirt "Taken from Lee Harvey Oswald"	"	
1	Pc Cardboard containing palm print of suspect	"	
3	Empty Cardboard Boxes marked A, B & C.	"	
1	Cardboard Box, empty, size: 11 3/4" x 13" x 17½" "From which thumb print of suspect was found"	"	
1	Partial palm print "off underside gun barrell near end of foregrip" on rifle C 2766	"	
3	Negatives of partial prints "found on trigger housing of rifle Ser #C 2766	"	

Arrested: Lee Harvey Oswald w/m/24
Dallas, Texas.

This inventory was made and invoice typed
~~In Crime Scene Search Section office in presence of:~~

Nº 11176 G

H. W. Hill
Property Clerk

116

If neither evidence nor recovered stolen property, write on face of this form in detail reason for police possession.

IDENTIFICATION BUREAU
CRIME SCENE SEARCH SECTION
POLICE DEPARTMENT, DALLAS, TEXAS

This is a list of evidence that was released to the FBI from our crime lab 11-28-63

__________ SUBMITTED TO

THE CSS OF THE IDENTIFICATION BUREAU THE FOLLOWING:

1- Grey mans jacket with "M" size in collar, laundry mark 30, and 030 in collar. Zipper opening, name tag (created in California by Maurice Holman) on lining of jacket. Bearing initials WEB and GMD placed by officers. Laundry tag B-9738 on bottom of jacket.

EXAMINATION REQUESTED:

LOCATION WHERE COMMITTED Found on parking lot w. of Patton between Tenth and Jefferson.

NATURE OF OFFENSE Murder DATE 11-22-63 OFFENSE# ______

COMPLAINANT ______

SUSPECT ______ RACE __ SEX __ AGE __ ID# ______

______ RACE __ SEX __ AGE __ ID# ______

SIGNATURE OF PERSON SUBMITTING SPECIMEN ______ ID# ______

SIGNATURE OF PERSON RECEIVING SPECIMEN ______ ID# ______

SPECIMEN RELEASED TO ______

DATE ______ TIME ______ BY ______

RESULTS:

Released to Vince Drain. FBI 11-28-63 10 PM

Also released:

5- live 38 cal. Western Special shells initialed EB which were found in the left front pocket of Lee Harvey Oswald.

4- live 38 cal. shells initialed [illegible] HILL (2 Western Special and 2 R P SPL. Removed from gun of Oswald at Tex[illegible] [illegible].

4- Hulls (RP SPL - 2 initialed ED) (1 Western initialed ED) and 1 Western found by Virginia Davis.

1- piece of window ledge 1 inch x 1 inch by 30 inches from window from which shots were thought to be fired.

Vince Drain
11/28/63

117

COMMISSION EXHIBIT No. 2003—Continued

Form No. CPS—GF—479

POLICE DEPARTMENT
CITY OF DALLAS
CASE REPORT

Disposition		Filed	
Date		Date	
Court		With	
Docket		By	
Method		Investigating Officers	J. R. Leavelle
Disposition		Arresting Officers	M. N. McDonald, T. A. Hutson
		Location of Defendant	Deceased

Defendant Lee Harvey OSWALD

Race W Age 24 Sex Male Residence 1026 N. Marsalis

Date of Arrest November 22, 1963 Identification No. 54018

Place of Arrest 231 W. Jefferson Arrest No. 63-98155

Date and Time of Offense November 22, 1963: 1:18 pm Offense No. F 85827

Complainant J. D. Tippit

Where and How Committed 400 Blk. E. 10th Street: with pistol

Charge Murder

Property Taken and Value ______

Evidence and Seizures Eyewitnesses and pistol used. Plus clothing of defendant.

Voluntary Statement no

Accomplices None

List Witnesses and What Each Can Testify to on Reverse Side.

Summary of Case The above defendant was walking west in the 400 blk. of East 10th when stopped by above complainant to be questioned. When Tippit got out of his squad car to walk around in front to further question the defendant, the defendant, Oswald, pulled a .38 pistol and shot Officer Tippit three times: one time each in the head, chest and stomach.

118

Any additional information may be placed on reverse side.

COMMISSION EXHIBIT No. 2003—Continued

WITNESSES:

Helen Markham 323 East 9th St. 1404 Main, RI8 2475-Bus.	This witness can testify that she was waiting on the corner for a bus near the shooting scene. She saw the officer stop Oswald and get out to question him, as Tippit got to the left front fender of squad car Oswald stepped back from the right side of squad car, pulled a pistol and fired several times at the officer. She ran to the sid of the officer and later identified Oswald in police lineup at city hall as the #2 man in 4-man 4:35 pm, 11-22-63. She gave affidavit.
Ted Calloway 501 E. Jefferson WH2 3530 and WH6 8045	Can testify he is manager of used car lot, 501 E. Jefferson just around corner from scene of shooting, that he heard the shots, ran out and saw Oswald running south on Patton Street with pistol in his hand. He ran to the scene and helped load Tippit on stretcher and ambulance then took Officer Tippit's gun, got in to cab with witness Scoggins and attempted to find Oswald. He was unable to do so. He identified Oswald in police lineup 11-22-63, 6:30 pm as #2 man in 4-man lineup, as the man he saw running from the scene of shooting. He also identified jacket in crime lab as the one worn by Oswald or one just like it.
W. W. Scoggins 3138 Alaska FRh 2955 wks: Yellow Cab	Can testify that he is a cab driver, that he was parked on Patton Street at the intersection of 10th St., that he saw the officer get out of his car and start around to question Oswald. He saw Oswald shoot the officer. Oswald then ran past him and heard Oswald say, "That poor dam cop." He later identified Oswald in a lineup as the #3 man in 4-man lineup 11-23-63, 2:15 pm. He also gave an affidavit.
Sam Guinyard c/m	Can testify thathe works as a porter at the used car lot at 501 E. Jefferson, that he was working 11-22-63 when he heard shots being fire, he ran out and saw Oswald running down the street with a pistol in his hand. Went to scene of shooting, saw the officer lying in the street. He later identified Oswald as the #2 man in 4-man lineup 6:30 pm, 11-22-63, as the same man he saw running from the scene of the shooting. This witness also identified the jacket in crime lab as the one suspect wore or one just like the one he wore. This jacket was found between the shooting scene and Texas Theater where arrest was made.
J. P. Leavelle 736 City Detective, Sta. 551	Can testify that he answered the call to 400 E. 10th Street, that he contacted the officers at the scene and interrogated the witnesses, took affidavits from them and held showups for Helen Markham, W. W. Scoggins, Ted Calloway and Sam Guinyard. Each of those people were able to positively identify Oswald as the man they saw at the scene of the Tippit shooting.

COMMISSION EXHIBIT No. 2003—Continued

witnesses continued---case report of Tippit's murder-Lee Oswald, defendant page 2

T. F. Bowley 1454 Summertime Lane FR6 5965	Can testify that he came up on the scene of the shooting just after it happened. He helped load the officer in the ambulance and used the police radio to call in to the dispatcher about the shooting. Gave affidavit.
M. N. McDonald 1178 Radio Patrol Officer Sta. 511	Can testify that he answered a call to the Texas Theatre at 231 W. Jefferson, 11-22-63 about 2:00 pm, thathe entered the rear door and proceeded to the rear of the theatre checking several people as he went. He came to Oswald seated in the center section in rear of theatre. When he approached him, he told Oswald to stand up. Oswald did, bringing his hands to shoulder height. He then struck McDonald in the face. He then grabbed Oswald and began struggling with him, hollering for help from other officers. While struggling for possession of Oswald's pistol it was snapped one time in his face. He did succeed in getting the pistol and giving it to another officer.
T. A. Hutson 1146 Traffic Officer City P. D., Sta. 515	Can testify thathe was looking for suspect in shooting of Officer Tippit when call came out that suspect was at Texas Theater. He went to rear of theater with Officer Hawkins. They entered through the rear door and were checking the patrons from the front to the back. Walked into the aisle behind Oswald as McDonald approach Oswald from opposite side. He saw Oswald stand up and strike McDonald. He grabbed Oswald around the neck. helped subdue him. Also heard the pistol snap as McDonald struggled for it.
Ray Hawkins 887 Patrolman, Traffic Div. City P. D., Sta. 515	Answered call to Texas Theatre, entered through rear door with OfficersWalker, Hutson and Baggett. Was near Oswald and McDonald when the struggle started. He put his handcuffs on Oswald. He also heard the snap of the pistol during the struggle for the gun.
Charles T. Walker 1592 Patrolman, Traffic Div. Sta. 515	Can testify he entered the theatre along with Officers Hawkins, Hutson and McDonald, that he was approaching Oswald from behind as he began grappling with Officer McDonald. He helped subdue him and assisted Officer Hawkins put the handcuffs on Oswald. He led him from the theatre and rode to City Hall with him in back seat of squad car.
Bob K. Carroll 923 Special Service Bureau City P. D., Sta. 566	Can testify that he was at the Texas Theatre,the scene of arrest, assisted in arrest, took pistol from McDonald and later turned it over to Sgt. Hill while enroute to city hall.

119

COMMISSION EXHIBIT No. 2003—Continued

Witnesses continued--case report of Tippit's murder - Lee Oswald, defendant page 3

Gerald Hill Sergeant City P. D., Sta. 513	Can testify he was at scene of arrest, received pistol from Carroll and released it to Det. T. L. Baker at City Hall, Homicide Office. Rode to City Hall in same car with Oswald.
K. E. Lyon 1276 Patrolman, Special Service Bureau, Sta. 566	Can testify that he was at scene of arrest, that he rode to city hall with Oswald along with other officers.
Det. Paul Bentley Identification Bureau City P. D., Sta. 525	Can testify that he was at the scene of the arrest, assisted in the arrest and rode in back seat of squad car with Oswald and C. T. Walker to city hall where the suspect Oswald was turned over to Homicide officers.
Lt. E. L. Cunningham CID, City P. D., Sta. 571	Was at the scene of arrest and along with other men under his command interrogated people in the theatre after the arrest of Oswald.
Julia Postal 2728 Seevers FR 6-5750	Can testify that she is employed at the Texas Theatre. That she saw a suspicious person duck into the theatre on November 22, 1963, just after the shooting of Officer Tippitt. That she called the Police and saw the man later identified as Oswald brought from the Theatre.
William Wayne Whaley 619 Pine Street Lewisville, Texas RI 2-9191	Can testify that he is a cab driver, and that on November 22, 1963, he took a man to the 500 Block of South Beckley. This was just a short time before the shooting of Officer Tippitt. He later identified Oswald as the man he took to the 500 Block of South Beckley.
Johnny C. Brewer 512 North Lancaster Apartment 102 WH 1-4793	Can testify that he saw Oswald come into his store, 213 West Jefferson when a police car came by. He was acting suspicious. He followed him to the theatre and told the cashier about him. She called the police.
Barbara Jennette Davis, w/f/22 400 East 10th WH 3-8120	Can testify she heard some shots on the afternoon of the Tippitt shooting. She jumped up, looked out the door and saw Oswald running across the yard unloading a pistol. After police arrived, she showed them the spot, and a empty shell was found. She later identified Oswald as #2 man in 4-man line up.
Mrs. Virginia Davis, w/f/16 400 East 10th WH 3-8120	Can testify that she heard the shots that killed Officer Tippit and saw Oswald running from the scene. She later that same day identified Oswald as #2 man in 4 man line up.

120

COMMISSION EXHIBIT No. 2003—Continued

Form No. CPS—GY—379

POLICE DEPARTMENT
CITY OF DALLAS
CASE REPORT

Disposition | Filed

Date________ Date________

Court________ With________

Docket________ By J. R. Leavelle and E. R. Beck

Method________ Investigating Officers

Disposition________ L. C. Graves - W. J. Harrison

Arresting Officers

County Jail

Location of Defendant

Defendant Jack Ruby

Race White Age 52 Sex Male Residence 223 South Ewing

Date of Arrest November 24, 1963 Identification No. 36398

Place of Arrest 2001 Commerce Basement Arrest No. 63-98531

Date and Time of Offense November 24, 1963 - 11:21 AM Offense No. F-86056

Complainant Lee Harvey Oswald

Where and How Committed 2001 Commerce Basement, City Hall - with pistol

Charge Murder

Property Taken and Value Life

Evidence and Seizures Bullet from the deceased and clothes of deceased, a .38 calibre revolver belonging to Ruby

Voluntary Statement No

Accomplices None

List Witnesses and What Each Can Testify to on Reverse Side.

Summary of Case Jack Ruby broke from the crowd of news reporters and television men as Oswald was being escorted to a waiting squad car for delivery to the County Jail. He fired from a distance of not more than 2 feet, the bullet hitting Oswald in the left side, going all the way through him, lodging just under the skin on the right side.

121

Any additional information may be placed on reverse side.

COMMISSION EXHIBIT No. 2003—Continued

WITNESSES:

1. J. R. Leavelle
DPD

Can testify to the summary and that he was handcuffed to Oswald's right arm. Saw Jack Ruby shoot Oswald. Also went to Parkland with Oswald in the ambulance and received the bullet recovered from Oswald's body. Witnessed it being marked with an "A" by Nurse Audrey Bue.

2. L. C. Graves
DPD

Can Testify to the summary and that he had hold of Oswald's left arm when he was shot by Ruby, that he took the gun from the hand of Ruby and arrested Ruby, also went to Parkland with Oswald.

3. Capt. W. Fritz
DPD

Can testify to the summary and saw the shooting from a few feet away. Interrogated Defendant Jack Ruby. Had charge of investigation.

4. C. N. Dhority
DPD

Can testify to the summary, also that he was backing the squad car into position to receive Oswald. Also went to Parkland in ambulance with Oswald and received Oswald's clothes at Parkland.

5. D. R. Peck
6. C. W. Brown
DPD

Was moving the lead car into position. Heard shot.

7. Lt. R. E. Swain
DPD - #561

Was in front of Capt Fritz. Was attempting to hold reporters and news media back on East side of ramp at time of shooting.

8. Det. W. J. Harrison
DPD - #576

Was standing in middle of drive way ramp on North side. Saw Ruby dash from his left with gun in hand and shoot Oswald. As Ruby was being subdued, he heard him say, "I hope I killed that SOB." Assisted in arrest of Ruby.

9. T. D. Mc Millian
DPD - #556

Can testify he was stationed just to the left of the jail office door, fell in behind Oswald, and his escorts. Saw Ruby dash from the crowd and heard him say, "You rat, Son of a Bitch, You shot the President." Assisted in arrest of Ruby and took him to fifth floor and stood guard over him.

10. L. D. Montgomery
DPD - #551

Can testify to summary and that he was behind Oswald, Graves and Leavelle heard the shot, helped arrest Ruby and heard him say, "I hope I killed the SOB".

11. Det. B. S. Clardy
DPD - #556

Can testify he was assigned to security in basement. After the shooting, assisted in arrest of Ruby, accompanied Ruby to fifth floor jail and stood guard over him.

12. R. L. Lowery
DPD - #576

Was assigned to security in basement. Observed TV crew moving equipment into place. Was just to the right of Det. Leavelle at time of shooting. Saw Ruby shoot Oswald. Assisted in arrest of Ruby.

CONTINUATION OF CASE REPORT - JACK RUBY, Defendant - LEE HARVEY OSWALD, Complainant

Witnesses (Continued)

13. W. J. Cutchshaw
DPD - #576

Was assigned to basement. Saw the movement of TV equipment into place. Was to the right and rear of Leavelle and Oswald at time of shooting. He saw shooting. Assisted in arrest of Ruby.

14. D. R. Archer
DPD - #556

Was stationed in basement. Saw the shooting. Heard Ruby say, "You SOB". Assisted in arrest. Took Ruby to fifth floor jail and stood guard until relieved by Homicide detective.

All of the below listed officers were in or near the scene of the shooting when Ruby shot Oswald. All are detectives assigned to C. I. D.

I. R. Stephens
H. L. Mc Gee
J. C. Watson
B. H. Combest
James K. Ramsey
D. L. Burgess
R. C. Wagner
W. E. Chambers
I. F. Van Cleave
D. G. Brantley
C. Goolsby
C. A. Gresson
Capt. J. C. Nichols
Lt. V. S. Smart
Lt. W. Wiggins

122

DUTY STATUS OFFICERS OF HOMICIDE AND ROBBERY BUREAU NOVEMBER 22, 1963

NAME	DUTY STATUS	TIME REPORTED FOR DUTY
CAPTAIN J. W. FRITZ	On duty	
LT. T. P. WELLS	ON DUTY	
LT. J. A. BOHART	DAY OFF	6:00 pm
DET. T. L. BAKER	OFF DUTY	1:30 pm
DET. J. P. ADAMCIK	OFF DUTY	2:00 pm
DET. K. L. ANDERTON	VACATION	2:00 pm
DET. E. R. BECK	DAY OFF	3:30 pm
DET. H. H. BLESSING	OFF DUTY	3:30 pm
DET. G. R. BOYCE	VACATION	——
DET. E. L. BOYD	ON DUTY (SPECIAL)	
DET. C. W. BROWN	ON DUTY	
DET. C. N. DHORITY	DAY OFF	2:00 pm
DET. L. C. GRAVES	DAY OFF	2:00 pm
DET. M. G. HALL	DAY OFF	3:00 pm
DET. MARVIN JOHNSON	ON DUTY	
DET. J. R. LEAVELLE	ON DUTY	
DET. V. D. MONAGHEN	OFF DUTY(GRAND JURY)	
DET. L. D. MONTGOMERY	ON DUTY	
DET. H. M. MOORE	DAY OFF	2:00 pm
DET. W. E. POTTS	DAY OFF	2:00 pm
DET. G. F. ROSE	OFF DUTY	2:00 pm
DET. B. L. SENKEL	ON DUTY(SPECIAL)	
DET. R. M. SIMS	ON DUTY (SPECIAL)	
DET. R. S. STOVALL	OFF DUTY	2:00 pm
DET. F. M. Turner	ON DUTY (SPECIAL)	

123

COMMISSION EXHIBIT No. 2003—Continued

DATES PERTINENT TO CASES INVOLVED IN PRESIDENT'S ASSASSINATION

President's assassination	November 22, 1963
Lee Oswald's arrest	November 22, 1963
Lee Oswald's arraignment	November 22, 1963
Murder cases filed	November 22, 1963
Oswald's shooting & death	November 24, 1963
Jack Ruby's arrest	November 24, 1963
Ruby's arraignment	November 24, 1963
Oswald's murder filed	November 24, 1963

124

COMMISSION EXHIBIT No. 2003—Continued

DISTANCES RELATED TO OSWALD'S ACTIVITIES AND TRANSFER

From:	To:	Distance
Elm & Murphy	Elm and Lamar	.2 mi
Elm & Lamar	Commerce & Lamar	3/20 mi.
Commerce & Lamar	500 Bl. N. Beckley	2.5 mi.
500 Blk. N. Beckley	1026 N. Beckley	.5 mi.
500 N. Beckley	404 E. 10th	.6 mi.
404 E. 10th	231 W. Jefferson (Texas Theatre)	.6 mi.
1026 N. Beckley	404 E. 10th	1.1 mi.
1026 N. Beckley	231 W. Jefferson (Texas Theatre)	1.7 mi.
Transfer from City Hall	Sheriff's Office	.9 mi.
Distance from the jail elevator door facing to facing of door of Homicide and Robbery Bureau		20 feet 3 3/4 in.
Ramp from Main Street to the center of the jailhouse doorway		90 ft. 8 inches
Ramp from Commerce St. to the center of the jailhouse doorway		90 ft. 8 inches
Width of ramp		10 ft. 9 inches
Entrance to parking basement from ramp		28 ft. wide
Inner measurements of Capt. Fritz's office		14 feet by 9 ft. 6 inches

125

COMMISSION EXHIBIT No. 2003—Continued

DISTANCES RELATED TO THE PRESIDENT'S MOTORCADE

From:	To:	Distance
Airport	Trade Mart Building	9.9 mi.
Airport	411 Elm	7.6 mi. by motorcade route
Airport	Parkland Hospital	11 mi. by motorcade route
Trade art Building	Parkland Hospital	1.1 mi.
Trade Mart Building	411 Elm	2.3 mi
Parkland Hospital by Captain Fritz's route	411 Elm	3.4 mi. Parkland to Hines to Industrial to Stemmons to Main to Houston to Elm.
411 Elm	Murphy & Elm	.4 mi.
411 Elm	City Hall	Between .9 and 1 mi.
Transfer from City Hall	Sheriff's Office	.9 mi.
Distance from jail elevator door facing to facing of door of Homicide and Robbery Bureau		20 feet 3 3/4 inches

126

COMMISSION EXHIBIT No. 2003—Continued

E

C, : FRITZ:
ALL contacted except as noted
Gannaway

22 November 1963

Captain W. P. Gannaway
Special Service Bureau
Dallas Police Department

Thru:
Lieutenant Jack Revill
Criminal Intelligence Section
Special Service Bureau
Dallas Police Department

SUBJECT: TEXAS SCHOOL BOOK DEPOSITORY
411 ELM

Sir:

The following is a list of the names and addresses of the employees of SUBJECT location.

	NAME	REF. INT.	ADDRESS
	HARVEY LEE OSWALD	NONE	605 ELSBETH
	AVERY DAVIS	NONE	903 WESMONT
	JUDY MCCULLY	NONE	4144 EMERSON
	RUTH NELSON	NONE	6118 GOLIAD
	MARY HOLLIS	NONE	BOX 5944 DALLAS
	VICKIE ADAMS	NONE	3651 FONTANA DRIVE
✓	CHARLES DOUGLAS GIVINS	NONE	NO ADDRESS
	O. V. CAMPBELL	NONE	7120 TWIN TREE LANE
	OTIS N. WILLIAMS	NONE	3429 SOUTHWESTERN BLVD.
	DORIS BURNS	NONE	2617 SHELBY
Not Home	MRS. JIM REESE WH8 9324	NONE	704 N. MADISON
Not Home	DENA CASE	NONE	1703 S. VERNON
	MRS H. G. WHITAKER	NONE	1035 GLEN PARK DRIVE
	PAT LAWRENCE	NONE	302 N. WINDOMERE
✓	DANNY GARCIA ARCE	NONE	1502 BENNETT
✓	BONNIE RAY WILLIAMS	NONE	1502 AVENUE B APT. B.
	RAY EDWARD LEWIS	NONE	2903 SOUTH BLVD.
	LAWRENCE S. FORD	NONE	303 N. FOREST CREST, GARLAND, TEXS
Not Home	RAY EDWARD LEWIS	NONE	2903 SOUTH BLVD. Apt 105
	TERRENCE S. FORD	NONE	303 N. FOREST CREST
Not Home	EDDIE PIPER	NONE	3402 MUNGER
✓	MRS. ROBERT A. REID	NONE	1914 ELMWOOD BLVD.
	JOE RODREQUEZ MOLINA	INT. 2370-9-49	4306 BROWN
Not Home	SANDRA SUE KRAMER	none	404 E. NINETH
	MRS. J. E. DEAN	INT. 2392-16	7727 BEARDEN LANE

✓ Roy S. Truly
~~[illegible]~~
✓ Jack E. Dougherty
✓ James Earl Jarman
✓ Billy Nolan Lovelady

PAGE 1

127

COMMISSION EXHIBIT No. 2003—Continued

- Page Two - TEXAS SCHOOL BOOK DEPOSITORY - 22 November 1963

	NAME	REF. INT.	ADDRESS
Not Home	HAROLD DEAN NORMAN	NONE	1858 BEULAH PLACE
	CARL EDWARD JONES	NONE	3709 SPRING
✓	BUELL WESLEY FRAZIER	NONE	2439 W. FIFTH IRVING, TEXAS
	JOE EARL JARMAN	NONE	3942 ATLANTA
	DOROTHY GARNER	NONE	911 ROYAL FORNEY, TEXAS
	JANE BERRY	NONE	3126 LEGION, APT. 2
Not Home	BETTY FOSTER	NONE	~~5723 MARQUETTA~~ 6827 LEWIS
	MRS. ELSIE DORMAN	NONE	1233 E. LOUISIANA
Not Home	MRS. OLIVER HOPSON	NONE WH2-4743	4717 WAVERLY Gone to Gatesville - be back Sun Even.
	BETTY THORNTON	NONE	3807 ROLINDA
Not Home	SANDRA STYLER	NONE	2102 GRAUWYLER IRVING, TEXAS
	MRS. R.A. REID	NONE	1914 ELMWOOD
✓	GENEVA L. HINE	NONE	2305 OAKDALE ROAD ✓
Not Home	MARTHA REED	NONE	338 W. TENTH
	SARA STANTON	NONE	227 N. EWING
	MRS. ROBERT E. SANDERS	NONE	4226 DELMAR
Not Home	HERBERT LESTER JUNKER	NONE	1709 LINDY LANE Gone to Shreveport be back Tues. IRVING, TEXAS
	L.R. VILES (Left building approximately 12:15 pm, was across the street when shots were fired returned to building at 3:10 pm)	NONE	3210 ST. CROIX CH-7-3854
	MRS. A.D. DICKERSON	NONE	7310 BRIERFIELD DRIVE CA-4-4792
	MARG LEE WILLIAMS	NONE	3718 INWOOD ROAD LA-8-1775
	MRS. HERMAN M. CLAY	NONE	6934 CASA LOMA DA-1-2761
Not Home	GEORGIA RUTH HENDRIX	NONE	2011 N. PRAIRIE TA-3-2615
	PEGGY BIGLER HAWKINS	NONE	2719 CUMBERLAND DRIVE MESQUITE, TEXAS, BR-9-3525

The below listed employees of SUBJECT organization left the building at 12:15 pm, and were standing across the street. They observed the assassination of President JOHN F. KENNEDY, and returned at 2:55 pm.

	NAME	REF. INT.	ADDRESS
	MRS. WILLIAM V. PARKER	NONE	5916 ELLSWORTH TA-3-7600
	DOLORES P. KOONAS	NONE	825 ARPEGE FR-4-7251
	VIRGIE RACKLEY	NONE	BOX 573, FERRIS, TEXAS 544-3827

128

COMMISSION EXHIBIT No. 2003—Continued

- Page Three - TEXAS SCHOOL BOOK DEPOSITORY - 22 November 1963

JAMES CLARK LARUE, 637 EDGE DALE DRIVE, CA-4-2563, found a coat on INDUSTRIAL BOULEVARD under the FT. WORTH TURNPIKE. This coat was given to Lieutenant E. Kaminski, who released it to the Homicide and Robbery Bureau. (LARUE is not an employee of SUBJECT organization).

Respectfully submitted,
R.W. Westphal
R.W. Westphal, Detective
Criminal Intelligence Section

P.M. Parks
P.M. Parks, Detective
Administrative Section

EVIDENCE

1	Italian make 6.5 rifle, serial # C 2766, blue steel, wood stock, brown leather sling with 4 x 18 Coated Ordinance Optics Inc. Hollywood California. O 10 Japan telescopic sight. Carcano carbine	Found by Dept. Sheriff Weitzman on 6th floor, 411 Elm, 5 ' from west wall and 8' from stairway.
1	Green and brown blanket	Found by Dets. Rose, Stovall, Adamcik 2515 W. 5th, Irving, Tex. taken from garage
1	.38 slug	(Taken from body of J. D. Tippit at (Methodist Hospital by Dr. Paul Moellenhoff
1	button	(at 1:30 pm. He gave them to R. A. Davenport
I	homemade paper bag resemblin gun case	Found by Johnson and Montgomery at 411 Elm and brought to Crime Lab.
1	.38 Cal pistol, 2" barrel, S&W, Rev. sandblast finish, brown wooden handles ser.# 510210. Rel. to FBI Agent 11-22-63 and again 11-26-63	M. N. McDonald, DPD, took it from Oswald at 231 W. Jefferson, gave it to Sgt. Jerry Hill who gave it to Det. Baker.
	Bullet fragments taken from body of Governor Connally	Mrs. Audrey Bell, Operating room nurse, to Bob Nolan, D.P.S., to Capt. Fritz, to Crime lab, to FBI.
	Live round 6.5	(Recovered by Dept. Sheriff Luke Mooney at (411 Elm, 6th floor, southeast window.
	6.5 spent rounds (3)	(
1	Man's brown sport shirt "Taken from Lee Harvey Oswald	

* 1 Piece cardboard containing palm print of suspect

* 3 Empty cardboard boxes marked A, B, & C

* 1 cardboard box, empty, size: 11 3/4" x 13" x 17½" "From which thumb print of suspect was found"

* 1 Partial palm print "off underside gun barrel near end of foregrip" on rifle C 2766

* 3 Negatives of partial prints "found on trigger housing of rifle ser. # C 2766.

* Taken from 6th floor, 411 Elm, by Lt. Day and Detective Studebaker and taken to Crime Lab, City Hall.

EVIDENCE (Page 2)

Post Office Box Records:

Post office box #2915 in the name of A. J. Hidell to which rifle was shipped March 20, 1963. Rented from October 9, 1962, to May 14, 1963.

Gave address as 3519 Fairmount.

Selective Service card in the name of Alex James Hidell found on Oswald at time of arrest.

Photostatic copy of money order sent to Klein's in Chicago from Oswald. (attached)

130-A

COMMISSION EXHIBIT No. 2003—Continued

138 ⌀159796 → *21|45 DOLLARS CENTS

2,202,130,462

U. S. Postal Money Order PAY THIS AMOUNT

MAXIMUM VALUE ONE HUNDRED DOLLARS

NOT VALID FOR MORE THAN THIRTY DOLLARS

WARNING DO NOT CASH IF ALTERED

PURCHASER—FILL IN INFORMATION BELOW

PAY TO Klein's Sporting Goods

FROM A. Hidell
PURCHASER'S NAME

P.O. Box 2915
PURCHASER'S STREET ADDRESS

Dallas, Texas
PURCHASER'S CITY AND STATE

DALLAS, TEX. MAR 12 1963

DO NOT FOLD, STAPLE, SPINDLE OR MUTILATE

COMMISSION EXHIBIT No. 2003—Continued

PAYEE MUST ENDORSE BELOW ON LINE MARKED "PAYEE"

OWNERSHIP OF THIS ORDER MAY BE TRANSFERRED TO ANOTHER PERSON OR FIRM IF THE PAYEE WILL WRITE THE NAME OF SUCH PERSON OR FIRM ON THE LINE MARKED "PAY TO" BEFORE WRITING HIS OWN NAME ON THE SECOND LINE. MORE THAN ONE ENDORSEMENT IS PROHIBITED BY LAW. BANK STAMPS ARE NOT REGARDED AS ENDORSEMENTS.

CAUTION

PAY TO THE ORDER OF
PAY TO The First National Bank of Chicago
50 91144
KLEIN'S SPORTING GOODS, INC.

RHJ 11-23-63
JHM 11-23-63
JEP 11-23-63

THIS ORDER BECOMES INVALID AFTER 20 YEARS. THEREAFTER NO CLAIM FOR PAYMENT WILL BE CONSIDERED.

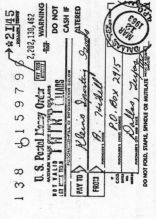

COMMISSION EXHIBIT No. 2003—Continued

7-1a (Rev. 9-7-60)

REPORT
of the
FBI LABORATORY

FEDERAL BUREAU OF INVESTIGATION
WASHINGTON, D. C.

To: Mr. Jesse E. Curry
Chief of Police
Dallas, Texas

November 23, 1963

This examination has been made with the understanding that the evidence is connected with an official investigation of a criminal matter and that the Laboratory report will be used for official purposes only, related to the investigation or a subsequent criminal prosecution. Authorization cannot be granted for the use of the Laboratory report in connection with a civil proceeding.

J. Edgar Hoover
John Edgar Hoover, Director

Re: ASSASSINATION OF PRESIDENT
JOHN F. KENNEDY

YOUR NO.
FBI FILE NO.
LAB. NO. PC-78243 BX
D-436461 AX

Examination requested by: Addressee

Reference: See below

Examination requested: Firearms - Spectrographic - Microscopic Analyes - Fingerprint - Document

Specimens:

Evidence received from Special Agent Elmer L. Todd, Washington Field Office of the FBI on 11/22/63:

Q1 Bullet from stretcher

Evidence received from Special Agent Orin Bartlett of the FBI on 11/22/63:

Q2 Bullet fragment from front seat cushion
Q3 Bullet fragment from beside front seat

2-Chief, U. S. Secret Service

2-FBI, Dallas

Page 1

(continued on next page)

Evidence received from Special Agent James W. Sibert and Special Agent Francis O'Neill, Jr., of the Baltimore Office of the FBI on 11/23/63:

Q4 Metal fragment from the President's head
Q5 Metal fragment from the President's head

Evidence received from Special Agent Vincent E. Drain of the Dallas Office of the FBI on 11/23/63:

Q6 6.5 millimeter Mannlicher-Carcano cartridge case from building
Q7 6.5 millimeter Mannlicher-Carcano cartridge case from building
Q8 6.5 millimeter Mannlicher-Carcano cartridge from rifle
Q9 Metal fragment from arm of Governor John Connolly
Q10 Wrapping paper in shape of a large bag
Q11 Suspect's shirt
Q12 Blanket
Q13 Bullet from Officer Tippett

K1 6.5 millimeter Mannlicher-Carcano rifle, with telescope sight, Serial No. C2766
K2 Paper and tape sample from shipping department, Texas Public School Book Depository
K3 .38 Special Smith and Wesson revolver, Serial No. V510210, Assembly No. 65248

Evidence obtained by FBI Laboratory personnel during examination of the President's limousine:

Q14 Three metal fragments recovered from rear floor board carpet
Q15 Scraping from inside surface of windshield

Also Submitted: Photograph of rifle, K1
Finger and palm prints of Lee Harvey Oswald

Results of examinations:

The bullet, Q1, is a 6.5 millimeter Mannlicher-Carcano rifle bullet. Specimen Q1 weighs 158.6 grains. It consists of a copper alloy jacket with a lead core.

PC-78243 BX

Page 2

(continued on next page)

Specimen Q2 is a portion of the core of a rifle bullet. Specimen Q2 weighs 44.6 grains and is composed of a portion of the copper alloy jacket and a portion of the lead core. Specimen Q3 is a portion of the base section of a copper alloy rifle bullet. Q3 weighs 21.0 grains and is composed of a section of the jacket from which the lead core is missing. It could not be determined whether specimens Q2 and Q3 are portions of the same bullet or are portions of two separate bullets.

The rifle, K1, is a 6.5 millimeter Mannlicher-Carcano Italian military rifle Model 91/38. Test bullets were fired from this rifle for comparison with specimens Q1, Q2 and Q3. As a result, Q1, Q2 and Q3 were identified as having been fired from the submitted rifle.

Specimens Q6 and Q7 are 6.5 millimeter Mannlicher-Carcano cartridge cases. They were manufactured by the Western Cartridge Company, East Alton, Illinois, as was the 6.5 millimeter Mannlicher-Carcano cartridge, Q8.

Test cartridge cases obtained from the submitted rifle were compared with specimens Q6 and Q7. As a result, specimens Q6 and Q7 were identified as having been fired in this rifle. The bullet, Q13, from Officer Tippett, is a .38 Special copper-coated lead bullet. Q13 weighs 156.6 grains and possesses the physical characteristics of 158 grain Western-Winchester revolver bullets. The surface of Q13 is so badly mutilated that there are not sufficient individual microscopic characteristics present for identification purposes. It was determined, however, that the .38 Special Smith and Wesson revolver, K3, is among those weapons which produce general rifling impressions of the type found on Q13.

The lead metal of Q4 and Q5, Q9, Q14 and Q15 is similar to the lead of the core of the bullet fragment, Q2.

A small tuft of textile fibers was found adhering to a jagged area on the left side of the metal butt plate on the K1 gun. Included in this tuft of fibers were gray-black, dark blue and orange-yellow cotton fibers which match in microscopic characteristics the gray-black, dark blue and orange-yellow cotton fibers composing the Q11 shirt of the suspect. These fibers could have originated from this shirt.

PC-78243 BX

Page 3

(continued on next page)

133

A single brown viscose fiber and several light green cotton fibers were found adhering to the Q10 paper bag. These fibers match in microscopic characteristics the brown viscose fibers and light green cotton fibers present in the composition of the Q12 blanket and could have originated from this blanket.

It is pointed out, however, that fibers do not exhibit sufficient individual microscopic characteristics to be positively identified as originating from a particular source to the exclusion of all others.

No fibers were found on the K1 gun that could be associated with the Q12 blanket and no fibers were found on the Q10 paper bag that could be associated with the Q11 shirt.

The debris, including foreign textile fibers and hairs, removed from the Q12 blanket and Q11 shirt has been placed in pillboxes for possible future comparisons. These pillboxes and the glass microscope slides containing fibers removed from K1 and Q10 are being temporarily retained in the Laboratory for possible future comparisons with additional items of the suspect's clothing should they be recovered.

The Q12 blanket has been folded double and one corner has been folded in and pinned with a safety pin. A length of white cotton cord has been tied around this corner giving it a triangular-shaped appearance as if it had once contained a long object.

The paper of the wrapping and the tape, Q10, were found to have the same observable physical characteristics as the known wrapping paper and tape, K2, from the Texas Public School Book Depository.

The inside surface of specimen Q10 did not disclose markings identifiable with the rifle, K1. A number of indentations, folds and extraneous markings appear on the inner surface of the Q10 wrapping.

The latent prints appearing in the photograph taken of the rifle, K1, by the Dallas Police Department, are too fragmentary and indistinct to be of any value for identification purposes. Photographs of this weapon taken by this Bureau also failed to produce prints of sufficient legibility for comparison purposes.

Page 4

PC-78243 BX

(continued on next page)

134

A latent fingerprint was developed on the wrapping paper, Q10, which was identified with the left index finger impression of Lee Harvey Oswald. In addition, one latent palm print developed on specimen Q10 was identified with the right palm print of Oswald.

No latent prints of value were developed on Oswald's revolver, the cartridge cases, the unfired cartridge, the clip in the rifle or the inner parts of the rifle.

Specimens Q1 through Q5, Q14 and Q15 are being retained in the Laboratory until called for by a representative of the U. S. Secret Service.

Specimens Q6 through Q13, K1, K2 and K3 are being returned to the Dallas Police Department by Special Agent Vincent E. Drain of the Dallas Field Office of this Bureau. The photograph of the latent print on the rifle is being returned separately. The fingerprints and palm prints of Oswald are being retained.

PC-78243 BX

Page 5

135

COMMISSION EXHIBIT NO. 2003—Continued

INTERROGATION OF LEE HARVEY OSWALD

We conducted the investigation at the Texas School Book Depository Building on November 22, 1963, immediately after the President was shot and after we had found the location where Lee Harvey Oswald had done the shooting from and left three empty cartridge cases on the floor and the rifle had been found partially hidden under some boxes near the back stairway. These pieces of evidence were protected until the Crime Lab could get pictures and make a search for fingerprints. After Lt. Day, of the Crime Lab, had finished his work with the rifle, I picked it up and found that it had a cartridge in the chamber, which I ejected. About this time some officer came to me and told me that Mr. Roy S. Truly wanted to see me, as one of his men had left the building. I had talked to Mr. Truly previously, and at that time he thought everyone was accounted for who worked in the building. Mr. Truly then came with another officer and told me that a Lee Harvey Oswald had left the building. I asked if he had an address where this man lived, and he told me that he did, that it was in Irving at 2515 W. 5th Street.

I then left the rest of the search of the building with Chief Lumpkin and other officers who were there and told Dets. R. M. Sims and E. L. Boyd to accompany me to the City Hall where we could make a quick check for police record and any other information of value, and we would then go to Irving, Texas, in an effort to apprehend this man. While I was in the building, I was told that Officer J. D. Tippit had been shot in Oak Cliff.

I 136A

Page 2

Immediately after I reached my office, I asked the officers who had brought in a prisoner from the Tippit shooting who the man was who shot the officer. They told me his name was Lee Harvey Oswald, and I replied that that was our suspect in the President's killing. I instructed the officers to bring this man into the office after talking to the officers for a few minutes in the presence of Officers R. M. Sims and E. L. Boyd of the Homicide Bureau and possibly some Secret Service men. Just as I had started questioning this man, I received a call from Gordon Shanklin, Agent in Charge of the FBI office here in Dallas, who asked me to let him talk to Jim Bookhout, one of his agents. He told Mr. Bookhout that he would like for James P. Hosty to sit in on this interview as he knew about these people and had been investigating them before. I invited Mr. Bookhout and Mr. Hosty in to help with the interview.

After some questions about this man's full name I asked him if he worked for the Texas School Book Depository, and he told me he did. I asked him which floor he worked on, and he said usually on the second floor but sometimes his work took him to all the different floors. I asked him what part of the building he was in at the time the President was shot, and he said that he was having his lunch about that time on the first floor. Mr. Truly had told me that one of the police officers had stopped this man immediately after the shooting somewhere near the back stairway, so I asked Oswald where he was when the police officer stopped him. He said he was on the second floor drinking a coca cola when the officer came in. I asked him why he left the building, and he said there was so much excitement he didn't think there would be any more work done that day, and

I 136 B

COMMISSION EXHIBIT NO. 2003—Continued

Page 3

that as this company wasn't particular about their hours, that they did not punch a clock, and that he thought it would be just as well that he left for the rest of the afternoon. I asked him if he owned a rifle, and he said that he did not. He said that he had seen one at the building a few days ago, and that Mr. Truly and some of the employees were looking at it. I asked him where he went to when he left work, and he told me that he had a room on 1026 North Beckley, that he went over there and changed his trousers and got his pistol and went to the picture show. I asked him why he carried his pistol, and he remarked, "You know how boys do when they have a gun, they just carry it."

Mr. Hosty asked Oswald if he had been in Russia. He told him, "Yes, he had been in Russia three years." He asked him if he had written to the Russian Embassy, and he said he had. This man became very upset and arrogant with Agent Hosty when he questioned him and accused him of accosting his wife two different times. When Agent Hosty attempted to talk to this man, he would hit his fist on the desk. I asked Oswald what he meant by accosting his wife when he was talking to Mr. Hosty. He said Mr. Hosty mistreated his wife two different times when he talked with her, practically accosted her. Mr. Hosty also asked Oswald if he had been to Mexico City, which he denied. During this interview he told me that he had gone to school in New York and in Fort Worth, Texas, that after going into the Marines, finished his high school education. I asked him if he won any medals for rifle shooting in the Marines. He said he won the usual medals.

I asked him what his political beliefs were, and he said he had none but that he belonged to the Fair Play for Cuba Committee and told me that

I 136 C

COMMISSION EXHIBIT NO. 2003—Continued

Page 4

they had headquarters in New York and that he had been Secretary for this organization in New Orleans when he lived there. He also said that he supports the Castro Revolution. One of the officers had told me that he had rented the room on Beckley under the name of O. H. Lee. I asked him why he did this. He said the landlady did it. She didn't understand his name correctly.

Oswald asked if he was allowed an attorney and I told him he could have any attorney he liked, and that the telephone would be available to him up in the jail and he could call anyone he wished. I believe it was during this interview that he first expressed a desire to talk to Mr. Abt, an attorney in New York. Interviews on this day were interrupted by showups where witnesses identified Oswald positively as the man who killed Officer Tippit, and the time that I would have to talk to another witness or to some of the officers. One of these showups was held at 4:35 pm and the next one at 6:30 pm. and at 7:55 pm. At 7:05 pm I signed a complaint before Bill Alexander of the District Attorney's office, charging Oswald with the Tippit murder. At 7:10 pm Tippit was arraigned before Judge Johnston. During the second day interviews I asked Oswald about a card that he had in his purse showing that he belonged to the Fair Play for Cuba Committee, which he admitted was his. I asked him about another identification card in his pocket bearing the name of Alex Hidell. He said he picked up that name in New Orleans while working in the Fair Play for Cuba organization. He said he spoke Russian, that he corresponded with people in Russia, and that he received newspapers from Russia.

I 136 D

COMMISSION EXHIBIT No. 2003—Continued

Page 5

I showed the rifle to Marina Oswald, and she could not positively identify it, but said that it looked like the rifle that her husband had and that he had been keeping it in the garage at Mrs. Paine's home in Irving. After this, I questioned Oswald further about the rifle, but he denied owning a rifle at all, and said that he did have a small rifle some years past. I asked him if he owned a rifle in Russia, and he said, "You know you can't buy a rifle in Russia, you can only buy shotguns." "I had a shotgun in Russia and hunted some while there." Marina Oswlad had told me that she thought her husband might have brought the rifle from New Orleans, which he denied. He told me that he had some things stored in a garage at Mrs. Paine's home in Irving and that he had a few personal effects at his room on Beckley. I instructed the officers to make a thorough search of both of these places.

After reviewing all of the evidence pertaining to the killing of President Kennedy before District Attorney Henry Wade and his assistant, Bill Alexander, and Jim Allen, former First Assistant District Attorney of Dallas County, I signed a complaint before the District Attorney charging Oswald with the murder of President Kennedy. This was at 11:26 pm. He was arraigned before Judge David Johnston at 1:35 am, November 23, 1963.

Oswald was placed in jail about 12:00 midnight and brought from the jail for arraignment before Judge David Johnston at 1:36 am.

I 137 A

COMMISSION EXHIBIT No. 2003—Continued

Page 6

On November 23 at 10:25 AM Oswald was brought from the jail for an interview. Present at this time was FBI agent Jim Bookhout, Forrest Sorrells, special agent and in charge of Secret Service, United States Marshall Robert Nash, and Homicide officers. During this interview I talked to Oswald about his leaving the building, and he told me he left by bus and rode to a stop near home and walked on to his house. At the time of Oswald's arrest he had a bus transfer in his pocket. He admitted this was given to him by the bus driver when he rode the bus after leaving the building.

One of the officers had told me that a cab driver, William Wayne Whaley, thought he had recognized Oswald's picture as the man who had gotten in his cab near the bus station and rode to Beckley Avenue. I asked Oswald if he had ridden a cab on that day, and he said, "Yes, I did ride in the cab. The bus I got on near where I work got into heavy traffic and was traveling too slow, and I got off and caught a cab." I asked him about his conversation with the cab driver, and he said he remembered that when he got in the cab a lady came up who also wanted a cab, and he told Oswald to tell the lady to "take another cab".

We found from the investigation the day before that when Oswald left home, he was carrying a long package. He usually went to see his wife of week ends, but this time he had gone on Thursday night. I asked him if he had told Buell Wesley Frazier why he had gone home a different night, and if he had told him anything about bringing back some curtain rods. He denied it.

During this conversation he told me he reached his home by cab and changed both his shirt and trousers before going to the show. He

I 137 B

COMMISSION EXHIBIT No. 2003—Continued

Page 7

said his cab fare home was 85 cents. When asked what he did with his clothing, he took off when he got home, he said he put them in the dirty clothes. In talking with him further about his location at the time the President was killed, he said he ate lunch with some of the colored boys who worked with him. One of them was called "Junior" and the other one was a little short man whose name he did not know. He said he had a cheese sandwich and some fruit and that was the only package he had brought with him to work and denied that he had brought the long package described by Mr. Frazier and his sister.

I asked him why he lived in a room, while his wife lived in Irving. He said Mrs. Paine, the lady his wife lived with, was learning Russian, that his wife needed help with the young baby, and that it made a nice arrangement for both of them. He said he didn't know Mr. Paine very well, but Mr. Paine and his wife, he thought, were separated a great deal of the time. He said he owned no car, but that the Paines have two cars, and told that in the garage at the Paine's home he had some sea bags that had a lot of his personal belongings, that he had left them there after coming back from New Orleans in September.

He said he had a brother, Robert, who lived in Fort Worth. We later found that this brother lived in Denton. He said the Paines were close friends of his.

I asked him if he belonged to the Communist Party, but he said that he had never had a card, but repeated that he belonged to the Fair Play for Cuba organization, and he said that he belonged to the American

I 137 C

COMMISSION EXHIBIT No. 2003—Continued

Page 8

Civil Liberties Union and paid $5.00 dues. I asked him again why he carried the pistol to the show. He refused to answer questions about the pistol. He did tell me, however, that he had bought it several months before in Fort Worth, Texas.

I noted that in questioning him that he did answer very quickly, and I asked him if he had ever been questioned before, and he told me that he had. He was questioned one time for a long time by the FBI after he had returned from Russia. He said they used different methods, they tried the hard and soft, and the buddy method, and said he was very familiar with interrogation. He reminded me that he did not have to answer any questions at all until he talked to his attorney, and I told him again that he could have an attorney any time he wished. He said he didn't have money to pay for a phone call to Mr. Abt. I told him to call "collect", if he liked, to use the jail phone or that he could have another attorney if he wished. He said he didn't want another attorney, he wanted to talk to this attorney first. I believe he made this call later as he thanked me later during one of our interviews for allowing him the use of the telephone. I explained to him that all prisoners were allowed to use the telephone. I asked him why he wanted Mr. Abt, instead of some available attorney. He told me he didn't know Mr. Abt personally, but that he was familiar with a case where Mr. Abt defended some people for a violation of the Smith Act, and that if he didn't get Mr. Abt, that he felt sure the American Civil Liberties Union would furnish him a lawyer. He explained to me that this organization helped people who needed attorneys and weren't able to get them.

I,37A

Page 9

While in New Orleans, he lived at 4907 Magazine Street and at one time worked for the William Riley Company near that address. When asked about any previous arrests, he told me that he had had a little trouble while working with the Fair Play for Cuba Committee and had a fight with some anti-Castro people. He also told me of a debate on some radio station in New Orleans where he debated with some anti-Castro people.

I asked him what he thought of President Kennedy and his family, and he said he didn't have any views on the President. He said, "I like the President's family very well. I have my own views about national policies." I asked him about a polygraph test. He told me he had refused a polygraph test with the FBI, and he certainly wouldn't take one at this time. Both Mr. Bookhout, of the FBI, and Mr. Kelley, and the Marshall asked Oswald some questions during this interview.

Oswald was placed back in jail at 11:33 am. At 12:35 pm Oswald was brought to the office for another interview with Inspector Kelley and some of the other officers and myself. I talked to Oswald about the different places he had lived in Dallas in an effort to find where he was living when the picture was made of him holding a rifle which looked to be the same rifle we had recovered. This picture showed to be taken near a stairway with many identifying things in the back yard. He told me about one of the places where he had lived.

Mr. Paine had told me about where Oswald lived on Neely Street. Oswald was very evasive about this location. We found later that this was the place where the picture was made. I again asked him about his property

I,38A

Page 10

and where his things might be kept, and he told me about the things at Mrs. Paine's residence and a few things on Beckley. He was placed back in jail at 1:10 PM.

At 6:00 PM I instructed the officers to bring Oswald back into the office, and in the presence of Jim Bookhout, Homicide officers, and Inspector Kelley, of the Secret Service, I showed Oswald an enlarged picture of him holding a rifle and wearing a pistol. This picture had been enlarged by our Crime Lab from a picture found in the garage at Mrs. Paine's home. He said the picture was not his, that the face was his face, but that this picture had been made by someone superimposing his face, the other part of the picture was not him at all and that he had never seen the picture before. When I told him that the picture was recovered from Mrs. Paine's garage, he said that picture had never been in his possession, and I explained to him that it was an enlargement of the small picture obtained in the search. At that time I showed him the smaller picture. He denied ever seeing that picture and said that he knew all about photography, that he had done a lot of work in photography himself, that the small picture was a reduced picture of the large picture, and had been made by some person unknown to him. He further stated that since he had been photographed here at the City Hall and that people had been taking his picture while being transferred from my office to the jail door that someone had been able to get a picture of his face and that with that, they had made this picture. He told me thathe understood photography real well, and that in time, he would

I 138 B

COMMISSION EXHIBIT No. 2003—Continued

Page 11

be able to show that it was not his picture, and that it had been made by someone else. At this time he said that he did not want to answer any more questions and he was returned to the jail about 7:15 pm.

At 9:30 on the morning of November 24, I asked that Oswald be brought to the office. At that time I showed him a map of the City of Dallas which had been recovered in the search of his room on North Beckley. This map had some markings on it, one of which was about where the President was shot. He said that the map had nothing to do with the President's shooting and again, as he had one in the previous interviews, denied knowing anything of the shooting of the President, or of the shooting of Officer Tippit. He said the map had been used to locate buildings where he had gone to talk to people about employment.

During this interview Inspector Kelley asked Oswald about his religious views, and he replied that he didn't agree with all the philosophies on religion. He seemed evasive with Inspector Kelley about how he felt about religion, and I asked him if he believed in a Diety. He was evasive and didn't answer this question.

Someone of the Federal officers asked Oswald if he thought Cuba would be better off since the President was assassinated. To this he replied that he felt that since the President was killed that someone else would take his place, perhaps Vice-President Johnson, and that his views would probably be largely the same as those of President Kennedy.

I again asked him about the gun and about the picture of him holding a similar rifle, and at that time he again positively

I 138 C

COMMISSION EXHIBIT No. 2003—Continued

Page 12

denied having any knowledge of the picture or the rifle and denied that he had ever lived on Neely Street, and when I told him that friends who had visited him there said that he had lived there, he said that they were mistaken about visiting him there, because he had never lived there.

During this interview, Oswald said he was a Marxist. He repeated two or three times, "I am a Marxist, but not a Leninist-Marxist. He told me that the station that he had debated on in New Orleans was the one who carried Bill Stakey's program. He denied again knowing Alex Hidell in New Orleans, and again reiterated his belief in Fair Play for Cuba and what the committee stood for.

After some questioning, Chief Jesse E. Curry came to the office and asked me if I was ready for the man to be transferred. I told him we were ready as soon as the security was completed in the basement, where we were to place Oswald in a car to transfer him to the County Jail. I had objected to the cameras obstructing the jail door, and the Chief explained to me that these have been moved, and the people were moved back, and the cameramen were well back in the garage. I told the Chief then that we were ready to go. He told us to go ahead with the prisioner, and that he and Chief Stevenson, who was with him, would meet us at the County Jail.

Oswald's shirt, which he was wearing at the time of arrest, had been removed and sent to the crime lab in Washington with all the other evidence for a comparison test. Oswald said he would like to have a shirt from his clothing that had been brought to the

I 138 D

Page 13

office to wear over the T-shirt that he was wearing at the time. We selected the best-looking shirt from his things, but he said he would prefer wearing a black Ivy League type shirt, indicating that it might be a little warmer. We made this change and I asked him if he wouldn't like to wear a hat to more or less camouflage his looks in the car while being transferred as all of the people who had been viewing him had seen him bareheaded. He didn't want to do this. Then Officer J. R. Leavelle handcuffed his left hand to Oswald's right hand, then we left the office for the transfer.

Inasmuch as this report was made from rough notes and memory, it is entirely possible that one of these questions could be in a separate interview from the one indicated in this report. He was interviewed under the most adverse conditions in my office which is 9 feet 6 inches by 14 feet, and has only one front door, which forced us to move this prisoner through hundreds of people each time he was carried from my office to the jail door, some 20 feet, during each of these transfers. The crowd would attempt to jam around him, shouting questions and many containing slurs. This office is also surrounded by large glass windows, and there were many officers working next to these windows. I have no recorder in this office and was unable to record the interview. I was interrupted many times during these interviews to step from the office to talk to another witness or secure additional information from officers needed for the interrogation.

I 138 E

ADMISSIONS OF JACK LEON RUBY IN CAPTAIN FRITZ'S OFFICE 11-24-63

Name is Jack Ruby. Formerly Rubinstein. Had name changed in Dallas Said attorneys were going to be one or more of the following: Tom Howard, Fred Brunner, Stanley Kaufman (civil attorney), Jim Arnton, and C. A. Droby.

Had gun (Colt snub-nose No. 2744-LW, .38 cal. equipped with hammer guard) for two or three years. Bout it from Ray's (possibly Ray's Hdw. and Sporting Goods, 730 Singleton) on Singleton.

Said roommate is George Senator.

Claimed he came in off of Main Street down ramp to basement of City Hall.

Felt Oswald was a red. Felt Oswald was alone in the assassination. cf Ruby statement wash Post 1/30/64 Had seen him in assembly room at showup. Knew who he was going for. Didn't want to be a martyr. Said it was a buildup of grievance.

Said he closed both is clubs; Vegas at 3508 Oak Lawn and Carousel at 1312½ Commerce Street.

Said he had never seen Oswald before he had seen him at the police station.

Said he was formerly in mail order business and had been a labor organizer.

Has nothing but fondness for the Police Department. Said that he felt very badly when officer "Slick" got killed.

Said that since President was killed he had seen people in night clubs laughing, no one in mourning, and had heard eulogies on TV. Saw the President's brother Bobby on TV. That all this created a moment of insanity. Read about the letter someone sent to little Carolyn.

Knows police department is wonderful and his heart is with the police department, and that if ever opportunity for participation in police battle, he would like to be a part of it.

139

COMMISSION EXHIBIT No. 2003—Continued

His mother and father separated for 25 years. Owes "Uncle Sam" a big piece of money. He has love for the city.

Sister operated on recently. She was hysterical about the President's being killed. That he had gone to the Synagogue Friday night - heard eulogy regarding the President. That he had been in mourning from that time on. That he went over where the wreaths were where the President was shot.

Wants Captain Fritz not to hate him. That he had been with the Union (Scrap Iron and Junk Dealers Assn.) and one of his dear friends, Leon Cook, was killed and that he had come to the place where it happened; that Jim Martin we killed Cook; that Martin was political and had affiliations and got out of it; that he had used the name "Leon" after his friend Leon Cook had been killed.

That his roommate, George Senator, sells postcards; that his politics is Democratic but votes for the man. Has brothers who are: Samuel Ruby, who services washaterias; Earl Ruby, who has cleaning plant in Detroit; and Hyman Rubenstein, salesman in Chicago. He said no one else was involved with him in the shooting of Oswald.

140

COMMISSION EXHIBIT No. 2003—Continued

POLICE DEPARTMENT
Dallas, Texas

THE JAILER IS HEREBY AUTHORIZED
TO RELEASE THE FOLLOWING PERSONS:

OUT: 11-23-63 (DATE) 12:35 AM. (TIME)
IN: 11-23-63 (DATE) 110A (TIME)

Lee H. Oswald

The above prisoners are in the custody of:

Jailer | Officer | Rank Lt. | Bureau or Dept. I. D.

POLICE DEPARTMENT
Dallas, Texas

THE JAILER IS HEREBY AUTHORIZED
TO RELEASE THE FOLLOWING PERSONS:

OUT: Nov. 23, 1963 (DATE) 10:25AM (TIME)
IN: Nov 23/63 (DATE) 11 33 (TIME)

Lee Harvey Oswald

The above prisoners are in the custody of:

Robinson (Jailer) | R. M. Sims, M. Hall, E. L. Boyd (Officer) | Det. (Rank) | H&R (Bureau or Dept.)

141

COMMISSION EXHIBIT No. 2003—Continued

POLICE DEPARTMENT
Dallas, Texas

THE JAILER IS HEREBY AUTHORIZED
TO RELEASE THE FOLLOWING PERSONS:

OUT: 11-23-63 (DATE) 6:00 PM (TIME)
IN: 11-23-63 (DATE) 7 15 PM (TIME)

Lee Henry Oswald

The above prisoners are in the custody of:

Jailer J. J. S. | Hall, Sims, Graves (Officer) | Dets (Rank) | Homicide (Bureau or Dept.)

POLICE DEPARTMENT
Dallas, Texas

THE JAILER IS HEREBY AUTHORIZED
TO RELEASE THE FOLLOWING PERSONS:

OUT: 11-24-63 (DATE) 9 30 am (TIME)
IN: 11-24-63 (DATE) (TIME)

Lee Oswald

DECEASED

The above prisoners are in the custody of:

Robinson (Jailer) | Graves (Officer) | Det (Rank) | H&R (Bureau of Dept.)

142

COMMISSION EXHIBIT No. 2003—Continued

POLICE DEPARTMENT
Dallas, Texas

THE JAILER IS HEREBY AUTHORIZED
TO RELEASE THE FOLLOWING PERSONS:

OUT: Nov. 24,1963 3:05 PM
DATE TIME

IN: 11-24-63 4P
DATE TIME

Jack Ruby

The above prisoners are in the custody of:

J.J.S. Jailer — E. L. Boyd Officer — Det Rank — H&R Bureau or Dept.

POLICE DEPARTMENT
Dallas, Texas

THE JAILER IS HEREBY AUTHORIZED
TO RELEASE THE FOLLOWING PERSONS:

OUT: 11/25/6 11:45 A
DATE TIME

IN: 11-25-63 12:05 P
DATE TIME

Jack Ruby

The above prisoners are in the custody of:

Blunkall Jailer — Leavelle Officer — Det Rank — H&R Bureau of Dept.

143

COMMISSION EXHIBIT No. 2003—Continued

[?]. DALLAS NEWS Thursday

Fulton Lewis, Jr.

The Washington Report

WASHINGTON, Dec. 12 -- The heretofore unidentified "top-ranking Communist" who swapped letters with Lee Harvey Oswald is a veteran revolutionary once convicted of teaching the violent overthrow of the U. S. government.

He is Arnold Samuel Johnson, who, it can be revealed on excellent authority, wrote Oswald from Communist Party headquarters in New York.

Johnson urged Oswald to "keep in touch" as he moved back and forth from Dallas to New Orleans. While the Johnson letters indicate Oswald was not under Communist discipline, they do show him to be a dedicated Marxist.

Johnson was indicted in 1951, and convicted in 1953, of violating the Smith Act. The prosecution showed that Johnson was loyal to a foreign power and that he had taught the violent overthrow of the federal government. He served three years in prison, getting out in 1957.

Johnson acts now as the Communist Party's legislative director and serves as a member of the party's national committee. When my associate, Bill Schulz, phoned Johnson to ask about the Oswald letters, an aide informed Mr. Schulz that Johnson was "unavailable for any comment."

It was not the first time that Johnson has clammed up. On May Day, 1962, the grey-haired party offic[...] scheduled to appear [...] York radio show. [...] gram host, Barr[...] arranged t[...] stein, a [...] munist, c[...] with the p[...] spokesman. Johnson stalked o[...] program when told he [...] share the mike with [...]stein, a former Com[...] who serves now as a[...] consultant to vari[...] gove[...] security agenci[...]

NOTE: Another Oswald pen pal was Vincent Theodore Lee, head of the Fair Play for Cuba Committee. Lee first denied any knowledge of Oswald, who was arrested once for passing out Fair Play leaflets in New Orleans.

Lee then discovered in his files six letters from Oswald, and turned them over to the FBI. Meanwhile, federal authorities had uncovered letters from Lee among Oswald's effects. The letters carried instructions on setting up local Fair Play chapters.

Lee has never been identified as a Communist. In an appearance before the Senate Internal Subcommittee, however, Lee took the Fifth Amendment more than 75 times in refusing to answer questions. He ducked queries on Communist Party membership and on Cuban assistance to his "[...] [...]nt" group.

Copyright 1963, King Features [...]ndicate, Inc.

Orphan Gets A Deer

The Park Cities Jaycees in cooperation with the Fowler's Orphans Home took two orphan boys to Abilene for a two day deer hunt. Clint Frank, Bob Campbell, and Greg Boss handled all the arrangements for the Jaycees. The boys flew out to Abilene in a private plane owned by W. C. Fain.

Nick Browndyke, treasurer of the Park Cities Jaycees escorted the boys, David Hopkins and Ben Haskel, from the orphans home to Abilene.

All the boys got a shot at many deer, but the only one to prove himself a marksman [...] David Hopkins who got a [...] size buck.

KEY TO DISTINC[...]

143 A

COMMISSION EXHIBIT No. 2003—Continued

403

FAIR PLAY FOR CUBA COMMITTEE

799 BROADWAY NEW YORK 3, N. Y. ORegon 4-8295

May 22, 1963

Lee H. Oswald
4907 1/c Magazine St.
New Orleans, La.

Dear Friend:

We received your notice of change of address and in looking for your old mailing plate and not finding one can only conclude that either it was pulled some time ago when mail was returned to us or that your subscription has long since expired.

In any event, We are enclosing a renewal form and a copy of our current literature catalog for you to catch up with. We hope to hea- from you soon so that we may again have your name amongst those who continue to support the efforts of our Committee.

Fraternally,

V. T. Lee

V. T. Lee,
National Director

Commission Exhibit No. 2003—Continued

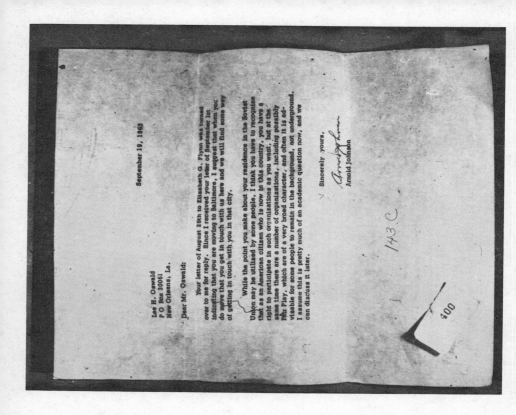

September 19, 1963

Lee H. Oswald
P O Box 30061
New Orleans, La.

Dear Mr. Oswald:

Your letter of August 28th to Elizabeth G. Flynn was turned over to me for reply. Since I received your letter of September 1st indicating that you are moving to Baltimore, I suggest that when you do move that you get in touch with us here and we will find some way of getting in touch with you in that city.

While the point you make about your residence in the Soviet Union may be utilized by some people, I think you have to recognize that as an American citizen who is now in this country, you have a right to participate in such organizations as you want, but at the same time there are a number of organizations, including possibly Fair Play, which are of a very broad character, and often it is advisable for some people to remain in the background, not underground. I assume this is pretty much of an academic question now, and we can discuss it later.

Sincerely yours,

Arnold Johnson

Arnold Johnson

143 C

400

Commission Exhibit No. 2003—Continued

COMMUNIST PARTY, U. S. A.

23 WEST 26th STREET • NEW YORK 10, N. Y. • MU. 5-5755

July 31, 1963

L. H. Oswald
P O Box 30061
New Orleans, La.

Dear Mr. Oswald:

Your letter to the WORKER has been referred to me for reply.

It is good to know that movements in support of fair play for Cuba has developed in New Orleans as well as in other cities. We do not have any organizational ties with the Committee, and yet there is much material that we issue from time to time that is important for anybody who is concerned about developments in Cuba.

Under separate cover we are sending you some literature.

Sincerely yours,

Arnold Johnson

Arnold Johnson, Director
Information and Lecture Bureau

406

143E

COMMISSION EXHIBIT No. 2003—Continued

FAIR PLAY FOR CUBA COMMITTEE

799 BROADWAY NEW YORK 3, N. Y. ORegon 4-8295

May 29, 1963

Lee H. Oswald
4907 L/C Magazine Street
New Orleans, Louisiana

Dear Friend:

Thank you for your prompt reply. Enclosed are your card and receipt, along with our thanks and welcome.

Your interest in helping to form an FPCC Chapter in New Orleans is gratefully received. I shall try to give you some basic information now so that you may have a better picture of what this entails.

For one thing, I am enclosing a copy of our Constitution and By-Laws for all Chapters and Student Councils. You will note that there is considerable autonomy for an organization our size. We try and let all Chapters operate according to the local requirements. Naturally, there a minimul regulations which must be met.

(All Chapters can receive literature in bulk at a discounted rate and resell at the retail price and use the proceeds for further Chapter activities. Credit is extended and payment is not required with the order. We do expect payment within a reasonable period so that we may continue our end of the operation.

It would be hard to concieve of a chapter with as few members as seem to exist in the New Orleans area. I have just gone through our files and find that Lousiana seems somewhat restricted for Fair Play activities. However, with what is there perhaps you could build a larger group if a few people would undertake the disciplined responsibility of concrete organizational work.

We certainly are not at all adverse to a very small Chapter but certainly would expect that there would be at least twice the amount needed to conduct a legal executive board for the Chapter. Should this be reasonable we could readily issue a charter for

COMMISSION EXHIBIT No. 2003—Continued

FAIR PLAY FOR CUBA COMMITTEE

799 BROADWAY NEW YORK 3, N. Y. ORegon 4-8295

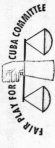

a New Orleans Chapter of FPCC. In fact, we would be very, very pleased to see this take place and would like to do everything possible to assist in bringing it about. We feel that the south-east is a very difficult area to work because of our lack of contacts. Our only southeastern Chapter right now is that in Tampa, Florida which I originally organized before coming up to work in the National Office.

I for one am convinced of the possibility of such an enterprise but know from experience that it is quite a problem and requires some sacrifice on the part of those involved.

You must realize that you will come under tremendous pressures with any attempt to do FPCC work in that area and that you will not be able to operate in the manner which is conventional here in the north-east. Even most of our big city Chapters have been forced to abandon the idea of operating an office in public. The national office here in New York is the only one in the country today and the New York City Chapter uses our office too so it is the only Chapter with an office. Most Chapters have discovered that it is easier to operate semi-privately out of a home and maintain a P.O. Box for all mailings and public notices. ((A P.O. Box is a must for any Chapter in the organization to guarnatee the continued contact with the national even if an individual should move or drop out.)) We do have a serious and often violent opposition and this proceedure helps prevent many unnecessary incidents which frighten away prospective supporters. I definitely would not recommend an office, at least not one that will be easily identifyable to the lunatic fringe in your community. Certainly, I would not recommend that you engage in one at the very beginning but wait and see how you can operate in the community through several public experiences.

We will be able to give you some assistence from here, but not much. It is up to the local Chapters to handle their own affairs. You shaould have at least access

COMMISSION EXHIBIT No. 2003—Continued

FAIR PLAY FOR CUBA COMMITTEE

799 BROADWAY NEW YORK 3, N. Y. ORegon 4-8295

to a mimeo machine to prepare public material if you are going to operate. A good typewriter is essential and above all people that will carry out the million and one mechanical functions necessary to make it a going operation.

(Note: when you contact people by mail we recommend that only first class be used and that no full name go on the return address on the outside of the envelope.) You will notice how we work our's here on the national level. Many people will respond better with this type of protection against nutty neighbors and over curious postment. These may sound like small things to you, but I can assure you that we have gone through thi a thousand and more time the length and breadth of the country and have learned a great deal over the last three years through some bitter experience.

Naturally, I would like to communicate with you a great deal more concerning yourself so that we can get to know you and possibly be of some assistence to you as we get more information.

We hope to hear from you very soon in this regard and are looking forward to a good working relationship for the future. Please fell free to discuss this matter quite thoroughly with me.

Fraternally,

V. T. Lee

V. T. Lee,
National Director.

COMMISSION EXHIBIT No. 2003—Continued

LITERATURE

NAME	PLACE FOUND	MICROFILM #
APPLICATION THE MILITANT	IRVING	#380
APPLICATION SLIP FOR FPCC	BECKLEY	416
APPLICATION SLIPS FOR FPCC (187)	IRVING	96
BOOKLET, "THE COMING AMERICAN REVOLUTION" by JAMES CANNON	IRVING	330
BOOKLET, CONTINENTAL CONGRESS OF SOLIDARITY WITH CUBA, BRAZIL BY FPCC	IRVING	319
BOOKLET, CUBAN COUNTER REVOLUTIONARIES TO THE U.S. PUBLISHED BY FPCC	IRVING	307
BOOKLET, DOBBS WEISS CAMPAIGN COMMITTEE, 116 UNIVERSITY PLACE, NYC, ENTITLED "APAMPHLAR"	IRVING	308
BOOKLET, FIDEL CASTRO DENOUNCES BUREAUCRACY AND SECTARIANISM	IRVING	304
BOOK, list of FPCC, NYC	IRVING	329
BOOK, FOREIGN LANGUAGE, 3PAGES	IRVING	201
BOOK, FOREIGN LANGUAGE, 2 PAGES	IRVING	202
BOOKLET, IDEOLOGY AND REVOLUTION BY JEAN PAUL SARTE	IRVING	313
BOOKLET, LIST OF RUSSIAN AND COMMUNIST LITERATURE PUBLICATIONS	IRVING	309
BOOKLET, "THE MCCARRAN ACT AND THE RIGHT TO TRAVEL	IRVING	311
BOOKLET, "THE NATION" DATED 1-23-60	IRVING	320
BOOKLET, THE PACT OF MADRID BY THE COMMITTED OF DEMOCRATIC SPAIN	IRVING	310
BOOK, RUSSIAN	IRVING	84
BOOKS, RUSSIAN (18)	IRVING	74-83
BOOK, Russian LANGUAGE # 732648	IRVING	112
BOOKLET, "SOCIALIST WORKERS PARTY" BY JOSEPH HANSEN	IRVING	305

144

COMMISSION EXHIBIT No. 2003—Continued

NAME	PLACE FOUND	MICROFILM #
BOOK, "SOFIA" DATED 1962	IRVING	324
BOOKLET, SPEECH AT THE UN BY FIDEL CASTRO	IRVING	318
BOOK, "THE SPY WHO LOVED ME" BY IAN FLEMING	BECKLEY	410
BOOK, "LIVE AND LET DIE" BY IAN FLEMING	BECKLEY	410
BOOK, "A STUDY OF USSR AND COMMUNISM HISTORICAL" BY KEIRER AND NELSON	BECKLEY	409
CIRCULARS, FPCC, BILL JONES PRINTING CO., NEW ORLEANS	BECKLEY	415
HANDBILL, FPCC, LEE H. OSWALD, 4907 MAGAZINE ST., NEW ORLEANS	IRVING	335
HANDBILL, FPCC, L. H. OSWALD, 4907 MAGAZINE ST., NEW ORLEANS, LA.	BECKLEY	414
HANDBILLS "HANDS OFF CUBA" (178) JOIN THE FPCC	IRVING	97
HANDBILLS, "HANDS OFF CUBA" (180) JOIN THE FPCC NEW ORLEANS BRANCH	IRVING	300
LETTER FROM JAMES J. FORNEY ON LETTERHEAD OF GUS HALL, BENJAMIN J. DAVIS, DEFENSE COMMITTEE, NYC, 12-13-62	BECKLEY	405
LETTER, FROM FARRELL DOBBS, NATIONAL SECRETARY OF SOCIALIST WORKERS PARTY TO LEE OSWALD11-5-62	BECKLEY	401
LETTER, SIGNED "GENE" TO "DEAR LEE" FROM JESUIT HOUSE OF STUDIES, MOBILE, ALABAMA LETTERHEAD 8-22-63	BECKLEY	412
LETTER, FROM JESUIT HOUSE OF STUDIES, MOBILE, ALABAMA TO LEE AND MARIE	BECKLEY	430
LETTER, FROM PETER P. GREGORY TO OSWALD RE: ABILITY TO TRANSLATE	BECKLEY	413
LETTER, FROM ARNOLD JOHNSON, P. O. BOX 30061, NEW ORLEANS, TO OSWALD	BECKLEY	400
LETTER, FROM ARNOLD JOHNSON, DIRECTOR INFORMATION AND LECTURE BUREAU CP 7-31-63 P. O. BOX 30061, NEW ORLEANS TO OSWALD	Beckley	406
LETTER, FROM V. T. LEE, NATIONAL DIRECTOR OF FPCC, NY TO OSWALD, 5-22-63	BECKLEY	403
LETTER, FROM V. T. LEE, NATIONAL DIRECTOR FPCC, N.Y.C., TO OSWALD 4907 MAGAZINE, NEW ORLEANS	BECKLEY	407

145

COMMISSION EXHIBIT No. 2003—Continued

LITERATURE-continued

page 3

NAME	PLACE FOUND	MICROFILM #
LETTER, FROM PAUL PIAZZA TO OSWALD, ON JESUIT HOUSE OF STUDIES, MOBILE, ALABAMA LETTERHEAD	BECKLEY	429
LETTER, FROM PIONEER PUBLISHERS 4-26-63	IRVING	363
LETTER, FROM JOSEPH TACK, SOCIALISTS WORKER PARTY TO OSWALD	BECKLEY	445
LETTER, FROM JOHNNY TACKETT ON FORT WORTH PRESS LETTERHEAD TO OSWALD	BECKLEY	438
LETTER, FROM LOUIS WEINSLOCK, GEN. MGR. OF THE WORKER 12-19-62 to OSWALD	BECKLEY	404
MAGAZINE, "FRIENDS WORLD NEWS"	IRVING	87
MAGAZINE, "THE MILITANT"	IRVING	85
MAGAZINE, "THE NEW REPUBLIC", REPRINT FROM 9-12-63	IRVING	322
MAGAZINE, COVER, GROUP OF MEN DRESSED IN BLACK STANDING BEHIND WHAT APPEARS TO BE A MASTER OF CEREMONIES DRESSED IN WHITE	IRVING	198
MAGAZINE, WRAPPER, ADDRESSED TO LEE OSWALD, MINSK, RUSSIA	IRVING	191
NEWSPAPER, "THE WORKER"	IRVING	86
NEWSPAPER, CLIPPING, RE: THE PRESIDENT	IRVING	120
NEWSPAPER, CLIPPING, NEW ORLEANS PAPER	IRVING	98
NEWSPAPER, CLIPPING, FORT WORTH PRESS, SHOWING PHOTO OF IRANIAN NATIVE, MRS. JOHN R. HALL	IRVING	270
NEWSPAPER, CLIPPING (OSWALD DEFECTION AND CARTOON REGARDING DEFECTORS)	BECKLEY	417
NEWSPAPER, CLIPPING (TIMES PICAYUNE, NEW ORLEANS, RE: OSWALD'S FINE FOR DISTURBING PEACE. SENT FROM ROOM 329, 799 BROADWAY, N. Y. C.	BECKLEY	413
NEWSPAPERS, (7) RUSSIAN LANGUAGE	IRVING	381
NEWSPAPER, SUBSCRIPTION FORMS (3) <u>THE WORKER</u> WITH RETURN ENVELOPES TO PUBLISHERS NEW PRESS	IRVING	380

146

COMMISSION EXHIBIT No. 2003—Continued

LITERATURE-continued

page 4

NAME	PLACE FOUND	MICROFILM #
PAMPHLET, " THE END OF THE COMINTERN", BY JAMES P. CANNON	IRVING	317
PAMPHLETS, "THE CRIME AGAINST CUBA" CURLISS LAMONT	IRVING	303
PAMPHLETS, "THE CRIME AGAINST CUBA" BY CURLISS LAMONT	IRVING	99
PAMPHLET, "THE REVOLUTION MUST BE A SCHOOL OF UNFETTERED THOUGHT" BY FIDEL CASTRO	IRVING	312
PAMPHLET, "THE ROAD TO SOCIALISM" BY BLAS ROCA N	IRVING	315
PAMPHLET, RUSSIAN BEARING #500 ON COVER	IRVING	325
PAMPHLETS, RUSSIAN	IRVING	89-94
PAMPHLET, #13, RUSSIAN DOCUMENT	IRVING	192
PAMPHLET, NEW YORK SCHOOL FOR MARXIST STUDY, FALL TERM 1963	BECKLEY	411
PAMPHLET, THE WEEKLY PEOPLE ENTITLED "AUTOMATION, A JOB KILLER"	IRVING	321
PHOTOS, "VISIT TO USSR" (4)	IRVING	366
PHOTOS, FIDEL CASTRO (6)	IRVING	367
PHOTO, FIDEL CASTRO	IRVING	368
PHOTO, FEMALE RUSSIAN WORKERS IN RADIO FACTORY	IRVING	332
PHOTO, RUSSIAN WORKERS	IRVING	331

147

COMMISSION EXHIBIT No. 2003—Continued

military and Far East

I served in the U.S.M.C. from Oct 1956-Sept 1959 during which time I served in San Diego, calif Oct 56-april 60 camp pendleton april-may 1957, Jacksonville fla may-June 1957, Santa anna calif June-august 1957, and in Japan August 1958-Dec 1958, Santa Anna, El toro air base Dec 1958-Sept 1959, 1 month on leave during Dec. 1958.

my stay in the far East included 8 months in Japan from Sept. 1957 to nov. 1957 and from may-Oct 1958 During Dec 57 to may 58 I was stationed at subic bay near manila, Philippine Islands.

I served in Electronics school Jacksonville fla., and advanced Radar school Biloxi mississippi. I also recived my high school level diploma at the same time as my schooling in Biloxi miss.

A. DISCHARGE DD 214
B. DIPLOMA - JACKSONVILLE FLA. SCHOOL
C " BILOXIE MISS. "
D. CERTIFICATE OF HIGH SCHOOL COMPLETION

148

Resident of USSR

I lived in moscow from Oct-16, 1959 to Jan 4, 1960 during which time I stayed at the Berlin and metropoles hotel. I then lived in minsk from Jan 5 1960 to July 1962. I visited moscow during June 1961 and June 1962 for a few weeks in minsk I was granted a small apartment on Kalinina St. later re-named Komunist St. I worked at the Belorussian Radio and T.V. plant as a metal worker.

A. CLIPPINGS

149

organizes

on may 29 1963 I requested permission from the FPCC headquarters at 799 Broadway New York 3, N.Y. to try to form a local branch in New Orleans. I received a cautionet but enthusiastic go-ahead from V.T. Lee national Director of FPCC. I than make a layouts and had printed public literature for the setting up of a local FPCC. I hired persons to distribute literature. I than organized persons who display receptive attitudes toward Cuba to distribute pamplets, I sough responses from latin american consuls of which there are many here in New Orleans, I infiltrated the Cuban Student directorate and that harrassed them with information I gained including having the N.O. city attorney general call them in a put a restraining order pending a hearing on some so-called bonds for invasion they were selling in the New Orleans area. I caused the formation of a small, active, FPCC organization of members and sympatizers where before there was none.

150

Photographes

I have worked in the Jaggers-Chiles-Stovall typographical co. 522 Browder St. Dallas, Texas, I worked from Oct 1, 1962 to April 1, 1962. I am proficient in the photographic arts known as reverses, transparencies, line, modification, squats, blowups, and miniaturization. I have submitted and been commended for photo work for the party. I am familiar with layout and art work and am aquainted with cold medel and hot medal process's in printing.

A. TAX RETURNS of JCS
B LETTERS COMMENDING PHOTO WORK
BY THE PARTY

151

marxist

I first read the communist manifesto and 1st volume of capital in 1954 when I was 15. I have study 18th century filosopher works by Lenin after 1959 and attend numerous marxist reading circles and groups at the factory where I worked some of which were complusory and others which were not. also in Russian through newspapers, radio and TV. I leared much of marx Engles and Lenins works. such articles are give very good coverage daily in the USSR.

after my stay in the Soviet Union upon my return to the USA I contined to recive by subsicbtion from "Kankini Inc." Soviet ideological and informative literature, "agitator" newspaper Soviet "Belorusia" "krockill" satrical polical magazine and the CPUSA newspaper "Worker" aslo I recive the well known Soviet Journal "Ogonyok". I also have recived literature from the Soviet Embassy, Washington D.C.

A. Proof of subsription to Soviet Journals

B. Subsription from 1962 of Worker

152

COMMISSION EXHIBIT No. 2003—Continued

11/23/63 H.m.m. & pa. Rdf. J.F.R

Russian

I leared the Russian language during my about three years residence in moscow and minsk USSR October 1959 - July 1962. I study russian elemantry and advanced grammar from text books with a English speaking Russian intourist teacher by the name of Rosa agafonava, minsk Jan-May 1960. I am totaly proficient in speaking conversational Russian. I can read non-technical Russian text without difficulty and can to a less extent write in the Russian language.

A. LETTER OF PROFICIENCY

153

COMMISSION EXHIBIT No. 2003—Continued

RADIO SPECKER AND LECTURER

B

on august 22 I was invited by
Gene murret, who is studing for
catholic priesthood, to give a leture
on Russia, Gene murret is the
son of my mother sister, mrs D.
murret 757 french st. N.O. La.
This Lecture took place July 27, 1963 7:00 P.M
at the university Jesuit House of Studies
Spring hill station mobile alabama over
50 student preist all of whom were college

154

11/23/63
H.M.M.
S.A.
(illegible)
GR

gruates taking the 4 years subsiquent
course for the priesthood attend several
of the college's professors also were
present. This leture lasted for 1 hr. 10 min
after which there was 20 minutes of questions
from the audience. This leture took
place in the setorium where women
are not allowed two an all-male
audience attend, the moderator of
this leture was Paul Piazza, Jesuit.

LETURE
A. invitation letter
B. comments letter

RADIO
NO RECORDS

155

A-B C D

SREET AGITATION

I am experienced in street agitation having done it in New Orleans in connection with the F.P.C.C. On Aug. 9 1963 I was accosted by three anti-Castro Cubans and was arrested for "causing a disturbance" I was interrogated by intelligence section of New Orleans Police Dept. and held overnight being bailed out the next morning by relatives I subsequently was fined 10$ charges against the three Cubans were droped by the judge.

On Aug 16 I organized a four man FPCC demonstration in front of the International trade mart in New Orleans. This demonstration was filmed by WDSU-TV and shown on the 6:00 news.

A / On August 17 I was invited by WDSU-Radio to appear on the August 17 radio program Latin American Focus at 7.30 PM. The moderator was Bill Stuckey who put questions to me for half an hour about FPCC attitudes and opinions.

B

After this program I was invited to take part in a radio debate between John Buttles of "Inca" anti communist propganda organization representative and Carlos Bringuier Cuban exile

156

COMMISSION EXHIBIT No. 2003—Continued

123/63 Am cit. 2 pp. [handwritten notations] E.F.R.

Student Revolutionary Directorate delegate in New Orleans. This Debate was broadcast at 6:05 to 6:30 August 21, 1963 after this program I made a 3 minute T.V. newsreel which was shown the next day (August 22.).

B

I recived advice, direction and literature from V.T. Lee national Director of the Fair Play for Cuba Committee of which I am a member. At my own expense I had printed "Hands off Cuba" handbills and New Orleans branch membership Blanks for the F.P.C.C. Local.

C

A. Letter from V.T. Lee
B. FPCC membership card

157

COMMISSION EXHIBIT No. 2003—Continued

LOCATION OF EVENTS RELATED TO PRESIDENT'S ASSASSINATION

President's assassination	Elm Street 150 feet west of Houston St.
Tippit, J. D. shooting	400 Blk. W. 10th
Tippit, J. D. hospital	Methodist Hospital
Oswald, Lee Harvey arrest	231 W. Jefferson (Texas Theatre)
Oswald, Lee Harvey death	Basement, Police Building, 2000 Main
Ruby, Jack arrest	Basement, Police Building, 2000 Main
President's Luncheon	2100 Stemmons Freeway, Trade Mart Bldg.

158

COMMISSION EXHIBIT No. 2003—Continued

FBI AND SECRET SERVICE MEN AT INTERROGATIONS OF OSWALD

FBI

WARREN C. de BRUEYS

JIM BOOKHOUT *

WILLIAM HOSTY

JOE MYERS **

GEORGE CARLSTON ***

NAT PINKSTON

SECRET SERVICE

MR. FORREST SORRELS

MR. KELLEY

WM. H. PATTERSON

ROGER WARNER

WINSTON LAWSEN

MIKE HOWARD

CHARLES KUNKEL

JOHN HOWLETT

DAVE GRANT

* Present for 1st, 2nd and other interrogations.

** Present at 1st interrogation.

*** Present at 2nd interrogation.

161

T. L. BAKER'S REPORT

Capt. J. W. Fritz, Dets. Boyd, Senkel, Sims, and Turner were assigned as part of the security force furnished by the Dallas Police Department for the President's visit to this city November 22, 1963.

At 9:00 AM on the 22nd of November, Capt. Fritz briefed each of these detectives on the specific duty that he was to perform. Capt. Fritz, Dets. Sims and Boyd were to assist in providing the security at the President's table and speaker's stand at the Trade Mart. Dets. Senkel and Turner were assigned to ride with Deputy Chief George Lumpkin in preceding the President's motorcade by approximately 1/2 mile and keep Chief Curry, who was with the motorcade, informed of conditions along the route.

At 10:10 AM Capt. Fritz, Dets. Sims and Boyd arrived at the Trade Mart and parked on the east parking lot. They entered the Trade Mart and met Dave Grant and Robert Stewart of the Secret Service. These men discussed the duties, and Capt. Fritz, Sims, and Boyd familiarized themselves with the area around the President's table and speaker's stand. Capt. Fritz and Mr. Robert Stewart of the Secret Service made the final inspection of the President's table at 12:30 PM.

Dets. Senkel and Turner arrived at Love Field at 11:40 AM with Chief Lumpkin, and Major Weiddemoyer, U. S. Army. After the President's party's planes had landed, they drove to the gate of Love Field at Cedar Springs and Mockingbird Lane. A Secret Service man had joined them at Love Field, and there were five people in their car. At 11:50 AM they received word via radio that the President's party was leaving, and they proceeded along the route and kept in constant radio contact with Chief Curry, who was accompanied by Sheriff Decker. They were on Stemmons Expressway when they heard on the radio "Notify Parkland

to stand by, I think he has been hit." They pulled off the Expressway, and when the President's car went by, they followed to Parkland and helped with the situation until the President and Governor were carried into the hospital. Then they, along with Forrest Sorrels, U. S. Secret Service, proceeded to the scene of the shooting at the Texas School Book Depository, 411 Elm, and arrived there at 12:50 PM. Det. Senkel, along with Deputy Sheriff Weatherford, entered the building and proceeded to search the building from the ground floor up. Det. Turner assisted in searching a box car and then proceeded to the Sheriff's office at Main and Houston to assist in questioning witnesses to the offense.

At 12:41 PM Deputy Chief Stevenson told Capt. Fritz that the President had been involved in an accident at the triple underpass and to go to Parkland. Capt. Fritz, Dets. Sims and Boyd left their assigned area, and Capt. Fritz had them verify the accident report to forestall a hoax. The dispatcher told them the President had been shot. They arrived at Parkland Hospital at 12:45 PM, which is 1 mile from the Trade Mart. On arrival, Chief Curry placed Capt. Fritz in charge of the crime scene and he, Dets. Sims, Boyd, and Sheriff Decker, proceeded to 411 Elm and arrived there at 12:58 PM. Capt. Fritz, Dets. Boyd and Sims and several other officers took the freight elevator and stopped on the second floor and found officers already on this floor. They also found officers on the 3rd, 4th, and proceeded to the 5th floor, and made a search along the front and west windows and then went up to the 6th floor. Some of the officers got off to search this floor and Capt. Fritz, Dets. Sims and Boyd went to the 7th floor and began the search there. At 1:15 PM Deputy Sheriff, Luke E. Mooney, found the empty rounds on the floor under the southeast window, and Capt. Fritz was notified. He inspected the scene and placed Dets. Johnson and Montgomery in charge of the scene where the empty rounds were found to await the arrival of Lt. Day of the Crime Lab. He then instigated a

-3-

thorough search of the entire floor from east to west. At 1:20 PM Lt. Day arrived and Johnson and Montgomery assisted him. At 1:25 PM Deputy Sheriff Weitzman found the rifle on the 6th floor, five feet from the west wall and eight feet from the stairway. About the time the rifle was found, Mr. Truly, manager of the Texas School Book Depository, gave Capt. Fritz the name and address of Lee Oswald, who was an employee of the company, but was now missing from the building. Capt. Fritz was then notified that Officer Tippit had been killed on West 10th Street in Oak Cliff. Capt. Fritz had instructed Det. Senkel and Det. Brown, who had reported to Capt. Fritz at the scene, to take some of the employees of the firm to the Homicide and Robbery office and question them. They left, and William H. Shelly, Bonnie Ray Williams, Danny Garcia Arce, employees, accompanied them to the Homicide and Robbery office. They were taking affidavits from these men when the suspect who had been arrested at the Texas Theater, 231 West Jefferson was brought into the office. They immediately identified him as an employee of the Texas School Book Depository, Lee Oswald. Capt. Fritz, Det. Sims and Boyd left 411 Elm and stopped by Sheriff Decker's office for a short time and then returned to the Homicide and Robbery office. They arrived shortly after Oswald was brought in, and Det. Baker told Capt. Fritz the suspect's name was Lee Oswald, the same as the one given to Capt. Fritz by Mr. Truly.

Lt. Wells, on the instructions of Capt. Fritz, had called all detectives of the Homicide and Robbery Bureau back from days off and vacations immediately after the President's shooting occurred. These were Dets. Hall, Adamcik, Anderton, Dhority, Graves, Beck, and Potts.

Det. Leavelle, who was assisting in the investigation at Elm (411) at the Sheriff's office, was instructed to investigate Officer Tippit's murder. He proceeded to the scene of the offense, and after the arrest of Oswald, returned to the office.

-4-

Capt. Fritz had Dets. Sims and Boyd bring Oswald to his office from the Interrogation Room, where he was being held by Dets. Stovall and Rose. This was at 2:20 PM. During this first interrogation period F. B. I. agents Bookout and Hosty, Dets. Sims and Boyd were present while Capt. Fritz talked to him.

At approximately 2:30 PM Capt. Fritz told Dets. Stovall, Rose, and Adamcik to meet the Sheriff Deputy Officers at 2515 West 5th Street in Irving, Texas. This is the home of Ruth Paine, with whom Lee Oswald's wife was staying. Deputy Sheriffs W. E. Walthers, and J. L. Oxford met these officers at this location and were invited into the house by Ruth Paine. She agreed for them to search the house, and these officers did so. While they were there, Ruth Paine's husband, Michael Ralph Paine, came in. These officers asked Oswald's wife, Marina Oswald, if her husband had a rifle, and she said she had seen a rifle wrapped in a blanket in the garage. Marina Oswald does not speak English, and the interpretation was done by Ruth Paine. The officers found the blanket used to wrap the rifle in the garage, but the rifle was gone. A Mrs. Bill Randall, 2439 East 5th Street, Irving, Texas, approached Det. Adamcik and told him that her brother, Wesley Frazier, took Lee Oswald to work this morning, and that she saw Oswald carry something over to her brother's car and put it in the back seat. It was long and wrapped in paper, or in a box. The officers confiscated several other objects belonging to Oswald and brought Mr. and Mrs. Paine and Marina Oswald to the Forgery Bureau because of the crowded conditions of the Homicide and Robbery Bureau.

At 2:30 PM Capt. Fritz also sent Dets. Senkel, Potts and Lt. Cunningham of the Forgery Bureau to 1025 North Beckley to search the room of Lee Oswald. They waited there until Justise of the Peace, David Johnson, Dets. Turner and Moore arrived, and searched the room. Oswald had the room rented under the name of O. H. Lee. While waiting for the search warrant, Mrs. Earlene Roberts, the landlady, and a Mrs. A. C. Johnson were watching television and saw a picture of Lee Oswald and immediately identified him as the same O. H. Lee, who had a room rented there. After the warrant arrive, the room was searched, and numerous Communist books and other literature was found, and all property taken to the Homicide and Robbery Bureau.

At 4:35 pm Helen Markham, who had witnessed the shooting of Officer Tippit, viewed a showup consisting of Lee Oswald, Bill Perry, R. L. Clark, and Dan Ables. She positively identified Lee Oswald as the one that had shot the officer. While searching Oswald again prior to the showup, Det. Boyd found 5 live rounds of .38 ammunition in his left front pocket, and Det. Sims found a bus transfer slip in his shirt pocket. After the showup he was again returned to the Homicide Office.

Det. Leavelle and Graves learned of two more witnesses to the Tippit murder, a Sam Guinyard and a Ted Calloway, and were instructed to have them come down and look at Oswald in a showup.

The street car transfer slip was traced, and Lt. Wells instructed Dets. Dhority and Brown to meet the Piedmont bus at Commerce and Harwood and have the bus driver, Mr. McWatters, look at Oswald in a showup. At 6:30 pm Mr. McWatters, Sam Guinyard, and Ted Calloway looked at Oswald in a showup, and all positively identified him: Ted Calloway and Sam Guinyard as being the person running from the scene of the shooting of Officer Tippit with a gun in his hand, and Mr. McWatters identified him as being a passenger on his bus shortly after the shooting of President Kennedy. McWatters said he caught the bus at approximately Elm and Murphy.

At 7:03 pm Lee Oswald was arraigned before Judge Johnston. He was also filed on at this time for the murder of Officer Tippit with Bill Alexander of the District Attorney's office. Captain Fritz signed the complaint.

After Mrs. Oswald and Mr. and Mrs. Paine were brought to the Forgery Bureau, she was shown the rifle found on the 6th floor of the Texas School Book Depository. She said it was like the one her husband had, but could not be sure. Det. Senkel, with Det. Adamcik, who understands a little Russian, and with Mrs. Paine and Mr. J. A. Brourantus interpreting, took an affidavit from Mrs. Oswald. This was approximately 7:00 PM.

At 7:55 PM Mrs. Jeanette and Virginia Davis looked at Lee Oswald and positively identified him as the man who walked across their lawn unloading a gun. A woman was standing nearby screaming, "He has killed him". She then saw the police car parked a short distance away.

At 8:55 PM Det. Hicks and Studebaker came to the Homicide and Robbery office and fingerprinted Lee Oswald. A few minutes later Det. Pete Barnes came in, and the three Crime Lab men made paraffin cast of Lee Oswald's hands.

At 9:00 PM Det. Mc Cabe, of the Irving Police Department, called and said they had picked up Wesley Frazier, who had carried Oswald to work that morning. Dets. Rose, Stovall, and Adamcik went to the Irving Police Department and with Frazier's permission searched his car and home. Later Wesley Frazier, his sister, Minnie Randle, and Rev. Campble of the Irving Baptist Church came with the officers to the Homicide and Robbery office, and Wesley Frazier and his sister, Minnie Randle, gave affidavits. Buell Wesley Frazier said that Lee Oswald had carried a package he described as curtain rods into the Texas Book Depository that morning.

Buell Wesley Frazier took a Polograph test, and the test showed he was telling the truth. This test was given between 11:20 PM on the 22nd and 12:10 AM on the 23rd of November.

During all interrogations there were representatives of the Secret Service and the F. B. I. present. Capt. Fritz was unable to interrogate Oswald for any great length of time at one time because of the many other duties that he had to attend to during period that Oswald was brought into the office at 2:15 pm until he was placed in jail for the night at 12:20 am, November 23, 1963.

Approximately 11:20 pm Chief Curry came to the Homicide and Robbery office and instructed us to take Lee Oswald to the showup room on the first floor for a press conference. While Chief Curry and Henry Wade were present at this time, it was decided to file on Oswald for the murder of President Kennedy. Henry Wade and Bill Alexander, of the District Attorney's office, accepted the complaint at 11:26 pm, November 22, 1963 signed by Capt. Fritz. Oswald was arraigned before Judge Johnston at 1:35 am, November 23, 1963 in the Identification Bureau.

Shortly after midnight Lee Oswald, accompanied by all the detectives in the Homicide and Robbery office and numerous other detectives and uniformed officers, was taken to the 1st floor showup room. There he remained for five minutes and was taken from there to the jail office elevator. He was taken upstairs to the 4th floor jail for searching and booking by Deputy Chief Lumpkin, Dets. Baker and Leavelle of the Homicide and Robbery Bureau. After booking and being searched, he was accompanied by the same officers to the 5th floor jail.

From this time until 2:00 am, November 23, 1963, the detectives of the Homicide and Robbery office remained on duty in the Homicide and Robbery office.

At 8:00 am, November 23, 1963, Detectives Beck and Leavelle returned to duty. All the rest of the Homicide and Robbery detectives reported back by

10:00 AM. At 10:30 AM Capt. Fritz instructed Dets. Sims, Hall, and Boyd to bring Lee Oswald from the jail to his office. After he was brought to Capt. Fritz's office, he interrogated him again with Jim Bookout, F. B. I., Mr. Kelly, Secret Service, Robert Nash, U. S. Marshall, and Dets. Boyd and Hall present. He was returned to the jail at 11:30 AM. At 11:30 AM Lt. Wells instructed Dets. Boyd, Hall, and Dhority to secure a search warrant from Justice of the Peace Joe B. Brown, Jr., and again search Lee Oswald's room at 1026 North Beckley.

At 12:30 AM Dets. Montgomery and Johnson were instructed by Lt. Wells to go to the Oak Cliff Cab Company at Davis and Tyler and contact a driver by the name of W. W. Scoggins and bring him to the City Hall. When they arrived at this location, they were advised that he was standing by at the cab station at the Adolphus Hotel at Commerce and Akard. The supervisor at this cab station said there was another driver we should talk to by the name of Bill Whaley. This driver was contacted, and they went to the cab company office at 610 South Akard and picked him up and brought him to the City Hall also. Mr. Scoggins witnessed the shooting of Officer Tippit. Mr. Whaley had picked up Lee Oswald at the Greyhound Bus station and had carried him to the 500 Block of North Beckley shortly after the President was shot. Both these men were shown Oswald in a line-up and both positively identified him. Both gave affidavits.

At 12:30 PM Dets. Rose, Stovall, Adamcik, and Moore secured a search warrant from Justice of the Peace Joe B. Brown, Jr., and went to 2515 West 5th Street. Det. Mc Cabe of the Irving, Texas, Police Department, accompanied them. They seized several articles belonging to Lee Oswald.

At 1:00 PM Capt. Fritz instructed Det. Hall to issue a visitor's pass to Lee Oswald's mother and wife to visit him. Juvenile police woman, Mildred Reeves kept the children while they visited him. Visit started at 1:10 PM and lasted for approximately 20 minutes, and they were returned to the Forgery Bureau at 1:30 PM.

At 2:15 PM a show-up was held, and the two taxi drivers, William Wayne Whaley and W. W. Scoggins, positively identified Oswald; Scoggins as the one he saw shoot Officer Tippit, and Whaley as being the passenger in his cab that he hauled from the Greyhound Bus Station, Lamar and Commerce, shortly after the President was shot.

At 3:30 PM Det. Hall, per instructions of Capt. Fritz, issued a pass to Robert Oswald, Lee Oswald's brother. This visit lasted for 5 minutes.

Dets. Moore and Adamcik went to Irving, Texas, accompanied by Det. Mc Cabe, of the Irving Police Department, brought Michael Paine to the Homicide and Robbery office, and took an affidavit from him, and he returned to his home at approximately 9:30 PM.

Dets. Graves, Sims, and Hall brought Oswald from the jail to Capt. Fritz's office at 6:00 PM. At 6:30 PM Capt. Fritz, with Bookout, F. B. I., and Mr. Kelly of the Secret Service, present interrogated Oswald again. He was returned to the jail at 7:50 PM.

Approximately 7:00 PM Mrs. Mary E. Bledsoe came to the office and said that she was on a bus and that Lee Oswald, who she knows because she used to live at the same place he did, got on the bus at Murphy and Elm, and when the traffic stopped the bus, he got off at Elm and Lamar. This was shortly after the President was shot. She gave an affidavit to these facts.

COMMISSION EXHIBIT No. 2003—Continued

All detectives were released from duty at 9:00 PM except Det. Sims, Boyd, and Hall, who remained on duty until 12:00 midnight.

On Sunday, November 24, 1963, Det. E. R. Beck arrived at the Homicide and Robbery office at 6:30 AM. Capt. Fritz arrived shortly after Det. Beck's arrival. By 9:00 AM Dets. Graves, Leavelle, Montgomery, Brown, Baker, and Dhority had arrived. Approximately 9:30 AM Capt. Fritz had Dets. Leavelle, Graves, and Dhority bring Oswald to his office from the jail. Present at this interrogation were Mr. Sorrels, Mr. Kelly of the Secret Service, Mr. Holmes of the U. S. Postal Service, Dets. Montgomery, Dhority, Leavelle, and Graves. Chief Curry was present for a few minutes at the beginning of the interrogation and returned again near the close. Capt. Fritz instructed Det. Dhority, Brown, and Beck to go to the basement and get the cars set up for Oswald's transfer. Det. Dhority was to put his car by the jail door and Beck to drive the lead car. At 11:15 AM Lee Oswald left Capt. Fritz's office on the 3rd floor with Det. Leavelle handcuffed to his left arm, and Det. Graves holding onto Lee Oswald's right arm, and Capt. Fritz, Det. Montgomery, and Lt. Swain of the Burglary and Theft Bureau accompanying them. The jail elevator was used to go to the basement jail office. Prior to leaving the office, Capt. Fritz told Det. Baker to notify the jail office they were leaving with Oswald and to have the cars ready. Det. Baker notified the jail office, and Lt. Wiggins said all was clear. When the elevator reached the basement jail office, Capt. Fritz, with Oswald and the other detectives, hesitated inside the jail elevator, and the all clear was given, and they moved out from the elevator into the jail office. At the door of the jail office that leads into the hallway, Dets. Graves, Leavelle, and Montgomery, who were with Lee Oswald, hesitated again until Capt. Fritz and Lt. Swain could determine that the hall way was clear, and then they moved into the hallway. Capt. Fritz and Lt. Swain preceded Dets. Graves, Leavelle, Montgomery, and Lee Oswald, and they moved into the basement from the hallway

COMMISSION EXHIBIT No. 2003—Continued

-11-

with Det. Leavelle handcuffed to Oswald's right wrist, and Graves on Oswald's left side, holding onto his arm. Det. Dhority was having trouble moving the car back because of the camera and newspaper men blocking the way. Capt. Fritz had opened the back door of the transfer car when a man broke quickly out of the large crowd of newspaper men and stepped up to Lee Oswald and fired one shot. Dets. Graves, Montgomery, and Leavelle, who were facing the brilliant lights of the cameras were unable to see until just as he fired. Lee Oswald fell, and Det. Graves grabbed the suspect, whose name was Jack Ruby. He was disarmed, and Lee Oswald was carried to Parkland, accompanied by Dets. Graves, Leavelle, and Dhority. Lee Oswald was shot at 11:21 AM, and died at 1:07 PM at Parkland Hospital. He was pronounced dead by Dr. Tom Shires. Capt. Fritz, Dets. Beck and Brown also went to Parkland. Before leaving for the hospital, Capt. Fritz instructed Det. Dhority to have Capt. Talbot get the names of everyone in the basement where the offense occurred.

Det. Graves accompanied Lee Oswald to the operating room to stand guard there. After he died, Dets. Dhority and Brown accompanied Dr. Rose to the morgue where he performed the autopsy. Det. Graves, who had disarmed Ruby, turned the gun over to Capt. Fritz in the basement before going to Parkland.

Judge Mc Bride ordered the post. At 3:00 PM Capt. Fritz had Dets. Hall, Boyd, Montgomery, and Senkel bring Ruby from his cell to his office. Present for this interrogation was Mr. Sorrells, and an unknown F. B. I. agent. At approximately 3:45 PM Peace Justice Mc Bride came in. He advised Ruby that he had been filed on and advised him of his rights. Ruby had been filed on for Lee Oswald's murder shortly before. Charges were accepted by Bill Alexander of the District Attorney's office. Ruby was returned to the jail at 4:00 PM.

On November 25, 1963, Jack Ruby was transfered at 11:45 AM by Detectives of the Homicide and Robbery Bureau to the County Jail.

172

G. F. ROSE - R. S. STOVALL - J. P. ADAMCIK - H. M. MOORE
REPORT ON INVESTIGATION OF THE PRESIDENT'S MURDER

November 23, 1963, Saturday, reported for duty 10:00 AM and spent first two hours checking and initialing the evidence. 12:30 PM called Judge Joe Brown, Jr., and obtained a Search Warrant to search the premises at 2515 West 5th, Irving, and Detectives R. S. Stovall, H. M. Moore, J. P. Adamcik, and G. F. Rose drove to Irving, Texas, and contacted Det. Mc Cabe of the Irving Police Department, who accompanied us to 2515 West 5th, Irving, home of Ruth Paine. We showed Mrs. Paine the Warrant and proceeded to search the premises, starting in the garage where we found two sea bags and three suit cases, and two cardboard boxes. We examined all of Lee Harvey Oswald's belongings and found numerous items of interest, among them found by Dets. Rose was two snapshots and negatives showing Oswald holding the rifle (murder weapon) and wearing a pistol in a holster on his right hip (Tippit murder weapon), also other papers of a Communist nature (See attached Property List). Also found by Det. Stovall was a cut out portion of a magazine advertisement from Kline Department Store in Chicago, showing an advertisement of the murder weapon. All these items were confiscated along with other items and marked for evidence.

177

REPORT ON INVESTIGATION OF THE PRESIDENT'S MURDER

J. P. ADAMCIK - #1548

I was off duty at home when I heard that President Kennedy had been shot. On Friday, November 22, 1963, I reported for work at 2:00 PM. I was starting to take an affidavit from one of the employees of the Texas School Depository Building when some officers brought Lee Harvey Oswald into the Homicide Bureau. A few minutes later Capt. Fritz asked Det. Rose, Stovall, and myself to go to 2515 West Fifth in Irving, Texas, and see what we could find. This was the address Oswald gave as his home address (See Detective's Rose and Stovall Report)

At about 5:45 PM, we came back to the Homicide Bureau with Mrs. Lee Oswald, Ruth Paine, and Michael Paine. Mrs. Oswald brought her two small children along. We put all these people in the Forgery Bureau Office, and I stayed with them. At about 7:30 PM, Capt. Fritz, along with a Russian interpreter and Det. Senkel came in and questioned Mrs. Oswald and Mrs. Paine. I listened to the questioning. During the interrogation, Lt. Day of the ID Bureau came in and brought a rifle in to see if Mrs. Oswald could identify it. She said that it looked like her husband's rifle. She said that it was dark. After Det. Senkel got through taking the affidavit from Mrs. Oswald, I took an affidavit from Mrs. Paine. In it she stated when she first met the Oswalds and the different times she saw them. She also/said that Oswald had spent Thursday night at her house (See affidavit).

Lee Oswald's mother and brother came in while I was taking the affidavit. I took the affidavit, and Capt. Fritz asked me to take these people home. Lt. Mc Kinney went with me on this trip. Oswald's mother also went with us to

178

COMMISSION EXHIBIT No. 2003—Continued

J. P. Adamcik - Page 2

Mrs. Paine's house. We took these people home and returned to the office at about 10:00 PM. At about 11:00 PM I talked to Oswald for about 15 minutes in Capt. Fritz's office. Det. L. D. Montgomery was also present at that time. Oswald would not mention anything about the President's or Officer Tippit's murder. I stayed at work until about 2:00 AM.

On Saturday, November 23, 1963, I reported for duty at 10:00 AM. At about 11:30 AM Detectives Rose, Stovall, Moore, and myself left the office to go to Mrs. Paine's house in Irving for a more complete search (See Detective Rose's report).

We came back to the office at about 4:00 PM. At about 5:00 PM, Capt. Fritz told Det. Moore and me to bring Michael Paine in and take an affidavit from him. We went by the Irving Police Station and took Det. John A. Mc Cabe of the Irving City Police Department to the house at 2515 West Fifth with us. We took Mr. Paine back to the Dallas Police Station with us. At about 9:30 PM, I took an affidavit from Mr. Paine. In it he told about seeing the blanket in which the rifle was wrapped in his garage a few times previous to the assassination (See affidavit). After finishing, I ended my tour of duty.

179

COMMISSION EXHIBIT No. 2003—Continued

G. F. ROSE - R. S. STOVALL - J. P. ADAMCIK
REPORT ON INVESTIGATION OF THE PRESIDENT'S MURDER

On November 22, 1963, the date of the assassination of the President, Detectives G. F. Rose and R. S. Stovall arrived at the Homicide Office at approximately 2:00 PM. This was as soon after the killing as we could get to the office. We were in the office about 10 or 15 minutes when at approximately 2:15 PM, Lee Harvey Oswald was brought into the Homicide Office. We (Rose and Stovall) talked to him briefly, obtaining his ID and name, and at about 2:30 PM, Capt. Fritz, R. M. Sims, and E. L. Boyd came into the office. Capt. Fritz instructed Detectives Rose and Stovall to get one additional man and to go Irving, Texas, meet the County Officers and make a search of the house at 2515 West 5th, Irving. This was the house where Lee Oswald's wife lived with Ruth Paine, and Oswald stayed there on week ends. We took Detective J. P. Adamcik and immediately drove to 2515 West 5th, Irving and parked about one-half block from the Paine home to await the arrival of the County Officers, after approximately a 40-minute wait, Detectives Harry K. Weatherford, E. W. (Buddy) Walthers, and J. L. Oxford of the Dallas County CID arrived. We instructed them of our mission and drove to the front of the Paine home. Detectives Adamcik and two of the County Officers went to the back door, and one county officer and Stovall and Rose went to the front door - time approximately 3:30 PM. Upon stepping onto the front porch, we could hear the TV and see two people sitting in the living room. Ruth Paine answered our knock on the door. She was very cordial, and her first statement after we presented our ID, was "Come on in, we were expecting you. Just as soon as we heard where it happened, we figured someone would be out." She invited us

to make a search of her home at which time we began a methodical search of the house, for a list of items we took from this house see the attached Property List. At approximately 3:45 PM Michael Ralph Paine walked up the walkway and entered the house without knocking. He told Ruth Paine, "I heard where the President was shot, and I came right on over to see if I could be of any help to you." He also told her that he had just walked off the job. At the suggestion of Marina Oswald, wife of Lee Harvey Oswald, we also made a search of the garage, which is attached to the Paine home. Mrs. Oswald was asked about her husband's rifle, and she stated that he had one, and that he kept it in the garage wrapped in a blanket. She was speaking in Russian, and Ruth Paine was interpreting for us. She pointed to a rolled-up blanket laying on the garage floor, and said, "That is where he keeps his rifle". (in Rusian, interpreted by Ruth Paine) Also see attached Property List. After some confusion as to what to do with the children, Ruth Paine agreed to accompany Marina Oswald to the City Hall, and we began loading the property that we were confiscating for evidence into our car and into the car of the Dallas County Sheriff's office. About this time Mrs. Bill Randall, who lives at 2439 West 5th, Irving, approached Det. Adamcik and told him that her brother Wesley Frazier took Oswald to work this morning, November 22, 1963, and that she saw Oswald carry something over to her brother's car and put it in the back seat. It was long and wrapped in paper or a box. She was suspicious. She said that her brother was visiting her father at Parkland Hospital, and we could reach him there.

We placed Michael Ralph Paine in the County Car, and Ruth Paine and Mariana Oswald and her two small children into our car. We drove immediately to the City Hall and parked our car in the basement of the City Hall. We brought Michael Paine, Ruth Paine, Mariana Oswald, and her two small children to the third floor, Homicide and Robbery Bureau Office, and then after a few minutes moved them to the Forgery Bureau Office, due to the crowded condition of the Homicide Office, time approximately 6:00 PM. After getting the Paines and Mrs. Oswald settled and while waiting for an interpreter, we started trying to locate Wesley Frazier. We contacted Parkland and found that Wesley Frazier was not at Parkland Hospital. We made a check of the Irving Clinics and found out via phone that Wesley was at the Irving Professional Center visiting his father. Det. Rose called the Irving Police Department and talked to Det. Mc Cabe, who stated that he would immediately go to the Irving Professional Center and take Wesley Frazier into custody and instructed us to call him back in 15 minutes to verify the arrest. We called Det. J. A. Mc Cabe back at about 6:45 PM, and he informed us that he had effected the arrest of Wesley Frazier, and we could pick Frazier up at the Irving Police Department. We (Dets. Rose and Stovall) drove immediately to Irving, arriving there at approximately 7:00 PM. We talked to Det. Mc Cabe, and he agreed to accompany us along with Wesley Frazier to the Irving Professional Center to make a search of Wesley Frazier's car, a 1954 black Chevrolet, 4 dr., License VK 3926. We made a thorough search of Frazier's car with negative results, then proceeded to Frazier's home, 2439 West 5th, Irving (1/2 block from the Paine home) and made a search of the Randle home (also Frazier home) and confiscated a 303 calibre rifle, full clip, and partial box 303 calibre ammunition belonging to Wesley Frazier (placed in Property Room). After a while Wesley Frazier's

sister, Linnie Randle, came in and she, Linnie Randle, Wesley Frazier, and a Rev. Campble, of the Irving Baptist Church, were brought to the City Hall, Homicide and Robbery Office, where affidavits were taken from Wesley Frazier and Linnie Randle - time approximately 9:00 PM. After finishing the affidavit, we (Dets. Rose and Stovall) started back to Irving, Texas, with the above witnesses. About midway we received a radio call to return to the office with the witnesses. We turned around at Irving Boulevard and Stemmons Expressway and drove back to City Hall, and Det. Rose called Capt. Fritz by telephone and Capt. Fritz asked that we run Wesley Frazier on the Polygraph machine. We took Frazier to the ID Bureau, and Capt. Dowdy called Det. R. D. Lewis at home. R. D. Lewis arrived on the fourth floor about 11:20 PM and conducted the Polygraph examination until approximately 12:10 AM, 11-23-63. This examination was witnessed by Dets. Stovall and Rose. The examination showed conclusively that Wesley Frazier was truthful, and that the facts stated by Frazier in his affidavit were true (See his Affidavit). We took Frazier, his sister, and their minister home and got off duty at 2:00 AM.'

G. F. Rose
R. S. Stovall
J. P. Adamcik

REPORT ON OFFICER'S DUTIES IN REGARDS TO THE PRESIDENT'S MURDER

K. L. ANDERTON - #1506

At about 12:00 noon on November 22, 1963, I was at my home at 709 Julia Lane, Garland, Texas, watching television. I saw a special news bulletin that the President of the United States had been shot during a motorcade in Dallas. I was on vacation from work on this day; however, I got ready to come back to work. I received a telephone call from Lt. Wells to come to work. When I got to work, Capt. Fritz had Lee Harvey Oswald and other people in his office.

My partner, J. P. Adamcik, was out with other detectives, so I stayed around the office to help transport Oswald through the hallway to the elevator, and to answer the telephones. I sat in Capt. Fritz's office with Detectives R. M. Sims and M. G. Hall with Lee Harvey Oswald for about an hour during the evening of November 22. While we were in the office with Oswald, we talked to him about his life in Russia. He talked freely about the living and working conditions in Russia, but would not talk about his family. I left the office for home between 1:30 AM and 2:00 AM, November 23, 1963.

I came to work at about 3:00 PM, November 23, 1963. At about 5:00 PM I took an affidavit of Fact from James Richard Worrell, Jr., w/m/20, 13510 Winterhaven, CH 7-2378, a student at Thomas Jefferson High School. James Worrell stated to me that at the time of the shooting of President J. F. Kennedy, he was watching the motorcade from the corner of Elm and Houston Streets. He said he was standing under the window where the shots were fired from and that he was looking at the rifle barrel when the second shot was fired. James Worrell said he got scared and ran down Houston Street to Pacific Street. When he stopped for breath, he stated he was on the North side of the Texas School Book Depository Building and he saw a man run out of the building in a southerly

direction. He said when he got home and saw pictures of Lee Harvey Oswald in the newspapers and on television, he recognized him as the man he saw run from the building.

I stayed in the office answering the telephone until I left for home at about 1:00 AM, November 24, 1963.

REPORT ON OFFICER'S DUTIES IN REGARDS TO OSWALD'S DEATH

K. L. ANDERTON - #1506

On the morning of November 24, 1963 at about 11:15 AM I was watching television at home and saw where Lee Harvey Oswald had been shot, while being transferred from the City Jail to the County Jail. When I got to the office at about 1:00 PM, Jack Ruby was in Capt. Fritz's office with several other men. I walked with Jack Ruby and several detectives from the office to the elevator on the third floor when Jack Ruby was placed in jail.

During the afternoon of November 24, 1963, Eva Grant, Jack Ruby's sister, came in the office with another white female and newsman, Jim Underwood. I took Eva Grant, the friend with her, and Jim Underwood into a back room and sat them down. I talked to Eva Grant, and she asked me questions about what her brother was charged with and how she could get him out on bond.

Eva Grant told me that Jack Ruby had changed his name from Jack Rubenstein to Jack Ruby while he was in the service. She said that she was afraid she had given Jack the idea to shoot Oswald by something she had said to him. She did not tell me what she had said to him. Eva said that Jack had talked to one of his brothers on the telephone on the night of Friday, November 22, 1963. She didn't tell me which brother, or what was said. She only said that Jack was crying.

I left the office at about 12:30 AM, November 25, 1963, and went home.

186

COMMISSION EXHIBIT No. 2003—Continued

REPORT ON OFFICER'S DUTIES IN REGARDS TO OSWALD'S MURDER

E. R. BECK - #45

On Sunday, November 24, 1963, I got to the office at 6:30 AM.

At about 9:30 AM, Det. Leavelle, Graves, and Dhority went to the Jail to bring Oswald to Capt. Fritz's office. Det. Brown, Montgomery and myself waited at the third floor Jail elevator door and helped get Oswald to our office.

At about 11:10 AM, Capt. Fritz told Dets. Dhority, Brown, and myself to go to the basement and get the cars set up for Oswald's transfer. He told Det. Dhority to put his car by the Jail door, and for me to drive the lead car. Capt. Fritz told me that we would go to Commerce, East on Commerce to Preston, North to Main, then West on Main, and when we got to the entrance of the Jail on Main, I was to drive past the entrance, so that they could drive into the Jail entrance.

When we got to the basement, we had some trouble lining up the cars because of the TV cameras and the press. Detective Dhority was backing Capt. Fritz's car into position. I was standing just to the rear of the lead car telling Det. Brown to back up just a little more, when a shot was fired, and I ran back and helped Lt. Swain get the crowd back. I went into the Jail office, and Oswald was lying on the floor on the North side of the office and several officers had a man on the floor that I later found out was Jack Ruby.

An ambulance arrived and Oswald was placed in the ambulance, and Det. Graves, Dhority, and Leavelle went in the ambulance to Parkland. I got my

187

COMMISSION EXHIBIT No. 2003—Continued

E. R. BECK - Page 2 - (Oswald Murder)

car and Capt. Fritz got in the front seat, and Det. Montgomery and Brown in the back, and we went to Parkland Hospital. We went to Emergency Room, and the doctors and nurses were working on Oswald. Shortly after we arrived, Oswald was taken from the Emergency Room to the Operating Room on the Second floor. Capt. Fritz and I left the second floor and returned to our office, along with Det. Montgomery.

After we had gotten back to the office, Jack Ruby was brought to Capt. Fritz's office at 3:25 PM, and I helped other officers get him from the Jail Elevator door to our office. After Capt. Fritz talked to Jack Ruby, I helped other officers get him back to the elevator door.

188

COMMISSION EXHIBIT No. 2003—Continued

REPORT ON OFFICER'S DUTIES IN REGARDS TO THE PRESIDENT'S MURDER

E. R. BECK - #45

Last Friday, November 22, 1963, I was on my regular day off when I heard a news report that the President had been shot, and later that he was dead. A later report said that Officer Tippit was shot and killed.

I reported to work at about 3:30 PM and helped in the office with the incoming telephone calls. I helped other officers in the Homicide Bureau move Oswald to the jail elevator and back several times. I went home about 2:00 AM.

On Saturday, November 23, 1963, I reported to work at 10:00 AM. At about 1:00 PM I took a statement, along with F. B. I. Agent Albert Sayers, from Mrs. Geneva L. Hine, 2305 OakDale Road, FR 6-7580, who is an employee of the Texas School Book Depository and has been there for 6½ years. She identified a picture of Oswald that Agent Sayers had as an employee there for about two months. She is a clerk in the office on the second floor, and Oswald worked on the first floor as a book filler. She states that she had not seen him speaking to anyone, and on the day of the shooting, she did not see him. She heard 3 shots, but did not know what had happened until officers came in the office and told her the President had been shot. I went off duty at 9:30 PM.

189

COMMISSION EXHIBIT No. 2003—Continued

REPORT ON OFFICER'S DUTIES IN REGARDS TO PRESIDENT'S MURDER

C. W. BROWN - #759

Last Friday, November 22, 1963, I reported for work at 10:00 AM. My partner, C. N. Dhority, was on a day off, and I was working alone. At approximately 11:00 AM, Det. J. R. Leavelle and myself started looking for a colored male that was wanted for armed robbery by this Bureau. At 12:15 PM, we arrested this subject at 2421 Ellis Street and brought him to the Homicide Office for booking. While Det. Leavelle and myself were booking this prisoner, we heard the police radio announce that the President had been shot and was enroute to Parkland Hospital. Det. Leavelle and I placed this prisoner in jail and proceeded to the location of the shooting at Elm and Houston. When we arrived at the location, we found that the Book Depository was sealed off for search. Det. Leavelle went in one direction, and I went to the rear of the building and entered. I saw several officers and proceeded to the sixth floor. I contacted Capt. Fritz. Capt. Fritz advised me and Det. B. L. Senkel, who was already there, to bring the employees of this building to the Homicide Office and get affidavits from them. Det. Senkel and I brought three of these employees to the office, and I took an affidavit from a William H. Shelley, w/m/37, of 126 South Tatum Street, FE 7-1969. While I was taking this affidavit from Mr. Shelley, a group of officers brought a Lee Harvey Oswald in, and these officers stated that he was the one that shot officer J. D. Tippit. Mr. Shelley saw this Oswald, and told me that he was one of his employees at the book store. After I took the affidavit from Mr. Shelley in regards to his whereabouts and action after the shooting, I took a second one from him relating to the employment and job supervision of Oswald. Det. Senkel took an affidavit from a

190

COMMISSION EXHIBIT No. 2003—Continued

C. W. Brown - 2

Bonnie Ray Williams, c/m/, of 1502 Avenue B, that we brought from the building. The rest of the night until 2:30 am, November 23, 1963, was spent in the Homicide and Robbery Bureau answering telephones. The next day, which was the 23rd of November, I took an affidavit from a Mr. Seymour Weitzman, w/m, of 2802 Oats Drive, DA 7-6624. This man is a deputy constable working out of Constable Robie Love's office, in the Court House Building. This man and a Deputy Boone of the Sheriff's office were on the sixth floor of the Book Depository Building and found the rifle used in the shooting of the President. Throughout the day and night I remained in the Homicide office continuing the investigation.

At approximately 6:00 pm Lt. T. P. Wells gave my partner, C. N. Dhority, and myself information that the bus driver that picked up Oswald near the scene of the President's murder was driving the Piedmont bus #50 and would be at the intersection of Commerce and Harwood at 6:15 pm. We walked over to the bus stop and stopped this bus which was driven by a Mr. McWatters, and he accompanied us to the Homicide Office where my partner took an affidavit from him. This suspect Oswald, when arrested, had a bus transfer slip in his pocket and Mr. McWatters identified this as being the one that he had punched earlier. After the affidavit was taken by my partner, we both took Mr. McWatters to the Police Assembly Room located in the basement of the city hall for a lineup. Mr. McWatters identified Oswald as #2 man in a 4-man lineup at 6:30 pm, numbering left to right on the stage. Mr. McWatters went back to his work, and my partner and I returned to the Homicide Office for further investigation.

191

COMMISSION EXHIBIT No. 2003—Continued

REPORT ON OFFICER'S DUTIES IN REGARDS TO OFFICER TIPPIT'S MURDER

C. W. BROWN - #759

Last Friday, November 22, 1963 I was at the Book Depository Store at Elm and Houston Streets investigating the murder of President Kennedy. About 1:30 pm I learned of Officer Tippit's death. At approximately 6:50 pm this same date Lt. T. P. Wells received a telephone call from a Mrs. Barbara Jeanette Davis of 400 E. Tenth stating that her sister-in-law of the same address had found an empty .38 cal. shell in their front yard. My partner, C. N. Dhority, and myself drove to the Davis residence where Mrs. Barbara Jeanette Davis handed my partner the spent shell at approximately 7:00 pm. Det. Dhority and I brought both Mrs. Barbara Davis and Mrs. Virginia Davis to the Homicide Office where I took an affidavit from Mrs. Barbara Jeanette Davis relating what she saw and heard at the time of the shooting of Officer J. D. Tippit. At 7:45 pm this same date, my partner and I held a lineup in the Police Assembly Room located in the basement of the city hall for both Mrs. Barbara Davis and Mrs. Virginia Davis. They both made positive identification of Lee Harvey Oswald as being the one that walked across their yard and was unloading a gun. The position of this Oswald in the lineup was #2 man in a 4-man lineup reading from left to right on the stage. After completion of the lineup and taking affidavits, my partner and I took both Mrs. Barbara Davis and Mrs. Virginia Davis back home and returned to the office to continue the investigation.

REPORT ON OFFICER'S DUTIES IN REGARDS TO OSWALD'S DEATH

C. W. BROWN - #759

On the 24th of November, 1963, I reported to work at 7:00 am driving Squad Car #376. After an interview of the suspect, Lee Harvey Oswald, by Captain Fritz, I was told to get my car and get in position in front of the other squad that was to carry Oswald to the County Jail. At approximately 11:40 am, I went to the City Hall basement and drove my car about half way up the south ramp, which leads out to Commerce Street, and my partner, Dhority, moved the other squad car up behind me. We both started attempting to back up to the jail office door when I heard a shot. I immediately put the emergency brake on and ran back to the other car. By this time, other officers had removed Lee Harvey Oswald and Jack Ruby into the jail office. I went back to my car and moved it back into the parking area so the ambulance could get through. When the ambulance arrived, Captain Fritz, Dets. E. R. Beck, L. D. Montgomery and I proceeded behind the ambulance to Parkland Hospital and set up security, first in the Emergency Room, then to the fourth floor, where Oswald underwent surgery. After Oswald died at 1:07 pm, the body was removed to the X-ray room on the ground floor. Judge Pierce McBride was contacted via telephone, and he reported to the morgue desk and gave authorization for a post mortem to be performed by Dr. Rose of the Parkland Staff. Dr. Rose took charge of the body, and I went with him and got the wife and mother of Oswald from the waiting room and let them view the body in the X-ray room. After the relatives viewed the body, I accompanied it along with my partner, C. N. Dhority, and Dr. Rose to the Morgue. At the Morgue, Dhority and I witnessed the preliminary photos taken of the body by Dr. Rose and his staff. After this, I returned to the office and continued our investigative work there.

REPORT ON OFFICER'S DUTIES IN REGARDS TO THE PRESIDENT'S MURDER

C. N. DHORITY - #476

Friday, November 22, 1963, I was on day off. I was called by Lt. T. P. Wells at 1:30 PM to come back to work, that the President had been killed. I got to work at 2:00 PM. I worked in the office answering telephone calls until 3:30 PM. At this time I received information from Lt. Wells that Mrs. Glenn S. Holcomb, 1000 Gilpin, FE 7-2488, had received a telephone call, and a woman said, "Repeat and report the information you heard. It ties in with what just happened." Mrs. Holcomb asked the woman what number she was calling, and she said FL 7-2488. This number was listed to Phillip Oliver, 5350 Surry Circle. I talked with Mrs. Oliver, who is a part time model. She said Mrs. Erma Austin, 1620 Cypress, BL 4-7998, had called her and was the woman who got the wrong number. The information that Mrs. Oliver gave to Mrs. Austin was as follows: Thursday, November 21, 1963, Mrs. Oliver called Mrs. Austin at BL 4-7998 and evidently was cut into a conversation that was going on between two men. They were talking about demanding some time from Governor Connally and Vice President Johnson to hear their side on a bond hearing or rezoning of property. Mrs. Oliver heard the name John Slaughter used and believed it to be one of the men that was talking. Mrs. Oliver made her call again to Mrs. Austin and told her what she had just heard. I returned to the office and worked in the office answering the telephone. About 6:00 PM, Lt. Wells gave C. W. Brown and myself information that Mr. C. J. Mc Watters was driving Piedmont Bus and was due at Commerce and Harwood at 6:15 PM. We met Mr. Mc Watters and carried him to the Detail Room. At 6:30 PM, Mr. Mc Watters made identification of Oswald as #2 man in four man line up. Mr. Mc Watter

194

COMMISSION EXHIBIT No. 2003—Continued

gave me an affidavit in the Homicide Office and identified the transfer that he had given Oswald positively.

About 9:00 PM, Capt. J. W. Fritz gave me three spent 6.5 rifle shells and advised me to take them to the Crime Lab to Lt. Day and return one of them back to him. Lt. Day examined all the shells for prints and put one in an envelope that I returned to Capt. Fritz. While I was at the Crime Lab., Lt. Day showed me the 6.5 rifle, and I wrote a description from the rifle. I returned to the office and was in Capt. Fritz's office when Det. J. B. Hicks, and Pete Barnes made paraffin cast of Lee Harvey Oswald's hands and face. I got off duty about 2:00 AM, November 23, 1963.

I returned to duty November 23, 1963, 9:45 AM and worked in the office answering telephone calls. At 2:15 PM I was present in the Assembly Room when cab driver, William W. Whaley, 619 Pine Street, Lewisville, Texas, identified Lee Harvey Oswald as the man he picked up at the Greyhound Bus Station, November 22, 1963, about 1:00 PM and carried to the 500 Block of North Beckley. Mr. Whaley identified Lee Harvey Oswald as #3 man in four man line up. Mr. Whaley came up to the third floor and gave an affidavit in the Auto Theft Office. Bill Alexander, Assistant District Attorney, was present at the show up, and when Mr. Whaley gave affidavit. Det. C. W. Brown and myself returned Mr. Whaley to 610 South Akard, and then took Bill Alexander to the District Attorney's office.

195

COMMISSION EXHIBIT No. 2003—Continued

REPORT ON OFFICER'S DUTIES IN REGARDS TO TIPPIT'S MURDER

C. N. DHORITY - #476

November 22, 1963, about 7:00 PM, Lt. T. P. Wells gave Det. C. W. Brown and myself information that Mrs. Virginia Davis, 400 East 10th, WH 3-8120, had found an empty .38 shell in her front yard. We went to her house and talked with her and her sister, Jeanette Davis, of the same address. We brought both of the women to the Detail Room of the Police Department, where they identified Lee Harvey Oswald as the man they saw walking across their front yard unloading his pistol after they had heard shots and saw the officer had been shot. They identified Lee Harvey Oswald as the #2 man in the line. We brought the Davis women to Homicide office where they gave affidavits. I took an affidavit ffom Virginia Davis, and Det. Brown took affidavit from Jeanette Davis. The spent .38 shell that Virginia Davis gave me was submitted to Lt. J. C. Day in the Crime Lab. We carried these women back to their home.

196

REPORT ON OFFICER'S DUTIES IN REGARDS TO OSWALD'S MURDER

C. N. DHORITY - #476

Sunday, November 24, 1963, about 9:30 AM, Capt. Fritz directed Dets. J. R. Leavelle, L. C. Graves and myself to go to the fifth floor jail and bring Lee Harvey Oswald to his office. We brought Oswald to Captain Fritz's office, where he was interrogated by Capt. Fritz, Mr. Kelly of the Secret Service, Mr. Sorrels of the Secret Service, and Mr. Holmes of the Postal Department. They talked to Oswald until about 11:10 AM. Chief Curry came into Capt. Fritz's office when the interrogation was going on. At the end of the interrogation, Capt. Fritz gave me the keys to his car, and told me to park it along the door from the jail office in the basement. I went to the basement and unlocked Capt. Fritz's car and proceeded to drive the car into the driveway. There was a plain black police car in front of me, and the officers who I could not recognize, drove this car up the ramp to Main Street exit. I was backing Capt. Fritz's car in front of the jail office, and was having trouble getting through the news reporters that had jammed the ramp driveway. While I was backing up, I was turned around in the seat looking back to keep from running over the reporters. Capt. Fritz came out of the jail door, followed by Det. J. R. Leavelle handcuffed to Oswald. Det. L. C. Graves was to Oswald's left. They were walking to the car while I was still moving the car back. Capt. Fritz opened the right rear door of the car I was driving, and I noticed a man move quickly across the right rear of the car. This man moved to Oswald and shot. I recognized this man as Jack Ruby, a man I had seen a few times before in previous years. When Ruby shot, Det. Graves grabbed the pistol Ruby had in his hand. The crowd of reporters closed in with the police officers, and I jumped out of the car, and went into the jail office.

197

The officers had Ruby, and Det. Leavelle was being unhandcuffed from Oswald. Capt. Fritz directed me to return to the basement and have the Supervisor Officer to obtain the names of everyone in the basement. I went to Capt. C. E. Talbert and gave him Capt. Fritz's message. I then moved Capt. Fritz's car out of the driveway where the ambulance could get to the jail office. When the ambulance came, I rode in the ambulance with Oswald to Parkland Hospital. I stayed at Parkland Hospital until Oswald was pronounced dead. Det. C. W. Brown and I went with Oswald's body to the morgue where we waited until Dr. Earl Rose made his preliminary pictures of the body prior to the autopsy. I turned over Oswald's clothing to Dr. Earl Rose, and returned to the Homicide Office in the City Hall approximately 5:30 PM. I stayed in the Homicide Office with Mr. Stewart and went through the property of Oswald. I made copies of letters and identification from Oswald's property for Mr. Stewart. I also made copies of all the affidavits that had been taken by the Homicide Office and Sheriff's Office for Mr. Sorrells of the Secret Service.

REPORT ON OFFICER'S DUTIES IN REGARDS TO THE PRESIDENT'S MURDER

L. C. GRAVES - 702

On Friday, November 22, 1963, I was called to duty from a day off at approximately 2:00 PM to assist in the investigation of the murder of President John F. Kennedy and Officer J. D. Tippit. At approximately 3:00 PM this same day a Helen Louise Markham of 328½ East 9th Street, telephone RI 8-2175 was brought to the City Hall by a uniform officer. I interviewed this woman and found that she was an eye witness to the shooting of Officer Tippit by Lee Harvey Oswald. Helen Markham gave an affidavit relating the facts of the shooting as they happened. We put Lee Harvey Oswald in a four man line up at the City Hall, November 22, 1963, at 4:30 PM and let Helen Markham view this line up. She was positive on the identification of Oswald, and he was the #2 man in the four man line up. The line up was held by Chief Curry, Capt. Fritz, J. R. Leavelle, C. W. Brown, and me. After the line up, Leavelle and I took Helen Markham to her East 9th address and let her out. From this location, we drove to 501 East Jefferson, where we interviewed Ted Calloway, Sam Guinyard, and Domingo Benavides regarding the murder of Officer Tippit. At a later time two of the three men came to City Hall and gave affidavits and viewed Oswald in a line up. Leavelle conducted the line up and took affidavits.

On Saturday, November 23, 1963, I took an affidavit from Mrs. Mary E. Bledsoe of 621 North Marsalis, telephone WH 2-1985. She knew Oswald and saw him get on and off of a bus on Elm Street shortly after President Kennedy was shot. (See affidavit).

REPORT ON OFFICER'S DUTIES IN REGARDS TO OSWALD'S MURDER

L. C. GRAVES - #702

Sunday, November 24, 1963, was the day set for the transfer of Lee Harvey Oswald to the County Jail. The time set for the transfer was 10:00 AM. Shortly before 9:30 AM, J. R. Leavelle, C. N. Dhority, and I brought Oswald down from the fifth floor jail for final questioning by Capt. Fritz, Agents Sorrel and Kelly from the Secret Service. Others present during the questioning were Mr. Holmes from the U. S. Post Office Department, Detectives L. D. Montgomery, C. N. Dhority, J. R. Leavelle, and I. Chief Curry was present only a few minutes at the beginning of the questioning and at the end just prior to Oswald's removal to the basement. Before leaving our office with Oswald, Capt. Fritz instructed J. R. Leavelle to handcuff his left arm to the right arm of Oswald. I was to walk by Oswald's left side, holding his left arm. Oswald's hands were handcuffed together in front of him. Det. Leavelle, Oswald, and I were escorted from this office via the jail elevator to the jail office by Capt. Fritz, Lt. Swain, and Det. L. D. Montgomery. At the jail office door that leads into the hall, we stopped for a few seconds until Capt. Fritz and Lt. Swain made sure the hall-way was clear. We got the all clear sign and made our way through the hall to the edge of the ramp where we had paused momentarily awaiting the arrival of our car, when suddenly out of the surging line of camera men and glaring camera lights, Jack Ruby sprang forward and fired one round from a pistol into the stomach of Lee Harvey Oswald before I could grab his pistol and disarm him.

Oswald was immediately placed in an O'Neal ambulance and rushed to Parkland Hospital, where he underwent surgery within 10 minutes after his

arrival. Oswald was pronounced dead at 1:07 PM, November 24, 1963, by Dr. Tom Shires, Parkland Staff. Detectives J. R. Leavelle, Burgess, and I, along with Dr. Bieberdorf, rode in the ambulance with Oswald to Parkland. At the hospital I changed into operating room clothing and accompanied Oswald to the Operating Room and stood guard until he was pronounced dead.

The pistol I took from Jack Ruby was turned over to Capt. Fritz at Parkland Hospital.

Dec... r 2, 1963

INFORMATION REGARDING OSWALD'S FIRING HIS RIFLE ON THE SPORTDOME GUN RANGE

This date, December 2, 1963, I went to 220 West 10th Street and interviewed Dr. Homer Wood. He stated that on November 16, 1963, he took his son, Sterling Charles Wood, w/m/13, to the Sportdome Gun Range, 8000 West Davis to zero in his rifle. Sterling was assigned the 4th booth and shortly after he got in the booth, he saw Oswald walk up and enter booth #5. After Oswald had fired a few rounds, Sterling noticed that his rifle was spitting a long stream of fire from the end of the barrel and that prompted Sterling to ask Oswald what kind of rifle and scope he was using. Oswald told Sterling he was using a 6.5 mm Italian make carbine with a 4 power scope. No other conversation transpired. Sterling and Dr. Wood observed that Oswald fired approximately 8 to 10 rounds and that each time he was careful in ejecting the hulls, that they were caught in his hand and put into his pocket. Oswald checked his target at least one time, then left the range by himself. He was driving some type of car, but Sterling does not remember what make or color it was. When Sterling and Dr. Wood checked Sterling's target, they also looked at Oswald's target and both concurred that he did some good shooting since all the rounds fired except one hit the bull's eye. Dr. Wood and Sterling are sure that Oswald was using the sling when firing his rifle.

Dr. Homer Wood's home address is 1326 Alaska and his home phone WH 1-5125, office phone WH 2-2067 and WH 2-1516.

Owner of the Sportdome Gun Range is Floyd Davis. He lives in the Sun Set Courts at Fort Worth Avenue and Westmoreland, right across in front of 2826 Byway.

202

COMMISSION EXHIBIT No. 2003—Continued

Continued - L. C. Graves - Page 2

Sterling Charles Wood was interviewed at Boude Story Jr High School.

Owner of the range has not been contacted at this time. He was not at the range today.

L. C. Graves

203

COMMISSION EXHIBIT No. 2003—Continued

Dec. 2, 1963

L. C. GRAVES:

We talked to Floyd Davis, owner of the Sportdrome Gun Range, at about 10:00 PM tonight. He lives in the Sun Set Trailer Park at 2825 By Way. By Way is South of 2800 Block Fort Worth Avenue. Mr. Davis and his wife say that they couldn't say that they had seen Oswald at the gun range. They said that they opened the range on October 16, 1963, and have been there every day except for three days. A Mr. Harold Price, who lives on Rice Street in Grand Prairie, works for Mr. Davis at the range. Price told Davis that Oswald had been out to the range on November 9th and 10th, as well as Sunday, November 17th. Price also told Davis that he had helped him set his scope. Price says that Oswald wouldn't talk to anyone at the range and that he would shoot his rifle three or four times real fast, wait a little while, and fire three or four more fast shots. Price said that Oswald had not carried his rifle into the range through the gate, that someone handed it over the fence to him after he got inside. The rifle was wrapped in something and tied with string. Davis doesn't know anything about the person who was supposed to have handed him the gun.

Price thinks that a white male, who looked like a foreigner 250 to 300 pounds with a "Beatnik" beard was with Oswald when he was at the range.

A Man named Mr. Slack, who works for the Water Department in the Urbandale Sub Station is also supposed to have seen Oswald at the range on the above dates.

Mr. Davis says that his records and some 605 brass was turned over to the F. B. I. man who contacted him on December 1, 1963.

J. P. Adamcik and K. L. Anderton

REPORT ON OFFICER'S DUTIES IN REGARDS TO THE PRESIDENT'S MURDER

M. G. HALL - #540
November 22, 1963

On Nov. 22, 1963, I was on a day off and was at home doing some work in my back yard. I went in the house sometime around 1:00 PM and turned the radio on and heard that the President had been shot. I tried to call the office, and the Riverside exchange was busy. I finally got the office and talked to Lt. Baker, and he told me to report for work at the office. I arrived at the office approximately 3:00 PM.

When I got to the office, my partners, R. M. Sims and E. L. Boyd, were in Capt. Fritz's office with Oswald. At approximately 3:30 PM I took an affidavit from Lee E. Bowers, 10508 Maplegrove.

At 4:05 PM, November 22, 1963, I assisted Sims and Boyd in taking Oswald down for a show up. We handled the line up from backstage behind the lights. The line up consisted of Bill Perry #1, Lee Oswald #2, R. L. Clark #3, and Don Ables #4. This show up was over at 4:20 PM, and Oswald was returned to Capt. Fritz's office, where he was questioned by Capt. Fritz and F. B. I. and Secret Service agents.

At 6:20 PM, November 22, 1963, Sims, Boyd, and I carried Oswald down for another show up. This show up consisted of the same people as the first. Bill Perry #1, Lee Oswald #2, R. L. Clark #3, and Don Ables #4. This show up was over at 6:37 PM, and Oswald was taken back to Capt. Fritz's office, where he was questioned by Capt. Fritz and F. B. I. and Secret Service agents.

At 7:03 PM, November 22, 1963, Capt. Fritz signed murder complaint with Bill Alexander, Assistant District Attorney, for the murder of Officer J. D. Tippit, Judge David Johnson was there and read the charge to Oswald.

At 7:40 PM, November 22, 1963, Sims, Boyd, and I took Oswald down for another show up. This show up consisted of Richard Walter Borchgardt #1, Lee Oswald #2, Ellis Carl Braswell #3, and Don Ables #4. This show up was over at 7:55 PM, and Oswald was taken back to Capt. Fritz's office. Just before this show up, F. B. I. Agent Clements, was talking to Oswald. Clements was getting Oswald's physical description, and where he had lived and worked before coming to Dallas. Clements also checked and listed the contents of Oswald's billfold. Clements's interrogation was discontinued until we had the show up. Agent Clements continued after we had brought Oswald back. Clements talked to him about 30 minutes more.

At 8:55 PM, Det. Hicks and Det. Studebaker of Crime Lab came to Capt. Fritz's office to make paraffin casts of Oswald.

At approximately 11:30 PM, November 22, 1963, Sims and Boyd wrote out arrest sheets on Oswald, and a short time later Cheif Curry and Capt. Fritz came in and told us to take Oswald to Show Up Room out in the front. Cheif Curry said for us not to let anyone get near him or touch him, and if they attempted to, for us to take him out immediately. Capt. Fritz told us he wanted all of his men to go with Oswald at this time. After a short time, we took Oswald down to the Show Up Room. The room was full of newsmen, and we kept him there about five minutes, and then we took Oswald to the Jail Office, and he was placed in jail.

REPORT ON OFFICER'S DUTIES IN REGARDS TO THE PRESIDENT'S MURDER

M. G. HALL - #540

November 23, 1963

I arrived at work at 9:30 AM. At 10:25 AM, November 23, 1963, Sims, Boyd, and I checked Oswald out of jail and brought him to Capt. Fritz's office for questioning. Capt. Fritz, F. B. I. agent Bookout, Secret Service Agent Kelly, U. S. Marshall Nash, Boyd, and I were in the office at this time. Sims, Boyd, and I returned Oswald to jail at 11:30 AM.

Sims, Boyd, Dhority, and I went to 1026 North Beckley to recheck Oswald's room. We arrived there at 11:59 AM and left at 12:30 PM, November 23, 1963.

At 1:00 PM, November 23, 1963, I issued a pass per Capt. Fritz for Oswald's mother and wife to visit him in jail. They were in the Forgery Bureau at this time. Juvenile Police Woman Reeves took care of the two Oswald children while I assisted the mother and wife to the fourth floor jail to visit Oswald. I remained outside the visitor's booth while they talked to Oswald. I returned them to the Forgery Bureauat 1:30 PM. The visiting time was approximately 20 minutes.

At 2:15 PM, November 23, 1963, Senkel, Potts, Brown, and I held show up with Oswald. He was brought down by jailers. The line up consisted of John Thurman Horn #1, David Knapp #2, Lee Oswald #3, Daniel Lujan #4. We handled the show up from the stage behind the lights.

At 3:30 PM, November 23, 1963, I issued a pass per Capt. Fritz to Robert Oswald to visit his brother, Lee Oswald. Robert was in the Forgery Bureau talking to Secret Service agent Howard at this time. I assisted Robert to the fourth floor jail, and he started talking to Lee Oswald at 3:35 PM. I remained outside the visitor's booth. At approximately 3:40 PM Agent Howard came to the fourth floor jail and said he wanted to talk to Robert again when he was through with the visit. The visit was over at 3:45 PM, and Secret Service Agent Howard and another agent who had come up assisted me in getting Robert Oswald back to the Forgery Bureau. I don't know this other agent's name. Secret Service Agent Howard was still talking to Robert Oswald in Forgery Bureau when I left them at approximately 3:55 PM.

At about 6:00 PM, November 23, 1963, Dets. L. C. Graves, Sims, and I checked Oswald out of jail and brought him to Capt. Fritz's office. Capt. Fritz was out, and we remained with Oswald until Capt. Fritz returned at 6:30. At this time Graves and Sims had gone out, and Dhority and Montgomery were in the office with me. F. B. I. Agent Bookout and Secret Service Agent Kelly was with Capt. Fritz. They talked to Oswald, and we put him back in jail at 7:15 PM.

REPORT ON OFFICER'S DUTIES IN REGARDS TO OSWALD'S DEATH

M. G. HALL - #540

On Sunday, November 24, 1963, I was in church at 821 West 10th when an usher came and told me Oswald had been shot. I went to the fire station across the street at 10th and Tyler and called the office, and Lt. Baker told me to report to the office. I arrived at the office shortly after 12:00 Noon. I assisted in routine office work until 3:00 PM. At 3:00 PM, Capt. Fritz sent Det. E. L. Boyd, L. D. Montgomery, B. L. Senkel, and me up to the fifth floor to bring Jack Ruby to his office. Det. Senkel waited in the room just outside of the elevator on the third floor while the other three of us went to the jail. When we arrived at the fifth floor jail, Ruby was stripped to his shorts, and F. B. I. Agent Hall was talking to him. We waited for Ruby to get dressed and then brought him to third floor on the elevator. There we were joined by Senkel and brought Ruby on into Capt. Fritz's office. Mr. Sorrels of the Secret Service was in Capt. Fritz's office, and some other officer from F. B. I., or Secret Service, was also there. After Capt. Fritz and Mr. Sorrels talked to Ruby awhile, Mr. Sorrels and this other officer left. In a few minutes, Justice of the Peace, Pierce Mc Bride and Assistant District Attorney Bill Alexander came in. Judge Mc Bride read the charge to Ruby that had been filed against him and advised him of his rights. At 4:00 PM Det. E. L. Boyd, B. L. Senkel, and I took Jack Ruby back to the fifth floor jail and turned him over to the jailers there.

REPORT ON OFFICER'S DUTIES IN REGARDS TO THE PRESIDENT'S MURDER

MARVIN JOHNSON - #879

Friday, November 22, 1963 at approximately 12:25 pm my partner, L. D. Montgomery, and myself stopped at Dales Cafe at Lemmon and McKinney to eat lunch. I went in and sat down at a table. My partner went to the phone to let our office know where we were. Approximately three minutes later he came back and said that Lt. Wells had told him the President had been shot and for us to come back to the office. We left the cafe immediately and returned to the office. As soon as we arrived at the office, Lt. Wells told us to go to Elm and Houston, the location of the shooting. We left the office and drove to Elm and Houston, arriving there at about 12:50 pm. We went immediately to the 6th floor of the Texas Book Depository Building and reported to Captain Will Fritz. Captain Fritz designated my partner and me to take charge of the scene where the assassin had done the shooting, to assist the crime lab and gather whatever evidence was available.

The window that the shot was fired from was open and we could hear the police radio from below. At approximately 1:20 I heard a call come out reporting a shooting at 10th and Patton Streets involving a police officer. We were not relieved of our assignment and did not answer this call. We remained where we were and continued to help Lt. Day and Det. Studebaker of the crime lab.

During the course of our search we found a brown paper bag which had been used for a lunch sack; a Dr. Pepper bottle and a long sack made from heavy wrapping paper. We suspected the long bag had been used to conceal the rifle that had been used in the shooting.

At approximately 2:30 pm we left the Book Depository and transported the above mentioned items to the crime lab located at city hall. We then returned to our office, arriving at the office at approximately 3:00 pm.

210

COMMISSION EXHIBIT No. 2003—Continued

Marvin Johnson-Page 2

I remained in the office from 3:00 pm, November 22, 1963 until 2:00 am on November 23, 1963. At 2:00 am I was dismissed from duty to go home by Captain Fritz. While in the office from 3:00 pm until 2:00 am I answered the phone and took an affidavit from Patrolman M. L. Baker. Patrolman Baker stated in his affidavit that he was riding escort on his motorcycle for the President's motorcade; that he heard the shots that killed the President and wounded Governor Connally; that he decided the shots were coming from the Texas Book Depository Building. After determining the origin of the shots, he jumped from his motor and ran into the building. He found a man that said he was the building manager. Officer Baker and the building manager then went to a stairway and started up the stairs to search the building. On about the 4th floor Officer Baker apprehended a man that was walking away from the stairway on that floor. Officer Baker started to search the man, but the building manager stated that the man was an employee of the company and was known to him. Officer Baker released the man and continued his search of the building. Officer Baker later identified Lee Harvey Oswald as the man he had seen on the 4th floor of the Texas Book Depository.

At 2:00 am I left city hall and went to my home. I returned to duty at 8:00 am Saturday, November 23, 1963. I remained in the office until approximately 12:30 pm. At this time my partner, L. D. Montgomery, and I were told by Lt. Wells to go to 610 S. Akard Street and pick up a cab driver by the name of Bill Whaley. He said this man had hauled Lee Harvey Oswald in his cab on Friday. We went to 610 S. Akard and picked up Whaley and returned with him to City Hall. We got back to City Hall at approximately 1:30 pm. I remained in the office from then until 9:30 pm. At this time Lt. Wells relieved me and I could go home. I arrived at my home at about 10:15 pm. At 10:30 pm I received a call from Lt. Bohart. Lt. Bohart stated that Sunday was my day off, and I could go ahead and take off,

211

COMMISSION EXHIBIT No. 2003—Continued

that I would not have to report for duty Sunday. I was off Sunday and Monday. I returned to duty Tuesday November 26, 1963 at 8:00 am.

When Patrolman M. L. Baker identified Lee Harvey Oswald as the man that he stopped in the Texas School Book Depository Building, Patrolman Baker was in the Homicide Bureau giving an affidavit and Oswald was brought into the room to talk to some Secret Service men. When Baker saw Oswald he stated, "That is the man I stopped on the 4th floor of the School Book Depository."

ADDITIONAL INFORMATION
ON
REPORT ON OFFICER'S DUTIES IN REGARDS TO THE PRESIDENT'S MURDER

M. JOHNSON - #879

Saturday, November 30, 1963, at 11:10 AM, I went to Market Hall on Industrial. I was driving Squad Car #376. I drove from Market Hall to Parkland Hospital. I measured the distance on the speedometer. The distance from Market Hall to Parkland Emergency entrance is exactly one mile.

I then measured the distance from Parkland Emergency to the front door of the Texas Book Depository Building. The distance is 3.9 miles. The route I traveled from Parkland was Hines to Industrial, Industrial to Stemmons Freeway, Stemmons Freeway to Triple Underpass, Triple Underpass on Main to Houston, then left on Houston to Elm and Houston.

At 2:05 PM, November 30, 1963, I walked from the Texas Book Depository Building at Elm and Houston to Elm and Murphy Streets, a distance of 7 blocks. This walk which was done at a fairly fast pace took 5 minutes, 10 seconds. I had to stop for one walk light on the way.

I then returned to Elm and Lamar and walked from the North side of Elm Street to the front of the Greyhound Bus Station at Lamar and Commerce Street, a distance of two blocks. This walk took 2 minutes 25 seconds. I had to stop for walk light at Main Street and at Commerce Street.

REPORT ON OFFICER'S DUTIES IN REGARDS TO OFFICER TIPPIT'S MURDER

MARVIN JOHNSON - #879

Saturday, November 23, 1963 at approximately 12:30 pm Lt. Wells told my partner L. D. Montgomery, and me to go to Oak Cliff Cab Co. in Oak Cliff and pick up a cab driver by the name of W. W. Scoggins. He said this man was a witness to the shooting of Officer J. D. Tippit.

When we arrived at the Cab Co. at Davis and Tyler in Oak Cliff, we were advised that Mr. Scoggins was on duty; that at that time he was at the Adolphus Hotel. Since we were going to bring Mr. Scoggins to city hall, he was advised by radio to meet us at 610 S. Akard, the main office of the Cab Co. We picked Mr. Scoggins up at 610 S. Akard and brought him to city hall. We arrived at city hall at approximately 1:30 pm. I took an affidavit from Mr. Scoggins in which he stated that he saw Officer Tippit stop on Tenth Street at Patton in Oak Cliff; that a man was walking down the sidewalk at this location. Officer Tippit stopped his squad car even with the man and got out of the car. As Officer Tippit started around in front of the squad car the man pulled a pistol and shot Officer Tippit three or four times. Mr. Scoggins further stated in his affidavit that he hotified the Cab Co. by radio to send an ambulance.

This is the extent of my investigation in the Tippit murder.

214

COMMISSION EXHIBIT No. 2003—Continued

REPORT ON OFFICER'S DUTIES IN REGARDS TO OSWALD'S DEATH

MARVIN JOHNSON - #879

When Lee Harvey Oswald was shot in the basement of the city hall Sunday, November 24, 1963 I was off duty. I was at my home all day on this date. I was also off duty Monday, November 25. I returned to duty at 8:00 am on Tuesday, November 26, 1963.

215

COMMISSION EXHIBIT No. 2003—Continued

REPORT ON OFFICER'S DUTIES IN REGARDS TO THE PRESIDENT'S MURDER

J. R. LEAVELLE - #736

I reported for work at 7:00 am on Friday November 22, 1963. My partners I normally work with, Detectives E. R. Beck and C. R. Boyce, were both off duty. At 10:00 am C. W. Brown reported in for duty. We got together to arrest a negro hijacker, Calvin Eugene Nelson. We located him at 12:15 pm, 2431 Ellis Street, and returned to our office and placed him in jail at 12:45 pm. I was told by Lt. Wells that the President had been shot and for us to report to Elm and Houston Streets.

On our arrival I went directly to the front of the Texas School Book Depository, 411 Elm Street. I met Inspector Sawyer who told me that the building was secure and that it was being searched. Inspector Sawyer also told me all witnesses were being taken to the Sheriff's Office for interrogation.

The uniform officers came up with a white man named William Sharp of 3439 Detonta, who the officers said had been up in the building across the street from the book depository without a good excuse. I took charge of this man and escorted him to the Sheriff's Office, where I placed him with other witnesses.

Several Burglary and Theft Bureau detectives came in and volunteered their services for interrogation. I told them if they would work with the Sheriff's deputies, questioning the witnesses, I would return to the scene of the shooting to assist in the search.

Just as I reached 411 Elm, the scene of the shooting of the President, a call came out on the police radio of a shooting of a police officer in the 400 Blk. of East 10th Street in Oak Cliff. I returned to the Sheriff's Office and called my office and talked with Lt. Wells who said there was no one covering the officer shooting. I told him I would make it. I borrowed a car from Det. A. L. Edwards who was questioning a witness in the sheriff's office and proceeded to Oak Cliff.

REPORT ON OFFICER'S DUTIES IN REGARDS TO OFFICER TIPPIT'S MURDER

J. R. LEAVELLE - #736

On my arrival in the 400 Blk. of E. 10th Street I talked with Sgt. Bud Owens and Officer J. M. Poe. At the same time a call came out that a person fitting the description of the suspect was seen entering the Texas Theatre on West Jefferson.

I attempted to reach the Texas Theatre in the 200 Blk. of West Jefferson but was unable to do so because of the traffic. Officer Poe had given me the name of a woman who was an eyewitness to the shooting. Her name was Helen Markham of 328 E. 9th Street, a waitress at the Eat Well Cafe on Main Street. Also that the manager of the used car lot, 501 E. Jefferson, had heard the shooting and seen the suspect running from the scene. Officer Poe also told me someone had picked up two empty .38 hulls from the street and given them to him, but he did not know who it was.

After the arrest of Oswald at the Texas Theatre I was told over the police radio that Squad 91 had the witness to the shooting and was enroute to the city hall. I then returned to the city hall and my office. I assisted other officers in taking affidavits and answering the telephone. I took affidavits from Charles Douglas Givins and Billy Nolan Lovelady.

I was then directed by Captain Fritz to locate the woman witness to Tippit's murder and take her to the showup room to view Lee Oswald in a lineup. I found Helen Markham in the Police Emergency Room with Det. L. C. Graves. She was suffering from shock. As soon as she was able, I took her to the showup room and called Captain Fritz who had Oswald brought down and placed in a lineup. At 4:35 pm, November 22, 1963 Helen Markham identified Oswald as the #2 man in a 4-man lineup as the man who had shot Officer Tippit. Also present was Chief Curry, Captain Fritz and Det. L. C. Graves. There may have been others in the room, I don't recall.

Det. L. C. Graves and I then took Helen Markham to her home in Oak Cliff. We stopped at the used car lot, 501 E. Jefferson, where we talked with the manager, Ted Calloway, who told me he had seen the suspect running from the scene with a gun in his hand and how he was dressed--with dark trousers, shirt light color, jacket and a T shirt; that the shirt and jacket were open and he could see the T shirt. A colored porter, Sam Guinyard, of Waxahachie, Texas said he also saw the suspect and could identify him. I also talked with another employee of the lot, Domingo Benavides, 509 E. Jefferson, who said he went to the scene of the shooting and picked up two empty hulls and gave them to Officer Poe.

We then returned to our office where Captain Fritz told me to call the above people to come down for a lineup. I called Mr. Calloway who came down and brought Sam Guinyard with him. We went directly to the showup room. While waiting for the showup I took an affidavit from both of the above men. At 6:30 pm Oswald was brought down, where he was identified by both Calloway and Guinyard as the same man they had seen running from the scene of Officer Tippit's killing with a gun in his hand. He was identified as #2 man in a 4-man lineup.

Mr. Calloway and Guinyard were then taken up to the crime lab on the 4th floor where Captain Doughty showed us a jacket that was found along the route taken by the suspect from the scene of the Tippit shooting. They identified it as the same one or one just like the one worn by the suspect.

I returned to the Homicide Office where I worked until 1:30 am Saturday morning. I went home and returned at 8:00 am Saturday, November 23, 1963. During the day I did general office work and took two more affidavits: one from R. S. Truly, supervisor at the Texas School Book Depository, 411 Elm Street and another employee of this business, Mrs. R. A. Reid. I also took an affidavit from W. W. Scoggins, a cab driver who was near the scene of the Tippit shooting and

COMMISSION EXHIBIT No. 2003—Continued

witnessed same. At 2:15 pm another showup was held where Scoggins identified Oswald as the man he saw shoot Officer Tippit.

Also at this same showup was William Wayne Whaley, another cab driver, who drove Oswald from the Greyhound Bus depot to the 500 Blk. of North Beckley. He also identified Oswald as the #3 man in a 4-man lineup. Others in the lineup were: #1 John Thurman Horn, #2 David Knapp, #3 Oswald, #4 Daniel Lujon.

I worked until 9:00 pm this date and was told to return about 8:30 am the next day, Sunday November 24, 1963 by Captain Fritz. He said we would transfer Oswald about 10:00 am.

COMMISSION EXHIBIT No. 2003—Continued

REPORT ON OFFICER'S DUTIES IN REGARDS TO OSWALD'S DEATH

J. R. LEAVELLE - #736

I arrived Sunday morning, November 24, 1963 about 8:00 am. We received word from Mr. Perry, Security Officer of the Statler-Hilton that they had a man check in who said he represented a munition company out of California. I went to the hotel in company with Det. C. N. Dhority and Mr. C. W. Brown. We talked with Robert W. Parker, 544 North Cypress, Orange, California. We satisfied ourselves he was O. K. and returned to the office.

At 9:30 am I was instructed, along with Det. L. C. Graves and Det. C. N. Dhority to go up in the jail and get Lee Oswald. I went to his cell and put the handcuff on him with his hands in front of him.

We returned to Captain Fritz's office where Captain Fritz, Mr. Sorrells and Mr. Thomas Kelly of the Secret Service questioned Oswald. Also in the room were Detectives L. D. Montgomery, L. C. Graves, C. N. Dhority and Inspector Holmes of the Post Office Department and myself.

Shortly after 11:00 am we began the transfer. Chief Curry had come to Captain Fritz's office. I had made a suggestion earlier to double cross the press and take Oswald out on the first floor via the Main Street door, leaving the press waiting in the basement and on Commerce Street.

Also it was suggested to go out the Main Street ramp and west on Main Street. These suggestions were turned down by Chief Curry who stated that we had better go ahead with the transfer as planned, since he had given his word on it.

Approximately 11:15 am we left the third floor office with Oswald handcuffed to my left arm with Det. L. C. Graves holding to Oswald's left arm, preceded to the jail elevator by Captain Fritz, Lt. Swain, Detective L. D. Montgomery. We reached the basement jail office with officers in front we headed to the automobile ramp just outside the jail office door. We hesitated just inside the jail door,

J. R. Leavelle-Page 2

then was given the all clear sign. We walked out and had just reached the ramp where the car we were to ride in was being backed into position by Detective Dhority when out of the mass of humanity composed of all the news media, which had surged forward to within six or seven feet of us, came the figure of a man with a gun in hand. He took two quick steps and double actioned a .38 revolver point blank at Oswald. I jerked back on Oswald, at the same time reaching out and catching Jack Ruby on the left shoulder, shoving back and down on him, bringing myself between Ruby and Oswald. I could see Det. Graves had Ruby's gun hand and gun in his hands. I turned my attention to Oswald and with the help of Det. Combest we took Oswald back into the jail office and laid him down. Handcuffs were removed and the city hall doctor, Dr. Bieberdorf was summoned. We also called O'Neal ambulance. Oswald was placed in the ambulance and rushed to Parkland Hospital. In the ambulance besides the crew was Dr. Bieberdorf, Det. L. C. Graves, Det. C. N. Dhority and myself.

He was rushed to surgery where he expired at 1:07 pm, November 24, 1963, pronounced by Dr. Tom Shires. Judge Pierce McBride was summoned. I gave him all the information needed to request an autopsy. When all necessary reports were made, I returned to the city hall where I made the offense report on Lee Harvey Oswald.

Form OPS-GF-355A-12
POLICE DEPARTMENT

SUPPLEMENTARY OFFENSE REPORT

CITY OF DALLAS

(1) LAST NAME OF COMPLAINANT (FIRM NAME)—FIRST NAME INITIAL	(2) OFFENSE AS REPORTED AND DATE	(3) THIS DATE	(4) OFFENSE SERIAL NO.
Oswald, Lee Harvey	Murder 11-24-63	12-17-63	F-

(5) ADDITIONAL DETAILS, PROGRESS OF INVESTIGATION, ETC.

I talked with a Don Campbell to-day who works for the Dallas Morning News, in the advertising department.

Don tells me that Jack Ruby is in the habit of comming to the office and drawing up his own copy for the advertising regarding the Carrosell and the Vagas [illegible] Club. That John Newman handles Ruby's account and that John's desk is just behind Mr Campbell's desk.

That on November 22, 1963 the day of the parade for the President Ruby came in and sat at John Newman's desk making out his copy. That John was not in the office at the time. Ruby came in around 12 Noon and was still there when Mr Campbell left about 12:20 PM

Mr Campbell says that Mr Newman told him later that he came in about 1 PM and that Jack Ruby was still there at his desk.

This would indicate that Jack Ruby did not see the parade or make any effort to see the President when he came by.

James R. Leavelle
Detective

(6) IF OFFENSE UNFOUNDED, GIVE REASON

H71

(7) LIST ADDITIONAL LOSS AND RECOVERED PROPERTY BELOW (Make Entry in Column (4) for Additional Loss Only)

(8) QTY.	(9) UNIT	(10) DESCRIPTION OF PROPERTY (USE STANDARD TERMS) SERIAL NOS.	(11) ESTIMATED VALUE	(12) DATE — RECOVERED — (13) VALUE

(14) RECOVERED BY | (15) RECOVERED AT

TOTAL VALUE	A	B	C	D	E	F	TOTAL
Leave Blank STOLEN							
Leave Blank RECOVERED							

(16) INVESTIGATING OFFICERS | I. D. NO. | (17) Bureau

(18) PERSONS ARRESTED—NAME, ADDRESS | (19) Race-Sex-Age | (20) ARRESTING OFFICERS I. D. NO. | (21) Dir. | (22) CHARGE

I RECOMMEND THIS OFFENSE BE DECLARED
(23) Unfounded ☐ (24) Pending ☐ (25) Cleared by Arrest ☐ | (26) DATE | (27) INVESTIGATING OFFICERS

(28) REPORTING OFFICERS | (I. D. NO.) | (I. D. NO.) | (29) DATE | (30) COMMANDING OFFICER

APPROVED:

INVESTIGATING BUREAU

COMMISSION EXHIBIT No. 2003—Continued

REPORT ON OFFICER'S DUTIES IN REGARDS TO THE PRESIDENT'S MURDER

V. D. MONAGHEN - #801

On November 22, 1963, I was off duty, but was summoned to Grand Jury at 10:00 AM. After I was released, I remained down town to watch the parade. At 12:40 PM I received word of the shooting of President Kennedy and reported to the Texas Book Depository Building to assist in the investigation. During this time I became ill and returned to my home.

On November 23, 1963, at approximately 10:00 AM, I was called to report for duty. I assisted in answering the telephones and again during the evening I became extremely ill and was taken home by Detectives Adamcik and Moore.

I did not return to duty until Monday, November 25, 1963, at 4:00 PM.

I did not make any further investigations on Mr. Kennedy, and I did not make any investigations on Mr. Oswald, or Mr. Ruby.

Respectfully submitted,
V.D. Monaghen
V. D. Monaghen, Detective

222

COMMISSION EXHIBIT No. 2003—Continued

REPORT ON OFFICER'S DUTIES IN REGARDS TO THE PRESIDENT'S MURDER

LESLIE D. MONTGOMERY - #1047

Friday, November 22, 1963 at 12:25 pm Marvin Johnson 879 and myself, while working as partners, went into the Dales Cafe, located at 3007 Lemmon Avenue, to eat lunch. Johnson and I sat down at the table and looked at the menu. I told Johnson to order for me that I was going to call the office and tell them that we would be out at this location. I called the office and talked to Lt. Wells. I told Lt. Wells that we would be out to eat, and the Lieutenant informed me that the President had been shot and to return to the office immediately. I hung up the phone, told Johnson that the President had been shot, and we were to return to the office immediately. We got into our car and returned to the city hall and our office.

Upon our return to the office Lt. Wells told us to report to Elm and Houston. We got into our car and drove to Elm and Houston and arrived there approximately 12:50 pm. Detective Johnson and myself entered the building, Texas Book Depository, and went directly to the 6th floor where we contacted Captain Fritz. Captain Fritz put Johnson protecting part of the scene on the 6th floor and myself protecting the part of the scene where the window was that the shooting took place. I remained at this location in the Texas Book Depository on the 6th floor until Det. Studebaker of the crime lab search section had dusted the windows and surrounding boxes for prints. I found a long brown paper sack looking item that looked homemade. It was beneath and to the left of the window where the shooting took place. I believed this to be the container that the rifle Oswald used was in. Det. Studebaker dusted this item and initialed it. Det. Johnson and myself initialed it also. Det. Johnson had a Dr. Pepper bottle that was in the area of the scene that he was protecting. Det. Studebaker dusted this item for prints. Approximately 2:30 pm upon completion of the work of

the Crime Scene Search Section, Det. Johnson and myself took the Dr. Pepper bottle and the brown paper sack looking item to crime laboratory on the 4th floor of the city hall. Det. Johnson carried the bottle and I carried the sack to the car. Det. Johnson was driving the car. I held all items from the Texas Book Depository to the crime lab. Upon our arrival at the crime lab, these two items were turned over to Det. H. R. Williams of the crime lab. Det. Johnson and myself then returned to our office on the 3rd floor of the city hall.

We arrived back at our office approximately 3:00 pm. From then until 2:00 am November 23, 1963 I answered the telephone and assisted in bringing Oswald from the jail to our office and back to the jail. At 2:00 am November 23, 1963 I was told by Captain Fritz to go home and return at 8:00 am. At 8:00 am on November 23, 1963 I returned to the office. I answered the phone and stood by for further orders. At 12:30 pm on November 23, 1963 Det. Johnson and myself were told by Lt. T. P. Wells to go to the Oak Cliff Cab Co. at Davis and Tyler Streets and contact a driver by the name of W. W. Scoggins and bring him to the city hall. Upon our arrival at the cab company we were advised that this driver was standing by the cab stand at the Adolphus Hotel at Commerce and Akard. This driver Scoggins was advised to meet us at the Yellow Cab Co. office at 610 S. Akard. Upon our arrival at 610 S. Akard we contacted W. W. Scoggins. The cab supervisor on duty at 610 S. Akard told Det. Johnson and myself that there was another driver on duty at this time that had said he had picked Oswald up at the Greyhound Bus Station. We advised this supervisor that we needed to talk with this driver also. The supervisor contacted the driver and had him to report to the office at 610 S. Akard. The driver, Bill Whaley, came to the office and Det. Johnson, W. W. Scoggins, Bill Whaley and myself returned to the city hall to our office at 1:30 pm.

Upon our arrival at our office I took Bill Whaley into Captain Nichols' office in the Auto Theft Bureau to take an affidavit of fact from him. Mr. Whaley gave an affidavit to the effect that he had picked Oswald up at the Greyhound Bus Station at 12:30 pm on November 22, 1963 and let Oswald out in the 500 Blk.of North Beckley at 12:45 pm on November 22, 1963. The affidavit was typed up by Patsy Collins and was notarized by her when Mr. Whaley signed it. Mr. Whaley and Mr. Scoggins were then returned to the Yellow Cab office at 610 S. Akard by other officers from our bureau.

I stood by the office answering the telephone and awaiting further orders. At 9:30 pm on November 23, 1963 I was advised by Captain Fritz to go home and return to the office at 8:00 am on November 24, 1963.

I returned to the office at 8:00 am and reported for duty. I answered the phone and stood by for further orders. At 9:30 am Detectives Leavelle and Graves went up to the 5th floor jail and brought Oswald down to Captain Fritz's office at which time Captain Fritz started interrogating him. Present at this interrogation, to the best of my knowledge, were Mr. Kelly of Secret Service; Mr. Holmes, Postal Inspector; Mr. Sorrells of Secret Service; Captain Fritz, Detectives C. N. Dhority, J. R. Leavelle, L. C. Graves and myself. This interrogation lasted until approximately 11:15 am at which time I, along with the others, was advised by Captain Fritz that we were going to transfer Oswald.

COMMISSION EXHIBIT No. 2003—Continued

REPORT ON OFFICER'S DUTIES IN REGARDS TO OSWALD'S DEATH

LESLIE D. MONTGOMERY - #1047

On Sunday November 24, 1963 at 11:15 am Captain Fritz, Lt. R. E. Swain, Det. J. R. Leavelle, Det. L. C. Graves and myself escorted Oswald from Captain Fritz's office to the jail elevator. Det. Leavelle had been handcuffed to Oswald. Patrolman C. G. Lewis, Jr., was the elevator operator as we carried Oswald down from the 3rd floor of the city hall to the basement. When we got off of the elevator in the basement, Lt. R. E. Swain walked out in front of Captain Fritz. Det. Leavelle was to Oswald's right and Det. Graves was to Oswald's left, and I was in back of Oswald about three feet as we approached the door leading from the basement and jail office. Captain Fritz told us to stop, that he was going to check one more time. The captain said, "All right, come on." We walked out of the door leading from the basement jail office to the ramp where the cars come down into the basement. We had to stop approximately five feet from the driveway of the ramp because the car was not in position. When we stopped I saw a blur of something and heard a shot. I went around Det. Graves and grabbed Jack Ruby by the head. At the time I grabbed Ruby by the head he was being held by W. J. Harrison, T. D. McMillon, R. L. Lowery and W. J. Cutshaw. We forced Ruby to the ground and a check was made for the weapon. We then moved Ruby into the basement jail office and put him back on the floor being held down by the same officers. While being held down on the floor of the basement jail office, Ruby said, "I hope I killed the son-of-a-bitch." I asked Chief Batchelor if we had better get Ruby on the elevator and get him up into the jail. Chief Batchelor said yes, and Ruby was taken to the elevator. I then went to where Oswald was lying on the jail office floor. A doctor was applying artificial respiration. The ambulance people arrived and loaded Oswald on the cot, and I went with the cot to the ambulance.

COMMISSION EXHIBIT No. 2003—Continued

Leslie D. Montgomery-Page 2

I then joined Captain Fritz, Detective E. R. Beck and C. W. Brown in their car and went with them to Parkland Memorial Hospital, 5201 Harry Hines Blvd. Upon our arrival at the hospital I was told by Captain Fritz to guard the east end of the hall of the Emergency Room. Oswald was taken to the operating room and I then moved up to the first floor main entrance to help maintain security. I was then relieved and returned to the outside entrance of the Emergency Room where I joined Captain Fritz and Det. E. R. Beck, and we all three returned to the city hall to our office. I answered the telephone and stood by for further orders. At 3:25 pm on Sunday November 24, 1963 Dets. E. L. Boyd, M. G. Hall and myself were told by Captain Fritz to get Ruby out of jail and bring Ruby to Captain Fritz's office. We checked Ruby out of the jail and brought him to Captain Fritz's office.

I then answered the telephone and stood by for further orders. I was told by Lt. Wells to interview a Bill DeMar (stage name)true name, William Delano Crowe, Jr. I interviewed this person and found him to be the master of ceremonies at the Carousel Club. The over-all content of the interview was the fact that this person was broke and that Ruby was supposed to pay him. He did also state that he thought Oswald was in the Carousel Club on November 20, 1963-Wednesday. DeMar said he could not be definite about this but he felt it was Oswald. This person was released without an affidavit taken. I then stood by for further orders and answered the telephone.

At 10:30 pm Sunday, November 24, 1963 I was told by Captain Fritz to go home and return at 8:00 am November 25, 1963.

REPORT ON OFFICER'S DUTIES IN REGARDS TO THE DEATHS OF PRESIDENT KENNEDY, OFFICER J. D. TIPPIT AND LEE HARVEY OSWALD

H. M. MOORE #679

On Friday November 22, 1963 I was off duty. I heard of the shooting of President Kennedy on the radio. I called the office and was instructed by Lt. Wells to report for duty. I arrived at the office shortly after 2:00 pm. I answered phones and helped in the office until approximately 4:20 pm. I then went with Det. F. M. Turner to the Sheriff's Office where we got with Judge David Johnston and secured a search warrant for 1026 N. Beckley. We then, F. M. Turner, Judge Johnston and Bill Alexander of the District Attorney's Office and myself proceeded to 1026 N. Beckley where we met Lt. Elmo Cunningham, Detectives Potts and Senkel. We then all searched the small room of Lee Harvey Oswald and confiscated all the property in the room that belonged to Oswald. See separate list. We then returned to the office where we went through the property we had seized and marked it. I ended my tour of duty just before 2:00 am.

Saturday November 23, 1963 I reported for duty at 10:00 am and worked in and around the office until approximately 12:30 pm when I went with Detectives Rose, Stovall and Adamcik to Judge Joe Brown, Jr.'s office to obtain a search warrant for the premises at 2515 W. 5th in Irving. We then went to Irving and contacted Det. McCabe, who accompanied us to the above address. We then made a search of these premises and seized several items belonging to Oswald. See separate list. We then returned to the office and marked several of these items. Approximately 5:00 pm Adamcik and myself were advised by Captain Fritz to return to Irving and bring in Michael Paine. We then contacted McCabe and returned and brought Michael Paine to our office and talked to him until approximately 9:30 pm when Adamcik and I took an affidavit from Paine. A ride was then secured for him so he could return home. I ended my tour of duty at 10:00 pm.Sunday, November 24, I was at home watching TV when the news of Oswald's being shot came on. I reported to the office as soon as I could get there, arriving approximately 1:30 pm. Shortly thereafter, Det. G. F. Rose and myself went to Judge Joe Brown, Jr.'s house and obtained a search warrant for Jack Ruby's apartment at 223 S. Ewing, Apt. 207. We then went to this apartment and searched it. Shortly after we arrived there Judge Brown, Jr. joined us and was present while search was completed. We took from this apartment some money (see property room invoice) and some telephone numbers. We then returned to the office, and I ended my tour of duty at approximately midnight.

COMMISSION EXHIBIT No. 2003—Continued

REPORT ON OFFICER'S DUTIES IN REGARDS TO THE PRESIDENT'S MURDER

W. E. POTTS - #576

On Friday, November 22, 1963, I was on my day off. At 1:00 PM I heard on the radio that the President had been shot. I called our office and talked to Det. T. L. Baker, and he told me to report for duty. I arrived at our office, Homicide and Robbery Bureau, at 2:00 PM. After arriving at the office, I took an affidavit from Danny Garcia Arce, w/m/18, and Jack E. Dougherty, w/m/40. Both of these men are employees of the Texas School Book Depository. I was in the process of taking an affidavit from Dougherty when the uniform officers brought in a white male they said killed Officer J. D. Tippit. I later learned that the man the officers brought in our office was Lee Harvey Oswald. Mr. Dougherty and Mr. Arce saw Oswald, and told me that he was employed at the same place they were employed, the Texas School Book Depository. It was about 2:40 PM when I finished taking affidavits from Dougherty and Arce.

Capt. Fritz told Det. B. L. Senkel and myself to go to 1026 North Beckley and search the room of Lee Harvey Oswald. Lt. E. L. Cunningham went with Det. Senkel and myself to this address. When we arrived at 1026 North Beckley, we contacted Mrs. Earlene Roberts, who is the landlady, and a Mrs. A. C. Johnson. This was at 3:00 PM, November 22, 1963. We checked the registration book for Alex Hidell or Lee Harvey Oswald, but could find neither of the names in the book.

The television was on, and they showed a picture of Lee Harvey Oswald, and Mrs. Johnson and Mrs. Roberts recognized the man as one of their roomers and said he had registered as O. H. Lee. They then directed us to his room which

COMMISSION EXHIBIT No. 2003—Continued

W. E. Potts - Page 2

is a small room just off the living room. We found that Lee Harvey Oswald had rented the room October 14, 1963, and used the name O. H. Lee.

We waited until Justice of the Peace, David L. Johnston, Det. F. M. Turner, Det. H. M. Moore, and Assistant District Attorney, Bill Alexander, arrived with the search warrant. This was about 4:30 or 5:00 PM when the above named men arrived at 1026 North Beckley. We then proceeded to search the room of Lee Harvey Oswald @ O. H. Lee. We recovered a City of Dallas Map with several locations marked on it, a leather holster, pair of binoculars, numerous letters addressed to Lee Harvey Oswald, several books and personal papers (See attached list for complete list). We then brought all this property to Room 317, City Hall.

On November 23, 1963, I reported to work at 10:00 AM and worked in the office answering telephone calls. I worked in the office until 12:00 midnight.

On November 25, 1963, Det. F. M. Turner and myself took a picture of Lee Harvey Oswald, DPD #54018, to 4007 Flamingo Street in Mesquite, Texas, to the home of Ronald Fischer, w/m/24, phone number BR 9-0950. Mr. Fischer's business address is the County Auditor's office. He stated that the picture looked like the person he saw looking out of a window on the sixth floor of the Texas School Book Depository, a few minutes before the President's motorcade arrived at Elm and Houston. He would not say definitely it was the man he saw, but he stated it looked like him.

W. E. Potts - Page 3

On November 23, 1963 at 2:15 PM Det. B. L. Senkel and I accompanied a show up, consisting of #1 John Thurman Horn, #2 David Knapp, #3 Lee Harvey Oswald, #4 Daniel Lujan, from the jail office to the show up room. I stood on the stage during the show up and could hear Det. Leavelle's voice, who was conducting the show up. I could not see Leavelle through the black screen. After the showup, Det. Senkel and I took the four above mentioned persons to the jail office elevator, and waited until they were safely on the elevator, before leaving.

REPORT ON OFFICER'S DUTIES IN REGARDS TO OSWALD'S DEATH

W. E. POTTS - #576

On November 24, 1963, at around 11:30 AM I went to the grocery store, and when I returned home, my wife told me that Lee Harvey Oswald had been shot. I then came to the City Hall and arrived about 12:30 PM. When I arrived, Det. Senkel, Turner, Lt. Smart, and Lt. Swain were in the squad room going through Jack Ruby's property. About 1:00 PM Jack Ruby was brought to Capt. Fritz's office, and I stood in the hallway to keep people back from Ruby. I also stood outside our office and kept the people back when Ruby was returned to the jail.

REPORT ON OFFICER'S DUTIES IN REGARDS TO THE PRESIDENT'S MURDER

R. M. SIMS -#629 and E. L. BOYD - #840

On November 22, 1963, at 9:00 AM, we arrived for duty at City Hall and reported to Capt. Fritz in his office. Capt. Fritz, E. L. Boyd, R. M. Sims, B. L. Senkel, and F. M. Turner discussed their assignments for the time President Kennedy was to be in Dallas. Capt. Fritz told Sims and Boyd that they were assigned with him to work the President's head table at the Trade Mart. At 10:00 AM Capt. Fritz, Boyd, and Sims left the City Hall in Capt. Fritz's city squad car. Sims drove to the Trade Mart and arrived there at 10:10 AM. We parked our car on the east parking lot. We walked directly to the Trade Mart and went to the President's table. We met Mr. Dave Grant and Mr. Robert Stewart of the U. S. Secret Service. We discussed our duties and familiarized ourselves with the area of the President's table. We discussed the route of the President to his table and who would be permitted in the roped off area around the President's table. We inspected the President's table and the roped off area. At 12:30 PM Capt. Fritz, along with Mr. Robert Stewart of the U. S. Secret Service, made the final inspection of the President's table. At about 12:40 PM Chief M. V. Stevenson came over to the west side of the roped off area and called Capt. Fritz. He told Capt. Fritz that President Kennedy had been involved in an accident at the triple underpass and was on his way to Parkland Hospital. He advised us to go to Parkland. Capt. Fritz, Sims, and Boyd rushed out to their car. Capt. Fritz said the report of the President's accident could be a hoax, so Sims checked with the police dispatcher by radio. The dispatcher told us the President had been shot. Sims drove Code 3 to Parkland, arriving there in less than 3 minutes.

COMMISSION EXHIBIT No. 2003—Continued

Chief Curry was out front of Parkland emergency entrance, and he told Capt. Fritz to go to the scene of the shooting. We rushed back to our car and Sheriff Decker went with us. Sims drove Code 3 to the Texas Book Depository Building at Elm and Houston and parked out front. We arrived there at approximately 12:58 PM and saw that the building was surrounded by Police officers, so we rushed on inside. We got on the elevator with several other officers. Lt. Jack Revill and Det. R. W. Westphal are the only ones that we can remember who rode the elevator with us. We stopped on the second floor, opened the elevator door, and saw officers there. We went on up to the third floor and got off the elevator. Westphal said he had a key to 305. We stayed there about 30 seconds and saw several other officers there, so we got back on the elevator and went to the fourth floor and got off. There were several officers on this floor so we caught the freight elevator and went to the fifth floor. We made a hurried search along the front and west side windows and then went on up to the sixth floor. Some officers stayed on the sixth floor, and we went on up to the seventh floor and started to search along the front windows. About this time someone yelled that some empty hulls had been found on the sixth floor. Capt. Fritz, Sims, and Boyd went to the southeast window on the sixth floor and saw three empty rifle hulls on the floor near the window. The empty hulls were found about 1:15 PM. Deputy Sheriff Luke E. Mooney said he found them and left them lay as they were. We stayed there with the empty hulls to preserve the scene and a methodical search was started by other officers going from east to west. About 1:20 PM, Lt. J. C. Day and Det. R. L. Studebaker arrived on the sixth floor. Capt. Fritz asked Lt. Day to take pictures of the hulls and the

COMMISSION EXHIBIT No. 2003—Continued

surrounding area. About 1:25 PM someone called for Capt. Fritz, and he left Det. L. D. Montgomery and Marvin Johnson to stay with the hulls. Capt. Fritz, Sims, and Boyd went over to near the stairway where one of the officers had called Capt. Fritz. Someone said the gun had been found. Capt. Fritz walked between a stack of books and over some books to where the gun was laying between some boxes and partially covered by some paper. The gun was about 5 feet from the west wall and about 8 feet from the west stairway. Sims went back to where Lt. Day was and told him the gun had been found. Lt. Day or Det. Studebaker took another picture of the hulls and said they had already taken pictures of the scene. Sims picked up the empty hulls, and Lt. Day held an envelope open while Sims dropped them in the envelope. Lt. Day then walked over to where the rifle had been found. Det. Studebaker and Lt. Day took pictures of the rifle. Mr. Pinkston of the F. B. I. and a Secret Service agent were there at the time pictures were being made. We don't know the Secret Service agent's name. Mr. Ellsworth and another officer from Alcohol Tax Department were also there. Lt. Day then picked up the rifle and dusted it for fingerprints. Some man then called Capt. Frtiz, and he walked over to where the man was. This man gave Capt. Fritz the name of Lee Harvey Oswald and his home address in Irving, Texas. We had just heard that Officer J. D. Tippit had been shot and killed in Oak Cliff. Capt. Fritz, Sims, and Boyd then left the Texas Book Depository and someone told Capt. Fritz that Sheriff Decker wanted to talk to him. Capt. Fritz went over to Sheriff Decker's office and stayed 10 or 15 minutes. Then Capt. Fritz, Sims, and Boyd left, and Sims drove Code 3 to City Hall. We arrived at Capt. Fritz's office approximately 2:15 PM. There were a lot of people in the Homicide

Bureau and Det. T. L. Baker told Capt. Fritz that the man who shot Officer Tippit was in the interrogation room. Capt. Fritz then found out that this man's name was Lee Harvey Oswald, the same name that he had received at the Texas Book Depository from the man there. At 2:20 PM Sims and Boyd took Oswald from the interrogation room and escorted him into Capt. Fritz's office. During the interrogation of Oswald, Mr. Jim Bookout and Mr. Hosty, F. B. I. agents, were in the office with Capt. Fritz, Sims and Boyd. There was also a Secret Service agent present and these F. B. I. and Secret Service agents took part in the interrogation of Oswald with Capt. Fritz. At 4:05 PM Sims, Boyd, and Det. M. G. Hall took Oswald down to the hold over in the jail office for a show-up. Down in the hold over, Boyd searched Oswald and found five live rounds of .38 calibre pistol shells in his left front pocket. Sims found a bus transfer slip in Oswald's shirt pocket. Oswald took his ring off and gave it to Sims. We put three other men in the show-up with Oswald. They were as follows: #1 Billy Perry, #2 Lee Harvey Oswald, #3 R. L. Clark, and #4 Don Ables. Sims, Hall, and Boyd went on the show-up stage with the men who were in the show-up. The four men were handcuffed together. After the show-up was over, at 4:20 PM, we took Oswald back to Capt. Fritz's office where Capt. Fritz, F. B. I. Agents, and Secret Service Agents talked to Oswald some more. At 6:20 PM Sims, Boyd, and Hall took Oswald back to the show-up room and held a line-up with the same men as were in the first one. They were also numbered the same as the first. At 6:37 PM, we left the show-up room and took Oswald back to Capt. Fritz's office. Shortly afterwards, Capt. Fritz, Justice of Peace David Johnston, and Assistant District Attorney, Bill Alexander, came to Capt. Fritz's office. Capt. Fritz signed a murder complaint against Lee Harvey Oswald which was accepted by Assistant district Attorney, Bill Alexander. This was for the murder of Officer J. D. Tippit. At approximately 7:30 PM, Hall and Boyd were sitting in the office with Oswald and Mr. Clements of the F. B. I came in and interrogated Oswald. At 7:40 PM Hall, Sims, and Boyd took Oswald back to show-up room. This time there was also three other men in the show up. They were as follows: #1 Richard Walter Borchgardt, #2 Lee Harvey Oswald, #3 Ellis Carl Braswell, #4 Don Ables. After the show-up, at 7:55 PM we took Oswald back to Capt. Fritz's office and Mr. Clements continued his interrogation of Oswald for about another half hour. At 8:55 PM Det. Johnny Hicks and R. L. Studebaker of the Crime Lab came to Capt. Fritz's office. Hicks started finger printing Oswald, then Sgt. Pete Barnes came in. Shortly afterward, Capt. George Doughty came in and stayed a few minutes. After Hicks finished Finger printing Oswald, he and Barnes made paraffin casts of both hands and also the right side of his face. Det. Studebaker assisted Hicks and Barnes. H. M. Moore, R. M. Sims, and E. L. Boyd were present most of the time while casts were being made. At approximately 11:30 PM Sims and Boyd made out arrest sheets on Oswald and shortly afterward Chief Curry and Capt. Fritz came to Capt. Fritz's office and told us to take Oswald down out in front of the stage at the show up room. Chief Curry gave us instructions not to let anyone touch Oswald, and if they attempted to do so, for us to take him to jail immediately. Capt. Fritz told us that he wanted all the officers in the Homicide Bureau to go down to the show-up room. After a short wait, we took Oswald down to the show-up room shortly after midnight. The show-up room was full of news men. We kept him there about 5 minutes then took him straight to the jail office at approximately 12:20 AM on November 23,

1963. Chief Lumpkin, Sims, Boyd, and Sgt. Warren took Oswald to fourth floor jail and turned him over to the jailers at 12:23 AM.

NOVEMBER 23, 1963

On November 23, 1963, we arrived for work at 9:30 AM. At 10:25 AM, Sims, Boyd, and Det. M. G. Hall checked Lee Harvey Oswald out of jail and brought him to Capt. Fritz's office for questioning. Mr. Bookout of the F. B. I., Mr. Robert Nash, U. S. Marshal, and Mr. Kelly of Secret Service were in the office with Capt. Fritz at the time. Boyd and Hall stayed in the office during the interrogation. After Capt. Fritz and the other officers finished their interrogation, Sims, Boyd, and Hall returned Oswald to jail at 11:30 AM. Shortly afterwards, Sims, Boyd, Hall, and Det. C. N. Dhority went to 1026 North Beckley to recheck Oswald's room. We arrived at 11:59 AM and left at 12:30 PM. At approximately 6:00 PM Sims assisted M. G. Hall and Det. L. C. Graves in checking Oswald out of jail and brought him to Capt. Fritz's office. Sims didn't stay in the office during the interrogation. After the interrogation, Sims assisted Hall and Graves in returning Oswald to jail at 7:15 PM.

REPORT ON OFFICER'S DUTIES IN REGARDS TO OSWALD'S DEATH

R. M. SIMS - #629

I was home on a regular off day November 24, 1963. I was watching T.V., and it was announced that Lee Harvey Oswald had been shot. I called the office and asked Lt. Baker if I could be of any help. He said, "Yes, come on in". I arrived at the office at 12:30 PM. I answered the phones and took an affidavit from George Senator, Jack Ruby's roommate. About 4:30 PM, Lt. Wells asked me to go to the jail and ask Ruby where his social security card was. Ruby had a visitor, so I waited on the fifth floor. Jack Ruby and F. B. I. Agent Hall got off the elevator, and I asked Jack Ruby about his social security card. He said he didn't know where it was.

240

REPORT ON OFFICER'S DUTIES IN REGARDS TO OSWALD'S DEATH

E. L. BOYD - #840

On Sunday, November 24, 1963, at 11:45 AM, I talked to Det.T.L. Baker by telephone from Irving, Texas, and he advised me to report to work as soon as I could get to the office. I had just heard about Jack Ruby shooting Lee Harvey Oswald while watching TV. I arrived at the office in the Homicide Bureau about 12:15 PM. At about 12:45 PM Patrolman R. E. Vaughn called our office and said he had a man down at the information desk in the basement who worked for Jack Ruby. I went down to the information desk and met Billy Joe Willis, w/m/34, of 6922 Forney Road, Phone #EV 1-3965, who was with Officer Vaughn. I searched Willis and then brought him to the Homicide Bureau. I talked to Willis awhile and then took an affidavit from him. After his affidavit was typed up, I took Willis downstairs to information desk and George Snyder notarized the affidavit at 2:27 PM after Willis signed it. Then I let Willis leave from the basement. At 3:00 PM Capt. Fritz sent Detectives M. G. Hall, L. D. Montgomery, B. L. Senkel, and me up to the fifth floor to bring Jack Ruby to his office. Det. Senkel waited in the room just outside of the elevator on the third floor while the other three of us went to the jail. When we arrived at the fifth floor jail, Ruby was stripped to his shorts and F. B. I. agent Hall was talking to him. We waited for Ruby to get dressed, and then brought him to third floor on the elevator. There we were joined by Senkel and brought Ruby on into Capt. Fritz's office. Mr. Sorrells of the Secret Service was in Capt. Fritz's office, and some other officer from F. B. I. or Secret Service was also there. After Capt. Fritz and Mr. Sorrells talked to Ruby awhile, Mr. Sorrells and this other officer left. In a few minutes Justice of the Peace, Pierce Mc Bride, and Assistant

241

District Attorney, Bill Alexander came in. Judge Mc Bride read the charge to Ruby that had been filed against him and advised him of his rights. At 4:00 PM Det. M. G. Hall, B. L. Senkel, and I took Jack Ruby back to the fifth floor jail and turned him over to the jailers there.

242

COMMISSION EXHIBIT No. 2003—Continued

STATEMENT OF B. L. SENKEL, DETECTIVE
RE: PRESIDENT'S ASSASSINATION

Reported on duty at 9:00 AM, November 22, 1963, the Homicide and Robbery Office, Dallas Police Department, Room 317. Talked with my partner Det. F. M. Turner, also Dets. Sims and Boyd. Capt. J. W. Fritz advised Det. Turner and I would report to Deputy Chief Lumpkin for assignment. Det. Turner and I had been issued beige colored lapel pins for identification. These were issued by Deputy Chief Stevenson on November 21, 1963. Deputy Chief Stevenson also showed us a complete list of identification badges and pins that would be used by all officers and members of the press. I secured a typewritten list of these items of identification.

9:30 AM, November 22, 1963, checked with Deputy Chief Lumpkin's Office, was advised that Deputy Chief Lumpkin was out at that time. Det. Turner and I returned to our office, and at about 9:40 AM, November 22, 1963, I received a call that Deputy Chief Lumpkin had returned and would meet Turner and me in the City Hall basement parking lot in 10 minutes.

9:50 AM, November 22, 1963, Det. Turner and I met Deputy Chief Lumpkin and another man that was with him. I believe his name was Weiddemeyer. The four of us drove to Love Field, arriving there around 10:30 AM. We drove the route that the motorcade would follow. Deputy Chief Lumpkin explained that we would be driving ahead of the motorcade about a half-mile. That we would look for any obstruction, or anything that might endanger the motorcade.

We waited at Love Field and saw both planes land. I saw the Presidential Party leave the plane. Deputy Chief Lumpkin told us there would be a Secret

243

COMMISSION EXHIBIT No. 2003—Continued

Service agent riding with us from Love Field. We left Love Field ahead of the motorcade. Deputy Chief Lumpkin driving, Det. Turner in front right seat. I was sitting in left rear seat, the Army Officer in center, and the Secret Service agent in right rear seat. Det. Turner checked radio contact with Chief Curry, who was leading the motorcade, and the dispatcher. We proceeded down the route to downtown, maintaining periodic checks by radio with Chief Curry. We turned off Main Street onto Houston Street, and I could see the motorcade at about Akard Street at this time. This was about 7 blocks behind us. We proceeded on Houston Street to Elm Street and then to the Stemmons Expressway. We were on Stemmons Expressway, nearing Oak Lawn Avenue when we learned of the shooting. The motorcade passed us on the service road near Oak Lawn Avenue. We followed the motorcade to Parkland Hospital. Saw the victims taken into the hospital. Left Parkland at about 12:45 PM, November 22, 1963. Had additional passenger, Forrest Sorrels, U. S. Secret Service. We proceeded to scene of the shooting. Arrived at the Texas School Book Depository, Houston and Elm Street, at about 12:50 PM, November 22, 1963. I met Deputy Sheriff Harry Weatherford at rear door. Weatherford and I entered building and proceeded to check building from ground floor upward. I got to the sixth floor about 1:10 PM. The empty hulls were found at window about 1:15 PM. Capt. Fritz, Dets. Sims and Boyd were present at this time. Capt. Fritz advised me to take the employees that had been on the sixth floor to the City Hall for statements. Officer C. W. Brown stated he had a car and would drive me to City Hall. Brown and I left the Texas School Book Depository with witnesses William H. Shelly, Bonnie Ray Williams, and Danny Garcia Arce (See affidavits).

Officer Brown and I arrived at Room 317, City Hall, at about 1:50 PM, November 22, 1963. I was in process of taking an affidavit from Bonnie Ray Williams when the uniform officers brought in a white male that they said killed Officer Tippit. I later learned the arrested subject was Lee Harvey Oswald. Shelly, Williams and Arce told us that Oswald was an employee of the Texas School Book Depository. Officer C. W. Brown talked to Capt. Fritz in my presence and advised him of Oswald's arrest. I completed the taking of the affidavit from Williams. This was at about 2:30 PM, November 22, 1963.

Capt. Fritz advised Det. W. E. Potts and me to proceed to 1026 North Beckley and search the room occupied by one Lee Harvey Oswald. Lt. E. L. Cunningham went with Det. Potts and me to this address. We contacted Mrs. Earlene Roberts, the landlady, and Mrs. A. C. Johnson. Checked registration book and did not find name of Lee Harvey Oswald, or name Hidell. Mrs. Johnson stated they had 17 rooms with 16 occupied. This was 3:00 PM, November 22, 1963. I called Det. T. L. Baker at City Hall, and he advised that he was sending out a Search Warrant. While we were waiting for the Search Warrant, the television was on, and a picture of Lee Harvey Oswald was put on the screen. Mrs. Johnson and Mrs. Roberts recognized him as O. H. Lee, a tenant, and directed us to his room. There was no number on this room, just the designation O, This being a small room off the living room of this large rooming house. We found that Lee Harvey Oswald had rented the room on October 14, 1963, and used the name O. H. Lee and still had the room rented, paying $8.00 per week. We waited until Justice of the Peace David L. Johnston, arrived with Det. Turner, and Det. H. M. Moore. The Search Warrant was shown to the owner of the house, and a search was made of the room occupied by Lee Oswald.

There was a City of Dallas map found, a leather holster, an address book with the name of Lee Harvey Oswald in it, numerous letters with his name on them, clothes, shoes, shaving kit, a paper back book entitled, "A Study of the U. S. S. R. and Communism", a pair of binoculars, several pamphlets, and handbills for the "Fair Play for Cuba", Undesirable Discharge from Marine Corps for Lee Harvey Oswald. This property was all taken to Room 317, City Hall.

I was in the process of looking through this property in Room 317, City Hall at about 7:00 PM, November 22, 1963, when I was advised by Capt. J. W. Fritz to talk to Mrs. Marina Oswald, wife of Lee Harvey Oswald. I talked to her in the presence of Mrs. Ruth Paine in Room 316, City Hall. With Mrs. Paine as interpreter, I took an affidavit from Marina Oswald. Miss Mary Rattan was the Notary and was present when a Mr. J. A. Brourantus and Mrs. Ruth Paine translated the affidavit. Det. J. P. Adamcik was also present. These persons, with the exception of Mary Rattan, were also present when the rifle found at the scene of the shooting was shown to Mrs. Marina Oswald. See her affidavit for her comments on the rifle.

On November 23, 1963 I talked to Mr. Joe Molina. See statement for information on him. He could not shed any light on Oswald's activity as he was not in close contact with Oswald during the day of November 22, 1963.

November 23, 1963 at 2:15 PM I was on stage in show up room when show up was held with #1 John Thurman Horn, #2 David Knapp, #3 Lee Harvey Oswald, #4 Daniel Lujan. I could not see into Assembly Room to see who was viewing the show up. I did recognize Det. J. R. Leavelle's voice, did not see him.

November 24, 1963 I came on duty at 12:00 Noon. I was returning from church services when I heard on a news broadcast that Lee Harvey Oswald had been shot. This was at 11:30 AM. I took my family home and reported for duty at 12:00 Noon. I was present when Jack Ruby was taken to Capt. Fritz's office at about 1:00 PM. I talked to Lts. Swain and Smart and listed property that they had taken from Jack Ruby's car. I went with Det. Turner and Lt. Swain and placed this property in Police Property Room. William F. Alexander of the Dallas District Attorney's office was also with us at the 1026 North Beckley address at time search warrant was executed.

REPORT ON OFFICER'S DUTIES IN REGARDS TO THE PRESIDENT'S MURDER

F. M. TURNER - #809

On Friday, November 22, 1963, Detectives Senkel and Turner reported to work at 9:00 AM. We were supposed to work with Chief Lumpkin and ride in his car to work the President's trip to Dallas. We got with Chief Lumpkin in the basement of the City Hall at approximately 9:45 AM. Chief Lumpkin had a U. S. Army Major with him that would ride in the car with us. All four of us drove to Love Field in Chief Lumpkin's car. The chief was driving. We drove to Love Field and to the area where the President would arrive. A Secret Service man met us at Love Field. He rode in Chief Lumpkin's car with us out in front of the motorcade. We stayed in this area until the President arrived at approximately 11:40 AM. We were to be the pilot car in this motorcade, after all the planes were on the ground, we drove to the outer gate at the parking lot near Cedar Springs and awaited word from Chief Curry in his car when they were about to pull out in the motorcade. We were on Channel 2 and were talking car-to-car as were all units involved in working the motorcade route. At approximately 11:50 AM, we received word from Chief Curry that they were ready to leave. We traveled the motorcade route and drove approximately 1 milesin front of the motorcade. We kept track of the location and speed of the motorcade by radio contact with Chief Curry. We were checking for any obstruction, or circumstance, that might impede the motorcade. The first time I saw the motorcade was after it turned on Main Street. I could see the red lights on the vehicles in the motorcade. When they turned on Main off Harwood, we were at approximately Main and Griffin. When we turned on Houston off Main, the motorcade was at approximately Main

and Akard. We turned on Elm and then onto the Stemmons Expressway. I do not recall noticing anyone in the windows of the Texas School Book Depository Building as we went by it. We drove on out Stemmons and were near Oak Lawn when we heard on the Police radio, "Tell Parkland to stand by". Then we heard Dallas one, which would be Sheriff Decker get on the radio and notify our dispatcher to notify all of his personnel to get over by the overpass on Elm Street and seal off the area until investigators could get there. Someone got back on the radio and said, "Notify Parkland to stand by, I think he has been hit." We were on the service road of Stemmons, near Oak Lawn when the President's car came by us on the way to Parkland. We followed the car to Parkland and helped with the situation until they got them carried into the hospital. I never did go in the hospital. In a couple of minutes Chief Lumpkin, Det. Senkel, the Army Major, and I proceeded to the location of the offense at Elm and Houston, arriving at approximately 12:50 PM. Chief Lumpkin advised to search a catoose of a freight car that was parked just behind the Lone Star School Book Depository Building. I looked through this car, apparently Chief Lumpkin and Senkel had gone in the building. I went in the first floor of the building. I talked shortly with a Mr. O. V. Campbell, the man in charge, and with R. S. Truly, warehouse superintendent, and with a Joe Molina who worked there. They were all of the opinion that the shots came from west of their building. They said they heard 3 shots at approximately 10-second intervals. Allen Sweat of the Sheriff's office came up and stated they had just sent a witness over to the Sheriff's office who might be able to give a description of the suspect. I went over to the Sheriff's office, where they had several witnesses in the Sheriff's office. Deputy Lum Lewis and

Ira Trantham of the Burglary and Theft Burea, Dallas Police Department, were interviewing the witnesses. Mr. Sorrels of the Secret Service was also talking with those witnesses. Affidavits were taken from these witnesses by various secretaries and court reporters from the County. I talked to the following listed witnesses: Charles F. Brehn, w/m, 1619 Kings Highway, WH 2-6893. He did not see suspect, or know where shots came from, was with his kid standing on Elm, west of Houston, saw something happen to the President. Also talked to Arnold Louis Rowland, w/m, and Barbara Walker Rowland, w/f, both of 3026 Hammerly. Have affidavits from them. Also interviewed Ronald B. Fischer, w/m/, 4007 Flamingo Drive, Mesquite, BR 9-0950, and Robert E. Edwards, w/m, 821 South Nursery, Irving. We have affidavits from them. On Monday, November 25, 1963, Detective Potts and I took a mug shot of Oswald and showed it to witness Fischer. He states he could not say definitely, but the photo of Oswald looked like the man he saw in the window less than a minute before the President's car arrived. I also interviewed at the Sheriff's office, John Arthur Chism, c/m, and Marvin Faye Chism, c/f, of 4502 Underwood. We have affidavits from them, also Jean Newman w/f, 3931 Clover Lane, FL 2-4222, have affidavit from her, also Julia Ann Mercer, w/f, 5200 Belmont, Apt. 208, we have affidavit from her. While at the Sheriff's office, I heard about Officer J. D. Tippit getting shot. Deputy Walthers told me some of the details. Sheriff Decker told me about them having Oswald arrested for shooting Tippit, and said Capt. Fritz had notified him that the suspect also worked at the Texas School Book Depository. I went over across the street to the building, hunting my partner, Detective Senkel. I went through the building and couldn't find him. Lt. Kaminski of the Special Service Bureau turned over a coat to me that had been turned in to

him by a James Clark La Rue. He found this coat on Industrial. As of this time, it has no part in the case. It was placed in the Property Room by me in Mr. La Rue's name as found property. I went back to the Sheriff's and called Lt. Wells at our office. He advised me to come to the office. I caught a ride to the office with an accident investigator. Upon arriving at the office, Lt. Baker was hunting a Justice of the Peace to get a search warrant. I told him of seeing Judge Dave Johnson at the Sheriff's office. He sent me, along with Detective H. M. Moore to get the warrant and go to 1026 North Beckley where Oswald had a room rented in another name. I think the name was O. H. Lee. We went to the Sheriff's office, where we picked up Judge Dave Johnson and Assistant District Attorney, Bill Alexander. Judge Johnson gave me the Search Warrant #295, which he had made out. All four of us drove to 1026 North Beckley, arriving at approximately 4:45 to 5:00 PM where we met Detectives Senkel and Potts and Lt. Cunningham. They were already at the location. We recovered the following listed property at this location on the warrant and brought it to the station, Room 317. Among the property recovered was a City of Dallas map that was marked at several locations, among them being the corner of Elm and Houston, a leather gun holster, numerous letters with Lee Harvey Oswald's name on them, several books, and pamphlets, and personal papers. (See attached list for complete list) Later in the evening on November 22, 1963, I took an affidavit from Linnie Mae Randle, w/f/30. She is the sister of the boy Oswald rode to work with and saw him carry the package and place it in the car on Friday morning, November 22, 1963. On or about November 23, 1963, I received information by telephone from an unknown caller who stated the December, 1963 issue of "Guns and Ammunition" has an exact picture of the gun like found at the scene, complete with scope. States this ad states that a mail order house, Klein's Sporting Goods,

Det. 487, 22 West Washington Street, Chicago 6, Illinois. This information was passed on to Capt. Fritz, who stated he already had that information.

On Sunday, November 24, 1963, I heard about the incident in the City Hall basement shortly after noon. I came on to the City Hall. I talked to Lt. Smart and Lt. Swain and helped them go through property they had recovered from Jack Ruby's car. We made a complete list of this property which has been typed up. Then Lt. Swain, Senkel, and I placed it in the Property Room. On Sunday night, November 24, 1963, a Ray John of Channel 8 News called this office stating that he had an anonymous phone call that stated they thought Oswald had the rifle sighted in on Thursday, November 21, 1963, at a gun shop at 211 or 212 Irving Boulevard. We checked and found an Irving Sport Shop at 221 East Irving Boulevard, BL 3-5309. A Woodrow Greener, BL 2-8492, owns this shop and has a man named Dial D. Ryder, 2028 Harvard, Irving, BL 3-4876, working for him. He states that he and Ryder have talked about this and have seen photos of Oswald and photos of the gun in the paper and neither can remember doing any work for this man, or any work on this gun. He will check his files for names and call back if he finds anything. He states that another reason that both of them think that they never worked on this gun is that in the photothe screws that hold the clamp that holds the scope on the rifle look like they are on top of the gun, and he thinks that neither of them ever saw a gun with a scope mounted with these screws on top.

On November 28, 1963, I talked to Mr. Greener again. He states that they found a work ticket back in the rear of the shop. This ticket has no date on it, but the best they can figure out this work probably came in November 4

to November 8, 1963. This ticket has the name Oswald on it and "Drill and Tap", $4.50 and Bore Sighting $1.50. He states that neither he nor Ryder can remember the face, or doing any work for this man. From the photo of the gun they still think that they did not work on the gun; however, he states that they will be glad to look at the rifle and see if they can recognize their work on it. The handwriting on the ticket is Mr. Ryder's. He states that they will check their cash register tapes and see if they can determine about when the rifle was picked up and when it was paid for.

We contacted Mr. Greener at his house in regards to picking up the work ticket that had been written up in the name of Oswald, Drill & Tap $4.50 and Bore Sighting, $1.50. Mr. Greener states that he has orders from a Mr. Horton of the F. B. I. to hold on to this ticket and not let it out. This ticket was written up in pencil by Mr. Ryder who works for Mr. Greener. This was Monday, November 25, when Mr. Horton of the F. B. I. first contacted them.

This phrase "drill and tap" as used by a gun smith means to drill a hole and using a tap to put threads in to attach a scope mount. They charge $1.50 a hole to bore these holes, this would mean that the mount on this scope would have three screws in it. The phrase "bore sights" means to attach a spud to the barrel of the rifle and then using a sight align tool they will attach this spud to this tool and align the cross hairs. Mr. Greener states that most mounting for scopes have to use 4 screws, states there are only two or three, the Springfield 03AM and the British 303 that use 3 screws in the mount. He states that they do not sell the ammunition that would fit the 6.5 calibre Italian gun. He is going to check his cash register tapes tomorrow and see if he can determine when approximately this order was picked up by the $6.00 service charge that would have been paid. Mr. Greener's home address is 2015 Rosebud Drive, BL 2-8492.

F. M. Turner - Page 7

We talked to Mr. Dial D. Rydor, 2028 Harvard, BL 3-1876. He states that he wrote the work ticket up with the name Oswald on it. We showed him a new mug shot of Oswald, and he states that he cannot identify the man as the one who left a rifle with him. He is going to check and see if he can find out tomorrow what day he did all of his business in pencil, as he usually writes with a pen, but does remember one day in the past when he used a pencil, and this tag was written in pencil. States that he can check because he remembers picking up some orders in Dallas on that day and will check this out tomorrow. He states that he will be glad to look at the rifle and see if he can remember working on it, but from the photos he has seen of it, he does not think that he has worked on it. He thinks from the photos he has seen of it, the scope mounting only has 2 screws in it, and he/states that he charged for 3 on this ticket. Also states that he thinks that he would remember a cheap scope like this and would have tried to sell the man another one and would remember this. He states that they do not sell ammunition that would fit a 6.5 calibre gun, but that he has found out that H. L. Green's does.

On November 25, 1963, we took a picture of Harvey Lee Oswald, DPD #54018 and showed it to witness Ronald Fischer, w/m/24, 4007 Flamingo Way, Mesquite, Texas, FR 9-0950. His business address is County Auditor's Office. An affidavit was taken from him at the Sheriff's office. He states the photo of Oswald looks like the man he saw at the window where the shots were fired from. States he saw this man in the window a minute or less before the motorcade arrived. He could not say definitely this was the man, but said that it looked like the man.

254

COMMISSION EXHIBIT No. 2003—Continued

NAMES AND ADDRESSES OF PRINCIPALS

President John F. Kennedy and Mrs. Kennedy, White House, Washington, D. C.

Governor John Connally and Mrs. Connally, Governor's Mansion, Austin, Texas

J. D. Tippit, 238 Glencairn, Dallas, Texas

Lee Harvey Oswald, 1026 N. Beckley, Dallas, Texas
& 2515 W. 5th, Irving, Texas

Jack Ruby, 223 S. Ewing, Apt. 207, Dallas, Texas

257

COMMISSION EXHIBIT No. 2003—Continued

POSITIONS ASSIGNED HOMICIDE AND ROBBERY BUREAU OFFICERS FOR THE SECURITY OF THE PRESIDENT

Captain J. W. Fritz	Market Hall-vicinity of President's table and Speaker's Stand.
R. M. Sims E. L. Boyd	Market Hall-vicinity of President's table and Speaker's Stand.
B. L. Senkel F. M.Turner	Reconnaissance car with Chief G. L. Lumpkin of the City Police Department, Major Weiddemeyer of the U. S. Army, and Secret Service They were to precede the Presidential Party approximately one-half mile and maintain radio contact with Chief J. E. Curry who was with the Presidential Party and advise him of the situation along the route in advance.

258

COMMISSION EXHIBIT No. 2003—Continued

Form CPS—PC—447

POLICE DEPARTMENT
CITY OF DALLAS

PROPERTY CLERK'S INVOICE OR RECEIPT

Nov 23 1963 ______ 19___

Received of R S Stovall & G R Rose the following described articles,

§ recovered stolen property:

Evidence in Offense No.______ Arrest No.______ Charge Confiscated, Evidence

QUANTITY	ARTICLE	BIN NO.	DISPOSITION
✓1	Rifle, British Enfield, P4 Mk 1, peep	AK-1	
	sight, ser #[illegible], 21 3/4" bl, black steel, wooden stock with brass butt,		
	bolt action, with 1 magazine clip and rings for fastening shoulder straps		
✓10	Rounds British R P 303 ammo	F-33	
	Tag Date: 11/22/63		
	Arr: FRAZIER, Buell Wesley		
	2439 W 5th, Irving, Texas		

W. M. Dickey
Property Clerk

Nº 11064 G

If neither evidence nor recovered stolen property, write on face of this form in detail reason for police possession.

259

COMMISSION EXHIBIT No. 2003—Continued

Form CPS—PC—447

POLICE DEPARTMENT
CITY OF DALLAS

PROPERTY CLERK'S INVOICE OR RECEIPT

25 Nov. 1963 ______ 19___

Received of Lt. Swain & Lt Smart the following described articles,

§ recovered stolen property:

Evidence in Offense No.______ Arrest No.______ Charge inv. murder

QUANTITY	ARTICLE	BIN NO.	DISPOSITION
	Rep. Nat'l Bank money bag with		
$124.87	one hundred twenty four dollars & eighty seven cents	Sf-dr-9	
	(50 ones, 602 dimes, 242 nickels, 257 pennies)		
	Envelope containing		
$131.41	one hundred thirty one dollars & forty one cents		
	(2 tens, 38 ones, 1 silver dollar, 47 halves, 154 quarters, 58 dimes, 86 nickels, 31 pennies)		
	First Nat'l money bag containing		
$795.50	seven hundred ninety-five & fifty cents		
	(80 fives, 320 ones, 47 halves, 82 quarters, 269 dimes, and 92 nickels)		
	(Total - $1051.78)		
1	blue canvas money bag		
1	khaki canvas money bag with leather trimmed top and fitted for locking seal missing the latch		
	tag dated 11-24		
	ARR: RUBY, Jack w/m/52		
	3929 Rawlins		

W M DICKEY & B J SMITH
Property Clerk

Nº 11105 G

If neither evidence nor recovered stolen property, write on face of this form in detail reason for police possession.

260

COMMISSION EXHIBIT No. 2003—Continued

Form CPS—PC—447

POLICE DEPARTMEN

CITY OF DALLAS

PROPERTY CLERK'S INVOICE OR RECEIPT

25 Nov 1963 19

Received of Lt. Smart & Lt Swain the following described articles,
§ recovered stolen property:

Evidence in Offense No. Arrest No. Charge inv. murder

QUANTITY	ARTICLE	BIN NO.	DISPOSITION
	paper sack containing		
1	blk. plastic briefcase with business	~~N-30~~	
	correspondence		
3	Newspapers dtd. 23 Nov. 1963,	N-18	
	2 The Dallas Morning News, & 1 The		
	Dallas Times Herald		
1	envelope containing		
	2 Polaroid pictures, 3 negatives		
	misc. receipts		
1	envelope containing		
	1 small notebook		
	1 tan plastic billfold with		
	1 Tex oper's license in name of		
	Jack Leon Ruby, 3929 Rawlins		
	1 passenger car lic. receipt, same name		
	misc. papers, cards		
1	envelope containing 1 newspaper page		
	from The Dallas Morning News, 22 Nov. 1963		
	1 pc. of paper with the word "Closed"		
1	small cardboard box with Carousel		
	Club passes & business papers		
	1 small btl. of brn. liquid		
1	envelope containing 2 razor blade		
	dispensers, 2 advertisement pictures		
1	carton of 18 razor blade dispensers		
1	book of 25 stamps (8¢)		
1	book of 20 stamps (5¢)		
2	pr. metal "Knuks"		
1	brn. lea. holster		
1	Wynnewood State Bank money bag		
1	Empire State Bank money bag with		
	misc. papers		
1	stack of envelopes		
1	Merchants State Bank money bag		
1	Rep. Nat'l Bank money bag w/		
	misc. papers		
1	lea. keycase with 4 keys		

tag dated 11-24 · ARR: RUBY, Jack Leon w/m/52
3929 Rawlins

Nº 11107 G

B J SMITH & W M DICKEY
Property Clerk

If neither evidence nor recovered stolen property, write on face of this form in detail reason for police possession.

261

COMMISSION EXHIBIT No. 2003—Continued

Form CPS—PC—447

POLICE DEPARTMEN

CITY OF DALLAS

PROPERTY CLERK'S INVOICE OR RECEIPT

25 Nov 1963 19

Received of jail the following described articles,
§ recovered stolen property:

Evidence in Offense No. Arrest No. Charge inv. murder

QUANTITY	ARTICLE	BIN NO.	DISPOSITION
$2015.33	two thousand fifteen dollars & thirty	Safe Dr 9	
	three cents		
1	man's "Le Coultre wrist watch w/clear stones on face ← A-13823		
3	Amer. Exp. Company ~~XXXX~~ travelers checks,		
	#DA49 990 257, DA49 990 258, DA49 990 259		
	all three in amt. of $20.00 - in name		
	of Samuel Baker		
1	Gents w/g ring with 3 clear stones	Safe dr 9 — A-13823	
1	envelope containing	G-25	
	1 pr. eyeglasses, blk. plastic frames		
3	ball pt. pens		
1	small "Trim-Trio" knife		
4	Polaroid pictures, "Impeach Earl Warren"		
	signs		
1	blk. lea. belt		
1	key		
1	blk. lea. belt		
1	necktie		
2	address book		
1	pr. blk. lea. shoes	~~N-30~~	
1	white dress shirt	N-18	
1	cot underwear		
1	brn. suit		
1	gray felt hat		
	tag dated 11-24		
	ARR: RUBY, Jack Leon w/m/52		
	3929 Rawlins		

Nº 11109 G

B J SMITH & W M DICKEY
Property Clerk

If neither evidence nor recovered stolen property, write on face of this form in detail reason for police possession.

261 A

COMMISSION EXHIBIT No. 2003—Continued

Form CPS—PC—447

POLICE DEPARTMENT
CITY OF DALLAS

PROPERTY CLERK'S INVOICE OR RECEIPT

November 26, 1963 19

Received of Police Lab Crime Scene Search Section #7992 the following described articles, § recovered stolen property:

Evidence in Offense No. F 85950 Arrest No. Charge Murder

QUANTITY	ARTICLE	BIN NO.	DISPOSITION
√1	Italian make 6.5 Rifle Ser. # C 2766 blue steel - wood stock - brn leather sling with 4 x 18 Coated Ordinance Optics Inc Hollywood California O 10 Japan tele scopic sight	Released	
√1	Green and Brown Wool Striped Blanket	"	
√1	Slug (believed to be 38 Cal)	"	
√1	Button off of Policeman's Uniform	"	
√1	Homemade paper bag resembling homemade gun case	"	
√1	38 Cal S & W Revolver - Sandblast brn wd hndles - 2" bbl Ser #510210	"	
√1	Bullet fragment taken from the body of Gov. John Connally	"	RECEIVED BY [signature] OF THE DALLAS POLICE DEPARTMENT
√1	Live round 6.5 mm shell	"	THIS 26th DAY OF Nov 196
√2	Spent 6.5 hulls ("found under window")	"	ALL OF THE ARTICLES OF PROPERTY LISTED HEREON.
√1	Mans brown sport shirt "Taken from Lee Harvey Oswald"	"	
√1	Pc Cardboard containing palm print of suspect	"	NAME [signature]
√3	Empty Cardboard Boxes marked A, B & C.	"	ADDRESS FBI
√1	Cardboard Box, empty, size: 11 3/4" x 13" x 17½" "From which thumb print of suspect was found"	"	
√1	Partial palm print "off underside gun barrell near end of foregrip" on rifle C 2766	"	
√3	Negatives of partial prints "found on trigger housing of rifle Ser #C 2766		
	Arrested: Lee Harvey Oswald w/m/24 Dallas, Texas.		

This inventory was made and invoice typed ~~in Crime Scene Search Section office in presence of:~~ [signature]

H. W. Hill
Property Clerk

Nº 11176 G

If neither evidence nor recovered stolen property, write on face of this form in detail reason for police possession.

262

COMMISSION EXHIBIT No. 2003—Continued

Form CPS—PC—447

POLICE DEPARTMENT
CITY OF DALLAS

PROPERTY CLERK'S INVOICE OR RECEIPT

November 26 1963

Received of G. F. ROSE, 1029 H. M. MOORE, 679; R.S.Stovall, J. P. Adamcik, Homicide Bureau 1031 the following described articles, § recovered stolen property:

Evidence in Offense No. Arrest No. Charge Murder

QUANTITY	ARTICLE	BIN NO.	DISPOSITION
√188	Photos and pictures #'s 1 thru 43	Released	
√67	Postcards # 44 - 64	"	
√6	Negatives # 65	"	
√25	Christmas cards # 66	"	
√1	Christmas card w. picture of mother # 67	"	
√1	Christmas card from mother #68	"	
√1	Russian Postcard #69 (with writing)	"	
√4	Photographs # 70	"	
√1	Marine Corps 2nd Btn. Class Book #71	"	
√1	Hammond Doubleday World Atlas #72	"	
√1	Modern Postage Stamp Album #73	"	
1	Texnika Russian Magazine #74	"	
√18	Russian Books #'s 75 thru 83	"	
√1	Russian Book # 84	"	
√1	Copy of Militant # 85 (10/7/63)	"	
√1	Copy of The Worker 10/20/63 #86	"	
√1	Copy of Friend's World News 4/63 #87	"	
√1	Copy of Pocketbook entitled GEORGE ORWELL, 1984 # 88	"	
√6	Russian Pamphlets #'s 89 - 94	"	
√1	Russian Telegram w. picture on front # 95	"	
√187	Applications for FPCC #96	"	
√173	Handbills entitled "Hands Off Cuba! Join the FPCC" #97	"	RECEIVED BY [signature]
√1	Receipt for fine from 2nd Mune Court, New Orleans, 8/12/63 #21902, and newspaper clipping #98	"	OF THE DALLAS POLICE DEPARTMENT THIS 26th DAY OF Nov 1963
√3	Pamphlets by CORLISS LAMONT "The Crime Against Cuba." #99	"	ALL OF THE ARTICLES OF PROPERTY LISTED HEREON.
√1	Roadmap "Eastern States" Cities Services #100	"	NAME [signature]
√1	Texas Highway Map Phillips 66 #101	"	ADDRESS Sp. Agt. FBI.
√1	Map of Moscow #102	"	
√1	Map of Minsk Russia #103	"	
√1	Map of City of New Orleans Bulf #104	"	

Arrested: Lee Harvey Oswald w/m/24 Dallas, Texas

This inventory was made & invoice typed in FBI Office, Dalas, Texas

Property Clerk
H. W. HILL

Nº 11177 G

If neither evidence nor recovered stolen property, write on face of this form in detail reason for police possession.

263

COMMISSION EXHIBIT No. 2003—Continued

Form CPS—PC—447

POLICE DEPARTMENT

CITY OF DALLAS

PROPERTY CLERK'S INVOICE OR RECEIPT

November 26 1963

Received of G. F. Rose, 1029 H. M. Moore, 679; R. S. Stovall, 1031 J.P. Adamcik, Homicide Bureau the following described articles

§ recovered stolen property:

Evidence in Offense No. Arrest No. Charge Murder

Continued from Inv. 11177G

QUANTITY	ARTICLE	BIN NO.	DISPOSITION
√1	Map of Beautiful Russia # 105	"	
√1	Map of the World #106	"	
√1	No Admittance Sign # 107	"	
√1	Notebook and contents in English #108	"	
√1	Notebook entitled "TETTADB" & Russian language contents #109	"	
√1	Notebook with designs #110	"	
√1	Red Russian Stamp Folder with stamps #111	"	
√1	4" x 7" blue book in Russian language bearing No. 732648 #112	"	
√1	Pocket size blue book apparently identification booklet with small photograph of OSWALD #113	"	
√1	Brown billfold with Marine Group photograph #114	"	
√159	Fair Play For Cuba Committee, New Orleans Chapter ID Cards #115	"	
√45	Sheets of English writing both sides which appears to be a diary #116	"	
√8½	Sheets of lined paper in green ink printing containing comments re CPUSA #117	"	RECEIVED BY H. W. Hill OF THE DALLAS POLICE DEPARTMENT
√1	Negative offset print of Russian City Moscow #118	"	THIS 26th DAY OF Nov 1963
√1	Penciled diagram #119	"	ALL OF THE ARTICLES OF PROPERTY LISTED HEREON.
√1	Newspaper clipping re "The President" #120	"	
√1	Brown Manila envelope from Dept. of the Navy directed to Mr. Lee H. Oswald Minsk, USSR. #121	"	NAME Warren C. deBrueys
√1	Single sheet in black ink printing entitled "The New Era" #122	"	ADDRESS Sp. Agt. FBI
	Arrested: Lee Harvey Oswald w/m/24 Dallas, Texas		

This inventory was made and invoice typed in FBI Office, Dallas, Texas.

11177G This invoice Search Warrant RUTH PAINE's, Irving, Texas 11/23/63

H. W. HILL
Property Clerk

No 11178 G

If neither evidence nor recovered stolen property, write on face of this form in detail reason for police possession.

264

COMMISSION EXHIBIT No. 2003—Continued

Form CPS—PC—447

POLICE DEPARTMENT

CITY OF DALLAS

PROPERTY CLERK'S INVOICE OR RECEIPT

November 26 1963

Received of G. F. ROSE, 1029 H. M. MOORE, 679; R. S. Stovall, 1031 J. P. Adamcik, Homicide Bureau the following described articles,

§ recovered stolen property:

Evidence in Offense No. Arrest No. Charge Murder

Continued from Inv. 11178G

QUANTITY	ARTICLE	BIN NO.	DISPOSITION
√11	Pages of blue ink handwriting No'd 1 - 11 on Holland American Lined Stationary #123	Released	
√4	Sheets of blue ink handwriting Holland American lined Stationary No'd 1A thru 4A #124	"	
√2	Sheets of blue ink handwriting on Holland American lined Stationary No'd 1B and 2B #125	"	
√1	Folder captioned "BLOKNOTS" #126	"	
√28	Letters in Russian script No. 127-through 155	"	
√6 √5	Envelopes and its contents and 5 empty envelopes in Russian language No's 156 through 167	"	
√2	Withholding Tax Statements for 1955 and 956 for Lee Oswald #168	"	
√2	Withholding Tax Statements for 1955 and 1956 for Lee Oswald #169	"	
√1	Deposit slip NO Public Service # 464792; Dallas City Water Works Deposit Slip K3331, and Texas Employment Commission Slip dated 4/16/63 allin name of L. H. OSWALD #170	"	RECEIVED BY H. W. Hill OF THE DALLAS POLICE DEPARTMENT THIS 26th DAY OF Nov 1963
√1	Rent receipt 8/9/63 signed I. DAWSON (New Orleans) #171	"	ALL OF THE ARTICLES OF PROPERTY LISTED HEREON.
√1	Receipt from U. S. Dept of Justice for $5 (I&NS) in name of MARINA N. OSWALD #172	"	NAME Warren C. deBrueys ADDRESS Sp. Agt, FBI
√1	Birth certificate for AUDREY MARINA RACHEL OSWALD born 10/20/63, No. 19133, Dallas, Texas #173	"	
	Arrested: Lee Harvey Oswald w/m/24 Dallas, Texas		

This inventory was made and invoice typed in FBI Office, Dallas, Texas

This invoice Search Warrant RUTH PAINE's, Irving, Texas 11/23/63

H. W. HILL
Property Clerk

No 11179 G

If neither evidence nor recovered stolen property, write on face of this form in detail reason for police possession.

265

COMMISSION EXHIBIT No. 2003—Continued

Form CPS—PC—447

POLICE DEPARTMENT

CITY OF DALLAS

PROPERTY CLERK'S INVOICE OR RECEIPT

Received of G. F. Rose, 1029 H. M. Moore, 679; R. S. Stovall, 1031, J. P. Adamcik, Homicide Bureau November 26 19 63 the following described articles,

§ recovered stolen property:

Evidence in Offense No. ______ Arrest No. ______ Charge Murder

Continued from Inv. 11179G

QUANTITY	ARTICLE	BIN NO.	DISPOSITION
√1	Soc. Sec. Receipt OSWALD, Soc. Sec. No. 433-54-3937 8/63 #174	Released	
√1	Withholding Tax for 1956 in name of Lee Harvey Oswald #175	"	
√1	Invoice No. 38210 USA, Dept. of State, in name OSWALD, transportation costs $435.71 #176	"	
√1	A promise by OSWALD to pay loan to Dept. of State #177	"	
√3	Remittance Slips State Department No's 298249; 298861; 299461 addressed OSWALD Box 2915, Dallas, Texas #178	"	
√4	Receipts from U.S. Dept. of State, No's 1152090;91, 95, 96 #179	"	
√1	Form I-90 I & NS in name of MARINA OSWALD #180	"	
√1	Incomplete Form FDI-130 (I&NS) in name of LEE HARVEY OSWALD #181	"	
√2	Russian Language Forms, one entitled "AHKETA" #182	"	H. W. Hill
√1	4-page form in Russian language which appears to be a questionnaire #183	"	OF THE DALLAS POLICE DEPARTMENT
√1	4-page form in Russian language which appears to be questionnaire #184	"	THIS 26th DAY OF Nov 19 63 ALL OF THE ARTICLES OF PROPERTY LISTED HEREON.
√2	Form DD293 Application for Review of Discharge from the Armed Forces of the U. S. #185	"	NAME Warren C. deBrueys ADDRESS Sp. Agt. FBI
√2	Booklets which appear to contain embroidery patterns #186	"	
√5	Color slides approx. 2" sq. #187	"	
√1	Pass dated 9/58 in name Sgt. OSWALD Zebra Co., Open Mess #188	"	
	Arrested: Lee Harvey Oswald w/m/24 Dallas, Texas		

This inventory was made and invoice typed in FBI Office, Dallas, Texas

This invoice Search Warrant RUTH PAINE's, Irving, Tex. 11/23/63

H. W. HILL
Property Clerk

No. 11180 G

If neither evidence nor recovered stolen property, write on face of this form in detail reason for police possession.

266

Form CPS—PC—447

POLICE DEPARTMENT

CITY OF DALLAS

PROPERTY CLERK'S INVOICE OR RECEIPT

Received of G. F. Rose, 1029; H. M. Moore, 679; R. S. Stovall, 1031, J. P. Adamcik, Homicide Bureau November 26 19 63 the following described articles,

§ recovered stolen property:

Evidence in Offense No. ______ Arrest No. ______ Charge Murder

Continued from Inv. 11180G

QUANTITY	ARTICLE	BIN NO.	DISPOSITION
√1	2-CMEHA #189 Russian Document	Released	
√1	Empty Enevelope to Mr. and Mrs. Lee H. Oswald from Vernon, Texas #190	"	
√1	Magaqine Wrapper Addressed to Lee H. Oswald frmm Minsk #191	"	
√1	Pamphlet #13 Russian Document #192	"	
√1	Russian Language Document #193	"	
√2	Hand Sketches on Plan Paper #194	"	
√1	Letter in Foreign language #195	"	
√2	One Letter and Envelope From John Connally to Lee H. Oswald #196	"	
√1	Letter in Foreign Language #197	"	
√1	Foreign Language Magazine Page #198	"	
√1	Note Paper bearing name Paul Gregory, Norman, Oklahoma. #199	"	H. W. Hill
√1	Subscription Coupon, Life Magazine #200	"	OF THE DALLAS POLICE DEPARTMENT THIS 26th DAY OF Nov 19 63
√3	Pages from Foreign Language Book #201	"	ALL OF THE ARTICLES OF PROPERTY LISTED HEREON.
√2	Pages of Foreign Language Book #202	"	NAME Warren C. deBrueys
√1	Note with name Ruth Paine, 2515 5th St., Irving, Texas #203	"	ADDRESS Sp. Agt. FBI
√1	Calling Card, McKay Secretarial Service #204	"	
√1	Film Exposure Instructions #205	"	
√1	Address Lable Advertisement #206	"	
√1	Negative bearing "Crime Against Cuba" #207	"	

This invoice Search Warrant RUTH PAINE's, Irving, Tex. 11/23/63

H. W. HILL
Property Clerk

No. 11181 G

If neither evidence nor recovered stolen property, write on face of this form in detail reason for police possession.

267

Form CPS—PC—247

POLICE DEPARTMENT
CITY OF DALLAS

PROPERTY CLERK'S INVOICE OR RECEIPT

November 26 1963

Received of G. F. ROSE, 1029 H. M. MOORE, 679; R. S. STOVALL, J. P. ADAMCIK, Homicide Bureau 1031 the following described articles, § recovered stolen property:

Evidence in Offense No. ______ Arrest No. ______ Charge Murder

QUANTITY	ARTICLE	DISPOSITION BIN NO.	
	Continued from Inv. 11181		
√1	Note bearing telephone no. #EM 31365 #208	Released	
√3	Postal Form, label bearing name George A. Bouhe, 4740 Homer St. Dallas, Tex., Postal Form bearing name Lee Oswald dated 11/20/63 #209	"	
√10	Empty Envelopes #210-218	"	
√2	Letter and Envelope bearing name Alex Klein Leror, PO Box 11277, Ft. Worth, Texas #219	"	
√5	Envelopes with contents #220-224	"	
√26	Negatives #225	"	
√5	Empty Envelopes #226-230	"	
√1	Slip of paper containing names Carlos J. Bungior, Magiul M. Cruz, and Lt. William Gaillot #231	"	Received ... of the Dallas Police Department this 26th day of Nov 1963 all of the articles of property listed hereon. Name Warren C. de Brueys Address Sp. Agt. F.B.I.
√17	Envelopes with contents #232-248	"	
√1	Manilla Envelope containing above stated letters and designated as letters during his stay in Soviet Union #249	"	
√1	Affadavit by Byron Phillips guaranteeing Marina Nikoliva Oswald will not be ward of state #250	"	
√1	Letter dated 10/8/62 at Minsk from Erick to Aleck #251	"	

This invoice Search Warrant RUTH PANE's, Irving, Tex. 11/23/63

H. W. Hill
Property Clerk

№ 11182 G

If neither evidence nor recovered stolen property, write on face of this form in detail reason for police possession.

268

COMMISSION EXHIBIT No. 2003—Continued

Form CPS—PC—247

POLICE DEPARTMENT
CITY OF DALLAS

PROPERTY CLERK'S INVOICE OR RECEIPT

November 26 1963

Received of G. F. ROSE, 1029 H. M. MOORE, 679; R. S. STOVALL, J. P. ADAMCIK, Homicide Bureau 1031 the following described articles, § recovered stolen property:

Evidence in Offense No. ______ Arrest No. ______ Charge Murder

QUANTITY	ARTICLE	DISPOSITION BIN NO.	
	Continued from Inv. 11182		
√1	Letter from Dept. of State, American Embassy Moscow 1/31/62 to LEE H. OSWALD, Minsk, Russia #252	Released	
√1	Letter from American Embassy, Moscow, 11/13/61 to Lee Harvey Oswald #253	"	
√1	A promise to repay Financial Assistance loan for Repatriation 6/1/62 signed by LEE HARVEY OSWALD to the Dept. of State #254	"	
√1	Letter from American Embassy, Moscow, 7/10/61, to Mrs. MARINA OSWALD, Minsk, for interview re her visa application #255	"	
√1	Form (Official) in Russian Language dated 12/1/62 #256	"	
√1	One page Russian language form No. UN-3/266 dated 3uas1961 #257	"	
√1	Letter from the Soviet Embassy, Washington, D.C., dated 6/4/63, directed to Mr. M. OSWALD, New Orleans, in Russian language #258	"	
√1	Single sheet containing typed Russian script and dated 25mas1962 #259	"	Received ... of the Dallas Police Department this 26th day of Nov 1963 all of the articles of property listed hereon. Name Warren C. de Brueys Address Sp. Agt. F.B.I.
√4	3 x 5 cards bearing respectively names G. Hall; A.J. Hidell; B. David, and V. T. Lee #260	"	
√1	No admittance sign #261	"	
√1	Green 4 x 8 sheet apparently a Russian form bearing No. 16-2U050 #262	"	
√1	International Smallpox Vacc. Certificate in name of MARINA Oswald #263	"	
√1	International Smallpox Vacc. Certificate in name of JUNE OSWALD #264	"	
	Arrested: Lee Harvey Oswald w/m/24, Dallas, Texas		

This inventory was made & invoice typed in FBI Office, Dallas, Texas.
This invoice Search Warrant RUTH PAINE's, Irving, Texas, 11/23/63

H. W. HILL
Property Clerk

№ 11183 G

If neither evidence nor recovered stolen property, write on face of this form in detail reason for police possession.

269

COMMISSION EXHIBIT No. 2003—Continued

Form CPS—PC—447

POLICE DEPARTMENT

CITY OF DALLAS

PROPERTY CLERK'S INVOICE OR RECEIPT

G. F. Rose, 1029; H. M. Moore, 679; R. S. Stovall, 1031; J. P. Adamcik, Homicide Bureau — November 26, 19 63

Received of ______ the following described articles,

§ recovered stolen property:

Evidence in Offense No. ______ Arrest No. ______ Charge Murder

Continued from Inv. 11183G

QUANTITY	ARTICLE	BIN NO.	DISPOSITION
√1	Russian language form executed in writing bearing No. 16-24424 #265	Released	
√1	Green Identification Booklet No. 3517282 in Russian language with photograph of Mrs. OSWALD #266	"	
√1	Red Russian language Identification Folder bearing Mrs. OSWALD's photo and No. 560123 #267	"	
√1	Small single sheet folder booklet bearing name OSWALD in Russian and No. 123610 #268	"	
√1	Lavender colored booklet in name of MARINA issued in 1960 in Russian language #269	"	
√1	Fort Worth Press news clipping showing photograph of Iranian native Mrs. JOHN R. HALL #270	"	
√1	Small white sheet bearing ink Russian script #271	"	
√1	Envelope Postmarked Minsk "24-462-7" addressed in Russian script to MARINA OSWALD #272	"	Received of [illegible]
√1	4 x 6 sheet of paper bearing Russian language script in blue ink #273	"	of the Dallas Police Department this 26th day of Nov 1963
√1	Letter by LEE H. OSWALD to Federal Income Tax #274	"	all of the articles of property listed hereon.
√1	Russian language form bearing No. 419128 #275	"	Name [illegible]
√2	Photographs portraying scenes in Russia #276	"	Address Sp. Agt. F.B.I.
√1	American Embassy letter, Moscow, 7/10/61, to Mrs. MARINA NIKILIEVA OSWALD, nee Proosakova, Minsk #277	"	
	Arrested: Lee Harvey Oswald w/m/24 Dallas, Texas		

This invoice was made & typed in FBI Office, Dallas, Texas. This invoice Search Warrant RUTH PAINE's, Irving, Texas, 11/23/63

H. W. HILL
Property Clerk

№ 11184 G

If neither evidence nor recovered stolen property, write on face of this form in detail reason for police possession.

270

COMMISSION EXHIBIT No. 2003—Continued

Form CPS—PC—447

POLICE DEPARTMENT

CITY OF DALLAS

PROPERTY CLERK'S INVOICE OR RECEIPT

G. F. Rose, 1029; H. M. Moore, 679; R. S. Stovall, 1031; J. P. Adamcik, Homicide Bureau — November 26, 19 63

Received of ______ the following described articles,

§ recovered stolen property:

Evidence in Offense No. ______ Arrest No. ______ Charge Murder

Continued from Inv. 11184G

QUANTITY	ARTICLE	BIN NO.	DISPOSITION
√1	Russian language form bearing writing and numerals (Numerals on last line 70.64; 25-63) #278	Released	
√2	Small sheets of paper bearing Russian language one carrying name of "LA VISTA" the other bearing dated 8/5 62 #279	"	
√1	Letter from Russian Embassy, Washington, to MARINA OSWALD, Box 2915, Dallas, 3/8/63 #280	"	
√1	Group of Sewing Patterns (6 pieces) #281	"	
√1	Top Value Stamp Book #282	"	
√1	Box containing Warrior Rubber Stamping Kit (Rubber date stamp, one printing block set to print OSWALD's New Orleans address and various rubber letters) #283	"	
√9	Various articles including small stamp pad, two marking devices, pocket flashlight, fountain pen, four small bottles of Pentids 400 Penicillin powder #284	"	
√1	Brown Identification Booklet bearing No. Y3095/K in the name of OSWALD in Russian script bearing dated 10/7/61 #285	"	Received of [illegible] the Dallas Police Department this 26th day of Nov 1963
√1	Small blue pouch containing Elgin pocket watch, tie clasp bearing letters CCCP, cuff links with hammer and sycle; stick pin with hammer sycle and star; one master lock key; one Benrus wristwatch 476343; one belt buckle; one tie clasp; one silver cuff link; one Marine Corps lapel button; one lapel button bearing Red flag with hammer and sycle; one Sharpshooters Medal; one die; one dog tag No. ~~1653230~~ 1653230, USMC #286	"	all of the articles of property listed hereon. Name [illegible] Address Sp. Agt. F.B.I.

Arrested: Lee Harvey Oswald w/m/24, Dallas, Texas. This inventory and invoice made and typed in FBI Office, Dallas, Texas. This invoice Search Warrant RUTH PAINE's, Irving, Texas, 11/23/63

H. W. HILL
Property Clerk

№ 11185 G

If neither evidence nor recovered stolen property, write on face of this form in detail reason for police possession.

271

COMMISSION EXHIBIT No. 2003—Continued

Form CPS—PC—447

POLICE DEPARTMENT

CITY OF DALLAS

PROPERTY CLERK'S INVOICE OR RECEIPT

November 26 1963

Received of G. F. Rose, 1029; H. M. Moore, 679; R. S. Stovall, 1031; J.P. Adamcik, Homicide Bureau the following described articles,

§ recovered stolen property:

Evidence in Offense No. ______ Arrest No. ______ Charge Murder

Continued from Inv. 11185G

QUANTITY	ARTICLE	BIN NO.	DISPOSITION
√9	Articles including small bottle alcoholic beverage; one small paint brush; two metal clips; one box of Gem clips; one bottle opener; one roll of 620 exposed film; one card board of some type; one small offset negative "Fair Play for Cuba" all contained in metal index card box approximately 12 x 6" x 6" including blank index cards with alphabetical indices #287	Released	Received of [signature] of the Dallas Police Department this 26th day of Nov 1963 all of the articles of property listed hereon. Name Warren C. deBrueys Address Spl Agt - FBI
√1	Blue suitcase (composition type) 28 x 16 x 8 #288		
	All property listed on invoices 11177G through 11186G in above suitcase.		
	Arrested: Lee Harvey Oswald w/m/24, Dallas, Texas		

This inventory made and invoice typed in FBI Office, Dallas, Texas.
This invoice Search Warrant RUTH PAINE's, Irving, Texas, 11/23/63

This Search Warrant issued by Judge JOE B. BROWN on 11/23/63 came out of garage attached to house, 2515 W. 5th, Irving, Texas.

This inventory made and typed in Dallas FBI Office.
Witnessed by: WARREN C. de BRUEYS, SA and Capt. J. M. ENGLISH, Dallas Police Dept.

H. W. HILL
Property Clerk

No 11186 G

Typed by Virginia G. McGuire

If neither evidence nor recovered stolen property, write on face of this form in detail reason for police possession.

272

COMMISSION EXHIBIT No. 2003—Continued

Form CPS—PC—447

POLICE DEPARTMENT

CITY OF DALLAS

PROPERTY CLERK'S INVOICE OR RECEIPT

November 26 1963

Received of Homicide Bureau, Dallas Police Department, J. P. Adamcik, R. S. Stovall, G. F. Rose the following described articles,

§ recovered stolen property:

Evidence in Offense No. ______ Arrest No. ______ Charge Murder

QUANTITY	ARTICLE	BIN NO.	DISPOSITION
√100	Handbills entitled "Hands Off Cuba" "Join The Fair Play for Cuba Committee, NO Charter Member Branch" #300	Released	
√108	Application form to the FPCC, New Orleans, Louisiana #301	"	
√100	FPCC New Orleans Chapter Identification Cards #302	"	
√17	Pamphlets entitled "The Crime Against Cuba" by CURLISS LAMONT #303	"	
√1	Booklet entitled "Fidel Castro Denounces Bureaucracy and Sectarianism: #304	"	
√1	Booklet entitled The Socialist Workers Party by Joseph Hansen #305	"	
√1	The Coming American Revolution by James P. Cannon #306	"	
√1	Cuban Counter Revolutionaries to the U.S. published by FPCC #307	"	
√1	Apamphler by the Dobbs Weiss Campaign Committee, 116 University Place, N. Y. #308	"	Received of [signature] of the Dallas Police Department this 26th day of Nov 1963 all of the articles of property listed hereon. Name Warren C. deBrueys Address Spl Agt FBI
√1	List of Russian and Communist Literature publications #309	"	
√1	Booklet entitled "The Pact of Madrid" by the Committee for a Democratic Spain #310	"	
√1	Booklet entitled The McCarran Act and The Right To Travel #311	"	
√1	Pamphlet entitled "The Revolution Must Be A school of Unfottered Thought -- Fidel Castro" #312	"	
√1	Booklet entitled "Ideology and Revolution" by Jean-Paul Sartre #313	"	
	Arrested LEE HARVEY OSWALD w/m/24, Dallas, Texas		

Voluntarily given Dallas PD by RUTH PAINE and Mrs. OSWALD at PAINE's residence, Irving, Texas, 11/22/63

H. W. HILL
Property Clerk

No 11187 G

Continued on Inv 11188G

If neither evidence nor recovered stolen property, write on face of this form in detail reason for police possession.

273

COMMISSION EXHIBIT No. 2003—Continued

Form CPS—PC—447

POLICE DEPARTMENT
CITY OF DALLAS

PROPERTY CLERK'S INVOICE OR RECEIPT

Homicide Bureau, Dallas Police Department, November 26 1963

Received of J. P. Adamcik, R. S. Stovall, G. F. Rose the following described articles,

§ recovered stolen property:

Evidence in Offense No. Arrest No. Charge Murder

~~Continued from Inv. 11187G~~

QUANTITY	ARTICLE	BIN NO.	DISPOSITION
√1	Pamphlet by the FPCC reflecting literature catalog spring, 1963, #314	Released	
√1	Pamphlet "The Road to Socialism" by BLAS ROCA N #315	"	
1	New Century Publishers 1961 Catalog #316	"	
√1	Pamphlet entitled "The End of the Comintern" by JAMES P. CANNON #317	"	
√1	Booklet "Speech at the U.N" by Fidel Castro #318	"	
√1	Continental Congress of Solidarity With Cuba, Brazil, 3/63 by FPCC, NY #319	"	
√1	Publicationentitled The Nation dated 1/23/60 #320	"	
√1	Pamphlet by The Weekly People entitled "Automation: A Job Killer" #321	"	
√1	Magazine entitled The New Republic reprint from 9/12/60 issued of The New Republic #322	"	RECEIVED OF Hurtled OF THE DALLAS POLICE DEPARTMENT THIS 26th DAY OF Nov 1963 ALL OF THE ARTICLES OF PROPERTY LISTED HEREON. NAME Warren C. de Brueys ADDRESS Sp. Agent FBI
√1	Russian booklet bearing OSWALD's name in Russian script "OSWALD L.H." #323	"	
√1	Russian book dated 1962 at Sofia #324	"	
√1	Brown covered Russian pamphlet bearing numbers 500 on its cover #325	"	
√1	Russian book dated 1961 at Kiev #326	"	
√1	Russian magazine bearing No. 15(1702) whose cover shows a group of men dressed in black standing behind what appears to be a master of ceremonies dressed in white #327	"	
	Arrested: Lee Harvey Oswald w/m/24, Dallas, Texas		
	Voluntarily given Dallas PD by RUTH PAINE and Mrs. OSWALD at PAINES residence, Irving, Texas, 11/22/63		

H. W. HILL
Property Clerk

No 11188 G

If neither evidence nor recovered stolen property, write on face of this form in detail reason for police possession.

274

COMMISSION EXHIBIT No. 2003—Continued

Form CPS—PC—447

POLICE DEPARTMENT
CITY OF DALLAS

PROPERTY CLERK'S INVOICE OR RECEIPT

Homicide Bureau, Dallas Police Department, November 26 1963

Received of J. P. Adamcik, R. S. Stovall, G. R. Rose the following described articles,

§ recovered stolen property:

Evidence in Offense No. Arrest No. Charge Murder

Continued from Inv. 11188G

QUANTITY	ARTICLE	BIN NO.	DISPOSITION
√1	Russian-English-Russian, pocketsize dictionary and stenographer's notebook containing Russian-Spanish vocabulary # 328	Released	
√1	Literature List of the FPCC, New York #329	"	
√1	Address book #330	"	
√1	Photograph Russian workers #331	"	
√1	photograph female Russian workers in what appears to be radio factory #332	"	
1	Photograph of Russian workers in factory #333	"	
√1	Photo of Fidel Castro #334	"	
√1	FPCC handbill bearing address L.H. Oswald, 4907 Magazine, New Orleans, Louisiana #335	"	
√1	Brown manila envelope containing return address in Russian at Moscow #336	"	RECEIVED OF Hurtled OF THE DALLAS POLICE DEPARTMENT THIS 26th DAY OF Nov 1963 ALL OF THE ARTICLES OF PROPERTY LISTED HEREON. NAME Warren C. de Brueys ADDRESS Sp. Agt. FBI
√17	Legal size typewritten deeds entitled "Part I D Collective" #337		
√1	32-page typewritten dissertation outlining political domestic and labor life of the Russian as well as other guides to the Russian political system #338	"	
√1	Letter from Embassy, Soviet Union, Washington, 4/18/63 to MARINA NIKOLILAVA (in Russian script) #339	"	
√1	Folded sheet representing some type of Russian Ident Card bearing No. 100584 & OSWALD's wife's name "MARINA" in Russian script #340	"	
√11	Pay vouchers of the Leslie Welding Co., 11241 West Melrose St., Franklin Park, Ill., covering employment between 7/21 and 9/29/62 #341	"	
	Arrested Lee Harvey Oswald w/m/24, Dallas, Texas		

Voluntarily given Dallas PD by RUTH PAINE and Mrs. OSWALD at PAINE's residence, Irving, Texas, 11/22/63

H. W. HILL
Property Clerk

No 11189 G

If neither evidence nor recovered stolen property, write on face of this form in detail reason for police possession.

[illegible]

COMMISSION EXHIBIT No. 2003—Continued

Form CPS—PC—647

POLICE DEPARTMENT

CITY OF DALLAS

PROPERTY CLERK'S INVOICE OR RECEIPT

November 26 1963

Received of Homicide Bureau, Dallas Police Department, J.P. Adamcik, R. S. Stovall, G. F. Rose the following described articles,

§ recovered stolen property:

Evidence in Offense No. ______ Arrest No. ______ Charge Murder

Continued from Inv. 11189G

QUANTITY	ARTICLE	BIN NO.	DISPOSITION
/23	Payroll vouchers of the Jaggars-Chiles-Stovall, Inc., Dallas, Tex., for the period 10/24/62 through 4/10/63 #342	Released	
√5	Payroll vouchers of the Wm. B. Reily and Co., Inc., Nola for the period 5/17/63 though 7/22/63 #343	"	
√1 √2	Birth certificate for JUNE OSWALD dob 3/15/62 Minsk, Russia and two Texas employment commission cards for LEE OSWALD #344	"	
√1	Alien Registration Card No. A12 530 645 MARINA N. OSWALD #345	"	
√1	Information and ID Card for the Division of Employment Security State of La. for Lee H. Oswald #346	"	
√1	Birth data re MARINA OSWALD 10/20/63 #347	"	
√1	Russian Identification Booklet with picture of MARINA OSWALD reflecting date of birth 7/17/29 (Passport) #348	"	RECEIVED BY [illegible] OF THE DALLAS POLICE DEPARTMENT THIS [illegible] DAY OF [illegible] 1963 ALL OF THE ARTICLES OF PROPERTY LISTED HEREON. NAME [illegible] ADDRESS Spec. Agt. FBI
√3	New Orleans Public Service Bills August-September, 1963, and one voucher from La. Div'n Employment Security #349	"	
√1	Petite notebook with Russian script #350	"	
√1	Booklet containing food recipes #351	"	
1	Pocketsize fashion magazine entitled Simplicity with a manila envelope #352	"	
√1	Sears Tower Automatic Slide Projector No. 9865 #353	"	
	Arrested: LEE HARVEY OSWALD w/m/24 Dallas, Texas		

Voluntarily given Dallas PD by RUTH PAINE and Mrs. OSWALD At PAINE's residence, Irving, Texas, 11/22/63

H. W. HILL
Property Clerk

No. 11190 G

If neither evidence nor recovered stolen property, write on face of this form in detail reason for police possession.

276

COMMISSION EXHIBIT No. 2003—Continued

Form CPS—PC—647

POLICE DEPARTMENT

CITY OF DALLAS

PROPERTY CLERK'S INVOICE OR RECEIPT

Received of Homicide Bureau, Dallas Police Department, J.P. Adamcik, R. S. Stovall, G. F. Rose November 26 1963 the following described articles,

§ recovered stolen property:

Evidence in Offense No. ______ Arrest No. ______ Charge Murder

Continued from Inv. 11190G

QUANTITY	ARTICLE	BIN NO.	DISPOSITION
√1	Sears Female Wearing Apparel Catalog #354	Released	
√1	Credit Card Lee H. Oswald, 2703 Mercedes St., Ft. Worth, for Public Library No. PE 23245; one return address Mrs. Arthur Young 35 E. 75th St., New York and one Russian language form No. 5099 #355	"	
√1	Envelope and letter in Russian directed to Mrs. Marina Oswald, New Orleans from Russia postmarked New Orleans 10/7/63 #356	"	
√1	3-page letter and envlope addressed to MARINA Oswald at NO from Loyda Ville in Russian language (Battles Wharf, Alabama) #357	"	
√1	Letter to Marina Oswald, New Orleans, in Russian language postmarked 25 763 13 Russia #358	"	
√1	2-page letter in Russian language in envelope directed to Marina Oswald, New Orleans, postmarked Taoli, Pennsylvania, 8/25/63, ret address Arthur Young #359	"	RECEIVED BY [illegible] OF THE DALLAS POLICE DEPARTMENT THIS [illegible] DAY OF [illegible] 1963 ALL OF THE ARTICLES OF PROPERTY LISTED HEREON. NAME [illegible] ADDRESS [illegible]
√2	Postcards one directed Lee Oswald New Orleans from Minsk, Russia, signed Erick; one directed to Lee Oswald in Minsk, Russia, from Vernon, Texas, signed Mother #360	"	
√1	Letter addressed to Mrs. RUTH PAINE (for Mrs. M. Oswald) Irving, Texas from Minsk, Russia postmarked 10/7/63, Irving #361	"	
√2	Envelopes one from Ruth Paine to Marine Oswald New Orleans the other directed from Minsk, Russia, to Ruth Paine, Irving, postmarked Irving, 10/7/63 (Letter for M. Oswald) #362	"	
	Arrested: LEE HARVEY OSWALD w/m/24, Dallas, Texas		

Voluntarily given Dallas PD by Ruth Paine and Mrs. Oswald at Paine's residente, Irving, Texas, 11/22/63

H. W. HILL
Property Clerk

No. 11191 G

If neither evidence nor recovered stolen property, write on face of this form in detail reason for police possession.

277

COMMISSION EXHIBIT No. 2003—Continued

Form CPS—PC—447

POLICE DEPARTMENT
CITY OF DALLAS

PROPERTY CLERK'S INVOICE OR RECEIPT

November 26 19 63

Received of Homicide Bureau, Dallas Police Department J.P. Adamcik, R.S. Stovall, G.F.Rose the following described articles,

§ recovered stolen property:

Evidence in Offense No. ______ Arrest No. ______ Charge Murder

Continued from Inv. 11191G

QUANTITY	ARTICLE	BIN NO.	DISPOSITION
1	Letter on Letterhead of Pioneer Publishers, 4/26/63 to L.H. Oswald, P.O.Box 2915, Dallas, Tex #363	Released	
1	Letter in Russian script addressed "Dear Marina (3 pages written on both sides) #364	"	
1	Letter from Dept. of State 1/11/63 to Oswald, Dallas, Tex #365	"	
4	Photographs and a tourist pamphlet "Visit the USSR" #366	"	
6	Photos #367	"	
12	Photos #368	"	
1	Photo house and car #369	"	
12	Photos (apparently Russia-mountainous) #370	"	
10	Boxes Kodaslide nine of which are stereo and 1 35mm. single slide #371	"	
1	Box of Kodachrome transparencies and two viewmaster reels entitled "Seven More Wonders of the World" (64) #372	"	
	Sorted medical items including pills lanacane, pentids "400", aspirins, Feenamint, 7 various containers of pills some labeled in Russian language, thermometer, nasal decongestant, two eye droppers, small container of white powder, numerous envelopes of powder and bottle of liquidlabeled in Russian #373	"	RECEIVED OF H. W. Hill OF THE DALLAS POLICE DEPARTMENT THIS 26th DAY OF Nov. 1963 ALL OF THE ARTICLES OF PROPERTY LISTED HEREON. NAME Warren C. de Brueys ADDRESS Sp. Agt. FBI
10	Foreign coins in a kodak film bag with address Corporal Michael Paine U.S. 51169740 Hdqtrs Btry #374	"	
8	One Minox camera; one pedometer; one compass; one Hansa self-timer; one lense in hood; one 15 power telescope, Wollensak; one stereo viewer one pocket knife in leather container #375	"	
	Arrested: LEE HARVEY OSWALD w/m/24, Dallas, Texas		

Voluntarily given Dallas PD by RUTH PAINE and Mrs. OSWALD at PAINE's residence, Irving, Texas, 11/22/63

H. W. HILL
Property Clerk

No. 11192 G

If neither evidence nor recovered stolen property, write on face of this form in detail reason for police possession.

278

Form CPS—PC—447

POLICE DEPARTMENT
CITY OF DALLAS

PROPERTY CLERK'S INVOICE OR RECEIPT

November 26 19 63

Received of Homicide Bureau, Dallas Police Dept., J. P. Adamcik, R.S. Stovall, G.F.Rose the following described articles,

§ recovered stolen property:

Evidence in Offense No. ______ Arrest No. ______ Charge Murder

Continued from Inv. 11192G

QUANTITY	ARTICLE	BIN NO.	DISPOSITION
9	Articles including one Nippon Kogaku binoculars; one and one Sunbeam 7 x 18 Ser. No. 12457; three rolls 35 mm. colored film exposed (?); two unexposed rolls 35 mm. colored film; one roll 620 plus X film exposed (?); one leather case with stereo realist filters #376	Released	
2	Rolls undeveloped Minox film ASA 50--DIN 17/10; two rolls of apparently exposed Minox film; one negative of baby in chair and one roll of 35 mm. exposed and developed #377	"	
3	Items including one stereo realist camera; one cuera-2 camera; and one stereo view-master #378)	"	
1	Flash assembly Ansco and one leather container (empty) #379)	"	
3	Applications for The Militant; one envelope containing three subscriptions forms for The Worker with the return envelope entitled Publishers New Press, Inc. #380	"	RECEIVED OF H. W. Hill OF THE DALLAS POLICE DEPARTMENT THIS 26th DAY OF Nov. 1963 ALL OF THE ARTICLES OF PROPERTY LISTED HEREON. NAME Warren C. de Brueys ADDRESS Sp. Agt. FBI
7	Russian language newspapers #381	"	
1 1	Red billfold; one scrap of white paper with Russian script in pencil #382	"	
	Arrested: LEE HARVEY OSWALD w/m/24 Dallas, Texas		
	Voluntarily given Dallas PD by RUTH PAINE and Mrs. OSWALD at PAINE's residence, Irving, Texas, 11/22/63		

This inventory typed at Dallas FBI Office, Dallas.

Witnessed by: Capt. J. M. ENGLISH
SA WARREN C. de BRUEYS

H. W. HILL
Property Clerk

No. 11193 G

Typed by Virginia G.McGuire

If neither evidence nor recovered stolen property, write on face of this form in detail reason for police possession.

279

COMMISSION EXHIBIT No. 2003—Continued

COMMISSION EXHIBIT No. 2003—Continued

Form CPS—PC—447

POLICE DEPARTMENT

CITY OF DALLAS

PROPERTY CLERK'S INVOICE OR RECEIPT

November 26 19 63

Received of H.M. Moore; W. E. POTTS; F. M. TURNER; BILL SENKEL, Homicide Bureau the following described articles,

§ recovered stolen property:

Evidence in Offense No. ______ Arrest No. ______ Charge Murder

QUANTITY	ARTICLE	BIN NO.	DISPOSITION
1	Letter from Arnold Johnson to Lee H. Oswald P.O. Box 30061, New Orleans, La., 9/19/63 #400	Released	
1	Letter on letterhead Socialists Workers Party 11/5/62 to Lee H. Oswald Box 2915, Dallas, signed by Farrell Dobbs, National Secretary #401	"	
1	Letter from BOB CHESTER to Lee H. Oswald Dallas, Tex., stating Oswald's letter turned over to him by SWP #402	"	
1	Letter from V.T. Lee, National Director, FPCC, New York, 5/22/63 to Lee H. Oswald, New Orleans #403	"	
1	Letter from Louis Weinsdock, Gen. Manager of The Worker dated 12/19/62 addressed to Lee H. Oswald P.O. Box 2915, Dallas, Texas #404	"	
1	Letter from James J. Tormey, dated 12/13/62 addressed to Lee H. Oswald Box 2915, Dallas, on letterhead of Gus Hall-Benjamin J. Davis, Defense Committee, New York #405	"	RECEIVED OF [handwritten signature] OF THE DALLAS POLICE DEPARTMENT
1	Letter from Arnold Johnson director Information and Lecture Bureau, CP, USA 7/31/63 to L.H. Oswald P.O.Box 30061, NO La #406		THIS 26th DAY OF Nov 63 ALL OF THE ARTICLES OF PROPERTY LISTED HEREON.
1	3-page letter from V.T. Lee, National Director, FPCC, New York, to Lee H. Oswald, 4907 Magazine St., New Orleans 5/29/63 #407		NAME Warren C. deBrueys ADDRESS Sp. Agt. FBI
3	Items: Gregg Shorthand dictionary; 20,000 Words; by Leslie; Roberts Rules of Order Revised 75th Anniv Edn #408	"	
	Arrested: Lee Harvey Oswald w/m/24 Dallas, Texas		
	Search Warrant dated 11/23/63, 1026 No. Beckley, Dallas, Texas		

This inventory was made & invoice typed in FBI Office, Dallas, Texas.

H. W. HILL
Property Clerk

№ 11194 G

Inv. continued on 11195G

If neither evidence nor recovered stolen property, write on face of this form in detail reason for police possession.

280

COMMISSION EXHIBIT No. 2003—Continued

Form CPS—PC—447

POLICE DEPARTMENT

CITY OF DALLAS

PROPERTY CLERK'S INVOICE OR RECEIPT

November 26 19 63

Received of H.M. Moore; W. E.Potts; F. M. Turner; Bill Senkel, Homicide Bureau the following described articles,

§ recovered stolen property:

Evidence in Offense No. ______ Arrest No. ______ Charge Murder

Continuation Inv. 11194G

QUANTITY	ARTICLE	BIN NO.	DISPOSITION
1	Book entitled "A Study of the USSR and Communism": and Historical" --Rieber and Nelson #409	Released	
2	Pocketbooks editions by Ian Fleming, one entitled "The Spy Who Loved Me" and the other "Live and Let Die" #410	"	
1	Pamphlet New York School for Marxist Study, Fall Term, 1963 #411	"	
1	Letter on letterhead of Jesuit House of Studies, Mobile, Alabama, 8/22/63 addressed "Dear Lee" and signed "GENE" #412	"	
1	Envelope addressed Mr. Lee H. Oswald 2703 Mercedes Avenue, Ft. Worth postmarked New York with return address Rm 329, 799 Broadway, and newspaper clipping Times Picayune, New Orleans, with article reflecting Oswald's fine of $10 or 10 days for disturbing peace #413	"	
1	Handbill FPCC New Orleans with address L.H. Oswald 4907 Magazine St., New Orleans, La., #414		RECEIVED OF [handwritten signature] OF THE DALLAS POLICE DEPARTMENT
1	Invoice of the Jones Printing Company, 422 Girod St., NO La. 6/4/63, billed to Mr. Osborne for 1,000 FPCC circulars, total $9.60, bal. 5.00, paid 6/4/63 #415		THIS 26th DAY OF Nov 63 ALL OF THE ARTICLES OF PROPERTY LISTED HEREON.
1	FPCC application slip #416	"	NAME Warren C. deBrueys
1	Envelope with news clippings regarding Oswald defection to Russia and other news clippings concerning Oswald and cartoon regarding defectors #417	"	ADDRESS Sp. Agent FBI
1	Drivers handbook state of Texas #418	"	
	Arrested: Lee Harvey Oswald w/m/24 Dallas, Texas		
	Search Warrant dated 11/23/63, 1026 No. Beckley, Dallas, Texas		

This inventory was made & invoice typed in FBI Office, Dallas, Texas.

H. W.HILL
Property Clerk

№ 11195 G

If neither evidence nor recovered stolen property, write on face of this form in detail reason for police possession.

281

COMMISSION EXHIBIT No. 2003—Continued

Form CPS—PO—647

POLICE DEPARTMENT

CITY OF DALLAS

PROPERTY CLERK'S INVOICE OR RECEIPT

November 26 1963

Received of H. M. Moore; W. E. Potts; F. M. Turner; Bill Senkel, Homicide Bureau the following described articles,

§ recovered stolen property:

Evidence in Offense No. ______ Arrest No. ______ Charge Murder

Continued from Inv. 11195G

QUANTITY	ARTICLE	BIN NO.	DISPOSITION
1	Identification booklet in Russian script contained in Oswald's Name and No. 01311655 #419	Released	
1	U.S. Marine Corps document appointing Lee Harvey Oswald 1653230/6741 Pvt.1st Cls 3/9/59 #420	"	
1	U.S. Air Force document certifying Oswald No. 1 653 230 satisfactorily passed specialized course in Aircraft Control and Warning Operator 18 June, 1957, Keisler AFB, #421	"	
2	Receipts Texas School Book Depository for salary Lee H.Oswald no date listed #422	"	
1	Typewritten promise to pay loan for repatriations with paid stamp Dept. of State 3/9/63 made out in name of Lee H. Oswald #423	"	
1	Letter from Embassy USSR, Washington, addressed to Mrs.Oswald, New Orleans, 8/5/63 in Russian language #424	"	
1	Undesirable Discharge USMC. 9/13/60 Lee Harvey Oswald 1653230 #425	"	
1	Letter U.S.Navy Lee Oswald Minsk, Russa, signed by R. McC. Thompkins Brigadier General, USMC 3/7/62 #426		RECEIVED OF [illegible] OF THE DALLAS POLICE DEPARTMENT THIS ___ DAY OF ___ 1963 ALL OF THE ARTICLES OF PROPERTY LISTED HEREON, NAME [illegible] ADDRESS Sp. Agt. FBI
1	Letter from Dept. of Navy 7/25/63 to Lee Oswald, New Orleans, stating no modifications to discharge warranted #427		
1	Form ID-14 La. Division Employment Security to Lee Oswald SSN 433 54 3937 pertinent date 4/29/63 address 757 France St., NO La. #428	"	
1	Letter from PAUL PIAZZA, S.J. 8/1/63 to Oswald on letterhead of Jesuit House of Studies, Mobile, Alabama, #429	"	
	Arrested: Lee Harvey Oswald w/m/24 Dallas, Texas		

Search Warrant dated 11/23/63, 1026 No. Beckley, Dallas, Texas
This inventory was made & invoice typed in FBI Office, Dallas, Texas.

H. W. HILL
Property Clerk

Nº 11196 G

If neither evidence nor recovered stolen property, write on face of this form in detail reason for police possession.

282

Form CPS—PO—647

POLICE DEPARTMENT

CITY OF DALLAS

PROPERTY CLERK'S INVOICE OR RECEIPT

November 26 1963

Received of H.M. Moore; W. E. Potts; F.M. Turner; Bill Senkel, Homicide Bureau the following described articles,

§ recovered stolen property:

Evidence in Offense No. ______ Arrest No. ______ Charge Murder

Continued from Inv. 11196G

QUANTITY	ARTICLE	BIN NO.	DISPOSITION
1	Letter on letterhead of Jesuit House of Studies Mobile, dated 7/6/63 and addressed to Dear Lee and Moreno signed GENE #430	Released	
1	Letter on stationary of Peter P. Gregory Ft. Worth, Tex., 6/19/62 attesting to Oswald's ability as Russian interpretor and translator #431	"	
1	Envelope containing receipt for Post Office Box 6225, Dallas, Tex. dated 11/11/63 for period ending 12/31/63 #432	"	
1	Single sheet in Russian script containing Oswald's name bearing No. 4-5408 #433	"	
1	Sheet folded in half which appears to be Russian identification document No. 332281 bearing the name of Oswald in Russian script #434	"	
1	Form bearing months and blank spaces for stamps in Russian language with no. 01311655 #435		RECEIVED OF [illegible] OF THE DALLAS POLICE DEPARTMENT THIS ___ DAY OF ___ 1963 ALL OF THE ARTICLES OF PROPERTY LISTED HEREON, NAME [illegible] ADDRESS Sp. Agt. FBI
1	Folded Russian language form bearing No. 01311655 with Oswald's name in Russian script #436		
1	Legal sized sheet in purple ink bearing dated 3/22/62 with an official stamp of #437		
1	Letter by Johnny Tackett on letterhead of Ft. Worth Press 6/22/62 addressed to Lee Oswald in envelope of Ft. Worth Press #438	"	
	Arrested: Lee Harvey Oswald w/m/24 Dallas, Texas		

Search Warrant dated 11/23/63 1026 No. Beckley, Dallas, Texas
This inventory was made & invoice typed in FBI Office, Dallas, Texas

H. W. Hill
Property Clerk

Nº 11197 G

If neither evidence nor recovered stolen property, write on face of this form in detail reason for police possession.

283

Form CPS—PC—647

POLICE DEPARTMENT

CITY OF DALLAS

PROPERTY CLERK'S INVOICE OR RECEIPT

November 26 19 63

Received of H.M. Moore; W. E. Potts; F. M. Turner; Bill Senkel, Homicide Bureau the following described articles,

§ recovered stolen property:

Evidence in Offense No. ______ Arrest No. ______ Charge Murder

Continued from Inv. 11197G

QUANTITY	ARTICLE	BIN NO.	DISPOSITION
2	Payroll vouchers, one from Jaggars Chiles Stovall, Inc., Dallas, 1/2/63; William B. Reiley, and Co., New Orleans, 5/31/63 #439	Released	
1	Letter from Dept. of Navy 4/2/62 to Lee H. Oswald Minsk, Russia #440	"	
2	Articles: One payroll voucher Leslie Welding Company, Inc., 11241 W. Melrose, Franklin Park, Illinois, No. 7619, dated 10/13/62; One withholding Fed. Tax slip addressed Lee H. Oswald 3519 Fairmont, Dallas, Texas #441	"	
1	U.S. Armed Forces Institute, Madison Certifying Oswald completed Highschool level tests 3/23/59 #442	"	
1	Dept. of Navy certification of 5/3/57 that Oswald Pvt. 1653230 USMC completed Elect-Electron. Occupational Group course, Jacksonville #443	"	
1	World Health Organization Vacc. Card bearing name Lee Oswald with name of vaccinator as A. J. Hidell P.O. Box 30016, New Orleans La., date stamped 6/8/63 #444	"	
1	Letter from Joseph Task on letterhead of Socialists Workers Party 3/27/63 directed to Lee H. Oswald P.O. Box 2915, Dallas #445		
1	Passport No. D092526 in the name of Lee Harvey Oswald dob 10/18/39 #446		
1	Separation form U.S. Marine Corps in name of Lee Harvey Oswald dated 11 Sept. 1959 #447		
1	Birth certificate No. 17034 for Lee Harvey Oswald reflecting birth 10/18/39 Folio 1321, Book No. 207 #448	"	
	Arrested: Lee Harvey Oswald w/m/24 Dallas, Texas		

RECEIVED OF H. W. Hill OF THE DALLAS POLICE DEPARTMENT THIS 26th DAY OF Nov 19 63 ALL OF THE ARTICLES OF PROPERTY LISTED HEREON.
NAME [illegible]
ADDRESS So. Cent. 282

Search Warrant dated 11/23/63, 1026 No. Beckley, Dallas, Texas
This inventory was made & invoice typed in FBI Office, Dallas, Texas

Nº 11198 G

H. W. HILL
Property Clerk

If neither evidence nor recovered stolen property, write on face of this form in detail reason for police possession.

281

COMMISSION EXHIBIT No. 2003—Continued

Form CPS—PC—647

POLICE DEPARTMENT

CITY OF DALLAS

PROPERTY CLERK'S INVOICE OR RECEIPT

November 26 19 63

Received of H.M. Moore; W. E. Potts; R. M. Turner; Bill Senkel, Homicide Bureau the following described articles,

§ recovered stolen property:

Evidence in Offense No. ______ Arrest No. ______ Charge Murder

Continued from Inv 11198G

QUANTITY	ARTICLE	BIN NO.	DISPOSITION
1	Passport No. 1733242 of the USA in the name of Lee H. Oswald #449	Released	
1	Application for Texas Driver's License #450	"	
6	Photos (6 of Oswald and one of his wife) two scenic shots, a Mexican Airmail Stamp and New Orleans Library card No. NA N8090 in the name of Lee H. Oswald #451	"	
1	Sewing kit with metal (religious) Mexican 20 cent piece, package of needles with fingernailfile #452	"	
1	World Atlas; The Catholic Geography Series #453	"	
1	Writing tablet (Fifth Avenue) #454	"	
1	Postcard City New Orleans; 5 Russian stamps and one 10 cent U.S. Postage stamp #455	"	
1	Blue plastic- 2 zipper compartments - AWOL Bag		
1	Man's tan sportshirt "Briarloom Traditionals by Enro"		
	Pair man's gray slacks		
	Pair man's faded gray slacks (torn & ripped)		
	Pair man's blue shorts		
	Pair man's white shorts		
1	White with flower design - light green trim pillow case		
2	Red, white & pink stripe hand towels		
2	Red & white stripe bath towels		
	White handkerchiefs		
1	2-tone gray with red stripe handkerchief		
	White cloth - approx 18 x 24"		
	Yellow & white wash rags		
3	White T-shirts		
	White undershirt		
	Pairs socks - brown-white-tan		
	Pair brown cloth work gloves		
	Pair man's brown low quarter shoes "Imchurst brand"		
	Pair man's black low quarter shoes "John Hardy Brand"		
	Pair man's shoes "Thongs style"		
	Brown & yellow gold Russian make portable radio		
1	Unknown electronic device - Brown plastic case - broken		
	Arrested: Lee Harvey Oswald w/m/24 Dallas, Texas		

RECEIVED OF H. W. Hill OF THE DALLAS POLICE DEPARTMENT THIS 26th DAY OF Nov 1963 ALL OF THE ARTICLES OF PROPERTY LISTED HEREON.
NAME [illegible]
ADDRESS So. Cent. 282

Search Warrant dated 11/23/63, 1026 No. Beckley, Dallas, Texas
This inventory was made & invoice typed in FBI Office, Dallas, Texas

Nº 11199 G

H. W. HILL
Property Clerk

If neither evidence nor recovered stolen property, write on face of this form in detail reason for police possession.

285

COMMISSION EXHIBIT No. 2003—Continued

Form CPS—PC—447

POLICE DEPARTMENT

CITY OF DALLAS

PROPERTY CLERK'S INVOICE OR RECEIPT

November 26 1963

Received of H. M. Moore; W. E. Potts; F. M. Turner; Bill Senkel, Homicide Bureau the following described articles,

§ recovered stolen property:

Evidence in Offense No. ______ Arrest No. ______ Charge Murder

Continued from Inv 11199G

QUANTITY	ARTICLE	BIN NO.	DISPOSITION
1	Zipper plastic shaving kit		
2	Bottles Squibbs "Pentids 400"		
1	Bar pink Lux soap		
3	Twelve Lina bean shaped pills in plastic box		
1	Single blade brown handle pocket knife		
1	Pair tweezers in plastic box		
1	Small plastic box		
1	Mirror in green folding case		
1	Can Tidy deodorant powder		
1	Gillette adjustable razor with blade		
1	Partial tube Colgate dental cream		
1	Plastic bottle Mum mist spray deodorant		
1	Toothbrush		
1	Partial cake pink soap		
1	Small hand brush		
1	Green & brown BB automatic ball point pen		
1	Small pair scissors		
1	Package Gillette blue blades		
1	Two blade pocket knife, plastic handle, screwdriver		
1	Pair black rim green lens sunglasses		
1	Farmers Electric Co-Op Inc Adv Ballpoint pen		
2	Small padlocks with keys		
1	Nail clippers		
1	Padlock key on key chain		
1	Bar soap La Luz, S. A. Mexico OF		
1	Plastic cup		
1	Partial tube foille		
1	Imperial hunting knife - tan scabbard		
1	Brown leather holster		
1	Small bottle Iodine		
2	Partial bottles with unknown liquid		
1	Roll Marcal wax paper		
1	Package phonics school aid flash cards		
1	Package Russian flash cards		
1	Package German [illegible] flashcards		
1	Pair Binoculars 6NT 4420 #591998, brown imitation alligator leather case		

RECEIVED BY [signature] OF THE DALLAS POLICE DEPARTMENT THIS 9th DAY OF Nov 1963 ALL OF THE ARTICLES OF PROPERTY LISTED HEREON.
NAME Warren C. de Brueys
ADDRESS Sp. Agt. FBI

Arrested: Lee Harvey Oswald w/m/24
Dallas, Texas

Search Warrant dated 11/23/63, 1026 No. Beckley, Dallas, Texas
This inventory was made & invoice typed in FBI Office, Dallas, Texas.

Witnessed by: Capt. J. M. ENGLISH
SA WARREN C. de BRUEYS

H. W. HILL
Property Clerk

Nº 11200 G

Typed by Virginia G. McGuire

If neither evidence nor recovered stolen property, write on face of this form in detail reason for police possession.

286

COMMISSION EXHIBIT No. 2003—Continued

Form CPS—PC—447

POLICE DEPARTMENT

CITY OF DALLAS

PROPERTY CLERK'S INVOICE OR RECEIPT

26 Nov 1963 19

Received of ______ the following described articles,

§ recovered stolen property:

Evidence in Offense No. F 85950 Arrest No. ______ Charge murder

QUANTITY	ARTICLE	BIN NO.	DISPOSITION
1	Enco map, "Fort Worth Dallas Map Visitor's Guide"	rel	

tag dated 11-26-63

Deceased: Kennedy, John F. w/m/47
Washington, D. C.

[illegible] by [illegible] Senkel & W. H. Moore, on 11-22-63

B J SMITH
Property Clerk

Nº 11209 G

If neither evidence nor recovered stolen property, write on face of this form in detail reason for police possession.

287

COMMISSION EXHIBIT No. 2003—Continued

Form CPS—PC—647

POLICE DEPARTMENT

CITY OF DALLAS

PROPERTY CLERK'S INVOICE OR RECEIPT

26 Nov 1963 19

Received of [illegible] the following described articles,

§ recovered stolen property:

Evidence in Offense No. F 85950 Arrest No. Charge Murder

QUANTITY	ARTICLE	DISPOSITION: BIN NO.	DISPOSITION
√4	copies of Dallas map, "Enco" by Humble Oil & Refining Company	C-1	
	(each copy has 8 sections taped together)		
	tag dated 11-26		
	DECEASED: KENNEDY, John F. w/m/47 Washington, D. C.		

No 11210 G

B J SMITH
Property Clerk

If neither evidence nor recovered stolen property, write on face of this form in detail reason for police possession.

288

COMMISSION EXHIBIT No. 2003—Continued

Form CPS—PC—647

POLICE DEPARTMENT

CITY OF DALLAS

PROPERTY CLERK'S INVOICE OR RECEIPT

30 November 1963

Received of E. L. Boyd #[illegible] the following described articles,

§ recovered stolen property:

Evidence in Offense No. Arrest No. Charge Inv Murder

QUANTITY	ARTICLE	DISPOSITION: BIN NO.	DISPOSITION
√ $0.87	Eighty-seven cents in money	Sf-dr-1	
	(1 half dollar, 3 dimes, 1 nickel, and 2 pennies)		
√ $13.00	Thirteen dollars in money		
	(1 five-dollar bill, 8 one dollar bills)		
√ 1	Dallas County bus transportation coupon or ticket for transfer dated Nov. 22, 1963		
1	Marine Corps, silver color		
√ 1	Chrome color ID bracelet with expansion band with the inscription 'Lee'		
√ 1	Brass key marked "Postoffice Department Do not Dup." #1126		
√ 1	paycheck voucher from American Bakeries Company dated 8/22/60		
√ 1	top of a small cardboard box with "Cox's Fort Worth" printed on top		
	Tag Date: 11/23/63		
	Arr: OSWALD, Lee Harvey w/m/24 1026 N Beckley		

No 11378 G

W. M. Dickey and D. W. Reuben
Property Clerk

If neither evidence nor recovered stolen property, write on face of this form in detail reason for police possession.

289

COMMISSION EXHIBIT No. 2003—Continued

Form CPS—PC—447

POLICE DEPARTMENT

CITY OF DALLAS

PROPERTY CLERK'S INVOICE OR RECEIPT

2 Dec 1963 19

Received of J R Adamcik, G F Rose, H M Moore, R S Stovall the following described articles, § recovered stolen property:

Evidence in Offense No. F 85827, 85950 Arrest No. Charge inv. murder

QUANTITY	ARTICLE	BIN NO.	DISPOSITION
✓ 47	pictures	C-dr-5	
✓ 2	magazine ads, "Klein's" Sporting Goods		
✓ 2	paper pencil written papers of qualifications		
[illegible handwriting]			
	tag dated 12-02-63		
	ARR: OSWALD, Lee Harvey w/m/24 2515 W. Fifth, Irving, Tex.		
	"Found at 2515 W. Fifth, Irving"		

B J SMITH
Property Clerk

No 11413 G

If neither evidence nor recovered stolen property, write on face of this form in detail reason for police possession.

290

COMMISSION EXHIBIT No. 2003—Continued

Form CPS—PC—447

POLICE DEPARTMENT

CITY OF DALLAS

PROPERTY CLERK'S INVOICE OR RECEIPT

3 Dec 1963 19

Received of Lt Swain & Lt. Smart the following described articles, § recovered stolen property:

Evidence in Offense No. Arrest No. Charge inv. murder

QUANTITY	ARTICLE	BIN NO.	DISPOSITION
$42.00	forty two dollars (all one dollar bills)	Sf dr 9	
[illegible handwriting]			
	tag dated 11-24-63		
	ARR: RUBY, Jack w/m/52 3929 Rawlins		
	money on invoice 111050 was recounted after F.B.I. agents recorded serial numbers on 12-2-63, and found to exceed the indicated total by the amount of $42.00. This $42.00 is shown on this invoice as a supplement to invoice 111050		

B J SMITH & D W REUBEN
Property Clerk

No 11474 G

If neither evidence nor recovered stolen property, write on face of this form in detail reason for police possession.

291

COMMISSION EXHIBIT No. 2003—Continued

Received from Capt. Will Fritz at approximately 1:00 a.m. on 11/27/63:

Billfold and 16 cards and pictures taken from Lee Harvey Oswald on 11/22/63.

One notebook recovered from room of Lee Harvey Oswald at 1026 No. Beckley on 11/22/63. with names and addresses.

One 6.5 mm rifle hull recovered at Texas School Book Depository, 411 Elm Street, Dallas, Texas, on 11/22/63.

James P. Hosty, Jr
Special Agent, F.B.I.

292

COMMISSION EXHIBIT No. 2003—Continued

SHOWUPS ON OSWALD

#1.

11-22-63, 4:35 pm

To: Helen Markham, positive identification.

Officers with Oswald: R. M. Sims, M. G. Hall, E. L. Boyd

Officers with witness: L. C. Graves, J. R. Leavelle, Chief Curry, C. W. Brown, Captain Fritz.

In the showup: #1, Bill Perry, #2 Lee Harvey Oswald #3 R. L. Clark #4 Dan Ables

#2.

11-22-63, 6:30 pm

To: Cecil J. McWatters, positive identification
Sam Guinyard, positive identification
Ted Calloway, positive identification

Officers with Oswald: R. M. Sims, E. L. Boyd, M. G. Hall

Officers with witnesses: J. R. Leavelle, C. . Brown, C. N. Dhority
In Showup: #1 Billy Perry, #2 Lee Harvey Oswald, #3 R. L. Calrk, #4 Dan Ables

#3.

11-22-63, 7:55 pm

To: Barbara Jeanette Davis, positive identification
Virginia Davis, positive identification

Officers with Oswald: M. G. Hall, R. M. Sims, E. L. Boyd, H. M. Moore

Officers with witnesses: C. W. Brown, C. N. Dhority
In showup: #1 Richard Walter Borchardt, #2 Lee Harvey Oswald #3 Ellis Carl Braswell, #4 Dan Ables

November 23, 1963, 2:15 pm

To: W. W. Scoggins, positive identification
William Wayne Whaley, positive identification

Officers with Oswald: B. L. Senkel, W. E. Potts, M. G. Hall, C. W. Brown

Officers with witnesses: J. R. Leavelle
In showup: #1 John Thurman Horn #2 David Knapp #3 Lee Oswald, #4 David Lujan

293

COMMISSION EXHIBIT No. 2003—Continued

SEARCHES AND SEIZURES

1026 N. Beckley (Oswald's room) searched by F. M. Turner, W. E. Potts, H. M. Moore, B. L. Senkel on 11-22-63, Search Warrant #295 issued by Judge Dave Johnston. Searched at 3:00 pm. (See attached list of property taken)

W.
2515 5th Street, Irving, Texas (Mrs. Paine's residence) searched at 3:30 pm 11-22-63 by R. S. Stovall, G. F. Rose, J. P. Adamcik. Information of owner. (see attached list of property taken.

W.
2515 5th Street, Irving, Texas (Mrs. Paine's residence) searched by H. M. Moore R. S. Stovall, and G. F. Rose on 11-23-63. Warrant issued by Judge Joe B. Brown, Jr. McCabe of Irving P. D. present. 12:30 pm. (see list attached.)

Car of Jack Ruby Searched 11-24-63 by Lt. R. E. Swain and Lt. V. S. Smart at 2035 Main Street, Dallas, a parking lot, at 1:00 pm. (see attached list of property taken)

223 S. Ewing, Apt. 207, Jack Ruby's residence, searched 11-24-63, 2:15 pm by H. M. Moore, G. F. Rose and J. P. Adamcik on a search warrant issued by Judge Joe B. Brown, Jr., who aided search.

Texas School Book Depository Building, November 22, 1963, 12:40 pm, Homicide and Robbery Bureau officers assisting in search were Captain J. W. Fritz, R. M. Sims, E. L. Boyd, Marvin Johnson, F. M. Turner, B. L. Senkel, L. L. Montgomery, V. D. Monaghen. (See attached list of property taken) Chief G. L. Lumpkin and other officers completed search of other floors.

Officers obtained search warrant for 1026 N. Beckley a second time. No recovery.

294

COMMISSION EXHIBIT No. 2003—Continued

The following items were recovered in Irving, Texas, at 2515 West 5th Street on November 23, 1963, by Moore, Rose, and Stovall:

Blue suitcase containing:

Sharp shooter medal

1 bag containing some old jewelry

2 watches

1 key

Dog tag

Envelope containing some 35mm negatives

Several miscellaneous Russian books and literature

1 gray metal box containing miscellaneous Russian literature and some slide negatives

Miscellaneous photographs and maps

Yellow envelope containing miscellaneous pictures and letters

Pamphlet on the Fair Play for Cuba Committee

1 candy box containing pictures, correspondence, and letters

1 notice of attempt to deliver mail, card dated November 20, 1963, to Mr. Lee Oswald, 2515 West 5th, Irving, Texas - a parcel to be picked up.

1 Book on Modern Postage Stamps

Miscellaneous personal papers and work receipts

1 copy of The Worker paper, dated October 20, 1963

Book containing World Atlas

Marine Corp Recruiting Depot Annual, Second Batallion, 2060 Platoon, San Diego, California.

Brown envelope containing hand written manuscripts of Lee Oswald.

295

List of property taken from Ruth Paine house at 2515 W. 5th, Irving, Texas

1 FairPlay for Cuba papers in envelope.
1 Leather folder camera filters
1 Immigrant card for Marina N. Oswald
2 White paper in Russian writing
1 Birth certificate for June Oswald
1 Passport b ok for June Oswald
1 Type A Kodachrome roll
1 Camera timer MANZA
2 Name tags black plastic Michael Paine, Irving, Texas
1 Sterio Realist Camera and case
1 Letter from Erick
1 Russell Stover candy box filled with drugs
1 Brown pasteboard box filled with camera films slides
1 Realist view master black plastic
1 Black plastic Sawyers view master
1 yellow box of Kodaslide single name of Ruth Hyde
1 Yellow box of Kodaslide single.
1 Small German camera and black case on chain and film
1 Yellow canvas sack of coins
1 Roll Kodak PX 135 film
1 7 x 18 Sun Beam glasses
1 New Haven Pedometer
1 Jap compas
1 Wollensak 15 power telescope
1 Box Sylvania flash bulbs
1 Russian-English dictionary
1 Telephone number (Anne TA3 2219)
1 Electric bill from New Orleans
1 Unemployment insurance stub
1 Russian mag.
1 Book from Sears Tower slide projector
1 Russian .35 mm camera and brown case
1 Plastic bag Russian papers and New Orleans paper
1 Blue notebook with Cuba papers and other papers of Communistic nature
1 Grey metal file box 12" x 6" youth pictures and literature
1 Black and grey metal box 10" x 4" letters, etc.
1 Box brown Keystone projector
3 Brown metal boxes 12" x 4" containing phonograph records
1 Blue check telephone index book (addresses)
1 Bracket (Instruction for mounting)
1 Book white paper back (Russian)
1 Roll Kodak film
1 Kodak Kodachrome film
1 Kodak Kodachrome film
1 View master reel (Glacier National Park)
1 View master reel (National Park Alaska)
1 Russian newspaper
(3 Kodachrome transparency slides
1 pictures from catalog of womens clothing
1 letter addressed to Mrs. Marina Oswald from Russia
1 Envelope to Marina Oswald from Ruth Paine postmarked Jul. 22, 1963
1 letter addressed to Marina Oswald from Fairhope, Ala.

296

COMMISSION EXHIBIT No. 2003—Continued

Page 2

List of property taken from Ruth Paine house at 2515 W. 5th, Irving.

1 Brown Russian booklet
1 Letter (in Russian)
1 Letter to Marina Oswald from Paoli, Pa.
2 Coil craft stenographer notebook
1 Texas employment comission card made to Lee H. Oswald
1 Pamphlet with "Minch & Minsk" also "Visit the USSR"
1 Russian letter
9 Pictures of Russia
1 Envelope with women's book entitled "Simplicity"
6 Roll film
1 Ansco flash attachment for camera
1 Brown case (camera) on long chain
1 Bottle of white powdered substance (red nail polish on the side)
1 Russian Book
1 Binoculars "Mikron 6X Coated" Tokyo and brown leather case
1 Letter to Lee from Minsk Sept. 30, 1963
1 Texas Employment Commission card to Lee Oswald
2 Cards with picture of stork for Oswald's baby
1 Instruction pamphlet for caring for baby.
1 Letter to Marina Oswald
1 Knife in leather case
1 Paper with green weeds
1 Letter addressed to Lee H. Oswald, PO Box 30061, New Orleans, La.
1 Picture of Oswald and wife
1 Wool blanket rolled up and tied at one end with a cord, open at the other end (released to the FBI and taken to Washington)

The above listed property was recovered from 2515 W. 5th, Irving by Detectives G. F. Rose, R. S. Stovall and J. P. Adamcik. All the property has been initialied and marked for evidence by Stovall and Rose.

297

COMMISSION EXHIBIT No. 2003—Continued

ovember 1963

Articles picked up at Suspect's house, 1026 North Beckley by Turner, Potts, Moore, and Senkel:

Search Warrant SW 295 issued by Judge David Johnston
1 pair black shoes
1 pair brown shoes
1 pair thong shoes
1 portable radio (Myduet)
1 roll wax paper (Kitchen charm)
Several articles of clothing, towels, wash cloths

1 pair brown cotton gloves
1 blue shaving kit, plastic-like cloth, with zipper containing miscellaneous shaving articles and two boxes of Pentids "400" flavored pencillin powder
1 brown leather holster, "38"
1 book paper back
"A Study of The USSR and Communism"
1 brown manilla envelope containing miscelaneous papers, books, and pamphlets

1 Dallas-Fort Worth City Map
1 Address and phone book
1 blue and black travel bag with zipper
1 pair of small binoculars, 6NT, 4 x 20, Serial #591998, in brown leatherette case with strap
1 brown envelope containing miscellaneous papers
3 packs flash cards, 1 German, 1 Russian, 1 Phonics
1 Hunting knife, black handle in brown sheath

List of papers recovered at 1026 North Beckley:

Letter to Lee Oswald, 4907 Magazine Street, New Orleans, August 2, 1963, from Jesuit House of Studies, Spring Hill Station, Mobile, Alabama.

Letter to L. H. Oswald, P. O. Box 30061, New Orleans, Louisiana, July 31, 1963, from Communist Party, U. S. A., 23 West 26th Street, New York 10, New York, MU-5-5755 regarding Fair Play for Cuba signed by Arnold Johnson. Another letter dated September 9, 1963.

A letter dated December 13, 1962 to Lee H. Oswald regarding photography from Gus Hall. Benjamin J. Davis Defense Committee, Room 1225, 22 East 17th Street, New York 3, New York.

A letter dated December 19, 1962 to Oswald at P. O. Box 2915, Dallas, letter from The Worker, 23 West 26th New York 11, New York, signed by Louis Weinstock.

A letter from Peter P. Gregory, 1503 Continental Building, Fort Worth 2, Texas, dated June 19, 1962, recommending Oswald as an interpreter of the Russian language.

A letter dated May 29, 1963, from Fair Play for Cuba Committee, 799 Broadway, New York 3, New York, Phone ORegan 4-8295. Oswald's address on Magazine Street in New Orleans. Another letter from same organization dated May 22, 1963.

Fair Play for Cuba circulars and receipt from Jone's Printing Company

298

November 22, 1963

Continuation of list of articles picked up at suspect's house:

Page 2 of 2

A letter from Socialist Worker Party, 116 University Place, New York, 3, New York, AL 5-7460, this letter dated November 5, 1962, regarding membership into party.

Miscellaneous photos in small envelope.

U. S. Passport dated June 25, 1963.

Russian passport.

Miscellaneous papers written in Russian.

Birth Certificate - #17034

Parish of Orleans - Carondelet and Lafayette Street, Lee Harvey Oswald, son of Robert E. Lee Oswald, (Dec.) and Marguerite Claverie, born 18th of October, 1939.

Letter dated June 22, 1962, from Johnny Tackett of Fort Worth Press regarding an interview.

Undesirable Discharge from U. S. M. C., 9-13-60.

1 brown shirt with button-down collar.

1 pair grey trousers and other miscellaneous men's clothing.

299

Property Recovered.

Recovered by R. S. Stovall and G. F. Rose on 11-22-63 at 2515 W. 5th Street, Irving, Texas.

1 Brown cardboard tube, five feet long, 2½" in diameter, label on it "Miss Ruth Hyde, 1308 Pine Street, Philadelphia 7, Pennsylvania," postage mark January 8, 1963, Columbus, Ohio, postage thirty-eight cents. Brown paper sacks tied with white string on each end. Contained one map of Asia and adjacent areas, compiled and drawn in the Cartographic Section of the National Geographic Society for the National Geographic Magazine, Gilbert Grosvenor, editor. Approximately size 4' x 4'.

1 Map of Africa Arabia peninsula, approximately 4' x 4' in size.

300

COMMISSION EXHIBIT No. 2003—Continued

TIME OF OCCURRENCES

November 22, 1963

11:40 am	President's Party arrived Love Field
11:50	Departed Love Field
12:35 pm	President shot. ([illegible] minutes of correct time)
12:43	President arrived Parkland Hospital
1:00	President pronounced
12:41	Captain Fritz notified
12:45	Captain Fritz arrived Parkland Hospital
12:58	Captain Fritz arrived scene of offense
1:15	Hulls found by Mooney of Sheriff's Office-showed Capt. Fritz where they were
1:18 pm	J. D. Tippit shooting reported
1:25	J. D. Tippit pronounced at Methodist
1:25	Rifle Oswald used found by Weitzman
1:40	Oswald arrested at Texas Theatre
2:15	Officers arrived Room 317 with Oswald

November 24, 1963

11:20 am	Oswald transfer
11:21	Ruby shot Oswald
11:21	Ruby arrested
1:07 pm	Oswald pronounced

301

COMMISSION EXHIBIT No. 2003—Continued

TRANSFER OF OSWALD ----personnel in office at time of transfer

Mr. Sorrells of the Secret Service

Thomas Kelly of the Secret Service

Jim Bookhout of the FBI

City Detective L. D. Montgomery

City Detective L. C. Graves

City Detective E. R. Beck

City Detective J. R. Leavelle

City Detective C. N. Dhority

City Detective C. W. Brown

Mr. Holmes of the Post Office Inspector's Office

City Detective T. L. Baker

Captain J. W. Fritz

302

COMMISSION EXHIBIT No. 2003—Continued

DUTY STATUS OFFICER OF HOMICIDE AND ROBBERY BUREAU NOVEMBER 24, 1963 (OSWALD'S TRANSFER

NAME	DUTY STATUS	TIME REPORTED FOR DUTY
CAPTAIN J. W. FRITZ	ON DUTY	
LT. J. A. BOHART	OFF DUTY	12:00 pm
LT. T. P. WELLS	DAY OFF	1:00 pm
DET. T. L. BAKER	ON DUTY	
DET. J. P. ADAMCIK	OFF DUTY	
DET. K. L. ANDERTON	VACATION	12:30 pm
DET. E. R. BECK	OFF DUTY	
DET. H. H. BLESSING	DAY OFF	
DET. G. R. BOYCE	VACATION	
DET. E. L. BOYD	OFF DUTY	12:15 pm
DET. C. W. BROWN	ON DUTY	
DET. C. N. DHORITY	ON DUTY	
DET. L. C. GRAVES	ON DUTY	
DET. M. G. HALL	OFF DUTY	12:00 noon
DET. MARVIN JOHNSON	DAY OFF	
DET. J. R. LEAVELLE	ON DUTY	
DET. V. D. MONAGHEN	SICK	
DET. L. D. MONTGOMERY	ON DUTY	
DET. H. M. MOORE	OFF DUTY	2:00 pm
DET. W. E. POTTS	OFF DUTY	12:30 pm
DET. G. F. ROSE	OFF DUTY	
DET. B. L. SENKEL	OFF DUTY	12:00 pm noon
DET. R. M. SIMS	OFF DUTY	12:30 pm
DET. R. S. STOVALL	OFF DUTY	
DET. F. M. TURNER	OFF DUTY	12:00 noon

303

COMMISSION EXHIBIT No. 2003—Continued

December 8, 1963

Mr. J. E. Curry
Chief of Police

Sir:

I wish to submit the following report relative to the transfer of Lee Oswald.

In the early afternoon of November 23, 1963 Chief Curry called me by telephone and asked me when we would be ready to transfer Oswald. Either this conversation or a later conversation I made some remark that I didn't know whether we were to transfer him or whether someone else was going to transfer him, and the Chief made some remark about talking to the Sheriff and that we were to transfer him. I told the Chief we were still talking to him, and he asked me if we could be ready to transfer him by 4:00 pm. I told him I didn't think we could finish our questioning by that time, and he asked me if we could be finished by 10:00 am the next morning. Chief Curry said, "I need to tell these people something definite." Who he was referring to I do not know. I told him I thought we could be ready by that time.

During the night or early morning hours of November 23, I received a telephone call from Captain W. P. Frazier, who told me that they were going to have to transfer Oswald as some threat had been received and that someone was going to try to kill him. I told Captain Frazier that no security had been set up for his transfer at that time and that he had better check with the Chief, as he was making some arrangements for the transfer. Later, Captain Frazier called me back and said that he was unable to reach the Chief and he was going to leave him where he was.

While interviewing Oswald on November 24 in conjunction with Harry D. Holmes, Post Office Inspector, Forrest Sorrels and Tom Kelly of the Secret Service, and in the presence of L. D. Montgomery, L. C. Graves, J. R. Leavelle and C. N. Dhority of the Homicide and Robbery Bureau, Chief Curry came to the office and

304

COMMISSION EXHIBIT No. 2003—Continued

asked if I was ready to transfer the prisoner to the Dallas County Jail. James Bookhout, F. B. I. and possibly other officers, who were assisting in the investigation and questioning, were standing in or just outside my office door. I told him I was ready to start any time the security was completed. Chief Curry advised me that the large cameras had been moved away from the jail office and that everything was prepared and that the people had been moved back across Commerce and that some newsmen would be in the basement, but would be well back in the garage.

Someone had ordered an armored truck, and it was agreed that we let a police car lead the armored truck as if the prisoner was in it, and when he turned to the left off Commerce where he was to go to Elm and turn left, while we would actually have the prisoner in an unmarked police car and turn to the left on Main Street followed by another group of officers in another police car and take him to the County Jail.

Security had been set up, we were told, at the County Jail, and I instructed the officers in the car that did not have the prisoner to drive just past the back entrance to the County Jail, and we would drive in the passageway made for unloading prisoners where a steel door could be dropped down behind us.

Chief Curry then told me that he and Chief Stevenson, who was with him, would go on to the County Jail and meet us there.

I instructed James R. Leavelle to handcuff his left hand to the prisoner's right hand. The prisoner was already handcuffed. I instructed L. C. Graves to walk to his left and L. D. Montgomery directly behind him, and I told them that I would walk in front of the prisoner out of the door to the car. We decided that the best route would be through the jail and out of the left door

305

COMMISSION EXHIBIT No. 2003—Continued

Captain Fritz - Transfer of Oswald Page 3

of the jail and then to the basement giving us but a few feet to the car.

As we were leaving to go to the jail elevator, I told Det. T. L. Baker to call downstairs and tell them we were on the way down and have the car ready. Det. Baker called and Lt. Wiggins said all was clear.

Before taking the man out of the jail office I asked one of the uniform officers who was standing to my right if everything was secure. I believe that two officers answered me that everything was all right. I then advised the officers following me to come on, and at this moment Officer Dhority, who was driving the police car for the prisoner, was backing into position with the police car we were to put the prisoner in. As I reached for the car door and told the officer to put him in the car, I heard a shot. On my left I saw Officer Graves and a number of officers grab this man and pull him to the pavement. Det. Graves twisted the gun from his hand and handed it to me. The prisoner was carried into the jail office and a doctor was summoned and arrived almost immediately and went to work with the prisoner until an ambulance arrived. Some of the other officers took the man that I found was Jack Ruby up into the jail.

I instructed Officers Dhority, Leavelle and Graves to ride with the prisoner in the ambulance. Dets. E. R. Beck, L. D. Montgomery, C. W. Brown and myself followed the ambulance to the hospital, where security was kept until he was released to an undertaker.

Immediately after the shooting, I asked Detective Dhority to contact the captain of the Uniform Division to secure the names of all of the people in the basement at the time of the shooting.

306

November 26, 1963

Mr. J. E. Curry
Chief of Police

Subject: Security Of Police Parking And Prisoner Loading Area Sunday, November 24, 1963

Sir:

At approximately 9:00 A.M., Sunday, November 24, 1963 I discussed the need for coverage against possible violence around the City Hall with Lieutenant R. S. Pierce. I instructed him to call three squads from their district assignments from the three stations and pull four from Headquarters Station, getting two man squads where possible. The officers were to be in Central Station with their squad cars parked on the street, available for immediate use but dispersed in parking, not later than 9:30 A.M. Out of thirteen squads we obtained a total of nineteen (19) patrolmen. Supervisors at the station for the security were Lieutenant Pierce, Sergeant P. T. Dean, Sergeant Putnam, Sergeant Steele, and I. Lieutenant Wiggins was in the Jail Office.

Lieutenant Pierce instructed Sergeant Dean to secure all entrances and exits to the parking and prisoner loading area, then clear the basement of all personnel other than police, and reserves. Sergeant Putnam was instructed to assist in the assignment.

The area in which the prisoner Oswald would be escorted was to be thoroughly searched. Areas searched were the cars parked in the basement, including their trunks, and engine compartments, the tops of all pipes, and air conditioning ducts, the service rooms opening into the basement were to be locked after clearing them of personnel. The building elevators were cut off on the first floor so they could not be used to reach the basement and the parking attendents were sent from the basement to the first floor of the City Hall with instructions to remain with the elevators to prevent tampering. The City Hall service elevator is a self-service type but had an operator. This man was instructed that he was not to go below the first floor until notified. The service elevator from the sub basement of the Police and Courts Building exit, into the basement parking area and has no doors to lock so a reserve officer was stationed there.

The sergeants used a total of seventeen2(17) regular and reserve officers to execute the search. The extra officers were held in the sergeant's room at my office and the reserves were retained in the assembly room. These officers were not permitted in the basement to incure no confusion in the systematic search.

307

After the area was secured and cleared only officers, reserves, and accredited news press were permitted to re-enter. Identification of the news personnel was made by their press credentials. All civilian employees of the Department were cleared from the basement lobby and instructed to remain at their desk.

Officer R. C. Nelson and a reserve officer were stationed in the hall leading to the jail service windows. The door from the jail to the lobby remained locked and the public used the first window, set at an angle, to conduct jail business.

Detective Beaty and Lowery remained with the officers during most of the period the parking and prisoner area was closed off. Everyone conducting business at the jail was scrutinized and if they did not appear to have legitimate business, they were conducted from the basement.

There was little traffic on Main and no one loitering. A large crowd was gathering on Commerce. I had everyone removed from the City Hall side (north) of Commerce to the south side. Sergeant Steele and Reserve Harrison checked the buildings opposite the basement drive for possible snipers.

The information received from the FBI by Captain Frazier was: two calls from males stated "one hundred of us will kill Oswald before he gets to the County Jail". Due to this and the crowds formation I built up my personnel on the Commerce Street side.

I called Homicide and told Detective Beck of the parking area check and asked if Captain Fritz wanted uniformed officers to proceed and follow the transfer vehicle. He said Captain Fritz was with the prisoner and they would let me know. I prepared three plain and three marked cars to use either type Homicide desired.

I was contacted by Chief Stevenson and Chief Lumpkin regarding an armored car. It was to back into the drive as far as possible from Commerce. When it arrived two more officers were stationed at the bottom of the Commerce Street ramp with instructions that no one was to pass up or down the ramp after the prisoner passed them. Due to its height, the armored car could only be backed in a short distance.

Before the arrival of the Armored Car, Chief Lumpkin, Chief Stevenson, and I discussed the route and traffic obstructions. They were reportedly six hundred (600) people around the County Jail. I instructed Sergeant Steele to place a regular officer at each traffic light with his squad car close by. The lead car would flash its lights as they approached and the officer would cut all opposing traffic. After the vehicle passed they were to enter their cars and follow to the County Jail to assist with any trouble. The entire traffic detail was in the County Jail Area.

308

COMMISSION EXHIBIT No. 2003—Continued

Sergeant Steele contacted Captain Lawrence for additional officers for intersection coverage. As the vehicle cleared the city hall all officers and reserves at the City Hall were to report by a parallel route to the County Jail. I would use Channel Two and tell Sergeant Steele to cut it. He had a motorcycle officer to send to Elm and Field to instfuct the officers on the corners to divert all traffic from Elm between Field and Houston. Regular traffic was heavy.

After the Armored Car arrived we sent a plain car out the Main Street side. This was the lead car and contained Lieutenant Pierce driving, Sergeant Putnam on the right front, and Sergeant B. J. Maxey in the rear.

A Homicide Detective pulled a plain car on the ramp behind the armored car then another Homicide Detective pulled in behind him and attempted to straighten his car and back up. Several reserve officers and I were attempting to push the news people back to give the vehicle room to manuever. I was pushing several people back at the left front fender when the shot was fired. I assisted the officers in clearing news personnel from the prisoner and officers who were down then ordered that no one was to be permitted out of the basement.

I checked the parking area several times and saw no unauthorized personnel. I removed a number of people from the first floor and basement lobby, this was acontinious check prior to the transfer.

After the prisoner entered the ambulance and I gathered my personnel from Elm and reported to Parkland Hospital, we secured the hospital.

Respectfully submitted,

Cecil E. Talbert
Captain of Police
Patrol Division

CET/bb

309

COMMISSION EXHIBIT No. 2003—Continued

December 6, 1963

Mr. J.E. Curry
Chief of Police

Subject: Threatening Call
Regarding Oswald

Sir:

At about 3:45 A.M. November 24, 1963 Mr. Newsome of the Federal Bureau of Investigation called this office and stated his office had received an anonymous call from a male individual indicating that a group was going to kill Oswald that day, that night or the following day. Caller stated that he did not want any officer hurt, that was the reason for the call, but they were going to kill Oswald and there was nothing anyone could do about it.

Subsequently about 5:00 A.M. or 5:30 A.M. I called Captain Fritz at home and related substance of the threatening call. Captain Fritz told me Chief Curry was handling the transfer of Oswald and suggested I call him.

Between 5:30 A.M. and 5:45 A.M. Deputy Cox or Coy, exact name unknown, of the Dallas Sheriff's Office called this office and stated that Sheriff Decker had instructed him to call the Dallas Police Department and request that Chief Curry call him about the transfer of Oswald. The Deputy Sheriff indicated Sheriff Decker wanted Oswald moved as soon as possible.

As I recall I had a second conversation with Captain Fritz regarding Decker wanting to move Oswald as soon as possible. Fritz stated that I should call Chief Curry.

About 6:00 A.M. I attempted to call Chief Curry at home. The telephone was busy, and after about fifteen minutes, I asked the operator to check the line for conversation. She reported trouble on the line.

By this time it was approximately 6:15 A.M., and Captain C.E. Talbort relieved me. I told Talbort of the threat, of the Deputy Sheriff's call, and my attempt to contact Chief Curry. Captain Talbert said he would send a squad by the residence of Chief Curry and have him call the office.

Respectfully submitted,

William B. Frazier
WILLIAM B. FRAZIER
CAPTAIN OF POLICE

WBF/4h

310

COMMISSION EXHIBIT No. 2003—Continued

November 27, 1963

Mr. J. E. Curry
Chief of Police

Subject: Murder of Lee H. Oswald

Sir:

On Sunday, November 24, 1963, my tour of duty was from 6:30 a.m. to 2:30 p.m. My assignment was the Jail Office and the Jail. I had no instructions to provide security outside the Jail and Jail Office.

I received a call, and I do not remember who called me, which told me they were bringing Oswald down from the third floor. I had hung up the phone when I noticed the elevator was enroute to the basement, and as the elevator opened at approximately 11:20 a.m., Captain Fritz and four detectives brought Lee H. Oswald from the jail elevator taking him into the basement to transfer him to the County.

Captain Fritz asked if everything was in readiness, and I stepped outside the Jail Office into the hallway leading to the basement where I stopped. Captain Fritz came out of the Jail Office, followed by the detectives and Oswald.

They had passed where I was standing approximately six or seven feet when I saw a man lunge toward Oswald and heard a shot. I saw several officers grab the man with the pistol and wrestle him to the floor. Immediately, they picked him up and brought him into the Jail Office and disarmed him. They then brought Oswald into the Jail Office and laid him on the floor. I called for a doctor and an ambulance, Code 3.

As they were taking the man who did the shooting from the floor, I recognized him as Jack Ruby, who is a night club operator and well known in police circles. Ruby was placed on the Jail elevator and taken upstairs.

The Jail Intern came into the Jail Office and tried to give Oswald some attention, but the ambulance arrived, he was placed in it and taken to Parkland Hospital.

I have known Ruby for several years. I have been in his businesses, The Silver Spur, 1717 S. Ervay, and The Vagas Club, 3508 Oak Lawn, both on and off duty. My visits to his places of business while on duty were for police business. My visits to his places of business while off duty were for personal recreation for my wife, myself and friends.

I have not been in his places of business, nor have I seen him, in the last three or four years. I did not see him in the basement prior to the shooting of Oswald.

Respectfully submitted,

W. Wiggins
W. Wiggins
Lieutenant of Police
Service Division

WW:fb

311

COMMISSION EXHIBIT No. 2003—Continued

REPORT ON OFFICER'S DUTIES IN REGARDS TO OSWALD'S MURDER

E. R. BECK - #45

On Sunday, November 24, 1963, I got to the office at 6:30 AM.

At about 9:30 AM, Det. Leavelle, Graves, and Dhority went to the Jail to bring Oswald to Capt. Fritz's office. Det. Brown, Montgomery and myself waited at the third floor Jail elevator door and helped get Oswald to our office.

At about 11:10 AM, Capt. Fritz told Dets. Dhority, Brown, and myself to go to the basement and get the cars set up for Oswald's transfer. He told Det. Dhority to put his car by the Jail door, and for me to drive the lead car. Capt. Fritz told me that we would go to Commerce, East on Commerce to Preston, North to Main, then West on Main, and when we got to the entrance of the Jail on Main, I was to drive past the entrance, so that they could drive into the Jail entrance.

When we got to the basement, we had some trouble lining up the cars because of the TV cameras and the press. Detective Dhority was backing Capt. Fritz's car into position. I was standing just to the rear of the lead car telling Det. Brown to back up just a little more, when a shot was fired, and I ran back and helped Lt. Swain get the crowd back. I went into the Jail office, and Oswald was lying on the floor on the North side of the office and several officers had a man on the floor that I later found out was Jack Ruby.

An ambulance arrived and Oswald was placed in the ambulance, and Det. Graves, Dhority, and Leavelle went in the ambulance to Parkland. I got my

car and Capt. Fritz got in the front seat, and Det. Montgomery and Brown in the back, and we went to Parkland Hospital. We went to Emergency Room, and the doctors and nurses were working on Oswald. Shortly after we arrived, Oswald was taken from the Emergency Room to the Operating Room on the Second floor. Capt. Fritz and I left the second floor and returned to our office, along with Det. Montgomery.

After we had gotten back to the office, Jack Ruby was brought to Capt. Fritz's office at 3:25 PM, and I helped other officers get him from the Jail Elevator door to our office. After Capt. Fritz talked to Jack Ruby, I helped other officers get him back to the elevator door.

REPORT ON OFFICER'S DUTIES IN REGARDS TO OSWALD'S DEATH

C. W. BROWN - #759

On the 24th of November, 1963, I reported to work at 7:00 am driving Squad Car #376. After an interview of the suspect, Lee Harvey Oswald, by Captain Fritz, I was told to get my car and get in position in front of the other squad that was to carry Oswald to the County Jail. At approximately 11:40 am, I went to the City Hall basement and drove my car about half way up the south ramp, which leads out to Commerce Street, and my partner, Dhority, moved the other squad car up behind me. We both started attempting to back up to the jail office door when I heard a shot. I immediately put the emergency brake on and ran back to the other car. By this time, other officers had removed Lee Harvey Oswald and Jack Ruby into the jail office. I went back to my car and moved it back into the parking area so the ambulance could get through. When the ambulance arrived, Captain Fritz, Dets. E. R. Beck, L. D. Montgomery and I proceeded behind the ambulance to Parkland Hospital and set up security, first in the Emergency Room, then to the fourth floor, where Oswald underwent surgery. After Oswald died at 1:07 pm, the body was removed to the X-ray room on the ground floor. Judge Pierce McBride was contacted via telephone, and he reported to the morgue desk and gave authorization for a post mortem to be performed by Dr. Rose of the Parkland Staff. Dr. Rose took charge of the body, and I went with him and got the wife and mother of Oswald from the waiting room and let them view the body in the X-ray room. After the relatives viewed the body, I accompanied it along with my partner, C. N. Dhority, and Dr. Rose to the Morgue. At the Morgue, Dhority and I witnessed the preliminary photos taken of the body by Dr. Rose and his staff. After this, I returned to the office and continued our investigative work there.

REPORT ON OFFICER'S DUTIES IN REGARDS TO OSWALD'S MURDER

C. N. DHORITY - #476

Sunday, November 24, 1963, about 9:30 AM, Capt. Fritz directed Dets. J. R. Leavelle, L. C. Graves and myself to go to the fifth floor jail and bring Lee Harvey Oswald to his office. We brought Oswald to Captain Fritz's office, where he was interrogated by Capt. Fritz, Mr. Kelly of the Secret Service, Mr. Sorrels of the Secret Service, and Mr. Holmes of the Postal Department. They talked to Oswald until about 11:10 AM. Chief Curry came into Capt. Fritz's office when the interrogation was going on. At the end of the interrogation, Capt. Fritz gave me the keys to his car, and told me to park it along the door from the jail office in the basement. I went to the basement and unlocked Capt. Fritz's car and proceeded to drive the car into the driveway. There was a plain black police car in front of me, and the officers who I could not recognize, drove this car up the ramp to Main Street exit. I was backing Capt. Fritz's car in front of the jail office, and was having trouble getting through the news reporters that had jammed the ramp driveway. While I was backing up, I was turned around in the seat looking back to keep from running over the reporters. Capt. Fritz came out of the jail door, followed by Det. J. R. Leavelle handcuffed to Oswald. Det. L. C. Graves was to Oswald's left. They were walking to the car while I was still moving the car back. Capt. Fritz opened the right rear door of the car I was driving, and I noticed a man move quickly across the right rear of the car. This man moved to Oswald and shot. I recognized this man as Jack Ruby, a man I had seen a few times before in previous years. When Ruby shot, Det. Graves grabbed the pistol Ruby had in his hand. The crowd of reporters closed in with the police officers, and I jumped out of the car, and went into the jail office.

The officers had Ruby, and Det. Leavelle was being unhandcuffed from Oswald. Capt. Fritz directed me to return to the basement and have the Supervisor Officer to obtain the names of everyone in the basement. I went to Capt. C. E. Talbert and gave him Capt. Fritz's message. I then moved Capt. Fritz's car out of the driveway where the ambulance could get to the jail office. When the ambulance came, I rode in the ambulance with Oswald to Parkland Hospital. I stayed at Parkland Hospital until Oswald was pronounced dead. Det. C. W. Brown and I went with Oswald's body to the morgue where we waited until Dr. Earl Rose made his preliminary pictures of the body prior to the autopsy. I turned over Oswald's clothing to Dr. Earl Rose, and returned to the Homicide Office in the City Hall approximately 5:30 PM. I stayed in the Homicide Office with Mr. Stewart and went through the property of Oswald. I made copies of letters and identification from Oswald's property for Mr. Stewart. I also made copies of all the affidavits that had been taken by the Homicide Office and Sheriff's Office for Mr. Sorrells of the Secret Service.

REPORT ON OFFICER'S DUTIES IN REGARDS TO OSWALD'S MURDER

L. C. GRAVES - #702

Sunday, November 24, 1963, was the day set for the transfer of Lee Harvey Oswald to the County Jail. The time set for the transfer was 10:00 AM. Shortly before 9:30 AM, J. R. Leavelle, C. N. Dhority, and I brought Oswald down from the fifth floor jail for final questioning by Capt. Fritz, Agents Sorrel and Kelly from the Secret Service. Others present during the questioning were Mr. Holmes from the U. S. Post Office Department, Detectives L. D. Montgomery, C. N. Dhority, J. R. Leavelle, and I. Chief Curry was present only a few minutes at the beginning of the questioning and at the end just prior to Oswald's removal to the basement. Before leaving our office with Oswald, Capt. Fritz instructed J. R. Leavelle to handcuff his left arm to the right arm of Oswald. I was to walk by Oswald's left side, holding his left arm. Oswald's hands were handcuffed together in front of him. Det. Leavelle, Oswald, and I were escorted from this office via the jail elevator to the jail office by Capt. Fritz, Lt. Swain, and Det. L. D. Montgomery. At the jail office door that leads into the hall, we stopped for a few seconds until Capt. Fritz and Lt. Swain made sure the hall-way was clear. We got the all clear sign and made our way through the hall to the edge of the ramp where we had paused momentarily awaiting the arrival of our car, when suddenly out of the surging line of camera men and glaring camera lights, Jack Ruby sprang forward and fired one round from a pistol into the stomach of Lee Harvey Oswald before I could grab his pistol and disarm him.

Oswald was immediately placed in an O'Neal ambulance and rushed to Parkland Hospital, where he underwent surgery within 10 minutes after his

L. C. Graves - Page 2 (Oswald's Murder)

arrival. Oswald was pronounced dead at 1:07 PM, November 24, 1963, by Dr. Tom Shires, Parkland Staff. Detectives J. R. Leavelle, Burgess, and I, along with Dr. Bieberdorf, rode in the ambulance with Oswald to Parkland. At the hospital I changed into operating room clothing and accompanied Oswald to the Operating Room and stood guard until he was pronounced dead.

The pistol I took from Jack Ruby was turned over to Capt. Fritz at Parkland Hospital.

COMMISSION EXHIBIT No. 2003—Continued

REPORT ON OFFICER'S DUTIES IN REGARDS TO OSWALD'S DEATH

LESLIE D. MONTGOMERY - #1047

On Sunday November 24, 1963 at 11:15 am Captain Fritz, Lt. R. E. Swain, Det. J. R. Leavelle, Det. L. C. Graves and myself escorted Oswald from Captain Fritz's office to the jail elevator. Det. Leavelle had been handcuffed to Oswald. Patrolman C. G. Lewis, Jr., was the elevator operator as we carried Oswald down from the 3rd floor of the city hall to the basement. When we got off of the elevator in the basement, Lt. R. E. Swain walked out in front of Captain Fritz. Det. Leavelle was to Oswald's right and Det. Graves was to Oswald's left, and I was in back of Oswald about three feet as we approached the door leading from the basement and jail office. Captain Fritz told us to stop, that he was going to check one more time. The captain said, "All right, come on." We walked out of the door leading from the basement jail office to the ramp where the cars come down into the basement. We had to stop approximately five feet from the driveway of the ramp because the car was not in position. When we stopped I saw a blur of something and heard a shot. I went around Det. Graves and grabbed Jack Ruby by the head. At the time I grabbed Ruby by the head he was being held by W. J. Harrison, T. D. McMillon, R. L. Lowery and W. J. Cutshaw. We forced Ruby to the ground and a check was made for the weapon. We then moved Ruby into the basement jail office and put him back on the floor being held down by the same officers. While being held down on the floor of the basement jail office, Ruby said, "I hope I killed the son-of-a-bitch." I asked Chief Batchelor if we had better get Ruby on the elevator and get him up into the jail. Chief Batchelor said yes, and Ruby was taken to the elevator. I then went to where Oswald was lying on the jail office floor A doctor was applying artificial respiration. The ambulance people arrived and loaded Oswald on the cot, and I went with the cot to the ambulance.

COMMISSION EXHIBIT No. 2003—Continued

REPORT ON OFFICER'S DUTIES IN REGARDS TO OSWALD'S DEATH

J. R. LEAVELLE - #736

I arrived Sunday morning, November 24, 1963 about 8:00 am. We received word from Mr. Perry, Security Officer of the Statler-Hilton that they had a man check in who said he represented a munition company out of California. I went to the hotel in company with Det. C. N. Dhority and Mr. C. W. Brown. We talked with Robert W. Parker, 544 North Cypress, Orange, California. We satisfied ourselves he was O. K. and returned to the office.

At 9:30 am I was instructed, along with Det. L. C. Graves and Det. C. N. Dhority to go up in the jail and get Lee Oswald. I went to his cell and put the handcuff on him with his hands in front of him.

We returned to Captain Fritz's office where Captain Fritz, Mr. Sorrells and Mr. Thomas Kelly of the Secret Service questioned Oswald. Also in the room were Detectives L. D. Montgomery, L. C. Graves, C. N. Dhority and Inspector Holmes of the Post Office Department and myself.

Shortly after 11:00 am we began the transfer. Chief Curry had come to Captain Fritz's office. I had made a suggestion earlier to double cross the press and take Oswald out on the first floor via the Main Street door, leaving the press waiting in the basement and on Commerce Street.

Also it was suggested to go out the Main Street ramp and west on Main Street. These suggestions were turned down by Chief Curry who stated that we had better go ahead with the transfer as planned, since he had given his word on it.

Approximately 11:15 am we left the third floor office with Oswald handcuffed to my left arm with Det. L. C. Graves holding to Oswald's left arm, preceded to the jail elevator by Captain Fritz, Lt. Swain, Detective L. D. Montgomery. We reached the basement jail office with officers in front we headed to the automobile ramp just outside the jail office door. We hesitated just inside the jail door,

320

COMMISSION EXHIBIT No. 2003—Continued

then was given the all clear sign. We walked out and had just reached the ramp where the car we were to ride in was being backed into position by Detective Dhority when out of the mass of humanity composed of all the news media, which had surged forward to within six or seven feet of us, came the figure of a man with a gun in hand. He took two quick steps and double actioned a .38 revolver point blank at Oswald. I jerked back on Oswald, at the same time reaching out and catching Jack Ruby on the left shoulder, shoving back and down on him, bringing myself between Ruby and Oswald. I could see Det. Graves had Ruby's gun hand and gun in his hands. I turned my attention to Oswald and with the help of Det. Combest we took Oswald back into the jail office and laid him down. Handcuffs were removed and the city hall doctor, Dr. Bieberdorf was summoned. We also called O'Neal ambulance. Oswald was placed in the ambulance and rushed to Parkland Hospital. In the ambulance besides the crew was Dr. Bieberdorf, Det. L. C. Graves, Det. C. N. Dhority and myself.

He was rushed to surgery where he expired at 1:07 pm, November 24, 1963, pronounced by Dr. Tom Shires. Judge Pierce McBride was summoned. I gave him all the information needed to request an autopsy. When all necessary reports were made, I returned to the city hall where I made the offense report on Lee Harvey Oswald.

321

COMMISSION EXHIBIT No. 2003—Continued

December 1, 1963

Mr. J. E. Curry
Chief of Police

Sir:

The following is a list of the personnel that were on duty in the basement, or proximity thereof, prior to or at the time Lee Harvey Oswald was shot:

ADMINISTRATIVE

Captain Glen D. King	519 Goldwood

CRIMINAL INVESTIGATION DIVISION

Captain Frank M. Martin	906 Five Mile Parkway
R. L. Lowery	838 W. Church, Grand Prairie, Tex.
W. J. Harrison	9223 Donnybrook
W. J. Cutchaw	401 N. W. 22nd, Grand Prairie, Tex.
L. D. Miller	1231 Ravina, Garland, Texas
Charles Goolsby	2911 Eisenhower
Lt. George Butler	6447 Velasco
Lt. V. S. Smart	2120 Balleycastle
D. R. Archer	2035 San Francisco
C. A. Greeson	1301 Ivy Lane, Arlington, Texas
B. S. Clardy	936 Ferncliff
T. J. McMillon	4929 Reiger
H. L. Dawson	428 Burnett, Richardson, Texas
J. C. Watson	3743 Clover Lane
Captain O. A. Jones	2603 Alco
W. E. Chambers	6521 Olcta Drive
R. C. Wagner	3048 Clover Drive, Mesquite, Texas
J. K. Ramsey	11621 Fernald
Lt. R. E. Swain	Route 1, Red Oak, Texas
V. C. Campbell	3306 Wise, Mesquite, Texas
H. L. McGee	3501 Sidney, Mesquite, Texas
I. F. VanCleave	226 S. Shore, Lewisville, Texas
D. G. Brantley	11919 Badger Drive, Mesquite, Texas
D. L. Burgess	2935 Milmar
H. B. Reynolds	1607 Pat Drive
L. R. Stephens	11306 Stallcup
Capt. J. W. Fritz	5121 Gaston Avenue
J. R. Leavelle	7703 Rilla
L. C. Graves	7611 Maxwell
C. W. Brown	General Delivery, DeSoto, Texas
C. W. Dhority	2110 Balleycastle

SPECIAL SERVICE

B. L. Beaty	404 Freeman, Garland, Texas
B. H. Combest	2803 Linhaven, Mesquite, Texas
J. D. Hutchinson	4950 Live Oak, Apartment H

322

COMMISSION EXHIBIT No. 2003—Continued

Mr. J. E. Curry Page 2

RADIO PATROL

M. L. Wise	6711 Latta
A. R. Brock	207 E. Baylor, Ennis, Texas
D. C. Patterson	3463 Caracas, Mesquite, Texas
L. E. Jez	7848 Claremont
R. E. Vaughn	3231 Loganwood
J. Raz	517 Hardy, Garland, Texas
D. L. Pate	1016 E. Allen, Carrollton, Texas
H. J. Wages	1639 Barlow
T. R. Gregory	502 Golden Meadow, Duncanville, Texas
L. L. Fox	554 Summit Ridge, Duncanville, Texas
L. C. Taylor	9420 Fairhope
T. R. Burton	2402 Glenbrook, Garland, Texas
D. K. Erwin	622 Milky Way, Garland, Texas
W. E. Hibbs	2345 Quinto
G. L. Tolbert	4346 Birch, Mesquite, Texas
M. E. Farris	2241 Tradewind, Mesquite, Texas
R. A. Watkins	1010 Calle Real, Mesquite, Texas
Lt. Rio S. Pierce	3227 S. Edgefield
Sgt. J. A. Putnam	2015 Joan Drive
Capt. C. E. Talbert	1211 Toltec
Sgt. D. F. Steele	1707 Kent, Arlington, Texas
Sgt. B. J. Maxey	8912 Freeport
K. K. Anderson	405 East College, Grapevine
P. T. Dean	2822 Nicholson Drive

SERVICE DIVISION

Lt. Woodrow Wiggins	319 W. Corning
W. B. Slack	5605 Sumatra
C. G. Lewis	Route 8, Box 331A
J. D. Slocum, Police Clerk	505 W. Melba
J. F. Newton, Police Clerk	8906 Angleton Place

Respectfully submitted,

W. R. Westbrook
Captain of Police
Personnel Bureau

WRW:RW

323

COMMISSION EXHIBIT No. 2003—Continued

DALLAS POLICE RESERVE OFFICERS ASSIGNED TO
CITY HALL BASEMENT SUNDAY, NOVEMBER 24, 1963

NAME / BUSINESS	HOME ADDRESS (ZONE) / BUSINESS ADDRESS	PHONE / PHONE	I.D.	BADGE
ARNETT, CHAS. O. (CPT.) Certain-Teed Prod.	1223 S. Waverly Dr. (8) 7910 S. Central Expy.	WH3-8065	301	955
BROCKWAY, JERRY D. L-T-V	2710 DOUGLASS, IRVING	BL5-7092 AN2-1311,482	703	398
Capps, Arthur W. Student	8406 Grovecrest (17) North Tex St. Collete	EX1-4541	954	258
Cox, Roland A. (Sgt) Sears Roebuck & Co.	Box 631, DeSoto, Tex.	CA3-6443 RI7-3011 - 336	80	803
Craig, Alvin B. Socony Mobil Res. Lab.	4310 Dawes Dr. (11)	FE1-8019 FE1-6531 563	657	285
Croy, Kenneth H. (Sgt.) Real Estate	2634 W. Illinois (33) 1720 S. Lamar	FE7-0621 RI8-2634	810	819
Davis, Robt. T. Student	115 N. Clinton (8) Arlington St. College	WH6-3272	957	101
Harrison, Oliver W. Wayne's Shell Sev. Sta.	6223 Old Ox Road 2100 E. Ledbetter	FR6-9095 FR4-9156	960	423
Hopkins, Jimmie R. (Sgt.) Braniff Airways	8643 Diceman Dr. (8)	DA8-1702 FL7-4061 395	378	855
Hunt, Jesse C. Int. Harvester Co.	520 S. Waverly Dr. (8) 1809 S. Lamar	WH1-0415 RI2-3413	920	229
Jacobs, Leslie H. Morton Foods Co.	2130 Shea Road (35)	FL2-4489 FL1-3291	760	382
Kasten, Jerome Bryan Adams	4611 Columbia 2101 Milimar	TA1-3866	963	333
Kriss, Harry M. (Lt.) Sweet Mfg. Co.	6906 Merrilee Lane (14 1100 Commerce	TA7-1578 RI2-8038	49	905
Mayo, Logan W. (Sgt) Sears Roebuck & Co.	7203 Casa Loma (14) 1409 S. Lamar	DA1-2264 RI7-3011 315	715	862
McCain, James C. (Sgt.) Ling-Temco-Vought	2332 Rosemario, Mesquit	AT5-8113	765	859
McCoy, Ben C. (Lt) T.P.&L. Company	1521 Dent.Garland Fidelity Union Bldg.	BR6-6562 RI8-5411 224	471	907

324

COMMISSION EXHIBIT No. 2003—Continued

NAME / BUSINESS	HOME ADDRESS (ZONE) / BUSINESS ADDRESS	PHONE / PHONE	I.D.	BADGE
Merrell, Barnie (Lt)	2928 Fondren Drive (5)	EM8-0427	90	901
Newman, Wm. J. Continental Electronics	10923 Cotillion Dr. (28) 4212 S. Buckner Blvd.	BR9-5923 EV1-7161 278	979	317
Suits, Donald T. (Lt) Lone Star Gas Co.	233 Sendero, Garland	BR6-1498 RI1-3711 669	399	927
Worley, Gano E., Jr. Lone Star Gas Co.	835 N. Ewing, Apt. D. 301 S. Harwood	WH3-8934 RI1-3711 323	876	516
Hatley, Hurshell H. Rem. Rand. Rep.	5223 Monticello (6)	TA7-7113 RI7-3111	313	310

325

COMMISSION EXHIBIT No. 2003—Continued

STATEMENT FROM LONNIE HUDKINS, HOUSTON POST

Attached is the information obtained from Lonnie Hudkins. I trust this is the information you wanted.

He tells me that he learned that Ruby reportedly was talking to Bill Alexander in the District Attorney's Office at 3:00 pm on November 21. It would save me a lot of work if this could be definitely verified.

If this office can be of further help to you, please contact us.

11:20 am Since talking to you via phone, talked to Lonnie. He just can't recall if he saw the card on the 22nd. Also will not state for certain that the card was issued by Glen Bird. Sorry. He is pulling photographs etc. having them reviewed in an effort to furnish you more details. Will let you know of anything developed.

326

COMMISSION EXHIBIT No. 2003—Continued

Alonzo Heidt Hudkins, III, Apartment 23, 7523 Highcrest Drive, Houston, Texas, employed by the Houston Post, a daily newspaper, was interviewed on December 10.

Mr. Hudkins stated that he was not present at the Dallas Police Department on November 24, 1963, when Lee Harvey Oswald was shot. He stated that he was in the Police Station on Friday evening of November 22 and observed Attorney Tom Howard, now representing Ruby, and his law partner Colley Sullivan and Attorney Bennie Henderson on the third floor of the Police Station near the office of Captain Fritz where Oswald was being interviewed. He stated that at approximately 11:00 Oswald was taken from Captain Fritz' Office to a police assembly room for a show-up and near the show-up room he saw Jack Ruby. He asked Ruby what he was doing there and as he recalls Ruby replied he was either writing for a Jewish paper or interpreting for someone who was writing for a Jewish paper. He advised that to the best of his knowledge Ruby had some sort of an identification card issued by Glenn Bird, now County Clerk who was formerly a Justice of the Peace. The card, as he recalls, read, "The Bearer is an Honorary Deputy of the Justice of the Peace." Mr. Hudkins stated that the third floor of the Police Station was full of newsmen and others and he felt that there was very little chance of obtaining a story there so his efforts were concentrated elsewhere.

He advised that on November 24 at the time Oswald was scheduled to be transferred from the police building to the County Sheriff's Office that he was in the office of County Sheriff Bill Decker, as he anticipated if there were any trouble, it would be at the entrance to the County Jail.

He states that one thing occurred while he was at the County Jail which was significant to him. He states that Attorney Tom Howard, who was allegedly at the Police Department at the time the shooting occurred, arrived at the County Sheriff's Office for the purpose of obtaining a writ for the release of Ruby two minutes before Oswald was delivered to the hospital. Mr. Hudkins states that this is significant to him. He states that later that day he asked Howard if Ruby had the gun with him on Friday night. He states Howard advised that Ruby did have the gun at that time. According to Mr. Hudkins, Howard

327

COMMISSION EXHIBIT No. 2003—Continued

later admitted that to a reporter on the Houston Post by long distance from Dallas. Mr. Hudkins was talking to the Houston Post in Houston and asked Mr. Howard to verify that statement directly to his paper, which Mr. Howard did.

Mr. Hudkins stated that on Friday night, November 22, near the police assembly room while Oswald was being taken for show-up he talked to Chief Curry of the Dallas Police Department, who was worried about Oswald's security. He states that at that time he observed many persons there who were not reporters, several of whom were attorneys and one, he noted, was a runner for a bondsman and is an ex-convict. He could not recall the runner's name.

Mr. Hudkins advised that he has known Ruby for quite some time as he was active as a judge at fights and that Ruby usually appeared at the fights, sitting in the front row. He has seen him on many occasions at fights and at other public gatherings. He stated it was common knowledge that Ruby went armed.

Mr. Hudkins and his staff are still actively running out leads which he states are being called in to the Houston Post. He agreed to advise this office of any information which he considers pertinent.

328

COMMISSION EXHIBIT No. 2003—Continued

December 18, 1963

Mr. J. E. Curry
Chief of Police

Subject: Jack Ruby

Sir:

Deputy Sheriff William L. Watkins was interviewed this date regarding the issuance of a Writ of Habeas Corpus on Jack L. Ruby, November 24, 1963. Mr. Watkins stated that Attorney Tom Howard entered the Dallas County Sheriff's Office approximately 30 or 45 minutes after the shooting of Lee Harvey Oswald. Attorney Howard used a public telephone to call Judge Joe B. Brown requesting a Writ of Habeas Corpus for subject.

Mr. Watkins stated that Sheriff Bill Decker then telephoned Judge Brown for verification of the issuance of a dry writ. Judge Brown gave this verification and the writ was returnable at 11:00 a.m., November 25, 1963, in Judge Joe B. Brown's Criminal District Court.

Judge Joe B. Brown telephoned the Sheriff's Office after hearing of the death of Lee Harvey Oswald and ordered Deputy Sheriff Watkins to cancel the writ application for Jack Ruby and he immediately complied with this order.

At the time of a writ application made with the Sheriff's Office, no record of the time of the issuance of a writ is recorded - only the date of issuance, the name of the attorney, the date and the time that the writ is returnable and the name of the court is recorded. The time given in this instance is the time furnished by Deputy Watkin's memory.

The application for this Writ of Habeas Corpus was made by Attorney Tom Howard and Attorney Colley Sullivan, local attorneys.

Respectfully submitted,

H M Hart

H. M. Hart, Detective
Special Service Bureau

HMH:nw

329

COMMISSION EXHIBIT No. 2003—Continued

December 17, 1963

Mr. J. E. Curry
Chief of Police

Subject: William Frank Coffney c/m/31
3132 Morgan Drive

Sir:

We received information that the above subject was arrested running from the City Hall after the shooting of Lee Harvey Oswald.

I contacted Sergeant J. F. Everett December 13, 1963. Sergeant Everett stated as follows:

"I was on duty in the Dispatcher's Office and had walked into the hall of the third floor at the time of the shooting. Someone shouted to secure the building and I ran down the steps to the first floor. There I saw the subject William Coffney run towards the Harwood Street exit. Sergeant Putnam, Officer R. T. Davis #1887 and myself apprehended the subject on the steps of the City Hall. He was taken to the Homicide Bureau and interrogated by Detective T. L. Baker. It was determined this subject was apparently sightseeing on the first floor. He was later released.

This person works for Cockrell and Winniford, 2712 Live Oak, Telephone TA4-6741 - Home Phone, CA4-3419."

This investigation of William Coffney has not been carried any farther at this time.

Respectfully submitted,

P. G. McCaghren, Lieutenant
Burglary & Theft Bureau

PGM:nw

330

Commission Exhibit No. 2003—Continued

December 18, 1963

Mr. J. E. Curry
Chief of Police

Subject: Jack Ruby

Sir:

On Saturday, November 23, 1963, Patrolman P. N. Cooper, #1283 was assigned as point-control at Elm and Houston Streets. About 3:00 p.m. that date subject walked up to Officer Cooper and stated that it was a terrible thing that President Kennedy had been killed. Officer Cooper stated that Ruby had walked from the curb at the corner of the Records Building, crossed the street to Dealey Plaza.

Patrolman Cooper is not personally acquainted with Jack Ruby, however, has seen him on numerous occasions.

Respectfully submitted,

H. M. Hart, Detective
Special Service Bureau

HMH:nw

331

Commission Exhibit No. 2003—Continued

WESTERN UNION TELEGRAM

W. P. MARSHALL, PRESIDENT

CLASS OF SERVICE: This is a fast message unless its deferred character is indicated by the proper symbol.

SYMBOLS: DL=Day Letter; NL=Night Letter; LT=International Letter Telegram

SF-1201 (4-60)

The filing time shown in the date line on domestic telegrams is LOCAL TIME at point of origin. Time of receipt is LOCAL TIME at point of destination

NOV 24 63 DG051 BA129
SSQ458 B STA126 PD STAMFORD CONN 24 307P EST
JACK RUBENSTEIN
1963 NOV 24 PM 4 58

C/O DALLAS POLICE DEPT
DAL
HORRAY FOR YOU JACK
FRANK AND ANDY

WESTERN UNION TELEGRAM

W. P. MARSHALL, PRESIDENT

CLASS OF SERVICE: This is a fast message unless its deferred character is indicated by the proper symbol.

SYMBOLS: DL=Day Letter; NL=Night Letter; LT=International Letter Telegram

SF-1201 (4-60)

The filing time shown in the date line on domestic telegrams is LOCAL TIME at point of origin. Time of receipt is LOCAL TIME at point of destination

155P CST NOV 24 63 DC258 LA096
L CPA011 PD TDCP LYNWOOD CALIF 24 1000A PST
JACK RUBY
DALLAS JAIL DAL
GOOD FOR YOU JACK RUBY
GENE OLSON 4157 FERNWOOD AVE LYNWOOD CALIF
(02).

332

COMMISSION EXHIBIT NO. 2003—Continued

WESTERN UNION TELEGRAM

W. P. MARSHALL, PRESIDENT

CLASS OF SERVICE: This is a fast message unless its deferred character is indicated by the proper symbol.

SYMBOLS: DL=Day Letter; NL=Night Letter; LT=International Letter Telegram

SF-1201 (4-60)

The filing time shown in the date line on domestic telegrams is LOCAL TIME at point of origin. Time of receipt is LOCAL TIME at point of destination

437P CST NOV 24 63 DC381 OA228
O SFN101 RX PD 3 EXTRA SAN FRANCISCO CALIF 24 104P PST
INMATE FRANK RUBENSTEIN
DALLAS CITY PRISON DAL
I WOULD BE HONORED TO CALL YOU FRIEND
ALICE ROSARIO
1300 GOLDEN GATE

1300
(47).

WESTERN UNION TELEGRAM

W. P. MARSHALL, PRESIDENT

CLASS OF SERVICE: This is a fast message unless its deferred character is indicated by the proper symbol.

SYMBOLS: DL=Day Letter; NL=Night Letter; LT=International Letter Telegram

SF-1201 (4-60)

The filing time shown in the date line on domestic telegrams is LOCAL TIME at point of origin. Time of receipt is LOCAL TIME at point of destination

440P CST NOV 24 63 DG067 OA133
O LBA075 PD LONG BEACH CALIF 24 1042A PST
JACK RUBY
DALLAS CITY JAL DAL
WELL DONE CONGRATULATIONS
FRANK GOODELL 13342 EL DORADO DR APT 191J LEISURE WORLD

333

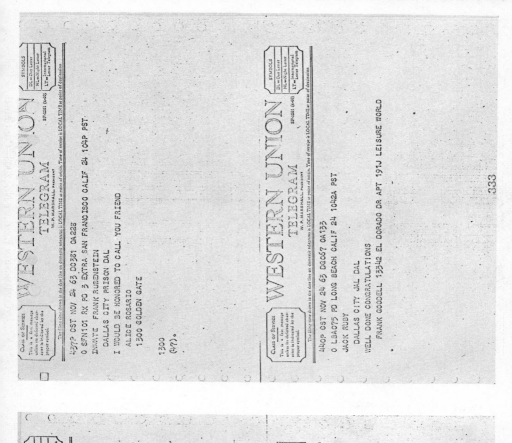

COMMISSION EXHIBIT NO. 2003—Continued

WESTERN UNION TELEGRAM

W. P. MARSHALL, PRESIDENT

CLASS OF SERVICE: This is a fast message unless its deferred character is indicated by the proper symbol.

SYMBOLS: DL=Day Letter; NL=Night Letter; LT=International Letter Telegram

SF-1201 (4-60)

The filing time shown in the date line on domestic telegrams is LOCAL TIME at point of origin. Time of receipt is LOCAL TIME at point of destination

DF091
SYA123 SY LLB183 PD DUNKIRK NY 24 513P EST
MR JACK RUBIN 1963 NOV 24 PM 5 52
DALLAS CITY JAIL
DAL
YOU DID WHAT MANY CITIZENS OF DALLAS WOULD HAVE DONE EXCEPT
YOU HAD COURAGE
JOSEPHINE DALLINGER TEACHER OF GERMAN DUNKIRK HIGH SCHOOL

(40).

WESTERN UNION TELEGRAM

W. P. MARSHALL, PRESIDENT

CLASS OF SERVICE: This is a fast message unless its deferred character is indicated by the proper symbol.

SYMBOLS: DL=Day Letter; NL=Night Letter; LT=International Letter Telegram

SF-1201 (4-60)

The filing time shown in the date line on domestic telegrams is LOCAL TIME at point of origin. Time of receipt is LOCAL TIME at point of destination

503P CST NOV 24 63 DF105 PA171
P SIA187 PD TDSI SILVER SPRING MD 24 424P EST
JACK RUBY
DAL
SO GLAD YOU HAD THE COURAGE AND CAREFUL DETERMINATION TO CARRY
OUT THE EXECUTION OF THE ASSASIN OF PRESIDENT KENNEDY JUSTICE
HAS TRULY VINDICATED BY ONE OF THE PEOPLE. I HOPE THIS MESSAGE
GIVES YOU CONSOLATION AND THAT YOU WILL GET THE SAME SUPPORT
FROM ALL OVER THE WORLD
ROBERT O'SHEA
3542 MADISON ST
HYATTSVILLE MD
(05).

334

Commission Exhibit No. 2003—Continued

WESTERN UNION TELEGRAM

W. P. MARSHALL, PRESIDENT

CLASS OF SERVICE: This is a fast message unless its deferred character is indicated by the proper symbol.

SYMBOLS: DL=Day Letter; NL=Night Letter; LT=International Letter Telegram

SF-1201 (4-60)

The filing time shown in the date line on domestic telegrams is LOCAL TIME at point of origin. Time of receipt is LOCAL TIME at point of destination

527P CST NOV 24 63 DF115 BA138 BA139
B NWA242 PD NEWTON MASS 24 434P EST
JACK RUBENSTEIN
THE COURT HOUSE
DAL
I DONT THINK HE SHOULD BE PROSECTUTED.
MRS RENA L JORDAN 905 WATERTOWN STREET WEST NEWTON
(00).

WESTERN UNION TELEGRAM

W. P. MARSHALL, PRESIDENT

CLASS OF SERVICE: This is a fast message unless its deferred character is indicated by the proper symbol.

SYMBOLS: DL=Day Letter; NL=Night Letter; LT=International Letter Telegram

SF-1201 (4-60)

The filing time shown in the date line on domestic telegrams is LOCAL TIME at point of origin. Time of receipt is LOCAL TIME at point of destination

DB151 PA166
P BRA602 (P SIA187) PD TDSI SILVER SPRING MD 24 424P EST 1963 NOV 24 PM 5 53
JACK RUBY
DAL
SO GLAD YOU HAD THE COURAGE AND CAREFUL DETERMINATION TO CARRY
OUT THE EXECUTION OF THE ASSASIN OF PRESIDENT KENNEDY. JUSTICE
HAS BEEN TRULY VINDICATED BY ONE OF THE PEOPLE. I HOPE THIS
MESSAGE GIVES YOU. CONSOLATION AND THAT YOU WILL GET THE SAME
SUPPORT FROM ALL OVER THE WORLD

ROBERT O'SHEA 3542 MADISON ST HYATTSVILLE MD
(15).

335

Commission Exhibit No. 2003—Continued

WESTERN UNION TELEGRAM

W. P. MARSHALL, PRESIDENT

CLASS OF SERVICE: This is a fast message unless its deferred character is indicated by the proper symbol.

SYMBOLS: DL=Day Letter; NL=Night Letter; LT=International Letter Telegram

SF-1201 (4-60)

The filing time shown in the date line on domestic telegrams is LOCAL TIME at point of origin. Time of receipt is LOCAL TIME at point of destination

652P CST NOV 24 63 DG133
SYA144 SY HEA779 PD TDHE MASSAPEQUA NY 24 722P EST
JACK RUBY
CARE OF CHIEF OF POLICE
DAL
IN GRATITUDE STAND READY TO ASSIST YOU IN WHATEVER WAY YOU
PERMIT ME
JOSEPH B LAMBERTA
(52).

WESTERN UNION TELEGRAM

W. P. MARSHALL, PRESIDENT

CLASS OF SERVICE: This is a fast message unless its deferred character is indicated by the proper symbol.

SYMBOLS: DL=Day Letter; NL=Night Letter; LT=International Letter Telegram

SF-1201 (4-60) TCP

The filing time shown in the date line on domestic telegrams is LOCAL TIME at point of origin. Time of receipt is LOCAL TIME at point of destination

DF078 LA193
L AYA138 PD ALBUQUERQUE NMEX 24 224P MST
1963 NOV 24 PM 5 53
JACK RUBY
CARE DALLAS POLICE STATION DAL
GOOD WORK MANY CONGRADULATIONS YOU DESERVE A MEDAL
JACK JORDAN 320 ALCAZAR NE
(48)

336

Commission Exhibit No. 2003—Continued

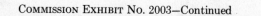

WESTERN UNION TELEGRAM

W. P. MARSHALL, PRESIDENT

CLASS OF SERVICE: This is a fast message unless its deferred character is indicated by the proper symbol.

SYMBOLS: DL=Day Letter; NL=Night Letter; LT=International Letter Telegram

SF-1201 (4-60)

The filing time shown in the date line on domestic telegrams is LOCAL TIME at point of origin. Time of receipt is LOCAL TIME at point of destination

529P CST NOV 24 63 DF117 LA240
L BHA366 PD FAX BEVERLY HILLS CALIF 24 259P PST
MR RUBY
CARE DALLAS JAIL DAL
HEARTIEST CONGRATULATIONS FOR A JOB WELL DONE
FRANK KINNEY
(05).

WESTERN UNION TELEGRAM

W. P. MARSHALL, PRESIDENT

CLASS OF SERVICE: This is a fast message unless its deferred character is indicated by the proper symbol.

SYMBOLS: DL=Day Letter; NL=Night Letter; LT=International Letter Telegram

SF-1201 (4-60)

The filing time shown in the date line on domestic telegrams is LOCAL TIME at point of origin. Time of receipt is LOCAL TIME at point of destination

648P CST NOV 24 63 DB197
MA110 M MWA388 PD MILWAUKEE WIS 24 628P CST
JACK RUBY
DALLAS CITY JAIL DAL
CONGRATULATIONS JACK FOR YOUR COURAGEOUS ACT YOU MERIT AND
HAVE GAINED THOUSAND OF AMERICAN FRIENDS
FRANK HOLT 739 SO 36 ST

337

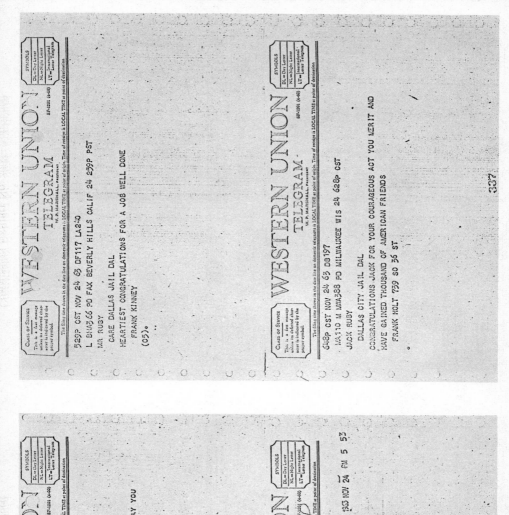

Commission Exhibit No. 2003—Continued

WESTERN UNION TELEGRAM

W. P. MARSHALL, PRESIDENT

CLASS OF SERVICE: This is a fast message unless its deferred character is indicated by the proper symbol.

SYMBOLS: DL=Day Letter; NL=Night Letter; LT=International Letter Telegram

SF-1201 (4-60)

The filing time shown in the date line on domestic telegrams is LOCAL TIME at point of origin. Time of receipt is LOCAL TIME at point of destination

625P CST NOV 24 63 DG117 KA209
K OCA221 PD OKLAHOMA CITY OKLA 24 423P CST
JACK RUBY
CARE DALLAS TEXAS CITY JAIL DAL
JACK, IF I CAN HELP, LET ME KNOW. WHEN YOU ARE ARRAIGNED AND YOUR BOND SET I AM A PROFESSIONAL BONDSMAN AND AM ASSOCIATED WITH ONE OF THE FINEST CRIMINAL ATTORNEYS IN THE WORLD. I WOULD BE WILLING TO PUT UP YOUR BOND FOR FREE. YOU DID WHAT BILLIONS OF PEOPLE WOULD HAVE DONE IF ONLY THEY HAD THE CHANCE. THE WORLD IS GRATEFUL TO YOU
JEEP O'NEAL OKLAHOMA CITY 2116 NORTHWEST 12 PHONE JA 85458
(11).

WESTERN UNION TELEGRAM

531P CST NOV 24 63 DG098
SYA131 SY ABA312 PD TDAB SCHENECTADY NY 24 620P EST
JACK RUBINSTEIN
MAN WHO SHOT OSWALD
DAL
YOU DID WHAT MILLIONS OF OTHERS WANTED TO DO IF I CAN HELP IN ANY WAY LET ME KNOW GOD HELP YOU
PATRICIA MILNE SCHENECTADY NY
(24).

338

COMMISSION EXHIBIT NO. 2003—Continued

WESTERN UNION TELEGRAM

533P CST NOV 24 63 DF119
NSA189 BA094 SSQ585 B WRA280 PD WORCESTER MASS 14 535P EST
JACK RUBENSTEIN
CITY JAIL DALLAS TEXAS
THANK YOU SIR GOD BLESS YOU
DON FITZMAURICE 16 HUNTINGTON AVE WORCESTER MASS
(40)

WESTERN UNION TELEGRAM

540P CST NOV 24 63 DF121 OA261
O LBA075 (HANDLE FLWG AS SUS DUP) PD LONG BEACH CALIF 24
1042A PST
JACK RUBY
DALLAS CITY JAIL
WELL DONE CONGRATULATIONS
FRANK GOODELL 13342 EL DORADO DR APT 191J LEISURE WORLD

339

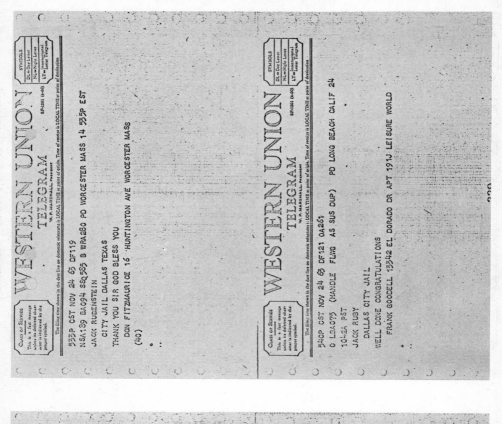

COMMISSION EXHIBIT NO. 2003—Continued

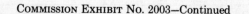

CLASS OF SERVICE
This is a fast message unless its deferred character is indicated by the proper symbol.

WESTERN UNION TELEGRAM

W. P. MARSHALL, PRESIDENT

SF-1201 (4-60)

SYMBOLS
DL=Day Letter
NL=Night Letter
LT=International Letter Telegram

The filing time shown in the date line on domestic telegrams is LOCAL TIME at point of origin. Time of receipt is LOCAL TIME at point of destination

518P CST NOV 24 63 DB157
AA178 A MZA561 PD MIAMI FLO 24 559P EST
MR RUBY
DAL.
WE LOVE YOUR GUTS AND COURAGE
CLAYTON T DODGE . MIAMI FLO.
(05).

CLASS OF SERVICE
This is a fast message unless its deferred character is indicated by the proper symbol.

WESTERN UNION TELEGRAM

W. P. MARSHALL, PRESIDENT

SF-1201 (4-60)

SYMBOLS
DL=Day Letter
NL=Night Letter
LT=International Letter Telegram

The filing time shown in the date line on domestic telegrams is LOCAL TIME at point of origin. Time of receipt is LOCAL TIME at point of destination

527P CST NOV 24 63 DC411 LA237
L LLT231 PD LOS ANGELES CALIF 24 218P PST
JACK RUBY
CITY JAIL DAL
GOD BLESS YOU THANK YOU VERY VERY MUCH
MRS LELAND 1984 LANDA ST LOS ANGELES CALIF
(05).

COMMISSION EXHIBIT No. 2003—Continued

CLASS OF SERVICE
This is a fast message unless its deferred character is indicated by the proper symbol.

WESTERN UNION TELEGRAM

W. P. MARSHALL, PRESIDENT

SF-1201 (4-60)

SYMBOLS
DL=Day Letter
NL=Night Letter
LT=International Letter Telegram

The filing time shown in the date line on domestic telegrams is LOCAL TIME at point of origin. Time of receipt is LOCAL TIME at point of destination

433P CST NOV 24 63 DC379 OA218
O VYB012 PD VAN NUYS CALIF 24 140P PST
JACK RUBY
DAL
CONGRATULATIONS. MY SINCERE THANKS. GOOD LUCK
ARTHUR SMITH 14422 RUNNYMEDE.

CLASS OF SERVICE
This is a fast message unless its deferred character is indicated by the proper symbol.

WESTERN UNION TELEGRAM

W. P. MARSHALL, PRESIDENT

SF-1201 (4-60)

SYMBOLS
DL=Day Letter
NL=Night Letter
LT=International Letter Telegram

The filing time shown in the date line on domestic telegrams is LOCAL TIME at point of origin. Time of receipt is LOCAL TIME at point of destination

422P CST NOV 24 63 DG060
SYA116 SY NC359 PD NEW YORK NY 24 447P EST
JACK RUBENSTEIN
DALLAS CITY JAIL DAL
GOD BLESS YOU FOR HAVING NERVE TO DO WHAT SO MANY PEOPLE WHO
LOVED KENNEDY WANTED
UNSIGNED
(12).

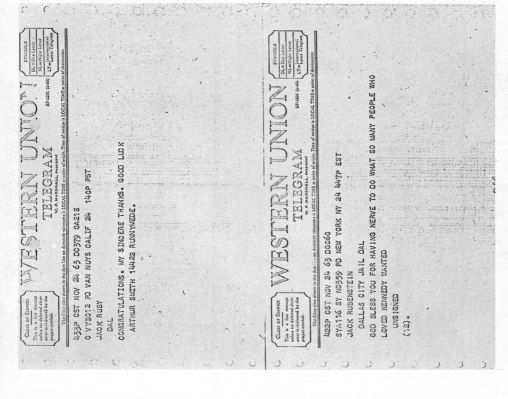

COMMISSION EXHIBIT No. 2003—Continued

WESTERN UNION TELEGRAM

W. P. MARSHALL, PRESIDENT

CLASS OF SERVICE: This is a fast message unless its deferred character is indicated by the proper symbol.

SYMBOLS: DL=Day Letter; NL=Night Letter; LT=International Letter Telegram

SF-1201 (4-60)

The filing time shown in the date line on domestic telegrams is LOCAL TIME at point of origin. Time of receipt is LOCAL TIME at point of destination

204P CST NOV 24 63 DC270 LA109
L AMA034 PD ALHAMBRA CALIF 24 1000AM PST
JACK RUBEY
CARE DALLAS JAIL DAL
I AS AN AMERICAN AM BACK OF YOU
CECILIA HAMILTON
(37).

WESTERN UNION TELEGRAM

W. P. MARSHALL, PRESIDENT

CLASS OF SERVICE: This is a fast message unless its deferred character is indicated by the proper symbol.

SYMBOLS: DL=Day Letter; NL=Night Letter; LT=International Letter Telegram

SF-1201 (4-60)

The filing time shown in the date line on domestic telegrams is LOCAL TIME at point of origin. Time of receipt is LOCAL TIME at point of destination

209P CST NOV 24 63 DB032 BA107
B LLM060 PD BOSTON MASS 24 239P EST
JACK RUBY
DONT FONE DLR CARE POLICE STATION DAL
CONGRATULATIONS. YOU DESERVE A MEDAL ALL THE WORLD IS IN BACK
OF YOU
N J WALDMAN DORCHESTER MASS
(52).

342

COMMISSION EXHIBIT No. 2003—Continued

WESTERN UNION TELEGRAM

W. P. MARSHALL, PRESIDENT

CLASS OF SERVICE: This is a fast message unless its deferred character is indicated by the proper symbol.

SYMBOLS: DL=Day Letter; NL=Night Letter; LT=International Letter Telegram

SF-1201 (4-60)

The filing time shown in the date line on domestic telegrams is LOCAL TIME at point of origin. Time of receipt is LOCAL TIME at point of destination

156P CST NOV 24 63 DC261 LA099
L BHA189 PD TDBH LOS ANGELES CALIF 24 100A PST
MR RUBY
DALLAS JAIL DAL
CONGRATULATIONS
MR AND MRS C H KINDRED
(04).

WESTERN UNION TELEGRAM

W. P. MARSHALL, PRESIDENT

CLASS OF SERVICE: This is a fast message unless its deferred character is indicated by the proper symbol.

SYMBOLS: DL=Day Letter; NL=Night Letter; LT=International Letter Telegram

SF-1201 (4-60)

T.G.P.

The filing time shown in the date line on domestic telegrams is LOCAL TIME at point of origin. Time of receipt is LOCAL TIME at point of destination

457P CST NOV 24 63 DB148 PA159
P ASA108 PD MANASQUAN NJER 24 330P EST
JACK RUBY
DALLAS POLICE HEADQUARTERS DAL
THANK GOD THERE IS ONE MAN IN AMERICA WHO KNOWS HOW TO DEAL
WITH PUNKS
THERESA BANNIGAN 428 EUCLID AVE MANASQUAN NJ
(38).

343

COMMISSION EXHIBIT No. 2003—Continued

WESTERN UNION TELEGRAM

CLASS OF SERVICE: This is a fast message unless its deferred character is indicated by the proper symbol.

W. P. MARSHALL, PRESIDENT — SF-1201 (4-60)

SYMBOLS: DL=Day Letter; NL=Night Letter; LT=International Letter Telegram

The filing time shown in the date line on domestic telegrams is LOCAL TIME at point of origin. Time of receipt is LOCAL TIME at point of destination

245P CST NOV 24 63 DB075
SYA091 SY TOA023 PD COHOES NY 24 332P EST
JACK RUBY
DALLAS TEXAS COUNTY JAIL DAL
CONGRATULATIONS THANK YOU
ED KANE CITY MARSHALL CITY OF COHOES NY
(32).

WESTERN UNION TELEGRAM

CLASS OF SERVICE: This is a fast message unless its deferred character is indicated by the proper symbol.

W. P. MARSHALL, PRESIDENT — SF-1201 (4-60)

SYMBOLS: DL=Day Letter; NL=Night Letter; LT=International Letter Telegram

The filing time shown in the date line on domestic telegrams is LOCAL TIME at point of origin. Time of receipt is LOCAL TIME at point of destination

148P CST NOV 24 63 DB003 PA105
P TDA169 CGN PD PHILADELPHIA PENN 24 1251P EST
JACK RUBY
DALLAS CITY JAIL DAL
CONGRATULATIONS MAY GOD BLESS YOU
MRS HARRY C WALSH
(51).

COMMISSION EXHIBIT No. 2003—Continued

WESTERN UNION TELEGRAM

CLASS OF SERVICE: This is a fast message unless its deferred character is indicated by the proper symbol.

W. P. MARSHALL, PRESIDENT — SF-1201 (4-60)

SYMBOLS: DL=Day Letter; NL=Night Letter; LT=International Letter Telegram

The filing time shown in the date line on domestic telegrams is LOCAL TIME at point of origin. Time of receipt is LOCAL TIME at point of destination

238P CST NOV 24 63 DB071 OA179
O PNA203 PD PASADENA CALIF 24 1225P PST
JACK RUBY RUBENSTEIN
CITY JAIL DAL
YOU HAVE ACCOMPLISHED SOMETHING THAT MILLIONS OF PEOPLE THROUGHOUT THE WORLD WOULD HAVE LOVED TO DO. IN SO DOING YOU HAVE EARNED YOURSELF A PLACE IN THE HISTORY OF THIS GREAT COUNTRY. I AM SURE THAT EVERYONE IN THE U.S. JOINS ME IN SAYING "THANK YOU" IF I CAN BE OF ANY HELP PLEASE HONOR ME WITH A CALL
JIM STONE PASADENA CALIF MURRAY 40282
(26).

WESTERN UNION TELEGRAM

CLASS OF SERVICE: This is a fast message unless its deferred character is indicated by the proper symbol.

W. P. MARSHALL, PRESIDENT — SF-1201 (4-60)

SYMBOLS: DL=Day Letter; NL=Night Letter; LT=International Letter Telegram

The filing time shown in the date line on domestic telegrams is LOCAL TIME at point of origin. Time of receipt is LOCAL TIME at point of destination

203P CST NOV 24 63 DB023
D LLM4 PD DALLAS TEX 24 105P CST
JACK RUBY
CITY JAIL DAL
DEAREST JACK, LOTS OF LUCK AND CONGRATULATIONS ON SHOOTING.
P.S. I USED TO WORK FOR YOU
VIRGINIA DITULLIO
(57).

COMMISSION EXHIBIT No. 2003—Continued

Class of Service — This is a fast message unless its deferred character is indicated by the proper symbol.

WESTERN UNION TELEGRAM

W. P. MARSHALL, PRESIDENT

SF-1201 (4-60)

Symbols — DL=Day Letter; NL=Night Letter; LT=International Letter Telegram

The filing time shown in the date line on domestic telegrams is LOCAL TIME at point of origin. Time of receipt is LOCAL TIME at point of destination

103P CST NOV 24 63 DE257 LA098
L LLA129 PD LOS ANGELES CALIF 24 942A PST
CHIEF OF POLICE
DAL
I WOULD LIKE TO PLEDGE $500 FOR THE DEFENSE OF THE MAN THAT
SHOT LEE OSWALD
JOHN E HUNTER 1421 WEST 45 ST LOS ANGELLS
(05).

Class of Service — This is a fast message unless its deferred character is indicated by the proper symbol.

WESTERN UNION TELEGRAM

W. P. MARSHALL, PRESIDENT

SF-1201 (4-60)

Symbols — DL=Day Letter; NL=Night Letter; LT=International Letter Telegram

The filing time shown in the date line on domestic telegrams is LOCAL TIME at point of origin. Time of receipt is LOCAL TIME at point of destination

224P CST NOV 24 63 DF007 OA162
O SJA142 PD TDSJ SANTA CLARA CALIF 24 1144A PST
JACK RUBINSTEIN
CARE DALLAS POLICE STATION DAL
COMMUNIST JUSTICE FOR A COMMUNIST THANK YOU I FEEL BETTER
ED LONG 293 MARIA ST SANTA CLARA CALIF.

Class of Service — This is a fast message unless its deferred character is indicated by the proper symbol.

WESTERN UNION TELEGRAM

W. P. MARSHALL, PRESIDENT

SF-1201 (4-60)

Symbols — DL=Day Letter; NL=Night Letter; LT=International Letter Telegram

The filing time shown in the date line on domestic telegrams is LOCAL TIME at point of origin. Time of receipt is LOCAL TIME at point of destination

CST NOV 24 63 DE244
SYA063 SY LLA062 CGN PD SYRACUSE NY 24 1259P EST
JACK RUBY, DALLAS CITY HALL
1963 NOV 24 PM 1 18
DAL
CONGRATULATIONS GOD BLESS YOU AND GOOD LUCK
MR AND MRS SAL ST ANGELO.

Class of Service — This is a fast message unless its deferred character is indicated by the proper symbol.

WESTERN UNION TELEGRAM

W. P. MARSHALL, PRESIDENT

SF-1201 (4-60)

Symbols — DL=Day Letter; NL=Night Letter; LT=International Letter Telegram

The filing time shown in the date line on domestic telegrams is LOCAL TIME at point of origin. Time of receipt is LOCAL TIME at point of destination

104P CST NOV 24 63 DE259
BA091 B QYA053 PD QUINCY MASS 24 107P EST
JOHN RUBY
DALLAS CITY JAIL DAI
CONGRATULATIONS
C C DECOSTE
(53).

Commission Exhibit No. 2003—Continued

WESTERN UNION TELEGRAM

W. P. MARSHALL, PRESIDENT

SF-1201 (4-60)

CLASS OF SERVICE: This is a fast message unless its deferred character is indicated by the proper symbol.

SYMBOLS: DL=Day Letter; NL=Night Letter; LT=International Letter Telegram

The filing time shown in the date line on domestic telegrams is LOCAL TIME at point of origin. Time of receipt is LOCAL TIME at point of destination

228P CST NOV 24 63 DB058 PA120
P RAA021 PD RAHWAY NJER 24 304P EST
JACK RUBY, NIGHT CLUB OWNER
CARE DALLAS POLICE HEADQUARTERS DAL
I KISS YOUR FEET BORN IN HUNGARY LOVE
KATHY BREWER
(05).

348

COMMISSION EXHIBIT No. 2003—Continued

WESTERN UNION TELEGRAM

W. P. MARSHALL, PRESIDENT

SF-1201 (4-60)

CLASS OF SERVICE: This is a fast message unless its deferred character is indicated by the proper symbol.

SYMBOLS: DL=Day Letter; NL=Night Letter; LT=International Letter Telegram

The filing time shown in the date line on domestic telegrams is LOCAL TIME at point of origin. Time of receipt is LOCAL TIME at point of destination

332P CST NOV 24 63 DF061
AA145 A KZA020 PD KEY WEST FLO 24 345P EST
JACK RUBY
CITY JAIL POLICE DEPT DAL
CONGRATULATIONS AND GOD BLESS YOU
GEORGE AND JACKIE FRANKLYN KEY WEST FLA

350

COMMISSION EXHIBIT No. 2003—Continued

WESTERN UNION TELEGRAM

W. P. MARSHALL, PRESIDENT

SF-1201 (4-60)

CLASS OF SERVICE: This is a fast message unless its deferred character is indicated by the proper symbol.

SYMBOLS: DL=Day Letter; NL=Night Letter; LT=International Letter Telegram

The filing time shown in the date line on domestic telegrams is LOCAL TIME at point of origin. Time of receipt is LOCAL TIME at point of destination

244P CST NOV 24 63 DB076
DEA094 DE LLA100 PD DETROIT MICH 24 247P EST
JACK RUBY
DALLAS COUNTY JAIL DAL
I KNOW YOU'RE WRONG IN WHAT YOU DID BUT PLEDGE MY SUPPORT
IN ANY WAY I CAN HELP
STUART WATSON 14100 SARASOTA DETROIT 39
(32).

349

COMMISSION EXHIBIT No. 2003—Continued

WESTERN UNION TELEGRAM

W. P. MARSHALL, PRESIDENT

SF-1201 (4-60)

CLASS OF SERVICE: This is a fast message unless its deferred character is indicated by the proper symbol.

SYMBOLS: DL=Day Letter; NL=Night Letter; LT=International Letter Telegram

The filing time shown in the date line on domestic telegrams is LOCAL TIME at point of origin. Time of receipt is LOCAL TIME at point of destination

1117A CST NOV 25 63 DG190
AA169 A PNA103 PD PENSACOLA FLO 25 1044A CST
JACK RUBY
DALLAS TEXAS JAIL DAL
IF YOU HAVE DIFFICULTY OBTAINING AN ATTORNEY TO REPRESENT YOU
IN YOUR CASE, I OFFER MY SERVICES.
DURING THE ALLEGED KLU KLUX DAYS, I, A JEW, REPRESENTED
A NEGRO WOMAN CHARGED WITH MAN SLAUGHTER, AFTER AN ALLEGED
ABORTION ON A VERY HIGH CLASS WHITE LADY. I WON THE CASE
J MONTROSE EDREHI SUITE 404, FIRST BANK & TRUST CO BLDG PENSACOLA
FLO
(52).

351

COMMISSION EXHIBIT No. 2003—Continued

CLASS OF SERVICE
This is a fast message unless its deferred character is indicated by the proper symbol.

WESTERN UNION
TELEGRAM
W. P. MARSHALL, PRESIDENT

SF-1201 (4-60)

SYMBOLS
DL=Day Letter
NL=Night Letter
LT=International Letter Telegram

The filing time shown in the date line on domestic telegrams is LOCAL TIME at point of origin. Time of receipt is LOCAL TIME at point of destination

929P CST NOV 24 63 DF289 LA352
L HPA253 NL PD HUNTINGTONPARK CALIF 24
JACK RUBY
DARE DALLAS CITY HALL DAL
WE FEEL YOU DID A VERY PATRIOTIC DEED IN REVENGING PRESIDENT KENNEDYS DEATH
DONALD BEAVSE AND FAMILY.

352

COMMISSION EXHIBIT No. 2003—Continued

CLASS OF SERVICE
This is a fast message unless its deferred character is indicated by the proper symbol.

WESTERN UNION
TELEGRAM
W. P. MARSHALL, PRESIDENT

SF-1201 (4-60)

SYMBOLS
DL=Day Letter
NL=Night Letter
LT=International Letter Telegram

The filing time shown in the date line on domestic telegrams is LOCAL TIME at point of origin. Time of receipt is LOCAL TIME at point of destination

733A CST NOV 25 63 DC059
SSB067 D CDU110 THLW 42 PD INGL CD BUENOSAIRES VIA WUCABLES
24 2330
LT JACK RUBISTEIN
CITY JAIL DAL
THANK YOU FOR DOING WHAT EVERY FREEDOM LOVING CITIZEN OF THE WORLD WANTED TO DO STOP WE WILL FORM FUND RAISING COMMITTEE TO HELP FINANCE YOUR DEFENSE STOP GOD BLESS YOU
MR AND MRS MARIO COHEN
(27).

353

COMMISSION EXHIBIT No. 2003—Continued

CLASS OF SERVICE
This is a fast message unless its deferred character is indicated by the proper symbol.

WESTERN UNION
TELEGRAM
W. P. MARSHALL, PRESIDENT

SF-1201 (4-60)

SYMBOLS
DL=Day Letter
NL=Night Letter
LT=International Letter Telegram

The filing time shown in the date line on domestic telegrams is LOCAL TIME at point of origin. Time of receipt is LOCAL TIME at point of destination

925P CST NOV 24 63 DF296
AA252 A LLA514 PD ATLANTA GA 24 1001P EST
JACK RUBINSTEIN, DALLAS CITY JAIL
DAL
CONGRATULATIONS FOR YOUR MOST HEROIC AND DYNAMIC ACT. IT TOOK GREAT COURAGE AND THOUGHT TO PERFORM THE ACT OF HEROISM WHICH YOU PERFORMED TODAY
LEON EPSTEIN
(15).

354

COMMISSION EXHIBIT No. 2003—Continued

QUICK SERVICE — **WESTERN UNION** — LOW RATES — Form 3NC (R5-61)

MONEY ORDER MESSAGE

Money Sent by Telegraph and Cable to All the World

W. P. MARSHALL, PRESIDENT

No. F ASAO34 — MF DALLAS, TEXAS (OFFICE) — NOV 24 1963 (DATE) 19

To JACK RUBY (MR., MRS. OR MISS)

DALLAS POLICE STATION (ADDRESS)

The Money Order paid you herewith is from ERA K DRAGOTTA (NAME)

at ASBURY PARK NJER (PLACE) and included the following message:

GET YOUR SELF A LAWYER WITH THIS WILL SEND ALL YOU NEED

THE WESTERN UNION TELEGRAPH COMPANY

THIS ORDER MAY BE CASHED BY ANYONE TO WHOM THE PAYEE IS KNOWN

WESTERN UNION MONEY ORDER — 32-1/1110

ISSUED AT ______ (CITY, ST.) ______ (DATE) 19__

PAY TO JACK RUBY ______ OR ORDER

THE SUM OF [illegible] HUNDRED AND NO/100 ---- DOLLARS $100.00

ASBURY PARK NJER NOV 24 1963 (ORIGINATING POINT) 19__ (DATE) UN15834

THE WESTERN UNION TELEGRAPH COMPANY

FIRST NATIONAL BANK IN DALLAS, DALLAS, TEXAS

COUNTERSIGNED [signature] (MONEY ORDER AGENT) — L. G. Aldred (TREASURER)

⑆1110⑆0001⑆ 00⑈0230⑈3⑈

355

COMMISSION EXHIBIT NO. 2003—Continued

QUICK SERVICE — **WESTERN UNION** — LOW RATES — Form 3NC (R5-61)

MONEY ORDER MESSAGE

Money Sent by Telegraph and Cable to All the World

W. P. MARSHALL, PRESIDENT

No. [illegible] — MF DALLAS, TEXAS (OFFICE) — NOV 24 1963 (DATE) 19

To JACK RUBY (MR., MRS. OR MISS)

CARE CITY JAIL (ADDRESS)

The Money Order paid you herewith is from PAUL L COMPERTHWAITE (NAME)

at LOS ANGELES CALIF (PLACE) and included the following message:

CONGRATULATIONS FOR ELIMINATING A RAT AND DOING THE COUNTRY A

A SERVICE MONEY IS TO HELP PROCURE A LAWYER

THE WESTERN UNION TELEGRAPH COMPANY

THIS ORDER MAY BE CASHED BY ANYONE TO WHOM THE PAYEE IS KNOWN

WESTERN UNION MONEY ORDER — 32-1/1110

ISSUED AT [illegible] (CITY AND STATE) NOV 24 1963 (DATE) 19__

PAY TO JACK RUBY ______ OR ORDER

THE SUM OF [illegible] ---------- DOLLARS $[illegible].00

TELEGRAPHED FROM [illegible] CALIF NOV 24 19 63 (ORIGINATING POINT, DATE) UN15860

THE WESTERN UNION TELEGRAPH COMPANY

FIRST NATIONAL BANK IN DALLAS, DALLAS, TEXAS

COUNTERSIGNED [signature] (MONEY ORDER AGENT) — L. G. Aldred (TREASURER)

⑆1110⑆0001⑆ 00⑈0230⑈3⑈

356

COMMISSION EXHIBIT NO. 2003—Continued

WESTERN UNION TELEGRAM
W. P. MARSHALL, PRESIDENT

CLASS OF SERVICE: This is a fast message unless its deferred character is indicated by the proper symbol.

SYMBOLS: DL=Day Letter; NL=Night Letter; LT=International Letter Telegram

SF-1201 (4-60)

The filing time shown in the date line on domestic telegrams is LOCAL TIME at point of origin. Time of receipt is LOCAL TIME at point of destination

246P CST NOV 24 63 DC326
SYA092 SY LLB145 PD SYRACUSE NY 24 315P EST
JACK RUBY
CITY JAIL DAL
YOU HAVE DONE WHAT MANY OF US HAVE WANTED TO DO
ARTHUR STASKO
(34).

WESTERN UNION TELEGRAM
W. P. MARSHALL, PRESIDENT

CLASS OF SERVICE: This is a fast message unless its deferred character is indicated by the proper symbol.

SYMBOLS: DL=Day Letter; NL=Night Letter; LT=International Letter Telegram

SF-1201 (4-60)

The filing time shown in the date line on domestic telegrams is LOCAL TIME at point of origin. Time of receipt is LOCAL TIME at point of destination

300P CST NOV 24 63 DF042 MA068
M CE101 PD CHICAGO ILL 24 216P CST
JACK RUBY
CAROUSEL LOUNGE DAL
WELL DONE SOLDIER MISSION ACCOMPLISHED
CARL C DEWEY MASTER SGT UNITED STATES ARMY
(28).

357

COMMISSION EXHIBIT No. 2003—Continued

WESTERN UNION TELEGRAM
W. P. MARSHALL, PRESIDENT

CLASS OF SERVICE: This is a fast message unless its deferred character is indicated by the proper symbol.

SYMBOLS: DL=Day Letter; NL=Night Letter; LT=International Letter Telegram

SF-1201 (4-60)

The filing time shown in the date line on domestic telegrams is LOCAL TIME at point of origin. Time of receipt is LOCAL TIME at point of destination

253P CST NOV 24 63 DC312 KA117
K LLD128 PD KANSAS CITY MO 24 140P CST
JACK RUBY
CITY JAIL DAL
YOUR ACT WAS NOT THE AMERICAN WAY TO DO IT NEITHER WAS THE
DISTORTEDLY ACT OF OSWALD AFTER 48 HOURS OF SHAME I AM AGAIN
PROUD TO BE AN AMERICAN TEXAS I'M SURE MY SENTIMENTS ARE FELT
BY OTHER AMERICANS GOOD LUCK
BOB CAIN
(59).

WESTERN UNION TELEGRAM
W. P. MARSHALL, PRESIDENT

CLASS OF SERVICE: This is a fast message unless its deferred character is indicated by the proper symbol.

SYMBOLS: DL=Day Letter; NL=Night Letter; LT=International Letter Telegram

SF-1201 (4-60)

The filing time shown in the date line on domestic telegrams is LOCAL TIME at point of origin. Time of receipt is LOCAL TIME at point of destination

225P CST NOV 24 63 DF008 OA163
O LBA093 PD LONG BEACH CALIF 24 1145A PST
JACK RUBY
DALLAS POLICE DEPT DAL
TO A JOB WELL DONE I KNOW THERE MUST BE MANY PEOPLE WHO FEEL
THE SAME AS I DO YOU ARE A GREAT MAN JACK RUBY
BILL OWENS.

358

COMMISSION EXHIBIT No. 2003—Continued

CLASS OF SERVICE
This is a fast message unless its deferred character is indicated by the proper symbol.

WESTERN UNION TELEGRAM
W. P. MARSHALL, PRESIDENT

SF-1201 (4-60)

SYMBOLS
DL=Day Letter
NL=Night Letter
LT=International Letter Telegram

The filing time shown in the date line on domestic telegrams is LOCAL TIME at point of origin. Time of receipt is LOCAL TIME at point of destination

1258P CST NOV 24 63 DE250
CEA054 DE TNA039 6 ONT ZE PICKERING ONT 24 108P EST
JACK RUBY
DALLAS COUNTY JAIL DALLAS TEX
THANKS AND A DEBT OF GRATITUDE
HAROLD L GARDINER.

CLASS OF SERVICE
This is a fast message unless its deferred character is indicated by the proper symbol.

WESTERN UNION TELEGRAM
W. P. MARSHALL, PRESIDENT

SF-1201 (4-60)

SYMBOLS
DL=Day Letter
NL=Night Letter
LT=International Letter Telegram

The filing time shown in the date line on domestic telegrams is LOCAL TIME at point of origin. Time of receipt is LOCAL TIME at point of destination

223P CST NOV 24 63 DF014
D LLM18 CGN PD DALLAS TEX 24 209P CST
LEON RUBENSTEIN
DALLAS CITY JAIL DAL
CONGRATULATIONS HAD I THE GUTS I'D HAVE DONE IT THANKS FOR
TRYING TO VINDICATE DALLAS
FARMERS BRANCH COWARD
(13).

359

COMMISSION EXHIBIT No. 2003—Continued

CLASS OF SERVICE
This is a fast message unless its deferred character is indicated by the proper symbol.

WESTERN UNION TELEGRAM
W. P. MARSHALL, PRESIDENT

SF-1201 (4-60)

SYMBOLS
DL=Day Letter
NL=Night Letter
LT=International Letter Telegram

The filing time shown in the date line on domestic telegrams is LOCAL TIME at point of origin. Time of receipt is LOCAL TIME at point of destination 16

1963 NOV 24

CST NOV 24 63 DE225 MA056
M CF059 PD CHICAGO ILL 24 1154A CST
JACK RUBY
THE DALLAS TEXAS COURT HOUSE BASEMENT DAL
CONGRATULATIONS - YOU HAD THE COURAGE TO DO WHAT THE REST OF
THE WORLD WOULD LIKE TO HAVE DONE
MRS G F GAGE 2151 EAST 68 STREET
(02).

CLASS OF SERVICE
This is a fast message unless its deferred character is indicated by the proper symbol.

WESTERN UNION TELEGRAM
W. P. MARSHALL, PRESIDENT

SF-1201 (4-60)

SYMBOLS
DL=Day Letter
NL=Night Letter
LT=International Letter Telegram

The filing time shown in the date line on domestic telegrams is LOCAL TIME at point of origin. Time of receipt is LOCAL TIME at point of destination

223P CST NOV 24 63 DD299
SYA086 SY NB443 RX PD NEW YORK NY 24 207P EST
MR RUBY
COUNTY JAIL DALLAS TEX
GOD BLESS YOU FOR YOUR HEROIC DEED YOU HAVE VINDICATED THE
PEOPLE OF THE GREAT CITY OF DALLAS AND OF THE NATION
MR AND MRS CHARLES SMITH BRONX NY.
(40).

360

COMMISSION EXHIBIT No. 2003—Continued

CLASS OF SERVICE
This is a fast message unless its deferred character is indicated by the proper symbol.

WESTERN UNION TELEGRAM

W. P. MARSHALL, PRESIDENT

SF-1201 (4-60)

SYMBOLS
DL=Day Letter
NL=Night Letter
LT=International Letter Telegram

The filing time shown in the date line on domestic telegrams is LOCAL TIME at point of origin. Time of receipt is LOCAL TIME at point of destination

241P CST NOV 24 63 DF022
D MDA020 PD MIDLAND-TEX 24 158P CST
JACK RUBY
DALLAS COUNTY JAIL DAL
DEAR JACK. WILL ARRIVE DALLAS THIS PM WILL HELP WITH LEGAL
COUNCIL ANYWAY I CAN. YOU KILLED THE SNAKE
SAM
(17).

CLASS OF SERVICE
This is a fast message unless its deferred character is indicated by the proper symbol.

WESTERN UNION TELEGRAM

W. P. MARSHALL, PRESIDENT

SF-1201 (4-60)

SYMBOLS
DL=Day Letter
NL=Night Letter
LT=International Letter Telegram

The filing time shown in the date line on domestic telegrams is LOCAL TIME at point of origin. Time of receipt is LOCAL TIME at point of destination

224P CST NOV 24 63 DB051 CTA116
CT AKA140 PD AKRON OHIO 24 229P EST
JACK RUBY DALLAS CITY JAIL
DAL
CONGRATULATIONS HISTORY WILL RECORD SOUTHERN JUSTICE AS THE
RIGHTER OF THIS DESPICABLE TRAGEDY HIGHEST REGARDS
JOE CURRIER
(34).

361

COMMISSION EXHIBIT No. 2003—Continued

CLASS OF SERVICE
This is a fast message unless its deferred character is indicated by the proper symbol.

WESTERN UNION TELEGRAM

W. P. MARSHALL, PRESIDENT

SF-1201 (4-60)

SYMBOLS
DL=Day Letter
NL=Night Letter
LT=International Letter Telegram

The filing time shown in the date line on domestic telegrams is LOCAL TIME at point of origin. Time of receipt is LOCAL TIME at point of destination

245P CST NOV 24 63 DC522 LA148
L BHA242 PD BEVERLY HILLS CALIF 24 1230P PST
JACK RUBY
DALLAS JAIL DAL
GOD BLESS YOU. PLEASE FEEL FREE TO CALL UPON MISS LAWSON FOR
ANY HELP NEEDED IN YOUR CLUB FREE OF CHARGE AT ANY TIME. SINGER.
EX-DANCER THANK YOU VERY. MUCH
MISS A L LAWSON 9187 BURTON WAY BEVERLY HILLS CALIF
(34).

CLASS OF SERVICE
This is a fast message unless its deferred character is indicated by the proper symbol.

WESTERN UNION TELEGRAM

W. P. MARSHALL, PRESIDENT

SF-1201 (4-60)

SYMBOLS
DL=Day Letter
NL=Night Letter
LT=International Letter Telegram

The filing time shown in the date line on domestic telegrams is LOCAL TIME at point of origin. Time of receipt is LOCAL TIME at point of destination

241P CST NOV 24 63 DG006
D LLR54 PD DALLAS TEX 24 237P CST
SENDER WAITING
JACK RUBY
CITY JAIL DAL
IF THERE IS ANYTHING WE CAN DO OR HELP IN ANY WAY NOTIFY 4617
SAMUELS. EVERGREEN 11560
WALLY WESTON
(40).

362

COMMISSION EXHIBIT No. 2003—Continued

WESTERN UNION TELEGRAM

W. P. MARSHALL, PRESIDENT

CLASS OF SERVICE: This is a fast message unless its deferred character is indicated by the proper symbol.

SYMBOLS: DL=Day Letter; NL=Night Letter; LT=International Letter Telegram

SF-1201 (4-60)

The filing time shown in the date line on domestic telegrams is LOCAL TIME at point of origin. Time of receipt is LOCAL TIME at point of destination

142P CST NOV 24 63 DE235

SYA077 SY BUA205 CGN PD BUFFALO NY 24 154P EST

JACK RUBY

CARE DALLAS COUNTY JAIL DAL

CONGRATULATIONS MR RUBY YOU REDEEMED THE STATE OF TEXAS

CAROL DEANE BRUNDO BUFFALO NY.

WESTERN UNION TELEGRAM

W. P. MARSHALL, PRESIDENT

CLASS OF SERVICE: This is a fast message unless its deferred character is indicated by the proper symbol.

SYMBOLS: DL=Day Letter; NL=Night Letter; LT=International Letter Telegram

The filing time shown in the date line on domestic telegrams is LOCAL TIME at point of origin. Time of receipt is LOCAL TIME at point of destination

NOV 24 63 DG057 PA149

P NB216 PD NEW YORK NY 24 320P EST

JACK RUBINSTEIN

CARE CAROUSEL DALLAS TEX

1963 NOV 24 PM 5 05

CONGRATULATIONS

ONS ON YOUR COURAGE FOR THE BRAVE DEED YOU PERFORMED THE FINGER

OF ALL THE NATIONWAS ON THE TRIGER YOU PULLED TODAY

THE BOYS THE MCLEANS BAR AND GRILL

WESTERN UNION TELEGRAM

W. P. MARSHALL, PRESIDENT

CLASS OF SERVICE: This is a fast message unless its deferred character is indicated by the proper symbol.

SYMBOLS: DL=Day Letter; NL=Night Letter; LT=International Letter Telegram

SF-1201 (4-60)

The filing time shown in the date line on domestic telegrams is LOCAL TIME at point of origin. Time of receipt is LOCAL TIME at point of destination

253P CST NOV 24 63 DG005.

AA158 A JNA266 PD JACKSONVILLE FLO 24 300P EST

JACK RUBY, CARE DALLAS POLICE HEADQUARTERS

DAL

THANK YOU. MAY THE LORD AND TEXAS JUSTICE HAVE MERCY ON YOU.

MAY YOU LIVE TO BE A THOUSAND SINCERELY YOURS.

A D PEEPLES

(59).

363

WESTERN UNION TELEGRAM

W. P. MARSHALL, PRESIDENT

CLASS OF SERVICE: This is a fast message unless its deferred character is indicated by the proper symbol.

SYMBOLS: DL=Day Letter; NL=Night Letter; LT=International Letter Telegram

SF-1201 (4-60)

The filing time shown in the date line on domestic telegrams is LOCAL TIME at point of origin. Time of receipt is LOCAL TIME at point of destination

229P CST NOV 24 63 DB060

SSB252 D AUA135 PD AUSTIN TEX 24 155P CST

CECIL RUBY

CARE CITY POL DAL

CONGRATULATIONS WISH YOU LUCK

ALBERT JOSEPH

2201 MANOR RD

(00).

364

COMMISSION EXHIBIT No. 2003—Continued

COMMISSION EXHIBIT No. 2003—Continued

WESTERN UNION TELEGRAM

W. P. MARSHALL, PRESIDENT

CLASS OF SERVICE: This is a fast message unless its deferred character is indicated by the proper symbol.

SYMBOLS: DL=Day Letter; NL=Night Letter; LT=International Letter Telegram

SF-1201 (4-60)

The filing time shown in the date line on domestic telegrams is LOCAL TIME at point of origin. Time of receipt is LOCAL TIME at point of destination

151P CST NOV 24 63 DB008

SYA082 SY TOA021 PD COHOES NY 24 238P EST

JACK RUBY

DAL

THANK YOU MY FRIEND AND FELLOW AMERICAN YOURS TRULY

JOHN C HALLORAN

(44).

WESTERN UNION TELEGRAM

W. P. MARSHALL, PRESIDENT

CLASS OF SERVICE: This is a fast message unless its deferred character is indicated by the proper symbol.

SYMBOLS: DL=Day Letter; NL=Night Letter; LT=International Letter Telegram

SF-1201 (4-60) T6P

The filing time shown in the date line on domestic telegrams is LOCAL TIME at point of origin. Time of receipt is LOCAL TIME at point of destination

NOV 24 63 DF073 OA212

O SDA226 PD TDSD LA JOLLA CALIF 24 127P PST

1963 NOV 24 PM 5 03

JACK RUBY

CITY JAIL CARE CAPTAIN WILL FRITZ DAL

OUR THOUGHTS ARE WITH YOU WILL VOUCH FOR YOUR CHARACTER ANY

TIME LOVE

HAL AND PAULINE COLLINS

(30).

WESTERN UNION TELEGRAM

W. P. MARSHALL, PRESIDENT

CLASS OF SERVICE: This is a fast message unless its deferred character is indicated by the proper symbol.

SYMBOLS: DL=Day Letter; NL=Night Letter; LT=International Letter Telegram

SF-1201 (4-60) T6P

The filing time shown in the date line on domestic telegrams is LOCAL TIME at point of origin. Time of receipt is LOCAL TIME at point of destination

CST NOV 24 63 DC264

1963 NOV 24 PM 2 07

BAC93 B LLJ022 PD TDB BRAINTREE MASS 24 151P EST

JACK RUBY

CARE DALLAS POLICE DEPT DAL

CONGRATULATIONS WE HOPE

HE DOESNT DIE JUST SUFFERS

W HARRIS AND A TANGHERLINI 82 MIDDLE ST BRAINTREE

(35).

COMMISSION EXHIBIT No. 2003—Continued

WESTERN UNION TELEGRAM

W. P. MARSHALL, PRESIDENT

CLASS OF SERVICE: This is a fast message unless its deferred character is indicated by the proper symbol.

SYMBOLS: DL=Day Letter; NL=Night Letter; LT=International Letter Telegram

SF-1201 (4-60) T6P

The filing time shown in the date line on domestic telegrams is LOCAL TIME at point of origin. Time of receipt is LOCAL TIME at point of destination

504P CST NOV 24 63 DC401 PA173

P TNA307 PD TDTN MARLTON NJER 24 305P EST

JACK RUBENSTEIN, CARE POLICE CHIEF JESSIE CURRY DAL

OUR FAMILY CANNOT FIND IT IN OUR HEARTS TO CENSOR YOU. WE SEND

YOU ALL OUR LOVE AND SUPPORT

JEAN SCATTERGOOD

(40).

COMMISSION EXHIBIT No. 2003—Continued

WESTERN UNION TELEGRAM

W. P. MARSHALL, PRESIDENT

CLASS OF SERVICE: This is a fast message unless its deferred character is indicated by the proper symbol.

SYMBOLS: DL=Day Letter; NL=Night Letter; LT=International Letter Telegram

SF-1201 (4-60)

The filing time shown in the date line on domestic telegrams is LOCAL TIME at point of origin. Time of receipt is LOCAL TIME at point of destination

200P CST NOV 24 63 DC265 LA102
L AHA028 PD CNG
ALHAMBRA CALIF 24 1015A PST
JACK RUBY
CAROUSEL LOUNGE NIGHT CLUB
DAL
CONGRATULATIONS
JOHN M SMITH
(15).

WESTERN UNION TELEGRAM

W. P. MARSHALL, PRESIDENT

CLASS OF SERVICE: This is a fast message unless its deferred character is indicated by the proper symbol.

SYMBOLS: DL=Day Letter; NL=Night Letter; LT=International Letter Telegram

SF-1201 (4-60)

The filing time shown in the date line on domestic telegrams is LOCAL TIME at point of origin. Time of receipt is LOCAL TIME at point of destination

NOV 24 63 DC2)4 OA133
O P CST
151

LBA075 PD LONG BEACH CALIF 24 1042A PST
JACK RUBY
DALLAS CITY JAL DAL
WELL DONE CONGRATULATIONS
FRANK GOODELL 13342 EL DORADO DR APT 191J LEISURE WORLD

367

COMMISSION EXHIBIT No. 2003—Continued

WESTERN UNION TELEGRAM

W. P. MARSHALL, PRESIDENT

CLASS OF SERVICE: This is a fast message unless its deferred character is indicated by the proper symbol.

SYMBOLS: DL=Day Letter; NL=Night Letter; LT=International Letter Telegram

SF-1201 (4-60)

The filing time shown in the date line on domestic telegrams is LOCAL TIME at point of origin. Time of receipt is LOCAL TIME at point of destination

CST NOV 24 63 DB005 PRA031
PR SEA142 PD SEATTLE WASH 24 1134A PST
JACK RUBY

1963 NOV 24 PM 2 06

DALLAS CITY JAIL DAL
CONGRATULATIONS YOU HAVE EXPRESSED AND ACCOMPLISHED WHAT THE AMERICAN PEOPLE FEEL IN OUR GREAT HOUR OF SADNESS
BETTY RAHCE
(43)

WESTERN UNION TELEGRAM

W. P. MARSHALL, PRESIDENT

CLASS OF SERVICE: This is a fast message unless its deferred character is indicated by the proper symbol.

SYMBOLS: DL=Day Letter; NL=Night Letter; LT=International Letter Telegram

SF-1201 (4-60)

The filing time shown in the date line on domestic telegrams is LOCAL TIME at point of origin. Time of receipt is LOCAL TIME at point of destination

200P CST NOV 24 63 DB019
SYA085 SY HVA104 CGN PD PLAINVIEW NY 24 235P EST
JACK RUBY
DALLAS TEXAS CITY JAIL DAL
CONGRATULATIONS JOB WELL DONE. GOD BLESS YOU
LEO FEINSTEIN 7 NAUTILUS AVE PLAINVIEW NY
(40).

368

COMMISSION EXHIBIT No. 2003—Continued

CLASS OF SERVICE
This is a fast message unless its deferred character is indicated by the proper symbol.

WESTERN UNION
TELEGRAM
W. P. MARSHALL, PRESIDENT

SYMBOLS
DL=Day Letter
NL=Night Letter
LT=International Letter Telegram

The filing time shown in the date line on domestic telegrams is LOCAL TIME at point of origin. Time of receipt is LOCAL TIME at point of destination

(SUSPECTED DUPLICATE)

DC254 OA133
O LBA075 PD LONG BEACH CALIF 24 1042A PST
JACK RUBY
DALLAS CITY JAIL DAL
WELL DONE CONGRATULATIONS
FRANK GOODELL 13342 EL DORADO DR APT 191J LEISURE WORLD

CLASS OF SERVICE
This is a fast message unless its deferred character is indicated by the proper symbol.

WESTERN UNION
TELEGRAM
W. P. MARSHALL, PRESIDENT
SF-1201 (4-60)

SYMBOLS
DL=Day Letter
NL=Night Letter
LT=International Letter Telegram

The filing time shown in the date line on domestic telegrams is LOCAL TIME at point of origin. Time of receipt is LOCAL TIME at point of destination

208P CST NOV 24 63 DC275
SSB231 D FWA182 CGN PD FORT WORTH TEX 24 125P CST
MR RUBY
POLICE DEPT DAL
CONGRATULATIONS
JIM RHODES

NTO MR RUBY
(08).

369

COMMISSION EXHIBIT No. 2003—Continued

CLASS OF SERVICE
This is a fast message unless its deferred character is indicated by the proper symbol.

WESTERN UNION
TELEGRAM
W. P. MARSHALL, PRESIDENT
SF-1201 (4-60)

SYMBOLS
DL=Day Letter
NL=Night Letter
LT=International Letter Telegram

The filing time shown in the date line on domestic telegrams is LOCAL TIME at point of origin. Time of receipt is LOCAL TIME at point of destination

NOV 24 63 DG179 OA307
O FVA164 PD FRESNO CALIF 24 529P PST
1963 NOV 24 PM 8 23
JACK RUBY
COUNTY JAIL DAL
MY PRAYERS ARE WITH YOU YOU DID WHAT EVERY AMERICAN WANTED TO DO. I AM A REPUBLICAN THIS WAS JUSTIFIABLE HOMICIDE
MARY A JOHNSON.

CLASS OF SERVICE
This is a fast message unless its deferred character is indicated by the proper symbol.

WESTERN UNION
TELEGRAM
W. P. MARSHALL, PRESIDENT
SF-1201 (4-60)
TGP

SYMBOLS
DL=Day Letter
NL=Night Letter
LT=International Letter Telegram

The filing time shown in the date line on domestic telegrams is LOCAL TIME at point of origin. Time of receipt is LOCAL TIME at point of destination

1012P CST NOV 24 63 DG288 LA372
L LLE077 NL PD TDL SOUTHGATE CALIF 24
JACK RUBY
CARE CHIEF OF POLICE DAL
CONGRATULATIONS ON A JOB WELL DONEYOUR ACTIN WHILE NOT WHOLLY CONDONED BY US IS EASILY UNDERSTOOD MAY WE WISH YOU THE BEST OF LUCK IN WHATEVER IS NOW TO BEFALL YOU
BOB BILL AND PETE SOUTHGATE CALIF.

370

COMMISSION EXHIBIT No. 2003—Continued

WESTERN UNION TELEGRAM

W. P. MARSHALL, PRESIDENT

CLASS OF SERVICE: This is a fast message unless its deferred character is indicated by the proper symbol.

SYMBOLS: DL=Day Letter; NL=Night Letter; LT=International Letter Telegram

SF-1201 (4-60)

The filing time shown in the date line on domestic telegrams is LOCAL TIME at point of origin. Time of receipt is LOCAL TIME at point of destination

```
636P CST NOV 24 63 DG125
DEA156 DE TNA073 17 NL ONT FD TORONTO ONT 24
JACK RUBY CARE DALLAS CITY JAIT  DALLAS TEXAS
CONGRATULATIONS YOU HAVE DONE WHAT EVERY LOYAL AMERICAN CITIZEN
WOULD LIKE TO HAVE DONE GOD BLESS YOU
 MRS MURIEL PIERCE WILLOWDALE ONT.
```

WESTERN UNION TELEGRAM

W. P. MARSHALL, PRESIDENT

CLASS OF SERVICE: This is a fast message unless its deferred character is indicated by the proper symbol.

SYMBOLS: DL=Day Letter; NL=Night Letter; LT=International Letter Telegram

SF-1201 (4-60)

The filing time shown in the date line on domestic telegrams is LOCAL TIME at point of origin. Time of receipt is LOCAL TIME at point of destination

```
        NOV 24 63 DG303
SA133  S LLG877 NL PD ST LOUIS MO 24            1963 NOV 24 PM 11 27
JACK RUBY
  CARE DALLAS CHEIFOF POLICE DAL
THE AMERICAN SOCIETY OF AUCTIONEERS LAUDS YOUR CORAGEOUS ACTION.
WE ARE 100 PERCENT BEHIND YOU. OUR MEMBERSHIP CONSISTS OF MEMBERS
IN ALL THE 50 STATES OF AMERICA
  COL JACK STINSON PRES AMERICAN SOCIETY OF AUCTIONEERS.
```

371

COMMISSION EXHIBIT No. 2003—Continued

WESTERN UNION TELEGRAM

W. P. MARSHALL, PRESIDENT

CLASS OF SERVICE: This is a fast message unless its deferred character is indicated by the proper symbol.

SYMBOLS: DL=Day Letter; NL=Night Letter; LT=International Letter Telegram

SF-1201 (4-60)

The filing time shown in the date line on domestic telegrams is LOCAL TIME at point of origin. Time of receipt is LOCAL TIME at point of destination

```
1222A CST NOV 25 63 DC010 CTA250
 CT LLA67 NL PD CINCINNATI OHIO 24
JACK RUBY
  CARE POLICE DAL
DURING THIS PERIOD OF UNAMINOUS BEREAVEMENT FOR OUR BELOVED
 PRESIDENT KENNEDY. YOUR ACTION WAS REFLECTION OF EVERY RED
 BLOODED AMERICANS FEELINGS. TO OBLITERATE THE MONSTER WHICH
HOUSED IDIOTIC SMIRKING FACE AND TWISTED MIND OF THE ASSASSIN
WOULD SEEM TO BE LIKE KILLING A WILD ANIMAL. HOWEVER AS A CIVILIZED
AND DEMCORATIC PEOPLE WE MUST TEMPER EMOTIONS WITH REASONING
AND COMMON SENSE THE ADMINISTRATION OF JUSTICE IS FOR THE COURTS
OF JUSTICE NOT THE INDIVIDUALS
  ORIVLLE GADD SYMPATHIZER 9671 WINTON RD CINCINNATI 31 OHIO.
```

WESTERN UNION TELEGRAM

W. P. MARSHALL, PRESIDENT

CLASS OF SERVICE: This is a fast message unless its deferred character is indicated by the proper symbol.

SYMBOLS: DL=Day Letter; NL=Night Letter; LT=International Letter Telegram

SF-1201 (4-60)

The filing time shown in the date line on domestic telegrams is LOCAL TIME at point of origin. Time of receipt is LOCAL TIME at point of destination

```
1244P CST NOV 24 63 DE252 CTA093
 CT CZA125 PD COLUMBUS OHIO 24 115P EST
JACK RUBY
  COUNTY JAIL DAL
CONGRATULATIONS AM SORRY YOU DIDN'T KILL HIM
  CARL DUNCAN 391 MAPLEWOOD AVE COLUMBUS OHIO
(19).
```

372

COMMISSION EXHIBIT No. 2003—Continued

WESTERN UNION TELEGRAM
W. P. MARSHALL, PRESIDENT

CLASS OF SERVICE: This is a fast message unless its deferred character is indicated by the proper symbol.

SYMBOLS: DL=Day Letter; NL=Night Letter; LT=International Letter Telegram

SF-1201 (4-60)

The filing time shown in the date line on domestic telegrams is LOCAL TIME at point of origin. Time of receipt is LOCAL TIME at point of destination

1218P CST NOV 24 63 DC215 BA084
B LLC029 PD BOSTON MASS 24 1245P EST
JACK RUBY
DALLAS TEXAS POLICE STATION DAL
GOOD BOY CONGRATULATIONS GOD BLESS YOU
TOMM HANTAKAS 31 CLAYBOURNE ST DORCHESTER MASS
(38).

WESTERN UNION TELEGRAM
W. P. MARSHALL, PRESIDENT

1115P CST NOV 24 63 DC562 KA301
K DVA746 PD DENVER COLO 24 946P MST
JACK RUBENSTEIN
DALLAS POLICE DEPT DAL
CONGRATULATIONS HOPE YOU RECEIVE CONGRESSIONAL MEDAL OF HONOR
PAT MCNAMARA
(12).

373

WESTERN UNION TELEGRAM
W. P. MARSHALL, PRESIDENT

1241P CST NOV 24 63 DC238
BPA089 D P JRB013 PD
JERSEYCITY NJER 24 1247P EST
CAROUSEL BAR
DAL
CONGRATULATIONS
AMBLE INN BAYONNE NJ
(59).

WESTERN UNION TELEGRAM
W. P. MARSHALL, PRESIDENT

1213P CST NOV 24 63 DE210
SYA055 SY PCA028 PD WEST SAYVILLE NY 24 1251P EST
JACK RUBIN
DALLAS JAIL DAL
CONGRATULATIONS YOU DESERVE A MEDAL NOT A JAIL CELL
DOROTHY FAZZINO
(53).

374

WESTERN UNION TELEGRAM

W. P. MARSHALL, PRESIDENT

CLASS OF SERVICE: This is a fast message unless its deferred character is indicated by the proper symbol.

SYMBOLS: DL=Day Letter; NL=Night Letter; LT=International Letter Telegram

The filing time shown in the date line on domestic telegrams is LOCAL TIME at point of origin. Time of receipt is LOCAL TIME at point of destination

1259P CST NOV 24 63 DC235 PRA020
PR SEA098 PD SEATTLE WASH 24 958A PST
JACK RUBY
CARE CARASEL NIGHT CLUB DAL
THANK YOU
MARY AND JOANN
(14).

WESTERN UNION TELEGRAM

W. P. MARSHALL, PRESIDENT

SF-1201 (4-60)

1246P CST NOV 24 63 DC246 OA129
O RNA007 PD TDRN VCOTTONWOOD CALIF 24 1035A PST
JACK RUBY
CARE DALLAS CITY JAIL DAL
YOU ASKED YOURSELF WHAT YOU COULD DO FOR YOUR COUNTRY AND YOU FOUND THE ANSWER BY SHOOTING THE DESPICABLE TRAITOR WHO KILLED OUR LEADER. YOU ARE A HERO, MR. RUBY. CONGRATULATIONS TO YOU
TOM AND DOROTHY PFIITZNER STAR ROUTE 1 COTTONWOOD CALIF

IN SIG PFIITZNER PPC
(36).

375

COMMISSION EXHIBIT No. 2003—Continued

WESTERN UNION TELEGRAM

W. P. MARSHALL, PRESIDENT

SF-1201 (4-60)

1242P CST NOV 24 63 DC259 RA047
R WA168 PD TDAX TDW HYATTSVILLE VIR 24 1250P EST
JACK RUBY
DALLAS CITY JAIL DAL
YOU ARE OUR HERO
SHELBY MCCLELLAN WHO DEARLY LOVED OUR PRESIDENT
(24).

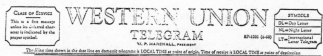

WESTERN UNION TELEGRAM

W. P. MARSHALL, PRESIDENT

SF-1201 (4-60)

CST NOV 24 63 DC193 PRA014
PR WEA004 CGN PD TDWE DRYDEN WASH 24 947A PST 1963 NOV 24 PM 12 44
JACK RUBY
DALLAS CITY JAIL DAL
CONGRATULATIONS AND GOD BLESS YOU
GARY OWEN
(47).

376

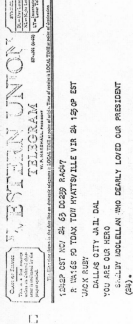

COMMISSION EXHIBIT No. 2003—Continued

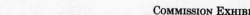

WESTERN UNION
TELEGRAM
W. P. MARSHALL, PRESIDENT

CLASS OF SERVICE: This is a fast message unless its deferred character is indicated by the proper symbol.

SYMBOLS: DL=Day Letter; NL=Night Letter; LT=International Letter Telegram

SF-1201 (4-60)

The filing time shown in the date line on domestic telegrams is LOCAL TIME at point of origin. Time of receipt is LOCAL TIME at point of destination

1214P CST NOV 24 63 DC210
SYA054 SY BUA166 PD BUFFALO NY 24 1250P EST
JACK RUBY
DALLAS JAIL DAL
CONGRATULATIONS FOR SHOOTING OSWALD
MRS COLOSI 4
VANWYCK BUFFALO NY.

377

COMMISSION EXHIBIT No. 2003—Continued

WESTERN UNION
TELEGRAM
W. P. MARSHALL, PRESIDENT

1205P CST NOV 24 63 DC201 PRA015
PR EUA002 FD TDEU SPRINGFIELD ORG 24 950A PST
JACK RUBY
DALLAS CITY HALL DAL
CONGRATULATIONS
BOB WRIGHT
(52).

379

COMMISSION EXHIBIT No. 2003—Continued

WESTERN UNION
TELEGRAM
W. P. MARSHALL, PRESIDENT

907P CST NOV 24 63 DG252
AA243 A TPA278 NL PD TAMPA FLO 24
RUBINSTEIN
COUNTY OR CITY JAIL DALLAS TEX
CONGRATULATIONS FOR YOUR ACT WE UPHOLD YOU IF THERE IS ANYTHING
WE CAN DO FOR YOU WILL BE GLAD TO DO IT
BRYAN PULLEN.

380

COMMISSION EXHIBIT No. 2003—Continued

WESTERN UNION
TELEGRAM
W. P. MARSHALL, PRESIDENT

CLASS OF SERVICE
This is a fast message unless its deferred character is indicated by the proper symbol.

SYMBOLS
DL=Day Letter
NL=Night Letter
LT=International Letter Telegram

SF-1201 (4-60)

The filing time shown in the date line on domestic telegrams is LOCAL TIME at point of origin. Time of receipt is LOCAL TIME at point of destination

710P CST NOV 24 63 DB212 CTA213
CT AKA256 CGN PD AKRON OHIO 24 750P EST
JOHN RUBY CITY JAIL DAL
CONGRATULATIONS ON A JOB WELL DONE
VERN TOMPKINS
(51).

381

Commission Exhibit No. 2003—Continued

WESTERN UNION
TELEGRAM
W. P. MARSHALL, PRESIDENT

CLASS OF SERVICE
This is a fast message unless its deferred character is indicated by the proper symbol.

SYMBOLS
DL=Day Letter
NL=Night Letter
LT=International Letter Telegram

SF-1201 (4-60)

The filing time shown in the date line on domestic telegrams is LOCAL TIME at point of origin. Time of receipt is LOCAL TIME at point of destination

922P CST NOV 24 63 DF293 MA155
M MWA459 PD MILWAUKEE WIS 24 912P CST
JACK RUBY
DALLAS COUNTY JAIL DAL
PERSONAL MESSAGE
JACK THANK GOD MY BEST HEARTFELT FEELINGS FOR YOU. YOU ARE YOUR OWN MAN AS YOU SEE YOUR KIND OF MAN SHOULD BE. THANK GOD FOR YOU
NORBERT W DIETRICH MILWAUKEE WIS
.

382

Commission Exhibit No. 2003—Continued

WESTERN UNION
TELEGRAM
W. P. MARSHALL, PRESIDENT

CLASS OF SERVICE
This is a fast message unless its deferred character is indicated by the proper symbol.

SYMBOLS
DL=Day Letter
NL=Night Letter
LT=International Letter Telegram

SF-1201 (4-60)

The filing time shown in the date line on domestic telegrams is LOCAL TIME at point of origin. Time of receipt is LOCAL TIME at point of destination

1205A CST NOV 25 63 DF005
SYA003 SY JAA029 PD JAMAICA NY 25 1256A EST
JACK RUBY
DALLAS TEXAS JAIL DAL
CONGRATULATIONS AND GOOD LUCK
A FALETTA.

383

Commission Exhibit No. 2003—Continued

QUICK SERVICE WESTERN UNION LOW RATES Form 3300C (R5-61)

MONEY ORDER MESSAGE

Money Sent by Telegraph and Cable to All the World

W. P. MARSHALL, PRESIDENT

No. DEARA053 341PEST MF DALLAS, TEXAS NOV 2 4 1963 19

To JACK RUDY

The Money Order paid you herewith is from J D HARRISON

at ANN ARBOR MICHIGAN and included the following message:

FOR YOUR LEGAL DEFENSE.

THE WESTERN UNION TELEGRAPH COMPANY

THIS ORDER MAY BE CASHED BY ANYONE TO WHOM THE PAYEE IS KNOWN

WESTERN UNION MONEY ORDER 32-1/1110

ISSUED AT ______ 19__

When Countersigned at Point of Issue PAY TO JACK-RUBY OR ORDER

THE SUM OF FIVE AND NO/100 - - - - - - - - DOLLARS $5.00

TELEGRAPHED FROM ANN ARBOR MICHIGAN NOVEMBER 24 UN15850

THE WESTERN UNION TELEGRAPH COMPANY

FIRST NATIONAL BANK IN DALLAS DALLAS, TEXAS

COUNTERSIGNED MONEY ORDER AGENT TREASURER

⑆1110⑈0001⑆ 00⑈0230⑈3⑈

384

COMMISSION EXHIBIT No. 2003—Continued

CLASS OF SERVICE This is a fast message unless its deferred character is indicated by the proper symbol.

WESTERN UNION TELEGRAM

W. P. MARSHALL, PRESIDENT

SYMBOLS DL=Day Letter NL=Night Letter LT=International Letter Telegram

SF-1201 (4-60)

The filing time shown in the date line on domestic telegrams is LOCAL TIME at point of origin. Time of receipt is LOCAL TIME at point of destination

252P CST NOV 24 63 DC332 PA133

"P CNA127 CGN PD WOODBURY NJER 24 310P EST

JACK RUBY

CITY JAIL DAL

CONGRATULATIONS ON A JOB WELL DONE

FRANK AND DOT PIKUL 319 WOODLBURY LAKE RD WOODLBURY NJER

(47).

CLASS OF SERVICE This is a fast message unless its deferred character is indicated by the proper symbol.

WESTERN UNION TELEGRAM

W. P. MARSHALL, PRESIDENT

SYMBOLS DL=Day Letter NL=Night Letter LT=International Letter Telegram

SF-1201 (4-60)

The filing time shown in the date line on domestic telegrams is LOCAL TIME at point of origin. Time of receipt is LOCAL TIME at point of destination

254P CST NOV 24 63 DB087

SYA098 MOA088 MO HMA007 2 EXTRA FDHM CNT CALEDONIA ONT 24

330PMEDT

JACK RUBENSTEIN

CARE DALLAS POLICE STATION DALLAS TEX

CONGRATULATIONS ON YOUR GREAT DEED

[illegible] CALEDONIA ONTARIO

385

CLASS OF SERVICE
This is a fast message unless its deferred character is indicated by the proper symbol.

WESTERN UNION TELEGRAM

W. P. MARSHALL, PRESIDENT

SF-1201 (4-60)

SYMBOLS
DL=Day Letter
NL=Night Letter
LT=International Letter Telegram

The filing time shown in the date line on domestic telegrams is LOCAL TIME at point of origin. Time of receipt is LOCAL TIME at point of destination

315P CST NOV 24 63 DG030
SA076 SBLA007 PD COLLINSVILLE ILL 24 210POST
JACK RUBENSTEIN
CARE CITY JAIL DAL
CONGRATULATIONS JOB WELL DONE
ROBERT BURNS COLLINSVILLE ILL
(22).

CLASS OF SERVICE
This is a fast message unless its deferred character is indicated by the proper symbol.

WESTERN UNION TELEGRAM

W. P. MARSHALL, PRESIDENT

SF-1201 (4-60)

SYMBOLS
DL=Day Letter
NL=Night Letter
LT=International Letter Telegram

The filing time shown in the date line on domestic telegrams is LOCAL TIME at point of origin. Time of receipt is LOCAL TIME at point of destination

327P CST NOV 24 63 DB105 BA122
B CAA213 CGN PD CAMBRIDGE MASS 24 401P EST
JACK RUBY (RUBINSTIEN)
CARE DALLAS CITY JAIL DAL
GOOD JOB. GOOD LUCK. ALL MINE AND MY FAMILYS PRAYERS ARE WITH
YOU. MOZELTOV
RONALD PETERS
(10).

386

COMMISSION EXHIBIT No. 2003—Continued

CLASS OF SERVICE
This is a fast message unless its deferred character is indicated by the proper symbol.

WESTERN UNION TELEGRAM

W. P. MARSHALL, PRESIDENT

SF-1201 (4-60)

SYMBOLS
DL=Day Letter
NL=Night Letter
LT=International Letter Telegram

The filing time shown in the date line on domestic telegrams is LOCAL TIME at point of origin. Time of receipt is LOCAL TIME at point of destination

331P CST NOV 24 63 DB110
DEA110 DE LLF006 PD DETROIT MICH 24 327P EST
JACK RUBY
CARE DALLAS POLICE STATION DAL
GOOD SHOOTING
SEDLER DETROIT
(23).

CLASS OF SERVICE
This is a fast message unless its deferred character is indicated by the proper symbol.

WESTERN UNION TELEGRAM

W. P. MARSHALL, PRESIDENT

SF-1201 (4-60)

SYMBOLS
DL=Day Letter
NL=Night Letter
LT=International Letter Telegram

The filing time shown in the date line on domestic telegrams is LOCAL TIME at point of origin. Time of receipt is LOCAL TIME at point of destination

335P CST NOV 24 63 DB113 LA184
L UDA088 PD LOS ANGELES CALIF
24 1201P PST
JACK RUBY
DAL
CONGRATULATIONS FOR A JOB WELL DONE MAY GOD HELP US ALL
LEON BURCHAM 1343 1/2 WEST 109 ST LOS ANGELES CALIF.(23).

387

COMMISSION EXHIBIT No. 2003—Continued

CLASS OF SERVICE
This is a fast message unless its deferred character is indicated by the proper symbol.

WESTERN UNION
TELEGRAM
W. P. MARSHALL, PRESIDENT

SF-1201 (4-60)

SYMBOLS
DL=Day Letter
NL=Night Letter
LT=International Letter Telegram

The filing time shown in the date line on domestic telegrams is LOCAL TIME at point of origin. Time of receipt is LOCAL TIME at point of destination

329P CST NOV 24 63 DC355
DEA109 DE RNA035 CRA080 MOA029 7 RX CPT FD EDMONTON ALTA 24
205PMST
MR JACK RUBIN
CITY POLICE JAIL DAL
HEARTIEST CONGRATULATIONS BUT HE DIED TOO FAST
JOE GUIDERE.

CLASS OF SERVICE
This is a fast message unless its deferred character is indicated by the proper symbol.

WESTERN UNION
TELEGRAM
W. P. MARSHALL, PRESIDENT

SF-1201 (4-60)

SYMBOLS
DL=Day Letter
NL=Night Letter
LT=International Letter Telegram

The filing time shown in the date line on domestic telegrams is LOCAL TIME at point of origin. Time of receipt is LOCAL TIME at point of destination

330P CST NOV 24 63 DF059 OA199
SSC060 O SFN058 RX PD TDSF SAN MATEO CALIF 24 1204P PST
JACK RUBY
DALLAS COUNTY JAIL DAL
CONGRATULATIONS JOB WELL DONE
ANDREW VERSEY
(29).

388

COMMISSION EXHIBIT No. 2003—Continued

CLASS OF SERVICE
This is a fast message unless its deferred character is indicated by the proper symbol.

WESTERN UNION
TELEGRAM
W. P. MARSHALL, PRESIDENT

SF-1201 (4-60)

SYMBOLS
DL=Day Letter
NL=Night Letter
LT=International Letter Telegram

The filing time shown in the date line on domestic telegrams is LOCAL TIME at point of origin. Time of receipt is LOCAL TIME at point of destination

NOV 24 63 DB106 OA195 — 1963 NOV 24 PM 3 50
O SDA210 PD SAN DIEGO CALIF 24 102P PST
RUBENSTEIN
. CITY JAIL DAL
THANKS RUBENSTEIN FOR DOING WHAT ALL LOYAL AMERICANS WANTED
TO DO
BETTY FELL AND WINNIE CRAIG

CLASS OF SERVICE
This is a fast message unless its deferred character is indicated by the proper symbol.

WESTERN UNION
TELEGRAM
W. P. MARSHALL, PRESIDENT

SF-1201 (4-60)

SYMBOLS
DL=Day Letter
NL=Night Letter
LT=International Letter Telegram

The filing time shown in the date line on domestic telegrams is LOCAL TIME at point of origin. Time of receipt is LOCAL TIME at point of destination

NOV 24 63 DF063 OA203 — 1963 NOV 24 PM 4 24
O SIA024 CGN PD SALINAS CALIF 24 123P PST
JACK RUBY
CITY JAIL DALLAS TEX
CONGRATULATIONS TO A GOOD AMERICAN
FRANK GUTH SALINAS CALIF.

389

COMMISSION EXHIBIT No. 2003—Continued

CLASS OF SERVICE
This is a fast message unless its deferred character is indicated by the proper symbol.

WESTERN UNION
TELEGRAM
W. P. MARSHALL, PRESIDENT

SF-1201 (4-60)

SYMBOLS
DL=Day Letter
NL=Night Letter
LT=International Letter Telegram

The filing time shown in the date line on domestic telegrams is LOCAL TIME at point of origin. Time of receipt is LOCAL TIME at point of destination

412P CST NOV 24 63 DC369 OA211
O SAA116 CGN PD TTDSA GARDENGROVE CALIF 24 100P PST
JACK RUBENSTEIN
CARE CITY JAIL DAL
CONGRATULATIONS TO A COURGEIOUS AMERICAN YOU HAVE DONE A REAL
SERVICE FOR ALL OF US THANK YOU
MR AND MRS RICHARD SCOTT 10602 BARBETT GARDENGROVE CALIF

CLASS OF SERVICE
This is a fast message unless its deferred character is indicated by the proper symbol.

WESTERN UNION
TELEGRAM
W. P. MARSHALL, PRESIDENT

SF-1201 (4-60)

SYMBOLS
DL=Day Letter
NL=Night Letter
LT=International Letter Telegram

The filing time shown in the date line on domestic telegrams is LOCAL TIME at point of origin. Time of receipt is LOCAL TIME at point of destination

613A CST NOV 25 63 DG042
SSB051 D HSA067 PD HOUSTON TEX 25 600A CST
JACK RUBY
DALLAS CITY JAIL DAL

JACK, THANK YOU AS AN EX CHICAGOAN AND MAY BE MOBSTER YOU HAVE
DONE WHAT EVERYONE WANTED THANK YOU IF YOU NEED MONEY YOU WILL
GET IT BOY. YOUR DEFENSE WILL BE THE BEST
ROB

(05).

390

COMMISSION EXHIBIT No. 2003—Continued

CLASS OF SERVICE
This is a fast message unless its deferred character is indicated by the proper symbol.

WESTERN UNION
TELEGRAM
W. P. MARSHALL, PRESIDENT

SF-1201 (4-60)

SYMBOLS
DL=Day Letter
NL=Night Letter
LT=International Letter Telegram

The filing time shown in the date line on domestic telegrams is LOCAL TIME at point of origin. Time of receipt is LOCAL TIME at point of destination

220A CST NOV 25 63 DB022 PRA001
PR VRA064 9/6 3 EX SCL FD CPR VANCOUVER BC 24 1158P PST
JACK RUBENSTIN
CARE COUNTY POLICE STATION DALLAS TEXAS
CONGRATULATIONS WELL DONE
RAYMOND CLARKE 5968 BATTISON STREET

CLASS OF SERVICE
This is a fast message unless its deferred character is indicated by the proper symbol.

WESTERN UNION
TELEGRAM
W. P. MARSHALL, PRESIDENT

SF-1201 (4-60)

SYMBOLS
DL=Day Letter
NL=Night Letter
LT=International Letter Telegram

The filing time shown in the date line on domestic telegrams is LOCAL TIME at point of origin. Time of receipt is LOCAL TIME at point of destination

758P CST NOV 24 63 DG194 KA249
K OMA258 PD OMAHA NEBR 24 737P CST
JACK RUBY RUBENSTEIN
DALLAS JAIL DAL
I, AS IM SURE, MILLIONS OF AMERICANS, AM FOR YOU 100 PERCENT.
AMERICANS ARE SENT OVERSEAS TO FIGHT COMMIES. WHY NOT HERE,
AS YOU HAVE DONE. YOU HAVE DONE A GREAT DEED FOR AMERICANS
REUBEN BARTH
(39).

391

COMMISSION EXHIBIT No. 2003—Continued

WESTERN UNION TELEGRAM

W. P. MARSHALL, PRESIDENT

CLASS OF SERVICE: This is a fast message unless its deferred character is indicated by the proper symbol.

SYMBOLS: DL=Day Letter; NL=Night Letter; LT=International Letter Telegram

SF-1201 (4-60)

The filing time shown in the date line on domestic telegrams is LOCAL TIME at point of origin. Time of receipt is LOCAL TIME at point of destination

437P CST NOV 24 63 DF035 OA223
O SJA200 NL PD TDSJ SANTA CRUZ CALIF 24
MR RUBY
DAL
AS A FORMER TEXAS I WISH TO THANK YOU FROM MY HEART AND I'M SURE FROM MOST AMERICANS AND EVERY POLICE OFFICER OF THE UNITED STATES FOR DOING WHAT EVERY RED BLOODED AMERICAN WISHES HE HAD THE COURAGE OR OPPORTUNTY TO DO WHAT YOU DID FOR US THANK AND GOD BLESS YOU
MRS GEORGE CALLICOTTE.

WESTERN UNION TELEGRAM

W. P. MARSHALL, PRESIDENT

CLASS OF SERVICE: This is a fast message unless its deferred character is indicated by the proper symbol.

SYMBOLS: DL=Day Letter; NL=Night Letter; LT=International Letter Telegram

SF-1201 (4-60)

The filing time shown in the date line on domestic telegrams is LOCAL TIME at point of origin. Time of receipt is LOCAL TIME at point of destination

:ST NOV 24 63 DC445 RA103 1963 NOV 24 PM 8 10
SSA480R WA325 PD TGT WASHINGTON DC 24 625P EST
JACK RUBY
DALLAS CITY JAIL DAL
CONGRATULATIONS ON A JOB WELL DONE

JERRY BARBER AND EILEEN KILDEA ROCHESTER NY.

COMMISSION EXHIBIT No. 2003—Continued

5th

PERMIT TO VISIT PRISONER IN CITY JAIL

Form No. CPS—JS—441 DALLAS POLICE DEPARTMENT

Date 11-23-63 19

Approval to see Lee Harvey Oswald Time 1:00 Pm

O. K'd by Capt Fritz Charge

This pass issued to Marguerite Oswald

Attorney ___ Bondsman ___ Relative ✓ Friend ___

Call received from

Prisoner desires to converse with above.

(Yes)___ (No)___ X Lee H. Oswald Prisoner's Signature

This card presented to

Prisoner by 1:15 Pm Stacy Jailer

3:37 P.

5

PERMIT TO VISIT PRISONER IN CITY JAIL

Form No. CPS—JS—441 DALLAS POLICE DEPARTMENT

Date 11-23-63 19

Approval to see Lee Harvey Oswald Time 3:30 Pm

O. K'd by Capt Fritz Charge Murder

This pass issued to Robert L Oswald

Attorney ___ Bondsman ___ Relative ✓ bro. Friend ___

Call received from

Prisoner desires to converse with above.

(Yes) ✓ (No)___ X Robert L Oswald Prisoner's Signature

This card presented to

Prisoner by Lee Jailer

COMMISSION EXHIBIT No. 2003—Continued

5th

PERMIT TO VISIT PRISONER IN CITY JAIL

Form No. CPS—JS—541

DALLAS POLICE DEPARTMENT

Date 11/24/63 19

Approval to see Jack Ruby Time 1:45 PM

O. K'd by Wells Charge Inv. Murd

This pass issued to Geon Martin

Attorney ✓ Bondsman____ Relative____ Friend____

Call received from____

Prisoner desires to converse with above.

(Yes)____ (No)____ X Jack Ruby

Prisoner's Signature

This card presented to

Prisoner by J. K. Stacy

Jailer

5th

PERMIT TO VISIT PRISONER IN CITY JAIL

Form No. CPS—JS—541

DALLAS POLICE DEPARTMENT

Date Nov 24 1963

Approval to see Jack Ruby Time 1 55 pm.

O. K'd by W E Potts Charge Inv. Murder

This pass issued to Tom Howard

Attorney ✓ Bondsman____ Relative____ Friend____

Call received from____

Prisoner desires to converse with above.

(Yes)____ (No)____ X Jack Ruby

Prisoner's Signature

This card presented to

Prisoner by J. K. Stacy

Jailer

5

PERMIT TO VISIT PRISONER IN CITY JAIL 6 P

Form No. CPS—JS—541

DALLAS POLICE DEPARTMENT

Date 11-24-63 19

Approval to see Jack Rubinsky Time 5 55 pm

O. K'd by Capt Fritz Charge murder

This pass issued to Pauline Hall - Eva L. Grant

Attorney____ Bondsman____ Relative ✓ Friend____

Call received from____

Prisoner desires to converse with above.

(Yes)____ (No)____ X Jack Ruby

Prisoner's Signature

This card presented to

Prisoner by BH

Jailer

394

COMMISSION EXHIBIT No. 2003—Continued

LIST OF WITNESSES

ADAMCIK, J. P.	DETECTIVE - CID
ANDERSON, K. K.	RADIO PATROL
ANDERTON, K. L.	DETECTIVE - CID
APPLIN, GEORGE JEFFERSON, JR.	W/M/21
ARCE, DANNY GARCIA	W/M/18
ARCHER, D. R.	POLICE DEPARTMENT - CID
ARNETT, CHARLES O.	RESERVE

B

BAKER, M. L.	PATROLMAN
BARNES, PETE	CITY POLICE CRIME LAB
BEATY, P. L.	SPECIAL SERVICE
BECK, E. R.	DETECTIVE - CID
BETZNER, HUGH WILLIAMS, JR.	AGE 22
BLEDSOE, MRS. MARY E.	W/F/67
BOONE, DEPUTY SHERIFF	FOUND RIFLE USED IN OFFENSE
BOWERS, LEE E., JR.	W/M/38
BOWLEY, T. F.	W/M/35
BOYD, E. L.	DETECTIVE - CID
BRADEN, JIM	AGE 49
BRANTLEY, D. G.	CID
BRENNAN, HOWARD LESLIE	AGE 44
BREWER, JOHNNY CALVIN	HARDY SHOE STORE
BROCK, A. R.	RADIO PATROL

BROCKWAY, JIMMY D.	RESERVE
BROWN, C. W.	DETECTIVE - CID
BROWN, JUDGE JOE B., JR.	JUSTICE OF THE PEACE
BURGESS, D. L.	CID
BURTON, T. R.	RADIO PATROL
BUTLER, LT. GEORGE	POLICE DEPARTMENT - CID

C

CALLAWAY, TED	W/M/40
CAMPBELL, V. C.	CID
CAPPS, ARTHUR W.	RESERVE
CARROLL, B. K.	SPECIAL SERVICE - CITY POLICE DEPT.
CHAMBERS, W. E.	POLICE DEPARTMENT
CHISM, JOHN ARTHUR	AGE 23
CHISM, MARVIN FAYE	AGE 19
CLARDY, B. S.	POLICE DEPARTMENT - CID
COMBEST, B. H.	SPECIAL SERVICE
COX, ROLAND A.	RESERVE
CRAIG, ALVIN R.	RESERVE
CROY, KENNETH H.	RESERVE
CUNNINGHAM, LT. ELMO	DETECTIVE - CID
CURRY, CHEIF	CHIEF OF POLICE DEPARTMENT
CUTSHAW, W. J.	POLICE DEPARTMENT - CID

D

DAVIS, BARBARA JEANETTE	W/F/22
DAVIS, ROBERT T.	RESERVE
DAVIS, MRS. VIRGINIA	W/F/16
DAWSON, H. L.	POLICE DEPARTMENT - CID

-3-

DAY, LT. CARL	CRIME LAB - POLICE
DEAN, P. T.	RADIO PATROL
DHORITY, C.N.	DETECTIVE - CID
DOUGHERTY, JACK E.	W/M/40
DOUGHTY, G. M. - CAPT.	CITY POLICE CRIME LAB.

E

EDWARDS, ROBERT E. (BOB)	AGE 22
ERWIN, D. K.	RADIO PATROL
EUINS, AMOS LEE	AGE 15

F

FARRIS, M. E.	RADIO PATROL
FISCHER, RONALD B.	AGE 24
FLORER, LARRY	AGE 23
FOX, L. L.	RADIO PATROL
FRAZIER, BUELL WESLEY	AGE 19
FRITZ, CAPT. J. W.	CID

G

GIVENS, CHARLES DOUGLAS	C/M/37
GOOLSBY, CHARLES	POLICE DEPARTMENT - CID
GRAVES, L. C.	DETECTIVE - CID
GREESON, C. A.	POLICE DEPARTMENT - CID
GREGORY, T. R.	RADIO PATROL
GUINYARD, SAM	

397

COMMISSION EXHIBIT No. 2003—Continued

-4-

H

HALL, M. G.	DETECTIVE - CID
HARRISON, OLIVER W.	RESERVE
HARRISON, W. J.	POLICE - CID
HATHAWAY, PHILIP BEN	AGE 28
HATLEY, HURSHELL H.	RESERVE
HAWKINS, RAY	CITY POLICE DEPARTMENT - TRAFFIC
HESTER, CHARLES	AGE 28
HIBBS, W. E.	RADIO PATROL
HICKS, JOHNNY	CITY POLICE - CRIME LAB
HILL, G. L.	SGT. - CITY POLICE - PATROL
HILL, JEAN	AGE 32
HOLLAND, S. M.	AGE 57
HOPKINS, JIMMY R.	RESERVE
HUDSON, EMMETT JOSEPH	AGE 56
HUNT, JESSE C.	RESERVE
HUTCHINSON, J. D.	SPECIAL SERVICE
HUTSON, T. A.	CITY POLICE - TRAFFIC

J

JACOBS, LESLIE H.	RESERVE
JARMAN, JAMES EARL, JR.	C/M/33
JEZ, L. E.	RADIO PATROL
JOHNSON, MARVIN	CITY POLICE DEPARTMENT - CID
JOHNSTON, JUDGE DAVE	JUSTICE OF PEACE
JONES, CAPT. O. A.	POLICE DEPARTMENT - CID

398

COMMISSION EXHIBIT No. 2003—Continued

-5-

K

KASTEN, JEROME	RESERVE
KING, CAPT. GLEN	POLICE DEPARTMENT - ADMINISTRATIVE
KRISS, HARRY M.	RESERVE

L

LAWRENCE, JOHN STEVENS BUTTER	AGE 23
LEAVELLE, J. R.	DETECTIVE - CID
LEWIS, C. G.	SERVICE DIV.
LOVELADY, BILLY NOLAN	W/M/26
LOWERY, R. L.	POLICE DEPARTMENT - CID

MC

MC BRIDE, JUDGE PIERCE	J. P. AT ARRAIGNMENT OF JACK RUBY
MC CABE, DETECTIVE JOHN A.	IRVING POLICE DEPARTMENT
MC CAIN, JAMES C.	RESERVE
MC COY, BEN. C.	RESERVE
MC DONALD, M. N.	CITY POLICE - PATROLMAN
MC GEE, H. L.	CID
MC MILLON, T. J.	POLICE DEPARTMENT - CID
MC WATTERS, CECIL J.	

M

Markham, HELEN LOUISE	
MARTIN, CAPT. FRANK	POLICE DEPARTMENT - CID
MAXEY, B. J.	RADIO PATROLMAN
MAYO, LOGAN W.	RESERVE
MERCER, JULIA ANN	AGE 23

Commission Exhibit No. 2003—Continued

-6-

MERRELL, BARNIE	RESERVE
MILLER, AUSTIN LAWRENCE	
MILLER, L. D.	POLICE DEPARTMENT - CID
MONAGHAN, V. D.	DETECTIVE - CID
MONTGOMERY, L. D.	POLICE - CID
MOONEY, DEPUTY SHERIFF LUKE E.	FOUND EMPTY RIFLE SHELL - 6th FLOOR TEXAS SCHOOL BOOK DEPOSITORY BUILDING
MOORE, H. M.	DETECTIVE - CID
MOORMAN, MARY ANN	AGE 31

N

NEWMAN, GAYLE	AGE 22
NEWMAN, JEAN	AGE 21
NEWMAN, WILLIAM EUGENE	AGE 22
NEWMAN, WILLIAM J.	RESERVE
NEWTON, J. F.	POLICE CLERK

O

OSWALD, MARINA	W/F/22
OWENS, ERNEST JAY	AGE 36

P

PAINE, MICHAEL RALPH	W/M/35
PAINE, RUTH HYDE	W/F/31
PATE, D. L.	RADIO PATROL
PATTERSON, B. G.	RADIO PATROL
PIERCE, RIO S.	RADIO PATROL
POSTAL, JULIA	W/F/39 - THEATRE CASHIER

Commission Exhibit No. 2003—Continued

-7-

POTTS, DET. W. E.	DETECTIVE - CID
PRICE, MR. J. C.	AGE 62
PUTNAM, J. A.	RADIO PATROL

R

RAMSEY, J. K.	CID
RANDLE, LINNIE MAE	W/F/30
RAZ, J.	RADIO PATROL
REID, MRS. R. A.	
REYNOLDS, H. B.	CID
ROSE, C. F.	DETECTIVE - CID
ROWLAND, ARNOLD LOUIS	AGE 18
ROWLAND, BARBARA WALKER	AGE 17

-S

SCOGGINS, W. W.	
SENATOR, GEORGE	W/M/50
SEWELL, R. L.	DETECTIVE - CID
SHELLEY, WILLIAM H. (#1)	W/M/37
SHELLEY, WILLIAM H. (#2)	W/M/37
SIMS, R. M.	DETECTIVE - CID
SKELTON, ROYCE GLENN	AGE 23
SLACK, W. R.	SERVICE DIVISION
SLOCUM, J. D.	POLICE CLERK
SMART, V. S.	POLICE DEPARTMENT
STEELE, D. F.	RADIO PATROL
STEPHENS, I. R.	CID
STOVALL, R. S.	DETECTIVE - CID
STUDEBAKER, R. L.	POLICE CRIME LAB
SUITS, DONALD T.	RESERVE
SWAIN, LT. R. E.	CID

401

COMMISSION EXHIBIT No. 2003—Continued

-8-

T

TALBERT, CAPT. C. E.	RADIO PATROL
TAYLOR, L. C.	RADIO PATROL
TRULY, ROY S.	W/M
TOLBERT, G. L.	RADIO PATROL
TURNER, F. M.	DETECTIVE - CID

V

VAN CLEAVE, I. F.	CID
VAUGHN, R. E.	RADIO PATROL

W

WAGES, H. J.	RADIO PATROL
WAGNER, R. C.	POLICE DEPARTMENT - CID
WALKER, C. T.	CITY POLICE DEPARTMENT - TRAFFIC
WATKINS, R. A.	RADIO PATROL
WATSON, J. C.	POLICE DEPARTMENT - CID
WHALEY, WILLIAM WAYNE	
WIGGINS, LT. WOODROW	SERVICE DIVISION
WILLIAMS, BONNIE RAY	
WILLIAMS, JESSE JAMES	AGE 40
WILLIS, BILLY JOE	
WISE, K. L.	RADIO PATROL
WORLEY, GANO E., JR.	RESERVE
WORRELL, JAMES RICHARD, JR.	W/M/20
WRIGHT, O. P.	SEC. OFF PARKLAND HOSPITAL

402

COMMISSION EXHIBIT No. 2003—Continued

White male 24 (DOB 10-18-1939)

1026 N. Beckley Ave. Dallas, Texas

Shorty

No. F-154

IN JUSTICE'S COURT, PRECINCT NO. 2
Dallas County, Texas.

THE STATE OF TEXAS

vs.

LEE HARVEY OSWALD

City Jail Dallas Police Dept.

Warrant of Arrest

ISSUED

This 22nd day of November, A. D. 1963

David L. Johnston
Justice of the Peace, Precinct No. 2
Dallas County, Texas.

Came to hand the........ day of........

19 ...., and executed the........ day of

.... 19 ...., by ....

........, Constable,

Precinct No........, Dallas County, Texas.

NO BOND

403

COMMISSION EXHIBIT No. 2003—Continued

Form 30 Warr... f Arr...

The State of Texas

No. F-154

IN THE JUSTICE'S COURT, PRECINCT NO. 2
Dallas County, Texas

TO ANY SHERIFF OR ANY CONSTABLE OF THE STATE OF TEXAS—GREETING:
YOU ARE HEREBY COMMANDED to arrest LEE HARVEY OSWALD

if to be found in your County and bring him before me, a Justice of the Peace in and for the said Dallas County, at my office in the City of ~~Dallas~~ Richardson, in said Dallas County, on the INSTANTER day of........ A. D. 19...., at........ o'clock........ M., then and there to answer THE STATE OF TEXAS for an offense against the laws of said State, to-wit:

MURDER WITH MALICE AFORETHOUGHT OF JOHN F. KENNEDY

of which offense he is accused by the written complaint, under oath of J. W. FRITZ, Dallas Police Dept. filed before me.

HEREIN FAIL NOT, but of this writ make due return, showing how you have executed the same.

WITNESS MY OFFICIAL SIGNATURE, This 22nd day of November A. D. 1963

David L. Johnston
Justice of the Peace, Precinct No. 2,
Dallas County, Texas.

404

COMMISSION EXHIBIT No. 2003—Continued

White MALE, 24 (DOB 10-18-1939)

1026 N. Beckley Ave. Dallas, Texas

No. F-153

IN JUSTICE'S COURT, PRECINCT NO. 2
Dallas County, Texas.

THE STATE OF TEXAS

vs.

LEE HARVEY OSWALD

City Jail Dallas Police Dept

Warrant of Arrest

405

ISSUED

This 22nd day of Novemb A. D. 1963

[signature]

Justice of the Peace, Precinct No. 2
Dallas County, Texas.

Came to hand the .... day of ....

19 ...., and executed the .... day

.... 19 ...., by ....

........, Constable,

Precinct No. ...., Dallas County, Texas.

NO BOND

COMMISSION EXHIBIT No. 2003—Continued

Form 30 Warr of Ar.

The State of Texas

No. F-153

IN THE JUSTICE'S COURT, PRECINCT NO. 2
Dallas County, Texas

TO ANY SHERIFF OR ANY CONSTABLE OF THE STATE OF TEXAS—GREETING:
YOU ARE HEREBY COMMANDED to arrest LEE HARVEY OSWALD

if to be found in your County and bring him before me, a Justice of the Peace in and for the said Dallas County, at my office in the City of ~~Dallas~~ Richardson, in said Dallas County, on the INSTANTER day of .... A. D. 19...., at .... o'clock .... M., then and there to answer THE STATE OF TEXAS for an offense against the laws of said State, to-wit:

MURDER WITH MALICE AFORETHOUGHT OF J.D. TIPPETT

of which offense he IS accused by the written complaint, under oath of J.W. FRITZ, DALLAS POLICE Dept. filed before me.

HERRIN FAIL NOT, but of this writ make due return, showing how you have executed the same.

WITNESS MY OFFICIAL SIGNATURE, This 22nd day of November, A. D. 1963

[signature]

Justice of the Peace, Precinct No. 2,
Dallas County, Texas.

COMMISSION EXHIBIT No. 2003—Continued

No. 18211

IN JUSTICE'S COURT, PRECINCT NO.......
Dallas County, Texas.

THE STATE OF TEXAS

vs.

JACK RUBY

MURDER

Warrant of Arrest

ISSUED

This 24 day of Nov A. D. 1963

Pierce McBride

Justice of the Peace, Precinct No.......
Dallas County, Texas.

Came to hand the........day of........

19...., and executed the........day of........

19...., by........

........, Constable,

Precinct No......., Dallas County, Texas.

<NO BOND>

State of Texas }

County of Dallas:

This is to certify that the above and foregoing Warrant of Arrest is a true and correct copy of the Warrant of Arrest issued for________charged with________ as the same appears to have been issued by this court.

Given under my hand officially this____day of________, 19____

Pierce McBride, Justice of the Peace
Precinct 1 — Place 2
Dallas, Dallas County, Texas

Subscribed and sworn to before me a notary public, this the____day of________, 19____

My Commission expires________

Notary Public in and for Dallas,
Dallas County, Texas

406

COMMISSION EXHIBIT No. 2003—Continued

Form 30 Warr[ant] [o]f Arr[est]

The State of Texas }

No........

IN THE JUSTICE'S COURT, PRECINCT NO........
Dallas County, Texas

TO ANY SHERIFF OR ANY CONSTABLE OF THE STATE OF TEXAS—GREETING:

YOU ARE HEREBY COMMANDED to arrest........

JACK RUBY

if to be found in your County and bring him before me, a Justice of the Peace in and for the said Dallas County, at my office in the City of Dallas, in said Dallas County, on the Instanter day of........A. D. 19...., at........o'clock........M., then and there to answer THE STATE OF TEXAS for an offense against the laws of said State, to-wit:

MURDER

of which offense........he is accused by the written complaint, under oath of ....

J. W. FRITZ ....filed before me.

HEREIN FAIL NOT, but of this writ make due return, showing how you have executed the same.

WITNESS MY OFFICIAL SIGNATURE, This 24 day of November A. D. 1963

Pierce McBride

Justice of the Peace, Precinct No. 1,
Dallas County, Texas.

<NO BOND>

COMMISSION EXHIBIT No. 2003—Continued

(1)

Marina OswaldW/F XX 22 2515 W. 5th Irving, Tex	Wife of def. see affidavit. #1
Seymour Weitzman W/M 2802 Oates Dr. DA7-6624 Bus: Robie Love RI1-1483	Was at place of affense See affidavit # 2
James Richard Worrell Jr. W/M20 13510 Winterhaven CH7-2378 Bus: Thomas Jefferson High	Was at place of offense See affidavit # 3
William Wayne Whaley W/M 619 Pine St. Lewisville, Tex Bus: 610 S. Akard RI2-9191	Cab driver who picked up Def. See affidavit #4
Mrs. Mary E. Bledsoe W/F 621 N. Marsalis WH2-1985	Saw Def. git on city Bus knows Def. See affidavit # 5
Lee E. Bowers Jr. W/M 38 10508 Maplegrove Ln. DA1-1909 Bus: Union Terminal Co, RI8-4698	Was at place of offense. See affidavit # 6
Cecil J. McW Watters W/M 2523 Blyth DA1-2909 Bus: Dallas Transit Co. RI1-1151	Picked up Def. on his bus. See affidavit # 7
Helen Louise Markham W/F 328½ E. 9th Bus: Eat Well Cafe RI8-2475	Saw officer Tippit killed by Def. See Affidavit # 8
Jeanette Davis W/F 22 400 E. Tenth WH3-8120	Saw officer Tippit killed rec. evidence See Affidavit # 9
Virginia Davis W/F16 400E. Tenth WH3-8120	Saw officer Tippit Killed rec. evidence See affidavit # 10
W. W. Scoggins W/M 3138 Alaska FR4-2955 Business:Oak Cliff Cab WH2-6203	Saw officer killed See affidavit # 11.
Ted Callaway W/M 40 805 W. 8th. St. WH6-8045 Bus: 501 E. Jefferson	Heard shots saw def run with pistol when officer was killed See Aff.# 12
George Jefferson Applin JR. W/M 21 3423 Weisenberger no phone or bus.	Saw def come into picture show See affidavit # 13

pages a, b, c, d, are also incorporated in case report on President

A 407

(2)

Ruth Hyde Paine W/F 31 2515 W. Fifth Street, Irving, Texas	Owns house where Def & his wife lived also lives there see affidavit # 14
Michael Ralph Paine W/M 35 2515 W. Fifth St. Irving, Texas	Owns house and lives where Def & his wife lived see affidavit # 15
Buell Wesley Frazier W/M 19 2439 W. 5th St. Irving, Texas Phone: BL3-8965	Works Texas School Book Depository See Affidavit (all listed below were there when offense happened) # 16
Roy S. Truly W/M 4932 Jade Dr. Phone: FR6-9893	Works Texas School Book Depository See Affidavit #17
William H. Shelley W/M 37 126 S. Tatum Phone: FE7-1969	Works Texas School Book Depository See Affidavit #18
Mrss R.A.Reid W/F 1914 Elmwood Phone: FE1-6617	Works Texas School Book Depository See Affidavit #19
Bonnie Ray Williams C/M 1502 Ave. B Apt. B	Works Texas School Book Depository See Affidavit #20
Linnie Mae Randle W/F 30 2439 W. 5th Irving, Texas BL3- 8965	Works Texas School Book Depository See Affidavit #21
Jack E. Dougherty W/M 40 1827 S. Marsalis Phone: WH6-7170	Works Texas School Book Depository See Affidavit #22
James E. Jarman, Jr. C/M33 3942 Atlanta St. Phone: HA8-1837	Works Texas School Book Depository See Affidavit #23
William H. Shelley W/M 37 126 S. Tatum FE7-1969	Works Texas School Book Depository See Affidavit #24
Danny Garcia Arce W/M 18 1502 Bennett Phone TA1-3289	Works Texas School Book Depository See Affidavit #25
Billy Nolan Lovelady W/M 26 7722 Hume Dr.	Works Texas School Book Depository See Affidavit #26
Charles Douglas Givens C/M 37 2511 Carpenter RI2-4670	Works Texas School Book Depository See Affidavit #27

B 408

COMMISSION EXHIBIT No. 2003—Continued

COMMISSION EXHIBIT No. 2003—Continued

(3)

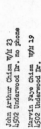

Affidavits from Sheriffs office

Howard Leslie Brennan W/M 44 6814 Woodard EV1-2713	Saw shooting Was at place of offense of JFK see ~~affense~~ Affidavit # 28
Amos Lee Euins U/M 15 411 Ave. F WH3-9701	Was at place of offense saw shooting See affidavit # 29
Ronald B. Fischer W/M 24 4007 Flamingo Dr. Mesquite, Tex BR9-0950 Bus. Dallas County Auditors office	Was at place of offense saw shooting See affidavit # 30
Robert E. Edwards W/M 22 821 S. Nursery Irving, Tex Bus: Dallas County Auditors office	Was at place of offense saw shooting See Affidavit # 31
Arnold Lewis Rowland W/M17 3026 Hammerly St FE7-1861 Student Adamson High	Was at place of offese saw shooting See affidavit # 32
Jesse James Williams W/M 40 1108 Allen St. Apt 114 Irving Tex or Phone PL3-7086 Longview Texas	Was at place of offense See Affidavit # 33 & 34
Hugh William Betzner Jr. W/M 22 5922 Velasco TA7-9761	Was at place of offense See affidavit # 35 & 36
Ernest Jay Owens W/M 36 3005 Peachtree Mesquite, Texas	Was at place of offense See affidavit # 37
Jim Braden W/M 49 621 S. Barington Dr. Los Angeles, Calif. Phone 4725301	Was at place of offense See affidavit # 38
Jean Newman W/F 3893 Clover Lane FL2-4222	Was at place of offense See affidavit # 39
Julia Ann Mercer W/F 23 5200 Belmont Apt. # 208 Bus: 1720 Canton	Was at place of offense See affidavit # 40 & 41
Philip Ben Hathaway W/M 28 11021 Quail Run DI8- 6532	Was at place of offense See af idavit # 42
John Stevens Rutter Lawrence W/M 23 709 Devonshire Richardson, Texas	Was at place of offense See affidavit # 43
Barbara Walker Rowland W/F 17 3026 Hammerly St. FE7- 1861	Was at place of offense See affidavit # 44
Jean Hill W/F 32 9402 Bluffcreek EV1-7419	Was at placeof offense See afficavit # 45

C 409

(4)

John Arthur Chism W/M 23 4502 Underwood Dr. no phone	Was at place of offense See affidavit # 46
Marvin Faye Chism W/M 19 4502 Underwood Dr.	See affidavit # 47
Mary Ann Moorman W/F 31 2832 Ripplewood DA1-9390	Was at place of offense See affidavit # 48
Austin Lawrence Miller W/M 1006 Powell Circle Mesquite, Tex AT5-2998	Was at place of offense see affidavit # 49
S.M. Holland W/M 57 1119 Lucille Irving , Tex BL3-2185	Was at place of offense See affidavit # 50
Gayle Newman W/M 22 718 W. Clarendon WH8-6082	Was at place of offense see affidavit #51
William Eugnne Newman W/M 22 718 W. Clarnedon WH8-6082	Was at place of affense see affidavat # 52
Larry Florer W/M 23 3609 Patomis LA1-7150	Was at plave of offense See affidavit # 53
Royce Glenn Skelton W/M 23 2509 Reagan LA1-2745 Bus: 215 Union Terminal RI1-1396	Was at place of offense See affidavit # 54
J.C. Price W/M 62 2602 Astor WH1-1940 Bus: Terminal Annex RI8- 5611 ext 3105	Was at place of offense see affidavit #55
Charles Hester W/M 28 2616 Keyhole Irving, Tex no phone	Was at place of offense see affidavit # 56
Emmett Joseph Hudaon W/M 56 107 S. Bishop WH2-2008 Bus. City of Dallas Park Dept.	Was at place of offnese see affidavit # 57

D 410

Commission Exhibit No. 2004

FD-302 (Rev. 3-3-59)

FEDERAL BUREAU OF INVESTIGATION

Date 11/27/63

1

DAVID A. TIMMONS, 900 Marigold Street, advised that he is Producer-Director for WBAP-TV, Channel 5, Fort Worth, and has worked for this station for the past fifteen years.

Mr. TIMMONS advised that he and JOHN H. TANKERSLEY, also of WBAP-TV, proceeded to Dallas, Texas, about 4:00 A.M., on November 23, 1963, and that he was floor director for Camera #1 with WBAP-TV for National Broadcasting Company. TIMMONS said that he and TANKERSLEY had their camera on the third floor of the Dallas City Hall during Saturday, November 23, 1963, until Sunday A.M., November 24, 1963, at which time it was learned that an armored car was being backed into the basement of the City Hall. TIMMONS said he and TANKERSLEY were directed to take their camera to the basement of the city hall as LEE HARVEY OSWALD would be leaving from that area.

TIMMONS stated that he and TANKERSLEY took the camera, which was on a tripod and was top heavy due to the fact that the camera had been set high on the tripod in order to take pictures over the crowd. He said that they left the third floor by elevator to the basement and upon entering the basement door the camera stated to "wobble". TIMMONS said that he was helping push the camera from the back and when the camera began to "wobble" that JAMES TURNER, also an employee of WBAP-TV and also a camera employee for WBAP-TV, came over and helped him and TANKERSLEY steady their camera and get it in through the door.

TIMMONS said that he did not see RUBY at any time in the basement of the City Hall and did not see the action that took place concerning the shooting of LEE HARVEY OSWALD because he, TIMMONS, at that particular time was on the right side of the camera holding the mike connections and the action was on the left side of the camera.

TIMMONS stated that he does not have any information or knowledge as to how JACK RUBY may have gotten into the basement of the City Hall.

on 11/27/63 at Fort Worth, Texas File # DL 44-1639

by Special Agent ROBLEY D. MADLAND and JOSEPH L. SCHOTT:jj Date dictated 11/27/63

138

This document contains neither recommendations nor conclusions of the FBI. It is the property of the FBI and is loaned to your agency; it and its contents are not to be distributed outside your agency.

COMMISSION EXHIBIT No. 2004

Commission Exhibit No. 2005

FD-302 (Rev. 3-3-59)

FEDERAL BUREAU OF INVESTIGATION

Date 11/27/63

1

Mr. JOHN H. TANKERSLEY, 1967 Milam Street, advised that he has been employed as an engineer for WBAP-TV, Channel 5, Fort Worth, since 1948.

Mr. TANKERSLEY stated that he was assigned to Dallas, Texas, by WBAP-TV for television coverage and arrived in Dallas for his assignment at about 4:00 A.M. on Saturday, November 23, 1963. TANKERSLEY said he and DAVID A. TIMMONS, Producer-Director for WBAP-TV, were on what was designated as Camera #1 for this television station and NBC.

TANKERSLEY said further that on Saturday, November 23, 1963, his camera was set up on the third floor at the Dallas City Hall and that they covered the third floor Saturday, Saturday night, until Sunday A.M., November 24, 1963. Shortly before Noon on November 24, 1963, TANKERSLEY said his crew received word that an armored car was being backed into the basement of the City Hall and that he was to discontinue coverage of the third floor and take the television camera to the basement. TANKERSLEY said that this television camera was on a tripod and was set very high in order to "shoot" film over the crowds and therefore, it was top heavy and was hard to handle. He said he and TIMMONS proceeded to the basement of the City Hall by elevator and believes that there were four other detectives in the elevator with them. Upon arriving in the basement, TANKERSLEY said the camera began to "wobble" as they started into the basement from being top heavy and that he and TIMMONS steadied it as they were going through the door to the basement and there was another person that helped them steady this camera and believes it possibly was a detective, however, he does not recall at this time.

TANKERSLEY said that he did not see JACK RUBY or JACK RUBENSTEIN in the basement until he saw RUBY appear to lunge toward LEE HARVEY OSWALD as OSWALD was being brought down the corridor.

TANKERSLEY advised that he does not have any information as to how RUBY may have gotten into the basement of the City Hall.

on 11/27/63 at Fort Worth, Texas File # DL 44-1639

by Special Agents ROBLEY D. MADLAND and JOSEPH L. SCHOTT:jj Date dictated 11/27/63

139

This document contains neither recommendations nor conclusions of the FBI. It is the property of the FBI and is loaned to your agency; it and its contents are not to be distributed outside your agency.

COMMISSION EXHIBIT No. 2005

FD-302 (Rev. 3-3-59) FEDERAL BUREAU OF INVE— Commission Exhibit No. 2006 —

Date January 10, 1964

1

Mr. HOWARD LESLIE BRENNAN, 6814 Woodard, was re-interviewed at his place of employment, Medical Arts Building Parking Lot, at which time he furnished the following information:

Mr. BRENNAN advised that on November 22, 1963, after finishing lunch at about 12:18 P.M., he sat on a retainer wall directly across from the Texas School Book Depository (TSBD) building, on Elm Street. While he was sitting there, he looked up at the TSBD building and noticed that there was a man standing in the sixth floor window; however, at this time, this man did not have a rifle. He said he then turned around and noticed that the man had left the window. Then he turned his head back toward the south where the Presidential motorcade would come. Approximately ten minutes after sitting down on this retaining wall, the Presidential motorcade turned onto Houston Street, and he was able to see President KENNEDY and his wife pass approximately thirty yards west on Elm from where he was seated. The car passed out of sight and shortly thereafter, he heard one shot, which he first believed to have been a firecracker, and he immediately looked toward the TSBD building and saw a man on the sixth floor in the same window, near the southeast corner of the building, and noticed that this man took deliberate aim and shot the rifle again. When he saw the man shoot the rifle this time, he realized it was the same man that he had seen standing in the window a few minutes before.

After the last shot, he immediately fell off the retaining wall and ran for an officer so that he could advise the police and Secret Service that the man whom he had seen take the last shot was in the TSBD building.

on 1/7/64 at Dallas, Texas File # DL 100-10461

by Special Agent WILLIAM G. BROOKHART:mja Date dictated 1/9/64

This document contains neither recommendations nor conclusions of the FBI. It is the property of the FBI and is loaned to your agency; it and its contents are not to be distributed outside your agency.

COMMISSION EXHIBIT No. 2006

2
DL 100-10461

Mr. BRENNAN estimated that it was approximately ninety yards from the window where the shots were fired to the area where the President's car had passed out of sight. He said that he did not see anyone else near him that he knew; however, there was a lady and a little girl approximately ten years old who had attempted to sit on a cement column attached to the southwest corner of the retainer wall, on Houston Street, close to where he was sitting.

He also noticed that a woman in her forties was taking pictures near him, but he could not tell whether she had a movie camera, or a still camera; although, he believed the size of this camera was approximately four inches by five inches.

Mr. BRENNAN added that after his first interview at the Sheriff's Office, on November 22, 1963, he left and went home at about 2 P.M. While he was at home, and before he returned to view a lineup, which included the possible assassin of President KENNEDY, he observed LEE HARVEY OSWALD'S picture on television.

Mr. BRENNAN said that this, of course, did not help him retain the original impression of the man in the window with the rifle; however, upon seeing LEE HARVEY OSWALD in the police lineup, he felt that OSWALD most resembled the man whom he had seen in the window.

COMMISSION EXHIBIT No. 2006—Continued

DL 100-10461
WRH:mam
1

106

On the following pages are listed various items of private and official correspondence and also public documentation of LEE HARVEY OSWALD. Some of these items are prepared in the English language, while others are prepared in the Russian language. The Russian language items have been translated by SA ANATOLE A. BOGUSLAV. The originals of all items have been forwarded to and examined by the FBI Laboratory at Washington, D. C. Each of these items is summarized as follows: (A notation is made in each case of the language in which the original document is written.)

1. Official documents pertaining to membership in a hunting and fishing club, registration of weapon, payment of dues, issuance of ammunition, which are prepared in the Russian language:

a. A hunting license, #28231, issued to ALIKSEI OSWALD, born in 1939, a resident at Kalinin Street #4, Apartment 24, Minsk, Russia. The license was issued by an organization of the Minsk Radio Plant and reflects membership of OSWALD in a club of hunters and fishermen.

b. A registration card of hunting equipment reflecting registration by OSWALD of a single barrel weapon, manufacturer's make IZHK-59. Under the column labeled "caliber" appears the written numbers 16. On the other side of this registration card appears the legend "registration of hunting dogs". There are no entries on this registration.

c. A card showing payment of membership dues to the Belorussian Society of Hunters and Fishermen in the amount of 51 rubles on July 18, 1960.

COMMISSION EXHIBIT No. 2007

FD-302 (Rev. 3-3-59)

FEDERAL BUREAU OF IN

1

Date 12/2/63

LINNIE MAE RANDLE, 2439 West Fifth Street, Irving, Texas, telephone BL 3-8965, furnished the following information:

On the morning of November 22, 1963, at approximately 7:10 AM to 7:15 AM, LINNIE MAE RANDLE was standing at her sink in the kitchen looking out the window, when she saw LEE HARVEY OSWALD walking diagonally across Westbrook Street toward the back yard of her house. Westbrook Street borders her home on the west, and OSWALD was proceeding from Fifth Street diagonally across Westbrook in a northeasterly direction. She noticed that he was walking west, and he came across the street toward the carport which adjoins the kitchen. She opened the back door a slight bit to see what he was doing and saw him go to the far side of her brother's car, which was parked just north of the carport and headed in an easterly direction toward Westbrook Street. She noticed OSWALD opened the right rear door of the car, and presuming he was getting in the car, she turned back to the sink after hearing the car door shut. She then looked up out the window and saw him looking in the window at her from the outside. She was startled and somewhat irritated and called to her brother, BUELL WESLEY FRAZIER, that OSWALD was waiting to ride to work with him.

Mrs. RANDLE stated that at the time she saw OSWALD walking across the street, he was carrying a long package wrapped in brown paper or a brown sack in his right hand. It appeared to contain something heavy. She stated that it was long but did not touch the ground as he walked across the street.

She examined a replica of the sack made by Special Agents BARDWELL D. ODUM and GIBBON E. MC NEELY on December 1, 1963, from 24-inch-wide brown wrapping paper with 4-inch gummed brown paper tape, from the Texas School Book Depository (TSBD) Building shipping room area at 411 Elm Street, Dallas. She stated that this was the same kind of paper that made up the sack or package that she saw OSWALD carrying and was the same heavy grade of paper, since she recalls noting that there

on 12/1/63 at Irving, Texas File # DL 89-43

by Special Agents BARDWELL D. ODUM AND GIBBON E. MC NEELY: mam Date dictated 12/2/63

This document contains neither recommendations nor conclusions of the FBI. It is the property of the FBI and is loaned to your agency; it and its contents are not to be distributed outside your agency.

COMMISSION EXHIBIT No. 2008

DL 89-43
BDO,GEM:mam
2

was something heavy in the sack when she saw it, and it was the same color paper as the sack she had seen on the morning of November 22, 1963.

She was shown the original paper sack which had been found by the sixth floor window of the TSBD Building, where empty cartridge cases were found and from which the shots were apparently fired that killed President JOHN F. KENNEDY on November 22, 1963. She stated that if that original sack was previously the same color as the replica sack, that the original sack could have been the one which she saw OSWALD carrying on the morning of November 22, 1963.

The action of OSWALD walking across Westbrook Street was re-enacted by Special Agent MC NEELY, carrying the replica sack with three scraps of wood in it to simulate weight until Mrs. RANDLE designated the proper path and the proper length of the sack as seen by her on November 22, 1963. The replica was shortened by folding the open top down to reach the desired length. Then, in accordance with Mrs. RANDLE's observations, Special Agent MC NEELY grasped the top of this sack with his hand, much like a right handed batter would pick up a baseball bat when approaching the plate. When the proper length of the sack was reached according to Mrs. RANDLE's estimate, it was measured and found to be 27 inches long. She demonstrated the width of the sack as it appeared to her, noting that it did have something bulky in it originally. Her designation on the replica sack was found to be 8½ inches for the width of the original package she had seen OSWALD carrying.

280

FD-302 (Rev. 3-3-59) FEDERAL BUREAU OF INV

Commission Exhibit No. 2009

1

Date 12/2/63

BUELL WESLEY FRAZIER was interviewed at his home, 2439 West Fifth Street, Irving, Texas, telephone BL 3-8965, and furnished the following information:

On November 21, 1963, sometime before noon, the exact time unrecalled to him, FRAZIER was approached by LEE OSWALD on the first floor of the Texas School Book Depository (TSBD) Building, 411 Elm Street, Dallas, Texas, where both were employed. They were standing toward the north side of the building near the stairs that lead to the basement. OSWALD asked FRAZIER if he could ride home with him that night, and FRAZIER told him he could but asked why he wanted to ride, since he usually rode home with FRAZIER on Friday nights, returning on Monday mornings. OSWALD replied that he wanted to get some curtain rods in Irving and take them to his room in Oak Cluff.

At about 4:45 PM, on November 21, 1963, FRAZIER and OSWALD departed the TSBD Building, walked to FRAZIER's car and drove to Irving. OSWALD did not have a package and was not carrying anything with him at that time. As FRAZIER recalls, OSWALD was wearing a reddish shirt and a grey jacket, waist length. Very little was said on the way home by OSWALD, and FRAZIER is unable to recall comments made by him. He let OSWALD off at 2515 West Fifth Street, Irving, Texas, where OSWALD's wife was living. He did not see OSWALD again that night.

At about 7:20 AM, November 22, 1963, FRAZIER recalls that OSWALD looked in the kitchen window at FRAZIER's home and waited outside the house until FRAZIER joined him to go to work. This was within a period of about 5 minutes from the time OSWALD first appeared.

FRAZIER went to his car, entered the left front door, while OSWALD entered the right front door, both getting into the front seat. As he started to drive out of the yard, FRAZIER glanced back and noticed a long package, light brown in color, lying on the back of the rear seat and extending from approximately the right rear door to about the center

on 12/1/63 at Irving, Texas File # DL 89-43

by Special Agents BARDWELL D. ODUM AND GIBBON E. MC NEELY: mam Date dictated 12/2/63

This document contains neither recommendations nor conclusions of the FBI. It is the property of the FBI and is loaned to your agency; it and its contents are not to be distributed outside your agency.

of the seat. He stated that he only glanced at this package, at the time, over his shoulder and said something to OSWALD about the package, and OSWALD explained that it was curtain rods. FRAZIER then remarked to OSWALD, "Oh, yes, you said you were going to get some curtain rods yesterday."

FRAZIER designated an approximate spot on the back seat where he felt the package extended to from the right rear door and measurement by Special Agents BARDWELL D. ODUM and GIBBON E. MC NEELY determined that this spot was 27 inches from the inside of the right rear door, indicating that FRAZIER estimates that as the length of the package.

FRAZIER stated that he and OSWALD drove to work, and he parked the car about two blocks north of the TSBD Building. OSWALD got out of the car first, and FRAZIER noticed him standing to the rear of the car at the time FRAZIER was about to get out of the front seat. As OSWALD turned to walk south toward the TSBD Building, FRAZIER observed that OSWALD had this package under his right arm, one end of the package being under his armpit and the other end apparently held with his right fingers. OSWALD then walked toward the building with his back to FRAZIER and continued in front of FRAZIER for the entire distance, possibly 200 or 300 yards. FRAZIER followed at a slower pace than OSWALD, watching some welders working on the railroad track. By the time OSWALD reached the TSBD Building, he was at least 50 feet ahead of FRAZIER, and when FRAZIER entered the building he did not see OSWALD and does not know where he went. He did not subsequently see him with the package again.

FRAZIER stated that when he saw this package under the arm of OSWALD, he reached the conclusion that the package was wrapped in a cheap, crinkly, thin paper sack, such as that provided by Five and Ten Cent Stores.

He stated that now upon reflecting upon this matter, he realizes that he reached this conclusion when he observed the package under OSWALD's arm as OSWALD was turned with his back toward him. FRAZIER indicated the approximate closest distance that OSWALD was to FRAZIER with the package under his arm, and this was found to be approximately 12 feet by Special Agent ODUM.

Special Agent ODUM placed the replica sack under his right armpit, and FRAZIER demonstrated how much of the package he could see. When this was completed to FRAZIER's satisfaction, Special Agent MC NEELY measured the part of the package visible, and it was found to measure 9" x 1".

The replica sack was made on December 1, 1963, at the TSBD Building by Special Agents ODUM and MC NEELY from 24-inch-wide wrapping paper found in the shipping area of the TSBD Building and 4-inch-wide gummed paper tape from the same area. The replica was made to the dimensions of the original which was available for reference. The original is the sack found near the sixth floor window of the TSBD Building on November 22, 1963, following the assassination of President JOHN F. KENNEDY.

FRAZIER advised after viewing the replica sack under the arm of Special Agent ODUM, that he now realizes that his conclusion that the sack was thin, crinkly paper, of the type used by Five and Ten Cent Stores, was based to a considerable extent upon the fact that the color of the sack was a very light brown as compared with the type of dark brown paper used for heavier grocery sacks. He noted that the color of the replica sack was the same color as the package which he had seen in possession of OSWALD on the morning of November 22, 1963.

FRAZIER examined the original found by the sixth floor window of the TSBD Building on November 22, 1963, and

DL 89-43/mam
4

stated that if that sack was originally the color of the replica sack, it could have been the sack or package which he saw in the possession of OSWALD on the morning of November 22, 1963, but that he does not feel he is in a position to definitely state that this original is or is not the sack.

FRAZIER indicated on the replica sack the estimated width of the package in possession of OSWALD on the morning of November 22, 1963, and this was found to be an approximate width of 6 inches.

FRAZIER recalls that at some time, probably on the way to work on the morning of November 22, 1963, OSWALD told him that he would not be going to Irving, Texas, on Friday night, November 22, 1963. He could recall no other conversation by OSWALD except that on the way to work that morning, he mentioned to OSWALD that he probably had a good time playing with his children, and OSWALD said that he did.

COMMISSION EXHIBIT No. 2009—Continued

Commission Exhibit No. 2010

FD-302 (Rev. 3-3-59)

FEDERAL BUREAU OF INVESTIGATION

Date December 11, 1963

1

CARL LINDSEY THOMPSON, Installer, OfficeDivision Plant Superintendent, Southwestern Bell Telephone Company, Life Building, 311 South Akard, residence 818 South Marlboro, telephone number WH 8-3311, furnished the following information:

On November 22, 1963, ALSTON RAMSEY, one of THOMPSON's supervisors, telephoned about 10:00 p.m., and requested THOMPSON to go to the Central Police Department as they needed someone to run the circuits.

He arrived at the Central Police Department around 10:30 p.m., and reported to GILES BERRY, Supervisor, Mobile Telephone Shop. He went to the third floor radio room located in the old City Hall Building. He remained at Central Police Department until approximately 10:00 p.m., November 23, 1963. He is known to most Police Department personnel since he has been employed by Southeastern Bell for 23 years and spends a great deal of time at the City Hall Building. He does not recall being requested to identify himself during the above period.

He arrived back at the Central Police Building at 8:00 a.m., on November 24, 1963, and reported to the telephone company trailer which was parked midway between Commerce Street and Main Street on the east side of Harwood Avenue. This was the command post for the telephone company operation at the Central Police Building. He reported to BERRY and was assigned to help in the installation of additional telephones in the office of the Chief of Police. He also checked the temporary wires which were taped to the floor in the area of the office of the Chief of Police.

At around 10:30 a.m., he rode the elevator to the basement from the third floor where he was required to identify himself by an unknown officer in police uniform, by exhibiting his telephone company identification card. The officer also looked through his tool pouch. A uniformed police sergeant, name unknown, who knew THOMPSON by sight, came up and asked THOMPSON his business in the basement at which time THOMPSON advised he desired to pass through the basement to the freight elevator and then up to the fifth floor of the new City Hall Building to the telephone room. He could not cross through from the old City Hall on the upper floors

on 12/11/63 at Dallas, Texas File # Dallas 44-1639

by Special Agent R. NEIL QUIGLEY:BL Date dictated 12/11/63

288

This document contains neither recommendations nor conclusions of the FBI. It is the property of the FBI and is loaned to your agency; it and its contents are not to be distributed outside your agency.

COMMISSION EXHIBIT No. 2010

DL 44-1639
2

since all the gates were closed and locked on the connecting hallways.

The Sergeant escorted THOMPSON through the basement to the freight elevator. The Sgt. advised THOMPSON they might have trouble getting the freight elevator to the basement since the Sergeant had ordered the elevator operator not to come to the basement.

After the elevator did come down to the basement, THOMPSON went to the fifth floor to the telephone room where he stayed about five minutes. He then returned to the basement via the freight elevator where the Sergeant was waiting for him. The Sergeant then escorted him to the Commerce Street entrance where THOMPSON left the building.

He then worked around the WBAP-TV trailer, located on the north side of Commerce Street near the ramp entrance; the KRLD trailer, located west of the WBAP trailer on the north side of Commerce; and the WFAA trailer, located on the east side of Harwood near the intersection of Commerce and Harwood. He also went to the third floor of the building during this time after leaving the basement he was required to identify himself approximately a half dozen times.

When the shooting of LEE HARVEY OSWALD took place THOMPSON was in the WBAP trailer viewing the three TV monitors. One set was monit ring the Chief of Police office area, one was monitoring the Commerce Street ramp entrance, and one was monitoring the center basement ramp area. He viewed the shooting of OSWALD by JACK RUBY on TV monitor.

He never returned to the basement of the building; however, he was on the third floor after the shooting. He estimated the security checks tripled after the shooting of OSWALD.

He does not know OSWALD or RUBY and never saw RUBY at any time.

He does not recall any other telephone company employees on duty who would have entered the building on November 24, 1963.

289

COMMISSION EXHIBIT No. 2010—Continued

UNITED STATES DEPARTMENT OF JUSTICE

FEDERAL BUREAU OF INVESTIGATION

In Reply, Please Refer to
File No.

Dallas, Texas
July 7, 1964

RE: LEE HARVEY OSWALD

By letter dated May 20, 1964, the President's Commission requested the tracing of various items of physical evidence. Pursuant to this request, the following information is submitted:

Three Rifle Cartridge Cases, C6, C7, C38

On June 9, 1964, Lieutenant J. C. Day, of the Crime Laboratory, Dallas Police Department, Dallas, Texas, was exhibited three rifle cartridge cases, C6, C7 and C38, by Special Agent Vincent E. Drain, of the Federal Bureau of Investigation. Lieutenant Day related he went to the sixth floor of the Texas School Book Depository, Dallas, Texas, immediately after the shooting of President Kennedy on November 22, 1963. Lieutenant Day arrived at the Texas School Book Depository building at 1:12 PM. He advised he observed these three rifle cartridge cases, C6, C7 and C38, lying on the floor near a window on the sixth floor of the Texas School Book Depository building. These cartridge cases were dusted for fingerprints by him, placed in an envelope, and delivered to the Dallas Police Department.

On November 22, 1963, Lieutenant Day stated he wrote his name on all three of the cartridge cases. On November 22, 1963, two of the rifle cartridge cases, C6 and C7, were given to Special Agent Drain for delivery to the Federal Bureau of Investigation Laboratory, Washington, D. C., for examination.

Lieutenant Day stated that on November 27, 1963, rifle cartridge case C38 was given to Special Agent Drain for delivery to the Laboratory of the Federal Bureau of Investigation, Washington, D. C., for examination.

COMMISSION EXHIBIT No. 2011

Re: LEE HARVEY OSWALD

Rifle Bullet, C1

On June 12, 1964, Darrell C. Tomlinson, Maintenance Employee, Parkland Hospital, Dallas, Texas, was shown Exhibit C1, a rifle slug, by Special Agent Bardwell D. Odum, Federal Bureau of Investigation. Tomlinson stated it appears to be the same one he found on a hospital carriage at Parkland Hospital on November 22, 1963, but he cannot positively identify the bullet as the one he found and showed to Mr. O. P. Wright. At the time he found the bullet, the hospital carriage was located in the Emergency Unit on the ground floor of the hospital.

On June 12, 1964, O. P. Wright, Personnel Officer, Parkland Hospital, Dallas, Texas, advised Special Agent Bardwell D. Odum that Exhibit C1, a rifle slug, shown to him at the time of the interview, looks like the slug found at Parkland Hospital on November 22, 1963, which he gave to Richard Johnsen, Special Agent of the Secret Service. He stated he was not present at the time the bullet was found, but on the afternoon of November 22, 1963, as he entered the Emergency Unit on the ground floor of the hospital, Mr. Tomlinson, an employee, called to him and pointed out a bullet, which was on a hospital carriage at that location. He estimated the time as being within an hour of the time President Kennedy and Governor Connally were brought to the hospital. He advised he could not positively identify C1 as being the same bullet which was found on November 22, 1963.

On June 24, 1964, Special Agent Richard E. Johnsen, United States Secret Service, Washington, D. C., was shown Exhibit C1, a rifle bullet, by Special Agent Elmer Lee Todd, Federal Bureau of Investigation. Johnsen advised he could not identify this bullet as the one he obtained from O. P. Wright, Parkland Hospital, Dallas, Texas, and gave to James Rowley, Chief, United States Secret Service, Washington, D. C., on November 22, 1963.

On June 24, 1964, James Rowley, Chief, United States Secret Service, Washington, D. C., was shown Exhibit C1, a rifle bullet, by Special Agent Elmer Lee Todd. Rowley advised he could

2

COMMISSION EXHIBIT No. 2011—Continued

Re: LEE HARVEY OSWALD

not identify this bullet as the one he received from Special Agent Richard E. Johnsen and gave to Special Agent Todd on November 22, 1963.

On June 24, 1964, Special Agent Elmer Lee Todd, Washington, D. C., identified C1, a rifle bullet, as being the same one he received from James Rowley, Chief, United States Secret Service, Washington, D. C., on November 22, 1963. This identification was made from initials marked thereon by Special Agent Todd at the Federal Bureau of Investigation Laboratory upon receipt.

3

COMMISSION EXHIBIT No. 2011—Continued

Re: LEE HARVEY OSWALD

Two rifle bullet fragments, C2 and C3

C2 - On June 2, 1964, Special Agent Orrin H. Bartlett, Federal Bureau of Investigation, displayed Exhibit C2, a rifle bullet fragment, to Thomas G. Mills, Chief Hospital Corpsman, United States Navy, assigned to the doctor's office, White House, Washington, D. C. Mills identified the fragment as the one he recovered from the space between the right front seat and the door panel of the right front door on the President's car. This recovery was made on the night of November 22, 1963, after the President's car was returned to Washington, D. C., from Dallas, Texas. This bullet fragment was turned over to Special Agent Bartlett on November 22, 1963.

C3 - On June 2, 1964, Special Agent Orrin H. Bartlett displayed Exhibit C3, a rifle bullet fragment, to Mr. Paul Paterni, Deputy Chief, United States Secret Service, Washington, D. C. Paterni identified this fragment as the one he recovered from the middle of the front seat of the President's car. This recovery was made on the night of November 22, 1963, after the car was returned to Washington, D. C., from Dallas, Texas. This bullet fragment was turned over to Special Agent Bartlett on November 22, 1963.

4

COMMISSION EXHIBIT No. 2011—Continued

Re: LEE HARVEY OSWALD

Rifle Cartridge, C8

On June 9, 1964, Lieutenant J. C. Day, of the Crime Laboratory, Dallas Police Department, Dallas, Texas, was exhibited rifle cartridge, C8, by Special Agent Vincent E. Drain, Federal Bureau of Investigation. Lieutenant Day related that rifle cartridge C8 was ejected from a 6.5 mm Mannlicher-Carcano rifle, having Serial Number C2766, which was found on the sixth floor of the Texas School Book Depository building on November 22, 1963. This rifle cartridge, C8, was ejected from this rifle by Captain Will Fritz, Dallas Police Department, in the presence of Lieutenant Day, who took the cartridge at the time it was ejected and dusted it for fingerprints. This cartridge was placed in an envelope and delivered by Lieutenant Day to the Dallas Police Department. This cartridge was marked by Lieutenant Day for identification purposes on November 22, 1963. This rifle cartridge was given to Special Agent Drain on November 22, 1963, for delivery to the Laboratory of the Federal Bureau of Investigation, Washington, D. C., for examination.

5

COMMISSION EXHIBIT No. 2011—Continued

Re: LEE HARVEY OSWALD

Bullet from the Walker Residence, C148

On June 12, 1964, Exhibit C148, a mutilated rifle slug, was shown to Billy Gene Norvell, former Dallas police officer, 1603 Darr Street, Apartment 147, Irving, Texas, by Special Agent Bardwell D. Odum, Federal Bureau of Investigation. He identified this exhibit as the same one which he had found at the residence of Major General Edwin A. Walker, Dallas, Texas, on April 10, 1963, and identified his marking on this slug.

6

Re: LEE HARVEY OSWALD

Revolver Cartridge Cases, C47 - C50

On June 18, 1964, Special Agents Kenneth R. Albert and Paul E. Wulff, Federal Bureau of Investigation, contacted Mrs. Troy (Barbara Jeanette) Davis at her residence, Kirk's Store, Route 2, Palestine Highway, Athens, Texas, at which time Special Agent Wulff exhibited to her four .38 Special cartridge cases, C47 - C50. Mrs. Davis stated on November 22, 1963, she resided at 400 East 10th Street, Dallas, Texas, and at approximately 2:00 PM or shortly thereafter she found a similar cartridge case in the front yard of her former residence. At the time she found the cartridge case, an unknown Dallas police officer was standing approximately five feet from her and she immediately gave the cartridge case to him. She cannot identify the cartridge case she found as being one of those exhibited to her.

On June 12, 1964, four .38 Special cartridge cases, designated as Exhibits C47 - C50, were shown to Captain G. M. Doughty of the Dallas Police Department by Special Agent Bardwell D. Odum, Federal Bureau of Investigation. Captain Doughty identified his marking on one of these cases which also bears a marking "Q76." Captain Doughty stated this is the same shell which he obtained from Barbara Jeanette Davis at Dallas, Texas, on November 22, 1963.

On June 18, 1964, Special Agents Kenneth R. Albert and Paul E. Wulff contacted Mrs. Charley Reagan (Virginia) Davis at 418 West Scott Street, Athens, Texas, at which time Special Agent Wulff exhibited to her four .38 Special cartridge cases, C47 - C50. Mrs. Davis stated on November 22, 1963, she resided at 400 East 10th Street, Dallas, Texas, and at approximately 3:30 PM that date she found a cartridge case in the front yard of that residence which she furnished to an unidentified officer of the Dallas Police Department at approximately 6:00 PM that same date. She advised she was unable to identify the cartridge case she found as being one of the four exhibited to her.

7

Re: <u>LEE HARVEY OSWALD</u>

On June 12, 1964, the same four cartridge cases, designated as Exhibits C47 - C50, were shown by Special Agent Bardwell D. Odum to Detective C. N. Dhority, Homicide Division Dallas Police Department. Detective Dhority identified his marking on one of these cartridge cases which also is marked "Q75." He stated this is the same cartridge case which he obtained from Virginia Davis, Dallas, Texas, on November 22, 1963.

On June 11, 1964, four .38 Special cartridge cases, C47 - C50, were exhibited by Special Agent Bardwell D. Odum to Domingo Benavides, 3112 June Drive, Dallas, Texas. Mr. Benavides stated these all resemble the two cartridge cases which he found on November 22, 1963, at Dallas, Texas, but stated he cannot identify any one of these as being the ones which he picked up and gave to an officer of the Dallas Police Department.

On June 12, 1964, four .38 Special cartridge cases, designated as Exhibits C47 - C50, were shown to Dallas Police Officer J. M. Poe at his home at 1716 Cascade, Mesquite, Texas, by Special Agent Bardwell D. Odum. Officer Poe stated he had received two similar cartridge cases on November 22, 1963, from Domingo Benavides at Dallas, Texas, and had on the same date given them to Pete Barnes, Crime Laboratory, Dallas Police Department. He stated he recalled marking these cases before giving them to Barnes, but he stated after a thorough examination of the four cartridges shown to him on June 12, 1964, he cannot locate his marks; therefore, he cannot positively identify any of these cartridges as being the same ones he received from Benavides.

On July 6, 1964, Officer J. M. Poe, Dallas Police Department, advised Special Agent Bardwell D. Odum that he marked the two cartridge cases on November 22, 1963, "J.M.P."

On June 15, 1964, the same cartridge cases, designated as Exhibits C47 - C50, were shown by Special Agent Bardwell D. Odum to Pete Barnes, an officer of the Dallas Police Department assigned to the Crime Laboratory, and he identified his marking on two of these cases, which also bear the markings "Q74" and "Q77." He advised these are the same two cartridge cases which he received from Officer J. M. Poe of the Dallas Police Department at Dallas, Texas, on November 22, 1963.

COMMISSION EXHIBIT No. 2011—Continued

Re: <u>LEE HARVEY OSWALD</u>

<u>Four Revolver Bullets Recovered From the Body of Officer Tippit, C13 and C251 -C253</u>

On June 11, 1964, Doctor Paul Moellenhoff, Methodist Hospital, Dallas, Texas, was shown the slug identified as Exhibit C13 by Special Agent Bardwell, Federal Bureau of Investigation. He advised this looks like the slug which he removed from the body of Officer J. D. Tippit at Methodist Hospital on November 22, 1963, but stated he cannot identify the slug positively. He stated Officer Davenport of the Dallas Police Department was with him when he removed this slug and he believes Davenport identified it.

On June 12, 1964, a slug identified as Exhibit C13 was shown by Special Agent Bardwell D. Odum to Patrolman R. A. Davenport of the Dallas Police Department. Officer Davenport identified his mark on this slug and stated it is the same slug which he obtained from Doctor Paul Moellenhoff on November 22, 1963, at Methodist Hospital, Dallas, Texas. He stated he was present and observed Doctor Moellenhoff remove this slug from the body of Officer J. D. Tippit.

On June 11, 1964, three slugs identified as Exhibits C251, C252, and C253 were exhibited by Special Agent Bardwell D. Odum to Doctor Earl Forrest Rose, Medical Examiner, Parkland Hospital, Dallas, Texas. He identified his mark on each of these slugs and stated these were the same slugs which he removed from the body of Officer J. D. Tippit at Parkland Hospital on November 22, 1963.

COMMISSION EXHIBIT No. 2011—Continued

LEE HARVEY OSWALD

Six Revolver Cartridges Found in the Revolver at the Time of Oswald's Arrest, C51 - C54 and C137 - C138

On June 11, 1964, Sergeant Jerry Hill, Dallas Police Department, Dallas, Texas, was exhibited revolver cartridges, C51 - C54 and C137 - C138, by Special Agent Vincent E. Drain, Federal Bureau of Investigation. Sergeant Hill identified these cartridges as being the cartridges he removed from the gun, a .38 revolver, which was in the possession of Lee Harvey Oswald at the time he was arrested at the Texas Theatre, Dallas, Texas, on November 22, 1963. Sergeant Hill stated he participated in the arrest with Dallas Patrolmen M. N. McDonald and B.K. Carroll. He stated at the time Oswald was seized in the Texas Theatre he was attempting to pull this gun from his clothing. The gun was seized by B. K. Carroll and M. N. McDonald in Hill's presence and was wrenched away from Oswald and handed to Sergeant Hill. Sergeant Hill stated he kept this gun in his personal possession until he arrived at the Dallas Police Department Headquarters where he placed his name on each of the cartridges. Sergeant Hill advised these were positively the cartridges he had removed from the gun in the possession of Oswald on November 22, 1963, at the time of Oswald's arrest.

Four of these cartridges bearing the name of Hill were subsequently delivered to Special Agent Vincent E. Drain by the Dallas Police Department on November 22, 1963, for delivery to the Laboratory of the Federal Bureau of Investigation, Washington, D. C., for comparison purposes. The other two cartridges bearing the name Hill were released to Secret Service on November 26, 1963.

Re: LEE HARVEY OSWALD

Five Revolver Cartridges Found in Oswald's Pocket at the Time of His Arrest, C55 - C59

On June 12, 1964, five revolver cartridges, designated as C55 through C59, were shown by Special Agent Bardwell D. Odum, Federal Bureau of Investigation, to Detective Elmer Boyd, Homicide Division, Dallas Police Department. He identified his marking on each of these five cartridges and stated these are the same five cartridges which he removed from the pocket of Lee Harvey Oswald at the Dallas Police Department on November 22, 1963.

Re: LEE HARVEY OSWALD

Green and Brown Blanket, C12

On June 19, 1964, Mrs. Marina Oswald was contacted at her home, 629 Belt Line Road, Richardson, Texas, by Special Agents Gary S. Wilson and Vincent E. Drain of the Federal Bureau of Investigation. Special Agent Drain exhibited a green and brown blanket, C12, to Mrs. Oswald, who stated this was the same blanket she had turned over to a representative of the Dallas, Texas, Police Department on the afternoon of November 22, 1963. Mrs. Oswald stated this was the same blanket that was removed from the garage at the residence of Mrs. Ruth Paine, 2515 West 5th Street, Irving, Texas. Mrs. Oswald stated this was the blanket she had observed her husband, Lee Harvey Oswald, wrap a rifle in previous to that time.

On June 11, 1964, Detective G. F. Rose, of the Homicide Bureau, Dallas Police Department, Dallas, Texas, advised he went to the address of 2515 West 5th Street, Irving, Texas, on the afternoon of November 22, 1963. He talked to Marina Oswald. He stated Marina Oswald, when questioned if her husband, Lee Harvey Oswald, owned a rifle, took Detective Rose to the garage at the back of the house at 2515 West 5th Street, Irving, where she pointed out a blanket which Detective Rose stated Marina Oswald thought contained a rifle. Detective Rose picked this blanket up, however, it contained no rifle. With Marina Oswald's permission, Detective Rose brought this blanket, C12, to the Dallas Police Department where it was turned over to Captain Will Fritz, Homicide Bureau, Dallas Police Department.

On June 11, 1964, Special Agent Vincent E. Drain exhibited this green and brown blanket to Detective Rose, and he identified this blanket as being the same blanket which he had obtained on November 22, 1963, from the garage at 2515 West 5th Street, Irving, Texas.

On June 11, 1964, Special Agent Vincent E. Drain exhibited this blanket, C12, to Captain Will Fritz of the Homicide Bureau, Dallas Police Department, and he advised this was the same blanket Detective G. F. Rose turned over to him on November 22, 1963. This blanket was subsequently delivered to Special Agent Vincent E. Drain on November 22, 1963, for delivery to the Laboratory of the Federal Bureau of Investigation, Washington, D. C., for examination.

COMMISSION EXHIBIT No. 2011—Continued

Re: LEE HARVEY OSWALD

Brownish Shirt, C11

On June 9, 1964, Detective Paul Bentley, of the Dallas Police Department, Dallas, Texas, was shown Exhibit C11, a brownish shirt, by Special Agent Vincent E. Drain, Federal Bureau of Investigation.

Upon examination, Detective Bentley advised he could positively identify this brownish shirt, C11, as being the shirt Lee Harvey Oswald was wearing at the time he was arrested in the Texas Theatre, Dallas, Texas, on November 22, 1963. Detective Bentley stated he participated in the arrest of Oswald and Oswald was never out of his custody until he was delivered to Captain Will Fritz, Homicide Bureau, Dallas Police Department, on November 22, 1963. Detective Bentley stated he had placed his initials on this shirt on November 22, 1963. The brownish shirt, C11, was delivered to Special Agent Vincent E. Drain on November 22, 1963, for transmittal to the Laboratory of the Federal Bureau of Investigation, Washington, D. C., for examination.

13

COMMISSION EXHIBIT No. 2011—Continued

Re: LEE HARVEY OSWALD

OSWALD's Hair Samples, C20 - C25

On November 23, 1963, Special Agent C. RAY HALL, Dallas Office of the Federal Bureau of Investigation, observed BOBBY G. BROWN, assisted by Officer JACK DONOHUE, Crime Scene Search Section, Dallas, Texas, Police Department, obtain hair samples from LEE HARVEY OSWALD. As each sample was obtained, it was placed in a pillbox container, which container was sealed, marked and identified by Special Agent HALL.

On June 11, 1964, a photograph (C18 - C25) of the original evidence was examined by Special Agent HALL, who identified the handprinting on the pillboxes as his.

14

COMMISSION EXHIBIT No. 2011—Continued

Re: LEE HARVEY OSWALD

The Wrapping-Paper Bag, C10

On June 9, 1964, Lieutenant J. C. Day, of the Crime Laboratory of the Dallas Police Department, Dallas, Texas, was exhibited the wrapping-paper bag, C10, by Special Agent Vincent E. Drain, Federal Bureau of Investigation. After examining this bag, Lieutenant Day advised he could positively identify this bag as the one he and Detective R. L. Studebaker found on the sixth floor of the Texas School Book Depository building immediately after the assassination of President Kennedy on November 22, 1963. Lieutenant Day stated this paper bag was marked on November 22, 1963, by him. This bag was subsequently delivered on November 22, 1963, to Special Agent Vincent E. Drain for transmittal to the Laboratory of the Federal Bureau of Investigation, Washington, D. C., for examination.

15

COMMISSION EXHIBIT No. 2011—Continued

Four Cartons Found in the Texas School Book Depository, C40

On June 9, 1964, Lieutenant J. C. Day of the Crime Laboratory of the Dallas Police Department, Dallas, Texas, was exhibited four cartons by Special Agent Vincent E. Drain of the Federal Bureau of Investigation. He advised these four cartons, C40, were observed by him on the sixth floor of the Texas School Book Depository building on November 22, 1963. Lieutenant Day stated after he had examined these cartons he instructed they be taken to the Dallas Police Department. Lieutenant Day stated he could identify these boxes as being the boxes he observed in the window and on the floor of the Texas School Book Depository building on November 22, 1963, inasmuch as he had placed his name on same. Lieutenant Day advised these boxes were subsequently delivered to Special Agent Vincent E. Drain on November 27, 1963, for delivery to the Laboratory of the Federal Bureau of Investigation, Washington, D. C., for examination.

COMMISSION EXHIBIT No. 2011—Continued

Oswald's Application for Dallas Post Office Box 2915, D17 (Q34)

On June 16, 1964, Special Agent C. Ray Hall, of the Federal Bureau of Investigation, exhibited to Mr. Harry Holmes, United States Post Office Inspector, Dallas, Texas, a photograph of Oswald's application for Dallas Post Office Box 2915. Inspector Holmes stated that this is a photograph of the original document, which bears his initials, which he had furnished to Special Agent Alfred C. Ellington, of the Federal Bureau of Investigation.

COMMISSION EXHIBIT No. 2011—Continued

LEE HARVEY OSWALD

Oswald's Change of Address Card for Dallas Post Office Box 2915, D18 (K18)

On June 16, 1964, Special Agent C. Ray Hall, of the Federal Bureau of Investigation, exhibited to Mr. Harry Holmes, United States Post Office Inspector, Dallas, Texas, a photograph of Oswald's change of address order for Dallas Post Office Box 2915, ordering the mail transferred to 4907 Magazine Street, New Orleans, Louisiana. Inspector Holmes stated that this is a photograph of the original document, which bears his initials, which he had furnished to Special Agent Alfred C. Ellington, of the Federal Bureau of Investigation.

Re: LEE HARVEY OSWALD

Oswald's Form POD 1093 For New Orleans Post Office Box 30061, D22 (Q36)

On June 23, 1964, Abraham Plough, Foreman of the Mails, Lafayette Square Station, United States Post Office, New Orleans, Louisiana, was contacted at his residence, 2404 Fenelon, Chalmette, Louisiana, by Special Agent Stephen M. Callender, Federal Bureau of Investigation.

Mr. Plough stated he recalled that at approximately 8:00 P.M. on November 22, 1963, he received a telephone call at his residence from Postal Inspector Joseph Zarza, instructing Plough to come to the Lafayette Square Station in order to open the premises. Mr. Plough stated he went to Lafayette Square Station where he met Mr. Zarza, who informed him Zarza desired the Post Office Department application form for Post Office box 30061. Mr. Plough went to a file containing the applications for post-office boxes and obtained the application card for box 30061, which he gave to Inspector Zarza.

A photograph of D22, an application for Post Office box, POD 1093, was exhibited to Mr. Plough. Mr. Plough stated that Post Office Department Form 1093 depicted in this photograph bearing the signature "L. H. Oswald" is the form he gave to Postal Inspector Joseph Zarza.

LEE HARVEY OSWALD

Oswald's Selective Service System
Notice of Classification, B1(2)

On June 11, 1964, Special Agent James W. Bookhout, Federal Bureau of Investigation, exhibited to Paul L. Bentley, Identification Bureau, Dallas Police Department, a photograph of a Selective Service System, Notice of Classification Card, bearing the name Lee Harvey Oswald, Selective Service No. 41-114-39-532, dated February 2, 1960. Bentley identified same as a photograph of a card found by him November 22, 1963, in the wallet, which he obtained from Lee Harvey Oswald, while en route with Oswald to the Dallas Police Department, following the arrest of Oswald at the Texas Theatre.

20

COMMISSION EXHIBIT No. 2011—Continued

LEE HARVEY OSWALD

Oswald's United States Marine
Corps Certificate of Service, B1(4)

On June 11, 1964, Special Agent James W. Bookhout, Federal Bureau of Investigation, exhibited to Paul L. Bentley, Identification Bureau, Dallas Police Department, a photograph of a United States Marine Corps, Certificate of Service Card, in the name of Lee Harvey Oswald, No. 1653230. Bentley identified same as a photograph of a card found by him November 22, 1963, in the wallet, which he obtained from Lee Harvey Oswald while en route with Oswald to the Dallas Police Department, following the arrest of Oswald at the Texas Theatre.

21

COMMISSION EXHIBIT No. 2011—Continued

LEE HARVEY OSWALD

Selective Service System Notice
of Classification in the Name of
Hidell, D207

On June 11, 1964, Special Agent James W. Bookhout, Federal Bureau of Investigation, exhibited to Paul L. Bentley, Identification Bureau, Dallas Police Department, a photograph of a Selective Service System, Notice of Classification Card, bearing the name Alek James Hidell and a photograph of Lee Harvey Oswald. Bentley identified same as a photograph of a card found by him November 22, 1963, in the wallet, which he obtained from Lee Harvey Oswald while en route with Oswald to the Dallas Police Department, following the arrest of Oswald at the Texas Theatre.

22

COMMISSION EXHIBIT No. 2011—Continued

LEE HARVEY OSWALD

United States Marine Corps
Certificate of Service in
the Name of Hidell, D206

On June 11, 1964, Special Agent James W. Bookhout, Federal Bureau of Investigation, exhibited to Paul L. Bentley, Identification Bureau, Dallas Police Department, a photograph of a United States Marine Corps Certificate of Service Card bearing the name Alex James Hidell. Bentley identified same as a photograph of a card found by him November 22, 1963, in the wallet, which he obtained from Lee Harvey Oswald, while en route with Oswald to the Dallas Police Department, following the arrest of Oswald at the Texas Theatre.

23

COMMISSION EXHIBIT No. 2011—Continued

Re: LEE HARVEY OSWALD

Fair Play for Cuba Committee
Card, Dated June 15, 1963, B1(8)

On June 11, 1964, Special Agent James W. Bookhout, Federal Bureau of Investigation, exhibited to Paul L. Bentley, Identification Bureau, Dallas Police Department, a photograph of a Fair Play for Cuba Committee Card, dated June 15, 1963, bearing the name of L. H. Oswald. Bentley identified same as a photograph of a card found by him November 22, 1963, in the wallet, which he obtained from Lee Harvey Oswald while en route with Oswald to the Dallas Police Department, following the arrest of Oswald at the Texas Theatre.

COMMISSION EXHIBIT No. 2011—Continued

Re: LEE HARVEY OSWALD

Vaccination Certificate Signed
Dr. Hideel, 444 (D47)

On June 11, 1964, Special Agent James W. Bookhout, Federal Bureau of Investigation, exhibited to H. M. Moore, Detective, Homicide and Robbery Bureau, Dallas Police Department, a photograph of an International Certificate of Vaccination bearing the name of Lee H. Oswald, New Orleans, Louisiana, dated June 8, 1963, and signed Dr. A. J. Hideel, P. O. Box 30016, New Orleans, Louisiana. Moore identified same as a photograph of a certificate found by him in a search of Lee Harvey Oswald's room at 1026 North Beckley, Dallas, Texas, November 22, 1963. Moore stated he placed his initials, "H.M.M.," and the date, "11/22/63," on same.

COMMISSION EXHIBIT No. 2011—Continued

Re: LEE HARVEY OSWALD

Negatives, B3

On June 11, 1964, Special Agent James W. Bookhout, Federal Bureau of Investigation, exhibited to G. F. Rose, Detective, Homicide and Robbery Bureau, Dallas Police Department, a photograph of the 35 mm negatives, six 2¼ x 2¼ negatives, one negative of Oswald's wife and one positive print of a building, as well as photographs numbered P1 through P33, which were developed from the above negatives.

Rose identified same as photographs of negatives found by him in a search of the garage at the residence of Mrs. Ruth Paine, 2515 West 5th Street, Irving, Texas, on November 23, 1963. Rose stated he had looked at some of the negatives against a light, at the time, and recalls having observed the negatives of the following numbered photographs: P2, P3, P7, P11, P17, P19, P22, P24, P27, P29, P32.

It is to be noted the "P" numbers referred to above are same numbers used in describing the various photographs, as set forth on pages 466 - 467, of the report of Special Agent Robert P. Gemberling, Dallas, dated March 10, 1964.

COMMISSION EXHIBIT No. 2011—Continued

Re: LEE HARVEY OSWALD

Two Photographs Showing Oswald
With a Rifle, D33

On June 11, 1964, Special Agent James W. Bookhout, Federal Bureau of Investigation, exhibited to G. F. Rose, Detective, Homicide and Robbery Bureau, Dallas Police Department, two photographs showing Lee Harvey Oswald with a rifle. Rose identified same as being two photographs in a packet of forty-seven photographs found by him in a box during a search of the garage at the residence of Mrs. Ruth Paine, 2515 West 5th Street, Irving, Texas, November 23, 1963.

Rose stated the following detectives of the Homicide and Robbery Bureau also participated in the search: H. M. Moore, R. S. Stovall and J. P. Adamcik.

On June 15, 1964, Special Agent James W. Bookhout exhibited the above-described photographs to J. P. Adamcik, Detective, Homicide and Robbery Bureau, Dallas Police Department. Adamcik stated these are two photographs from a packet of forty-seven photographs found in the search described above and turned over to the Federal Bureau of Investigation, December 2, 1963, by Captain J. W. Fritz. Adamcik stated since he was present during the search he had numbered each photograph on the back and placed his initials thereon.

Commission Exhibit No. 2011—Continued

Re: LEE HARVEY OSWALD

Application For Employment With
Cosmos Shipping Company, Inc., D28

On June 23, 1964, Ralph C. Hirdes, Manager, Cosmos Shipping Company, Inc., Balter Building, 404 St. Charles Avenue, New Orleans, Louisiana, was contacted by Special Agent Stephen M. Callender, Federal Bureau of Investigation.

Mr. Hirdes informed he personally found the employment application made by Lee H. Oswald with his company, which is dated August 6, 1963. This application, which he furnished to the Federal Bureau of Investigation in November 1963, had been found in a file he maintains which contains employment applications made by various individuals.

A photograph of D28 was exhibited to Mr. Hirdes, at which time he advised the employment application depicted in this photograph is the same as the original application for Lee H. Oswald which he previously furnished to the Federal Bureau of Investigation.

Commission Exhibit No. 2011—Continued

LEE HARVEY OSWALD

Affidavit of Support and
Three Letters, D6

On June 23, 1964, James L. Gribble, Investigator, Immigration & Naturalization Service, 701 Loyola Avenue, New Orleans, Louisiana, was contacted by Special Agent Stephen M. Callender, Federal Bureau of Investigation.

Mr. Gribble advised that on November 23, 1963, he was contacted by representatives of the Federal Bureau of Investigation for the purpose of obtaining samples of the known handwriting of Lee Harvey Oswald which might be contained in his agency's file for Marina Nikolaeva Oswald, who has Immigration and Naturalization Service File No. A12530645. Mr. Gribble personally obtained an Affidavit of Support, dated January 17, 1962, as well as three undated letters date stamped July 2, 6 & 10, 1962, respectively, from the file of Marina Nikolaeva Oswald, which he gave to a representative of the Federal Bureau of Investigation.

Photographs of D6 were exhibited to Mr. Gribble, who stated the Affidavit of Support and the three letters depicted in the photographs are the same documents he furnished to the Federal Bureau of Investigation on November 23, 1963.

Re: LEE HARVEY OSWALD

Jaggars-Chiles-Stovall Checks, D11

Mr. S. L. MALONE, Secretary-Treasurer, Jaggars-Chiles-Stovall, Inc., 522 South Browder Street, Dallas, Texas, was shown photographs of twenty-six checks, on June 11, 1964, by Special Agent C. RAY HALL, of the Dallas Office of the Federal Bureau of Investigation. These checks are drawn on the Jaggars-Chiles-Stovall, Inc., account at the Mercantile National Bank at Dallas, Dallas, Texas, payable to LEE H. OSWALD, signed by S. L. MALONE, and have the following numbers: 2101, 2255, 2408, 2560,2714, 2864, 3016, 3169, 3322, 3472, 3620, 3767, 3912, 4058, 4203, 4348, 4492, 4639, 4781, 4922, 5072, 5217, 5364, 5511, 5663, 5811.

Mr. MALONE stated the signature,"S. L. MALONE," appearing on each of these checks is his signature.

LEE HARVEY OSWALD

New Orleans Library Card, D16

On June 23, 1964, Miss Theresa Militello, Acting Librarian, Main Office, New Orleans Public Library, New Orleans, Louisiana, was contacted by Special Agent Stephen M. Callender, Federal Bureau of Investigation.

Miss Militello advised the original application for a library card in the name of Lee H. Oswald indicating Library Card N8640 had been issued to Oswald which she furnished to the Federal Bureau of Investigation on November 23, 1963, was originally located by Geraldine Vaucresson, an Assistant Librarian at the Napoleon Branch of the New Orleans Public Library. Miss Militello stated she actually obtained this application from a supply cabinet of Mrs. Vaucresson.

On June 24, 1964, Mrs. Geraldine Vaucresson, Assistant Librarian, Napoleon Branch of the New Orleans Public Library, New Orleans, Louisiana, was contacted by Special Agent Stephen M. Callender.

Mrs. Vaucresson stated that on November 23, 1963, at the request of Jacob Liechner, part-time library assistant, she checked the application cards on file and located an application for a library card made by Lee H. Oswald. After locating this application card, she advised Miss Theresa Militello that the application card of Oswald had been placed in the supply cabinet of Mrs. Vaucresson at the Napoleon Branch of the New Orleans Public Library.

A photograph of D16 was exhibited to Mrs. Vaucresson, at which time she stated the application depicted in this photograph was identical to the one she had removed from the application file at the Napoleon Branch of the New Orleans Public Library and thereafter placed in her supply cabinet.

COMMISSION EXHIBIT No. 2011—Continued

Re: LEE HARVEY OSWALD

Notes, The Communist Party of the United States Has Betrayed Itself, 117 (D43)

On June 11, 1964, Special Agent James W. Bookhout, Federal Bureau of Investigation, exhibited to H. M. Moore, Detective, Homicide and Robbery Bureau, Dallas Police Department, photographs of hand printed notes pertaining to "The Communist Party of the United States has betrayed itself." Moore identified same as photographs of notes which he found in a search of the garage at the residence of Mrs. Ruth Paine, 2515 West 5th Street, Irving, Texas, November 23, 1963.

Moore stated the following detectives of the Homicide and Robbery Bureau also participated in the search: G. F. Rose, R. S. Stovall and J. P. Adamcik.

COMMISSION EXHIBIT No. 2011—Continued

Re: LEE HARVEY OSWALD

U. S. Marine Corps File, D5

Special Agent Edward C. Palmer, Federal Bureau of Investigation, displayed a photograph of U. S. Marine Corps file pertaining to Lee Harvey Oswald, Marine Serial Number 1653230, to Captain E. P. Yates, Office of the Secretary of the Navy, Room 4E689, Pentagon Building, on June 1, 1964. Captain Yates identified the photograph of this file as being identical to documents located in the Navy Discharge Review Board Case Number 8812, which case pertains to Oswald.

Captain Yates informed this file had been secured from the closed section of the Navy Discharge Review Board on November 23, 1963, delivered to Captain Robert W. Drewelow, U. S. Navy Duty Officer, Navy Flag Plot Room, Pentagon, for subsequent delivery to a Special Agent of the Federal Bureau of Investigation on November 23, 1963.

COMMISSION EXHIBIT No. 2011—Continued

Re: LEE HARVEY OSWALD

Passport Application, June 24, 1963, D3

On June 1, 1964, Special Agent Eugene C. Gies, Federal Bureau of Investigation, displayed a photograph of a passport application pertaining to Lee Harvey Oswald to Murray E. Bellman, Legal Advisor's Office, United States Department of State (USDS), Washington, D. C. Bellman identified this photograph as being identical to the original passport application located by him in the USDS file relating to Lee Harvey Oswald. Bellman noted the original passport application was made available to a Special Agent of the Federal Bureau of Investigation on November 23, 1963.

Re: LEE HARVEY OSWALD

State Department File, D67

Special Agent Eugene C. Gies, Federal Bureau of Investigation, displayed a photograph of United States Department of State file pertaining to Lee Harvey Oswald to Murray E. Bellman, Legal Advisor's Office, United States Department of State (USDS), Washington, D. C., on June 1, 1964. Bellman identified the photographs as being identical to material located by him in the USDS file relating to Lee Harvey Oswald on November 22, 1963. Bellman noted the original documents were photographed by Special Agents of the Federal Bureau of Investigation on November 23, 1963, and the originals of the documents were left in the possession of the USDS.

Bellman said he believes the complete USDS file relating to Lee Harvey Oswald has since been made available to the President's Commission investigating the assassination of President John F. Kennedy.

COMMISSION EXHIBIT No. 2011—Continued

Re: LEE HARVEY OSWALD

Letter to ACLU, D46

D46 - On May 27, 1964, Assistant Director COURTNEY A. EVANS, Federal Bureau of Investigation, displayed a photograph of Exhibit D46, a letter to the American Civil Liberties Union (ACLU) bearing the signature of Lee H. Oswald and a membership application bearing the name Lee H. Oswald to Mrs. Susan Newman, Assistant Secretary to the Attorney General of the United States. Mrs. Newman stated she recalled receiving this exhibit in a letter received from an official of the ACLU on November 27, 1963. Mrs. Newman stated the original letter from the ACLU was returned and the Exhibit D46 was turned over to Assistant Director Evans.

Re: LEE HARVEY OSWALD

Letter to Secretary of Navy, D4

On June 1, 1964, Special Agent Edward C. Palmer, Federal Bureau of Investigation, displayed to William Earle Odom, Director, Office of News Service, Department of Defense, Room 2E757, Pentagon, a photograph of a handwritten letter from Lee H. Oswald to John B. Connally, Jr., Secretary of Navy, Fort Worth, Texas, dated January 30, 1962. Odom identified this photograph as being identical to the original letter located in the personnel file of Lee Harvey Oswald, Marine Serial Number 1653230.

Odom stated Oswald's file was maintained at the Marine Corps Section of the Federal Records Center (FRC), St. Louis, Missouri. He said this file was telephonically requested on November 22, 1963, from FRC, and was delivered to Adam Yarmolinsky, Special Assistant to Secretary of Defense, and John T. McNaughton, General Counsel, Department of Defense, who in turn made it available to him on November 23, 1963.

Odom noted he had furnished the original of the above letter to Special Agent Palmer on November 23, 1963.

COMMISSION EXHIBIT No. 2011—Continued

Re: LEE HARVEY OSWALD

Letter from Oswald to Brigadier General Tompkins, D4

Special Agent Edward C. Palmer, Federal Bureau of Investigation, displayed to William Earle Odom, Director, Office of News Service, Department of Defense, Room 2E757, Pentagon, on June 1, 1964, a photograph of a handwritten letter from Lee H. Oswald to R. McC. Tompkins, Brigadier General, U. S. Marine Corps, Assistant Director of Personnel, dated March 22, 1962. Odom identified this photograph as being identical to the original letter located in the personnel file of Lee Harvey Oswald, Marine Serial Number 1653230.

Odom stated Oswald's file was maintained at the Marine Corps Section of the Federal Records Center (FRC), St. Louis, Missouri. He said this file was telephonically requested on November 22, 1963, from FRC, and was delivered to Adam Yarmolinsky, Special Assistant to Secretary of Defense, and John T. McNaughton, General Counsel, Department of Defense, who in turn made it available to him on November 23, 1963.

Odom noted he had furnished the original of the above letter to Special Agent Palmer on November 23, 1963.

COMMISSION EXHIBIT No. 2011—Continued

Re: LEE HARVEY OSWALD

Commission Exhibits 55, 56 & 66
(Letters in Russian), 156, 157, 159

On June 11, 1964, Special Agent James W. Bookhout, Federal Bureau of Investigation, exhibited to G. F. Rose, Detective, Homicide and Robbery Bureau, Dallas Police Department, photographs of Federal Bureau of Investigation Exhibits 156, 157 and 159 (Letters in Russian). Rose stated he recognized same as being photographs of letters found in the search of the garage at the residence of Mrs. Ruth Paine, 2515 West 5th Street, Irving, Texas, November 23, 1963, by Detective R. S. Stovall.

On June 15, 1964, Special Agent James W. Bookhout exhibited these same photographs to R. S. Stovall, Detective, Homicide and Robbery Bureau, Dallas Police Department, at which time he identified them as being photographs of letters found by him in the search of the garage at the residence of Mrs. Ruth Paine, 2515 West 5th Street, Irving, Texas, on November 23, 1963.

COMMISSION EXHIBIT No. 2011—Continued

FD-302 (Rev. 1-25-60)

FEDERAL BUREAU OF INVESTIGATION

1

Date 11/26/63

Dr. FRANCIS T. FLOOD, Acting Deputy Medical Officer In Charge, Public Health Service Hospital, 210 State Street, New Orleans, advised the name of LEE HARVEY OSWALD does not appear in the files of that institution, including the clinic vaccination book for June 8, 1963.

He likewise advised Public Health Service Form 731 (Revised January 1, 1957) was again revised on June 1, 1961, and that all copies of the old form have been destroyed. He continued by saying primary vaccinations are given for smallpox but that only legal beneficiaries are entitled to receive them at the Public Health Service Hospital. He pointed out, however, that anyone can obtain a blank Form 731 through the following sources: Government Printing Office, Washington, D. C.; various quarantine stations maintained by Public Health Service, The State Department and various travel agencies.

Dr. FLOOD concluded by stating that there is not now nor has there ever been a doctor in the Public Health Service at New Orleans by the name of A. J. HIDEEL or HIDELL.

On 11/26/63 at New Orleans, Louisiana File # NO 89-69

by SA ROBERT M. WHOMSLEY /bda Date dictated 11/26/63

458

This document contains neither recommendations nor conclusions of the FBI. It is the property of the FBI and is loaned to your agency; it and its contents are not to be distributed outside your agency.

COMMISSION EXHIBIT No. 2012

FD-302 (Rev. 1-25-60) FEDERAL BUREAU OF INVESTIGATION

Date 11/25/63

1

Dr. CHARLES A. STERN, Public Health Service Hospital, New Orleans, reported that to his knowledge there has been no doctor previously employed nor is there a doctor currently employed at that institution named A. J. or ART HIDEEL. He informed appropriate administrative personnel were not available at instant hospital at the time of interview to substantiate information relating to the vaccination of LEE H. OSWALD on June 8, 1963.

On 11/25/63 at New Orleans, Louisiana File # NO 89-69

by SA ROBERT M. WHOMSLEY /jm Date dictated 11/25/63

459

This document contains neither recommendations nor conclusions of the FBI. It is the property of the FBI and is loaned to your agency; it and its contents are not to be distributed outside your agency.

COMMISSION EXHIBIT No. 2012—Continued

FD-302 (Rev. 3-3-59) FEDERAL BUREAU OF INVESTIGATION Commission Exhibit No. 2013

Date 11/24/63

1

At 2:30 AM, I received a telephone call at the office of the Dallas FBI from an unknown male who spoke in a calm voice and asked, "I would like to talk to the man in charge."

I told the caller that the SAC was not present at that time and asked him if someone else could help him. The caller then said, "Wait a minute.", and apparently turned the phone over to another man. I am not certain there were two different voices, however, the tone of the unknown caller's voice changed somewhat at this point.

The voice at this point was calm and mature in sound and this person stated as follows: "I represent a committee that is neither right nor left wing, and tonight, tomorrow morning, or tomorrow night, we are going to kill the man that killed the president. There will be no excitement and we will kill him. We wanted to be sure and tell the FBI, Police Department, and Sheriff's Office and we will be there and we will kill him."

The unknown caller hung up without any other statement and without identifying himself in any manner.

I immediately prepared a memorandum reflecting this information and furnished same to SA MILTON L. NEWSOM. I was present when SA NEWSOM furnished this information to the Dallas County Sheriff's Office at approximately 3:00 AM, and to the Dallas Police Department at 3:20 AM.

on 11/24/63 at Dallas, Texas File # DL 89-43 ~~44-1639~~

by SPC VERNON R. GLOSSUP/cah Date dictated 11/25/63

140

This document contains neither recommendations nor conclusions of the FBI. It is the property of the FBI and is loaned to your agency; it and its contents are not to be distributed outside your agency.

COMMISSION EXHIBIT No. 2013

1
NO 100-16601
MRK/gml

The following investigation was conducted by SA MILTON R. KAACK on January 24, 1964.

The 1964 Directory for the City of New Orleans, does not list an address at 705 Polk Street, nor is there a Polk Street, in the City of New Orleans.

Mr. and Mrs. FRED L. MC COMBS, 711 Polk Avenue, advised that there was no such number as 705 Polk Avenue and that they knew no one in the neighborhood named GEORGE HIDELL.

On January 29, 1964, the following individuals advised that they had no record of GEORGE HIDELL as a student at their respective institutions:

Miss AUDREY BISSO, Registrar's Office, Tulane University.

Dean HARRY J. ENGLER, Loyola University

Miss MARY HOGAN, Registrar's Office, Louisiana State University, in New Orleans.

The 1962 and the 1964 New Orleans City Directories, which are the most recent city directories, and the current directory of the Southern Bell Telephone and Telegraph Company do not list GEORGE HIDELL.

The following investigation was conducted by IC C. L. MURRAY:

On January 29, 1964, Mr. JOSEPH B. TONER, Manager, New Orleans Retailers Credit Bureau, Mrs. GLORIA WATSON, clerk, record room, New Orleans Police Department, and Mrs. CLARE ZIEGLER, clerk Bureau of Identification, New Orleans Police Department, advised that they have no record on anyone named HIDELL.

COMMISSION EXHIBIT No. 2014

— Commission Exhibit No. 2015 —

(11)

NY 105-38431

On December 13, 1963, Miss ROSALEEN QUINN, 214 East 84th Street, Apartment 2D, New York City, New York, advised SA ROGER H. LEE that she has been a stewardess for Pan American Airlines for the past seven years. She stated that during the summer of 1959 she took a leave of absence from Pan American and accompanied her nephew, HENRY ROUSELL, Baton Rouge, Louisiana, to Santa Anna, California. She remained in Santa Anna for approximately one week and resided in a private boarding house. She stated that during the period that she was in Santa Anna she would occasionally visit her nephew, who was in the Marine Corps and stationed in Santa Anna. She remarked that her nephew had arranged two dates for her and the first one of these dates was with LEE HARVEY OSWALD, who was an acquaintance of her nephew's and also a member of the Marine Corps. She advised that her nephew had told her that OSWALD was studying the Russian language and since she had taken a Berlitz course in this language her nephew felt that it would give both of them an opportunity to practice speaking the language. She stated that on the night of the date with subject her nephew brought subject to the boarding house where she was residing, introduced subject to her and then both subject and she had dinner and attended a movie.

Miss QUINN recalled that OSWALD was a quiet individual and that it was difficult to converse with him. She commented that she thought OSWALD spoke Russian well for someone who had not attended a formal course in the language. She stated that she could not recall any statement made by OSWALD which indicated that he was dissatisfied with the United States Government or the United States Marine Corps. She stated that in her opinion the evening date with subject did not prove to be a very interesting one and in fact she could not recall whether OSWALD accompanied her back to her boarding house or whether she returned alone. Miss QUINN stated that the only other date she had while visiting at Santa Anna was with one Lieutenant DONOVAN, described as OSWALD's Company Commander. She concluded by stating that she has never seen nor heard from OSWALD since the above-described meeting and was unable to furnish any additional information regarding him.

COMMISSION EXHIBIT No. 2015

REVIEW OF DISCHARGE
NAVEXOS-2409 (REV. 6-61)

DEPARTMENT OF THE NAVY
NAVY DISCHARGE REVIEW BOARD

TO: SECRETARY OF THE NAVY JAP:gjc DOCKET NO. 8812

REVIEW OF THE DISCHARGE OF				CHARACTER OF DISCHARGE RECEIVED	
OSWALD, Lee Harvey Ex-Pfc 1653230 USMC				UNDES(UNFIT)	
COUNSEL NONE	PETITIONER PRESENT [ ] YES [x] NO		RECORD OF PROCEEDINGS OF REVIEW MADE [ ] YES [x] NO	DATE OF REVIEW 10Jul63	

FINDINGS

DATE OF ENTRY IN NAVAL SERVICE	AGE	[illegible] HELD			TRAITS	GCT
24Oct56	17/0	02X 101 17D	Pvt-Pfc-Pvt-Pfc	3.94 / 4.1		105

SUMMARY OF PETITIONER'S CLAIM: [illegible] case and appropriate action. He submitted a brief which essentially states that his discharge was improperly issued. Also included was pet's statement and two letters from the U.S. Embassy, Moscow. As requested by pet, his lengthy statement was read to the board. It contained his contention that the Undesirable Discharge Board found against him primarily on the grounds that he went to USSR and allegedly renounced his U.S. citizenship to become a citizen of that country. Pet denied this allegation and claimed that since he had a choice of residence as an American citizen, such action could not be judged as being fair or impartial. He further stated that he did not violate any U.S. laws by his actions and quoted in part, an American Embassy, Moscow letter which stated: "Meanwhile, your continued retention of your present Soviet passport or an extension thereof does not prejudice in any way your claim to American citizenship."

SUMMARY OF SERVICE, COMMENDATIONS, AND OFFENSES:

Enl for 3 years. No prior service claimed. Attained equiv of High School grad through USAFI; Grad 46/54 AvnFundScol, JAX and completed AC&WOperCrse, Keesler AFB.

1May57 Pro to PFC.
MACS-1, MAG-11, 1stMAW, FMF

11Apr58 SumCM Violate a lawful general order by having in his possession a privately-owned weapon that was not registered. Sent as appr: CHL for 20 days and forf $25.00 per mo for two mos and red to PVT. (Confinement suspended for 6 mos etc., but vacated on 27Jun58)

27Jun58 SumCM 1. Wrongfully use provoking words to a Staff NCO. (found guilty)
2. Assault a Staff NCO (found not guilty)
Sent as appr: CHL for 28 days and forf $55.00 per mo for 1 month.
SubUnit 1, H&MS 11, MAG-11, 1stMAW

17Oct58 SRB JAG found that injury received by pet on 27Oct57 as a result of an accidental discharge of a weapon, was incurred in line of duty and not result of misconduct. (Upon opening his locker, a .22 cal pistol fell to the floor and discharged, wounding pet in the left elbow.)
MACS-9, MWHG, 3dMAW, AirFMFPac

1Mar59 Pro to PFC

17Aug59 Pet submitted a request for dependency discharge, by reason of hardship on the part of his mother. Pet appeared before the Hardship/Dependency discharge Board who recommended that he be released from active duty for reason of dependency. Appr by CG, 3dMAW on 31Aug59.

(SEE ATTACHED SHEET)

COMMISSION EXHIBIT No. 2016

II - 13

JAP:gjc D# 8812

REVIEW OF THE DISCHARGE OF	CHARACTER OF DISCHARGE RECEIVED
OSWALD, Lee Harvey Ex-Pfc 1653230 USMC	UNDES(UNFIT)

CONCLUSION

REMARKS

The service record of petitioner shows that he was discharged as unfit for good and sufficient reasons. This was based on reliable information which indicated that he had renounced his U.S. citizenship with the intentions of becoming a permanent citizen of the Union of Soviet Socialist Republics. Further, that petitioner brought discredit to the Marine Corps through adverse newspaper publicity, which was generated by the foregoing action, and had thereby, in the opinion of his commanding officer, proved himself unfit for retention in the naval service.

After careful consideration of the facts presented in all available records of the Department of the Navy and of the claims and evidence submitted, the Board finds that the discharge was proper and equitable under standards of law and discipline applicable at the time, or since made applicable, and that the discharge accurately reflects petitioner's conduct and character during the period of service which was terminated by the discharge. Not finding sufficient evidence to support a contrary conclusion, the Board concludes that no change, correction or modification should be made in the type or character of the discharge.

DECISION: NO CHANGE. [illegible]

It is the decision of the Board that the character of the discharge originally issued is proper and that no change, correction or modification be made in the Undesirable Discharge.

(Auth: Sec. 301, Servicemen's Readjustment Act of 1944, P.L. 346 - 78th Congress)

BOARD MEMBERS

President JOHN H. CARROLL, LTCOL, USMC	MEMBER LYLE W. EADS, LCDR, USN
MEMBER R. O. CARLOCK, LTCOL, USMC	MEMBER VIRGIL G. BOWEN, MAJ, USMCR
	RECORDER - CERTIFIED TO BE CORRECT J. A. POLIDORI, MAJ, USMCR

Forwarded

Reviewed and Approved JUL 19 1963
PAUL B. FAY, Jr.
Under Secretary of the Navy

C. W. TRAVIS, CAPT, USN
Director, Navy Council of Personnel Boards

Secretary of the Navy

REVIEW OF DISCHARGE
NAVEXOS-2409 (REV. 6-61)

COMMISSION EXHIBIT No. 2016—Continued

II - 14

JAP:gjc DJ 8812

OSWALD, Lee Harvey Ex-Pfc 1653230 USMC

Summary of Service, Commendations and Offenses: (CONT'D)

11Sep59 Released from active duty (Honorable) and assigned to Ready Reserve, Class XIX, Transferred to MARTC, NAS, Glenview, Ill., for completion of 6 years obligated service ending 8Dec62.

MEDICAL RECORD: Contains nothing pertinent.

HQ, MARTC, NAS, Glenview, Ill.

29Jul60 Mobilization Planning Officer, recommended pct be discharged by reason of unfitness based on reliable information which indicated that pct had renounced his U.S. citizenship with the intentions of becoming a permanent citizen of the Union of Soviet Socialist Republics. Pct's case was heard (in absentia) by the Hardship, Retention and Desirability Board who recommended discharge by reason of unfitness. Pct was notified by certified mail that a board would convene to determine his fitness, and afforded him his rights. The correspondence was returned unclaimed. The findings, opinions and recommendations of the Board were approved by CGMART on 9Aug60, and forwarded to CMC for final determination.

17Aug60 CMC approved and directed discharge.

13Sep60 Discharged by HQ, MARTC, NAS, Glenview, Ill., Auth para 10277.2f, MCM.

Commission Exhibit No. 2016—Continued

Form No. 1588 (Revised) Memorandum Report (7-1-60)

Commission Exhibit No. 2017

UNITED STATES SECRET S.
TREASURY DEP

ORIGIN TYPE OF CASE: Field	OFFICE: Dallas, Texas	FILE NO. CO-2-34,030
Assassination of President Kennedy	STATUS: Continued	TITLE OR CAPTION: Bus Routes
INVESTIGATION MADE AT: Dallas, Texas	PERIOD COVERED: 7-28-64	
INVESTIGATION MADE BY: SA Roger C. Warner		

SYNOPSIS

Bus stops near Oswald's former address, 1026 Beckley Avenue.

DETAILS OF INVESTIGATION

Reference is made to phone call from Inspector Kelley at 12:15 pm, 7-28-64, in which he requested the location of the nearest bus stop utilized by the southbound bus on the Beckley route. He further requested the information when gathered be called back to him at Washington. This was done at 2 pm, same date.

Other Investigations

On 7-28-64 physical inspection was made of the area surrounding 1026 Beckley. The nearest bus stop was found to be located on the northwest corner of the Zangs-Beckley-Eldorado Streets intersection. The next closest bus stop for southbound Beckley bus was at the intersection of 5th Street and Beckley, one block south of the above intersection.

A sketch of the Zangs-Eldorado-Beckley intersection with southbound and northbound Beckley bus stop is attached.

It is noted that the southbound Beckley bus stops at each intersection on Beckley Ave. traveling south.

It is suggested that because the Eldorado-Zangs-Beckley intersection is wide and heavily traveled and equipped with traffic lights, the southbound bus stop at the intersection of 5th and Beckley would be more convenient to reach, even though it is slightly further from the 1026 Beckley address.

DISPOSITION

This phase of the investigation is considered closed.

DISTRIBUTION	COPIES	REPORT MADE BY	DATE
RCW:VS Chief	Orig.& 2 co's W/Sketch	Roger C. Warner, SPECIAL AGENT	7-28-64
Dallas	2 co's	APPROVED: Forrest V. Sorrels, SPECIAL AGENT IN CHARGE	7-28-64

(CONTINUE ON PLAIN PAPER)

SS Control #1719

Commission Exhibit No. 2017

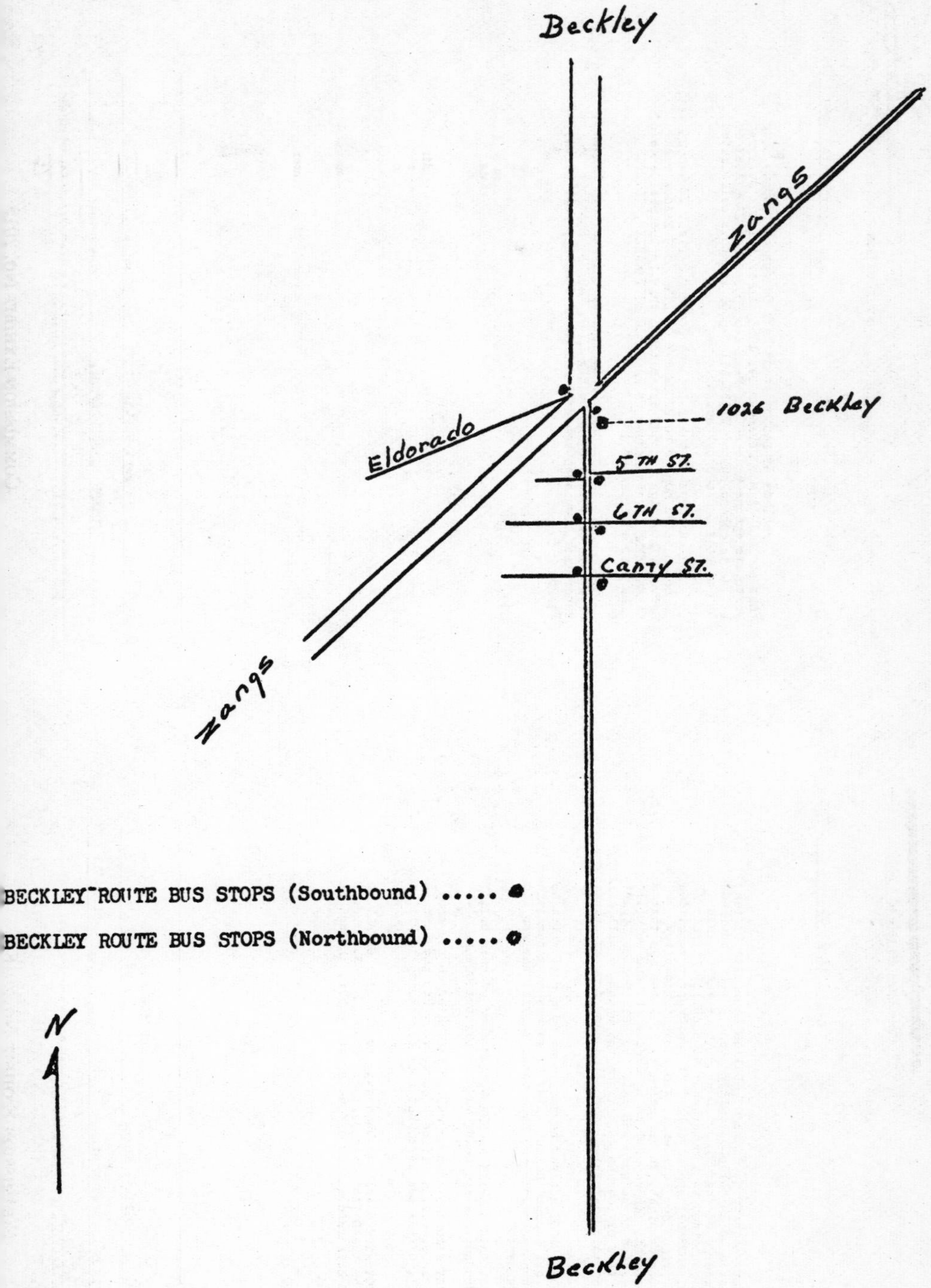

COMMISSION EXHIBIT No. 2017—Continued

[redacted]

Commission Exhibit No. 2018

FD-302 (Rev. 3-3-59)

FEDERAL BUREAU OF INVESTIGATION

Date 11/25/63

1

Deputy Sheriff,C. C. McCOY, Dallas Sheriff's Office, was contacted at 3:00 AM telephonically. Deputy McCOY advised he was man in charge at that time. Deputy McCOY was advised of information contained in a memorandum of Security Patrol Clerk VERNON R. GLOSSUP, specifically, "I represent a committee that is neither right nor left wing, and tonight, tomorrow morning, or tomorrow night, we are going to kill the man that killed the President. There will be no excitement and we will kill him. We wanted to be sure and tell the FBI, Police Department, and Sheriff's Office and we will be there and we will kill him." McCOY was told that this information came from an unknown male caller.

Deputy McCOY advised he had received a call which he believed identical except the man said, "I represent a committee of around one hundred people who have voted to kill the man who killed the President."

McCOY said Sheriff DECKER was advised of this call and security precautions are being made to protect OSWALD.

McCOY said the unknown caller indicated to him they were advising the Sheriff's Office because they did not want any of the Sheriff's Office men hurt, but they were going to kill the man anyway.

McCOY said plans had been made to transfer OSWALD to the County Jail from the Dallas City Jail at 10:00 AM on November 24, 1963. He said this information had been made public through news releases.

on 11/24/63 at Dallas, Texas File # DLfile 44-1639 DL 89-43

by Special Agent MILTON L. NEWSOM/mfr Date dictated 11/24/63

147

This document contains neither recommendations nor conclusions of the FBI. It is the property of the FBI and is loaned to your agency; it and its contents are not to be distributed outside your agency.

COMMISSION EXHIBIT No. 2018

FD-302 (Rev. 3-3-59)

FEDERAL BUREAU OF INVESTIGATION

1

Date December 12, 1963

Records of Southwestern Bell Telephone Company show that at 10:19 A.M., November 24, 1963, an individual at Fort Worth, telephone number JEfferson 4-8525, called JACK RUBY at Dallas telephone number WHitehall 1-5601 and this call lasted two minutes and twenty seconds.

Records of the Telephone Company reflect JE 4-8525 is an unlisted number to BRUCE RAY CARLIN, 3809 Meadowbrook Drive. (Investigation has established this is the residence of KAREN BENNETT, also known as KAREN BENNETT KARLIN, "LITTLE LYNN", an entertainer.)

This information is obtainable only through issuance of a subpoena duces tecum to RONALD G. NAPLES, Exchange Supervisor, Southwestern Bell Telephone Company, Fort Worth, Texas.

on 12/10/63 at Fort Worth, Texas File # DL 44-1639

by Special Agent JOSEPH L. SCHOTT/jn Date dictated 12/10/63

509

This document contains neither recommendations nor conclusions of the FBI. It is the property of the FBI and is loaned to your agency; it and its contents are not to be distributed outside your agency.

COMMISSION EXHIBIT No. 2019

WU 4370 (R 9-54) THE WESTERN UNION TELEGRAPH COMPANY

RECEIPT

MF DALLAS, TEXAS Nov 2 1963

OFFICE DATE

RECEIVED FROM Jack Ruby

ADDRESS 1313 1/2 Commerce

Twenty Five Dollars $ 25.00

☐ Account for the month of ____________ 19__

☐ Telegraphic Money Order

☐ Telegram or Cable

☐ Deposit on Collect Telegram Returnable after 24 hours

☐ Account No. ____________

FOR REMITTANCE

TO Karen Bennett

Address WC

Place Ft Worth Texas

MONEY ORDER CHARGES PAID		
Chgs	$	55
Tolls	$	1.20
Tax	$	12
TOTAL	$	1.87

THE WESTERN UNION TELEGRAPH COMPANY

BY [signature]

P 404

COMMISSION EXHIBIT No. 2020

... TEXAS

1963 NOV 24 AM 11 16

P 404 a

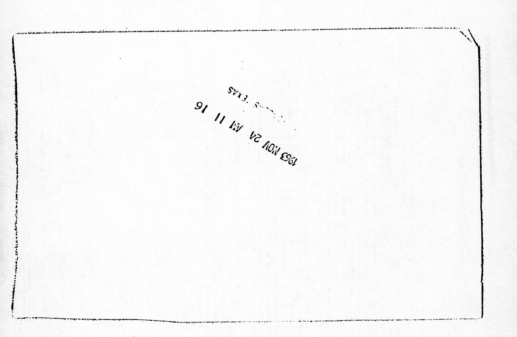

COMMISSION EXHIBIT No. 2020—Continued

Commission Exhibit No. 2021

FD-302 (Rev. 3-3-59)

FEDERAL BUREAU OF INVESTIGATION

1

Date 11/25/63

Shortly after 8:00 AM November 24, 1963 I called Chief of Police JESSE E. CURRY and was unable to reach him. At 8:15 AM, Chief JESSE CURRY called me and first mentioned another matter regarding the evidence which his Department had given us for the FBI Laboratory. I then relayed to him the following, which was given to Security Patrol Clerk VERNON R. GLOSSUP by an unknown caller at 2:30 AM on November 24, 1963: "I represent a committee that is neither right nor left wing, and tonight, tomorrow morning, or tomorrow night, we are going to kill the man that killed the President. There will be no excitement and we will kill him. We wanted to be sure and tell the FBI, Police Department, and Sheriff's Office and we will be there and we will kill him."

Chief CURRY advised me that he had already received this information from one of his officers and that he was taking all precautions. He stated that he had changed his schedule for the moving of OSWALD. He stated he was not going to give this out to the press and that he had two armored cars and that OSWALD would be placed in one of the armored cars and that both of them would go out, which would mean that one of the cars was being used for diversion purposes.

I mentioned to Chief CURRY that according to the employee who received this information from the anonymous caller, that he seemed very calm while talking and could have possibly been reading the statement; he had a very mature sounding voice, and possibly there was another voice heard in the background.

on 11/24/63 at Dallas, Texas DL File 44-1639 DL File # 89-43

by Special Agent in Charge J. GORDON SHANKLIN/mfr Date dictated 11/24/63

150

This document contains neither recommendations nor conclusions of the FBI. It is the property of the FBI and is loaned to your agency; it and its contents are not to be distributed outside your agency.

Commission Exhibit No. 2022

FD-302 (Rev. 3-3-59)

FEDERAL BUREAU OF IN

1

Date 6/10/64

On November 24, 1963, SAs IVAN D. LEE and ROBERT M. BARRETT were contacting EDDIE BARKER, Director of KRLD-TV and Radio News, at his office. In Mr. BARKER's office was a television monitor and BARKER explained it was set on a closed-circuit channel and that in a few moments the Agents could observe the removal of LEE HARVEY OSWALD from the Dallas City Jail to the Dallas County Jail via this closed-circuit television.

After observing a man later identified as JACK L. RUBY shoot OSWALD in the basement of the City Hall, and within 30 seconds of the shooting, SA BARRETT telephonically reported what he and SA LEE had observed via television to Special Agent in Charge J. GORDON SHANKLIN at the Dallas FBI Office. SAC SHANKLIN has advised SAs BARRETT and LEE that immediately upon receiving their report he placed a telephone call via direct dialing to FBI Headquarters in Washington, D. C., telephone No. EXecutive 3-7100, to report the incident.

After telephonically reporting the incident to SAC SHANKLIN, SAs BARRETT and LEE made notes of what they had observed to be used later in the dictation of a report of the matter. Preparation of the notes took place about 8 to 10 minutes after the shooting and the Agents had to approximate the time of the shooting as 11:25 a.m. This approximation was based on estimation of time lapse and the Agents' own personal wristwatches, the accuracy of which is unknown.

on 6/8/64 at Dallas, Texas File # DL 44-1639

by Special Agent ROBERT M. BARRETT and IVAN D. LEE:vm 130 Date dictated 6/9/64

This document contains neither recommendations nor conclusions of the FBI. It is the property of the FBI and is loaned to your agency; it and its contents are not to be distributed outside your agency.

FD-302 (Rev. 3-3-59)

FEDERAL BUREAU OF INVESTIGATION

Date 6/10/64

1

Records of Southwestern Bell Telephone Company, Dallas, Texas, show that a telephone call was placed from a number assigned to the FBI Office, Dallas, via direct dialing, to EXecutive 3-7100, Washington, D. C., at 11:22 a.m., November 24, 1963.

The above information can be made public only through the issuance of a subpoena duces tecum directed to Mr. R. A. BURROW, Chief Special Agent, Southwestern Bell Telephone Company, Dallas, Texas.

on 6/8/64 at Dallas, Texas File # DL 44-1639

by Special Agent ROBERT M. BARRETT and IVAN D. LEE:vm 131 Date dictated 6/9/64

This document contains neither recommendations nor conclusions of the FBI. It is the property of the FBI and is loaned to your agency; it and its contents are not to be distributed outside your agency.

COMMISSION EXHIBIT No. 2022—Continued

FD-302 (Rev. 3-3-59)

FEDERAL BUREAU OF INVESTIGATION

1

Date 11/24/63

Mr. BOBBY G. BROWN, Crime Scene Search Section of the Identification Bureau, Dallas, Texas, Police Department, advised that at 2:45 P.M., November 23, 1963, he, accompanied by Officer JACK DONAHUE, and with the consent of LEE HARVEY OSWALD, obtained scrapings from under the fingernails of the right and left hands of LEE HARVEY OSWALD; specimens of hair from the head, right armpit, chest, right forearm, pubic area, and right leg of LEE HARVEY OSWALD. BROWN made these specimens available to SA C. RAY HALL.

on 11/23/63 at Dallas, Texas File # DL 89-43

by Special Agent C. RAY HALL/ejg/sah Date dictated 11/23/63

143

This document contains neither recommendations nor conclusions of the FBI. It is the property of the FBI and is loaned to your agency; it and its contents are not to be distributed outside your agency.

COMMISSION EXHIBIT No. 2023

Commission Exhibit No. 2024

FD-302 (Rev. 3-3-59)

FEDERAL BUREAU OF INVESTIGATION

1

Date 11-25-63

On November 25, 1963, Mr. C. J. PRICE, Administrator, Parkland Memorial Hospital, Dallas, Texas, advised that a statement concerning resuscitative efforts, LEE HARVEY OSWALD had been prepared at 5:00 p.m., November 24, 1963, by M. T. JENKINS, MD, Professor and Chairman, Department of Anesthesiology. This statement, a copy of which has been given the FBI, reflects that at approximately 11:27 a.m., November 24, 1963, Dr. RONALD JONES, Senior Resident in general surgery after being notified through the Office of the Administrator of Parkland Memorial Hospital informed a surgical and anesthesiology team that LEE HARVEY OSWALD had sustained a gunshot wound and was being brought to the emergency operating room at Parkland Memorial Hospital for emergency and definitive treatment. By the time the patient OSWALD was reported in the emergency operating room at 11:32 a.m., there was assembled a resuscitation team in E.O. R. Surgical Room #2. Statement further reflects a time table description of medical treatment administered up to 1:05 p.m. when statement indicates it was apparent that the lens had become opaque and retinal circulation was not observed. At 1:07 p.m. the patient OSWALD was pronounced dead.

It should be noted that the statement reflects the bullet which had palpable in the right posterior axillary line was removed and sent out by Dr. ROBERT SHAW and Miss AUDREY BELL to be turned over to the law authorities.

Mr. PRICE further advised that report of emergency case number 48162 dated April 18, 1945, reflects that OSWALD, LEE, 4801 Victor, Dallas, Texas, at the age of five was treated for an injury sustained when he was hit in the left eye by a rock. Patient was treated with ice packs and discharged on April 19, 1945.

410

on 11-25-63 at Dallas, Texas File # DL 44-1639 DL 89-43

by Special Agent JAMES W. SWINFORD md Date dictated 11-25-63

This document contains neither recommendations nor conclusions of the FBI. It is the property of the FBI and is loaned to your agency; it and its contents are not to be distributed outside your agency.

5 410

Commission Exhibit No. 2025

FD-302 (Rev. 3-3-59)

FEDERAL BUREAU OF INVESTIGATION

1

Date 12/7/63

CONVERSATION BETWEEN ATTORNEY TOM HOWARD AND CAPTAIN J. W. FRITZ, HOMICIDE AND ROBBERY BUREAU, DALLAS POLICE DEPARTMENT, ON DECEMBER 6, 1963, AND PRESENCE OF AGENTS.

On December 6, 1963, SAs JAMES W. BOOKHOUT and GEORGE W. H. CARLSON were called into the office of Captain J. W. FRITZ, Homicide and Robbery Bureau, Dallas Police Department, at which time Captain FRITZ made available two postcards from JOSEPHINE BRYGGS, 2100½ Crenshaw Blvd., Los Angeles, California. While discussing the above with Captain FRITZ, Attorney TOM HOWARD came into the office and spoke to Captain FRITZ.

Captain FRITZ asked HOWARD if he had obtained any information from JACK RUBY that might be helpful in the investigation, specifically had RUBY told him how he got into the City Hall building on November 24, 1963.

HOWARD stated RUBY had told him how he (RUBY) got in the basement, and the facts were the same as he (HOWARD) had released to the newspaper. HOWARD related that on November 24, 1963, at about 10:30 AM, RUBY was at his (RUBY's) home when he received a long-distance telephone call from some woman in Fort Worth who wanted RUBY to send her some money. HOWARD stated (FNU) SENATOR, RUBY's roommate, was present at the time RUBY received the call and corroborates same. HOWARD said RUBY thereafter dressed and went directly to the Western Union and sent $25 to the girl in Fort Worth. HOWARD stated he understood Western Union records reflect same sent at 11:16 AM, November 24, 1963. HOWARD said RUBY told him that after leaving the Western Union RUBY walked up Main Street to the Main Street ramp leading to the basement of the City Hall building. HOWARD said that RUBY said that as RUBY approached the ramp, an automobile was at the entrance of the ramp, and the driver of this automobile called the officer, standing at the ramp entrance, over to the automobile. While this officer was talking to the driver of the automobile, RUBY walked behind the officer and down the ramp into the basement of the City Hall building.

on 12/6/63 at Dallas, Texas File # DL 44-1639

by Special Agents SAs GEORGE W. H. CARLSON and JAMES W. BOOKHOUT :lp Date dictated 12/7/63

This document contains neither recommendations nor conclusions of the FBI. It is the property of the FBI and is loaned to your agency; it and its contents are not to be distributed outside your agency.

21

Commission Exhibit No. 2024 Commission Exhibit No. 2025

DL 44-1639

2

Captain FRITZ asked HOWARD how long RUBY had been in the basement before the killing. HOWARD stated that RUBY told him (HOWARD) that after walking down the ramp he stood in the basement only a very short time when he saw Captain FRITZ walk out and then saw OSWALD and the other officers. HOWARD pointed out that he had heard that the time of the killing had been fixed as 11:21 AM or 11:26 AM, and therefore, he (RUBY) could not have been in the basement very long.

Captain FRITZ asked HOWARD if RUBY had given him any indication that he (RUBY) knew the officer stationed at the head of the ramp. HOWARD said no. FRITZ asked why, then, had RUBY refused to discuss this point with him (FRITZ). HOWARD stated the reason was because RUBY did not want to get the officer in trouble.

FRITZ asked HOWARD if RUBY had said why he shot OSWALD. HOWARD stated that from talking to RUBY, he (HOWARD) feels that RUBY probably thought that he would be a hero and would be carried out on the shoulders of those present.

FRITZ asked HOWARD if there was any possibility of RUBY having any communist connections or Cuban connections. HOWARD said "absolutely no."

FRITZ asked HOWARD if RUBY knew OSWALD prior to the killing. HOWARD stated RUBY had not known OSWALD.

FRITZ asked HOWARD if RUBY had ever killed anybody before. HOWARD said no, but he understood at one time in the past, an associate of RUBY's had been killed, but that RUBY was not involved in the killing; HOWARD did not elaborate further.

HOWARD stated RUBY indicated he had been active in the past in some union in Chicago.

HOWARD said that he was leaving town this weekend to confer with the attorney who was going to take the lead in RUBY's murder trial (name of attorney not disclosed). HOWARD said that he (HOWARD) and the unnamed attorney will decide whether there is any reason why an interested agency should not interview RUBY and get all the background concerning RUBY first-hand. HOWARD said in his opinion, it would be to RUBY's advantage to give complete information concerning his (RUBY's) past so it could be definitely established beyond anyone's doubt that RUBY had no communist connections or prior acquaintance with OSWALD.

22

COMMISSION EXHIBIT No. 2025—Continued

FD-302 (Rev. 3-3-59)

FEDERAL BUREAU OF [ ] Commission Exhibit No. 2026

Date 12/5/63

1

SA LEO L. ROBERTSON, who is 6 feet, 3 inches tall, walking at a normal rate of speed, took the following set out time to cover these distances:

From the far entrance at the front of the Western Union office down Main Street ramp leading into the basement of the Dallas Police Department--105 steps--63 seconds.

From the near Western Union door to the middle of the Main Street entrance--101 steps--58 seconds.

From the middle of the sidewalk of the Main Street ramp to the place where the shooting occurred--33 steps--22 seconds.

SA JAMES C. KENNEDY is 5 feet, 10 inches tall, and walking at a normal rate of speed, covered the distance from the nearest WEstern Union door to the middle of the sidewalk of the Main Street ramp in 107 steps--62 seconds.

From the middle of the sidewalk of the ramp to the place where the shooting occurred--37 steps--22 seconds.

The Western Union Building is located at 2034 Main Street, and Central Expressway, going south, runs by the east side of the building. Main Street runs on the north side of the building, and the building is in the same block with the police station. The above-mentioned doors open on the north, or on Main Street.

Captain O. A. JONES, of the Dallas Police Department, had the man in the Police Crime Laboratory measure the actual distance from the east end of the Western Union Building to the center of the Main Street ramp and found that it was 356 feet and 6 inches. It is to be noted that there are two doors opening on Main Street from the Western Union Building.

He stated the first door, or the one farthest from the police station, was 18 feet from the east side of the Western Union Building to the center of the first door of this

on 12/4/63 at Dallas, Texas File # DL 44-1639

by Special Agents JAMES C. KENNEDY and LEO L. ROBERTSON - LAC Date dictated 12/4/63

This document contains neither recommendations nor conclusions of the FBI. It is the property of the FBI and is loaned to your agency; it and its contents are not to be distributed outside your agency.

23

COMMISSION EXHIBIT No. 2026

DL 44-1639
2

building. He stated the first door, or the one farthest from the police station, was 10 feet from the east side of the Western Union Building to the center of the first door of this building. He stated it was 17 feet from the center of the first door to the center of the second door of the Western Union Building. By steel tape, it measured 99 feet from the center of the sidewalk to the corner of the wall on the east side of the corridor that goes to the jail office, where OSWALD was led out at the time he was shot. It is approximately 8 feet from the center of the driveway on a line with this east wall to the point where OSWALD was shot.

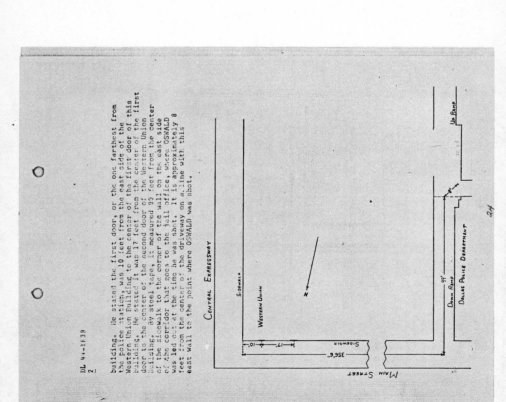

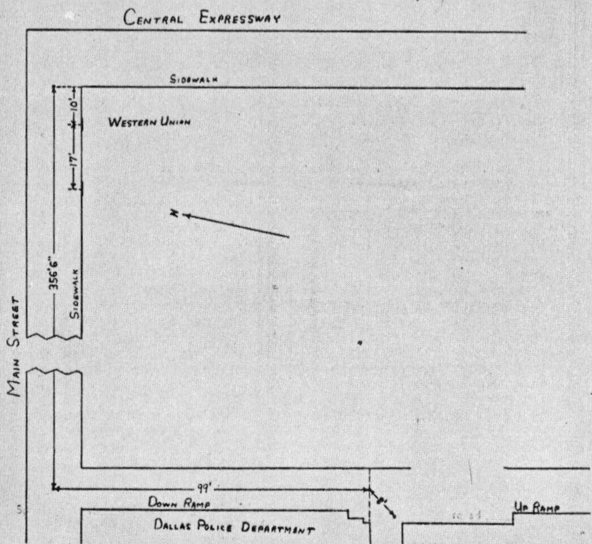

24

FD-302 (Rev. 3-3-59)

[redacted]

Commission Exhibit No. 2027

...ber 4, 1963

(1)

Detective DANIEL G. BRANTLEY advised that he is in the Burglary and Theft Detail of the Dallas Police Department. He was advised that he did not have to make a statement; that any statement he made could be used against him in a court of law, and that he was entitled to talk to an attorney. BRANTLEY voluntarily furnished the following information:

On November 24, 1963, he was assigned by Lieutenant SWAIN of the Burglary Detail to go to the basement of the Dallas Police Department. He and other detectives were told to "spread out and be inconspicuous and watch the crowd in the lobby." The lobby is the area between the information desk and the jail windows. BRANTLEY was instructed to do this shortly before LEE HARVEY OSWALD was brought out from the jail to be taken to the County Jail.

When BRANTLEY arrived in the lobby area there were two uniformed officers at the door leading from the lobby to the ramp. BRANTLEY believes that he would not have been allowed to go through that door without identifying himself. BRANTLEY went to the lobby and observed the crowd and also saw OSWALD when he was being taken from the elevator to the ramp area. He lost sight of OSWALD and the detectives transporting OSWALD within a short time after they left the elevator and did not see OSWALD further and did not see him shot.

Shortly after OSWALD was taken through a door onto the ramp area, he heard a shot and he ran to the ramp to see what was going on. He saw considerable struggling going on and only saw JACK RUBY's face. He heard someone say that it was JACK RUBY who had shot OSWALD.

BRANTLEY estimated there were 40 to 50 persons on the outside ramp area where the shooting took place and approximately half of those persons were probably people from the news media. There were television cameras and other cameras set up out on the ramp area. He does not know what the entire security picture was or what other persons' orders were in connection with security of the basement area. He does recall that when he rode down on the elevator two men pushing a television camera were trying to get on the elevator and he helped them get the camera on the elevator. When he arrived in the basement, he heard one man say to the other "I believe we can push through this crowd and go up the ramp." BRANTLEY does not believe that they would have been challenged or that anyone else appearing with a camera would have been challenged if they appeared to be working for a news media.

on 12/3/63 at Dallas, Texas File # DL 44-1639

by Special Agents JAMES E. CARRIS and JACK B. ... Date dictated 12/4/63

This document contains neither recommendations nor conclusions of the FBI. It is the property of the FBI and is loaned to your agency; it and its contents are not to be distributed outside your agency.

37

BRANTLEY was not told to check identification himself. He was instructed only to watch the crowd in the lobby.

BRANTLEY has heard rumors that JACK RUBY was around the Police Department for the two previous days and he is of the opinion that on this day RUBY just walked in.

Every person that he personally saw inthe lobby appeared to be either with a news media or with the Police Department. There were uniformed officers at practically every door and he does not believe that he would have been allowed to pass those officers unless he identified himself. However, he felt that if he had had a camera and had looked as if he were with some TV station or newspaper he would probably have been allowed to pass without displaying identification.

Detective BRANTLEY informed that he had been in JACK RUBY's place, the Carousel, on two or three occasions, but he said RUBY does not know him by name and he has never worked for RUBY. He said that when he was in RUBY's place he would have talked with RUBY because RUBY makes a special point of being friendly with officers of the Police Department.

BRANTLEY said he did not see RUBY any time between November 22 and November 24, and he does not have any information indicating that RUBY and OSWALD were acquainted prior to the shooting.

3-8

COMMISSION EXHIBIT No. 2027—Continued

FD-302 (Rev. 3-3-59)

FEDERAL BUREAU OF INVESTIGATION

Date December 1, 1963

1

Mr. JAMES K. RAMSEY was advised that he was being interviewed by Agents of the FBI and he did not have to make a statement. He was advised that any statement during course of this interview could be used against him or in a court of law. He was advised of his right to consult with an attorney before submitting to the interview and no threats or promises were given to Mr. RAMSEY during course of interview.

RAMSEY advised he is a Detective assigned to the Forgery Bureau of the Dallas Police Department and was working his regular duty schedule of 8:00 a.m. to 4:00 p.m. on the day of November 24, 1963. Detective RAMSEY said he is under the direction of Captain O. A. JONES and on the day of November 24 was asked to standby in the Forgery Bureau which is located on the third floor of City Hall in the Police Department.

Detective RAMSEY stated about 10:30 a.m. he and Detective R. C. WAGNER, who is also in the Forgery Bureau, left the third floor of the Police Department and went down into the basement of City Hall which is located below the level of the street.

Detective RAMSEY stated there had been information circulating among detectives and photographers this day that LEE HARVEY OSWALD, the alleged assassin of President KENNEDY who was confined at the City Jail, was going to be transferred from City police custodyto the custody of the Dallas County Sheriff's Office, located in Dallas. He stated it was obvious at the time that they went to the basement ofe the City Hall that OSWALD had not been transferred at that time.

Mr. RAMSEY stated after arriving in the basement about 10:30 a.m., he went into the area used to park police cars, squad cars and other vehicles in the city hall where there were a group of uniformed police officers stationed with whom he had formerly worked. He stated among these officers he can recall seeing and talking with Officers GERALD L. TOLBERT, D. K. ERWIN, Badge 1849, and MAX FARRIS. He stated there were a number of uniformed officers in the parking area posted at various places; however, he could not recall others than he mentioned above. He stated there were approximately 25 uniformed officers stationed in the general area of the parking area portion of the basement. He stated at this time he would estimate the

on 11/30/63 at Dallas, Texas File # Dallas 44-1639

by Special Agents WARREN A. LARSON & RAYMOND M. LESTER, JR.:BL Date dictated 12/1/63

207

This document contains neither recommendations nor conclusions of the FBI. It is the property of the FBI and is loaned to your agency; it and its contents are not to be distributed outside your agency.

COMMISSION EXHIBIT No. 2028

Commission Exhibit No. 2029

FD-302 (Rev. 3-3-59)

FEDERAL BUREAU OF INVESTIGATION

Date December 4, 1963

(1)

Detective H. BARON REYNOLDS, Dallas, Texas, Police Department, who resides at 1607 Pat Drive, Dallas, was contacted concerning the shooting of LEE HARVEY OSWALD on the morning of November 24, 1963, at the Dallas City Hall. REYNOLDS was advised he did not have to make a statement; that any statement he did make could be used against him in a court of law, and that he could consult an attorney at any time he desired. REYNOLDS voluntarily advised as follows:

On the morning of November 24, 1963, he was assigned by Lieutenant (FNU) SWAIN, Burglary and Theft Division, Dallas Police Department, to security duty in the lobby of the basement at City Hall, which area is adjacent to the basement ramp where OSWALD was shot and killed. REYNOLDS said he did not arrive at his duty station until approximately 11 a.m. He said to the best of his knowledge all exits to the basement were secure, but added he had no occasion to personally observe the basement ramp or the two exits to the ramp leading to Commerce and Main Streets. He stated that everyone in the lobby where he was assigned was required to properly identify himself and there was no unauthorized person in the lobby, to his knowledge.

He said at approximately 11:20 a.m. that morning he saw OSWALD leave the basement elevator, accompanied by two plain clothesmen. He and others in the lobby were able to see OSWALD as he left the elevator, through windows on one side of the lobby, but no one in the lobby could see OSWALD as he was led on to the basement ramp since the view was blocked shortly after OSWALD left the elevator. He said moments later he heard what sounded like a revolver being fired. He then heard someone yell that OSWALD had been shot, and he immediately proceeded to the Commerce Street side of the basement and instructed a uniformed officer, name unknown, on duty there to block the exit.

REYNOLDS said at the very moment he heard the shot he also heard Dallas Police Detective J. R. LEAVELLE, who was one of the two plain clothesmen escorting OSWALD on to the ramp, yell "You S.O.B." REYNOLDS later heard from unrecalled sources that Dallas Police Officer (FNU) VAUGHN of the Radio Patrol Division was on duty at the time of the shooting at the Main Street entrance to the basement ramp.

He also heard later from unrecalled sources there was a rumor to the effect that shortly before the shooting of OSWALD, JACK RUBY was seen getting out of an unattended Dallas police squad car parked in the basement parking area. He knew nothing further concerning this matter.

on 12/3/63 at Dallas, Texas File # DL 44-1639

by Special Agents JAMES E. GARRIS and JACK B. PEDEN:bnm Date dictated 12/4/63

This document contains neither recommendations nor conclusions of the FBI. It is the property of the FBI and is loaned to your agency; it and its contents are not to be distributed outside your agency.

FD-302 (Rev. 3-3-59)

1

FEDERAL BUREAU OF INVESTIGATION

Other Individuals and Organizations Involved or Interviewed

Date Dec. 11, 1963

Patrolman GERALD K. SPRINGER, 12211 Sunland, Dallas Police Department, was interviewed and was immediately advised of the official identity of Special Agent LEO L. ROBERTSON. He was advised that he did not have to make a statement, that any statement he did make could be used against him in a court of law and that he had the right to consult an attorney prior to making any statement. He then furnished the following information:

He advised that on November 24, 1963, he was in a patrol car in the downtown area. He stated a call came on the radio for any cars who were unassigned to check in the radio. He stated his call number was 111, and when he checked in, he was instructed to come to Central Headquarters and report to the Chief's office for assignment.

He stated that he drove into the Main Street ramp, that Patrolman VAUGHN was on duty along with a couple of reserve policemen, whose names he did not know. He stated he observed 10 or 15 people standing back a few feet from either side of the ramp but they were not trying to go down into the basement. He did not pay much attention to the crowd and did not recognize anyone standing there on the sidewalk. He stated he parked his car near the First Aid Station, which is located on the northeast corner of the basement garage and proceeded to the 3rd floor of the building to the Chief's office. He stated this was at approximately 10:30 a.m. as nearly as he can recall and that when he arrived on the 3rd floor, Patrolman ART HAMMETT advised him to pick up some telegrams and other mail and deliver it to Mrs. TIPPIT, the wife of the slain policeman.

When he left the 3rd floor and started back to his car, he noticed several newsmen, cameras, photographers and other persons there, but he did not pay too much attention to them and did not recognize any of them. He stated there could have been 8 or 10 or possibly more, but he was not thinking about how many were there and could not give a more accurate estimate.

on 12/10/63 at Dallas, Texas File # DL 44-1639

by Special Agent LEO L. ROBERTSON/csh Date dictated 12/10/63

This document contains neither recommendations nor conclusions of the FBI. It is the property of the FBI and is loaned to your agency; it and its contents are not to be distributed outside your ag[redacted]

Commission Exhibit No. 2030

DL 44-1639

He advised he got in his car, pulled out of the police station, and was in the vicinity of Ervay and Jackson Streets when he received a call on the radio to report back to the Central Police Station. He stated he again drove through the Main Street entrance, was admitted by Patrolman VAUGHN and the same two reserve officers and parked his car in the same place as before in the basement. He stated he went back to the 3rd floor and Patrolman HAMMETT told him to disregard his assignment, that they would take the mail and so forth out to Mrs. TIPPIT later on.

He went back to the basement, contacted Sergeant PUTNAM and asked if there was anything he wanted him to do. Sergeant PUTNAM told him there was nothing for him to do, that all of the men had been assigned so he got back in his car, drove out the Commerce Street exit and left on a burglary investigation.

He stated he was in South Dallas approximately at the intersection of Hatcher and Scyene Streets when he heard on the radio that OSWALD had been shot. He stated he had formerly been on assignment where he worked downtown and made periodic checks in the Carousel Club and other "joints" of that nature, and he knew JACK RUBY when he saw him. He estimated it had been two or three months since he had seen RUBY and he did not see him in the basement or on Main Street the day of the shooting.

He advised he had never heard any information concerning a relationship between RUBY and OSWALD. He further advised he had never worked for RUBY and did not know of any police officers who had, stating it was against departmental regulations for a Dallas police officer to work in an establishment where alcoholic beverages were served.

221

COMMISSION EXHIBIT No. 2030—Continued

Date December 4, 1963

(1)

Detective IVAN R. STEPHENS, Burglary and Theft Detail, Dallas Police Department, residing at 11306 Stalcup, Dallas, Texas, was advised that he did not have to make a statement; that any statement he made could be used against him in a court of law, and that he was entitled to talk with an attorney. He furnished the following information:

STEPHENS was instructed, on the morning of November 24, 1963, which is the day that LEE HARVEY OSWALD was shot in the Dallas Police Department, to go to the lobby of the basement area of the Dallas Police Department. Lieutenant SWAIN of the Burglary Detail, ordered him and approximately two or three other officers, whose identities he cannot recall at this time, to go to the lobby and "help any way we could." These instructions came just prior to the transfer time of OSWALD. STEPHENS and the other unidentified officers got to the lobby of the basement, and he thought there would be a supervisor there to give him instructions, but there was no supervisor to tell him what to do.

He stood in the lobby in front of the windows through which one can look and see the booking desk of the Sergeant. He had to show his badge on several occasions during the day, but when he arrived in the lobby he does not believe he was required to identify himself.

He estimated that there were 8 or 9 photographers and cameramen in the lobby which is a small area, and the area was quite crowded. He did not try to go on to the ramp area at that time but saw through the windows that OSWALD was being brought out of the elevator and on to the ramp area. Immediately after he heard the pistol shot he went to the swinging doors leading from the lobby area to the ramp area. He saw only turmoil and then realized that the officers were trying to get OSWALD back inside the booking room. He helped keep the crowd back as they returned OSWALD and got RUBY through the door into the booking area.

STEPHENS said he did not know of the entire security taken by the Dallas Police Department or what the overall plan was. He did notice approximately eight or nine photographers and four or five detectives in the lobby area, which area he had been sent to observe. He would estimate there were

on 12/3/63 at Dallas, Texas File # DL 44-1639

by Special Agent s JAMES E. GARRIS and JACK B. PEDEN:bnm Date dictated 12/4/63

224

*This document contains neither recommendations nor conclusions of the FBI. It is the property of the FBI and is loaned to your agency; it and its contents are not to be distributed outside your agency.

COMMISSION EXHIBIT No. 2031

Commission Exhibit No. 2032

FD-302 (Rev. 3-3-59)

FEDERAL BUREAU OF INVESTIGATION

Date 12/4/63

1

DONALD T. SUITS, 233 Sendero, Garland, Texas, advised that he was a Dallas Reserve Policeman who was on duty the day OSWALD was shot in the Central Police Station. He advised that Lieutenant BEN MC COY, Police Reserve Lieutenant, called and told him to report to the Assembly Room in the Central Police Station between 9:00 and 9:15 AM, on November 24, 1963. He stated his assignment was to check the reserve men in as they reported for duty. He recalled there were about twenty-six of them.

He stated that Sergeant DEAN, of the regular Police Department, came in about 9:20 AM and asked the reserves to help "shake" the basement down. He stated that the reserves, as well as regular police officers, checked every car and newsmen in the basement and found everything in order.

SUITS advised he did not see the shooting, as he was standing on the west side of the first car that was parked in the driveway just outside the corridor where they led OSWALD out. He stated he was trying to keep the crowd back on the east side of the driveway at the time the shooting occurred and, therefore, was unable to see it. He stated he looked around immediately after hearing a noise, which he thought was a flash bulb popping at the time, and saw several plain-clothes men struggling with a man whom he later found out was RUBY. He advised he had heard of RUBY, but had never met him and would not have known him had he seen him. He never heard of any reserves or regular police officers who had worked for RUBY.

SUITS estimated there were probably at least 100 people in the basement besides the police officers and he assumed that most of them were newsmen, photographers, and television cameramen. He stated he saw a few people, probably five or six, come down the south ramp where the armored truck was parked prior to the time of the shooting and, in each instance, the officers standing there required them to show identification before they allowed them to pass. He stated that about five or six minutes before the shooting they apparently had stopped everyone from coming in, as he did not see anyone coming down during that interval.

on 12/3/63 at Dallas, Texas File # DL 44-1639

by Special Agents LEO L. ROBERTSON & PAUL L. SCOTT/eah Date dictated 12/3/63

This document contains neither recommendations nor conclusions of the FBI. It is the property of the FBI and is loaned to your agency; it and its contents are not to be distributed outside your agency.

Commission Exhibit No. 2033

MARK LANE
ATTORNEY AT LAW
654 MADISON AVE.
NEW YORK 21, N. Y.
TEMPLETON 8-1900

Rec'd. Pres. Comm.
DEC 24 1963

December 17, 1963

Hon. Earl Warren
Justice of the United States Supreme Court
Washington, D.C.

Dear Justice Warren:

As an attorney who witnessed the destruction of almost every right ordinarily available to a person charged with the commission of a crime in the matter of the arrest, interrogation and subsequent killing of Mr. Lee H. Oswald, I felt constrained to comment upon the serious breaches of law and ethics that took place. Accordingly, I drafted an article for publication dealing with these and other related questions. It has been suggested that I submit that article to you for whatever use you may be able to make of it. I submit it herewith.

May I respectfully request that your Commission give consideration to the appointment of defense counsel in order that in your inquiry an advocate zealously protecting his client's rights may be present; an advocate who may examine documents and cross examine witnesses. It would be appropriate, I suggest, that Mr. Oswald, from whom every legal right was stripped, be accorded counsel who may participate with the single purpose of representing the rights of the accused.

Respectfully,

Mark Lane

ML/jc

COMMISSION EXHIBIT No. 2033

CNS/sw

Dec. 30, 1963

Mark Lane, Esquire
654 Madison Avenue
New York 21, New York

Dear Mr. Lane:

The Commission has asked me to thank you for your letter of December 24, 1963 and the enclosed brief relating to Lee Harvey Oswald. The Commission appreciated your making this material available to it, and in order to minimize any inconvenience to you, we have made a copy and are returning herewith the original to you.

As you know, President Johnson on November 29, 1963 established this Commission to study and report upon all the facts and circumstances relating to the assassination of the late President, John F. Kennedy, and the subsequent killing of the man charged with the assassination. The views contained in your letter will be given appropriate consideration by the Commission prior to the preparation of any final report. I can assure you that the Commission and its staff are determined to implement President Johnson's directive as completely and quickly as possible.

Thank you for your thoughtfulness in writing to the Commission.

Sincerely,

Enclosure

J. Lee Rankin
General Counsel

COMMISSION EXHIBIT No. 2033—Continued

~~Investigation and Evidence~~

LANE MARK

JLR:HPW:al
1/22/64

JAN 23 1964

Mr. Mark Lane
164 West 79th Street
New York, New York

Dear Mr. Lane:

On behalf of the Commission I wish to acknowledge receipt of your recent telegram informing the Commission that you have been retained by Mrs. Marguerite C. Oswald to represent her deceased son.

As you know, the Commission is interested in developing all the pertinent facts relating to the assassination of President John F. Kennedy and the subsequent killing of Lee Harvey Oswald by Jack L. Ruby. Any documentary material which Mrs. Marguerite C. Oswald or others wish to submit to the Commission will receive careful consideration.

The Commission does not believe that it would be useful or desirable to permit an attorney representing Lee Harvey Oswald to have access to the investigative materials within the possession of the Commission or to participate in any hearings to be conducted by the Commission. I can assure you that every effort will be made to ascertain the facts regarding Lee Harvey Oswald's implication in the assassination of President Kennedy as accurately and fairly as possible.

Sincerely,

J. Lee Rankin
General Counsel

HPW
1/22
JLR

COMMISSION EXHIBIT No. 2033—Continued

FD-302 (Rev. 3-3-59)

FEDERAL BUREAU OF INVESTIGATION

Date December 11, 1963

1

GEORGE THOMAS CHABOT, Mechanic, Police Garage, Young Street and Pearl Expressway, residence 5336 Bonita, telephone number TA 4-6040, Dallas, Texas, furnished the following information:

He has been employed with the City of Dallas in his present position for 8-9 years. Part of his duties involve the basement garage at the Central Dallas Police Department.

He was at the Central Dallas Police Department basement garage on November 22, 1963, and November 23, 1963, and was not at any time required to identify himself. He moved freely in and out of the garage area. However, he knows the majority of policemen by sight as well as a number of the reserve policemen.

On November 24, 1963, he was duty mechanic in charge at the police garage, Young and Pearl Expressway, and around 10:00 a.m., drove a police car to the Central Police Department Building, parked it about midway in the block east of Main and Harwood Streets intersection on the south side of the street. He walked to the Main Street ramp entrance and spoke with Officer VAUGHN, who was on duty keeping unauthorized individuals out of the basement and then he proceeded down the ramp to the basement.

His purpose in going to the Central Police Department basement was to determine if more than one attendant would be required due to the transfer of LEE HARVEY OSWALD that morning. The attendant on duty that morning in the basement was HAROLD FUQUAY (phonetic), a Negro male whose job it is to handle the parking of the vehicles.

He spoke with Sgt. P. T. DEAN for about two minutes regarding any need for further attendants and was advised no one else would be required. Sgt. DEAN then told him to leave the basement.

He proceeded up the Main Street ramp and held a conversation for over 20 minutes with Officer VAUGHN. The time was probably around 11:00 a.m. when he left and drove the car back to the police garage, Young and Pearl Expressway.

on 12/10/63 at Dallas, Texas File # Dallas 44-1639

by Special Agent R. NEIL QUIGLEY & JOHN E. DALLMAN:BL Date dictated 12/11/63

272

This document contains neither recommendations nor conclusions of the FBI. It is the property of the FBI and is loaned to your agency; it and its contents are not to be distributed outside your agency.

DL 44-1639
2

While in the basement he also spoke with a reserve policeman who he knows by sight only.

While speaking with Officer VAUGHN he noticed several police vehicles enter the basement after being checked by VAUGHN. VAUGHN also allowed one newspaperman to enter down the ramp after showing proper identification.

VAUGHN was in the immediate area of the ramp entrance at all times and did not at any time walk into the street or even to the sidewalk in front of the ramp.

No vehicles came out of the ramp while he was there talking to VAUGHN.

After he returned to the police garage, Young and Pearl Expressway, he heard on a commercial radio of the shooting of OSWALD. He cannot recall the exact time which elapsed from the time he returned to the garage to the radio broadcast of the shooting.

He returned to the Central Police basement around 3:00 p.m. and worked in the basement until around 6:00 p.m. He remained in the police garage, Young and Pearl Expressway, except for a short trip home for lunch around 12 noon, and that period of time as he returned from lunch until going to the Central Police Building around 3:00 p.m. He does not personally know OSWALD or JACK RUBY. He did not see RUBY while at the Central Police Building on November 22, 1963, through November 24, 1963.

He advised he is a white male, 5'7" tall, blond crew cut hair, and on November 24, 1963, he was wearing gray khaki trousers and a yellow jacket.

273

Commission Exhibit No. 2035

FD-302 (Rev. 3-3-59)

FEDERAL BUREAU OF INVESTIGA JN

1

Date 12-6-63

HARRY T. TASKER, Cab Driver, was interviewed at his place of employment, City Transportation Company, 610 S. Akard Street, Dallas. He advised that on November 24, 1963, he was retained by a newsman to stand by in his cab outside of the Dallas Police Station from 9:40 a.m. to 12:25 p.m. He parked his cab on Main Street across the street from the "in" ramp to the basement of the police station. He advised that while waiting for the newsman, he occasionally walked across the street and talked with the police officer, who was standing at the top of the ramp. He said that the police officer checked the credentials of numerous persons going in and out of the ramp entrance.

TASKER advised that he heard the shot fired in the basement which killed OSWALD; that prior to the shot he had been standing at the "in" ramp entrance for about five minutes. He was shown a photo of JACK RUBY and he advised that he did not observe anyone resembling RUBY enter the basement through the "in" ramp during the period of time which he was standing there. He advised that he probably would have remembered RUBY had he seen him enter during that five minute period.

on 12-6-63 at Dallas, Texas File # DL 44-1639

by Special Agent ALVIN J. ZIMMERMAN & JOSEPH G. PEGGS - md/jn Date dictated 12-6-63

This document contains neither recommendations nor conclusions of the FBI. It is the property of the FBI and is loaned to your agency; it and its contents are not to be distributed outside your agency.

COMMISSION EXHIBIT No. 2035

Commission Exhibit No. 2036

FD-302 (Rev. 3-3-59)

FEDERAL BUREAU OF INVESTIGATION

1

Date 7/20/64

JOSEPH RODRIGUEZ MOLINA, 4306 Brown Street, Dallas, was interviewed at his place of employment, Neuhoff Brothers Packers, 2821 Alamo, Dallas.

He stated that between 1:30 A.M. and 2:00 A.M., on November 23, 1963, a large group of police officers came to his home. He was questioned by Captain WILLIAM P. GANNAWAY and Lieutenant JACK REVILL, primarily about his connection with the American GI Forum. They asked him about his acquaintance with several fellow members of that organization. They also asked him about his acquaintance with LEE HARVEY OSWALD, a fellow employee of the Texas School Book Depository, whom he had seen but did not know. He was not accused at that time, by Captain GANNAWAY or Lieutenant REVILL, of being subversive or of having subversive affiliations, and despite the late hour, MOLINA assumed they were conducting routine investigation in the assassination case because of his employment by the Texas School Book Depository.

During and after this questioning, other officers were searching his home. He does not remember that a search warrant was mentioned, but believes he was asked if he minded if they "looked around," and he gave permission for the search.

The officers never did say what they were searching for, but they spent from thirty to forty minutes searching his home. To the best of his knowledge, the only thing they found which appeared to interest them, and which they carried away, was a list of names his wife had been given by the Holy Trinity Mothers' Club of women to be contacted to help serve dinner at the Trade Mart in Dallas.

After the search, the group went into the kitchen, out of the presence of Mr. and Mrs. MOLINA, where they held a brief discussion. He was then asked if he would be willing to accompany them to Police Headquarters at that time, or if he preferred to come to Police Headquarters on his own later

on 7/15/64 at Dallas, Texas File # DL 100-9847

by Special Agent W. JAMES WOOD and JAMES P. HOSTY, JR./ds Date dictated 7/16/64

-12-

This document contains neither recommendations nor conclusions of the FBI. It is the property of the FBI and is loaned to your agency; it and its contents are not to be distributed outside your agency.

COMMISSION EXHIBIT No. 2036

in the morning. He told them he would prefer to come to Police Headquarters later in the day, and the officers left.

At about 9:50 A.M., he arrived at Dallas Police Headquarters. He first went to the office of the Special Service Bureau, where he waited for about forty minutes in a small office there. Representatives of the news media kept coming in and out of the office, and photographs of him were taken by such individuals. None of these pictures, however, appeared in the paper.

Captain WILLIAM P. GANNAWAY then came into the office and started questioning him about the American GI Forum and his connection with it. Lieutenant JACK REVILL was also present. This questioning was rather brief, and he was told he was going to be sent for questioning to Captain WILL FRITZ of the Homicide Bureau.

MOLINA then went to the Homicide Bureau, where he waited for about forty-five minutes to be interviewed. He was then interviewed for from twenty to thirty minutes by a Detective and by a Special Agent of the Federal Bureau of Investigation concerning his knowledge of OSWALD, his work at the Texas School Book Depository, and his whereabouts during the pertinent period surrounding the assassination.

He was then told by the Agent that he could leave, but when he tried to leave the Homicide Bureau a police officer stationed at the door, whose identity he did not know, told him to go back in and sit down. He was kept waiting in the office another thirty to forty-five minutes.

A police officer then came and told MOLINA to follow him, taking him to the Special Service Bureau. Here he was interrogated by Lieutenant JACK REVILL and another officer whom he did not know. This questioning had to do with the American GI Forum, apparently trying to prove that MOLINA was acquainted

with a number of people therein who had records of subversive activities. For instance, he was asked if he was acquainted with JOHN STANFORD, a State official of the Communist Party. He said he was not acquainted with STANFORD. He was asked to write a statement as to the political sympathies of the various members of the American GI Forum, which he declined to do, stating he had no first-hand knowledge as to which of them, if any, were Communist Party members or had communist sympathies.

Lieutenant REVILL and the other officer then wrote an affidavit concerning the American GI Forum based on his statements to them, which he signed. He was then permitted to leave Police Headquarters, and was driven home by a police officer.

MOLINA said he was at Police Headquarters from about 10:00 A.M. to 5:00 P.M. He was never told he was under arrest. The only indication he had that he might have been under some form of restraint was his one effort to leave the Homicide Bureau, and his having been told by a police officer at that time not to leave.

He said there is no question in his mind that his discharge from his 16 years' employment with the Texas School Book Depository was a direct result of publicity following his questioning by the police, and alleged subversive affiliations on his part. He said that immediately following his questioning by the police, and the attendant publicity, there was no mention of this made at his place of employment. About ten days thereafter, he was told he could no longer sign outgoing letters, which he had done previously. Shortly thereafter, all letterheads which bore his name were taken from him.

He then went to the office of O. V. CAMPBELL, the Vice-President of the Texas School Book Depository, where he objected to the action being taken against him and asked CAMPBELL the reason for it. CAMPBELL told him that the allegations made about his loyalty would have to be cleared up, that the company had been getting a lot of crank calls, several customers had said they would not buy books from the company as long as the company had a subversive working for them. MOLINA said no one else was present when CAMPBELL made these statements.

Shortly thereafter, he was told studies had been and were being made with a view to automating the operation of the Accounting Department, that the publishers and customers demanded faster service, and that as a result of the coming automation, MOLINA's job was being eliminated. MOLINA stated he believed this claim to be completely false, that a credit manager's job could not be eliminated by automation, and that this was just a convenient way to discharge him because of allegations made against his loyalty.

He said CAMPBELL offered him a severance contract which he refused to sign until he contacted his attorney, one MULLINAX. The latter told MOLINA he could not see that MOLINA had any recourse but to agree to the terms of the contract, and on December 12, 1963, he signed this contract calling for full pay for three months, half-pay for three months, and other benefits.

He said he stayed at his employment until December 30, 1963, but in the interim constantly sought employment at such places as Sears, Roebuck and Company, Texas Instruments, and through the Texas Employment Commission. He had no success, and when prospective employers found from his application forms that he had been discharged from the Texas School Book Depository job as credit manager, after sixteen years of employment there, coupled with the fact that that place had been the site of the assassination of President KENNEDY, they had no further interest in hiring him. One woman connected with the Texas Employment Commission questioned him as to whether he was a "subversive," and thereafter told him the Commission had no work for him because of his lack of a college education, although she had known about this lack of a college education from the outset.

He said he was acquainted, through his work in the Parent Teachers Association at the Holy Trinity School in Dallas, with MARTIN MC REDMOND, an official of the Neuhoff Packing Company. He asked MC REDMOND if he had any work MOLINA might be able to do, and was told that there was a vacancy anticipated in the Credit Union of his company. He went to work on a part-time basis there in January 1964, and full-time in February 1964. There has never been any mention there of the adverse publicity he received following the assassination.

He said that in his work at the Texas School Book Depository, he had been earning $6,000 a year, while in his present employment his salary is only $4,500 a year.

He said the only police official who he knows made statements detrimental to him was Chief of Police JESSE CURRY of the Dallas Police Department. He said when he returned home on November 23, 1963, his wife told him she had seen Chief CURRY on television, and heard him make a statement to the effect that police were investigating a man who had been in their subversive files since 1957, and mentioned MOLINA by name as being the individual in question. MOLINA believes this telecast was carried on all local television channels as a part of a pool operation. He said he does not know whether any other police officials made statements to the press concerning his alleged subversive affiliations.

He also said that in one of the local newspapers there was a news item quoting Chief CURRY to the effect that the Dallas Police were investigating a man who had been in the police subversive files since 1957.

He said that on the night of November 23, 1963, he had called the Police Department in an effort to get a retraction of the statements made by Chief CURRY. He talked with Captain GLEN D. KING, who told him Chief CURRY was the only official who could make an official retraction of such statements, but MOLINA was never successful in contacting Chief CURRY.

He said he mentioned to a friend, HECTOR GARCIA, a founder of the American GI Forum, the troubles he was having as a result of the publicity concerning his alleged subversive affiliations. GARCIA told him he could write the various radio and television stations and demand copies of texts or recording tapes of all broadcasts and telecasts in which MOLINA was mentioned, and he did so. The only station which furnished any information to him was Dallas Radio Station WRR, which furnished the text of a broadcast by Chief CURRY making the above allegations. Dallas Radio Station KRLD stated the matter was being referred to their New York office because the networks were responsible for any broadcasts, and he never heard anything further from them.

His attorney filed suit against WRR for damages on MOLINA's behalf because of derogatory statements carried by that station, but in reply his attorney was told that the station was city-owned and that under the city charter, such a suit had to be filed within thirty days of the occurrence, which had not been done. MOLINA said, however, that plans for a lawsuit have not been dropped, and his attorney is still exploring means of suing the station for damages on his behalf.

MOLINA furnished the following descriptive data concerning himself:

Sex	Male
Race	White
Age	40 years
Born	June 18, 1924, at Dallas, Texas
Height	5'7½"
Weight	164 pounds
Eyes	Brown

Hair	Brown, graying, balding in front
Build	Stocky
Complexion	Fair
Marks and Scars	Large mole in left eyebrow
Wife	SOLEDAD MOLINA
Children	JOE MOLINA, JR., aged 17; JOHN MOLINA, aged 10; LINDA MOLINA, aged 14; and, adopted daughter SYLVIA, aged 14
Education	Crozier Technical High School, Dallas
Military Service	U. S. Navy, 1943-46, NSN 1891658
Residence	4306 Brown, Dallas, Texas

FD-302 (Rev. 1-25-60) FEDERAL BUREAU OF INVESTIGATION

1

Date December 2, 1963

Mr. STEVEN L. ALEXANDER, news cameraman, KTAL-TV, Channel 6, Shreveport, Louisiana, furnished the following information:

On November 22, 1963, ALEXANDER was on vacation at Waco, Texas, when he heard the President had been shot at Dallas, Texas. He immediately drove to Dallas, arriving about 3:30 p.m. on the same day. He stayed in Dallas until 6:10 p.m. on November 24, 1963, during which time he was working for NBC, having been hired by Mr. DONALD C. ROBERTS, NBC of Los Angeles, California, to cover the incident.

During this time ALEXANDER did not talk to JACK RUBY. He has no information RUBY knew LEE HARVEY OSWALD, or was associated with OSWALD. There was a rumor going around the basement of the City Hall in Dallas on the afternoon of November 24, 1963, that RUBY's roommate, a bartender of Ruby, or an entertainer at RUBY's night club, had said OSWALD had been in RUBY's club a day or two before November 22, 1963. ALEXANDER does not know who started this rumor and can not furnish the name of any person he heard repeat the rumor. He did not check into the truth of the rumor and does not know if any representative of news media checked into the rumor.

On November 23, 1963, about 6 p.m., the Chief of Police, Dallas, held a press conference at which time he stated LEE OSWALD would be moved from the city jail to the county jail in Dallas the next morning at 10 a.m. The Chief of Police said the news media could cover the transfer and obtain photographs of OSWALD.

The next morning, Sunday, November 24, 1963, ALEXANDER entered City Hall, Dallas, at 7:30 a.m. He immediately went to the basement. He does not recall if he entered the basement by walking down the ramp or if he entered the building on the main floor and took an elevator to the basement. No one asked for his identification and business appeared to be going on as usual in the basement. There were four officers on duty at the Bail Out Desk located

On 12/2/63 at Shreveport, Louisiana File # NO 44-2064

by SA JAMES A. WOOTEN :gas Date dictated 12/2/63

This document contains neither recommendations nor conclusions of the FBI. It is the property of the FBI and is loaned to your agency; it and its contents are not to be distributed outside your agency.

368

2

NO 44-2064
JAW:gas

in the basement. Two of the employees were uniformed officers and two were in civilian clothing. Several persons were standing at the desk obtaining the release of inmates of the jail. ALEXANDER asked the police lieutenant in charge of the desk about OSWALD and was told OSWALD would not be moved until 10 a.m. There was no other representative of news media in the basement yet.

ALEXANDER stated he walked in various parts of the basement from 7:30 a.m. until the shooting of OSWALD which occurred about 11:30 a.m. He was carrying a camera but wore no identification of any kind. At no time was he asked for identification by any police officer and he doubts that any other newsmen were asked for identification. He noticed several representatives of news media had press cards on their coat lapels but most did not have any identification showing. He knows of no person other than police and representatives of news media who were in the area, except for JACK RUBY and he was not aware RUBY was there until after the shooting of OSWALD. ALEXANDER is of the opinion the police did not ask for identification from persons entering the basement of City Hall and just assumed everyone there was a representative of news media.

During the time between 7:30 a.m. and 11:30 a.m., many representatives of news media entered the basement. About 9:30 a.m., a crew of camermen from KSLD - TV, Dallas, and WBAP - TV, Fort Worth, Texas, manned two live cameras which cameras had been left in the hall way of the basement overnight. The two crews were told by officers to move the cameras and moved eastward to the area of the basement at the entrance of the police garage. There were some 15 to 20 uniformed officers in the area along with about 17 reserve policemen. About half of the reserve policemen were sent outside the building. About 10 a.m., ALEXANDER went outside and observed the police enter and apparently search a red brick building across

369

COMMISSION EXHIBIT No. 2037—Continued

3

NO 44-2064
JAW:gas

the street south from the south ramp entrance into the basement. He observed one officer on the roof of this building. ALEXANDER re-entered the basement without being asked for identification. About 9 a.m., ALEXANDER observed several officers searching the area of the basement. The officers were looking in the trunks of cars located in the police garage as well as looking in air conditioning grills in the hall ways. ALEXANDER asked one of the officers the reason for the search and was told the police had received a threat on OSWALD's life. During all of this time no part of the basement was closed off and business appeared to be going on as usual at the Bail Out Desk ALEXANDER did observe some police officers to move several city employees out of the area of this police garage and to seal off the two elevators in that side of the building.

ALEXANDER observed the following representatives of news media who were known to him in the basement prior to the shooting:

JACK BEERS, Photographer, Dallas Morning News, Dallas, Texas.

GENE BARNES, NBC cameraman, Burbank, California, who was working in conjunction with ALEXANDER, but who did not arrive at the basement of City Hall until about 9:30 a.m.

JAMES R. DAVIDSON, AIE Studios, 2510 Tangley, Houston, Texas, who was working for ABC.

TOM PETTIT, NBC, Burbank, California.

Camera crew of WBAP - TV, Fort Worth, Texas.

Camera crew of KRLD - TV, Dallas, Texas.

370

COMMISSION EXHIBIT No. 2037—Continued

Date 12/2/63

1

GENE BARNES, Cameraman for National Broadcasting Company, Inc. (NBC) News Staff, Hollywood, California, telephone 845-7000, residing at 12942 Bloomfield Street, Van Nuys, California, telephone CRestview 4-3062, furnished the following information:

He left Los Angeles, California, at 12:20 p.m., November 22, 1963, by American Airlines for Dallas, Texas, and was present on official duties at the Dallas City Hall on November 24, 1963, when LEE HARVEY OSWALD was shot. His plan was to photograph OSWALD as he was brought into the basement by law officers and then to exit the basement, while other NBC cameras picked up camera continuity, and prepare to follow the armored truck, parked in one of the two basement ramps, as it transported OSWALD to the County Jail. He photographed OSWALD as the latter was brought by officers out of the basement elevator doors in the City Hall and was walking some fifteen feet towards a corridor. At that time BARNES exited through a tunnel being used for television cables and other equipment. As he was leaving the building, he heard a shot but continued on to his rented car parked nearby in order to be ready to follow the armored truck. Dallas Police Department Officer SPEARS was standing by the rented car and was to serve as driver. He had obtained three days off from duty and had been employed by BARNES to act as driver for BARNES for the first two of those days.

BARNES saw Sergeant PUTNAM, Dallas Police Department, run up to a Police Department Lieutenant stationed at the armored truck and heard him say, "I got me a nigger." Upon seeing a microphone close by he said, "I'm sorry. I have me a Negro." He then explained to the Lieutenant that the Negro had been climbing over the tops of cars in the City Hall basement.

OSWALD was brought out very shortly thereafter and taken in an ambulance to a nearby hospital at a speed approximating ninety miles per hour, with BARNES and SPEARS following closely in the rented car, which had no radio.

On 12/1/63 at 12942 Bloomfield Street Van Nuys, California File # Los Angeles 44-895

by SAs EUGENE P. PITTMAN & JOHN C. OAKES:JM Date dictated 12/2/63

This document contains neither recommendations nor conclusions of the FBI. It is the property of the FBI and is loaned to your agency; it and its contents are not to be distributed outside your agency.

COMMISSION EXHIBIT No. 2038

LA 44-895
2

BARNES was the first newsman to arrive at the hospital from the City Hall, although other newsmen were there as they had been stationed previously at the hospital. As BARNES started setting up his equipment, Officer SPEARS came up to him and whispered, "Do you want the name of the guy who shot OSWALD?" BARNES answered, "Sure." SPEARS said, "You'll have to grease his palm." Because of SPEARS' accent, BARNES asked him to repeat what he had said and SPEARS did so. BARNES asked, "What does he want - $5.00?" SPEARS answered, "You're the newsman - you ought to know." BARNES asked, "How good is your source?" SPEARS answered, "He's only the guy who was handcuffed to him." BARNES understood this to refer to an officer who was handcuffed to OSWALD. BARNES answered, "I'll have to check my office" and just as he was receiving information on the telephone from his "office," his NBC colleagues in WBAP-TV in Fort Worth, Texas, that JACK RUBY had shot OSWALD, SPEARS, who had stood guard for him at the telephone booth, stuck his head in the booth and said, "It's JACK RUBY." BARNES noted that the "Dallas Times-Herald" of November 25, 1963, carried a large front-page photograph of officers escorting OSWALD down a corridor in the City Hall basement and that a detective in a light suit, believed to be JACK LAVEL, appeared to be the only officer handcuffed to OSWALD. BARNES is at a loss to understand how Officer SPEARS knew so quickly who had shot OSWALD or what officer was handcuffed to OSWALD or why he believed that officer would give out any information. BARNES noted that when he telephoned his colleagues as to paying for information as to who shot OSWALD, he was advised that they had learned less than three minutes before from their technicians on the mobile remote truck that it was JACK RUBY; that the technicians had recognized RUBY immediately when his picture was telecast at the very moment OSWALD was shot, and before RUBY's name had been announced over the air.

BARNES has no personal knowledge of any person conspiring to kill OSWALD or the existence of any such conspiracy. He did not know OSWALD or RUBY or know of any connection between them. He did not talk to RUBY at any time.

374

COMMISSION EXHIBIT No. 2038—Continued

LA 44-895
3

BARNES heard rumors but cannot pinpoint any source that the man who let RUBY into the Dallas City Hall basement just before OSWALD was shot was in a Dallas Police Department Reserve uniform. BARNES recalled seeing this man on guard duty at elevators in Dallas City Hall basement at some time on the day OSWALD was shot and described him as being in his 60's, having white hair and a slender build. BARNES believes it possible he might have heard this through CLYDE GOODSON or GODSON, an off-duty Dallas Police Department officer who drove for BARNES on November 26, 27 and 28, 1963.

BARNES said BOB MULHOLLAND, NCB News, Chicago, talked in Dallas to one FAIRY, a narcotics addict now out on bail on a sodomy charge in Dallas. FAIRY said that OSWALD had been under hypnosis from a man doing a mind-reading act at RUBY's "Carousel." FAIRY was said to be a private detective and the owner of an airplane who took young boys on flights "just for kicks." MULHOLLAND may be located at Room 1537, Statler Hotel, Dallas, WBAP-TV, Fort Worth, Texas, or through his Chicago headquarters.

Officer HAMMIL or HAMMEL, Dallas Police Department, of the office of the Chief of Police, Dallas, said he knew many Dallas Police Department officers who frequented RUBY's "Carousel" on a "free-loading" basis.

BARNES was told by one BOGARD, salesman for Downtown Lincoln-Mercury dealer, Dallas, that about two weeks prior to the OSWALD shooting, he gave OSWALD a demonstration ride in a Comet automobile, which ride covered about seventeen miles instead of the usual twelve or fourteen blocks. BOGARD said OSWALD drove, accelerating on expressways, decelerating in city traffic, and indicating he knew where he wanted to drive. OSWALD refused to sign any papers, saying he wanted to pay cash for the car, the price of which was $3,500.00, and that he would be back in about ten days to pay cash. He gave BOGARD the name of LEE OSWALD and BOGARD gave him a business card.

375

Commission Exhibit No. 2039

FD-302 (Rev. 3-3-59)

FEDERAL BUREAU OF INVESTIGATION

1

Date December 2, 1963

ISADORE BLECKMAN, Apartment 101, 6002 North Kenmore, Chicago, was interviewed at his residence. BLECKMAN said he has been employed as a photographer by United Press International (UPI), for a little over a month. BLECKMAN stated that he was sent to Dallas Friday, November 22, 1963, immediately after news of President KENNEDY's death was received.

On Sunday, November 24, 1963, he stated that he went to Dallas, Texas Police Department about 8:00 a.m. His reason, he added, for being at the Police Department, was because of the department's announcement to the press that LEE HARVEY OSWALD would be moved from the Police Department to the County Jail at 10:00 a.m., November 24, 1963. He said he entered the Police Department through the main entrance doors and took an elevator to the third floor of the building where heretofore the press, photographers, etc., had previously been accomodated. As he emerged from the elevator BLECKMAN said he was asked by a uniformed armed policeman to identify himself which he did by exhibiting his press credentials before he was permitted to enter the third floor. He said he remained a little while on the third floor before taking the elevator to the booking room in the basement where he remained until 10 or 15 minutes prior to OSWALD's being brought out of the elvator by police.

About 10 to 15 minutes prior to OSWALD's appearance, he said he and other photographers and newsmen were all asked to vacate the booking room which they did. BLECKMAN said he then took up a position in front of a window in the booking room so he could photograph OSWALD as OSWALD emerged from the elevator. As OSWALD emerged he said he got his photographs and then raced to the far side of the ramp so he could continue to photograph OSWALD as he emerged from the booking room and presumably would be led therefrom to the waiting armored car which would be used to transport him to the county jail. BLECKMAN stated that he was in this position as OSWALD was led out of the booking room and that he had his camera going from that time on.

An individual later identified as JACK RUBY cut through photographers, TV cameramen, etc., a short distance to BLECKMAN's right and proceeded to shoot OSWALD. BLECKMAN said he continued to take action photos throughout. This film which BLECKMAN stated recorded all activity from the time OSWALD emerged from the

on 11/24/63 at Chicago, Ill. File # Chicago 44-645 Dallas 44-1639

by Special Agents GEORGE D. GATINS & WILLIAM J. SMITH, JR.:BL Date dictated 12/4/63

390

This document contains neither recommendations nor conclusions of the FBI. It is the property of the FBI and is loaned to your agency; it and its contents are not to be distributed outside your agency.

elevator into the booking room and from that room to where he was shot is presently in the hands of his employer, UPI, in New York City or Washington, D. C.

BLECKMAN stated that between 9:00 and 10:00 a.m., the same morning he proceeded from the booking room to the ramp and left the police department premises and was permitted to do so only after identifying himself. His reason for leaving he told the officer at the Main Street entrance of the ramp that he had to leave to get equipment. On his return he was permitted to re-enter the police department premises by the same route without identifying himself but that he presumed the armed officer on duty recognized him as having left the ramp shortly before. BLECKMAN said he saw no one in the Police Department or in the ramp who was not believed by him to be a member of the department or theworking press. He said he had no knowledge of anyone permitted to gain entry to the police department on Sunday, November 24, 1963, without properly identifying himself, and neither did he have any knowledge or indication that any police officer or official conspired or permitted the unauthorized presence of anyone in the basement.

BLECKMAN said that to his knowledge he had never seen RUBY prior to RUBY's actual shooting of OSWALD although on Friday evening November 22, 1963, when OSWALD was brought to the lineup room of the Police Department, according to various persons (identities unknown) RUBY was alleged to havebeen present and allegedly asked a question of OSWALD. The exhibition of OSWALD in the lineup room was apparently for the convenience of the press and photographers than for any police function according to BLECKMAN.

BLECKMAN stated that at Parkland Memorial Hospital later on Sunday, November 24, 1963, an individual described as in his early thirties, 5'8" tall, 180-200 pounds, sturdy build, blond hair who was either a director of a TV station in Dallas or in charge of a TV crew from a Dallas TV station told him in the presence of HENRY A. KOKOJAN, 9009 Freeport Drive, Dallas, telephone DAvis 8-1043, that an upper window of a building on either Main or Commerce Streets overlooking the police department ramp was open Friday after the President's assassination, all day Saturday and Sunday but that shortly after OSWALD's murder the window was shut. BLECKMAN stated that he could recall being

391

told nothing additional by this individual, but that the above caused speculation among themselves as to whether RUBY had an accomplice or whether others besides RUBY were interested in doing away with OSWALD.

392

Commission Exhibit No. 2040

FD-302 (Rev. 1-25-60)

FEDERAL BUREAU OF INVESTIGA

Other Individuals and Organizations Involved or Interviewed

1

Date 12/5/63

GENE COFFEY advised that he is a Sound Technician employed in the News Section of the National Broadcasting Company located at 3000 West Alameda Street in Burbank, California.

He stated that he arrived at Dallas, Texas, before 5:00 p.m. on Friday, November 22, 1963, having been sent there from Los Angeles. He stated that for about the first hour and a half, he was able to make several trips from the street into the police building and up into the third floor of the police building without being asked for any identification. He did not notice anyone being asked for identification during this period of time. After this first hour and a half, he was challenged by uniformed officers and had to show his identification. The only place he did have to show his identification, however, was on the third floor of the police building.

At about 11:00 p.m. on Friday, the news people were informed that there would be a press conference attended by LEE HARVEY OSWALD held in the auditorium in the basement of the police building. He attended this conference along with all the other news people and he does not recall being stopped entering this conference room and asked to show any identification. He believes that anybody could have attended this press conference.

COFFEY said that his assignment on November 24, 1963 was at the Dallas County Jail and, therefore, he was not in the vicinity of the police building on November 24, 1963.

COFFEY knows of no connection between OSWALD and JACK RUBY and knows of no one who aided or abetted either in committing their crimes. He stated that he never interviewed RUBY and only attended one press conference early Saturday morning, at which OSWALD was present.

On 12/4/63 at Burbank, California File # Los Angeles 44-895

by SA JAMES L. CLOAR, JR. and SA GERALD F. LONERGAN/bje Date dictated 12/5/63

This document contains neither recommendations nor conclusions of the FBI. It is the property of the FBI and is loaned to your agency; it and its contents are not to be distributed outside your agency.

397

COMMISSION EXHIBIT No. 2040

FD-302 (Rev. 3-3-59)

EDERAL BUREAU OF I[redacted]

Commission Exhibit No. 2041

1

Date 12-1-63

JOE CUMMING, Correspondent, Newsweek Magazine, telephonically advised that although he was in Dallas, Texas, at the time that JACK LEON RUBY shot LEE HARVEY OSWALD, he was at his hotel and not at the Police Department and did not witness the shooting.

Mr. CUMMING stated that every time he went to the Police Department starting on the evening of November 22, 1963, he was required to identify himself with his press credentials. He stated even though some of the officers who guarded the different entrances recognized him, they still required him to produce his credentials. He stated he knows of no unauthorized person who was permitted to enter any area of the Police Department, including the basement without showing proper identification.

Mr. CUMMING stated he does not know of any information which would indicate that a police officer or other official conspired with RUBY or willfully permitted the killing. He stated that he did not see or talk to RUBY from November 22, through November 24, 1963, and did not know who RUBY was until after the shooting and the resultant publicity. He stated further that he has no knowledge of any relationship or prior acquaintance between RUBY and OSWALD.

on 12-1-63 at Atlanta, Georgia File # DL 44-1639 AT 105-3193

by Special Agent CHARLES S. HARDING/jkw/jn Date dictated 12-1-63

This document contains neither recommendations nor conclusions of the FBI. It is the property of the FBI and is loaned to your agency; it and its contents are not to be distributed outside your agency.

398

COMMISSION EXHIBIT No. 2041

FD-302 (Rev. 3-3-59)

FEDERAL BUREAU OF INVESTIGATION

1

Date 12/6/63

JAMES R. DAVIDSON, operator, A.I.E. Studios, 2510 Tangley Road, Houston, Texas, advised that he was in Dallas, Texas, as a motion picture photographer with sound man WARREN FERGUSON, 5406 Windswept, Houston, Texas, as a photo sound free-lance crew operating with reporter BILL LORD of the ABC Staff, New York, in connection with news coverage at the Dallas City Hall on the morning of November 24, 1963, when OSWALD was shot.

He, LORD and WARREN, arrived at the City Hall as a 3-man crew at about 8:30 AM that day. They may have gone up to the press room on the third floor but, if not, went directly to the basement area of the City Hall. They had to exhibit their press credentials on the third floor if they went to the press room, and exhibited their credentials if they entered the basement area. DAVIDSON explained that he had been at the City Hall on a number of occasions since Friday night, November 23, 1963, and that in all instances they had to exhibit their credentials prior to gaining entry to the building.

Shortly after 8:30 AM on November 24, 1963, they set up in the jail office in the basement, intending to photograph OSWALD as he walked from the jail elevator across the jail office out into the ramp area. At about 10:00 AM a police officer directed them and other newsmen in the jail office to vacate this area. He, LORD and FERGUSON left the jail office from a rear door and entered the hallway behind the double doors from the ramp area. LORD went into a public telephone booth in that area and remained in that booth, holding the line open and talking with ABC, New York, until after the shooting of OSWALD. DAVIDSON and FERGUSON took up a position in this hallway behind the double doors where he would be able to photograph through some barred windows to get pictures of OSWALD walking from the jail elevator, across the jail office and out into the ramp area. FERGUSON remained close to him at all times because his sound equipment was electrically connected with DAVIDSON and his camera. They remained in this area watching the jail office area from shortly after 10:00 AM until OSWALD came down on the elevator.

As OSWALD walked from the elevator through the jail office area, he took photographs. When OSWALD was taken through the jail office door into the ramp area, he and FERGUSON went through the

on 12/4/63 at Dallas, Texas File # DL 44-1639

by Special Agent s JAMES F. GLONEK and RALPH E. RAWLINGS - LAC Date dictated 12/4/63

This document contains neither recommendations nor conclusions of the FBI. It is the property of the FBI and is loaned to your agency; it and its contents are not to be distributed outside your agency.

399

COMMISSION EXHIBIT No. 2042

DL 44-1639
2

jail office door into the ramp area, he and FERGUSON went through the double doors and followed along behind. There were detectives or there were police officers behind OSWALD so that he did not actually see him. Just after he got through the double doors, he heard the shot, following which there was a commotion. His cameraman's instinct told him that OSWALD and the officers would be returning to the jail office, so he immediately turned around and proceeded back down the hall through the double doors where he could photograph action in the jail office. In the commotion his electrical connection with FERGUSON was broken, and FERGUSON was kept in the ramp area for a period of time.

He photographed the jail area as RUBY and OSWALD were brought back into the jail office. RUBY was taken up on the jail elevator and OSWALD taken out on a stretcher from the jail office.

After RUBY had been taken up on the elevator and it appeared OSWALD/was taken out of the building in an ambulance, FERGUSON came back through the double doors. Then he and FERGUSON went into the jail office, where he shot pictures of the area and briefly interviewed a police lieutenant. Then he and FERGUSON left the jail office area and joined LORD in the hall behind the double doors. The three of them then proceeded to Commerce Street, where he filmed LORD while LORD explained on a news reel the ramp area where it was intended that OSWALD would have been brought out for transfer to the County Jail. They then conducted several short interviews with people who had gathered in the area.

DAVIDSON explained that throughout the time he was in the City Hall basement, his interest was in securing photographs of OSWALD in the jail office area. He did not look down into the ramp area from about 10:00 AM until the time that OSWALD was shot because he did not want to miss a picture. Consequently, he has no impression as to how many newsmen and police officers were in the ramp area at the time OSWALD was shot. DAVIDSON explained that although he had been in the Police Department on a number of occasions from Friday night, November 23, 1963, he has no recollection of ever seeing RUBY in that area, either on the morning of the shooting or prior to that time. The only time he would have seen RUBY was in the jail office after the shooting when the police officers brought him into that area and then took him upstairs.

DAVIDSON advised that on Friday night, November 22, 1963, when OSWALD was first made available to the press for photographing in an assembly room at the City Hall, he took photographs

400

COMMISSION EXHIBIT No. 2042—Continued

DL 44-1639
3

of OSWALD, which photos included other people. He has reviewed these photographs and is unable to identify any individual in these photographs as RUBY.

DAVIDSON explained that he had not been acquainted with either RUBY or OSWALD prior to that time and had no information as to any possible association or connection between these two individuals.

401

Commission Exhibit No. 2043

FD-302 (Rev. 3-3-59) FEDERAL BUREAU

Date 12-4-63

1

Mr. CURTIS GANS, 7714 Eastern Avenue, Dallas, Texas, advised that he is employed as a newsman for the United Press International Office Office (UPI) located at 2523 McKinney Avenue, Dallas.

GANS stated that on November 24, 1963, he traveled to the Police Department with other UPI newsmen by the name of TERRANCE McGARRY, arriving at the police department at approximately 10:00 a.m. GANS stated that he entered the Police Department at the Main Street police car ramp after being questioned by a policeman. GANS stated that he displayed his press card which reflects his identity and the news service he is working for.

GANS stated that he remained in the basement for approximately 20 minutes and then left the building via the Main Street car ramp. He stated that after attempting to interview several people standing on the opposite side of the street from the Police Department, he returned to the basement using the police car ramp entrance. GANS stated that another policeman on duty at this ramp entrance made him display his identification before allowing him to enter. He advised that after entering the basement, he observed a police officer holding McGARRY and he immediately went to McGARRY's assistance and identified him as a member of the UPI staff. He advised that after displaying his card to the policeman, McGARRY was allowed to enter the building.

GANS stated that he again departed the basement, going out the Commerce Street police car ramp exit. After taking several photographs of the crowd, he again entered the basement without showing his identity to the policeman. He advised that he did not go too far from the ramp to take the photographs and the policeman possibly observed his entire activities from the time he left the basement and this is possibly the reason he did not require him to

on 11-30-63 at Dallas, Texas File # DL 44-1639

by Special Agent IVAN D. LEE - md Date dictated 12-2-63

410

This document contains neither recommendations nor conclusions of the FBI. It is the property of the FBI and is loaned to your agency; it and its contents are not to be distributed outside your agency.

2

DL 44-1639

identify himself agin. GANS related that after returning to the basement, he talked with McGARRY a few minutes and then departed the building for the Sheriff's Office to cover the activities in the area for a possible news story.

GANS stated that after learning of the shooting while at the Sheriff's Office, he immediately returned to the Police Department and entered the basement from the police car entrance located on Main Street. He advised to the best of his knowledge, he did not identify himself on this occasion, but due to the excitement, he could have displayed his press card to gain admittance. GANS stated that he remained in the Police Department Building until approximately midnight, November 24, 1963, going between the basement and the third floor. He stated that on several occasions he was stopped by police officers requesting him to display his press card.

GANS stated that outside of McGARRY's being admitted to the basement, he has no knowledge of any other press officials or any other individuals being admitted to the building without showing their identification. He advised that to the best of his knowledge, there were approximately 100 newsmen and police officers in the basement at the the time he departed the building for the Sheriff's Office. He stated that to the best of his knowledge, he did not see RUBY in the building at any time nor does he have anyknowledge of a newsman or police officer assisting RUBY to enter the building. GANS advised that he does not have any knowledge of RUBY's activities any time prior to the shooting of OSWALD, nor does he have any knowledge of anyone being involved with RUBY in the killing of OSWALD.

COMMISSION EXHIBIT No. 2043—Continued

FD-302 (Rev. 1-25-60)

FEDERAL BUREAU OF INVESTIGAT

1

Date 12/5/63

EDMONDE HADDAD advised he is a news broadcaster at Radio Station KPOL at 5700 Sunset Boulevard, Hollywood, California.

HADDAD said he arrived in Dallas, Texas, at about 4:00 p.m. on November 22, 1963, and he left Dallas to return to Los Angeles at about 7:00 p.m. on Saturday, November 23, 1963. He was, therefore, back in Los Angeles at the time LEE HARVEY OSWALD was shot by JACK RUBY.

HADDAD stated that all the time he was in the police building in Dallas on Friday and Saturday, he was never once asked for any identification.

HADDAD did not interview RUBY and he knew nothing concerning RUBY's associates and does not know of any conspiracy to slay OSWALD.

HADDAD was in attendance in the police basement auditorium when OSWALD was brought in early Saturday morning for his general news interview. HADDAD knew of no conspiracy to assassinate the President and he knows of no connection existing between RUBY and OSWALD.

HADDAD stated that the scene on the third floor of the Police Department building on Friday and Saturday resembled a circus. Whenever the police officials would take OSWALD out of one room and along in the corridor, everyone would press in close to OSWALD to try and take a picture of him and to interview him and to shove microphones into his face. HADDAD said that anyone could have entered the room in the basement of the police building on Saturday morning for OSWALD's general press interview for there was no security set up as far as he could notice and he did not notice anyone being asked to show any identification. HADDAD was of the opinion that OSWALD could easily have been slain on Friday or Saturday for anyone could move freely throughout the building.

HADDAD knows nothing concerning the security measures taken by the police on Sunday, November 24, 1963.

On 12/4/63 at Hollywood, California File # Los Angeles 44-895

by SA JAMES L. CLOAR, JR. and SA GERALD F. LONERGAN/bje Date dictated 12/5/63

This document contains neither recommendations nor conclusions of the FBI. It is the property of the FBI and is loaned to your agency; it and its contents are not to be distributed outside your agency.

COMMISSION EXHIBIT No. 2044

CITY OF DALLAS
TEXAS
POLICE DEPARTMENT

August 4, 1964
A-2

Mr. Norman Redlick
President's Commission on the
Assassination of President Kennedy
200 Maryland Avenue, N.E.
Washington, D.C. 20002

Dear Mr. Redlick:

This refers to your inquiry by telephone as to the location of police car number 107 on November 22, 1963.

Investigation reveals that the Dallas Police Department did not have a car with this number on the date in question. We had a 1962 model Ford carrying this number which was sold on April 17, 1963, to Mr. Elvis Blount, a used car dealer in Sulphur Springs, Texas. Before sale, all signs and numbers were removed from the car and the areas involved were repainted.

We did not resume using this number (107) until February, 1964.

Yours very truly,

Charles Batchelor
Assistant Chief of Police

CB:cp

COMMISSION EXHIBIT No. 2045

UNITED STATES DEPARTMENT OF JUSTICE
FEDERAL BUREAU OF INVESTIGATION

In Reply, Please Refer to File No.

Dallas, Texas
March 28, 1964

LEE HARVEY OSWALD
ALSO KNOWN AS
INTERNAL SECURITY - RUSSIA - CUBA

On March 20, 1964, Mrs. A. C. (GLADYS) JOHNSON, 1026 North Beckley Street, Dallas, Texas, was interviewed by representatives of the Federal Bureau of Investigation in an effort to establish additional information concerning LEE HARVEY OSWALD's statement to BUELL WESLEY FRAZIER on November 21, 1963, that he wanted to return to Irving, Texas, to pick up curtain rods. At the time of the interview with Mrs. JOHNSON, a thorough examination was made of the room occupied by LEE HARVEY OSWALD immediately prior to the assassination.

Mrs. JOHNSON advised that she is the owner of the residence at 1026 North Beckley where she and her husband reside and that, in addition, they rent several rooms to the public.

Mrs. JOHNSON exhibited the room which had been occupied by LEE HARVEY OSWALD prior to November 22, 1963.

This room is located on the north side of the house and access to it is gained from the dining room through two thirty-two inch solid wooden double doors. The room measures approximately five feet in width and approximately thirteen and one-half feet in length.

The entry doors are located on the south wall of the room and the north wall is comprised of four double-hung wooden sash windows, each approximately thirty-two inches in width and equally spaced along the wall.

The five-foot east wall likewise has one thirty-two inch double-hung wooden sash window centered in the wall.

COMMISSION EXHIBIT No. 2046

The west wall is solid and the entire room is painted a light aqua color.

All of the five windows are fitted with venetian blinds and the entire north wall is spanned with a room-length traverse rod on which are hung floor length draperies covering the entire north wall. The east wall is similarly spanned by a floor length drapery of the same material.

The room is furnished with a single iron-rail bed located in the northeast corner of the room, a large wooden movable wardrobe in the southwest corner of the room, a small plastic-top table north of the wardrobe, and a night stand next to the head of the bed in the southeast corner on which sits a table lamp. On the linoleum-tiled floor are two small throw rugs. A light fixture containing only a light bulb and no shade is fastened in the center of the north wall.

Mrs. JOHNSON advised the room is in essentially the same condition as when occupied by LEE HARVEY OSWALD with the exception of the new draperies.

Mrs. JOHNSON advised that the room formerly occupied by LEE HARVEY OSWALD at that address had curtains over all the windows at the time OSWALD occupied it. Mrs. JOHNSON said double doors opened into OSWALD's room and directly across from these doors running the entire length of the room were a series of wooden double-hung windows. Above these windows, Mrs. JOHNSON stated, was one flat-type curtain rod composed of a number of sections of the five and ten-cent store variety, which was fastened above the windows and extended the entire length of the room. At each end of the rod thirty-inch pink side-drapes were hung with white lace curtains in between. She advised that venetian blinds covered each window. Mrs. JOHNSON said upon entering this room there was on the right, or end, wall one wooden double-hung window which was also covered by a

venetian blind and over which hung a white lace curtain. Mrs. JOHNSON said that because of all of the windows in this small room, it was very light and cheerful.

Mrs. JOHNSON stated that when the Dallas, Texas, Police searched this room following OSWALD's arrest, they bent the rod which held the drapes and curtains. Consequently, she stated, she had the old rod taken down and replaced it with a traverse rod and aqua-colored acetate drapes. A traverse rod and the same color drapes replaced the lace curtain which was on the end wall window.

Mrs. JOHNSON said OSWALD had not been engaged by her to hang any curtain rods nor did he ask her permission to hang any curtain rods. Further, she stated, OSWALD did not at any time make any mention to her of replacing the curtains in his room.

Commission Exhibit No. 2047

FD-302 (Rev. 1-25-60)

FEDERAL BUREAU OF INVESTIGAT

Date 12/3/63

WILLIAM EDWARD LORD, News Correspondent for the American Broadcasting Company (ABC), 7 West 66th Street, New York, New York, advised that he was in the basement of the Municipal Building at Dallas, Texas at the time that LEE HARVEY OSWALD was shot.

Mr. LORD said he entered the basement of the Municipal Building at about 9:00 a.m. by public elevator from the third floor of that building. He said no one asked him to identify himself and he did not observe that anyone was responsible for identifying those persons entering the basement.

Mr. LORD was unable to furnish the names of any unauthorized persons in the basement; however, he said it was his opinion that it would not have been difficult for unauthorized persons to have entered the basement.

Mr. LORD advised that he has no reason to believe that anyone conspired with JACK RUBY in the murder of OSWALD.

Mr. LORD advised that he did not see or talk to JACK RUBY during the period November 22 through November 24, 1963, and he advised that he has no knowledge of any relationship or prior acquaintance between RUBY and OSWALD.

On 12/2/63 at NYC File # NY 44-974

by SAS LELAND F. LOWERY and JOSEPH C. HESTER/rea Date dictated 12/2/63

This document contains neither recommendations nor conclusions of the FBI. It is the property of the FBI and is loaned to your agency; it and its contents are not to be distributed outside your agency.

445

FD-302 (Rev. 1-25-60)

FEDERAL BUREAU OF INVESTIGATION Commission Exhibit No. 2048

1

Date 12/5/63

TED MANN advised that he is a Sound Technician employed by the National Broadcasting Company working out of the News Department at 3000 West Alameda Street, Burbank, California, telephone 845-7000.

MANN stated that he works as a team with GENE BARNES, a cameraman. They were sent from Los Angeles to Dallas, Texas and arrived there at about 5:00 p.m. on November 22, 1963. He does not recall being asked for any identification while in the Dallas Police building on Friday or Saturday. They were carrying equipment clearly marked NBC and got to be known by several officers on sight. He believed that anyone carrying sound or camera equipment could have moved throughout the building at will on Friday or Saturday.

On Saturday evening, the Chief of the Dallas Police Department, in reply to an inquiry as to when LEE HARVEY OSWALD would be moved from the City Jail to the County Jail, told the newsmen to be on hand by 10:00 a.m. the following morning.

MANN and BARNES returned to the Dallas Police building at about 9:00 a.m. on Sunday, November 24, 1963. They had hired an off-duty Dallas police officer to drive for them, and they parked their car near the Commerce Street exit ramp from the police building basement. MANN and BARNES were stopped at the entrance to the ramp and they had to show their identification before being allowed into the building. They took up positions in the vicinity of the booking office in the basement of the building. With them were camera crews from CBS and ABC and one still cameraman. MANN said that he and BARNES were able to get pictures of OSWALD as he walked from the elevator until he entered the corridor going out toward the ramp. OSWALD was out of MANN's vision when he was shot. MANN was at that time making his way with BARNES out of the building by another exit so that they could follow the vehicle which was to carry OSWALD to the County Jail. It was not until they had reached the street that they realized that OSWALD had been shot.

MANN believed that the security in the police building on Sunday, November 24, 1963, was good but he has heard from several individuals whom he does not know that JACK RUBY was well known to the Dallas Police officers and that RUBY even

On 12/4/63 at Burbank, California File # Los Angeles 44-895

by SA JAMES L. CLOAR, JR. and SA GERALD F. LONERGAN/bje Date dictated 12/5/63

This document contains neither recommendations nor conclusions of the FBI. It is the property of the FBI and is loaned to your agency; it and its contents are not to be distributed outside your agency.

446

2
LA 44-895

had parked his vehicle right next to the Police building. He was also told that RUBY had a press sticker on his vehicle.

MANN does not know of any conspiracy that existed as to the assassination or to the slaying of OSWALD. He knows of no connection between OSWALD and RUBY although he had heard rumors that OSWALD had lived for awhile in a Dallas YMCA where RUBY worked out. He did not interview either OSWALD or RUBY.

MANN said that he and BARNES had received word that OSWALD, a few weeks prior to the assassination, had talked to an automobile salesman by the name of BOGARDE about buying a car. They determined that BOGARDE was in Shreveport, Louisiana, and they flew there in order to interview him. MANN believes that BOGARDE has been interviewed by the FBI.

BOGARDE told them that OSWALD had taken a demonstration ride in a red Comet over the route followed by the motorcade in which President KENNEDY later rode. BOGARDE was employed as a salesman by the Downtown Lincoln Mercury which is located near the building in which OSWALD was employed in Dallas, Texas. When they talked about financing of the car, the price of which was $3,500.00, OSWALD told BOGARDE that he would not finance it and it would be a cash transaction.

MANN said there was a rumor, unconfirmed, that RUBY had a large amount of money in his possession at the time of his arrest.

COMMISSION EXHIBIT No. 2048—Continued

FD-302 (Rev. 3-3-59)

FEDERAL BUREAU OF INVESTIGATION

Date August 18, 1964

1

JOE RODRIGUEZ MOLINA, Bookkeeper, Neuhoff Employees' Credit Union, 2821 Alamo, Dallas, Texas, was reinterviewed to identify, if possible, the employee of the Texas School Book Depository who told him he could no longer sign outgoing letters and who took from him letterheads which bore his name. He advised that his full and correct name is JOE RODRIGUEZ MOLINA, and that he has never had the name JOSEPH.

He stated O. V. CAMPBELL, Vice President, Texas School Book Depository, in their conversation in December, 1963, told him that it would be better if he (MOLINA) did not sign any more letters with things being the way they were. CAMPBELL thought it would be better if he did not sign letters anymore. MOLINA said he agreed at that time to continue his work and to dictate letters to the same stenographers who had regularly been taking his dictation, but that letters dictated by him would be sent out over the signature of BONNIE ______, last name not remembered, one of the stenographers. Immediately after his discussion with Mr. CAMPBELL, he (MOLINA) told BONNIE to thereafter prepare letters dictated by him under her signature and for her to sign them after they were typed. He stated BONNIE ______ and CAROLYN ______, last name not remembered, were the two stenographers who regularly took his dictation, as well as Mr. CAMPBELL's dictation.

MOLINA stated he did not question Mr. CAMPBELL's request because he thought he knew the reason why the request was made of him. MOLINA said it is his opinion the Texas School Book Depository wanted to disassociate his name with that company because Mr. CAMPBELL had already told him the company had received telephone calls and letters from people who announced they would not do business with a firm that hired

on 8/14/64 at Dallas, Texas File # DL 100-9847

by Special Agent ALFRED C. ELLINGTON and EDWIN D. KUYKENDALL /jtf Date dictated 8/18/64

-18a-

This document contains neither recommendations nor conclusions of the FBI. It is the property of the FBI and is loaned to your agency; it and its contents are not to be distributed outside your agency.

COMMISSION EXHIBIT No. 2049

48-380 O—64—vol. XXIV——31

communists or persons of subversive backgrounds. MOLINA stated it appeared to him the firm was trying to keep from losing customers. MOLINA said the things that had been said on radio and television about him were never retracted.

MOLINA stated that later in December, 1963, BONNIE and CAROLYN, identified above, both asked him for the blank letterhead forms that he had in his possession. He believes BONNIE first asked him for the forms, but he did not know what she meant, and later CAROLYN asked him for them. He did not understand what they meant, and it was not until later he realized they were trying to obtain from him letterhead forms that bore his name. He realized that about ten days later when he observed a pile of these forms on the desk of SARAH STANTON, a pricer employed by that firm. He does not know what official caused these employees to gather up the forms bearing his name. He recalled that the gathering up of these forms and Mr. CAMPBELL's request to him that he no longer sign letters had been completed by December 13, 1963, the date when forms were filled out leading toward his termination by that firm.

MOLINA stated he went to the Texas Employment Commission in the United Fidelity Building, Dallas, on December 19, 1963, prior to his termination with the Texas School Book Depository, and registered for employment as a credit manager or bookkeeper. After signing up, he was referred to the Professional Office of that agency on the Seventh Floor of the United Fidelity Building where a Mrs. LOGAN interviewed him. She possessed his application and asked him questions as to why he was leaving his previous employment. He told her he was terminating from the Texas School Book Depository because things had been said on radio and television to the effect that he was supposed to be a subversive or had associated with persons of a subversive background, which statements had not been retracted. She then asked if there was any truth to those

allegations. He told her there was no truth to those comments. She then told him she was sorry but that he did not have the educational qualifications to be a credit manager and referred him back to the First Floor at the Texas Employment Commission where he had registered for employment.

FD-302 (Rev. 3-3-59)

FEDERAL BUREAU OF INVESTIGATION

Date 12-4-63

1

Mr. TERRANCE McGARRY, 3517 Cole Avenue, Dallas, Texas, advised that he is a newsman - reporter for United Press International Office (UPI), Dallas, with his business address being 2523 McKinney Avenue.

McGARRY related that on Sunday, November 24, 1963, he arrived in the area of the Police Department at approximately 10:00 a.m. with CURTIS GANS, another newsman for UPI. McGARRY stated that GANS entered the Police Department Building. After parking the automobile, McGARRY related that he remained outside the building near the car exit ramp from the basement on the Commerce Street side of the building. After being there five minutes, a policeman advised that he would have to leave the immediate area of the basement exit and stand across the street. McGARRY stated that instead of crossing the street he entered the building through the Main Street pedestrian entrance and went down to the basement using the basement stairway.

McGARRY related that at the bottom of the steps he was questioned by a policeman concerning his identity and when failing to have the proper press identification, he was told he would have to leave the building. McGARRY stated at that instance he observed GANS and another UPI newsman by the name of RAYBON, who were standing in a crowd of newsmen nearby. After he had vouched for his identity, the policeman then allowed him to enter the building.

McGARRY stated that KARL KING, another UPI newsman, was stationed in the telephone booth of the building to keep a telephone line open to the UPI Office. He advised after speaking to KING, he made a quick observation of the basement area to look for a spot where he could be and observe OSWALD's departure from the City Jail area.

McGARRY stated that just prior to OSWALD coming out, the police made an announcement that he was on his way and they

on 11-30-63 at Dallas, Texas File # DL 44-1639

by Special Agent IVAN D. LEE - md Date dictated 12-2-63

453

This document contains neither recommendations nor conclusions of the FBI. It is the property of the FBI and is loaned to your agency; it and its contents are not to be distributed outside your agency.

COMMISSION EXHIBIT No. 2050

2

DL 44-1639

would have to clear the hallway and the pertinent area of the car ramp. He stated that he immediately moved to a spot in the middle of the car ramp just north of the hallway where they would be bringing OSWALD from the jail. He advised that he believes that he remained in this spot for at least five minutes prior to OSWALD being shot.

McGARRY stated that he does not recall seeing RUBY prior to the shooting nor does he recall anyone coming down the ramp from the Main Street entrance to join the other newsmen.

McGARRY related that when OSWALD came into the basement area, he was able to observe him for a few seconds and then he heard a shot and with the activity and commotion of the policemen, he did not observe the person who shot OSWALD nor did he see OSWALD fall.

McGARRY stated that most of the time he was in the basement area, he was concentrating on OSWALD's departure and does not recall seeing any other newsmen or persons being admitted to the basement area without proper identification.

McGARRY stated that after the shooting of OSWALD, he remained in the building until approximately 4:00 p.m., and at no time was he questioned by a Police Department Officer concerning his identity.

McGARRY advised that he did not see RUBY prior to the shooting, nor is he personally acquainted with RUBY. He also stated that to his knowledge, he has never talked to RUBY, nor did he know of RUBY's activities prior to the shooting. McGARRY advised that he has no information concerning any newsmen or police officers being friends of RUBY. He also stated

454

COMMISSION EXHIBIT No. 2050—Continued

FD-302 (Rev. 3-3-59)

FEDERAL BUREAU OF INVESTIGATION

Commission Exhibit No. 2051

1

Date December 2, 1963

OLIVER OAKES, 5514 Monroe Street, Morton Grove, Illinois, was interviewed on December 1, 1963, at his residence. He advised as follows:

He is employed by United Press International (UPI), News Films as a sound engineer. He, PAUL SISCO and ISADORE BLECKMAN, as a UPI team, went to Dallas Friday, November 22, 1963, via plane, arriving Dallas in the evening of that day.

On November 22 and 23, 1963, he entered and left the Dallas police department building several times and on occasion had his press pass inspected by uniformed policemen but added, "they got to know us." Initials "UPI" are on all news gear carried by OAKES and he sometimes entered the building without showing press card with police officers assuming he was a news person based on identification on news gear.

He arrived at Dallas police department at 9:30 a.m., November 24, 1963, and entered the basement of the police department via the Main Street ramp. It had been previously announced by the Chief of Police that if newsmen arrived at the Police Department by 10:00 a.m., that day, that would be early enough to cover OSWALD's transfer to the County Jail.

He was carrying several pieces of equipment and suitcases containing photographic equipment, all bearing initials UPI and cannot recall whether or not he had to show press pass or not. He believes he was possibly permitted to enter by young neatly dressed uniformed officer based on UPI identification on equipment.

OAKES left the police department at 10:40 a.m., that day to cover the news conference being held by the wife of Governor CONNALLY at Parkland Hospital. He was advised of OSWALD's shooting while at the hospital and waited at the hospital a while in an attempt to cover OSWALD's arrival at the hospital but was instructed by SISCO to return to the police department and did not shoot any film of OSWALD at the hospital. Upon returning to the police department, he entered via the Main Street ramp to the basement and had to exhibit press pass to uniformed officer to gain entrance. A second officer approached and also demanded to see press pass

on 12/1/63 at Morton Grove, Ill. File # Chicago 44-645 Dallas 44-1639

by Special Agents EUGENE J. McKINNEY and DUNCAN J. EVERETTE:BL Date dictated 12/1/63

This document contains neither recommendations nor conclusions of the FBI. It is the property of the FBI and is loaned to your agency; it and its contents are not to be distributed outside your agency.

CG 44-645
DL 44-1639
2

not taking word of first officer that he was a newsman.

OAKES stated he believed the Dallas Police Department maintained strict security measures and that any time he was permitted entrance without exhibiting press pass it occurred when his news equipment was clearly marked "UPI." OAKES has no knowledge of unauthorized persons in basement of police department or persons present who did not have proper identification, other than the fact that PAUL SISCO of UPI team, commented during press conference with Chief of Police on November 26, 1963, that JACK RUBY was present at OSWALD's press conference at 1:00 a.m., November 23, 1963.

OAKES has no knowledge of anyone conspiring to kill OSWALD or any police officers or other officials permitting unauthorized persons to be present in the police department during this time. The only time OAKES recalls seeing RUBY is after the shooting of OSWALD when he was in police custody on the third floor of the Dallas Police Department. However, he understands from other newsmen that RUBY was passing out tickets for free drinks at his night club to newsmen present. OAKES did not see RUBY do this nor did he receive a free ticket and knows of no one receiving one.

The only films shot by OAKES were of Mrs. CONNALLY and this was given to SISCO which he forwarded to New York.

464

FD-302 (Rev. 3-3-59)

FEDERAL BUREAU OF INVESTIGATION

Date December 3, 1963

1

JEREMIAH O'LEARY, better known as JERRY O'LEARY, reporter for the "Washington Evening Star," 225 Virginia Avenue, Washington, D. C., telephone LI 3-5000, residence 405 Prince Street, Alexandria, Virginia, telephone TE 6-7063, furnished the following information:

He was sent to Dallas to cover the story of the assassination of President JOHN F. KENNEDY on November 22, 1963.

At about 9:00 p.m., November 22, 1963, O'LEARY stepped off the elevator on the third floor of the old building, Dallas City Hall, where he observed an individual he now knows to be JACK L. RUBY standing by the elevator giving out cards to the members of the press advertising his night club. RUBY was flashily dressed, including a sport coat and a felt hat and O'LEARY knew immediately he was not a member of the press. He recalls seeing RUBY handing one of his cards to IKE PAPPAS, an out-of-town correspondent. He does not recall where PAPPAS is from.

At this time there were a number of correspondents and representatives of other news media in the city hall and he does not recall anyone asking for his identification as a member of the press.

He observed no one standing guard or checking credentials except that there were two detectives apparently standing guard outside the door to the Homicide and Robbery Division of the Dallas Police Department, keeping out those who were not entitled to admission.

On this night, O'LEARY noted that RUBY appeared to be familiar with the city hall and was what O'LEARY described as a "hanger on."

On November 22, 1963, O'LEARY was at the City Hall in Dallas during a part of the day. He stated occasionally he was requested to show his identification as a member of the press but that there seemed to be no definite organization about the security of the building.

He recalled seeing OSWALD that night about 10:00 p.m. or

on 11/30/63 at Dallas, Texas File # Dallas 44-1639

by Special Agent BARDWELL D. ODUM:BL Date dictated 12/3/63

This document contains neither recommendations nor conclusions of the FBI. It is the property of the FBI and is loaned to your agency; it and its contents are not to be distributed outside your agency.

466

DL 44-1639
2

11:00 p.m. in the show up room in the basement of the City Hall old building. OSWALD was not behind the screen but was out in the witness area of the show-up room, and when the press crowded around him the police removed OSWALD from the room.

O'LEARY recalled he was not stopped in the entrance to the show-up room or asked for his identification at that time.

On November 23, 1963, word was passed from correspondent to correspondent that they should be back at the police department at 10:00 a.m. the next morning, November 24, 1963.

On November 24, 1963, slightly before 10:00 a.m., O'LEARY went to the Dallas City Hall to observe the transfer of LEE HARVEY OSWALD from the city hall to the county jail. He did not see any policemen at the Commerce Street door of the city hall but he did see a policeman in uniform standing on the corner of Harwood and Commerce. O'LEARY entered on the first floor level of the old building on the Commerce Street side and was not challenged or asked for identification. He went to the self-service elevator in the center and on the west side of the building and used this elevator to go to the third floor. As soon as he stepped off the elevator on the third floor of the old building, he was challenged by a uniformed officer of the Dallas Police Department and he exhibited his identification as a newspaper correspondent.

About 10:20 a.m., he and 15 or so other representatives of news media gathered in the anteroom of the office of the Chief of Police and heard a few words from Chief JESSE CURRY. CURRY stated to the newsmen who had gathered that he could have moved OSWALD the night before but he did not want to double cross "you people," meaning the representatives of the press. Someone in the group asked CURRY if there had been any threats against OSWALD and Chief CURRY answered in the affirmative saying that threats had been made against OSWALD's life to the effect that OSWALD would not arrive at the county jail alive. O'LEARY recalled that he asked Chief CURRY about security measures being taken and Chief CURRY stated that they were using an armored car. O'LEARY asked him where they had obtained the armored car and Chief CURRY stated it was obtained from a commercial firm in Dallas. CURRY also stated, "We think we have enough men to handle it." Someone in the group asked Chief CURRY how they were going to get OSWALD down to the basement from

467

DL 44-1639
3

the jail which is located on the fourth floor. Chief CURRY stated that they would use the elevator.

At about 11:16 a.m., there was a buzz of activity throughout the third floor and O'LEARY sensed that OSWALD was coming out. He then hurried from the Chief's anteroom to the lobby by the elevator on the third floor. There he observed a line of uniformed officers and detectives keeping the reporters who were in considerable number against the west wall of the corridor outside of the entrance to the Homicide and Robbery Division. OSWALD appeared in the corridor under guard and the newsmen were ordered by an officer not to move up against or to try to move up against him. He also told them not to ask questions of OSWALD or to shout at him as he passed through the corridor to the elevator.

A minute or so later OSWALD walked out the door of Homicide with two officers, the name of one being LEAVELLE as O'LEARY recalls, immediately followed by several other officers. He stated that the entire group was preceded by Captain WILL FRITZ, Dallas Police Department and that there were perhaps 12-15 policemen in the hall of the third floor in the corridor of the third floor of city hall as OSWALD was brought out of Homicide and Robbery Division and taken to the elevator which is a special elevator used by prisoners and not the public service elevator. In spite of the instructions not to ask questions, several reporters shouted questions at OSWALD and he made a comment to the group, apparently in response to a question, stating, "Yes, I want to get in touch with the American Civil Liberties..." following which his words were broken off by his being taken inside in the anteroom toward the jail elevator. He was only in the corridor for about a minute and as soon as he went into the anteroom to the jail elevator, O'LEARY and IKE PAPPAS ran down the stairs on the third floor to the basement and waited outside the corridor in the garage area of the basement. O'LEARY recalls that there was no attempt to stop them as they went down, although he recalls he had an identification card as a member of the press on hand. He cannot recall anyone looking at it at any time.

When he arrived in the basement OSWALD had not yet arrived on the jail elevator in the basement. He estimated there were at least 50 policemen in the basement and most of them were in uniform. He estimated there was a policeman every three feet on the route that OSWALD was to

468

DL 44-1639
4

travel between the door coming out from behind the booking counter and the ramp where he was to be loaded into a car or an armored car. O'LEARY did not recall seeing anyone who appeared to be other than a member of the press or an officer. He stated that he recalls there was an automobile at the foot of the ramp coming down from the Commerce Street side and that there was an armored car further up toward Commerce Street. He stated that there was a solid double line of officers and press representatives curving from the exit to the door coming from behind the booking counter to the ramp where OSWALD would be loaded.

O'LEARY stated he was standing almost directly in front of the double doors coming out of the public corridor of the basement and to the east side of the automobile ramp. About the time that OSWALD appeared coming through the door into the ramp and garage area the driver of the automobile backed up suddenly and O'LEARY's attention was diverted to this car since he wondered if the driver would stop the car before he rammed the line of people directly behind him toward the Main street side of the ramp.

At this time O'LEARY became vaguely aware of a short fat man moving in a gliding motion from O'LEARY's right starting possibly 8 - 10 feet from O'LEARY and moving across an area possibly a distance of ten feet directly to OSWALD who was between two police officers. This man who as O'LEARY recalls was wearing a brown hat put his entire body up against LEE HARVEY OSWALD's body as in a shoulder block and O'LEARY heard a muffled "bang." He at first thought it might be a flash bulb exploding since there were many photographers in the basement area. He then saw OSWALD's mouth open in pain or astonishment and saw OSWALD clutch his stomach and double over going down with the man who had shot him on top of him immediately followed by a number of officers to the extent that no single body could be distinguished from another.

From that point on O'LEARY stated he could not see the principals and that the entire mass of men appeared to pick up and move into the basement of the city hall. He never did see the face of the assailant but recalls him as a little old man with shaggy hair. He later learned that this assailant was JACK L. RUBY, but recalls he did not recognize RUBY since he did not see his face.

469

O'LEARY advised that at least one officer preceded OSWALD as he came out of the basement door into the ramp and garage area, that there were two officers at his side, several officers behind him and that the way was apparently almost completely lined with officers. He stated that RUBY approached from the side at a diagonal direction to that being traveled by OSWALD and the officers holding him in custody and that their attention seemed to be focused ahead of them and along the line of people that they were still to come to. He stated that this apparently kept them from seeing RUBY before it was too late.

O'LEARY advised that since the shooting of OSWALD by RUBY, TOM HOWARD, attorney for RUBY, has stated that RUBY has stated that RUBY had been to the Western Union Office on the morning of November 24, 1963, and had wired $25 to a girl in FortWorth. According to HOWARD, RUBY then returned to the Main Street side of the ramp under the Dallas city hall where two officers were on guard.

These officers were apparently keeping unauthorized individuals from entering the basement area via the ramp. According to HOWARD, Officer R. E. VAUGHN walked to a police car which was about to enter the ramp and then while VAUGHN was busy at the police car, RUBY walked down the ramp unchallenged. He had apparently been standing talking to VAUGHN before the police car appeared.

O LEARY advised that he recalls that SETH KANTOR of United Press International (UPI), Washington Bureau and TONY RIPLEY of the Detroit "NEWS" were in the basement of the courthouse. He also recalled that BOB JACKSON and JOE BEERS of either the Dallas "News" or the Dallas "Times Herald" made pictures of the shooting and TV cameras from NBC and CBS filmed the murder while NBC was broadcasting it simultaneously. CBS broadcast it at a later time according to O'LEARY.

O'LEARY stated that he does not recall where IKE PAPPAS is from although he represents a radio network. He met him while in Dallas and he was sure PAPPAS was not from Dallas as PAPPAS had rented a car while in Dallas.

470

COMMISSION EXHIBIT No. 2052—Continued

FD-302 (Rev. 3-3-59)

FEDERAL BUREAU OF INVESTIG. ON

Date December 8, 1963

1

JEREMIAH O'LEARY, JR., "Washington Evening Star," Washington, D. C., advised that following the Presidential assassination, he had been assigned to proceed to Dallas, Texas, and cover events concerning same. In this regard, he stated he was present in Dallas on November 24, 1963, and was a witness to the murder of LEE HARVEY OSWALD by night club owner JACK LEON RUBY. He related the following events which took place on the day of the murder, November 24, 1963:

He recalled that on the evening of November 23, 1963, a rumor had circulated among the press that the Dallas Chief of Police might transfer OSWALD from the Dallas Municipal Building to the County Jail on the following day without advising the press. In view of this, he proceeded to the Dallas Municipal Building on the morning of November 24, 1963, arriving at 10 a.m. He entered the building from the Commerce Street side, where a police officer was stationed. He was alone and this officer gave him an inquiring look, so he exhibited his press identification card. The officer gave a cursory look at same and permitted him to enter. He then proceeded directly to the third floor, where the Dallas Police Department Homicide Division is located and where OSWALD had been interrogated subsequent to his arrest. Upon leaving the elevator, he noted an officer stationed at this location who nodded recognition, apparently from the previous day, and permitted him access to the floor. At this time, there were approximately fifteen or twenty press and television representatives in the hallway, none of whom he recognized other than IKE PAPPAS, a representative from a radio station. He had met PAPPAS on the previous day and does not know what radio station he represents, but feels that it is probably a local Dallas station.

At 10:15 a.m., the Chief of Police emerged from his office and announced that OSWALD would be moved to the County Jail very shortly. The Chief commented that he could have moved OSWALD on the previous night, but had decided not to because this would be double-crossing the press. Reporters

on 12/4/63 at Washington, D. C. File # Dallas 44-1639 WFO 44-520

by Special Agent RICHARD WOOD KAISER:sch:BL Date dictated 12/4/63

This document contains neither recommendations nor conclusions of the FBI. It is the property of the FBI and is loaned to your agency; it and its contents are not to be distributed outside your agency.

471

COMMISSION EXHIBIT No. 2053

DL 44-1639
2

asked the Chief whether any threats had been made against OSWALD's life. He replied in the affirmative, but refused to discuss the nature or the source of these threats. In reply to questions concerning protective measures, the Chief said that a commercial armored car would be used to transport OSWALD to the County Jail. The Chief explained that OSWALD would be taken from the Homicide Squad Room to a non-public elevator located approximately twenty paces from this room. He would then be taken directly to the basement where the armored car was waiting to transport him.

O'LEARY stated that at this point, he and PAPPAS determined that they could remain on the third floor to observe OSWALD's exit from the Homicide Squad Room and would have sufficient time to quickly descend the stairs to the basement, arriving there before OSWALD would in the elevator. He and PAPPAS then had arranged to use the latter's car in order to follow the police and OSWALD to the County Jail.

At approximately 11:15 a.m., Captain FRITZ, head of the Homicide Division, Dallas Police Department, emerged from his office with OSWALD, who was flanked by two other detectives, one of whom was handcuffed to OSWALD. At this point, the press representatives were lined up on one side of the corridor leading to the elevator and the police on the other. All of the representatives began shouting unintelligible questions to OSWALD, who was quickly taken to the elevator. O'LEARY could only hear one comment that OSWALD made to the press, which was, "Yes, I want to see the American Civil Liberties Union." He and PAPPAS immediately took the stairway to the basement where a large contingent of police, television and press representatives awaited. He noted that they did not encounter any police officers guarding the stairway or its entrance to the garage. The elevator where OSWALD was to arrive from the third floor was located in a separate security room. Outside of this room there was a twenty foot wide channel leading to the armored car, with police and press representatives milling about freely on both sides. O'LEARY, upon crossing from one side to the other of this corridor, exhibited his press identification very quickly to an officer and was waved on.

At approximately 11:19 a.m., OSWALD emerged from the security room, flanked by the previously mentioned officers, paused briefly and then proceeded toward an unmarked police

472

DL 44-1639
3

car which had been placed in the garage for the purpose of transporting OSWALD to the garage entrance where the armored car was waiting, due to the fact that it was too large to gain access to the garage.

O'LEARY stated that at this moment, the police car was backed further into the garage toward OSWALD and the operator accelerated the motor, causing considerable noise and confusion. He noted that he, as well as other individuals present, including OSWALD, had momentarily focused their attention upon this car. From the corner of his eye, he noted an individual emerge from the crowd about five yards to his side. This individual, subsequently identified as JACK RUBY, quickly ran up to OSWALD and appeared to throw his body directly against OSWALD, at which time the shot was fired, OSWALD's face first registered surprise and then pain as he collapsed on top of JACK RUBY. At this point, a complete state of bedlam existed, with officers drawing their weapons and shouting to seal off the building and permit no one to leave.

O'LEARY stated that he immediately detached himself from the crowd and took a public elevator up to the third floor in search of a telephone. He noticed that the Chief of Police was in his office preparing correspondence and apparently was unaware of the recent events. He quickly informed the Chief of the shooting and proceeded to the telephone to call his paper.

O'LEARY stated that in his opinion, the Dallas Police Department was very relaxed in their security precautions, based upon the fact that they appeared to be accepting any identification from the press representatives and in his own case, he was permitted access to various areas, apparently from previous recognition. He stated that he does not personally know of any unauthorized person who was permitted to enter the basement area, but due to the number of people and disorganization, it was possible there were some. Due to his concentration on events which were taking place at that time, he can recall recognizing only one other press representative in the basement and that was TONY RIPLEY, who he believed to be with a Detroit paper.

O'LEARY stated that he had no information which would indicate that any person, police officer or Dallas government official conspired with RUBY in committing this murder.

473

On the contrary, he believes that RUBY committed this act on the spur of the moment. He based this on the fact that he had observed RUBY on the previous day, November 23, 1963, present in the Municipal Building when OSWALD was being taken to and from the Homicide Division for questioning. At such times, RUBY was in close proximity to OSWALD and would have had ample opportunity to shoot him at that time. O'LEARY stated that in addition, several days subsequent to the murder, he had occasion to talk with TOM HOWARD, Defense Attorney for RUBY. HOWARD informed him that RUBY had arrived at the Municipal Building only moments before OSWALD emerged into the garage. O'LEARY noted that only very few top police officials knew the exact time when OSWALD was to be trasnsported and that if RUBY had arrived a few minutes later, OSWALD would not have been present. HOWARD also informed that RUBY had entered the Municipal Building from the Main Street entrance, directly past two police officers who were conversing and who did not challenge him.

O'LEARY stated that he had not personally conversed with JACK RUBY, but had observed him on various occasions prior to the shooting, circulating among the various press representatives, passing out his business card and inviting them to visit his night club.

O'LEARY stated that he has no information indicating any prior relationship or acquaintance between OSWALD and RUBY.

O'LEARY stated that he had no knowledge of any unauthorized persons being present in the garage at the time of the shooting, nor has he received information concerning any relationship or prior acquaintance between RUBY and OSWALD.

O'LEARY advised that prior to his departure from Dallas, Texas, on November 30, 1963, he had been in contact with FBI Agents on several occasions and furnished considerable information concerning the events of November 24, 1963, as well as other matters relating to the Presidential assassination, which he had obtained both prior and subsequent to that date.

474

1

Date 12/10/63

HENRY MICHAEL RABUN, 8015 Westchester, Apartment G, Dallas, Texas, a newsman for United Press International, related the following:

On November 24, 1963, he went to the basement of the building housing the Dallas Police Department, about 7:00 AM. There were about three newsmen already there at this time. He sat in the Jail Office waiting for LEE HARVEY OSWALD to be transferred from the City Jail to the Dallas County Jail. He occasionally went to the third floor during the waiting period to ascertain any new developments. When he first entered the basement, he was not asked to exhibit any credentials by anyone but, on numerous occasions during the day, he was asked to show his credentials to both uniformed and plain-clothes police officers. His credentials were also checked on one occasion on the third floor by a police officer.

About twenty minutes before LEE HARVEY OSWALD was shot, he went upstairs to the third floor and while he was there suddenly everyone went downstairs. He said he did not recall hearing any announcement, but all of a sudden everyone seemed to know it was time to transfer OSWALD. As he came down in the elevator, he was checked by police officers standing in the little hallway in front of the windows in the Jail Booking Office. His credentials were examined at this point and he continued on through this hall or lobby and took up a position in the basement. Since he is of rather short stature, he stood on a railing around the parking area just in front of the swinging door leading to the hallways of the Jail Office. He saw OSWALD being brought from the Jail Office into the basement.

With regard to the actual shooting, he stated he recalled seeing a moving blur to his right and heard the shot, but everything happened so quickly he did not even see the man who had shot OSWALD, because this man was almost instanteously surrounded by police officers, who bore him to the ground.

November 24, 1963, was the first time he had been in the Dallas Police Department or the City Hall. He

on 12/10/63 at Dallas, Texas File # DL 44-1639

by Special Agents ALLEN H. SMITH & TOM E. CHAPOTON Date dictated 12/10/63
JR./eah

This document contains neither recommendations nor conclusions of the FBI. It is the property of the FBI and is loaned to your agency; it and its contents are not to be distributed outside your agency.

491

DL 44-1639

2

was not aware of any announced or security procedures of the Police Department, but does know he was required to identify himself on several occasions, which he did by use of his press card. He has no personal knowledge of any unauthorized persons being permitted in the basement, assuming that everyone was checked as he was by the Police Department.

He had no knowledge that anybody in the Police Department or elsewhere conspired with RUBY to shoot OSWALD. RABUN had never seen RUBY at any time and particularly between November 22 - 24, 1963, and had no knowledge of any association or relationship between JACK RUBY and LEE HARVEY OSWALD.

RABUN is not acquainted with RUBY and has never been in the Carousel Club or the Vegas Club. He stated there was such a mob of people in the basement that it would be difficult for him to give any estimate as to the number who were there, but did state it was very crowded and it was necessary for the Police Department to hold the newsmen back since there were so many of them.

492

FD-302 (Rev. 1-25-60)

FEDERAL BUREAU OF INVESTIGA

Date December 5, 1963

1

WILLIAM RAILEY, Manager, United Press International, Press Building, 2100 Rusk Avenue, Houston, Texas, advised SA EDWARD G. STORK, that on November 22, 1963, he was in his office at Houston, when he learned of the assassination of President KENNEDY. He said that he immediately proceeded to Dallas, Texas, via the airlines, arriving there around 3:00 P. M. Central time the same date.

RAILEY advised that at that time suspect OSWALD was being held on the third floor of Dallas Police Jail, and that he had to display his Texas State Press Card, to officers at the entrance to the Police Department, before he was allowed to enter the building. Further, that on reaching the third floor of the building, he was again requested to display his press card to two officers before he was permitted to go in the hall where members of the news media were congregated.

RAILEY said that he is in possession of numerous "press cards" issued by various news organizations and anyone of which is usually sufficient for identification to police authorities, but the Dallas officers were concerned mainly with the card issued by the State of Texas, and that anyone not having this card was not permitted into the building. He cited one case of a newsman (unidentified) who did not have a Texas State Press Card who was denied entrance to the Police Department when it was "quite obvious that the person was a newsman". He said that this person was "loaded down" with photographic equipment and was displaying all sorts of press cards, but lacking the aforementioned card was denied entrance.

RAILEY said that, in his estimation, the security measures of the Dallas Police Department, were as "tight" as he had ever encountered.

RAILEY said that as of 12:10 A. M., November 24, 1963, security measures were extended to all entrance ways to the basement of the Dallas Police Department, where

On 12/5/63 at Houston, Texas File # HO 44-939

by SA EDWARD G. STORK:bp Date dictated 12/5/63

This document contains neither recommendations nor conclusions of the FBI. It is the property of the FBI and is loaned to your agency; it and its contents are not to be distributed outside your agency.

493

OSWALD was to be taken out for removal to the County Jail. RAILEY thinking that the Police Department would remove OSWALD prior to the announced hour, positioned himself in the basement at midnight and remained there until approximately 6:00 A. M., November 24, 1963, at which time he was relieved by his associate, FRANK JOHNSON, Photographer, UPI, American Stationary Building, Austin, Texas.

RAILEY advised that he then returned to his hotel to sleep, since he had been awake some seventeen straight hours. On awakening at noon he learned that OSWALD had been killed. RAILEY then returned to the basement of the Dallas Police Department, gaining entrance via the ramp, and was again "checked out" by Officers.

RAILEY stated that he has never known RUBY or OSWALD, and did not recall seeing RUBY at the Dallas Police Department at any time. Further, that he has never interviewed RUBY or OSWALD; knows of no possible connection between RUBY or OSWALD, or of any relationship between RUBY and the Dallas Police Department.

RAILEY advised that the only persons that he could recall seeing at the Police Department, on November 22, 23 or 24, 1963, were FRANK JOHNSON (previously mentioned) JACK BEERS, Dallas Morning News and BOB JOHNSON, Dallas Times Herald.

494

COMMISSION EXHIBIT No. 2055—Continued

FD-302 (Rev. 1-25-60)

FEDERAL BUREAU OF INVESTIGATION

Date 11/30/63

ANTHONY (no middle name) RIPLEY, 414 West Harrison, Royal Oak, Michigan, was interviewed at his residence.

He stated he is a reporter for "The Detroit News", a daily Detroit publication, which is located at 615 West Lafayette, Detroit, Michigan. He has been employed as a reporter for this publication since November, 1956. He stated he arrived at Dallas, Texas, at 7:30 PM, on November 22, 1963, having been sent to cover the assassination of President KENNEDY. He said he did not know the identity of President KENNEDY's assassinator at the time he left Detroit. He said his assignment was to cover the investigation to apprehend the assassinator of President KENNEDY.

He advised that en route to Dallas, Texas, from Detroit, he changed planes at Atlanta, Georgia, and on this plane he met JOE CUMMINGS or CUMMING, who represented the Newsweek Magazine and who is stationed in Atlanta. He said he also met one STEWART LOORY of the "New York Herald Tribune", New York, New York. He said he is not certain if either CUMMINGS or LOORY were at the scene of the shooting of LEE HARVEY OSWALD.

RIPLEY said he was actually present in the basement of the Dallas Municipal Building (DMB), which houses the Dallas Police Department and other city offices. He said he assumed, but does not know of his own personal knowledge, that everyone present in the basement of the DMB was either a representative of the news media, police officer or other law enforcement agency of the State of Texas.

He said that the only other individual that may have been present in the basement of the DMB was one TOM HOWARD, who is now the defense attorney from Dallas for JACK RUBY. He said he could not now recall who stated this, but it might have been one GERALD O'LEARY, reporter, "Washington Star," Washington, D.C. He stated HOWARD's office is located across the street from the DMB.

He advised that at about 9:45 AM, on November 24, 1963, he was proceeding to the DMB, arriving at the corner of the DMB, which is closest to the Statler Hilton Hotel, where he was staying. He said one of the cross streets was Commerce Street. He stated as he arrived at this corner, he was immediately challenged by an officer of the Dallas Police Department, identity unknown. He advised he immediately displayed his press card to this officer and was allowed to proceed.

On 11/30/63 at Royal Oak, Michigan File # Detroit 44-563

by SA CHARLES I, ROBICHAUD and SA JACK G. WILSON / MOS Date dictated 11/30/63

This document contains neither recommendations nor conclusions of the FBI. It is the property of the FBI and is loaned to your agency; it and its contents are not to be distributed outside your agency.

497

COMMISSION EXHIBIT No. 2056

DE 44-563
2

He reported he then entered the DMB, Commerce Street entrance, and as soon as he entered he was again asked to identify himself by officers of the Dallas Police Department. He stated he again identified himself by showing his press card and proceeded to the third floor of the DMB, which is the main office of the Dallas Police Department. He stated he then found out that OSWALD had not as yet been transferred to the Dallas County Jail. He said that he then left the DMB via the same way that he had entered. He stated he then walked to the entrance of the ramp leading to the basement of the DMB, where the armored car was parked, and was hesitant at first about entering the basement via the ramp, thinking that the Police Department did not want newsmen in the basement. He said he noticed that two or three individuals entered the basement via the ramp, identities unknown, but presumed by RIPLEY to be newsmen, and he decided to enter the basement. He said he also noticed a cable running down the ramp, which he was sure was a television cable, and immediately thought that there was news coverage of this event. He said he then proceeded down this ramp into the basement and, thereafter, was never challenged as to his identity until after the shooting of OSWALD.

He said there was no specific stations for reporters to stand, but he, as well as others, were told by the Dallas Police Department to keep out of the way. He stated as a result, most reporters positioned themselves along the walls of the basement.

He said there were no security instructions or procedures outlined to the reporters as far as he knows. He reiterated that neither he, nor as far as he knows anyone else, was required to identify himself in the basement of the DMB.

He said he was about twenty feet away from the actual spot where OSWALD was shot. He stated that the assailant of OSWALD was not clearly seen by him and all he recalled is a "blur" of someone moving into the vicinity of where OSWALD was at the time of the shooting.

Within five minutes after the shooting of OSWALD, RIPLEY said he was approached by a plainclothesman of the Dallas Police Department and was asked to identify himself. He said he again displayed his press credential, which was examined minutely by this plainclothesman. He said that he then immediately left the basement and went to the third floor, which was the office of the Dallas Police Department and, thereafter, left the building.

498

DE 44-563
3

He said he has no knowledge whatsoever of anyone entering the basement without identification.

He said he had no knowledge whatsoever, either by direct knowledge or hearsay, of any conspiracy between any individual and RUBY regarding the shooting.

He said he has no indication that there was any conspiracy between RUBY or any police officer of the Dallas Police Department or any other individual that would allow or permit RUBY to perform the killing.

He said he never officially interviewed or spoke to JACK RUBY and cannot recall seeing RUBY prior to the OSWALD shooting. He said he only noticed him and knew his identity after he had been apprehended by the Dallas Police Department, which was after RUBY shot OSWALD.

He said he had no personal knowledge that there was any connection between JACK RUBY and OSWALD. He did state that on November 24, 1963, there was a television interview with BILL DE MAR, a ventriloquist and master of ceremonies at the Carousel Club, Dallas, Texas. He also conducted a "memory act" at the Carousel Club. During this interview, it was alleged that DE MAR had seen OSWALD at the Carousel Club.

On November 26, 1963, according to RIPLEY, JOYCE EGGERTON, a reporter for the "London Sunday Observer," London, England, who was staying at the Statler Hilton Hotel, suggested to RIPLEY that they interview DE MAR. He said he believed that EGGERTON's office was located in either Washington, D.C., or New York City.

As a result, on November 26, 1963, he and EGGERTON interviewed DE MAR at the Carousel Club. DE MAR stated, as a result of this interview, that he had seen OSWALD at the club on a week night several weeks prior to the shooting. He said DE MAR reported that he was doing his "memory act" and claimed that OSWALD was part of the audience participation in this act. He said DE MAR was from Evansville, Indiana. RIPLEY advised he was not enthusiastic nor did he pursue to any great extent this interview of DE MAR because he had been convinced in his own mind that DE MAR had not seen OSWALD at the Carousel Club. The only reason RIPLEY could offer for this opinion was from his experience

499

DE 44-563
4

in the newspaper business. He did state that DE MAR seemed to be sincere, but for the above reasons it appeared that he might be seeking publicity.

RIPLEY advised that the following are the only individuals he knows by name to have actually been in the basement of the DMB at the time of the OSWALD shooting:

JOHN MC CULLOUGH
Reporter
"Philadelphia Bulletin"
Philadelphia, Pennsylvania

PEGGY SIMPSON
Associated Press
Dallas, Texas

FRANCOIS PELOU
Reporter
France Press
believed stationed at Washington, D.C.

TOM PETIT
NBC-TV
believed to be stationed in New York City

RIPLEY advised from overall observation the security offered by the Dallas Police Department was rather "relaxed" and offered this observation in comparing other important affairs which he covered with the security taken by other police departments. He based this mostly on the fact he, RIPLEY, was allowed down the ramp without being challenged, even though he was previously challenged elsewhere.

500

COMMISSION EXHIBIT No. 2056—Continued

Commission Exhibit No. 2057

FD-302 (Rev. 3-3-59) FEDERAL BUREAU OF INVESTIGATION

Date Dec. 11, 1963

JAMES N. STANDARD, reporter, Oklahoma Publishing Company, advised he traveled to Dallas, Texas, at approximately 12:00 noon, November 22, 1963, to cover the assassination of President KENNEDY for his newspaper. He stated on November 22 and 23, 1963, he spent his time talking to witnesses concerning the assassination and attempting to locate other eye witnesses and photographs of the assassination.

STANDARD advised during this period of time he did not see JACK RUBY at any time in the Dallas Police Department or that vicinity. He stated some of the reporters, names unrecalled, had mentioned RUBY was present at the District Attorney's conference regarding OSWALD and the assassination and had asked the District Attorney a question concerning OSWALD and the assassination. He stated he could not verify this information because he was not present himself at the District Attorney's press conference.

STANDARD stated he was present in the Dallas Police Department basement alleyway on the morning of November 24, 1963, when OSWALD was to be transported to the Dallas County Jail. He advised he gained entrance to the alleyway through the door from the Police Department Identification Section adjacent to the jail elevator door from which OSWALD was removed. He stated as he entered the door to the alleyway he was confronted by two policemen requesting he exhibit press credentials. He informed these policemen he had no press card and exhibited a credit card and a group insurance card which identified him as an employee of the Oklahoma Publishing Company. He said one of the policemen did not want to permit him to pass; however, the other officer agreed to pass him only after a complete search of his person. STANDARD was of the opinion the security measures set up at the Dallas Police Department were very rigid and he knew of no one present in the basement alleyway who had not exhibited credentials to gain entrance.

STANDARD stated he saw no one present in the alleyway who was not connected with law enforcement or news media.

on 12/10/63 at Oklahoma City, Oklahoma File # DL 44-1639
OC 44-430

by Special Agents GLENN E. SILVEY & DAVID W. McCLUGAGE/csh Date dictated 12/10/63

521

This document contains neither recommendations nor conclusions of the FBI. It is the property of the FBI and is loaned to your agency; it and its contents are not to be distributed outside your agency.

COMMISSION EXHIBIT No. 2057

FD-302 (Rev. 3-3-59) FEDERAL BUREAU OF — Commission Exhibit No. 2058

Date 12/2/63

1

JAMES ROBERT THORNTON, newsman, WFAA Radio, Dallas, who resides at 7819 Milstone Drive, Dallas, advised he arrived at the City Hall, Dallas, on November 24, 1963, shortly before 10:00 A.M. He carried a portable tape recorder and planned to cover events there when and if LEE HARVEY OSWALD was transferred from the City Jail to the Dallas County Jail. He said he had learned from press reports several hours earlier that he might be transferred that morning.

Another newsman, one CHURCH IRWIN, also of WFAA, was stationed at the Dallas County Jail in order to work with him in covering that event.

That morning he entered the building through the first floor and took an elevator to the basement, entering same without exhibiting his press pass, no inquiry being made of same. He explained that he is at the City Hall almost daily and is well-known to all the police officers there. He walked around a few minutes and then walked out of the building to the Main Street entrance of the police department garage. There he entered the garage by the Main Street ramp. A police officer, name unknown, asked for his press pass and he exhibited same. His pass was issued by Chief of Police J. E. CURRY in July, 1961, and bears number 259. He then walked through the garage and back to the entrance to the corridor through which it was expected OSWALD would walk. Soon an unidentified Dallas Police Department detective required all newsmen with the exception of two network television men to move to the East side of the ramp in the garage. He took his position about five feet from the numerous television cameras and was there when he heard a shot fired which he later found out was a shot fired by JACK RUBY which killed LEE HARVEY OSWALD.

So far as he knows the two television network men were the only newsmen allowed in the basement corridor at the time OSWALD was brought out of the City Jail. He identified those two men as TOM PETTIT of New York (NBC representative) and BOB HUFFAKER of KRLD, Dallas, who was serving for CBS.

on ~~11/30/63~~ at ~~Dallas, Texas~~ File # ~~DL 44-1639~~

by Special Agent EDWIN D. KUYKENDALL and ~~LEO L. ROBERTSON~~:jj Date dictated 12/2/63

This document contains neither recommendations nor conclusions of the FBI. It is the property of the FBI and is loaned to your agency; it and its contents are not to be distributed outside your agency.

523

2
DL 44-1639

He advised he ~~had~~ did not see JACK RUBY in the basement, garage or City Hall prior to the shooting. He is not personally acquainted with JACK RUBY. He does not know how RUBY gained access to the area. He noticed there was an armored car on the ramp and two police cars had been brought to the south ramp. It appeared the police were taking considerable security precautions because he saw several officers asking some of the other newsmen for their press passes. He did not observe anyone in the area where OSWALD was shot other than police officers and newsmen. He remembers, however, there was either a utility man or electrician who appeared for the purpose of doing some kind of work and was checked out by the police after which the electrician or utility man proceeded with his task in that vicinity. He could not tell that person's identity but presumed he was some kind of a building employee. He said all of the news representatives were required to exhibit their passes before they were allowed to leave the City Hall basement after the shooting had occurred. He said the police, therefore, undoubtedly learned if any unauthorized persons were there at that time. He has not heard any other individuals give any explanation as to how JACK RUBY came to be there.

He has no information that would indicate any individual has conspired with JACK RUBY concerning the shooting of OSWALD. He has no knowledge that RUBY talked to any other individuals there prior to the shooting and he only saw RUBY for the first time just momentarily before the shot was fired. He has no information that would indicate any police officer has been closely associated with RUBY or allowed RUBY permission to be in the area. He has no knowledge of any relationship or prior acquaintance between RUBY and OSWALD.

524

FD-302 (Rev. 1-25-60)

'EDERAL BUREAU OF INVESTIGAT

Date 12/9/63

INTERVIEW WITH NEWSMEN

MAURICE CARROLL, 14 Symor Drive, Convent Station, New Jersey telephone Jefferson 8-7694 was interviewed at the office of the New York Herald Tribune, 230 West 41st Street, where he is employed as a news reporter. He indicated he is generally known as "MICKEY" CARROLL. He furnished the following information:

He arrived Dallas, Texas from New York the night of November 22, 1963. He was in and around the Dallas Municipal Building, Dallas, Texas on Saturday, November 23, 1963. He spent the majority of his time on the third floor of this building where the Homicide Bureau of the Dallas Police Department was located and where LEE HARVEY OSWALD was being held. He recalled that when he went to the third floor of this building, his credentials were always checked by a police officer stationed in the corridor on the third floor.

JESSE CURRY, Chief of the Dallas Police Department at an informal press conference on the night of November 23, 1963, indicated that OSWALD would be moved into the County Jail about 10:00 a.m. on the following morning. CURRY told those present at the conference that they need not show up before 10:00 a.m. the following day, but that they should not be much later than 10:00 a.m. CURRY said there had been threats made against the life of OSWALD, and that an armored car would be used to transport OSWALD to the County Jail.

CARROLL arrived at the Dallas Municipal Building shortly before 10:00 a.m. on Sunday, November 24, 1963. He went to the third floor of the building. His credentials were checked by an officer of the Dallas Police Department. There were other newsmen on the third floor, but most of them wandered down to the basement of the building, as they knew OSWALD would be taken through the basement to an armored car parked on the ramp in the basement.

On 12/6/63 at New York, New York File # NY 44-974

by SAS TIMOTHY B. LAGRONE AND JAMES J. ROGERS:aam Date dictated 12/9/63

This document contains neither recommendations nor conclusions of the FBI. It is the property of the FBI and is loaned to your agency; it and its contents are not to be distributed outside your agency.

52

CARROLL remained on the third floor and with him were "IKE" PAPPAS, reporter for New York City Radio Station WNEW, and a newpaper reporter named, "JERRY" Last Name Unknown. CARROLL did not know what newspaper "JERRY" worked for or of the city he worked out of.

At about 10:00 a.m. OSWALD was lead out of the room on the third floor by three or four Dallas Police Department officers. CARROLL was unable to state exactly how many officers there were. OSWALD was lead down the hall to an elevator.

CARROLL, PAPPAS, and "JERRY" ran down the stairway to the basement. In the basement corridor leading to the garage, he was required to show identification by a uniformed officer stationed in this corridor.

When he entered the basement, OSWALD had not yet appeared. CARROLL explained this was probably due to the fact that the elevator was very slow moving.

CARROLL noticed that there were two rows of people who had formed in the corridor leaving from a doorway from which OSWALD was expected to appear.

CARROLL started toward the side of the corridor where the television camera was located, but he was directed by a plain clothes policeman to stand back on the other side. There were newsmen standing two and three deep on this side, and CARROLL was behind them.

Within a very short time, which CARROLL estimated to be less than one minute, OSWALD emerged from the doorway. About this same time, CARROLL saw a blue car backing down the ramp behind the armored car.

53

NY 44-974

When OSWALD emerged into the basement, the crowd of newsmen and television reporters on both sides surged forward toward OSWALD, and one man appeared to thrust a microphone towards him. Just then CARROLL heard a "pop" and then there was a lot of confusion. OSWALD was then taken back through the doorway from which he had emerged.

CARROLL had been leaning forward trying to get a look at OSWALD and to hear anything that OSWALD might say. He was not able to have a good view of OSWALD. He did not actually see OSWALD get shot. He did not see RUBY prior to the time that OSWALD was shot, and only had a fleeing glimpse of a man being lead out of the basement garage by the police.

CARROLL does not know of any unauthorized person who may have entered the basement of the Dallas Municipal Building, nor does he know of any authorized person permitted to enter the basement without identification.

CARROLL did not have any information that any person conspired with RUBY, or any information that a police officer, or other official conspired with RUBY or wilfully committed the killing of OSWALD.

CARROLL did not see or talk to RUBY at any time from November 22 through November 24, 1963.

CARROLL has no knowledge of any relationship or prior acquaintance between RUBY and OSWALD.

The following is a list of persons whom CARROLL recalled were in the basement at the time of the shooting of OSWALD:

NY 44-974

"IKE" PAPPAS

FRANK JOHNSTON
United Press International Photographer

NBC-Television newsman who was broadcasting "live"

Reporter name unknown, who worked for a French newspaper.

HANK MACHIRELLA
Reporter for the New York Daily News

There were other newsmen present whom CARROLL did not know. In addition, there were a number of officers of the Dallas Police Department whom CARROLL did not know.

Commission Exhibit No. 2060 CO-2-34,030

U. S. Secret Service

Chief November 29, 1963

Inspector Kelley

Preliminary Special Dallas Report # 3
Covers third interview with Oswald and
circumstances immediately following his murder

This interview started at approximately 9:30 AM on Sunday, November 24, 1963. The interview was conducted in the office of Captain Will Fritz of the Homicide Bureau, Dallas Police. Present at the interview in addition to Oswald were Captain Fritz, Postal Inspector Holmes, SAIC Sorrels, Inspector Kelley and four members of the Homicide Squad. The interview had just begun when I arrived and Captain Fritz was again requesting Oswald to identify the place where the photograph of him holding the gun was taken. Captain Fritz indicated that it would save the Police a great deal of time if he would tell them where the place was located. Oswald refused to discuss the matter. Captain Fritz asked, "Are you a Communist?" Oswald answered, "No, I am a Marxist but I am not a Marxist Leninist". Captain Fritz asked him what the difference was and Oswald said it would take too long to explain it to him. Oswald said that he became interested in the Fair Play for Cuba Committee while he was in New Orleans; that he wrote to the Committee's Headquarters in New York and received some Committee literature and a letter signed by Alex Hidell. He stated that he began to distribute that literature in New Orleans and it was at that time that he got into an altercation with a group and he was arrested. He said his opinions concerning Fair Play for Cuba are well known; that he appeared on Bill Stukey's television program in New Orleans on a number of occasions and was interviewed by the local press often. He denies knowing or ever seeing Hidell in New Orleans, said he believed in all of the tenets of the Fair Play for Cuba and the things which the Fair Play for Cuba Committee stood for, which was free intercourse with Cuba and freedom for tourists of the both countries to travel within each other's borders.

Among other things, Oswald said that Cuba should have ~~folded~~ full diplomatic relationship with the United States. I asked him if he thought that the President's assassination would have any effect on the Fair Play for Cuba Committee. He said there would be no change in the attitude of the American people toward Cuba with President Johnson becoming President because they both belonged to the same political party and the one would follow pretty generally the policies of the other. He stated that he is an avid reader of Russian literature whether it is communistic or not; that he subscribes to "The Militant", which, he says, is the weekly of the Socialist party in the United States (it is a copy of "The Militant" that Oswald is shown holding in the photograph taken from his effects at Irving Street). At that time he asked me whether I was an FBI Agent and I said that I was not that I was a member of the Secret Service. He said when he was standing in front of the Textbook Building and about to leave it, a young crew-cut man rushed up to him and said he was from the Secret Service, showed a book of identification, and asked him where the phone was. Oswald said he pointed toward the pay phone in the building and that he saw the man actually go to the phone before he left. 177

U S SECRET SERVICE
RECEIVED

COMMISSION EXHIBIT No. 2060

2.
CO-2-34,030

I asked Oswald whether as a Marxist he believed that religion was an opiate of the people and he said very definitely so that all organized religions tend to become monopolistic and are the causes of a great deal of class warfare. I asked him whether he considered the Catholic Church to be an enemy of the Communist philosophy and he said well, there was no Catholicism in Russia; that the closest to it is the Orthodox Churches but he said he would not further discuss his opinions of religion since this was an attempt to have him say something which could be construed as being anti-religious or anti Catholic.

Capt. Fritz displayed an Enco street map of Dallas which had been found among Oswald's effect at the rooming house. Oswald was asked whether the map was his and whether he had put some marks on it. He said it was his and remarked "My God don't tell me there's a mark near where this thing happened". The mark was pointed out to him and he said "What about the other marks on the map?- I put a number of marks on it. I was looking for work and marked the places where I went for jobs or where I heard there were jobs".

Since it was obvious to Captain Fritz that Oswald was not going to be cooperative, he terminated the interview at that time.

I approached Oswald then and, out of the hearing of the others except perhaps one of Captain Fritz's men, said that as a Secret Service agent, we are anxious to talk with him as soon as he had secured counsel; that we were responsible for the safety of the President; that the Dallas Police had charged him with the assassination of the President but that he had denied it; we were therefore very anxious to talk with him to make certain that the correct story was developing as it related to the assassination. He said that he would be glad to discuss this proposition with his attorney and that after he talked to one, we could either discuss it with him or discuss it with his attorney, if the attorney thought it was the wise thing to do, but that at the present time he had nothing more to say to me. Oswald was then handed some different clothing to put on. The clothing included a sweater. Captain Fritz made a number of telephone calls to ascertain whether the preparations he had placed into effect for transferring the prisoner to the County Jail were ready and upon being so advised, Captain Fritz and members of the Detective Bureau escorted Oswald from the Homicide Office on the third floor to the basement where Oswald was shot by Jack Ruby.

On the completion of the interview, SAIC Sorrels and I proceeded to the office of the Chief of Police on the third floor and were discussing the interview when we heard that Oswald had been shot. We both ran down the steps to the basement. I arrived in the ante-room where they had dragged Oswald. SAIC Sorrels located and interviewed Ruby. Someone was bending over Oswald with a stethoscope and he appeared to be unconscious in very serious condition at that time. I asked Captain Fritz what had happened and he said Oswald had been shot by one Jack "Rubio" whom the police knew as a tavern operator. Shortly thereafter a stretcher arrived and I accompanied the stretcher to the ambulance which had been hastily backed into the garage. I observed that during the transfer that Oswald was unconscious; when the ambulance drove away from the building, I attempted to board a cruiser that apparently was going to follow the ambulance but I was unable to get into the car before it pulled away. Special Agents Warner and Patterson had heard of the shooting on their radio, proceeded to Parkland Hospital where Oswald was being taken and arrived very shortly after Oswald had arrived at the emergency entrance and was 177

RECEIVED

COMMISSION EXHIBIT No. 2060—Continued

being taken into the emergency treatment room. One or the other of these agents was in close proximity to Oswald while he was being treated. When I arrived at the hospital, I rode up on the elevator with Dr. Shaw who had looked at Oswald as he had come in and was being recalled to the operating room where Oswald had been taken. While Oswald was in the operating room, no one other than medical personnel was present but a Dallas policeman who had accompanied Oswald in the ambulance was standing in the doorway of the operating room in operating room scrub clothes. No other investigating personnel were in the vicinity. In the immediate vicinity of the detective was Special Agent Warner. Oswald made no statements from the time he was shot until the time of his death. He was unconscious during the ambulance run to the hospital which I verified through Detective Daugherty, who accompanied him. He did not regain consciousness at any time during the treatment until he died. At the time of his death, myself, Detective Daugherty and Colonel Garrison of the Texas State Police were on the fifth floor of the hospital arranging a security room in which to take Oswald, in the event he survived the operating room treatment. It was never necessary to use this room and upon learning of his death, I proceeded to the morgue to arrange for his family to view the body. When the family heard of the death they were in the process of being interviewed by Special Agents Kunkel and Howard, and requested to be brought to the hospital. Oswald's brother, Robert, who had also come to the hospital, was being interviewed by Special Agent Howlett. Before the post mortem was performed, Oswald's family, with the exception of Robert, viewed the body. Robert arrived too late to view the body before the autopsy had started and was not permitted by hospital authorities to view the body. The family was accompanied during the viewing by the hospital chaplain.

After making arrangements through the chaplain and another clergyman for the burial of the body, the family was returned to a secluded spot under the protection of Special Agents Kunkel and Howard, and the Irving Texas police. Precaution was taken to insure their safety in view of the excitement caused by the killing of Oswald. Special Agents Howard and Kunkel did an excellent job in handling the security of this family detail and insuring their safety. Thereafter, I was called by SAIC Bouck who advised me that the President and the Attorney General were concerned about the safety of this family and instructed that all precautions should be taken to insure that no harm befell them. SAIC Bouck was advised that the family was presently under our protection; we would continue providing protection until further notice.

Later that same day, I was contacted by SA Robertson of the FBI who asked whether we had someone with the family. He was assured that we had. He requested to be advised where the family had been taken. Since their ultimate destination was unknown to me at the time, I assured him that when I learned of their whereabouts I would relay it to him. He said that they received instructions from the Attorney General and President Johnson that precaution should be taken to insure the family safety.

At 11 pm, Sunday, November 24th, I was advised of the location of the family and immediately notified Robertson and inquired whether they now wished to take over their protection. He said no they had no such instructions, they merely wished to be assured that someone was looking out for their safety. I assured them that

U S SECRET SERVICE
RECEIVED

adequate protection was being provided and that they were available for interviews by the FBI. He stated that they did not wish to interview the family at this time; that they merely wanted to make sure they were in safe hands.

TJK:VS

OFFICE OF THE CHIEF

U S SECRET SERVICE
RECEIVED

Commission Exhibit No. 2061 CO-2-34,030

U. S. Secret Service

Chief, Washington Dec. 1, 1963

Inspector Kelley

Interviews with Lee Harvey Oswald

There are attached reports of the interviews with Lee Harvey Oswald.

TJK:VS

338

COMMISSION EXHIBIT No. 2061

INTERVIEWS WITH LEE HARVEY OSWALD
ON NOVEMBER 23, 1963

At about 12:35 P.M., November 23, 1963, Lee Oswald was interviewed in the office of Captain Will Fritz of the Homicide Division, Dallas Police Department. Among those present at this interview were Inspector Kelley, Captain Fritz, Detectives Senkel and Tiernon of the Homicide Division and SA James Bookout, FBI. Captain Fritz conducted the interview which was concerned mostly with Oswald's places of residence in Dallas and was an attempt to ascertain where the bulk of Oswald's belongings were located in Dallas. As a result of the interview, Oswald furnished information to Captain Fritz that most of his personal effects, including a sea bag, were in the garage at the address of Mrs. Paine, 2515 West 5th Street, Irving, Texas.

The interview was concluded about 1:10 P. M. and immediately thereafter members of the Homicide Division secured a search warrant and recovered Oswald's effects from the home of Mrs. Paine. Found among the effects were two different poses in snapshot type photographs taken of Oswald holding a rifle in one hand and holding up a copy of a paper called the Militant and "The Worker" in the other hand. Oswald was wearing a revolver in a holster on his right side. This photograph was enlarged by the Dallas Police Laboratories and was used as a basis of additional questioning of Oswald at approximately 6:00 P.M. that same evening.

On November 23, 1963, at 6:00 P.M., in the office of Captain Fritz, Homicide Division, Dallas Police Department, I was present at an interview with Oswald. Also present were Captain Fritz, FBI Agent Jim Bookhoutt, and four officers from the Homicide Division. This interview was conducted with Oswald for the purpose of displaying to him the blow-ups of photographs showing him holding a rifle and a pistol which were seized as a result of the search warrant for the garage of Mrs. Paine at 2515 West 5th Street, Irving, Texas. When the photographs were presented to Oswald, he sneered at them saying that they were fake photographs; that he had been photographed a number of times the day before by the police and apparently after they photographed him they superimposed on the photographs a rifle and put a gun in his pocket. He got into a long argument with Captain Fritz about his knowledge of photography and asked Fritz a number of times whether the smaller photograph was made from the larger or whether the larger photograph was made from the smaller. He said at the proper time he would show that the photographs were fakes. Fritz told him that the smaller photograph was taken from his effects at the garage. Oswald became arrogant and refused to answer any further questions concerning the photographs and would not identify the photographs as being a photograph of himself. Captain Fritz displayed great patience and tenacity in attempting to secure from Oswald the location of what apparently is the backyard of an address at which Oswald formerly lived, but it was apparent that Oswald, though slightly shaken by the evidence, had no intention of furnishing any information.

The interview was terminated at about 7:15 P.M.

Thomas J. Kelley
Inspector

338

COMMISSION EXHIBIT No. 2061—Continued

FIRST INTERVIEW OF
LEE HARVEY OSWALD

At about 10:30 A.M., November 23, 1963, I attended my first interview with Oswald. Present during the interview at the Homicide Division, Dallas Police Department, were Special Agent Jim Bookhout, FBI; Captain Will Fritz, Homicide Division, Dallas Police Department; U. S. Marshal Robert Nash; SA David Grant and SAIC Sorrels; and Officers Boyd and Hall of Captain Fritz's detail. The interview was not recorded. Mr. Sorrels and my presence was as observers, since Oswald was being held for murder and his custody and interrogation at that time was the responsibility of the Dallas Police Department.

In response to questions put by Captain Fritz, Oswald said that immediately after having left the building where he worked, he went by bus to the thea er where he was arrested; that when he got on the bus he secured a transfer and thereafter transferred to other buses to get to his destination. He denied that he brought a package to work on that day and he denied that he had ever had any conversation about curtain rods with the boy named Wesley who drove him to his employment. Fritz asked him if he had ridden a taxi that day and Oswald then changed his story and said that when he got on the bus he found it was going too slow and after two blocks he got off the bus and took a cab to his home; that he passed the time with the cab driver and that the cab driver had told him that the President was shot. He paid a cab fare of 85¢.

In response to questions, he stated that this was the first time he had ever ridden in a cab since a bus was always available. He said he went home, changed his trousers and shirt, put his shirt in a drawer. This was a red shirt, and he put it with his dirty clothes. He described the shirt as having a button down collar and of reddish color. The trousers were grey colored.

He said he ate his lunch with the colored boys who worked with him. He described one of them as "Junior", a colored boy, and the other was a little short negro boy. He said his lunch consisted of cheese, bread, fruit, and apples, and was the only package he had with him when he went to work.

He stated that Mrs. Paine practices Russian by having his wife live with her. He denied that he had ever owned a rifle. He said he does not know Mr. Paine very well but that Paine usually comes by the place where his wife was living with Mrs. Paine on Friday or Wednesday. He stated that Mr. Paine has a car and Mrs. Paine has had two cars. He said in response to questions by Captain Fritz that his effects were in Mrs. Paine's garage and that they consisted of two sea bags with some other packages containing his personal belongings and that he had brought those back from New Orleans with him sometime in September. He stated that his brother, Robert, lived at 7313 Davenport Street, Fort Worth, and that the Paines were his closest friends in town. He denied that he had ever joined the Communist party; that he never had a Communist card. He did belong to the American Civil Liberties Union and had

paid $5 a year dues. He stated that he had bought the pistol that was found in his possession when he was arrested about seven months ago. He refused to answer any questions concerning the pistol or a gun until he talked to a lawyer.

Oswald stated that at various other times he had been thoroughly interrogated by the FBI; that they had used all the usual interrogation practices and all their standard operating procedure; that he was very familiar with interrogation, and he had no intention of answering any questions concerning any shooting; that he knew he did not have to answer them and that he would not answer any questions until he had been given counsel. He stated that the FBI had used their hard and soft approach to him, they used the buddy system; that he was familiar with all types of questioning and had no intention of making any statements. He said that in the past three weeks when the FBI had talked to his wife, they were abusive and impolite; that they had frightened his wife and he considered their activities obnoxious. He stated that he wanted to contact a Mr. Abt, a New York lawyer whom he did not know but who had defended the Smith Act "victims" in 1949 or 1950 in connection with a conspiracy against the Government; that Abt would understand what this case was all about and that he would give him an excellent defense. He stated in returning a question about his former addresses that he lived at 4907 Magazine Street in New Orleans at one time and worked for the William Riley Company; that he was arrested in New Orleans for disturbing the peace and paid a $10 fine while he was demonstrating for the Fair Play for Cuba Committee; that he had a fight with some anti-Castro refugees and that they were released while he was fined.

Upon questioning by Captain Fritz, he said, "I have no views on the President." "My wife and I like the President's family. They are interesting people. I have my own views on the President's national policy. I have a right to express my views but because of the charges I do not think I should comment further." Oswald said "I am not a malcontent; nothing irritated me about the President." He said that during 1962 he was interviewed by the FBI and that he at that time refused to take a polygraph and that he did not intend to take a polygraph test for the Dallas police. At this time Captain Fritz showed a Selective Service Card that was taken out of his wallet which bore the name of Alex Hidell." Oswald refused to discuss this after being asked for an explanation of it, both by Fritz and by James Bookhout, the FBI Agent. I asked him if he viewed the parade and he said he had not. I then asked him if he had shot the President and he said he had not. I asked him if he had shot Governor Connally and he said he had not. He did not intend to answer further questions without counsel and that if he could not get Abt, then he would hope that the Civil Liberties Union would give him an attorney to represent him. At that point Captain Fritz terminated the interview at about 11:30 A.M., 11-23-63.

Thomas J. Kelley (signature)
Thomas J. Kelley
Inspector

FD-204 (Rev. 3-3-59)

UNITED STATES DEPARTMENT OF JUSTICE
FEDERAL BUREAU OF INVESTIGATION

Copy to:

Report of: SA EUGENE J. MC KINNEY Office: Chicago
Date: December 1, 1963

Field Office File No.: 44-645 Bureau File No.: 44-24016

Title: JACK L. RUBY;
LEE HARVEY OSWALD -
VICTIM - DECEASED

Character: CIVIL RIGHTS

Synopsis: Results of interviews with PAUL SISCO, ISADORE BLECKMAN and OLIVER OAKES, members of a UPI news film team all present at the Dallas Police Department on 11/24/63 are set forth.

\- P -

DETAILS: AT CHICAGO, ILLINOIS

This document contains neither recommendations nor conclusions of the FBI. It is the property of the FBI and is loaned to your agency; it and its contents are not to be distributed outside your agency.

COMMISSION EXHIBIT No. 2062

FD-302 (Rev. 1-25-60)

FEDERAL BUREAU OF INVESTIGATION

Date December 1, 1963

PAUL SISCO was interviewed at the Chicago Office of the FBI on November 30, 1963. SISCO advised that he is an employee of the News Film Department of UPI. He stated that, in this capacity, he was present in the basement of the Dallas Police Department Building on the morning of November 24, 1963. SISCO advised that he entered the basement area through the ramp entrance on Main Street at about 9 a.m. On his initial entry he was required to exhibit his Chicago Police Department press card to a police officer on duty at the entrance. He stated that there was only one policeman on duty at this entrance. He had noticed several officers on the Commerce Street side of the Police Department building. During the next few hours SISCO departed the ramp via the Main Street entrance on two occasions. On both occasions he told the officer on duty that he was going out to get equipment and would be back momentarily. He stated that on these two occasions the policeman let him re-enter the ramp without again showing his press card. SISCO stated that he felt that this was due to the fact that the police officer recognized him as having identified himself on his intial entrance. SISCO could describe this officer only as about 6'3", husky, probably dark complected. SISCO stated that he did not notice any other police officers on the Main Street side at this time. SISCO stated that he had no knowledge of any unauthorized persons in the basement area.

SISCO stated he had no knowledge or reason to believe that any person conspired with JACK RUBY in the killing of LEE HARVEY OSWALD. SISCO related that he had no knowledge that any police officer or other official conspired or permitted the unauthorized presence of anyone in the basement. SISCO said that he cannot positively say that he saw RUBY until after OSWALD had been shot and RUBY was in custody of the Dallas Police Department in the basement area. SISCO said that during the press conference held at the police station about 1 a.m. Saturday morning, November 23, 1963, which SISCO attended, he remembers some unrecalled person point to an individual standing on a table and say, "What's a night club owner doing here". SISCO said he looked at the person standing on the table and recalls only

On 11/30/63 at Chicago, Illinois File # CG 44-645

by SAs JOSEPH M. CULKIN and CHARLES SETAR/kah Date dictated 12/1/63

This document contains neither recommendations nor conclusions of the FBI. It is the property of the FBI and is loaned to your agency; it and its contents are not to be distributed outside your agency.

2 -

COMMISSION EXHIBIT No. 2062—Continued

2

CG 44-645

that the person was wearing dark glasses. SISCO stated that he cannot definitely say it was RUBY, but feels in retrospect that it must have been him. SISCO said that before OSWALD was brought from the elevator into the basement about six police officers armed with rifles came out of the interior area of the building and went out the Main Street entrance, presumably, according to SISCO, to take up guard on Main Street.

SISCO stated that he was one of a three man UPI team from Chicago present at the Dallas Police Department on November 24, 1963. He identified the others as OLIVER OAKES and ISADORE BLECKMAN. BLECKMAN was with SISCO in the basement until after the shooting. OAKES left about 10:30 a.m. to cover the press conference being held by the wife of Governor JOHN B. CONNALLY. SISCO stated his UPI team got good film of the shooting and also possibly film of the police department exterior area as it appeared a few hours prior to the shooting. He stated some of this film may have been cut or edited as a part of the normal routine. This film was sent to UPI News Film Department 448 West 56th Street, New York 19, New York.

SISCO stated he had retained a Yellow Cab to stand by outside the Main Street entrance of the Police Department building for expedite transportation of the film. He believes the cab number may have been 932. The driver was described as probably in his 50's, gray hair, no hat. This cab stood by on Main Street from about 9:30 a.m. to 1 p.m. on November 24, 1963. SISCO recalls the meter for the waiting period was about $8.50 and he gave the driver $10.00.

FD-302 (Rev. 1-25-60)

FEDERAL BUREAU OF INVESTIGATION

Date December 1, 1963

ISADORE BLECKMAN, Apartment 101, 6002 North Kenmore Avenue, Chicago, on November 30, 1963, advised:

He has been employed as a photographer by UPI for a little over a month. BLECKMAN stated that he was sent to Dallas, Texas, Friday, November 22, 1963, immediately after news of President KENNEDY's death was received.

On Sunday, November 24, 1963, he stated that he went to the Dallas, Texas Police Department about 8 a.m. His reason, he added, for being at the police department was because of the department's announcement to the press that LEE HARVEY OSWALD would be moved from the police department to the county jail at 10 a.m., November 24, 1963. He said he entered the police department through the main entrance doors and took an elevator to the third floor of the building where heretofore the press, photographers, etc. had previously been accommodated. As he emerged from the elevator BLECKMAN said he was asked by a uniformed armed policeman to identify himself which he did by exhibiting his press credentials before he was permitted to enter the third floor. He said he remained a little while on the third floor before taking the elevator to the booking room in the basement where he remained until ten or fifteen minutes prior to OSWALD being brought out of the elevator by police.

About ten to fifteen minutes prior to OSWALD's appearance he said he and other photographers and newsmen were all asked to vacate the booking room, which they did. BLECKMAN said he then took up a position in front of a window in the booking room so he could photograph OSWALD as OSWALD emerged from the elevator. As OSWALD emerged he said he got his photographs and then raced to the far side of the ramp so he could continue to photograph OSWALD as he emerged from the booking room and presumably would be led from there to the waiting armored car which would be used to transport him to the county jail. BLECKMAN stated that he was in this position as OSWALD was led out of the booking room and that he had his camera going from that time on.

On 11/30/63 at Chicago, Illinois File # CG 44-645

by SAs GEORGE D. GATINS and WILLIAM J. SMITH, Jr./kzh Date dictated 12/1/63

This document contains neither recommendations nor conclusions of the FBI. It is the property of the FBI and is loaned to your agency; it and its contents are not to be distributed outside your agency.

An individual later identified as JACK RUBY cut through photographers, television cameramen, etc., a short distance to BLECKMAN's right and proceeded to shoot OSWALD. BLECKMAN said he continued to take action photos throughout. This film which BLECKMAN stated recorded all activity from the time OSWALD emerged from the elevator into the booking room and from that room to where he was shot is presently in the hands of his employer, UPI, in New York City or Washington, D.C.

BLECKMAN stated that between 9 to 10 a.m. the same morning he proceeded from the booking room to the ramp and left the police department premises and was permitted to do so only after identifying himself. His reason for leaving he told the officer at the Main Street entrance of the ramp was that he had to leave to get equipment. On his return he was permitted to re-enter the police department premises by the same route without identifying himself but that he presumed the armed officer on duty recognized him as having left the ramp shortly before. BLECKMAN said he saw no one in the police department or in the ramp who was not believed by him to be a member of the department or the working press. He said he had no knowledge of anyone permitted to gain entry to the police department on Sunday, November 24, 1963, without properly identifying himself, and neither did he have any knowledge or indication that any police officer or official conspired or permitted the unauthorized presence of anyone in the basement.

BLECKMAN said that to his knowledge he had never seen RUBY prior to RUBY's actual shooting of OSWALD although on Friday evening, November 22, 1963, when OSWALD was brought to the lineup room of the police department, according to various persons, identities unknown, RUBY was alleged to have been present and allegedly asked a question of OSWALD. The exhibition of OSWALD in the lineup room was apparently for the convenience of the press and photographers than for any police function, according to BLECKMAN.

BLECKMAN stated that at Parkland Memorial Hospital later on Sunday, November 24, 1963, an individual described as in his early thirties, 5'8", 180 to 200 lbs., sturdy build, blond hair who was either a director of a television station in Dallas or in charge of a television crew from a

Dallas television station told him in the presence of HENRY A. KOKOJAN, 9009 Freeport Drive, Dallas, Texas, telephone DAvis 8-1043, that an upper window of a building on either Main or Commerce Streets overlooking the police department ramp was open Friday after the President's assassination, all day Saturday and Sunday but that shortly after OSWALD's murder the window was shut. BLECKMAN stated that he could recall being told nothing additional by this individual but that the above caused speculation among themselves as to whether RUBY had an accomplice or whether others besides RUBY were interested in doing away with OSWALD.

FD-302 (Rev. 1-25-60)

FEDERAL BUREAU OF INVESTIGATION

Date December 1, 1963

OLIVER OAKES was interviewed on December 1, 1963, at his residence, 5514 Monroe Street, Morton Grove, Illinois. He advised that he is employed by UPI News Film as a sound engineer and in this capacity was sent with a news team comprised of PAUL SISCO, ISADORE BLECKMAN and himself to Dallas, Texas. He departed Chicago on Friday afternoon, November 22, 1963, by plane and arrived in Fort Worth, Texas after 5 p.m. This news team rented an automobile and drove to Dallas. During the week end of November 22-24, 1963, he was in and out of the Dallas Police Department building on numerous occasions and on several occasions had to exhibit his press pass to gain entrance to the police department building. However, after a while he was recognized and permitted by the policemen to enter without exhibiting his press pass.

OAKES stated, however, that he was always carrying his news equipment with him which is contained partially in suitcases and which is all marked with the initials UPI. On occasion when he entered the police officers would look him over, recognize him, note the initials UPI on his press gear and would not request that he exhibit a press pass. He stored his equipment on the third floor near the elevator right next to the police guards and because of this he believes they came to recognize him on sight.

On Sunday, November 24, 1963, he arrived at the Dallas Police Department at approximately 9:30 a.m. and entered the basement of the police department building by way of the Main Street ramp. It had been previously announced by the chief of police that if newsmen arrived at the police department by 10 a.m. on Sunday it would be early enough to cover OSWALD's transfer to the county jail. When he entered the police department basement he was carrying several pieces of equipment clearly marked UPI and he does not recall whether or not he was requested to exhibit a press pass. He believes he was possibly admitted based on the UPI identification on his news equipment by a young, neatly dressed uniformed officer. At this time there were approximately 12 newsmen present and everything appeared to be orderly and there was no confusion. At approximately 10:20 a.m.

On 12/1/63 at Morton Grove, Illinois File # CG 44-645

by SAs EUGENE J. MC KINNEY and DUNCAN J. EVERETTE/kmh Date dictated 12/1/63

This document contains neither recommendations nor conclusions of the FBI. It is the property of the FBI and is loaned to your agency; it and its contents are not to be distributed outside your agency.

CG 44-645

on November 24, 1963, PAUL SISCO, who was in charge of the news team, instructed OAKES to go to the Parkland Hospital to cover a news conference which was to be held by Governor CONNALLY's wife and he left the police department building at approximately 10:20 am.

While at the Parkland Hospital he was advised of the fact that LEE HARVEY OSWALD had been shot and he waited at the hospital for a time in an effort to cover OSWALD's arrival at Parkland Hospital. However, he received a telephone message from SISCO to return to the police department and did so. Upon returning to the police department he attempted to enter the Main Street ramp entrance to the basement at approximately 1 p.m. and a police officer demanded that he exhibit his press pass. He did so and this officer was about to permit him to enter the basement when a second uniformed officer walked up to the ramp and also demanded to see his press pass. The first officer told the second officer that he had already seen the pass and that OAKES was a newsman but the second officer demanded to see the press pass for himself, not taking the word of the first officer. Upon exhibiting his press pass he was permitted to enter the basement.

OAKES stated that during his presence at the Dallas Police Department he felt that they employed strict security measures and he was not permitted entrance to the police department without specifically showing his press pass or unless he was carrying equipment clearly marked UPI. He had no knowledge of unauthorized persons in the basement of the police department on November 24, 1963, or other days who did not have proper identification. However, he was informed by PAUL SISCO that JACK RUBY was in attendance at the press conference held at approximately 1 a.m. on November 23, 1963, with LEE HARVEY OSWALD.

In addition, at a news conference held with the Chief of Police, Dallas, Texas, on Tuesday, November 26, 1963, SISCO mentioned to the chief of police that RUBY was in attendance at this press conference on November 23, 1963. The chief of police did not acknowledge or deny the fact that RUBY was there.

It was his understanding that RUBY was passing out tickets for free drinks at his night club to news personnel at the Dallas Police Department. However, he did not see him do this nor did he receive any free tickets and could not furnish the names of any reporters who did obtain these free drink tickets.

OAKES stated that he has no knowledge of anyone conspiring to kill OSWALD nor did he have any knowledge or indication that any police officers or other officials conspired or permitted unauthorized persons to be present at the police department.

OAKES stated that he saw JACK RUBY during the afternoon of November 24, 1963, on the third floor of the Dallas Police Department after the shooting of LEE HARVEY OSWALD. This was the only time that he saw RUBY.

OAKES stated that the only film that he shot in Dallas was of the wife of Governor CONNALLY and this was given to PAUL SISCO and forwarded to New York.

COMMISSION EXHIBIT No. 2062—Continued

FEDERAL BUREAU OF INVESTIGATION

Date December 1, 1963

PAUL SISCO, News Film Photographer for UPI was interviewed on December 1, 1963. He advised that he interviewed the Dallas Chief of Police on November 26, 1963, and that during this interview he may have mentioned to the Chief of Police that JACK RUBY was present at a press conference at the police station on November 23, 1963, at approximately 1 a.m. However, if he did refer to this individual as RUBY it was strictly an assumption on his part based on the fact that he saw an individual standing on a table at this conference and an unrecalled individual stated, "What's a night club owner doing here". It was the opinion of all newsmen covering the press conference on November 23, 1963, that this individual was actually JACK RUBY and that he was of the strong opinion that this was JACK RUBY. However, he stated that he could not definitely say it was RUBY and that any reference to this individual as RUBY by him was strictly based on an assumption on his part.

On 12/1/63 at Berwyn, Illinois File # CG 44-645

by SA EUGENE J. MC KINNEY/kmh Date dictated 12/1/63

This document contains neither recommendations nor conclusions of the FBI. It is the property of the FBI and is loaned to your agency; it and its contents are not to be distributed outside your agency.

COMMISSION EXHIBIT No. 2062—Continued

Commission Exhibit No. 2063

FD-302 (Rev. 3-3-59)

FEDERAL BUREAU OF INVESTIGATION

Date December 13, 1963

1

HARRY T. TASKER, cab driver, was recontacted at his place of employment, City Transportation Company, 610 South Akard Street, Dallas, Texas, to determine if he recalled a uniformed officer of the Dallas Police Department stop traffic so that a police car could leave the Main Street ramp on November 24, 1963. After being furnished the information concerning the police car, TASKER furnished the following additional information:

TASKER recalled that he had been standing at the Main Street ramp for about 5 minutes prior to hearing the gunshot in the basement. TASKER now recalls a police car coming out of the Main Street ramp and the uniformed officer at the ramp walked almost to the middle of Main Street to stop the traffic so that the police car could make a left turn on to Main Street. TASKER could not recall the officers talking with the occupants of this car nor could he recall the number of occupants in the car or a description of the car, although he indicated that he was under the impression that it was a police car similar to the one used in connection with traffic investigations.

TASKER could not recall whether the police car left the Main Street ramp prior to or after the shooting. However, he assumes that the car left the ramp prior to the shooting because the police officer on duty at the Main Street ramp drew his gun and ordered everyone to the other side of the street after the shot was fired. Since TASKER was standing near the ramp where the officer was assigned he now concludes that the police car must have left the ramp prior to the shooting. TASKER indicated that he does not recall anyone entering the ramp who resembled RUBY enter the basement through the Main Street ramp during the period of time when he was standing near the ramp.

on 12/9/63 at Dallas, Texas File # Dallas 44-1639

by Special Agent ALVIN E. ZIMMERMAN & JOSEPH G. PEGGS:BL Date dictated 12/12/63

9

This document contains neither recommendations nor conclusions of the FBI. It is the property of the FBI and is loaned to your agency; it and its contents are not to be distributed outside your agency.

1
DL 100-10461
RPG:gmf

On December 19, 1963, Mr. HARRY HOLMES, Postal Inspector U. S. Post Office, Terminal Annex, Dallas, Texas, made available to Special Agent CHARLES T. BROWN, JR., a copy of a memorandum reflecting results of interview by Inspector HOLMES with LEE HARVEY OSWALD on November 24, 1963, which memorandum is quoted as follows:

"Dallas, Texas December 17, 1963

"MEMORANDUM OF INTERVIEW

"Informal memorandum furnished by Postal Inspector H. D. Holmes, Dallas, Texas, of an interview he took part in with Lee H. Oswald on Sunday morning, November 24, 1963, between the approximate hours of 9:25 a.m. to 11:10 a.m. Those present, in addition to Inspector Holmes, were Captain Will Fritz, Dallas Police, Forrest V. Sorrels, Local Agent in Charge, Secret Service, and Thomas J. Kelly, Inspector, Secret Service. In addition, there were three Detectives who were apparently assigned to guarding Oswald as none of them took part in the interrogation.

"Oswald at no time appeared confused or in doubt as to whether or not he should answer a question. On the contrary, he was quite alert and showed no hesitancy in answering those questions which he wanted to answer, and was quite skillful in parrying those questions which he did not want to answer. I got the impression that he had disciplined his mind and reflexes to a state where I personally doubted if he would ever have confessed. He denied, emphatically, having taken part in or having had any knowledge of the shooting of the policeman Tippitt or of the President, stating that so far as he is concerned the reason he was in custody was because he 'popped a policeman in the nose in a theater on Jefferson Avenue.'

173

COMMISSION EXHIBIT No. 2064

"P. O. BOXES---He was questioned separately about the three boxes he had rented, and in each instance his answers were quick, direct and accurate as reflected on the box rental applications. He stated without prompting that he had rented Box 2915 at the Main Post Office for several months prior to his going to New Orleans, that this box was rented in his own name, Lee H. Oswald, and that he had taken out two keys to the box, and that when he had closed the box, he directed that his mail be forwarded to him at his street address in New Orleans.

"He stated that no one received mail in this box other than himself, nor did he receive any mail under any other name than his own true name; that no one had access to the box other than himself nor did he permit anyone else to use this box. He stated it was possible that on rare occasions he may have handed one of the keys to his wife to go get his mail but certainly nobody else. He denied emphatically that he ever ordered a rifle under his name or any other name, nor permitted anyone else to order a rifle to be received in this box. Further, he denied that he had ever ordered any rifle by mail order or bought any money order for the purpose of paying for such a rifle. In fact, he claimed he owned no rifle and had not practiced or shot a rifle other than possibly a .22, small bore rifle, since his days with the Marine Corp. He stated that 'How could I afford to order a rifle on my salary of $1.25 an hour when I can't hardly feed myself on what I make.'

"When asked if he had a post office box in New Orleans he stated that he did, for the reason that he subscribed to several publications, at least two of which were published in Russia, one being the hometown paper published in Minsk where he met and

married his wife, and that he moved around so much that it was more practical to simply rent post office boxes and have his mail forwarded from one box to the next rather than going through the process of furnishing changes of address to the publishers. When asked if he permitted anyone other than himself to get mail in box 30061 at New Orleans, he stated that he did not. It will be recalled that on this box rent application he showed that both Marina Oswald and A. J. Hidell were listed under the caption 'Persons entitled to receive mail through box'. After denying that anyone else was permitted to get mail in the box, he was reminded that this application showed the name Marina Oswald as being entitled to receive mail in the box and he replied 'well so what, she was my wife and I see nothing wrong with that, and it could very well be that I did place her name on the application'. He was then reminded that the application also showed the name A. J. Hidell was also entitled to receive mail in the box, at which he simply shrugged his shoulders and stated 'I don't recall anything about that'.

"He stated that when he came back to Dallas and after he had gone to work for the Texas School Book Depository, he had rented a box at the nearby Terminal Annex postal station, this being Box 6225, and that this box was also rented in his name, Lee H. Oswald. He stated he had only checked out one key for this box, which information was found to be accurate, and this key was found on his person at the time of his arrest. He professed not to recall the fact that he showed on the box rental application under name of corporation 'Fair Play For Cuba Committee' and 'American Civil Liberties Union'. When asked as to why he showed these organizations on the application, he simply shrugged and said that he didn't recall showing them.

When asked if he paid the box rental fee or did the organizations pay it, he stated that he paid it. In answer to another question, he also stated that no one had any knowledge that he had this box other than himself.

"ORGANIZATIONS- MEMBERSHIP IN --- With respect to American Civil Liberties Union he was a little evasive stating something to the effect that he had made some effort to join but it was never made clear whether he had or had not been accepted. He stated that he first became interested in the Fair Play for Cuba Committee, after he went to New Orleans, that it started out as being a group of individuals who, like him, who thought and had like political opinions. They did decide to organize, and did organize after a fashion, but denied that they had any president or any elected officers. He stated that he, himself, could probably be considered the secretary since he wrote some letters on their behalf and attempted to collect dues, which, if I recall, were $1.00 per month. He also stated that there was a 'Fair Play for Cuba Committee' in New York which was better organized. He denied that he was sent to Dallas for the purpose of organizing such a cell in Dallas.

"When asked if he was a communist, he stated emphatically not, that he was a Marxist. Someone asked the difference and he stated that a communist is a Lenin-Marxist, that he himself was a pure Marxist, and when someone asked the difference, he stated that it was a long story and if they didn't know, it would take too long to tell them. He stated further that he had read about everything written by or about Karl Marx.

"When asked as to his religion, he stated that Karl Marx was his religion, and in response to further questioning he stated that

some people may find the Bible interesting reading, but it was not for him, stating further that even as a philosophy there was not much to the Bible.

"MARINE CORP_ SERVICE---Captain Fritz made some mention of his dishonorable discharge from the Marine Corp_ at which point he bristled noticeably, stating that he had been discharged with an 'honorable' discharge and that this was later changed due to his having attempted to denounce his American Citizenship while he was living in Russia. He stated further that since his change of citizenship did not come to pass, he had written a letter to Mr. Connally, then Secretary of the Navy, and after considerable delay, received a very respectful reply wherein Connally stated he had resigned to run for Governor of Texas, and that his letter was being referred to the new Secretary, a Mr. Cork, Kurth, or something like that. He showed no particular animosity toward Mr. Connally while discussing this feature.

"MAP---Captain Fritz advised him that among his effects in his room, there was found a map of the City of Dallas that had some marks on it and asked him to explain this map. Oswald said he presumed he had reference to an old City map which he had on which he had made some X's denoting location of firms that had advertised job vacancies. He stated that he had no transportation and either walked or rode a bus and that as he was constantly looking for work, in fact had registered for employment at the Texas Employment Bureau, and that as he would receive leads either from newspaper ads or from the Bureau or from neighbors, he would chart these places on the map to save time in his traveling. He said to the best of his recollection, most of them were out Industrial, presumably meaning Industrial Blvd. When asked as to why the X at the location of the Texas School Book Depository at Elm and Houston, he stated that 'Well, I interviewed there for a job, in fact, got the job, therefore the X'.

"When asked as to how he learned about this vacancy, he stated that'Oh, it was general information in the neighborhood, I don't recall just who told me about it, but I learned it from people in Mrs. Paynes' neighborhood' and that all the people around there were looking out for possible employment for him.

"ACTIVITY JUST PRIOR TO AND IMMEDIATELY FOLLOWING ASSASSINATION ATTEMPT---To an inquiry as to why he went to visit his wife on Thursday night, November 21, whereas he normally visited her over the weekend, he stated that on this particular weekend he had learned that his wife and Mrs. Payne were giving a party for the children and that they were having in a 'houseful' of neighborhood children and that he just didn't want to be around at such a time. Therefore, he made his weekly visit on Thursday night.

"When asked if he didn't bring a sack with him the next morning to work, he stated that he did, and when asked as to the contents of the sack, he stated that it contained his lunch. Then, when asked as to the size or shape of the sack, he said 'Oh, I don't recall, it may have a small sack or a large sack, you don't always find one that just fits your sandwiches.' When asked as to where he placed the sack when he got in the car, he said in his lap, or possibly the front seat beside him, as he always did because he didn't want to get it crushed. He denied that he placed any package in the back seat. When advised that the driver stated that he had brought out a long parcel and placed it in the back seat, he stated 'Oh, he must be mistaken or else thinking about some other time when he picked me up.'

"When asked as to his whereabouts at the time of the shooting, he stated that when lunch time came, and he didn't say which floor he was on, he said one of the Negro employees invited him to eat lunch with him and he stated 'You go on down and send the elevator back up and I will join you in a few minutes." Before he could finish whatever he was doing, he stated, the commotion surrounding the assassination took place and when he went down_stairs, a policeman questioned him as to his identification and his boss stated that 'he is one of our employees' whereupon the policeman had him step aside momentarily. Following this, he simply walked out the front door of the building. I don't recall that anyone asked why he left or where or how he went. I just presumed that this had been covered in an earlier questioning.

"A. J. HIDELL IDENTIFICATION CARD---Captain Fritz asked him if he knew anyone by the name of A. J. Hideil and he denied that he did. When asked if he had ever used this name as an alias, he also made a denial. In fact, he stated that he had never used the name, didn't know anyone by this name, and never had heard of the name before. Captain Fritz then asked him about the I.D. card he had in his pocket bearing such a name and he flared up and stated 'I've told you all I'm going to about that card. You took notes, just read them for yourself, if you want to refresh your memory.' He told Captain Fritz that 'You have the card. Now you know as much about it as I do.'

"About 11:00 a.m. or a few minutes thereafter, someone handed through the door several hangers on which there were some trousers, shirts, and a couple of sweaters. When asked if he wanted to change any of his clothes before being transferred to the County jail, he said, 'Just give me one of these sweaters.'

8
DL 100-10461
RPG:gmf

"He didn't like the one they handed him and insisted on putting on a black slip-over sweater that had some jagged holes in it near the front of the right shoulder. One cuff was released while he slipped this over the head, following which he was again cuffed. During this change of clothing, Chief of Police Curry came into the room and discussed something in an inaudible undertone with Captain Fritz, apparently for the purpose of not letting Oswald hear what was being said. I have no idea what this conversation was, but just presume they were discussing the transfer of the prisoner. I did not go downstairs to witness the further transfer of the prisoner."

"s/ H. D. Holmes
H. D. HOLMES
Postal Inspector
Dallas 22, Texas"

COMMISSION EXHIBIT No. 2064—Continued

FD-302 (Rev. 3-3-59)

FEDERAL BUREAU OF INVESTIGATION

1

Date 7/17/64

ROY S. TRULY, Director of the Texas School Book Depository, Dallas, advised that in the Fall of 1963, his company was having various firms conduct surveys with a view to automating much of their operation. He said it was decided, as a result of these studies, to install automated devices handled by the Frieden Company, and it became apparent that automation would make it necessary for the Texas School Book Depository to get rid of at least one employee on a supervisory level, in the Accounting Department.

He said there were two men in the Accounting Department from which to choose. One was OTIS WILLIAMS, who was in charge of the Bookkeeping Department, and the other was JOE MOLINA, the Credit Manager. Both were good employees, both had been with the company for about the same length of time. Officials of the company did not feel that MOLINA had as good an over-all knowledge of the operations of the Accounting Department as did WILLIAMS, and, accordingly, chose to retain WILLIAMS rather than MOLINA.

MOLINA was given advance notice of the plans of the company, and considerable severance pay, so that he would have an opportunity to seek work elsewhere before automation actually began.

Mr. TRULY stated that O. V. CAMPBELL, Vice-President of the firm, was MOLINA's direct supervisor, and would have complete information concerning this matter. He said, however, that although they heard some allegations immediately following the assassination of President KENNEDY that MOLINA had ha.. some subversive affiliations, he could not recall the specific allegations made, or exactly when or where he heard them, other than through local news media. He said MOLINA had been an efficient and trusted employee of the firm for sixteen years, had never given any indication of disloyalty, and the allegations of subversive affiliations on the part of MOLINA did not play a part in his discharge by the Texas School Book Depository.

on 7/14/64 at Dallas, Texas File # DL 100-9847

by Special Agent W. JAMES WOOD/ds Date dictated 7/15/64

This document contains neither recommendations nor conclusions of the FBI. It is the property of the FBI and is loaned to your agency; it and its contents are not to be distributed outside your agency.

COMMISSION EXHIBIT No. 2065

DL 100-9847

He said he felt MOLINA's period of unemployment was brief, that he drew unemployment compensation for a brief period, and then secured work in the Credit Union of the Neuhoff Brothers Packers in Dallas.

COMMISSION EXHIBIT No. 2065—Continued

Date December 27, 1963

GENE MILLER, Reporter, "Miami Herald" advised that on November 24, 1963, he was in Dallas, Texas, covering news events subsequent to the assassination of President JOHN F. KENNEDY. During the morning of November 24, 1963, he was on the third floor of the Dallas Municipal Building with other reporters and proceeded to the basement of this building to observe the transfer of prisoner LEE HARVEY OSWALD. About the time that OSWALD was removed from the elevator in the basement of the building, MILLER proceeded up the ramp and had arrived at the left side of the armored car parked there, when he heard a shot behind him. His back was to the scene and he did not observe OSWALD being shot by JACK RUBY. He said that following the shot, the police immediately sealed the area and no one was permitted to leave.

MILLER said that numerous police officers were present in the basement during the attempted transfer of OSWALD and these officers carefully examined credentials of the various members of the press. MILLER said he showed his credentials on two occasions and they were very closely scrutinized by officers. He said that, in addition, officers searched all the cars in the basement, physically searched the air conditioning ducts and rain spouts outside the building. He said he felt the security in the basement was excellent.

MILLER said he was a stranger in Dallas and had no way of knowing who was authorized to be in the basement or who was not authorized. It was his understanding that only police officers and members of the press were supposed to be in the basement, but it appeared that everyone in the Dallas Police Department knew JACK RUBY and simply accepted him as belonging with the police. MILLER said that as a matter of fact, RUBY had attended a press conference prior

On 12/26/63 at Miami, Florida File # Miami 44-1412

by SA ROBERT K. LEWIS:jlt Date dictated 12/27/63

This document contains neither recommendations nor conclusions of the FBI. It is the property of the FBI and is loaned to your agency; it and its contents are not to be distributed outside your agency.

39

COMMISSION EXHIBIT No. 2066

DM 44-1412
2.

to November 24, 1963, and actually answered some questions which were put to the Chief of Police and the District Attorney. MILLER said he felt the Dallas police were so used to seeing RUBY that they accepted him as "part of the scenery."

He said he had no actual facts one way or another as to an association between OSWALD and RUBY, but it was his personal feeling that they never had previously met.

.40

COMMISSION EXHIBIT No. 2066—Continued

THE NEW YORK TIMES, SUNDAY, MAY 24, 1964.

Kennedy's Car in Dallas Is Refitted for Johnson

Special to The New York Times

DETROIT, May 16—The car in which President Kennedy was assassinated, equipped with nearly a ton of bullet-proof glass and armor plating, will be shipped to Washington this week for use by President Johnson.

Owned by the Ford Motor Company and leased to the Government, the Continental has been transformed from a bubbletop convertible into a hardtop limousine with three-inch bulletproof windows eight panels thick.

Formerly powered with a 275-horsepower engine, the car was equipped in Dearborn with a 500-horsepower engine to handle its increased weight.

The vehicle now weighs more than five tons and is believed to be one of the heaviest autos ever constructed.

COMMISSION EXHIBIT No. 2067

UNITED STATES DEPARTMENT OF JUSTICE

FEDERAL BUREAU OF INVESTIGATION

In Reply, Please Refer to
File No.

Dallas, Texas
June 12, 1964

JACK L. RUBY;
LEE HARVEY OSWALD

The investigation in the attached document was based on a request of the President's Commission on the Assassination of President Kennedy that determination be made of the approximate driving times over five specified routes in Dallas, Texas.

Attachment

COMMISSION EXHIBIT No. 2068

FD-302 (Rev. 3-3-59)

FEDERAL BUREAU OF INVESTIGATION

1

Date 6/11/64

The following times and distances were computed at the times indicated by driving at legal speed limits and via the routes indicated:

1. From the Temple Shearith Israel, 9401 Douglas, to Phil's Delicatessen, 3531 Oak Lawn, a distance of 4.9 miles, it required 13 minutes to drive via the Club Bali Hai, 8200 Douglas Street, and the Gaylife Club, 6135 Sherry Lane. This is a reasonable direct route from 9401 Douglas Street, to 3531 Oak Lawn.

   It should be noted that the Club Bali Hai and the Gay Life Club are not on a reasonable direct route from the Temple Shearith Israel to Phil's Delicatessen at 11111 North Central Expressway. It should also be noted that the Club Bali Hai is located on the northeast corner of the intersection of Douglas Street and Sherry Lane.

2. From 223 South Ewing to the parking lot at the northwest corner of Main Street and Pearl Expressway, a distance of 4.1 miles, it required 15½ minutes to drive, starting at 10:30 AM, and via the Thornton Expressway, Industrial Boulevard and Main Street.

3. From 4611 Cole Avenue to 1312½ Commerce Street (Carousel Club), a distance of 3.8 miles, it required nine minutes to drive, late at night in light traffic and via Knox Street to Central Expressway, south to Elm Street, west to Murphy Street, south to Commerce Street, then east to 1312½ Commerce Street.

   (It should be noted that the Pago Club is no longer located at 4611 Cole Avenue).

on 6/9/64 at Dallas, Texas File # DL 44-1639

by Special Agent s ROBERT M. BARRETT & IVAN D. LEE Date dictated 6/11/64
eah

This document contains neither recommendations nor conclusions of the FBI. It is the property of the FBI and is loaned to your agency; it and its contents are not to be distributed outside your agency.

COMMISSION EXHIBIT No. 2068—Continued

2
DL 44-1639

From 4611 Cole Avenue to 1312½ Commerce Street, via Knox Street, west to Abbott Avenue, south to Armstrong Avenue, west to Turtle Creek Boulevard, then south via Turtle Creek Boulevard, Cedar Springs Road and Field Street to Ross Avenue, west to Griffin Street, south to Commerce Street, then east to 1312½ Commerce Street (Carousel Club), a distance of 4.2 miles, it required 17 minutes to drive late at night and in light traffic.

From 223 South Ewing to 1312½ Commerce Street (Carousel Club), via Thornton Expressway and Commerce Street, a distance of 3.6 miles, it required 5 minutes to drive, late at night and in light traffic.

From 223 South Ewing to 4611 Cole Avenue, via the Thornton Expressway, Commerce Street, North Central Expressway and Knox Street, a distance of 7.3 miles, it required 19 minutes to drive, late at night and in light traffic. From 223 South Ewing to 4611 Cole Avenue, via the Thornton and Stemmons Expressways, Oak Lawn Avenue, Armstrong Avenue, Abbott Avenue, Knox Street, a distance of 7.3 miles, it required 15 minutes to drive, late at night and in light traffic.

(It should be noted that it is 5.5 miles from 223 South Ewing to the Vegas Club at 3508 Oak Lawn, it required 10 minutes to drive at 2:30 PM, via the Thornton and Stemmons Expressways and Oak Lawn Avenue).

4. From the Dallas Morning News Building, Young and Houston Streets, to Parkland Memorial Hospital rear entrance, 5201 Harry Hines Boulevard, a distance of 3.7 miles, it required 10 minutes to drive, starting at 1:00 PM, via Houston Street to Elm Street, Stemmons Expressway, Industrial Boulevard and Hines Boulevard.

3
DL 44-1639

5. From Parkland Memorial Hospital rear entrance, 5201 Harry Hines Boulevard, to 1312½ Commerce Street (Carousel Club), via Harry Hines Boulevard, Cedar Springs Road, Ross Avenue, Griffin Street and Commerce Street, a distance of 3.7 miles, it required ten minutes to drive, starting at 1:30 PM. From the hospital to the Carousel Club via Hines Boulevard, Industrial Boulevard, Stemmons Expressway and Commerce Street, a distance of 4.1 miles, it required 9 minutes to drive.

It should be noted that the traffic conditions at 1:00 and 1:30 PM, on November 22, 1963, cannot be duplicated, in view of the emergency situation which existed at those times on that date.

UNITED STATES DEPARTMENT OF JUSTICE

FEDERAL BUREAU OF INVESTIGATION

In Reply, Please Refer to
File No.

Dallas, Texas

June 29, 1964

JACK L. RUBY;
LEE HARVEY OSWALD

The investigation reported herein was based on a request from the President's Commission on the Assassination of President Kennedy, dated June 18, 1964, for interviews with appropriate personnel of Armored Motor Service, Inc., concerning the role of this firm in connection with the proposed transfer of Lee Harvey Oswald from Dallas City Jail to Dallas County Jail on November 24, 1963.

Attached are reports of interviews in the above connection.

COMMISSION EXHIBIT No. 2069

FD-302 (Rev. 3-3-59)

FEDERAL BUREAU OF INVESTIGATION

Date 6/29/64

1

HAROLD FLEMING, Operations Manager and Corporate Counsel, Armored Motor Service, Inc., 1020 West Seventh Street, Fort Worth, advised that between 9:30 and 9:40 AM, on November 24, 1963, he received a telephone call at his home in Dallas from Assistant Chief of Police BATCHELOR, Dallas Police Department, asking if the company could loan the city an armored truck for transportation of LEE HARVEY OSWALD from City Hall to the County Court House. FLEMING asked Chief BATCHELOR if there was any limitation as to the size of the vehicle he wanted to use, and asked Chief BATCHELOR to measure the Commerce Street entrance to the City Hall Garage, which Chief BATCHELOR stated the truck should enter, to determine if the truck would fit into that entrance. He told Chief BATCHELOR he would recontact him later to ascertain the measurements.

Chief BATCHELOR told FLEMING the armored truck was needed in order to handle the transportation of OSWALD with the utmost security. He also told FLEMING he wanted the truck backed into the Commerce Street entrance.

FLEMING told Chief BATCHELOR there would be some delay, because it would be necessary to contact two employees, each of whom had a key to the armored transport terminal, two keys being necessary to open the terminal. Chief BATCHELOR asked him to get to City Hall as soon as he could. He made no mention of the details of the transportation, such as the route that would be taken, the time OSWALD would be put into the truck, the size of the guard, or any other details.

FLEMING then attempted to call BERT HALL, manager of the Dallas Office of his firm, but was unable to locate him at home. He then called TOM MASTIN, JR., the company President, in Fort Worth, and told him of Chief BATCHELOR's request. MASTIN gave his okay for the furnishing of an armored truck to the Police Department.

FLEMING then called TOM JAMES, a Vice President of the firm, who lives near the church BERT HALL attends, and asked JAMES

on 6/26/64 at Fort Worth, Texas File # DL 44-1639

by Special Agent W. JAMES WOOD/eah Date dictated 6/26/64

This document contains neither recommendations nor conclusions of the FBI. It is the property of the FBI and is loaned to your agency; it and its contents are not to be distributed outside your agency.

COMMISSION EXHIBIT No. 2069—Continued

2
DL 44-1639

to go to the church, attempt to locate HALL, and have him call FLEMING. He told JAMES at that time of the Police Department's request to furnish a truck for the transporting of OSWALD.

A few minutes later, at around 9:45 to 9:55 AM, HALL telephonically contacted FLEMING. The latter asked HALL who had the two keys to the Dallas terminal of the company. HALL told him they were in possession of employees DONALD GOIN and ED DIETRICH. FLEMING called DIETRICH and it took him another ten minutes, approximately, to contact DIETRICH. He did not tell DIETRICH of the plans to move OSWALD, but merely told him to meet FLEMING and HALL at the terminal immediately. FLEMING said DONALD GOIN was telephonically contacted by HALL and given similar instructions.

FLEMING then proceeded to the Dallas terminal of the company. By the time he arrived, HALL, GOIN and DIETRICH were already there. FLEMING, from the terminal, telephonically recontacted Chief BATCHELOR and ascertained the dimensions of the Commerce Street entrance to the City Hall garage. FLEMING said that by this time such information was unnecessary, because the other men had been at that garage and knew that the larger truck would not go all the way into the entrance.

FLEMING and HALL discussed what truck to take. HALL was in favor of using an ordinary armored truck, but FLEMING was in favor of taking the larger, two-ton Chevrolet truck, because he felt this larger truck would be necessary to accommodate the many persons who he felt would accompany OSWALD on the transfer. It was decided that the larger truck would be used.

FLEMING said he had left his wrist watch at home, and could not even estimate the time that their conference broke up, the time they left the terminal, or the time they arrived at City Hall. He added parenthetically that his company was most anxious to extend complete cooperation to the Police Department in this or

COMMISSION EXHIBIT No. 2069—Continued

3
DL 44-1639

any other matter, because the company was seeking the issuance of fifty special officers' permits for its employees to carry guns.

They then left the terminal, with HALL driving the larger armored vehicle and FLEMING riding as passenger. GOIN and DIETRICH followed in the smaller vehicle. FLEMING believes GOIN drove the smaller vehicle, and believes GOIN was the only member of the group in uniform. They left the parking lot on Flora Street, drove west on Flora to Leonard, south on Leonard to Ross, west on Ross to Pearl south on Pearl to Main, west on Main to Harwood, south on Harwood to Commerce, and east on Commerce to the entrance of the City Hall garage.

HALL backed the truck into the Commerce Street entrance of the garage, and was only able to get the rear end in, the cab and the four front doors of the truck protruding outside the garage. FLEMING got out the passenger side, while HALL remained in the truck the entire time, with the motor running. The truck fit very snugly into the entrance and was so close to the entrance on the passenger side that FLEMING had to go around the front of the truck and enter the garage on the driver's side of the truck. He recalls there was a policeman on guard duty on the passenger side of the garage entrance. He was not a part of the OSWALD guard force, but was merely on duty to prevent unauthorized persons from entering and leaving the garage. FLEMING does not know the identity of this officer.

When FLEMING tried to enter the garage he was challenged by a police officer just inside the garage. During the course of the period he spent there, he was in and out of the garage on three occasions, conferring with the other employees of his firm, and he was challenged on three occasions, having to identify himself and explain the reason for his presence in the garage.

When FLEMING got in the garage, he located and conferred with Chief BATCHELOR. They got into the rear of the truck and checked

COMMISSION EXHIBIT No. 2069—Continued

4
DL 44-1639

the locks and other security devices for protecting the prisoner. Chief BATCHELOR did not tell FLEMING when OSWALD would be brought down, the route they should take in going to the County Court House, or any other details of the proposed transfer. FLEMING said he entered into no discussion with any other police official or employee.

He said the smaller armored vehicle parked across the street from the garage entrance, on the south side of Commerce Street, and during the period he was in and out of the garage he was checking their position, and conferring with GOIN and DIETRICH in that truck. He instructed them to follow the larger truck when they departed for the Court House, so that should anything go wrong with the larger truck OSWALD could be immediately transferred to the smaller vehicle and the transfer could be accomplished with a minimum of trouble and a maximum of security.

FLEMING said he did not see any police officer conferring with HALL while the truck was parked in the entrance. He said that when the shooting occurred he, FLEMING, was outside the garage. He said the shooting sounded like a cap pistol. He said he was not in a position to see into the garage at the time or immediately after the shooting, but he did enter the garage soon thereafter and was told by a newspaper reporter that OSWALD had been shot.

FLEMING said he never knew OSWALD or RUBY, and did not see either of them at any time. He said he could not estimate the length of time they were at the City Hall garage before the shooting. Shortly after the shooting, an ambulance entered the Main Street side of the garage to pick up OSWALD, at which time their armored truck was kept from leaving the Commerce Street side because it was barred by a police cruiser parked in front of it. However, in a short time, the police cruiser was moved and the truck then pulled out of the garage entrance, and parked across the street on the south side of Commerce Street.

FLEMING then located Chief BATCHELOR, told him it did not

COMMISSION EXHIBIT No. 2069–Continued

5
DL 44-1639

look as though the services of the armored truck would be needed any longer, to which Chief BATCHELOR agreed, and the four individuals from the armored transport firm left in the two trucks. He estimated that they left about seven or eight minutes after the shooting of OSWALD.

COMMISSION EXHIBIT No. 2069–Continued

FD-302 (Rev. 3-3-59)

FEDERAL BUREAU OF INVESTIGATION

1

Date 6/29/64

TOM MASTIN, JR., 912 Alta Drive, Fort Worth, President of Armored Motor Service, Inc., 1020 West Seventh Street, Dallas, said that on the morning of November 24, 1963, shortly before 10:00 AM, he had received a call from HAROLD FLEMING, Operations Manager for his firm, who told him of the request by Assistant Chief of Police BATCHELOR, Dallas, for an armored truck to be used in transporting LEE HARVEY OSWALD from the City Hall to the County Court House. They briefly discussed how FLEMING should go about getting hold of the two keys necessary to get into the Dallas terminal of the firm. FLEMING told MASTIN of his unsuccessful attempts to locate BERT HALL. MASTIN told FLEMING to call TOM JONES, a Vice President of the firm, and ask him to personally try to locate HALL.

MASTIN said he had been going out the front door of his home to church when FLEMING's call was received, that he then went directly to church without discussing this matter with anyone. The pastor at his church made an accouncement during the sermon that OSWALD had been shot.

MASTIN said he never knew JACK RUBY or LEE HARVEY OSWALD and had never seen either of them, to the best of his knowledge.

on 6/26/64 at Fort Worth, Texas File # DL 44-1639

by Special Agent W. JAMES WOOD/eah Date dictated 6/26/64

This document contains neither recommendations nor conclusions of the FBI. It is the property of the FBI and is loaned to your agency; it and its contents are not to be distributed outside your agency.

COMMISSION EXHIBIT No. 2070

FD-302 (Rev. 3-3-59)

FEDERAL BUREAU OF INVESTIGATION

1

Date 6/25/64

BERT HALL, 4112 Sun Valley, Dallas, Dallas Manager of Armored Motor Service, Inc., 1800 Leonard, Dallas, was interviewed at his place of business. He said that HAROLD J. FLEMING is Operations Manager and Corporate Counsel for that firm, and has offices in Fort Worth, Texas.

HALL said that at about 9:45 A.M. on the morning of November 24, 1963, he was called from the Sunday School class he was teaching to take a telephone call from FLEMING. FLEMING told him that Assistant Chief of Police CHARLES BATCHELOR had requested the Armored Motor Service to furnish an armored truck. FLEMING asked HALL to meet him at their Dallas office and to call two other employees to meet with them there.

HALL said he does not now recall whether FLEMING said he had received the call from Chief BATCHELOR, or whether Chief BATCHELOR called TOM MASTIN, President of the company, who in turn called FLEMING. He also said he cannot now recall whether FLEMING told him the reason the truck was needed at the time the call was made.

HALL said he immediately called DONALD GOIN, Assistant Vault Manager, and ED DIETRICH, Assistant Crew Chief, and asked them to meet him at the Dallas office of the company. He does not recall whether he explained the reason for this request at that time.

HALL said his wife was also teaching Sunday School at the time, and before leaving the church he merely told her he had to go to work and would meet her at home later.

FLEMING, GOIN, DIETRICH and HALL then met at the Dallas office of the firm, arriving at various times from about 10:15 A.M. to 10:30 A.M. There was a brief discussion as to which truck to use. HALL said FLEMING told them the larger armored truck would be used to transport LEE HARVEY OSWALD from City Hall to the County Court House. This truck is described as a two-ton Chevrolet, two compartment, over-the-road truck.

on 6/24/64 at Dallas, Texas File # DL 44-1639

by Special Agent W. JAMES WOOD and MANNING C. CLEMENTS/ds Date dictated 6/25/64

This document contains neither recommendations nor conclusions of the FBI. It is the property of the FBI and is loaned to your agency; it and its contents are not to be distributed outside your agency.

COMMISSION EXHIBIT No. 2070—Continued

It is a large truck with two bunks in it. FLEMING explained that the larger truck was needed because of the large number of people it would be transporting, including OSWALD and a number of police officers.

HALL stated he was familiar with the basement at City Hall and knew that the truck was too large to get into the entrance on the Main Street side of City Hall, so it was agreed to back the truck into the entrance on the Commerce Street side.

The four of them left their Dallas office at about 10:45 A.M. HALL drove the larger truck, with FLEMING riding in the passenger side. GOIN and DIETRICH went in an accompanying smaller armored truck, with GOIN driving.

They left their parking lot located next to the building, on Flora Street, proceeding west on Flora Street to Leonard, south on Leonard to Ross Avenue, west on Ross to Pearl, south on Pearl to Main Street, west on Main Street to Harwood, south on Harwood to Commerce, and then east on Commerce to the Commerce Street entrance to the City Hall Garage.

HALL said the entrance to the garage was too small for their truck to enter, so he backed into the garage, leaving the rear end of the truck inside the garage, and the cab protruding outside. He said the truck almost completely blocked the entrance to the garage. GOIN and DIETRICH, in the smaller armored truck, parked immediately adjacent to the garage entrance, on the north side of Commerce Street, just east of the garage entrance.

HALL estimated that they parked in the garage entrance at about 11:00 A.M. on November 24, 1963. FLEMING got out of the passenger side of the truck and entered the garage to talk with Chief BATCHELOR and other police officials. HALL was not told when OSWALD was to be placed in the truck or any other arrangements which had been planned for his transportation at that time.

HALL said that at no time was he told that the truck would be used as a decoy, and another automobile used for the actual transportation of OSWALD, and he did not hear this report until at least two weeks after the shooting of OSWALD.

Shortly after he parked the truck in the garage entrance, a police officer, whose identity HALL never knew, got into the passenger side of the truck, armed with a shotgun. This policeman told HALL they would leave the garage, turn left onto Commerce Street, go in an easterly direction on Commerce to Central Expressway, north on Central Expressway one block to Main Street, and then proceed west on Main to the Court House.

HALL said he recalls that FLEMING and the patrolman with the shotgun were the only persons to enter or leave the garage through the Commerce Street entrance while his truck was parked there. He also said he kept his motor running all the time he was parked there. He said the patrolman did not mention any specific time as to when OSWALD and his guard would enter the truck.

About twenty minutes after he parked the truck in the garage entrance he heard a shot, and someone yelled that OSWALD had been shot. He remained in place, however, until someone asked him to move his truck out of the garage entrance. By this time, an ambulance had entered the Main Street side of the garage to pick up OSWALD. HALL was unable to immediately drive the truck from the garage because parked immediately in front of the truck was a police car. He yelled to the driver of the police car to move it, and when this was done he pulled the truck across the street where he parked it on the south side of Commerce Street, until he was told by Chief BATCHELOR that the truck would no longer be needed, at which time he and FLEMING, accompanied by GOIN and DIETRICH in the other truck, returned to their parking lot.

HALL estimated that not more than two minutes could have elapsed from the time of the shooting until he actually pulled out of the garage entrance.

4

DL 44-1639

HALL said he had never met or known either LEE HARVEY OSWALD or JACK RUBY, and that he did not see either of them on November 24, 1963, and does not recall having ever seen either of them.

He said he did not enter into any discussions with any police officials about the arrangements, other than the instructions he received from the patrolman with the shotgun who got into the truck with him.

COMMISSION EXHIBIT No. 2070—Continued

Commission Exhibit No. 2071

UNITED STATES DEPARTMENT OF JUSTICE

FEDERAL BUREAU OF INVESTIGATION

In Reply, Please Refer to File No.

Dallas, Texas
July 8, 1964

JACK L. RUBY;
<u>LEE HARVEY OSWALD</u>

The investigation reported in the attachment hereto was based on a request in a letter of the President's Commission on the Assassination of President Kennedy dated June 22, 1964, that a time check be made as to possible modes of entry of Jack L. Ruby into the Dallas Police Department.

Attached is a report of investigation regarding this matter.

COMMISSION EXHIBIT No. 2071

FEDERAL BUREAU OF INVESTIGATION

1

Date 6/29/64

SA IVAN D. LEE, walking at a normal rate of speed, took the following set out times to cover the distances listed below:

From the counter at the Western Union office at which RUBY transacted business on November 24, 1963, via the eastern exit of the office onto Main Street, west on Main Street to the alleyway located behind the Police Courts Building, south in the alley to the loading platform doors, pass through the elevator and walk down the stairway entering the garage, walk through the auto parking area, crawl through the ramp railing approximately ten feet from where the Main Street ramp levels off and walk to a point where OSWALD was shot -- 189 steps -- 2 minutes, 25 seconds.

From the counter at the Western Union office, leaving the Western Union office via the Main Street exit, south on Pearl Expressway, west on Commerce Street, walk down the Commerce Street ramp leading to the Police Department basement into the police garage area, cross over to the Main Street ramp approximately ten feet from where it levels off by going through the ramp railing and walk to the spot where OSWALD was shot -- 286 steps -- 2 minutes, 50 seconds.

It was noted that the alleyway behind the Police Courts Building is located approximately one hundred forty feet east of the Main Street ramp leading to the Police Department basement.

It was also noted that the route via Pearl Expressway and Commerce Street took only 25 seconds more; however, there were no doors to go through or other obstructions as found when entering the building via the loading dock entrance.

As to the visibility to the base of the Main Street ramp at approximately 11:15 A.M. from the top of the ramp at Main Street, it was noted that the level part of the ramp area can be observed without any difficulty. It was also noted that

on 6/26/64 at Dallas, Texas File # DL 44-1639

by Special Agent IVAN D. LEE/ds Date dictated 6/26/64

This document contains neither recommendations nor conclusions of the FBI. It is the property of the FBI and is loaned to your agency; it and its contents are not to be distributed outside your agency.

COMMISSION EXHIBIT No. 2071—Continued

2

DL 44-1639

as to observation at the base of the ramp from the curbline that most of the level part of the ramp area can be observed from this point.

From standing in a position in the middle of Main Street, it was noted that an area of the basement can be observed from this point; however, the view does not give a person a good view of the level area of the ramp in the basement. It was also noted that from the three different positions it was impossible to observe any activity in the parking area of the garage or observe activity in the hallway leading to the City Jail office.

COMMISSION EXHIBIT No. 2071—Continued

Commission Exhibit No. 2072

OFFICE OF THE DIRECTOR

UNITED STATES DEPARTMENT OF JUSTICE

FEDERAL BUREAU OF INVESTIGATION

WASHINGTON 25, D. C.

July 16, 1964

BY COURIER SERVICE

Honorable J. Lee Rankin
General Counsel
The President's Commission
200 Maryland Avenue, Northeast
Washington, D. C.

Dear Mr. Rankin:

Reference is made to your letter of July 14, 1964.

Special Agent Manning C. Clements advises that when he arrived at the office of Chief Curry at approximately 1:00 p.m. on November 22, 1963, Chief Curry was not in his office and the Agent's best present estimate as to the time Chief Curry arrived is approximately 3:30 or 4:00 p.m. He recalled specifically that Curry's arrival was after Oswald was on the premises of the Dallas Police Department. When he observed Chief Curry in his office, he conveyed the message to Chief Curry personally in substantially the language set forth in his report dated November 30, 1963. Agent Clements had been instructed to deliver this message by Mr. J. Gordon Shanklin, Special Agent in Charge of the Dallas Office of the FBI. No other person is recalled by Agent Clements as having been present when he spoke to Chief Curry.

With respect to Mr. Clements' testimony before the President's Commission, Mr. Clements has advised that it is his recollection that he did not make a direct statement that he was not a "conduit for any information that the FBI had concerning Oswald to the Dallas Police Department," but rather when the question, "Did you serve as a conduit for

COMMISSION EXHIBIT No. 2072

Honorable J. Lee Rankin

any information from FBI files to the Police Department relative to Oswald?" was put to him by Mr. Samuel A. Stern of the President's Commission, he replied "No" without further comment.

Mr. Clements states that his answer is factual in that he was at no time instructed to furnish and he did not furnish to the Police Department or anyone else information from prior investigation concerning Oswald.

With regard to my testimony before the President's Commission wherein I referred to a message I sent to Chief Curry requesting that the Dallas Police refrain from announcing to the press details regarding the progress of the investigation into the assassination, Mr. Shanklin states that at 3:15 p.m. on November 24, 1963, he personally telephoned Chief Curry and talked to him concerning the amount of publicity that was being afforded the case. He pointed out to Chief Curry that the President of the United States was concerned over the amount of publicity that was being given out by Chief of Police Curry and Captain Fritz. Chief Curry stated that he was in full agreement that too much publicity was being given out and that he personally would cease answering further questions concerning the matter and would assure that Captain Fritz who had been giving additional statements would do likewise.

Mr. James R. Malley, who was in Dallas at the time, states that on November 25, 1963, Chief Curry was in telephonic contact with him and referred to the fact that the City Manager of Dallas had been in touch with Chief Curry and was insisting that he make a release to the press concerning the case that the Police Department had against Oswald. The release was to be to the effect that at a proper time when the investigation had reached a status where it would be proper to do so evidence against Oswald would be documented and made available to the public. Curry stated he was getting considerable pressure from the City Manager and desired to clear the matter with Mr. Malley. At that time Mr. Malley pointed out to Chief Curry that he had been in touch with Captain Fritz on the evening of November 24, 1963, in Chief Curry's absence and had passed on the President's grave concern over the amount of publicity that was emanating from Dallas.

- 2 -

COMMISSION EXHIBIT No. 2072—Continued

Honorable J. Lee Rankin

Mr. Malley again contacted Chief Curry at 12:50 p.m. on November 27, 1963, and brought to his attention the President's concern over the publicity that was still being released. Chief Curry advised that he was not making any press releases of any kind, that he had specifically requested individuals in his Department to refrain from making comments to the press, but was having difficulty in controlling this phase of the Police Department's activities. Chief Curry assured Mr. Malley that he would make every effort to see that no comments were made and said that he personally had not made any comments since this matter had been discussed with him on Sunday, November 24, 1963.

Sincerely yours,

J. Edgar Hoover

- 3 -

COMMISSION EXHIBIT No. 2072—Continued

OFFICE OF THE DIRECTOR Commission Exhibit No. 2073

UNITED STATES DEPARTMENT OF JUSTICE

FEDERAL BUREAU OF INVESTIGATION

WASHINGTON 25, D.C.

February 4, 1964

Honorable J. Lee Rankin
General Counsel
The President's Commission
200 Maryland Avenue, N. E.
Washington, D. C.

Dear Mr. Rankin:

Reference is made to my letter of February 3, 1964, setting forth information concerning a slip of paper bearing four telephone numbers which was found in one of the pockets of the trousers worn by Oswald at the time he was shot by Jack Ruby. Inquiry concerning this matter has been made by our Dallas Office and the following information is submitted:

Captain J. W. Fritz, Homicide and Robbery Bureau, Dallas, Texas, Police Department, advised that Oswald requested permission to call Attorney John Abt in New York City but did not have his telephone number. Captain Fritz told Oswald he could call collect and that he would have to give the operator the name of the person he wanted without the number and it being an attorney in New York, the operator would locate Abt and furnish the telephone number to him. Captain Fritz also told Oswald the operator would want to know the number he was calling from. In this connection, it is noted the telephone number RI 8-9711 appears on the dial of the telephone in the jail and this was one of the four numbers on the piece of paper found in Oswald's trousers.

Captain Fritz advised that when Oswald was permitted to use the telephone, one of the jail officers, Jim Poppelwell, took Oswald from his cell to the phone and Oswald tried to call his attorney collect. He obtained the telephone number from the operator and Oswald then commented he could not recall the number and asked Poppelwell to get him paper and a pencil in order to write the number down. Captain Fritz stated that the calling of an attorney and the furnishing of a pencil and paper to the prisoner to write were all within the regulations of the city jail.

COMMISSION EXHIBIT No. 2073

Honorable J. Lee Rankin

Officer Poppelwell advised he tore off a small piece of paper from the corner of what is called a Telephone Contact Slip and, after receiving permission from his superior officer, furnished the piece of paper and pencil to Oswald so Oswald could write down the telephone number. Poppelwell advised that Oswald again attempted to call Abt but was unable to get the call through. He states he later took Oswald to the phone again and Oswald made two or three attempts to call. He states he does not know if the calls were completed or the identity of the person Oswald was trying to call. The police department kept no records of the numbers Oswald tried to call. Captain Fritz advised that the following morning, November 23, 1963, he talked with Oswald and inquired if Oswald had made his call. Oswald told Captain Fritz he had been allowed to make the call but had been unable to contact Attorney Abt. With reference to the piece of paper furnished by Officer Poppelwell to Oswald, it is noted this paper was two and one-fourth inches long by one and a quarter inches wide and that two telephone numbers were written down each side.

Our New York Office has advised that the office address for Attorney John J. Abt is 320 Broadway, New York City, the same address as the law firm of David Freedman and Abraham Unger. The telephone number for the law firm of Freedman and Unger is CO 7-3110 and this same telephone number is listed in the New York telephone directory for John J. Abt.

It is noted that the telephone number AC 2-4611, which appeared on the slip of paper in Oswald's trousers, is listed to Attorney John J. Abt, 444 Central Park West, New York City.

Telephone number RI 8-9711 is the general telephone number for the City of Dallas, Texas, and it is noted Captain Fritz states that this number appears on the dial of the telephone which was utilized by Oswald in making his calls.

The reason why the telephone number OR 9-9450, the number for "The Worker," 23 West 26th Street, New York City (East Coast Communist Party newspaper), appears on this slip of paper is not known. The possibility exists that the operator, at Oswald's request or on her own initiative, may have attempted to reach Attorney Abt at this number.

- 2 -

COMMISSION EXHIBIT No. 2073—Continued

Honorable J. Lee Rankin

The foregoing is submitted to you for your assistance in the inquiry you are conducting.

Sincerely yours,

J. Edgar Hoover

COMMISSION EXHIBIT No. 2073—Continued

Th_s is the report of an interview with Deputy Chief N. T . Fisher commencing on March 23 at approximately 5:30 P.M. and ending at approximately 6:30 P.M.

Fisher stated that he was at home and off duty at the time that Ruby shot Oswald. He states that he had no information concerning the movement of Lee Harvey Oswald.

Fisher further states that it is his understanding that Captain Talbert acted under his own initiative in setting up the security in the basement. Fisher stated that when he arrived at the Police Department Building from Love Field at approximately 5:00 P.M. on Friday evening no procedures had been established for excluding persons from the third floor.

Fisher stated that he has known Ruby since about 1947 when he was a Detective with the Juvenile Bureau. Fisher was in charge of places like Ruby's. He was a Lieutenant in the CID. He does not recall Ruby as having been a hanger-on around the Police Department in the sense that he came to the Police Department out of curiosity. Although he does recall seeing Ruby on numerous occasions at the Police Department it was always his understanding that Ruby was down there for specific reasons since he recalls no occasion when Ruby simply stopped into his office for social conversation. Fisher remembers seeing Ruby in the third floor hallway somewhere between Chief Curry's office and the elevators on Friday night prior to the Press conference in the assembly room. Fisher believes that there were other unauthorized persons in the same area at the same time. He stated that he thought there was no positive effort being made to exclude everybody even on Saturday. He said that anybody could come up with a plausible reason for going to one of the third floor bureaus and was able to get in.

Fisher is in charge of the Patrol Division of the Police Department. He says this comprises approximately one-half of the personnel in the Department. He said that on Friday and Saturday he was concerned almost entirely with the operation of his own department and only collaterally assisted with the other events going on. Fisher, like Chief Batchelor, spent much of his time in connection with the Oswald investigation answering phone calls from persons outside the Police Department. Although he received no information of value on these telephone calls, it is his recollection that some citizen provided useful information with respect to Oswald's rifle. I did not question him about this but I presume that he was referring to information provided by Linnie Mae Randall or Buel Wesley Fraden. He commented that many of the phone calls were from people who were criticizing the Police Department or from people who were suggesting that Oswald's stomach ought to be pumped to see if he were the man who had been eating chicken on the sixth floor of the School Book Depository Building.

COMMISSION EXHIBIT No. 2074

Fisher stated that he knew Officer Tippitt and in fact had been in charge of the platoon in which Tippitt served some years ago. He stated that Tippitt had been called in from an outlying area and that the area that he was patrolling was not his normal one. He estimated that he was normally assigned some four or five miles from the spot at which he was killed. It is his understanding that the dispatcher's office sent out dispatches to particular cars to move to particular areas. He stated that he believed that Captain Talbert would have the most information as to how these various cars were assigned and moved.

Fisher was also questioned about any conversations he might have had with Officer Vaughn. He stated first that he did not believe that Officer Vaughn told him on the occasion of their first talk that he has stepped out into the street at the time that the Pierce Maxey car emerged onto Main Street. He almost immediately corrected this statement to say that he couldn't remember if Vaughn first stated that he left the entrance way and moved out into Main Street.

Fisher
Vaughn also stated that sometime between 10:00 and 11:00 o'clock the crowd which had been congregating on the North side of Commerce Street had moved to the South side.

He was questioned concerning whether he saw Tom Howard in the building on either Friday or Saturday. He first indicated that he had seen him t here on Friday or Saturday then he stated that he was not sure if he saw him on Friday or Saturday but knew he saw him Sunday after the shooting. I mentioned to him in particular that some of their people stated that Howard was in the building shortly before the shooting of Oswald, and Fisher stated that he had not heard such story. He described Howard as a man who handled drunk cases and other minor crimes.

I attempted to learn how the decision to move Oswald might have been communicated to someone outside. Fisher said that he did not participate in any discussion in connection with the movement of Oswald. He also said he heard nothing concerning the route which Oswald was to take until after Oswald was shot. Fisher also said that the television and radio people were on the third floor of the Police Department, seemed to be in constant contact with their control room and that movements on the third floor were being quickly communicated to the control center. He remembers that there were news men in the jail office just prior to the moving of Oswald.

I asked Chief Fisher if he had any particular suggestions for the further protection of the President. He stated that he believed that one of the greatest problems was the poor liaison between the Secret

COMMISSION EXHIBIT No. 2074—Continued

Secret, the F.B.I., and the local Police Departments. He commented in particular about the fact that the Police Department was never told about Oswald. He said that if the Police Department had known that Oswald was in that Elm Street Building they most certainly would have had someone in that building with Oswald or that they would have placed him under arrest for investigation on some phony charge.

He further commented that he thought the decision to go out the Freeway was a bad one, that he had suggested prior to the announcement of the decision as to the President's route that the caravan proceed down Main Street to Industrial and then go out Industrial to the Trade Mart. He told me that this was rejected because the section of town along Industrial was not particularly attractive.

COMMISSION EXHIBIT No. 2074—Continued

(PLEASE TYPE OR PRINT)

DEPARTMENT OF STATE
FORM APPROVED BUDGET BUREAU NO. 47-R081.1

PASSPORT APPLICATION

(Before Completing this Application, Read Information for Passport Applicants on Page 4)

(Passport Office Use Only)

D 0 9 2 5 2 6

PASSPORT ISSUED
JUN 25 '63
DEPARTMENT OF STATE NEW ORLEANS, LA.

R D O OF

A

PART I - TO BE COMPLETED BY ALL APPLICANTS

I, (First name) LEE (Middle name) HARVEY (Last name) OSWALD, a citizen of the United States, do hereby apply to the Department of State for a passport.

MAIL PASSPORT TO
STREET P.O. BOX 30061
CITY NEW ORLEANS STATE LA.
IN CARE OF (IF NECESSARY)

DATE OF BIRTH (Month, day, year)	PLACE OF BIRTH		
OCT. 18, 1939	NEW ORLEANS, LA		
HEIGHT	HAIR	EYES	APPROXIMATE DATE OF DEPARTURE
5 FT. 11 IN.	BR.	GREY	OCT-JAN

VISIBLE DISTINGUISHING MARKS: NONE
OCCUPATION: Photographer

MY PERMANENT RESIDENCE (Street address, City, State) (If same as in mailing block, write "Same"): 757 FRENCH ST. NEW ORLEANS, LA
COUNTY OF RESIDENCE: USA

B

PERSONS TO BE INCLUDED IN PASSPORT

This section to be completed only if wife or husband is to be included in applicant's passport (Include photographic likenesses in group photo)

(WIFE'S) (HUSBAND'S) FULL LEGAL NAME

(WIFE'S) (HUSBAND'S) LAST U. S. PASSPORT WAS OBTAINED FROM

LOCATION OF ISSUING OFFICE	DATE OF ISSUANCE	NUMBER
		☐ SUBMITTED HEREWITH ☐ OTHER DISPOSITION (STATE)

This section to be completed only if children are to be included in applicant's passport (Include photographic likenesses in group photo)

NAME IN FULL	PLACE OF BIRTH (City, State)	DATE OF BIRTH	RESIDED IN THE U. S. FROM TO

TO BE PRINTED IN FULL: (LAST NAME) (FIRST NAME) (MIDDLE NAME)

C

STAPLE ONE PHOTO BELOW DO NOT MAR FACE

(STAPLE HERE)

HAVE YOU PREVIOUSLY APPLIED FOR A U. S. PASSPORT? (If answer is "Yes", complete box below) ☐ YES ☐ NO

MY LAST U. S. PASSPORT WAS OBTAINED FROM (Note: If included in another's passport, state name bearer):

LOCATION OF ISSUING OFFICE	DATE OF ISSUANCE
LOS ANGELES, CALIF	SEPT 10, 1959

NUMBER 1733242 : C+A-m
☑ SUBMITTED FOR CANCELLATION
☐ OTHER

Commission Exhibit No. 2075

JUN-24-63 600004 LT ACAPPT 9.00

(Passport Office Use Only)

Lee H. Oswald

FEE ___ EXEC. ___ TAX ___ POST. ___ JUN-24-63 600004 LT ACLLXN 1.00

FORM DSP-11 5-62

(OVER - YOU MUST COMPLETE PAGE 2)

D-3

COMMISSION EXHIBIT NO. 2075

D

FATHER'S NAME	FATHER'S PLACE OF BIRTH	FATHER'S DATE OF BIRTH	
ROBERT LEE OSWALD	NEW ORLEANS, LA	1895	☑ U. S. CITIZEN ☐ NOT U. S. CITIZEN
MOTHER'S MAIDEN NAME	MOTHER'S PLACE OF BIRTH	MOTHER'S DATE OF BIRTH	
MARGRET, CLAVIER	NEW ORLEANS, LA	1907	☑ U. S. CITIZEN ☐ NOT U. S. CITIZEN

E

☐ I WAS NEVER MARRIED
☑ I WAS LAST MARRIED ON APRIL 31 1961 TO (Full legal name - complete whether widowed or divorced) MARINA PROSSAKAVA
WHO WAS BORN AT ARXANGIES, USSR ON (Date of birth) JULY 17, 1941
☐ WHO IS A U. S. CITIZEN
☑ WHO IS NOT A U. S. CITIZEN
☑ MARRIAGE NOT TERMINATED
☐ MARRIAGE TERMINATED BY (DEATH) (DIVORCE) ON
☑ I WAS NEVER PREVIOUSLY MARRIED
☐ I WAS PREVIOUSLY MARRIED ON TO (Full legal name)
WHO WAS BORN AT ON (Date of birth)
☐ FORMER HUSBAND OR WIFE WAS U. S. CITIZEN
☐ FORMER HUSBAND OR WIFE WAS NOT U. S. CITIZEN
PREVIOUS MARRIAGE TERMINATED BY (DEATH) (DIVORCE) ON
(IF MARRIED MORE THAN TWICE, SET FORTH FACTS IN A SUPPLEMENTAL STATEMENT)

F

PROPOSED TRAVEL PLANS

TRAVELING BY ORGANIZED TOUR? ☐ YES ☑ NO
PURPOSE OF TRIP: TOURIST
LIST EACH COUNTRY TO BE VISITED: ENGLAND, FRANCE, GERMANY, HOLLAND, USSR, FINLAND, ITALY, POLAND
PORT OF DEPARTURE: NEW ORLEANS
APPROXIMATE DATE OF DEPARTURE: OCT-DEC 1963
NAME OF SHIP OR AIRLINE: LYKES LINE
NUMBER OF PREVIOUS TRIPS ABROAD WITHIN LAST 12 MONTHS: —

MEANS OF TRANSPORTATION	SHIP	AIR	OTHER
DEPARTURE	☑	☐	☐
RETURN	☑	☐	☐

PLEASE INDICATE WHETHER YOU EXPECT TO TAKE ANOTHER TRIP ABROAD: ☑ YES ☐ NO; IF YES, WITHIN ☐ YEAR ☑ 2 YEARS ☐ 5 YEARS
PROPOSED LENGTH OF STAY: 3 MONS - 1 YR.

IN THE EVENT OF DEATH OR ACCIDENT NOTIFY
NAME IN FULL: LILIAN MURRETT RELATIONSHIP: AUNT STREET ADDRESS, CITY, STATE: 757 FRENCH ST. NEW ORLEANS, LA

G

I have not (and no other person to be included in the passport has), since acquiring United States citizenship, been naturalized as a citizen of a foreign state; taken an oath or made an affirmation or other formal declaration of allegiance to a foreign state; entered or served in the armed forces of a foreign state; accepted or performed the duties of any office, post, or employment under the government of a foreign state or political subdivision thereof; voted in a political election in a foreign state or participated in an election or plebiscite to determine the sovereignty over foreign territory; made a formal renunciation of nationality either in the United States or before a diplomatic or consular officer of the United States in a foreign state; ever sought or claimed the benefits of the nationality of any foreign state; been convicted by a court or court martial of competent jurisdiction of committing any act of treason against, or attempting by force to overthrow, or bearing arms against, the United States, or conspiring to overthrow, put down or to destroy by force, the Government of the United States; or departed from or remained outside of the jurisdiction of the United States for the purpose of evading or avoiding training and service in the military, air or naval forces of the United States; and I am not and have not been at any time during the period of 12 full calendar months preceding the date of this application (and no other person to be included in the passport is or has been at any time during the said period) a member of any organization registered or required to register as a Communist organization under Section 7 of the Subversive Activities Control Act of 1950, as amended. (50 U.S.C. 786)*

(If any of the above-mentioned acts or conditions have been performed by or apply to the applicant, or to any other person to be included in the passport, the portion which applies should be struck out, and a supplementary explanatory statement under oath (or affirmation) by the person to whom the portion is applicable should be attached and made a part of this application.)

I solemnly swear (or affirm) that the statements made on all the pages of this application are true and that the photograph attached is a likeness of me and of those persons to be included in the passport.

OATH OF ALLEGIANCE

Further, I do solemnly swear (or affirm) that I will support and defend the Constitution of the United States against all enemies, foreign and domestic; that I will bear true faith and allegiance to the same; and that I take this obligation freely, without any mental reservation, or purpose of evasion; So help me God.

Lee H. Oswald
(To be signed by Applicant in presence of a Clerk of Court or Passport Agent)

Subscribed and sworn to (affirmed) before me this ___ day of ___, 19 ___

AGENT DEPARTMENT OF STATE
JUN 24 1963
NEW ORLEANS, LOUISIANA

(SEAL OF COURT) Clerk of the ___ Court at ___

* See paragraph 6 of instructions.

D-3

COMMISSION EXHIBIT NO. 2075—Continued

DEPARTMENT OF STATE
BUREAU OF INTELLIGENCE AND RESEARCH
TRANSMITTAL OF DOCUMENT FOR RETENTION OR DESTRUCTION

TO: INR/CS - Mr. McAfee

DATE: October 11, 1963

The attached information is for confidential utilization. It is NOT to be disseminated outside the Department.

The communication may be RETAINED or DESTROYED; it should NOT be returned to INR. If DESTROYED, security procedures as outlined in Section 1985, Vol. 5, Foreign Affairs Manual must be followed.

CLASSIFICATION OF ENCLOSED DOCUMENT

IF SECRET, THE DOCUMENT: consists of 1 pages; Number 2 of 4 copies, Series SY/A.

SCA (No. 3 of 4 Copies, SY/A)
✓PPT (No. 4 of 4 Copies, SY/A)
cc: CIA/Mexico (No. 1 of 3 Copies, SY/B)
SOV (No. 2 of 3 Copies, SY/B)
RAR/P (No. 3 of 3 Copies, SY/B)

SY has file on subject which will be made available if you so desire.

OCT 16 1963

INR/DDC: JCrowley:jcm

PT/LS

This Transmittal Form Becomes UNCLASSIFIED Upon Removal of Any Classified Enclosures.

FORM DS-1514a 4-63

Form No. 1588 (1[redacted]
MEMORANDUM REPORT (7-1-60)

UNITED STATES SECRET SERVICE
TREASURY DEPARTMENT

ORIGIN: Field (Dallas)	OFFICE: Dallas, Texas	FILE NO. CO-2-34,030
TYPE OF CASE: Protective Research	STATUS: Continued	TITLE OR CAPTION: Assassination of President Kennedy
INVESTIGATION MADE AT: Dallas, Texas	PERIOD COVERED: 11-24-63	Jack Leon Ruby - slayer of Lee Harvey Oswald, charged with murder of President Kennedy
INVESTIGATION MADE BY: SAIC Forrest V. Sorrels		

DETAILS

SYNOPSIS

Jack Ruby questioned by SAIC Forrest V. Sorrels shortly after Ruby shot Lee Harvey Oswald in basement of police station, Dallas, Texas, about 11:20 A.M., Nov. 24, 1963.

DETAILS OF INVESTIGATION

On the morning of November 24, 1963, Inspector Tom Kelley and I were in the office of Assistant Chief of Police Charles Batchelor on the third floor of the City Hall, Dallas, Texas, shortly after 11 A.M. We observed the crowd across the street on Commerce Street south of the City Hall. Some twenty or thirty minutes later we heard that Lee Harvey Oswald had been shot by Jack Ruby, night club operator. Inspector Kelley and I went to the basement of the city hall where we heard that Oswald had been shot and I observed Oswald on the floor of the jail office and someone appeared to be administering artificial respiration. I then went to a nearby phone and called Deputy Chief Paul Paterni in Washington and informed him in re to the above.

I then went to office of Capt. Will Fritz, Homicide Bureau, but found that he was not there. I made inquiries as to whereabouts of Jack Ruby and was informed that he had been taken to the city jail. I then went to the jail elevator and after identifying myself was taken to the fifth floor of the jail and to a cell where Jack Ruby was standing with two uniformed officers, one on each side of him. Ruby only had on his shorts as his clothes had apparently been taken from him. I identified myself to Ruby and informed him that I would like to ask him some questions. He wanted to know if it was for newspapers or magazines and I told him it was not. He seemed to hesitate and I told him that I had seen Honest Joe (Rubin Goldstein, a well known Jewish pawn broker and used tools dealer on Elm Street) across the street just a short time before and that I knew a number of the Jewish

(continued)

DISTRIBUTION	COPIES	REPORT MADE BY	DATE
Chief	Orig. & 2 ccs	------ SPECIAL AGENT	------
Dallas	1 cc	APPROVED: [signature] SPECIAL AGENT IN CHARGE	2-3-64

(CONTINUE ON PLAIN PAPER)

U. S. GOVERNMENT PRINTING OFFICE 16-61500-1

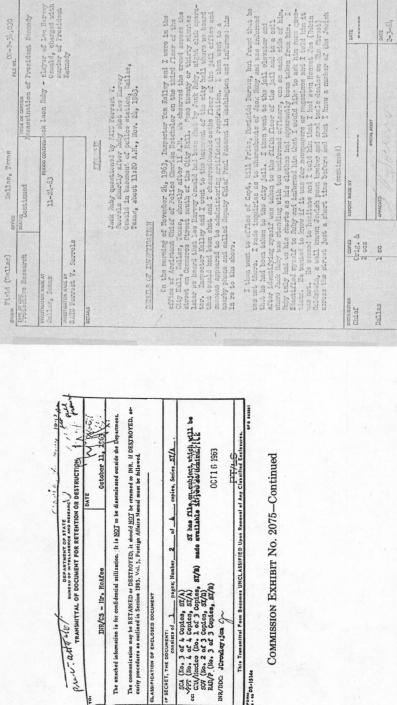

COMMISSION EXHIBIT No. 2075—Continued

business men in the city and he stated that that was good enough for him and what was it I wanted to know.

Ruby, in answer to my questions, stated that his name is Jack Ruby and that his last name was originally Rubenstein; that he was in the entertainment business, operating the Carousel Club (1312½ Commerce Street) and the Vegas Club,(3508 Oak Lawn), and that he lived at 223 S. Ewing St., Apt. 207, Dallas, Texas.

Ruby was then asked the question: "Jack, why?" To this question he replied that on the morning that President Kennedy was assassinated that he had been to the newspaper office (Dallas Morning News) and put an advertisement for his business and that when he heard that the President had been shot that he had cancelled the ad and that his business had been closed for three days; that when he read an article about Mrs. Kennedy having to come to Dallas for the trial he thought why should she be brought down here and have to go through the ordeal on account of that no good ------ (Oswald); that he had seen about a letter to little Caroline (Kennedy); that he had been to the Synagogue on Friday night (Nov. 22, 1963) and heard an eulogy on President Kennedy; that his sister, who had recently had an operation, had been hysterical, and that he guessed he had worked himself up to a state of insanity to where he just had to do what he had done, and that he guessed he felt that he had "to show the world that a Jew had guts". He also stated that he was afraid that he (Oswald) might not get just punishment as he had known instances where just punishment had not been given.

Ruby stated that he had been a labor organizer years ago. When asked if he had ever been convicted of a felony he replied that he had not. He stated that he had been arrested and taken before a Justice of the Peace in 1954 and was released (investigation of violation of State Liquor Laws).

When Ruby was asked why he had the gun (with which he shot Oswald) he stated that he usually carried a gun as he often carried large amount of money taken in his business.

In answer to questions concerning his parents, he stated that his father is Joseph Rubenstein, born in Russia and that his mother is deceased and that she was born in Poland. He stated that his civil attorney is Stanley Kaufman.

Ruby was asked the specific question as to whether or not anyone else was involved in this case and he stated that there was not and that he acted alone and that he had not known Oswald before.

Ruby stated that he had very high regard for the Dallas Police Department and that they all knew him (or some similar remark). There were some detectives standing in back of me when I was questioning Ruby. I do not recall that I asked him how he got down in the basement where he shot Oswald. That question may have been asked by one of the detectives and he may have stated that he came down the ramp. This I do not recall for sure as my main interest at the time was to get to Ruby as soon as possible for the purpose of determining if he was involved with others and if he knew or had any connection with Oswald.

Later on, at about 3:15 PM, on Nov. 24, 1963, I was in Capt. Fritz's office where Ruby was being questioned by Capt. Fritz at which time, in answer to questions, he stated he might get attorneys Tom Howard, Fred Bruner, Stanley Kaufman, civil attorney, Jim Arnton or C. A. Droby to represent him; that he had his name

COMMISSION EXHIBIT No. 2076—Continued

legally changed in Dallas from Rubenstein to Ruby; that the revolver (Colt 2 inch barrel, .38 Cal., serial #2744-LW) had been purchased by him from Ray on Singleton (Ray's Hardware & Sporting Goods, 730 Singleton, Dallas, Texas) about three years ago. (NOTE: the above described revolver is equipped with a hammer guard). He stated that his room-mate is George Senator. He stated that he had come into the basement of the police station from the Main Street ramp; that he felt that Oswald was a "red" and that he was alone; that he saw him (Oswald) in show-up room and that he knew who he was going for.

Ruby stated that he didn't want to be a martyr and that it was a build-up of grievance. (Ruby told me when I talked to him in the jail cell that he had been grieving ever since the President had been shot). He stated that he had closed both of his clubs, the Vegas at 3508 Oak Lawn and the Carousel at 1312½ Commerce Street; that he had never seen Oswald before; that he, Ruby, had at one time been in the mail order business, that he had been a labor organizer in Chicago; that he has a fondness for the police department and that when officer Slick had gotten killed sometime ago that he grieved about it; that Saturday night he had driven around and that people were in clubs laughing and no one seemed to be in mourning; that he saw eulogies of President Kennedy on TV and that he has seen President Kennedy's brother Bobby on TV; that he felt that all this had created a moment of insanity; that he had read about the letter someone sent to "little Carolyn"; that he knows the Police Department is wonderful and that his heart is with the Police Department and that he had hopes that if ever there was an opportunity for participation in police battle that he could be a part of it with them.

Ruby further stated that his mother and dad were separated for 25 years; that he owes "Uncle Sam" a big piece of money (income tax); that he loves the city (Dallas); that his sister was operated on recently and she was hysterical about the President being killed; that he went to the Synagogue Friday night (Nov. 22nd); that he went over where the wreaths were where President was shot; and that he wants Captain Fritz to not hate him.

He further stated that in Chicago when he was with the union that one of his dear friends was killed and that he had come to place where it happened; that Leon Cook was the man; that he, Ruby, was so upset about this that his mother told him to leave; that man named Martin is one that killed Cook and that Martin was political and had affiliations and got out of it.

When questioned as to what union he, Ruby, was with he stated that it was the Scrap Iron & Junk Dealers Association. Ruby stated that his politics are Democratic but that he votes for the man. He stated that he has brothers Samuel Ruby, who services washeterias in Dallas, Earl Ruby, who operates a cleaning plant in Detroit, Michigan, and Hyman Rubenstein, a salesman, in Chicago.

Ruby stated that he would not think of committing a felony; that he has a high regard for the police and that he had called Detective Sims and wanted to bring them sandwiches as he knew they were having a tough time but was informed that they were all right and didn't need them; that he was trying to locate some of the TV people to give them to and that was when he went to the show-up room and that when he went there he saw Oswald and that was first time he had ever seen anyone like that; that there was no one else but him (Ruby) involved in this case. He refused to answer some of the questions asked him by Capt. Fritz and at one time asked Capt. Fritz if he didn't think he (Ruby) would make a good actor.

COMMISSION EXHIBIT No. 2076—Continued

CO-2-34,030
Page 4.

Ruby stated that after his friend Leon Cook was killed that he took Cook's middle name "Leon" for his own middle name.

When Ruby was questioned by me in the jail cell he appeared to be somewhat emotionally upset but gave prompt answers to the questions asked him. He seemed more composed when he was questioned in Captain Fritz's office and gave quick answers to questions put to him. In response to some questions he would very quickly reply "I will not answer that".

DISPOSITION

This case remains pending in the Dallas District.

S

FD-302 (Rev. 3-3-59)

FEDERAL BUREAU OF INVESTIGATION

Date 11/29/63

On November 26, 1963, material of various types which had been recovered by the Dallas Police Department from the residence of LEE HARVEY OSWALD at 1026 Beckley, Dallas, Texas, and from the home of Mrs. MICHAEL R. (RUTH) PAINE, 2515 West 5th Street, Irving, Texas, where OSWALD's wife resided and where he periodically visited, was turned over to SA's KENNETH C. HOWE, JAMES P. HOSTY, JR., and WARREN C. DE BRUEYS of the Federal Bureau of Investigation.

The above material was brought by the above agents, Captain J. M. ENGLISH of the Dallas Police Department, and H. W. HILL, an employee of the Dallas Police Department Property Room, to the Dallas FBI Office.

The above material at the Dallas Office of the FBI was photographed and inventoried and items pertinent to the investigation subsequently were personally transported by air to FBI headquarters in Washington, D.C., by SA DE BRUEYS, along with a complete copy of the inventory.

A copy of the inventory of the above material is being maintained in the Dallas file on LEE HARVEY OSWALD. This inventory is marked to indicate those items not believed pertinent to the investigation at this time and these items are being retained in the Dallas Office.

on 11/26/63 at Dallas, Texas File # DL 89-43

by Special Agents KENNETH C. HOWE, JAMES P. HOSTY, JR., and WARREN C. DE BRUEYS / mac Date dictated 11/29/63

139

This document contains neither recommendations nor conclusions of the FBI. It is the property of the FBI and is loaned to your agency; it and its contents are not to be distributed outside your agency.

ADMISSIONS OF JACK LEON RUBY IN CAPTAIN FRITZ'S OFFICE 11-24-63

Name is Jack Ruby. Formerly Rubinstein. Had name changed in Dallas

Said attorneys were going to be one or more of the following: Tom Howard, Fred Brunner, Stanley Kaufman (civil attorney), Jim Arnton, and C. A. Droby.

Had gun (Colt snub-nose No. 2744-LW, .38 cal. equipped with hammer guard) for two or three years. Bout it from Ray's (possibly Ray's Hdw. and Sporting Goods, 730 Singleton) on Singleton.

Said roommate is George Senator.

Claimed he came in off of Main Street down ramp to basement of City Hall.

Felt Oswald was a red. Felt Oswald was alone in the assassination. (cf Ruby statement Wash Post 1/30/64) Had seen him in assembly room at showup. Knew who he was going for. Didn't want to be a martyr. Said it was a buildup of grievance.

Said he closed both is clubs; Vegas at 3508 Oak Lawn and Carousel at 1312½ Commerce Street.

Said he had never seen Oswald before he had seen him at the police station.

Said he was formerly in mail order business and had been a labor organizer.

Has nothing but fondness for the Police Department. Said that he felt very badly when officer "Slick" got killed.

Said that since President was killed he had seen people in night clubs laughing, no one in mourning, and had heard eulogies on TV. Saw the President's brother Bobby on TV. That all this created a moment of insanity. Read about the letter someone sent to little Carolyn.

Knows police department is wonderful and his heart is with the police department, and that if ever opportunity for participation in police battle, he would like to be a part of it.

139

COMMISSION EXHIBIT No. 2078

Jack Ruby's talk to Capt. Fritz--page 2

His mother and father separated for 25 years. Owes "Uncle Sam" a big piece of money. He has love for the city.

Sister operated on recently. She was hysterical about the President's being killed. That he had gone to the Synagogue Friday night - heard eulogy regarding the President. That he had been in mourning from that time on. That he went over where the wreaths were where the President was shot.

Wants Captain Fritz not to hate him. That he had been with the Union (Scrap Iron and Junk Dealers Assn.) and one of his dear friends, Leon Cook, was killed and that he had come to the place where it happened; that Jim Martin [illegible] killed Cook; that Martin was political and had affiliations and got out of it; that he had used the name "Leon" after his friend Leon Cook had been killed.

That his roommate, George Senator, sells postcards; that his politics is Democratic but votes for the man. Has brothers who are: Samuel Ruby, who services washaterias; Earl Ruby, who has cleaning plant in Detroit; and Hyman Rubenstein, salesman in Chicago. He said no one else was involved with him in the shooting of Oswald.

140

COMMISSION EXHIBIT No. 2078—Continued

2
DL 89-43

9. Front and back of U.S. Forces, Japan, identification card in name of LEE H. OSWALD, Private, SN 1653230, bearing signature of LEE H. OSWALD, issued May 8, 1958.

10. Photograph of MRS. LEE HARVEY OSWALD.

11. Front and back, street map, compliments of Ga-Jo-Enkanko Hotel, bearing telephone number ED 50755, and figure or telephone number 92463.

12. Front and back of Selective Service System notice of classification card in name ALEK JAMES HIDELL, which bears photograph of LEE HARVEY OSWALD and signature of ALEK J. HIDELL.

13. Front and back of Certificate of Service, U.S. Marine Corps, in name of ALEK JAMES HIDELL.

14. Front and back of Selective Service System Notice of Classification in name LEE HARVEY OSWALD, SSN 41-114-39-532, dated February 2, 1960.

15. Front and back of Selective Service System Registration Certificate in name LEE HARVEY OSWALD, SSN 41-114-39-532, bearing signature LEE H. OSWALD, dated October 18, 1939.

16. Slip of paper (Embassy USSR, 1609 Decatur St., N.W., Washington, D.C., Consular Pezhuyehko".

17. Slip of paper "The worke, 23 W. 26th St., New York 10, NY"; "The Worker, Box 28 Madison Sq. Station, New York 10, NY".

141

— Commission Exhibit No. 2080 —

FD-302 (Rev. 3-3-59)

FEDERAL BUREAU OF INVESTIGATION

1

Date 11/25/63

JACK RUBY was observed by SA JOSEPH M. MYERS at the Dallas City Jail, Fifth Floor, from 5:06 p.m., November 24, 1963, to 1:20 a.m., November 25, 1963.

At 5:40 p.m., November 24, 1963, RUBY was taken by Jailer G. WILLIAMS, Badge #1098, to the Identification Bureau, where he was fingerprinted and photographed by ED CARLSON, Identification Bureau. He gave as his next of kin, EARL RUBY, Cobo Cleaners, Detroit, Michigan. He appeared to be extremely friendly with CARLSON and other officers around the Identification Bureau, calling them by their first names and he specifically inquired about an officer named BLANKENSHIP.

At 6:01 p.m., Dr. FRED BEAVERDORF administered a rectal finger test in search of any pills that he might have hidden. He was allowed to talk to two visitors through the visitors' room on a communication system and the permit allowing these visitors was signed by WILL FRITZ, 5:55 p.m. The visitors were PAULINE HALL and EVA L. GRANT. RUBY kept talking to his sister, EVA GRANT, about all of his attorneys, naming FRED BRUNER, TOM HOWARD, GEORGE SANDERS, JIM MARTIN and another named KAUFMAN. He made the following remarks to his sister:

"BRUNER is my man. I have friends here so don't worry about me. Something happens inside of you and then you crack and then it happens. FRED BRUNER will come down in the morning and arrange bonds and have a hearing. I have nothing else to say and I've got the strength to stand up. I got lots of friends here so don't make a scene and get hysterical. JACK came up and said 'we don't care how much the bonds are we'll make them.' You can't live forever so they will let any of my relatives come up to see me any time. The judge is real nice and they don't bother me here."

RUBY stated PAULINE HALL manages the Vegas Club, whose address is 1606 Pratt and his sister, EVA, resides at 3929 Rawlins, Dallas.

From about 6 p.m. to 1:20 a.m., RUBY slept off and on, both in a lying down and sitting position. He did not talk very much.

on 11/24/63 at Dallas, Texas File # DL 44-1639

by Special Agent JOSEPH M. MYERS/tjd Date dictated 11/25/63

19

This document contains neither recommendations nor conclusions of the FBI. It is the property of the FBI and is loaned to your agency; it and its contents are not to be distributed outside your agency.

FD-302 (Rev. 3-3-59)

FEDERAL BUREAU OF INVESTIGATION

1

Date 11/25/63

It was noted at the time that RUBY appeared at the Identification Division of the Dallas Police Department for fingerprinting and photographing that RUBY appeared very cordial towards EDWARD E. CARLSON, Detective, Identification Division of the Dallas Police Department. They greeted each other warmly and exchanged pleasantries.

It is noted that at the conclusion of the photographing and fingerprinting of RUBY, CARLSON approached the agents and advised that he still had a liking for RUBY and would shake hands with him at any time.

on 11/24/63 at Dallas, Texas File # DL 44-1639

by Special Agents JOSEPH J. HANLEY & WILLIAM G. JOHNSON/sah Date dictated 11/24/63

20

This document contains neither recommendations nor conclusions of the FBI. It is the property of the FBI and is loaned to your agency; it and its contents are not to be distributed outside your agency.

COMMISSION EXHIBIT No. 2080—Continued

FD-302 (Rev. 3-3-59)

FEDERAL BUREAU OF INVESTIGATION

J

1 — Commission Exhibit No. 2081

Date 12/11/63

Mr. ELMER MOORE, Special Agent, U. S. Secret Service, 505 North Ervay Street, Dallas, Texas, advised Agents of the Secret Service had interviewed JACK LEON RUBY on the following occasions, at which time the following information was obtained. Mr. MOORE stated in conducting these interviews he was present on each interview and he was accompanied by various other Secret Service Agents on the interviews:

On November 30, 1963, RUBY was interviewed regarding information received by Secret Service that RUBY owned or possessed a Minifon, which MOORE described as a small wire recorder. MOORE said the Secret Service Office at Dallas received a long distance telephone call from the Los Angeles Secret Service Office regarding this Minifon. On that date, RUBY denied owning a Minifon.

On December 1, 1963, Agent MOORE again interviewed RUBY regarding the Minifon since the Secret Service Office at Dallas had received additional information regarding the background of the Minifon machine. The information had been supplied to Secret Service in Los Angeles by VIVIAN CURRY, 4855 Elmwood Avenue, Hollywood, California. CURRY had furnished information that in 1958 and 1959 she was working in Dallas and she sold wire recording equipment on the side. Agent MOORE said this interview was negative as to his ownership of the Minifon and Secret Service subsequently ascertained BARNEY WEINSTEIN, Owner of the Theater Lounge Night Club in Dallas, was the one who actually bought a Minifon from VIVIAN CURRY. MOORE said apparently CURRY was confused on having sold a Minifon to RUBY when it was actually WEINSTEIN. CURRY was interviewed by Los Angeles Agents of the Secret Service on November 29, 1963.

In the interview on December 1, 1963, which was conducted at the Dallas County Jail, RUBY was questioned regarding information furnished to Secret Service by Assistant to the Commissioner of Narcotics, Mr. GEORGE GAFFNEY. With regard to the interview with RUBY concerning information furnished by Mr. GAFFNEY, RUBY advised the Secret Service Agents as follows:

"He was first asked if he knew a TAYLOR CROSSLAND

5

on 12/9/63 at Dallas, Texas File # DL 44-1639

by Special Agent CHARLES T. BROWN/eah Date dictated 12/11/63

This document contains neither recommendations nor conclusions of the FBI. It is the property of the FBI and is loaned to your agency; it and its contents are not to be distributed outside your agency.

COMMISSION EXHIBIT No. 2081

"and he replied in the negative as he did to the same question regarding MORRIS MELTON. When he was asked if he knew PAUL JONES he said 'I know what you are getting at now. Yes, I know him. I'll tell you all about that. About 1947 I met Paul Jones at the Silver Spur, it was the Singapore Club first, on Ervay Street here in Dallas - my sister, Eva, was running it then. Later I heard that I had a phone call from Paul Jones at the Congress Hotel in Chicago where I was staying but I wasn't there at the time and I didn't talk to him. Later some Narcotics Agents came to see me and showed me some pictures. I think the only one I knew was JONES. I told the agents all I knew but I didn't know anything about narcotics or what those fellows were doing. I know that HYMIE, my brother in Chicago, had some kind of a deal with PAUL JONES. I think it was something to do with iron pipe. Everyone was trying to make a buck in those days after the war when things were short. For all I know, maybe they were shipping narcotics in iron pipe but I didn't know anything about it.'

"RUBY said that he couldn't remember anymore about the incident but he was sure that he did not meet with JONES, MELTON or CROSSLAND in Chicago and that he was not 'propositioned' on narcotics by JONES. He acknowledged that he was introduced to JONES by his sister, EVA GRANT."

On December 2, 1963, RUBY was interviewed by Agent MOORE, at which time he was questioned concerning a trip he reportedly made to Cuba in 1959. RUBY admitted to Agent MOORE that he did make a trip to Cuba, which was supposed to last for ten days, on an invitation from LOUIS MC WILLIE, described by Agent MOORE as a gambler who is well known in Fort Worth and Dallas, Texas. MC WILLIE was known to run gambling games in Dallas prior to 1959, according to MOORE. RUBY became acquainted with him in Dallas. RUBY told Secret Service Agents he and MC WILLIE had mutual friends and MC WILLIE left Dallas in about 1958 to move to Havana, Cuba. In 1959, MC WILLIE was pit boss or had a similar job at a Havana casino. MC WILLIE, according to RUBY, wrote RUBY or sent word to RUBY in Dallas that

6

he, MC WILLIE, would like for RUBY to visit with him in Havana. MC WILLIE reportedly sent RUBY plane tickets to Havana and RUBY went down as a guest. RUBY told Agent MOORE, although he was supposed to spend ten days in Cuba, following his arrival, he found he did not have as good time as he expected, he was not a gambler, and after several days in Havana with nothing to do, he was glad to return to Dallas.

On December 4, 1963, RUBY was interviewed by Agent MOORE, at which time RUBY was questioned regarding his whereabouts and movements on the day preceding the visit of President JOHN F. KENNEDY to Dallas. Agent MOORE said RUBY at first stated that the only thing he could think of at this time was that he had talked to a bartender named MICKEY RYAN and that the conversation took place at his club, probably in the early afternoon hours. Later in the conversation, RUBY recalled that he had been in downtown Dallas when he went to the Merchants State Bank and got a $500 Cashier's check which he gave to Miss MARY LEWANDOWSKI, secretary of LEO F. CORRIGAN, JR., for rental of one of his clubs. Agent MOORE advised this interview with RUBY was interrupted due to a visit with RUBY by his attorney, Mr. TOM HOWARD, and RUBY's brother, Mr. EARL RUBENSTEIN. The interviewed was discontinued when Mr. HOWARD and Mr. RUBENSTEIN appeared.

On December 4, 1963, RUBY was also questioned by Secret Service Agents regarding his alleged presence in Houston, Texas, on November 21, 1963. RUBY denied being in Houston, Texas, on that date. Agent MOORE said that the information RUBY was in Houston on November 21, 1963, was false and did not come from Secret Service. He stated the information came from a photograph of RUBY which was observed in a Houston paper by an unidentified complainant.

MOORE said in interviews conducted with RUBY by Secret Service Agents RUBY was asked a specific question, after which RUBY would talk profusely. MOORE said efforts were made to confine RUBY to an answer to the question.

7

which had been the basis for the Secret Service interview, but RUBY continued talking long after the question had been answered. MOORE said RUBY talked about the family of President JOHN F. KENNEDY, his grief over their loss, and RUBY claimed he killed LEE HARVEY OSWALD because he is an American and he did not want Mrs. KENNEDY brought back to Dallas as a witness in the trial of a "no good bastard like OSWALD." RUBY told Secret Service Agents as a Jew he knew right from wrong and "he had the guts to do something about it." He further stated he "wanted to prove to the world that a Jew has guts." Agent MOORE said the foregoing statement was as close to RUBY's actual statement as he could recall, stating it was "something of that nature."

Agent MOORE said in the interviews with RUBY he was advised on several occasions that the Secret Service was not interviewing him on a Dallas police matter; however, RUBY would continue to talk about different phases of the case. Agent MOORE said that RUBY jumped around a lot in his answers, and he would ramble from one subject to another in the interviews.

Agent MOORE furnished the results of an interview with RUBY's sister as follows:

"Eva Grant, 3929 Rawlins Avenue, Apt. I, telephone LA 6-6258, was interviewed December 1, 5, and 6, 1963 and stated that sometime in 1947 while she was preparing to open the Singapore Supper Club, 1717 S. Ervay St., Dallas, she met Paul Roland Jones through a chiropractic doctor, Waldon Duncan, with whom she was going at the time. She understood that Jones was in the brokerage business and that he dealt in eggs and metals. Jones frequently used her telephone, paying her for any long distance calls.

8

"During this time Jack Ruby met Jones. Jones advised Mrs. Grant against going into the night club business as he believes it was too tough for her and suggested that she stick to selling. He suggested several business deals to her, one of which involved iron pipe which was in demand at the time. Jones said he had access to thousands of feet of 1½' pipe which was stored in a warehouse at Ardmore, Oklahoma. He gave her a sample about 6' long which she mailed to her brother, Hyman Rubenstein, in Chicago. As a result of this transaction, both Jack and Hyman were questioned by Narcotics Agents. An agent interrogated Mrs. Grant at Dallas and suggested that she contact the Chicago Narcotics office on her next visit to that city. She did so, possibly four or five months later. At Chicago, she stated, she was shown books of photographs but recognized only one - that of Jones. She recalled that she was questioned regarding a Benny Weinberg whom she did not know but remembers the incident as she has relatives named Weinberg. Hyman was called as a witness to either Austin or Houston for the trial.

"Eva Grant, who now operates the Vegas Club, 3508 Oaklawn Avenue, Dallas, with Jack Ruby, stated that he has never been involved in any narcotic deals and that she is 'absolutely positive' that none of her brothers have ever been engaged in the narcotic business. None have had any association with Mexicans or persons in Mexico."

9

— Commission Exhibit No. 2082

[redacted]

Form No. 1580 (Revised) Memorandum Report (7-1-60)

UNITED STATES SECRET SERVICE
TREASURY DEPARTMENT

ORIGIN Field (Dallas)	OFFICE Dallas, Texas	FILE NO. CO-2-34030
TYPE OF CASE Protective Research	STATUS Continued	TITLE OR CAPTION Assassination of President Kennedy Jack Ruby
INVESTIGATION MADE AT Dallas, Texas	PERIOD COVERED 12/1- 12/6/63	
INVESTIGATION MADE BY Special Agent Elmer W. Moore		

DETAILS

SYNOPSIS

Jack Ruby interviewed regarding 1947 narcotics case involving Mexican contacts. Denies any implication.

DETAILS OF INVESTIGATION

Reference is made to Chief's office memorandum dated 11-29-63, file 601.0, captioned Jack Ruby.

On December 1, 1963 Jack Ruby was interviewed at the Dallas County jail regarding the information furnished by Assistant to the Commissioner of Narcotics George Gaffney.

He was first asked if he knew a Taylor Crossland and he replied in the negative as he did to the same question regarding Morris Melton. When he was asked if he knew Paul Jones he said "I know what you are getting at now. Yes, I know him. I'll tell you all about that. About 1947 I met Paul Jones at the Silver Spur, it was the Singapore Club first, on Ervay Street here in Dallas - my sister, Eva, was running it then. Later I heard that I had a phone call from Paul Jones at the Congress Hotel in Chicago where I was staying but I wasn't there at the time and I didn't talk to him. Later some Narcotics Agents came to see me and showed me some pictures. I think the only one I knew was Jones. I told the agents all I knew but I didn't know anything about narcotics or what those fellows were doing. I know that Hymie, my brother in Chicago, had some kind of a deal with Paul Jones. I think it was something to do with iron pipe. Everyone was trying to make a buck in those days after the war when things were short. For all I know, maybe they were shipping narcotics in iron pipe but I didn't know anything about it."

Ruby said that he couldn't remember anymore about the incident but he was sure that he did not meet with Jones, Melton or Crossland in Chicago and that he was

DISTRIBUTION	COPIES	REPORT MADE BY	DATE
→Chief Dallas	Orig.&2cc 2 cc	Elmer W. Moore SPECIAL AGENT Elmer W. Moore	12-6-63
		APPROVED Forrest V. Sorrels SPECIAL AGENT IN CHARGE	DATE 12-6-63

(CONTINUE ON PLAIN PAPER) U. S. GOVERNMENT PRINTING OFFICE 16-61508-1

COMMISSION EXHIBIT No. 2082

CO-2-34030
12-6-63

not "propositioned" on narcotics by Jones. He acknowledged that he was introduced to Jones by his sister, Eva Grant.

Eva Grant, 3929 Rawlins Avenue, Apt. I, telephone LA 6-6258, was interviewed December 1, 5 and 6, 1963 and stated that sometime in 1947 while she was preparing to open the Singapore Supper Club, 1717 S. Ervay St., Dallas, she met Paul Roland Jones through a chiropractic doctor, Waldon Duncan, with whom she was going at the time. She understood that Jones was in the brokerage business and that he dealt in eggs and metals. Jones frequently used her telephone, paying her for any long distance calls. During this time Jack Ruby met Jones. Jones advised Mrs. Grant against going into the night club business as he believed it was too tough for her and suggested that she stick to selling. He suggested several business deals to her, one of which involved iron pipe which was in demand at the time. Jones said he had access to thousands of feet of 1½" pipe which was stored in a warehouse at Ardmore, Oklahoma. He gave her a sample about 6" long which she mailed to her brother, Hyman Rubenstein, in Chicago. As a result of this transaction, both Jack and Hymen were questioned by Narcotics Agents. An agent interrogated Mrs. Grant at Dallas and suggested that she contact the Chicago Narcotics office on her next visit to that city. She did so, possibly four or five months later. At Chicago, she stated, she was shown books of photographs but recognized only one - that of Jones. She recalled that she was questioned regarding a Benny Weinberg whom she did not know but remembers the incident as she has relatives named Weinberg. Hyman was called as a witness to either Austin or Houston for the trial.

Eva Grant, who now operates the Vegas Club, 3508 Oaklawn Avenue, Dallas, with Jack Ruby, stated that she has never been involved in any narcotic deals and that she is "absolutely positive" that none of her brothers have ever been engaged in the narcotic business. None have had any association with Mexicans or persons in Mexico.

DISPOSITION

Inquiry closed at Dallas unless otherwise directed.

EWM:mla

463

COMMISSION EXHIBIT No. 2082—Continued

OFFICE OF THE DIRECTOR

UNITED STATES DEPARTMENT OF JUSTICE

FEDERAL BUREAU OF INVESTIGATION

WASHINGTON 25, D.C.

February 28, 1964

BY COURIER SERVICE

Honorable J. Lee Rankin
General Counsel
The President's Commission
200 Maryland Avenue, N. E.
Washington, D. C.

Dear Mr. Rankin:

Reference is made to my letter dated February 19, 1964, which reported that Marina Oswald had expressed the belief that she took the photograph of Lee Harvey Oswald with the rifle and pistol using her husband's American camera. She described the camera as grayish in color, something like aluminum.

On February 24, 1964, Mr. Robert Lee Oswald, brother of Lee, furnished to a Special Agent of the Dallas Office of this Bureau a Duo-lens Imperial reflex camera which he stated was the property of Lee. This camera is aluminum colored, uses roll film, number 620, has a matching gray plastic carrying strap and is equipped for use with a flash attachment. Robert advised that he obtained this camera from the residence of Mrs. Ruth Paine, Irving, Texas, in December, 1963. At that time it did not contain film. He advised that this camera was purchased by Lee in about 1957 and Lee subsequently left it with Robert in about 1959 when Lee went to Russia. After Lee returned from Russia, he regained possession of this camera and, as far as Robert is aware, retained possession of it until his death. Robert stated that, although this camera is equipped for use with a flash attachment, he had no knowledge that Lee had such an attachment.

On February 25, 1964, this camera was displayed to Marina Oswald and she immediately identified it as the American camera which belonged to her husband and the one which she used to take the photograph of him with the rifle and the pistol.

— Commission Exhibit No. 2083 —

XERO COPY

Commission Exhibit No. 2083

Honorable J. Lee Rankin

On February 24, 1964, Robert also made available to a Special Agent of this Bureau an Eastman Baby Brownie box camera which is currently in an inoperable condition. According to Robert, this camera also belonged to Lee and Robert first saw it in about 1953 in New York City when Robert visited his mother at her home in New York City. Robert last saw this camera in about 1958 when Lee gave it to Robert's daughter Cathy. To the best of Robert's knowledge, Lee did not have this latter camera in his possession subsequent to 1958.

Both of the above-mentioned cameras will be retained by this Bureau along with the other items of evidence in this case.

Sincerely yours,

J. Edgar Hoover

- 2 -

XERO COPY

XERO COPY

Commission Exhibit No. 2083—Continued

FD-302 (Rev. 3-3-59) FEDERAL BUREAU OF II

Date December 7, 1963

1

MARY ELIZABETH WOODWARD, 4812 Alcott, employee, Women's News, "Dallas Morning News," Dallas, Texas, advised that she, AURELIA ALONZO, MARGARET BROWN and ANNE DONALDSON, on November 22, 1963 left the office of the "Dallas Morning News" just about 12:00 noon to observe the Presidential Motorcade.

They walked to Elm Street and stopped in front of the Texas School Book Depository building, but were located a short distance down the street near the second light post. They were standing in this spot when the Presidential Motorcade came by. She stated she was watching President and Mrs. KENNEDY closely, and all of her group cheered loudly as they went by. Just as President and Mrs. KENNEDY went by, they turned and waved at them. Just a second or two later, she heard a loud noise. At this point, it appeared to her that President and Mrs. KENNEDY probably were about one hundred feet from her. There seemed to be a pause of a few seconds, and then there were two more loud noises which she suddenly realized were shots, and she saw President KENNEDY fall over and Mrs. KENNEDY jumped up and started crawling over the back of the car. She stated that her first reaction was that the shots had been fired from above her head and from possibly behind her. Her next reaction was that the shots might have come from the overpass which was to her right. She stated, however, because of the loud echo, she could not say where the shots had come from, other than they had come from above her head. She stated that she had seen about five or six persons standing on top of the overpass, and possibly this is why her first reaction was to look at the top of this overpass. She never at any time saw anything in the hands of the people on the overpass. She never looked at any time toward the Texas School Book Depository building, and stated she could not furnish any information regarding anyone who appeared to be leaving the area, as there was a lot of confusion and everyone was running around.

She and her friends stayed for a few minutes under a tree on the grounds of the Texas School Book Depository building, as she thought that she was going to be sick. After

on 12-6-63 at Dallas, Texas File # DL 89-43

by Special Agent s HENRY J. OLIVER
DAVID H. BARRY Date dictated 12-6-63
mvs

This document contains neither recommendations nor conclusions of the FBI. It is the property of the FBI and is loaned to your agency; it and its contents are not to be distributed outside your agency.

2
DL 89-43

standing under this tree for a few minutes, they returned to their office. She stated she does not know RUBY or OSWALD and stated to her knowledge she did not see either RUBY or OSWALD at the scene of the assassination.

18

FD-302 (Rev. 3-3-59) FEDERAL BUREAU OF

1

Date 12/4/63

Mrs. ALVIN HOPSON, residence 4717 Waverly, Dallas, Texas, employed by Scott Foresman Book Company, Fourth Floor of Texas School Book Depository (TSBD) Building, furnished the following information:

On November 22, 1963, she was looking out a window on the south side of the fourth floor of the TSBD Building when the motorcade of President JOHN F. KENNEDY passed in front of the building going west on Elm Street toward the Triple Underpass. She stated that she was standing at a window which could not be opened and thus was looking through the glass rather than through an open window. She stated that she was standing at this window from about 12 o'clock noon until President KENNEDY's car passed in front of the building. Immediately after he passed, she heard two or more loud sounds which she thought were firecrackers. She stated that she thought they had been set off on the street below, and she saw people on the street running toward the underpass and the railroad track.

She stated at the time she heard these sounds she could not see the Presidential car since there were some trees along the edge of the street which blocked her view.

She and the other people on the fourth floor milled around in the office, and for a few minutes could not determine what was going on.

She stated that from where she was she did not see anyone going downstairs. She pointed out that the fourth floor is partitioned off into office space, and the elevator she normally uses does not run higher than the fourth floor and is located on the east end of the building.

on 12/1/63 at Dallas, Texas File # DL 8943

by Special Agent BARDWELL D. ODUM: mam Date dictated 12/3/63

This document contains neither recommendations nor conclusions of the FBI. It is the property of the FBI and is loaned to your agency; it and its contents are not to be distributed outside your agency.

21

COMMISSION EXHIBIT No. 2085

DL 89-43
BDO:mam
2

Mrs. HOPSON stated that she did not see the Presidential car at the time of the shooting and thus did not see the President shot. She stated that it did not sound to her like the sounds were coming from her building, and that she was not alert to the possibility of someone fleeing that building after the shots. She advised that she does not know LEE HARVEY OSWALD and does not recall ever having seen him, and she specifically does not recall seeing him or anyone resembling him on the day of the shooting, November 22, 1963.

22

COMMISSION EXHIBIT No. 2085—Continued

FD-302 (Rev. 3-3-59)

FEDERAL BUREAU OF

1

Date 12/5/63

Mrs. ERIC (CAROLYN) WALTHER, 4118 Shelley, Dallas, Texas, stated she is employed in the cutting room for Miller and Randazzo, a dress factory, on the third floor of the Dal-Tex Mart Building, 501 Elm Street, Dallas.

On November 22, 1963, she and another employee, Mrs. PEARL SPRINGER, ate lunch at 12:00 noon and left the lunch room at about 12:20 PM to go down on the street to see President KENNEDY ride by. They walked out of the front door of the building, crossed the street, and stopped at a point on the east side of Houston Street, about fifty or sixty feet south of the south curb of Elm Street. They stopped next to the curb to await the passing of the President. While standing there, she started looking around, and looked over toward the Texas School Book Depository (TSBD) Building. She noticed a man wearing a brown suit and a very dark red shirt leaning out a window of the third floor, somewhere about the middle window of the third floor. Shortly after this, a man in the crowd across the street to the west of where she was standing apparently had an epileptic seizure, and an ambulance came by and took the man away. Shortly after the ambulance left, she looked back toward the TSBD Building and saw a man standing on either the fourth or fifth floor in the southeast corner window. This would be the most easterly window of either the fourth or fifth floors, of the windows on the south side of the building, which faces toward Elm Street. This man had the window open and was standing up leaning out the window with both his hands extended outside the window ledge. In his hands, this man was holding a rifle with the barrel pointed downward, and the man was looking south on Houston Street. The man was wearing a white shirt and had blond or light brown hair. She recalled at the time that she had not noticed the man there a few moments previously when she looked toward the building and thought that apparently there were guards everywhere. The rifle had a short barrel and seemed large around the stock or end of the rifle. Her impression was that the gun was a machine gun. She noticed nothing like a telescopic sight on the rifle or a leather strap or sling on the rifle. She said she knows nothing about rifles or guns of any type, but

on 12/4/63 at Dallas, Texas File # DL 89-43

by Special Agents C. RAY HALL AND MAURICE J. WHITE: mam Date dictated 12/5/63

This document contains neither recommendations nor conclusions of the FBI. It is the property of the FBI and is loaned to your agency; it and its contents are not to be distributed outside your agency.

24

DL 89-43
CRH,MJW:mam
2

thought that the rifle was different from any she had ever seen. This man was standing in about the middle of the window. In the same window, to the left of this man, she could see a portion of another man standing by the side of this man with a rifle. This other man was standing erect, and his head was above the opened portion of the window. As the window was very dirty, she could not see the head of this second man. She is positive this window was not as high as the sixth floor. This second man was apparently wearing a brown suit coat, and the only thing she could see was the right side of the man, from about the waist to the shoulders.

Almost immediately after noticing this man with the rifle and the other man standing beside him, someone in the crowd said "Here they come," and she looked to her left, looking south on Houston Street, to see the Presidential Party. As soon as President KENNEDY's car passed where she was standing, she and Mrs. SPRINGER turned away and started walking north toward Elm Street. At about the time they reached the curb at Elm Street, she heard a loud report and thought it was fireworks. There was a pause after this first report, then a second and third report almost at the same time, and then a pause followed by at least one and possibly more reports. The noise seemed to come from up in the air, but she never looked up in any direction. When the second report sounded, she decided it was gunfire, so she and Mrs. SPRINGER started diagonally across the street toward the TSBD Building. About the time she got across the street, she heard someone yell that the President had been hit. She stopped a moment and listened to the police radio on a motorcycle, then returned to the building across the street where she works. She returned to her job at about 12:45 PM.

25

FD-302 (Rev. 3-3-59) FEDERAL BUREAU OF

Date December 5, 1963

1

Mrs. PEARL SPRINGER, 8218 Elkton Circle, Dallas, Texas, telephone EX 1-1803, advised she is employed in the cutting room for Miller and Randazzo on the third floor of the Dal-Tex Mart Building, 501 Elm Street, Dallas, Texas.

On November 22, 1963, she and another employee, Mrs. CAROLYN WALTHER, left the building where they work after they hrrriedly ate lunch at about 12:15 p.m., to see the Presidential parade. They walked out of the building, crossed Elm Street and walked south on Houston Street on the east side of Houston Street, stopping just south of a sign post. (This sign post is seventeen steps south of the Elm Street Curb.) They stood there for about fifteen minutes waiting for the parade. During that time, she looked around at the crowd but never looked up above the ground floor of the Texas School Book Depository building located diagonally across the street from where she was standing. She recalled some commotion across the street from her, and an ambulance came and carried a man away. She heard a police officer say that the man carried away in the ambulance had an epileptic seizure. After the Presidential party passed her and turned the corner going west on Elm Street, she heard what she thought was a shot. At first she thought it was some kind of salute, but this shot was followed by two more. She recalled that after the first shot there was a pause, then two more shots were fired close together. She and Mrs. WALTHER ran across the street for a moment toward the Texas School Book Depository building to see if they could see anything down toward the Elm Street underpass, but they could not, so they returned to the building where they work.

Mrs. SPRINGER said that she noticed no one standing in the windows on the upper floors of the Texas School Book Depository building, and Mrs. WALTER did not mention to her anything about seeing a man standing in a window of that building holding a rifle.

on 12/4/63 at Dallas, Texas File # DL 89-43

by Special Agents C. RAY HALL and MAURICE J. WHITE/gm Date dictated 12/5/63

26

This document contains neither recommendations nor conclusions of the FBI. It is the property of the FBI and is loaned to your agency; it and its contents are not to be distributed outside your agency.

COMMISSION EXHIBIT No. 2087

FD-302 (Rev. 3-3-59) FEDERAL BUREAU

Date November 25, 1963

1

Mrs. CHARLES HESTER, 2619 Keyhold Street, Irving, Texas, advised that sometime around 12:30 p.m., on November 22, 1963, she and her husband were standing along the street at a place immediately preceding the underpass on Elm Street, where President KENNEDY was shot. Mrs. HESTER advised she heard two loud noises which sounded like gunshots, and she saw President KENNEDY slump in the seat of the car he was riding in. Her husband then grabbed her and shoved her to the ground. Shortly thereafter they then went across to the north side of the street on an embankment in an attempt to gain shelter. She stated that she believes she and her husband actually had been in the direct line of fire. She did not see anyone with a gun when the shots were fired and stated she could not furnish any information as to exactly where the shots came from. After the President's car had pulled away from the scene, she and her husband proceeded to their car and left the area as she was very upset.

on 11/24/63 at Irving, Texas File # DL 89-43

by Special Agents J. DOYLE WILLIAMS and HENRY J. OLIVER/gm 30 Date dictated 11/25/63

This document contains neither recommendations nor conclusions of the FBI. It is the property of the FBI and is loaned to your agency; it and its contents are not to be distributed outside your agency.

COMMISSION EXHIBIT No. 2088

FD-302 (Rev. 3-3-59) FEDERAL BUREAU OF INV.

Date December 6, 1963

Mrs. TONEY (RUBY) HENDERSON, 1434 Prairie Creek, Dallas, Texas (EX 1.2474), furnished the following information:

On November 22, 1963 at approximately 12:15 P.M., she was standing on the east side of Elm Street just north of Houston Street awaiting the passing of the Presidential Motorcade at that site. She said shortly after she arrived at this location, and just prior to the arrival of the motorcade, she recalls an ambulance arriving and departing the area to pick up an individual whom she understood had an epileptic fit. Mrs. HENDERSON said after the ambulance departed the area, she heard a woman in the record building located on the southwest corner of Elm and Houston, yell "Yeah, Woodman," which is a Dallas High School, and she looked in the direction from which the yell emanated. She said she thereafter swung around and looked in the building in which she works, the building located on the southeast corner of Elm and Houston and thence around to the Texas School Book Depository Building.

She said she observed numerous people on various floors looking out of the windows of the Texas School Book Depository Building, and recalls that she saw two men on one of the upper floors of the building. She said she recalls one of the men had on a white shirt and one had on a dark shirt. She said she only observed these men from the waist up and does not know what their other attire consisted of. She said these men were standing back from the window and she got the impression they were working and yet looking out the window in anticipation of the motorcade passing that building. She said she saw these men before the motorcade reached Houston and Elm, but doesn't have any idea how long it was prior to the motorcade arriving at that location. She said she believes the person in the white shirt had dark hair and was possibly a Mexican, but could have been a Negro as he appeared to be dark-complexioned. She said she couldn't describe the other person other than the fact he was taller than the aforementioned individual.

Mrs. HENDERSON said at the time the motorcade passed where she was standing, she heard what she initially thought was

on 12-5-63 at Dallas, Texas File # DL 100-10461

by Special Agent s JAMES J. WARD & ROBERT E. BASHAM /mvs Date dictated 12-5-63

35

This document contains neither recommendations nor conclusions of the FBI. It is the property of the FBI and is loaned to your agency; it and its contents are not to be distributed outside your agency.

COMMISSION EXHIBIT No. 2089

DL 100-10461

2

a firecracker and saw what she thought was paper fly out of the Presidential car. She said she now realized it was a shot she heard and what she thought was paper was probably flesh. She said after the first shot, she believes she heard two more in rapid succession, and then a fourth shot.

Mrs. HENDERSON said after the shooting she stood transfixed for some time before returning to work. She said she returned to her place of employment at approximately 12:43 P.M.

Mrs. HENDERSON said she became extremely upset, and nervous, after the President's assassination and it was necessary for her to take the following Monday off her job. She said she hesitated to mention anything about her observations but felt she should relate same as they might possibly be of some benefit.

Mrs. HENDERSON reiterated she could not definitely state one of the men she saw in the window of the Texas School Book Depository was not a Negro. She said she does not know what floor of the building the men were on, but doesn't recall seeing anyone on a floor higher up than the one they were on.

36

COMMISSION EXHIBIT No. 2089—Continued

1 Date 11/25/63

Mrs. JACK FRANZEN, 11572 Cromwell Circle, contacted at 1900 Main Street, advised she was with her husband and small son viewing the motorcade of President KENNEDY from the park area near the intersection of Houston and Elm Streets at approximately 12:30 PM, November 22, 1963.

She advised shortly after the President's automobile passed by on Elm Street near where she and her family were standing, she heard a noise which sounded to her as if someone had thrown a firecracker into the President's automobile. She advised at approximately the same time she noticed dust or small pieces of debris flying from the President's automobile.

She advised she heard two other sounds which sounded like shots from a firearm and noticed blood appearing on the side of President KENNEDY's head.

She does not remember looking at the building housing the Texas School Book Depository (TSBD); however, she stated this building was across Elm Street from the position where she was standing, and she may have looked toward the building. She advised the President's automobile continued on down Elm Street at a higher rate of speed, and she observed police officers and plain-clothes men, whom she assumed were Secret Service Agents, searching an area adjacent to the TSBD Building, from which area she assumed the shots which she heard had come.

She advised her small son called her attention to the fact that some of the men in the automobile behind the President's car were holding guns in their hands shortly after the shots which apparently struck President KENNEDY and stated she assumed these men were Secret Service Agents.

She advised she has no additional information which she feels might be helpful to this investigation.

on 11/22/63 at Dallas, Texas File # DL 100-10461

by Special Agent ALFRED C. ELLINGTON AND JOSEPH J. LOEFFLER: mam 35 Date dictated 11/25/63

This document contains neither recommendations nor conclusions of the FBI. It is the property of the FBI and is loaned to your agency; it and its contents are not to be distributed outside your agency.

COMMISSION EXHIBIT No. 2090

1 Date 12/18/63

JOHN ARTHUR CHISM, 4502 Underwood Drive, advised he was employed as a cook at the Marriott Motel, 2101 Stemmons Freeway, Dallas, Texas. According to CHISM, he was standing on the curb in front of the concrete memorial on Elm Street which is just east of the triple underpass where Elm, Commerce and Main join in Dallas on November 22, 1963. He was standing at this location when the Presidential motorcade passed this point. As it passed in front of him he heard at least two shots and possibly three but no more. The first shot he thought was a firecracker until the second shot sounded and at the same instant he saw the President slump over in the back seat of the Presidential limousine. On hearing the second shot he definitely knew the first was not a firecracker and was of the opinion the shots came from behind him.

At this point Mr. CHISM advised he would be looking south and, therefore, immediately turned towards the north but did not see anyone who appared to be doing the shooting either in the aforementioned concrete memorial or in the Texas School Book Depository. He also advised that since the day of the shooting he has seen both LEE HARVEY OSWALD and JACK L. RUBY's photograph in the news media but is positive he does not know either of these two men and also did not possess any information which might indicate these two men were associated with each other.

on 12/18/63 at Dallas, Texas File # 89-43

by Special Agents WILLIAM K. BOCK and JAMES R. GRAHAM/EJD 36 Date dictated 12/18/63

This document contains neither recommendations nor conclusions of the FBI. It is the property of the FBI and is loaned to your agency; it and its contents are not to be distributed outside your agency.

COMMISSION EXHIBIT No. 2091

FD-302 (Rev. 3-3-59)

FEDERAL BUREAU OF I   Commission Exhibit No. 2092

1

Date 12/4/63

Mrs. JOHN C. INGRAM, 1806 Durham Street, Irving, Texas, telephone number BL-5-2717, was interviewed concerning a telephone call which she was reported to have made at 1:26 p.m. on that date to telephone number JE 6-8321 in Fort Worth, Texas.

Mrs. INGRAM stated she had contacted her husband at this telephone number, which number is listed to George W. Childs Construction Company, by which firm her husband is employed.

She advised she is a Democrat and her husband is a Republican, which situation has lead to numerous good-natured jibes between them.

She stated during her telephone conversation with her husband on this date she had used language which, if misinterpreted, would seem very suspicious. In this connection she said she had called her husband to advise him of the assassination of President KENNEDY in the event he had not previously heard of it, and she inquired of him, "Will his assassin receive the loot" or some similar wording. She pointed out as background for this comment that her husband had jokingly said in teasing her that the citizens of Fort Worth were "offering a pot" to the person who poisoned President KENNEDY. She said this statement by her husband grew out of a newspaper article which referred in some manner to precautions being taken to prevent the President's poisoning in connection with the food served to him. She said this comment was made by her to, in turn, shame her husband for having ever made such a comment, even though she knew at the time he made the comment, he was merely teasing her.

188

on 11/22/63 at Irving, Texas File # DL 89-43

by Special Agent S ALFRED C. ELLINGTON and JAMES W. ANDERTON /cv Date dictated 11/28/63

This document contains neither recommendations nor conclusions of the FBI. It is the property of the FBI and is loaned to your agency; it and its contents are not to be distributed outside your agency.

COMMISSION EXHIBIT No. 2092

Commission Exhibit No. 2093

1

DL 89-43
GWC:rmb

Re: VIRGIL "TOMMY" MITCHELL

On November 26, 1963, Houston Office furnished information related by Detective TED BULLARD, Corpus Christi, Texas, Police Department, that one PATRICK G. CONNOR was arrested for a traffic violation at approximately midnight, November 24, 1963, at Corpus Christi, Texas. Prior to his release he advised that on November 21, 1963, he was in San Antonio, Texas, in a bar across the street from the Greyhound Bus Station, where he met two unknown persons, one of whom claimed to be from Dallas, Texas. This individual from Dallas said he owned two bars in Dallas. During the conversation with these two unknown individuals, one of them brought up the question about President KENNEDY's trip to Texas, and asked in effect, "How much do you think it would be worth to kill KENNEDY?" The other unknown individual replied "CASTRO would pay a lot". Then one of these individuals said it should be easy to do it with a high-powered rifle.

CONNOR said that one of both of the unknown individuals requested employees of the bar, believed to be a barmaid waiting their table, to call the airport to see what time a plane left for Dallas.

187

COMMISSION EXHIBIT No. 2093

HO 62-2115
ED:djw
1

RE: JACK NICHOLAS PAYTON

On November 25, 1963 JACK NICHOLAS PAYTON was contacted at his residence, 4325 Betty Street, Bellaire, Texas, by Special Agents LEVERETTE A. BAKER and EDWIN DALRYMPLE. PAYTON's wife and children were present and were informed in the presence of PAYTON he was not being placed under arrest but it was merely desired that he be interviewed in complete privacy. PAYTON was informed that his cooperation was desired in connection with a matter under investigation and it would be appreciated if he would proceed to the Houston Office of the Federal Bureau of Investigation for this purpose. PAYTON stated he would gladly proceed to the Houston FBI Office and he considered it his "Christian duty" to assist the FBI in connection with any official investigation.

This interview began at the Houston FBI Office at 8:00 p.m. and was concluded at 9:03 p.m.

PAYTON stated his true name was JACK NICHOLS PAYTON, although he has frequently been known as JACK NICHOLAS PAYTON. He stated he was born August 30, 1918 at Joplin, Missouri and served in the United States Air Force from 1941 to 1945, having Air Force Serial Number 37016015. He resides with his wife and three children at 4325 Betty Street, Bellaire, Texas, and has telephone number MA 3-6217. PAYTON stated he has been self employed as a photographer, specializing in photographs of small children and has been so employed in the Houston, Texas area for over ten years, except for a period of two or three years when he resided in Austin, Texas. He indicated he returned to Houston, Texas from Austin, Texas on approximately September 1, 1963.

PAYTON was informed that his assistance was desired in connection with the investigation of the recent assassination of President KENNEDY, and he was requested to furnish any factual information in his possession which he felt might remotely have a bearing on this matter. He was specifically asked if he had been acquainted with LEE OSWALD or JACK RUBIN or RUBY, and whether he had heard any statements or remarks prior to the assassination that such a thing might take place. PAYTON was questioned as to whether he had any knowledge that any person or group of persons might hav been involved in the planning of this assassination and whether he had ever heard of any efforts to raise money or assemble funds for the possible purpose of paying someone to assassinate the President

246

COMMISSION EXHIBIT No. 2094

HO 62-2115
2

PAYTON stated in reply that he had absolutely no information which he felt could remotely be related to this matter, that he was not acquainted with OSWALD or JACK RUBY and the only thing he knew about them or about the assassination was what he had learned through the news media. PAYTON stated it was his belief that JACK RUBY was a Communist who had been sent to do away with the evidence which OSWALD might have furnished and that RUBY would undoubtedly be set free on an insanity plea.

PAYTON was asked whether he had discussed the assassination of President KENNEDY with any persons other than his family and personal friends in the Houston area and whether he had discussed this matter with anyone outside the Houston area. PAYTON replied that he had discussed this assassination with only one person outside of Houston and that occurred during a lengthy telephone conversation he had on the evening of November 24, 1963 with one GENE O'DOHERTY in Ohio. PAYTON explained that O'DOHERTY had worked for him in Austin, Texas as a photographer for a short period about one year previously and on approximately November 17, 1963 he had telephoned O'DOHERTY in Ohio and asked his assistance during the Christmas rush in the photography business. O'DOHERTY could not give him an answer at that time but agreed to call PAYTON back within a few days. PAYTON stated he could not even recall the city in Ohio where O'DOHERTY resided but he had O'DOHERTY's address and telephone number at his residence. He stated that O'DOHERTY left Austin shortly after Christmas 1962 and proceeded to Ohio and has written PAYTON occasionaly since that time. PAYTON met O'DOHERTY through a mutual acquaintance, BILL FLANAGAN, in Austin, Texas approximately 18 months ago.

PAYTON related that O'DOHERTY initiated the telephone call to him on the evening of November 24, 1963 and declined to accept his employment offer. PAYTON could recall discussing the assassination in general terms with O'DOHERTY but stated he could not recall the exact statements made by either. He recalled that this conversation lasted about ten or fifteen minutes and he noticed when he left the telephone it was approximately 8:45 p.m. PAYTON realized that O'DOHERTY was in bad financial condition and stated in the middle of this telephone call he signaled the operator in Ohio and requested her to reverse the charges to his telephone in Bellaire, Texas.

247

COMMISSION EXHIBIT No. 2094—Continued

HO 62-2115
3

PAYTON was informed that he must realize his conversation with O'DOHERTY could have been related by O'DOHERTY to a number of persons in Ohio and he was then questioned concerning the following specific statements.

PAYTON was asked whether he made a statement to O'DOHERTY to the effect that "Its a good thing they got him before we were implicated." PAYTON at first denied making any statement along that line but then advised he probably made such a statement and if so, he was not referring to President KENNEDY's death but was simply stating it was a good thing that LEE OSWALD was apprehended and charged with this crime because otherwise the "Liberal elements" would try to place the blame for the assassination on the John Birch Society.

In connection with the above, PAYTON had been a member of the John Birch Society and also other conservative groups, such as the Austin Anti-Communism League of Austin, Texas. He stated he had attempted unsuccessfully to get O'DOHERTY to join the John Birch Society. PAYTON talked at some length about what he considered the important work done by these organizations in fighting Communism and stated flatly the John Birch Society was the only organization which was attempting to get the truth to the American people, whereas all other organizations, and particularly all the news media had sold out to the communists and were helping bring about the gradual move to communism in the United States.

PAYTON was asked whether he made any references in his talk with O'DOHERTY to some groups having been associated with the assassination. He replied that if he used the word groups he intended to refer to the John Birch Society but that he made no reference to the John Birch Society being connected in any way with the assassination.

PAYTON was asked whether he told O'DOHERTY something to the effect "Our next move will be to get behind them so we can overthrow JOHNSON." PAYTON replied that he possibly made such a statement, although he could not recall it and if he made such a statement, such a remark did not even suggest violence or physical opposition but merely that he hoped the conservative organizations would get together and have President JOHNSON thrown out of office through the election processes. PAYTON stated that the John Birch Society was "fighting with truth - words are bullets". He stated that the immediate goal of all conservative groups is to defeat the Democratic Party at the ballot box.

248

COMMISSION EXHIBIT No. 2094—Continued

HO 62-2115
4

PAYTON was asked whether any mention had been made in his conversation with O'DOHERTY concerning JACK RUBIN or JACK RUBY. PAYTON at first denied any mention of this person but later stated this name was undoubtedly mentioned. PAYTON denied any acquaintance with RUBY and stated in fact his only personal acquaintance in the Dallas area was General EDWIN A. WALKER, for whom he had campaigned in 1962 at Austin, Texas when General WALKER ran for the office of Governor of Texas. PAYTON stated as well as he could recall he had not talked with General WALKER by telephone during the past two months and the only telephone calls he could remember making to Dallas were a number of calls he made to the Gavert Company of America, which he described as a photo supply company from which he ordered most of his supplies.

PAYTON was asked whether he had told O'DOHERTY something to the effect that it was a good thing people thought of OSWALD as an ultra-leftist and he replied he probably made such a statement which again he would have intended to mean that this would tend to keep people from thinking the John Birch Society was connected with the assassination. PAYTON was asked whether there was any reason why people might reasonably believe the John Birch Society was involved and he replied there was no good reason for such beliefs but that the liberals will undoubtedly try to make people believe that.

PAYTON commented that he strongly opposed the current and past Federal administrations and had been active for years in distributing literature and similar activities but that he emphatically opposed all violence, sincerely regreted the assassination of President KENNEDY and had no information concerning it.

PAYTON was advised that our interests were restricted to any possible information bearing on the criminal act of the President's assassination and that no investigation of the John Birch Society, as such, should be implied from the questions asked him. PAYTON was informed that charges had been made by persons whose identity could not be revealed to him that the John Birch Society may have collected money and attempted to hire someone to assassinate the President. PAYTON was advised that he should not assume that the FBI believed this charge to be true but it was the FBI's duty to exploit every questionable bit of evidence and he was requested to advise whether he had ever received any indication from any source whatever that the John Birch Society, individual members or any other persons, had been engaged in such activities. PAYTON replied that he considered

249

COMMISSION EXHIBIT No. 2094—Continued

HO 62-2115
5

this charge ridiculous and that he had never heard anyone associated with the John Birch Society or anyone else discuss any plans for, agreement with, or scheme for financing any assassination or violence against any elected official.

258

COMMISSION EXHIBIT No. 2094—Continued

DL 89-43
VM/gm

On November 23, 1963, the Los Angeles Division furnished the following information:

On the evening of November 22, 1963, Mrs. ERNESTINE WHITE, Fullerton, California, telephonically advised that a young German identified as JAOCHIM RUDOLPH ROEHRICHT, an employee of Knotts Berry Farm, Buena Park, California, in a conversation with her on November 16, 1963, commented she would be surprised to know how many young men in Texas wore the Swastika. He allegedly said that if the President came to Texas, he would be assassinated. He went on that in San Antonio there are a number of young men who believe the Negroes should be killed. He allegedly said, "We need a GOERING to get rid of the Negro in the United States like they did the Jews in Germany."

BARBARA WICKWARE, an employee of Knotts Berry Farm, telephonically advised on the evening of November 22, 1963, that a German alien, identified as ROEHRICHT, employee at Knotts, went to Texas on vacation and returned approximately November 13, 1963. Upon his return, he told KEN KNOTT that if President KENNEDY insists on continuing his trip to Texas, he will not come out alive. After hearing of the President's assassination, he laughed and stated that he knew all about it.

JAOCHIM RUDOLPH ROEHRICHT, 7641 Filmore Drive, Apartment C, Anaheim, California, was interviewed by SAs HARVEY D. KUTZ and SAM J. SHOEMAKER on November 23, 1963, and furnished the following information:

He stated he met GEORGE E. STRAUCH of 455 North Drive, San Antonio, Texas, while STRAUCH attended University at Heidelberg, Germany, and while STRAUCH residing at ROEHRICHT's parents' home at Siekerlad Strasse Seventeen, Ahrensburg, Germany. STRAUCH, an American citizen, attended University in Germany. STRAUCH now attends law school of San Antonio and resides with his parents at above address.

256

COMMISSION EXHIBIT No. 2095

DL 89-43

ROEHRICHT visited STRAUCH in San Antonio recently and met STRAUCH's law school friends. They talked about many subjects including the political situation in Texas in a "university atmosphere." ROEHRICHT stated the general thought was it was not safe for KENNEDY to come to Texas because the people there hated him. ROEHRICHT stated he thought these discussions were purely academic and had nothing to do with the assassination. ROEHRICHT denied making statements attributed to him. He claims no pertinent knowledge of assassination.

During interview, ROEHRICHT's sister, ANNA MARIE HARVARD, came in and she commented she had told ROEHRICHT not to talk so much. He admitted that he had talked loosely but that it was idle talk without malice. ROEHRICHT spoke very broken English.

257

COMMISSION EXHIBIT No. 2095—Continued

1

DL 89-43
DHB:BJD

HERMAN ESCAR SHEFFIELD

On November 23, 1963, Houston advised of the following concerning HERMAN ESCAR SHEFFIELD:

On November 23, 1963, HERMAN ESCAR SHEFFIELD was interviewed at 510 Louise Street, Houston. He admitted being member of John Birch Society, an ultra-conservative and opposed to practically all of the programs of the present Federal administration. He stated he disliked late President of the United States but certainly would not take part in assassinating him and has no knowledge of anyone who did. SHEFFIELD denied that he recalled having made the statement that the John Birch Society planned to hire anyone to kill the President. He stated he may have made the statement "something along that line as a joke" but certainly had no knowledge that this was true, and stated the John Birch Society did not advocate violence.

277

COMMISSION EXHIBIT No. 2096

FD-302 (Rev. 3-3-59) FEDERAL BUREAU OF INVESTIGATION

1

Date 12/4/63

LEONARD G. WIDNER, 2302 Hanover Avenue, Northwest, barber at Cave Spring Barber Shop, Roanoke, Virginia, advised that on November 25, 1963, between 10:15 AM and 10:45 AM, an unknown white male in his early 40's, 5'10" to 5'11", weighing 200 pounds, husky build, medium blond hair, thinning on top, blue-gray eyes, had a haircut. While in the shop, this individual stated that about two weeks before, he was at a convention in Chicago, Illinois, the nature of which was not stated, but was attended by one or more city councilmen of Dallas, Texas. One councilman stated President KENNEDY was going to Dallas but he, the President, would not know when he left.

This unknown individual remarked to WIDNER, "OSWALD was killed because he knew too much and besides, he was only a little man in the plot." This same individual indicated he was happy with the President's death since KENNEDY was going to bring the Pope to this country.

It was WIDNER's opinion this unknown individual was anti-KENNEDY since he also stated that during the President's election in 1960, KENNEDY supporters in California gave $5 in wine to "winos" and transported them to the polls.

The unknown individual stated he was not a salesman but owned two small businesses and a part of a third, the location of same not being furnished. He also claimed he was reared in Kansas and spoke with a Mid-western accent.

WIDNER has no idea as to this unknown individual's identity nor anyone in the area who might know him. He stated, however, should this individual return to the barber shop, he would immediately notify the FBI.

321

on 11/26/63 at Roanoke, Virginia File # DL 89-43

by Special Agent PAUL W. YENGST/cah Date dictated 11/29/63

This document contains neither recommendations nor conclusions of the FBI. It is the property of the FBI and is loaned to your agency; it and its contents are not to be distributed outside your agency.

COMMISSION EXHIBIT No. 2097

FD-302 (Rev. 3-3-59) FEDERAL BUREAU OF I.

Date January 10, 1964

1

LILLIAN MOONEYHAM, Deputy District Court Clerk, 95th Court, Records Building, advised that she watched the Presidential Motorcade on November 22, 1963 from the windows of the court house. She, along with Mrs. ROSE CLARK and JEANNETTE E. HOOKER, observed the Presidential Motorcade proceeding down Main Street from the window of Judge J. FRANK WILSON's courtroom, overlooking Main Street. As the motorcade passed them on Main Street, MOONEYHAM, CLARK and HOOKER ran to Judge HENRY KING's courtroom window, which faces Houston Street, in time to see the motorcade turn west from Elm Street on Houston. Mrs. MOONEYHAM believes that BOB REID, Deputy District Court Clerk, Dallas, Texas, was in Judge KING's courtroom watching the motorcade at the same time as was MOONEYHAM, CLARK and HOOKER.

Mrs. MOONEYHAM heard a gunshot and observed President KENNEDY slump to the left of the seat of the car. At the time of the initial shot, Mrs. MOONEYHAM believed that a firecracker had gone off. Following the first shot, there was a slight pause and then two more shots were discharged, the second and third shots sounding closer together. Mrs. MOONEYHAM observed Mrs. KENNEDY climb up on the back of the car and her eyes were then diverted toward the left of the Presidential Motorcade on Elm Street toward a bystander, a man who had fallen to the ground.

Mrs. MOONEYHAM and Mrs. CLARK left Judge KING's courtroom and went to the office of Judge JULIEN C. HYER on the third floor of the Records Building, where they continued to observe the happenings from Judge HYER's window. From Judge HYER's window, Mrs. MOONEYHAM noted a number of bystanders running toward the cement pavilion which borders Elm Street between the railroad viaduct and the Texas School Book Depository (TSBD). Mrs. MOONEYHAM estimated that it was about 4½ to 5 minutes following the shots fired by the assassin, that she looked up towards the sixth floor of the TSBD and observed the figure of a man standing in a sixth floor window behind some cardboard boxes. This man appeared to Mrs. MOONEYHAM to be looking out of the window, however, the man was not close up to the window but was standing slightly back from it, so that

on 1-8-64 at Dallas, Texas File # DL 100-10461

by Special Agent GEORGE T. BINNEY - mvs Date dictated 1-9-64

This document contains neither recommendations nor conclusions of the FBI. It is the property of the FBI and is loaned to your agency; it and its contents are not to be distributed outside your agency.

COMMISSION EXHIBIT No. 2098

2
DL 100-10461

Mrs. MOONEYHAM could not make out his features. She stated that she could give no description of this individual except to say that she is sure it was a man she observed, because the figure had on trousers. She could not recall the color of the trousers.

Mrs. MOONEYHAM stated she could not furnish any additional identifying information regarding the figure she observed in this window.

Mrs. MOONEYHAM stated that following the assassination of President JOHN FITZGERALD KENNEDY, she observed a re-enactment of the assassination on two separate occasions on one day, and it was her impression that the Presidential Motorcade was going slower than the re-enactment motorcade. She stated that it was her estimation that the Presidential car was going approximately five or six miles per hour at the time of the assassination, however, she noted that her estimation was based upon her observation of the Presidential car as it moved west on Elm away from the position where she was located.

COMMISSION EXHIBIT No. 2098—Continued

Commission Exhibit No. 2099

FD-302 (Rev. 3-3-59)

FEDERAL BUREAU OF

Date January 10, 1964

1

ROBERT REID, Deputy District Court Clerk, Dallas District Court, Clerk's Office, Records Building, advised that on November 22, 1963 he was observing the Presidential Motorcade from the window of Judge HENRY KING's court room, and followed the progress of the Presidential Motorcade from the second floor windows of the court house as it progressed down Main Street on to Houston Street and west on Elm Street from Houston Street.

Mr. REID believes that Mrs. LILLIAN MOONEYHAM and CECIL AULT, Deputy District Court Clerks, Criminal Courts Building, as well as others not recalled, were also observing the Presidential Motorcade from Judge KING's court room window.

Mr. REID heard the three gunshots fired and took his eyes from the President's car because he noticed people who were lining the streets were either running or dropping to the ground after the shots were fired. He observed people running or dropping to the ground and noticed policemen running up the grass toward the railroad tracks between the Texas School Book Depository (TSBD) and the railroad overpass. Mr. REID stated he observed nothing significant and at no time did he observe the windows of the TSBD building.

on 1-8-64 at Dallas, Texas File # DL 100-10461

by Special Agent GEORGE T. BINNEY
mvs
Date dictated 1-9-64

This document contains neither recommendations nor conclusions of the FBI. It is the property of the FBI and is loaned to your agency; it and its contents are not to be distributed outside your agency.

COMMISSION EXHIBIT No. 2099

FD-302 (Rev. 3-3-59)

FEDERAL BUREAU OF INVESTIGATION

1

Date January 10, 1964

Mrs. ROSE CLARK, Deputy District Court Clerk, 44th Court, Records Building, Dallas, Texas, advised that on November 22, 1963, she was with LILLIAN MOONEYHAM and Mrs. JEANNETTE E. HOOKER in the court building, and observed the Presidential Motorcade from windows of the court house. She observed the motorcade come down Main Street and turn in to Houston Street. From the window of Judge HENRY KING's courtroom on the second floor of the court house, she heard the three shots, and it was her impression that the first shot was louder than the second and third shots. She noted that the second and third shots seemed closer together than the first and second shots. It was her impression that bystanders on the sidewalk on Elm Street ran toward the cement pavilion on the north side of Elm Street, and she noticed that the President's automobile came almost to a halt following the three shots, before it picked up speed and drove away. Mrs. CLARK did not see the President following the shots because she was watching the bystanders running away.

Following the gunshots, Mrs. CLARK and Mrs. MOONEYHAM left Judge KING's court room and went to Judge JULIEN C. HYER's office window, where they observed what was occurring outside on Elm Street.

Mrs. CLARK stated that she did not observe anything else of consequence, except that it was her impression that less than five minutes following the shots, she observed a crowd of people and policemen gathering around the entrance to the Texas School Book Depository (TSBD).

Mrs. CLARK stated that JAMES CRAWFORD, Deputy District Court Clerk, Dallas District Court, had advised her that on November 22, 1963, he had observed what appeared to be a gun protruding from one of the windows of the TSBD building. Mrs. CLARK stated she had no additional information regarding Mr. CRAWFORD having observed a gun on November 22, 1963.

on 1-8-64 at Dallas, Texas File # DL 100-10461

by Special Agent GEORGE T. BINNEY 21 Date dictated 1-9-64
mvs

This document contains neither recommendations nor conclusions of the FBI. It is the property of the FBI and is loaned to your agency; it and its contents are not to be distributed outside your agency.

COMMISSION EXHIBIT No. 2100

FD-302 (Rev. 3-3-59)

FEDERAL BUREAU OF INVESTIGATION

Date January 10, 1964

1

Mrs. JEANNETTE E. HOOKER, Deputy District Court Clerk, Criminal Court of Dallas, Records Building, advised that on November 22, 1963 she was watching the Presidential Motorcade from the window of Judge J. FRANK WILSON's court room, having followed the progress of the Presidential Motorcade down Main Street, Dallas, from the window of Judge HENRY KING's court room. From Judge WILSON's court room window, she observed the Presidential Motorcade turn west on Elm Street.

Mrs. HOOKER estimated that the President's car was almost to the R. L. THORNTON Freeway when she heard three gunshots. From the sound of the shots, she could not tell from where they had been fired. Mrs. HOOKER observed Mrs. KENNEDY stand up in the Presidential car and observed a man jump on to the back of the car, whom she assumes was a Secret Service Agent. She then observed the car speed away.

At no time did Mrs. HOOKER observe the windows of the Texas School Book Depository. During her observations of the Presidential Motorcade, Mrs. HOOKER was accompanied by Mrs. LILLIAN MOONEYHAM and Mrs. ROSE CLARK, fellow employees in the Records Building.

on 1-8-64 at Dallas, Texas File # DL 100-10461

by Special Agent GEORGE T. BINNEY 21 Date dictated 1-9-64
mvs

This document contains neither recommendations nor conclusions of the FBI. It is the property of the FBI and is loaned to your agency; it and its contents are not to be distributed outside your agency.

COMMISSION EXHIBIT No. 2101

Commission Exhibit No. 2102

FD-302 (Rev. 3-3-59)

FEDERAL BUREAU OF INVESTIGATION

Date January 10, 1964

1

T. E. MOORE, Deputy District Court Clerk, Records Building, advised that on November 22, 1963, he took his lunch hour to observe the Presidential Motorcade. He was standing at the southeast corner of Elm and Houston and observed the motorcade going by, turning west from Houston to Elm Street. By the time President KENNEDY had reached the Thornton Freeway sign, a shot was fired and Mr. MOORE observed the President slumping forward in the Presidential car. Mr. MOORE heard two more shots fired, however, the President was out of Mr. MOORE's sight at the time the last two shots were fired. Mr. MOORE noticed some of the bystanders on the north side of Elm Street below the concrete pavilion, rushing away from the street across the grass towards the concrete pavilion in the direction of some railroad tracks behind the concrete pavilion. Mr. MOORE stated that at the sound of the first shot, he looked up toward the Texas School Book Depository because the shot sounded like it had come from a high area, however, he did not observe anything noteworthy at the Texas School Book Depository.

He stated that approximately ten minutes later, the Texas School Book Depository was surrounded by police officers.

on 1-8-64 at Dallas, Texas File # DL 100-10461

by Special Agent GEORGE T. BINNEY MVB Date dictated 1-9-64

This document contains neither recommendations nor conclusions of the FBI. It is the property of the FBI and is loaned to your agency; it and its contents are not to be distributed outside your agency.

COMMISSION EXHIBIT No. 2102

Commission Exhibit No. 2103

FD-302 (Rev. 3-3-59)

FEDERAL BUREAU OF INVESTIGATION

1

Date 1/10/64

CECIL AULT, Deputy District Court Clerk, Dallas District Court, 505 Main Street, advised that on November 22, 1963 he had put up the shades of the windows in the courtroom of Judge HENRY KING, Dallas District Court, in order to look through the windows onto Main Street to observe the Presidential motorcade as it came down Main Street. Mr. AULT observed the President pass the courthouse on Main Street turning onto Houston and observed the President's automobile as it moved down Houston to the intersection of Houston and Elm Streets where the Presidential motorcade turned west on Elm Street. After the Presidential car had turned the corner onto Elm Street, Mr. AULT heard three loud reports which Mr. AULT immediately recognized as shots from a high-powered rifle. He noted that the first and second shots sounded to him to be close together and the third shot was spaced more after the second shot, the first two shots sounding close enough to be from an automatic rifle. Mr. AULT could not tell from what direction the rifle shots came.

Following the first shot Mr. AULT noted that President KENNEDY appeared to raise up in his seat in the Presidential automobile and after the second shot the President slumped into his seat.

Mr. AULT could not recall what other persons were present in Judge HENRY KING's courtroom at the time the above observations were made by Mr. AULT, however, he was of the belief that several other persons were present at the time.

Mr. AULT advised that he did not look toward the Texas School Book Depository at the time of the firing of the three shots and immediately thereafter because his attention was directed toward a policeman who got off his three-wheeler on Elm Street and ran toward a hedge to the left of the cement pavilion which is immediately north of Elm Street.

on 1/9/64 at Dallas, Texas File # DL 100-10461

by Special Agent GEORGE T. BINNEY/sah Date dictated 1/9/64

This document contains neither recommendations nor conclusions of the FBI. It is the property of the FBI and is loaned to your agency; it and its contents are not to be distributed outside your agency.

COMMISSION EXHIBIT No. 2103

FD-302 (Rev. 3-3-59)

FEDERAL BUREAU OF I

Date 1/9/64

1

STEVEN F. WILSON, Office Manager, Allyne and Bacon, Inc., 301 Texas School Book Depository Building, advised at approximately 12:30 p.m. on the afternoon of November 22, 1963, employees of his office had gone to view the Presidential Motorcade on the corner of Elm and Houston Streets, and due to a heart condition which he has had, he opened the blinds on the third floor opposite from his reception desk and viewed the Presidential Motorcade as it proceeded north on Houston Street and then west on Elm Street. Due to a large tree being in the way, he could not view the entire procession, but as his view became obstructed, he heard three distinct shots which he thought came from a rifle, and subsequently it was determined that the President had been shot.

WILSON advised he discovered later that the President had been shot, but he had not seen or heard anything unusual in the immediate area surrounding his office, and when questioned as to any knowledge he might have concerning LEE HARVEY OSWALD, he stated he did not know OSWALD and did not, in fact, subsequently remember seeing him in the Texas School Book Depository Building. However, he noted he could have possibly seen him on one or two occasions in the lunchroom located on the second floor of the building.

Mr. WILSON could offer no information of subsequent value in this matter.

on 12/30/63 at Dallas, Texas File # DL 100-10461

by Special Agent S RICHARD E. HARRISON & ALLAN D. BRAY/jt Date dictated 1/3/64

This document contains neither recommendations nor conclusions of the FBI. It is the property of the FBI and is loaned to your agency; it and its contents are not to be distributed outside your agency.

COMMISSION EXHIBIT No. 2104

FD-302 (Rev. 3-3-59)

FEDERAL BUREAU OF

Date January 8, 1964

1

Mr. JOHN J. SOLON, 4153 Beachwood Lane, was interviewed at his residence.

Mr. SOLON advised he is no longer in private law practice, but is employed as an attorney by the Texas Highway Department, at Mesquite, Texas.

Mr. SOLON advised that on November 22, 1963, he was in the Main Street entrance of the Old Courthouse, on the south side of Main Street, looking north toward the Dallas County Jail, when the Presidential motorcade passed by. Mr. SOLON advised he observed President JOHN FITZGERALD KENNEDY, Mrs. KENNEDY, and other officials in the Presidential car, which was moving at approximately 35-40 miles per hour. The Presidential car slowed down to turn north on Houston Street from Main, and a few moments later, he heard three shots which sounded as follows:

First shot; pause; two shots; then echoes of the shots.

Mr. SOLON advised he would judge that approximately five and one-half seconds was taken for all three shots.

Mr. SOLON advised he did not have any further specific information about the assassination of President JOHN FITZGERALD KENNEDY. Mr. SOLON advised that on December 10, 1963 he addressed a post card to the FBI. Mr. SOLON said these comments were merely an opinion of his and he had no idea that there was any information available concerning the date that the Presidential trip to Dallas was first planned; the date OSWALD obtained a job at the Texas School Book Depository; nor did he have any information or proof that the "Dallas Morning News" was the connecting link between these two facts.

on 1/4/64 at Dallas, Texas File # DL 100-10461

by Special Agents WILLIAM G. BROOKHART and GEORGE T. BINNEY:mja Date dictated 1/7/64

This document contains neither recommendations nor conclusions of the FBI. It is the property of the FBI and is loaned to your agency; it and its contents are not to be distributed outside your agency.

COMMISSION EXHIBIT No. 2105

2
DL 100-10461

Mr. SOLON advised he also addressed a post card, dated December 17, 1963, to the Southwestern Bell Telephone Company. He said his comments on this post card were only his opinion that someone at the "Dallas Morning News" must have called Caracas, Venezuela, so that the kidnapping of the U. S. Army Colonel could have been reported at the same time of the assassination of President KENNEDY to push the news of his death off the front pages.

Mr. SOLON said he felt that if such a call was made, the Southwestern Bell Telephone Company should report this to the FBI and that if this was not done, then this was "treason".

Mr. SOLON advised he had been a great admirer of President KENNEDY and was deeply shocked by his death. He said he had thought about this very much and just wished that he could help in some way, so he wrote the post cards as a means of suggestion and help. Mr. SOLON advised, however, the only thing he really knew of positively was having heard the three shots of the assassination.

36

COMMISSION EXHIBIT No. 2105—Continued

Commission Exhibit No. 2106

FD-302 (Rev. 3-3-59)

FEDERAL BUREAU OF INVESTIGATION

Date January 20, 1964

1

Mr. SAMUEL BURTON PATERNOSTRO, Assistant District Attorney, Dallas County, Texas, advised he resides at 3050 Cridelle, Dallas, Texas, and his telephone number at home is FL. 7-2900. He said his office is in the Dallas County Records Building, and his telephone number there is RI. 7-6351. He said he recalled that on November 22, 1963, he viewed the Presidential parade in Dallas, Texas from the second floor of the Dallas County Criminal Courts Building in Criminal District Courtroom No. 2, with RUTH THORNTON, a clerk for Criminal District Court No. 4, and he believed that a Dallas Police Officer, E. R. GADDY, was possibly present when he and Mrs. THORNTON were watching the Presidential car and they heard a report or shot which he believed came from the Texas School Book Depository (TSBD) building or the Criminal Courts Building or the triple overpass.

He said he estimated several seconds, possibly four or five or more, elapsed between the first report and the second and third reports. He said he observed President JOHN F. KENNEDY when he appeared to grab his head and thought at the time "he is well-trained"; then when the other reports followed in quick succession, he realized that the President had been shot and it was not a practiced action on the part of the President when he fell against Mrs. KENNEDY and later into the rear part of the vehicle he was riding in. Mr. PATERNOSTRO said he did not observe any person or persons in the window of the TSBD building; in fact, he said he doubted that he could have seen anyone in the window where the alleged assassin was reported to have fired the shots from.

He said he knew nothing more about the assassination of the President. He said he had discussed the fact that he viewed the parade with ARTHUR STEVENS, Deputy District Court Clerk, Dallas County, but he had not been interviewed by any FBI Agents regarding his viewing the assassination.

Mr. PATERNOSTRO advised he has never known LEE HARVEY OSWALD or JACK RUBY personally. He does know RUBY when he sees him and has spoken to him personally, but has no knowledge concerning RUBY's background.

on 1-20-64 at Dallas, Texas File # DL 100-10461

by Special Agent ARTHUR E. CARTER AEC ~~EVC~~ Date dictated 1-20-64

This document contains neither recommendations nor conclusions of the FBI. It is the property of the FBI and is loaned to

COMMISSION EXHIBIT No. 2106

2
DL 100-10461

He said he knew of no association between LEE HARVEY OSWALD and JACK RUBY.

12

COMMISSION EXHIBIT No. 2106—Continued

FD-302 (Rev. 3-3-59)

F.DERAL BUREAU OF IN

Commission Exhibit No. 2107

Date January 20, 1964

1

Mrs. U. L. "JACK" THORNTON (RUTH THORNTON), advised that she is a Deputy District Clerk in Criminal District Court No. 4, Dallas County, and she recalled that on November 22, 1963, she observed the Presidential parade from Criminal District Courtroom No. 2 in the Dallas County Court Building, and had been observing it for about ten minutes before the motorcade turned off of Main Street. She said she was looking out of a window on the Main Street side of the building and then walked over to a window on the Houston Street side, as the Presidential car drove toward the triple overpass.

She said she heard a report which she believed was a car backfiring, until somebody said "that was a shot!" Then she said two more reports followed in quick succession and she observed Mrs. KENNEDY as she stood up in the rear seat of the Presidential car, and about that same time she observed a plainclothes officer jump on the rear part of the Presidential car just before it was rushed away.

She said she did not look toward the Texas School Book Depository building, and after thinking the event over, she doubted that she could have seen the window ~~from~~ where the assassin is alleged to have fired the shot that killed President KENNEDY. She said the only person that she recalled that was present while she was watching the shooting of the President was SAM PATERNOSTRO.

Mrs. THORNTON said she has never known LEE HARVEY OSWALD or JACK RUBY. She said she had never visited either the Carousel or the Vegas Club and that she knows of no association between OSWALD and RUBY except that released by the news media subsequent to the assassination of President JOHN FITZGERALD KENNEDY.

on 1-20-64 at Dallas, Texas 14 File # DL 100-10461

by Special Agent ARTHUR E. CARTER AEC /mvs Date dictated 1-20-64

This document contains neither recommendations nor conclusions of the FBI. It is the property of the FBI and is loaned to your agency; it and its contents are not to be distributed outside your agency.

COMMISSION EXHIBIT No. 2107

FD-302 (Rev. 1-25-60) FEDERAL BUREAU OF IN

Commission Exhibit No. 2108

Date 1/28/64

Mr. F. LEE MUDD, Route 1, Box 109, Keithville, Louisiana, advised as follows:

On November 22, 1963, he was in Dallas, Texas, on a business trip to purchase clothing for his store. He operates the Southside Ranch, 9066 Mansfield Road, Shreveport, Louisiana, a western store. While in Dallas he decided to watch the parade for President KENNEDY. At about noon he was watching the parade from a position on the north side of Elm Street and some 75 to 100 feet west of a building, which he later learned was the Texas School Book Depository. He saw the President's car approaching from the east on Elm Street in the parade, and he recognized President KENNEDY and saw him waving to the crowd. When the President's car was some 50 or more feet away from him, he heard what sounded to him like two gunshots, and he saw the President slump. Immediately thereafter, he observed the President's car pull out of the line of the parade and continue west on Elm Street toward the underpass. When the President's car came abreast of MUDD, he could see the President slumped down toward his wife, who was leaning over him. He recalled seeing another man in the car, whom he did not recognize at the time but whom he later learned was Governor CONNALLY and this man appeared to be holding one arm to his side. However, he did not notice this man much because his attention was focused on the President.

Mr. MUDD stated he definitely recalls hearing two shots, probably less than a second apart. He said there may have been a third shot fired, but he could not be sure of this. He stated that immediately after the shots were fired, some of the spectators along the side of the street dropped to the ground, and he did so himself, inasmuch as the shots alarmed him and he did not know what had happened or where the shots had come from. He looked around him, and he recalled that in looking toward the building nearby, he noticed several broken windows on about the fourth floor, and the thought occurred to him that possibly the shots had been fired through these broken windows. However, he did not observe any smoke, nor did

On 1/24/64 at Shreveport, Louisiana File # 89-69

by SA DONALD R. BELMONT /dmk 19 Date dictated 1/24/64

This document contains neither recommendations nor conclusions of the FBI. It is the property of the FBI and is loaned to your agency; it and its contents are not to be distributed outside your agency.

COMMISSION EXHIBIT No. 2108

NO 89-69
2

he see anyone at the windows, nor did he notice any motion within the building. He said the building appeared to be abandoned. Subsequent to the shooting, he did not notice anyone enter or leave the building. Mr. MUDD stated that when the shots were fired, they sounded as if they came from the direction of the building.

Mr. MUDD stated that he remained in the vicinity for possibly three or four minutes, after which he walked back toward the main part of town, where he had parked his car. He did not remain to talk to police or Secret Service men because he did not feel he had seen anything that would be of assistance to them.

Mr. MUDD said he was not with anyone else at the time this occurred. He said he later made another trip to Dallas, accompanied by his wife, and he showed her the place where the assassination occurred, and he observed the Texas School Book Depository building and he is confident this is the same building he was standing near at the time of the assassination.

Mr. MUDD said he could furnish no further information regarding this matter.

19

COMMISSION EXHIBIT No. 2108—Continued

FD-302 (Rev. 3-3-59)

FEDERAL BUREAU OF INVESTIGATION

1

Date 12/3/63

ORVILLE O. NIX, 2527 Donley Drive, employee General Service Administration, voluntarily turned over to SA JOE B. ABERNATHY an 8 millimeter colored movie film taken by him near the northwest corner of the intersection of Main and Houston Streets in Dallas on November 22, 1963. The film depicts the Presidential motorcade making the turn on Houston Street and approaching the Elm Street intersection to the north. NIX then moved west on Main Street and the film picks up the motorcade subsequent to the firing of the first two shots. NIX believed the film depicts the third shot hitting President KENNEDY and the sequence of events immediately after including Mrs. JACQUELINE KENNEDY reaching out over the back trunk lid to assist a Secret Service Agent who is running to her aid.

NIX further advised that the camera speed with which he took the above movie was believed to be 40 frames per second. He was using a Keystone Zoom lens, 8 millimeter camera and had the speed set on normal. It was also set on automatic eye.

on 12/1/63 at Dallas, Texas File # DL 100-10461

22

by Special Agent JOE B. ABERNATHY - gj Date dictated 12/2/63

This document contains neither recommendations nor conclusions of the FBI. It is the property of the FBI and is loaned to your agency; it and its contents are not to be distributed outside your agency.

COMMISSION EXHIBIT No. 2109

FD-302 (Rev. 3-3-59)

FEDERAL BUREAU OF INVESTIGATION

1

Date 1/29/64

Mr. ORVILLE O. NIX, 2527 Denley, Dallas, Texas, made available for examination by the FBI Laboratory his Keystone Auto Zoom, Model K-810, 8-mm movie camera in a black leather carrying case, Keystone No. 702.

In addition to information previously furnished by him on December 1, 1963, he said the setting was at 40 and he was using the zoom lens with Type A film when he photographed the Presidential Motorcade in Dallas on November 22, 1963.

He recalled that the first series were made at the corner of Main and Houston just as the Motorcade turned north on Houston and he was at a position near the curb on the southwest corner of the intersection and made the pictures of the left side of the Presidential car.

After the car got by, he then proceeded to a point about 20 feet west of Houston Street on the south side of Main Street and made the latter series across an open area which was in view of his position, using the zoom lens completely open.

As to whether or not the camera was wound tightly, he pointed out that he could not recall specifically, but his experience had been that it would only run at a slower speed when the spring was almost run down.

Mr. NIX advised the FBI was welcome to use the camera for experimental purposes and that he would be available as a witness if needed.

on 1/29/64 at Dallas, Texas 3 File # DL 100-10461

by Special Agent JOE B. ABERNATHY - LAC Date dictated 1/29/64

This document contains neither recommendations nor conclusions of the FBI. It is the property of the FBI and is loaned to

COMMISSION EXHIBIT No. 2110

OPTIONAL FORM NO. 10
MAY 1962 EDITION
GSA GEN. REG. NO. 27

UNITED STATES GOVERNMENT

Memorandum

Commission Exhibit No. 2111

U. S. Secret Service

TO : Chief
Attn.: Inspector Kelley

DATE: February 13, 1964

FROM : SAIC Sorrels, Dallas

SUBJECT: Identification of Photograph

Reference is made to Chief's O/M of 1-14-64 to SA John Joe Howlett to which was attached a photograph of the concrete slab where a bullet was thought to have hit, which photograph was taken by the Bureau of Identification, Dallas Police Department. You instructed that a report be submitted setting forth in detail exactly where this slab is located and the circumstances which prompted the police to take the photograph.

This concrete slab and manhole cover is located on the south side of Elm Street almost opposite to where the President's car was located when the last shot that killed President Kennedy was fired. Someone reported that a bullet had ricocheted off the concrete slab in the corner next to the word "sewer" stamped on the manhole cover and for this reason the photograph was taken. However, it was never verified that any bullet hit it.

The spot was personally examined by me and I did not see any mark that in my opinion could have been caused by a bullet and I did not see how it could have been possible for any fragment of any of the three bullets that were fired to have hit this concrete slab.

The photograph is returned as requested.

FVS:LR

COMMISSION EXHIBIT No. 2111

COMMISSION EXHIBIT No. 2111—Continued

Commission Exhibit No. 2112

TREASURY DEPARTMENT
UNITED STATES SECRET SERVICE
WASHINGTON 25, D.C.

OFFICE OF THE CHIEF

May 14, 1964

Mr. J. Lee Rankin
General Counsel
President's Commission on the
Assassination of President Kennedy
Washington, D. C.

Dear Mr. Rankin:

There is forwarded herewith a copy of the original notes made by Special Agent Bennett concerning his recollection of the incidents surrounding the assassination of President Kennedy on November 22, 1963.

A statement by SA Bennett was included in our original report to the Commission as Exhibit 18. The significance of the attached notes is that they were prepared by SA Bennett on the President's plane during its return flight to Washington on November 22, before the details of President Kennedy's wounds became general knowledge.

The notes have been marked as Secret Service Control 1496.

Very truly yours,

James J. Rowley

James J. Rowley

Attachments

COMMISSION EXHIBIT No. 2112

AF 2 LANDED AT 11:35 Am.
at LOVE FIELD, DALLAS, TEXAS,
I COVERED THE PRESS AREA
UNTIL THE BOSS ARRIVED AT
APPROXIMATELY 11:38 Am. I stayed
with THE BOSS AND FIRST LADY
AFTER THEY DEPLANED. THEY, BOSS
AND FIRST LADY, GREETED people
ON THE APRON AND ALONG THE
FENCE FOR APPROXIMATELY 5 to
8 MINUTES. THE BOSS, FIRST
LADY, GOVERNOR CONNELLY & MRS
CONNELLY ENTERED THE
PRESIDENTIAL CAR AT APPROX-
IMATELY 11:50. THE PRESIDENT'S
AUTO WAS DRIVEN BY BILL GREER
AND THE COVERING AGENT
WAS ROY KELLERMAN. I ASKED,
while moving to the follow-
up CAR, EMERY ROBERT WHAT
POSITION I should TAKE IN
THE follow-up CAR. MR. ROBERTS
SAID HE WANTED ME TO BE
SEATED IN THE REAR SEAT of
THE follow-up CAR. I TOOK
THIS POSITION AND HELD THIS
POSITION WITH THE EXCEPTION
of LEAVING THE follow-up AND
ASSISTING in disbanding WEL
WISHERS WHO RAN from THE
CROWD AND ATTEMPTED TO

COMMISSION EXHIBIT No. 2112—Continued

SHAKE HANDS WITH THE PRESIDENT. THE PRESIDENT'S CAR, THE MOTORCADE, HAD BEEN TRAVELING FOR APPROXIMATELY 30 MINUTES ENROUTE TO THE TRADE-MART, WHEN WE MADE A LEFT HAND TURN AND THEN A quick RIGHT. THE PRESIDENT'S AUTO MOVED DOWN A SLIGHT GRADE AND THE CROWD WAS VERY SPARSE. AT THIS POINT I HEARD A NOISE THAT IMMEDIATELY REMINDED ME OF A FIRE-CRACKER. I IMMEDIATELY, UPON HEARING THE SUPPOSED FIRE CRACKER, LOOKED AT THE BOSS'S CAR. AT THIS EXACT TIME I SAW A SHOOT THAT HIT THE BOSS ABOUT 4 INCHES DOWN FROM THE RIGHT SHOULDER; A SECOND SHOOT FOLLOWED IMMEDIATELY AND HIT THE RIGHT REAR HIGH OF THE BOSS'S HEAD. I IMMEDIATELY HOLLERED TO SPECIAL AGENT HICKEY, SEATED IN THE SAME SEAT, TO GET THE AR-15. I DREW MY REVOLVER AND LOOKED TO THE REAR AND TO THE LEFT high left BUT WAS

COMMISSION EXHIBIT No. 2112—Continued

UNABLE TO SEE ANY ONE PERSON THAT COULD HAVE RENDERED THIS TERRIBLE TRAGEDY. THE PRESIDENT'S AUTO IMMEDIATE KICKED INTO HIGH GEAR AND THE FOLLOW-UP CAR DEPARTED THE SCEAN. THE PRESIDENT WAS TAKEN TO A NEAR-BY HOSPITAL AND WAS RUSHED THEREIN. AT THIS TIME, I WAS INSTRUCTED TO PROTECT THE VICE PRESIDENT WHO FOLLOWED THE PRESIDENT'S AUTO AND FOLLOW-UP TO THE HOSPITAL. I THEN HELPED IN ACCOMPANYING THE VICE PRESIDENT TO A ROOM ON THE GROUND FLOOR OF SAID HOSPITAL.

Glen A. Bennett
Written on Plane (5:30 pm 11-22-63) to Wash.

COMMISSION EXHIBIT No. 2112—Continued

FREEWAY CONVERGENCE AT TRIPLE UNDERPASS
DALLAS, TEXAS—

Commission Exhibit No. 2113

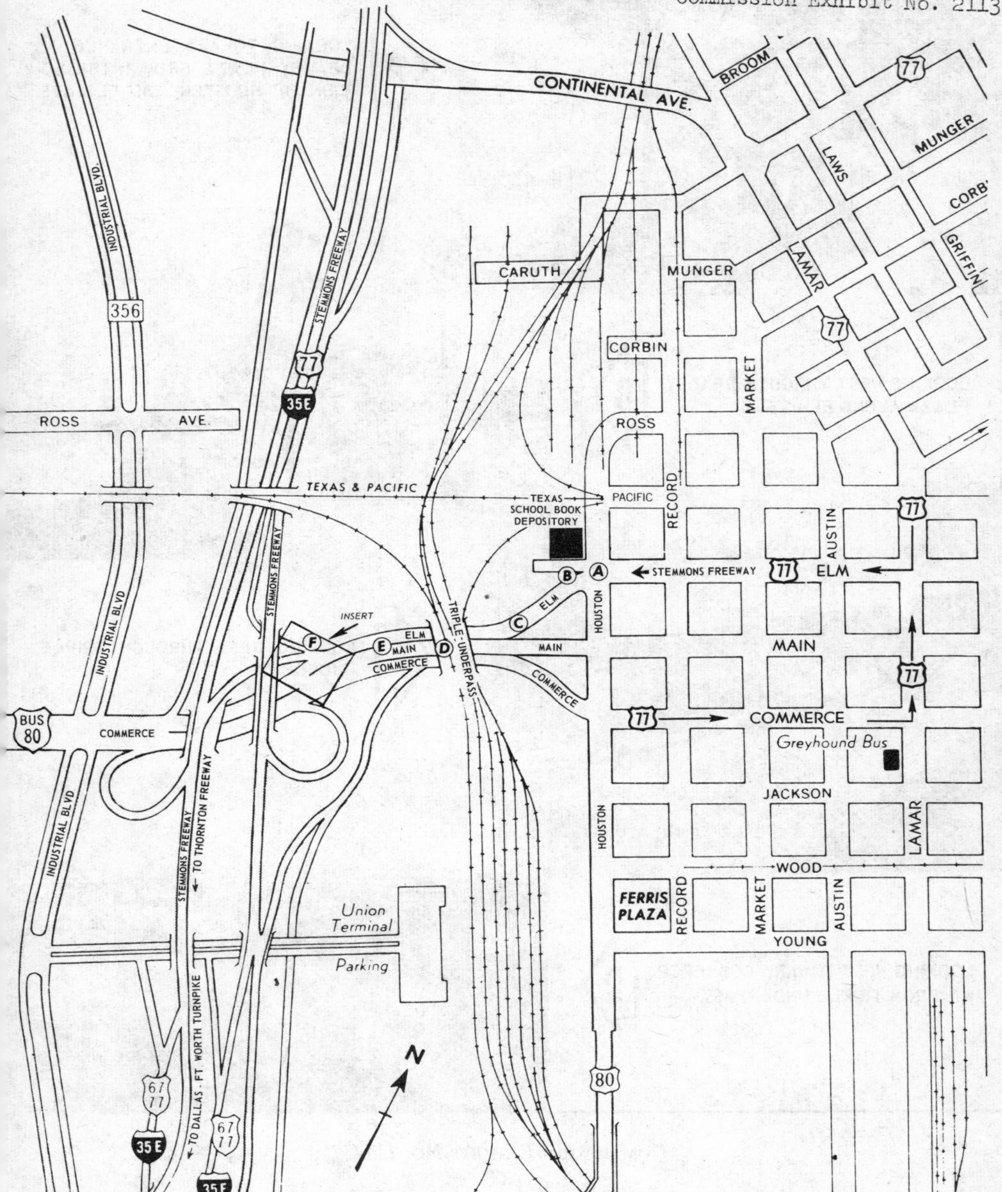

COMMISSION EXHIBIT No. 2113

Commission Exhibit No. 2114

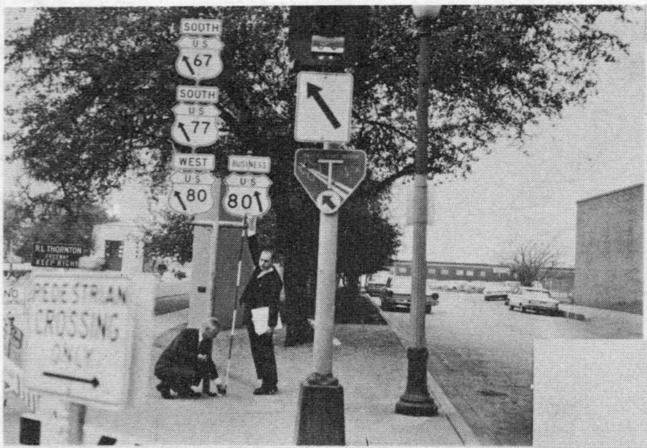

A LOOKING TOWARD ENTRANCE TO DEALEY PLAZA FROM INTERSECTION OF HOUSTON AND ELM STS.

LOOKING WEST THROUGH DEALEY PLAZA ALONG ELM ST. B

C LOOKING WEST THROUGH TRIPLE UNDERPASS

LOOKING WEST TOWARD COMMERCE ST. FROM TRIPLE UNDERPASS D

COMMISSION EXHIBIT No. 2114

Commission Exhibit No. 211)

PLAN VIEW OF FREEWAY CONVERGENCE WEST OF TRIPLE UNDERPASS DALLAS, TEXAS

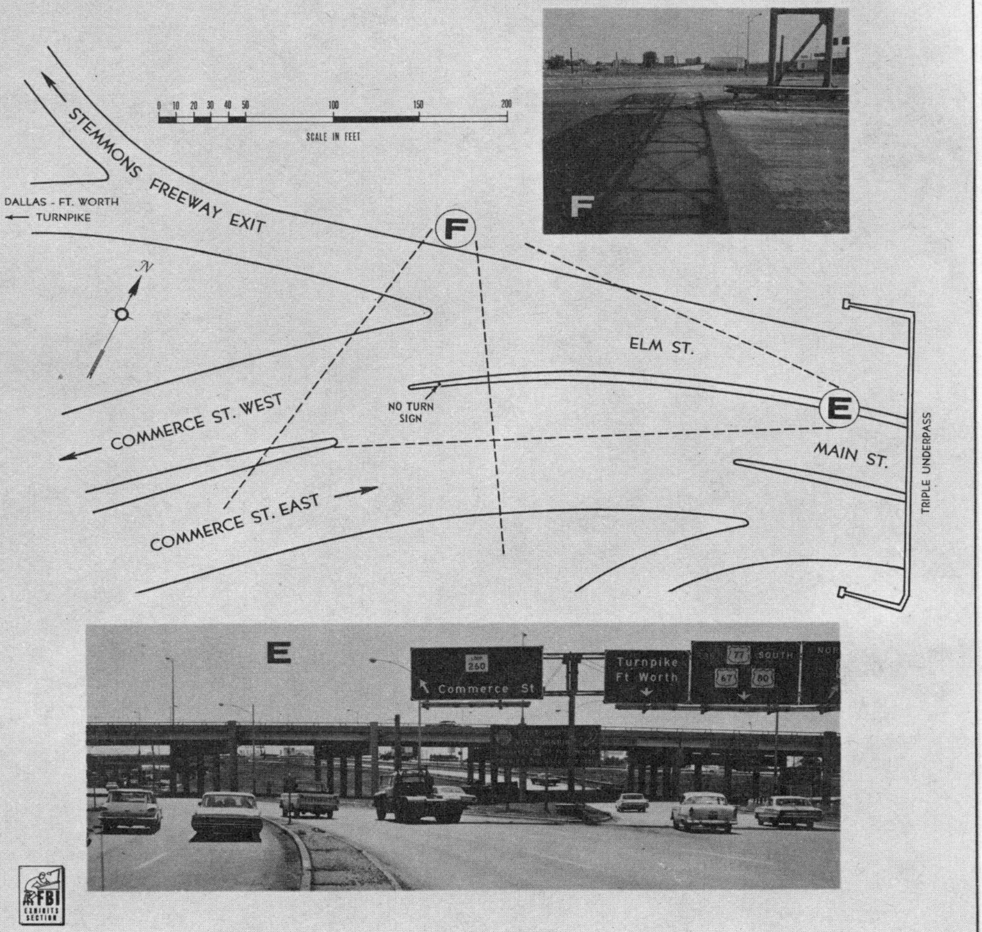

COMMISSION EXHIBIT No. 2115

AERIAL VIEW (500 FT. ALTITUDE) OF FREEWAY CONVERGENCE WEST OF TRIPLE UNDERPASS, DALLAS, TEXAS

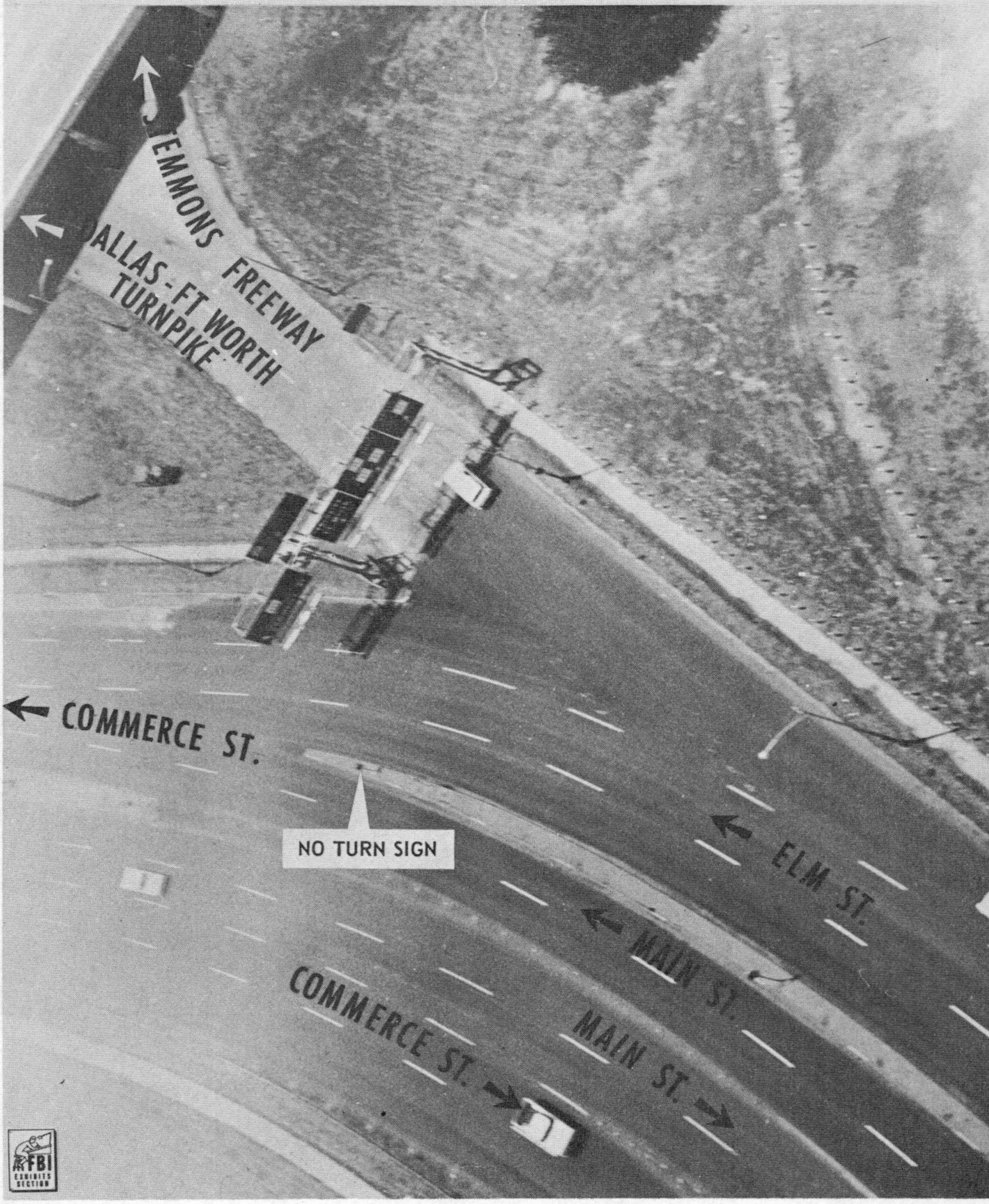

Commission Exhibit No. 2116

COMMISSION EXHIBIT No. 2117

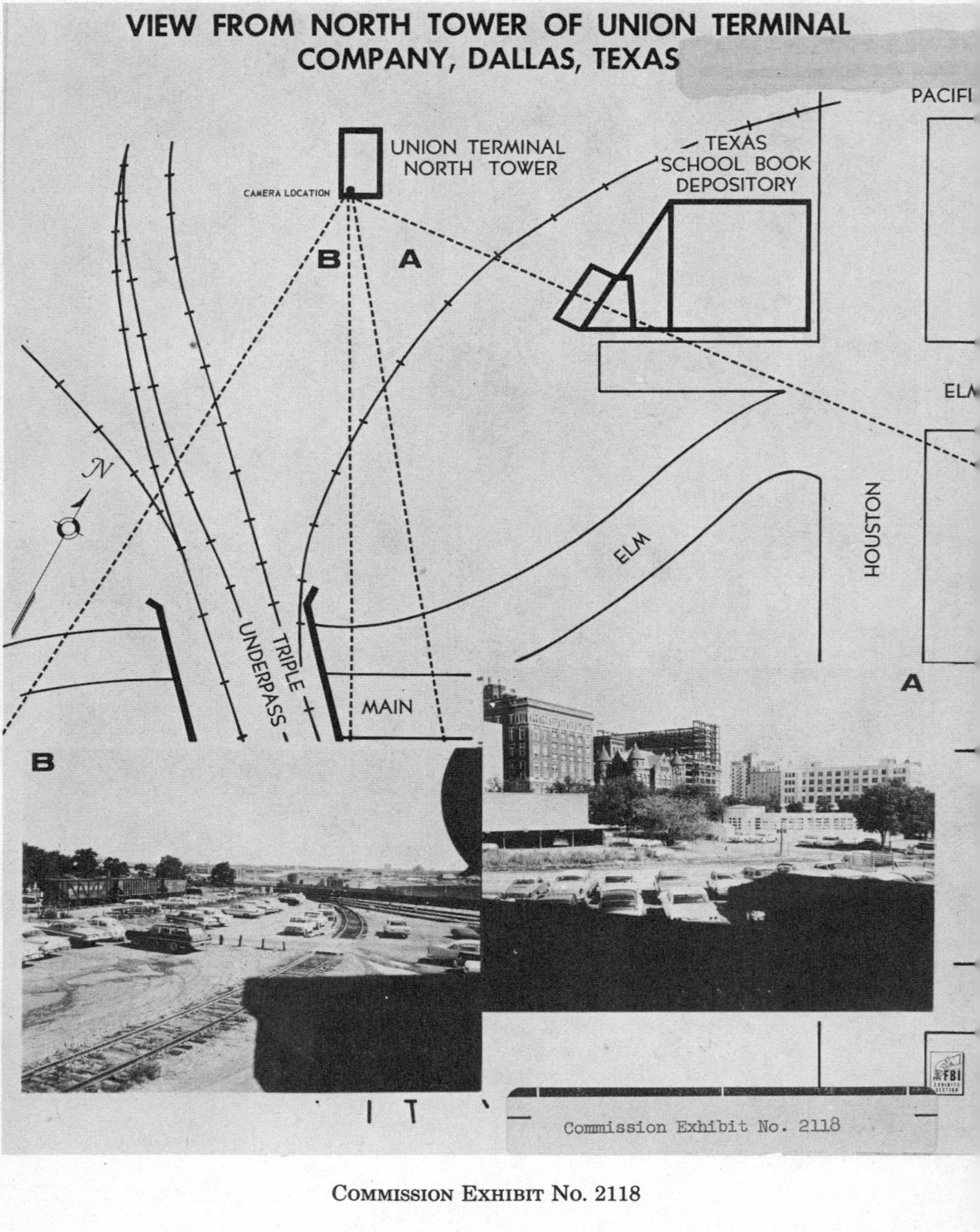

Commission Exhibit No. 2118

UNITED STATES DEPARTMENT OF JUSTICE

FEDERAL BUREAU OF INVESTIGATION

In Reply, Please Refer to
File No.

WASHINGTON 25, D. C.

March 16, 1964

LEE HARVEY OSWALD

A confidential source abroad who is thoroughly familiar with the workings of the Mexican Ministry of Gobernacion (Interior) has furnished the following information concerning the procedures utilized by the Mexican Immigration Service in connection with the entry and departure of non-Mexican citizens into and out of Mexico. It is to be noted that the Mexican Immigration Service is a part of the Mexican Ministry of Gobernacion.

Tourists usually enter Mexico on a Mexican tourist card. There are two types of such cards, one being called the FM-8 which is valid for a stay in the country of only fifteen days and one called the FM-5 which has a validity for 180 days' stay in Mexico. Both types of tourist cards are issued in duplicate. Both types are issued at Mexican Consulates throughout the world and can also be obtained from the Mexican Immigration Service at border ports of entry.

At the time of entry into Mexico the traveler surrenders the duplicate portion of the tourist card and both the duplicate and the original, which remains in possession of the traveler, are stamped with a rubber stamp which shows the name of the Mexican representative handling the entry, the date of the entry and the name of the port of entry.

- 1 -

COMMISSION EXHIBIT No. 2119

When the traveler leaves Mexico he surrenders the original portion of the tourist card and it is stamped with a rubber stamp which carries the name of the Mexican representative, the date of the departure and the name of port of departure.

Each Mexican port of entry is required on a continuing basis to prepare a form called Form FM-11. This form is a recapitulation which covers non-Mexican citizens entering and departing Mexico as tourists. Entries and departures are maintained on separate lists of FM-11. The FM-11 for both entries and departures is prepared each "quincena" (fifteen-day period). Entries and departures are set up on the FM-11 in chronological order and thereafter, within each date, the names of the tourists are listed in alphabetical order. Basic information appearing on the FM-11 is taken from the tourist card presented by the traveler. At the time the FM-11 is prepared a number is placed on the tourist card, these numbers being in sequence according to the alphabetical order of the names within each date and thereafter by date. By way of example, the first traveler in alphabetical order entering at a port of entry on the first day of the month or a "quincena" is assigned number one. Thereafter all travelers entering that port on that date are assigned numbers in sequence according to alphabetical order. This sequence continues on the second day of the month and throughout the remaining days of the "quincena."

Investigation in instant case has disclosed that subject OSWALD entered Mexico at Nuevo Laredo, State of Tamaulipas, on September 26, 1963. OSWALD's entry into Mexico was handled by Mexican Immigration Service employee HELIO TUEXI MAYDON at Nuevo Laredo and his departure from Mexico at Nuevo Laredo on October 3, 1963, was handled by Mexican Immigration Service employee ALBERTO ARZAMENDI CHAPA.

This source made available for examination the forms FM-5 and FM-8 for all non-Mexican citizens entering Mexico at Nuevo Laredo as tourists on September 26, 1963, as well as the copies of forms FM-11 containing the recapitulation of the entries to Mexico at Nuevo Laredo on this date.

- 2 -

COMMISSION EXHIBIT No. 2119—Continued

From the tourist cards (FM-5 and FM-8) and the copies of the form FM-11 the following summary of information concerning each person who entered Mexico at Nuevo Laredo on September 26, 1963, has been obtained. The summaries have been divided into those persons traveling on forms FM-5 and those traveling on forms FM-8 since the forms FM-11 are so set up. The number appearing before each name is the number which appears on the form FM-11. The names of the Mexican Immigration Service employees handling the entry have been set forth in each case in order that it can be seen what travelers were handled by HELIO TUEXI MAYDON, the Immigration Service employee who handled OSWALD's entry and in order that it can be determined which traveler entered Mexico in the Mexican Immigration Service shift when OSWALD was reported to have entered Mexico:

Entry into Mexico on September 26, 1963, at Nuevo Laredo, State of Tamaulipas, of non-Mexican Citizens Traveling on Form FM-5 <u>Tourist Cards</u>

368. MARGARITA ALANIS, FM-5 No 4329957, issued by Mexican Immigration Office, Nuevo Laredo, September 26, 1963. Entry was by autobus with final destination in Mexican indicated as both Monterrey, Nuevo Leon and Mexico, D F. Described as female American citizen, 45 years of age, born McAllen, Texas, single, housekeeping, residence San Antonio, Texas, with no street address indicated. Presented birth certificate as proof of citizenship. Entry handled by ALBERTO ARZAMENDI CHAPA.

369. JOSE R. ALFARO, FM-5 No. 4496450, issued by Mexican Consulate, Dallas, Texas, September 19, 1963. Entry was by automobile with final destination of Mexico, D F. Described as male American citizen, 55 years of age, divorced, office worker, born Waco, Texas; residence 2204 Olive St., Dallas, Texas Presented "identification card" as proof of citizenship. Entry handled by ANTONIO RAMON GUAJARDO.

370. NORBERTA AVILA, FM-5 No 4329958, issued by Mexican Immigration Office, Nuevo Laredo, September 26, 1963. Entry was by autobus with final destination in Mexico of Monterrey, Nuevo Leon. Described as female American citizen, 32 years of age, single, privately employed, born Bryan, Texas; residence San Antonio, Texas, with no street address indicated. Presented "American identification document" as proof of citizenship Entry handled by ALBERTO ARZAMENDI CHAPA.

371. WINFRED BARNES, FM-5 No. 4516631, issued by Pan American Airways, Miami, Florida, September 5, 1963. Upon entry travel was indicated to be by plane with final destination of Monterrey, Nuevo Leon. Described as male American citizen, 51 years of age, married, executive, born Gatesville, Texas; residence 5350 SW 76th St., Miami, Florida. Presented U S Passport No. B108531 as proof of citizenship. Entry handled by EDUARDO DE LEON SILLER.

372. JOHN H. BOWEN, FM-5 No. 4329926, issued by Mexican Immigration Office, Nuevo Laredo, September 26, 1963. Mode of travel not indicated. Final destination in Mexico given as Mexico, D. F. Described as male American citizen, 60 years of age, married, office worker, born Houston, Texas; residence Houston, Texas, with no street address indicated. Presented birth certificate as proof of citizenship. Entry handled by HELIO TUEXI MAYDON.

373. SARA MARQUELA YANIS DE CHAMPSAUR, FM-5 No. 4212610, issued by Mexican Embassy, Panama, Republic of Panama, August 14, 1963. Entry was made by autobus with final destination of Mexico, D. F. Described as female Panamanian citizen, 39 years of age, married, office clerk, born Panama, Province of Panama; residence Calle 93, Paitilla, Panama. Presented Panamanian Passport No. 50.632, bearing Visa No. 1719, as proof of nationality. Entry handled by HECTOR RAGA LOPEZ.

374. MARJORIE FERN CHARLES, FM-5 No. 4234731, issued by Mexican Consulate, Kansas City, Missouri, September 19, 1963. Described as female American citizen, 35 years of age, single, office worker, born Harlan, Kansas; residence Topeka, Kansas, no street address given. Presented birth certificate as proof of citizenship. Entry handled by FRUMENCIO GONZALEZ PEREZ.

375. ANDREW WEBSTER CHRISTOPHER, FM-5 No. 4052670, issued by Mexican Consulate, Laredo, Texas, September 25, 1963. Entry was by autobus with final destination of Mexico, D. F. Described as male American citizen, 59 years of age, married, office worker, born Denver, Colorado; residence 1295 Race St., Denver, Colorado. Presented birth certificate as proof of citizenship. Entry handled by ALBERTO ARZAMENDI CHAPA.

376. SAMUEL ESTRADA, FM-5 No. 4329955, issued by Mexican Immigration Office, Nuevo Laredo, September 26, 1963. Entry was by automobile with final destination of Mexico, D. F. Described as male American citizen, 51 years of age, divorced, privately employed, born Penjamo, Guanajuato, Mexico; residence Chicago, Illinois, no street address given. Presented Naturalization Certificate No. 6148803, dated June 2, 1944, as proof of citizenship. Entry handled by ALBERTO ARZAMENDI CHAPA.

- 5 -

COMMISSION EXHIBIT No. 2119—Continued

377. BENNIE H. FABER, FM-5 No 4329980, issued by Mexican Immigration Office, Nuevo Laredo, September 26, 1963. Entry was by railroad with final destination of Mexico, D. F. Described as male American citizen, 70 years of age, widower, civil engineer, born E. Lake, Tex.; residence Normangee, Texas, no street address given. Presented birth certificate as proof of citizenship. Entry handled by RAUL LUEVANO TRUJILLO.

378. OSCAR ENRIQUE GALLARDO, FM-5 No. 4363772, issued by Mexican Consulate General, New Orleans, Louisiana, September 9 (possibly 19), 1963. Entry was by autobus with destination of Mexico, D. F. Notation appears that departure from Republic of Mexico would be at Ciudad Cuauhtemoc or Tapachula, Chiapas. Described as male Guatemalan citizen, 44 years of age, married, dressmaker, born Guatemala City, Guatemala; residence Pasaje Espinola 317, San Salvador, El Salvador. Presented Guatemalan Passport No. 20926, bearing Visa No. 306, issued Mexican Consulate, San Antonio, Texas, July 12, 1963, as proof of nationality. Entry handled by RAUL LUEVANO TRUJILLO.

379. ELSIE GIBBS, FM-5 No. 4329708, issued by Mexican Immigration Office, Nuevo Laredo, September 26, 1963. Entry by automobile with final destination of Mexico, D. F. Described as female American citizen, 44 years of age, single, office worker, born El Paso, Texas; residence Zapata, Texas, no street address given. Presented birth certificate as proof of citizenship. Entry handled by PEDRO CASTRO ROMERO.

380. LUISA MAGUER, FM-5 No. 4158246, issued by Mexican Consulate General, San Antonio, Texas, September 24, 1963. Entry by railroad with destination of Mexico, D. F. Described as female Argentine citizen, 28 years of age, single, occupation indicated as "home," born Buenos Aires, Argentina; residence Av. San Martin 6195, Buenos Aires, Argentina. Presented Argentine Passport No. 32425, bearing Visa No. 438, issued by Mexican Consulate General, San Antonio, Texas, September 24, 1963, as proof of nationality. Entry handled by RAUL LUEVANO TRUJILLO.

381. Miss J. M. HENDRICKSE, FM-5 No. 4359974, issued by Mexican Consulate, Toronto, Canada, August 19, 1963. Entry was by autobus with destination of Mexico, D. F. Described as female British subject, 32 years of age, single, secretary, born Cape Town, South Africa; residence 25 Lamport Avenue, Toronto. Presented Passport (British, apparently) No. 962247,

- 6 -

COMMISSION EXHIBIT No. 2119—Continued

valid until September 28, 1966, as proof of nationality. Entry handled by FRUMENCIO GONZALEZ PEREZ.

382. MARIA CONSUELO MATA GONZALEZ, FM-5 No. 4329707, issued by Mexican Immigration Office, Nuevo Laredo, September 26, 1963. Entry was by automobile with final destination of Mexico, D. F. Described as female American citizen, 18 years of age, single, office worker, born Hidalgo, Texas; residence Waukesha, Wisconsin, no street address indicated. Presented birth certificate as proof of citizenship. Entry handled by PEDRO CASTRO ROMERO.

383. JOHN BRYAN McFARLAND, FM-5 No. 4363754, issued by Mexican Consulate General, New Orleans, Louisiana, September 14, 1963. Entry was by autobus with final destination of Mexico, D. F. Described as male British subject, 32 years of age, married, surgeon, born Liverpool, Lancaster; residence 10 Fulwood Park, Liverpool. Presented British Passport No. L0243714, valid until July 18, 1965, as proof of nationality. Entry handled by ANTONIO RAMON GUAJARDO.

384. ANNA MERYL REID McFARLAND, FM-5 No. 4363755, issued by Mexican Consulate General, New Orleans, Louisiana, September 14, 1963. Entry was by autobus with final destination of Mexico, D. F. Described as female British subject, 34 years of age, married, housewife, born Liverpool, Lancashire; residence Apt. 50, 760 Lakeland Dr., Jackson, Miss. Presented British Passport No. L0516307, valid until September 29, 1964, as proof of nationality. Entry handled by ANTONIO RAMON GUAJARDO.

385. MICHAEL A. NOVOA, FM-5 No. 4351992, issued by Honorary Mexican Consulate, Newark, N. J., September 18, 1963. Entry was by railroad with final destination of Mexico, D. F. Described as male American citizen, 18 years of age, single, student, born Jersey City, N. J.; residence 175 Virginia Ave., Jersey City, N. J. Presented birth certificate as proof of citizenship. Entry handled by RAUL LUEVANO TRUJILLO.

386. TOMAS JERIEL OWENS, FM-5 No. 4329625, issued by Mexican Immigration Office, Nuevo Laredo, September 26, 1963. Mode of travel not indicated. Final destination indicated as Mexico, D. F. Described as male American citizen, 21 years of

- 7 -

COMMISSION EXHIBIT No. 2119—Continued

age, single, student, born Polk, Minnesota; residence listed only as "Minnesota." Presented birth certificate as proof of citizenship. It is to be noted that instant individual appeared to have signed form FM-5 as JERRY T. OWENS. Entry handled by HELIO TUEXI MAYDON.

387. JUANITA A. PEREZ, FM-5 No. 4496449, issued by Mexican Consulate, Dallas, Texas, September 19, 1963. Entry was by automobile with announced final destination of Mexico, D. F. Described as female American citizen, 52 years of age, divorced, merchant, born San Felipe, Guanajuato, Mexico; residence 2210 Olive St., Dallas, Texas. Presented voter's registration as proof of citizenship. Accompanied by children JUANITA PEREZ, five years of age, and RICHARD CRUZ, two years of age. Entry handled by ANTONIO RAMON GUAJARDO.

388. ANIBAL PLEITEZ, FM-5 No. 4363773, issued by Mexican Consulate General, New Orleans, Louisiana, September 9 (possibly 19), 1963. Entry was by autobus and travel was en route Mexico, D. F., with departure from Republic of Mexico indicated as via Ciudad Cuauhtemoc or Tapachula, Chiapas. Described as male Salvadoran citizen, 40 years of age, single, motorman, born San Salvador, El Salvador; residence 4 Calle Oriente No. 132, San Salvador. Presented Salvadoran Passport No. 66802, bearing Mexican Visa No. 709, issued Mexican Consulate General, New Orleans, La., September 19, 1963, as proof of nationality. Entry handled by RAUL LUEVANO TRUJILLO.

389. JOSE HUMBERTO PLEITEZ, FM-5 No. 4363774, issued by Mexican Consulate General, New Orleans, Louisiana, September 19, 1963. Entry was by autobus en route Mexico, D. F., with departure from Republic of Mexico indicated as via Ciudad Cuauhtemoc or Tapachula, Chiapas. Described as male Salvadoran citizen, 35 years of age, single, mechanic, born San Salvador, El Salvador. Presented Salvadoran Passport No. 51852, bearing Mexican Visa No. 708, issued by Mexican Consulate General, New Orleans, La., September 19, 1963, as proof of nationality. Entry handled by RAUL LUEVANO TRUJILLO.

390. EMIL SAINZ, FM-5 No. 4455632, issued by Mexican Tourism Department, New York, N. Y., September 20, 1963. Entry

- 8 -

COMMISSION EXHIBIT No. 2119—Continued

was by railroad with announced destination in Mexico of Mexico, D. F. Described as male American citizen, 64 years of age, married, hotel manager, born Santander, Spain; residence 7424 88th Rd., Woodhaven, N. Y. Presented voter's registration and Naturalization Certificate No. 6726383, dated March 1, 1949, as proof of citizenship. Entry handled by RAUL LUEVANO TRUJILLO.

391. TERESA CACCIATORE SAINZ, FM-5 No. 4455631, issued by Mexican Tourism Department, New York, N. Y., September 20, 1963. Entry was by railroad with final destination given as Mexico, D. F. Described as female American citizen, 60 years of age, born Yonkers, N. Y.; residence 7424 88th Rd., Woodhaven, N. Y. Presented U. S. Passport No. 235152, which notation appeared to indicate was dated August 10, 1935, as proof of citizenship. Entry handled by RAUL LUEVANA TRUJILLO.

392. MATTHEW SCHILLER, FM-5 No. 4329624, issued by Mexican Immigration Office, Nuevo Laredo, September 26, 1963. Mode of travel not indicated. Final destination given as Mexico, D. F. Described as male American citizen, single, retired, born in Austria (place not indicated), 69 years of age; residence San Antonio, Texas, with no street address given. Presented U. S. Passport No. 2004931 as proof of citizenship. Entry handled by HELIO TUEXI MAYDON.

393. RICHARD RALPH SCHWARZE, FM-5 No. 4381251, issued by Mexican Consulate, Detroit, Michigan, September 23, 1963. Entry was by autobus with final destination of Mexico, D. F. Described as male American citizen, 19 years of age, single, student, born in Michigan (no place indicated); residence given only as Birmingham, Michigan. Presented birth certificate as proof of citizenship. Entry handled by HECTOR RAGA LOPEZ.

394. CHESTER STANLEY STEMP, FM-5 No. 4449875, issued by Mexican Tourism Department, Houston, Texas, September 25, 1963. Mode of travel upon entry not indicated. Final destination given as Mexico, D. F. Described as male American citizen, 22 years of age, single, teacher, born Hammond, Indiana; residence 7223 Jarnecke Ave., Hammond, Ind. Presented U. S. Passport No. D544826, dated July 10, 1963, as

proof of citizenship. Entry handled by HELIO TUEXI MAYDON.

395. TEODORO OSCAR TREVINO, FM-5 No. 4329956, issued by Mexican Immigration Office, Nuevo Laredo, September 26, 1963. At time of entry was traveling by plane with announced destination in Mexico of Mexico, D. F. Described as male American citizen, 36 years of age, married, privately employed, place of birth appeared to be indicated as Lima, Peru; residence Lima, Peru. Presented American Passport No. C-002627, issued in 1962 and indicated as still valid, as proof of citizenship. Entry handled by ALBERTO ARZAMENDI CHAPA.

396. VIOLA MARIA YANIS DE VIGGIANO, FM-5 No. 4212612, issued by Consular Section of Mexican Embassy, Panama, Republic of Panama, August 14, 1963. Entry was by autobus with announced destination in Mexico as Mexico, D.F. Described as female Panamanian citizen, 48 years of age, married, office clerk, born Panama, Republic of Panama; residence Calle Gerardo Ortega No. 5 (apparently Panama City, Panama, as no other town or city mentioned on form). Presented Panamanian Passport No. 50.604, Visa No. 1721, as proof of nationality. Entry handled by ALBERTO ARZAMENDI CHAPA.

397. ANTONY S. WATNE, FM-5 No. 4484229, issued by Mexican Consulate, Phoenix, Arizona, September 23, 1963. Entry was by autobus with final destination in Mexico of Mexico, D. F. Described as male British subject, 27 years of age, single, engineer, born London, England; residence given only as New York City, N. Y. Presented British Passport No. 34596 as proof of nationality. Entry handled by HECTOR RAGA LOPEZ.

398. FLOR DE MARIA SUCRE DE YANIS, FM-5 No. 4212611, issued by Consular Section of Mexican Embassy, Panama, Republic of Panama, August 14, 1963. Entry was by autobus with Mexico, D. F., given as final destination in Mexico. Described as female Panamanian citizen, 58 years of age, married, telegraph operator, born Pocri Los Santos, Panama; residence given only as Calle 83 No. 9 (possibly Panama City, Panama). Presented Panamanian Passport No. 32.694, bearing Visa No. 1720, as proof of citizenship. Entry handled by HECTOR RAGA LOPEZ.

399. TOBIAS ROZENZEW ZAREMBER, FM-5 No. 4052668, issued by Mexican Consulate, Laredo, Texas, September 25, 1963.

Entered by autobus with announced destination in Mexico of Tampico, Tamaulipas. Described as male Colombian citizen, 25 years of age, single, office worker, born Barranquilla, Colombia; residence 14-6n Grand Conurse (thought possibly to be 14-61 Grand Concourse), N. Y. Presented Colombian Passport No. C-05587, bearing Mexican Visa No. 416 issued by Mexican Consulate General, San Antonio, Texas, September 11, 1963, as proof of nationality. Entry handled by PEDRO CASTRO ROMERO.

Entry into Mexico on September 26, 1963, at Nuevo Laredo, State of Tamaulipas, of non-Mexican Citizens Traveling on Form FM-8 Tourist Cards

762. FELIX ALONZO, FM-8 No. 626144, issued by Mexican Immigration Office, Nuevo Laredo, September 26, 1963. Mode of travel at time of entry not indicated. Final destination in Mexico given as Monterrey, Nuevo Leon. Described as male American citizen, 37 years of age, married, occupation not indicated, proceeding from San Antonio, Texas; accompanied by minor son FELIX, JR., of nine years of age. Presented birth certificate as proof of citizenship. Entry handled by HELIO TUEXI MAYDON.

763. APOLONIO ALVARES, FM-8 No. 626133, issued by Mexican Immigration Office, Nuevo Laredo, September 26, 1963. Mode of travel at time of entry not indicated. Final destination given as Monterrey, Nuevo Leon. Described as male American citizen, 42 years of age, married, no data as to occupation, proceeding from San Antonio, Texas. Presented birth certificate as proof of citizenship. Entry handled by HELIO TUEXI MAYDON.

764. CAMILA ALVARES, FM-8 No. 626134, issued by Mexican Immigration Office, Nuevo Laredo, September 26, 1963. Mode of travel at time of entry not indicated. Final destination given as Monterrey, Nuevo Leon. Described as female American citizen, 39 years of age, married, no employment data indicated, proceeding from Laredo, Texas; accompanied by minor

children GUADALUPE, YOLANDA, JESUS, MARIA, RICARDO and BERNARDINO. Presented birth certificate as proof of citizenship. Entry handled by HELIO TUEXI MAYDON.

765. JUAN ALVARES, FM-8 No. 626135, issued by Mexican Immigration Office, Nuevo Laredo, September 26, 1963. Mode of travel not indicated. Final destination given as Monterrey, Nuevo Leon. Described as male American citizen, 16 years of age, single, no employment data recorded, proceeding from Laredo, Texas. Presented birth certificate as proof of citizenship. Entry handled by HELIO TUEXI MAYDON.

766. BERTHA AVILA, FM-8 No. 626242, issued by Mexican Immigration Office, Nuevo Laredo, September 26, 1963. Travel was indicated as by autobus with Monterrey, Nuevo Leon, as final destination in Mexico. Described as female American citizen, 32 years of age, single, occupation given only as "home," proceeding from San Antonio, Texas. Entry was indicated as handled by ALBERTO ARZAMENDI CHAPA. It is to be noted that instant tourist card bears the notation that same was cancelled in accordance with AVILA's wish this regard.and was not utilized by her.

767. BERTHA AVILA, FM-8 No. 626242. It is noted that this listing carries identical information as set forth under No. 766. It appears that the two listings of the name of BERTHA AVILA on the FM-11 was done in error since apparently she did not enter Mexico.

768. TED C. BLAND, FM-8 No. 624673, issued by Mexican Immigration Office, Nuevo Laredo, September 26, 1963. Entry was by auto with final destination of Monterrey, Nuevo Leon. Described as male American citizen, 29 years of age, single, contractor, proceeding from Hillsboro, Texas. Presented voter's registration as proof of citizenship. Entry handled by ANTONIO RAMON GUAJARDO.

769. STEPHEN ALAN BRILL, FM-8 No. 47905, issued by Miami Office of Mexican Tourism Department August 13, 1963. No data given as to mode of travel or final destination in Mexico. Described as male American citizen, 25 years of age, married, engineer, presented birth certificate as proof of

citizenship. FM-11 indicates instant individual was proceeding from Miami, Florida, at time of entry. Entry handled by HELIO TUEXI MAYDON.

770. ELAINE ESTERMAN BRILL, FM-8 No. 47906, issued by the Miami Office of Mexican Tourism Department August 13, 1963. No data given as to mode of travel or final destination in Mexico. Described as female American citizen, 24 years of age, married, teacher, presented birth certificate as proof of citizenship. FM-11 indicates instant individual was proceeding from Miami, Florida, at time of entry. Entry handled by HELIO TUEXI MAYDON.

771. HARVEY M. CAMPBELL, FM-8 No. 626139, issued by Mexican Immigration Office, Nuevo Laredo, September 26, 1963. Final destination indicated as Monterrey, Nuevo Leon, but mode of travel not given. Described as male American citizen, 71 years of age, single, occupation not indicated, proceeding from Longview (believed Texas). Presented birth certificate as proof of citizenship. Entry handled by HELIO TUEXI MAYDON.

772. FRANK CANTERBURY, FM-8 No. 624669, issued by Mexican Immigration Office, Nuevo Laredo, September 26, 1963. Entry was by automobile with final destination given as Salinillas, Nuevo Leon. Described as male American citizen, 72 years of age, married, salesman, proceeding from San Antonio, Texas. Presented voter's registration as proof of citizenship. Entry handled by ANTONIO RAMON GUAJARDO.

773. FERNANDO CARRILLO, FM-8 No. 626230, issued by Mexican Immigration Office, Nuevo Laredo, September 26, 1963. Entry was by automobile with final destination of Monterrey, Nuevo Leon. Described as male American citizen, 18 years of age, single, student, proceeding from Duval, Texas. Presented "document of identity" as proof of citizenship. Entry handled by ALBERTO ARZAMENDI CHAPA.

774. R. ALECOR CAVAZOS (possibly ALECOR CAVAZOS R.), FM-8 No. 626140, issued by Mexican Immigration Office, Nuevo Laredo, September 26, 1963. Final destination given as

- 13 -

COMMISSION EXHIBIT No. 2119—Continued

Monterrey, Nuevo Leon, but mode of travel not indicated. Described as male American citizen, 47 years of age, married, occupation not indicated, proceeding from Dallas, Texas. Presented Naturalization Certificate No. 5533230, dated February 24, 1943, as proof of citizenship. Entry handled by HELIO TUEXI MAYDON.

775. N. ARNALDO CAVAZOS (possibly ARNALDO CAVAZOS N.), FM-8 No. 626141, issued by Mexican Immigration Office, Nuevo Laredo, September 26, 1963. Final destination given as Monterrey, Nuevo Leon, but mode of travel not indicated. Described as male American citizen, 45 years of age, married, occupation not indicated, proceeding from Dallas, Texas. Presented Naturalization Certificate No. 6109277, dated June 5, 1944, as proof of citizenship. Entry handled by HELIO TUEXI MAYDON.

776. TIM PRADO CHAPA, FM-8 No. 626365, issued by Mexican Immigration Office, Nuevo Laredo, September 26, 1963. Entry was by autobus with final destination of Monterrey, Nuevo Leon. Described as male American citizen, 24 years of age, married, butcher, proceeding from Taylor, Texas. Presented "military identification" as proof of citizenship. Entry handled by PEDRO CASTRO ROMERO.

777. CHARLES DEWWEY, FM-8 No. 626231, issued by Mexican Immigration Office, Nuevo Laredo, September 26, 1963. Entry was made by automobile with final destination of Monterrey, Nuevo Leon. Described as male American citizen, 31 years of age, cook, proceeding from Treasure Island, Florida. Presented "sworn document" as proof of citizenship. Entry handled by ALBERTO ARZAMENDI CHAPA.

778. ROBERT V. DUBLIN, JR., FM-8 No. 133158, issued by Mexican Consulate, Laredo, Texas, September 26, 1963. Travel at time of entry was indicated as by plane with final destination of Mexico, D. F. Described as male American citizen, 57 years of age, married, merchant. FM-11 indicates this individual was proceeding from Laredo, Texas, at time of entry. Presented birth certificate as proof of American citizenship. Entry handled by HECTOR RAGA LOPEZ.

- 14 -

COMMISSION EXHIBIT No. 2119—Continued

779. JOSE BENITO ESCOBAR, FM-8 No. 133155, issued by Mexican Consulate, Laredo, Texas, September 26, 1963. Entry was by autobus with final destination of Mexico, D. F. Described as male Salvadoran citizen, 51 years of age, married, occupation not indicated, proceeding from Laredo, Texas. Presented Salvadoran Passport No. 67375, bearing Mexican Visa No. 4014, issued September 10, 1963, at Mexican Embassy in El Salvador, as proof of nationality. Entry handled by HECTOR RAGA LOPEZ.

780. OLIMPIA BENITEZ DE ESCOBAR, FM-8 No. 133154, issued by Mexican Consulate, Laredo, Texas, September 26, 1963. Described as female Salvadoran citizen, 49 years of age, married, occupation not indicated, proceeding from Laredo, Texas. Presented Salvadoran Passport No. 67373, bearing Mexican Visa No. 4015, issued September 10, 1963, at Mexican Embassy in El Salvador, as proof of nationality. Entry handled by HECTOR RAGA LOPEZ.

781. REINA ESCOBAR, FM-8 No. 133153, issued by Mexican Consulate, Laredo, Texas, September 26, 1963. Entry was by autobus with final destination of Mexico, D. F. Described as female Salvadoran citizen, 19 years of age, single, no occupation indicated, proceeding from Laredo, Texas. Presented Salvadoran Passport No. 67374, bearing Mexican Visa No. 4016, issued September 10, 1963, at Mexican Embassy in El Salvador, as proof of nationality. Entry handled by HECTOR RAGA LOPEZ.

782. JENNIFER JULIA FELLOWES, FM-8 No. 624676, issued by Mexican Immigration Office, Nuevo Laredo, September 26, 1963. Entry was by automobile with indicated final destination of Monterrey, Nuevo Leon. Described as female British subject, 23 years of age, single, office worker, proceeding from New York, N. Y. Presented British Passport 676491, visa exempt, valid until March 14, 1966, as proof of nationality. Entry handled by ANTONIO RAMON GUAJARDO.

783. SUSANA SELINA FOSTER, FM-8 No. 624677, issued by Mexican Immigration Office, Nuevo Laredo, September 26, 1963. Entry was by automobile with final destination of

- 15 -

COMMISSION EXHIBIT No. 2119—Continued

Mexico, D. F. Described as female British subject, 22 years of age, single, office worker, proceeding from New York, N. Y. Presented British Passport No. 32181, visa exempt, valid until October 9, 1967, as proof of nationality. Handled by ANTONIO RAMON GUAJARDO.

784. LUCIANO G. GARCIA, FM-8 No. 626229, issued by Mexican Immigration Office, Nuevo Laredo, September 26, 1963. Entry was by automobile with final destination of Monterrey, Nuevo Leon. Described as male American citizen, 18 years of age, single, student, proceeding from Duval, Texas. Presented "American document of identity" as proof of citizenship and was indicated to be traveling with his parents. Handled by ALBERTO ARZAMENDI CHAPA.

785. AGAPITO GONZALEZ, FM-8 No. 626234, issued by Mexican Immigration Office, Nuevo Laredo, September 26, 1963. Entry was by autobus with final destination of Monterrey, Nuevo Leon. Described as male American citizen, 63 years of age, married, privately employed, proceeding from Victoria, Texas, Presented "American document of identity" as proof of citizenship. Handled by ALBERTO ARZAMENDI CHAPA.

786. ELVIRA GONZALEZ, FM-8 No. 626235, issued by Mexican Immigration Office, Nuevo Laredo, September 26, 1963. Entry was by autobus with final destination of Monterrey, Nuevo Leon. Described as female American citizen, 62 years of age, married, housekeeper, proceeding from Victoria, Texas. Presented "American document of identity" as proof of citizenship. Handled by ALBERTO ARZAMENDI CHAPA.

787. ROBERTO GONZALEZ, FM-8 No. 626238, issued by Mexican Immigration Office, Nuevo Laredo, September 26, 1963. Entry was by autobus with final destination of Monterrey, Nuevo Leon. Described as male American citizen, 39 years of age, married, privately employed, proceeding from Victoria, Texas. Presented birth certificate as proof of citizenship. Entry handled by ALBERTO ARZAMENDI CHAPA.

788. DOLORES GUARDIOLA, FM-8 No. 626241, issued by Mexican Immigration Office, Nuevo Laredo, September 26, 1963.

- 16 -

COMMISSION EXHIBIT No. 2119—Continued

Entry was by automobile with final destination of Monterrey, Nuevo Leon. Described as female American citizen, 27 years of age, married, housekeeper, place from which proceeding indicated as F. Wath (possibly Ft. Worth), Texas. Entry handled by ALBERTO ARZAMENDI CHAPA.

789. H. ARTURO GUERRA, FM-8 No. 624668, issued by Mexican Immigration Office, Nuevo Laredo, September 26, 1963. Entry was by automobile with final destination of Salinillas, Nuevo Leon. Described as male American citizen, 55 years of age, married, manager of service station, proceeding from San Antonio, Texas. Presented voter's registration as proof of citizenship. Entry handled by ANTONIO RAMON GUAJARDO.

790. JODEYE (last three letters questionable) BRANS HANDS, FM-8 No. 626138, issued by Mexican Immigration Office, Nuevo Laredo, September 26, 1963. Mode of travel not indicated. Final destination indicated as Monterrey, Nuevo Leon. Described as female American citizen, 36 years of age, married, no occupation given, proceeding from Fort Worth, Texas. Presented birth certificate as proof of citizenship. Entry handled by HELIO TUEXI MAYDON. Instant individual appeared to sign her name as Mrs. JODENE HANDS.

791. ERNESTINE WHITE HANDS, FM-8 No. 626137, issued by Mexican Immigration Office, Nuevo Laredo, September 26, 1963. Mode of travel not indicated. Final destination indicated as Monterrey, Nuevo Leon. Described as female American citizen, 34 years of age, married, no occupation indicated, proceeding from Fort Worth, Texas. Presented birth certificate as proof of citizenship. Entry handled by HELIO TUEXI MAYDON.

792. NELLIE L. HARDIN, FM-8 No. 626364, issued by Mexican Immigration Office, Nuevo Laredo, September 26, 1963. Entry was by automobile with final destination as Monterrey, Nuevo Leon. Described as female American citizen, 29 years of age, married, housewife, proceeding from Laredo, Texas. Presented birth certificate as proof of citizenship. Accompanied by ARACELE, DAVID and LINDA, age 11 years, five years and one month respectively. Entry handled by PEDRO CASTRO ROMERO.

793. BRIAN JAQUES, FM-8 No. 330187, issued by Mexican Consulate, San Diego, California, September 18, 1963.

COMMISSION EXHIBIT No. 2119—Continued

Entry was by automobile and final destination in Mexico was indicated as being Nuevo Laredo. It is noted, however, that FM-11 gave his final destination in Mexico as Mexico, D. F. Described as male British subject, 25 years of age, married, professor, proceeding from San Diego, California. Presented British Passport No. LO 293041 as proof of nationality. Entry handled by FELIPE GONZALEZ ECHAZARRETA.

794. FRANK JIMENEZ, FM-8 No. 626233, issued by Mexican Immigration Office, Nuevo Laredo, September 26, 1963. Entry was by automobile with final destination of Monterrey, Nuevo Leon. Described as male American citizen, 32 years of age, married, privately employed, proceeding from Fort Worth, Texas. Presented "American document of identity" as proof of citizenship. Entry handled by ALBERTO ARZAMENDI CHAPA.

795. ABRAHAM KAPLAN, FM-8 No. 626226, issued by Mexican Immigration Office, Nuevo Laredo, September 26, 1963. Entry was by autobus with final destination of Guadalajara, Jalisco. Described as male American citizen, 58 years of age, married, privately employed, proceeding from Buffalo, N. Y. Presented birth certificate as proof of citizenship. Entry handled by ALBERTO ARZAMENDI CHAPA.

796. RENATE KRAMER, FM-8 No. 447251, bearing the stamp of Mexican Consulate General, San Francisco, California, but no date indicated. This form bears a typed date of September 26, 1963, apparently inserted upon bearer's arrival Nuevo Laredo. Entry was made by car with final destination in Mexico of Mexico, D.F. Described as female German citizen, 23 years of age, married, housewife, place from which proceeding not indicated other than by fact tourist card bears stamp of Mexican Consulate General, San Francisco. Presented German Passport No. 2293/54, dated November 19, 1959, as proof of nationality. Entry handled by PEDRO CASTRO ROMERO.

797. DIETRICH KRAMER, FM-8 No. 447250, bearing the stamp of Mexican Consulate General, San Francisco, California, but no date indicated. This form bears a typed date of September 26, 1963, apparently inserted upon bearer's arrival Nuevo Laredo. Entry was indicated as by autobus (FM-11 shows entered by automobile) with final destination of Mexico, D. F.

COMMISSION EXHIBIT No. 2119—Continued

Described as male German citizen, 24 years of age, married, student, place from which proceeding not indicated other than by fact tourist card bears stamp of Mexican Consulate General, San Francisco. Presented German Passport No. B-3018960, dated November 19, 1959, as proof of nationality. Entry handled by PEDRO CASTRO ROMERO.

798. EDITH W. KUNTZ, FM-8 No. 510259, issued San Antonio, Texas (issuing office not identified), September 26, 1963. Final destination given as Monterrey, Nuevo Leon, but mode of travel not indicated. Described as female American citizen, 63 years of age, married, occupation not given, proceeding from San Antonio, Texas. Presented certificate of naturalization (no further data indicated) as proof of citizenship. Entry handled by EDUARDO DE LEON SILLER.

799. FERNANDO LOZANO GARCIA, FM-8 No. 626132, issued by Mexican Immigration Office, Nuevo Laredo, September 26, 1963. Mode of travel not indicated. Final destination given as Monterrey, Nuevo Leon. Described as male American citizen, 31 years of age, single, occupation not listed, proceeding from Laredo, Texas. Presented birth certificate as proof of citizenship. Entry handled by HELIO TUEXI MAYDON.

800. WILLIAM HENRY MASON, FM-8 No. 626232, issued by Mexican Immigration Office, Nuevo Laredo, September 26, 1963. Entry was by automobile with final destination of Monterrey, Nuevo Leon. Described as male American citizen, 27 years of age, single, privately employed, proceeding from Treasure Island, Florida. Presented "sworn document" as proof of citizenship. Entry handled by ALBERTO ARZAMENDI CHAPA.

801. ANGELINA MA. GONZALEZ MENDEZ, FM-8 No. 626037, issued by Mexican Immigration Office, Nuevo Laredo, September 26, 1963. Entry was by autobus with final destination of Monterrey, N. L. Described as female American citizen, 52 years of age, married, housewife, proceeding from Laredo, Texas. Presented birth certificate as proof of citizenship. Entry handled by HECTOR RAGA LOPEZ.

802. HARRY J. MITCHELL, FM-8 No. 624674, issued by Mexican Immigration Office, Nuevo Laredo, September 26, 1963. Entry was by autobus with final destination of Mexico, D. F. Described as male American citizen, 41 years of age, married, attorney, proceeding from Palmyra, Missouri. Presented birth certificate as proof of citizenship. Entry handled by ANTONIO RAMON GUAJARDO.

803. ANN MARIE MITCHELL, FM-8 No. 624675, issued by Mexican Immigration Office, Nuevo Laredo, September 26, 1963. Entry was by autobus with final destination of Mexico, D. F. Described as female American citizen, 22 years of age, married, housewife, proceeding from Palmyra, Missouri. Presented birth certificate as proof of citizenship. Entry handled by ANTONIO RAMON GUAJARDO.

804. ADOLIO MORALES, FM-8 No. 626145, issued by Mexican Immigration Office, Nuevo Laredo, September 26, 1963. Final destination given as Monterrey, N. L., but mode of travel not indicated. Described as male American citizen, 54 years of age, married, occupation not given, proceeding from Laredo, Texas. Presented birth certificate as proof of citizenship. Entry handled by HELIO TUEXI MAYDON.

805. MARTINA MORENO, FM-8 No. 626236, issued by Mexican Immigration Office, Nuevo Laredo, September 26, 1963. Entry was by autobus with final destination of Monterrey, N. L. Described as female American citizen, 59 years of age, married, housewife, proceeding from Victoria, Texas. Presented birth certificate as proof of citizenship. Entry handled by ALBERTO ARZAMENDI CHAPA.

806. BUELL MOORE, FM-8 No. 625566, issued by Mexican Immigration Office, Nuevo Laredo, September 26, 1963. Final destination indicated as Monterrey, N. L., but mode of travel not given. Described as male American citizen, 48 years of age, single, occupation not listed, proceeding from Houston, Texas. Presented "sworn declaration" as proof of citizenship. Entry handled by JORGE LUIS SOLALINDE L.

807. HARVEY OSWALD LEE, FM-8 No. 24085, issued by Mexican Consulate General, New Orleans, La., September 17,

1963. Final destination given as Mexico, D. F., but mode of travel not indicated. Described as male American citizen, 23 years of age, married, photographer, place from which proceeding not indicated on FM-8 other than fact same issued New Orleans. FM-11 indicated proceeding from New Orleans, La. Presented birth certificate as proof of citizenship. Entry handled by HELIO TUEXI MAYDON.

808. MAURICE OUELLET, FM-8 No. 32060/196, issued by Mexican Consulate General, Montreal, Que., Canada, September 19, 1963. Entry was by autobus with final destination of Mexico, D. F. Described as male Canadian citizen, 22 years of age, single, social worker, place from which proceeding not indicated on FM-8 other than fact same issued in Montreal. Presented Canadian Passport No. 5-101459, visa exempt, as proof of nationality. Entry handled by PEDRO CASTRO ROMERO.

809. KENNETH GRENIER PECK, FM-8 No. 625567, issued by Mexican Immigration Office, Nuevo Laredo, September 26, 1963. Travel at time of entry indicated as by plane with final destination of Monterrey, N. L. Described as male American citizen, 43 years of age, married, no occupation indicated, proceeding from Houston, Texas. Presented "sworn declaration" as proof of citizenship. Entry handled by JORGE LUIS SOLALINDE L.

810. YOLANDA A. DE RAMOS, FM-8 No. 623793, issued by Mexican Immigration Office, Nuevo Laredo, September 26, 1963. Final destination given as Mexico, D. F., but mode of travel not indicated. Described as female American citizen, 36 y ars of age, married, housewife, proceeding from San Antonio, Texas. Presented birth certificate as proof of citizenship. Entry handled by ZEFERINO ESPINOZA RAMOS.

811. ROESLY ROBERT, FM-8 No. 623924, issued by Mexican Immigration Office, Nuevo Laredo, September 26, 1963. Entry was by railroad with final destination of Mexico, D. F. Described as female American citizen, 75 years of age, widow, no occupation indicated, place from which proceeding given as "A. Bech" (thought possibly to be Atlantic Beach), N. Y. Presented American Passport No. 2363c30,d/f, dated July 27, 1960, as proof of citizenship. Entry handled by RAUL LUEVANO TRUJILLO.

- 21 -

COMMISSION EXHIBIT No. 2119—Continued

812. FLORENCE S. ROCLEVITCH, FM-8 No. 623795, issued by Mexican Immigration Office, Nuevo Laredo, September 26, 1963. Final destination at time of entry given as Mexico, D. F., but mode of travel not indicated. Described as female American citizen, age 40 years, married, occupation not given, proceeding from Hyattsville, Maryland. Presented birth certificate as proof of citizenship. Entry handled by ZEFERINO ESPINOSA RAMOS.

813. ANTHONY PAUL ROCLEVITCH, FM-8 No. 623794, issued by Mexican Immigration Office, Nuevo Laredo, September 26, 1963. Final destination at time of entry given as Mexico, D. F., but mode of travel not indicated. Described as male American citizen, age 43 years, married, technician, proceeding from Hyattsville, Maryland. Presented "sworn declaration" as proof of citizenship. Entry handled by ZEFERINO ESPINOZA RAMOS.

814. RAFAEL RUBEN RODRIGUEZ, FM-8 No. 625625, issued by Mexican Immigration Office, Nuevo Laredo, September 26, 1963. Final destination at time of entry given as Monterrey, N. L., but mode of travel not indicated. Described as male American citizen, 58 years of age, married, retired, proceeding from Laredo, Texas. Presented Naturalization Certificate No. 6829172, dated July 18, 1950. Accompanied by child, REBECA, seven years of age. Entry handled by JESUS GOVEA HERRERA.

815. ROBERTO GONZALO RODRIGUEZ ESPINOSA (carried on FM-11 as ROBERTO GONZALO ESPINOZA RODRIGUEZ), FM-8 No. 133156, issued by Mexican Consulate, Laredo, Texas, September 26, 1963. Final destination at time of entry given as Mexico, D. F., but mode of travel not indicated. Described as male Costa Rican citizen, 25 years of age, occupation not given, place from which proceeding likewise not given. Presented Costa Rican Passport No. 6057-63, Visa No. 964, as proof of nationality. Entry handled by RAUL LUEVANO TRUJILLO.

816. JORGE ANTONIO RODRIGUEZ ESPINOSA, FM-8 No. 133157, issued by Mexican Consulate, Laredo, Texas, September 26, 1963. Final destination at time of entry given as Mexico, D. F., but mode of travel not indicated. Described as male Costa Rican, 21 years of age, single, no occupation, place from which proceeding not given. Presented Costa Rican Passport No. 6075-63, Visa No. 963, as proof of nationality. Entry handled by RAUL LUEVANO TRUJILLO.

- 22 -

COMMISSION EXHIBIT No. 2119—Continued

817. JOSEFA RODRIGUEZ INMAN, FM-8 No. 626131, issued by Mexican Immigration Office, Nuevo Laredo, September 26, 1963. Final destination at time of entry given as Monterrey, N. L., but mode of travel not indicated. Described as female American citizen, 75 years of age, single, no occupation given, proceeding from San Antonio, Texas. Presented birth certificate as proof of citizenship. Entry handled by HELIO TUEXI MAYDON.

818. MINO ROMERO CRUZ, FM-8 No. 626143, issued by Mexican Immigration Office, Nuevo Laredo, September 26, 1963. Final destination given at time of entry as Monterrey, N. L., but mode of travel not indicated. Described as male American citizen, 64 years of age, married, no occupation given, proceeding from San Antonio, Texas. Presented Naturalization Certificate No. 7596537, dated April 27, 1956, as proof of citizenship. Entry handled by HELIO TUEXI MAYDON.

819. RICARDO SANDOVAL, FM-8 No. 626363, issued by Mexican Immigration Office, Nuevo Laredo, September 26, 1963. Entry was by automobile with final destination of Monterrey, N. L. Described as male American citizen, 29 years of age, married, office worker, proceeding from San Antonio, Texas. Presented birth certificate as proof of citizenship. Entry handled by PEDRO CASTRO ROMERO.

820. GEORGES ALBERT SPINNER, FM-8 No. 626362, issued by Mexican Immigration Office, Nuevo Laredo, September 26, 1963. Entry was by autobus with final destination of Mexico, D. F. Described as male American citizen, 23 years of age, single, student, proceeding from Metz, France. Presented American Passport No. 556/62, dated March 7, 1962, as proof of citizenship. Entry handled by PEDRO CASTRO ROMERO.

821. RICHARD STRETTON, FM-8 No. 626239, issued by Mexican Immigration Office, Nuevo Laredo, September 26, 1963. Entry was by automobile with final destination of Monterrey, N. L. Described as male American citizen, 30 years of age, married, privately employed, proceeding from San Francisco, California. Presented "American document of identity" as proof of citizenship. Entry handled by ALBERTO ARZAMENDI CHAPA.

- 23 -

822. NANCY STREETT (tourist card signed as NANCY C. STRETTON), FM-8 No. 626240, issued by Mexican Immigration Office, Nuevo Laredo, September 26, 1963. Entry was by automobile with final destination of Monterrey, N. L. Described as female American citizen, 25 years of age, married, housewife, proceeding from San Francisco, California. Presented birth certificate as proof of citizenship. Entry handled by ALBERTO ARZAMENDI CHAPA.

823. M. JOHN SZUCHY, JR., FM-8 No. 625632, issued by Mexican Immigration Office, Nuevo Laredo, September 26, 1963. Entry was by autobus with final destination of Mexico, D. F. Described as male American citizen, 35 years of age, single, privately employed, proceeding from Ambridge (state illegible, believed Pennsylvania). Presented birth certificate as proof of citizenship. Entry handled by FRUMENCIO GONZALEZ PEREZ. This individual appeared to sign his name as JOHN M. SZUCHY, JR., on instant tourist card.

824. THOMAS J. ROGER, FM-8 No. 626142, issued by Mexican Immigration Office, Nuevo Laredo, September 26, 1963. Final destination given at time of entry as Monterrey, N. L., but mode of travel not indicated. Described as male American citizen, 42 years of age, married, occupation not indicated, proceeding from Dallas, Texas. Presented birth certificate as proof of citizenship. Entry handled by HELIO TUEXI MAYDON.

825. MAURICIA VALLE DE TORRES, FM-8 No. 510398, issued by Mexican Tourism Department, San Antonio, Texas, September 25, 1963. Entry was by autobus with final destination of Monterrey, N. L. Described as female American citizen, 53 years of age, married, housewife, proceeding from San Antonio, Texas. Presented birth certificate as proof of citizenship. Entry handled by ANTONIO RAMON GUAJARDO.

826. VICENTE V. TORRES, FM-8 No. 510399, issued by Mexican Tourism Department, San Antonio, Texas, September 25, 1963. Entry was by autobus with final destination of Monterrey, N. L. Described as male American citizen, 23 years of age, single, musician, proceeding from San Antonio, Texas. Presented birth certificate as proof of citizenship. Entry handled by ANTONIO RAMON GUAJARDO.

- 24 -

COMMISSION EXHIBIT No. 2119—Continued

827. JUSTINO TREVINO, FM-8 No. 626227, issued by Mexican Immigration Office, Nuevo Laredo, September 26, 1963. Entry was by autobus with final destination of Monterrey, N. L. Described as male American citizen, 62 years of age, married, privately employed, proceeding from Laredo, Texas. Presented "American card of identity" as proof of citizenship. Entry handled by ALBERTO ARZAMENDI CHAPA.

828. ABELINA P. DE TREVINO, FM-8 No. 626228, issued by Mexican Immigration Office, Nuevo Laredo, September 26, 1963. Entry was by autobus with final destination of Monterrey, N. L. Described as female American citizen, 61 years of age, married, housewife, proceeding from Laredo, Texas. Presented "American card of identity" as proof of citizenship. Entry handled by ALBERTO ARZAMENDI CHAPA.

829. ALFREDO TREVINO, FM-8 No. 626554, issued by Mexican Immigration Office, Nuevo Laredo, September 26, 1963. Entry was by railroad with final destination of Monterrey, N. L. Described as male American citizen, 46 years of age, married, occupation not indicated, proceeding from Laredo, Texas. Presented birth certificate as proof of citizenship. Entry handled by MANUEL BUENTELLO ORTEGON.

830. ESTELA S. TREVINO, FM-8 No. 626555, issued by Mexican Immigration Office, Nuevo Laredo, September 26, 1963. Entry was by railroad with final destination of Monterrey, N. L. Described as female American citizen, 70 years of age, married, occupation not indicated, proceeding from Laredo, Texas. Presented birth certificate as proof of citizenship. Entry handled by MANUEL BUENTELLO ORTEGON.

831. ESPERANZA DE VALDEZ S., FM-8 No. 624671, issued by Mexican Immigration Office, Nuevo Laredo, September 26, 1963. Entry was by autobus with final destination of Monterrey, N. L. Described as female American citizen, 39 years of age, married, housewife, proceeding from Carrizo S. (believed Carrizo Springs), Texas. Presented Naturalization Certificate No. 39740 as proof of citizenship. Entry handled by ANTONIO RAMON GUAJARDO.

COMMISSION EXHIBIT No. 2119—Continued

832. BENITO TOMAS VALDEZ, FM-8 No. 624670, issued by Mexican Immigration Office, Nuevo Laredo, September 26, 1963. Entry was by autobus with final destination of Monterrey, N. L. Described as male American citizen, 40 years of age, married, carpenter, proceeding from Carrizo S. (believed Carrizo Springs), Texas. Presented birth certificate as proof of citizenship. Entry handled by ANTONIO RAMON GUAJARDO.

833. JUANA VALDEZ, FM-8 No. 626136, issued by Mexican Immigration Office, Nuevo Laredo, September 26, 1963. Final destination at time of entry given as Monterrey, N. L., but mode of travel not indicated. Described as female American citizen, 38 years of age, married, occupation not indicated, proceeding from Laredo, Texas. Presented birth certificate as proof of citizenship. Accompanied by children HECTOR, ARTURO and ROSALINDA, seven, six and four years of age. Entry handled by HELIO TUEXI MAYDON.

834. MARIA ELSA VALDEZ, FM-8 No. 624672, issued by Mexican Immigration Office, Nuevo Laredo, September 26, 1963. Entry was by autobus with final destination of Monterrey, N. L. Described as female American citizen, 16 years of age, single, student, proceeding from Carrizo S. (believed Carrizo Springs), Texas. Presented Naturalization Certificate No. 67356 as proof of citizenship. Notation on instant form to effect this individual was traveling with her parents who were documented separately. Entry handled by ANTONIO RAMON GUAJARDO.

835. OLIVIA VILLARREAL, FM-8 No. 626237, issued by Mexican Immigration Office, Nuevo Laredo, September 26, 1963. Entry was by autobus with final destination of Monterrey, N. L. Described as female American citizen, 62 years of age, married, housewife, proceeding from Victoria, Texas. Presented birth certificate as proof of citizenship. Entry handled by ALBERTO ARZAMENDI CHAPA.

COMMISSION EXHIBIT No. 2119—Continued

It should be noted that in connection with cases involving travel of other Americans, it has been found not unusual for errors to be committed in connection with the entry shown on the form FM-11 for travelers entering Mexico. As pointed out above, the original of the tourist card is surrendered by the traveler at the time of departure from Mexico. This original shows the place of issuance of the tourist card and the principal error that has been noted is showing final destination as the place where the tourist card was originally issued. In other cases final destination is shown as the point from which the person was proceeding at the time he entered Mexico. Several specific cases have occurred in which airline passenger manifests clearly showed a final destination different from the place where the tourist card was issued; nevertheless, the form FM-11 showed a final destination of this latter place.

- 27 -

COMMISSION EXHIBIT No. 2119—Continued

THE LEGAL ADVISER
DEPARTMENT OF STATE
WASHINGTON

May 28, 1964

Dear Mr. Rankin:

I am enclosing a copy of a note and a confidential memorandum, dated May 14, 1964, from the Mexican Government of Foreign Affairs to the United States Embassy in Mexico City, sent in response to the United States note dated April 10, 1964. Also enclosed are two copies of a translation of the note and memorandum prepared by the Division of Language Services in the Department of State.

As you will see, the note states that the Mexican Government "understands that the enclosed confidential memorandum will not be published, either partially or in full, without the consent of the Government of Mexico."

Sincerely,

Abram Chayes

Abram Chayes

Enclosures:

As stated.

Mr. J. Lee Rankin,
General Counsel,
President's Commission on the
Assassination of President Kennedy,
200 Maryland Avenue, N.E.,
Washington, D.C.

COMMISSION EXHIBIT No. 2120

UNITED MEXICAN STATES)
FEDERAL DISTRICT)
CITY OF MEXICO) ss:
EMBASSY OF THE UNITED)
STATES OF AMERICA)

I, Pierre M. Hartman, Vice Consul of the United States of America at Mexico, Federal District, United Mexican States, duly commissioned and qualified, do hereby certify that the annexed copy of Note No. 504826, dated May 14, 1964, from the Secretariat of Foreign Relations of the United Mexican States, with a memorandum of the same date attached thereto, is a true copy of the original note and memorandum, the same having been examined by me and found to agree word for word and figure for figure with the said original.

IN WITNESS WHEREOF I have hereunto set my hand and seal of the Consular Service of the United States of America at México, D. F., México, this twenty-second day of May, 1964.

Pierre M. Hartman
Pierre M. Hartman
Vice Consul of the United States of America

Ite 3
No

504826

ACTION		
TAKEN		
DATE		
BY		
AMB	DCM	S/A
A/A	CCA	P
P/R	LAB	USIS
A/C	AG/A	IRS
AIR	ARMY	NAVY
E	L	US/TS
C	E/PAT	C/PAQ
C/VIS	C/VETS	INS
GS	GUS	NAR
ADM	PERS	[illegible]
BF	SY	[illegible]
R/LTS	E/LIB	FG/COM
CS		
CR.P	CR/T	CR/F

La Secretaría de Relaciones Exteriores saluda atentamente a la Embajada de los Estados Unidos de América y tiene el honor de referirse a su nota número 1349, fechada el 10 de abril próximo pasado, en la que indica que sería útil al Gobierno de los Estados Unidos de América disponer de una información sobre la investigación realizada por los organismos mexicanos competentes respecto de las actividades que el presunto asesino del señor Presidente John F. Kennedy, Lee Harvey Oswald, realizó durante el tiempo que estuvo en México en septiembre de 1963.

La Embajada también manifiesta en la nota de referencia que interesaría igualmente una descripción de las medidas que el Gobierno mexicano hubiese tomado inmediatamente después de que tuvo noticia del atentado contra la vida del señor Presidente Kennedy, como por ejemplo el establecimiento de una vigilancia especial en los puertos fronterizos u otras medidas similares.

En obsequio de los deseos de la Embajada, la Secretaría se complace en transmitirle con la presente nota un memorándum confidencial que contiene la información solicitada sobre los dos puntos arriba mencionados.

De acuerdo con el ofrecimiento hecho por la Embajada en el último párrafo de su nota, la Secretaría

cueda en

A la Embajada de los Estados Unidos de América,
C i u d a d .

EMBASSY OF THE
UNITED STATES OF AMERICA
MEXICO, D. F. MEXICO
MAY 21 1964

2

queda en el entendimiento de que el memorándum confidencial anexo no será publicado, ni total ni parcialmente, sin el consentimiento del Gobierno de México.

La Secretaría de Relaciones Exteriores aprovecha la ocasión para renovar a la Embajada de los Estados Unidos de América el testimonio de su más alta consideración.

México, D. F., a 14 de mayo de 1964.

COMMISSION EXHIBIT No. 2120—Continued

M E M O R A N D U M

El Gobierno de México, tan pronto como tuvo noticia del atentado contra la vida del señor Presidente John F. Kennedy, ocurrido el 22 de noviembre de 1963 en la ciudad de Dallas, Texas, adoptó por conducto de la Secretaría de Gobernación ciertas medidas para impedir que el autor del magnicidio pudiera buscar refugio en territorio mexicano.

De inmediato, a las 15:00 horas de ese mismo día, se ordenó el cierre de la frontera entre México y los Estados Unidos de América y, a pesar de los problemas que ocasionó esta medida, se mantuvo en vigor hasta el momento en que se supo que el presunto asesino se hallaba ya detenido por la policía de Dallas.

Asimismo, la Secretaría de la Defensa Nacional, en colaboración con la Secretaría de Gobernación, envió tropas con el fin de estrechar la vigilancia en la zona fronteriza, especialmente en Reynosa, Ciudad Miguel Alemán, Nuevo Laredo y Matamoros.

Al conocerse el nombre y filiación del presunto asesino Lee Harvey Oswald, se inició una investigación que condujo al conocimiento de que dicho individuo había estado en México en 1963. En efecto, pudo establecerse con certeza que Oswald se internó a la República Mexicana por Nuevo Laredo, Tamaulipas, el día 26 de septiembre de 1963, con una tarjeta de turista con límite de quince días que le había sido expedida por el Consulado de México en Nueva Orleans

EMBASSY OF THE
UNITED STATES OF AMERICA
MEXICO, D. F. MEXICO
MAY 21 1964

COMMISSION EXHIBIT No. 2120—Continued

co en Nueva Orleans el día 17 del mismo mes y año.

Al día siguiente, o sea el 27 de septiembre, Oswald tomó la habitación número 18 en el "Hotel del Comercio", ubicado en la calle de Fray Bernardino de Sahagún número 19 de la ciudad de México.

Durante su estancia de cinco días en la capital mexicana, Oswald se dedicó a tratar de obtener del Consulado de la República de Cuba una visa para viajar a La Habana en tránsito hacia la Unión Soviética. Sus gestiones resultaron infructuosas, ya que el Consulado cubano condicionó la expedición de la visa al previo otorgamiento por la Embajada soviética del permiso necesario para que pudiera dirigirse a Moscú.

A este respecto se transcribe, en su parte pertinente, la declaración hecha el 23 de noviembre de 1963 por la señora Silvia Tirado de Durán, empleada del Consulado de Cuba en esta capital, ante las autoridades investigadoras mexicanas:

"ya cerca de la hora de salida, al mediodía, una compañera comentó que acababa de escuchar en el radio una noticia relativa a que el Presidente KENNEDY había sufrido un atentado, en el que le habían disparado tres balazos, por lo que le llamó por teléfono a su esposo y comentaron acerca de tal noticia, contestándole éste que ya lo sabía, calificando a dicho atentado de "monstruoso" y acordando que al reunirse en su domicilio platicarían sobre ese particular, lo hicieron a la hora de la comida pero en forma breve, ya que desconocían los incidentes del atentado y nombre y señas del presunto autor del mismo, siendo hasta por la noche cuando leyeron en una "extra" la nota relativa y posteriormente, en el radio de su domicilio, escuchó la de la voz el nombre de LEE HARVEY OSWALD, el cual le hizo recordar que este nombre corresponde a un norteamericano que en los últimos días de Septiembre o primeros días del mes de Octubre del año en curso, se presentó al Consulado Cubano solicitando una visa para Cuba, en

tránsito hacia

tránsito hacia Rusia, y apoyando su solicitud con la exhibición de su pasaporte en el que constaba que había estado viviendo en este último País por espacio de tres años, su carnet de trabajo del propio País, escrito en idioma ruso y cartas en igual idioma, así como comprobaba estar casado con una mujer de nacionalidad rusa así como ser dirigente al parecer en la ciudad de Nueva Orleans, de la organización denominada "Trato Justo para Cuba", con la pretensión de que se le aceptaba como "amigo" de la Revolución Cubana, por lo que la dicente cumpliendo con sus funciones le tomó todos sus datos y escribió el lleno de la solicitud respectiva, y la dicente, aceptando que se excedió en sus funciones, oficiosamente llamó por teléfono al Consulado Ruso, con el interés por su parte de facilitar el trámite del visado Ruso a LEE HARVEY OSWALD, pero de ahí le contestaron que el trámite duraría cuatro meses aproximadamente, lo que molestó al solicitante, porque según afirmó tenía suma prisa en obtener las visas que le permitieran viajar a Rusia, insistiendo en su derecho a ello por sus antecedentes y su partidarismo y actividades personales en pro del Movimiento Cubano, sin que pueda precisar por no recordarlo la declarante, si le dijo o no, que fuera miembro del Partido Comunista, y que su esposa ya mencionada de nacionalidad rusa estaba en ese entonces en la ciudad de Nueva York, de donde lo seguiría, siendo su procedencia de la citada ciudad de Nueva Orleans; que una vez que OSWALD entendió que no era posible darle la visa Cubana, sin obtener previamente la Rusa, porque aquella era en tránsito, se exhaltó o enojó mucho, por lo que la dicente llamó al Cónsul ASCUE, quien en ese momento se encontraba en su privado en compañía de su posterior sustituto MIRAVAL, saliendo el primero, comenzó a alegar en inglés con OSWALD, en forma muy alterada, terminando por decirle ASCUE, que "de ser por él no le daría la visa", y que "un individuo como él en vez de beneficiar a la Revolución Cubana, le causaba daño", en la inteligencia de que en su discusión se referían a la Revolución Socialista Rusa y no a la Cubana, aduciendo OSWALD que tenía dos razones para solicitar con toda premura la visa y que eran, una, que se le vencía su permiso de estancia en México y otra, que con toda urgencia necesitaba llegar a Rusia; que a pesar del disgusto, la de la voz le entregó a OSWALD un papel igual al que en este momento manuscribe en el que le anotó su nombre "SILVIA DURAN." y el número del teléfono del Consulado que es el "11-28-47", y de todas maneras se le dió trámite a la solicitud de visa,

enviándola

4

enviándola al Ministerio de Relaciones de Cuba, de donde se obtuvo respuesta en forma ordinaria, de quince a treinta días después, aceptando la concesión de la visa, pero condicionándola a que previamente obtuviera la Rusa, aunque no recuerda si OSWALD con posterioridad llamó o no a la declarante al Teléfono del Consulado que le proporcionó; que toda la plática que sostuvo la dicente con OSWALD, al igual que la del Cónsul ASCUE, fue en idioma inglés, ya que aquel no habla nada de español, y que al tener a la vista su fotografía que apareció en los periódicos de hoy, precisamente en el Periódico "El Día", desde luego lo reconoció e identificó como el mismo al que se ha venido refiriendo como LEE HARVEY OSWALD."

Oswald canceló su habitación en el Hotel del Comercio el día lo. de octubre y reservó un asiento en la empresa de autobuses "Transportes Frontera", de segunda clase, para hacer el viaje de regreso a Nuevo Laredo el día siguiente.

Sin embargo, aparentemente no utilizó esa reservación y sin que haya podido establecerse la forma como viajó a Nuevo Laredo, aparece en dicha población fronteriza el 3 de octubre y atraviesa la frontera regresando a territorio norteamericano.

De las investigaciones realizadas por las autoridades mexicanas quedó establecido, por otra parte, que Oswald no hizo contacto dentro de la República Mexicana con persona o grupo alguno afiliado a tendencias políticas de ninguna naturaleza.

México, D. F., a 14 de mayo de 1964. 19

DEPARTMENT OF STATE
DIVISION OF LANGUAGE SERVICES

(TRANSLATION)

LS NO. 15638
T-39/T-90/R-XVII
Spanish

[Embossed seal of the Mexican Department of Foreign Relations]

504826

The Department of Foreign Relations presents its compliments to the Embassy of the United States of America and has the honor to refer to its note No. 1349, dated April 10 last, in which it states that it would be helpful to the Government of the United States of America to have information on the investigation made by the competent Mexican agencies regarding the activities of Lee Harvey Oswald, the alleged murderer of President John F. Kennedy, while he was in Mexico in September 1963.

The Embassy also stated in the note in question that it would be of interest to have a description of the measures which the Mexican Government took immediately after it received news of the attempt on the life of President Kennedy, as for example the establishment of special surveillance at the border ports, or other similar measures.

In compliance with the wishes of the Embassy, the Department is happy to send herewith a confidential memorandum containing the information requested on the two points mentioned above.

Embassy of the United States of America,
City.

- 2 -

In accordance with the offer made by the Embassy in the last paragraph of its note, the Department understands that the enclosed confidential memorandum will not be published, either partially or in full, without the consent of the Government of Mexico.

The Department of Foreign Relations avails itself of the opportunity to renew to the Embassy of the United States of America the assurance of its highest consideration.

Mexico City, May 14, 1964

[Initialed]

COMMISSION EXHIBIT No. 2120—Continued

[Embossed seal of the Mexican Department of Foreign Relations]

MEMORANDUM

As soon as the Government of Mexico received news of the attempt on the life of President John F. Kennedy, which took place in the city of Dallas, Texas, on November 22, 1963, it took certain measures through the Department of the Interior to prevent the assassin of the great man from being able to seek refuge in Mexican territory.

The border between Mexico and the United States of America was immediately ordered closed at 3:00 p.m. on that same day and, despite the problems created by this measure, it was kept in effect until it became known that the alleged assassin had been arrested by the Dallas police.

Likewise, the Department of National Defense, in cooperation with the Department of the Interior, sent troops in order to tighten the surveillance in the border area, especially at Reynosa, Ciudad Miguel Alemán, Nuevo Laredo, and Matamoros.

When the name and personal description of the alleged assassin, Lee Harvey Oswald, became known, an investigation was initiated which led to the discovery that the said individual had been in Mexico in 1963. Indeed, it was established with certainty that Oswald entered the Mexican Republic by way of Nuevo Laredo, Tamaulipas, on September 26, 1963, with a tourist card having a fifteen-day limit, which had been issued to him by the Mexican Consulate in New Orleans on the 17th day of the same month and year.

The following day, that is on September 27, Oswald took room Number 18 at the Hotel del Comercio located at No. 19, calle de Fray Bernardino de Sahagún, Mexico City.

COMMISSION EXHIBIT No. 2120—Continued

During his five-day stay in the Mexican capital Oswald made every effort to obtain a visa from the Consulate of the Republic of Cuba to travel to Habana in transit to the Soviet Union. His efforts proved fruitless since the Cuban Consulate would not issue the visa unless the Soviet Embassy first granted the necessary permission so that he could go to Moscow.

In this connection, the pertinent section of a statement made on November 23, 1964 by Mrs. Silvia Tirado Durán, an employee of the Cuban Consulate in this capital, before the Mexican investigating authorities, is transcribed below:

"Around noon, the time she usually left, a friend told her that she had just heard a news flash on the radio that President Kennedy had been the victim of an attempted assassination in which three shots had been fired at him. Accordingly, she telephoned her husband and they discussed the report. He told her that he had already heard about it. He called the attack 'monstrous,' and they agreed that they would discuss the matter later when they reached home, which they did at the dinner hour, but only briefly, since they did not know the details of the attack and the name and description of the alleged perpetrator of the crime. It was only in the evening that they read the report on the occurrence in an 'extra' and when later, on the radio at home, the declarant heard the announcer mention the name of Lee Harvey Oswald, she remembered this was the name of an American who had come to the Cuban Consulate to obtain a visa to travel to Cuba

in transit to Russia, the latter part of September or the early part of October of this year, and in support of his application had shown his passport, in which it was noted that he had lived in that country for a period of three years; his labor card from the same country written in the Russian language; and letters in that same language. He had presented evidence that he was married to a Russian woman, and also that he was apparently the leader of an organization in the city of New Orleans called 'Fair Treatment for Cuba,' claiming that he should be accepted as a 'friend' of the Cuban Revolution. Accordingly, the declarant, complying with her duties, took down all of the information and completed the appropriate application form; and the declarant, admittedly exceeding her responsibilities, informally telephoned the Russian Consulate, with the intention of doing what she could to facilitate issuance of the Russian visa to Lee Harvey Oswald. However, they told her that there would be a delay of about four months in processing the case, which annoyed the applicant since, according to his statement, he was in a great hurry to obtain visas that would enable him to travel to Russia, insisting on his right to do so in view of his background and his loyalty and his activities in behalf of the Cuban Movement. The declarant was unable to recall accurately whether or not the applicant told her he was a member of the Communist Party, but he did say that his wife, mentioned above, who was of Russian nationality was then in New York City, and would follow him, having come from the city of New Orleans.

[The affiant stated] that when Oswald understood that it was not possible to give him a Cuban visa without his first having obtained the Russian visa, since the Cuban visa would be a transit visa, he became very excited or angry, and accordingly, the affiant called Consul Ascue, who was then in his private office with his subsequent replacement, Miraval, and the former came out and began a heated discussion in English with Oswald, that concluded by Ascue telling him [Oswald] that 'if it were up to him, he would not give him the visa,' and 'a person of his type was harming the Cuban Revolution rather than helping it,' it being understood that in their conversation they were talking about the Russian Socialist Revolution and not the Cuban. Oswald maintained that he had two reasons for requesting that his visa be issued promptly, and they were: one, that his tourist permit in Mexico was about to expire; and the other, that he had to get to Russia as quickly as possible. Despite her annoyance, the declarant gave Oswald a paper identical to the one she is now signing in which she put down her name, 'Silvia Durán,' and the number of the telephone at the Consulate, which is '11-28-47' and the visa application was processed anyway. It was sent to the Ministry of [Foreign] Relations of Cuba, from which a routine reply was received some fifteen to thirty days later, approving the visa, but on the condition that the Russian visa be obtained first, although she does not recall whether or not Oswald later telephoned her at the Consulate number that she gave him.

She stated that all of the conversation she had with Oswald, as well as that with Consul Ascue, was in the English language since Oswald did not speak any Spanish, and when she saw the photograph that came out in the newspapers today, to be specific, in the newspaper El Día, she immediately recognized and identified him as the same person to whom she had been referring as Lee Harvey Oswald."

Oswald checked out of his room at the Hotel del Comercio on the first of October and reserved a second-class bus seat on the "Transportes Frontera," for the return trip to Nuevo Laredo the next day.

However, he apparently did not use that reservation; and although it has not been possible to ascertain by what means he traveled to Nuevo Laredo, he appeared in that town on October 3, and crossed the border, returning to American territory.

From the investigation conducted by the Mexican authorities, it was established, however, that, while in the Mexican Republic, Oswald did not get in touch with any person or group affiliated with any political movement of any kind.

México, D.F., May 14, 1964

[Initialed]

UNITED STATES DEPARTMENT OF JUSTICE
FEDERAL BUREAU OF INVESTIGATION

In Reply, Please Refer to
File No.

WASHINGTON, D.C. 20535

May 18, 1964

LEE HARVEY OSWALD

COMMISSION EXHIBIT No. 2121

I. INTRODUCTION

That portion of the information recorded herein relating to inquiries in Mexico was furnished by confidential sources abroad who, subsequent to the assassination of President John F. Kennedy, were requested to conduct investigation designed to develop all aspects of the activity of Lee Harvey Oswald in Mexico.

II. TRAVEL TO MEXICO BY LEE HARVEY OSWALD (September 26-27, 1963)

(A) OSWALD's Application for United States Passport, June 24, 1963

United States State Department records disclose that on June 24, 1963, OSWALD applied for a United States passport at New Orleans, Louisiana, stating that he intended to depart from New Orleans during the period from October to December, 1963, for proposed travel as a tourist of three months' to a year's duration to England, France, Germany, Holland, Russia, Finland, Italy and Portugal. He was issued United States Passport No. DO 92526 at New Orleans on June 25, 1963.

This passport was valid for three years for travel to all countries except Albania, Cuba and those portions of China, Korea and Vietnam under communist control.

This passport was found among OSWALD's effects following his arrest at Dallas, Texas, on November 22, 1963.

(B) OSWALD's Mexican Tourist Visa

On November 23, 1963, T-1, a confidential source abroad, advised that the official records of the Mexican Government reflected that one LEE, HARVEY OSWALD had entered

COMMISSION EXHIBIT No. 2121—Continued

Mexico on September 26, 1963, at Nuevo Laredo, Tamaulipas, and had departed Mexico at the same place on October 3, 1963.

On November 24, 1963, source made available a copy of the Mexican form FM-8 (tourist card) used for the entry of this person into Mexico. The FM-8 is reproduced on the following page.

The FM-8 bears No. 24085 and was issued on September 17, 1963, by the Mexican Consulate General in New Orleans, Louisiana. As noted above, it was issued in the name of LEE, HARVEY OSWALD. It would appear that the comma was placed on the card in error inasmuch as the signature appearing on the original and duplicate portions of the FM-8 is LEE H. OSWALD. OSWALD listed his profession as "photographer," stated that he was 23 years of age and married, and presented a birth certificate as proof of his citizenship. The FM-8 was valid for a single journey to Mexico for a period of fifteen days.

According to the rubber-stamp impression appearing on both the original and the duplicate copy of the FM-8, OSWALD was admitted at Nuevo Laredo on September 26, 1963, by Mexican Immigration Service employee HELIO TUEXI MAYDON. A rubber-stamp impression on the original of the FM-8 indicated that he departed Mexico at Nuevo Laredo on October 3, 1963, his departure having been handled by Mexican Immigration Service employee ALBERTO ARZAMENDI CHAPA.

By way of general information, T-1 has stated that Mexican tourist cards are issued in duplicate. The duplicate copy of the card is picked up at the time of entry into Mexico of the bearer of the card. The latter retains the original of the card until departure from Mexico, at which time the original is picked up at the port of departure. Both the original and the duplicate copies of the card are date-stamped at the port of entry and, in addition, the original is date-stamped at the port of departure.

- 2 -

COMMISSION EXHIBIT No. 2121—Continued

F.M.-8

ESTADOS UNIDOS MEXICANOS
SECRETARIA DE GOBERNACION

ORIGINAL Nº 24085

VALIDA POR 15 DIAS

BUENA PARA UN SOLO VIAJE POR ... DIAS

Apellidos y nombre LEE, HARVEY OSWALD

FOTOGRAFO

Sexo H [X] M [ ] Edad 23 AÑOS Estado Civil S [ ] C [X]

Documento con el que acredita su nacionalidad: ACTA NACIMIENTO

Menores que lo acompañan:

Destino MEXICO, D. F.

NUEVA ORLEANS, LA., EUA., 17 SEPTIEMBRE DE 1963.

Lugar y fecha

ENTRADA
SET 26 1963
Sello fechador
NUEVO LAREDO, TAMPS.

SALIDA
ALBERTO ARZAMENDI CHAPA
Nuevo Laredo, Tamps
OCT. 1963

Reproduced above is the original portion of the Mexican FM-8 with which LEE HARVEY OSWALD entered Mexico on September 26, 1963, and departed therefrom on October 3, 1963. Although he is known to have traveled by bus from Nuevo Laredo to Mexico City, his mode of travel is not recorded on the FM-8, which was retrieved and cancelled by ALBERTO ARZAMENDI CHAPA at the time of his departure. No space is provided on the card for recording means of travel upon departure, and no such information appears on the above card. The back of the FM-8 contains no information other than printed instructions and warnings to the traveler in Spanish, English and French.

- 3 -

COMMISSION EXHIBIT No. 2121—Continued

On November 27, 1963, Father ANTONIO MORENO, Sacred Heart Catholic Church, 215 North 16th Street, Edinburg, Texas, advised in Edinburg, Texas, that Father RICHARD LAWRENCE PHILION, who formerly resided at this address, obtained a Mexican tourist card on about September 17, 1963, with which to enter Mexico. He added that Father RICHARD LAWRENCE PHILION is now assigned to the Santa Maria Magdalena Church in Tequixistlan, Oaxaca, Mexico, and that his mailing address is Apartado Postal No. 93, Salina Cruz, Oaxaca, Mexico.

T-2, a confidential source abroad, advised that Father PHILION stated at Salina Cruz, Oaxaca, Mexico, on December 13, 1963, that he had obtained his Mexican tourist card, form FM-5 No. 4373765, at the Mexican Consulate in New Orleans, Louisiana, on September 17, 1963.

Father PHILION examined various photographs of OSWALD, and he could not recall any person of OSWALD's description being present at the Mexican Consulate in New Orleans when he obtained his Mexican tourist card.

Father PHILION advised that it was his best recollection that he was in the Mexican Consulate in New Orleans at about 1:30 p.m. on September 17, 1963, and that he arrived shortly before the Mexican Consulate was scheduled to close. He recalled that his tourist card was the last one issued on the day of September 17, 1963, and that one man and a woman were present at the Mexican Consulate when he was securing his tourist card. He did not recall any individual resembling OSWALD while he was at the Mexican Consulate in New Orleans.

(C) Results of FBI Laboratory Examination of OSWALD's Tourist Card

Mexican tourist card, FM-8 No. 24085, issued on September 17, 1963, by the Mexican Consulate General in New Orleans, Louisiana, was forwarded to the FBI Laboratory, Washington, D. C., for examination, and on December 6, 1963, the FBI Laboratory concluded the following, after examination of the tourist card issued to OSWALD:

"It was concluded that handwritten OSWALD signatures on the two portions of the tourist card, FM-8 No. 24085, issued to OSWALD by the Mexican Consulate General at New Orleans, Louisiana, on September 17, 1963, were written by LEE HARVEY OSWALD.

"No latent fingerprint impressions of value were developed on OSWALD's Mexican tourist card."

(D) Closing of United States-Mexican Border

Immediately upon receipt of information of the assassination of President KENNEDY, the Mexican Government closed all border traffic between the United States and Mexico for the specific purpose of forestalling the escape of the assassin.

The Mexican border was reopened following the apprehension of OSWALD.

(E) Mexican Newspaper, "Excelsior," November 25, 1963, Issue re: OSWALD's Trip to Mexico

On November 25, 1963, Mexican newspaper "Excelsior" published at Mexico, D. F., Mexico (Federal District of Mexico which encompasses Mexico City), contained on page 1-A an article in the Spanish language, a translation of which is as follows:

"THE APPARENT ASSASSIN OF KENNEDY SOLICITED VISAS HERE (MEXICO, D. F., MEXICO) IN ORDER TO GO TO MOSCOW VIA HAVANA.

"LEE HARVEY OSWALD, alleged murderer of President KENNEDY and who was assassinated by JACK RUBINSTEIN, entered Mexico on September 26, last, with a tourist card which our Consul in New Orleans issued him on the seventeenth of the same month, with his birth certificate, which he presented, accrediting him as an American citizen.

"Excelsior has confirmed that on September 26, 1963, he crossed the border at Nuevo Laredo, Tamaulipas, and the following day arrived at this capital by vehicle highway.

"According to inquiries made, on the same September 27, OSWALD went to the Consul General of Cuba in Mexico in order to obtain a transit visa because he was thinking of traveling to Moscow via Havana.

"The Consul, EUSEBIO AZCUE, indicated to him that in order to issue him the visa which he was soliciting, he had to consult directly with his own government. The operation, therefore, would require from ten to twelve days.

"LEE HARVEY OSWALD, because of his irritable temperament, had an argument with Consul AZCUE and departed from his office giving a hard slam to the door as he left.

"The following day, or on the 28th of September, OSWALD interviewed the Consul General of the Soviet Union, accredited in Mexico, in order to solicit his corresponding visa for entry into the USSR.

"He supported his petition with the fact that his wife was a Soviet citizen; that he was a militant communist; and that he had lived for three years in Russia.

"OSWALD told the Consul of the Soviet Union in Mexico that they could easily verify his words by communicating telephonically with his wife, who could be found lodging in a hotel in New Orleans.

"Following the normal procedure carried out in these cases, the Soviet Consul indicated to him that he would first have to consult with his own government and that the lapse of time for obtaining an answer was from three to four months.

"The apparent murderer of President KENNEDY again became angry and repeated the scene which he had made the day before at the Cuban Embassy, arguing with the Soviet Consul, and departing highly disgusted from his office.

"OSWALD returned to Texas on the third day of October through the border at Nuevo Laredo, Tamaulipas.

"The inquiries which have been made to the present in Mexico apparently indicate that LEE HARVEY OSWALD had no interviews with highly placed officials at the Soviet Embassy or at the Cuban Embassy accredited to our government."

(F) Checks Made on Compania de Aviacion Passenger Manifests for September 26-27, 1963

T-3, a confidential source abroad, advised that on November 25, 1963, FERNANDO FARIAS, Assistant Sales Manager for Compania Mexicana de Aviacion (CMA), Balderas 36, Mexico, D. F., stated that he had caused a careful check to be made of all CMA passenger manifests for CMA flights between Nuevo Laredo, Tamaulipas, Mexico, and Mexico, D. F., and for all CMA flights between Monterrey, Nuevo Leon, Mexico, and Mexico, D. F., for September 26 and 27, 1963.

FERNANDO FARIAS stated that there were no passengers listed on these manifests using the name LEE HARVEY OSWALD or any name variation thereof.

(G) Check at OSWALD's Port of Entry into Mexico

On November 25, 1963, HELIO TUEXI MAYDON, Mexican Immigration Service employee, advised at Nuevo Laredo, Mexico, that OSWALD entered Mexico at Nuevo Laredo on September 26, 1963, using a fifteen-day tourist card issued September 17, 1963, by the Mexican Consulate General at New Orleans, Louisiana.

TUEXI MAYDON had no independent recollection of OSWALD but considered that OSWALD may have been in the company of a young American couple.

An exhaustive search was made of Mexican Immigration records at Nuevo Laredo, which disclosed that there was only one young American couple whose entry into Mexico may have coincided with that of OSWALD. This couple was named BILL and ELAINE ALLEN of Miami, Florida.

On November 27, 1963, TUEXI MAYDON advised that no information had been developed regarding the exact time or specific mode of travel of OSWALD at the time he entered Mexico. He stated that OSWALD's entry into Mexico on September 26, 1963, took place between 6:00 a.m. and 2:00 p.m. as he had handled OSWALD's entry and he worked this shift at the border port of entry at Nuevo Laredo. He added that OSWALD's departure from Mexico was at Nuevo Laredo, Mexico, on October 3, 1963, between 12:01 a.m. and 8:00 a.m. and that this shift was supervised by ALBERTO ARZAMENDI CHAPA, Mexican Immigration Service employee.

On November 27, 1963, MARIO DEL VALLE PLATA, Mexican Immigration Service employee, Nuevo Laredo, Mexico, advised that no Mexican Immigration Service employee who was on duty at Nuevo Laredo when OSWALD entered or departed from Mexico had any independent recollection of OSWALD by photograph or otherwise with regard to his entry or departure from Mexico.

(H) Check of Flecha Roja (Red Arrow) Baggage List for Passengers for September 26, 1963, Trip <u>from Nuevo Laredo to Mexico, D. F.</u>

The baggage list for passengers for September 26, 1963, of the Mexican bus line Flecha Roja (Red Arrow) for the bus which left Nuevo Laredo, Tamaulipas, Mexico, at 2:00 p.m. on this same date, reflects that there was a total of 18 pieces of baggage. The baggage list reflects the following:

1. PABLO VASQUEZ
2. Second piece of luggage attributed to PABLO VASQUEZ
3. S. MOROU
4. ALFREDO BRISENO
5. ROIG SORQUIS
6. T. GONZALEZ
7. ANDRES MORALES
8. Second piece of luggage attributed to ANDRES MORALES
9. Gpe. MARTINEZ (possibly GUADALUPE or Capt. MARTINEZ)
10. (FNU) BOWEN
11. HARRY J. MITCHELL
12. Second piece of luggage attributed to HARRY J. MITCHELL
13. Third piece of luggage attributed to HARRY J. MITCHELL
14. LEE H. OSWALJ
15. (FNU) BOWEN (believed identical with JOHN H. BOWEN)
16. Second piece of luggage attributed to BOWEN
17. JOHN McFARLAND
18. Second piece of luggage attributed to JOHN McFARLAND

The driver of this bus was listed as ROBERTO MORALES.

The baggage list has the number "18" at the bottom, which, according to the Mexico City terminal manager of Flecha Roja, signifies that 18 pieces of luggage had been checked and ticketed on that bus.

T-4, a confidential source abroad advised on December 16, 1963, that ROBERTO MORALES, driver of the Flecha Roja bus No. 516 on September 26, 1963, could not recall the passengers on the trip of September 26, 1963, because so much time had elapsed; and since he makes two round trips between Nuevo Laredo and Mexico, D. F., each week, he could not recall any information regarding OSWALD or any other passengers who were on the bus.

JOHN H. BOWEN was identified from Mexican Immigration records as 60 years of age, born Houston, Texas, a United States citizen, residence Houston, Texas. Mexican tourist card was issued to him at Nuevo Laredo, Mexico, on September 26, 1963, upon presentation of his birth certificate.

HARRY J. MITCHELL was identified as 41 years of age, a United States citizen, a lawyer, residence Palmyra, Missouri. Mexican tourist card was issued to him at Nuevo Laredo on September 26, 1963.

ANNIE MARIE MITCHELL was identified as apparently being the wife of HARRY J. MITCHELL, above, 22 years of age, a United States citizen, residence same as husband, above.

Dr. JOHN BRYAN McFARLAND and his wife, Mrs. ANNA MERYLE REID McFARLAND, 10 Fulwood Park, Liverpool, England, were interviewed in England and advised they were on the Flecha Roja bus from Nuevo Laredo, Tamaulipas, Mexico, to Mexico, D. F., September 26-27, 1963. They stated that they observed the following during this trip:

> OSWALD was on this bus trip traveling alone and he sat next to an 80-year-old man, described as a United States citizen, who appeared to be 60 years of age and who resides in Cuernavaca, State of Morelos, Mexico, and in the State of Tennessee in the United States. This individual was identified further as a school teacher who taught in India and Arabia and currently was writing a book on the Lisbon, Portugal, earthquake of 1775.

- 10 -

COMMISSION EXHIBIT No. 2121—Continued

During this trip, OSWALD spoke to two Australian girls in their mid-twenties who boarded this bus in Monterrey, State of Nuevo Leon, Mexico, and these two girls got off at Mexico, D. F., Mexico.

OSWALD left the bus alone at Mexico, D. F.

With regard to the first individual described by the McFARLANDs, JOHN HOWARD BOWEN, listed above with tourist card FM-5 No. 4329926, was considered possibly to be the elderly United States citizen who sat next to OSWALD, and he could be contacted in care of Calle Carranza No. 4-A, San Martin de Texmelucan, State of Puebla, Mexico. Extensive investigation to locate JOHN HOWARD BOWEN was made, and the results are set forth hereinafter.

With regard to the two Australian girls in their mid-twenties, these girls were considered identical with PATRICIA CLARE ROSHLEIGH WINSTON, 22 years of age, Australian citizen, native of Fiji Islands, bearer of Mexican tourist card FM-5 No. 4225835, issued August 24, 1963, by the Mexican Consulate in New York, New York, home address listed as 222 West 23rd Street, New York, New York, and PAMELA LILLIAN MUMFORD, 21 years of age, English citizen, born Fiji Islands, bearer of Mexican tourist card FM-5 No. 4225836, issued the same date and place as that of WINSTON. According to Mexican Immigration records, WINSTON and MUMFORD entered Mexico at Nuevo Laredo on September 25, 1963, one day before OSWALD entered Mexico.

PATRICIA WINSTON and PAMELA MUMFORD advised the following on December 17, 1963, when interviewed in the United States:

> WINSTON and MUMFORD boarded a bus at Monterrey, State of Nuevo Leon, Mexico, on September 26, 1963, at 7:30 p.m., en route to Mexico, D. F. Both identified OSWALD as a passenger on this bus and both observed him sitting next to an Englishman who had lived in Mexico for thirty years. This latter individual was described as being in his late sixties, heavy build, gray hair - balding, with a distinctive English accent, and both believed him to be retired from business.

- 11 -

COMMISSION EXHIBIT No. 2121—Continued

WINSTON and MUMFORD recalled that OSWALD introduced himself and exhibited to them his United States passport. OSWALD advised WINSTON and MUMFORD that he had lived in Russia for two years and that he had had a hard time getting out of Russia. OSWALD stated that he had been in Japan.

OSWALD made no comment concerning communism or Cuba. He did not state why he was traveling to Mexico, where he was going, and he did not advise concerning his occupation or future plans.

OSWALD stated that he was from Fort Worth or Dallas, Texas. He was observed to be traveling alone. He had only one piece of luggage and a small zipper bag. He wore a gold wedding ring.

OSWALD recommended that WINSTON and MUMFORD stay at the Hotel Cuba, Mexico, D. F., where he claimed that he had stayed several times before. He pointed out that this hotel was inexpensive but that he was not staying at the Hotel Cuba on this trip.

WINSTON and MUMFORD recalled an English couple aboard the bus. This couple is considered identical with Dr. JOHN BRYAN McFARLAND and his wife, Mrs. ANNA MERYLE REID McFARLAND, mentioned above.

JOHN HOWARD BOWEN, who has been known as Reverend ALBERT OSBORNE and has resided at Calle Emilio Carranza No. 4-A, San Martin de Texmelucan, State of Puebla, Mexico, and 4114 Drummond Street, Montreal, Canada, was determined to be the holder of Canadian Passport No. 5-605377. T-2 advised on January 7, 1964, that BOWEN, while posing as Reverend ALBERT OSBORNE, stated in Mexico that he was acquainted with Reverend JOHN HOWARD BOWEN and furnished misleading information concerning the alleged whereabouts of BOWEN.

On January 28, 1964, T-5, a confidential source who has furnished reliable information in the past, advised the records at the Mexican Ministry of Gobernacion (Ministry of the Interior) reflect that ALBERT OSBORNE was ordered deported from Mexico on April 5, 1958, through Laredo, Texas. OSBORNE had been charged with selling an automobile in the Oaxaca, Mexico, area without paying the import duties. These records reflect also that, in 1958, OSBORNE was known as JOHN HOWARD BOWEN and was located in Mexico and determined to be without proper Mexican immigration papers.

On January 30, 1964, T-6, a confidential source abroad, advised that inasmuch as ALBERT OSBORNE had been illegally in Mexico, he would be detained for deportation if located in Mexico.

BOWEN was interviewed at Florence, Alabama, on February 8, 1964, and advised that he recalled making a bus trip from Nuevo Laredo, Mexico, to Mexico, D. F., on September 26-27, 1963, and sitting next to a young man whom he described as 29 years of age, 5 feet 8 inches tall, 150 pounds in weight, with thin, blond hair and a dark complexion, who appeared to be of Mexican or Puerto Rican descent. This individual went to sleep soon after boarding the bus, and, after a lunch stop at Sabinas Hidalgo, Mexico, this person moved to the back of the bus where he reclined on a seat and went to sleep. BOWEN claimed that he did not talk to the above person and was unable to identify press photographs of OSWALD.

BOWEN stated that he is acquainted with an ALBERT OSBORNE, described as a Baptist preacher or missionary from Canada, and while in Oaxaca, Mexico, in 1958, BOWEN misplaced his identification papers and during a census taken at Oaxaca he borrowed OSBORNE's identification papers. BOWEN claimed that he had never before or afterward used the name of OSBORNE.

Interviewed further at Nashville, Tennessee, on March 3, 1964, OSBORNE admitted that he had used dual identities as OSBORNE and JOHN H. BOWEN for many years in Mexico and the United States. He continued to deny any knowledge of OSWALD, however.

(I) List Obtained of Entry of All Non-Mexican Citizens on September 26, 1963, at Nuevo Laredo, Tamaulipas, Mexico

T-1, who is thoroughly familiar with the workings of the Mexican Ministry of Gobernacion (Interior), furnished the following information concerning the procedures utilized by the Mexican Immigration Service in connection with the entry and departure of non-Mexican citizens into and out of Mexico. It is to be noted that the Mexican Immigration Service is a part of the Mexican Ministry of Gobernacion.

Tourists usually enter Mexico on a Mexican tourist card. There are two types of such cards, one being called the FM-8, which is valid for a stay in the country of only 15 days, and one designated as FM-5, which has validity for a 180 days' stay in Mexico. Both types are issued at Mexican Consulates throughout the world and can also be obtained from the Mexican Immigration Service at border ports of entry. FM-8 tourist cards also are available at airlines ticket offices and tourist agencies.

At the time of entry into Mexico, the traveler surrenders the duplicate portion of the tourist card, and both the duplicate and the original, which remains in the possession of the traveler, are stamped with a rubber stamp which shows the name of the Mexican representative handling the entry, the date of the entry and the locality of the port of entry. When the traveler leaves Mexico, he surrenders the original portion of the tourist card and it is stamped with a rubber stamp which carries the name of the Mexican representative, the date of the departure and the locality of the port of departure.

Each Mexican port of entry is required on a continuing basis to prepare a form called form FM-11. The FM-11 for both entries and departures is prepared each "quincena" (fifteen-day period). Entries and departures are set up on the FM-11 in chronological order and thereafter, within each date, the names of the tourists are listed in alphabetical order. Basic information appearing on the FM-11 is taken from the tourist card presented by the traveler. At the time the FM-11 is prepared, a number is placed on the tourist card, these

numbers being in sequence according to the alphabetical order of the names within each date and thereafter by date. By way of example, the first traveler in alphabetical order entering at a port of entry on the first day of the month or a "quincena" is assigned number 1. Thereafter, all travelers entering that port on that date are assigned numbers in sequence, according to alphabetical order. This sequence continues on the second day of the month and throughout the remaining 15 days of the "quincena."

T-1 made available for examination the forms FM-5 and FM-8 for all non-Mexican citizens entering Mexico at Nuevo Laredo as tourists on September 26, 1963, as well as the copies of forms FM-11 containing the recapitulation of the entries to Mexico at Nuevo Laredo on this date.

From the tourist cards (FM-5 and FM-8) and the copies of the forms FM-11, the following summary of information concerning each person who entered Mexico at Nuevo Laredo on September 26, 1963, has been obtained. The summaries have been divided into those persons traveling on form FM-5 and those traveling on form FM-8, since the forms FM-11 are so set up. The number appearing before each name is the number which appears on form FM-11. The following is a brief resume regarding each person who entered Mexico on September 26, 1963. Information was available regarding the mode of transportation on entry, a brief description of the person, the residence listed, proof of citizenship was shown and the Mexican Immigration Service employee who handled the entry, and this information was set out in detail in memorandum dated March 16, 1964.

368. MARGARITA ALANIS, FM-5 No. 4329957, issued by Mexican Immigration Office, Nuevo Laredo, September 26, 1963.

369. JOSE R. ALFARO, FM-5 No. 4496450, issued by Mexican Consulate, Dallas, Texas, September 19, 1963.

370. NORBERTA AVILA, FM-5 No. 4329958, issued by Mexican Immigration Office, Nuevo Laredo, September 26, 1963.

371. WINFRED BARNES, FM-5 No. 4516631, issued by Pan American Airways, Miami, Florida, September 5, 1963.

372. JOHN H. BOWEN, FM-5 No. 4329926, issued by Mexican Immigration Office, Nuevo Laredo, September 26, 1963.

373. SARA MARQUELA YANIS DE CHAMPSAUR, FM-5 No. 4212610, issued by Mexican Embassy, Panama, Republic of Panama, August 14, 1963.

374. MARJORIE FERN CHARLES, FM-5 No. 4234731, issued by Mexican Consulate, Kansas City, Missouri, September 19, 1963.

375. ANDREW WEBSTER CHRISTOPHER, FM-5 No. 4052670, issued by Mexican Consulate, Laredo, Texas, September 25, 1963.

376. SAMUEL ESTRADA, FM-5 No. 4329955, issued by Mexican Immigration Service, Nuevo Laredo, September 26, 1963.

377. BENNIE H. FABER, FM-5 No. 4329980, issued by Mexican Immigration Service, Nuevo Laredo, September 26, 1963.

378. OSCAR ENRIQUE GALLARDO, FM-5 No. 4363772, issued by Mexican Consulate General, New Orleans, Louisiana, September 9 (possibly 19), 1963.

379. ELSIE GIBBS, FM-5 No. 4329708, issued by Mexican Immigration Service, Nuevo Laredo, September 26, 1963.

380. LUISA MAGUER, FM-5 No. 4158246, issued by Mexican Consulate General, San Antonio, Texas, September 24, 1963.

381. Miss J. M. HENDRICKSE, FM-5 No. 4359974, issued by Mexican Consulate, Toronto, Canada, August 19, 1963.

382. MARIA CONSUELO MATA GONZALEZ, FM-5 No. 4329707, issued by Mexican Immigration Office, Nuevo Laredo, September 26, 1963.

383. JOHN BRYAN McFARLAND, FM-5 No. 4363754, issued by Mexican Consulate General, New Orleans, Louisiana, September 14, 1963.

384. ANNA MERYL REID McFARLAND, FM-5 No. 4363755, issued by Mexican Consulate General, New Orleans, Louisiana, September 14, 1963.

385. MICHAEL A. NOVOA, FM-5 No. 4351992, issued by Honorary Mexican Consulate, Newark, New Jersey, September 18, 1963.

386. TOMAS JERIEL OWENS, FM-5 No. 4329625, issued by Mexican Immigration Office, Nuevo Laredo, September 26, 1963.

387. JUANITA A. PEREZ, FM-5 No. 4496449, issued by Mexican Consulate, Dallas, Texas, September 19, 1963.

388. ANIBAL PLEITEZ, FM-5 No. 4363773, issued by Mexican Consulate General, New Orleans, Louisiana, September 9 (possibly 19), 1963.

389. JOSE HUMBERTO PLEITEZ, FM-5 No. 4363774, issued by Mexican Consulate General, New Orleans, Louisiana, September 19, 1963.

390. EMIL SAINZ, FM-5 No. 4455632, issued by Mexican Tourism Department, New York, New York, September 20, 1963.

391. TERESA CACCIATORE SAINZ, FM-5 No. 4455631, issued by Mexican Tourism Department, New York, New York, September 20, 1963.

392. MATTHEW SCHILLER, FM-5 No. 4329624, issued by Mexican Immigration Office, Nuevo Laredo, September 26, 1963.

393. RICHARD RALPH SCHWARZE, FM-5 No. 4381251, issued by Mexican Consulate, Detroit, Michigan, September 23, 1963.

394. CHESTER STANLEY STEMP, FM-5 No. 4449875, issued by Mexican Tourism Department, Houston, Texas, September 25, 1963.

395. TEODORO OSCAR TREVINO, FM-5 No. 4329956, issued by Mexican Immigration Office, Nuevo Laredo, September 26, 1963.

396. VIOLA MARIA YANIS DE VIGGIANO, FM-5 No. 4212612, issued by Consular Section of Mexican Embassy, Panama, Republic of Panama, August 14, 1963.

397. ANTONY S. WATNE, FM-5 No. 4484229, issued by Mexican Consulate, Phoenix, Arizona, September 23, 1963.

398. FLOR DE MARIA SUCRE DE YANIS, FM-5 No. 4212611, issued by Consular Section of Mexican Embassy, Panama, Republic of Panama, August 14, 1963.

399. TOBIAS ROZENZEW ZAREMBER, FM-5 No. 4052668, issued by Mexican Consulate, Laredo, Texas, September 25, 1963.

- 18 -

COMMISSION EXHIBIT No. 2121—Continued

762. FELIX ALONZO, FM-8 No. 626144, issued by Mexican Immigration Office, Nuevo Laredo, September 26, 1963.

763. APOLONIO ALVARES, FM-8 No. 626133, issued by Mexican Immigration Office, Nuevo Laredo, September 26, 1963.

764. CAMILA ALVARES, FM-8 No. 626134, issued by Mexican Immigration Office, Nuevo Laredo, September 26, 1963.

765. JUAN ALVARES, FM-8 No. 626135, issued by Mexican Immigration Office, Nuevo Laredo, September 26, 1963.

766. BERTHA AVILA, FM-8 No. 626242, issued by Mexican Immigration Office, Nuevo Laredo, September 26, 1963. AVILA's tourist card was cancelled at her request and was not utilized.

767. BERTHA AVILA, FM-8 No. 626242. It is noted that this listing carries identical information as set forth under No. 766. It appears that the two listings of this individual on the FM-11 were done in error since she apparently did not enter Mexico.

768. TED C. BLAND, FM-8 No. 624673, issued by Mexican Immigration Office, Nuevo Laredo, September 26, 1963.

769. STEPHEN ALAN BRILL, FM-8 No. 47905, issued by Miami Office of Mexican Tourism Department, August 13, 1963.

770. ELAINE ESTERMAN BRILL, FM-8 No. 47906, issued by the Miami Office of the Mexican Tourism Department, August 13, 1963.

771. HARVEY M. CAMPBELL, FM-8 No. 626139, issued, by Mexican Immigration Office, Nuevo Laredo, September 26, 1963.

- 19 -

COMMISSION EXHIBIT No. 2121—Continued

772. FRANK CANTERBURY, FM-8 No. 624669, issued by Mexican Immigration Office, Nuevo Laredo, September 26, 1963.

773. FERNANDO CARRILLO, FM-8 No. 626230, issued by Mexican Immigration Office, Nuevo Laredo, September 26, 1963.

774. R. ALECOR CAVAZOS (possibly ALECOR CAVAZOS R.), FM-8 No. 626140, issued by Mexican Immigration Office, Nuevo Laredo, September 26, 1963.

775. N. ARNALDO CAVAZOS (possibly ARNALDO CAVAZOS N.), FM-8 No. 626141, issued by Mexican Immigration Office, Nuevo Laredo, September 26, 1963.

776. TIM PRADO CHAPA, FM-8 No. 626365, issued by Mexican Immigration Office, Nuevo Laredo, September 26, 1963.

777. CHARLES DEWWEY, FM-8 No. 626231, issued by Mexican Immigration Office, Nuevo Laredo, September 26, 1963.

778. ROBERT V. DUBLIN, JR., FM-8 No. 133158, issued by Mexican Consulate, Laredo, Texas, September 26, 1963.

779. JOSE BENITO ESCOBAR, FM-8 No. 133155, issued by Mexican Consulate, Laredo, Texas, September 26, 1963.

780. OLIMPIA BENITEZ DE ESCOBAR, FM-8 No. 133154, issued by Mexican Consulate, Laredo, Texas, September 26, 1963.

781. REINA ESCOBAR, FM-8 No. 133153, issued by Mexican Consulate, Laredo, Texas, September 26, 1963.

782. JENNIFER JULIA FELLOWES, FM-8 No. 624676, issued by Mexican Immigration Office, Nuevo Laredo, September 26, 1963.

783. SUSANA SELINA FOSTER, FM-8 No. 624677, issued by Mexican Immigration Office, Nuevo Laredo, September 26, 1963.

784. LUCIANO G. GARCIA, FM-8 No. 626229, issued by Mexican Immigration Office, Nuevo Laredo, September 26, 1963.

785. AGAPITO GONZALEZ, FM-8 No. 626234, issued by Mexican Immigration Office, Nuevo Laredo, September 26, 1963.

786. ELVIRA GONZALEZ, FM-8 No. 626235, issued by Mexican Immigration Office, Nuevo Laredo, September 26, 1963.

787. ROBERTO GONZALEZ, FM-8 No. 626238, issued by Mexican Immigration Office, Nuevo Laredo, September 26, 1963.

788. DOLORES GUARDIOLA, FM-8 No. 626241, issued by Mexican Immigration Office, Nuevo Laredo, September 26, 1963.

789. H. ARTURO GUERRA, FM-8 No. 624668, issued by Mexican Immigration Office, Nuevo Laredo, September 26, 1963..

790. JODEYE (last three letters questionable) BRANS HANDS, FM-8 No. 626138, issued by Mexican Immigration Office, Nuevo Laredo, September 26, 1963. Instant individual appeared to sign her name as Mrs. JODENE HANDS.

791. ERNESTINE WHITE HANDS, FM-8 No. 626137, issued by Mexican Immigration Office, Nuevo Laredo, September 26, 1963.

792. NELLIE L. HARDIN, FM-8 No. 626364, issued by Mexican Immigration Office, Nuevo Laredo, September 26, 1963.

793. BRIAN JAQUES, FM-8 No. 330187, issued by Mexican Consulate, San Diego, California, September 18, 1963.

794. FRANK JIMENEZ, FM-8 No. 626233, issued by Mexican Immigration Office, Nuevo Laredo, September 26, 1963.

795. ABRAHAM KAPLAN, FM-8 No. 626226, issued by Mexican Immigration Office, Nuevo Laredo, September 26, 1963.

796. RENATE KRAMER, FM-8 No. 447251, bearing the stamp of Mexican Consulate General, San Francisco, California, but no date indicated. This form bears a typed date of September 26, 1963, apparently inserted upon bearer's arrival Nuevo Laredo.

797. DIETRICH KRAMER, FM-8 No. 447250, bearing stamp of Mexican Consulate General, San Francisco, California, but no date indicated. This form bears a typed date of September 26, 1963, apparently inserted upon bearer's arrival Nuevo Laredo.

798. EDITH W. KUNTZ, FM-8 No. 510259, issued at San Antonio, Texas (issuing office not identified), September 26, 1963.

799. FERNANDO LOZANO GARCIA, FM-8 No. 626132, issued by Mexican Immigration Office, Nuevo Laredo, September 26, 1963.

800. WILLIAM HENRY MASON, FM-8 No. 626232, issued by Mexican Immigration Office, Nuevo Laredo, September 26, 1963.

801. ANGELINA MA. GONZALEZ MENDEZ, FM-8 No. 626037, issued by Mexican Immigration Office, Nuevo Laredo, September 26, 1963.

802. HARRY J. MITCHELL, FM-8 No. 624674, issued by Mexican Immigration Office, Nuevo Laredo, September 26, 1963.

803. ANN MARIE MITCHELL, FM-8 No. 624675, issued by Mexican Immigration Office, Nuevo Laredo, September 26, 1963.

804. ADOLIO MORALES, FM-8 No. 626145, issued by Mexican Immigration Office, Nuevo Laredo, September 26, 1963.

805. MARTINA MORENO, FM-8 No. 626236, issued by Mexican Immigration Office, Nuevo Laredo, September 26, 1963.

806. BUELL MOORE, FM-8 No. 625566, issued by Mexican Immigration Office, Nuevo Laredo, September 26, 1963.

807. HARVEY OSWALD LEE, FM-8 No. 24085, issued by Mexican Consulate General, New Orleans, Louisiana, September 17, 1963.

808 MAURICE OUELLET, FM-8 No. 32060/196, issued by Mexican Consulate General, Montreal, Que., Canada, September 19, 1963.

809. KENNETH GRENIER PECK, FM-8 No. 625567, issued by Mexican Immigration Office, Nuevo Laredo, September 26, 1963.

810. YOLANDA A. DE RAMOS, FM-8 No. 623793, issued by Mexican Immigration Office, Nuevo Laredo, September 26, 1963.

811. ROESLY ROBERT, FM-8 No. 623924, issued by Mexican Immigration Office, Nuevo Laredo, September 26, 1963.

812. FLORENCE S. ROCLEVITCH, FM-8 No. 623795, issued by Mexican Immigration Office, Nuevo Laredo, September 26, 1963.

813. ANTHONY PAUL ROCLEVITCH, FM-8 No. 623794, issued by Mexican Immigration Office, Nuevo Laredo, September 26, 1963.

814. RAFAEL RUBEN RODRIGUEZ, FM-8 No. 625625, issued by Mexican Immigration Office, Nuevo Laredo, September 26, 1963.

815. ROBERTO GONZALO RODRIGUEZ ESPINOSA (carried on FM-11 as ROBERTO GONZALO ESPINOZA RODRIGUEZ), FM-8 No. 133156, issued by Mexican Consulate, Laredo, Texas, September 26, 1963.

816. JORGE ANTONIO RODRIGUEZ ESPINOSA, FM-8 No. 133157, issued by Mexican Consulate, Laredo, Texas, September 26, 1963.

817. JOSEFA RODRIGUEZ INMAN, FM-8 No. 626131, issued by Mexican Immigration Office, Nuevo Laredo, September 26, 1963.

818. MINO ROMERO CRUZ, FM-8 No. 626143, issued by Mexican Immigration Office, Nuevo Laredo, September 26, 1963.

819. RICARDO SANDOVAL, FM-8 No. 626363, issued by Mexican Immigration Office, Nuevo Laredo, September 26, 1963.

820. GEORGES ALBERT SPINNER, FM-8 No. 626362, issued by Mexican Immigration Office, Nuevo Laredo, September 26, 1963.

821. RICHARD STRETTON, FM-8 No. 626239, issued by Mexican Immigration Office, Nuevo Laredo, September 26, 1963.

COMMISSION EXHIBIT No. 2121—Continued

822. NANCY STREETT (tourist card signed as NANCY C. STRETTON), FM-8 No. 626240, issued by Mexican Immigration Office, Nuevo Laredo, September 26, 1963.

823. M. JOHN SZUCHY, JR., FM-8 No. 625632, issued by Mexican Immigration Office, Nuevo Laredo, September 26, 1963. (This individual appeared to sign his name as JOHN M. SZUCHY, JR., on instant tourist card.)

824. THOMAS J. ROGER, FM-8 No. 626142, issued by Mexican Immigration Office, Nuevo Laredo, September 26, 1963.

825. MAURICIA VALLE DE TORRES, FM-8 No. 510398, issued by Mexican Tourism Department, San Antonio, Texas, September 25, 1963.

826. VICENTE V. TORRES, FM-8 No. 510399, issued by Mexican Tourism Department, San Antonio, Texas, September 25, 1963.

827. JUSTINO TREVINO, FM-8 No. 626227, issued by Mexican Immigration Office, Nuevo Laredo, September 26, 1963.

828. ABELINA P. DE TREVINO, FM-8 No. 626228, issued by Mexican Immigration Office, Nuevo Laredo, September 26, 1963.

829. ALFREDO TREVINO, FM-8 No. 626554, issued by Mexican Immigration Office, Nuevo Laredo, September 26, 1963.

830. ESTELA S. TREVINO, FM-8 No. 626555, issued by Mexican Immigration Office, Nuevo Laredo, September 26, 1963.

831. ESPERANZA DE VALDEZ S., FM-8 No. 624671, issued by Mexican Immigration Office, Nuevo Laredo, September 26, 1963.

COMMISSION EXHIBIT No. 2121—Continued

832. BENITO TOMAS VALDEZ, FM-8 No. 624670, issued by Mexican Immigration Office, Nuevo Laredo, September 26, 1963.

833. JUANA VALDEZ, FM-8 No. 626136, issued by Mexican Immigration Office, Nuevo Laredo, September 26, 1963.

834. MARIA ELSA VALDEZ, FM-8 No. 624672, issued by Mexican Immigration Office, Nuevo Laredo, September 26, 1963.

835. OLIVIA VILLARREAL, FM-8 No. 626237, issued by Mexican Immigration Office, Nuevo Laredo, September 26, 1963.

(J) Persons Interviewed in Mexico Who Entered Mexico September 26, 1963, at Nuevo Laredo

T-7, a confidential source abroad, advised that SOLOMON BANDECK, residence 18652 Kelly Road, Detroit, Michigan, stated at Monterrey, Nuevo Leon, Mexico, on December 11, 1963, that he is a retired jeweler and he traveled from Monterrey to Nuevo Laredo on September 26, 1963, in his personally-owned automobile. He again entered Mexico at Nuevo Laredo on September 26, 1963, and returned to Monterrey.

He had no contact with OSWALD and he could not furnish any information concerning him.

T-8, a confidential source abroad, advised that ANDREW WEBSTER CHRISTOPHER, residence Lerdo de Tejada 320-A, Guadalajara, State of Jalisco, Mexico, stated on December 16, 1963, that he entered Mexico at Nuevo Laredo, on September 26, 1963, in his personally-owned automobile.

He was unable to identify photographs of OSWALD and stated he had not observed OSWALD in Nuevo Laredo at the time he entered Mexico.

T-9, a confidential source who has furnished reliable information in the past, advised on December 13, 1963, that CARLOS ALMAGUER ECHARTEA, residence Calle Lic. Jose

Maria Bocanegra No. 1105, Colonia Industrial, Monterrey, Nuevo Laredo, Mexico, had stated that he and his wife entered Mexico at Nuevo Laredo on September 26, 1963, in their personally-owned automobile and that they had not seen or heard anything about OSWALD until November 22, 1963.

T-4 advised on December 18, 1963, that GUILLERMO HEVIA VILLAR, residence 217 West Johnson Street, San Antonio, Texas, and Mrs. MARIA OTERO PABLOS, residence 1101 Pecan Street, McAllen, Texas, who had entered Mexico by automobile on September 26, 1963, at Nuevo Laredo, had no pertinent information concerning OSWALD and they had not observed him.

T-8 advised that HARVEY TUTTLE, residence Calle 6 No. 208, Atemajac, State of Jalisco, México, stated on January 4, 1964, that he entered Mexico at Nuevo Laredo by bus on or about September 26, 1963, which exact date he could not recall because he did not have in his immediate possession his tourist card.

He could not recall anyone resembling OSWALD at Nuevo Laredo or on the bus on which he traveled.

T-10, a confidential source abroad, advised that CHESTER STANLEY STEMP, residence 7223 Jarnecke Avenue, Hammond, Indiana; employed as a mathematics teacher, American High School, San Salvador, El Salvador, stated in San Salvador, El Salvador, on January 14, 1964, that he entered Mexico at Nuevo Laredo, on September 26, 1963, on the first bus which crossed the border on this date at about 6:00 a.m. He traveled to Laredo, Texas, by Greyhound bus from San Antonio, Texas, and boarded a Transportes del Norte bus in Nuevo Laredo, Mexico. He traveled from Nuevo Laredo to Monterrey, Nuevo Leon, by bus, arriving at the latter place at about noon on September 26, 1963. He took a train from Monterrey to San Luis Potosi, State of San Luis Potosi, Mexico, and Mexico, D. F., arriving at noon on September 28, 1963.

He could not identify a photograph of OSWALD and stated that he had not seen him.

(K) Interview of ROBERTO MORALES, Driver of Flecha Roja (Red Arrow) Bus No. 516 from Nuevo Laredo to Mexico City on trip for September 26 and 27, 1963.

T-11, a confidential source abroad, advised as follows:

On March 14, 1964, ROBERTO MORALES, driver of Flecha Roja bus No. 516 on September 26-27, 1963, from Nuevo Laredo to Mexico, D. F., Mexico, furnished the following information:

He could not recall specifically the trip which he made on September 26-27, 1963, from Nuevo Laredo to Mexico City, because he has made numerous trips and seen a large number of passengers since that time. He was shown the baggage list recording the names of some of the passengers on that trip and stated he is not acquainted with any of the names and does not know any of the persons listed. He was unable to identify photographs of OSWALD and of JOHN HOWARD BOWEN, true name ALBERT OSBORNE. MORALES stated that his codriver from Monterrey to Mexico City usually is ALFREDO GARCIA CERVANTES, who resides in Mexico City, address unknown to him.

On May 14, 1964, ALEJANDRO SAUCEDO, manager of the Mexico City terminal of "Servicios Unidos Autobuses Blancos Flecha Roja, S. A. de C. V." (The Unified Services of White Autobuses Red Arrow, Incorporated), Calle Heroes Ferrocarrileros 45, provided the following information with respect to the Flecha Roja baggage manifest mentioned above:

The baggage list reflects it was prepared for bus No. 516, which departed from Nuevo Laredo, Tamaulipas, at 2:00 p.m., September 26, 1963, driven by ROBERTO MORALES. The number "18" encircled at the bottom of the list indicates that 18 pieces of baggage were checked and baggage claim checks issued for storage and handling in the baggage compartment of the bus and revision by Mexican Customs.

.SAUCEDO affirmed that the number of passengers departing on the bus from Nuevo Laredo is not specified on the baggage list and that only the persons who check and become responsible for one or more articles of baggage are listed thereon. He pointed out that unaccompanied baggage also may be sent in this manner and the presence of a name on the baggage list does not insure that the person actually traveled on the bus.

(L) Interview of ERNESTO HERNANDEZ, codriver of Flecha Roja (Red Arrow) Bus No. 516 from Nuevo Laredo to Mexico City on September 26 to 27, 1963

T-12, a confidential source abroad, advised on April 21, 1964, that ERNESTO HERNANDEZ, codriver of Flecha Roja (Red Arrow) bus No. 516 on September 26 to 27, 1963, from Nuevo Laredo to Mexico, D. F., Mexico, furnished the following:

He resides at Aldama No. 4, Tizayuca, Hidalgo, Mexico, and for the past nine years he has been employed as a bus driver for the Flecha Roja bus company.

He has no independent recollection of having been the codriver of bus No. 516 on September 26 to 27, 1963, but when his recollection was refreshed, he stated that for the first and only time he had been the codriver for ROBERTO MORALES on bus No. 516 on the trip from Nuevo Laredo to Mexico, D. F., on September 26 to 27, 1963. He normally does not work as a codriver with MORALES but did recall having substituted for MORALES' regular partner, ALFREDO GARCIA CERVANTES.

He was unable to identify the photographs of OSWALD and JOHN HOWARD BOWEN. He could not associate OSWALD with anyone he might have seen in the past. He had seen photographs of OSWALD in the newspapers following the assassination of President KENNEDY but he did not associate OSWALD with anyone he has seen.

He was shown the baggage list for passengers for the above trip and he did not know any of the names on this list, He advised that it was difficult for him to distinguish one trip from another or to recall individual passengers in the absence of a particular incident which might occur on a trip. He could not recall the above-mentioned trip made by bus No. 516, the portions of the trip during which MORALES had operated the bus or between what points he, HERNANDEZ, had driven the bus,

He could not furnish any data to assist in identifying OSWALD as being a passenger aboard Flecha Roja bus No. 516 on September 26 to 27, 1963.

III. OSWALD IN MEXICO CITY

(A) "New York Times" Newspaper Account

The Western Edition of the "New York Times," dated December 3, 1963, carried an article by Correspondent PETER KIHSS, which is reproduced hereinunder and reports information purportedly gleaned by the correspondent in Mexico City:

"OSWALD FOLLOWED LONELY PATH DURING RECENT VISIT TO MEXICO

"Inquiry Finds $30 Could Have Covered All Expenses of Month-Long Trip

-- His Travels Are Detailed

"By PETER KIHSS

"Special to The New York Times

"MEXICO CITY, Dec. 2--More lonely steps along the trail of LEE H. OSWALD in the last autumn of his life came to light today.

"Evidence turned up concerning the trip that OSWALD made here in late September and early October presented a picture consistent with that pertaining to other periods in the life of the accused assassin of President KENNEDY.

"The Mexican Ministry of the Interior disclosed that the results of its intensive police investigation had indicated that OSWALD was alone here. The ministry's findings have been transmitted to United States authorities.

"Indeed few mysteries remained as to OSWALD's trip here, following painstaking inquiry. The investigation disclosed that the often impecunious OSWALD could have financed his entire trip to Mexico Sept. 26 to Oct. 23 with less than $30--

thus apparently disposing of the question of where he could have obtained substantial funds for the trip.

"Newsmen identified the bus line on which OSWALD traveled from Nuevo Laredo, across the (border) to this capital and back. It was Transportes Frontera.

"At its office on Buenavista Street, a clerk, LUCIO LOPEZ, said the Mexican police had been given the lists of passengers on that run that the line keeps.

"Investigators were understood also to have checked a number of the guests who were at the Hotel Comercio, the hotel where OSWALD stayed. He was the only American among a clientele composed mostly of Mexicans and a few Cubans, the latter apparently exiles.

"The Cuban Foreign Ministry has confirmed that OSWALD, while in Mexico City, sought a Cuban visa on Sept. 27 as a transit traveler to the Soviet Union. The ministry said that when OSWALD was told the consulate could not issue such a visa without Havana authorization, he left 'visibly displeased.' The ministry also said such a visa would not be granted unless a visa had been previously issued by the country of destination.

"Met Delay on Soviet Visa

"The Mexican Interior Ministry said OSWALD's effort later to get a Soviet visa had also been met with a consular statement that there would have to be a delay. A Mexican official said OSWALD told the Cubans and the Russians he was a Communist who had lived two years in the Soviet Union and had married a Russian woman.

The police investigation was reported to have found no indication that OSWALD had visited anyone else of political interest.

"Cuban exiles opposed to the regime of Premier FIDEL CASTRO have been trying to check on OSWALD's activities here. So far they have not turned up anything of consequence. This is a sprawling city of nearly five million inhabitants but even in this multitude OSWALD's tracks have been uncovered.

"OSWALD took a 2:30 P.M. bus Thursday, Sept. 26, from Nueva Laredo for the 750-mile trip scheduled to end here Friday, Sept. 27, at 8:30 P.M. The one-way fare on the Frontera line is $5.71 at the exchange rate of 12½ Mexican pesos a dollar.

"There are at least two-score of what Mexicans call humble hotels within a radius of five blocks of the bus terminal. OSWALD appears to have been fortunate to have found the well-kept Comercio on block-long Bernardo de Sahaguan Street, named for a Spanish colonial missionary who befriended Indians.

"For 16 pesos a day--$1.28--he got room No. 18, with private bath, in the four-story glazed red brick hotel.

"SEBASTIAN PEREZ HERNANDEZ, desk clerk, said OSWALD had arrived alone and had left early in the morning and come back late at night. He had no visitors.

"The hotel proprietor, GUILLERMO GARCIA, was shocked when investigators found OSWALD's signature on the registry. Mr. GARCIA admired President KENNEDY as a friend of Mexico and a Roman Catholic. He had never connected the name of his guest with the assassination.

OSWALD had one leather suitcase, about two feet long. He wore short-sleeved shirts. He talked only briefly with the night watchman and the chambermaid, in Spanish.

"Next to the hotel is the lunchroom La Esperanza. Mrs. DOLORES RAMIREZ DE BARRERO, a widow who has run the neat eating place for six months, remembered having seen OSWALD three or four days. She said he had eaten there only once.

"A Chop for 21 Cents

"He had a lunch of steak and rice, which came to about 26 cents. The costliest item on the bill of fare is a chop, cooked to taste, for about 21 cents.

"Mrs. BARRERO said OSWALD's Spanish had been hard to understand and he had eaten alone, in silence.

"Newsmen calculated that OSWALD could have stayed within $8 for meals in Mexico for eight days. He paid $11.42 for bus fare, $6.40 for five days' rent and 50 cents for a special 15-day tourist card he got in New Orleans Sept. 17. These figures add up to $26.32.

"On the same block with the hotel are a number of modest apartment houses. Across the way is a parking lot. At the end of the street is a typical little park, with stone benches. The neighborhood is the Guerrero District, largely commercial.

"OSWALD left Mexico City on Wednesday, Oct. 2, on a Frontera bus that was scheduled to depart at 1 P.M. and arrive at Nueva Laredo at 6:30 A.M. Thursday, Oct. 3.

"A Mexican Interior Ministry official suggested that OSWALD might have spent most of his time here, which included a weekend, as a tourist, perhaps also taking in some movies.

"It is believed OSWALD left New Orleans on Sept. 24, after having sent his wife to Dallas the previous day with a friend. He vanished from his cheap apartment there on that day without having paid his rent.

"He is believed to have hitchhiked to Laredo on the American side of the border, where he arrived Sept. 26. It was his custom to travel by hitch-hiking wherever possible.

"It was presumed that he probably hitchhiked north to Dallas from Laredo on his return from Mexico City. He arrived in Dallas the evening of Oct. 3 and checked into the Dallas YMCA. The distance from Laredo to Dallas is 475 miles."

(B) OSWALD's Visits to Cuban and Soviet Diplomatic Establishments - Investigation by Mexican Authorities

A signed statement which had been made by SILVIA DURAN to the Federal Security Police on November 23, 1963, as translates from Spanish is recorded hereinunder:

"At the City of Mexico, Federal District, at 6:00 p.m. of November 23, 1963, the undersigned, Captain FERNANDO GUTIERREZ BARRIOS, Assistant Director of the Federal Security (Police), proceeding legally with witnesses present, makes record: that with the presentation in this office of Mrs. SILVIA TIRADO DE DURAN for the purpose of being interrogated concerning the matters which are herein set forth, this document was prepared:

"Promptly upon the presentation of the person who under normal conditions is called SILVIA TIRADO DE DURAN, having been warned to tell the truth and advised of the penalties which are incurred by those who furnish false testimony, described herself as follows: that her name is as recorded, 25 years of age, married, without religious preference, an employee, literate, a native and resident of this city, with domicile at Constituyentes #143, Apartment #3, with respect to the matters under investigation declares: that she has been legally married to Mr. HORACIO DURAN NAVARRO since November 5, 1958, and is the mother of a child named PATRICIA, who, at the present time, is three and one-half years of age; that in the month of July or August of 1961 the deponent was invited to join the Mexican-Cuban Institute of Cultural Relations, which at that time, was directed by Attorney AGUSTIN CUE CANOVAS, as a Coordinator, and, although she does not recall specifically who it was that recommended her, she can clarify that for some time previously she was friendly and visited with frequency the employees of the Cuban Embassy, being a personal friend of Ambassador PORTUONDO, as well as the Cultural Attaches, TERESA PROENZA and LUIS ALVERU, as well as with the female employees, but principally with the secretary of Consul EUSEBIO ASCUE, Miss MARICARMEN OLAVARRI, of Spanish nationality but a relative of ASCUE; that at the Institute the activities were exclusively of a cultural nature and were attended on occasions by the afore-mentioned Cultural Attaches and some Cubans, but in a greater number by Mexicans, always artists and intellectuals, without any political discussions, although she recalls that at the time of the October Cuban crisis in connection with the threatened invasion of Cuba and the subsequent blockade of the island by the North American Government, they listened by shortwave radio to the news from the 'Prensa Latina' (Latin Press), on the basis of which they made up a bulletin which was read of the news that they had listened to directly from Havana, agreeing also to the effect that Cubans and Mexicans attending said meetings discussed the political problem of Cuba on a private basis without doing so in any official character; that the declarant was receiving a salary of 500 pesos ($40 U.S.) monthly in her capacity as Coordinator at the Institute, with her work schedule being from 4:00 to 8:00 p.m. daily, and the money for the maintenance of the Institute itself coming from a monthly subsidy from the Cuban Embassy, the amount of which she is not aware, but also with each one of the members paying a quota, and also contributions were received from persons whose names she does not recall because usually they were made anonymously,

being unable to fix the monthly receipts, although she was the person who personally received all of the funds received at the Institute; that in addition to the speaker, only Mr. FELIPE ROJAS, who worked as a secretary at the Institute during the morninge, received any monthly salary in the same amount of 500 pesos ($40 U.S.), with the remainder of the money which was received being used for the payment of rent and other expenses connected with its operation. That in the month of December of 1961, the declarant and her husband made a trip by air to Havana, Cuba, paying for their own transportation, but all of their expenses of their visit to that city and the greater number of the cities of the island being paid by the Cuban Institute of Friendship with the People and the House of Culture, so-called, 'of the Americas,' the trip having lasted fifteen days without their having any contact or connection during this trip with officials of the Cuban Government. That as the speaker has already stated, she has been a sympathizer of socialism and Marxist doctrine for several years, having studied philosophy and existentialism, and particularly she has sympathized since its inception and sympathizes with the Cuban Revolution. That approximately three months ago she began to occupy the position of Secretary to the Cuban Consul in this city, Mr. EUSEBIO ASCUE, who ceased to function in that capacity some five days ago on Monday, the 18th of this month, having been substituted by Mr. ALFREDO MIRAVAL Y DIAZ, clarifying at this time that from the beginning she began to work in that capacity as a temporary measure as a result of the death in a traffic accident of her friend, MARICARMEN OLAVARRI, who had been occupying that position, until some person should arrive from Cuba who would assume the same, having had under her responsibility the administrative operation and preparing the visas which are issued, as well as handling the applications for such visas which invariably are sent to the

Ministry of Foreign Relations, Government of Cuba, for its approval, having obtained this position directly from former Consul ASCUE, with whom she is very friendly, and for whom the speaker even organized a farewell party in her home, which was attended by almost all of the officials and employees of the Embassy and the Consulate, except the Ambassador. That the speaker does not belong to any political party and never has attended manifestations or meetings, nor has she given lectures or speeches, which her husband has done, since he has written several articles for the newspaper 'El Dia' (The Day) (pro-Communist Spanish language newspaper published in Mexico City); that she has never been arrested for any reason, nor even on the occasion of the visit to Mexico of Mr. JOHN F. KENNEDY, which caused her a great deal of personal satisfaction because of the benefits which it would represent to the country. That yesterday while she was working at the Cuban Consulate, where she is employed from 10:00 to 2:00 and from 4:00 to 6:00 p.m. daily and where she receives a salary of 1,500 pesos ($120 U.S.) monthly, just before their time of departure at noon, a friend commented to her that she had been listening to the radio and heard a news item to the effect that President KENNEDY had suffered an attack in which they had fired three shots at him, as a result of which she called her husband on the telephone and they discussed this news, and he advised her that he already knew about it and referred to said attack as 'monstrous,' and they agreed that upon meeting at their home they would discuss the matter, which they did during their dinner hour, but in a very brief manner since they did not know all the circumstances of the attack and the name and description of the presumed author of the same, its having been only that night that they read in the extra (edition) the news relating thereto, and subsequently on the radio at her residence she heard the name of LEE HARVEY OSWALD, which caused her to remember that this name refers to a North

American who in the last days of September or the first days of the month of October of the present year appeared at the Cuban Consulate and applied for a visa to Cuba in transit to Russia and based his application on his presentation of his passport in which it was recorded that he had been living in the latter country for a period of three years, his work permit from that same country written in the Russian language and letters in the same language, as well as proof of his being married to a woman of Russian nationality and being the apparent Director in the city of New Orleans of the organization called 'Fair Play for Cuba' with the desire that he should be accepted as a 'friend' of the Cuban Revolution, as a result of which the speaker, in compliance with her duties, received all of his data and filled out the appropriate application, and he left to return in the afternoon, this time with his photographs, and the speaker, recognizing that she exceeded her duties, semi-officially called the Russian Consulate by telephone because of her interest in facilitating the handling of the Russian visa for LEE HARVEY OSWALD, but from there they answered her that the operation would require approximately four months, which annoyed the applicant, since as he affirmed he was in a great hurry to obtain the visas which would permit him to travel to Russia, insisting that he was entitled to them because of his background and his partisanship and personal activities in favor of the Cuban movement, the declarant's not being able to specify because she does not remember whether or not he said that he was a member of the Communist Party, but that his wife, of Russian nationality, was at that time in the city of New York from where she would follow him, although his place of origin was the afore-mentioned city of New Orleans; that as soon as OSWALD understood that it was not possible to give him a Cuban visa without his previously obtaining a Russian one, because the former was for transit, he became highly agitated and angry, as a result of which the speaker called Consul ASCUE, who, at that time, was in his private office in company of his ultimate replacement, MIRAVAL, but came out and began to argue in English with OSWALD in a very angry manner and ASCUE concluded by saying to him that, 'As far as he was concerned, he would not give him a visa,' and that 'A person like him, in place of aiding the Cuban Revolution, was doing it harm,' its being noted that in their discussion they had been referring to the Russian socialist revolution and not the Cuban, its being stated by OSWALD that he had two reasons to request the visa with urgency, which were, one, that his permit to be in Mexico was expiring and the other that he had urgent necessity of reaching Russia; that in spite of the argument the speaker handed to OSWALD a piece of paper similar to that which she writes at this time in which she recorded her name, 'SILVIA DURAN,' and the telephone number of the Consulate, which is '11-28-47,' and, at any rate, she initiated the handling of his visa application by sending it to the Cuban Ministry of (Foreign) Affairs, from which a reply was received in the normal manner some fifteen to thirty days later approving the issuance of a visa, but conditioning it on his previously obtaining the Russian (one), although she does not recall whether OSWALD subsequently called her or not on the telephone for the Consulate which she had given him; that all of the conversation which the speaker had with OSWALD, as well as that of Consul ASCUE with him, was in the English language since he did not speak any Spanish, and that upon seeing his photograph which appears in today's newspapers, specifically in the newspaper 'El Dia,' she immediately recognized and identified it as being the same person that she has been referring to as LEE HARVEY OSWALD. That on only one occasion the declarant attended a reception ceremony at the Russian Embassy which was given on the occasion of the visit of the astronauts, GAGARIN and TERESHKOVA, on the personal invitation which the

speaker received from the Russian Consul YACKSOV when the latter visited ASCUE and MIRAVAL and delivered to them their respective invitations at the Cuban Consulate. That with respect to her in-laws, LIDIA and RUBEN DURAN NAVARRO, the former on various occasions attended with the declarant the meetings which were being held at the Institute, whereas the latter only did so on one or two occasions in connection with exhibits of paintings and with respect to BETY SERRATO AZUCAR, the wife of RUBEN, she has always remained aloof from these activities, although all of them are of leftist ideology but do not actively participate in any activities; that BARBARA ANN BLITS TRESMOND ESQUIVEL and AGATA ROSENO GARCIA are friends of BETY and the speaker has known them very little and superficially, as a result of which she knows nothing about their activities and ideologies, and in connection with the gentleman who she now knows is named BENTLEY, she had never seen him before and supposes that he is a friend of BARBARA, since she noticed that he was talking to BARBARA when they were dining at the home of the deponent, being present her husband, AGATA and LIDIA, whereas the others were at the home of her brother-in-law, RUBEN. That she has nothing further to declare and after reading the above, she ratifies and signs the margins in evidence thereof. The above document is closed authorized and witnessed.

Signed, Assistant Director of Federal Security,
Captain FERNANDO GUTIERREZ BARRIOS.
Witnesses: Lic. (Atty.) FERNANDO ORTIZ DE LA PENA;
Lic. CARLOS DURAN LANZ."

(C) Other Inquiries by Mexican Federal Security Police

On November 29, 1963, T-17 obtained a copy of a report dated November 25, 1963, recording the results of investigation by Agents of the Mexican Federal Security Police (Direccion Federal de Investigaciones - DFS). A translation from Spanish of that report follows hereinunder:

"In connection with the assassination of the President of the United States, JOHN F. KENNEDY, it was reported that LEE HARVEY OSWALD had previously been in Mexico, as a consequence of which appropriate investigation was conducted, the results of which are as follows:

"1. LEE HARVEY OSWALD was in Mexico, having entered at Nuevo Laredo, Tamaulipas (State), on September 26 last, as a tourist, proceeding from New Orleans and departing at the same place on last October 3rd.

"2. It was confirmed that he had come to Mexico to apply for a visa at the Cuban Embassy, for transit enroute to Moscow.

"3. Toward this objective, he established contact with SILVIA TIRADO DE DURAN, a Mexican 'SILVIA DURAN,' whom he interviewed on two occasions, since she is an employee of the Consulate, responsible for making the arrangements necessary for this type of visa and completing the cards with data concerning the applicant, an indispensable requisite for obtaining a Cuban visa.

"4. Through her, he made contact with the Russian Consulate for the same purpose.

"When it was learned that the above-mentioned SILVIA DURAN had been one of the contacts made by LEE HARVEY OSWALD in Mexico, said lady and her husband were arrested in order that they

- 42 -

COMMISSION EXHIBIT No. 2121—Continued

might be interrogated, advising in their statements as follows:

"INTERVIEW OF HORACIO DURAN NAVARRO: Mexican by birth, son of a Chilean father and Mexican mother. He said that his occupation is that of Industrial Designer, holding a teaching position on this subject in the National School of Plastic Arts, a dependency of the UNAM (Universidad Nacional Autonoma de Mexico - National Autonomous University of Mexico), where he receives a salary of 1,400 pesos ($112 U.S.) monthly; 40 years of age, married, without religious preference, domiciled at Constituyentes (street) #143, Apartment #3, in this city; that the first eight years of his life were spent in Los Angeles, California, and subsequently he came to this capital with his parents, RUFINO DURAN and LIDIA NAVARRO DE DURAN, and later they went to Santiago, Chile, to live, remaining there for a period of a year and one-half, later returning with his brother, RUBEN, to Mexico, being followed later by his sister, LIDIA, and his mother; that he entered the National Agricultural School at Chapingo, where he studied for five years for a career as an Agronomist and as he had learned drawing in the San Carlos Academy, he chose to continue studying that art, which served him as a basis for specializing in Industrial Designing, which he now follows, being a teacher in that subject in the School of Fine Arts of the UNAM, spending his free time in private work as a Designer, for which he receives an income of approximately 5,000 pesos ($400 U.S.) monthly; that in 1950 he was married to a French woman, LUCILLE DEJARDIN, with whom he fathered a son named PAUL DURAN DEJARDIN, who at the present time is 10 years of age, and with that marriage having lasted more or less six years, and with the breaking up of that matrimony, on November 5, 1958, he entered into a new marriage contract with his present wife, SILVIA TIRADO DE DURAN, with whom he fathered a

- 43 -

COMMISSION EXHIBIT No. 2121—Continued

girl named PATRICIA, now 3½ years of age; that when he became acquainted with his present wife, she was working as a Secretary in the Proteo Gallery and later she and other persons, among them Prof. AGUSTIN CUE CANOVAS, the Cultural Attache of the Cuban Embassy, and others, began to organize the Mexican Cuban Institute of Cultural Relations 'Jose Marti,' in which she served as a Coordinator, and for about the last four months, she has been employed as a Secretary in the Consulate General of Cuba in this city, first having worked with the Consul, EUSEBIO AZCUE, and now with MIRABAL, receiving a monthly salary of 1,500 pesos. He acknowledged that his ideology is leftist and in sympathy with the Cuban Revolution, adding that this is the reason why he permits his wife to work and engage in her present activities. He stated that when he discussed with his wife the assassination of President KENNEDY, having heard the name of the presumed perpetrator, LEE HARVEY OSWALD, she immediately told him that she believed that he was the same individual who in the latter part of September or early October had been in the Cuban Consulate applying for a Cuban visa in transit to Russia; that she had attended him herself and handled his visa application papers, but when she notified him that he would first need a Russian visa and that his application would have to be sent to the Cuban Ministry of Foreign Relations, which, of course, would require several days, OSWALD became angry and lost his self control, as a result of which SILVIA called the Consul AZCUE, with whom the applicant had a violent argument. He added that he had not seen nor had he personally known LEE HARVEY OSWALD, and in December of 1961 he (DURAN) made a trip to Cuba, accompanied by his wife, paying for their tickets himself.

"It is pointed out that at the home where the DURAN couple was detained at Herodoto #14, Apartment A, the home of the brother-in-law of SILVIA DURAN, named RUBEN DURAN NAVARRO, the

persons who were visiting at that residence were arrested and their background data is recorded below:"

(None of the individuals listed below as having been interviewed admitted knowing OSWALD or having any information concerning him. Therefore, the data concerning them is being summarized rather than recorded in full.)

RUBEN DURAN NAVARRO advised that he was born in Los Angeles, California, is married to BETTY SERRATOS, is 38 years of age, a decorator by profession, and has applied for Mexican citizenship. He related that Calle Herodoto #14, Apartment A, is his residence.

BETTY SERRATOS DE DURAN related that she was born in the Republic of Honduras and has resided in Mexico for the past ten years, is 33 years of age, and has never belonged to any political party or entertained leftist ideas. She explained that she resides with her husband, RUBEN DURAN NAVARRO, at Herodoto #14, Apartment A.

LIDIA DURAN NAVARRO VDA. (widow) DE FLORES advised that she is 35 years of age, having been born in Chihuahua, Chihuahua; that she resides at Luz Savinon Street No. 1211, Apartment 2, and is employed in the Tourism Department and the Mexican Sports Federation. She denied having political affiliations or sympathies. She explained that she is the sister of RUBEN DURAN NAVARRO and had been visiting them at the time the investigators arrived at their apartment.

AGATA ROSENA GARCIA related that she was born in the Capital (of Mexico) and resides at Rivera Street No, 63, Colonia Las Aguilas. She denied having any political affiliations or being of leftist ideology and explained that she is a friend of the DURANs and visits them frequently at their home.

BARBARA ANN BLISS stated that she was in Mexico as a tourist and has been living in the country for the past eight years, and resides at Bahia de Magdalena #125; that she is divorced from JUAN ESQUIVEL, a Costa Rican citizen who presently lives in the United States, and has a monthly income of $800 per month from the estate of her father, which is administered by a firm in Washington, D. C. She explained that her father, ALONSO BLISS, formerly owned a sugar plantation on Trinidad, but presently resides at 2585 Bayshore Drive, Coconut Grove, Miami, Florida. She explained that she had become acquainted with BETTY SERRATOS some three months earlier at the apartment of CARMEN PINO, and they had exchanged visits with each other thereafter because of their mutual liking for recorded music. She also stated that she had met SILVIA TIRADO DE DURAN at a concert, but had no friendship with her.

CHARLES E. BENTLEY explained that he is 27 years of age and was in Mexico as a tourist, having resided for the previous three months at Palermo Street No. 9, Colonia Hipodromo, in Mexico City; that he had been trying to obtain employment as a salesman for the Sonora Cattle Company; that he had served in the United States Marine Corps from 1954 to 1957 and had no political affiliations or leftist ideas. He explained that he had met BARBARA ANN BLISS and BETTY SERRATOS some two months earlier and was visiting at Herodoto No. 14-7 because of his friendship with them.

(D) <u>Hotel Accommodations of LEE HARVEY OSWALD in Mexico City</u>

On November 26, 1963, T-14, a confidential source who has furnished reliable information in the past, advised that, following a check of the registration records of numerous middle and lower class hotels in the downtown area of Mexico City, he had ascertained that on September 27, 1963, LEE HARVEY OSWALD had registered at the Hotel del Comercio, located at Calle (Street) Bernardino de Sahagun No. 19 and approximately eight blocks from the commercial heart of the Mexican capital. The records disclosed that OSWALD was registered as the occupant of room No. 18 until October 1, 1963, and was deleted from the hotel guest list on October 2, 1963.

According to source, there were only three employees at the hotel, and some of them were able to recognize OSWALD's photograph as having been a guest at that establishment but could recall virtually no information concerning the circumstances relating thereto.

1. <u>OSWALD's Registration at Hotel</u>

T-1 made available photocopies of the registration records of the Hotel del Comercio, Calle Bernardino de Sahagun No. 19, Mexico, D. F., which reflect that on September 27, 1963, OSWALD registered at that hotel as "LEE, HARVEY OSWALD, USA, Texas, PHOTO, US citizen" and was assigned room No. 18.

The owner and manager of the hotel, GUILLERMO GARCIA LUNA, explained on March 3, 1964, that upon arrival a guest is required to register in his own handwriting; however, as long as he remains at the hotel thereafter, the name is transferred to the registration list for subsequent days by the manager or his assistant.

2. <u>Examination of Handwriting on Hotel Register by FBI Laboratory</u>

On December 11, 1963, a photocopy of the above-described page of the Hotel del Comercio registration book was submitted to the FBI Laboratory for examination of the "LEE, HARVEY OSWALD" signature appearing thereon.

In a laboratory report dated December 18, 1963, the FBI Laboratory stated that examination of "Qc333, photocopy of page of registry book of Hotel del Comercio, Calle Sahagun 19, Mexico City, with signatures of guests registering on September 27, 1963, Line 18, bearing signature 'Lee Harvey Oswald'" had been made with the following result:

"It was concluded that the LEE HARVEY OSWALD signature on Line 18 of Qc333 was written by LEE HARVEY OSWALD, whose known writing appears as K4 and K5 in this case."

The information recorded hereinunder was furnished by T-13.

3. Identities of Persons at Hotel During Same Period as OSWALD

A review of copies of the pages of the Hotel del Comercio registration book for individuals who registered or remained at the hotel from September 26, 1963, through the night of October 1-2, 1963, revealed the following with respect to their names, city and state of origin, room or rooms occupied, and date or dates of occupancy.

Because of the fact that some of the names were abbreviated and others not decipherable, Hotel del Comercio owner, GUILLERMO GARCIA LUNA, assisted in clarifying those names.

Name and Residence	Room No.	Dates of Occupancy
ISABEL SALAZAR y comp. Durango, Durango	1	September 26 and 27, 1963
J. ASCENCION HERRERA Durango, Durango	2	September 26 and 27, 1963
POLO DUENAS Aguascalientes, Ags.	3	September 26 and 27, 1963
ANTONIO OLIVA y Sra. Mexico, D. F., Mex. (Musician)	4	September 26, 27, 28, 29 and 30, and October 1, 1963
POLO DUENAS Aguascalientes, Ags.	5	September 26, 1963
FERNANDO VALENZUELA Chihuahua, Chihuahua	6	September 26 through October 1, 1963
ANGELICA PEREYRA Torreon, Coahuila (Housewife)	7	September 26 through October 1, 1963
ERNESTO LIMA JUAREZ Reynosa, Tamaulipas	8	September 26, 1963

COMMISSION EXHIBIT No. 2121—Continued

Name and Residence	Room No.	Dates of Occupancy
MARTIN GUERRERO San Luis Potosi, S.L.P.	9	September 26 through October 1, 1963
JOSE LUIS MACIAS Chihuahua, Chihuahua	10	September 26 through October 1, 1963
PEDRO QUIJANO Torreon, Coahuila	11	September 26 through October 1, 1963
MANUEL SANTOS Saltillo, Coahuila (Farmer)	12	September 26, 27, 28 and 30, and October 1, 1963
URBANO TORRES Guanajuato, Guanajuato	13, 22	September 26 and October 1, 1963
GABRIEL CONTRERAS Ciudad Juarez, Chihuahua	14	September 26 through October 1, 1963
JULIO LINAN San Luis Potosi, S.L.P.	15	September 26 through October 1, 1963
POLO DUENAS Aguascalientes, Ags.	16	September 26, 1963
RODOLFO RODRIGUEZ Chihuahua, Chihuahua	17, 16 and 17	September 26 through October 1, 1963
POLO DUENAS Aguascalientes, Ags.	18	September 26, 1963
PEREZ PLIEGO San Luis Potosi, S.L.P.	19	September 26, 27 and 28, 1963
SANTOS PEDROZA Leon, Guanajuato	20	September 26 through October 1, 1963
MARIO RESENDIZ Saltillo, Coahuila (Businessman)	21	September 26 through October 1, 1963

COMMISSION EXHIBIT No. 2121—Continued

Name and Residence	Room No.	Dates of Occupancy
POLO DUENAS Aguascalientes, Ags.	22	September 26, 1963
ENRIQUE GARZAT Monterrey, Nuevo Leon	23	September 26, 1963
OSCAR LOZA	25	September 26, 1963
POLO DUENAS	26	September 26, 1963
ARTURO CHAVEZ Ciudad del Maiz, S.L.P.	27	September 26, 1963
POLO DUENAS	28	September 26, 1963
MANUEL SERRALDE Monterrey, Nuevo Leon	29	September 26 through October 1, 1963
LEOPOLDO DIAZ Guadalupe, Guanajuato	30	September 26, 1963
MARTIN SUMAYA Nuevo Laredo, Tamaulipas	5	September 27, 1963
FRANCISCO MORALES Reynosa, Tamaulipas	8	September 27 through October 1, 1963
RAFAEL ROCHA Torreon, Coahuila	13	September 27, 1963
LEE, HARVEY OSWALD (Photo.)	18	September 27 through October 1, 1963
ROBERTO LOPEZ Mexico, D. F., Mexico	22	September 27, 1963
JUAN FCO. ROCHA Durango, Durango	24	September 27, 1963
OSCAR SANCHEZ DE LA ROSA Monterrey, Nuevo Leon	25	September 27 through 30, 1963

- 50 -

COMMISSION EXHIBIT No. 2121—Continued

Name and Residence	Room No.	Dates of Occupancy
ALFREDO GARCIA Guadalajara, Jalisco	26	September 27 through 29, 1963
JOSE GAMES Aguascalientes, Ags. (Chauffeur)	28, 30 and 24	September 27 and 30 and October 1, 1963
ALICIA PLAZA Aguascalientes, Ags. (Housewife)	1, 23	September 28, 29 and 30, 1963
JORGE ROQUE Puebla, Puebla	2	September 28, 1963
Sr. VILLA Puebla, Puebla	3	September 28, 1963
Sr. RAMOS y Sra. Queretaro, Queretaro	5	September 28, 1963
FIDENCIO GARCIA San Luis Potosi, S.L.P.	13	September 28, 1963
CARLOS MARQUES Veracruz, Veracruz	16	September 28, 1963
Sr. PEREZ y fam. Chihuahua, Chihuahua (Businessman)	22, 19	September 28 and October 1, 1963
Sr. RAMIREZ Torreon, Coahuila	23	September 28, 1963
SILVINO MARTINEZ Queretaro, Queretaro	24	September 28, 1963
MARIO ALATORRE Puebla, Puebla (Businessman)	28, 3	September 28 and 29, 1963

- 51 -

COMMISSION EXHIBIT No. 2121—Continued

Name and Residence	Room No.	Dates of Occupancy
LEONARDO BEZERRA Guanajuato, Guanajuato (Businessman)	2	September 29 and 30 and October 1, 1963
RAUL RAMIREZ Veracruz, Veracruz	12	September 29, 1963
RAUL RAMIREZ Veracruz, Veracruz	13	September 29 and 30 and October 1, 1963
FERNANDO MARTINEZ Guadalajara, Jalisco	16	September 29, 1963
ALFONSO BELTRAN Chihuahua, Chihuahua	19	September 29, 1963
TOMAS GALVAN Queretaro, Queretaro	24	September 29, 1963
JESUS GOMEZ y fam.	1	September 30, 1963
JUAN PEDRAZA (JULIAN PEDRAZA) San Luis Potosi, S.L.P.	3	September 30 through October 1, 1963
JESUS GOMEZ	5	September 30, 1963
MANUEL SANTOS Saltillo, Coahuila	12	September 30 through October 1, 1963
SALVADOR HERNANDEZ Puebla, Puebla	16	September 30, 1963
Cap. ESQUIVEL Veracruz, Veracruz (Military)	19	September 30, 1963
GUILLERMO FLORES Queretaro, Queretaro	22	September 30, 1963
TEOFIL. (TEOFILO) VELAZQUEZ Irapuato, Guanajuato	24	September 30, 1963

Name and Residence	Room No.	Dates of Occupancy
ARMANDO RODRIGUEZ San Luis, Guanajuato (San Luis de la Paz)	26	September 30, 1963
GREGORIO PEREZ Puebla, Puebla	28	September 30 through October 1, 1963
RAMIREZ Monterrey, Nuevo Leon	1	October 1, 1963
Cap. DOMINGUEZ Guadalajara, Jalisco	5	October 1, 1963
ROSAS RAMIREZ Celaya, Guanajuato	16	October 1, 1963
Sr. MONTOYA Puebla, Puebla	23	October 1, 1963
FRANCISCO GUTIERREZ Puebla, Puebla (Chauffeur)	25	October 1, 1963
FELIPE ESCOBEDO	26	October 1, 1963
ALFONSO GARCIA Monterrey, Nuevo Leon	27	October 1, 1963

4. Interview of Manager and Other Personnel at Hotel

GUILLERMO GARCIA LUNA advised on March 3, 1964, that he is the owner and manager of the Hotel del Comercio, which is located approximately five blocks north of the main east-west thoroughfare of Mexico City, Paseo de la Reforma, and two blocks east of the principal north-south artery, Avenida Insurgentes. He explained that his hotel caters to commercial travelers, most of whom are Mexican citizens; that it has a total of thirty rooms, most of which are equipped with a private bath; that for a single room the minimum rate, without bath, is 13.00 pesos ($1.04 U.S.) and the maximum, with bath, is 20.00 pesos ($1.60 U.S.). He added that the hotel is in the heart of the area of many of the bus terminals in Mexico City and also is only a few blocks from the passenger railroad station.

GARCIA LUNA furnished the following observations concerning the stay of LEE HARVEY OSWALD at the Hotel del Comercio. He received OSWALD and caused him to sign the hotel registration book, which is utilized in place of registration cards. He believed OSWALD's arrival had occurred between 10:00 and 11:00 a.m. The guest makes the initial entry in the registration book with data which includes his name, place of origin, occupation, and nationality; thereafter, so long as the guest remains at the hotel, his name and identifying data are transferred to the registration book page for the current date, after he has made payment in advance for his room for the ensuing night. Inasmuch as payment is made in advance, no effort is made to obtain an exact home address for the registrant.

The hotel has four floors, and OSWALD was assigned room No. 18 (with bath) on the third floor at a daily rate of 16.00 pesos ($1.28 U.S.) The rooms on the latter floor are numbered from 18 through 23. The hotel registration book reflects that OSWALD paid for his room on October 1, 1963, which, according to GARCIA LUNA, indicates he was entitled to and probably slept at the hotel the night of October 1-2, 1963, and departed therefrom during the day of October 2, 1963. GARCIA LUNA stated he could not recall the circumstances of OSWALD's departure nor the hour thereof, but merely was judging normal procedure on the basis of information in his record.

GARCIA LUNA advised that he speaks a few words of English and received the impression that OSWALD neither spoke nor understood any Spanish. He had not observed OSWALD in the hotel during the day nor had he ever seen him accompanied by any individual or individuals. He recalled that OSWALD had been carrying a medium-size, brown handbag, which he believed had a zipper and was either of Naugahyde or canvas material. He did not remember that OSWALD had ever worn a coat and believed he usually appeared in a short-sleeved shirt of a knit variety.

Inquiry was made of GARCIA LUNA as to other personnel at the hotel who might recall OSWALD on the basis of having any reason to notice or contact him, and he stated that those persons would be his assistant, SEBASTIAN PEREZ, and the maid who cleans the rooms on the upper two floors, MATILDE GARNICA.

GARCIA LUNA stated that he was acquainted with a few of the guests who were at the hotel during the same period as OSWALD but did not have home addresses for any of them. He mentioned that several of the guests of that period are commercial travelers and return to the hotel from time to time.

MATILDE GARNICA, maid at the Hotel del Comercio, advised on March 3, 1964, that she recognized the photographs of OSWALD as being of the young American who had occupied room No. 18 for almost a week during the latter part of last year. She explained that she handles the daily housekeeping duties for the third and fourth floors of the hotel, comprising rooms numbered 18 through 30, and ordinarily arrives at work between 9:00 a.m. and 10:00 a.m., leaving at 9:00 p.m., upon completion of her working day.

Mrs. GARNICA related that she clearly recalls OSWALD, as few Americans stay at the hotel, and was somewhat intrigued by his presence there. He had very few personal effects, which he carried in what she described as a "small, brown, zippered handbag," which was either of canvas or imitation leather material. She did not believe she had seen OSWALD in the hotel on more than two occasions, the day of his arrival and the following Saturday as he was still in his room when she checked to determine which rooms were available for cleaning. She remembered that when she saw him in the room on the Saturday morning in question, he said "good morning" to her in English, and a short time later left the hotel.

She never saw him with any other person and had no conversation with him, having received the impression that he neither spoke nor understood Spanish.

SEBASTIAN PEREZ HERNANDEZ, desk clerk and assistant to the owner of the Hotel del Comercio, advised on March 10, 1964, that he had not conversed with OSWALD but remembered him clearly inasmuch as very few Americans have stayed at the hotel. To the best of his recollection, OSWALD left the hotel each morning and did not return until evening, possibly after PEREZ HERNANDEZ had completed his working day and left the hotel. He stated OSWALD was alone whenever he noticed him at the hotel and usually wore a knit, short-sleeved sport shirt and no coat or jacket.

PEREZ HERNANDEZ advised that since OSWALD paid his rent in advance for the night of October 1, 1963, there would have been little reason for contact with him on the presumed date of his departure, October 2, 1963, and he was unable to remember any details in this connection.

On April 18, 1964, PEDRO RODRIGUEZ LEDESMA advised that he resides at Santa Clara, State of Mexico, and for many years has been the night watchman at the Hotel del Comercio, his working hours being from 9:00 p.m. to 9:00 a.m. He explained, however, that he often is able to leave the hotel by 8:00 a.m. or earlier if the owner and manager, GUILLERMO GARCIA LUNA, has arrived to relieve him and handle reception duties. With respect to LEE HARVEY OSWALD's stay at the hotel, he furnished the following information.

He clearly recalls the young American whom he later identified in his mind as OSWALD and remembers that on the date of the latter's departure from the hotel and on the basis of sign language and the word "taxi," which he interpreted to indicate that OSWALD wanted a taxicab, RODRIGUEZ walked around the corner from the Hotel del Comercio to Orozco y Berra and Bernal Diaz Streets where he obtained a taxicab which had just left a passenger at the "Estrella Blanca" (White Star) bus terminal. He stated definitely that he did not know the taxi driver and had not known or discussed with the driver or OSWALD the latter's intended destination. He said OSWALD carried his own luggage downstairs and waited in front of the hotel with the luggage until RODRIGUEZ returned with the taxicab.

He believed OSWALD left the hotel between 6:30 and 7:00 a.m., since it was getting light when he went in search of the taxicab. He could not be more precise concerning the time. He believed that OSWALD gave him a small tip of one or two pesos ($.08 or $.16 U.S.) for his assistance in calling

a taxi. RODRIGUEZ commented that while he had little difficulty obtaining a taxi at the early hour, it becomes very difficult to secure taxi transportation between 7:30 and 8:30 a.m. because of the heavy traffic at that time.

RODRIGUEZ related that to the best of his recollection OSWALD always arrived at the hotel late at night, "midnight or thereafter," but he never noticed any indication that OSWALD had been drinking. He never observed OSWALD in the company of any person and did not recall his ever using the only telephone at the hotel, which is located at the reception desk.

5. Other Inquiries in the Area of the Hotel del Comercio, Taxi Stands, and Bus Terminals

On March 4 and again on April 10, 1964, DOLORES RAMIREZ DE BARREIRO advised that she is the owner, manager and sometimes cook at the small restaurant on Calle Bernardino de Sahagun (no number) immediately adjacent to the Hotel del Comercio. She explained that there is no commercial connection between the hotel and her restaurant, but because of its proximity many hotel guests eat some meals at the restaurant.

Upon viewing photographs of OSWALD, Mrs. BARREIRO affirmed that she remembered him as a young American who had eaten several meals at the restaurant in the late afternoon over a period of approximately one week. She said he appeared at the restaurant after the noon rush hour or some time after 2:00 p.m., always alone, and ordered his food by pointing on the menu, apparently with some consideration of costs. He always ate the soup of the day, rice, and either meat or eggs, but always rejected dessert and coffee. She thought this unusual, as the dessert and coffee ordinarily are included in the price of the daily lunch, but he did not appear to understand this and always waved the waitress away if she tried to serve those items. She recalled that he also rejected any efforts to sell him soft drinks, which she described as an important item in her business. She estimated that OSWALD spent from five to six pesos ($.40 to $.48 U.S.) for his meals. She had assumed he was a guest at the hotel but never observed him contact or talk to anyone while at the restaurant.

6. Inquiries in Neighborhood of Hotel del Comercio

T-15, a confidential source who has furnished reliable information in the past, advised that he had interviewed a large number of persons in the area of the Hotel del Comercio, among them car watchers, taxi drivers, restaurant operators, ambulatory salesman, shoeshine boys, newspaper vendors, and others, displaying to them a photograph of OSWALD. According to source, he had been unable to locate anyone who recalled OSWALD.

7. Interviews of Guests at Hotel del Comercio

T-2 and T-13 advised that interviews of the following persons, who were guests at the Hotel del Comercio during the same period as OSWALD, had failed to identify anyone who was able to remember him:

ALFONSO PEREZ PLIEGO
Captain SALVADOR ESQUIVEL SEGURA
URBANO TORRES MENDOZA
MARTIN GUERRERO
JULIO LINAN
MANUEL SERRALDE

Sources advised that GUILLERMO GARCIA LUNA, owner of the Hotel del Comercio, had been able to furnish some identifying data concerning hotel guests ANTONIO OLIVA, FERNANDO VALENZUELA, ANGELICA PEREYRA, PEDRO QUIJANO, GABRIEL CONTRERAS, RODOLFO RODRIGUEZ, MARTIN SUMAYA, RAFAEL ROCHA, JOSE GAMES, FIDENCIO GARCIA, Captain CARLOS DOMINGUEZ, and MARIO RESENDIZ, and efforts are being made to locate those individuals as well as identify and locate others who were guests at the Hotel del Comercio during the same period as OSWALD.

8. Reputation of Hotel del Comercio

On April 22, 1964, inquiry was made of GUILLERMO GARCIA LUNA by T-13 as to his opinion of how OSWALD had selected and appeared at his hotel, and he stated that even though the hotel is three blocks and "around three corners" from the Red Arrow bus terminal, he considers his hotel to have the best general aspect and appearance of any of several in the area; furthermore, it is known by personnel in other hotels that GARCIA LUNA can understand and speak a little English. He also mentioned that his hotel is filled to approximately ninety per cent of capacity at all times because he makes every effort to provide superior accommodations to commercial travelers at competitive prices.

On April 17, 1964, T-16, a confidential source who has furnished reliable information in the past and is in a position to be informed with respect to the activities in Mexico of Cubans and individuals of other nationalities who are sympathetic to the Castro revolutionary regime in Cuba, advised that the Hotel del Comercio is not known to him as being frequented by pro-Castro Cubans.

On April 23, 1964, T-14, who is well acquainted with hotel operations in Mexico City, reported that he knows nothing unfavorable with respect to the character and reputation of GUILLERMO GARCIA LUNA or the Hotel del Comercio and considers the latter to be a reputable establishment usually frequented by commercial travelers and individuals of modest means.

IV. OSWALD'S DEPARTURE FROM MEXICO

The information recorded below was made available by T-17, a confidential source abroad.

The files of the Department of Immigration, Mexican Ministry of "Gobernacion" (Interior or Government), reveal that LEE HARVEY OSWALD departed from Mexico on October 3, 1963, at Nuevo Laredo, Tamaulipas. The records of the Mexican Immigration Office at Nuevo Laredo reveal that on October 3, 1963, from 12:00 midnight until 8:00 a.m., Immigration official ALBERTO ARZAMENDI CHAPA was in charge of the "Kilometer 26" highway checking station, where tourist cards are picked up from aliens leaving Mexico by highway travel through Nuevo Laredo. An official of the Department of Immigration stated that the name and date stamp of ARZAMENDI CHAPA on the original tourist card surrendered by OSWALD upon his departure from Mexico on that date were evidence of the fact that his exit from Mexico occurred during those hours.

The official added that considerable investigation had been conducted by several different agencies of the Mexican Government for the purpose of ascertaining subject's method of travel on departure and that, in view of the fact the name "OSWLD" had been located on a passenger list for the 1:00 p.m. trip of the Transportes Frontera bus line from Mexico City to Nuevo Laredo, Tamaulipas, on October 2, 1963, it was considered that OSWALD had traveled thereon.

Considerable investigation with respect to the passenger list mentioned above, including a check of the ticket stubs at the Monterrey, Nuevo Leon, headquarters of the company, interviews of bus drivers and passengers, and numerous interviews of employees of the Mexico City terminal of the bus line, failed to confirm that OSWALD, in fact, had been a passenger on the Transportes Frontera bus in question.

(A) Interview of HERBERT ROBERT VOORHEES, Passenger on Transportes del Norte Bus Traveling from San Luis Potosi to Nuevo Laredo on October 2 to 3, 1963

T-11 advised on March 26, 1964, that HERBERT ROBERT VOORHEES, true name HERBERT FRANCIS VOORHEES, who resides at Calle Masones No. 19, Apartment 10, San Miguel de Allende, Guanajuato, Mexico, furnished the following:

On October 2, 1963, he left San Miguel de Allende, Guanajuato, at 7:30 a.m. by a "second-class yellow bus" for San Luis Potosi, San Luis Potosi, Mexico, where at about 2:40 p.m. on the same date he departed for Nuevo Laredo, Tamaulipas, Mexico, via a Transportes del Norte bus.

His bus arrived at Laredo, Texas, at approximately 2:00 a.m. on October 3, 1963, and following his going through United States Customs and United States Immigration at Laredo, Texas, he disembarked from the bus in Laredo, rested at the Southland Hotel, and thereafter proceeded to San Antonio, Texas, via Greyhound bus.

He was certain that the Transportes del Norte bus, while en route to Laredo, Texas, stopped in Mexico at about 1:00 a.m. on October 3, 1963, at the "Mexican Immigration check station about twelve miles from the Mexican-American border," where the lights were turned on and a Mexican Immigration official boarded the bus to check each passenger's identification and travel documents.

At this point, the Mexican Immigration official ushered off the bus a young American, whom he described as about 20 years of age, five feet nine inches tall, of medium build, clean-shaven, bareheaded, coatless, and cleanly attired in shirt, slacks and shoes. The young American, who had carried one small bag, had been sitting at the back of the bus. Upon his return to the bus, after apparently being questioned for a few minutes, he walked again to the back of the bus. As he passed VOORHEES, he mumbled in good English, in a grumbling manner, something like, "My papers were in order before and I don't know why they bother me now -- they took my pass before."

He clearly recalled seeing the American at the United States Customs checking station in Laredo, Texas, at about 1:30 a.m. on October 3, 1963, when a Mexican woman's luggage was being examined and the young American was standing by. The American was trying to dispose of a banana by eating it hurriedly, "gulping it down," and he was told by a Customs officer that he could carry the banana into the United States and did not have to gulp it down so fast.

He recalled talking with a "Mexican-American" man who sat across the aisle from him. This man was traveling with his wife and spoke English and Spanish. He could recall neither his name nor his destination.

He furnished as many other details about the above-described trip as he could recall and claimed he could not definitely state that the young American was identical with OSWALD; however, he considered photographs of OSWALD to be similar in every detail with the young American who was on the bus.

(B) Checks of Records of Other Bus Lines

T-13 provided the following information:

On March 30, 1964, officials of the Autobuses Blancos Flecha Roja, S. A. bus line made available passenger lists for the four scheduled trips of that company from Mexico City to Nuevo Laredo of October 2, 1963, and no information identifiable with OSWALD by any of the names he was known to have used was located on those lists. It was determined, however, that if the time schedules of that company are maintained, none of its trips to Nuevo Laredo would arrive at the "Kilometer 26" highway checking station between midnight and 8:00 a.m.

Mr. Ricardo Medina Beltran, manager of the Mexico City terminal of the Autobuses Transportes del Norte bus line (hereinafter referred to as Transportes del Norte), advised that his company provides bus service between Mexico City, Mexico, and Laredo, Texas. He said that in connection with this service, a passenger list is normally prepared for each of the bus trips of his company between the above points.

MEDINA explained that the passenger list actually is a card form on which reservations and ticket sales are recorded and that after the particular trip for which it was prepared has left the terminal, it is cancelled to avoid further confusion, as the reverse side of the form is utilized for a similar record at a later date. He stated that the cancelled lists are not a permanent record and are maintained only for a short period of time following their use. He stated that he had set aside the lists for early October, 1963, in the event there should be further need for them; nevertheless, he was unable to locate them. He pointed out that apparently they had been placed inadvertently in a storeroom where tires, spare parts, boxes of obsolete files and records, and other materials

are maintained and that only a thorough review of all material in the storeroom would reveal whether or not the list for October 2, 1963, was still in existence. He related that his company has two direct trips daily to Nuevo Laredo, Tamaulipas, and Laredo, Texas, and that the bus which departs from Mexico City at 8:30 a.m. is scheduled to arrive in Nuevo Laredo at 2:00 a.m. the following morning and would arrive at the "Kilometer 26" checking station at approximately 1:00 a.m.

(C) Transportes del Norte Passenger List for October 2, 1963

On March 30, 1964, Mr. MEDINA advised that he had located the passenger-reservations list for the 8:30 a.m. bus of October 2, 1963, and on the basis of consultation with him and with several reservations and ticket clerks who recognized their handwriting thereon, the following data was obtained therefrom as translated from Spanish:

TRANSPORTES DEL NORTE

Wednesday Wednesday

MEXICO TO LAREDO

Bus No. 332 October 2, 1963 8:30

Drivers R. (ROGELIO) CUEVAS - R. (RAMON) GONZALEZ

Seat No.	Name of Passenger	Destination	Ticket No.
2	Miss COSIO	S.A.	13920
3	Mr. A. MARTINEZ	N. Ldo.	12619
4	MARGARET A. WOLFF	Ldo.	61840 exchange
5	ROBERTO P. GONZALEZ	Mty.	7915
6	M. H. VILLANUEVA	Mty.	99232
7	PAULA RUSIONI	Ldo.	9511
8	J. M. DE CUBA	Ldo.	8940
9	" "	"	41
10	Operator		
11	AUGUSTO AGUILAR	Houston	13742

Seat No.	Name of Passenger	Destination	Ticket No.
12	Chihuahuenses	Laredo, Tex.	13688
13			
14	Mr. EULALIO RODRIGUEZ	Houston	13921
15	A Viajes	Ldo.	13619
16	PH. VAN DER VORM	Laredo, Tex.	13927
17	JORGE DAVILA	Mty.	716
18	JOSE BARRIGA	Dallas	13740
19	and wife	"	741
20			
21	Mr. or Miss AGAPITO DEL RIO	S.A.	13928
22	Guadalajara	Laredo	
23	"		
24	"		
25	"		
26	"		
27	"		
28	"		
29	"		

MEDINA explained that seats No. 12 and No. 15 had been reserved for another bus line or travel agency and that the company would have no record with respect to the identities of the occupants of those seats.

On March 31, 1964, Miss ROSA MARIA OROZCO, auditor of the Auto Viajes Internacionales, S. A. travel agency (International Auto Travels, Inc.), Lafragua No. 4, Mexico, D. F., advised that she had located a record of the sale by that firm of a ticket for travel on seat No. 15 of the 8:30 a.m., October 2, 1963, bus of Transportes del Norte to Laredo to ANASTACIO RUIZ MEZA. She stated that the company had sold this transportation to RUIZ MEZA for travel via the Transportes del Norte bus line to Laredo and from Laredo to Chicago, Illinois, by Greyhound Line.

(D) Record of Location of Transportation Sold to H. O. LEE

T-11 provided the information recorded hereinunder:

On April 1, 1964, MACLOVIO PORTILLO G., Superintendent of the Mexico City terminal of the bus line Transportes Chihuahuenses, S. A. de C. V. (Chihuahuenses Transportation, Incorporated with Variable Capital), Bernal Diaz No. 5, Mexico, D. F., and his clerk, MARIA TERESA CASARES, caused the records of that bus line to be searched for all tickets issued for travel on October 2, 1963, in an effort to locate the names LEE HARVEY OSWALD, O. H. LEE, ALEK JAMES HIDELL, and V. L. LEE, with particular attention to ticket No. 13688.

PORTILLO advised that no information had been located which could be identified with the foregoing, explaining that tickets sold by his company during that period were in the eighty and ninety thousand series, eliminating the possibility that ticket No. 13688 might have been sold at that office.

PORTILLO suggested that the transportation concerning which inquiry was being made might have been sold at the Agencia de Viajes, Transportes Chihuahuenses, S. A. de C. V. (Chihuahuenses Transportation Travel Agency, Inc.), with offices at Paseo de la Reforma No. 52, Room 5. He telephoned to that agency and was advised by a clerk, ALEJANDRINA M. DE BUTCHER, that the reservation order under No. 13688 was available at that office.

On April 1, 1964, Miss TERESA SCHAEFFER BEQUERISSE, manager of the above-mentioned travel agency, located the reservation and purchase order No. 13688, and it was determined to be in blank, never having been utilized. She reviewed the Transportes del Norte passenger list for bus No. 332 for October 2, 1963, considering that the order number might be 12688, and this order No. 12688 was located and also found to be blank. She insisted that her office had not handled the reservation noted on the Transportes del Norte passenger list shown her for October 2, 1963. She was requested to review all reservation and purchase orders issued for October, 1963, by her office.

A review of the carbon copies of these reservation and purchase orders was made by the confidential source abroad in the presence of Miss SCHAEFFER, which revealed that reservation and purchase order No. 14618 was issued to Transportes del Norte in Mexico City for Mr. H. O. LEE for seat No. 12 from

Mexico City to Laredo, Texas, on Wednesday, October 2, 1963, at 8:30 a.m. This information was printed in Spanish, and the reservation was confirmed by a Mr. SAUCEDO. At the bottom of this printed order the date was indicated to be September 30, 1963, and the cost was listed as 93.75 "moneda nacional" (national money or Mexican pesos comparable to $7.50 U.S.) Also at the bottom of this printed order was the printed notice that the Agencia de Viajes, Transportes Chihuahuenses, is an agent for the Greyhound Bus Line.

Miss SCHAEFFER advised that former employee ROLANDO BARRIOS had signed the reservation and purchase order and apparently made the sale to Mr. H. O. LEE. She stated the original of this form was given to the purchaser in order that he could then obtain his ticket at Transportes del Norte, explaining that an original and two copies of the reservation and purchase order are made and the original is given to the purchaser, one copy is kept at her office, and the third copy is forwarded to the main office of the travel agency, which is Transportes Chihuahuenses, S. A. de C. V., Avenida 16 de Septiembre No. 274, Ciudad Juarez, Chihuahua, Mexico. She made available the carbon copy of the above-mentioned purchase order and stated she would search her files for any other pertinent records.

Subsequently she advised on the same date by telephone that she had located Greyhound International Exchange Order No. 43599 for presentation to the Greyhound agent at Laredo, Texas, and issued to Mr. H. O. LEE. This order was issued against the Western Greyhound Lines, 371 Market Street, San Francisco 5, California, for travel from Laredo, Texas, to Dallas, Texas, via San Antonio, Texas.

T-12 advised that on April 1, 1964, Miss SCHAEFFER made available a copy of the Greyhound International Exchange Order mentioned above, which noted that Mr. H. O. LEE was traveling to the port of exit via Transportes del Norte. The order reflected it was issued on October 1, 1963, for $12.80 U. S. by the Agencia de Viajes, T. Ch. S. A. de C. V., Reforma 52-5, Mexico City. According to Miss SCHAEFFER, the signature of the issuing agent on this order form was that of ROLANDO BARRIOS.

Miss SCHAEFFER's bookkeeper, Miss NORMA ROMAN, made available the agency's cash receipt and disbursement ledger which Miss SCHAEFFER described as a record of cash receipts and disbursements of the business on a daily basis. These records disclosed that on October 1, 1963, an entry was made in the ledger reflecting receipt of 253.75 pesos ($20.30 U.S.) from Mr. H. O. LEE which was paid to cover the cost of a bus trip from Mexico City to Dallas via Laredo. Miss SCHAEFFER explained that the entry reflecting receipt of cash is made in the cash receipt and disbursement ledger on the day following the actual transaction. She added that of the total 253.75 peso amount, 93.75 pesos ($7.50 U.S.) applied to the portion of the trip from Mexico City to Laredo and 160.00 pesos ($12.80 U.S.) applied to the travel from Laredo to Dallas.

The above record reflected that the total amount of 253.75 pesos was paid on Agencia de Viajes T. Ch. reservation and purchase order No. 14618 and that H. O. LEE was also issued Greyhound International Exchange Order No. 43599 to cover the trip from Laredo to Dallas.

The above-mentioned cash ledger reflected that the letter "B" appeared beside the name of H. O. LEE, and Miss SCHAEFFER explained that the letter "B" represents the surname initial of ROLANDO BARRIOS, the former employee of the firm who handled the transaction with H. O. LEE.

The cash ledger also revealed that under the figure of 253.75 pesos, the amount of the cash transaction, were illegible handwritten initials, and Miss SCHAEFFER stated that those are the initials of ELSA MAYNEZ, another former employee of the firm, acknowledging receipt of the 253.75 pesos by MAYNEZ from BARRIOS for entry in the cash ledger book.

Miss SCHAEFFER advised that ROLANDO BARRIOS was involved in a financial problem with her agency for which she discontinued his services. She furnished his home address as Bahia de Santa Barbara No. 20-209, Mexico, D. F., and stated he was last known to be employed at the Mauna Loa Restaurant in Mexico City.

On April 1, 1964, Miss SCHAEFFER made available a copy of a form captioned: "Western Greyhound Lines (Division of the Greyhound Corporation), 371 Market Street, San Francisco, California, International Sales Report." This sales report covers the period from October 1, 1963, to October 31, 1963, and Miss SCHAEFFER advised that recorded on this form is a recapitulation of travel sales during the month of October, 1963, made by the agency as agents for the Western Greyhound Lines in connection with which Greyhound International Exchange Orders were issued to the travelers. There were twelve such sales recorded on the above-mentioned sales report, which reflects that the second entry or sale made involved the issuance of Greyhound International Exchange Order No. 43599 to one passenger, Mr. H. O. LEE, for travel from Laredo, Texas, to Dallas, Texas, total fare for that portion of the trip being recorded as $12.80 U. S.

Miss SCHAEFFER advised that the foregoing must be maintained as a matter of permanent record in her office because of Mexican Government regulations.

On April 2, 1964, T-11 was advised by Miss SCHAEFFER that MARGARITA LABASTIBA, who also worked in the front office while BARRIOS was present, had informed her that she remembered an American who purchased a travel order but could not recall the date nor could she state it was OSWALD. Upon interview, Miss LABASTIBA could only recall that the American was tall, wore disheveled clothing, and had a great deal of hair. She could not be more specific about the date or the description of the American.

Photographs of LEE HARVEY OSWALD were exhibited to TERESA SCHAEFFER BEQUERISSE, ALEJANDRINA M. DE BUTCHER, NORMA ROMAN and MARGARITA LABASTIBA at the Agencia de Viajes, Transportes Chihuahuenses, S. A. de C. V. offices and these persons were unable to identify OSWALD.

(E) Interview of ROLANDO BARRIOS RAMIREZ

On April 2, 1964, the following information was furnished to T-13.

ROLANDO BARRIOS RAMIREZ, Bahia de Santa Barbara No. 20, Apartment 209, Mexico, D. F., advised that formerly he was

employed at the Chihuahuenses Travel Agency and now is employed as a cashier at the Mauna Loa Restaurant in Mexico City. BARRIOS reviewed the copy of the reservation and purchase order No. 14618 of the travel agency reflecting the sale on September 30, 1963, of seat No. 12 on the 8:30 a.m. trip of Transportes del Norte from Mexico City to Laredo, Texas, on October 2, 1963, and definitely identified the handprinting and signature thereon as his own. He also viewed a copy of International Exchange Order No. 43599 dated October 1, 1963, recording the sale to Mr. H. O. LEE of transportation by Greyhound Lines from Laredo, Texas, to Dallas, Texas. He stated that the handprinting and signature on this document were his and that undoubtedly he had handled the transaction represented by the two documents.

BARRIOS viewed photographs of LEE HARVEY OSWALD and advised that he was unable to affirm positively that he recalled OSWALD in connection with the travel agency. He related that at the time OSWALD's photographs were being published widely in newspapers and magazines he was impressed by the feeling that he had known or met OSWALD at some time, but had been unable to associate the feeling with any particular incident or time.

(F) Interview of Personnel at Transportes del Norte Terminal, Mexico City

On April 3, 1964, the Mexico City Terminal Manager for Transportes del Norte, RICARDO MEDINA BELTRAN, reiterated that he had no recollection whatsoever with respect to OSWALD and explained that he has no contact with passengers except under unusual circumstances since his office is removed from the passenger area of the terminal.

On the same date, bus drivers ROGELIO CUEVAS and RAMON GONZALEZ were contacted upon their arrival at the Mexico City terminal and advised that they reside in Monterrey, Nuevo Leon, Mexico, at Magna Vista No. 232 and at Juan Mendez No. 1407 Altos, respectively. Although they had no independent recollection in connection therewith, they were aware of the fact that the company's records reflect that they were the drivers of bus No. 332 between Mexico City and Monterrey on

October 2, 1963. They stated that they usually leave the bus at Monterrey, and it was their understanding that on October 2, 1963, all passengers from bus No. 332 were transferred to another unit which transported them to Nuevo Laredo with a relief driver. They viewed all available photographs of LEE HARVEY OSWALD and stated they were unable to recall his having been a passenger. They pointed out that they rarely notice the passengers and would not remember one of them unless an incident or special circumstance created a special reason for noticing and recalling them.

On April 2, 1964, ANGEL CURIEL informed that he is a ticket salesman at the Mexico City terminal of Transportes del Norte and that he recognized his handwriting on the October 2, 1963, passenger list for bus No. 332 in connection with the items listed under "destination" and "ticket number." He explained that he undoubtedly exchanged ticket No. 13688 for the travel agency purchase order and recorded the number of the ticket before delivering it to the passenger. CURIEL viewed available photographs of OSWALD and stated he could not recall him in connection with his duties at the bus line.

On the same date, salesman MIGUEL SAUCEDO advised that the handwriting on the passenger list under "name of passenger" of the word "Chihuahuenses" opposite seat No. 12 indicated that he received the telephonic reservation of the space by the travel agency. SAUCEDO did not recall the matter and was unable to identify photographs of OSWALD in connection therewith.

Ticket salesmen CANUTO S. ROJAS and JUAN GASCON advised that they recognized their handwriting on the October 2, 1963, manifest in connection with some of the reservations and ticket sales, but upon viewing photographs of OSWALD could not recall having seen him at the Mexico City terminal of Transportes del Norte.

MEDINA and the four ticket salesmen mentioned above explained that the diversity of serial numbers for tickets sold on the passenger list in question is occasioned by the fact that they each sell from different blocks of tickets for the various destinations involved.

(G) Interviews of Personnel at Transportes del Norte Bus Terminal Restaurant, Monterrey, Nuevo Leon

On April 6, 1964, T-7 interviewed the following personnel of the restaurant located in the Transportes del Norte terminal at Monterrey, Nuevo Leon:

DAVID SANCHEZ GONZALEZ, manager and cashier
MARIA OTILLA TOVAR, waitress
RAFAEL ZAVALA CASTILLO, counterman
MANUEL CUELLAS GARCIA, counterman

All four of these persons advised that they work a 2:00 p.m. to 2:00 a.m. shift and that all were on duty during that shift on October 2-3, 1963. No one else worked during this shift.

Upon being shown various photographs of OSWALD, none was able to recall having seen him in the restaurant at any time.

According to T-7, the restaurant is located within the Transportes del Norte terminal in Monterrey, there being a ticket counter at one end of the terminal, a waiting room in the center, and the restaurant at the opposite end of the waiting room from the ticket counter.

(H) Inquiry at Monterrey, Nuevo Leon Main Offices of Transportes del Norte

T-18, a confidential source abroad, provided the following information:

On April 2, 1964, RAMON TREVINO QUEZADA, Vice President and General Manager of Transportes del Norte at Monterrey, Nuevo Leon, caused a search to be made for and succeeded in locating an envelope containing the tickets surrendered by the passengers to the bus drivers for the Mexico City-Monterrey travel in bus No. 332 on October 2, 1963. Among those tickets was No. 13688 which reflected thereon that it had been used for seat No. 12 on that trip.

TREVINO advised that the company records reflect that following the arrival of bus No. 332 in Monterrey at 9:15 p.m., October 2, 1963, all passengers destined for Nuevo Laredo or beyond were transferred to bus No. 373, which was driven by ALVARO IBARRA and departed from Monterrey at 9:50 p.m. He explained further that because the company has thirteen trips daily between Monterrey and Nuevo Laredo, no effort is made to maintain a record of the passengers who board the bus at Monterrey in connection therewith. Mr. TREVINO explained that IBARRA recently married and resides at Nuevo Laredo, Tamaulipas.

On April 3, 1964, Mr. TREVINO stated he had located the portion of ticket No. 13688 for travel from Monterrey to Laredo and that its presence in the envelope for that trip of October 2-3, 1963, was definite indication that the travel was performed.

(I) Bus Passenger ANASTASIO RUIZ MEZA
Identified Photographs of LEE HARVEY OSWALD

T-13 advised as follows:

On March 30, 1964, RICARDO MEDINA BELTRAN, manager of the Mexico City terminal of the Transportes del Norte bus line, advised that seat No. 15 of Transportes del Norte bus No. 332 for the trip of October 2, 1963, had been reserved for another bus line or travel agency and that the company would have no record with respect to the identity of the occupant of that seat.

On March 31, 1964, Miss ROSA MARIA OROZCO, auditor of the Auto Viajes Internacionales, S. A. (International Auto Travels, Inc.) travel agency, Lafragua No. 4, Mexico, D. F., located a record of the sale by that firm of a ticket for travel in seat No. 15 of the 8:30 a.m., October 2, 1963, bus of Transportes del Norte to Laredo to ANASTACIO RUIZ MEZA. This transportation was sold to RUIZ MEZA for travel via Transportes del Norte bus line to Laredo and from Laredo to Chicago, Illinois, by Greyhound line.

T-19, a confidential source abroad, advised as follows:

On April 5, 1964, ANASTASIO RUIZ MEZA, who resides at Sullana No. 710, Mexico, D. F., and who is employed in the Auditor's Office, Customs Section, Mexican Ministry of the Treasury and Public Credit, advised as follows:

He was a passenger on a Transportes del Norte bus which departed Mexico City at 8:30 a.m., October 2, 1963, en route to Laredo, Texas, and occupied seat No. 15 on that bus. Following his arrival in Laredo, he departed on a Greyhound Line bus with his final destination being Chicago, Illinois.

RUIZ MEZA still had the Transportes del Norte ticket stub for the Mexico City-Laredo, Texas, portion of the trip, the number of the ticket being 13619.

As nearly as he could recall, the bus departed without delay at 8:30 a.m., October 2, 1963. He believed there were about fourteen or fifteen other passengers who boarded the bus with him.

He could not remember whether or not any Americans had boarded the bus in Mexico City but stated that seated next to him on the bus was an individual whom he described as being tall, heavy and about 54 years of age. This individual, whose name he did not know, was of Mexican extraction and was traveling to Houston, Texas. This person sat next to RUIZ MEZA on the several buses from Mexico City to San Antonio, Texas, where he departed the bus. Changes of buses had occurred at Monterrey, Nuevo Leon, Mexico, and at Laredo, Texas on the trip north. (The Transportes del Norte manifest for the trip of October 2, 1963, bus No. 332, lists space for one EULALIO RODRIGUEZ in seat No. 14, which adjoins seat No, 15, with final destination for RODRIGUEZ listed as Houston.)

Directly across the aisle to his rear, the seating arrangements of the bus being staggered on either side, was a young "Ecuadorian" couple, assumed to be man and wife (seats No. 8 and No. 9). He was not certain that this couple was from Ecuador, but believed they were South Americans. RUIZ identified a photograph of JUAN MATEO DE CUBA, as it appears on Mexican Government tourist form FM-5 No. 3625296, as identical with the above-described "Ecuadorian." RUIZ also viewed a photograph of ADA FRANCISCA BISLIP DE DE CUBA, as it appears on Mexican Government tourist form FM-5 No. 3625295, which depicts Mrs. DE CUBA wearing eyeglasses. RUIZ could not be sure this woman is identical with the woman traveling in the company of the person whom he identified as being JUAN MATEO DE CUBA. He stated that the woman who was seated next to DE CUBA was not wearing eyeglasses.

(The above-described tourist forms describe Mr. and Mrs. DE CUBA as being residents of Aruba, Dutch West Indies. The Transportes del Norte manifest for the above-described trip lists space for J. M. DE CUBA and one other person in seats No. 8 and No. 9.)

After departure from Mexico City at 8:30 a.m. on October 2, 1963, the bus did not stop until its arrival in San Luis Potosi, San Luis Potosi, Mexico, at about 1:00 p.m. the same day. After about a half-hour stop, everyone again boarded the bus for the trip to Monterrey, arriving at the Transportes del Norte terminal there about 9:30 p.m. on October 2, 1963.

RUIZ recalled that upon arrival in the bus terminal in Monterrey, everyone debarked and many of the passengers went to the restaurant located at the Transportes del Norte bus terminal to eat. While RUIZ was eating at one of the tables in the restaurant at the Transportes del Norte bus terminal in Monterrey, a young American was seated alone at a table a few yards away from him to his rear. He advised this was the first time he had noted the presence of this person, whom he described as being about 27 years of age, weighing approximately 130 to 135 pounds, with brown hair, about five feet seven or five feet eight inches in height, and of slender build. He recalled this same individual's boarding the bus in Monterrey a few minutes after him.

RUIZ viewed several photographs of LEE HARVEY OSWALD and positively identified two profile photographs of OSWALD as being of the above-described American youth who was seated to his rear in the restaurant of the Transportes del Norte bus terminal in Monterrey. He advised he had no doubt in his mind with respect to this identification.

One of the photographs identified by RUIZ was a photograph of OSWALD which had appeared in "Life" magazine depicting OSWALD passing out pro-Cuban literature on a street in New Orleans, Louisiana. (This is a profile photograph of OSWALD showing his right arm extended and his torso.)

The other photograph identified by RUIZ was a profile view of OSWALD taken at the New Orleans Police Department on August 9, 1963, under New Orleans Police Department No. 112723.

He had seen front-view photographs of OSWALD in the newspapers following the assassination of President KENNEDY; however, he pointed out that he did not associate the photographs with the above-described American nor did he give any careful or studied thought to their being identical to the American youth.

The American youth, whom he described as being OSWALD, was dressed in a light-colored, perhaps white, open-collared, short-sleeved sport shirt, and was bareheaded. According to RUIZ, this individual was not wearing a coat. He did not recall the color or type of trousers this person was wearing, his shoes, or the luggage he might have been carrying.

After the meal stop in Monterrey, which lasted approximately one-half hour, the passengers boarded a different bus of the Transportes del Norte line, and he observed there also had been a change of bus drivers at that time. He recalled that the individual whom he identified as OSWALD boarded the bus in Monterrey after he did, and after he had taken his seat, No. 15, he noticed the American youth go down the aisle past him. He believed this person had taken a seat in the right rear section of the bus or on the same side of the bus where RUIZ was seated.

He believed the bus arrived at "Kilometer 26," the Immigration and Customs control point located about sixteen miles south of Nuevo Laredo, Tamaulipas, Mexico, at about 1:00 a.m. on October 3, 1963. Upon reaching "Kilometer 26," the bus stopped and an official, whom RUIZ assumed to be a

Mexican Immigration officer, boarded the bus and proceeded to review the travel documents of the passengers on board. He recalled seeing the Immigration official in the aisle on his way from the rear to the front of the bus and hearing him exclaim in English, "Come on with me," apparently directing his remarks to someone in the rear of the bus. He then saw the Mexican Immigration official go to the front of the bus followed by the American identified by him as being OSWALD. He assumed some question had arisen as to the American's travel documents.

The interior lights of the bus were on at the time, and he saw the Immigration official and the American get off the bus and enter the small Immigration office located at the side of the road a few feet from the bus. RUIZ estimated that from the time the American left the bus with the Immigration official until the time he boarded the bus and again went to the rear of the vehicle a period of perhaps three or four minutes may have transpired.

He recalled that after the American again boarded the bus, Mr. DE CUBA left the bus and went to the Immigration office, and he assumed that there was some question with respect to DE CUBA's travel documents. He believed that about one minute later DE CUBA returned and seated himself in the bus. The only two passengers he recalled having left the bus at "Kilometor 26" were the American and Mr. DE CUBA.

He estimated that the entire operation of the Immigration check at "Kilometer 26" lasted from ten to fifteen minutes, and shortly after Mr. DE CUBA boarded the bus, the driver continued the journey to Nuevo Laredo, where the bus arrived at the Transportes del Norte bus terminal about 1:30 a.m., October 3, 1963.

All of the passengers left the bus in Nuevo Laredo, remaining at the bus terminal for a period of from twenty minutes to one-half hour. During the period the passengers were in the Transportes del Norte terminal in Nuevo Laredo, he recalled seeing OSWALD waiting near the bus alone. He did not recall observing the American speaking to anyone.

He recalled that after a short stop in Nuevo Laredo, the passengers boarded the same bus on which they had traveled from Monterrey to Nuevo Laredo. He recalled the American whom he identified as OSWALD boarding the bus at Nuevo Laredo for the trip across the International Bridge to Laredo, Texas, as he remembered seeing the American go down the aisle to the rear of the bus after he, RUIZ, was in his seat. From that point on, he does not recall seeing the American again.

The Transportes del Norte bus proceeded across the International Bridge and in several minutes was in Laredo, Texas, on the United States side of the bridge. The bus stopped on the south side of the United States Government building adjacent to the steps which lead into the offices where, according to RUIZ, he was vaccinated.

All passengers left the bus and proceeded up the stairway leading to what he assumed were Immigration offices. He stated that he and another person, whom he described as a short Mexican male of advanced age and who he believed had boarded the bus at Monterrey, were the only persons who remained behind to be vaccinated.

RUIZ estimated that the entire United States Government processing operation at the port of entry was about one-half hour in duration. Everyone already had boarded the bus by the time he had been processed by United States Immigration, and he was the last of the passengers to board the bus for the short trip to the Laredo bus terminal.

Upon reaching the Laredo bus terminal, everyone again left the bus. After about one-half hour, he boarded a two-tiered Greyhound Line bus in the Laredo bus terminal and automatically seated himself in seat No. 15, since he had been in that seat all the way from Mexico City. He estimated that there might have been a total of from fifteen to twenty passengers who boarded the Greyhound bus at Laredo.

RUIZ estimated the departure from Laredo of the Greyhound bus as being about 3:00 a.m., October 3, 1963, and the arrival in San Antonio, Texas, as about 8:00 a.m. that same morning. He observed that everyone got off the bus at

San Antonio, and he believed the stop in San Antonio lasted about one-half hour, after which the passengers boarded the same bus and proceeded to Dallas, Texas, arriving at about 1:00 p.m. on the same day.

RUIZ recalled that the stop in Dallas lasted about two hours, and it was approximately 3:00 p.m. when the same bus departed Dallas for the journey to Chicago, Illinois, via Tulsa, Oklahoma.

RUIZ recalled seeing for the last time the American whom he identified as OSWALD when the latter boarded the bus at Nuevo Laredo prior to the trip across the International Bridge to Laredo, Texas. RUIZ believed that the American had boarded the same Greyhound bus at Laredo on the morning of October 3, 1963, and continued the trip to Dallas, Texas, but stated he did not notice him nor did he pay particular attention to the other passengers.

RUIZ did not recall having seen the American speak to anyone at any time, and it appeared to RUIZ that the American was traveling alone. He commented that the American had given him the impression of being a quiet individual of a retiring nature.

RUIZ viewed a photograph of PHILIPPE PITER E. VAN DER VORM, as it appears on Mexican Government tourist form FM-8 No. 624820, which VAN DER VORM utilized upon entry to Mexico in September, 1963. RUIZ did not recall having seen this person as a passenger on either of the Transportes del Norte buses on the trip from Mexico City to Laredo in October, 1963.

(J) Interview of Transportes del Norte Passenger JOSE BARRIGA BERNAL

On April 6, 1964, Captain JOSE BARRIGA BERNAL advised T-13 that he is a retired officer of the Mexican Army and resides in Mexico City at Gabino Barreda 104, Apartment No. 3. He recalled that on October 2, 1963, he and his wife had traveled from Mexico City to Laredo on Transportes del Norte, and after entering the United States, had continued to Dallas, Texas, via Greyhound bus. He viewed available photographs of OSWALD and

stated emphatically that he could not recall him as a passenger. He mentioned that the only passenger he could recall was AGAPITO DEL RIO, with whom he conversed while they were passing through United States Customs at Laredo, Texas.

(K) List Obtained of Departure of Non-Mexican Citizens on October 3, 1963, at Nuevo Laredo, Tamaulipas

T-1, who is familiar with the workings of the Mexican Ministry of Gobernacion (Interior), made available for examination the forms FM-5 and FM-8 for all non-Mexican citizens departing Mexico at Nuevo Laredo, Tamaulipas, as tourists on October 3, 1963, as well as the copies of forms FM-11 containing the recapitulation of the departures from Mexico at Nuevo Laredo on this date.

Investigation in this case disclosed that OSWALD departed from Mexico at Nuevo Laredo on October 3, 1963. OSWALD's departure was handled by Mexican Immigration Service employee ALBERTO ARZAMENDI CHAPA.

According to T-1, ARZAMENDI CHAPA worked the 12:00 midnight to 8:00 a.m. shift on October 3, 1963.

From the tourist cards (forms FM-5 and FM-8) and the copies of the forms FM-11, the following is a list of the individuals who departed Mexico at Nuevo Laredo on October 3, 1963, the list's having been divided into those individuals traveling on forms FM-5 and those traveling on forms FM-8, since the forms FM-11 are so set up.

The number appearing before each name is the number which appears on the form FM-11.

1. Holders of Forms FM-5

79. TEODORA HERRERA ALVAREZ, FM-5 No. 4049060, issued by Mexican Consulate at Lubbock, Texas, September 25, 1963.

80. PABLO CALAMATEO, FM-5 No. 4049059, issued at Mexican Consulate, Lubbock, Texas, September 25, 1963.

81. JUAN CANALES, FM-5 No. 4049058, issued at Mexican Consulate, Lubbock, Texas, September 25, 1963.

82. MANUEL CAPIZ, FM-5 No. 4329753, issued by Mexican Immigration Office, Nuevo Laredo, September 12, 1963.

83. GUADALUPE CAPIZ, FM-5 No. 4329756, issued by Mexican Immigration Service, Nuevo Laredo, September 12, 1963.

84. JUAN MATEO DE CUBA, FM-5 No. 3625296, issued by the Honorary Mexican Consul in Curacao, Dutch West Indies, July 18, 1963.

85. ADA FRANCISCA BISLIP DE DE CUBA, FM-5 No. 3625295, issued by the Honorary Mexican Consul, Curacao, July 18, 1963.

86. IGNACIA CHAVEZ, FM-5 No. 4496345, issued by Mexican Consulate, Dallas, Texas, September 12, 1963.

87. TOMASA GARZA DE ESCAMILLA, FM-5 No. 4329952, issued by Mexican Immigration Service, Nuevo Laredo, September 23, 1963.

88. RAY FOK, FM-5 No. 4326296, issued by Mexican Immigration Service, Nuevo Laredo, June 12, 1963. (It is to be noted that this individual appeared to sign her name on instant form FM-5 as RAY FOX.)

89. EMMA ELISABETH GOERITZ FRANK, FM-5 No. 4307615, issued by Mexican Tourism Department, New York, New York, June 10, 1963.

90. MARCELINO RAMON GARCIA CASTRO, FM-5 No. 4478227, issued by Mexican Consulate General, Chicago, Illinois, September 7, 1963.

91. ERNESTINA A. DE GARZA, FM-5 No. 4327720, issued by Mexican Immigration Service, Nuevo Laredo, July 23, 1963.

92. EUGENE EVERALD HUNTER, FM-5 No. 4193457, issued by Honorary Mexican Consul, Kingston, Jamaica, British West Indies, September 12, 1963.

93. VICTOR JOSEPH KIMM, FM-5 No. 4097447, issued by Mexican Tourism Department, Houston, Texas, April 10, 1963.

94. PATRICIA ANN KIMM, FM-5 No. 4097446, issued by Mexican Tourism Department, Houston, Texas, April 10, 1963. Accompanied by minor children, KEVIN, 3 years of age, and TERRY, 2 years of age.

95. MARIA LUISA CRUZ DE LOPEZ, FM-5 No. 4346726, issued by Mexican Consulate, Corpus Christi, Texas, August 31, 1963.

96. LAWRENCE LOPEZ, FM-5 No. 4381039, issued by Mexican Consulate, Detroit, Michigan, August 8, 1963.

97. CORNELIUS D. LeFEVRE, FM-5 No. 4027798, issued by Mexican Consulate, Fort Worth, Texas, June 4, 1963.

98. JESSIE E. LeFEURE, FM-5 No. 4027799, issued by Mexican Consulate, Fort Worth, Texas, June 4, 1963.

99. WILLIAM G. LOPEZ, FM-5 No. 4381128, issued by Mexican Consulate, Detroit, Michigan, August 27, 1963.

100. MAMIE A. MILLER, FM-5 No. 4329147, issued by Mexican Immigration Service, Nuevo Laredo, September 7, 1963.

101. CHARLES L. MILLER, FM-5 No. 4455353, issued by Mexican Tourism Department, New York, New York, September 4, 1963.

102. MA. MAGDALENA MORENO, FM-5 No. 4329635, issued by Mexican Immigration Service, Nuevo Laredo, September 15, 1963.

103. MATILDE MURACCIOLE DAVILA, FM-5 No. 3461434, issued by Mexican Embassy, Caracas, Venezuela, March 4, 1963.

104. JOSE NERI, FM-5 No. 4120593, issued by Mexican Immigration Service, Nuevo Laredo, April 4, 1963.

105. MA. CRISTINA CARACCIOLE DAVILA DE PIEDRA, FM-5 No. 3461432, issued March 4, 1963, at Caracas, Venezuela, by Mexican Embassy.

106. MANUEL VICENTE PORRAS RIVERA, FM-5 No. 4377279, issued by Mexican Embassy, San Jose, Costa Rica, September 13, 1963.

107. AGAPITO DEL RIO, FM-5 No. 4158202, issued by Mexican Consulate General, San Antonio, Texas, September 13, 1963.

108. GLORIA ROMERO, FM-5 No. 4329755, issued by Mexican Immigration Service, Nuevo Laredo, September 12, 1963.

109. FRANCES MAUD ROSS, FM-5 No. 4234718, issued by Mexican Consulate, Kansas City, Missouri, September 11, 1963.

110. RICHARD T. SCHUBERT, FM-5 No. 4496471, issued by Mexican Consulate, Dallas, Texas, September 23, 1963.

111. Mrs. BEATRICE L. SCHUBERT, FM-5 No. 4496472, issued by Mexican Consulate, Dallas, Texas, September 23, 1963.

112. SALVADOR SEGOBIANO, FM-5 No. 4366853, issued by Mexican Consulate, St. Louis, Missouri, September 12, 1963.

113. MARIA SEGOBIANO, FM-5 No. 4366852, issued by Mexican Consulate, St. Louis, Missouri, September 12, 1963.

114. PHILLIP TRITSCHLER STEFFEN, FM-5 No. 4328866, issued by Mexican Immigration Service, Nuevo Laredo, August 7, 1963.

115. OTELLO MERICHI TADDIA, FM-5 No. 4050009/900, issued by Mexican Embassy, Caracas, Venezuela, May 15, 1963.

116. HARVEY H. TUTTLE, FM-5 No. 4121947, issued by Mexican Immigration Service, Nuevo Laredo, April 6, 1963.

117. HERBERT ROBERT VOORHEES, FM-5 No. 4325846, issued by Mexican Immigration Service, Nuevo Laredo, June 5, 1963.

118. ANTONY S. WATNEY, FM-5 No. 4484229, issued by Mexican Consulate, Phoenix, Arizona, September 23, 1963.

2. Holders of Forms FM-8

76. MARIA JUANA ALANIZ, FM-8 No. 626392, issued by Mexican Immigration Office, Nuevo Laredo, October 1, 1963.

77. ORALIA GARCIA MARTINEZ AYALA, FM-8 No. 626310, issued by Mexican Immigration Office, Nuevo Laredo, September 28, 1963.

78. ROBERTO BALDAZO, FM-8 No. 623799, issued by Mexican Immigration Office, Nuevo Laredo, September 28, 1963.

79. DOLORES BALDAZO ROMERO, FM-8 No. 626318, issued by Mexican Immigration Office, Nuevo Laredo, September 30, 1963.

80. RALPH A. BANNIGAN, FM-8 No. 667990, issued by Mexican Immigration Office, Ciudad Miguel Aleman, Tamaulipas, October 2, 1963.

81. DARLENE L. BANNIGAN, FM-8 No. 667991, issued by Mexican Immigration Office, Ciudad Miguel Aleman, Tamaulipas, October 2, 1963.

82. EDUARD BASTIEN, FM-8 No. 362357, issued by Mexican Consulate General, Guatemala City, Guatemala, October 1, 1963.

83. JOHN H. BENNETT. Departed utilizing form FM-17 No. 518151, issued by Mexican Immigration Office, Nuevo Laredo, October 3, 1963. The form FM-17 is not used ordinarily by tourists but rather by Mexicans and foreigners having permanent residence in Mexico. Attached to the form FM-17 was an official statement drawn up by the Mexican Immigration Office in Nuevo Laredo which set forth that BENNETT, a resident of 10250 Haitian Drive, Miami, Florida, had been stopped on October 3, 1963, at a Mexican Immigration check station located 26 kilometers south of Nuevo Laredo. At that time BENNETT claimed that he had lost his tourist documentation and stated he had originally entered Mexico at Nuevo Laredo. A check of the Mexican Immigration records at Nuevo Laredo disclosed that BENNETT had entered Mexico at that port of entry on September 8, 1963, on FM-8 No. 625114. From this, it was obvious that BENNETT had overstayed his fifteen-day permission granted by the FM-8 and, accordingly, he was required to deposit 200 pesos to cover any fine that might grow

out of his overstay in Mexico, and he was permitted to depart Mexico using the form FM-17. This form described him as 53 years of age, born in Nutley, New Jersey, married, accountant, and proceeding from Guadalajara, Jalisco, to Houston, Texas, by automobile. The same information appeared on the FM-11. Departure was handled by JOSE REBOLLEDO LARA.

84. ELENA S. DE CORONADO, FM-8 No. 668002, issued by Mexican Immigration Office, Ciudad Miguel Aleman, Tamaulipas, October 2, 1963.

85. DALLAS ZELMA CLINE, FM-8 No. 51047, issued by Mexican Tourism Department, San Antonio, Texas, September 27, 1963.

86. PHILIPPE PITER E. VAN DER VORM, FM-8 No. 624820, issued by Mexican Immigration Office, Nuevo Laredo, September 24, 1963.

87. LEO CHRIS EHLINGER, FM-8 No. 609060, issued by Mexican Immigration Office, Piedras Negras, Coahuila, September 28, 1963.

88. HENRY OLIVER EMERSON, FM-8 No. 624041, issued by Mexican Immigration Office, Nuevo Laredo, October 1, 1963.

89. ADRIENNE M. J. EMERSON, FM-8 No. 624040, issued by Mexican Immigration Office, Nuevo Laredo, October 1, 1963.

90. ENRIQUETA GARZA GARZA, FM-8 No. 609132, issued by Mexican Immigration Office, Piedras Negras, Coahuila, October 1, 1963.

91. CRISTEL G. DE GONZALEZ, FM-8 No. 624970, issued by Mexican Immigration Office, Nuevo Laredo, September 23, 1963.

92. MA. LUISA DE GUERRERO GARCIA, FM-8 No. 625650, issued by Mexican Immigration Office, Nuevo Laredo, September 28, 1963.

93. LEIGHTON COLIN HINKSON, FM-8 No. 454694, issued by Mexican Consulate, Belize, British Honduras, September 24, 1963.

94. EDUARDO LUIS MARTINEZ, FM-8 No. 510350, issued by Mexican Tourism Department, San Antonio, Texas, September 23, 1963.

95. ILDEFONSO MUNOZ, FM-8 No. 622097, issued by Mexican Immigration Office, Nueva Ciudad Guerrero, Tamaulipas, September 29, 1963.

96. JOSEPH MICHAEL McDANIEL, FM-8 No. 625603, issued by Mexican Immigration Office, Nuevo Laredo, September 21, 1963.

97. MARY LOUISE McDANIEL, FM-8 No. 625604, issued by Mexican Immigration Office, Nuevo Laredo, September 21, 1963.

98. JOHN O. BRIAN, FM-8 No. 626185, issued by Mexican Immigration Office, Nuevo Laredo, September 30, 1963. (It is to be noted this individual appeared to sign his name as JOHN O'BRIEN.)

99. As has been previously reported, this traveler was OSWALD. He was in possession of Mexican tourist card form FM-8 No. 24085, issued September 17, 1963, by the Mexican Consulate General, New Orleans, Louisiana, under the name of LEE, HARVEY OSWALD. The card was signed LEE H. OSWALD. The card described him as 23 years of age, married and a photographer by profession. It indicated that he presented a birth certificate as proof of citizenship. Entry was at Nuevo Laredo on September 26, 1963, with an announced final destination of Mexico City. No means of travel was shown on the tourist card, either at the time of entry or at departure on October 3, 1963. The FM-11 listed his name as HARVEY OSWALD LEE, showed he was proceeding from Mexico City

with a final destination of New Orleans, Louisiana, and that he was traveling by auto. Records of the Mexican Immigration Service in Mexico City contain no information to substantiate that he actually was traveling by automobile. As has been previously reported, the departure of OSWALD was handled by an employee of the Mexican Immigration Service named ALBERTO ARZAMENDI CHAPA.

100. LUCAS PERALES, JR., FM-8 No. 625584, issued by Mexican Immigration Office, Nuevo Laredo, October 2, 1963.

101. MA. LUISA PEREZ, FM-8 No. 626610, issued by Mexican Immigration Office, Nuevo Laredo, October 2, 1963.

102. ANTONIO B. QUIMBAR, FM-8 No. 826020, issued by Mexican Immigration Office, Nuevo Laredo, September 21, 1963.

103. BERTA ALICIA RAMOS, FM-8 No. 668003, issued by Mexican Immigration Office, Ciudad Miguel Aleman, Tamaulipas, October 2, 1963.

104. PABLO REYES GONZALEZ, FM-8 No. 626181, issued by Mexican Immigration Office, Nuevo Laredo, September 30, 1963.

105. ARNOLD RIOJAS, FM-8 No. 622168, issued by Mexican Immigration Office, Nueva Ciudad Guerrero, Tamaulipas, October 2, 1963.

106. RICARDO ROCHA, FM-8 No. 609133, issued by Mexican Immigration Office, Piedras Negras, Coahuila, October 2, 1963.

107. CELIA MARTINEZ DE RUMSEY, FM-8 No. 510349, issued by Mexican Tourism Department, San Antonio, Texas, September 23, 1963.

108. CLEMENTE SAENZ, FM-8 No. 625609, issued by Mexican Immigration Office, Nuevo Laredo, September 24, 1963.

109. CHARLES SCHMEDZ, FM-8 No. 626186, issued by Mexican Immigration Office, Nuevo Laredo, September 30, 1963.

110. ROBERT L. TARIN, FM-8 No. 609130, issued by Mexican Immigration Service, Piedras Negras, Coahuila, October 1, 1963.

111. ELISABETH TARIN, FM-8 No. 609129, issued by Mexican Immigration Service, Piedras Negras, Coahuila, October 1, 1933

112. BONIFACIO URDIALES, FM-8 No. 626390, issued by Mexican Immigration Office, Nuevo Laredo, October 1, 1963.

113. HOMER VAUHAN (possibly VAUGHAN), FM-8 No. 625158, issued by Mexican Immigration Office Nuevo Laredo, October 2, 1963.

114. MARTIN L. WILSON, FM-8 No. 626019, issued by Mexican Immigration Office, Nuevo Laredo, September 21, 1963.

(L) Additional List of Persons Who Departed on October 3, 1963, and Entered on September 26, 1963, at Nuevo Laredo, Tamaulipas, Mexico

T-20, a confidential source abroad, advised as follows:

In order to ascertain the identities of other persons who entered Mexico at Nuevo Laredo on September 26, 1963, and departed Mexico at Nuevo Laredo on October 3, 1963, utilizing travel documents other than FM-5 and FM-8 tourist cards, the following inquiry was conducted:

On April 20 and 29, 1964, source examined the original Mexican Immigration Department FM-11 forms recording data concerning persons who entered Mexico at Nuevo Laredo on September 26, 1963, and departed from Mexico at Nuevo Laredo on October 3, 1963, with various types of travel documents. The original FM-11 forms relating thereto were reviewed inasmuch as separate lists are maintained for each type of travel document issued to travelers. The following is the complete list of persons of record who entered Mexico at Nuevo Laredo on September 26, 1963, and who departed Mexico through that city on October 3, 1963, utilizing travel documents other than FM-5 and FM-8 tourist cards. It was explained to source that these persons and those previously recorded as having entered and departed with forms FM-5 and FM-8 do not include all persons who entered and departed at Nuevo Laredo on September 26, 1963, and October 3, 1963, respectively, as there are numerous individuals who cross the United States-Mexico border daily who are not documented by Mexican authorities, including many Mexican nationals traveling from the interior of Mexico to the United States.

T-21, a confidential source abroad, compiled the following from a review of the forms FM-11 described above:

Departures - October 3, 1963

Departures of October 3, 1963, of Non-Mexican Citizens Traveling on Form FM-6 Tourist Cards

FRANK WOODROW BLADES, FM-6 No. 077307.

Departures of October 3, 1963, of Non-Mexican Citizens (Children Under 15 Years of Age) Traveling on Form FM-7

JESUS DE MARK (this child is listed alphabetically on the FM-11 form to indicate his name is JESUS DE MARK; however, the name could possibly be MARK DE JESUS), FM-7 No. 89790.

MONICA JULIA CASTRO, FM-7 No. 152138.

JUAN JOSE CASTRO, FM-7 No. 152137.

FEDERICO DIAZ, FM-7 No. 94256.

MARGARITA GARZA, FM-7 No. 151335.

FERNANDO GARZA, FM-7 No. 151334.

Departures of October 3, 1963,
of Non-Mexican Citizens
Traveling on Form FM-17

WILLIAM ALBERT SCHMIDT HUSEBO, FM-17 No. 106517.

MARIO CHUCA REYNOSO, FM-17 No. 51325.

WALTER SCOTT TURNPAUGH, FM-17 No. 11019.

LAURA LAUTERBACH DE TURNPAUGH, FM-17 No. 11020.

KEVIN KIMM, FM-17 No. 566256.

TERRY KIM, FM-17 No. 566257.

Departures of October 3, 1963,
of Mexican Nationals,
Traveling on Form FM-17

LEONOR CASTILLO TORROELLA, FM-17 No. 459400.

MARIO DE COTE MUNOZ SOTO, FM-17 No. 693742.

CONCEPCION NUNEZ RODRIGUEZ, FM-17 No. 693743.

FERNANDO BALDAZO FLORES, FM-17 No. 521780.

RAUL DAVILA CHAVARRIA, FM-17 No. 521022.

ARCADIO ESCAMILLA MARTINEZ, FM-17 No. 521647.

GUADALUPE GARZA ARRAMBIDE, FM-17 No. 526583.

ANTONIO GOMEZ GOVEA, FM-17 No. 521638.

RENATO GONZALEZ TALAVERA, FM-17 No. 281694.

CARLOS AMADO MAYAUDON LOPEZ, FM-17 No. 681641.

MICAELA DE JESUS MONTEMAYOR, FM-17 No. 632203.

HECTOR OROZCO ESQUIVEL, FM-17 No. 521758.

HELIODOR PEREZ GUEVARA, FM-17 No. 519391.

SIMON TAPIA, FM-17 No. 521701.

Entries - September 26, 1963

Entries of September 26, 1963,
of Non-Mexican Citizens
Traveling on Form FM-6

NUNO TEOTONIO PEREIRA, FM-6 No. 005361.

Entries of September 26, 1963,
of Non-Mexican Citizens
(Children Under 15 Years of Age)
Traveling on Form FM-7

RICHARD CRUZ, FM-7 No. 96364.

JUANITA PEREZ, FM-7 No. 96363.

Entries of September 26, 1963,
of Non-Mexican Citizens
Traveling on Form FM-14

PAULA MARTA LAWRIE, FM-14 No. 111332.

Entries of September 26, 1963,
of Non-Mexican Citizens
Traveling on Form FM-17

MANUEL FLORES, FM-17 No. 089392.

FRANCISCO MAJEWSKI MADRAK, FM-17 No. 089393.

HOWARD WILLIAM REYNOLDS, FM-17 No. 60079.

LILY DE CHICUREL BEJA, FM-17 No. 74182.

ISAAC LEVY LEON, FM-17 No. 74903.

MARIO O. MENDIVIL, FM-17 No. 4160.

IRENE ESTELA MENDIVIL, FM-17 No. 4161.

Entries of September 26, 1963, of Non-Mexican Citizens Traveling on Form FM-9

LOUISE KNOWLES, FM-9 No. 5844.

ROGER A. KONCZAL, FM-9 No. 5896.

PHYLLIS JEAN JENSK, FM-9 No. 2000.

DONALD CHARLES SOLOMME, FM-9 No. 1752.

Entries of September 26, 1963, of Mexican Nationals Traveling on Form FM-17

RODOLFO ACEVEDO GUEVARA, FM-17 No. 521689.

CARLOS ALMAGUER ECHRTEA, FM-17 No. 521687.

AGUSTIN CERDA REYES, FM-17 No. 521685.

MANUEL ESCALANTE GONZALEZ, FM-17 No. 521692.

APOLINAR GARCIA GUARDIOLA, FM-17 No. 521691.

RODOLFO HERNANDEZ MENDIOLA, FM-17 No. 521694.

JOSE MARCOS MATA GALVAN, FM-17 No. 521686.

ANTONIO MORENO GARZA, FM-17 No. 521690.

ALVARO ONTIVEROS CANTU, FM-17 No. 521693.

ELVA VALLE RENDON, FM-17 No. 521677.

JUAN M. SALAZAR ESPINOZA, FM-17 No. 521648.

JUAN RODRIGUEZ SAUCEDO, FM-17 No. 521678.

PABLO SILVA GARZA, FM-17 No. 521679.

PEDRO VILLARREAL GARCIA, FM-17 No. 521688.

ALICIA ARGUELLES ARRATIA, FM-17 No. 651598.

CELIA ALICIA MARQUEZ DE CHAVEZ, FM-17 No. 667155.

ABRAHAM CHERNOVICH, FM-17 No. 655719.

ODETTE CHICUREL Y BEJA, FM-17 No. 669402.

SYLVIA CHICUREL BEJA, FM-17 No. 669401.

CAROLINA GONZALEZ DE ESPARZA, FM-17 No. 693068.

YOLANDA FIGUEROA ARGUELIES, FM-17 No. 651599.

MARIA FELICITAS GALLARDO DE FINLEY, FM-17 No. 693436.

MARGARET YOLANDA FINLEY GALLARDO, FM-17 No. 693423.

DONNA CAROLINA FINLEY GALLARDO, FM-17 No. 693437.

JOSE LUIS LLAMOSAS GUTIERREZ, FM-17 No. 521342.

RICHARD HANS SPECK STHAMER, FM-17 No. 648799.

OLGA RIEFKOHL VIUDA DE STAHMER, FM-17 No. 648800.

LISOLETTE ESTHAMER DE SPECK, FM-17 No. 635119.

FERNANDO ANASTACIO TREVINO GONZALEZ, FM-17 No. 635119.

MARIA OTERO PABLOS, FM-17 No. 521676.

Entries of September 26, 1963, of Non-Mexican Citizens in Miscellaneous Categories

NELSON ULISES ESCOBAR BENITEZ, traveling with special document "Circular No. 1091."

HEINZ KARL TZCHENTKE, traveling with form FM-1. Described as being a returning non-immigrant of German nationality.

CATALINA ADA DEL CARMEN CANIZARES, traveling with document classified as an "Oficio Bueno Para Salir y Regresar al Pais" (Memorandum of Authorization Valid for Exit and Entry into the Country.)

(M) OSWALD's Travel Documents and Mexican Government Records

The following information was furnished by T-13 on March 17, 1964:

The travel document with which LEE HARVEY OSWALD entered Mexico on September 26, 1963, is described as a Mexican Ministry of "Gobernacion" (Interior) FM-8 and is commonly referred to as a tourist card, which consists of two sections, an original and a carbon copy duplicate. At the time of OSWALD's travel to Mexico, the FM-8 was valid for a single entry to the interior of Mexico and residence therein for no longer than fifteen days. The original tourist card utilized by OSWALD records the following data:

FM-8 No.:	24085, valid for 15 days
Full Name:	LEE, HARVEY OSWALD
	Photographer
Sex:	Male
Marital Status:	Married
Document with which nationality was established:	Birth Certificate
Final Destination:	Mexico, D. F.

COMMISSION EXHIBIT No. 2121—Continued

Date and Place (of issuance):	New Orleans, La., USA, September 17, 1963
Signature of Bearer:	LEE H. OSWALD

It bears the stamp of the Consulate General of Mexico at New Orleans, Louisiana, indicating issuance by that agency, and the date stamp of Mexican Immigration official HELIO TUEXI MAYDON, reflecting entry into Mexico at Nuevo Laredo, Tamaulipas, September 26, 1963. The stamp for departure is that of Immigration official ALBERTO ARZAMENDI CHAPA and the date shown is October 2, 1963. Under normal procedures, the means of travel of the bearer upon entry to Mexico is recorded with a stamped, typed, or handwritten notation; however, this record does not appear on the FM-8 for OSWALD.

A review of the original tourist cards (FM-5, FM-8, and one FM-17, the latter explained above) in the possession of the Immigration Department of the Mexican Ministry of "Gobernacion" revealed that 79 persons documented with those forms had departed from Mexico at Nuevo Laredo, Tamaulipas, on October 3, 1963, among them LEE HARVEY OSWALD.

On March 23, 1964, Mr. MACLOVIO HERRERA, Chief of the Travel Control Files of the Mexican Immigration Department described the Immigration form "FM-11" as a "statistical record to be prepared every two weeks on nationals and aliens entering and leaving the country." Mr. HERRERA explained that separate FM-11 forms are submitted semimonthly by all Mexican Immigration stations for entries and departures from Mexico. He explained that separate lists are prepared in connection with the various types of travel documents presented and are submitted in duplicate (an original and one carbon copy) to the Travel Control Files for checking and comparison with the tourist cards or other travel documents on which they are based.

Under current procedures, twenty names are placed on each page of the FM-11 in alphabetical order by date, and prior to final filing these are reviewed by a clerk who may make corrections and report possible discrepancies which might require investigation in order to make certain that the immigration laws of Mexico are not being violated. The items of information which are recorded on the FM-11 in horizontal columns are: chronological number (chronological listing number

COMMISSION EXHIBIT No. 2121—Continued

during fifteen-day period), identification document number, complete name, sex, age, marital status, nationality, occupation, place and country of origin, final destination, date of entry or departure, type of vehicle in which traveling, date of entry, date of departure (latter columns to determine period of residence), and remarks.

A review of the original tourist cards for persons traveling as tourists who departed from Mexico at Nuevo Laredo on October 3, 1963, disclosed that in no instance did any notation appear on the travel documents to indicate the manner of travel of the bearer or the destination in the United States upon departure from Mexico.

It was observed that on the FM-11 forms, the "destination" of the traveler at the time of departure was completed invariably with the same information as appeared on the tourist card as to place of residence, place of issuance thereof, or a notation that the information was not available.

FM-11 Preparation and Utilization by Mexican Immigration

Inspector JOSE MARIO DEL VALLE of the Inspection Department of the Mexican Ministry of "Gobernacion," who conducted investigation at Nuevo Laredo concerning the travel in Mexico of LEE HARVEY OSWALD, advised on March 12, 1964, that the typist who prepares the FM-11 has no information available to her other than that which appears on the tourist cards. He stated the typist prepares the FM-11 for persons entering the country from the duplicate copies of the tourist cards which are surrendered to the Immigration official at the time of entry of the traveler. The duplicate tourist cards are then transmitted to the headquarters of the Immigration Department in Mexico, D. F., with the FM-11 form for the fifteen-day period.

In the same manner, the FM-11 form for departures is prepared on the basis of data taken from the original of the tourist card, which is surrendered by the traveler to the Immigration official upon departure from the country.

DEL VALLE acknowledged that the Mexican Immigration Department does not have any major interest in "method of travel" or "destination" of the departing traveler, other than to make certain that the individual who enters the country with an automobile is removing the vehicle upon departure. He added that the typist who prepares the departure FM-11 usually records the means of travel as being the same as that appearing on the tourist card in connection with the traveler's entry to the country; however, in some instances she may "guess" at the means of travel on the basis of the usual assignment at the airport, railroad station, or highway checking station of the Immigration official whose cancellation stamp appears on the tourist card.

On March 13, 1964, MACLOVIO HERRERA, Chief of the Travel Control Files of the Mexican Department of Immigration, Ministry of "Gobernacion," and his assistant, EDUARDO RIVAS, made the following comments concerning Mexican Immigration records and procedures:

The "means of travel" and "destination" data appearing on the departure FM-11 forms are not information in which the Mexican Immigration Department has any substantive interest and are filled out by the typist only because the same form is used to record both arrival and departure information. This information with respect to "arrivals" is most essential to assist the Immigration Department in maintaining a record and control of aliens who are in Mexico as temporary residents without authorization to be gainfully employed. There is no source of information from which the typist preparing the FM-11 can obtain data for it other than the tourist cards, data provided to her by the Immigration official who may bundle a group of cards together and label them as having been taken up on a departing train or other vehicle, or her own knowledge of the Immigration station where the cancelling official may have been working during a particular period of time.

Inquiry was made of HERRERA with respect to certain horizontal lines which appear on the FM-11, and he explained that such lines are drawn to delineate between different dates on the same page and also to designate an individual concerning whom some research is being done or a report has been submitted to some section or department of the Ministry of "Gobernacion."

With respect to the fact that on the copies of the FM-11 which were made available for study and review there appeared under the "Remarks" (No. 16) column considerable data concerning the date and place of issuance of the tourist cards, HERRERA advised that this information did not appear on the originals of the FM-11 which were in his possession, and he was certain that this information had been added only on the carbon copy.

On March 23, 1964, T-1 produced the carbon copies of the FM-11 forms relating to OSWALD's travel in Mexico, and it was observed that column 16 thereof had been completed in original typing with data from the tourist cards as to date and agency where each tourist card had been issued. T-1 said that the entries in column 16 were made to be of possible assistance in the investigation with respect to Oswald. T-1 added that the information in column 16 was taken from the tourist cards of the travelers who were recorded in the FM-11 forms.

With regard to the observation that the date of issuance of OSWALD's tourist card was recorded in column 16 as having taken place on "Sept. 16/63," T-1 stated very definitely that this had been a typographical error on the part of the stenographer, who should have copied the information from OSWALD's tourist card to the effect that it had been issued on September 17, 1963.

V. OTHER INQUIRIES CONCERNING OSWALD'S TRAVEL

(A) Transportes Frontera Bus Line

The original passenger list or manifest relating to departure No. 2 of bus No. 340 on October 2, 1963, of the Transportes Frontera, S. A. de C. V. bus line, which has its headquarters in Monterrey, Nuevo Leon, Mexico, and its Mexico, D. F. terminal at Calle Buenavista No. 7, was obtained.

The information recorded on the passenger list is handwritten; the names are not complete; and portions of it are not legible; however, the following constitutes an effort to reproduce as clearly as possible the information which appears on the list.

Seat No.	Ticket No.	Name of Passenger	Destination
1	39633	Fco. Saucedo	Monterrey
2			
3	39634	Fco. Saucedo	Monterrey
4		Oswld	Lared
5	10347	Sra. Landeros	Laredo
6	39648	Adrian Hernandez	Mty.
7	10357	Juana	Laredo
8	39649	Angel Gallegos	Monterrey
9	10348	Sra. Morales	Laredo
10	Pase	Nicolas Gonzalez	Torreon
11	10351	Rafael Flores	Laredo
12	10354	Gautier ? (Ganstine)	Laredo
13		Angel Perez	
14	39650	Antonio Cazarez	Mty.
15	10356	Sra. Aguilar	Laredo

Seat No.	Ticket No.	Name of Passenger	Destination
16	10355	Sra. Franco	Laredo
17	10352	Constantino Garcia	Laredo
18	39659	Eliasar Gonzalez	Monterrey
19	10353	Constantino Garcia	Laredo
20	39661	Ynignes (Inigues ?)	Mty.

At the top of the manifest the name, Transportes Frontera, is handwritten, and in Spanish the following headings are printed:

RESERVATIONS FOR 13 O'CLOCK,

DESTINATION Laredo , DEPARTURE NO. 2 ,

ON BUS NO. 340 , DATE 2, MONTH, October of 1963.

The underlined portions are blanks which had been completed in ink.

Following the list of passengers is the notation: "9 Laredo, 7 Monterrey."

Handprinted at the bottom of the page appears: "DRIVER, DIONISIO REYNA, FCO. SAUCEDO," as well as the numbers "13 - 2."

On the left-hand margin of the manifest are the handwritten figures, "78" and "16." At the top right-hand corner thereof are the numerals "186," "41" and under these "227." On the backside of the document are the numbers "146.30" and "108.80" and thereunder, as though a column of addition, "255.10."

The following information was made available by T-13 on March 9, 1964:

On March 5, 1964, GILBERTO LOZANO GUIZAR advised that he is the manager of the Mexico City terminal of the Transportes Frontera bus company, Calle Buenavista No. 7, which has a franchise for "through service" between Mexico,

D. F., Monterrey, and Nuevo Laredo, Mexico, but is not permitted to sell tickets or pick up passengers at intermediate localities.

LOZANO stated a complete study of Transportes Frontera bus company records and procedures had been made which resulted in the conclusion that the person designated as "OSWLD" on the October 2, 1963, passenger manifest did not purchase a ticket and could not have traveled on the trip to which it relates. He pointed out that the passenger reservations, tickets sold, and passengers actually boarding the bus in Mexico, D. F., are recorded on the form which is provided for that purpose and maintained on a clip board on the counter from which ticket sales normally are made by the ticket salesman and dispatcher, FRANCISCO ALVARADO. He admitted that ALVARADO occasionally is assisted during rush hours or a temporary absence from the counter by the baggage handler, LUCIO LOPEZ MEDINA, who may receive and record reservations on the manifest but does not handle the actual receipt of payment for tickets.

FRANCISCO ALVARADO, ticket salesman and dispatcher for Transportes Frontera, advised that he prepared most of the handwriting on the October 2, 1963, manifest on which the name "OSWLD" and destination "Lared" appear opposite seat No. 4. He stated he did not write the "OSWLD" reservation information and it was his opinion the reservation had been made and the information recorded by the baggage handler, LUCIO LOPEZ. With respect to the manifest for October 2, 1963, ALVARADO furnished the following explanation:

He was quite certain that the individual designated on the list as "OSWLD" did not purchase a ticket and did not travel on the trip relating to that manifest. No ticket number was recorded for that person, and a search of the company's records in Monterrey had failed to locate a ticket stub which was not otherwise accounted for in connection with that particular trip.

ALVARADO and GILBERTO LOZANO stated the notations on the back of the manifest referred to advances of funds made by ALVARADO to LOZANO from the cash for repairs, parts, or other requirements. They related that the passenger lists are not kept as a permanent record, and, when the manifest was located in the "trash" at the request of investigators of the Mexican Presidential Staff, the blanks at the top of the form had not been filled in as to time, destination, trip number, bus number, and date, but they had completed those blanks from their personal knowledge in order to make that data clear to the investigators. They also had listed the names of the drivers on the form at that time. They affirmed that the handwritten "Transportes Frontera" at the top of the document had been added by some official of the Mexican Government after the document was borrowed from them. Both LOZANO and ALVARADO stated they had no recollection of LEE HARVEY OSWALD, could not recognize his photograph as being of an individual who had been at the terminal or traveled on that bus line, and had no personal knowledge with respect to his contacts and activities in Mexico. They could offer no explanation as to how Mexican authorities had arrived at the conclusion that OSWALD traveled on the Transportes Frontera bus of October 2, 1963, but pointed out that, after the name was located on the manifest, they had not been given an opportunity of reviewing or checking the data thereon.

LUCIO LOPEZ MEDINA, baggage and freight handler at Transportes Frontera, related that he often assists the ticket salesman by recording reservations and is quite certain he wrote "OSWLD" and "Lared" opposite seat No. 4 on the passenger manifest of October 2, 1963. He stated he also recorded the reservations and ticket sales to "FCO. SAUCEDO," one of the drivers, opposite seats Nos. 1 and 3, "ANGEL GALLEGOS," seat No. 8, and possibly other items on the manifest. He had no personal recollection of OSWALD, could not recognize his photograph as being of anyone who had been at the bus terminal, and did not believe OSWALD had embarked on the bus in question.

T-12 furnished the following information:

On March 31, 1964, GILBERTO LOZANO GUIZAR, manager of the Mexico City terminal of the Transportes Frontera bus company, Calle Buenavista No. 7, Mexico, D. F., emphatically advised that the original passenger list or manifest relating to departure No. 2 of bus No. 340 on October 2, 1963, of the Transportes Frontera bus company, is an authentic record of data pertaining to that particular trip.

- 102 -

COMMISSION EXHIBIT No. 2121—Continued

LOZANO pointed out that a passenger list is compiled at the Mexico City terminal of the company for trips originating in Mexico City and that following the departure of the bus, information relating to the number of passengers destined to particular points, is radioed ahead to one of the main offices located along the point of travel. In case of the above-described trip, the information was reported by radio to their Monterrey office. LOZANO advised that once the information is relayed ahead and the trip is completed, for all practical purposes, they have no further need of conserving the passenger lists as a permanent record.

He advised that officers of the Presidential Staff appeared at the bus terminal shortly after the assassination of President KENNEDY, seeking to review passenger lists of the bus company for early October, 1963, and it was found at that time that the completed block of forms for most of the month of October, 1963, which included the above-described passenger list, was still in the baggage room at the terminal prior to being discarded. He stated he had torn the October 2, 1963, manifest from the block of forms and furnished it to one of the officers. LOZANO advised that one Lieutenant ARTURO BOSCH, an investigator of the Presidential Staff, had reviewed the above-described manifest.

LOZANO expressed the opinion that ARTURO BOSCH had filled in the blanks in ink at the top of the form as to the time, destination, trip number, bus number, and date, and had crossed out the date "November 1," replacing it with the notation "October 2" which appeared on the manifest. LOZANO stated BOSCH had done so on the basis of information he and FRANCISCO ALVARADO, the ticket salesman, had furnished to BOSCH as an aid to his investigation of the matter.

LOZANO stated the handprinted notation appearing at the bottom of the manifest, "Driver, DIONISIO REYNA, FCO. SAUCEDO," was also filled in by BOSCH.

LOZANO advised that there definitely was only one section of bus No. 340 which departed Mexico City at 1:00 p.m. on October 2, 1963, en route Monterrey, Mexico, and Nuevo Laredo, Mexico. He explained that the notation "Departure 2" appearing on the top of the manifest, which he believed BOSCH

- 103 -

COMMISSION EXHIBIT No. 2121—Continued

had filled out, merely indicates the second departure of a Transportes Frontera bus on that particular day, October 2, 1963. The first departure of one of their buses on that day from the Mexico City terminal occurred at 9:00 a.m. with the terminal point being Monterrey, Mexico. He stated the second departure of a Transportes Frontera bus from the Mexico City terminal on October 2, 1963, was the departure at 1:00 p.m. with the terminal point being Nuevo Laredo, Mexico, and the passengers on this bus were recorded on the above-mentioned manifest of October 2, 1963. He stated there were three other departures on that day from the Mexico City terminal, the third departure having occurred at 2:30 p.m. with the terminal point being Matamoros, Tamaulipas, Mexico; the fourth departure having occurred at 9:00 p.m. with terminal point at Nuevo Laredo; and the fifth departure at 10:00 p.m. with terminal point being Ciudad Juarez, Chihuahua, Mexico. LOZANO advised the only bus operating on their line which would have arrived at Nuevo Laredo between the hours of 12:00 a.m. and 8:00 a.m. on October 3, 1963, is bus No. 340, which departed from the Mexico City terminal at 1:00 p.m. on October 2, 1963.

T-13 and T-21 furnished the information which follows:

On March 25, 1964, FRANCISCO ALVARADO, ticket salesman and dispatcher for the Transportes Frontera bus company at Mexico City, advised that the above-described manifest is an authentic document. He stated he had prepared most of the handwriting on the manifest. With regard to the notations appearing at the top of the manifest as to time, destination, trip number, bus number, and date, he expressed the opinion that those notations were filled in by one of the Presidential Staff investigators who reviewed the manifest at the bus terminal shortly after President KENNEDY's assassination. He advised that the handprinted notation appearing at the bottom of the page of the manifest, "Driver, DIONISIO REYNA, FCO. SAUCEDO," also was made by one of the President Staff investigators, and he believed this person was Lieutenant ARTURO BOSCH.

On March 25, 1964, FRANCISCO SAUCEDO, bus driver for the Transportes Frontera bus company, advised in Mexico City that he had been one of the bus drivers who had driven the Transportes Frontera bus No. 340 on October 2, 1963,

which departed Mexico City at 1:00 p.m. on that day en route to Monterrey and Nuevo Laredo. He stated seats No. 1 and No. 3 on that bus had been reserved by him under tickets No. 39633 and No. 39634; however, he did not recall for whom he had made the reservations. He said that on occasion he reserves seats in advance for friends or relatives but never does so for anyone with whom he is not acquainted. He could not recall who had utilized those seats on that particular day. He stated he was certain that seats No. 1 and No. 3 were not used by OSWALD or ANGEL PEREZ.

On March 25, 1964, DIONISIO REYNA, who was co-driver with SAUCEDO on Transportes Frontera bus No. 340 of October 2, 1963, advised at Mexico City that he could furnish no information regarding the individuals who had utilized seats No. 1 and No. 3 on the trip in question. REYNA stated he was quite certain that OSWALD did not travel on that particular bus.

(B) Inquiry at Flecha Roja Bus Terminal

On March 7, 1964, JESUS SAUCEDO, comptroller at the terminal of the Flecha Roja (Red Arrow) bus company, Heroes Ferrocarrileros No. 45, Mexico City, advised that the full and complete name of the company is Servicios Unidos Autobuses Blancos, Flecha Roja, S. A. de C. V. (The Unified Services of White Autobuses Red Arrow, Incorporated) and that it provides bus service to numerous localities within Mexico, as well as to Nuevo Laredo, Tamaulipas, and Laredo, Texas. He explained that two trips daily are made to Nuevo Laredo and Laredo, where the line makes connection with the Continental Trailways Bus System of the United States, departures from Mexico City being scheduled for 3:15 p.m. and 7:30 p.m. each day and arrival at Nuevo Laredo 19 hours later.

SAUCEDO advised that a passenger list is prepared in duplicate for reservations and ticket sales for a given trip; the original is carried by the driver, and the carbon copy is transmitted to him for final checking and auditing of the operation in connection with each bus.

With the assistance of SAUCEDO, a search was made of the passenger manifests of the company for all trips to

Laredo for October 1, 2, and 3, 1963, without locating any information identifiable with the name LEE HARVEY OSWALD.

(C) OSWALD's Time of Arrival in Mexico City

T-12 advised as follows:

On April 16, 1964, JULIO CASTRO, employee of the accounting department in the offices of the Flecha Roja bus line, Mexico, D. F., made available the ledger of arrivals at Mexico, D. F., for the Flecha Roja buses. The ledger records separate entries for each day, with the exact time of arrival of each bus in Mexico, D. F., at the terminal.

This ledger disclosed that bus No. 516 of the Flecha Roja bus line, which made the trip from Nuevo Laredo, to Mexico, D. F., on September 26-27, 1963, arrived at the Flecha Roja bus terminal, Heroes Ferrocarrileros No. 45, Mexico, D. F., at 10:00 a.m. on September 27, 1963.

(D) Efforts to Locate Flecha Roja Passenger List

T-12 furnished the following information:

On March 19, 1964, ALEJANDRO SAUCEDO, manager of the Flecha Roja bus terminal, Mexico, D. F., advised that the original passenger manifest of bus No. 516 which had traveled from Nuevo Laredo to Mexico, D. F., on September 26-27, 1963, had been borrowed by investigators of the Mexican Government soon after the assassination of President JOHN F. KENNEDY. He could not recall the identities of the investigators and did not know whether or not they intended to return the list. SAUCEDO stated the duplicate copy of this passenger list was maintained in the office of the Flecha Roja bus line at Nuevo Laredo and he would attempt to obtain this copy.

On March 24, 1964, ALEJANDRO SAUCEDO stated he had determined from the Flecha Roja bus line office in Nuevo Laredo that the duplicate copy of the passenger list for bus No. 516 also had been borrowed by unidentified investigators of the Mexican Government and had not been returned.

COMMISSION EXHIBIT No. 2121—Continued

SAUCEDO stated he had assisted the Mexican Government investigators in searching for the passenger list relating to the trip of September 26-27, 1963, and was quite certain the name of LEE HARVEY OSWALD did not appear thereon. He added, however, that the Flecha Roja bus line makes connection at Laredo, Texas, with the Continental Trailways bus line in the United States, and if a passenger who had purchased a through ticket to Mexico, D. F., from a point within the United States were to board the Flecha Roja line at Laredo or Nuevo Laredo, no record of that passenger by name would be made on the passenger list. He explained that the passenger list would include a seat designation and ticket number in the name of "Continental."

T-12 advised that on April 2, 1964, and thereafter, ALEJANDRO SAUCEDO furnished the following additional data:

He recalled that shortly after the assassination of President JOHN F. KENNEDY two investigators, whom he described as being with the "Policia Federal Judicial" (Federal Judicial Police), appeared at the Flecha Roja terminal, Mexico, D. F., and requested the original passenger list of bus No. 516 of September 26, 1963, for review. SAUCEDO remembered that the two investigators examined the passenger lists, filed by dates, in a storeroom at the offices of the Flecha Roja bus terminal and found the original copy for the pertinent date and borrowed same. He could not recall the names of the investigators or the exact date they appeared at the office.

SAUCEDO now recalled clearly that these two investigators, whom he could only describe as being "in their thirties," had the duplicate copy of the passenger list which apparently had been at the Flecha Roja bus terminal office in Nuevo Laredo when the trip for September 26, 1963, began. The investigators stated they wanted the original list because the duplicate copy was not completely legible. SAUCEDO stated they had the original and duplicate copy of the passenger manifest for Flecha Roja bus No. 516 for September 26, 1963, when they left.

SAUCEDO stated the investigators did exhibit to him government credentials, agency not recalled, and advised they were interested only in finding the passenger list for the incoming trip of bus No. 516 on September 26, 1963. When

COMMISSION EXHIBIT No. 2121—Continued

SAUCEDO asked them if they were interested in locating a departure trip, they stated they were not, explaining they had just been at the bus terminal of Transportes Frontera in Mexico, D. F., where they had located the passenger list for OSWALD's departure from Mexico.

On April 9, 1964, JULIO CASTRO, an employee of the accounting department in the offices of the Flecha Roja bus line terminal, Mexico, D. F., made available on instructions of ALEJANDRO SAUCEDO the original passenger lists of the Flecha Roja bus line, which were kept in a storeroom across the hall from the accounting office and were maintained in a disorganized manner, bound with heavy string in bundles and stored in bins.

The available bundles for the period September and October, 1963, were reviewed without locating a passenger list for bus No. 516 relating to September 26, 1963.

During this search and review, an untied, loose bundle dated October 5, 1963, was located thrown aside in a cardboard box on the floor of the storage room outside the bin area. This bundle was reviewed and found to include passenger lists for dates September 21, 1963, to October 5, 1963, but no passenger list for bus No. 516 for September 26, 1963, was found.

The information hereinunder was furnished by T-13:

On March 24, 1963, Captain FERNANDO GUTIERREZ BARRIOS, Assistant Director of the Mexican Federal Security Police (DFS), advised that his agency had conducted no investigation in connection with the travel in Mexico of LEE HARVEY OSWALD and did not have in its possession any passenger lists from any bus lines.

On April 14, 1964, the fact the passenger lists of the September 26, 1963, Flecha Roja trip from Nuevo Laredo to Mexico, D. F., had never appeared and were alleged to be in the hands of an unidentified investigative agency of the Mexican Government was brought to the attention of the Acting Minister of Government, Attorney LUIS ECHEVERRIA, who issued instructions to the Chief of the Inspection Department of the Immigration Service, Attorney SANTIAGO IBANEZ LLAMAS, to make every effort to locate the passenger list described above.

On May 1, 1964, Inspector JOSE MARIO DEL VALLE advised that he had been instructed to attempt to locate the Flecha Roja passenger list and was making every effort to do so.

(E) Transportes del Norte Passengers Originating in Guadalajara

On April 3, 1964, T-8 advised that the Linea Azul (Blue Line) bus company affords service from Guadalajara, Jalisco, Mexico, to San Luis Potosi, State of San Luis Potosi, Mexico, to make connections with Transportes del Norte for possible further travel to Monterrey and Nuevo Laredo, Mexico. According to T-8, a reservations list for the October 2, 1963, 8:00 a.m. departure of the Blue Line bus from Guadalajara with San Luis Potosi as its destination reflects the following information as best the names and other data thereon could be deciphered:

Name of Passenger	Destination	Ticket No.
HILDA QUEZADA	N. Laredo	77898
----- (*)	-----	99
JOSE CRUZ	Monterrey	00751
HILDA QUEZADA	N. Laredo	77900 ½ (**)
CECILIO CARDENAZ	Monterrey	00749
JOSE MAZO	San Luis	14128
VICTORIA MAGALLANES	(apparently did not travel)	
MAXIMINO ESQUIVEL	Monterrey	00752
PEDRO GLEZ. (GONZALEZ)	Monterrey	00753
AURELIO HDEZ. (HERNANDEZ)	San Luis	1362

(* Lines indicate second passenger or seat reserved in name of preceding passenger)
(** ½ indicates half fare paid)

Comprehensive investigation, including a check of the files of the United States Consulate visa records, a check of telephone directories, and numerous interviews of persons listed in the telephone directories with similar names, were conducted at Guadalajara for the above names of persons traveling beyond San Luis Potosi, without identifying anyone who had been a passenger of Transportes del Norte on October 2, 1963,

(F) Transportes del Norte Bus Line Operation, Monterrey

The following information was furnished by T-18.

On April 19, 1964, RAMON TREVINO QUEZADA, vice president and manager of the Monterrey, Nuevo Leon, terminal of Transportes del Norte bus line, advised that tickets are taken up by the driver from passengers at the time they board the bus, and he deposits them in a mahila envelope, which is provided for that purpose in connection with each trip of a unit and driver. He stated the driver makes a notation on the outside of the envelope as to the number of passengers traveling over a determined section of the route, and the tickets inside the envelope should coincide or balance with the notation by the driver on the envelope.

With respect to the records of the company for the trip of bus No. 373 on October 2, 1963, from Monterrey to Nuevo Laredo, Tamaulipas, and Laredo, Texas, TREVINO advised that he was unable to explain the fact that the envelope carries the figure of "12" passengers from Monterrey, Nuevo Leon, to Nuevo Laredo, Tamaulipas, and Laredo, Texas, and "1" passenger from Nuevo Laredo to Laredo, although a total of "20" ticket sections were in the envelope for that particular trip. He stated, however, that the notation by the driver is a clerical function which he handles during the trip, often at night and under considerable stress and pressure, and he can only conclude that the driver made an error in writing "12" rather than "19" upon completing his collection of tickets and delivering the envelope at the conclusion of his run.

It was mentioned to TREVINO that the baggage manifest for the bus which arrived at Nuevo Laredo in the early morning of October 3, 1963, had listed the number of that bus as No. 396, and he advised that this notation could only be a clerical error by the baggage handler. He displayed a copy of a document referred to as a "traffic report" for Transportes del Norte at its Nuevo Laredo terminal for October 3, 1963, which recorded that bus No. 373 had arrived at that terminal at 1:35 a.m. with A. IBARRA as the driver. The "traffic report" for October 2, 1963, registered the arrival of bus No. 396

at Nuevo Laredo as having taken place at 15:30 (3:30 p.m.) on that date and its departure from Nuevo Laredo for Monterrey was recorded on the report for the following day as having occurred at 2:30 a.m. He pointed out that on the basis of the foregoing records, bus No. 396 would still have been at the Nuevo Laredo terminal at the time of arrival on October 3, 1963, of bus No. 373, and he assumed the baggage handler had become confused between them when he made the erroneous notation on the baggage manifest.

(G) Ticketing Procedures by Transportes del Norte Bus Line

The following information was furnished by T-13.

On April 20, 1964, RAMON MEDINA BELTRAN, manager of the Mexico City terminal of the Transportes del Norte bus line, advised that this company is affiliated with the Greyhound Lines in the United States and is authorized and in a position to sell transportation to any point in the United States. He stated that until approximately one year ago the sale of bus transportation in the United States in behalf of Greyhound Lines had been effected through a system of exchange or purchase orders; however, in the interest of simplifying the sales and accounting procedures, Transportes del Norte ticket counters are now stocked with Greyhound Lines tickets and make direct sales in behalf of Greyhound, as well as its own facilities. He stated very definitely that the only record as to the identity of any person purchasing Greyhound transportation through a Transportes del Norte ticket counter would be the recording of the seat reservation on a passenger list at the point of origin or purchase of the ticket.

VI. MISCELLANEOUS INQUIRIES AT MEXICO CITY CONCERNING OSWALD

(A) Telephone Numbers in Oswald's Address Book

The following notations appeared in the personal address book of LEE HARVEY OSWALD (translations of the Spanish language items appear in parentheses):

Mexico City

Consulado de Cuba
(Cuban Consulate)
Zamora y F. Marquez
11-28-47
SYLVIA DURAN
Embajada de la Union de las Republicas Sovietilas Socialistas
(Embassy of the Union of the Soviet Socialist Republics)

15-61-55 (15-60-55)

Depto. de Asuntos Consulares
(Department of Consular Affairs)

Cubano Airlines
Paseo de la Reforma 56
35-79-00

The directory of the Mexican Telephone Company for the Federal District (Mexican Federal Capital, which includes Mexico City) published in September, 1963, column 2, page 119, records: "CONSULADO de Cuba, Zamora y F. Marquez (names of cross Streets), (telephone) 11-28-47."

Column 1, page 157, of the same directory reflects: "EMBAJADA de la Union de las Republicas Sovieticas Socialistas en Mexico (Embassy of the Union of the Soviet Socialist Republics in Mexico), Czda, Tacubaya (Calzada meaning highway

or street) 204, Agregado Militar (Military Attache)...(telephone) 15-69-37, Depto. de Asuntos Consulares (Department of Consular Affairs), C. B. Zetina (Street name) 12...(Telephone) 15-61-55."

Column 4, page 112, of the above-mentioned directory records the following: "CIA. CUBANA DE AVIACION, S. A., (Cuban Aviation Company, Incorporated) PASEO DE LA REFORMA 56... (telephone) 35-79-00." In addition to the foregoing, which is indicated as being equipped with two direct lines, the following additional telephone numbers are listed: 46-75-04, 46-61-64, 46-61-27, and 35-79-09.

The April 1,1964, issue of the "Diario Oficial" ("Official Daily"), which states on the cover that it is the "Organ of the Constitutional Government of the United States of Mexico," records as emanating from the Ministry of Foreign Affairs the "List of the Diplomatic Corps Accredited to the Government of the United States of Mexico." On page 15 of the above-described publication under "Union de Republicas Socialistas Sovieticas" (Union of the Soviet Socialist Republics) is recorded the data: "Cancilleria y residencia: (Chancellery and residence) Calzada de Tacubaya 204, Telefonos: (Telephones) 15-60-55 y (and) 15-61-55." The foregoing data is followed by a listing of names and residence addresses of the Soviet diplomatic officials and their wives.

T-16, who is in a position to be well-informed with respect to the day-to-day operations of the Mexico City ticket offices of the "Compania Cubana de Aviacion" (Cuban Aviation Company - commonly referred to as "Cubana Airlines"), furnished the following information on April 18, 1964:

Most of the office employees at the Cubana Airlines ticket office, Paseo de la Reforma 56, Mexico City, are Mexican citizens. Source would have an excellent possibility of being informed of any visits or inquiries made at the Cubana Airlines offices by an American, and is thoroughly convinced that LEE HARVEY OSWALD did not appear at those offices during late September and early October, 1963, within the regular working hours. Source viewed various photographs of OSWALD and also consulted with associates at the Cubana Airlines office and reiterated the conviction that

OSWALD had not been at those offices at any time.

This source confirmed that the published and most used telephone number for the Cubana Airlines office is 35-79-00.

(B) Possibility OSWALD Sent or Received Money

T-11 reported that on January 13, 1964, ALFONSO FRIAS, Assistant Chief of the Bank of Mexico Police at Mexico, D. F., Mexico, advised that a check of the records of "Telegrafos Nacionales" failed to disclose any record of money sent or received by OSWALD during the time he was in Mexico through use of communications channels handled by that telegraph system.

On March 6, 1964, FRIAS advised that all banks in Mexico, including all branch banks, were checked officially for LEE HARVEY OSWALD and his aliases of O. H. LEE and ALEK JAMES HIDELL, and no information was developed that OSWALD had received or sent any money through those banks during the time he was in Mexico.

(C) Inquiries at Hotel Cuba

PATRICIA WINSTON and PAMELA MUMFORD, who were passengers on the same bus with OSWALD from Monterrey, Nuevo Leon, Mexico, to Mexico, D. F., September 26-27, 1963, when interviewed on December 17, 1963, related that during the bus trip OSWALD recommended that they stay at the Hotel Cuba in Mexico City. They related that OSWALD claimed he had stayed at that hotel several times before and pointed out that the hotel was inexpensive, mentioning, however, that he was not staying at the Hotel Cuba during his current trip.

Inquiry was conducted to establish whether OSWALD had, in fact, stayed at the Hotel Cuba during a period following his return to the United States from Russia in June, 1962 to November, 1963.

On December 27, 1963, T-4 advised that an exhaustive search of the records of the Hotel Cuba located at Calle Republica de Cuba No. 69, Mexico City, for the period June, 1962, to October, 1963, failed to disclose any registration

for OSWALD under his name or known aliases.

T-12 advised as follows:

On March 11, 1964, ANGEL CELORIO, manager, Hotel Cuba, made available records of that hotel, which were rechecked for the period June 9, 1962, to November 22, 1963, and no record could be located for the name of LEE HARVEY OSWALD or his known aliases O. H. LEE and ALEK JAMES HIDELL. The records did contain a registration for one ROBERTO LEE, who registered at the hotel on August 11, 1963, was assigned room No. 27, and checked out of the hotel on August 21, 1963. No further identifying data regarding this LEE was contained in the records. (OSWALD had been reported as being at New Orleans, Louisiana, during that period.)

CELORIO advised he has been at the Hotel Cuba only since November 11, 1963, when he became manager, and prior thereto, JOSE SANCHEZ, who is presently associated with another hotel in Mexico City, served as manager for about a four-month period and Mr. RAFAEL AVALOS, also now employed at another hotel in Mexico City, had served as manager for a number of years.

On March 12, 1964, both RAFAEL AVALOS, manager, Hotel Congreso, Calle de Allende No. 18, Mexico, D. F., and JOSE SANCHEZ, manager, Hotel Catedral, Calle Donceles No. 95, Mexico, D. F., viewed a photograph of OSWALD, and both advised they could not recognize the photograph as being of anyone who stayed at the Hotel Cuba during the time they were managing the hotel. Both were of the opinion that if OSWALD had stayed at the Hotel Cuba during the time they were in charge there, they would have recalled him. Neither could furnish any pertinent information regarding the possibility OSWALD may have stayed at the Hotel Cuba in the past.

AVALOS related he had served as manager at the Hotel Cuba for a number of years until July, 1962, and SANCHEZ stated he had managed the Hotel Cuba from June 1, 1963, to November 11, 1963. SANCHEZ stated that during the period July, 1962, to June 1, 1963, when he became manager, the administration of the hotel had been disorganized and there was no permanent manager. He stated that JESUS HERNANDEZ SANCHEZ and his brother, HIGINIO HERNANDEZ SANCHEZ, both of whom he believed were still employed at the Hotel Cuba, would most logically be the persons in the best position to know whether or not OSWALD stayed at the Hotel Cuba during the period July, 1962, to June 1, 1963.

JESUS HERNANDEZ SANCHEZ, room clerk, Hotel Cuba, advised on March 13, 1964, that he has been employed as room clerk at that hotel for several years. He stated that during the period from July, 1962, to June 1, 1963, when the hotel had no permanent manager, he and his brother, HIGINIO HERNANDEZ SANCHEZ, performed the administrative functions at the hotel and had most contact with the guests.

HERNANDEZ viewed a photograph of OSWALD and stated he could not recall ever seeing him. He further stated he could not recognize the photograph as being of any person who had been at the Hotel Cuba during the time he has been employed there. He advised that several months ago he and his brother, HIGINIO, had been shown a photograph of OSWALD by a local police official, and at that time both he and his brother were unable to recognize the photograph of OSWALD as being of any person who had stayed at the hotel during the period they had been working there. He added that following the publicity arising from the assassination of President KENNEDY, seeing OSWALD's photograph in the newspapers, and after viewing a photograph of OSWALD exhibited by the police official mentioned above, he and his brother had discussed the matter and had agreed they could not recall OSWALD's ever having stayed at the Hotel Cuba.

(D) <u>Jai Alai in Mexico City</u>

T-12 advised in connection with the possibility that OSWALD might have attended a jai alai game in Mexico, D. F., that the "Mexico City Daily Bulletin," a free English publication circulated at hotels, motels, drug stores, and tourist-type stores in Mexico, D. F., lists daily the following as a sport event of interest:

"Jai alai, the ancient game from Spain, can be seen every day but Monday at Fronton Mexico, Plaza de la Republica, at 7:30 p.m. (men players) and every afternoon except Thursday at 4:30 p.m. at Fronton Metropolitano, Bahia Todos Santos 190 (women players). Parimutuel betting at both."

T-12 provided the following data:

On March 19, 1964, GUADALUPE GAYTAN SANCHEZ, caretaker and resident at the Fronton Mexico, Plaza de la Republica No. 3, Mexico, D. F., for thirty years, was unable to identify the photograph of OSWALD. GAYTAN SANCHEZ stated that ENRIQUE MARTINEZ DE VILLAGRAN has been the doorman at the Fronton Mexico for twenty years and, as such, observes every person who enters to determine that this person is properly dressed and not the type who might cause a disturbance at the jai alai game.

On March 19, 1964, ENRIQUE MARTINEZ DE VILLAGRAN was unable to identify OSWALD's photograph, but stated the photograph appeared similar to an American who had entered the Fronton Mexico five or six months previously on several occasions for a period of a week and a day. He was not certain the American could be identical with OSWALD nor did he have any specific information about the American, his whereabouts, or his background.

On March 20, 1964, IGNACIO VADILLO B., the general cashier for the Fronton Metropolitano, Bahia Todos Santos No. 190, Mexico, D. F., stated jai alai is not played at this Fronton. The game played there is <u>Fron-Tenis</u>, which differs from jai alai in that the players <u>do not use</u> a <u>cesta</u> (a basket fastened to the hand of the player), but a <u>racket similar</u> to a tennis racket is used.

VADILLO B. stated few, if any, Americans frequent the Fronton Metropolitano and those who do so are usually remembered. VADILLO B. was unable to identify the photograph of OSWALD as an American who might have been at the Fronton Metropolitano. He suggested that OSWALD's photograph be displayed to ESQUIEL TAPIA ROMERO, an Inspector for the Treasury

Department of the Federal District of Mexico, because TAPIA ROMERO is always on duty at the front door of the Fronton Metropolitano to observe all customers as they enter.

ESQUIEL TAPIA ROMERO viewed the photograph of OSWALD on March 20, 1964, and stated definitely that OSWALD had not been at the Fronton Metropolitano.

(E) OSWALD's Luggage

The following information was furnished by T-13:

On May 4, 1964, JUAN PEREZ GONZALEZ advised that he is the chief of the baggage department at the terminal of the Flecha Roja bus line, Calle Heroes Ferrocarrileros No. 45, Mexico, D. F. PEREZ viewed photographs of an olive-colored, "B-4" bag with yellow chalk or crayon markings on one side which appeared to be "9/23" and possibly an initial, of fragments of stickers and tags thereon, and of a blue, zippered handbag and affirmed that he has no recollection of those pieces of luggage and did not recognize any of the markings, stickers or tags as being in any way connected with the Flecha Roja operations. He stated, however, that he recently entered Mexico at Nuevo Laredo with a small, zippered handbag of canvas material, and when he went through Mexican Customs, the Inspector placed a green chalk or crayon marking on the bag to indicate it had been inspected.

PEREZ displayed the various photographs to the baggage handlers on duty at the terminal, and they stated they were unable to recall the luggage in question or make any explanation of the tags, stickers and inscriptions on them.

On May 8, 1964, the manager of the Mexico City terminal of the Transportes del Norte bus line, Insurgentes Sur No. 137, viewed the photographs mentioned above and advised that he did not have any recollection with respect to the two pieces of luggage described above nor did he believe that any of the fragments of stickers and tags thereon were connected in any way with the Transportes del Norte baggage handling procedures. He expressed the belief that the yellow chalk markings on the olive-colored bag were typical of the method used by Mexican Customs Inspectors at Nuevo Laredo to mark luggage upon completing examination thereof in lieu of a sticker which they sometimes use.

- 118 -

COMMISSION EXHIBIT No. 2121—Continued

The manager, RICARDO MEDINA BELTRAN, displayed the photographs to the baggage handlers on duty, and they affirmed that they were unable to recognize either piece of luggage in connection with any passenger but stated unanimously that they recognized the crayon or chalk markings on the olive-colored bag as typical of the inspection procedure of Mexican Customs at Nuevo Laredo. MEDINA also displayed the photographs to several Transportes del Norte drivers, and they were of the opinion that the yellow inscriptions on the olive-colored bag had been placed there by the Mexican Customs Inspector at Nuevo Laredo.

On May 4, 1964, SEBASTIAN PEREZ HERNANDEZ, assistant desk clerk at the Hotel del Comercio, Calle Bernardino de Sahagun No. 19, Mexico City, advised that he could not recognize the photographs of either the olive-colored or the blue-colored luggage as having been in the possession of a guest at that hotel.

On May 8, 1964, GUILLERMO GARCIA LUNA, owner of the Hotel del Comercio, affirmed that he was unable to recognize the photographs of the two bags as having any connection with OSWALD or any other guest at the Hotel del Comercio.

MATILDE GARNICA, maid at the Hotel del Comercio, who claimed to remember OSWALD as a guest at the hotel in room No. 18, examined the photographs of the luggage on May 8, 1964, and stated she recognized the small, blue, zippered handbag as the luggage which OSWALD had in his room at the hotel. She pointed out that she had been impressed by the fact that he had very few personal effects, had noticed he did some laundry each day and left the wet articles hanging in the bathroom, and she was quite certain she had not seen the larger, olive-colored bag.

On May 9, 1964, PEDRO RODRIGUEZ LEDESMA, night watchman at the Hotel del Comercio, examined the photographs referred to above and stated he was quite certain OSWALD had been carrying the blue handbag on the morning of his departure from the hotel. He claimed to be unable to definitely affirm that OSWALD had been carrying the olive-colored bag, as he could not remember several of its characteristics, but he expressed the firm conviction that OSWALD had been carrying two pieces of luggage. He related that on the morning of his departure, OSWALD carried his own luggage down the two flights of stairs and waited in the reception area while RODRIGUEZ went in search of a taxi.

- 119 -

COMMISSION EXHIBIT No. 2121—Continued

When RODRIGUEZ returned with the taxi, he carried the luggage from the reception area to the taxi, but still has the strong impression that he had a bag in each hand. RODRIGUEZ admitted his recollection of the type and color of the luggage is very hazy, and he does not wish to state definitely that he recognizes the photograph of either piece of luggage in connection with OSWALD.

(F) Arrest, Interrogation and Physical Condition of SILVIA DURAN

With respect to the alleged arrest of SILVIA T. DURAN, the Mexico City daily newspaper "Novedades" for November 30, 1963, page 1, published an article, translated from Spanish as follows:

"Gobernacion (Interior) advises concerning case of Mrs. SILVIA T. DURAN

"The Ministry of Gobernacion advised last night that Mrs. SILVIA TIRADO DE DURAN, who was interviewed concerning the possibility that she might have had dealings with LEE HARVEY OSWALD during his stay in our country as a tourist, was not located at the Cuban Consulate, nor did she request authorization to serve a foreign government, and that in view thereof, the investigation which was made was not in respect to her status as an employee of the Cuban Consulate in Mexico.

"It (the announcement) concluded by saying that the woman in question agreed to go to the office to which she was summoned and she was interrogated without any force whatsoever."

On December 9, 1963, DAVID ALKON appeared voluntarily at the United States Embassy, Mexico City, identified himself as an architect residing at Calle Fernandez Gonzalez Roa No. 47, Ciudad Satelite, State of Mexico, and furnished the following information:

ALKON is a designer of residential homes and has a business arrangement with one HORACIO DURAN for the interior decoration of houses designed by ALKON. DURAN is the husband of SILVIA TIRADO DE DURAN.

ALKON stated he has no social association with DURAN but understands DURAN is procommunist and often holds Marxist discussions in his home. ALKON advised that DURAN had mentioned to him that his wife had been detained and questioned by Mexico City police about her knowledge of LEE HARVEY OSWALD. DURAN told ALKON his wife knew OSWALD because the latter had been to the Cuban Embassy in an attempt to secure a visa for travel to Cuba. ALKON gained the impression that the wife was not well-acquainted with OSWALD, but only recalled he had been at the Cuban Embassy after she read of the assassination of President KENNEDY. ALKON advised that it was his impression that the wife's contact with OSWALD related only to the application for a visa and that her contact with him was very slight.

ALKON said that DURAN commented to him that he thought it was a mistake for Cuba to protest to Mexico about his wife's being questioned by Mexican authorities, since the latter had a perfect right to question her about her knowledge of OSWALD. According to press reports, the Cuban Government presented a very strong note of protest to the Mexican Ambassador in Havana with regard to the detention and questioning of SILVIA TIRADO DE DURAN by Mexican authorities, and this note was rejected by the Mexican Government because of the unacceptable language utilized therein.

On April 4, 1964, the following information was provided by T-13:

WILLIAM D. SHANAHAN, Editor of the Mexico City daily English-language newspaper, "The News," related that on April 3, 1964, DANIEL NAVA RAMOS, reporter for the Mexico City daily, "Novedades," had attempted to contact SILVIA DURAN and her husband, HORACIO DURAN, at their residence in an effort to obtain human interest material for a newspaper article he was writing with respect to the OSWALD case. NAVA had experienced considerable difficulty in seeing the DURANs and was allowed to enter their apartment with the understanding that he remain no longer than fifteen minutes. He was not permitted to speak directly to SILVIA DURAN and was advised by her husband that she had suffered a nervous breakdown following her interrogation by Mexican authorities and had been prohibited by her physician and DURAN, himself, from discussing the OSWALD matter further.

(G) Information Concerning CHARLES SMALL; <u>Bracelet, Post Cards, Race Track Pamphlet</u>

T-22 reported that as a result of the assassination of President KENNEDY and the publication of the facts concerning OSWALD's leftist connections and his prior residence in the Soviet Union, many members of the American Communist Group in Mexico (ACGM) were extremely fearful, expecting police harassment of all leftists.

Source identified CHARLES SMALL, true name CHARLES NELSON SMOLIKOFF, who was born in Brooklyn, New York, on March 16, 1911, as being one of the most prominent associates of the ACGM. According to the source, SMALL is a United States citizen who resides in Mexico, D. F., and operates a tourist-type store at Calle Niza No. 47, where he sells silver jewelry and other gift items.

Source advised that in the past some, but not all, American communists visiting Mexico, D. F., have appeared at SMALL's place of business, and SMALL has assisted these individuals in connection with their problems while in Mexico, D. F.

T-22 learned that in mid-December, 1963, SMALL had expressed concern that OSWALD might have visited his store in Mexico, as many American communists, when in Mexico, D. F., appear at his store.

In early January, 1964, according to source, SMALL continued to worry that he might have known OSWALD at some time and that OSWALD might have visited his store while in Mexico, D. F. Source stated SMALL had no definite information in this regard and was only speculating on the matter. Source was unable to develop any specific information to indicate that SMALL might actually have known OSWALD, that SMALL knew anyone who knew OSWALD, or that OSWALD had visited SMALL's store in Mexico, D. F. Source considered SMALL's concern about the possibility that OSWALD might have visited his store to be part of the general concern of members of the ACGM after reading that OSWALD had been in Mexico.

The ACGM is a loose association of a predominantly social nature of present and/or past members of the Communist Party, USA, and their friends and associates who share a common sympahty for communism and the Soviet Union.

In connection with the possibility that a silver-colored bracelet considered to be of Japanese origin was given by OSWALD to his wife, MARINA NIKOLAEVNA OSWALD, upon his return to Dallas, Texas, from Mexico, about October 3, 1963, T-22 advised that SMALL was not known to handle imported Japanese merchandise in his store in Mexico, D. F., which merchandise would be similar to the type of bracelet given to Mrs. OSWALD and added as follows:

Post cards had never been observed on sale in SMALL's store at any time, and this would seem to obviate OSWALD's having purchased at SMALL's store six colored post cards depicting scenes in Mexico, which reportedly were among OSWALD's possessions. SMALL had not been known to have available for sale or distribution any pamphlets exactly like or similar to the pamphlet reportedly located among OSWALD's possessions with the inscription on the cover page: "Hipodromo de las Americas, S. A., Mexico, D. F."

Source advised that additional inquiries would be made at SMALL's store for any possibility that OSWALD could have purchased or obtained the above-mentioned bracelet, post cards, and/or pamphlet at his store and that a check also would be made for these items at the four known outlets of Japanese merchandise in Mexico, D. F.

Source subsequently advised that careful review had been made of all the bracelets in SMALL's store, and none of these was of Japanese origin or appeared in any way similar to a photograph of the above-mentioned bracelet.

According to T-22, complete verification had been made of previous observations that no post cards exist and none are sold at SMALL's store in Mexico, D. F.

T-22 advised that the six colored post cards depicting various scenes in Mexico which were in OSWALD's possession were designed and manufactured by one FISCHGRUND, one of the two largest manufacturers of post cards in Mexico and that these post cards are sold in a great number of stores in Mexico.

Source stated that a check of four known outlets of Japanese merchandise in Mexico, D. F., was made and that these outlets do not handle any type of bracelet which would be similar to the one which OSWALD gave his wife.

T-23, a confidential source who has furnished reliable information in the past, advised that 244 stores, including jewelry stores, tourist-type gift shops, and stores handling silverware in Mexico, D. F., were contacted during the period March 6 through 13, 1964, without locating any store which carries the type of bracelet which OSWALD gave his wife.

This source concluded that OSWALD could not have purchased the bracelet in Mexico since the import tax on such an article not manufactured in Mexico would be prohibitive for resale at a profit, unless OSWALD bought it from an ambulatory street vendor, in which case the bracelet might have been smuggled into Mexico by a Japanese sailor at the port of Acapulco, Guerrero, Mexico. If the latter occurred, OSWALD might have had a problem upon presenting the bracelet to an engraver in Mexico because he would have been handling smuggled merchandise.

T-24, a confidential source who has furnished reliable information in the past, contacted 59 stores in Mexico, D. F., during the period March 7 through 14, 1964, which included jewelry stores, stores selling silverware, and stores handling

engraving, and was unable to locate any store which carried the type of bracelet OSWALD gave his wife. As a result, source did not believe OSWALD could have purchased the bracelet in Mexico because the import tax on a bracelet not manufactured in Mexico would prohibit resale at a profit. T-24 stated that if OSWALD bought the bracelet in Mexico, he could have purchased it from a street vendor, who could have obtained it from a Japanese seaman in Acapulco, Guerrero, Mexico, in which case OSWALD would have had a problem getting the bracelet engraved because it would have been smuggled into Mexico.

T-13 advised that on March 19, 1964, DANIEL GALINDO, assistant manager of the Hipodromo de las Americas, S. A., Mexico, D. F., a thoroughbred race track, stated he was familiar with the pamphlet entitled "Hipodromo de las Americas, S. A., Mexico, D. F." GALINDO related that this pamphlet was published by the race track three or four years ago, explaining in English and in Spanish the "Rules for Betting in 1-2 Selection and Quinielas."

This pamphlet was given wide distribution at the race track and at souvenir shops, hotels, motels, drug stores, and restaurants and for a time was inserted in the programs on racing days for patrons of the track. The race track still has some copies of this pamphlet on hand but has not distributed it during recent years. The same information recorded in the pamphlet is now published in the racing program for a given day whenever space is available for that purpose.

GALINDO stated such a pamphlet could possibly have been picked up from any of the numerous localities in Mexico, D. F., where the pamphlet was previously distributed if copies are still available, but all the localities are now unknown to him.

VII. ALLEGATION BY PEDRO GUTIERREZ VALENCIA

(A) Basis for Inquiry

On January 23, 1964, ELDRIDGE A. SNIGHT, Regional Security Officer, United States Embassy, Mexico, D. F., Mexico, made available a letter, written in the Spanish language, dated December 2, 1963, which had been directed to President LYNDON B. JOHNSON by PEDRO GUTIERREZ VALENCIA, who described himself as a credit investigator for a Mexico City department store.

The letter states that he was at the Cuban Embassy in Mexico City on September 30, 1963, or October 1, 1963, to conduct a credit investigation concerning an employee of that Embassy and, upon leaving, he observed a Cuban in the company of a person he judged to be an American also leaving the premises of the Cuban Embassy. According to this letter, these two individuals were engaged in a heated discussion in English involving "CASTRO, Cuba and KENNEDY." GUTIERREZ alleged that the Cuban observed by him at that time was counting American currency, and both persons departed from the area in an automobile. The letter continued that he had later seen photographs of LEE HARVEY OSWALD and had concluded that the American seen with the Cuban was LEE HARVEY OSWALD.

Inquiry on January 27, 1964, at the credit department of the Mexico City department store known as "Palacio de Hierro," Calle Durango No. 230, revealed that GUTIERREZ is known there as a credit investigator.

T-2 furnished the information which follows:

(B) Interviews of GUTIERREZ VALENCIA

On January 29, 1964, PEDRO GUTIERREZ VALENCIA, who resides in Mexico City at Calle Florida No. 9, Colonia Napoles, Mexico, D. F., advised that he currently is employed at the Palacio de Hierro department store as a credit investigator and during the period from 1947 to 1949, he was the Assistant Commandant of the Penitentiary of the Federal District, located on Calle Lecumberri. During the period from 1943 to 1946, he was connected with the management of the restaurant "Le Rendez

Vous," in Mexico, D. F.

GUTIERREZ related that when he was Assistant Commandant of the Penitentiary, Dr. ESTHER CHAPA, whom he described as a "well-known communist," was the Parole Board Director at the prison. He said that Dr. CHAPA formally accused him of being anti-communist at that time, which was a correct charge, since he "most certainly was anti-communist." He stated that Dr. CHAPA was finally dismissed from her position by her superiors.

GUTIERREZ explained he had offered the above facts for the purpose of substantiating his avowed anti-communist sentiments during a long period of time.

GUTIERREZ acknowledged that he was the author of the aforementioned letter dated December 2, 1963, directed to President LYNDON B. JOHNSON.

GUTIERREZ stated that on September 30, 1963, or October 1, 1963, he had occasion to go to the Cuban Embassy in Mexico, D. F., in connection with a credit investigation of a female employee of that Embassy, and needing to interview this woman at the Cuban Embassy at about 10:30 a.m., he had parked his car on Calle Francisco Marquez just outside the parking area reserved for the use of Cuban Embassy vehicles.

On February 3, 1964, GUTIERREZ stated that he now estimates that he entered the premises of the Cuban Embassy at about 10:30 or 10:35 a.m. on October 1, 1963, and departed about 10:50 a.m., explaining that he had been able to fix the time rather closely because he had located a credit report on an individual he was investigating that date in Coyoacan (municipality in the Federal District) and estimated he was in Coyoacan at about 11:15 a.m. on October 1, 1963.

On January 29, 1964, GUTIERREZ related that upon entering the Cuban Embassy on October 1, 1963, he was able to locate the woman about whom he was inquiring and she displayed to him a card which identified her as a "Second Counselor" of the Cuban Embassy, but when he asked her to show him her carnet to identify her as an employee of the Cuban Embassy accredited to the Mexican Government, she said that an application had been made to the Mexican Foreign Office but that her status had not, at that time, been recognized or accredited by the Mexican Government. GUTIERREZ explained that this was an obvious falsehood as he had checked at the Mexican Foreign Office previously and had found that no information was on record for this female employee of the Cuban Embassy, and the Mexican Foreign Office had no knowledge of her presence in Mexico.

GUTIERREZ stated that he told the credit applicant that she would require a "fiador" (guarantor) in order to have her credit application approved, and she indicated she could not furnish a "fiador," for which reason the credit application was not approved by the department store and no further action was taken in connection therewith.

On February 3, 1964, GUTIERREZ advised that an exhaustive search of the credit reports made by him in September and October, 1963, revealed that the credit report he made on a female employee of the Cuban Embassy at Mexico City on or about October 1, 1963, had been destroyed because of the fact her credit application had been rejected. He believed she was employed in the Commercial Department of the Cuban Embassy, that being the section he visited when he went there to contact her.

GUTIERREZ further related as follows:

Upon leaving the Cuban Embassy he paused in the courtyard which leads to the outside sidewalk and, while in the process of lighting his cigarette lighter, was bumped by a person who was also leaving the Cuban Embassy and was accompanied by an adult male American. GUTIERREZ subsequently viewed photographs of OSWALD and advised that it is his opinion OSWALD was the aforementioned American. It was his opinion that the person accompanying the American was a Cuban, basing this assumption on an expression used by this person after bumping into GUTIERREZ in the courtyard, as when GUTIERREZ excused himself, the person responded in Spanish, "Esta bien Chico" (that's all right, buddy), a common expression used by Cubans to indicate no harm was done.

He described this Cuban as follows:

Sex	Male
Race	White
Nationality	Cuban
Age	Appeared to be about 33 years of age
Height	Short, about 5 feet 3 inches to 5 feet 5 inches
Build	Very stocky and appeared to be a person of considerable physical strength
Hair	Black and curly
Complexion	Very light for a Cuban
Dress	Wore dark colored business suit, with sport shirt open at collar, and no necktie
Remarks	Wore no hat; spoke English fluently and rapidly; also spoke Spanish with a Cuban accent.

GUTIERREZ described the American who was accompanying this Cuban as follows:

Sex	Male
Race	White
Citizenship	Presumed to be United States citizen
Age	27 to 30 years
Complexion	Very light
Eyes	Unknown
Height	5 feet 9 inches to 5 feet 10 inches
Build	Slender
Weight	GUTIERREZ claimed to be unable to estimate weight but stated American was not at all fat or stocky
Hair	Dark brown
Dress	Wore beige or khaki-colored slacks and shirt of unrecalled type, with short jacket or windbreaker; wore no hat

Remarks	Appeared nervous and had appearance of being aggressive; was heard to speak only English

GUTIERREZ said that when they passed him, the two individuals were engaged in a heated discussion in English, and GUTIERREZ heard the words "CASTRO" and "KENNEDY" mentioned. He claimed he noticed that the Cuban had some American currency in his hand and appeared to be examining or counting this money. He said that after the Cuban and the American exited through the gate to the sidewalk on Calle Francisco Marquez, he observed the Cuban hand the money to the American, and the American took this money with his left hand, folded it and pushed it into his left-hand trouser pocket.

GUTIERREZ related that this exchange interested him, and he followed the two individuals along Calle Francisco Marquez until they turned left at the corner where he observed that they entered an automobile which he described as being a "Dina Renault," light beige in color and a fairly new or current model. The Cuban was on the driver's side. The license plates had white numerals on a black background, the coloring of the 1962-63 Mexican plates, but GUTIERREZ could furnish no information as to whether the plates were for the Federal District of Mexico, whether the plates may have been "diplomatic" plates, or whether they may have been from some state or territory of Mexico. After the American and the Cuban got into the car, they apparently drove away, and he did not see them further.

GUTIERREZ advised he believes that the person he considered to be OSWALD referred to the Cuban as "ERNIE" on at least two occasions during the conversation which he overheard. He expressed the opinion that the use of the name "ERNIE" may indicate that the Cuban's name may be "ERNESTO," which would be the normal Spanish name for a person who might be known as "ERNIE" or ERNEST.

(C) Character and Reputation of GUTIERREZ

On February 17, 1964, T-5 advised that a check of the Identification Division of the Metropolitan Police of the Federal District revealed that one PEDRO GUTIERREZ VALENCIA had a driver's license issued to him in 1938 and again in 1942.

It was also determined that a thumb print of PEDRO GUTIERREZ VALENCIA, which he had affixed to his letter dated December 2, 1963, directed to President LYNDON B. JOHNSON, is identical with the right thumb print of GUTIERREZ which is on file at the Identification Division of the Metropolitan Police in connection with a request by GUTIERREZ to carry a firearm and also in connection with the issuance to him of driver's licenses.

T-5 advised on February 20, 1964, that the records of all Mexican police and investigative agencies at Mexico City do not contain any information of a derogatory nature concerning GUTIERREZ.

On February 20, 1964, T-25, a confidential source, stated that PEDRO GUTIERREZ VALENCIA enjoys a good reputation in his neighborhood and is considered to be a person of good conduct and wholesome habits.

(D) Information Concerning ARTURO GAONA ELIAS

On February 25, 1964, T-2 received information that a beige-colored Renault automobile with 1962-63 Federal District of Mexico license plates No. 26-58-61 was observed on that date entering the premises of the Cuban Embassy at Mexico, D. F.

On February 27, 1964, T-4 advised that he ascertained through a check of the records of the Traffic Department of the Federal District of Mexico that a 1959 Renault, Motor No. 744492, was registered on April 11, 1962, in the name of ARTURO GAONA ELIAS, Calle Tolteca No. 53, Colonia Morelos, Mexico, D. F., with 1962-63 license plates No. 26-58-61 for the Federal District of Mexico. The only other data appearing in the Traffic Department file is that the 1959 Renault is a sedan model, as the color of the vehicle was not specified.

On February 27, 1964, T-25 advised that inquiries at Calle Tolteca No. 53, Colonia Morelos, and at various business establishments in the immediate vicinity of that address, failed to develop any information concerning GAONA ELIAS or the above-described 1959 Renault automobile. Source advised that the structure numbered 53 on Calle Tolteca is actually a cow stable and unsuitable for human habitation. The address is located in an extremely poor, low-class area of Mexico City which is frequented by thieves.

Inquiry was also conducted at Calle Tolteca No. 53, Colonia Industrial, at Calle Tolteca in Colonia Ixtapalapa, and at Calle Tolteca in Colonia San Pedro de los Pinos, without obtaining information which would aid in identifying ARTURO GAONA ELIAS.

T-5 advised that a check of driver's license records at the Federal District Traffic Department revealed no evidence that anyone identifiable with ARTURO GAONA ELIAS had been issued a driver's license in the Federal District of Mexico. Source further advised that Traffic Department records do not show that license number 26-58-61 had been issued as of that date for the current 1964-65 Federal District license plates and that license number 26-58-61 is a 1962-63 Federal District license number.

Source further reported that no record could be located at the Ceremonial Division of the Mexican Ministry of Foreign Affairs that anyone by the name of ARTURO GAONA ELIAS had been reported to that Division as a representative of any foreign nation in Mexico.

The source also advised that no information identifiable with ARTURO GAONA ELIAS could be located in the files of the Identification Division Metropolitan Police of the Federal District.

T-2 advised on March 2, 1964, that PEDRO GUTIERREZ VALENCIA stated that he had never known or heard of ARTURO GAONA ELIAS.

The information which follows was furnished by T-2:

Additional investigation at Mexico City, which included a check of the United States Visa records and the files of the National Automobile Theft Bureau, failed to develop further identifying information concerning ARTURO GAONA ELIAS until on March 4, 1964, ANTONIO SERVIN DE LA MORA, official of the Mexican Social Security Institute, reported that the files of that agency included a record for ARTURO GAONA ELIAS and his wife, IRMA MENDIVIL DE GAONA, as residents in the year 1957 at Calle Zaragosa No. 800, Colonia Plano Oriente, Ciudad Obregon, Sonora.

T-26, a confidential source who has furnished reliable information in the past, advised that on March 11, 1964, ARTURO GAONA ELIAS had been located in Ciudad Obregon, Sonora, where he now resides at Calle Nuevo Leon 743 Norte. He advised source that he had sold the 1959 Renault automobile, motor No. 744492, to REYNALDO ROMERO FELIX, who lives at Calle Sinaloa No. 234 Sur, Ciudad Obregon.

Source advised that on March 11, 1964, REYNALDO ROMERO FELIX was located in Ciudad Obregon and advised he had sold the above-mentioned Renault automobile in July, 1961, to CLAUDIO OLIVEROS of Mexico City. He described OLIVEROS as having a questionable reputation as an automobile dealer and related that OLIVEROS took the Renault to Mexico, D. F., where he was believed to have turned it over to ERNESTO MITRANI, a Cuban, who was engaged in the automobile business. He advised that ERNESTO MITRANI has a brother by the name of ISAAC MITRANI, who also might be an automobile buyer.

According to ROMERO, this automobile was to have been sold by ERNESTO MITRANI at Mexico, D. F., or to have been sent to an American by the name of GUILLERMO WILLY, who deals in automobiles at Chihuahua, Chihuahua.

(E) Inquiry Concerning ERNESTO MITRANI

On March 13, 1964, MARGARITA MUNGUIA, Visa Section, United Stated Embassy, Mexico, D. F., made available visa file data concerning ERNESTO MITRANI LEVY, reflecting that he was born December 29, 1936, at Havana, Cuba, and that he was the holder of Cuban passport No. 26367, issued December, 1959, with expiration date in 1964.

The visa card contained a photograph of ERNESTO MITRANI, and he was described on this card in January, 1961, as being five feet seven inches in height, weighing 176 pounds, of fair complexion, brown hair and green eyes.

On March 17, 1964, photographs of ERNESTO MITRANI LEVY were exhibited to PEDRO GUTIERREZ VALENCIA, who stated that the photographs of MITRANI definitely do not depict the Cuban he saw in the company of an American at the Cuban Embassy about October 1, 1963.

GUTIERREZ advised he believes that the Cuban observed by him at the Cuban Embassy was not an employee of that Embassy, because this person had his late model Renault automobile parked on Calle Tacubaya in an area which is used by the general public for parking. He pointed out that many officials and employees of the Cuban Embassy park their cars on Calle Francisco Marquez in an area reserved for their use.

GUTIERREZ stated he believes that he would have no difficulty whatsoever identifying the Cuban if he ever observed a photograph of this person, because he has the appearance of the Cuban better fixed in his mind than the appearance of the American he considered to have been OSWALD.

T-19 advised on March 18, 1964, that ERNESTO MITRANI LEVY, employee of the "Casa Vogue" (Ladies' wear shop), Calle Madero No. 20, Mexico, D. F., advised that about two years ago he was engaged in buying and selling used automobiles in Mexico. He affirmed, however, that he is certain he did not buy a 1959 Renault sedan from CLAUDIO OLIVEROS, explaining that OLIVEROS formerly operated a used car lot in Mexico City but, due to OLIVEROS' bad character and alleged fraudulent activities, he had been forced to close down the business and reportedly had left Mexico, D. F., for his home in Guadalajara, Jalisco, Mexico.

MITRANI also mentioned that he had been employed in the Cuban Embassy in Mexico, D. F., until 1959; however, he was unable to furnish any information concerning any possible employee of the Cuban Embassy who might have had a 1959 beige-colored Renault in his possession in October, 1963, or in February, 1964.

MITRANI stated that it is common practice for persons in Mexico to buy an automobile and leave it regis-tered in the name of a prior owner to avoid payment of sales taxes. He said that the 1959 Renault may have changed hands many times since it originally was purchased by ARTURO GAONA ELIAS of Ciudad Obregon, Sonora, in 1959.

Upon recontact on March 24, 1964 MITRANI advised he had checked the incomplete records he still possesses for the period he was in the used car business and had located no record of a purchase of a 1959 Renault from CLAUDIO OLIVEROS or anyone else. MITRANI advised he had spoken with his brother, ISAAC MITRANI, in an effort to determine whether he might have a record of a transaction involving the afore-mentioned Renault, but his brother likewise could locate no record involving the 1959 Renault automobile.

(F) Further Interviews of GUTIERREZ

T-2 advised as follows:

On February 20, 1964, GUTIERREZ was shown a photograph of LEE HARVEY OSWALD which had appeared in "Life" magazine and which depicts OSWALD passing out pro-Cuban literature on a street in New Orleans, Louisiana. With respect to a profile photograph of OSWALD showing his right arm extended and his torso from the waist up, GUTIERREZ advised that it does not appear familiar to him and that he cannot say that this photograph in any way resembles the American seen by him at the Cuban Embassy on October 1, 1963. He explained that during his brief encounter with the American and Cuban on October 1, 1963, he at no time observed the profile view of either the American or the Cuban.

GUTIERREZ agreed that a mistaken identification from newspaper photographs of OSWALD which he saw almost two months later would be very possible. He insisted, however, that he does not believe he is mistaken in his identification of OSWALD.

In order to more readily pinpoint the date he had been at the Cuban Embassy and observed the Cuban and the American, on March 2, 1964, GUTIERREZ made available a listing of 260 names of individuals concerning whom he had conducted credit investigations for the Palacio de Hierro department store for the period September 1, 1963, to October 25, 1963, who were approved for credit. He stated this list represents the basis for his pay as a credit investigator because he is paid on an individual case basis for each person investigated. He pointed out that he is paid only for those applicants who are approved for credit and that no records are maintained by the department store of names of persons who are rejected for credit. Among those names mentioned are the names of 30 persons investigated for credit by GUTIERREZ during the period from September 27 to October 3, 1963. GUTIERREZ explained that no specific data appears on this list which would identify the exact date he conducted the individual investigation on each of the 30 persons listed but that he has estimated that the names of the 17th and 18th individuals listed would have been conducted on or about October 1, 1963. He advised that the

names of JOSEFINA LORENZANA HERNANDEZ and her "fiador," RICARDO LORENZANA RUBIN, are the 17th and 18th names on this listing.

GUTIERREZ pointed out that the names of LORENZANA HERNANDEZ and LORENZANA RUBIN are significant in that these persons were the subjects of his investigation in Coyoacan on October 1, 1963, and the appearance of these names on the pay sheet in a numerical sequence indicating that the investigations were conducted on or about October 1, 1963, further substantiates information to the effect he conducted the credit investigation of these persons on October 1, 1963, as he recalled that he had been at the Cuban Embassy just prior to conducting the investigation on the LORENZANAs.

GUTIERREZ stated he had given much thought to any other possible means of pinpointing the exact date he was at the Cuban Embassy but had not arrived at any additional means of establishing that he was there on October 1, 1963, other than from his personal recollection and the fact he conducted a credit investigation of the aforementioned JOSEFINA LORENZANA HERNANDEZ and her father, RICARDO LORENZANA RUBIN, on that date.

In furnishing further details regarding his reported visit to the Cuban Embassy on or about October 1, 1963, GUTIERREZ advised he had departed from the Consular Section of the Cuban Embassy through the rear door leading into the patio or garden section of the premises and departed from the patio area through the main entrance on Calle Francisco Marquez, GUTIERREZ stated it was his impression that the unidentified Cuban and the person identified by him as OSWALD had left the building in the Embassy compound where the Cuban Ambassador has his quarters rather than the Consular building, which is a separate edifice. He said he could not be sure that the

Cuban and the American had not left the Consular building, but when he was bumped by the Cuban, it seemed to him that the Cuban and the American were coming more from the direction of the residence than from the Consular building.

On April 25, 1964, front view and profile photographs of HORACIO DURAN NAVARRO were exhibited to PEDRO GUTIERREZ VALENCIA, who stated that these photographs of DURAN in no way resemble the unknown Cuban he observed on or about October 1, 1963, in the company of the American exiting the premises of the Cuban Embassy in Mexico, D. F.

GUTIERREZ pointed out that he feels that the data he had previously provided had exhausted his means of substantiating his allegation.

T-2 advised as follows:

On March 7, 1964, an official of the Mexican Federal Automobile Registration Bureau (MFARB), Mexico, D. F., advised that the MFARB file No. 193630 contains the following information concerning ARTURO GAONA ELIAS and a 1959 Renault automobile registered to him.

A 1959 Renault "Dauphine" four-door sedan, motor No. 744492, serial No. 5401098, was assembled in Mexico by the automobile assembly factory known as "Autos Franceses, S. A." (incorporated), Avenida Cuauhtemoc No. 393, Mexico, D. F.

This vehicle, a model 1090, was sold in 1959 to an

automobile agency known as "Distribuidores Sonorenses de Autos Franceses, S. A." (French Automobile Distributors of Sonora, Inc.), located at Avenida Miguel Aleman No. 242, Ciudad Obregon, Sonora, Mexico.

According to the MFARB file, this vehicle was sold by the aforementioned automobile distributor in Ciudad Obregon, Sonora, on December 5, 1959, to ARTURO GAONA ELIAS, Calle Tolteca No. 53, Mexico, D. F.

(H) Information From CLAUDIO OLIVEROS

The information which follows was provided by T-19:

On April 7, 1964, CLAUDIO OLIVEROS was located at a Mexico City automobile parking lot at Parque Espana No. 5, and advised as follows:

OLIVEROS stated emphatically that he did not buy a 1959 Renault automobile from REYNALDO ROMERO, a used car dealer of Ciudad Obregon, Sonora, in 1961. OLIVEROS said that during 1961, he was hospitalized in Mexico, D. F., for an operation, and during that period he made no trips to Ciudad Obregon, Sonora, to buy used cars.

OLIVEROS stated that he could only recall having purchased two Renault automobiles in the Ciudad Obregon area in the past. One of these automobiles was a used Renault which he purchased during 1960 from the Renault car agency in Ciudad Obregon, and the other was a Renault automobile he purchased from an unknown farmer in the Ciudad Obregon area, also during the year 1960.

OLIVEROS claimed that he is well acquainted with REYNALDO ROMERO and that this individual is known locally around Ciudad Obregon by the nickname "El Rey." OLIVEROS advised that REYNALDO ROMERO is mistaken if he stated that he sold a Renault automobile to OLIVEROS in 1961, because he,

OLIVEROS, has never purchased a Renault automobile from REYNALDO ROMERO.

The following data was provided by T-2:

On April 15, 1964, CLAUDIO OLIVEROS, who stated he resides at Avenida Ejercito Nacional No. 1049, Apartment No. 301, Mexico, D. F., related that following his previous interview on April 7, 1964, he had recalled that he purchased a Renault automobile in Ciudad Obregon, Sonora, Mexico, in about July, 1961, and transported this vehicle to Mexico, D. F., where he sold the car to a "Mr. DURAN," who was employed at a furniture manufacturing establishment. OLIVEROS vaguely recalled that the buyer of this vehicle either resided or had his place of business in the "Colonia Del Valle" section of Mexico City. He also recalled this individual had a brother who claimed he was married to an American girl.

T-23 advised that it had been determined from observation that HORACIO DURAN NAVARRO, the husband of SILVIA TIRADO DE DURAN, operates a 1962 maroon, four-door Volvo automobile, bearing 1964-65 Federal District of Mexico license plates number 30-51-18.

T-2 advised that on April 24, 1964, CLAUDIO OLIVEROS stated he had learned from a former associate in the used car business that an automobile sales receipt still in the possession of the latter clearly shows that OLIVEROS sold a 1959 Renault, motor No. 7444492, to a "Mr. DURAN" at Mexico, D. F., in 1961. OLIVEROS stated that this sales receipt was signed by DURAN, but the signature was somewhat illegible and he was unable to read the full name. It was brought to the attention of OLIVEROS that records of the Mexican Federal Automobile Bureau indicate the motor number of the 1959 Renault under consideration is 744492. OLIVEROS stated that he is certain that the motor number he provided is correct according to the sales receipt which he personally had examined, and he indicated that he is convinced that this is the vehicle which formerly was the property of ARTURO GAONA ELIAS of Ciudad Obregon, Sonora, Mexico, which he, OLIVEROS, had purchased in 1961 in Ciudad Obregon.

On April 25, 1964, OLIVEROS advised that he had recalled that the 1959 Renault automobile had been sold to the aforementioned "Mr. DURAN" at a lamp manufacturing and sales establishment known as "Lamparas Duran" (Duran Lamps) located in the Colonia Del Valle area of Mexico, D. F.

(I) <u>Inquiries Concerning DURAN Family</u>

On April 27, 1964, T-25 ascertained that "Lamparas Duran" is located at Calle Amores No. 327-A, Mexico, D. F., and is operated by one MARIO CARAZO, who stated he had purchased the business from LIDIA DURAN. Source advised that the business apparently employed only three persons.

On April 29, 1964, T-25 advised that he had ascertained that LIDIA DURAN is a widow and has one or two brothers.

On April 27,1964, T-5 advised he had established that LIDIA DURAN was born March 18, 1928, at Chihuahua, Chihuahua, Mexico, and that her full name, according to Spanish usage, is LIDIA DURAN NAVARRO. At the time of the issuance of a Mexican Passport in 1959, she was married to one RAUL FLORES GUERRERO.

T-2 advised that on May 7, 1964. CLAUDIO OLIVEROS examined front view and profile photographs of HORACIO DURAN NAVARRO and immediately identified these photographs as those of the individual to whom he had sold a 1959 Renault automobile at Mexico, D. F., in July, 1961. OLIVEROS also examined a photograph of RUBEN DURAN NAVARRO and identified this photograph as that of a brother of HORACIO DURAN NAVARRO. After examining these photographs, OLIVEROS recalled he had known the DURAN family about ten years ago when they resided on

Calle Panuco in Mexico, D. F., and late in 1962 he had encountered RUBEN DURAN NAVARRO at the International Airport in Mexico, D. F., and was told by DURAN at that time that he was taking a flight to visit some of the European "Iron Curtain" countries, possibly including Russia.

On May 7, 1964, DAVID ALKON, a Mexico City resident with residence at Calle Fernandez Gonzalez Roa No. 47, Ciudad Satelite, State of Mexico, advised that HORACIO DURAN NAVARRO, the husband of SILVIA TIRADO DE DURAN, currently operates a red, four-door Volvo automobile. ALKON stated that DURAN also owns a 1959 Renault automobile which was from Ciudad Obregon, Sonora, and had been purchased by DURAN at Mexico, D. F., in 1961. ALKON recalled that DURAN experienced difficulty in licensing the vehicle and mentioned that he had to correspond with the previous owner in Ciudad Obregon in order to secure additional data concerning the vehicle. ALKON affirmed that this 1959 Renault is a light grey color and definitely is not beige in color. He said this car is currently stored at a Mexico City repair garage after having been involved in an accident, and DURAN has indicated he was not able financially to pay for the repairs on the vehicle. ALKON stated that to the best of his knowledge, DURAN has maintained possession of this car since he purchased it in 1961.

ALKON stated that he maintains a contractual relation with HORACIO DURAN NAVARRO for the interior decoration of houses designed by ALKON and also is well acquainted with RUBEN DURAN NAVARRO, a brother, as well as with one sister who is known to ALKON as "LIN." Concerning "LIN," ALKON related that she is a widow and until about one year ago operated a lighting fixture firm known as "Lamparas Duran."

ALKON stated that SILVIA TIRADO DE DURAN, the wife of HORACIO DURAN NAVARRO, was formerly employed in the Consular Section of the Cuban Embassy at Mexico City, and the 1959 Renault which had been the property of HORACIO DURAN NAVARRO since 1961 had undoubtedly been used by the family for transportation to and from the Cuban Embassy on numerous occasions.

ALKON made reference to th e fact that he voluntarily had appeared at the United States Embassy, Mexico, D. F., on December 9, 1963, at which time he reported that his contacts

with HORACIO DURAN NAVARRO had left him with the impression that contacts between SILVIA TIRADO DE DURAN and OSWALD related only to the latter's application for a visa and that her contact with him was slight. On May 7, 1964, ALKON advised that his subsequent contacts with HORACIO DURAN NAVARRO have not led him to believe the latter ever had any contact with OSWALD and SILVIA DURAN's contacts with OSWALD related to anything more than OSWALD's application for a visa at the Cuban Embassy.

VIII <u>ALLEGATION BY YLARIO ROJAS VILLANUEVA</u>

(A) <u>Basis for Inquiry</u>

In an undated letter directed to Attorney General ROBERT F. KENNEDY, which was contained in an envelope postmarked December 31, 1963, at Guadalajara, Jalisco, Mexico, the following was recorded as translated from the Spanish language:

"I ask you to forgive these few bold lines addressed to so distinguished a person.

"Mr. ROBERT, I am a Mexican by race and nationality. Also, Mr. ROBERT, I am communicating with you because I do not trust anyone in the matter I intend to deal with.

"I am referring to the death of your brother. Perhaps, my information may prove quite helpful even though various officials of the United States may be involved and affected by it. I, your servant, am willing to identify them. I will tell you only later; however, with patience. It concerns the plan which I never thought would be carried out.

"I used to be a friend of LEE OSWALD, and also of ALBERT, as well as three more people. I knew about the plan, but I never thought that it would turn out to be a true plan.

"I lost their friendship because I did not accept to introduce Communist propaganda into my Mexico. To be more specific, I separated from them and never saw them again until I found out about the death of the President, your brother.

"Forgive me for not explaining any more, but it is an extremely delicate subject for you and for me. I ask you to see to it that justice is done now that this is in your possession.

"(Signed) YLARIO ROJAS,
Manuel Acuna 1367,
Guadalajara"

(B) Initial Interviews of YLARIO ROJAS

T-8 advised as follows:

Upon interview on January 10, 1964, at Guadalajara, Jalisco, Mexico, YLARIO ROJAS VILLANUEVA, Manuel Acuna 1367, Guadalajara, advised that in June or July, 1962, he was approached by an unidentified Cuban in a park in Mexico City. He claimed this Cuban talked to him about smuggling Cuban propaganda into Mexico and promised to see him later in Guadalajara.

ROJAS related that the Cuban arrived in Guadalajara by automobile about the middle of August, 1962, and the two of them drove by automobile to Ciudad Juarez, Chihuahua, Mexico, across the border from El Paso, Texas. On this trip to Ciudad Juarez, he was introduced by this Cuban to an individual, whose name he could not recall but whom he recognized later by photograph as LEE HARVEY OSWALD. He stated that after their meeting, the three of them discussed the introduction of pro-CASTRO propaganda into Mexico via Cozumel, an island located off the coast of the Yucatan Peninsula of Mexico.

ROJAS claimed that the following morning they left Ciudad Juarez on a flight of Aeronaves de Mexico Airlines and flew to Guadalajara, after a stop at Monterrey, Nuevo Leon. After their arrival in Guadalajara, the Cuban gave him 400 pesos ($32 U.S.) and told him he would receive further instructions at a later date.

ROJAS continued as follows:

The latter part of December, 1962, the Cuban visited him in Guadalajara, gave him 900 pesos ($72 U.S.), and on the instructions of the Cuban, he proceeded to Cozumel by bus, arriving there shortly after Christmas, 1962. In Cozumel, ROJAS was met by two Cubans, whose names he could not recall, and also by a Cuban woman whose first name was CRISTINA. Although he could not recall the names of the Cubans, he claimed to have them written in a notebook which he left with DANIEL SOLIS, a municipal policeman in Cozumel, and he affirmed SOLIS would not deliver the notebook to anyone but him.

About December 28, 1962, OSWALD arrived in Cozumel, having proceeded there from Jamaica via Compania Mexicana de Aviation (CMA) Airlines. OSWALD, the three Cubans and ROJAS discussed the introduction of Cuban propaganda into Mexico. During the time of these discussions, OSWALD and the three Cubans stayed at the Hotel Playa in Cozumel and ROJAS resided at the home of DANIEL SOLIS. OSWALD remained in Cozumel for two or three days and returned to Jamaica by air, and ROJAS and the three Cubans remained in Cozumel until about February 15, 1963, when OSWALD again appeared in Cozumel from Jamaica and on this occasion stayed three days. The day following OSWALD's arrival, an American by the name of ALBERT arrived from Jamaica.

ROJAS claimed the Cuban woman, CRISTINA, told him that she, the other two Cubans, OSWALD and ALBERT had discussed the elimination of President KENNEDY. According to ROJAS, she stated OSWALD was in favor of killing President KENNEDY, but ALBERT and the Cubans did not agree with OSWALD. ROJAS was told by CRISTINA that OSWALD had stated to the Cubans that he and ALBERT had laid plans to eliminate the President. ALBERT had stayed at the Hotel Isleno in Cozumel and returned to the United States via Jamaica the day after his arrival in Cozumel.

ROJAS claimed to have stayed in Cozumel until early March, 1963, when he returned by bus to Guadalajara.

T-20 advised as follows:

On January 21, 1964, a check of Mexican immigration records pertaining to arrivals and departures at the Island of Cozumel, Quintana Roo, Mexico and at Merida, Yucatan, Mexico, for the period from December 25, 1962, through February, 1963, disclosed no information for anyone with the name of LEE HARVEY OSWALD and the aliases of O. H. LEE and ALEK JAMES HIDELL, or any information identifiable with the ALBERT referred to by ROJAS or the unidentified Cubans.

(C) Reinterview of ROJAS

T-27, a confidential source abroad, advised as follows:

On January 22-23, 1964, YLARIO ROJAS VILLANUEVA advised that he was born in Ciudad Manuel Doblado in the State of Guanajuato, Mexico, but he did not know the year and guessed it was about 1932 or 1933.

He stated he also uses the name ELADIO VILLANUEVA ROJAS and explained that his mother's name was ESTEFANIA ROJAS and that his father, whose surname was VILLANUEVA, was not known by him, for which reason most of the time he prefers to use his mother's maiden name, ROJAS, rather than his true name from his father of VILLANUEVA.

At this time he furnished further background information concerning himself, as follows: He completed the sixth grade at a ranch school and in about 1949 he traveled to the United States border and crossed illegally into the United States where he was employed at El Centro, California, by a man named MacILVANEY (phonetic), who had a drainage and irrigation business. He was arrested by the United States Immigration authorities but this agency allowed him to leave the United States voluntarily. Upon his return from the United States, he went to the ranch where his mother resides and remained there for approximately three years, after which, in about 1957, he went to Tijuana, Mexico, where he was employed for approximately a year by a bottling firm which handled "7-Up." Prior to his departure from Tijuana, he had married his present wife, MARIA YOLANDA CORDOVA DE VILLANUEVA. After about 1958, ROJAS had only odd jobs and stated he has worked part-time during the period 1958 to 1964.

With specific reference to his alleged knowledge of OSWALD and ALBERT and other unidentified Cubans, on this occasion ROJAS advised as follows:

About August 14, 1962, he traveled to Mexico City and while waiting in a park near the bus station of the bus line "Estrellas de Oro" and the hotel where he stayed, he was contacted by an unidentified individual, who he later learned was a Cuban, and at that time this person proposed that ROJAS assist him in smuggling Cuban propaganda into Mexico.

About August 19, 1962, the Cuban and ROJAS departed from Guadalajara by air to the United States border at Nuevo Laredo, Tamaulipas, where he was introduced to a person who he later learned was LEE HARVEY OSWALD. At that time OSWALD was accompanied by two other Americans. ROJAS claimed that the Cuban and OSWALD discussed amounts to be paid for smuggling Cuban propaganda into Mexico; thereafter, about August 21, 1962, he and the Cuban departed from Nuevo Laredo to Monterrey by bus, where the Cuban separated from him, going to Mexico City, while he, ROJAS, continued to Guadalajara.

About three or four months latter, the Cuban arrived in Guadalajara, gave him 700 pesos ($56 U.S.) and instructed him to proceed to Cozumel for further contacts in connection with the smuggling of Cuban propaganda into Mexico.

ROJAS departed for Cozumel and claimed that upon arrival in Cozumel by accident he met DANIEL SOLIS, a policeman whose wife is ROJAS' niece, and he resided at SOLIS' home during the entire time he was in Cozumel.

During his stay in Cozumel, he again met OSWALD, the unidentified Cubans, one of whom was a woman by the name of CRISTINA, and also met with the American named ALBERT. During this period OSWALD came to Cozumel by plane on two occasions, and during OSWALD's two trips to Cozumel, the plot to murder President KENNEDY was discussed.

During his stay in Cozumel, he was friendly with a Mexican Air Force sergeant whose name he could not recall and whose assistance he sought to help him follow the activities of the Cubans, OSWALD and ALBERT. This person later was identified as LEOPOLDO TORRES CORTES, Mexican Air Force sergeant, who is based at Cozumel airport.

He claimed to have left at the home of SOLIS a notebook which he alleged contained the names of the unidentified Cubans and the full name of the unidentified American named ALBERT.

He stated that the Cubans and OSWALD stayed at the Hotel Playa in Cozumel and that ALBERT stayed at the Hotel Isleno in Cozumel.

(D) Discrepancies in ROJAS' Story

T-20 advised that on February 24, 1964, a review of the register of the Hotel Playa at Cozumel failed to reveal any record of OSWALD or any information identifiable with the Cubans mentioned by ROJAS for the period March 20, 1963, through July, 1963. It also was determined that the Hotel Isleno in Cozumel was closed from April to August, 1963.

On the same date, a review of the records of CMA airlines at Cozumel was conducted for the period from March 20 through August, 1963, and no record could be located for anyone with the name of LEE HARVEY OSWALD or his known aliases.

When interviewed on January 22-23, 1964, the discrepancies with regard to the information he had furnished on January 22-23, 1964, with relation to the information he had furnished on January 10, 1964, were pointed out to ROJAS, who merely attributed the discrepancies to his "lack of education."

T-8 advised as follows:

On February 6, 1963, ROJAS produced a slip of paper which he claimed he had obtained from under the inner sole of an old pair of shoes, and he alleged the paper had recorded thereon the names of certain unidentified individuals concerning whom he had furnished information previously, as follows:

The Cuban woman whom ROJAS had formerly identified as CRISTINA is listed on this slip of paper as CRISTINA GADEA.

The unidentified Cuban whom he claimed to have met in Mexico City and with whom he later claimed to have traveled to Nuevo Laredo and to Cozumel is listed as TONI FERREA.

The individual referred to as the American named ALBERT is listed as ADVVIN WALKER, and the name of LEE HARVEI OSVVOL is listed.

A review of the manifest of Aeronaves de Mexico airlines at Guadalajara for August 3, 1962, included a listing for HILARIO ROJAS as having flown from Guadalajara to Monterrey on an Aeronaves de Mexico flight; however, this manifest failed to reflect a listing for one TONI FERREA, whom ROJAS identified as the Cuban who traveled to the border with him.

T-20 advised as follows:

On February 24, 1964, at Cozumel, DANIEL SOLIS advised he knows ROJAS as ELADIO VILLANUEVA RAMIREZ. SOLIS produced ROJAS' notebook, and it was observed that it did not contain the names of the unidentified Cubans as claimed by ROJAS.

SOLIS advised that during the period of time he stayed in Cozumel, ROJAS did not engage in any unusual activities of any kind. He said he never saw ROJAS in the company of any unusual strangers nor in the company of any Americans or Cubans.

LEOPOLDO TORRES CORTES, a Mexican Air Force sergeant, Cozumel airport, was contacted on February 25, 1964. TORRES advised he became acquainted with ROJAS when the two of them arrived in Cozumel together in March, 1963. He related that he associated with ROJAS once or twice a week and that he had never observed ROJAS in the company of a Cuban or an American. TORRES stated that he never was requested by ROJAS to keep watch over or cover the activities of anyone in Cozumel. (ROJAS had previously claimed that TORRES had been of assistance to him in watching over the unidentified Cubans and the Americans.)

(E) ROJAS Involved in JACOB S. FLOYD Matter

On February 21, 1964, MARIA ESPERANZA GARCIA, manager, Sanborns airlines office, Hamilton Hotel, Laredo, Texas, advised Special Agent ROBERT L. CHAPMAN of the Federal Bureau of Investigation that she handled ticket purchase order No. A37240 with CMA on July 31, 1962, which reflected that the purchase order was made out to HILARIO ROJAS for an airline ticket from Guadalajara, Mexico, to Nuevo Laredo, Mexico, which was utilized by ROJAS on August 4, 1962. GARCIA stated that she had received a telephone call during the latter part of July, 1962, from Attorney JACOB S. FLOYD, Alice, Texas, concerning the purchase of a round-trip ticket from Guadalajara to Nuevo Laredo for YLARIA V. ROGAS.

GARCIA stated that on July 31, 1962, she received a letter dated July 30, 1962, from FLOYD enclosing a check for $60.64 (U. S. currency). This letter stated, "I enclosed herewith a check for $60.64 covering a round trip ticket for YLARIA V. ROGAS, Chilarde 665, Guadalajara, Jalisco. This trip is to begin on August 4, 1962, and is from Guadalajara to Nuevo Laredo and return." The letter requested a refund if the ticket was not used and gave a residence telephone number of Mohawk 4-6823 and office telephone as Mohawk 4-6561, Alice, Texas. The letter was signed "JACOB S. FLOYD" and is on stationery of the law offices of Perkins, Floyd, Davis, and Oden.

GARCIA stated that she had also received a copy of a letter written by JACOB S. FLOYD to ROJAS dated July 30, 1962. This letter advised ROJAS that arrangements had been made for the District Attorney and a good interpreter to meet with ROJAS on Sunday afternoon, August 5, 1962, at the Plaza Hotel, Laredo, and that a round-trip airline ticket was being sent to him through Sanborns as agent for Aeronaves airlines. It was pointed out in the letter that a ten-dollar bill was being enclosed to ROJAS to cover expenses for food and hotel in the event he could not make airlines connections on the trip to Nuevo Laredo and had to stay in Monterrey overnight.

According to T-17, on February 28, 1964, District Attorney SAM H. BURRIS and Assistant District Attorney JOHN C. CAMPOS at Alice, Texas,

advised as follows regarding their association with YLARIO ROJAS:

BURRIS and CAMPOS have been investigating the murder of BUDDY FLOYD since 1952. ROJAS initially contacted the FLOYD family in July, 1962, by letter addressed to Jim Wells County, Texas officials, claiming knowledge of a conspiracy by ALFREDO CERVANTES and others to murder FLOYD and suggested a meeting with JACOB FLOYD, SR.

On July 23, 1962, ROJAS wrote FLOYD from Guadalajara offering to meet FLOYD at the Mexican border if his expenses were furnished, as a result of which airline travel tickets were sent to ROJAS.

On August 5, 1962, FLOYD, BURRIS and CAMPOS met ROJAS at the Nuevo Laredo Motel, Nuevo Laredo, Mexico. At that time ROJAS stated he owned a bar at Chapala, Mexico, where he knew CERVANTES as a customer. ROJAS stated CERVANTES held a meeting with two Americans, NORMAN NEOCON and LOUIS FEANO, who allegedly had hired CERVANTES to kill JACOB (BUDDY) FLOYD, JR. ROJAS furnished detailed descriptions of these men. Before this conference with FLOYD and his associates began, ROJAS demanded money, but this was refused until information of value was received. At the end of the conference, ROJAS was paid $40.00 by FLOYD, in addition to expenses, and was left at the Nuevo Laredo Motel.

The investigation of this matter was turned over to BURRIS by FLOYD. BURRIS then wrote to ROBERT ADAMS, American Consul, Mexico City, in this regard.

On September 13, 1962, ADAMS reported investigation in this matter failed to verify the story related by ROJAS. He advised that no information was developed concerning NEOCON, FEANO or anyone fitting their descriptions, driving a red Buick as described by ROJAS.

ADAMS further reported that inquiry revealed ROJAS was considered irresponsible and lazy and that he had apparently learned of the CERVANTES case through an associate at Guadalajara.

On August 16, 1962, ROJAS in a letter to BURRIS claimed that United States Customs officers had beaten him up on August

5, 1962, which allegation BURRIS subsequently determined to be false. ROJAS again demanded more money, and constantly did so, which money was not furnished.

BURRIS stated ROJAS did not furnish any information which could be verified. The last letter received from ROJAS was dated November 5, 1963, in which he again pleaded for money, but this letter was not acknowledged.

BURRIS and CAMPOS considered ROJAS to be "a liar" and a person who attempts to exploit others for money.

District Attorney BURRIS advised he has in his files all correspondence and records pertaining to this matter which he would gladly furnish if needed and that he would be willing to testify at any time concerning these matters if such testimony would be needed.

(F) ROJAS' Admission of Fabrication

T-29, a confidential source abroad, advised as follows:

On March 5, 1964, at Guadalajara, Jalisco, Mexico, ROJAS orally admitted that he had never known or met OSWALD anywhere.

On March 5, 1964, GENARO ALFARO LOPEZ and Captain ESTEBAN LOPEZ GARCIA, agents of the Mexican Federal Security Police at Guadalajara, Jalisco, interviewed ROJAS.

They questioned ROJAS concerning his allegations of knowledge of an alleged assassination plot against President KENNEDY and of having met OSWALD, ALBERT and other unidentified Cubans in relation to this matter. At that time ROJAS admitted that he had fabricated the information.

On March 5, 1964, at Guadalajara, ALFARO and LOPEZ obtained a signed statement from ROJAS, who, as has been pointed out, also uses the name ELADIO VILLANUEVA RAMIREZ. His statement as translated from Spanish is as follows:

"At Guadalajara, Jalisco, 1:30 p.m., March 5, 1964, before GENARO ALFARO LOPEZ and Captain ESTEBAN LOPEZ GARCIA, Agents of the Federal Security Police, a

statement was taken from ELADIO VILLANUEVA RAMIREZ, who stated his name is ELADIO VILLANUEVA RAMIREZ, born Rancho Guayabo de Santa Rita, Municipality of Ciudad Manuel Doblado, Guanajuato, that he is married, 30 years of age, of Mexican nationality, presently engaged at his home in the making of 'huaraches' (Mexican native footwear). With respect to the letter which he had written to ROBERT F. KENNEDY, Attorney General of the United States of America, VILLANUEVA stated as follows:

"The information in said letter, as well as his oral statements to various United States Government officials at Guadalajara, are false and were fabricated by him personally; that he obtained the various names and details of said information from local newspapers; further, that the foregoing was done in the hope of obtaining a reward, he is willing to testify to this statement, if necessary, and places his signature and fingerprint on this statement to confirm its veracity.

"/s/ GENARO ALFARO LOPEZ
"/s/ Captain ESTEBAN LOPEZ GARCIA"

VILLANUEVA signed to this statement the name ELADIO VILLANUEVA RAMIREZ, on the margin thereof, and also placed an inked fingerprint impression on the same margin.

ALFARO and Captain LOPEZ advised that ROJAS had admitted that the trip he had made to the border in August, 1962, was for the purpose of contacting JACOB S. FLOYD, details of which have been previously recorded herein.

IX. ALLEGATION BY T-32

On November 25, 1963, T-32 made contact with the United States Embassy at Mexico, D. F., and advised the following:

T-32 entered Mexico illegally from Guatemala on August 29, 1963, traveled to Mexico, D. F., and subsequently made contact with a Nicaraguan communist residing in Mexico City. From this contact a plan was developed for T-32 to travel to Cuba to study guerrilla warfare tactics. He had occasion to visit the Cuban Consulate in Mexico, D. F., several different times for the purpose of obtaining travel documentation for Cuba by furnishing false identification papers as a Mexican citizen.

He stated that on September 18, 1963, he went to the Cuban Consulate, and while sitting in the waiting room saw a group of approximately eight persons enter the Consulate and the office of Cuban Consul EUSEBIO AZCUE. A person unknown to him was sitting at AZCUE's desk. A short time later, while source was standing near the door to the men's room at the Cuban Consulate, he noticed three men conversing a few feet away from him. One of them was a tall, thin Negro with reddish hair; the second was a man whom T-32 had seen previously holding a Canadian passport in the waiting room of the Cuban Consulate; and the third person was LEE HARVEY OSWALD.

Source stated that a tall Cuban joined the above group momentarily and passed some United States currency to the Negro.

The following conversation between the Negro and OSWALD was overheard by source:

Negro (in English): I want to kill the man.

OSWALD: You're not man enough. I can do it.

Negro (in Spanish): I can't go with you. I have a lot to do.

OSWALD: The people are waiting for me back there.

T-32 stated that the Negro then gave OSWALD $6,500 in United States currency of large denominations, saying: "This isn't much." Of this sum, $1,500 was for extra expenses. The Negro also gave OSWALD about 200 Mexican pesos.

In a later interview, source stated that the United States bank notes were in a small pack about one fourth of an inch thick, bound with a paper band, which the Negro broke before counting out $1,500 extra for expenses and $5,000 as "advance payment."

T-32 stated that Oswald had carried a green passport in his pocket, and he believed he saw OSWALD wearing a pistol in a shoulder holster, but he was not sure of this point. He stated that OSWALD had long shoes and a wrist watch with a yellow-metal band. According to source, OSWALD appeared to be completely at home at the Consulate and to know and to be known by Cuban Consulate personnel.

T-32 was arrested and interrogated by Mexican authorities on November 28, 1963, and a copy of the interrogation report by the Mexican authorities revealed the following:

At the outset source's story generally resembled that recorded above. He repeated to the Mexican authorities the details of the scene in which he saw the Negro, the Canadian and the American conversing together, the delivery of the money to the American by the Negro, and the conversation he overheard.

T-32 advised the interviewing Mexican officials that upon seeing the photograph of OSWALD in the newspapers following the assassination of President JOHN F. KENNEDY, he recognized OSWALD as the American he had seen at the Cuban Consulate.

An excerpt from source's statement to Mexican authorities, as translated from Spanish, is as follows:

".....spontaneously and after reconsidering he desires to state that the American to whom he referred in the body of his statement and whom he saw the 18th of September of this year in the Cuban Consulate had a certain resemblance, about sixty per cent, to LEE HARVEY OSWALD (assassin of the President of the United States). That after the assassination of President KENNEDY the witness took advantage of this fact in his favor to exploit it, furnishing versions such as those initially set forth, for the purpose of provoking an energetic reaction from the political point of view on the part of the United States of America against the government of FIDEL CASTRO RUZ and that he had no motive other than the profound hatred he feels for communism. That all his life the witness had dedicated himself to combating communism and he regrets at this moment not having accomplished his objective in the sense of causing a reaction on the part of the American Government against FIDEL CASTRO."

Because of the fact that subsequent to making the above-mentioned statement to Mexican authorities, source claimed that he had changed his statement because of fear, he was interviewed at considerable length on December 5 and 6, 1963, in Mexico, D. F.

After reiterating his story, T-32 was afforded a polygraph examination on December 6, 1963. During the course of the examination he was asked, "Is this the American you saw in the Cuban Consulate?" At the time he was shown photographs of OSWALD.

Each time he was asked this question, he definitely responded, "Yes," but it was noted that the polygraph indicated a "deception response" on these answers. These responses and those with respect to other questions led to the conclusion that T-32 was a fabricator. It was specifically pointed out to him that the polygraph indicated that he was not being

truthful in identifying photographs of OSWALD as being of a person he saw in the Cuban Consulate, and he was asked for his explanation thereof.

He replied that he had full faith in the polygraph and would not attempt to refute its results. He went on to say that the only explanation he could offer was that he had seen an American in the Cuban Consulate on September 18, 1963, who resembled OSWALD, and that upon seeing the photograph of OSWALD in the newspaper, he built up within himself, either consciously or subconsciously, a complete belief that the person he had seen in the Cuban Consulate was OSWALD.

X. MISCELLANEOUS INQUIRIES AND ALLEGATIONS RELATING TO OSWALD

(A) Allegation by SALVADOR DIAZ VERSON Concerning OSWALD and SILVIA DURAN

The White House at Washington, D. C., received a paper entitled "Possible Psychological Motivations in the Assassination of President KENNEDY" written by JOSE I. LASAGA, 2340 N. E. 7th Avenue, Apartment 4, Miami, Florida.

This speculative paper attempted to establish that the motivation of OSWALD in the assassination of President KENNEDY was FIDEL CASTRO or a CASTRO agent and that OSWALD was so motivated during his trip to Mexico between September 27 and October 2, 1963. The paper included the allegation that OSWALD had an extended interview with the Cuban Ambassador to Mexico, whom he met at a restaurant on the outskirts of Mexico, D. F., from where they departed together in the Cuban Ambassador's automobile for a private conversation.

LASAGA had advised the White House that he received the above report from ANGEL FERNANDEZ VARELA, an employee of the Voice of Cuba in Miami, Florida, who received the information from SALVADOR DIAZ VERSON, who reportedly was in

Mexico, D. F., doing some investigative work after the assassination of President KENNEDY.

SALVADOR DIAZ VERSON was interviewed at Miami, Florida, and stated that while in Mexico, D. F., from November 20 to 29, 1963, attending the Congress of the International Federation of Professional Newspaper Organizations, he was at the offices of the newspaper "Excelsior" on the night of November 25, 1963. He learned through the Mexican press that the Mexican Government had arrested one SILVIA DURAN, that DURAN allegedly had OSWALD as a guest in her house during his visit to Mexico, and that DURAN had placed OSWALD in contact with officials of the Cuban Embassy in Mexico, D. F.

DIAZ VERSON claimed Dr. BORRELL NAVARROS, an exiled Cuban newspaperman employed by "Excelsior," told him that on the day following OSWALD's arrival in Mexico, D. F., OSWALD and DURAN went to a restaurant called the "Caballo Blanco" or possibly the "Caballo Bayo," where they met an official of the Cuban Embassy. DIAZ VERSON claimed he knew nothing about OSWALD and the Cuban official's having left the restaurant together in a car.

T-3 advised that on January 11, 1964, Dr. EDUARDO BORRELL NAVARRO, a former Cuban cabinet minister who on occasions writes feature articles for the Mexico City daily newspaper "Excelsior," and resides at 1303 Homero Street, Apartment 301, Mexico, D. F., furnished the following:

SALVADOR DIAZ VERSON was in Mexico, D. F., as he had claimed and discussed OSWALD with BORRELL and other Cuban exiles. DIAZ VERSON also visited BORRELL at the latter's home.

BORRELL did not corroborate the story credited to him by DIAZ VERSON concerning the visit to a Mexico City restaurant by OSWALD and SILVIA DURAN. BORRELL stated he had never heard this story or anything similar.

BORRELL knew of no meeting between OSWALD and Cuban Embassy officials other than the meetings which allegedly occurred at the time OSWALD visited the Cuban Consulate in Mexico, D. F. BORRELL knew nothing concerning any visit by OSWALD to the home of DURAN.

On January 17, 1964, T-5 advised that he had been unable to locate a "Caballo Blanco" restaurant in Mexico, D. F., but stated that there is a "Caballo Bayo" restaurant located on the outskirts of Mexico, D. F. Source stated that it is a very large, typical, Mexican restaurant which does a thriving business. Source advised that on January 11, 1964, the photographs of former Cuban Consul EUSEBIO AZCUE LOPEZ, who was in charge of the Cuban Consulate at the time of OSWALD's visit, of Cuban Ambassador JOAQUIN HERNANDEZ ARMAS, of SILVIA DURAN, and of OSWALD were shown to the employees of the "Caballo Bayo" restaurant and extensive interviews among the employees of this restaurant were conducted without locating anyone who could recognize any of the photographs of the persons mentioned above as having been at this restaurant.

(B) Information Furnished by ROBERT KAFFKE

On February 27, 1964, ROBERT KAFFKE appeared at the United States Embassy in Mexico City and identified himself as having been a member of a student group which visited Cuba in 1963 and he explained that he had come to Mexico, D. F., to seek contact with the Cuban Embassy in the hope of arranging another trip to Cuba or to obtain assistance in making arrangements to travel to Communist China as an observer of a teacher. He mentioned that he had made some inquiries with respect to the visit to Mexico, D. F., of LEE HARVEY OSWALD in the hope that he could develop an angle which would enable him to write a saleable magazine article.

KAFFKE furnished the following background data concerning his interest in OSWALD's activities in Mexico:

He stated that within the recent past, MARK LANE, an attorney for Mrs. MARGUERITE OSWALD, LEE HARVEY OSWALD's mother, had visited San Francisco, California, on a lecture tour, and KAFFKE had attended the lecture and had spoken to LANE at some length after the lecture.

LANE told KAFFKE that "the FBI is so convinced that OSWALD was responsible for the assassination of President KENNEDY that it has ignored other witnesses and failed to follow up various leads." LANE claimed to have seen an affidavit in the possession of the Dallas Police Department reflecting that the paraffin tests made of OSWALD had disclosed powder burns on his hands but not on his cheek, suggesting from this that he might have fired a hand gun on the day of the assassination but not a rifle.

LANE advised KAFFKE that he had located four women newspaper reporters who were between the underpass and the point from which the assassination shots allegedly were fired, and these women had expressed the belief that the shots they heard had seemed to originate from the opposite direction from the Texas School Book Depository where OSWALD reportedly was employed. According to LANE, the four reporters had claimed that upon hearing the shots from the direction of the underpass, they turned in time to see a puff of smoke and figures running along the bridge over the underpass.

LANE also told KAFFKE that he had seen (or had in his possession) a second affidavit to the effect that five spent bullets had been located following the assassination rather than the three bullets which had been publicized in the United States press. He referred to those alleged projectiles as follows:

(1) A bullet which appeared on the stretcher which was utilized in removing President KENNEDY from the official limousine.

(2) One bullet which lodged in the thigh of Governor CONNALLY.

(3) One bullet which struck Governor CONNALLY in the chest.

(4) A bullet which was found imbedded in the presidential limousine.

(5) A bullet which was found on the grass adjacent to where the automobile had been at the time of the shooting.

KAFFKE quoted LANE further to the effect that the latter had information that two days prior to the assassi-

nation a "huddle" had taken place at JACK RUBY's "Carousel Club" with the participants being RUBY, TIPPIT (the Dallas policeman allegedly killed by OSWALD) and an individual whose name KAFFKE was unable to recall but whom he described as the "man who had published a full-page advertisement in a Dallas newspaper shortly prior to the assassination, charging President KENNEDY with being a communist."

KAFFKE expressed reluctance to discuss the above-described meeting, stating that the information had been obtained by LANE from a very confidential source, the identity of whom he was not aware, and he referred to the information concerning the meeting as being "real dynamite." He commented that if the meeting had taken place, it suggested a conspiracy of the "radical Left" or "radical Right" and added that perhaps TIPPIT had meant to shoot OSWALD. He stated that possibly OSWALD killed TIPPIT contrary to the "conspiracy" and it became necessary for JACK RUBY to kill OSWALD.

KAFFKE denied that his trip to Mexico had been financed in any way by Attorney LANE but stated that he had advised LANE of his intention of traveling to Mexico, to which LANE replied that he would be "interested in anything he might pick up."

(C) Allegation by ROBERT EDMOND GALLANT, Santa Clara Prison Farm, Santa Clara, California, that OSWALD was in the Cuban Embassy in Mexico, D. F., on July 12, 1963.

On November 16, 1963, ROBERT EDMOND GALLANT, also known as ROBERT JAMES GALLANT, ROBERT EDWARD GALLANT and General ROBERTO EDMONDO CORTEZ, addressed a letter to United States Attorney General ROBERT F. KENNEDY from Milpitas, California, where GALLANT was incarcerated in a jail farm.

In this letter, GALLANT alleged that he had been supplying the United States Government "with vital information as to the communist movement in Latin American Countrys. Mainly Cuba, Brazil, Argentina and Mexico." He wrote that he held the rank of a general in the "Secret Underground movement in Mexico;" that he was known as "General ROBERTO DE EDMONDO CORTEZ, Director of the Secret Army of Mexico; and that the Mexican Government did not approve of this movement because its top brass is 100% communist, both in the Government Party and the Military."

In the letter, GALLANT advised that he had sent a long letter to President J. F. KENNEDY pertaining to this matter. He then furnished information regarding the alleged shipment of arms and ammunition to Cuba. He stated that he had been risking his life for the last four years to obtain information on the inside of the communist movement and that if he were given his freedom to carry on his work, he would do all in his "power to aid the United States Government in obtaining information from Cuba throughout to Mexico."

GALLANT was interviewed at the Santa Clara County Jail on January 7, 1964, and advised the following:

After stating that he was born on March 19, 1922, and furnishing background information to the effect that he was arrested by Texas authorities at Houston, Texas, for burglary and served for seven years at the Texas State Prison at Huntsville, Texas, he related other experiences of his life until in 1960 he moved to Mexico where he resided until the fall of 1963, at which time he was arrested by Mexican authorities and deported to the United States for having written fraudulent checks.

GALLANT stated further that he had been active in an anti-FIDEL CASTRO underground in Mexico for the past few years under the name of General ROBERTO DE EDMONDO CORTES; that he had under his command a secret army of 3,500 men throughout Mexico, and that this group was an anti-CASTRO force concentrating its activities against Cuban communists in Mexico. He claimed to have a "secret agent" working in the Cuban Embassy in Mexico, D. F., and alleged that OSWALD was in the Cuban Embassy on July 12, 1963, to obtain a visa to Cuba and had stayed in Mexico for about one week at that time.

GALLANT's allegations concerning his underground movement were unknown in Mexico, and the results of a polygraph

examination of GALLANT were furnished on January 8, 1964, it's being the opinion of the examiner that GALLANT was suffering from delusions and that his story, as summarized above, was untrue.

(D) Allegation by HECTOR FRANCISCO SERRANO

T-17 advised as follows:

On November 26, 1963, a local newspaper editor at Guadalajara, Jalisco, Mexico, was reported to have stated that on Monday, November 25, 1963, he was visited by one HECTOR FRANCISCO SERRANO, a news photographer from Culiacan, Sinaloa, Mexico, who told the newspaper editor that in late September, 1963, he traveled by bus from Culiacan to Mexico City with "LEE OSWALD." SERRANO related that they had attempted to converse though "OSWALD's Spanish was poor," and "OSWALD" gave SERRANO a personal card and pamphlet in English with many pictures of FIDEL CASTRO, both of which later were discarded. SERRANO reportedly told the newspaper editor that upon arrival in Mexico City he noted "OSWALD's" baggage included a rifle in a leather case.

T-23, a confidential source abroad, advised as follows:

On December 2, 1963, HECTOR FRANCISCO SERRANO, Calle Rosales No. 477, Culiacan, Sinaloa, advised that in September, 1963, he had taken a Tres Estrellas de Oro (Three Gold Stars) bus from Culiacan to Mexico City, arriving about September 29, 1963. On the way to Mexico City, a person took a seat next to him near Guadalajara. He described this person as having facial characteristics similar to OSWALD and the same apparent age. He related that this person had talked to him in very poor Spanish on the trip from Guadalajara to Mexico City. He stated that he had seen OSWALD on television.

SERRANO related that he is a newspaper photographer, and when the Soviet Astronaut GAGARIN arrived in Mexico about October 10, 1963, he went to the airport to meet him. Being in the crowd, SERRANO was pushed to the front and personally talked to GAGARIN. SERRANO stated that he was surprised to see the same individual who had been next to him on the bus at the airport reception for GAGARIN.

SERRANO advised that many photographs were taken of the GAGARIN airport reception, and among the photographs which were taken was one which appeared on the front page of the October 12, 1963, issue of "Ovaciones," a Mexico City daily newspaper, in which SERRANO appeared with GAGARIN. SERRANO expressed the belief that in the background of one of the photographs is the person he saw on the bus and again at the airport reception.

T-17 advised that a review of the photographs appearing in the October 12, 1963, issue of "Ovaciones" revealed that OSWALD definitely does not appear in any of the photographs.

SERRANO advised that the above-mentioned bus from Culiacan to Mexico City arrived in Mexico City about September 29, 1963; however, OSWALD apparently entered Mexico at Nuevo Laredo, Tamaulipas, Mexico, on September 26, 1963, and is reported to have traveled by bus from Nuevo Laredo to Mexico City where he arrived on September 27, 1963, and was registered at a Mexico City hotel from September 27, 1963, until October 1-2, 1963.

(E) Allegation by LUIS FERNANDEZ GONZALEZ

On December 2, 1963, a person who identified himself as LUIS FERNANDEZ GONZALEZ contacted the United States Embassy, Mexico, D. F., and advised that he had some information of interest concerning LEE HARVEY OSWALD.

FERNANDEZ claimed he resided at the Hotel Yale, Calle Mosqueta No. 200, Mexico, D. F., that he was born on September 28, 1936, at Tegucigalpa, Honduras, and that his only living relative is his mother, AURORA GONZALEZ, who resides at Avenida 28 de Marzo No. 1300, Tegucigalpa, Honduras. He indicated that he is in Mexico illegally, having entered the country at Tapachula, Chiapas, on or about September 19, 1963.

FERNANDEZ claimed to be a member of the Movimiento de Liberacion Nacional (National Liberation Movement) in Mexico, D. F., and in connection therewith was acquainted

with one SAUL LOPEZ, whom he described as Press Chief of the National Liberation Movement.

> The Movimiento Liberacion Nacional (National Liberation Movement), which was formally organized at Mexico, D. F., in August, 1961, is an anti-United States, procommunist organization under the partial influence of the Partido Comunista Mexicano (Communist Party of Mexico).
>
> The published statutes of the Partido Comunista Mexicano (Communist Party of Mexico) state: "The Communist Party of Mexico has as its final objective to construct socialism and to build the communist society in Mexico."

FERNANDEZ related that on or about September 28, 1963, he met an American whom he came to know as JOHN WHITE on the street in front of the Hotel Reforma in Mexico City and again saw this person on September 29, 1963, in front of the same hotel. FERNANDEZ stated he has seen newspaper photographs of OSWALD and was of the opinion JOHN WHITE greatly resembled OSWALD.

On September 29, 1963, he accompanied WHITE and SAUL LOPEZ in LOPEZ' 1959 Ford Galaxie to Cuernavaca, Morelos, where they spent the day swimming and entertaining themselves at the Hotel Casino de la Selva but did not register at that hotel.

FERNANDEZ stated that he last saw JOHN WHITE on September 30, 1963, when WHITE and LOPEZ left Mexico, D. F., traveling to Monterrey, Nuevo Leon, in LOPEZ' automobile.

FERNANDEZ described WHITE as being about 23 to 24 years of age, about 5 feet 6 inches in height, and weighing about 110 pounds. He claimed that WHITE could speak fairly good Spanish and seemed very familiar with the Mexico City area.

FERNANDEZ stated he had nothing further to offer bearing on LEE HARVEY OSWALD but added that he was in need of assistance to go to the United States or elsewhere out of Mexico because he feared that he would be apprehended by the police in Mexico, D. F., and jailed if he were found in Mexico without proper documentation. He advised he was without funds and had no gainful employment. He was badly in need of a shave and had an unkempt appearance.

On December 4, 1963, FERNANDEZ presented an undated passenger ticket stub, No. 46218, of the bus line known as Transportes del Norte, which he claimed had been given to him by WHITE on September 28, 1963, to have his baggage picked up at the Transportes del Norte bus station.

FERNANDEZ at this time again related he was in need of assistance to leave Mexico and enter the United States.

T-7 advised on December 4, 1963, that inquiry at the Transportes del Norte bus line in Monterrey revealed that ticket No. 46218 had been sold on November 30, 1963. (FERNANDEZ claimed to have been furnished the ticket stub with that number on September 28, 1963.)

On December 19, 1963, T-6 reported that FERNANDEZ had been detained by Mexican Immigration authorities in Mexico, D. F., for investigation concerning his alleged illegal entry into Mexico and to clarify his citizenship status. It was subsequently learned from T-6 that on January 15, 1964 FERNANDEZ had been deported from Mexico to Honduras in view of his continued claim of Honduran citizenship.

On March 17, 1964, source advised that investigation by the Mexican Government had revealed that LUIS FERNANDEZ GONZALEZ actually was a Mexican citizen and that he was considered to be insane. Source also stated that FERNANDEZ' mother had been an inmate of a mental institution in Mexico.

On March 23, 1964, T-6 advised that FERNANDEZ had returned to Mexico from Honduras without permission of Mexican Immigration authorities and again had been detained

on March 4, 1964, for questioning as a result of information received by Mexican authorities that he had claimed to have information concerning a planned attempt against the life of French President CHARLES DE GAULLE incidental to DE GAULLE's March 16-19, 1964, visit to Mexico.

Source related that investigation by the Mexican Ministry of Government had established that FERNANDEZ' true name is MANUEL SANTAMARINA MENDEZ. He stated that two Mexico City attorneys, AUGUSTIN SANTAMARINA, JR., Avenida Reforma No. 76, Office No. 3, and FERNANDO ARCE SANTAMARINA, Avenida Reforma No. 76, Office No. 1, Mexico, D. F., personally' identified FERNANDEZ as their cousin and informed the Mexican investigators that FERNANDEZ' mother, AURORA MENDEZ DE SANTAMARINA, is mentally afflicted and his father, CARLOS SANTAMARINA, is deceased. The two attorneys described their cousin as mentally unbalanced and as a person who is well known for inventing fantastic falsehoods.

Source stated that FERNANDEZ or SANTAMARINA had been released from custody on March 20, 1964, after inquiries had clearly established his Mexican citizenship, and Mexican authorities were convinced that most of his statements were unreliable or completely false.

(F) Allegation by ROBERT HIMES

On December 13, 1963, ROBERT HIMES, 301 Isaac Garza Sur, Monterrey, Nuevo Leon, Mexico, furnished the following information:

On or about November 6, 1963, OSWALD allegedly entered Mexico at Ojinaga, Chihuahua, and proceeded south through the Republic of Mexico to the State of Michoacan where he converred with General LAZARO CARDENAS.

HIMES stated this information was given to his son, DAVID, by General SILICIA, Commandant of the Military Garrison at Ojinaga, Chihuahua. HIMES had no further particulars as to how OSWALD was traveling or any additional information regarding the matter.

HIMES advised that his son, DAVID, was engaged to marry the daughter of General SILICIA, and during his early December visit to Ojinaga, the General had made the above statement.

In connection with the allegation, it is noted that Mr. H. S. AIKEN, bookkeeper, Texas School Book Depository, Dallas, Texas, on November 25, 1963, made available official payroll records for the Texas School Book Depository, which reflected that OSWALD first worked for this company on October 16, 1963, and worked continuously eight hours per day from October 16, 1963, through November 22, 1963, without missing a day's work. During this period of time he was off duty on Saturdays, Sundays and November 11, 1963, which was a company holiday. It is noted in this connection that November 6, 1963, was a Wednesday.

(G) Allegation by ANDREW CHAMPION that a Friend of FRANCIS H. FIEDLER of New Orleans, Louisiana, was OSWALD

T-7, who had occasion to interview ANDREW CHAMPION of Donna, Texas, at Calle Parras No. 213, Montemorelos, Nuevo Leon, Mexico, advised that on January 2, 1964, CHAMPION made the following statement:

CHAMPION, who was born October 14, 1900, in Santa Maria, Texas, and served in the United States Marines in World Wars I and II, in 1952 or 1953 became acquainted with FRANK H. FIEDLER, also known as FRANCIS H. FIEDLER, at the Buena Vista Hotel in Cuernavaca, Morelos, Mexico. FIEDLER had stated that he was working on his doctor's thesis at the University of California, Berkeley, California; that he was a teacher; that his studies were in "space work;" and that he was mistreated in the United States because he was Jewish.

In November, 1960, CHAMPION received a letter from FIEDLER dated October 8, 1960, which was addressed from 912 North Rampart Street, New Orleans, Louisiana, and in this letter FIEDLER stated that he was going to visit the Rio Grande; that he was "an American refugee from Cuba"; and that he had given up his position as professor of literature at the University of Hawaii "because of CASTRO."

On November 7, 1962, CHAMPION received another letter from FIEDLER, and on January 1, 1963, two men suddenly appeared at CHAMPION's home in Donna, Texas. One of the men was identified later as JACK J. FRAZIER, 910 North Rampart Street, New Orleans, Louisiana, a neighbor of FIEDLER's. FRAZIER presented a letter to CHAMPION from FIEDLER in which the latter asked CHAMPION to assist the two men in parking their car and in obtaining instructions concerning travel in Mexico.

The second man, whose name CHAMPION never learned, stated that the two of them possibly were going to spend their vacation in Veracruz or Tampico and asked for the names of some inexpensive hotels at these places. The two men took two sea bags, presumably full of clothes, and on the afternoon of January 1, 1963, departed on foot toward the Mexican border, stating they were going to cross into Mexico at Brownsville, Texas.

On January 29 and 30, 1963, FRAZIER returned by himself, stating that he had been in Tampico and that his friend had decided to stay another month. FRAZIER left in his automobile after he had identified himself as the owner of the Ryder Coffee House, Home and Gallery, 910 Rampart Street, New Orleans.

With the publication of OSWALD's picture in the national press on the day of President KENNEDY's assassination, CHAMPION concluded that LEE HARVEY OSWALD was identical with the second man who visited his home on January 1, 1963.

CHAMPION stated that on December 1, 1963, on his return from a trip to Mexico, he learned that he had received a letter from FIEDLER advising that he probably would visit the Rio Grande Valley in the near future, and CHAMPION's wife had dispatched a letter to FIEDLER stating that CHAMPION would not be home for four months. This letter was mailed on November 23, 1963, to 1123 Burgundy Street, New Orleans.

From the "Time" magazine issued after the assassination of President KENNEDY, CHAMPION had clipped an article wherein it was set out that a WESLEY FRAZIER had driven OSWALD to work on the morning of the assassination, and CHAMPION had wondered if there was any association between the two FRAZIERs and the information that OSWALD had resided in New Orleans. CHAMPION stated that with this information he became more convinced that the man who visited his home on January 1, 1963, was OSWALD.

Subsequent to the foregoing, JACK J. FRAZIER, 2106 Chartres Street, New Orleans, Louisiana, advised in January, 1964, that he had made a trip into Mexico in late December, 1962, accompanied by HOWARD COHEN, 611 Esplanade, New Orleans, Louisiana. He stated that he and COHEN toured the east coast of Mexico, went to Acapulco, Guerrero, Mexico, and then returned to New Orleans about February 1, 1963.

FRAZIER advised that he did not know LEE HARVEY OSWALD and that HOWARD COHEN in no way resembled OSWALD.

(H) Allegation by ALBERTO GODOY That Film in His Possession Might Depict LEE HARVEY OSWALD and JACK RUBY Together

On January 13, 1964, SANDERS F. ROSENBLUM of the United States Information Service, United States Embassy, Mexico, D. F., advised that a Mexican attorney named ALBERTO GODOY appeared at the United States Embassy and related the following:

At 9:30 a.m. on January 14, 1964, he was planning a private showing at the Cine Versalles, Mexico, D. F., of a film on the Cuban revolution which he had in his possession.

GODOY had seen this film two years previously, and although he was not certain, he thought it possible that the film depicted an individual who possibly was identical with LEE HARVEY OSWALD and another person who possibly was identical with JACK RUBY.

GODOY was not certain that the individuals in the film were identical with OSWALD and RUBY and was anxious that an observation of the film be made on January 14, 1964.

- 170 -

COMMISSION EXHIBIT No. 2121—Continued

T-2 advised on January 14, 1964, that when contacted on the morning of that date, GODOY advised that the film had been shown on January 13, 1964, and that there was no one available at the Cine Versalles to run the film again.

He stated that reel No. 4 of the film was important because it depicted Cuban Premier FIDEL CASTRO's entry to Havana, Cuba, at the conclusion of the Cuban revolution and includes shots of throngs of people which could be enlarged to possibly identify OSWALD or RUBY as being in the crowd.

He made no allegation of having seen or identified OSWALD or RUBY in these crowds because he had seen the film two years before this. He stated that many communists were present when FIDEL CASTRO entered Havana, and he believed that OSWALD and RUBY could have been members of these crowds in HAVANA.

On January 14, 1964, he was shown photographs of OSWALD and he was not familiar in any way with the appearance of OSWALD. He also was shown a photograph of RUBY and could furnish no information reflecting that RUBY was shown in the film.

On January 14, 1964, GODOY reappeared at the United States Embassy, Mexico, D. F., with reel No. 4 of his film and stated that his primary interest was to sell the film to the United States Embassy for a price of $1,000 (United States currency) for the four reels of film.

GODOY furnished no concrete data to substantiate the allegation made by him on January 13, 1964, that OSWALD and RUBY might be depicted in his film.

GODOY, who appeared to be from 65 to 70 years of age, was unshaven and shabbily dressed and furnished his address as 128 Calle Bucareli, Mexico, D. F.

(I) Letter to Attorney General ROBERT F. KENNEDY from ERNESTO FLORES LUNA

A typewritten letter in Spanish, postmarked January 17, 1964,

- 171 -

COMMISSION EXHIBIT No. 2121—Continued

at Mexico, D. F., was sent to Attorney General ROBERT F. KENNEDY by one ERNESTO FLORES LUNA, not further identified.

This letter alleged that there possibly were certain documents at the residence of VICTOR COHEN, owner of a shoe store in Tapachula, Chiapas, Mexico, and allegedly an intimate friend of FIDEL CASTRO of Cuba, which concerned contacts by a clerk of COHEN's shoe store and an unidentified man who delivered shipments of documents from him (COHEN) to OSWALD and three other persons, not named, who were to assassinate President ADOLFO LOPEZ MATEOS of the Republic of Mexico. This letter stated that the writer of same was taking "the liberty of reproducing with care certain documents which arrived from Tapachula addressed to OSWALD." The writer of the letter alleged that COHEN was FIDEL CASTRO's treasurer and that COHEN had kept individuals of different nationalities in his house, including OSWALD.

There were no enclosures to the above letter and the identity of the writer could not be established.

T-30, a confidential source abroad, advised as follows:

On February 11, 1964, A. R. GEHRKE, British Vice Consul at Tapachula, advised that he was not acquainted with VICTOR COHEN but would make inquiries concerning him.

GEHRKE subsequently advised that COHEN is the owner of the store, "La Nacional," at 3a Calle Poniente No. 35 (35 West 3rd Street), Tapachula, which handles shoes, cloth, clothing and general merchandise. He stated COHEN is considered to be a respectable businessman but is suspected of dealing in contraband.

On February 11, 1964, Lieutenant JORGE AGUILAR PEREZ of the Mexican Federal Highway Police at Tapachula, advised that he knew COHEN well and that COHEN would not involve himself personally in illegal activities for political reasons. He knew of no pro-CASTRO groups or activities in the Tapachula area.

JOSE POLITO MORALES, head of Mexican Immigration Service at Tapachula, advised on February 11, 1964, that he was well-acquainted with COHEN, whom he described as a prosperous local merchant. He stated that because of COHEN's alleged contraband activities, he has tried without success to follow COHEN's activities and establish evidence of violation of Mexican laws. He stated that during the course of his investigation, he learned of no contacts by COHEN with North Americans or other foreigners. He stated he believed it to be ridiculous to believe that COHEN would do anything for political motivation. He was certain that COHEN was not pro-FIDEL CASTRO and that there were no pro-CASTRO groups in Tapachula.

VICTOR COHEN CHARAFF, who is the son of ISAAC COHEN and considered identical with VICTOR COHEN SCHARAFF, a white, male Mexican, born July 19, 1933, at Tuxtepēc, Oaxaca, Mexico, 5 feet 7 inches tall, weighing 147 pounds, with brown hair and eyes, of fair complexion, by occupation a clothing merchant, bearer of Mexican passport No. 282800, issued September 7, 1959, advised as follows on February 11, 1964, at his store in Tapachula:

He is not interested in politics concerning the United States, Cuba or any other nation; he is not pro-FIDEL CASTRO and has never belonged and never will belong to any pro-CASTRO organization.

He stated that because he is a prosperous businessman and Jewish, he has many enemies in Tapachula.

The name ERNESTO FLORES LUNA had no significance for him.

He claimed he had had no contact with any North Americans or other foreigners during the previous year; that no North Americans or other foreigners have been in his house or rental units; and that none of his forty employees are pro-CASTRO.

He was unfamiliar with OSWALD and unable to identify OSWALD from a group of photographs exhibited to him.

He recalled reading that OSWALD had visited Mexico but knew nothing further concerning this visit.

VICTOR COHEN CHARAFF was cooperative in furnishing samples from his typewriter for determination as to whether this typewriter was used in preparing the letter forwarded to Attorney General KENNEDY.

Result of FBI Laboratory
Examination of Typewriter Samples

The original and carbon copy samples from the typewriter of VICTOR COHEN were submitted to the FBI Laboratory for comparison with the typewritten letter directed to ROBERT F. KENNEDY by ERNESTO FLORES LUNA.

The FBI Laboratory concluded in a report dated March 3, 1964, that the typewriter used to type the samples submitted from VICTOR COHEN's typewriter was not used to type the envelope and accompanying letter forwarded to "Sr. ROBERT KENNEDY" from ERNESTO FLORES LUNA.

Additional Efforts to Identify
ERNESTO FLORES LUNA in Mexico, D. F.

T-4 advised that throughout February, March and April, 1964, the following efforts were made to locate and identify ERNESTO FLORES LUNA in Mexico:

The only reference which could be located in the files of the numerous Mexican Government agencies checked for the name ERNESTO FLORES LUNA was a December 15, 1959, application for Mexican Social Security registration as an employee of the "Constructora Valle de Bravo, S. A." (Brave Valley Construction Co., Inc.), Calle Oaxaca 93, Colonia Roma, Mexico, D. F., Mexico. This individual indicated he was born in 1922 and resided at Sierra Mojada, Lot 51, San Isidro Tecamachalo, State of Mexico, Mexico. His wife was listed as MARGARITA DELGADO PEDRAZA. He was registered with Mexican Social Security No. 153-22-157.

T-4 conducted the following inquiry:

At the "Constructora Valle de Bravo, S. A." it was determined that no record could be located of the employment of ERNESTO FLORES LUNA. The "Constructora Valle de Bravo, S. A."

was formed in 1959 when this concern was engaged in the construction of a housing development known as "San Esteban" in Mexico, D. F., and the firm and its subcontractors employed thousands of temporary workers. It was suggested at the "Constructora Valle de Bravo, S. A." that ERNESTO FLORES LUNA might have been employed by one of the subcontractors as he was unknown to the parent firm.

Neighborhood inquiries in San Isidro Tecamachalco, State of Mexico, which immediately adjoins the Federal District, failed to locate any information relative to ERNESTO FLORES LUNA.

According to T-4, no documentation is necessary to apply for Social Security registration in Mexico, and any identity may be assumed in making such an application. Source pointed out that the fact there has been no other activity or entry with respect to this registration may indicate the registration of ERNESTO FLORES LUNA was fictitious, since efforts to identify LUNA through numerous other sources had been unsuccessful.

(J) Information from JOSE GARCIA LUCHICHI
That American Woman in Monterrey, Mexico,
Telephoned Dallas Before and After
Assassination of President KENNEDY

On January 3, 1964, JOSE GARCIA LUCHICHI, a former employee of the United States Embassy, Mexico, D. F., and a reporter for "The News," an English language daily newspaper published in Mexico, D. F., furnished the following information to the Regional Security Office, United States Embassy, Mexico, D. F.

An unidentified American woman, who had rented a room in Monterrey, Nuevo Leon, Mexico, from GUADALUPE DAVILA REYES at Colombia 345, Vista Hermosa, Monterrey, had telephoned Dallas, Texas, from Monterrey several times prior to the assassination of President JOHN F. KENNEDY and again following the assassination

The unidentified woman allegedly revealed that she was very happy upon learning of President KENNEDY's death and allegedly played "happy tunes on the piano" thereafter.

The woman's conduct reportedly was so offensive to Miss GUADALUPE DAVILA REYES that she was asked to leave and the woman's whereabouts was not known.

T-31, a confidential source abroad, advised on January 15, 1964, at Monterrey, Mexico, that Miss GUADALUPE DAVILA REYES stated that the above allegations were completely unfounded and without any basis whatsoever.

(K) Allegation That STEVE KENNAN Might Have Met OSWALD in Mexico

T-2 advised as follows:

On January 22, 1964, HOMOBONO ALCARAZ ARAGON, a graduate student of the Universidad Nacional Autonoma de Mexico (National Autonomous University of Mexico), Mexico, D. F., commented on an alleged statement he made the latter part of December, 1963, that a young American, STEVE KENNAN, described by ALCARAZ ARAGON as procommunist and from some city in Pennsylvania, might have had something to do with OSWALD.

ALCARAZ ARAGON advised that when KENNAN was in Mexico in 1962 and 1963, he apparently was unsuccessful in securing a visa from Cuban authorities for travel to Cuba.

ALCARAZ ARAGON stated he could not identify photographs of OSWALD as identical with anyone he ever observed in KENNAN's company in Mexico or as anyone he had ever seen.

ALCARAZ ARAGON claimed to have no knowledge which would place KENNAN in contact with OSWALD.

On April 27, 1964, ALCARAZ ARAGON was reinterviewed and stated very positively that he had never seen OSWALD and had no personal knowledge whatsoever concerning OSWALD's travel to and activities and contacts in Mexico City. He advised that he can be located in Mexico City at Calle Chiapas No. 160.

(L) Information From ARTURO ALCOCER RUIZ

T-10 advised that on November 27, 1963, Attorney ARTURO ALCOCER RUIZ, Calle Masaryk No. 51, Mexico, D. F., furnished the following information:

At approximately 9:00 a.m., November 21, 1963, he and his wife, DOLORES AHEDO DE ALCOCER, upon departing the Gunter Hotel in San Antonio, Texas, for a shopping tour, had observed a very obese woman who was wearing glasses and a green cotton dress, was about 50 years of age, about 5 feet 7 inches in height, with dyed blond hair and weighing about 200 pounds. This woman was standing in front of "Carl's" store near the Gunter Hotel.

Upon returning to the vicinity of the Gunter Hotel about 1:00 p.m., they again saw the same woman still standing at the same location. At that time President JOHN F. KENNEDY was passing down the street in a caravan, and they observed the woman leave the area after the Presidential procession had gone by.

On November 22, 1963, following the assassination of President KENNEDY, while still in San Antonio and while watching a television interview of the manager of the guest house where OSWALD stayed in Dallas, Texas, the television camera, during the course of that interview, picked up the same fat woman they had seen in San Antonio the previous day.

On November 24, 1963, ALCOCER and his wife were watching a television program in San Antonio, following the shooting of OSWALD by JACK RUBY, and while RUBY's sister was being interviewed on television, they became certain that RUBY's sister was identical with the fat woman.

ALCOCER expressed the belief that the foregoing information might possibly indicate involvement of JACK RUBY and his sister as conspirators in the assassination of President KENNEDY.

(M) Information That ERNESTO RODRIGUEZ, New Orleans, Louisiana, Possessed Tape Recordings of OSWALD's Spanish

T-17 advised as follows:

On November 27, 1963, a widow named Mrs. MARIA RODRIGUEZ DE LOPEZ made the statement in Mexico, D. F., Mexico, that her son-in-law, a Cuban named ERNESTO RODRIGUEZ, 212 Jefferson Parish, New Orleans, Louisiana, telephone No. Vernon 5-9658, operates a Spanish school in New Orleans and had tape recordings of Spanish conversations by OSWALD. Mrs. RODRIGUEZ DE LOPEZ stated her son is opposed to Cuban Premier FIDEL CASTRO.

According to T-17, ERNESTO RODRIGUEZ, President of the Modern Language Institute, New Orleans, Louisiana, advised that OSWALD contacted him on one occasion during the last week of July or early August, 1963, and inquired concerning a Spanish language course offered at the Institute. OSWALD did not take any courses, and RODRIGUEZ had no taped recordings of OSWALD's voice. He had no knowledge of OSWALD's Spanish-speaking ability.

COMMISSION EXHIBIT No. 2121—Continued

UNITED STATES DEPARTMENT OF JUSTICE
FEDERAL BUREAU OF INVESTIGATION

In Reply, Please Refer to
File No.

WASHINGTON 25, D.C.

March 12, 1964

LEE HARVEY OSWALD

BACKGROUND OF INQUIRY

On November 28, 1963, and again on March 6, 1964, a confidential source abroad made available the original of a passenger list or manifest relating to departure No. 2, Bus No. 340, October 2, 1963, of the "Transportes Frontera, S. A. de C. V." bus line, which has its headquarters in Monterrey, Nuevo Leon, Mexico, and its Mexico City Terminal at Buenavista Street No. 7.

The confidential source abroad advised that the above-mentioned passenger list or manifest was clear evidence that LEE HARVEY OSWALD had departed from Mexico City on the bus connected therewith, which had left Mexico City at 1:00 p.m. and was scheduled to have arrived at Nuevo Laredo, Tamaulipas (across the border from Laredo, Texas), at 5:30 a.m., October 3, 1963.

The information recorded on the passenger list is handwritten; the names are not complete; and portions of it are not legible; however, the following constitutes an effort to reproduce as closely as possible the information which appears on the list:

COMMISSION EXHIBIT No. 2122

Seat No.	Ticket No.	Name of Passenger	Destination
1	39633	Fco. Saucedo	Monterrey
2			
3	39634	Fco. Saucedo	Monterrey
4		Oswld	Lared
5	10347	Sra. Landeros	Laredo
6	39648	Adrian Hernandez	Mty.
7	10357	Juana	Laredo
8	39649	Angel Gallegos	Monterrey
9	10348	Sra. Morales	Laredo
10	Pase	Nicolas Gonzalez	Torreon
11	10351	Rafael Flores	Laredo
12	10354	Gautier ? (Ganstine)	Laredo
13		Angel Perez	
14	39650	Antonio Cazarez	Mty.
15	10356	Sra. Aguilar	Laredo
16	10355	Sra. Franco	Laredo
17	10352	Constantino Garcia	Laredo
18	39659	Eliasar Gonzalez	Monterrey
19	10353	Constantino Garcia	Laredo
20	39661	Ynignos (Iniguez ?)	Mty.

At the top of the manifest the name "Transportes Frontera " is handwritten, and in Spanish the following headings are printed:

RESERVATIONS FOR 13 O'CLOCK,

DESTINATION Laredo , DEPARTURE NO. 2 ,

ON BUS NO. 340 , DATE 2, MONTH, October of 1963.

The underlined portions are blanks which had been completed in ink.

Following the list of passengers are the notations: "9 Laredo, 7 Monterrey."

Handprinted at the bottom of the page is: "DRIVER, DIONISIO REYNA, FCO. SAUCEDO." There also appear the numbers "13 - 2."

On the left-hand margin of the manifest are the handwritten figures "78" and "16." At the top right-hand corner thereof are the numerals "186" and "41" and under these "227." On the back side of the document are the numbers "146.30" and "108.80" and thereunder, as though a column of addition, "255.10."

INQUIRY AT TRANSPORTES
FRONTERA BUS TERMINAL

The information which follows was made available by a second confidential source abroad on March 9, 1964:

On March 5, 1964, GILBERTO LOZANO GUIZAR advised that he is the Manager of the Mexico City Terminal of Transportes Frontera Bus Company, Buenavista Street No. 7, which has a franchise for "through service" between Mexico City, Monterrey and Laredo, Mexico, but is not permitted to sell tickets or pick up passengers at intermediate localities.

LOZANO stated that the Transportes Frontera Company has made a complete study of its records and procedures and has now arrived at the conclusion that the person designated as "OSWLD" on the October 2, 1963, passenger manifest did not purchase a ticket and could not have traveled on the trip to which it relates. He pointed out that the list of passenger reservations, tickets sold, and passengers actually boarding the bus in Mexico City are recorded on the form which is provided for that purpose and is maintained on a clip board on the counter from which ticket sales normally are made by the ticket salesman and dispatcher, FRANCISCO ALVARADO. He admitted that ALVARADO occasionally is assisted during rush hours or a temporary absence from the counter by the baggage handler, LUCIO LOPEZ MEDINA, who may receive and record reservations on the manifest but does not handle the actual receipt of payment for tickets.

According to Mr. LOZANO, a reservation is recorded by assigning a seat number as available and recording opposite the seat number assigned, the name and destination of the individual requesting the reservation. That reservation is respected under normal conditions until two hours before departure time; however, in the event all seats are not filled, it may be held until the actual departure of the bus. Prior to the departure of the bus, a final check is made of passengers in connection with tickets sold for that particular trip, and at that time the dispatcher communicates by radio to the company headquarters in Monterrey the number of "paying" passengers on the bus in relation to the Monterrey or Laredo destinations for which they purchased tickets.

FRANCISCO ALVARADO, ticket salesman and dispatcher for Transportes Frontera, advised that he prepared most of the handwriting on the October 2, 1963, manifest on which the name "OSWLD" and destination "Lared" appear opposite Seat No. 4. He stated that he did not write the "OSWLD" reservation information and it was his opinion that the reservation had been made and the information recorded by the baggage handler, LUCIO LOPEZ. With respect to the manifest for October 2, 1963, ALVARADO furnished the following explanations:

He is quite certain at the present time that the individual designated on the list as "OSWLD" did not purchase a ticket and did not travel on the trip relating to that manifest. No ticket number was recorded for that person, and a search of the company's records in Monterrey had failed to locate a ticket stub which was not otherwise accounted for in connection with that particular trip.

The notations by ALVARADO of "9 Laredo, 7 Monterrey" reflected that he had reported by radio to the Monterrey office of the company that the bus had departed with nine "paying" passengers for Laredo and seven "paying" passengers destined for Monterrey. Listed under "NAME OF PASSENGERS" were "OSWLD" with no ticket number, indicating he did not travel; "ANGEL PEREZ" with no ticket number or destination, which confirmed that he had not purchased a ticket and had not boarded the bus; and "NICOLAS GONZALEZ," Seat No. 10, listed as having traveled on a pass to Torreon.

ALVARADO explained that the passenger manifest was merely a worksheet, and he often used it for extraneous notations, usually arithmetical. He was unable to account for the number "78" on the left-hand margin of the manifest. He believed that the number "16" was his summation of the total number of paying passengers on the bus. The numbers in the upper right-hand corner appear to represent the addition of "136" and "41," but ALVARADO could offer no explanation for the notations. The "13" and "2" at the bottom of the manifest were his notations to the effect that the bus departed at 13:00 hours on October 2, 1963.

ALVARADO and GILBERTO LOZANO stated that the notations on the back of the manifest referred to advances of funds made by ALVARADO to LOZANO from the cash for repairs, parts or other requirements. They related that the passenger lists are not kept as a permanent record, and, when the manifest was located in the "trash" at the request of investigators of the Mexican Presidential Staff, the blanks at the top of the form had not been filled in as to time, destination, trip number, bus number, and date, but they had completed those blanks from their personal knowledge in order to make that data clear to the investigators. They also had listed the names of the drivers on the form at that time. They affirmed that the handwritten "Transportes Frontera" at the top of the document had been added by some official of the Mexican Government after the document was borrowed from them.

Both LOZANO and ALVARADO stated that they had no recollection of LEE HARVEY OSWALD, could not recognize his photograph as being of any individual who had been at the terminal or travelled on that bus line, and have no personal knowledge with respect to his contacts and activities in Mexico. They could offer no explanation as to how Mexican authorities had arrived at the conclusion that OSWALD had travelled on the Transportes Frontera bus of October 2, 1963, but pointed out that after the name was located on the manifest, they had not been given an opportunity of reviewing, analyzing or checking out the data thereon.

LUCIO LOPEZ MEDINA, baggage and freight handler at

Transportes Frontera, related that he often assists the ticket salesman by recording reservations and is quite certain that he wrote the "OSWLD" and "LARED" opposite Seat No. 4 on the passenger manifest of October 2, 1963. He stated that he also had recorded the reservations and ticket sales to "FCO. SAUCEDO," one of the drivers, opposite Seats Nos. 1 and 3, "ANGEL GALLEGOS," Seat No. 8, and possibly other items on the manifest. He acknowledged that he had no personal recollection of OSWALD, could not recognize his photograph as being of anyone who had been at the bus terminal, and did not believe that OSWALD had embarked on the bus of October 2, 1963.

LOPEZ MEDINA expressed the belief, however, that the reservation was made by the individual in person, as he did not recall having received a reservation by telephone from any person who spoke very little Spanish. He stated that he has no knowledge of English.

GILBERTO LOZANO stated that his company, the Flecha Roja, and Transportes del Norte are the only bus lines which afford direct service between Mexico City and Nuevo Laredo, Tamaulipas.

INQUIRY AT FLECHA ROJA BUS TERMINAL

On March 7, 1964, JESUS SAUCEDO, Comptroller at the terminal of the Flecha Roja (Red Arrow) bus company, Heroes Ferrocarrileros Street No. 45, Mexico City, Mexico, advised that the full and complete name of the company is Servicios Unidos Autobuses Blancos, Flecha Roja, S.A. de C.V. (The Unified Services of White Autobuses Red Arrow, Incorporated) and that the company provides bus service to numerous localities within Mexico, as well as to Nuevo Laredo, Tamaulipas, and Laredo, Texas. He explained that two trips daily are made to Nuevo Laredo and Laredo, where the line makes connection with the Continental Trailways Bus System of the United States, departures from Mexico City being scheduled for 3:15 p.m. and 7:30 p.m. each day and arrival at Nuevo Laredo 19 hours later.

SAUCEDO advised that a passenger list is prepared in duplicate for reservations and ticket sales for a given trip; that the original is carried by the driver, and the carbon copy is transmitted to him for final checking and auditing of the operation in connection with each bus.

With the assistance of Mr. SAUCEDO, a search was made of the passenger manifests of the company for all trips to Laredo for October 1, 2 and 3, 1963, without locating any information identifiable with the name LEE HARVEY OSWALD.

INQUIRY AT TRANSPORTES DEL NORTE BUS TERMINAL

On March 9, 1964, RICARDO BELTRAN MEDINA, Manager of the Mexico City terminal of the bus line known as Transportes Del Norte at Avenida Insurgentes Sur 137, reported that his company provides bus transportation to and from various localities of Northern Mexico but principally to Nuevo Laredo and Laredo, Texas, where it makes connections with the Greyhound Lines in the United States. He explained that the company makes two trips daily from Mexico City to Laredo with departures scheduled at 8:30 AM and 9:00 PM, and arrivals in Laredo at 2:00 AM and 2:30 PM, respectively.

Mr. BELTRAN stated that his office makes passenger reservations and ticket sales manifests in duplicate and maintains a copy thereof as a permanent record. He stated very emphatically that those records had been searched by agents of the Mexican Presidential Staff, the Ministry of Government, the Federal Judicial Police, and himself, and no record had been located which might be identifiable with LEE HARVEY OSWALD. He mentioned that he had assisted with the various searches made of the company's records and that he, personally, had extended the search to include lists for several days prior to and following October 1, 1963, with completely negative results.

BELTRAN advised that his company, the Flecha Roja, and Transportes Frontera are the only bus lines which are chartered for direct service between Mexico City and Nuevo Laredo, Tamaulipas, or Laredo, Texas.

WASHINGTON

June 23, 1964

Dear Mr. Rankin:

I am enclosing a certified copy of a note dated June 9, 1964, together with a number of attachments, from the Mexican Ministry of Foreign Affairs to the United States Embassy in Mexico City, supplementing the May 14, 1964 note and memorandum which I sent to you on May 28, 1964. Also enclosed is a translation of the note prepared by the Division of Language Services in the Department of State.

As you will see, the note states that the Mexican Department of Foreign Affairs "wishes to emphasize . . . [the] confidential nature" of the enclosed documents "for which reason it is understood, according to the promise made in the last paragraph of Embassy note No. 1349, that they will not be published, either in their entirety or in part, without the consent of the Government of Mexico."

Sincerely,

Leonard C. Meeker
Acting Legal Adviser

Enclosures:

1. Certified copy of note dated June 9, 1964, from Mexican Department of Foreign Affairs w/enclosures.
2. Translation of above note.

The Honorable
J. Lee Rankin,
General Counsel,
President's Commission on the
Assassination of President Kennedy.

COMMISSION EXHIBIT No. 2123

MEXICO

UNITED MEXICAN STATES)
FEDERAL DISTRICT)
COTY OF MEXICO) ss:
EMBASSY OF THE UNITED)
STATES OF AMERICA)

I, Piers L. Williams, Vice Consul of the United States of America at Mexico, Federal District, United Mexican States, duly commissioned and qualified, do hereby certify that the annexed copy of Note No. 505503 dated June 9, 1964, transmitting a number of photostatic copies of documents, is a true copy of the original note and photostatic copies, the same having been examined by me and found to agree word for word and figure for figure with the said original.

IN WITNESS WHEREOF I have hereunto set my hand and seal of the Consular Service of the United States of America at México, D. F., México, this fifteenth day of June, 1964.

Piers L. Williams
Vice Consul of the United States of America

COMMISSION EXHIBIT No. 2123—Continued

ENCL NO. 1
A-1461
MEXICO D.F.

CONFIDENCIAL.

505503 La Secretaría de Relaciones Exteriores saluda atentamente a la Embajada de los Estados Unidos de América y tiene el honor de hacer referencia tanto a la nota de la Embajada número 1349, de fecha 1o. de abril próximo pasado, como a la nota de la Secretaría número 504826, fechada el 14 de mayo último, las cuales se relacionan con la investigación realizada por los organismos mexicanos competentes respecto de las actividades que Lee Harvey Oswald, presunto asesino del señor Presidente John F. Kennedy, realizó durante el tiempo que estuvo en México en septiembre de 1963.

Como complemento de las informaciones transmitidas a la Embajada en la nota número 504826, la Secretaría se complace en enviarle ahora los siguientes documentos que le han sido transmitidos por las autoridades que intervinieron en la investigación:

1.- Copia fotostática certificada de la tarjeta de turista (F.M.8) número 24085, válida por 15 días, que sirvió a Lee Harvey Oswald para entrar a México el día 26 de septiembre de 1963 por Nuevo Laredo, Tamaulipas.

2.- Copia fotostática certificada de diversas hojas del libro de registro de pasajeros del Hotel "Comercio", ubicado en la calle de Fray Bernardino de Sahagún número 19 de esta capital, en el cual se alojó

La Embajada de los Estados Unidos de América,
Ciudad.

alojó Lee Harvey Oswald el 27 de septiembre de 1963.

3.- Copia fotostática certificada de la hoja de reservaciones de la empresa de camiones de pasajeros "Transportes Frontera" correspondiente al día 2 de octubre de 1963 en la que aparece bajo el número 4 el nombre de Oswald.

4.- Copias fotostáticas certificadas de las relaciones de entrada y salida de pasajeros (F.M.11) por Nuevo Laredo, Tamaulipas, correspondientes a los días 26 de septiembre y 3 de octubre de 1963 en las que figuran la entrada a México de Oswald en la fecha primeramente indicada y su salida del país.

5.- Copia fotostática certificada de la declaración rendida el 23 de noviembre de 1963 por la señora Silvia Tirado de Durán ante autoridades mexicanas.

6.- Copia fotostática certificada del informe rendido el 30 de noviembre de 1963 por el Inspector José Mario del Valle respecto de las investigaciones que practicó en Nuevo Laredo, Tamaulipas, sobre el paso por ese lugar de Oswald.

Al transmitir los anteriores documentos a la Embajada, la Secretaría desea señalar a su atención que tienen el carácter de confidenciales por lo que está en el entendimiento, de acuerdo con lo ofrecido en el último párrafo de la nota número 1349 de la Embajada,

Embajada, que no serán publicados ni total ni parcialmente sin el consentimiento del Gobierno de México.

La Secretaría de Relaciones Exteriores aprovecha esta oportunidad para renovar a la Embajada el testimonio de su más alta consideración.

México, D. F., a 9 de junio de 1964.

SECRETARIA DE GOBERNACION

DUPLICADO Nº 24085

VALIDA POR 15 DIAS

BUENA PARA UN SOLO VIAJE POR ~~.......~~ DIAS

Apellidos y nombre LEE, HARVEY OSWALD

FOTOGRAFO

Sexo H ☒ M ☐ Edad 23 AÑOS Estado Civil S ☐ C ☒

Documento con el que acredita su nacionalidad:

ACTA NACIMIENTO

Menores que lo acompañan:

Destino MEXICO, D. F.

NUEVA ORLEANS, LA., EUA.,

17 SEPTIEMBRE DE 1963.

Lugar y fecha

Lee H Oswald

Firma del interesado

PARA SER LLENADO EXCLUSIVAMENTE POR LAS AUTORIDADES

ENTRADA	SALIDA
SET 26 1963	Sello fechador
NUEVO LAREDO, TAMPS.	

T. G. N.—4508-62

ADVERTENCIAS

1. EL IMPUESTO QUE CAUSA ESTE DOCUMENTO ES DE $ 6.25.
2. Autoriza al titular a permanecer en México 5 (cinco) días improrrogables, a partir de la fecha de su entrada al país.
3. No podrá desarrollar actividades distintas a las de recreo.
4. Si el titular se internó con menores, deberá salir acompañado de ellos.
5. Este documento deberá ser entregado a las Autoridades de Migración del lugar por donde efectúe su salida del país.

ATTENTION

1. TAX APPLICABLE TO THIS DOCUMENT: $ 6.25 MEXICAN CURRENCY (DLS. 0.50).
2. The legal holder of this permit is authorized to remain in Mexico for a period not to exceed 5 (five) days (not renewable) starting from the date of his entry into the country.
3. Issued only for pleasure trips.
4. If bearer enters the country accompanied by minors, upon departure he must leave with them.
5. This document must be surrendered to the Migration Authorities at the time and place of departure from the country.

OBSERVATION IMPORTANTE

1. CE DOCUMENT EST SOUMIS A UN IMPOT DE $ 6.25 PESOS MEXICAINS (U.S. $ 0.50).
2. Le titulaire de ce document est autorisé à séjourner au Mexique pendant une période qui ne pourra, en aucun cas, dépasser 5 (cinq) jours à partir de la date de son entrée dans le pays.
3. Il ne pourra exercer aucune activité autre que celle de touriste.
4. Si le titulaire est entré au Mexique accompagné de mineurs, ceux-ci devront obligatoirement quitter le pays en même temps que lui.
5. Ce document devra être remis aux Autorités Mexicaines du port de sortie au moment du départ du pays.

SECRETARIA DE GOBERNACION

ORIGINAL Nº 24085

VALIDA POR 15 DIAS

BUENA PARA UN SOLO VIAJE POR ~~5 (CINCO)~~ DIAS

Apellidos y nombre LEE, HARVEY OSWALD

FOTOGRAFO

Sexo H ☒ M ☐ Edad 23 AÑOS Estado Civil S ☐ C ☒

Documento con el que acredita su nacionalidad:

ACTA NACIMIENTO

Menores que lo acompañan:

Destino MEXICO, D. F.

NUEVA ORLEANS, LA., EUA.,

17 SEPTIEMBRE DE 1963.

Lugar y fecha

Firma del interesado

PARA SER LLENADO EXCLUSIVAMENTE POR LAS AUTORIDADES

ENTRADA	SALIDA
SET 26 1963	SRIA. DE GOBERNACION OFICINA DE POBLACION AUTORIZO
Sello fechador	ALBERTO ARZAMENDI CHAPA Nuevo Laredo, Tamps.
NUEVO LAREDO, TAMPS.	OCT. 1963

ADVERTENCIAS

1. EL IMPUESTO QUE CAUSA ESTE DOCUMENTO ES DE $ 6.25.
2. Autoriza al titular a permanecer en México 5 (cinco) días improrrogables, a partir de la fecha de su entrada al país.
3. No podrá desarrollar actividades distintas a las de recreo.
4. Si el titular se internó con menores, deberá salir acompañado de ellos.
5. Este documento deberá ser entregado a las Autoridades de Migración del lugar por donde efectúe su salida del país.

ATTENTION

1. TAX APPLICABLE TO THIS DOCUMENT: $ 6.25 MEXICAN CURRENCY (DLS. 0.50).
2. The legal holder of this permit is authorized to remain in Mexico for a period not to exceed 5 (five) days (not renewable) starting from the date of his entry into the country.
3. Issued only for pleasure trips.
4. If bearer enters the country accompanied by minors, upon departure he must leave with them.
5. This document must be surrendered to the Migration Authorities at the time and place of departure from the country.

OBSERVATION IMPORTANTE

1. CE DOCUMENT EST SOUMIS A UN IMPOT DE $ 6.25 PESOS MEXICAINS (U.S. $ 0.50).
2. Le titulaire de ce document est autorisé à séjourner au Mexique pendant une période qui ne pourra, en aucun cas, dépasser 5 (cinq) jours à partir de la date de son entrée dans le pays.
3. Il ne pourra exercer aucune activité autre que celle de touriste.
4. Si le titulaire est entré au Mexique accompagné de mineurs, ceux-ci devront obligatoirement quitter le pays en même temps que lui.
5. Ce document devra être remis aux Autorités Mexicaines du port de sortie au moment du départ du pays.

COMMISSION EXHIBIT No. 2123—Continued

EL C. LIC. NOE PALOMARES, Oficial Mayor de la Secretaría de Gobernación, por Ac. del C. Subsecretario Enc. del Despacho, CERTIFICA: que la presente copia fotostática concuerda fiel y exactamente con su original que obra en los archivos de la Oficina del Control Migratorio del Departamento de Migración de esta propia Secretaría. No se causa el Impuesto del Timbre por expedirse para usos oficiales.

México, D.F., a 7 de mayo de 1964.

SECRETARIA DE GOBERNACION OFICIALIA MAYOR

COMMISSION EXHIBIT No. 2123—Continued

Anexo 2.

Viernes. 27 de septiembre 1963

Nº	Nombres.	Procedencia	Ocupación	Nacionalidad
1	Fr. Isabel Salazar -	Durango Dgo	Empleado	mex
2	[illegible]	Durango Dgo	Empleado	mex
3	Rito Guerrero	Aguascalientes	medico	mex
4	Antonio Avila -	D. F.	musico	mex
5	Martin Quiroga	N. Laredo Tamps	Comte	mex
6	Fernando Valenzuela	Chihuahua	Empleado	mex
7	Angelica Gereyda -	Torreon Coah	Hogar	mex
8	Francisco Morales -	Reynosa Tamps	Empleado	mex
9	Martin Guerrero	S. L. Potosi	Empleado	mex
10	Jose Luis Muñoz	Chihuahua	Empleado	mex
11	Pedro Quijano	Torreon -	Empleado	mex
12	Manuel Santos	Saltillo Coah	Empleado	mex
13	Fidencio Garcia -	Torreon Coah	Empleado	mex
14	Gabriel Contreras	C. Juarez Chih	Empleado	mex
15	Julio Liñan	San Luis Pot	Empleado	mex
16	Rodolfo Rodriguez	Chihuahua	Empleado	mex
17	Rodolfo Rodriguez	Chihuahua	Empleado	mex
18	Lee, Harvey Oswald	U S A Texas	Photo.	US citizen
19	[illegible]	S. L. Pot	Empleado	mex
20	Daniel Pedrero -	Leon Gto	Empleado	mex
21	[illegible] Resendiz	Saltillo Coah	Empleado	mex
22	Roberto Lopez	D F	—	—
23				
24	Juan Fco Pcha.	Durango Dgo	Empleado	Mex
25	[illegible] Loza -	Monterrey N.L.	Empleado	mex
26	Alfredo Garcia	Guadalajara	Empleado	mex
27				
28	Jose Gomez	Aguascalientes	Chofer	mex
29	Manuel Sorrelo -	Monterrey N.L.	Empleado	mex
30				

OFICINA DE LICENC. TENDER

Anexo 3.

Sabado 28 de Sep. 1963

Nº	Nombres	Procedencia	Ocupación	Nacionalidad
1	Alicia Plaza	Aguascalientes Ags		
2	Jorge Roblez -	Puebla Pue	Empleado	mex
3	Sr. Lilla	Puebla Puebla	Empleado	mex
4	Arlango Avila y Sra	D. F.	musico	mex
5	Sr Ramirez y Sra	Queretaro Qro	Empleado	mex
6	Fernando Valenzuela	Chihuahua	Empleado	mex
7	Angelica Gereyda	Torreon Coah	Hogar	mex
8	Ernesto Limon -	Reynosa Tamps	Empleado	mex
9	Martin Guerrero	San Luis Pot	Empleado	mex
10	Jose Luis Muñoz	Chihuahua	Empleado	mex
11	Pedro Quijano	Torreon Coah	Empleado	mex
12	Manuel Santos	Saltillo Coah	Empleado	mex
13	Fidencio Garcia	San Luis Pot	Empleado	mex
14	Gabriel Contreras	C. Juarez Chih	Agricultor	mex
15	Julio Liñan -	San Luis Pot	Empleado	mex
16	Carlos Marquez	Veracruz Ver	Empleado	mex
17	Rodolfo Rodriguez	Chihuahua	Empleado	mex
18	LEE HARVEY	USA TEXAS		
19	Perez Gallego	San Luis Pot	Empleado	mex
20	Daniel Pedrero -	Leon Gto	Empleado	mex
21	Dionicio Resendiz	Saltillo Coah	Empleado	mex
22	Sr. Reyes y Familia	Chihuahua	Comte	mex
23	Sr. Ramirez -	Torreon Coah	Empleado	mex
24	Silvino Martinez	Queretaro Qro	Empleado	mex
25	Sr. C. Sanchez de la Rosa	Monterrey N.L.	Empleado	mex
26	Alfredo Garcia -	Guanajuato Gto	Empleado	mex
27				
28	Mario Alatorre -	Puebla Pue	Comte	mex
29	Manuel Sorrelo -	Monterrey N.L.	Empleado	mex
30				

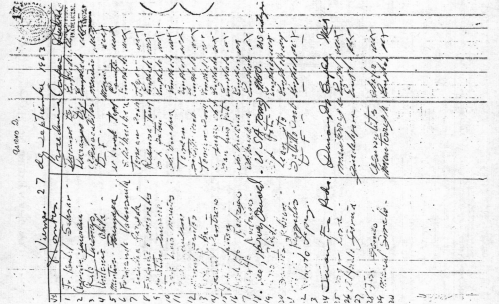

COMMISSION EXHIBIT No. 2123—Continued

DEPARTAMENTO DEL DISTRITO FEDERAL
OFICINA DE LICENCIAS
SEC. TERCERA

9323

Esta Oficina autoriza el presente libro de registro de pasaportes del Hotel "Comercio" ubicado en la calle de Sahagún #19, de esta ciudad propiedad del Sr. Guillermo Garcia Luna.

México D.F. a 4 de abril 1963.

El Jefe de la Oficina

COMMISSION EXHIBIT No. 2123—Continued

Comercio - 29 de Sep 196[illegible]

No	Nombre	Procedencia	Ocupación	
1				
2	Leonardo Becerra	Guanajuato	Empleado	mex
3	Maria Cela Torre -	Puebla Pue	Empleado	mex
4	Antonio Oliva -	D.F. -	Musico	mex
5				
6	Fernando Valenzuela -	Chihuahua -	Empleado	mex
7	Angelica Pereyda -	Torreon Coah	Empleado	mex
8	Ernesto Luna -	Reynosa Tamp	Empleado	mex
9	Martin Guerrero	S. L. Potosi	Empleado	mex
10	Jose Luis Macias -	Chihuahua -	Empleado	mex
11	Pedro Quijano	Torreon Coah	Empleado	mex
12	Raul Ramirez -	Veracruz Ver	Empleado	mex
13	Raul Ramirez -	Veracruz-Ver	Empleado	mex
14	Gabriel Contreras -	C. Juarez Chih	Empleado	mex
15	Julio Lizan -	San Luis Potosi	Empleado	mex
16	Fernando Macias [illegible]	Guadalajara Jal		
17	Rodolfo Rodriguez -	Chihuahua -	Empleado	mex
18	Lee, Harvey	USA Texas		Americano
19	Alfonso Beltran -	Chihuahua -	[illegible]	mex
20	Santos Pedano	Leon Gto	Empleado	mex
21	Mario Recendiz -	Saltillo Coah	Empleado	mex
22				
23	Alicia Plaza -	Aguascalientes -	Hogar	mex
24	Tomas Gallegos -	Queretaro Q.	Empleado	mex
25	Sangelas de la Rosa -	Monterrey	Empleado	mex
26	Alfredo Garcia	Guanajuato Gto	Empleado	mex
27				
28				
29	Manuel Serrati	Monterrey NL	Empleado	mex
30				

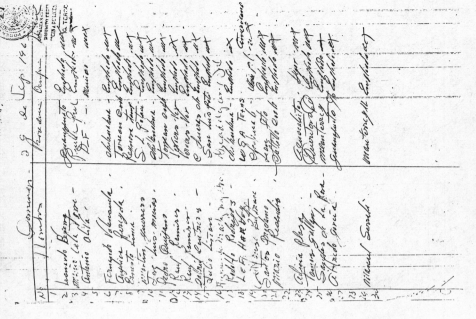

COMMISSION EXHIBIT No. 2123—Continued

78

Anexo 5.

Lunes, 30 de Septiembre 1963

No.	Nombres	Procedencia	Ocupación	Nacionalidad
1	Jesus Gomez y Familia			
2	Leonardo Becerra	Leon Gto	Comerciante	Mex
3	Juan Pedraza	S L P.		Mex
4	Antonio Avila	D. F.	Musico	mex
5	Jesus Gomez			
6	Fernando Valenzuela	Chihuahua	Empleado	mex
7	Evangelina Pereyra	Torreon Coah	Hogar	Mex
8	Ernesto Luna	Reynosa Tamps	Empleado	mex
9	Martin Guerrero	S L Poti	Empleado	mex
10	Jose Luis Macias	Leon Gto	Empleado	mex
11	Pedro Quijano	Torreon Coah		Mex
12	Manuel Santos	Saltillo Coah	Empleado	mex
13	Raul Ramirez	Veracruz Ver	Empleado	mex
14	Gabriel Contreras	C Juarez Chih	Empleado	mex
15	Julio Limon	S L Poti	Empleado	mex
16	Filiberto Hernandez	Puebla Pue	Empleado	mex
17	Rodolfo Rodriges	Chihuahua	Empleado	mex
18	Lee HARVEY	SUA		
19	Cap Espinosa	Veracruz Ver	Cap marina	Mex
20	Santos Pedroza	Leon Gto	Empleado	mex
21	Mario Resendiz	Saltillo Coah	Empleado	
22	Guillermo Flores	Queretaro	Empleado	mex
23	[illegible] Raza	Aguascalientes	Empleado	mex
24	Leopoldo Ortega	Irapuato Gto		Mex
25	Sanchez de la Rosa	Monterrey NL	Empleado	mex
26	Armando Rodriges	San Luis Poti	Empleado	mex
27				
28	Gregorio Perez	Puebla Pue	Empleado	mex
29	Manuel Gomez	Monterrey	Empleado	mex
30	Jose Gomes	Aguascalientes	Chofer	mex

Anexo 6.

Martes 1o de Octubre 196[illegible]

No.	Nombres	Procedencia	Ocupación	Nacionalidad
1	Ramirez	Monterrey	Empleado	
2	Leonardo Becerra	Leon Gto	Empleado	Mex
3	Juliana Pedroza y Familia	S L P.	Comerciante	mex
4	Antonio Avila	D F	Musico	mex
5	Jose Gomez	Guadalajara	Empleado	mex
6	Fernando Valenzuela	Chihuahua	Empleado	mex
7	Evangelina Pereyra	Torreon Coah	Hogar	mex
8	Ernesto Luna	Reynosa Tamps	Empleado	mex
9	Martin Guerrero	S L Poti	Empleado	Me
10	Jose Luis Macias	Leon Gto	Empleado	Mex
11	Pedro Quijano	Torreon Coah	Empleado	Me
12	Manuel Santos	Saltillo Coah	Agente	Mex
13	Raul Ramirez	Veracruz Ver	Empleado	Mex
14	Gabriel Contreras	C Juarez Chih	Empleado	Mex
15	Julio Limon	S L Poti	—	Mex
16	Rogelio Ramirez	Celaya Gto		
17	Rodolfo Rodriguez	Chihuahua	Empleado	Mex
18	Lee Harvey	USA, Texas	Photo.	American
19	[illegible] Perez	Aguascalientes	Empleado	Mex
20	Santos Pedroza	Leon Gto	Empleado	Mex
21	Mario Resendiz	Saltillo	Empleado	Mex
22	Antonio Torres	Guanajuato Gto	Empleado	Mex
23	Sr Montoya	Puebla Pue	Empleado	mex
24	Jose Gomez	Aguascalientes	Chofer	mex
25	Francisco Gutierrez	Puebla Pue	Chofer	Mex
26	Felipe Escobedo			
27	Alfonso Garcia	Monterrey NL		Mex
28	Gregorio Perez	Puebla Pue	Empleo	Mex
29	Manuel Sanchez	Monterrey NL	Empleo	Mex
30				

COMMISSION EXHIBIT No. 2123—Continued

EL C. LIC. NOE PALOMARES, Oficial Mayor de la Secretaría de Gobernación, por Ac. del C. Subsecretario Enc. del Despacho, CERTIFICA: que las presentes copias fotostáticas fueron tomadas de las fojas correspondientes -- del libro de registro de viaj-eros del "Hotel del Comercio", que se tuvo a la vista.- No se causa el Impuesto del Timbre por expedirse para usos oficiales.

México, D.F., a 7 de mayo de 1964.

COMMISSION EXHIBIT No. 2123—Continued

-----En la Ciudad de México, Distrito Federal, siendo las -- 18 dieciocho horas del día 23 veintitres de Noviembre de - - 1963 mil novecientos sesenta y tres, el suscrito Capitán FERNANDO GUTIERREZ BARRIOS, Subdirector Federal de Seguridad, que actúa legalmente con testigos de asistencia, HACE CONSTAR: - Que habiendo sido presentada en esta Oficina la señora SIL-- VIA TIRADO DE DURAN, con el objeto de ser interrogada sobre los hechos que a continuación se expresan, se procedió a levantar la presente, acta: - - - - - - - - - - - - - - - - - -

-----En seguida, presente la que en su estado normal manifestó llamarse SILVIA TIRADO DE DURAN, y protestada para que se conduzca con verdad y después de hacérsele saber las penas - en que incurren quienes declaran falsamente, por sus generales dijo: llamarse como está escrito, de 26 veintiseis años de edad, casada, sin religión, empleada, con instrucción, originaria y vecina de esta ciudad, con domicilio en Constitu-- yentes Número 143 Departamento 3 tres, y sobre los hechos que se investigan DECLARO: Que la de la voz está legalmente casada con el señor HORACIO DURAN NAVARRO, desde el 5 cinco de Noviembre de 1958 mil novecientos cincuenta y ocho, habiendo -- procreado una niña de nombre PATRICIA, que a la fecha cuenta con tres años y medio de edad; que en el mes de julio o agosto de 1961 mil novecientos sesenta y uno, la dicente fué invitada a ingresar al Instituto Mexicano Cubano de Relaciones -- Culturales, que entonces presidía el Lic. AGUSTIN CUE CANO--- VAS, como Coordinadora, y aún cuando no recuerda concretamente la persona que la recomendó, sí puede aclarar que desde -- hacía tiempo, tenía relaciones y visitaba con frecuencia a -- los funcionarios de la Embajada Cubana, teniendo personal - - amistad con el Embajador PORTUONDO, así como con los Agrega-- dos Culturales TERESA PROENZA y LUIS ALVERU, así como con las empleadas, pero principalmente con la Secretaria del Cónsul - EUSEBIO ASCUE, señorita MARICARMEN OLAVARRI, de nacionalidad española, pero pariente de ASCUE; que en el Instituto se desarrollaban exclusivamente actos de carácter cultural, a los -

COMMISSION EXHIBIT No. 2123—Continued

que asistían en ocasiones los mencionados Agregados Culturales y algunos cubanos, pero en mayor número eran mexicanos,- siempre artistas e intelectuales, sin que nunca discutieran- temas políticos, recordando que únicamente cuando la crisis- cubana de Octubre, relativa a la pretendida invasión de Cuba y posterior bloqueo de la Isla por el Gobierno Norteamericano, en un radio de onda corta escuchaban las noticias que daba Prensa Latina, de las cuales formaba un boletín al que se daba lectura, siendo las noticias que escuchaban procedentes directamente de La Habana, aceptando que también a dichas - reuniones asistían cubanos y mexicanos que en lo personal - discutían sobre el problema político de Cuba, pero sin que - se hiciera en forma oficial; que la declarante disfrutaba de un sueldo de $ 500.00 quinientos pesos mensuales, por su función de Coordinadora en el Instituto, siendo sus horas de labores de las dieciseis a las veinte horas, diariamente, obteniendo el dinero para el sostenimiento del propio Instituto- de una subvención mensual dela Embajada Cubana, cuyo importe desconoce, pero además cada uno de los socios cubría una- cuota y se recibían aportaciones de personas cuyos nombres - no recuerda, porque la mayoría lo hacía sin identificarse, - sin poder precisar el ingreso mensual, no obstante que la declarante era quien personalmente recibía todas las cantidades que ingresaban al Instituto; que además de la de la voz, únicamente el señor FELIPE ROJAS, quien trabajaba en las mañanas en el Instituto, como Secretario, percibía un sueldo mensual-- de igual cantidad de $500.00 quinientos pesos, empleándose el resto del dinero que ingresaba en el pago de la renta del local y otros gastos inherentes al funcionamiento. Que en el - mes de Diciembre de 1961 mil novecientos sesenta y uno, la declarante y su esposo hicieron un viaje por avión a La Habana, Cuba, del cual cubrieron sus respectivos pasajes, pero todos- los gastos que ocasionó su visita a dicha ciudad y a la mayor parte de las ciudades de la Isla, fueron costeados por el - - Instituto Cubano de Amistad con los Pueblos y la Casa de Cul-

- 2 -

tura denominada de Las Américas, cuyo viaje duró quince -- días, sin que tuvieran contacto ni relaciones en este viaje con funcionarios del Gobierno Cubano. Que como ya dijo - la dicente es simpatizante del socialismo y la doctrina Marxista, desde hace varios años, habiendo estudiado filosofía y existencialismo, y en particular ha simpatizado y -- simpatiza desde sus inicios con la Revolución Cubana. Que - desde hace tres meses más o menos, comenzó a prestar sus -- servicios como Secretaria del Cónsul de Cuba en esta ciudad, señor EUSEBIO ASCUE, quien dejó de fungir como tal hace cinco días, o sea el lunes 18 dieciocho del actual, siendo sustituído por el señor ALFREDO MIRAVAL Y DIAZ, haciendo la -- aclaración que desde un principio entró a prestar sus servicios con el carácter de provisional y con motivo de la muerte en un accidente de tránsito de su amiga MARICARMEN OLAVARRI, que era quien desempeñaba dicho puesto, y en tanto llega alguna persona de Cuba que deberá hacerse cargo del mismo, teniendo a su cargo el trámite administrativo y el lleno de las visas que se expiden, así como el darle curso a - las solicitudes de tales visas, que invariablemente son enviadas al Gobierno de Cuba, Ministerio de Relaciones Exteriores para su aprobación, habiendo obtenido este cargo directamente del ex Cónsul ASCUE, con quien la liga una buena amistad, por lo que inclusive la dicente organizó una fiesta de despedida a éste, en el domicilio de la que habla, a la que asistieron casi todos los funcionarios y empleados - de la Embajada y el Consulado, exceptuando al Embajador. -- Que la de la voz no pertenece a ningún Partido Político y - nunca ha asistido a manifestaciones o mítines, ni tampoco - ha dictado conferencias ni pronunciado discursos, lo que sí ha hecho su esposo, ya que éste ha escrito varios artículos en el Periódico "El Día"; que nunca ha estado detenida- por ningún motivo, sin hacer excepción al hacer esta referencia en ocasión de la visita a México del señor JOHN F. - KENNEDY, la que en lo particular le causó gran satisfacción por los beneficios que acarrearía al País. Que el día de -- ayer cuando se encontraba trabajando en el Consulado Cubano, en donde presta sus servicios de diez a catorce, y de diez y seis a dieciocho horas, diariamente, por el cual percibe un- sueldo de $1,500.00 mil quinientos pesos mensuales, ya cerca de la hora de salida, al mediodía, una compañera comentó que acababa de escuchar en el radio una noticia relativa a que - el Presidente KENNEDY había sufrido un atentado, en el que - le habían disparado tres balazos, por lo que le llamó por te léfono a su esposo y comentaron acerca de tal noticia, con-- testándole éste que ya lo sabía, calificando a dicho atentado de "monstruoso" y acordando que al reunirse en su domicilio - platicarían sobre ese particular, lo cual hicieron a la hora- de la comida pero en forma muy breve, ya que desconocían los- incidentes del atentado y nombre y señas del presunto autor - del mismo, siendo hasta por la noche cuando leyeron en una -- "extra" la nota relativa y posteriormente, en el radio de su- domicilio, escuchó la de la voz el nombre de LEE HARVEY OS- - WALD, el cual le hizo recordar que este nombre corresponde a- un norteamericano que en los últimos dias de Septiembre o -- primeros días del mes de Octubre del año en curso, se presen- tó al Consulado Cubano solicitando una visa para Cuba, en - - tránsito hacia Rusia, y apoyando su solicitud con la exhibi-- ción de su pasaporte en el que constaba que había estado vi-- viendo en este último País por espacio de tres años, su car-- net de trabajo del propio País, escrito en idioma ruso y car- tas en igual idioma, asi como comprobaba estar casado con una mujer de nacionalidad rusa asi como ser dirigente al aparecer en la ciudad de Nueva Orleans, de la organización denominada- "Trato Justo para Cuba", con la pretensión de que se le acep- taba como "amigo" de la Revolución Cubana, por lo que la di-- cente cumpliendo con sus funciones le tomó todos sus datos y- escribió el lleno de la solicitud respectiva, y se retiró re- gresando por la tarde, ya con sus retratos, y la dicente, - - aceptando que se excedió en sus funciones, oficiosamente - -

COMMISSION EXHIBIT No. 2123—Continued

llamó por telefono al Consulado Ruso, con el interés por -- su parte de facilitar el trámite del visado Ruso a LEE HAR- VEY OSWALD, pero de ahí le contestaron que el trámite dura- ría cuatro meses aproximadamente, lo que molestó al solici- tante, porque según afirmó tenía suma prisa en obtener las- visas que le permitieran viajar a Rusia, insistiendo en su- derecho a ello por sus antecedentes y su partidarismo y ac- tividades personales en pro del Movimiento Cubano, sin que- pueda precisar por no recordarlo la declarante, si le dijo- o no, que fuera miembro del Partido Comunista, y que su es- posa ya mencionada de nacionalidad rusa estaba en ese enton ces en la ciudad de Nueva York, de donde lo seguiría, sien- do su procedencia de la citada ciudad de Nueva Orleans; que una vez que OSWALD entendió que no era posible darle la vi- sa Cubana, sin obtener previamente la Rusa, porque aquella- era en tránsito, se exhaltó o enojó mucho, por lo que la di cente llamó al Cónsul ASCUE, quien en ese momento se encon- traba en su privado en compañía de su posterior sustituto - MIRAVAL, saliendo el primero, comenzó a alegar en inglés -- con OSWALD, en forma muy alterada, terminando por decirle - ASCUE, que "de ser por él no le daría la visa", y que "un - individuo como él en vez de beneficiar a la Revolución Cuba na, le causaba daño", en la inteligencia de que en su discu sión se referían a la Revolución Socialista Rusa y no a la- Cubana, aduciendo OSWALD que tenía dos razones para solici- tar con toda premura la visa y que eran, una, que se le ven cía su permiso de estancia en México y otra, que con toda - urgencia necesitaba llegar a Rusia; que a pesar del disgus- to, la de la voz le entregó a OSWALD un papel igual al que- en este momento manuscribe en el que le anotó su nombre - - "SILVIA DURAN." y el número del telefono del Consulado - - que es el "11-28-47", y de todas maneras se le dió trámite a la solicitud de visa, enviándola al Ministerio de Rela - - ciones de Cuba, de donde se obtuvo respuesta en forma ordi- naria, de quince a treinta días después, aceptándo la - - -

COMMISSION EXHIBIT No. 2123—Continued

concesión de la visa, pero condicionándola a que previamente obtuviera la Rusa, aunque no recuerda si OSWALD con posterioridad llamó o no a la declarante al Teléfono del Consulado que le proporcionó; que toda la plática que sostuvo la dicente con OSWALD, al igual que la del Cónsul ASCUE, fué en idioma inglés, ya que aquel no habla nada de español, y que al tener a la vista su fotografía que apareció en los periódicos de hoy, precisamente en el Periódico "El Día", desde luego lo reconoció e identificó como el mismo al que se ha venido refiriendo como LEE HARVEY OSWALD. Que en una sola ocasión, la declarante asistió a una ceremonia de recepción, en la Embajada Rusa que se les dió en ocasión de su visita a los astronautas GAGARIN y TERESHKOVA, por invitación personal que le hizo a la de la voz, el Consul Ruso YACKSOV, al visitar a ASCUE y MIRAVAL, llevándoles sus respectivas invitaciones en el Consulado Cubano. Que respecto a sus cuñados LIDIA y RUBEN DURAN NAVARRO, la primera en varias ocasiones asistió en compañía de la declarante a las reuniones que se celebraban en el Instituto, en tanto que el segundo únicamente lo hizo en una o dos ocasiones y con motivo de exposiciónes de pinturas, y por cuanto a BETY SERRATO AZUCAR, esposa de RUBEN, siempre se ha mantenido al márgen de estas actividades, aunque todos son de ideología de izquierda, pero sin participar activamente en ningunas actividades; que BARBARA ANN BLITS TRESMOND ESQUIVEL y A GATA ROSENO GARCIA, son amigas de BETY, y la de la voz las ha tratado muy poco y superficialmente, por lo que desconoce sus actividades e ideología y en lo que respecta al señor que ahora sabe se apellida BENTLEY, antes de ahora nunca lo había visto y supone que sea amigo de BARBARA, ya que se dió cuenta que a esta era la que trataba, y se encontraban comiendo en la casa de la deponente, ésta, su esposo, AGATA y LIDIA, en tanto que en la casa de su cuñado RUBEN se encontraban los demás. - Que es todo lo que tiene que declarar, y previa lectura de lo ex-

Anexo 10.

- 4 -

puesto, ratifica y firma al margen para constancia.---------

-----Se cierra y autoriza lo actuado.----Damos fé.----------

EL SUBDIRECTOR FEDERAL DE SEGURIDAD.

CAP. FERNANDO GUTIERREZ BARRIOS.

T. de A. T. de A.

Lic. FERNANDO ORTIZ DE LA PEÑA. Lic. CARLOS DURAN LANZ.

EL C. LIC. NOE PALOMARES, Oficial Mayor de la Secretaría de Gobernación, por Ac. del C. Subsecretario Enc. del Despacho, CERTIFICA: que la presente copia fotostática concuerda fiel y exactamente con su original que obra en los archivos del Departamento de Inspección de Migración de esta propia Secretaría.- No se causa el impuesto del timbre por expedirse para usos oficiales.

México, D.F., a 7 de mayo de 1964.

SECRETARIA DE GOBERNACION
Dirección General de Gobierno

RESERVACIONES PARA LAS 13. HORAS, CON DESTINO A LAREDO
SALIDA No. 2º EN BUS No. 340 EL DIA 2º MES Octubre de 1963

Asiento No.	Boleto No.	NOMBRE DEL PASAJERO	LUGAR DE DESTINO
1	39633	[illegible]	[illegible]
2			
3	39634	[illegible]	[illegible]
4		[illegible]	[illegible]
5	10347	[illegible]	[illegible]
6	39648	[illegible]	Mty
7	10357	[illegible]	[illegible]
8	39649	[illegible]	[illegible]
9	10348	[illegible]	[illegible]
10	[illegible]	[illegible]	[illegible]
11	10351	[illegible]	Laredo
12	10350	[illegible]	[illegible]
13		[illegible]	
14	39650	[illegible]	Mty
15	10356	[illegible]	[illegible]
16	10355	[illegible]	[illegible]
17	10352	[illegible]	[illegible]
18	39659	[illegible]	Mty
19	10353	[illegible]	Laredo
20	39661	[illegible]	Mty
21			
22			
23			
24			
25			
26		[illegible]	
27			
28		[illegible]	
29			
30			
31			
32			
33			
34			
35			
36			
37			
38			
39			
40	CHOFER	Dionisio Reyna: Fco. Saucedo.	

13 — [illegible]

2 OCT 1963

COMMISSION EXHIBIT No. 2123—Continued

EL C. LIC. NOE PALOMARES, Oficial Mayor de la Secretaría de Gobernación, por Ac. del C. Subsecretario Enc. del Despacho, CERTIFICA: que la presente copia fotostática concuerda fiel y exactamente con el original de la lista de pasajeros de la linea de autobuses de segunda clase " Transportes - Frontera", correspondiente al día dos de octubre de 1963 la cual se tuvo a la vista.- No se causa el impuesto del timbre por expedirse para usos oficiales.

México, D.F., a 7 de mayo de 1964.

SECRETARIA DE GOBERNACION OFICIALIA MAYOR

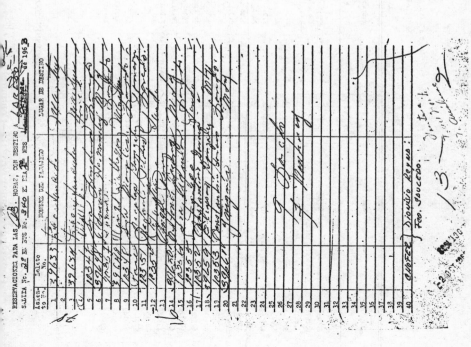

COMMISSION EXHIBIT No. 2123—Continued

F. M. 11.

ESTADOS UNIDOS MEXICANOS [illegible] 12.

SECRETARIA DE GOBERNACION

NUM. ....

Reg. de Coord. 1085.

OFICINA EN NVO. LAREDO TAMPS. MOVIMIENTO DE [illegible]

2da. QUINCENA DE SEPTIEMBRE DE 1963. EXTRANJEROS CLASIFICACION [illegible] SIN CANCELAR.

Imp. E. O. V.

Núm. Progresivo 1	Documento de identidad número 2	APELLIDOS Y NOMBRE 3	Sexo 4	Edad Años 5	Edad Meses 6	Edo. Civil 7	NACIONALIDAD ACTUAL 8	OCUPACION 9	LUGAR Y PAIS DE PROCEDENCIA 10	DESTINO FINAL 11	Día Ent. o salida 12	CLASE DE VEHICULO EN QUE VIAJA 13	PERMANENCIA ENTRADA 14	PERMANENCIA SALIDA 15	OBSERVACIONES 13
801	626057	Mendez González de Angelina Ma.	M	52		C	N. Americana.	Su hogar.	Laredo Tex.	Mont. N.L.	[illegible]	autobus.	h.r.l.		
802	624674	Mitchell Harry J.	H	41		C	"	Abogado.	Palyra Mis.	Méx. D.F.	'	autobus.	a.r.g.		
803	624675	Mitchell Ann Marie.	-	22		C	"	Su hogar.	"	"	"	"	"		
804	626145	Morales Adolio	H	54		C	"	S.D.	Laredo Tex.	Mont. N.L.	"	s.d.	h.t.m.		
805	626236	Moreno Martina.	M	59		C	"	Su hogar.	Victoria Tex.	"	"	autobus.	a.a.ch.		
806	625566	Moore Buell.	H	48		S	"	S.D.	Houston Tex.	"	"	s.d.	j.s.l.		
807	24085	Oswald Lee Harvey	H	23		C	"	Fotógrafo.	N.Orleans La.	Méx. D.F.	"	s.d.	h.t.m.		
808	32060	Cuellet Maurice.	H	22		S	Canadiense.	T. Social.	Montreal Ca.	"	"	autobus.	p.c.r.		
809	625567	Peck Kenneth Grenier.	H	43		C	N. Americana.	S.D.	Houston Tex.	Mont. N.L.	"	avión.	j.sl.		
810	623793	Ramos Yolanda A. de	M	36		C	"	Su hogar.	S. Ant. Tex.	Méx. D.F.	"	s.d.	z.e.r.		
811	623924	Robert Roesley	M	75		V	"	S.D.	A. Bech NY.	"	"	ff.cc.	r.l.t.		
812	623795	Roclovich Florence S.	M	40		C	"	Su hogar.	Hyattavil Mar.	"	"	s.d.	z.e.r.		
813	623794	Roclovich Anthony Paul.	H	43		C	"	Técnico.	"	"	"	"	"		
814	625625	Rodríguez Rafael Ruben. (1)	H	58		C	"	Pensionado.	Laredo Tex.	Mont. N.L.	"	"	j.g.h.		
815	133156	Rodríguez Roberto Gonzalo Espinoza.	H	25		S	Costarricense	S.D.	"	Méx. D.F.	"	s.d.	r.l.t.		
816	133157	Rodríguez Espinoza Jorge Antonio	H	21		S	"	"	"	"	"	"	"		
817	626131	Rodríguez Inman Josefa.	M	75		S	N. Americana.	"	S. Ant. Tex.	Mont. N.L.	"	s.d.	h.t.m.		
818	626143	Romero Cruz Mino	H	64		C	"	"	"	"	"	"	"		
819	626363	Sandoval Ricardo.	H	29		C	"	Empleado.	"	"	"	auto.	p.c.r.		
820	626362	Spinner Georges Robert.	H	23		S	"	Estudiante.	Metz Francia.	Méx. D.F.	"	autobus.	p.c.r.		

pfa.

COMMISSION EXHIBIT No. 2123—Continued

EL C. LIC. NOE PALOMARES, Oficial Mayor de la Secretaría de Gobernación, por Ac. del C. Subsecretario Enc. del Despacho, CERTIFICA: que la presente copia fotostática concuerda fiel y exactamente con su original que obra en los Archivos de la Oficina del Control Migratorio del Departamento de Migración de esta propia Secretaría; No se causa el Impuesto del Timbre por expedirse para usos oficiales.

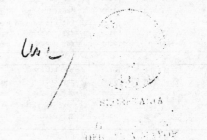

México, D.F., a 7 de mayo de 1964.

COMMISSION EXHIBIT No. 2123—Continued

ESTADOS UNIDOS MEXICANOS *Ano 13.*

SECRETARIA DE GOBERNACION

F. M. 11

NUM. ....

Reg. de Coord. 1085.

OFICINA EN NVO LAREDO TAMPS. MOVIMIENTO DE S [illegible] 5.

.... OFICINA EN .... OCTUBRE DE 1963. EXTRANJEROS. CLASIFICACION NO INMIGRANTES [illegible] FRAC. I, [illegible] 8 CANCELADOS.

Imp. E. O. V.

Núm. Progresivo 1	Documento de identidad número 2	Apellidos y nombre 3	Sexo 4	Edad Años 5	Edad Meses 6	Edo. Civil 7	Nacionalidad actual 8	Ocupacion 9	Lugar y pais de procedencia 10	Destino final 11	Dia Ent o salida 12	Clase de vehiculo en que viaja 13	Permanencia Entrada 14	Permanencia Salida 15	Observaciones 16
81	667991 ✓	Banning Darlene [illegible]	[illegible]	29		C	N. Americana.	S/D.	Mont. N.L.	Springfield M3		Auto.	Oct.2-63	j.p.c.	
82	362357 ✓	Bastien Eduard.	H	56		S	"	"	Monte N.L.	Guatemala Gta"		Auto.	Oct.1 "	t.s.e.	
83	518161 / 625114 ✓	Bennett John H.	H	53		C	"	Contador.	Guada Jal.	HoustonTex. "		Auto.		j.r.l.	
84	668002 ✓	Coronado Elena S. [illegible]	M	26		C	"	Su hogar.	Mont. N.L.	Laredo Tex. "		Auto.	Oct.2-63	a.a.ch.	
85	510457 ✓	Dallas Zelma Cline.	M	61		S	"	Emp.Cia.	"	S.Ant. Tex. "		Avion.	Sep.30 "	t.s.e.	
86	510457	Dallas Zelma Cline.	M	61		S		Emp.Cia.	"	"	"	"	" 30 "	t.s.e.	La data circulada se dio de baja en virtud de estar doblemente considerada.
87	624820 ✓	Der Vorm Phillippe [illegible] de.	M	23		S	*FRANCESA*	Estudiante.	Mont. N.L.	Laredo Tex. "		Autobus.	Sep.24 "	a.a.ch.	
87	609060 ✓	Ehlinger Leo Chris.	H	37		C	"	S/D.	Guada Jal.	S.Ant. Tex.	2	Auto.	Sep.28 "	j.g.n.	
88	624041 ✓	Emerson Henry Oliver.	H	70		C	"	Empleado.	Mexico DF.	Austin Tex. "		Autobus.	Oct.1 "	j.g.h.	
89	624040 ✓	Emerson Adrienne I. J.	M	59		C	"	Su hogar. M	Mexico DF.	Austin Tex. "		Autobus.	Oct.1 "	j.g.h.	
90	609132 ✓	Garza Garaza Enriqueta.	M	32		C	"	Su hogar.	Mont. N.L.	S.Ant. Tex. "		Auto.	Oct.1 "	j.g.h.	
91	624970 ✓	Gonzalez Cristela Gonzalez de.	M	32		C	"	S/D.	"	Lared Tex. "		FF.CC.	Sep.23 "	j.g.h.	
92	625650 ✓	Guerrero Garcia Ma. Luisa.de.	M	35		C	"	Su hogar.	"	C.Christi Tex"		Autobus.	Sep.28 "	j.g.h.	
94	510350 ✓	Martinez Eduardo Luis.	H	62		C	"	Jefe Ofna.	Leon Gto.	S.Ant. Tex. "		FF.CC.	Sep.23 "	e.l.s.	
95	622097 ✓	Muñoz Ildefons .	H	50		S	"	Comerciante.	Mont. N.L.	S.Ant. Tex. "		Auto.	Sep.29 "	j.g.h.	
96	625603 ✓	McDanile Joseph Michael.	H	42		S	"	S/D. M	Mexico DF.	Floyd Nobbs Ind		Avion.	Sep.27 "	t.s.e.	
97	625604 ✓	McDaniel Mary Louise.	M	42		C	"	Su hogar.	Mexico DF.	Floyd Nobbs Ind. "			Sep.21 "	t.s.e.	
98	626185 ✓	Brian John C.	H	37		C	"	S/D.	Mont. N.L.	El Encinal T "		Auto.	Sep.30 "	j.p.c.	
99	24085 ✓	Harvey Oswald Lee.	H	23		C	"	Fotografo.	Mexico DF.	N.Orelans La."		Auto.	Sep.26 "	a.a.ch.	
100	625584 ✓	Perales Lucas Jr.	H	25		C	"	S/D.	Mexico DF.	Sotula Tax. "		Auto.	Oct.2 "	j.j.c.	
93	45469	Hinkson Leighton	H	35			N. Americana.		México, D.F.		3				

rmsr.

COMMISSION EXHIBIT No. 2123—Continued

SECRETARIA DE GOBERNACION
Dirección General de Gobierno

EL C. LIC. NOE PALOMARES, Oficial Mayor de la Secretaría de Gobernación, por Ac. del C. Subsecretario Enc. del Despacho, CERTIFICA: que la presente copia fotostática concuerda fiel y exactamente con su original que obra en los Archivos de la Oficina del Control Migratorio del Departamento de Migración de esta propia Secretaría. No se causa el Impuesto del Timbre por expedirse para usos oficiales.

México, D.F., a 7 de mayo de 1964.

COMMISSION EXHIBIT No. 2123—Continued

Anexo 14.

DIRECCION GENERAL DE
POBLACION.
DEPTO. DE INSPECCION.

Se rinde informe. Dc3/1644

C. JEFE DEL DEPTO. DE INSPECCION
P r e s e n t e.

En cumplimiento a la orden que recibí para trasladarme a la Ciudad de Nuevo Laredo, Tamps. con el objeto de practicar una investigación relacionada con el extranjero de nacionalidad norteamericana LEE HARVEY OSWALD, a continuación me permito rendir a usted el siguiente INFORME:

E[illegible].- El extranjero de referencia se internó al País por Nuevo L[illegible], Tamps. al amparo de la FM8 # 24085 el 26 de Septiembre de 1963. El Agente de Migración Helio Tuexi Maydon que lo atendió, omitió anotar tres datos esenciales: la hora de la entrada, el medio de transporte que usó y la nacionalidad. Interrogado sobre el particular, admitió esos errores, agregando que no podía aportar ningún dato que ayudara a esta investigación en vista del tiempo transcurrido. No pudo recordar absolutamente nada que tuviera relación con el extranjero Oswald.

Pudo establecerse con certeza que fué atendido en la Oficina de Migración entre las 6 a.m. y las 14 p.m. de ese día, ya que el registro del personal indica que el Agente Tuexi Maydon cubrió ese turno.

SALIDA.- El extranjero citado abandonó el País con fecha 3 de Octubre de 1963, habiendo sido atendido por el Agente de Migración Alberto Arzamendi Chapa en el Kilómetro 26 de la carretera. A su salida dicho Agente observó las omisiones en la forma migratoria y subsanó, en forma manuscrita, la referente a la nacionalidad escribiendo la palabra "Americano".

El Agente Arzamendi tiene dos Auxiliares de nombres Luis de la Peña y Eduardo García, pero al igual que el primero no pudieron aportar ningún dato.

Pudo establecerse también que dicho extranjero cruzó por el Kilómetro 26 entre las o hrs. a.m. y las 8 a.m. del día mencionado.

ESTANCIA EN NUEVO LAREDO, Tamps.- Fueron checados varios hoteles de la localidad sin que apareciera en ninguno haberse hospedado el 26 de septiembre. Sin embargo, tomando en cuenta que al día siguiente, o sea el 27, se registró en el Hotel del Comercio en el Distrito Fe

COMMISSION EXHIBIT No. 2123—Continued

Anexo 15.

GOBERNACION
al de Gobierno

Hoja # 2.

deral, debe concluírse que hizo el viaje inmediatamente sin detenerse en Nuevo Laredo, Tamps.

MEDIO DE TRANSPORTE.- Fueron revisadas las listas de pasajeros de la Cía. Mexicana de Aviación y no aparece que el mencionado OSWALD hiciese el viaje por ese medio. Además, siendo el 27 de septiembre día Viernes, tampoco pudo abordar avión en vista de que en ese mes la compañía citada no hacía vuelos diarios a México.

En la línea de camiones Transportes del Norte no puede establecerse si viajó por ella a México, en vista de que no formulan listas de sus pasajeros. Por otra parte, a pesar de que dicha línea es la conexión con la "Greyhound", tampoco puede afirmarse que viajó por ella, ya que esta última solamente estampa la anotación de "Ocupado" en sus hojas de viaje.

Es de suponerse que Oswald viajó en autobús, lo que le permitió hospedarse en el Hotel en México al día siguiente de su internación al País, pues por ferrocarril tampoco queda huella alguna de los pasajeros. Cabe la posibilidad de que hubiese hecho el viaje en auto, pero esto sólo sería admisible si personas conocidas le hubieren permitido acomodarse con ellos, pues como más adelante se verá no entró con auto propio al País.

DIVORCIO DE OSWALD.- Existen rumores en esa población de Nuevo Laredo, Tamps. en el sentido de que anteriormente dicho extranjero había estado allí con el objeto de obtener un divorcio. Respecto de lo anterior, pudo investigarse en el Juzgado de Primera Instancia de Nuevo Laredo, Tamps. a cargo del Lic. Pinto, que fué otro extranjero de nombre Harvey Larry Hudson quien tramitó allí y obtuvo un divorcio en el año de 1963, de su esposa Jane Marie Huber Hudson. Del estudio del expediente se concluye que no se trata del extranjero Oswald.

En una población cercana llamada Colombia, Nuevo León, igualmente se tramitan divorcios de ciudadanos norteamericanos, con dispensa de trámites. En vista de las lluvias que azotaron aquella población fué imposible trasladarse por carretera, que es el único medio de comunicación, para verificar si existe algún antecedente del citado divorcio. Sin embargo, se giró Telegrama urgente al C. Ciro Manuel Riojas, encargado del Registro Civil en ese lugar solicitando dichos informes y hasta el día 29 del mes en curso no había dado contestación. El Jefe de la Oficina de Migración en Nuevo Laredo, Tamps. Sr. Gilberto Cáceres Pérez ofreció informar inmediatamente que tuviese alguna contestación.

Igualmente, sobre este particular se entrevistaron a los Lic.

COMMISSION EXHIBIT No. 2123—Continued

Queso 16.

Hoja # 3.

José Tenene Ramos y Marcos Trinidad Salinas, así como al Guía de Turistas Mateo Reyes, quienes informaron no haber patrocinado al extranjero OSWALD en algún juicio de esa naturaleza.

INTERNACION FAMILIARES.- Se hizo una búsqueda minuciosa con el objeto de determinar si la esposa de Oswald de nombre MARINA NIKOLAEVNA - OSWALD se internó al País, pero sin resultados positivos. Igualmente, con respecto a su madre de nombre MARGUERITE CLAVIRE OSWALD, con los mismos resultados por la frontera de Nuevo Laredo, Tamps.

PERMISOS DE IMPORTACION DE AUTOS.- Según se desprende de las - Relaciones F.M. 11 de salida, el extranjero Oswald abandonó el País el 3 de Octubre de 1963 por Nuevo Laredo, Tamps. a bordo de un auto. Sin embargo, tal dato constituye otro error, esta vez de la Srta. Solalindo, mecanógrafa encargada de hacer dichas relaciones, quien admitió haberse equivocado, pues la F.M. 8 que tuvo a la vista correspondiente al extranjero Oswald no contiene en ninguna parte la anotación respectiva que indicase que viajó en auto.

Por otra parte, se acompaña una relación de los Permisos Temporales de Importación de Autos expedidos el día 26 de septiembre de 1963 por las autoridades aduanales de Nuevo Laredo, Tamps., complementada con los datos migratorios de cada persona. Estudiada esta relación no se encuentra nada que pueda ligarlos con el extranjero Oswald.

TARJETAS F.M. 8 LOCALIZADAS.- Se llevó a cabo una búsqueda, - habiéndose localizado las F.M. 8 24086 y 24087, o sean las dos posteriores a la del extranjero Oswald y que contienen los siguientes datos:

FLO[redacted]SON DE MEN, 38 años, casada, hogar, domiciliada - en Nueva Orleans, La., con destino a Monterrey, N.L. habiéndose internado con auto por C. Miguel Alemán, Tamps. y de nacionalidad norteamericana.

GEORGE HENRY DE MEN, 42 años, casado, Obrero, domiciliado en Nueva Orleans, La., con destino a Monterrey, N.L. y con el mismo lugar de internación y nacionalidad que la anterior.

Al igual que Oswald solicitaron su Tarjeta en Nueva Orleans,- La. y la importancia de tal dato radica en que habiendo obtenido su forma migratoria el mismo día, quizás pudieran proporcionar algún informe, ya - que en el Consulado Mexicano su turno fué el inmediato posterior al del - referido extranjero. Para obtener mayores datos de ambas personas deberá consultarse el Permiso de Importación del Auto por C. Miguel Alemán,Tams.

También se localizaron las F.M. 8 24082 y 24083 que corresponden a SAMUEL THOMAS NORTH y JUDITH MARIE MUTH NORTH, ambos norteamericanos

COMMISSION EXHIBIT No. 2123—Continued

Hoja # 4.

y domiciliados en Nueva Orleans, La. habiéndose internado con auto por - C. Miguel Alemán, Tams. Para obtener mayores datos de ambos, también - deberá consultarse el Permiso de Importación respectivo.

Atentamente,
México, D.F., oviembre 30 de 1963.
Inspector # 16.

José Mario del Valle.

SECRETARIA DE GOBERNACION
DIC 3 1963
DEPARTAMENTO DE INSPECCION

COMMISSION EXHIBIT No. 2123—Continued

EL C. LIC. NOE PALOMARES, Oficial Mayor de la Secretaría de Gobernación, por Ac. del C. Sub-Secretario Enc. del Despacho, CERTIFICA: que la presente copia fotostática concuerda fiel y exactamente con su original que obra en los archivos del Departamento de Inspección de Migración de esta propia Secretaría.- No se causa el impuesto del timbre por expedirse para usos oficiales.

México, D.F., a 7 de mayo de 1964.

SECRETARIA DE GOBERNACION
Dirección General de Gobierno

SECRETARIA DE GOBERNACION OFICIALIA MAYOR

COMMISSION EXHIBIT No. 2123—Continued

DEPARTMENT OF STATE
DIVISION OF LANGUAGE SERVICES

(TRANSLATION)

LS NO. 16257
T-52/R-XX
Spanish

Encl. No. 1
A-1461
México, D.F.

505503

The Department of Foreign Affairs presents its compliments to the Embassy of the United States of America and has the honor to refer to Embassy note No. 1349, dated April 10, and note No. 504826, dated May 14, of the Department of Foreign Affairs, which pertain to the investigation conducted by the competent Mexican authorities of the activities of Lee Harvey Oswald, alleged assassin of President John F. Kennedy, while he was in Mexico in September 1963.

Supplementing the information transmitted to the Embassy in note No. 504826, the Department takes pleasure in sending now the following documents, which have been transmitted to it by the authorities who conducted the investigation:

1. Certified photostatic copy of tourist card (F.M.8) No. 24085, valid for 15 days, used by Lee Harvey Oswald to enter Mexico on September 26, 1963, at Nuevo Laredo, Tamaulipas.

2. Certified photostatic copy of several pages from the register of the Comercio Hotel at No. 19 Fray Bernardino de Sahagún Street, Mexico City, where Lee Harvey Oswald stayed on September 27, 1963.

3. Certified photostatic copy of the reservation sheet of the bus company "Transportes Frontera" for October 2, 1963, on which Oswald's name appears as No. 4.

Embassy of the United States of America,

City.

COMMISSION EXHIBIT No. 2123—Continued

4. Certified photostatic copies of the records of passenger entry and departure (F.M. 11) at Nuevo Laredo, Tamaulipas, for September 26 and October 3, 1963, which show that Oswald entered Mexico on September 26 and departed on October 3.

5. Certified photostatic copy of the statement made before Mexican authorities on November 23, 1963, by Mrs. Silvia Tirado Durán.

6. Certified photostatic copy of the report made November 30, 1963, by Inspector José Mario del Valle of the investigations conducted in Nuevo Laredo, Tamaulipas, regarding Oswald's passage through that city.

In transmitting the above documents to the Embassy, the Department wishes to emphasize their confidential nature, for which reason it is understood, according to the promise made in the last paragraph of Embassy note No. 1349, that they will not be published, either in their entirety or in part, without the consent of the Government of Mexico.

The Department of Foreign Affairs avails itself of this opportunity to renew to the Embassy the assurance of its highest consideration.

México, D.F., June 9, 1964

Enclosures

COMMISSION EXHIBIT No. 2123—Continued

CENTRAL INTELLIGENCE AGENCY
WASHINGTON 25, D.C.

23 JUL 1964

MEMORANDUM FOR: Mr. J. Lee Rankin
General Counsel
President's Commission on the
Assassination of President Kennedy

SUBJECT: Lee Harvey Oswald

Attached are the translations requested in your letter of 3 July 1964. The original documents are also returned herewith.

Richard Helms
Richard Helms
Deputy Director for Plans

Attachments - a/s

COMMISSION EXHIBIT No. 2123—Continued

17 July 1964

Lee Harvey OSWALD

The following is a translation of information contained in the attachments to Note No. 505503 of the Mexican Ministry of Foreign Affairs to the United States Embassy in Mexico City, 9 June 1964.

Item 1

Certified photostat of tourist card (FM 8) No. 24085, valid for 15 days, used by Lee Harvey Oswald to enter Mexico on 26 September 1963 at Nuevo Laredo, Tamaulipas. Oswald is listed as a photographer, married, 23 years old. Card was issued at New Orleans on 17 September 1963. The entry stamp bears the name of agent Helio (Tuexi?) Maydon, and the exit stamp that of agent Alberto Arzamendi Chapa.

Item 2

ertified photostats of several pages from the guest register of the Comercio Hotel at 19 Fray Bernardino de Sahagun Street in Mexico City, where Oswald registered on 27 September 1963. The dates are given as 27, 28, 29, and (30?) September, and 1 October. The name (listed as #18) is given as Lee, Harvey Oswald on 27 September and as Lee Harvey thereafter.

Item 3

Certified photostat of reservation sheet of Transportes Frontera bus company for 2 October 1963, reportedly listing Lee Harvey Oswald as passenger No. 4. The attached print is not good enough for the name or initials to be legible. The sheet, in three columns, gives some sort of identifying number for each passenger as well as the passenger's name and destination. Dionisio Reyna and Francisco Saucedo are listed as drivers.

COMMISSION EXHIBIT No. 2123—Continued

Item 4

Certified photostat of list of persons entering Mexico through Nuevo Laredo on the second half of September 1963. Oswald is listed as entry 807, by his tourist card number, name, sex, age, marital status, nationality, occupation (photographer), point of departure, destination, day of the month (26th), means of travel (not indicated), and agent's initials (H.T.M.). Certified photostat of list of persons departing from Mexico through Nuevo Laredo in October 1963. His nationality is given as French (by ditto marks), his means of travel as "auto," and the agent as A.A. Ch.

Item 5

Certified photostat of the statement made by Silvia Duran to the Mexican Federal Security Police on 23 November 1963 (Translation is given in FBI memorandum of 26 March 1964 and therefore is not repeated).

Item 6

Certified report of 30 November 1963 by Jose Mario del Valle of the Department of Inspection, Directorate-General of Population (see Attachment A).

-2-

COMMISSION EXHIBIT No. 2123—Continued

ATTACHMENT A

DIRECTORATE-GENERAL OF POPULATION
DEPARTMENT OF INSPECTION

REPORT

To the Chief of the Inspection Department
in his office

In compliance with the order I received to go to the city of Nuevo Laredo, Tamaulipas, to conduct an investigation in relation to the foreigner of US nationality, Lee Harvey Oswald, I hereby submit the following report:

ARRIVAL. The subject foreigner came into the country through Nuevo Laredo, Tamaulipas, under FM8 No 24085 on 26 September 1963. Migration Agent Helio Tuexi Maydon, who attended to him, failed to note three essential facts: the hour of entry, the means of transportation he used, and his nationality. Under questioning concerning the facts, he admitted those mistakes, adding that he was unable to supply any data which might help in this investigation, in view of the time elapsed. He was unable to remember anything at all related to the foreigner Oswald.

It was possible to establish with certainty that he was attended to at the Migration Office between 0600 and 1400 hours of that day, as the personnel register shows that agent Tuexi Maydon was on that shift.

EXIT. The above-mentioned foreigner left the country on 3 October 1963, and was attended to by Migration Agent Alberto Arzamendi Chapa

at Kilometer 26 of the highway. Upon his exit the agent observed the omissions on the migration form and corrected in writing the one with reference to nationality by entering the word "American."

Agent Arzamendi has two assistants named Luis de la Peña and Librado García, but they, like him, were unable to supply any information.

It was possible to establish also that the subject foreigner crossed over by Kilometer 26 between 0001 and 0800 hours of the day in question.

STAY IN NUEVO LAREDO, TAMAULIPAS. Several local hotels were checked but it was not found that he had stayed at any of them on 26 September. However, in view of the fact that the following day, the 27th, he registered at the Hotel del Comercia in the Federal District, it must be concluded that he made the trip immediately without stopping at Nuevo Laredo, Tamaulipas.

MEANS OF TRANSPORTATION. [I have checked] the passenger lists of the Compania Mexicana de Aviacion and it does not appear that the [foreigner] Oswald made the trip by that means. Also, since 27 September was Friday, he could not have boarded a plane in view of the fact that during that month the above-mentioned airline did not have daily flights to Mexico City.

At the Transportes del Norte bus line it was not possible to establish whether he traveled on it to Mexico City, in view of the fact that they do not make lists of their passengers. In addition, despite

-2-

the fact that the above-mentioned bus line is the connection [sic] with the Greyhound Line, it was not possible to assert that he traveled on it, since the latter only stamps the notation "Occupied" on its way bill.

It is to be supposed that Oswald traveled by bus, which enabled him to stay at the Hotel in Mexico City the day after his entry into the country, since there is no trace of a record of railroad passengers either. There is the possibility that he may have made the trip by automobile, but his would be possible only if persons of his acquaintance would have permitted him to go along with them, since, as will be seen further on, he did not enter into the country with his own automobile.

DIVORCE IN MEXICO. There are rumors in this town of Nuevo Laredo, Tamaulipas, to the effect that, previously, the above-mentioned foreigner had been there for the purpose of obtaining a divorce. With respect to the former, it was possible to determine at the Court of First Instance of Nuevo Laredo, Tamaulipas, which is under Lic. Pinto, that it was another foreigner named Harvey Larry Hudson who applied for and obtained a divorce there in 1960, from his wife June Marie [name illegible] Hudson. A study of the record leads to the conclusion that the person involved is not the foreigner Oswald.

In a near-by town named Colombia, Nuevo Leon, divorce suits by US citizens also are handled, with dispensation of [illegible word]. In

-3-

view of the rains which fell in that town it was impossible to go there by road, the only means of transportation, to verify whether there is any record of the above-mentioned divorce. However, a priority telegram was sent to Ciro Manuel Riojas, who is in charge of the Vital Statistics Office in the town, requesting such information, and until the 29th of this month there had not been any reply. The chief of the Migration Office in Nuevo Laredo, Tamaulipas, Gilberto Cámaros Pérez, promised to report immediately that he had any reply.

Also, on this subject, interviews were held with attorneys José Tenene Ramos and Marcos Trinidad Salinas, as well as the tourist guide Mateo Reyes, who reported that they had not sponsored foreigner Oswald at any trial of that nature.

ENTRY OF RELATIVES. A detailed search was made to determine whether Oswald's wife, Marina Nikolaevna Oswald entered the country, but without positive results. Likewise, with respect to his mother, Marguerite Ciavire Oswald, the same result was obtained [as to her entry] through the border at Nuevo Laredo, Tamaulipas.

AUTOMOBILE IMPORT PERMIT. According to F. M. 11 Reports of exits, the foreigner Oswald left the country on 3 October 1963 through Nuevo Laredo, Tamaulipas, in an automobile. However, that entry is another mistake, this one committed by Miss Solalindo, the typist in charge of preparing such reports, who admitted having made a mistake, since the F. M. 8, which she had in front of her, with reference to the foreigner Oswald, does not contain anywhere an entry to indicate that he traveled by automobile.

-4-

In addition, there is attached a list of the Temporary Automobile Import Permits issued on 26 September 1963 by the customs authorities of Nuevo Laredo, Tamaulipas, together with the migration data of each person. Upon examination, this list shows nothing that might connect them to the foreigner Oswald.

F. M. 8 CARDS LOCATED. A search was made, which resulted in locating F. M. 8 cards No 24086 and 24087, the two cards after that of the foreigner Oswald, and which contain the following information:

[illegible female name] de Men, 38 years old, married, housewife, a resident of New Orleans, Louisiana, destination Monterrey, Nuevo Leon, who entered with an automobile through Ciudad Miguel Aleman, Tamaulipas, and who is of US nationality.

George [name illegible] de Men, 42 years old, married, blue collar worker, a resident of New Orleans, Louisiana, destination Monterrey, Nuevo Leon, who entered through the same place and has the same nationality as the above-mentioned person.

Like Oswald, they applied for their card at New Orleans, Louisiana, and the importance of this fact lies in that, since they obtained their migration form the same day, they might be able to furnish some information, since their turn at the Mexican Consulate was the one immediately prior to that of the subject foreigner. For further information on both persons, the permit to import the automobile through Ciudad Miguel Aleman, Tamaulipas, should be consulted.

Also located were F. M. 8 No 24082 and 24083, corresponding to Samuel Thomas North and Judith Marie Muth North, both US nationals and residents of New Orleans, Louisiana, who entered with an automobile through Ciudad Miguel Aleman, Tamaulipas. For further information on both, the respective import permit should be consulted.

Respectfully,

Jose Mario del Valle
Inspector No 16,
Mexico, D. F., 30 November 1963

[Receipt stamp of the Directorate-General of Population, Secretariat of Migration, Department of Inspection, 3 December 1963.]

Lic. Noe Palomares, Chief Clerk of the Secretariat of Interior, for the Undersecretary in Charge of the Office, certifies: That the present photostatic copy agrees faithfully and exactly with its original in the files of the Department of Inspection of Migration of this Secretariat. No tax is levied because this is issued for official use.

Mexico, D. F., 7 May 1964

[Signature]

[NOTE: This translation has been prepared from a very poor print and may contain some error in the transcription of names.]

DEPARTMENT OF STATE
DIVISION OF LANGUAGE SERVICES

(TRANSLATION)

LS NO. 16285
T-52/R-XX
Spanish

Annex 1

[Stamp of Executive Branch of Mexico]

UNITED MEXICAN STATES

Department of the Interior

Original No. 24085

Valid for 15 days

Good for one trip only for --- days

Full name: Lee Harvey Oswald

Photograph

Sex M X Age 23 Marital status Unmarried
F
Married X

Document certifying nationality: Birth certificate American

[Note: the word "American" is handwritten]

Destination: Mexico City

New Orleans, Louisiana, U.S.A.

September 17, 1963

Place and Date

[s] Lee H. Oswald

Signature of Bearer

To be filled out by the Immigration authorities:

Department of the Interior, Population Division	Dept. of the Interior, Population Division
Entered:	Departed:
September 26, 1963	October 3, 1963
date stamp	Alberto Arzamendi Chapa
Helio Tuexi Maydon	Nuevo Laredo, Tamaulipas
Nuevo Laredo, Tamaulipas	

[Remainder of page contains duplicate of tourist card and notes concerning the tax applicable to the tourist card]

[Certification follows]

Annex 7

At 6 p.m. on November 23, 1963, in Mexico City, Federal District, I, the undersigned, Captain Fernando Gutiérrez Barrios, Deputy Federal Director of Security, acting legally, in the presence of witnesses, certify that Mrs. Silvia Tirado Durán, having appeared for questioning concerning the events stated below, drew up this instrument:

Mrs. Silvia Tirado Durán, being present and having sworn to tell the truth after being informed of the penalties for perjury, stated that her name was as written, that she was 26, married, no religion, clerk, literate, a native and resident of this city, her address being Apt. 3, No. 143 Constituyentes, who declared, with respect to the events being investigated:

That she had been legally married to Mr. Horacio Durán Navarro since November 5, 1958, and had one child, a girl named Patricia, 3-1/2 years old; that in July or August 1961, she was invited to take the position of Coordinator with the Instituto Mexicano Cubano de Relaciones Culturales, [Mexican-Cuban Cultural Relations Institute] at that time headed by Mr. Agustin Cue Canovas, and although she did not remember exactly who recommended her, she could state that for some time she had been in contact with, and frequently visited, officials of the Cuban Embassy, being a personal friend of Ambassador Portuondo and of the Cultural Attachés, Teresa Proenza and Luis Alveru, as well as of the clerks, chiefly the Consul's secretary, Miss Maricarmen Olavarri, of Spanish nationality but a relative of the Consul, Eusebio Ascué;

That the Institute engaged in purely cultural activities, which were sometimes attended by the above-mentioned Cultural Attachés and various Cubans, although most of those attending were Mexicans, always artists and intellectuals. Politics were never discussed. She remembered only that during the Cuban crisis in October in connection with the attempted invasion of Cuba and later the blockade of the Island by the United States Government, they listened by short-wave radio to the reports being announced by Prensa Latina and made up a bulletin of those reports, which was read. The reports they heard came directly from Habana. She admitted that some Cubans and Mexicans also attended these meetings who discussed the Cuban political problem among themselves but not officially;

That the declarant had received a salary of 500 pesos a month as Coordinator of the Institute; that her working hours were 4 to 8 p.m. daily; that the money to support the Institute was received from a monthly subsidy from the Cuban Embassy, the amount of which she did not know. In addition, each of the members paid dues, and contributions were received from individuals whose names she did not remember, because most of them contributed anonymously. She could not give the monthly amount, despite the fact that she was the one who personally received all the money that came into the Institute;

That the only other person who received a monthly salary of 500 pesos was Mr. Felipe Rojas, who worked at the Institute in the mornings as Secretary; the rest of the money received was used for rent for the premises and other operating expenses;

That in December 1961, the declarant and her husband flew to Habana, Cuba, paying for their own tickets. However, all their expenses while in Habana and several other cities of Cuba were paid by the Instituto Cubano de Amistad con los Pueblos [Cuban Friendship Institute] and the Cultural Club known as "The Americas." The trip lasted 15 days. The declarant and her husband had no contact with officials of the Cuban Government on this trip;

That, as she had already stated, the declarant had been a follower of Socialsim and the Marxist doctrine for several years, having studied philosophy and existentialism; and in particular, she had supported the Cuban Revolution since its beginning, and continued to support it;

That about three months ago, she began to work as Secretary to Mr. Eusebio Ascué, the Cuban Consul in this city, who terminated his duties in that capacity five days ago, that is to say, Monday, November 18, when he was replaced by Mr. Alfredo Miraval y Diaz. She stated that from the beginning she had taken the position on a temporary basis because of the death in an automobile accident of her friend, Maricarmen Olavarri, the Consul's Secretary, until someone else could come from Cuba to fill the position. She was responsible for the administrative work,

filling out the visas issued, and processing applications for such visas, which are invariably sent to the Ministry of Foreign Affairs of Cuba for approval. She obtained this position directly through former Consul Ascué, with whom she was very friendly, even having given him a farewell party in her home, which was attended by almost all the officials and employees of the Embassy and Consulate, except the Ambassador;

That she did not belong to any political party and had never attended any demonstrations or meetings, nor had she ever given any lectures or speeches, although her husband had, since he had written several articles in the newspaper El Dia;

That she had never been arrested for any reason, including the time of Mr. John F. Kennedy's visit to Mexico, which visit had made her very happy because of the benefits it would bring to her country;

That yesterday, while she was working at the Cuban Consulate, where she is employed from 10 a.m. to 2 p.m. and from 4 p.m. to 6 p.m. daily, for which she receives a monthly salary of 1,500 pesos, at about the time for her to leave for lunch, a colleague remarked that she had just heard on the radio that President Kennedy had been attacked, and that three shots had been fired at him. She called her husband by telephone and commented on the news. He replied that he already knew it and called the attack "monstrous". He agreed that when they reached home they would talk about it, and they did that, when they went home for lunch, but only briefly, since they did not know the details of the attack or the name and description of the alleged assailant. It was not until that night that they read in an "extra" a report on the matter, and later, on their radio at home, the declarant heard the name of Lee Harvey Oswald, which made her remember that that was the name of an American who, at the end of September or beginning of October, had come to the Cuban Consulate and applied for transit visa for Cuba, en route to Russia. In support of his request, he had presented his passport, which showed that he had lived in Russia for three years, his work card from that country, in Russian, and letters in that language. He also presented evidence showing that he was married to a Russian woman, and that he appeared to be the leader in New Orleans of the organization known as "Fair Treatment for Cuba," claiming that he was accepted as a "friend" of the Cuban Revolution. In view of all that, the declarant, performing her duties, took all his data and filled out the necessary application. He then left the office but returned in the afternoon with his photographs, and the declarant, admitting that she exceeded her duties, unofficially called the Russian Consulate in a desire to facilitate the processing of the Russian visa for Lee Harvey Oswald. However, she was told by that Consulate that it would take approximately four months to process his application, which annoyed the applicant, because, he said, he was in a hurry to obtain the visas to go to Russia. He insisted on his right to them because of his background and his support and personal activities in behalf of the Cuban Movement. The declarant could not state--because she did not remember--whether he said he was a member of the Communist Party. He did say that his Russian wife was at that time in New York, from where she would follow him, having come from the above-mentioned city of New Orleans;

That when Oswald heard that a Cuban visa, being a transit visa, could not be issued to him until after he had obtained a Russian visa, he became excited and very angry, and so the declarant called Consul Ascué, who was in his private office with Mr. Miraval, who later replaced him. The Consul came out of his office and began to argue with Oswald in English. Ascué finally said, "If it were up to me, I would not give you a visa," and "people like you, instead of helping the Cuban Revolution, only do it harm," it being understood that in their argument, they were referring to the Russian Socialist Revolution and not the Cuban Revolution. Oswald maintained that he had two reasons for wanting a visa so urgently, and they were: his permit to stay in Mexico was about to expire; and he needed to reach Russia right away. Despite the dispute, the declarant gave Oswald a piece of paper identical to the one on which she was writing in the proceedings, on which she wrote her name "Silvia Durán" and the

telephone number of the Cuban Consulate "11-28-47," and his visa application was processed in any case. It was sent to the Ministry of Foreign Affairs of Cuba, which sent a reply in the routine manner, 15 to 30 days later, granting the visa on condition that the applicant first obtained a Russian visa. The declarant did not remember whether or not Oswald later called the declarant on the Consulate telephone. She said that her entire conversation with Oswald, as well as the conversation the Consul had with him, was in English, since Oswald did not speak Spanish at all;

That when she saw the photograph that appeared in today's newspapers, precisely in El Dia, she immediately recognized him and identified him as the one whom she had been calling Lee Harvey Oswald;

That, only once, the declarant went to a reception at the Russian Embassy when astronauts Gagarin and Tereshkova were there, having received a personal invitation from Russian Consul Yacksov when he went to the Cuban Consulate, to see Ascué and Miraval and gave them their invitations;

That, with resepct to her brother- and sister-in-law, Lidia and Rubén Durán Navarro, Lidia Durán went several times with the declarant to meetings at the Institute, but Rubén Durán went only once or twice, and then it was to see exhibitions of paintings; that Bety Serrato Azúcar, Rubén's wife, had always stayed out of these activities, although all of them are Lefists, but do not actively participate in any activities; that Barbara Ann Blits Tresmond Esquivel and Agata Roseno García are friends of Bety; that the declarant had only very infrequent, casual contacts with them, and do did not know about their activities or ideology. As for the gentleman whose name she knew to be Bently, she had never seen him before and assumed that he was a friend of Barbara, since she noticed that she was the one to whom he was talking; and that she, her husband, Agata, and Lidia were dining at her home, while the others were at the home of her brother-in-law, Rubén;

That she had nothing further to declare, and after her statement had been read to her, she approved the contents and signed in the margin in witness thereof.

The proceedings were closed and attested. Certified.

[Initialed]
Capt. Fernando Gutiérrez Barrios

Deputy Federal Director of Security

[Signature]
Fernando Ortiz de la Peña
Witness

[Signature]
Carlos Durán Lans
Witness

[Certified May 7, 1964, by Noé Palomares, Chief Administrative Officer, Department of the Interior, Mexico.]

COMMISSION EXHIBIT No. 2123—Continued

Population Division
Office of Inspection

Report

Chief of the Office of Inspection
City

Pursuant to the order I received to go to Nuevo Laredo, Tamaulipas, to conduct an investigation of the American, Lee Harvey Oswald, I take the liberty of submitting to you the following report:

Entry. The above-mentioned alien entered the country via Nuevo Laredo, Tamaulipas, with FM8 No. 24085 [tourist card] on September 26, 1963. The Immigration Officer, Helio Tuexi Maydon, who attended him, failed to record three essential facts: the time of his entry, the means of transportation he used, and his nationality. When asked about this, he admitted his mistakes and added that he could not furnish any information that would help in this investigation because of the time that had elapsed. He could not remember anything at all relating to Oswald.

It was possible to establish, beyond any doubt, that Oswald passed through the Immigration Office between 6 a.m. and 2 p.m. on that day, since the time sheet shows that Officer Tuexi Maydon was on duty during that shift.

Departure. The alien in question left the country on October 3, 1963, having been checked by Immigration Officer Alberto Arzamendi Chapa at Kilometer 26 on the highway.

COMMISSION EXHIBIT No. 2123—Continued

When he departed, the Immigration Officer noted the omissions on the tourist card and corrected, by hand, the mistake referring to his nationality, writing in the word "American."

Officer Arzamendi has two assistants, Luis de la Peña and Librado García, but like Officer Arzamendi, they could not furnish any information.

It was also established that the alien in question passed Kilometer 26 between midnight and 8 a.m. of the date stated.

Stay in Nuevo Laredo, Tamaulipas. Several hotels in the locality were checked, but no evidence was found that he stayed in any of them on September 26. However, since the next day, September 27, he registered at the Comercio Hotel in the Federal District, it must be concluded that he continued on his way without stopping in Nuevo Laredo, Tamaulipas.

Means of Transportation. The passenger lists of the airline, Cía. Mexicana de Aviacion, were checked, but apparently Oswald did not travel by that means. In any case, since September 27 was a Friday, he could not have flown, because in the month of September, the airline did not have daily flights to Mexico City.

There is no way of establishing whether or not he used the bus line "Transportes del Norte" to go to Mexico City, since it does not prepare passenger lists. And, although that company connects with the Greyhound, it could not be established whether or not he used the latter company either, since it merely stamps the notation "Taken" on its travel sheets.

It is to be assumed that Oswald traveled by bus, which would have enabled him to stay at the hotel in Mexico City the next day after he entered the country, since there is no evidence of his having traveled by rail either. He may have made the trip by car, but this would be admissible only if acquaintances had permitted him to accompany them, since, as will be shown later, he did not enter Mexico with a car of his own.

Oswald divorce. There are rumors in the town of Nuevo Laredo, Tamaulipas, that the alien in question had gone there previously to obtain a divorce. In this connection, it was ascertained from the Court of First Instance of Nuevo Laredo, Tamaulipas, under the direction of Mr. Pinto, that it was another alien by the name of Harvey Larry Hudson, who filed for and obtained a divorce there in 1960 from his wife June Marie Huber Hudson. It was concluded from a study of the file that this was not the alien, Oswald.

In a nearby town called Colombia, in the State of Nuevo León, divorces of American citizens are also granted without the usual requirements. Because of the heavy rains that had struck that town, it was impossible to go there by road--which is only way to reach there--to find out if there is any record of the divorce. However, an urgent telegram was sent to Ciro Manuel Riojas, Officer of the Civil Register in that town, requesting the information needed, but by November 29, no reply had been received. Gilberto Cázares Pérez, Immigration Officer at Nuevo Laredo,

Tamaulipas, promised to notify us as soon as he had a reply. Messrs. Jose Teneno Ramos and Marcos Trinidad Salinas, as well as Mateo Reyes, a tourist guide, were also questioned, but they said that they had not assisted the alien Oswald in any legal proceeding of that kind.

Family information. A detailed search was made to determine whether Oswald's wife, Marina Nikolaevna Oswald, entered Mexico, but without results. The same was done with respect to his mother, Marguerite Clavire Oswald, with the same results, at the border at Nuevo Laredo, Tamaulipas.

Automobile import permits. According to the lists, form F.M. 11 for departure, Oswald left Mexico October 3, 1963 via Nuevo Laredo, Tamaulipas, in an automobile. However, that information also proved to be a mistake, this time made by Miss Solalinde, the typist responsible for making out such forms, who admitted that she had made a mistake, since the form F.M. 8 she had before her, which referred to Oswald, did not have a notation anywhere showing that he traveled by automobile.

Enclosed is a list of Temporary Automobile Import Permits, issued September 26, 1963, by the customs authorities at Nuevo Laredo, Tamaulipas, supplemented by the immigration data of each person. An examination of that list did not disclose anything that could connect them with the alien Oswald.

F.M. 8 Cards Located. A search was made and the two tourist cards [form F.M. 8], 24086 and 24087, that followed Oswald's tourist card were found. They contain the following information:

Florence Johnson [?] de Men, 38, married, housewife, residing at New Orleans, La., destination, Monterrey,

Nuevo León, having entered by private car via Miguel Alemán, Tamaulipas, American citizen; and George Henry de Men, 42, married, worker, address, New Oreleans, La., destination, Monterrey, Nuevo León, same port of entry and nationality as the former.

Like Oswald, they applied for their tourist cards in New Orleans, La. The significance of that fact is that, having obtained their immigration papers on the same day, perhaps they could furnish some information, since their appointment at the Mexican Consulate was immediately after that of the alien in question. To obtain more data concerning these two persons, the automobile import permit issued at Miguel Alemán, Tamaulipas, should be consulted.

Tourist cards F.M. 8 24082 and 24083, issued to Samuel Thomas North and Judith Marie Muth North, both Americans, residing at New Orleans, La., were also found. They entered Mexico by automobile via Miguel Alemán, Tamaulipas. To obtain more information on these two persons, their import permit should also be consulted.

Respectfully,

[Initialed]

José Mario del Valle
Inspector No. 16
México, D.F, November 30, 1963

[Certified May 7, 1964, by Noe Palomares, Chief Administrative Officer, Department of the Interior, Mexico.]

Commission Exhibit No. 2124

FD-302 (Rev. 3-3-59)

FEDERAL BUREAU OF INVESTIGATION

1

Date 11/28/63

Mrs. RUTH PAINE, 2515 W. 5th, furnished the following information regarding the day by day location of LEE HARVEY OSWALD:

February 22, 1963 ?	-	Mrs. PAINE believes this is the date she first met LEE and MARINA OSWALD at a party at the home of EVERETT GLOVER, Dallas, Texas.
March 20, 1963	-	Mrs. PAINE visited MARINA OSWALD at their residence, 214 W. Neeley. LEE was not present.
April 2, 1963	-	Mrs. PAINE had LEE and MARINA OSWALD for dinner at PAINE's home, Irving, Texas. Mr. MICHAEL PAINE, husband of RUTH, picked OSWALDs up at their apartment, 214 W. Neeley.
April 8, 1963	-	RUTH visited MARINA at MARINA's apartment. LEE was not present.
April 11, 1963	-	RUTH brought MARINA to her home in Irving. On this occasion or possibly on April 8, 1963, MARINA told RUTH that LEE OSWALD had asked her to return to Russia and indicated that LEE OSWALD was tired of the marriage. MARINA indicated she wanted to stay in the United States.
April 20, 1963	-	RUTH picnicked with LEE and MARINA at Oak Cliff near their residence.
April 24, 1963	-	RUTH went to the OSWALD residence. LEE OSWALD was packed and asked RUTH to take him to the bus station saying he was leaving to look for work in New Orleans. RUTH and MARINA took LEE to the bus station believed to be Trailways, Dallas. LEE bought a ticket for himself and one for MARINA. RUTH asked MARINA to stay with her in Irving while LEE was looking for a job. MARINA agreed to stay and LEE got a refund on her bus ticket. MARINA and her child moved into the PAINE residence, 2515 W. 5th,

381

on 11/26/63 at Irving, Texas File # DL 89-43

by Special Agents BARDWELL D. ODUM and JAMES P. HOSTY:vm Date dictated 11/27/63

This document contains neither recommendations nor conclusions of the FBI. It is the property of the FBI and is loaned to your agency; it and its contents are not to be distributed outside your agency.

COMMISSION EXHIBIT No. 2124

2

DL 89-43

Irving, Texas. On leaving the bus station, PAINE took LEE back to the OSWALD apartment. He had shipped some things at the bus station and was to pack up the rest of his things and return to the bus station in time to catch a night bus to New Orleans. PAINE let him off at his apartment about 4:00 or 5:00 p.m.

May 9, 1963	-	LEE OSWALD called MARINA at PAINE's home and stated he was living with his aunt and uncle in New Orleans and was working.
May 10, 1963	-	MARINA and RUTH PAINE drove from Dallas to Shreveport staying in a run-down motel across the street from the Holiday Inn on the north side of Highway 80 West.
May 11, 1963	-	MARINA and RUTH drove from Shreveport to New Orleans arriving about supper time at LEE OSWALD's uncle's home. PAINE believes his name was JOHN MURET. They went directly to an apartment LEE had rented at 4709 or 4907 Magazine.

On the morning of May 14, 1963, RUTH PAINE left New Orleans leaving MARINA and LEE in this apartment.

May 14, 1963, to September 20, 1963	-	During this period RUTH PAINE did not see LEE or MARINA OSWALD. She received one letter probably about June, 1963, in which MARINA stated she would soon have to return to Russia. RUTH wrote to tell her she could stay with her (RUTH).

Sometime probably in July, 1963, RUTH PAINE received a second letter from MARINA in which she stated she was in good health.

382

COMMISSION EXHIBIT No. 2124—Continued

About the end of August, 1963, RUTH received a letter from MARINA stating LEE was out of work again. RUTH wrote back asking if she could stop by New Orleans and see them when she returned to Texas after visiting her family in Philadelphia, Pennsylvania.

September 21, 1963 ? - RUTH PAINE arrived in New Orleans and visited the OSWALDs still living in the same apartment. LEE had been working previously but had lost his job. LEE mentioned that he had been in jail. RUTH asked MARINA if LEE had lost his job because of his political views. MARINA stated she did not know.

September 22, 1963 - RUTH PAINE remained at OSWALDs' apartment.

September 23, 1963 - MARINA left New Orleans with RUTH PAINE. LEE OSWALD stated he would go to Houston where he had a friend and look for work. He also mentioned he might go to Philadelphia. On that night MARINA and RUTH stayed in a motel just across the line in Texas.

September 24, 1963 - MARINA and RUTH PAINE arrived at Irving.

October 4, 1963 - LEE OSWALD called MARINA at Mrs. PAINE's home in Irving. He wanted MARINA to have Mrs. PAINE pick him up. MARINA told him that Mrs. PAINE could not come because she had just given blood. Mrs. PAINE produced a receipt for blood donated on October 4, 1963, at Parkland Hospital for MARINA OSWALD, by which Mrs. PAINE fixed the date that LEE OSWALD contacted MARINA. This card is signed B. WHITNEY.

LEE OSWALD arrived at the PAINE residence, Irving, while RUTH PAINE was gone. She returned from grocery shopping before dark

383

COMMISSION EXHIBIT No. 2124—Continued

and found him at the house. He stated he had been in Houston but had not found work. He also claimed to have been in Dallas for a few days before coming out to the house.

October 5 and 6, 1963 - LEE OSWALD remained at the PAINE residence throughout this period.

October 7, 1963 - RUTH PAINE took LEE OSWALD to the bus station in Irving. At this time she gave him an Enco map with Dallas on one side and Fort Worth on the other side. She recalled that sometime during this time LEE stated he stayed at the YMCA.

Either on this date or some time in the next day or two, LEE OSWALD called the PAINE residence to report that he had moved to a $7.00 a week room. He gave MARINA OSWALD a telephone number and MARINA contacted him at that telephone number at least once.

October 12, 1963 - LEE OSWALD arrived at the PAINE residence and spent the night.

October 13, 1963 - LEE OSWALD was at the PAINE home all during this day and night.

October 14, 1963 - RUTH PAINE took LEE OSWALD to the bus station in Irving.

October 15, 1963 - RUTH PAINE did not see LEE OSWALD on this date but she learned through telephone conversations that LEE had started to work at the Texas School Book Depository. Mrs. PAINE had located this job for him through a sister of WESLEY FRAZIER with whom RUTH was having coffee at her nextdoor neighbor's. WESLEY FRAZIER lives a few doors away and works at the Texas School Book Depository.

384

COMMISSION EXHIBIT No. 2124—Continued

5
DL 89-43

October 18, 1963	-	LEE OSWALD arrived at the PAINE home having obtained a ride with WESLEY FRAZIER from work. This was LEE's birthday.
October 19, 1963	-	LEE spent entire day and night at PAINE's residence.
October 20, 1963	-	MARINA OSWALD had labor pains and Mrs. PAINE took her to Parkland Hospital while LEE OSWALD babysat with his older child and Mrs. PAINE's children. MARINA gave birth to a girl, named AUDREY MARINA RACHEL OSWALD, at 10:41 p.m., Parkland Hospital in Dallas.
October 21, 1963	-	LEE OSWALD left for work with WESLEY FRAZIER. He returned that night to the PAINE residence and Mrs. PAINE finally got him to go visit his wife and the baby at the Parkland Hospital. LEE OSWALD did not want to go and RUTH PAINE's theory was that he did not want the hospital to find out he was working for fear they would bill him for the cost of delivery.
October 22, 1963	-	LEE OSWALD went to work with WESLEY FRAZIER. MARINA came to RUTH PAINE's home from the hospital with her new baby.
October 25, 1963	-	LEE OSWALD came out after work with WESLEY FRAZIER and saw his wife and baby for the first time after they had left the hospital.
October 26 and 27, 1963		LEE spent the day and night at the PAINE home.
October 28, 1963	-	LEE went to work in the morning with WESLEY FRAZIER. During this period LEE called and talked with his wife almost every night.

385

6
DL 89-43

November 1, 1963	-	LEE OSWALD came to the PAINE residence after work with WESLEY FRAZIER.
November 2 and 3, 1963		LEE spent entire day and night both dates at the PAINE home.
November 4, 1963	-	LEE went to work in the morning with WESLEY FRAZIER.
November 8, 1963	-	LEE OSWALD came to the PAINE home after work with WESLEY FRAZIER.
November 9, 1963	-	Mrs. PAINE drove to the driver's license office located in Oak Cliff to try to help LEE OSWALD get a learner's permit. LEE was not able to drive a car and had never learned. He had never held a driver's license. He told RUTH PAINE that once he had driven his uncle's car in New Orleans but RUTH PAINE recalls helping him try to learn how to drive and park the car. They were unable to get a learner's permit on this date since the office was closed due to it being an election day.
November 10, 1963	-	LEE spent the entire day at the PAINE home watching television. He spent that night there also.
November 11, 1963	-	This was a holiday. He stayed at the PAINE residence this entire day and night. He practiced parking for a short period with Mrs. PAINE's car. Mrs. PAINE was gone for two or three hours this date but LEE was there when she left and there when she came back.
November 12, 1963	-	LEE OSWALD left with WESLEY FRAZIER in the morning to go to work.
November 18, 1963	-	Mrs. PAINE placed a call for MARINA OSWALD to a WHitehall number which LEE had given her as his residence telephone number.

386

Mrs. PAINE asked for Mr. OSWALD and was told that no one by that name lived there. She asked if this was the number repeating it and was told it was. She then asked if this was a rooming house and was told it was.

November 19, 1963 ? - LEE OSWALD called MARINA at the PAINE residence and bawled her out for trying to call him the previous day. He instructed MARINA, according to what she told RUTH PAINE, to get hold of RUTH PAINE's address book and scratch out the WHitehall number which was written there.

November 20, 1963 - Whereas LEE had usually called his wife once a day he did not call on this date.

November 21, 1963 - LEE OSWALD arrived about 5:15 p.m. at the PAINE residence having come out with WESLEY FRAZIER. He was not expected and it was unusual since he had never come before on Thursday night and had very seldom come on a weekday and had never come before without calling to ask if he could come out. On this night he said to MARINA that they should get their own apartment. Mrs. PAINE did not see him in the garage of her home but someone had been moving things around in the garage. LEE OSWALD went to bed early, about 8:00 or 9:00 p.m.

November 22, 1963 - Mrs. PAINE was up at 7:30 a.m. and found that LEE OSWALD had already arisen and departed. She found a coffee cup which had been used in the kitchen and believes he fixed himself a cup of coffee before leaving.

November 23, 1963 - LEE OSWALD called RUTH PAINE twice in rapid succession telling her he wanted her to get in touch with a Mr. ABT, an attorney in New York City, and ask him to defend OSWALD in his trial for the murder of President JOHN

387

KENNEDY. These calls were received some time in the evening probably around 7:30 p.m.

Mrs. PAINE maintains a calendar with notations made on certain dates and she referred to this calender in fixing many of the dates set forth above.

Mrs. RUTH PAINE advised that LEE OSWALD received about $50.00 per week gross from his employer, Texas School Book Depository, and that he was paid twice a month by them, the first pay being October 29, 1963. She stated she recalls seeing him cash what she believes was a pay check at the A & P in Irving while she was buying groceries. This check was for about $50.00 and was some time in the period between October 29 and November 2, 1963.

She stated she knew of no bank account he might have used and she knows of no other income he had other than unemployment compensation and wages. She stated she had never observed him in possession of any sizeable amount of money and that he spent very little.

388

FD-302 (Rev. 3-3-59)

FEDERAL BUREAU OF INVESTIGATION

1

Date 2/7/64

Mr. MIKE CARRIER, Rambler Motel, Waskom, Texas, while being contacted on another matter, volunteered that he and his brother, EUGENE CARRIER, operate this motel and are assisted by Mrs. EUGENE CARRIER.

After reading in the newspaper about the assassination of President JOHN F. KENNEDY, his brother, EUGENE, while looking through registration cards for the year 1963, discovered the following described registration card: RUTH PAINE, 2515 W. 5th St., Irving, Texas, driving a Chevrolet with Texas License NK 4041, registered on September 23, 1963, for two persons in Room 10 at the rate of $6. The identity of the second person is not recorded on the registration card.

Mr. CARRIER said the writing on the above registration card is in the handwriting of the motel guest, with the exception of "9-23-63", which is in his handwriting.

Mr. CARRIER said he is unable to recall RUTH PAINE or the other guest who occupied Room 10, and has discussed it with Mr. and Mrs. EUGENE CARRIER, and they also were unable to recall these particular guests. Further, he stated all of them have seen photographs of LEE HARVEY OSWALD, his wife, and JACK RUBY, and cannot recall any of them as having been a guest of the motel at any time.

Mr. CARRIER furnished the above-described registration card, requesting it be returned to him when no longer needed.

– Commission Exhibit No. 2125 –

475

on 2/5/64 at Waskom, Texas File # DL 100-10461

by Special Agent ROBERT J. STEVENS/nc Date dictated 2/6/64

This document contains neither recommendations nor conclusions of the FBI. It is the property of the FBI and is loaned to your agency; it and its contents are not to be distributed outside your agency.

COMMISSION EXHIBIT No. 2125

FD-302 (Rev. 3-3-59)

FEDERAL BUREAU OF INVESTIGATION

1

Date 2/11/64

On February 5, 1964, while contacting Mr. MIKE CARRIER, Rambler Motel, Waskom, Texas, it was observed that the Rambler Motel is several years old and is located on the south side of U. S. Highway 80 in the east end of the business district of Waskom, Texas, approximately three blocks from the Texas-Louisiana State line. This motel is of one story brick construction, approximately twenty connected units, in an "L" shape, with one section running north and south and the other going east from this section. The motel is on raised ground with the "L" open to Highway 80.

476

on 2/5/64 at Waskom, Texas File # DL 100-10461

by Special Agent ROBERT J. STEVENS:vm Date dictated 2/7/64

This document contains neither recommendations nor conclusions of the FBI. It is the property of the FBI and is loaned to your agency; it and its contents are not to be distributed outside your agency.

COMMISSION EXHIBIT No. 2125—Continued

FD-302 (Rev. 3-3-59) FEDERAL BUREAU OF INVESTIGATION

Date 3/2/64

1

Mrs. RUTH PAINE, 2515 W. 5th Street, Irving, Texas, was exhibited a motel registration card obtained from Mr. MIKE CARRIER, Rambler Motel, Waskom, Texas, which is identified as Item DL-39.

Mrs. PAINE identified the handwriting on the above-described registration card as being her handwriting. She stated the car license number NK 4041 for the State of Texas is the license number on her 1955 Chevrolet four door, two tone green, station wagon.

Mrs. PAINE described the motel, the name of which motel and the city in which located she could not recall, as being located on the south side of the road shortly after leaving the State of Louisiana coming into Texas.

Mrs. PAINE stated that MARINA OSWALD was with her at the time she visited this motel on September 23, 1963, as indicated on the registration card but that MARINA OSWALD stayed in the car while she (Mrs. PAINE) registered.

Mrs. PAINE described the motel as a 10-15 unit motel, "L" shaped with one portion running north and south, and the other running east from the south end of the first portion. She does not remember the color of the motel. Mrs. PAINE stated she and MARINA OSWALD occupied a room in this motel near the middle section which runs east from the south end of the portion that runs north and south. The entire motel is one story. She stated it was not a new motel and that the only parking was that in front of the entrance to the motel rooms.

477

on 2/28/64 at Irving, Texas File # DL 100-10461

by Special Agent BARDWELL D. ODUM and JAMES P. HOSTY, Jr.:vm Date dictated 2/29/64

This document contains neither recommendations nor conclusions of the FBI. It is the property of the FBI and is loaned to your agency; it and its contents are not to be distributed outside your agency.

FD-302 (Rev. 3-3-59) FEDERAL BUREAU OF INVESTIGATION

Date 3/2/64

1

There was observed on the afternoon of February 28, 1964, parked at 2515 W. 5th Street, Irving, Texas, which is the residence of Mrs. RUTH PAINE, a 1955 Chevrolet four door, two tone green, station wagon, bearing 1963 Texas license NK 4041, which automobile was identified by Mrs. PAINE as belonging to her.

on 2/28/64 at Irving, Texas File # DL 100-10461

by Special Agent BARDWELL D. ODUM and JAMES P. HOSTY, Jr.:vm Date dictated 2/29/64

This document contains neither recommendations nor conclusions of the FBI. It is the property of the FBI and is loaned to your agency; it and its contents are not to be distributed outside your agency.

FD-302 (Rev. 1-25-60) FEDERAL BUREAU OF INVESTIGATION

Date 12/11/63

1 .

— Commission Exhibit No. 2126 —

EARL SPENCER ANDERSON, Badge 171, residence address 6554 Jefferson Highway (Harahan), New Orleans 23, Louisiana, advised that he knew where the OSWALD apartment was located at 4905 Magazine Street, near Upperline. He stated that he did not recognize a photograph of OSWALD and cannot recall seeing him. He recalled seeing a station wagon parked in front of the OSWALD apartment for one or two days several months ago. He cannot state when he saw the station wagon, but remembered that it was parked in front of the OSWALD apartment for one or two days. He further recalled one evening on a trip toward Canal Street where he had stopped at the corner of Magazine and Upperline Streets to pick up a passenger. He observed a man walking on the lake side of Magazine Street at the corner of Upperline, carrying two suitcases and walking toward the bus. ANDERSON said he waited for this individual to get on the bus and that this person asked if he could put his two suitcases by the driver's seat. This individual had one small suitcase which he placed alongside the bus driver's seat and a larger suitcase which he placed in the space behind the bus driver's seat. After this individual paid his fare, he inquired as to the best route to the Greyhound Bus Station. ANDERSON said that he told him that he should stay on the Magazine bus until he got to Canal Street at which point he should transfer to a Canal streetcar going toward the lake. When this streetcar got to Elks Place, he instructed the individual to get off the streetcar and transfer to a Tulane bus at Elks Place and Canal Street which would take him to the Greyhound Bus Station, which is located on Tulane Avenue and South Claiborne Avenue. ANDERSON was unable to describe the color of the suitcases but recalled that they, although they were not new, were not in a dilapidated condition. They bore no tags or stickers to the best of his recollection. He said the small suitcase was rectangular shaped piece of luggage approximately 22 inches long. The larger suitcase was the same shape as the smaller one and it was about 29 inches long.

ANDERSON could not describe this individual except to state that he spoke in a pleasant voice and that

On 12/11/63 at New Orleans, Louisiana File # NO 100-16601

by SA MILTON R. KAACK and SA ROBERT M. WHOMSLEY :lav Date dictated 12/11/63

This document contains neither recommendations nor conclusions of the FBI. It is the property of the FBI and is loaned to your agency; it and its contents are not to be distributed outside your agency.

10

NO 100-16601/lav
2

he believes he had some sort of jacket or sweater on, since he does not recall that he was just in his shirt sleeves.

11

UNITED STATES DEPARTMENT OF JUSTICE

FEDERAL BUREAU OF INVESTIGATION

In Reply, Please Refer to
File No.

Dallas, Texas
May 7, 1964

LEE HARVEY OSWALD

The following investigation was conducted concerning two traveling bags believed to have been the property of LEE HARVEY OSWALD, which have been designated Commission Exhibits A-1 and C-254. These articles are described as follows:

A-1 is a cloth zipper bag, blue in color, with black plastic edgings and two plastic handles. This bag has a zipper at the top and on one side. It measures approximately 21" long, by 11" high, by 9 1/2" wide. There are no markings on this bag.

Exhibit C-254 is a cloth bag, green in color, known as a "Bee 4" bag. It measures approximately 24" long, by 18" high, by 11" wide. Exhibit C-254 has markings in yellow on one side of the bag. These markings are the date "9/26" and an unreadable mark above the numeral "26" which may be an initial.

On the top portion of C-254 are two fragments of what appear to be bus company stickers and a small decal believed to be the trademark of the bag. The printing on the fragments of the stickers is red in color and the fragment located above the decal appears to be a form of the Continental Trailways Company. Attached to the handle of C-254 is the top portion of a baggage check of the Continental Trailways.

On April 30, 1964, SHAN BENTLEY, Supervisor, Stationery Supplies, Continental Trailways, 1500 Jackson Street, Dallas, Texas, was exhibited photographs of the two above-described traveling bags. Upon viewing photographs depicting portions of two paper stickers affixed to the top surface of Exhibit C-254, and a photograph depicting the top portion of a baggage check

COMMISSION EXHIBIT No. 2127

Re: LEE HARVEY OSWALD

tied to the handle of Exhibit C-254, BENTLEY identified the adhesive stickers as sensitized identification labels utilized by Continental Trailways for customers' convenience in further identifying their baggage, and BENTLEY identified the baggage check tied to the handle of Exhibit C-254 as the top portion of a Continental Trailways baggage check.

BENTLEY furnished samples of the adhesive-backed identification labels and it was noted they are printed on slick white paper in red ink and the words "Continental Trailways" appear across the top of the sticker, followed by three ruled lines and the words "Name, Address, City." Printed across the bottom of the sticker are the words "Route of the SILVER EAGLES." BENTLEY advised these stickers have a sensitized adhesive back, indicating the stickers are affixed to the baggage by peeling off a paper backing which protects the adhesive surface. BENTLEY advised the adhesive-backed identification label has been in use by Continental Trailways since May 1962 and that previously the company utilized string-tie identification labels similar to the baggage checks.

BENTLEY stated his records reflected that the first order for the new sensitized identification label was placed in April 1962 for one million labels, and that delivery was made on May 23, 1962, at which time the labels were immediately dispersed to all Continental Trailways outlets. The labels are described as 1 1/4" x 2 7/16" in size and are shipped 1,000 per roll. BENTLEY stated these labels are purchased from the Printer, Allen, and Company, Post Office Box 169, Arlington, Texas.

With regard to the photograph depicting a torn upper portion of a baggage check, BENTLEY advised that the baggage check affixed to the handle of Exhibit C-254 in the photograph bears the number 2-1125-2 in the upper right-hand portion and the note "Form No. T-13" in the upper left-hand portion, indicating that this is a portion of a baggage check discontinued since January 1964.

BENTLEY stated the baggage check now in use is identical in format with the exception that the printer's mat number set

- 2 -

COMMISSION EXHIBIT No. 2127—Continued

forth in the upper right-hand corner is now Number 2-4672-3, and that the upper left-hand corner now bears the Continental Trailways symbol instead of the note "Form No. T-13." BENTLEY added that in addition, the new tag is printed in black ink, whereas the discontinued tag was printed in blue ink. BENTLEY advised the first order for new baggage check number 2-4672-3 was first placed with the printer August 31, 1963; however, due to the large backlog of old tags in the hands of the printer, this baggage tag was still in use as of January 1964, and, in fact, the last order of the old tag was received in early January 1964. BENTLEY was unable to advise as to the significance of the printer's mat number located in the upper right-hand corner of the baggage check; however, BENTLEY stated baggage checks for the Continental Trailways system are printed by the Ennis Business Forms Company, Ennis, Texas.

BENTLEY observed further that the brown manila patch at the top portion of the baggage check bears the words "Continental Trailways, Dallas, Texas." BENTLEY advised that all baggage checks for the Continental Trailways system which are dispersed through the Stationery Supply Center in Dallas bear the same designation, "Continental Trailways, Dallas, Texas," and that this indicates simply that the baggage checks are handled through the Dallas Stationery Supply Center. BENTLEY stated that the Dallas Stationery Supply Center supplies all Continental facilities throughout the States of Texas and Arkansas and the Rocky Mountain area. He stated that other Stationery Supply Centers are located in Omaha, Nebraska; Alexandria, Virginia; Wichita, Kansas; and, Los Angeles, California, and that supplies, including baggage checks, dispersed through those centers would accordingly bear the name of the supplying city.

With regard to the photograph of Exhibit C-254 depicting yellow chalk markings on the side, BENTLEY advised he is sure the Continental Trailways, within the realm of his experience, does not utilize such system. He feels sure this method of identification is not in use by any other bus company.

On April 30, 1964, Mr. CYRUS H. TOLMAN, Director of Traffic and Sales, Continental Trailways, 315 Continental Avenue,

Dallas, Texas, was exhibited photographs of the two above-described traveling bags. Upon viewing the photographs depicting two partial stickers affixed to the top surface of Exhibit C-254, Mr. TOLMAN readily identified these stickers as portions of sensitized adhesive identification labels which are furnished to customers at the time they check their baggage into the bus station, preparatory to their departure. The customer is requested at that time to fill in his name, address and city on the face of the label and to affix the adhesive-backed label to his baggage. Mr. TOLMAN advised that these sensitized labels are the only such labels utilized by Continental Trailways in the general course of business, and that the two photographs of the portions of the top surface of Exhibit C-254 may be the top right-hand portion of one label and the other portion represents the lower left-hand corner of an identification label.

TOLMAN pointed out further that the sensitized adhesive identification label has only been in use by Continental Trailways Company since the spring of 1962. Prior to that time, TOLMAN advised, the company had utilized a string-tie identification tag similar in appearance to the baggage check.

With respect to the baggage check, TOLMAN advised the torn baggage check portion depicted in the photograph as being affixed to Exhibit C-254 is of a type discontinued by Continental Trailways about January 1964, indicating this tag was undoubtedly issued to a customer prior to that time.

TOLMAN advised the format of both tags is identical with the exception that the note "Form No. T-13" set forth in the upper left-hand corner of the discontinued tag have been replaced with a Continental Trailways symbol and the new tag is now printed in black ink, whereas the previous tag was printed in blue ink.

TOLMAN viewed the photograph of Exhibit C-254 reflecting markings in yellow chalk consisting of the numerals "9/26" and a third indistinguishable mark above the "26". TOLMAN advised that Continental Trailways has a strict policy against marking or defacing the customers' bags in any way, and all identifying markings and data are affixed to the customers' bags by string-ties or adhesive labels. TOLMAN stated further that he was not aware of any system of marking customers' bags with chalk utilized by any bus company, railroad, or airline operating in the Continental United States. TOLMAN suggested, however, that this system of marking would be unique in itself and might possibly be prevalent in Mexico or used by other foreign travel services.

On May 1, 1964, LEONARD F. GEHRIG, Financial Vice President, Ennis Business Forms, 214 Knox Street, Ennis, Texas, advised that for the last two years his company has been commissioned by Continental Trailways to print baggage checks, as well as other material for that company, in accordance with a nationally adopted format. GEHRIG exhibited a Continental Trailways baggage check formerly printed for and utilized by Continental Trailways bearing in the upper right-hand corner of the tag the number 2-1125-2 and bearing in the upper left-hand corner "Form No. T-13." GEHRIG explained that the note "Form No. T-13" represent a format recommended by the Interstate Commerce Commission for use by all common carriers and is a generally accepted and widely used form. GEHRIG explained that the number set forth in the upper right-hand corner represents a printing mat number and that all baggage checks printed according to that format bear a printer's mat number for reference purposes.

GEHRIG stated the initial order for this tag was received by his firm from Continental Trailways on March 14, 1962, requesting a printing of 600,000 baggage check tags using printer's mat number 2-1125-2 for format. GEHRIG advised there was a total of two orders under printing mat number 2-1125-2 and that periodic shipment of these orders was made in 1962 and 1963, as follows:

Order of March 14, 1962 - For 600,000 tags - blue ink
Series 300-001 through 900-000

Shipments	Amount	For
4/11/62	200,000 tags	Dallas Continental Trailways
5/25/62	200,000 tags	Dallas Continental Trailways
5/28/62	200,000 tags	Dallas Continental Trailways

COMMISSION EXHIBIT No. 2127—Continued

Order of January 11, 1963 - For 750,000 tags - blue ink
Series 100-001 through 850-000

Shipments	Amount	For
3/29/63	250,000 tags	Dallas Continental Trailways
7/15/63	250,000 tags	Dallas Continental Trailways

Third shipment completed
10/30/63 - Break-down as follows:

10/8/63	-	Two cartons	-	Shipped	-	10,000 tags
10/9/63	-	Two cartons	-	Shipped	-	15,000 tags
10/18/63	-	Seven cartons	-	Shipped	-	70,000 tags
10/30/63	-	Sixteen cartons	-	Shipped	-	155,000 tags
		TOTAL				250,000 tags

GEHRIG advised that the initial order for the new tag under printer's mat number 2-4672-3 was placed August 31, 1963, by Continental Trailways and indicated only minor changes from the previous baggage check in that Continental requested the new tag be printed in black ink and that the note "Form No. T-13" in the upper left-hand corner be replaced with the Continental Trailways copyrighted symbol. GEHRIG advised the first shipment of the new baggage check was made on January 13, 1964, for 175,000 tags which were shipped to Continental Trailways, Dallas.

GEHRIG advised that the printer's mat number 2-1125-2 has no significance in establishing when a particular tag was issued or through what Continental Trailways station other than to signify the tag was furnished to a customer sometime between April 1962 and January 1964. GEHRIG advised that all baggage checks furnished to the Dallas Office of Continental Trailways likewise bear the words "Continental Trailways, Dallas, Texas," on the brown reinforcing patch at the top portion of the baggage check.

COMMISSION EXHIBIT No. 2127—Continued

Re: LEE HARVEY OSWALD

On May 1, 1964, Mr. JOE R. MC REE, Secretary of Residence, Young Men's Christian Association (YMCA), 605 North Ervay Street, Dallas, Texas, advised that a check of his receipts for October 3, 1963, reflect that RAE G. BARKER, Desk Clerk, registered LEE HARVEY OSWALD on October 3, 1963. MC REE stated that to the best of his recollection he did not see LEE HARVEY OSWALD when he registered at the YMCA on October 3, 1963, or when he checked out on October 4, 1963.

MC REE was exhibited color photographs of Commission Exhibits A-1 and C-254, after which he stated to the best of his recollection he has never seen either of these traveling bags.

On May 1, 1964, Mr. RAE G. BARKER, Desk Clerk, Young Men's Christian Association (YMCA), 605 North Ervay Street, Dallas, Texas, advised he was on duty as Desk Clerk from 4:00 P.M. to 12:00 Midnight, on October 3, 1963. BARKER said, upon a review of receipts for October 3, 1963, he would estimate that he registered LEE HARVEY OSWALD into that YMCA, Room 601, between the hours of 4:00 P.M. and 4:30 P.M. He said he could not recall registering OSWALD, inasmuch as he registers numerous people throughout the day.

Mr. BARKER was exhibited color photographs of Commission Exhibits A-1 and C-254, described above, after which he stated he could not recall ever seeing these bags, and stated he does not know what type luggage LEE HARVEY OSWALD had at the time he registered into the YMCA on October 3, 1963.

On May 1, 1964, Mrs. EVA MARSHALL, 5932½ Oram, Dallas, Texas, advised she worked part-time as a Desk Clerk at the Young Men's Christian Association (YMCA), 605 North Ervay, Dallas, Texas. Mrs. MARSHALL said she was so employed between the hours of 8:00 A.M and 4:00 P.M., on October 4, 1963. Mrs. MARSHALL said she recalls the name LEE HARVEY OSWALD and recalls she checked him out of the YMCA sometime between noon and 4:00 P.M., to the best of her recollection. She said she recalls the incident because she thinks the name OSWALD is a very ugly name. She said to the best of her recollection OSWALD was alone.

- 7 -

COMMISSION EXHIBIT No. 2127—Continued

Re: LEE HARVEY OSWALD

Mrs. MARSHALL was exhibited color photographs of Commission Exhibits A-1 and C-254 and, after viewing same, stated she does not recall what bags OSWALD might have had with him when he checked out of the YMCA on October 4, 1963. She stated he probably placed any bags he had on the floor on the other side of the four-foot high desk from where she was standing. She stated she would not have been able to see any bags so placed.

On April 30, 1964, Mrs. MARY BLEDSOE, 621 North Marsalis, Dallas, Texas, advised that LEE HARVEY OSWALD formerly rented a room at her residence from October 7 through 14, 1963.

Mrs. BLEDSOE viewed photographs of two traveling bags identified as Commission Exhibits A-1 and C-254. She stated she recalls that at about 3:30 P.M. on Monday, October 7, 1963, OSWALD entered the house at 621 North Marsalis, Dallas, Texas, carrying a small, zipper-type bag similar in appearance to Commission Exhibit A-1; however, she was unable to state positively the bag in his possession at that time was identical to the photograph of Commission Exhibit A-1. She stated she could not recall any name tags or other identifying data being affixed to the bag and has no way of further identifying such bag.

Mrs. BLEDSOE stated that same Monday afternoon OSWALD left the rooming house shortly thereafter and returned in a short while, carrying a second, larger bag, but she stated she is unable to state if this bag was identical to the photograph of Commission Exhibit C-254. Mrs. BLEDSOE stated she paid little attention to the second bag and would be unable to state whether the bags were of the same type. She further stated she does not recall observing any tags or labels or other markings on the other bag which she observed OSWALD carrying, and has no way to further identify it.

On April 30, 1964, Mrs. GLADYS JOHNSON, 1026 North Beckley Street, Dallas, Texas, owner of a rooming house at that location where LEE HARVEY OSWALD formerly resided in October and November 1963, was exhibited photographs of two traveling bags identified as Commission Exhibits A-1 and C-254. She stated she

- 8 -

COMMISSION EXHIBIT No. 2127—Continued

recalls seeing OSWALD in possession of a bag similar in size, type and color to Commission Exhibit A-1. She does not recall observing OSWALD in possession of this bag at the time he rented the room, but stated she believes she observed him leaving the rooming house at about 11:30 A.M., Saturday morning, November 16, 1963, which she believes was the only weekend OSWALD spent at the rooming house. She stated she observed him walk across the street in the direction of a coin-operated laundromat. She was of the impression at that time that the bag contained dirty laundry and that OSWALD was taking the bag and contents to the laundry to wash his clothes. She stated OSWALD returned to the rooming house about forty-five minutes to one hour later and took the bag to his room. Mrs. JOHNSON stated she does not recall any tags or other marks of identification on this bag.

Mrs. JOHNSON advised she does not ever recall seeing a large bag similar to Commission Exhibit C-254 at any time in her rooming house in the possession of LEE HARVEY OSWALD.

On May 1, 1964, Mrs. RUTH PAINE, 2515 West 5th Street, Irving, Texas, furnished the following information after examining colored photographs of Commission Exhibits A-1 and C-254, previously described herein:

On October 4, 1963, when Mrs. PAINE arrived at her residence in Irving, Texas, LEE HARVEY OSWALD had already arrived at her home and she did not see what luggage, if any, he brought with him at that time.

On October 7, 1963, when OSWALD left Mrs. PAINE's home for Dallas, Texas, he had with him a bag similar to that depicted in the photograph of Commission Exhibit C-254, and she believes this is a photograph of the bag which he had with him at that time.

Mrs. PAINE advised she does not recall seeing the figures "9/26" at any time on the bag carried by OSWALD on October 7, 1963, or on a similar bag at any time.

At the time RUTH PAINE and MARINA OSWALD moved some of the OSWALD effects from New Orleans, Louisiana, to Irving, Texas, in Mrs. PAINE's Chevrolet Station Wagon, she does not specifically recall any bags resembling Commission Exhibits A-1 and C-254.

COMMISSION EXHIBIT No. 2127—Continued

FD-302 (Rev. 1-25-60)

FEDERAL BUREAU OF INVESTIGATION

Date May 6, 1964

EMILIO CASTILLO, Mexican Customs Inspector, viewed the photograph of the "Bee 4" bag, Commission Exhibit C 254 and advised that the yellow markings made on the side of the "Bee 4" bag were made by a Customs Inspector at the time the bag was checked into Mexico.

CASTILLO stated that the Customs Inspector who checked the bag would have written "9/26" to show that the bag was passed through Mexican Customs on that date and was okayed for entry into Mexico.

— Commission Exhibit No. 2128 —

On 5/5/64 at Nuevo Laredo, Mexico File # SA 105-2909

by SA ROBERT L. CHAPMAN / njs Date dictated 5/5/64

This document contains neither recommendations nor conclusions of the FBI. It is the property of the FBI and is loaned to your agency; it and its contents are not to be distributed outside your agency. -15-

COMMISSION EXHIBIT No. 2128

FD-302 (Rev. 1-25-60)

FEDERAL BUREAU OF INVESTIGATION

1

Date May 6, 1964

MIGUEL MORENO IBARRA, Chief of Mexican Customs Inspectors, International Bridge, Nuevo Laredo, Mexico, viewed the photograph of the "Bee 4" bag marked Commission Exhibit C 254, and stated that the yellow markings on the side of the bag were made by a Mexican Customs Inspector at Nuevo Laredo, Mexico, and denotes that this particular bag passed through Customs on September 26, 1963.

IBARRA explained that the yellow crayon marking system was one of two methods of marking luggage used by the Mexican Customs Inspectors. The other method is to seal the bag with tape or with a Customs sticker.

When the Mexican Customs official is busy with a lot of people passing through Customs, he will usually use the yellow crayon marking system. If the Customs official has more time he will use a sticker or colored tape and will initial the tape or sticker.

IBARRA explained that on September 26, 1963, there were six persons on duty in addition to the chief, and any of these persons could have checked the bag and made the yellow markings thereon.

On 5/5/64 at Nuevo Laredo, Mexico File # SA 105-2909

by SA ROBERT L. CHAPMAN/dnb Date dictated 5/5/64

This document contains neither recommendations nor conclusions of the FBI. It is the property of the FBI and is loaned to your agency; it and its contents are not to be distributed outside your agency.

-16-

COMMISSION EXHIBIT No. 2128—Continued

FD-204 (Rev. 3-3-59)

UNITED STATES DEPARTMENT OF JUSTICE
FEDERAL BUREAU OF INVESTIGATION

Copy to:

Report of: JOHN M. KEMMY Office: SAN ANTONIO
Date: April 30, 1964

File Number: 105-2909 Bureau File: 105-82555

Title: LEE HARVEY OSWALD

Character: INTERNAL SECURITY - RUSSIA - CUBA

Synopsis:

Investigation Greyhound Bus Station, U. S. Agencies, International Bridge, Laredo, Texas, as well as at Transportes del Norte, Nuevo Laredo, Texas, concerning 10/3/63 travel of OSWALD negative. Explanation of Flecha Roja Bus Line baggage guide list set out. Interviews with some persons who departed Mexico at Nuevo Laredo, Mexico, on 10/3/63 negative regarding OSWALD. Interviews with some persons who rode Greyhound Bus early a.m., on 10/3/63 for portions of trip between San Antonio, Texas, and Dallas, Texas, negative regarding OSWALD. DEWEY C. BRADFORD, Austin, Texas, observed an individual in Morgan's Gun Shop, Fort Worth, Texas, on the day before Texas-SMU football game played in Dallas, Texas, on 11/2/63, which individual was considered by BRADFORD to be rude and impertinent. This individual, who told BRADFORD he had been in Marine Corps, purchased rifle ammunition. BRADFORD could not recall caliber requested. At that time BRADFORD was with his wife and brother-in-law, H. V. WHITSON; when photographs of OSWALD were published in Life magazine all three agreed individual in Morgan's Gun Shop was OSWALD. WHITSON informed BRADFORD he knew this individual who had hung out at WHITSON's used car lot. Efforts to determine if OSWALD rented safety deposit box, Laredo, Texas, negative.

\- P -

— Commission Exhibit No. 2129 —

DETAILS:

I. TRAVEL

This document contains neither recommendations nor conclusions of any kind. It is the property of the FBI, and is a loan to your agency; it and/or its contents are not to be distributed outside your agency.

COMMISSION EXHIBIT No. 2129

FD-302 (Rev. 1-25-60) FEDERAL BUREAU OF INVESTIGATION

1

Date April 15, 1964

HARRY SMITH, Manager, Greyhound Bus Station, Laredo, Texas, advised that Greyhound Bus records at Laredo, Texas, disclosed a record of Exchange Order Number 43599 and shows this order processed at Laredo in the amount of $12.80. Mr. SMITH stated that $12.80 is the price of a one-way Greyhound Bus ticket from Laredo, Texas, to Dallas, Texas. Exchange Order Number 43599 was issued for Greyhound Bus ticket Number 8256009 and was issued by RAUL TIJERINA, Ticket Agent on duty from 12:00 midnight to 8:30 a.m. on October 3, 1963.

Mr. SMITH advised that according to Greyhound records, this was the only International Exchange order ticket issued on October 3, 1963. Mr. SMITH further advised that RAUL TIJERINA was on duty with REYMUNDO VERA, a porter, and that bus driver J. C. ROBISON was the driver of the Greyhound Bus that departed Laredo, Texas, at 3:00 a.m. on the morning of October 3, 1963, enroute to San Antonio and Dallas, Texas.

On 4/6/64 at Laredo, Texas File # SA 105-2909

by SA ROBERT L. CHAPMAN/dnb Date dictated 4/10/64

This document contains neither recommendations nor conclusions of the FBI. It is the property of the FBI and is loaned to your agency; it and its contents are not to be distributed outside your agency.

2

COMMISSION EXHIBIT No. 2129—Continued

FD-302 (Rev. 1-25-60) FEDERAL BUREAU OF INVESTIGATION

1

Date April 15, 1964

RAUL TIJERINA, Ticket Agent, Greyhound Bus Station, was interviewed and shown a photograph of LEE HARVEY OSWALD. TIJERINA advised that he was the Ticket Agent on duty at the Greyhound Bus Station, Laredo, Texas, from midnight to 8:30 a.m. on the morning of October 3, 1963, and that he issued Ticket Number 8256009 on International Exchange Order Number 43599. TIJERINA states that he does not recall this transaction specifically, and, after viewing a photograph of LEE HARVEY OSWALD, advised that he does not recall having issued a Greyhound Ticket Number 8256009 specifically to LEE HARVEY OSWALD and that the photograph did not appear to be familiar to him, TIJERINA.

TIJERINA advised that he had been previously interviewed concerning this matter and could not recall LEE HARVEY OSWALD having passed through the Greyhound Bus Station at Laredo, Texas, on the morning of October 3, 1963.

TIJERINA verified that the porter on duty with him the early morning of October 3, 1963, was REYMUNDO VERA.

On 4/6/64 at Laredo, Texas File # SA 105-2909

by SA ROBERT L. CHAPMAN/dnb Date dictated 4/10/64

This document contains neither recommendations nor conclusions of the FBI. It is the property of the FBI and is loaned to your agency; it and its contents are not to be distributed outside your agency.

3

COMMISSION EXHIBIT No. 2129—Continued

FD-302 (Rev. 1-25-60)

FEDERAL BUREAU OF INVESTIGATION

1

Date April 15, 1964

REYMUNDO VERA, Porter, Greyhound Bus Station, Laredo, Texas, was interviewed and was exhibited a photograph of LEE HARVEY OSWALD.

VERA advised that from the Greyhound Bus records, he had verified that he was on duty between midnight and 8:30 a.m. of October 3, 1963, but that he does not recall LEE HARVEY OSWALD as having been in the Greyhound Bus Terminal on the morning of October 3, 1963.

On 4/6/64 at Laredo, Texas File # SA 105-2909

by SA ROBERT L. CHAPMAN/dnb Date dictated 4/10/64

This document contains neither recommendations nor conclusions of the FBI. It is the property of the FBI and is loaned to your agency; it and its contents are not to be distributed outside your agency.

6

FD-302 (Rev. 1-25-60)

FEDERAL BUREAU OF INVESTIGATION

1

Date April 15, 1964

J. C. ROBISON, Bus Driver, Greyhound Bus Station, Laredo, Texas, advised that he was the driver of the Greyhound bus that departed Laredo, Texas, at 3:00 a.m. on the morning of October 3, 1963, enroute to San Antonio and Dallas, Texas. ROBISON advised that he was the driver of the bus only from Laredo, Texas, to San Antonio, Texas. ROBISON checked the "Dispatcher's Sheet" for October 3, 1963, which showed that he, ROBISON, departed Laredo, Texas, at 3:00 a.m. enroute to San Antonio, and that he had 21 passengers aboard, 20 of whom were enroute to San Antonio, Texas. Of the 20 going to San Antonio, 7 were continuing on north of San Antonio which could be to Dallas, and 3 were going east of San Antonio, which could be to Houston, Texas.

ROBISON viewed the photograph of LEE HARVEY OSWALD and advised that he could not recall LEE HARVEY OSWALD having been on the bus that he was driving from Laredo, to San Antonio, Texas, and further stated that he did not recall any person with a sack of bananas on the October 3, 1963, bus, from Laredo to San Antonio, Texas.

On 4/6/64 at Laredo, Texas File # SA 105-2909

by SA ROBERT L. CHAPMAN/dnb Date dictated 4/10/64

This document contains neither recommendations nor conclusions of the FBI. It is the property of the FBI and is loaned to your agency; it and its contents are not to be distributed outside your agency.

5

FD-302 (Rev. 1-25-60)

FEDERAL BUREAU OF INVESTIGATION

1

Date April 15, 1964

PEDRO MOLANO, Terminal Manager, Transportes del Norte , advised that Bus Number 373 arrived in Nuevo Laredo, Mexico, from Mexico City at 1:35 a.m., October 3, 1963, and was driven by ALVARO IBARRA whom, Mr. MOLANO stated, was presently in Monterrey, Mexico, but would return to Nuevo Laredo, Mexico, on April 7, 1964.

On 4/6/64 at Nuevo Laredo, Mexico File # SA 105-2909

by SAs ROBERT L. CHAPMAN and LEOPOLDO E. ARMIJO/dnb Date dictated 4/10/64

This document contains neither recommendations nor conclusions of the FBI. It is the property of the FBI and is loaned to your agency; it and its contents are not to be distributed outside your agency.

FD-302 (Rev. 1-25-60)

FEDERAL BUREAU OF INVESTIGATION

1

Date April 15, 1964

ALVARO IBARRA, Driver of Transportes Del Norte Bus Number 373 from Monterrey, Nuevo Leon, Mexico, to Nuevo Laredo, Tamaulipas, Mexico, the early morning of October 3, 1963, was interviewed at Multifamiliar Apartment Building, Nuevo Laredo, Mexico. Police Officer RODOLFO GUZMAN, Nuevo Laredo Police Department, was present during the interview.

IBARRA advised that he could not recall any incident with Mexican Immigration that he could place as being on October 3, 1963. IBARRA stated that Bus Number 373 that he drives from Monterrey to Nuevo Laredo, Mexico, is the direct connection for Chicago, Illinois, and almost daily Mexican Immigration takes persons off the bus to check their papers since people of all nationalities ride this bus.

IBARRA could recall no one with bananas and stated that he drove Bus Number 373 all the way to the Greyhound Terminal in Laredo, Texas, and was with the bus and the passengers as they checked through the Mexican and American authorities.

IBARRA viewed a photograph of LEE HARVEY OSWALD, and he stated that he had commented when he first saw OSWALD's photograph in newspapers following the assassination of President KENNEDY that the "face of OSWALD did not appear unfamiliar." IBARRA continued that he was not sure if he had ever seen OSWALD and could not place him on Bus Number 373 from Monterrey, Nuevo Leon, Mexico, to Nuevo Laredo, Mexico, and Laredo, Texas, on the morning of October 3, 1963.

IBARRA advised that he, IBARRA, was the only driver and the entire run from Monterrey is at night and only covers a period of approximately four hours, whereas the trip from Mexico City to Monterrey, Mexico, on the connecting bus covers a much longer period, including daylight hours, and has two bus drivers.

On 4/7/64 at Nuevo Laredo, Mexico File # SA 105-2909

by SAs LEOPOLDO E. ARMIJO and ROBERT L. CHAPMAN/dnb Date dictated 4/13/64

This document contains neither recommendations nor conclusions of the FBI. It is the property of the FBI and is loaned to your agency; it and its contents are not to be distributed outside your agency.

FD-302 (Rev. 1-25-60)

FEDERAL BUREAU OF INVESTIGATION

1.

Date April 15, 1964

WALTER SEAWELL, Inspector in Charge, U. S. Customs, Laredo, Texas, advised that the normal procedure at the International Bridge on the midnight to 8:00 a.m. shift concerning the checking of busses from Mexico is that the bus will pull into the U. S. Customs check points at the International Bridge and all passengers will unload. Those persons who have been to the interior of Mexico and do not have smallpox vaccinations must report to the United States Public Health Service for vaccinations. Those passengers who are not citizens must report to Immigration and Naturalization Service and produce proper documents for entrance into the United States. All baggage is checked through the U. S. Customs by the Customs Inspector. The United States Department of Agriculture Inspector checks for plants and helps Customs or other Inspectors. All Inspectors on duty, that is, U. S. Department of Agriculture, U. S. Public Health, Immigration and Naturalization Service, or U. S. Customs Service, may assist each other since they are the only authorities on duty at the International Bridge between midnight and 8:00 a.m.

Mr. SEAWELL advised that Customs records disclose that two busses entered the United States from Mexico between midnight and 8:00 a.m. on the morning of October 3, 1963, and that these two busses contained a total of 15 passengers and 32 pieces of luggage. Mr. SEAWELL advised that the passengers are not identified and that only the baggage claim ticket number is listed on the Customs record and that this record is actually filled out by the employees of the Mexican Bus service prior to the bus entering the United States and that this baggage form that is filled out by the bus company employees is turned over to the U. S. Customs Inspector by the driver of the bus.

On 4/6/64 at Laredo, Texas File # SA 105-2909

by SA ROBERT L CHAPMAN/dnb Date dictated 4/10/64

This document contains neither recommendations nor conclusions of the FBI. It is the property of the FBI and is loaned to your agency; it and its contents are not to be distributed outside your agency.

FD-302 (Rev. 1-25-60)

FEDERAL BUREAU OF INVESTIGATION

1

Date April 15, 1964

VICTOR GUNNOE, U. S. Customs Inspector, International Bridge, Laredo, Texas, advised that he was on duty at the International Bridge from midnight, October 3, 1963, until 8:00 a.m., October 3, 1963.

GUNNOE was shown photograph of LEE HARVEY OSWALD, and he advised that he did not recall LEE HARVEY OSWALD having checked through the International Bridge, Laredo, Texas, during his shift from 12:00 midnight to 8:00 a.m., October 3, 1963.

GUNNOE advised he did not recall any incident where an individual had checked with the Customs Inspector or any authorities on duty concerning the entry of bananas into the United States. GUNNOE advised that it is legal for people to bring bananas into the United States and that any inquiry concerning the entry of bananas would have been answered by any American authorities on duty at the International Bridge with the statement that the bananas could be brought into the United States.

On 4/6/64 at Laredo, Texas File # SA 105-2909

by SA ROBERT L. CHAPMAN/dnb Date dictated 4/10/64

This document contains neither recommendations nor conclusions of the FBI. It is the property of the FBI and is loaned to your agency; it and its contents are not to be distributed outside your agency.

FD-302 (Rev. 1-25-60)

FEDERAL BUREAU OF INVESTIGATION

1

Date April 15, 1964

WILLIAM S. HUNTER, U. S. Immigration Inspector, Immigration and Naturalization Service, International Bridge, Laredo, Texas, advised that he was on duty between midnight and 8:00 a.m. on the morning of October 3, 1963.

HUNTER was exhibited the photograph of LEE HARVEY OSWALD, and he advised that he did not recall OSWALD having passed through the U. S. Immigration and Naturalization Service on the morning of October 3, 1963.

HUNTER further advised that he did not recall any incident where a person had made inquiry concerning the entry of a sack of bananas into the United States on the morning of October 3, 1963.

On 4/6/64 at Laredo, Texas File # SA 105-2909

by SA ROBERT L. CHAPMAN/dnb Date dictated 4/10/64

This document contains neither recommendations nor conclusions of the FBI. It is the property of the FBI and is loaned to your agency; it and its contents are not to be distributed outside your agency.

10

COMMISSION EXHIBIT No. 2129—Continued

FD-302 (Rev. 1-25-60)

FEDERAL BUREAU OF INVESTIGATION

1

Date April 15, 1964

ABRAHAM DILLY, U. S. Border Quarantine Inspector, U. S. Public Health, International Bridge, Laredo, Texas, advised that he was the U. S. Quarantine Inspector on duty at the International Bridge from 12:00 midnight to 8:00 a.m. on October 3, 1963.

DILLY was exhibited a photograph of LEE HARVEY OSWALD, and he advised that he did not recall LEE HARVEY OSWALD having been checked through the International Bridge between 12:00 midnight and 8:00 a.m. on October 3, 1963.

DILLY advised that he did not recall any incident where anyone had asked concerning the entry of bananas on the morning of October 3, 1963.

On 4/6/64 at Laredo, Texas File # SA 105-2909

by SA ROBERT L. CHAPMAN/dnb Date dictated 4/10/64

This document contains neither recommendations nor conclusions of the FBI. It is the property of the FBI and is loaned to your agency; it and its contents are not to be distributed outside your agency.

11

COMMISSION EXHIBIT No. 2129—Continued

FD-302 (Rev. 1-25-60)

FEDERAL BUREAU OF INVESTIGATION

1

Date April 15, 1964

RAY W. BAKER, Plant Quarantine Inspector, U. S. Department of Agriculture, International Bridge, Laredo, Texas, advised that he was on duty at the International Bridge from 12:00 midnight until 8:00 a.m. the morning of October 3, 1963.

BAKER viewed a photograph of LEE HARVEY OSWALD, and he advised that he did not recall OSWALD having passed through the International Bridge during his shift from midnight to 8:00 a.m. on October 3, 1963.

BAKER advised that the situation concerning the entry of bananas into the United States is that they can be brought into the United States by anyone and that inquiries concerning the entry of bananas would have been answered to the effect that the bananas could be brought into the United States. BAKER advised that he did not specifically recall anyone asking or making any inquiry concerning the entry of bananas on the morning of October 3, 1963.

On 4/6/64 at Laredo, Texas File # SA 105-2909

by SA ROBERT L. CHAPMAN/dnb Date dictated 4/10/64

This document contains neither recommendations nor conclusions of the FBI. It is the property of the FBI and is loaned to your agency; it and its contents are not to be distributed outside your agency.

12

FD-302 (Rev. 1-25-60)

FEDERAL BUREAU OF INVESTIGATION

1

Date April 15, 1964

M. L. MURPHY, U. S. Customs, Laredo, Texas, furnished a copy of "Inward Manifest of Baggage Car, Bureau of Customs," Form 7533-A. Mr. MURPHY stated that this form is filled out by the Mexican transportation company on all passengers coming from Mexico to the United States. Mr. MURPHY furnished the "Inward Manifest of Baggage Car" form filled out by Transportes Del Norte for Bus Number 396 (note this should be for Bus Number 373) from Monterrey, Mexico, to Laredo, Texas, for October 3, 1963. The driver of the Transportes Del Norte bus was A. IBARRA, who surrendered the Form 7533-A to U. S. Customs Inspector VDG (VICTOR D. GUNNOE) who marked this form "cleared 10/3/63, VDG 2:30 AM." This form lists the baggage by claim check number and reflects that 18 pieces of baggage were on the bus.

On 4/8/64 at Laredo, Texas File # SA 105-2909

by SA ROBERT L. CHAPMAN/dnb Date dictated 4/13/64

This document contains neither recommendations nor conclusions of the FBI. It is the property of the FBI and is loaned to your agency it and its contents are not to be distributed outside your agency.

13

COMMISSION EXHIBIT No. 2129—Continued

1

Date April 16, 1964

LEOBARDO MEDELLIN, Assistant Manager, Transportes Del Norte Bus Company, Nuevo Laredo, Mexico, advised that on the morning of October 3, 1963, between the hours of 12:00 midnight and 8:00 a.m. only two busses arrived at Nuevo Laredo, Mexico, and crossed to Laredo, Texas. These two busses should have been Bus Number 352 from Monterrey, Nuevo Leon, Mexico, and Bus Number 373 from Monterrey, Nuevo Leon, Mexico. Transportes Del Norte Bus Number 352 arrived at Laredo, Texas, at 1:25 a.m.

MEDELLIN stated Transportes Del Norte Bus Number 373 arrived from Monterrey, Nuevo Leon, Mexico, at approximately 1:25 a.m. and crossed into Laredo, Texas, at approximately 2:30 a.m. and the driver was ALVARO IBARRA.

MEDELLIN stated that the "Inward Manifest of Baggage Car," Form Number 7533-A, showing Bus Number 396 arriving in Laredo, Texas, at 2:30 a.m. and being driven by A. IBARRA is in error as to the number of the bus since it definitely should have been marked Bus Number 373.

MEDELLIN further advised that Transportes Del Norte Bus Number 396 on October 3, 1963, departed Nuevo Laredo, Mexico, for Monterrey and Mexico City at 2:30 a.m. and was driven by bus driver RUBEN GONZALEZ. This same bus, Number 396, had arrived in Nuevo Laredo, Mexico, from Monterrey on October 2, 1963, at 3:30 p.m. Bus Number 396 did not return to Nuevo Laredo, Mexico, until October 5, 1963, at 3:00 p.m., and it was driven by A. IBARRA.

On 4/15/64 at Nuevo Laredo, Mexico File # SA 105-2909

by SA ROBERT L. CHAPMAN/dnb Date dictated 4/15/64

This document contains neither recommendations nor conclusions of the FBI. It is the property of the FBI and is loaned to your agency; it and its contents are not to be distributed outside your agency.

COMMISSION EXHIBIT No. 2129—Continued

FD-302 (Rev. 1-25-60)

FEDERAL BUREAU OF INVESTIGATION

1

Date April 17, 1964

On April 7, 1964, GILBERTO CAZARES GARZA, Chief of Mexican Immigration, Nuevo Laredo, Mexico, advised that HELIO TUEXI MAYDON and ZEFERINO ESPINOSA RAMOS were the Immigration Inspectors on duty at the Mexican Immigration headquarters, International Bridge, Nuevo Laredo, Mexico, on the 6:00 a.m. to 2:00 p.m. shift on September 26, 1963. ZEFERINO ESPINOSA RAMOS was in charge of the shift. The stamp of RAMOS or of HELIO TUEXI MAYDON would appear on the entry permits of all persons entering Mexico at Nuevo Laredo, Mexico, between, 6:00 a.m. and 2:00 p.m. on September 26, 1963, by bus or automobile, according to GILBERTO CAZARES GARZA.

On 4/7/64 at Nuevo Laredo, Mexico File # SA 105-2909

by SA ROBERT L. CHAPMAN/dnb Date dictated 4/13/64

This document contains neither recommendations nor conclusions of the FBI. It is the property of the FBI and is loaned to your agency; it and its contents are not to be distributed outside your agency.

COMMISSION EXHIBIT No. 2129—Continued

FD-302 (Rev. 1-25-60)

FEDERAL BUREAU OF INVESTIGATION

1

Date April 17, 1964

On April 7, 1964, ROBERTO RAMOS, Manager of Flecha Roja (Red Arrow) Bus Lines, Nuevo Laredo, Mexico, advised that Red Arrow Bus from Nuevo Laredo, Mexico, to Mexico City, Mexico, normally carries a total of 41 passengers and is normally loaded to capacity. RAMOS advised that no passenger manifest is made, and the only record is the baggage guide that contains the names of only those persons on the bus with baggage.

Mr. RAMOS stated that the baggage guide for Bus Number 516 that departed Nuevo Laredo, Mexico at 2:00 p.m. on September 26, 1963, enroute to Mexico, D. F., was prepared by ALEJANDRO CONTRERAS, and the person who drives all of the busses that operate between Nuevo Laredo, Mexico, and Laredo, Texas, connecting Continental passengers with Flecha Roja or Red Arrow Bus Lines for trips into Mexico is EDUARDO CERVERA.

On 4/7/64 at Nuevo Laredo, Mexico File # SA 105-2909

by SA ROBERT L. CHAPMAN/dnb Date dictated 4/13/64

This document contains neither recommendations nor conclusions of the FBI. It is the property of the FBI and is loaned to your agency; it and its contents are not to be distributed outside your agency.

SA 105-2909

Baggage Guide List of Red Arrow Bus No. 516

Nuevo Laredo to Mexico City

9/26-27/63

EXHIBIT D-107

17

Exhibit D-107 is the baggage guide list or manifest (Guia de Equipajes) dated September 26, 1963, at Nuevo Laredo, Mexico, for Red Arrow bus number 516. This manifest shows that bus 516 departed from Nuevo Laredo, Mexico, at 2:15 p.m. en route to Monterrey, Mexico, and Mexico City. The driver of the bus was listed as ROBERTO MORALES.

The baggage guide list (D-107) was originally reported on pages 10 and 11 of San Antonio report in this case dated December 17, 1963, in which it was reported that the list disclosed that 18 passengers boarded the bus at Nuevo Laredo on September 26, 1963, 6 of whom were destined to Monterrey and 12 to Mexico City. As a result of the information developed from Mr. ROBERTO RAMOS as previously reported and from Mr. ALEJANDRO CONTRERAS which is to be reported hereinafter, it has now been established that the baggage list indicates the number of pieces of luggage checked on the bus rather than the number of passengers.

As a matter of ready reference, exhibit D-107 is set forth as follows:

Seat No.	Person	Destination	Baggage Claim Check	Type of Baggage	Customs Check
1	PABLO VASQUEZ	Mexico City	#257512	Veliz	Marked
2	--------------	Mexico City	#257513	"	"
3	S. MORAN	Mexico City	#257580	"	"
4	ALFREDO BRESENO	Mexico City	#257577	"	"
5	ROSA SORQUIS	Mexico City	#257578	"	#7318061

Seat No.	Person	Destination	Baggage Claim Check	Type of Baggage	Customs Check
6.	T. GONZALES	Mexico City	#257579	"	#7318060
7.	ANDRES MORALES	Monterrey	#257575	"	Marked
8.	--------------	Monterrey	#257574	Caja (box)	"
9.	GPE. MARTINEZ	Monterrey	#257576	Veliz	Marked
10.	(FNU) ROWEN (NOTE: Probably should have been Bowen per entry at Seat 15).	Mexico City	#320438	Maletin (small handbag)	"
11.	HARRY J. MITCHELL	Monterrey	#320200	"	"
12.	--------------	Monterrey	#320202	Veliz	"
13.	--------------	Monterrey	#320201	"	"
14.	LEE H. OSWALJ	Mexico City	#320435	"	"
15.	(FNU) BOWEN	Mexico City	#320441	"	"
16.	--------------	Mexico City	#320440	"	"
17.	JOHN MC FARLAND	Mexico City	#320437	"	#7317276
18.	--------------	Mexico City	#320436	"	#7317277

Mexican Customs Inspector of baggage into Mexico placed the notation "marked" when luggage or veliz contained clothing and articles of small value. Whenever luggage contained clothing or other articles of great value, it was given a customs inspection number for entry into Mexico, thus accounting for the customs inspection numbers as opposed to the customs notation "marked."

The correct baggage claim checks for entries at seats 17 and 18 should have been previously reported as checks number 320437 and 320436 and the numbers 7317276 and 7317277 should have appeared as indicated above in the Customs Check column at seats 17 and 18 respectively. The number 7318061 should have appeared in the Customs Check column at seat 5.

The afore-mentioned baggage list when previously recorded in the December 17, 1963, report made at San Antonio indicated that the lines appearing in the list at seats 2, 8, 12, 13, 16 and 18 denoted that individuals were aboard the bus traveling with the persons listed in the seats immediately preceding the seats in question.

In light of the revelations of Messrs. RAMOS and CONTRERAS, it has been ascertained that the lines drawn at the points in question, in fact, represent additional pieces of luggage belonging to the individuals listed in the preceding seats or to members of their party.

In addition, the baggage list as set forth herein has been amended from the list appearing in the December 17, 1963, report made at San Antonio in that the name "ROIG" for the person recorded at seat 5 has been changed to "ROSA" in light of the comments of Mr. CONTRERAS.

The abbreviated first name "APE." for the person recorded at seat 9 as reported in the earlier report has been amended to "GPE.," most likely the abbreviation of the female name GUADALUPE. In this connection, the first letter in the abbreviation of the name at seat 9 on D-107 appears to more closely resemble the letter "G" in the name "GONZALES" for the person recorded in seat 6. The name OSWALT in the list as previously reported has been changed to OSWALJ as the best possible interpretation of the hand printing.

COMMISSION EXHIBIT No. 2129—Continued

FD-302 (Rev. 1-25-60)

FEDERAL BUREAU OF INVESTIGATION

Date 4/9/64

L. H. YARBROUGH, dispatcher, Greyhound Bus Terminal, 500 North St. Mary's Street, advised the records of his office reflect that Greyhound Bus #1265 was used in making the Laredo-Chicago run which left Laredo, Texas, at 3:00 a.m. on October 3, 1963, and arrived in San Antonio at about 6:20 a.m., October 3, 1963, with 20 passengers. It carried seven passengers going north of San Antonio. The bus was operated by J. C. ROBISON, 119 Ferncliff, Apartment B, San Antonio.

The records reflect that Greyhound Bus #1265 left San Antonio at 7:10 a.m., October 3, 1963, with a total of 30 passengers. The driver of this bus from San Antonio to Dallas was BEN JULIAN, an extra operator who resides in Dallas, Texas. After viewing the photograph of LEE HARVEY OSWALD, Mr. YARBROUGH stated he does not recall ever seeing this individual or anyone fitting his description.

On 4/7/64 at San Antonio, Texas File # SA 105-2909

by SA BRUNO F. DREYER/csh Date dictated 4/9/64

This document contains neither recommendations nor conclusions of the FBI. It is the property of the FBI and is loaned to your agency; it and its contents are not to be distributed outside your agency.

COMMISSION EXHIBIT No. 2130

UNITED STATES DEPARTMENT OF JUSTICE

FEDERAL BUREAU OF INVESTIGATION

In Reply, Please Refer to
File No.

San Antonio, Texas

April 1, 1964

RE: LEE HARVEY OSWALD

JACK BURCHAM, Texas Employment Commission, Austin, Texas, on April 1, 1964, advised Special Agent H. T. BURK Texas warrant dated September 23, 1963, payable to LEE HARVEY OSWALD, Post Office Box 30061, New Orleans, Louisiana, in payment of his unemployment claim, was mailed in a window envelope direct to OSWALD at above post office box in New Orleans, Louisiana, on September 23, 1963, via regular mail which was picked up about 5:15 p.m., September 23, 1963, at Texas Employment Commission Building, Austin, Texas, by U. S. Post Office Department.

The above unemployment check and all others issued to OSWALD by the Texas Employment Commission, Austin, Texas, while he was in Louisiana, were mailed direct to him at his New Orleans, Louisiana, post office box address, and at no time were any checks sent to him in care of the Louisiana Employment Commission.

COMMISSION EXHIBIT No. 2131

UNITED STATES DEPARTMENT OF JUSTICE

FEDERAL BUREAU OF INVESTIGATION

In Reply, Please Refer to
File No.

New Orleans, Louisiana
April 7, 1964

LEE HARVEY OSWALD

Mr. Germinal Messina, District Supervisor, Louisiana Division of Employment Security, Room 200, 442 Canal Street, New Orleans, Louisiana, advised on April 1, 1964, that according to regulations, Oswald was required to report weekly in person in order to continue his claim for benefits. Additionally, Oswald was required at these weekly appearances to furnish information regarding his earnings, his availability for work and efforts made by him to secure employment.

Mr. Messina said that according to his records, Oswald appeared on September 24, 1963 and signed for benefit assistance for the week ending September 27, 1963. He said the benefit checks were mailed by the Texas Employment Commission directly to Oswald at his residence address and that no checks were obtained by Oswald on his weekly visits to the Louisiana Division of Employment Security Office.

Mr. Frederick Christen, Claims Interviewer, Louisiana Division of Employment Security, 630 Camp Street, New Orleans advised on April 1, 1964, that Oswald's weekly visits to his office were to qualify for payments and to show what efforts he had made to obtain employment. On Oswald's visit on September 24, 1963, the claimant filled out a yellow form, IB-2 (Continued Interstate Claim) which form Oswald signed in Christen's presence. He said that Oswald did not receive any benefit checks on his visits to his office, since these checks were mailed directly to Oswald at his residence by the Texas Employment Commission.

Lee W. Robertson, Postal Inspector, Room 2002, Main Post Office Building, New Orleans, Louisiana, on April 2, 1964, observed photographs of FBI Exhibit #D-22 and furnished the following information:

COMMISSION EXHIBIT No. 2131—Continued

LEE HARVEY OSWALD

The "Change of Address Order" signed by Lee H. Oswald bears the stamped mark of 11:00 AM, September 25, 1963 on the reverse side. This is a cancelling machine impression which shows that this card was received at the main Post Office, New Orleans, Louisiana at 11:00 AM on September 25, 1963. This card could have been delivered personally at the main Post Office as late as 10:00 AM to 10:30 AM on September 25, 1963 depending on the volume of mail received at the Post Office at that time and receive the 11:00 AM machine cancelling impression. However, if the Change of Address Card was placed in a collection box on the street, in some outlying section of the City of New Orleans, it could have been deposited as early as 5:00 PM on September 24, 1963.

Inspector Robertson observed that there is a collection box at the Lafayette Square Substation where Post Office Box 30061 is located and that the mail is picked up at this collection box at 10:20 AM and brought directly to the main Post Office which would be in sufficient time to enable the card to bear the cancelling machine impression of 11:00 AM, September 25, 1963.

Inspector Robertson said that the date stamped on the front side of the Change of Address Order of September 26, 1963, is the cancellation stamp of the Lafayette Square Substation showing that the Change of Address Order was received at the Lafayette Square Substation on September 26, 1963. This stamp was also used to cancel the 5¢ postage stamp attached to the card.

The perforated card which has been torn along the perforated edge is an Application For Post Office Box, Form 1093. This application is made out at the Post Office and is not mailed. The application was probably made out at the Lafayette Square Substation when Oswald applied for the box. The perforated card bears two postal marks for the following reason: When Oswald made application for the Post Office Box, he indicated by check mark, that he

-2-

LEE HARVEY OSWALD

desired "all except special delivery mail in box", which required the Post Office not to place special delivery mail in the box, but to deliver it to the address furnished. This card was sent to the main Post Office to the Special Delivery Section which handles all special delivery mail. There a notation was made to deliver all special delivery mail to the residence address and the card was stamped with the special delivery stamp "June 11, 1963", indicating that this action had been taken and the card returned to the Lafayette Square Substation. The second date stamp, namely October 3, 1963, is the stamp made by the Special Delivery Section noting that the box had been closed and thereby removing its notice to forward special delivery mail to the residence address.

Investigation has determined that the latest available air travel from New Orleans, Louisiana to Houston, Texas on September 25, 1963, which would have enabled Oswald to board a Continental Trailways Bus at Houston, Texas at approximately 2:00 AM, on September 26, 1963, was Eastern Air Lines Flight #543, which was scheduled to depart from New Orleans at 11:40 PM on September 25, 1963 and scheduled to arrive in Houston, Texas at 12:37 AM, September 26, 1963.

It has been determined that Oswald received a warrant from the Texas Employment Commission, Austin, Texas, addressed to his Post Office Box 30061, New Orleans, Louisiana, which warrant was dated September 23, 1963 and was mailed at 5:15 PM on that date and arrived in New Orleans at 6:00 PM on September 24, 1963. Investigation has shown that the earliest time Oswald could have obtained this warrant from his Post Office Box was subsequent to 5:00 AM on September 25, 1963. The Winn-Dixie Store, #1425, 4303 Magazine Street, New Orleans, Louisiana, the place where the warrant dated September 23, 1963 was cashed, was not open to the public on September 25, 1963 until 8:00 AM. J. D. Fuchs, Manager, Winn-Dixie Store #1425, who approved the warrant for cashing, worked from 6:00 AM until noon and from 1:00 PM to 5:30 PM, on September 25, 1963. Mrs. Thelma F. Fisher, Cashier #3, Winn-Dixie Store #1425, who actually cashed the warrant, worked

-3-

from 8:00 AM until 1:00 PM on September 25, 1963.

Investigation has further determined that only three busses departed from New Orleans after 8:00 AM on September 25, 1963, and arrived at Houston, Texas prior to 2:00 AM on September 26, 1963. The drivers of these busses have failed to identify a photograph of Oswald as a passenger on these busses. There is no record of Oswald as a passenger on any air flight from New Orleans, Louisiana to Houston, Texas on September 25, 1963.

The only conductor, flagman, and porter assigned to the one train departing New Orleans after 8:00 AM on September 25, 1963 and arriving at Houston, Texas prior to 2:00 AM, September 26, 1963, do not recall Oswald as a passenger.

COMMISSION EXHIBIT No. 2131—Continued

HO 105-1291
TDD:pak

RE: TRAVEL OF LEE HARVEY OSWALD TO MEXICO

The following investigation was conducted by SA TERENCE D. DINAN:

AT HOUSTON, TEXAS

This investigation was conducted in an effort to locate and interview those Greyhound Bus drivers who drove portions of the following trips:

Leave New Orleans, 5:45 P.M., September 24, 1963,
Arrive Laredo, Texas, 3:45 P.M., September 25, 1963.

Leave New Orleans 10:45 P.M., September 24,
Arrive Laredo, Texas, 6:50 P.M., September 25.

Leave New Orleans, 12:45 A.M., September 25,
Arrive Laredo 10:10 P.M., September 25.

Leave New Orleans 7:00 A.M., September 25,
Arrive Laredo 5:30 A.M., September 26.

Leave New Orleans 2:45 P.M., September 25,
Arrive Laredo 12:20 P.M., September 26.

On December 7, 1963, JOHN FLANAGAN, Terminal Manager, Greyhound Bus Lines Depot, 1402 Texas, furnished the following list of drivers who drove the Houston to San Antonio leg of the above mentioned trips:

Leaving Houston 6:00 A.M., September 25, 1963,
MEL W. NOWOTNY, San Antonio, Texas.

Leaving Houston 9:30 A.M., September 25, 1963,
T. PAT TOLAND, San Antonio, Texas.

Leaving Houston, 12:40 P.M., September 25, 1963,
T. C. JONES, San Antonio, Texas.

COMMISSION EXHIBIT No. 2132

Leaving Houston 7:40 P.M., September 25, 1963,
DENNIS C. WARREN, 1806 Chippendale, Houston, Texas

Leaving Houston 1:30 A.M., September 26, 1963,
A. L. COPELAND, San Antonio, Texas;
E. P. WILLARD, San Antonio, Texas.

FLANAGAN further advised that the Lake Charles, Louis to Houston, Texas, portions of the above mentioned trips were made by the following drivers:

Leaving Lake Charles 1:00 A.M., September 25, 1963,
W. L. HALL, 5914 Bretshire Drive, Houston, Texas.

Leaving Lake Charles 4:00 A.M., September 25, 1963,
R. W. MURPHY, 8039 Bonner Drive, Houston, Texas.

Leaving Lake Charles 6:41 A.M., September 25, 1963,
RALPH ASHFORD, 1007 Magnolia, Rosenburg, Texas.

Leaving Lake Charles 2:15 P.M., September 25, 1963,
J. M. SHOFNER, 5517 Pagewood, Houston, Texas;
B. R. ALLEN, 1112 Ashland, Houston, Texas.

Leaving Lake Charles 8:40 P.M., September 25, 1963,
J. D. KENNEDY, 6607 Stearnes, Houston, Texas;
E. E. SIMMONS, Beaumont, Texas.

On December 7, 1963, the following persons at the Greyhound Bus Terminal, 1402 Texas, viewed a photograph of LEE HARVEY OSWALD and all stated that they were unable to identify him as a person they had ever seen at the Houston, Texas, terminal:

OLGA NORRIS, Cashier,
Post House Cafeteria

MARGARET KING, Waitress,
Post House Cafeteria

P. J. CRAMER, Ticket Agent

DAISEY SANDERS,
Post House Newsstand

On the following dates the below listed bus drivers for Greyhound Bus Lines all advised that they were unable to definitely identify LEE HARVEY OSWALD as a person who had traveled on a bus which they were driving. All of these drivers advised that because of the multitude of persons which they carry daily, it would be virtually impossible to so identify one person unless some particular incident such as a fight had arisen which would cause the driver to pay particular attention.

DATE	NAME
12/7/63	JAMES MERVEL SHOFNER; J. D. KENNEDY; RALPH ASHFORD; WATSON LEWIS HALL; ELRAY E. SIMMONS
12/8/63	BILLY R. ALLEN
12/9/63	RICHARD W. MURPHY; DENNIS C. WARREN

COMMISSION EXHIBIT No. 2132—Continued

1

HO: 105-1291
PWH:gn

Re: Oswald Travel to Mexico City, September 26, 1963

On December 7, 1963, Mr. R. S. COBB, Station Manager, Continental Trailways Bus Terminal, 1114 McKinney, Houston, Texas, advised that the following schedule and drivers are all of the Continental drivers which transport buses from Houston, Texas to Victoria, Texas, from Victoria, Texas to Alice, Texas, and from Alice, Texas to Laredo, Texas:

Even numbered days

HOUSTON TO VICTORIA, TEXAS

Leave Houston	Operator	Run #	Bus #
2:35 AM	J. C. LINTON	2801	1703
7:40 AM	EVERETT WARD	2851 (via Bay City)	1712
7:40 AM	KENNETH R. LLOYD	2803 (via Victoria, Texas)	1140
11:30 AM	R. L. BUTTERFIELD	2853	1137
*12:30 PM	R. M. GOODWIN	2805	1142

*Through bus to Laredo

VICTORIA TO ALICE

JOSEPH C. SPEER, JR.

13

COMMISSION EXHIBIT No. 2132—Continued

2

HO 105-1291

ALICE TO LAREDO

L. H. THOMAS 326

Odd Numbered Days

Leave Houston	Operator	Run #	Bus #
2:35 AM	CHARLES E. REED	2801	1714
7:40 AM	C. R. SUTTLE (via Bay City)	2851	1700
7:40 AM	JOE T. GREER	2803	1103
11:30 AM	C. E. WILLIAMS	2853	1137
*12:30 PM	FRANK EDGAR	2805	1133

*Through bus to Laredo

VICTORIA TO ALICE

JOE C. SPEER, JR.

ALICE TO LAREDO

R. H. THOMAS 326

On December 9, 1963, Mr. C. W. CARLILE, Assistant Division Superintendent, Continental Trailways Bus Terminal, 1114 McKinney, gave the following addresses for the Houston to Laredo drivers:

14

COMMISSION EXHIBIT No. 2132—Continued

8-380 O—64—vol. XXIV——47

3

HO 105-1291

J. C. LINTON
7802 Camwood, Houston
MI 5-6889

EVERETT WARD
415 Heights Boulevard, Houston
UN 2-9383

KENNETH R. LLOYD
10326 Bretton Drive, Houston
HI 2-9074

R. L. BUTTERFIELD
449 Fairmount
Corpus Christi, TU 2-1304

JOE C. SPEER, JR.
116 N. Park, Alice, Texas
MO 4-5224

R. H. THOMAS, Laredo, Texas

R. M. GOODWIN
702 S. Liberty
Victoria, Texas

CHARLES E. REED
1415-22nd Street, Huntsville, Texas
CA 5-2844

CAROL R. SUTTLE
7470 Lakehurst Drive, Houston
MI 5-8166

JOE T. GREER
242 Red Ripple Road, Houston
OX 4-2512

CONWAY E. WILLIAMS
1310 Story, Houston
OV 2-0464

A. FRANK EDGAR
2510 Nightengale Street, Victoria, Texas
HI 5-2580

15

FD-302 (Rev. 1-25-60)

1

FEDERAL BUREAU OF INVESTIGATION

Date December 11, 1963

Mr. HARRY MILLER, Manager, Greyhound Bus Lines Depot, Laredo, Texas, furnished the following schedule of buses that arrive in Laredo daily and which make connections with those buses leaving New Orleans Louisiana.

Leave New Orleans 5:45 p.m., September 24, 1963 - Arrive Laredo, Texas, 3:45 p.m., September 25, 1963.

Leave New Orleans 10:45 p.m., September 24, 1963 - Arrive Laredo, Texas, 6:50 p.m., September 25, 1963.

Leave New Orleans 12:45 a.m., September 25, 1963 - Arrive Laredo 10:10 p.m., September 25, 1963.

Leave New Orleans 7 a.m., September 25, 1963 - Arrive Laredo 5:30 a.m., September 26, 1963.

Leave New Orleans 2:45 p.m. , September 25, 1963 - Arrive Laredo 12:20 p.m., September 26, 1963.

Mr. SMITH added that all Greyhound buses pass through San Antonio and bus drivers in above schedules change in Lake Charles, Louisiana, Houston and San Antonio, Texas.

He stated that bus drivers from San Antonio to Laredo on dates indicated above were ROUNDTREE, W. H. HAGENS, McNABB, W. J. FLOYD, C. D. MONTGOMERY, respectively.

P 8

On 12/6/63 at Laredo, Texas File # SA 105-2909

by SA LEOPOLDO E. ARMIJO/cbl Date dictated 12/9/63

This document contains neither recommendations nor conclusions of the FBI. It is the property of the FBI and is loaned to your agency; it and its contents are not to be distributed outside your agency.

FEDERAL BUREAU OF INVESTIGATION

1

Date December 18, 1963

The information set forth hereinafter was furnished by Mr. ELMER E. BILBRAY, Supervisor of Revenue Accounting, Continental Trailways Bus Company, 425 Bolton Avenue.

Mr. BILBRAY furnished Xerox copies of two trip reports and time slips for the scheduled Continental Trailways Bus run from New Orleans, Louisiana, to Houston, Texas, on September 25, 1963, which departed New Orleans at 12:20 p.m.

Referring to the trip report and time slip of bus operator CONRAD ROBERTS, Mr. BILBRAY stated that ROBERTS drove Bus No. 5121 which left New Orleans at 12:20 p.m., September 25, 1963 and arrived at Beaumont, Texas, at 8:10 p.m., the scheduled arrival at Beaumont is 8:15 p.m. When ROBERTS arrived at Beaumont he had eleven passengers.

ROBERTS was released from the hospital December 16, 1963, and is recuperating at his home, 421 Cummins, Pineville, Louisiana, telephone 5-4967.

The only major scheduled stops from New Orleans to Houston are a 15 minute stop at Baton Rouge, Louisiana, at about 2:20 p.m. and a 30 minute stop at Kinder, Louisiana, at approximately 5:40 p.m. for supper. At Beaumont, Texas, the stop is only long enough for the transfer of drivers. In this case ROBERTS got off the bus and the new driver was T. R. HENDERSON.

According to HENDERSON's trip report and time slip, he had eleven passengers on the bus at Beaumont, Texas and he picked up another passenger at Baytown, Texas; consequently, there were twelve passengers on the bus destined for Houston, Texas. HENDERSON shows on his report that he left Beaumont at 8:15 p.m. and arrived Houston, Texas 10:50 p.m.

On 12/17/63 at Alexandria, Louisiana File # NO 100-16601

by SA PAUL R. LANCASTER :gas Date dictated 12/17/63

13

This document contains neither recommendations nor conclusions of the FBI. It is the property of the FBI and is loaned to your agency; it and its contents are not to be distributed outside your agency.

COMMISSION EXHIBIT No. 2134

2

NO 100-16601
PRL:gas

T. R. HENDERSON resides at 111 Garrotsville Street, Houston 22, Texas, telephone number OX 2-0064.

14

COMMISSION EXHIBIT No. 2134—Continued

FD-302 (Rev. 1-25-60)

FEDERAL BUREAU OF INVESTIGATION

Date 12/18/63

1

The information set forth hereinafter was telephonically furnished by Mr. CONRAD ROBERTS, 421 Cummins, Pineville, Louisiana.

Mr. ROBERTS advised he was released from the hospital on December 16, 1963 and is recuperating at home and requested that if possible any information he might furnish be given over the telephone.

Mr. ROBERTS' memory was refreshed with a Zerox copy of his trip report and time slip which he executed on September 25, 1963 in his position as bus driver for Continental Trailways Bus Company.

ROBERTS regularly makes a scheduled run on Wednesdays to Beaumont, Texas. On September 25, 1963, he left New Orleans at 12:20 PM driving Continental Bus #5121 and arrived at Beaumont, Texas, at 8:10 PM where he was relieved by bus driver T. R. HENDERSON, who drove the bus from Beaumont, Texas, to Houston, Texas.

ROBERTS has seen many pictures of LEE HARVEY OSWALD and does not recall ever seeing OSWALD in person at any time. ROBERTS cannot recall any of the passengers on his bus because he does not pay any attention to them unless they might appear to be foreigners or say or do something to impress him. ROBERTS said he handles hundreds of passengers during a week and there was nothing that would cause him to remember anything at all about the passengers that were on his bus on September 25, 1963.

ROBERTS has one regular passenger who is a nurse living in Gonzales, Louisiana, who boards the bus at Gonzales at about 1:45 PM and gets off in front of the Baton Rouge, Louisiana General Hospital where she works in the Recovery Room from 3:00 to 11:00 PM. This nurse is a white female about 35 years old, 140 pounds, 5'7", dark hair with gray mixed in. This nurse usually sits in the front seat of the bus if this seat is vacant.

ROBERTS could not remember if this nurse was on

On 12/17/63 at Alexandria, Louisiana File # NO 100-16601

by SA PAUL R. LANCASTER /jm 15 Date dictated 12/18/63

This document contains neither recommendations nor conclusions of the FBI. It is the property of the FBI and is loaned to your agency; it and its contents are not to be distributed outside your agency.

NO 100-16601
2

his bus on September 25, 1963. It was pointed out to ROBERTS that according to his trip report there was a passenger who boarded his bus at Gonzales, Louisiana, and ROBERTS stated that in all probability this was the above described nurse.

On his scheduled run from New Orleans to Beaumont, Texas, ROBERTS stated that there is usually a fifteen minute stop at Baton Rouge, Louisiana at about 2:20 PM and a thirty minute stop at Kinder, Louisiana, at about 5:40 PM for supper. The stop at Beaumont, Texas, is only long enough to change bus drivers.

COMMISSION EXHIBIT No. 2134—Continued

FD-302 (Rev. 1-25-60)

FEDERAL BUREAU (

Date February 6, 1964

Mr. HENRY MATHEWS, Vice President, Kerrville Bus Co., 306 East Fourth Street, Austin, Texas, advised that company operated the only direct bus service between Austin, Texas, and Houston, Texas. The schedule of Kerrville Bus Co. with drivers on the schedule for September 25, 1963, after 12:00 noon was furnished by MATHEWS as follows:

DEPARTURE TIME FROM AUSTIN, TEXAS	ARRIVAL TIME IN HOUSTON, TEXAS	NAME OF DRIVER
2:10 p.m.	6:10 p.m.	W. C. SUTTON
5:25 p.m.	9:45 p.m.	A. P. SCHWARTZ
6:15 p.m. (Express)	9:55 p.m.	L. O. INGRAM

All ticket sales for Kerrville Bus Co. on the Austin, Texas, to Houston, Texas, route are handled by the ticket agents at the Greyhound Bus Terminal, 118 East 10th Street, Austin, Texas.

7

On 2/5/64 at Austin, Texas File # SA 105-2909

by SA H. T. BURK/mkd Date dictated 2/5/64

This document contains neither recommendations nor conclusions of the FBI. It is the property of the FBI and is loaned to your agency; it and its contents are not to be distributed outside your agency.

COMMISSION EXHIBIT NO. 2135

FD-302 (Rev. 1-25-60)

FEDERAL BUREAU OF INVESTIGATION

Date February 6, 1964.

Mr. LELAND O. INGRAM, 2322 Westrock Drive, Austin, Texas, advised he is a bus driver for the Kerrville Bus Co. and as such, drove a Kerrville bus from Austin, Texas, to Houston, Texas, on September 25, 1964, departing from Austin, Texas, at 6:15 p.m., and arriving at Houston, Texas, at 9:55 p.m.

He observed a photograph of LEE HARVEY OSWALD and also of JACK RUBY and advised that he is not personally acquainted with either of them and does not recognize the photograph of either of them as having ever ridden on a bus of which he was the driver. He explained that it is possible that OSWALD or RUBY either one could have been a passenger on his bus, but he does not pay sufficient attention to the average passengers to be able to identify them after they leave the bus at destination.

He was unable to furnish any positive information to indicate that OSWALD did or did not ride on his bus on September 25, 1963, because he did not recognize his photograph as being familiar to him.

8

On 2/5/64 at Austin, Texas File # SA 105-2909

by SA H. T. BURK/mkd Date dictated 2/5/64

This document contains neither recommendations nor conclusions of the FBI. It is the property of the FBI and is loaned to your agency; it and its contents are not to be distributed outside your agency.

COMMISSION EXHIBIT NO. 2135—Continued

FD-302 (Rev. 1-25-60)

FEDERAL BUREAU OF INVESTIGATION

Date February 6, 1964

WILLIAM CLELL SUTTON, 1113 Walton Lane, Austin, Texas, advised he is a bus driver for the Kerrville Bus Co., and as such, drove a Kerrville bus from Austin, Texas, to Houston, Texas, on September 25, 1964, departing from Austin, Texas, at 2:10 p.m., and arriving at Houston, Texas, at 6:10 p.m.

He observed a photograph of LEE HARVEY OSWALD and also of JACK RUBY and advised that he is not personally acquainted with either of them and does not recognize the photograph of either of them as having ever ridden on a bus of which he was the driver. He explained that it is possible that OSWALD or RUBY either one could have been a passenger on his bus, but he does not pay sufficient attention to the average passengers to be able to identify them after they leave the bus at destination.

He was unable to furnish any positive information to indicate that OSWALD did or did not ride on his bus on September 25, 1963, because he did not recognize his photograph as being familiar to him.

9

On 2/5/64 at Austin, Texas File # SA 105-2909

by SA H. T. BURK/mkd Date dictated 2/5/64

This document contains neither recommendations nor conclusions of the FBI. It is the property of the FBI and is loaned to your agency; it and its contents are not to be distributed outside your agency.

FD-302 (Rev. 1-25-60)

FEDERAL BUREAU OF INVESTIGATION

Date February 6, 1964

Mr. ALBERT POMEROY SCHWARTZ, 4520 Frontier Trail, Austin, Texas, advised he is a bus driver for the Kerrville Bus Co. and as such, drove a Kerrville bus from Austin, Texas, to Houston, Texas, on September 25, 1964, departing from Austin, Texas, at 5:25 p.m. and arriving at Houston, Texas, at 9:45 p.m.

He observed a photograph of LEE HARVEY OSWALD and also of JACK RUBY and advised that he is not personally acquainted with either of them and does not recognize the photograph of either of them as having ever ridden on a bus of which he was the driver. He explained that it is possible that OSWALD or RUBY either one could have been a passenger on his bus, but he does not pay sufficient attention to the average passengers to be able to identify them after they leave the bus at destination.

He was unable to furnish any positive information to indicate that OSWALD did or did not ride on his bus on September 25, 1963, because he did not recognize his photograph as being familiar to him.

10

On 2/5/64 at Austin, Texas File # SA 105-2909

by SA H. T. BURK/mkd Date dictated 2/5/64

This document contains neither recommendations nor conclusions of the FBI. It is the property of the FBI and is loaned to your agency; it and its contents are not to be distributed outside your agency.

FEDERAL BUREAU OF INVESTIGATION

1

Date February 12, 1964

Mr. C. R. BROWNING, home address 1119 Mission Ridge, Austin, Texas, Greyhound Bus Terminal Ticket Agent, advised he was on duty during the afternoon on September 25, 1963, until after the departure of Kerrville Bus Company bus that departed at 6:15 p.m. and was on duty at all times after 12:00 noon. He observed a photograph of LEE HARVEY OSWALD and one of JACK RUBY and stated he could not state that he had ever sold a bus ticket to either on September 25, 1963, or at any other time. He pointed out that due to the large number of tickets sold to passengers enroute to Houston, Texas, from Austin, Texas, it would be almost impossible to recall any one passenger who purchased a ticket as far back as September, 1963.

He admitted it would have been possible for him to have sold a ticket to OSWALD or RUBY and him not be able to identify either of their pictures at this time.

BROWNING pointed out that he and Miss LOUISE HAMILTON were the only ticket agents on duty from noon to after 6:15 p.m. on September 25, 1963.

11

On 2/7/64 at Austin, Texas File #SA 105-2909

by SA H. T. BURK/dnb Date dictated 2/7/64

This document contains neither recommendations nor conclusions of the FBI. It is the property of the FBI and is loaned to your agency; it and its contents are not to be distributed outside your agency.

COMMISSION EXHIBIT No. 2135—Continued

FEDERAL BUREAU OF INVESTIGATION

1

Date February 12, 1964

Miss LOUISE HAMILTON, 1802 Bremen Street, Austin, Texas, Greyhound Bus Terminal Ticket Agent, advised she was on duty during the afternoon of September 25, 1963, until after the departure of Kerrville Bus Company bus that departed at 6:15 p.m. and was on duty at all times after 12:00 noon. She observed a photograph of LEE HARVEY OSWALD and one of JACK RUBY and stated she could not state that she had ever sold a bus ticket to either of them, either on September 25, 1963, or at any other time. She pointed out that due to the large number of tickets sold to passengers enroute to Houston, Texas, from Austin, Texas, it would be almost impossible to recall any one passenger who purchased a ticket as far back as September, 1963.

She admitted it would have been possible for her to have sold a ticket to OSWALD or RUBY and her not be able to identify either of their pictures at this time.

12

On 2/7/64 at Austin, Texas File #SA 105-2909

by SA H. T. BURK/dnb Date dictated 2/7/64

This document contains neither recommendations nor conclusions of the FBI. It is the property of the FBI and is loaned to your agency; it and its contents are not to be distributed outside your agency.

COMMISSION EXHIBIT No. 2135—Continued

FD-204 (Rev. 9-23-58)

UNITED STATES DEPARTMENT OF JUSTICE
FEDERAL BUREAU OF INVESTIGATION

Copy to:

Report of: SA EDWIN DALRYMPLE   Office: Houston
Date: 1/14/64

File Number: Houston 105-1291   105-82555

Title: LEE HARVEY OSWALD

Character: INTERNAL SECURITY - R - CUBA

Synopsis: Reinterviews of Mr. and Mrs. HORACE TWIFORD, Houston, Texas, indicate OSWALD believed to have telephoned TWIFORD residence between 7 and 9 PM prior to 9/26/63. Ticket agents at Continental Trailways bus terminal, Houston, Texas, could not recall selling ticket to OSWALD. Records of this company indicate only one ticket sold between 9/24/63 and 9/26/63 for travel between Houston and Laredo. HENRY OTIS CHENYWORTH, Jasper, Texas, denied making any statement that he had any information regarding assassination of President KENNEDY. CHENYWORTH states there is "remote possibility" he made statement he would learn who assassinated the President, but if so, such statement was made "in jest." CHENYWORTH stated did not know LEE HARVEY OSWALD and had never engaged in shooting practice in area of Dallas or Grand Prairie, Texas.

\- P -

DETAILS: AT HOUSTON, TEXAS:

This document contains neither recommendations nor conclusions of any kind. It is the property of the FBI, and is a loan to your agency; it and/or its contents are not to be distributed outside your agency.

COMMISSION EXHIBIT No. 2136

1

HO 105-1291
ED:yk

The following investigation was conducted in an effort to develop specific information concerning the time and date that LEE HARVEY OSWALD was in Houston, Texas, during his reported travel from New Orleans, Louisiana, to Laredo, Texas, on September 25, 1963 - September 26, 1963. It was previously reported that OSWALD was in New Orleans on September 25, 1963, and that he boarded a Continental Trailways bus at 2 AM on September 26, 1963, at Houston, Texas, traveling on this bus from Houston to Laredo, Texas.

On January 6, 1964, HORACE TWIFORD, 7018 Schley, Houston, Texas, advised he and his wife ESTELLE TWIFORD had searched further in their records in an effort to determine the exact date on which Mrs. TWIFORD had received a telephone call from an individual who identified himself as LEE HARVEY OSWALD. TWIFORD stated he and his wife had located a slip of paper which had been used by Mrs. TWIFORD on the evening on which she received the above telephone call, and this slip of paper carried a notation of OSWALD's name and contained the words "Fair Play for Cuba Committee." TWIFORD stated his wife had made these notations on this slip of paper in order to remember to mention this telephone call to TWIFORD when he returned home from duty on a merchant vessel which was then traveling between Houston and other Gulf Coast ports.

TWIFORD stated he could recall that while on a coast-wise trip as a seaman during September, 1963, he made a quick trip from New Orleans, Louisiana, to Houston, Texas, by air in order to visit his wife. TWIFORD stated to the best of his recollection he made this trip to Houston on September 26, 1963, and his wife mentioned to him at that time of having received the telephone call from OSWALD.

On January 7, 1964, Mrs. ESTELLE TWIFORD, 7018 Schley, confirmed the above information and stated she had also been attempting to recall more specifically the time at which she received the telephone call from OSWALD which she previously reported. Mrs. TWIFORD stated she feels sure this telephone call was received after dark but

2

COMMISSION EXHIBIT No. 2136—Continued

HO 105-1291

not in the late evening. She stated if this call had been received at 10:00 PM or 11:00 PM, she would have considered this fact unusual and believes she would have recalled it. Mrs. TWIFORD stated the best she could do toward fixing the hour of this call was to estimate that it was received in the period between 7:00 PM and 9:00 PM.

The following investigation was conducted in an effort to locate an employee at the Continental Trailways bus terminal, Houston, Texas, who might recall having sold a ticket to LEE HARVEY OSWALD:

3

COMMISSION EXHIBIT No. 2136—Continued

HO 105-1291
PWH:yk

The following investigation was conducted by SA PAUL W. HUCKERIEDE:

On the dates indicated, the following Continental Trailways ticket agents in Houston, Texas, were interviewed but none could recall selling a ticket to LEE HARVEY OSWALD:

1/10/64	ROBERT STEVENSON 8909 Lockwood
1/9/64	RAY DYAL 7901 Easton
1/9/64	MORGAN LAIRD, JR. 9234 Tallyho
1/9/64	BILL PRATT 5806 Dryad

On January 9, 1964, ANN LINDSEY, 2243 Harwell Lane, Houston, Report Clerk, Continental Trailways, Houston, advised that for the period September 24 through September 26, 1963, one ticket, numbered 112230, was sold from Houston to Laredo, Texas, for $10.60. She advised this was the only ticket sold from Houston to Laredo during these dates, and there were no tickets sold through to Mexico City.

Miss LINDSEY stated the portion of the above ticket retained by Continental Trailways Bus Company was subsequently mailed to the Dallas office of that company for permanent filing. She stated there should be rubber stamp impressions on this ticket stub which would show the date on which the ticket was sold and the identity of the employee who sold it.

4

COMMISSION EXHIBIT No. 2136—Continued

FD-302 (Rev. 1-25-60)

FEDERAL BUREAU OF INVESTIGA ON

1

Date 1/6/64

HENRY OTIS CHENYWORTH, Route 2, Box 171, was advised of the identity of JOHN T. KELLY as a Special Agent of the Federal Bureau of Investigation, that he did not have to make any statement, that any statement he made might be used against him in a court of law, and that he had the right to the services of an attorney. No threats or promises were made to CHENYWORTH, who furnished the following information:

He was born April 27, 1943, in Troy, Texas, and served in the U. S. Air Force from September 9, 1960, until November 2, 1961, when he received a General Discharge under Honorable Conditions. Since his discharge from the Air Force, he has been employed in approximately twenty-five or thirty different jobs and has never held steady employment. His most recent employment was at Strangi Manufacturing Company in Dallas, Texas, until approximately two weeks ago. Prior to that period, during the month of November, 1963, he was employed by the Thompson Tool Company, 2328 Langford, Dallas, Texas.

On November 22, 1963, the day of the assassination of President JOHN F. KENNEDY, he recalls being at work at the Thompson Tool Company as he remembers listening to the reports of the assassination on the radio in the company shop. He worked all day Friday, November 22, 1963, was off on Saturday and Sunday, which is customary at this firm, and then he did not go to work on Monday, November 25, 1963, as he recalls watching the Presidential burial on television, at the residence of E. R. COLLIER, 306 East 7th Street, Dallas, Texas. To the best of his recollection, he returned to Jasper, Texas, on Tuesday, November 26, 1963, to stay with his stepbrother, JOE WILLIANS, who was ill, and after staying in Jasper for two days he returned to Dallas, Texas.

He denies making any statement concerning or implying that he had any information as to who killed the President, or a statement that he did not know whether he would be around by morning as he might be in jail. He stated there is a remote possibility he might have said

On 1/3/64 at Jasper, Texas File # HO 105-1291

by SA JOHN T. KELLY:yk Date dictated 1/3/64

This document contains neither recommendations nor conclusions of the FBI. It is the property of the FBI and is loaned to your agency; it and its contents are not to be distributed outside your agency.

5

2

HO 105-1291

"I bet I will know who did it by morning," in regard to who might have killed KENNEDY, but stated if he said this then the statement was made in jest as he does not recall saying this and could not see why he would have made this statement as he "would have no way in the world of finding out who did it."

He advised that he did not know LEE HARVEY OSWALD, nor did he have a gun or do any practice shooting in Dallas, Texas. He does not know where the practice range is near Grand Prairie and stated he never practiced on this area.

CHENYWORTH has no ill feeling toward KENNEDY and thought it "terrible that he was assassinated."

The following description was obtained by observation and interview:

Name	HENRY OTIS CHENYWORTH
Born	April 27, 1943, Troy, Texas
Race	White
Height	6'3"
Weight	160 pounds
Eyes	Hazel
Hair	Brown
Social Security No.	450-66-5211
Army service number	AF 18 60 16 65
Education	Completed high school in service
Residence	Route 2, Box 171, Jasper, Texas
Marital status	Single
Occupation	Unemployed

6*

FD-263 (Rev. 5-65)

UNITED STATES DEPARTMENT OF JUSTICE
FEDERAL BUREAU OF INVESTIGATION

Copy to:

Report of: JOHN M. KEMMY — Office: SAN ANTONIO
Date: January 6, 1964

Field Office File No.: 105-2909 — BUREAU FILE: 105-8255

Title: LEE HARVEY OSWALD

Character: INTERNAL SECURITY - R - CUBA

Synopsis:
Efforts to locate persons with knowledge of travel by OSWALD set forth. Mrs. LEE DANNELLY, Selective Service Headquarters, Austin, Texas, believes she was contacted by OSWALD on 9/25/63. Negative results of miscellaneous investigation set forth.

\- P -

DETAILS:

This document contains neither recommendations nor conclusions of any kind. It is the property of the FBI, and is a loan to your agency; it and/or its contents are not to be distributed outside your agency.

COMMISSION EXHIBIT NO. 2137

SA 105-2909

I. TRAVEL

The following investigation was conducted in an effort to determine travel OSWALD may have made on or about September 26, 1963, and October 3, 1963.

\- 2 -

COMMISSION EXHIBIT NO. 2137—Continued

1

SA 105-2909

The following investigation was conducted by SA ROBERT L. CHAPMAN:

AT LAREDO, TEXAS

On December 3, 1963, AUGUST O. HEIN, Assistant Principal, Martin High School, the only public high school in Laredo, Texas, was contacted to locate an ALICIA BERTHA RAMOS who departed Mexico on October 3, 1963, by unknown means and who was listed in the Mexican Immigration records as being 16 years of age. Mr. HEIN advised that he had two girls by the name of ALICIA RAMOS in Martin High School and both of them were in school on October 2 and 3, 1963. Mr. HEIN stated he questioned both girls and neither had been to Monterrey, Nuevo Leon, Mexico, which was the city that Mexican Immigration records indicated that RAMOS had visited.

The Laredo Telephone and City Directories contain a list of approximately 50 families by the name of RAMOS residing in Laredo, Texas.

No ALICIA RAMOS could be located in the Holding Institute or St. Augustine High Schools, the only other high schools in Laredo, Texas.

3

1

SA 105-2909

The following investigation was conducted by SA DON R. ROSE:

AT SAN ANTONIO, TEXAS

Current San Antonio telephone and city directories were examined and found to contain no names identifiable with C. ERVING, (FNU) NIETO, R. GOMEZ, or E. GUTIERREZ.

On December 17, 1963, records of the Retail Merchants Association were examined by IC JOHN C. SMITH and found to contain no records identifiable with the above individuals.

On December 11, 1963, JOE KENDRICKS, Detachment Commander, Office of Special Investigations, Lackland Air Force Base, advised SA DON R. ROSE that he had referred to appropriate records at Lackland Air Force Base and ascertained that no R. GOMEZ arrived at that base on October 3, 1963, or anywhere near this date. He said there is an R. GOMEZ presently stationed at Lackland Air Force Base whom he identified as RAUL N. GOMEZ but explained that this GOMEZ was a basic trainee who arrived at Lackland Air Force Base on November 6, 1963. According to him there is no other R. GOMEZ stationed at that base.

Mr. KENDRICKS further advised that he could find no record concerning a (FNU) NIETO.

On December 12, 1963, Mr. R. JAMES CUNNINGHAM, Joint Airlines Military Ticket Office (JAMTO), Lackland Air Force Base, advised after referring to appropriate records that Airman Third Class REYNALDO GOMEZ was assigned to Lackland Air Force Base during the period in question but had been transferred to Gettysburg Air Force Station, Gettysburg, South Dakota, recently. He said that REYNALDO GOMEZ' residence is listed as Bruni, Texas, which is close to Laredo, Texas, and he quite probably is the R. GOMEZ that was on Trans-Texas Airways Flight 290 from Laredo, Texas, to San Antonio, Texas, on October 3, 1963.

4

Mr. CUNNINGHAM also made known that he had determined that two NIETOs had been assigned to Lackland Air Force Base. He identified these individuals as DONALD E. NIETO who is presently in Officer's Training School, Medina Base, in class 64E. He identified the other NIETO as FRANCISCO A. NIETO who recently was transferred to the 340th Bomber Wing, Bergstrom Air Force Base, Texas.

On December 12, 1963, Officer Candidate DONALD E. NIETO, Class 64E, Officer's Training School, Medina Base, advised SA DON R. ROSE that he was not in the Air Force as of October 3, 1963, and was not on Flight 290 of Trans-Texas Airways, flight from Laredo, Texas, to San Antonio, Texas, on October 3, 1963. According to him he was in California on this date.

On December 19, 1963, FRANCISCO A. NIETO, 340th Bomber Wing, Bergstrom Air Force Base, advised SA H. T. BURK that he entered the Air Force on September 13, 1963, as a recruit and finished his basic training at Lackland Air Force Base on November 13, 1963. He said he has never been to Laredo, Texas, and was not on Flight 290 of Trans-Texas Airways from Laredo, Texas, to San Antonio, Texas, on October 3, 1963.

On December 20, 1963, FRANK M. DRAIN, 918 Manor Drive, San Antonio, Texas, advised SA DON R. ROSE that he has taken a number of flights on Trans-Texas Airlines from Laredo, Texas, to San Antonio, and he recalls the flight from Laredo to San Antonio on October 3, 1963. He said that he does not recall seeing anyone on this flight resembling the photograph of LEE HARVEY OSWALD.

On December 20, 1963, Mr. A. RAFFAELE, Base Locator, Kelly Air Force Base, Texas, advised SA DON R. ROSE that the records of his office contain no mention of any military officer or enlisted man by the name of NIETO. He added that his records contain the names of those individuals who have been transferred from that base since October 3, 1963.

Mr. RAFFAELE pointed out that had an Air Force member been assigned to Kelly Air Force Base on temporary duty (TDY) he would have no record of this individual.

On December 20, 1963, Airman First Class RICHARD F. GAFFNEY, Base Locator, Randolph Air Force Base, Texas, advised that his records make no mention of any individual by the name of NIETO.

On December 20, 1963, Airman First Class JAMES A. CURRY, Base Locator, Brooks Air Force Base, Texas, advised that his records make no mention of an individual by the name of NIETO.

FD-302 (Rev. 1-25-60)

FEDERAL BUREAU OF INVESTIGATION

Date December 20, 1963

Mrs. LEE DANNELLY, Assistant Chief of the Administrative Division, State Selective Service Headquarters, Austin, Texas, prepared a memorandum concerning her recollection concerning a contact with LEE HARVEY OSWALD which memorandum reads as follows and which was prepared specifically for Special Agent H. T. BURK:

"At your request, following is a resume of information the undersigned furnished to Mr. RONNIE DUGGER, publisher of the "Texas Observer" and representative of a Washington, D.C., daily newspaper, on 17 December 1963.

"Mr. DUGGER called at this Headquarters at approximately 4:30 PM, 17 Dec 63; he showed me an identification card from the Department of Public Safety and stated he wished to obtain any information I knew relative to a visit by LEE HARVEY OSWALD to this Headquarters. Before I gave him any information, my supervisor, Lt. Col. WILLIAM BOYD SINCLAIR walked up to my desk and the two greeted one another. Colonel SINCLAIR asked Mr. DUGGER to come on in to his office and Mr. DUGGER told him that as soon as he asked me a few questions he would come in.

"Mr. DUGGER asked if I could furnish in detail everything in connection with the visit of LEE HARVEY OSWALD to this Headquarters and I advised him as follows: On 24 Nov 63 (Sunday), it was announced over TV that at that time there was no definite record as to Mr. OSWALD's whereabouts from May 1963 until the time of the assasination of President KENNEDY. I was at home at the time and I called Colonel SINCLAIR and advised him I was positive this man had been to our office, approximately 6 or 8 weeks prior to that date (24 Nov 63). I could not recall any information that would make me positive about a specific date but that I was positive that it had been on a Wednesday. I have been having quite a bit of trouble with my back and

8

On 12/19/63 at Austin, Texas File # SA 105-2909

by SA H. T. BURK/als Date dictated 12/27/63

This document contains neither recommendations nor conclusions of the FBI. It is the property of the FBI and is loaned to your agency; it and its contents are not to be distributed outside your agency.

legs for quite sometime, and the only times I have gone to town during my lunch hour was on our pay days to cash a check--we are paid on alternate Wednesdays. I was a few minutes late getting back to the office that day and Mr. OSWALD was waiting to see me when I got back. Mr. OSWALD stated that he had just come from the Governor's office to try to straighten out his discharge from the Marine Corps, which had been under 'other than honorable conditions.' The Governor's office told him they did not have anything to do with such things but that maybe this office would be able to assist him. Mr. OSWALD stated that at the time he was given the discharge under 'other than honorable conditions' he was told that if he lived an upright life for the next two years, he could then make application to have the type of discharge changed to 'honorable.' He told me that he was having difficulty in obtaining a job, and holding a job, with that type discharge. Also, he said it was embarrassing to his family. I asked him where he was registered and he said he registered in Florida but that he was living in Ft. Worth at the present time. I checked our locator file for HARVEY OSWALD (the name he gave me), but did not check any of the other OSWALD cards for possible identification since I presumed he was correct and was registered in Florida. I did not find a card for HARVEY OSWALD. We do have a card for LEE HARVEY OSWALD. Mr. OSWALD did not remember whether he had given his address in Fort Worth (at time of separation from the Marine Corps) as place of entry into service or not. I advised him to check with our local boards in Fort Worth when he got back and maybe they would have a copy of his Report of Separation (DD Form 214).

"This Headquarters maintains sets of military regulations from the various armed forces which jointly concern the Selective

9

3.

SA 105-2909

Service System. I checked these regulations in an attempt to learn the exact procedure Mr. OSWALD should follow in making application for a change in 'type' of discharge. I did not find the regulation covering this subject. I then gave Mr. OSWALD a copy of an information sheet (RC-1229) (copy attached) which lists the location of various types of military records, so that he could write direct and request the procedure for making the application for change in 'type' of discharge.

"During this entire interview, which lasted for approximately 30 minutes, Mr. OSWALD was very courteous.

"---"

"Mr. DUGGER advised me to inform the FBI of my knowledge of this case.

"---"

"Mr. DUGGER called me on the telephone sometime during the morning of 18 December and asked if Mr. OSWALD at any time mentioned to me that he had lived in Russia at one time. I told him no. Mr. DUGGER asked me if I saw Mr. OSWALD at the time he was supposedly at the Trek Cafe, 3100 South Congress. I told him no. Mr. DUGGER also asked if Mr. OSWALD had at any time during the interview mentioned anything as to his mode of transportation. I told him no. Mr. DUGGER advised me that he was now ready to mail his report in to the Washington, D.C., newspaper he represents.

"/s/ LEE DANNELLY

Mrs. LEE DANNELLY
Asst Chief
Administrative Division"

10

COMMISSION EXHIBIT No. 2137—Continued

4.

SA 105-2909

Mrs. DANNELLY further related orally that she is of firm belief at this time that the date on which LEE HARVEY OSWALD contacted her was September 25, 1963.

Mrs. DANNELLY advised that she cannot establish this date from any official record at the State Selective Service Headquarters due to the fact that no record was made at the time she interviewed OSWALD or at the time OSWALD called upon her. She advised that the date is established in the following manner. She advised that she brings her lunch to work each day and has lunch in the office with exception of the days on which she is paid which is every other Wednesday. She advised that on these so called pay days that she frequently goes to the bank for the purpose of withdrawing money from her account. She does not deposit her salary check in the bank due to the fact that these checks are mailed direct to the bank and she is not required to make these deposits, the checks being mailed direct from the office. She does business at the Capital National Bank, Austin, Texas, and on the date in question she advised that she recalls coming back to work slightly after 1:00 p.m., perhaps at about 1:05 p.m., and on that date had been to the main branch of the Capital National Bank, Austin, Texas, and cashed a check in the amount of $100 and in addition she had had lunch elsewhere other than the office where she normally had lunch. She advised that there is a possibility that the date on which OSWALD was in Austin, Texas, could have been September 11, 1963, because from her cancelled checks which she personally carried to the Capital National Bank she had the bank employee look at all of her cancelled checks for the last six months and he picked out only three of these checks that according to the bank stamp had been cashed inside the main Capital National Bank. The first of these checks, the more recent of them rather, was September 25, 1963; the second was September 11, 1963; and the third was July 31, 1963. Of these three checks Mrs. DANNELLY feels that the September 25, 1963, date is the more accurate date of the visit of OSWALD.

Mrs. DANNELLY further pointed out that her other banking operations and withdrawals from the bank are done at the drive-in window of the Capital National Bank which is directly across the street from the State Selective Service Headquarters on the south side of her building and

11

COMMISSION EXHIBIT No. 2137—Continued

5.

SA 105-2909

that she frequently did business at that drive-in window after normal banking hours and other checks cashed by her would bear a stamp indicating they were cashed at the drive-in window rather than at the main bank proper.

A photograph of LEE HARVEY OSWALD was exhibited to Mrs. DANNELLY and she stated that in her opinion the photograph looks like the man who came to State Selective Service Headquarters on the day in question inquiring concerning the discharge mentioned above.

Mrs. DANNELLY advised that she recalls being at the Trek Cafe on South Congress Avenue, Austin Texas, on November 24, 1963, at which time she was engaged in conversation with a man who is employed as a printer for the Austin daily paper and at that time this individual whose name is not known to her at this time advised her that he believed that he had seen LEE HARVEY OSWALD at the Trek Cafe sometime in the past. This man had seen OSWALD's photograph on television at that time and due to this conversation, Mrs. DANNELLY recalled her experience of having been contacted by the individual using the name of HARVEY OSWALD and recalled that the photograph seen on television resembled the individual who had contacted her using the name of HARVEY OSWALD.

Mrs. DANNELLY advised that the printer whom she engaged in conversation at the Trek Cafe was a white male, age 45, of slender build, approximate 5' 6" to 5' 8", 135 to 140 pounds, and during the course of conversation had mentioned that he had been recently divorced and had a home in the country where he kept a considerable number of dogs. Mrs. DANNELLY advised that she had seen this printer in the Trek Cafe on numerous other occasions and knew him by sight but not by name.

Mrs. DANNELLY likewise recalled as best she could remember at this time Mr. RONNIE DUGGER is a friend of the son of the printer referred to above. She also recalls that a waitress at the Trek Cafe made some comment indicating that she was of the opinion that OSWALD had been in that cafe at one time or another. She seems to recall

12

SA 105-2909

that this waitress was named BOBBIE, last name unknown, and that she was a sister-in-law of one BILL COVINGTON, manager of the Trek Cafe.

13

COMMISSION EXHIBIT No. 2137—Continued

FD-302 (Rev. 1-25-60)

FEDERAL BUREAU OF INVESTIGATION

1.

Date December 30, 1963

Mr. LARRY TEMPLE, Administrative Assistant to the Governor of Texas, Capital Building, Austin, Texas, advised a thorough search of all the guest registers maintained in the Governor's Office in Austin, Texas, back for the last preceeding six months failed to reveal a registration for LEE HARVEY OSWALD, or HARVEY OSWALD, or any other individual that can be possibly identical with LEE HARVEY OSWALD. He advised that as a general rule all individuals or guests coming to or calling on the Governor or any of the Administrative Assistants to the Governor are required to sign these guest registers. He advised that there is no record of OSWALD having signed such a register.

TEMPLE further pointed out that any individual contacting the Governor's Office with respect to a matter concerning the military, for example a military discharge, would under normal conditions have been referred to him, TEMPLE, for handling and interview. He advised that he at no time recalls ever having contacted LEE HARVEY OSWALD concerning any matter either concerning a U. S. Marine Corps Discharge or any other type matter. He advised that a thorough search of all of the records and indices maintained in the Governor's Office failed to reveal any information whatsoever concerning LEE HARVEY OSWALD and has no record of any correspondence ever having been carried on between Governor's Office of Texas and LEE HARVEY OSWALD.

14

On 12/19/63 at Austin, Texas File # SA 105-2909

by SA H. T. BURK/als Date dictated 12/27/63

This document contains neither recommendations nor conclusions of the FBI. It is the property of the FBI and is loaned to your agency; it and its contents are not to be distributed outside your agency.

COMMISSION EXHIBIT No. 2137—Continued

FD-302 (Rev. 1-25-60)

FEDERAL BUREAU OF INVESTIGATION

Date December 31, 1963

Mrs. LEE DANNELLY, Assistant Chief of the Administrative Division, State Selective Service Headquarters, Austin, Texas, advised the State Selective Service Headquarters at Austin, Texas, maintains a three inch by five inch locator card on all registrants with all boards located throughout the State of Texas and that these locator cards reveal that one LEE HARVEY OSWALD, Selective Service Number 41-114-39-532, born October 18, 1939, is a registrant with Local Board Number 14, which is located at Fort Worth, Texas. This card contains no other information whatsoever concerning LEE HARVEY OSWALD and any information concerning him in the possession of the Selective Service System would be located in the files of Local Board Number 114, Fort Worth, Texas.

Mrs. DANNELLY further pointed out that the locator cards in the State Selective Service Headquarters indicates that there are fifteen individuals with the last name OSWALD in the locator files and that she recalls having searched for a name HARVEY OSWALD in these files when the individual known to her as HARVEY OSWALD contacted her on or about September 25, 1963, and finding no name listed therein for HARVEY OSWALD she did not search for a LEE HARVEY OSWALD.

Mrs. DANNELLY further pointed out that she recalls that another employee of the State Selective Service Headquarters, namely Mr. JESSE E. SKRIVANEK, had brought HARVEY OSWALD back to her desk on the day in question which she thought to be September 25, 1963. She advised that she had checked and rechecked with JESSE E. SKRIVANEK who was on Christmas leave as of December 26, 1963, but that SKRIVANEK could not recall OSWALD by name and had made no notation concerning him at the time he came to State Selective Service Headquarters. She advised that as far as she knows Colonel SINCLAIR never at any time observed the individual using the name of HARVEY OSWALD and that JESSE E. SKRIVANEK is the only other employee that she can recall personally at this time who may have observed OSWALD.

Mrs. DANNELLY further pointed out that since she was last interviewed on December 19, 1963, she has since learned that the name of the printer whom she referred to

15

On 12/26/63 at Austin, Texas File # SA 105-2909

by SA H. T. BURK/als Date dictated 12/27/63

This document contains neither recommendations nor conclusions of the FBI. It is the property of the FBI and is loaned to your agency; it and its contents are not to be distributed outside your agency.

COMMISSION EXHIBIT No. 2137—Continued

2

SA 105-2909

in previous interview was a Mr. L. B. DAY who is a printer for the Austin American Statesman, a daily newspaper published in Austin, Texas. She likewise advised that she has learned that the name of the waitress in question whom she previously thought to be named BOBBIE is actually Mrs. STELLA NORMAN, a waitress employed at the Trek Cafe, Austin, Texas. She states that she cannot at this time think of any other information of a pertinent nature concerning the visit of LEE HARVEY OSWALD. She cannot recall him having made any statement whatsoever as to his mode of travel into or how he expected to depart from Austin, Texas, or his destination. She states that she has read a news item in the Texas Observer written by RONNIE DUGGER referred to in prior interview wherein DUGGER reported information reading as follows, "OSWALD had been in New Orleans last summer on September 23, 1963 Mrs. OSWALD and Mrs. RUTH PAINE of Irving drove to Irving and OSWALD left shortly thereafter.

"He turned up in Mexico City applying for travel papers to Russia via Cuba on September 27, 1963. He could have stopped in Austin, Texas, on his way to Mexico through Laredo, Texas."

Mrs. DANNELLY pointed out that the information referred to above apparently is information gathered by DUGGER himself and that she at no time ever furnished any such information to DUGGER. She stated that the information set out in the memorandum previously prepared for Special Agent H. T. BURK is the only information she had at the time of interview by DUGGER.

16

COMMISSION EXHIBIT No. 2137—Continued

FD-302 (Rev. 1-25-60)
1.

FEDERAL BUREAU OF INVESTIGATION

Date December 30, 1963

Lieutenant Colonel WILLIAM B. SINCLAIR, Chief of the Administrative Division, State Selective Service Headquarters, Austin, Texas, advised that he had never heard of or seen LEE HARVEY OSWALD until his name was mentioned on newscast and television programs on November 22, 1963, in connection with the assassination of President KENNEDY. He advised further that on November 24, 1963, his Assistant Chief of the Administrative Division, Mrs. LEE DANNELLY, called him at home and advised him that after observing the photographs of OSWALD on television and hearing his name announced that she recalled that this individual had contacted her at State Selective Service Headquarters sometime in the past six or eight weeks and that he had inquired at that time for information concerning a Marine corps discharge which he desired to have changed from "other than honorable" to an honorable discharge. Colonel SINCLAIR pointed out that at the time of this contact on November 24, 1963, Mrs. DANNELLY was unable to recall any specific date of this contact and that it did not appear to be pertinent at that time, but he advised Mrs. DANNELLY that she should use her own discretion about whether or not the matter should be reported to the proper authorities.

Colonel SINCLAIR was allowed to observe a photograph of LEE HARVEY OSWALD and he advised that he could not recall ever having seen that individual inside the State Selective Service Headquarters in Austin, Texas.

Colonel SINCLAIR further pointed out that there are a large number of callers at State Selective Service Headquarters and no register is maintained of the individuals who call at that office concerning routine matters which would have been the category of the inquiry referred to by Mrs. DANNELLY on behalf of OSWALD.

SINCLAIR advised that he has no further information of any sort that would have any bearing upon where OSWALD actually did visit the State Selective Service Headquarters or whether he did not. He pointed out that there is always a possibility that the individual who contacted the State Selective Service Headquarters may have been an individual by the name of OSWALD and been one other than LEE HARVEY OSWALD, subject of this investigation.

17

On 12/27/63 at Austin, Texas File # SA 105-2909

by SA H. T. BURK/als Date dictated 12/27/63

This document contains neither recommendations nor conclusions of the FBI. It is the property of the FBI and is loaned to your agency; it and its contents are not to be distributed outside your agency.

FD-302 (Rev. 1-25-60)

FEDERAL BUREAU OF INVESTIGATION

Date December 29, 1963

Mr. RONNIE DUGGER, Editor, The Texas Observer, Austin Texas, newspaper, 504 W. 245h Street, advised he learned from Mrs. LEE DANNELLY, State Selective Service Headquarters, Austin, Texas, that she was contacted by a person believed to be identical with LEE HARVEY OSWALD on about September 25, 1963, at Austin, Texas. DUGGER feels Mrs. DANNELLY's information is reliable and that she is a very capable individual of good judgment.

In addition, DUGGER pointed out that he had interviewed Mrs. STELLA NORMAN, waitress at Trek Cafe, South Congress Avenue, Austin, Texas, who advised she had waited on a customer "about two months ago" who looked just like the pictures she had seen of LEE HARVEY OSWALD. She had reported the man believed to be OSWALD drank two or three cups of coffee and stayed at the cafe thirty or forty minutes and was alone. She further advised DUGGER that she had Wednesday off each week and the day she believes she saw OSWALD could not have been on September 25, 1963, since this date was on Wednesday.

DUGGER also had talked to L. B. DAY, a pressman for the American Statesman, Austin, Texas, newspaper. DAY claimed to have seen the man referred to by Mrs. NORMAN, and he also was convinced the man was identical with OSWALD.

DUGGER pointed out that while he feels the information furnished by Mrs. DANNELLY is reliable the information furnished by STELLA NORMAN and L. B. DAY is possibly a case of mistaken identity. His reason for this latter opinion was due to the statement of STELLA NORMAN that she did not work on Wednesday and Mrs. DANNELLY is positive the interview she had with the person believed to be OSWALD was on Wednesday.

On 12/28/63 at Austin, Texas File # SA 105-2909

by SA H. T. BURK/cbl Date dictated 12/28/63

This document contains neither recommendations nor conclusions of the FBI. It is the property of the FBI and is loaned to your agency; it and its contents are not to be distributed outside your agency.

18

SA 105-2909

III. MISCELLANEOUS

19

Commission Exhibit No. 2137—Continued

FD-302 (Rev. 1-25-60)

FEDERAL BUREAU OF INVESTIGATION

1

Date December 20, 1963

OREN PUGH, Agent in Charge, U. S. Customs Investigators, Laredo, Texas, advised SA ROBERT L. CHAPMAN on 12/20/63 that two days ago, December 18, 1963, Mr. (First Name Unknown) GONZALEZ, Customs Administrator, Miguel Aleman, Mexico, stated that the FBI had been checking for information on OSWALD and that he (GONZALEZ) had found the information the FBI wanted concerning the re-entry at Miguel Aleman the same day OSWALD's brother who had entered Mexico at Miguel Aleman the same day OSWALD entered Mexico at Laredo, Texas.

Mr. GONZALEZ advised PUGH that he was holding these records at his office in Miguel Aleman.

PUGH could furnish no additional information.

20

On 12/20/63 at Laredo, Texas File # SA 105-2909

by SA ROBERT L. CHAPMAN/dte Date dictated 12/20/63

This document contains neither recommendations nor conclusions of the FBI. It is the property of the FBI and is loaned to your agency; it and its contents are not to be distributed outside your agency.

Commission Exhibit No. 2137—Continued

SA 105-2909

The following investigation was conducted by SA CHRISTOPHER C. ISBELL.

On December 24, 1963, CARLOS RAMOS, Mexican Customs Administration and MIGUEL ALEMAN Mexico, stated that EDUARDO GONZALEZ, the customs administrator, would not return from Mexico City until January 2, 1964. RAMOS stated he had located the original copy of the Temporary Entry Permit showing the entry of ANTHONY W. OSSWALD into Mexico at that port of Entry on September 27, 1963. RAMOS and the other employee stated this was believed to be the information which GONZALEZ wanted to furnish the FBI.

It is to be noted that inquiry has previously been made concerning the entry into Mexico of ANTHONY W. OSSWALD.

21X

COMMISSION EXHIBIT No. 2137—Continued

UNITED STATES DEPARTMENT OF JUSTICE
FEDERAL BUREAU OF INVESTIGATION

Copy to:

Report of: SA JOHN M. KEMMY Office: SAN ANTONIO
Date: February 28, 1964

File Number: 105-2909 Bufile 105=82555

Title: LEE HARVEY OSWALD

Character: INTERNAL SECURITY - RUSSIA - CUBA

Synopsis:

FLORENCE NORMAN and L. B. DAY believe OSWALD was in Austin, Texas, in October and/or November, 1963. Further investigation does not substantiate this. Efforts to locate persons for knowledge of travel by OSWALD negative. JOHN H. BOWEN reported to have passed through Laredo. Texas, from Mexico on or about 1/1/64. Reverend WALTER L. HLUCHAN has known ALBERT OSBORNE, aka., JOHN HOWARD BOWEN since 1939. HLUCHAN states OSBORNE years ago lost or misplaced his Mexican Tourist card and BOWEN, who was leaving Mexico, gave OSBORNE BOWEN's card to use for identification. HLUCHAN furnished background information concerning OSBORNE. Results of miscellaneous investigation set forth.

- P -

DETAILS:

— Commission Exhibit No. 2138 —

This document contains neither recommendations nor conclusions of any kind. It is the property of the FBI, and is a loan to your agency; it and/or its contents are not to be distributed outside your agency.
16—74635-1 GPO

COMMISSION EXHIBIT No. 2138

I. TRAVEL

COMMISSION EXHIBIT No. 2138—Continued

Date January 9, 1964

JESSE A. SKRIVANEK, resident of 5909 Carleen Drive, employed as purchasing clerk, Procurement Division, State Headquarters, Selective Service System, 515 Western Republic Building, advised the following:

The Monday following the assassination of President JOHN F. KENNEDY, Mrs. DANNELLY of his office asked him if he could recall an individual who she believed to be HARVEY OSWALD having visited that office.

Thereafter he "racked his brain" but could not recall having ever seen anyone resembling OSWALD, having seen several photographs of OSWALD in the newspapers as well as having observed him on television.

More specifically he could not recall the individual or instance referred to by Mrs. DANNELLY.

On 1/2/64 at Austin, Texas File # SA 105=2909

by SA ROBERT W. CARNES/jb;cbl Date dictated 1/4/64

This document contains neither recommendations nor conclusions of the FBI. It is the property of the FBI and is loaned to your agency; it and its contents are not to be distributed outside your agency.

COMMISSION EXHIBIT No. 2138—Continued

FEDERAL BUREAU OF INVESTIGATION

Date February 5, 1964

LORINE SHULER, Cashier, Trek Cafe, 3100 South Congress, advised the following:

STELLA NORMAN was no longer employed as a waitress at this cafe. NORMAN's last known residence was the second house on the east side of Bannister Street, running north off of Ben White Boulevard.

During NORMAN's employment at the Trek Cafe her hours were from three until eleven p.m., except on Fridays and Saturdays when she worked from five p.m., until one a.m.

NORMAN's day off was Wednesday.

She could not recall an instance during NORMAN's employment when NORMAN had been the only waitress on duty at the Trek Cafe. The work schedules were set up so there would always be two waitresses on duty at all times, but one might be temporarily preoccupied by answering the telephone or using the washroom normally for very few minutes at a time.

SHULER advised that on three or four different occasions within a week's span of time shortly after the assassination of President JOHN F. KENNEDY, NORMAN mentioned to her that she had seen LEE HARVEY OSWALD as a customer in the Trek Cafe sometime prior to the assassination. However, she did not pay too much attention to NORMAN and could not recall the details of what NORMAN had told her but that each time the story was told by NORMAN she varied from the previous story or stories. These remarks by NORMAN were made while on duty at the cafe. To her recollection NORMAN made these remarks to her, SHULER, and to her alone.

In conclusion SHULER said she did not place any faith in the stories related by NORMAN hence more or less dismissed the matter from her mind.

- 4 -

On 1/2/64 at Austin, Texas File # SA 105-2909

by SA ROBERT W. CARNES & H. T. BURK/cbl Date dictated 2/3/64

This document contains neither recommendations nor conclusions of the FBI. It is the property of the FBI and is loaned to your agency; it and its contents are not to be distributed outside your agency.

COMMISSION EXHIBIT No. 2138—Continued

FEDERAL BUREAU OF INVESTIGATION

Date January 9, 1964

FLORENCE ESTELLA NORMAN, widow, 4301 Bannister, advised the following:

She began employment at the Trek Cafe, 3100 South Congress, the latter part of August, 1963, and was so employed until the Monday before Thanksgiving.

From the beginning of this employment until October, 1963, her hours were from 5:00 p.m., until 1:00 a.m., seven days a week. Her hours were changed and she began work either at 1:00 or 3:00 p.m., and worked until either 11:00 p.m., or midnight except Fridays and Saturdays when her hours were from 5:00 p.m., until 1:00 a.m.

The Sunday after the assassination of President KENNEDY while at the Trek Cafe she saw a picture of LEE HARVEY OSWALD in an Austin paper and recognized him as a customer she had served at the Trek Cafe.

This customer was at the cafe in the midafternoon so by the above working hours she concluded this individual was present at the Trek Cafe either the latter part of October or the early part of November 1963.

She recalled the following concerning this incident:

She was alone in the restaurant, neither any other employee nor customer being present. The cook was in the kitchen. This individual came into the restaurant and ordered coffee. He appeared very nervous. He kept fooling with the paper napkins and appeared to be writing or doodling on these napkins. He used three or four napkins and must have put these in his pocket before leaving as the napkins were not left on the table, ashtray or floor.

The customer remained 30 or 45 minutes and had either three or four cups of coffee. He paid 10¢ for each coffee as the Trek does not give refills on coffee.

- 5 -

On 1/2/64 at Austin, Texas File # SA 105-2909

by SA ROBERT W. CARNES/jb;cbl Date dictated 1/4/64

This document contains neither recommendations nor conclusions of the FBI. It is the property of the FBI and is loaned to your agency; it and its contents are not to be distributed outside your agency.

COMMISSION EXHIBIT No. 2138—Continued

This customer was alone at all times. She did not notice his mode of transportation on leaving and neither did she notice the direction in which he left.

Seeing he was nervous she tried to start a conversation with him but he did not respond.

On seeing the photograph of the accused assasin in the paper that Sunday she exclaimed out loud, "My God I know him."

A Mr. DAY who is employed at a local newspaper was in the cafe as a customer.

Mr. DAY asked her how she knew the accused assasin and she told him, "As a customer."

Mr. DAY then said he thought he too had seen this individual in the Trek Cafe.

She could not recall Mr. DAY being in the cafe when this customer whom she believed to be identical with the accused assassin of President KENNEDY was there, but Mr. DAY could have been present.

NORMAN advised she could not recall having discussed this matter with anyone other than Mr. DAY and the newspaper reporter who had contacted her about two weeks prior to this interview at her then place of employment, Bill's Grill, located at South Congress and Riverside Drive. As a matter of fact she had not even discussed this with her parents.

In conclusion NORMAN said she did not know who had directed the newspaper reporter to her.

Date 2/5/64

WILLIAM COVINGTON, owner, Trek Cafe and Motel, 3100 South Congress, Austin, Texas, advised as follows:

FLORENCE NORMAN, who was commonly known as STELLA NORMAN began employment as a waitress at the Trek Cafe on July 26, 1963, with her hours being from three o'clock p.m. until eleven o'clock p.m., Sunday, Monday, Tuesday and Thursday and from five o'clock p.m., until one o'clock a.m., on Friday and Saturday.

Wednesday was NORMAN'S day off.

Her last day of employment was on Monday of the week ending Saturday, November 30, 1963.

He determined these dates of employment by referring to his payroll book and the hours of her employment he recalled from memory.

Specifically concerning the date of September 25, 1963, his payroll record showed that NORMAN had been paid for the usual six days work for the week ending September 28, 1963, indicating to him that NORMAN had her regular day off on Wednesday September 25, 1963.

According to his records, NORMAN worked on only two Wednesdays during her employment, these being the Wednesdays of weeks ending on Saturdays, August 31, 1963, and October 19, 1963, on those occasions NORMAN was paid for full seven days of work.

NORMAN was not related to him. To his knowledge NORMAN was not related with anyone connected with the Trek Cafe.

He had heard NORMAN make mention of having seen LEE HARVEY OSWALD, reputed assassinator of President JOHN F. KENNEDY in the Trek Cafe, though he could not recall the party to whom she made this statement and she had never discussed the matter with him directly.

- 7 -

On 1/22/64 at Austin, Texas File # SA 105-2909

by SAs ROBERT W. CARNES & H. T. BURK/cbl & cas Date dictated 2/3/64

This document contains neither recommendations nor conclusions of the FBI. It is the property of the FBI and is loaned to your agency; it and its contents are not to be distributed outside your agency.

He did not pay too much attention to NORMAN in this regard as he felt it was "foolishness" on NORMAN'S part.

He believed NORMAN to be somewhat irresponsible and unreliable for the following reason. In terminating this employment, NORMAN did not resign, but, for several days she would call in and say she was ill and could not report for work. It seemed that each time some other employee would mention having seen NORMAN at a night club the previous evening "living it up." After several days she quit calling in and just did not show for work again.

Mr. COVINGTON advised that in his manner of operating the Trek Cafe there are always at least two waitresses on duty in the cafe and one waitress should not be left alone by the other for a period of more than ten minutes for he would not permit this. Such an absence should be only to use the wash room or answer the telephone.

In conclusion, Mr. COVINGTON advised that the guests in the Trek Motel for the nights of September 24 and 25, 1963, were all regular customers who were known to him, and not identifiable by name or photograph with LEE HARVEY OSWALD.

FEDERAL BUREAU OF INVESTIGATION

Date 1/23/64

L. (only) B. (only) DAY, 4524 Duval Street, Austin, Texas, was contacted after attempts had been made to contact him on January 2, 5, 7, 9, 10, and 13, 1964, at various times of the day. DAY advised as follows:

When he first saw the photograph of LEE HARVEY OSWALD in the newspaper a day or two after the assassination of President JOHN F. KENNEDY, he was in the Trek Cafe located on South Congress in Austin. Present was STELLA, the waitress at the cafe, whose last name was not known to him.

On seeing the photograph, he said, "Gol dang, STELLA, don't you remember him?" Whereupon she answered, she did not.

He then told STELLA she had waited on that man, there in the Trek Cafe, about six weeks prior to this occurrence. He then told STELLA that OSWALD was sitting in the cafe one day when he, DAY, was "ragging her" and reminded her that on that occasion he told her, "If I could find a wife who would make me a living, I'd marry her," and that STELLA had said not to try to trap her, that she was already married and making a living for that husband.

He reminded STELLA that OSWALD had been sitting on the third or fourth stool from the cash register and that he, DAY, had sat on the last stool in the rear of the cafe.

He reminded STELLA that OSWALD had what appeared to be a pencil in his hand and seemed to be "jotting" on something; that OSWALD kept looking in the direction of the kitchen.

After reminding STELLA of the above, STELLA sat down and after appearing to give the "matter some deep thought," told him she too recalled seeing OSWALD in the

On 1/17/64 at Austin, Texas File # SA 105-2909

by SA ROBERT W. CARNES/dnb & cas Date dictated 1/17/64

This document contains neither recommendations nor conclusions of the FBI. It is the property of the FBI and is loaned to your agency; it and its contents are not to be distributed outside your agency.

cafe on that occasion.

He supposed he recalled OSWALD'S appearance in the Trek so vividly because OSWALD, to him, resembled two of his friends, BERNIE BALKY, who would be known to TOMMY ATTRA, and BILL, who operates Bill's Wrecking Yard on the Old San Antonio Highway out of Austin.

He did not mention this resemblance to a reporter who talked to him about this matter as he had already told the reporter that OSWALD resembled a "cedar chopper," a not too favorable comparison, and did not want to embarrass BERNIE BALKY and BILL by extending such a comparison to them for their resemblance to OSWALD.

He did not tell STELLA to joke with OSWALD, as related by the reporter in the Texas Observer, and this was a misunderstanding on the reporter's part.

Refering back to the incident of OSWALD'S appearance in the Trek Cafe, he advised that OSWALD was sitting at the counter on his arrival there and estimated this was some six or seven weeks prior to President KENNEDY'S assassination. He said OSWALD remained thirty or forty minutes; that he did not notice OSWALD on his departure as to what direction he took or his mode of travel.

Normally, there are at least two waitresses present at the Trek Cafe, but on this occasion he could recall only STELLA being present.

While OSWALD was there, two or three people came in and had coffee, though he could not recall who they were, or even if he knew them.

This must have occurred after 3:00 p.m. as at that time STELLA was reporting for work at 3:00 p.m.

In conclusion, he wished to say that he was wrong as many times as he was right, but that he believed the man at the Trek Cafe was, in fact, OSWALD.

COMMISSION EXHIBIT No. 2138—Continued

FEDERAL BUREAU OF INVESTIGATION

Date 1/23/64

TOM ATTRA, Street Circulation, Austin American newspaper, Austin, Texas, advised the following:

He has known L. B. DAY for a number of years. In the last few years DAY has had several different wives and has given the appearance of being a bit unstable.

He was of this opinion as in his infrequent conversations with DAY, DAY had conversed "in a wandering manner" and really appeared to have imagined some of the things he related.

As a result thereof, he has accepted things told to him by DAY with "a grain of salt."

On 1/17/64 at Austin, Texas File # SA 105-2909

by SA ROBERT W. CARNES/dnb & cas Date dictated 1/17/64

This document contains neither recommendations nor conclusions of the FBI. It is the property of the FBI and is loaned to your agency; it and its contents are not to be distributed outside your agency.

COMMISSION EXHIBIT No. 2138—Continued

FEDERAL BUREAU OF INVESTIGATION

Date January 30, 1964

Colonel VANCE E. MURPHY, Director, Department of Aviation, City of Austin, Municipal Airport, 3600 Manor Road, Austin, Texas, advised the following:

There were no direct scheduled commercial flights between Austin, Texas, and New Orleans, Louisiana, in September of 1963.

Continental Airlines had direct flights between Austin, Texas, and Houston, Texas, in September, 1963. This was the only direct scheduled service available between Austin and Houston at that time.

More recently, Continental Airlines has moved its entire service from Austin Municipal Airport.

Records of Continental Airlines Company are maintained at the home office located at the Los Angeles International Airport, Los Angeles 9, California.

In conclusion, MURPHY advised he had not retained a schedule of Continental Airlines, Austin - Houston service, which would have been in effect on September 25, 1963; however, he said from memory he believed flights to Houston departed Austin at 10:30 a.m., 3:00 or 4:00 p.m., and 8:00 or 9:00 p.m., with return flights departing Houston 7:00 a.m., 1:00 p.m., and 5:30 or 6:00 p.m.

On 1/22/64 at Austin, Texas File # SA 105-2909

by SA ROBERT W. CARNES/dnb/cbl Date dictated 1/25/64

This document contains neither recommendations nor conclusions of the FBI. It is the property of the FBI and is loaned to your agency; it and its contents are not to be distributed outside your agency.

FEDERAL BUREAU OF INVESTIGATION

Date February 6, 1964

ROY T. BARNES, District Sales Manager, Braniff International Airways advised that no name record is maintained of passengers arriving in Austin by Braniff.

He advised that the only records maintained of passengers leaving Austin by Braniff Airways is the reservation card filed on each passenger. He said these cards after one month are sent to Braniff International Airways, Love Field, Dallas, Texas, for filing.

On 1/29/64 at Austin, Texas File # SA 105-2909

by SA ROBERT W. CARNES/cbl Date dictated 2/3/64

This document contains neither recommendations nor conclusions of the FBI. It is the property of the FBI and is loaned to your agency; it and its contents are not to be distributed outside your agency.

FEDERAL BUREAU OF INVESTIGATION

Date February 6, 1964

TOM SMITH, Station Manager, Trans-Texas Airways, Inc., made available his reservation cards for September 24, 25 and 26, 1963, for all flights departing Austin on those dates.

These reservation cards were reviewed in the name of known aliases of LEE HARVEY OSWALD and all variations of the name and aliases and none was identified with him.

SMITH advised that no lists are maintained of passengers on incoming flights.

- 14 -

On 1/29/64 at Austin, Texas File # SA 105=2909

by SA ROBERT W. CARNES/cbl Date dictated 2/3/64

This document contains neither recommendations nor conclusions of the FBI. It is the property of the FBI and is loaned to your agency; it and its contents are not to be distributed outside your agency.

COMMISSION EXHIBIT No. 2138—Continued

FEDERAL BUREAU OF INVESTIGATION

Date February 6, 1964

Mrs. LEE DANNELLY, Assistant Chief of the Administrative Division, State Selective Service Headquarters, Austin, Texas, advised as best she can recall the person who contacted her giving his name as HARVEY OSWALD on or about September 25, 1963, was wearing grey trousers and a light colored shirt, not white, but possibly a faded blue. His clothes were wrinkled but clean and otherwise neat but worn looking. She could not recall the type of shoes he wore and pointed out that his shoes would not have been visible to her during her interview with him, although she could have observed his shoes when he walked up to her desk and as he left. She cannot recall his having a hat although he may have left one in the waiting room when he came in.

- 15 -

On 1/31/64 at Austin, Texas File # SA 105-2909

by SA H. T. BURK/cbl Date dictated 2/1/64

This document contains neither recommendations nor conclusions of the FBI. It is the property of the FBI and is loaned to your agency; it and its contents are not to be distributed outside your agency.

COMMISSION EXHIBIT No. 2138—Continued

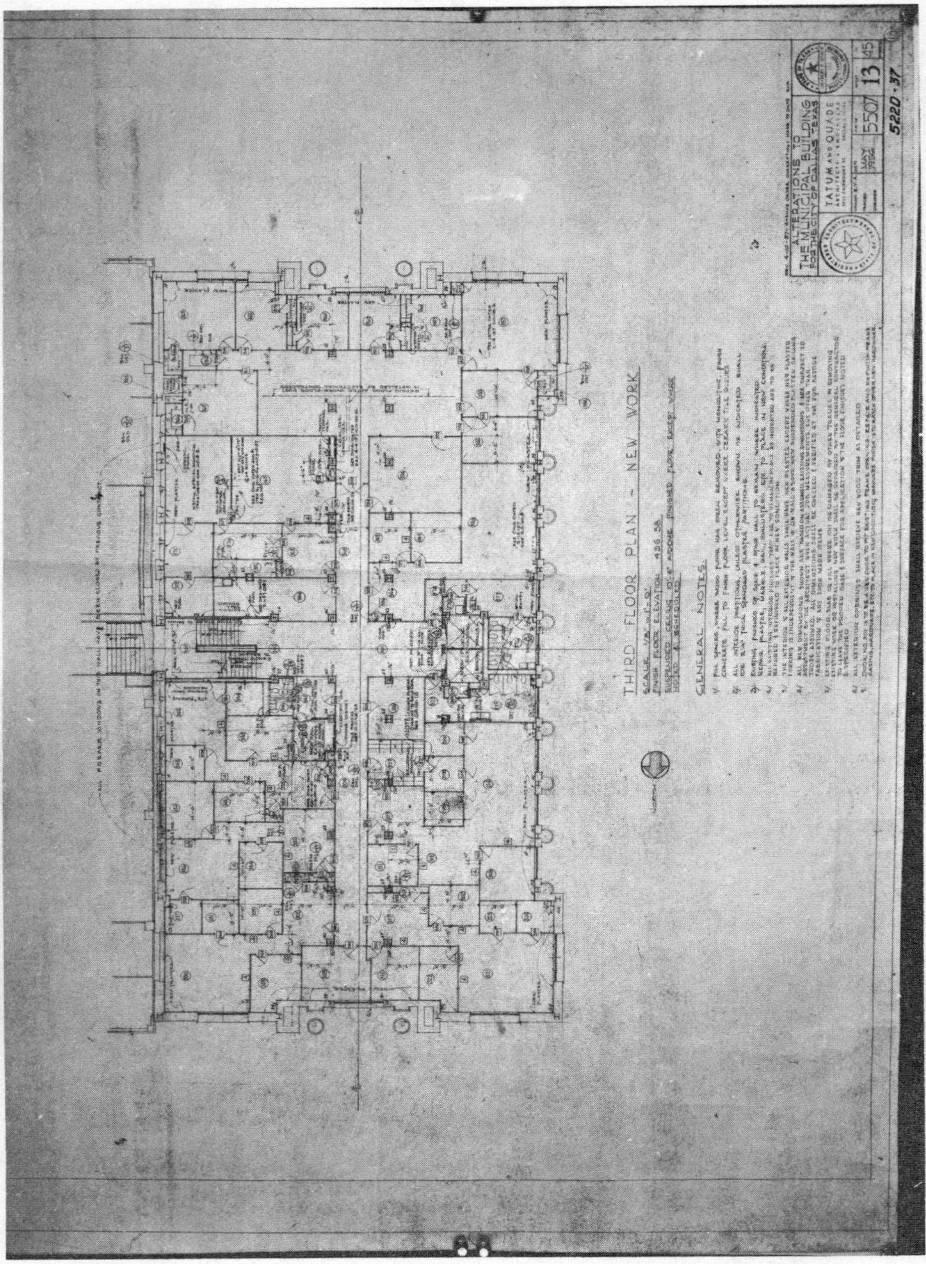

COMMISSION EXHIBIT No. 2139

ROOM FINISH SCHEDULE • THIRD FLOOR

Nº	NAME	FLOOR	BASE	WALLS	WAINSCOT MATERIAL	WAINSCOT HT.	CEILING MATERIAL	CEILING TYPE	CEILING HT	TRIM	REMARKS
301	ELEVATOR LOBBY	ASPHALT TILE	6' METAL	PLASTER	NONE	—	PLASTER	SUSPENDED	10'-6"	METAL	
302	STAIR HALL	" "	EXIST'G MARBLE	EXIST PLASTER	EXIST MARBLE	—	EXIST PLASTER	———		WOOD ON WDS.	RUBBER TILE TREADS ON STAIRS
303	BUILD'G CONN'G PASSAGE	" "	" "	" "	" "	—	NEW SF PLASTER	SUSPENDED.	13'-0"		
304	PUBLIC CORRIDOR	" "	5' METAL	PLASTER	NONE	—	SF PLASTER	SUSPENDED.	10'-6"	METAL	
305	PUBLIC CORRIDOR	" "	" "	"	"	—	" "	"	10'-6"	"	
306	~~[illegible]~~ Stolen Property Bur.	" "	" "	"	"	—	ACOUS TILE	CONCEALED SUSP	10'-6"	"	
307	RECORDING ROOM	" "	" "	"	"	—	" "	" "	10'-6"	"	COUNTER DET
308	RECORDING TYPIST	" "	" "	"	"	—	" "	" "	10'-6"	"	
309	SECTY. BURGLARY, THEFT.	" "	" "	"	"	—	" "	" "	10'-6"	"	
310	SUPPLY CLOSET	" "	" "	"	"	—	SF PLASTER	SUSPENDED.	10'-6"	"	SHEET DET —
311	LIEUT. BURGLARY THEFT.	" "	" "	"	"	—	ACOUS TILE	CONCEALED SUSP	10'-6"	"	
312	DESK OFFICER " "	" "	" "	"	"	—	" "	" "	10'-6"	"	
313	CAPTAIN " "	" "	" "	"	"	—	" "	" "	10'-6"	" & WOOD	
314	SQUAD RM " "	" "	" "	"	"	—	" "	" "	10'-6"	" " "	
315	INTERVIEW " "	" "	" "	"	"	—	" "	" "	10'-6"	"	
316	INTERVIEW " "	" "	" "	"	"	—	" "	" "	10'-6"	"	
317	SECRETARY JUVENILE	" "	" "	"	"	—	" "	" "	10'-6"	"	
318	SUPPLY CLOSET "	" "	" "	"	"	—	SF PLASTER	SUSPENDED	10'-6"	"	SHEET DET
319	CAPTAIN JUVENILE	" "	" "	"	"	—	ACOUS TILE	CONCEALED SUSP	10'-6"	" & WOOD	
320	LIEUT "	" "	" "	"	"	—	" "	" "	10'-6"	"	
321	SQUAD RM. "	" "	" "	"	"	—	" "	" "	10'-6"	" & WOOD	
322	HOLD RM "	" "	" "	"	"	—	" "	" "	10'-6"	"	
323	INTERVIEW "	" "	" "	"	"	—	" "	" "	10'-6"	"	
324	INTERVIEW "	" "	" "	"	"	—	" "	" "	10'-6"	"	
325	PRESS ROOM.	" "	" "	"	"	—	" "	" "	10'-6"	" & WOOD	
326	SECRETARY AUTO-THEFT	" "	" "	"	"	—	" "	" "	10'-6"	"	
327	SUPPLY CLOSET "	" "	" "	"	"	—	SF PLASTER	SUSPENDED	10'-6"	"	SHEET DET
328	CAPTAIN AUTO-THEFT	" "	" "	"	"	—	ACOUS TILE	CONC'L'D SUSP	10'-6"	"	
329	LIEUT " "	" "	" "	"	"	—	" "	" "	10'-6"	"	
330	SQUAD "	" "	" "	"	"	—	" "	" "	10'-6"	" & WOOD	
331	INTERVIEW "	" "	" "	"	"	—	" "	" "	10'-6"	"	
332	SECRETARY FORGERY	" "	" "	"	"	—	" "	" "	10'-6"	"	
333	SUPPLY CLOSET "	" "	" "	"	"	—	SF PLASTER	SUSPENDED	10'-6"	"	SHEET DET
334	LIEUT — FORGERY	" "	" "	"	"	—	ACOUS TILE	CONC'L'D SUSP	10'-6"	"	
335	CAPTAIN "	" "	" "	"	"	—	" "	" "	10'-6"	"	
336	SQUAD ROOM "	" "	" "	"	"	—	" "	" "	10'-6"	"	
337	INTERVIEW "	" "	" "	"	"	—	" "	" "	10'-6"	"	
338	SECRETARY HOMICIDE	" "	" "	"	"	—	" "	" "	10'-6"	"	
339	SUPPLY CLOSET "	" "	" "	"	"	—	SF PLASTER	SUSPENDED	10'-6"	"	SHEET DET
340	CAPTAIN HOMICIDE	" "	" "	"	"	—	ACOUS TILE	CONC'L'D SUSP	10'-6"	"	
341	LIEUT. " "	" "	" "	"	"	—	" "	" "	10'-6"	"	
342	SQUAD ROOM "	" "	" "	"	"	—	" "	" "	10'-6"	"	
343	INTERVIEW "	" "	" "	"	"	—	" "	" "	10'-6"	"	
344	INTERVIEW "	" "	" "	"	"	—	" "	" "	10'-6"	"	
345	HOLD ROOM "	" "	" "	"	"	—	SF PLASTER	SUSPENDED	9'-6"	"	
346	SECRETARY PERSONNEL	" "	" "	"	"	—	ACOUS TILE	CONC'L'D SUSP.	10'-6"	"	
347	SUPPLIES "	" "	" "	"	"	—	SF PLASTER	SUSPENDED	10'-6"	"	
348	CAPTAIN "	" "	" "	"	"	—	ACOUS TILE	CONC'L'D SUSP	10'-6"	"	
349	SQUAD ROOM "	" "	" "	"	"	—	" "	" "	10'-6"	"	
350	RECORDS	" "	" "	"	"	—	" "	" "	10'-6"	"	
351	SECRETARIES CHIEFS	" "	" "	"	"	—	" "	" "	10'-6"	" & WOOD	
352	SUPPLY CLOSET	" "	" "	"	"	—	SF PLASTER	SUSPENDED.	10'-6"	"	SHEET DET
~~353~~	~~SUPPLY CLOSET~~	~~" "~~	~~" "~~	~~"~~	~~"~~		~~" "~~	~~" "~~	~~10'-6"~~	~~"~~	~~SHEET DET~~ THIS CLOSET ELIMINATED SEE C.O. NO. 2
354	CONFERENCE RM.	" "	" "	"	"	—	ACOUST TILE	CONC'L'D SUSP	10'-6"	"	
355	CAPTAIN ADMIN. ASST	" "	" "	"	"	—	" "	" "	10'-6"	" & WOOD	
356	SECRETARIES	" "	" "	"	"	—	" "	" "	10'-6"	"	
357	CHIEF OF POLICE	" "	" "	"	"	—	" "	" "	10'-6"	" & WOOD	
~~358~~	~~WARDROBE CLOSET~~	~~" "~~	~~" "~~	~~"~~	~~"~~		~~SF PLASTER~~	~~SUSPENDED.~~	~~10'-6"~~	~~"~~	~~SHEET DET~~ THIS CLOSET ELIMINATED SEE C.O. NO. 2
359	DEPUTY CHIEF	" "	" "	"	"	—	ACOUS TILE	CONC'L'D SUSP	10'-6"	"	
360	DEPUTY CHIEF	" "	" "	"	"	—	" "	" "	10'-6"	" & WOOD	
361	DEPUTY CHIEF	" "	" "	"	"	—	" "	" "	10'-6"	" " "	
362	DEPUTY CHIEF	" "	" "	"	"	—	" "	" "	10'-6"	" " "	
363	ASSISTANT CHIEF	" "	" "	"	"	—	" "	" "	10'-6"	" " "	
364	SUPPLY CLOSET	" "	" "	"	"	—	SF PLASTER	SUSPENDED	10'-6"	"	SHEET DET
365	INSPECTORS	" "	" "	"	"	—	ACOUS TILE	CONCEALED SUSP	10'-6"	"	
366	SUPPLY CLOSET	" "	" "	"	"	—	SF PLASTER	SUSPENDED	10'-6"	"	SHEET DET
367	DISPATCH ROOM.	" "	" "	ACOUS TILE ON PLASTER	"	—	ACOUS TILE	CONCEALED SUSP	10'-6"	"	SPECIAL ACOUSTICAL TREATMENT ON ROOM 367A - WALLS & CLG. SEE C.O. # 2
368	DISPATCH SUPERVISOR	" "	" "	SF PLASTER.	"	—	" "	" "	10'-6"	"	
369	SUPPLY CLOSET	" "	" "	" "	"	—	SF PLASTER	SUSPENDED	10'-6"	"	
370	TELETYPE ROOM	" "	" "	ACOUS TILE ON PLASTER	"	—	ACOUS TILE	CONCEAL'D SUSP	10'-6"	"	
371	RADIO KKB EQPT. RM	" "	" "	S.F. PLASTER	"	—	" "	" "	10'-6"	"	
372	COMMUNICATIONS EQPT	" "	" "	" "	"	—	SF PLASTER	SUSPENDED	10'-6"	"	
373	VESTIBULE MENS TLT	CERAMIC TILE	3/8" COVE WALL TILE	" "	GL WALL TILE	4'-3 5/8"	" "	"	10'-0"	"	
374	" " WOMENS TLT	" "	3/8" " "	" "	" " "	4'-3 5/8"	" "	"	10'-0"	"	
375	MENS TOILET	" "	3/8" " "	" "	" " "	4'-3 5/8"	" "	"	10'-6"	" & WOOD	CLG. 7'-6" OVER W.C. DET
376	WOMENS TOILET	" "	3/8" " "	" "	" " "	4'-3 5/8"	" "	"	10'-6"	" " "	" 7'-6" OVER W.C. DET
377	WOMENS LOUNGE	ASPHALT TILE	5' METAL	" "	NONE	—	ACOUS TILE	CONC'L'D SUSP	10'-6"	" " "	
378	JANITORS CLOSET	MONO FIN CONC FILL	6" CEM FL	CEM. PLAS	"	—	SF PLASTER	SUSPENDED	10'-6"	"	
379	JANITORS CLOSET	" " " "	6" " "	CEM. PLAS.	"	—	" "	"	10'-6"	"	
380	PRISONERS TOILET	CERAMIC TILE	3/8" COVE WALL TILE	S.F. PLAS.	GL WALL TILE	4'-3 5/8"	" "	"	9'-6"	"	SHEET DET.
381	" " "	" "	3/8" " "	" "	" " "	4'-3 5/8"	" "	"	9'-6"	"	SHEET DET.
382	MECH SPACE	CONCRETE	NONE	FIBER. PLAS.	NONE	—	STRUCTURAL	———	——	———	
383	MECH. SPACE	" "	"	" "	"	—	" "	———	——	———	
384	UNASSIGNED	ASPH. TILE		PLASTER	NONE	—	S.F. PLAS.	SUSPENDED	10'-0"	MET. & WOOD	
	MAIN STAIR (EXISTING)	RUBBER TILE OVER EXISTING MARBLE	EXISTING MARBLE BASE	EXIST. PLAS.	EXIST. MARBLE	—	EXIST. PLAS.	VARIES	——	EXISTING	

COMMISSION EXHIBIT NO. 2140

2605

WFAA-TV reel PKT 30
Sunday a.m., November 24, 1963

REPORTERS' DESCRIPTION OF OSWALD TRANSFER
AND POLICE PREPARATION

BOB THORNTON. The story of Oswald from city jail to county jail. And for that report, here is ABC's Bill Lord at the city jail. Bill, what's the situation?

BILL LORD. Well, I am presently in the basement of the Dallas Municipal Building, and it is like an armed camp. For the past half hour, scores of police have been filing past me, carrying riot guns and rifles. Police officials are frankly worried. They don't want anything to happen to Oswald. They firmly believe that he is the man who killed the President. They want to make sure he is safely transferred to the county jail and that he does stand trial and is convicted. The elevator that will bring him down from the fifth floor to the basement is just several feet away from me. When he comes through here, I will be able to see him and describe to you the same. And that's the latest from City Hall.

BOB THORNTON. Thank you, Bill. We have other remote facilities at the county jail now, awaiting the arrival of Lee Oswald from the city jail to the county jail. And for the situation there now, here is ABC's Roger Sharp reporting.

ROGER SHARP. At the scene of last Friday's assassination, heavy Sunday traffic is filing by along the Elm Street approach to the Triple

COMMISSION EXHIBIT No. 2141

2

Underpass. A crowd of several hundred Dallas citizens has gathered along the Houston Avenue side of the Dallas County Courthouse, the route of the Presidential motorcade, the area where President Kennedy passed moments before the fatal shots rang out. This is a curious crowd--no obvious anger in their faces--but all possible security precautions have been taken. Policemen are stationed at every fifteen feet along the entire block. This crowd, by the way, is considerably larger than the crowd that lined this very same street more than forty-six hours ago, when the Presidential motorcade moved by. Police have blocked off the Courthouse building itself. Sheriff Bill Decker, Dallas County Sheriff Bill Decker, has done everything possible to assure strict security. No one is inside the Courthouse building, which houses the county jail, other than authorized personnel of the County Sheriff's Department, authorized Federal officials, police officials, or accredited newsmen.

This is the Texas School Book Depository Building directly catercorner across Elm Street from the Courthouse. It was on the sixth floor of this building, from the corner window, that the assailant--the assassin--fired the fatal shots from the bolt-action 6.5 millimeter Italian rifle. From that window the shots covered a distance of approximately 250 to 300 feet down to the point along the Elm Street approach to the underpass where the President was shot.

From inside the Courthouse compound, the corner entrance to the County Sheriff's office, our cameras will show the approach of the car that will carry Lee Harvey Oswald into the Courthouse building. He

COMMISSION EXHIBIT No. 2141—Continued

will be housed in the jail of this building. He may possibly be in the cell that will face the assassination scene. He will be within 100 yards of where President Kennedy died. Lee Harvey Oswald will spend most likely the next couple of months in this building. He will be here through his arraignment and through his trial, which will probably come sometime in early January.

PAUL GOOD. We are inside the County Courthouse, which the presumed assassin, Lee Harvey Oswald, is soon to enter. He will be taken immediately to a booking room, and a very historic booking will be made; next into an I.D. room, where he will be photographed and fingerprinted. And then representatives of the press will have their first opportunity for a real front-to-front confrontation. Now our big television cameras can't fit in that room, but we'll shoot that on sound film and, just as soon as that's processed, you'll be able to see it. After the press has its time with Oswald, he perhaps will be given a set of prison clothing or he may be allowed to retain his own. Then he'll be brought to a cell. It probably--it will probably be a special cell about 10 feet by 10 feet, with a steel cot and a wash basin, and that's about all. There's a possibility--only a possibility--that that cell may have a window giving out on the assassination site.

This is Paul Good, returning you to WFAA.

BOB THORNTON. And we are still standing by, awaiting on the movement of the prisoner Oswald. We still have ABC's Bill Lord on

the phone from City Hall, so, once again, Bill Lord, what is the situation at ABC at the City Hall?

BILL LORD. Well, Bob, we are waiting and waiting. It is anticipated that he will be moved, because extreme precautions have been taken. As I said before, the police are worried; they are so worried they've talked about the possibility of moving him in an armored vehicle, not just the normal Sheriff's vehicle. And when this arrives, we'll know that this is the cue for Mr. Oswald to be brought downstairs and transferred to the car.

BOB THORNTON. Bill, what about the armed precautions down there? Are there weapons visible?

BILL LORD. There are many weapons visible. Riot guns and rifles are on display; the officers have them in their hands. They are ready to prevent anything they possibly can. There are perhaps two or three hundred people outside the City Hall waiting to see the transfer of Oswald.

BOB THORNTON. All right. Very good, Bill. Thank you very much, Bill Lord. ABC standing by at City Hall.

Now, I think once again we'll go down to the county jail and where Roger Sharp is standing by outside. Roger.

ROGER SHARP. Outside of the County Courthouse here, in the distance, some 300 feet from where I am standing, the area directly

5

adjacent to the assassination point, the park area where, during the past 24 hours, numerous floral wreaths have been laid by various Dallas citizens and organizations. . . .

COMMISSION EXHIBIT No. 2141—Continued

NBC-TV reels 22 and 24
Friday night, November 22, 1963

INTERVIEW WITH CHIEF OF POLICE CURRY, DISTRICT ATTORNEY WADE, CAPTAIN FRITZ BY THE PRESS, THIRD FLOOR, POLICE AND COURTS BUILDING

CURRY. --the Dallas Police Department, Captain Fritz has been in charge.

Q. Has he confessed, sir? Has he made a statement?

CURRY. He has not confessed. He has made no statement. Charges of murder have been accepted against him.

Q. Any particular thing that he said that caused you to file the charges regarding the President's death, against him?

CURRY. No, sir.

CURRY. Physical evidence is the main thing that we are relying upon.

Q. Can you name that physical evidence?

Q. When will he appear before the grand jury, sir?

CURRY. I don't know.

Q. --is that the next step?

CURRY. The next step would be that.

COMMISSION EXHIBIT No. 2142

CURRY. We will continue with the investigation. There are still many things that we need to work on.

WADE. --evidence gathered by the four agencies mentioned.

Q. Do you think you have got a good case?

WADE. I figure we have sufficient evidence to convict him.

Q. Was this, was there any indication that this was an organized plot or was there just one man?

WADE. We--there's no one else but him.

Q. Do you know whether he will be tried in Federal court, county court, or where he will be tried because this was a Presidential murder? Do you care to comment on the jurisdictional dispute which has been arising?

WADE. He has been charged in the State court with murder with malice. The charge carried the death penalty which my office will ask in both cases.

Q. Is there a similar Federal charge?

WADE. I don't know of any.

Q. Attorney General?

WADE. No.

COMMISSION EXHIBIT No. 2142—Continued

Q. What's the next step?

WADE. Tomorrow.

WADE. Well, there's a lot of the physical evidence that was gathered in--

Q. Mr. Wade, within 48 hours do you think he might be before the jury?

CURRY. Let Mr. Wade make a statement.

WADE. There are still some more ends that we're working on. This will be presented immediately to the grand jury as soon as some of the evidence is examined. It will be examined today, tonight, and tomorrow. He has been filed before, filed in Judge David Johnston's, Justice of the Peace, Precinct 2 of Dallas, and been held without bond on this case and the other case too. It will probably be the middle of next week before it goes to the Grand Jury because of some more evidence that has to be examined by the laboratory.

Q. Has he engaged a lawyer, sir?

Q. Mr. Wade, could you elaborate on the physical evidence?

WADE. Well, we've gone on into some other things that were gathered; the gun is one of them.

COMMISSION EXHIBIT No. 2142—Continued

Q. Mr. Wade, can you tell us if he has engaged a lawyer?

CURRY. We don't know that. His people have been here but we don't--

Q. Are there any fingerprints on the gun?

Q. Mr. Wade, can we get a picture of him?

Q. Are you going to bring him out?

WADE. I--

Q. Could we get a room where we could get a picture of him?

Q. Can we get a press conference where he could stand against a wall and we could talk to him?

Q. Has where he will be tried been determined yet?

WADE. It will be in the Dallas County Grand Jury.

Q. Where did he say he was when the President was killed?

COMMENTATOR. Captain Fritz, Chief Curry and Henry Wade are in conference right now to determine whether--

Q. Wade! Henry--

Q. Captain Fritz, can we go to the Assembly Room, sir?

WADE. We will get in a larger room here, that's what we're talking about.

[Wade, Curry and Fritz still conferring but cannot make out words.]

Q. What about the Assembly Room?

WADE. Is that all right?

FRITZ. That's--

WADE. Let's go down there where--

Q. O.K. Down to the assembly room.

Q. Will there be a way to make any pictures?

Q. -- make pictures right then and there?

WADE. I don't know, I don't even know where he is.

Q. --

WADE. I will, but I don't see any reason to take any picture of him.

Q. Of Lee?

WADE. Yes.

- 6 -

Q. Well, the whole world's only waiting to see what he looks like.

Q. Was there evidence enough to--?

WADE. Oh, is that all, the whole world.

Q. That's all.

Q. Just the world.

Q. We're crazy if we--

WADE. What?

Q. When will the preliminary hearing or arraignment be?

WADE. It hasn't been set. He's already been before the J.P. here but hasn't been arraigned yet.

Q. Will the indictment call--?

WADE. He has been taken before the J.P. right here.

COMMISSION EXHIBIT No. 2142—Continued

NBC-TV reel 43
Saturday, November 23, 1963

PRESS INTERVIEW WITH POLICE CHIEF JESSE CURRY
DALLAS POLICE AND COURTS BUILDING

Q. Will you hold it up again, sir, please.

Q. Would that paraffin test be valid on a rifle also or just-- ?

Q. Chief Curry, how would you describe this man? Is he a prime suspect?

CURRY. Yes.

Q. Is he the only suspect?

CURRY. Yes.

Q. Does he confess anything?

CURRY. No.

Q. What does he say?

CURRY. [Unintelligible]

Q. Has he admitted killing the policeman?

CURRY. No.

Q. Will he be questioned for an indeterminate period of time? How long will you question him?

COMMISSION EXHIBIT No. 2143

- 2 -

CURRY. I don't know that. It will be left up to the District Attorney.

Q. He was yelling and complaining about no attorney. Does he have an attorney here now?

CURRY. Not that I know of.

Q. Chief, --

CURRY. Not in the near future, I don't believe.

Q. Chief, are you convinced that this is the man?

CURRY. Well, we don't have positive proof. We feel he is a prime suspect.

Q. What do you think, personally?

CURRY. Personally, I think we have the right man.

Q. Chief, what--

Q. What is the name of the rifle that was found in the sixth floor of the Depository Building?

CURRY. That was--

COMMISSION EXHIBIT No. 2143—Continued

WFAA-TV reel PKT 14
Saturday, November 23, 1963

POLICE CHIEF JESSE CURRY TALKING TO PRESS CONCERNING RELATIONS BETWEEN THE F.B.I. AND DALLAS POLICE DEPARTMENT

CURRY. There has been some information that has gone out. I want to correct anything that might have been misinterpreted or misunderstood and that is regarding information that the FBI might have had about this man. I do not know if and when the FBI has interviewed this man; the FBI is under no obligation to come to us with any information concerning anyone. They have cooperated with us in the past 100 percent. Anytime there is any information that they feel might be helpful to us they have always come to us. Last night someone told me, I don't even know who it was, that the FBI did know this man was in the city and had interviewed him. I wish to say this, of my knowledge, I do not know this to be a fact and I don't want anybody to get the wrong impression that I am accusing the FBI of not cooperating or of withholding information because they are under no obligation to us, but have always cooperated with us 100 percent.

Q. Chief, just to make this--

CURRY. And I do not know if and when they have ever interviewed this man.

COMMISSION EXHIBIT No. 2144

Q. Just to make this clear, Chief, you were talking about Oswald and the reports that the FBI had information about him before the assassination.

CURRY. That's correct. And I wish to make this statement: I do not know to my knowledge whether they have anything on this man or not or whether or not they have ever interviewed him. I do say this, that they have always in the past, if they had information that they thought would be helpful to us they have come to us with it.

Q. Have you been given an erroneous or unreliable report that they had some information on him?

CURRY. I don't know. Someone last night told me this and I don't even know who told me. But they just said last night that the FBI did know this man was here. I wish to make this statement that I do not know whether they knew it or not and I certainly am not saying that the FBI knew something that we should have known and didn't tell us. They are under no obligation to us--that they have always cooperated.

Q. Chief, can you tell us when Oswald was questioned this morning if he continued to deny his guilt, to deny that he had anything to do with the killing?

CURRY. That I don't know because I haven't contacted the Captain since he's been with him.

Q. Now that you have made the record clearer as to the matter of FBI cooperation, can you tell us where you now stand in the matter of prosecuting this man?

CURRY. Well, so far as I know we are right where we were last night because I don't know what has developed in the questioning this morning. We are still trying to establish a verification on the gun--where it came from--and we are still--

Q. Is it the rifle you are talking about?

CURRY. Yes, the rifle. We are still interviewing many witnesses that were in the area. We have appealed to any citizens who might have been in the area that might have taken any pictures, that might have seen anything, to come to us. And actually we probably will have--well, there is no way of estimating how many statements we will take. We have several people taking statements now.

Q. Chief, was the subject of a polygraph, a lie detector test, broached with Oswald, and if so, what was the outcome?

CURRY. I understood that it was offered to him and he refused it.

- 4 -

Q. Do you know when this occurred, sir?

CURRY. Yesterday, I understand.

Q. Did he give any reason for refusing to take the lie detector test?

CURRY. I understand he said he didn't have to take it and he didn't want to.

Q. There were some pop bottles being found up there on that floor up there. Was there one, were there caps on?

CURRY. I don't know. That's the first I'd heard of that.

Q. Chief Curry, what are your plans now in dealing with Oswald himself? Will he be interrogated here further or will he be transferred to the county jail to await presentment to the grand jury?

CURRY. He will go to the county jail. I don't know just when. But I am thinking probably sometime today. I couldn't be sure. It is more convenient here to have him near us where we can talk to him when we need to, but we will probably transfer him soon.

Q. You may then question him again before he is transferred to the county jail?

COMMISSION EXHIBIT No. 2144—Continued

- 5 -

CURRY. It's possible, yes.

Q. --

CURRY. I have not heard from him. I understood that his mother was obtaining an attorney for him this morning, but I don't know.

Q. Is his mother here now?

CURRY. I don't know.

Q. He told us that as he left this morning that he would like to contact a Mr. Abt of New York City to serve as his attorney. Do you know who he was referring to?

CURRY. No, I don't.

Q. The information in question on the rifle--

CURRY. No, sir, we haven't had a return yet.

Q. As far as you know so far, was there any evidence that there was anybody else involved in this?

CURRY. No, sir, not that we know of.

Q. Molina--had he been arrested or just picked up?

COMMISSION EXHIBIT No. 2144—Continued

CURRY. He came in voluntarily this morning. They went to his home last night, he invited them in, they had a search warrant, but it wasn't necessary to use it because he invited them in and told them they could look around, the officers, and then after they had talked to him last night they left him at home and he had agreed to come in this morning and I think he is somewhere in the building now.

Q. Chief, as far as you are concerned, does the investigation at this hour point toward the possibility of accomplices?

CURRY. We don't believe so at this time.

Q. You have no information linking Mr. Molina with the case?

CURRY. No. The only reason that we wanted to talk to him was the fact that we do have him listed in some of our subversive files and he did work in the building.

Q. Did Molina admit knowing Oswald?

CURRY. I don't know whether he admitted knowing him or not.

Q. Is there any indication from the investigation to date that would indicate motive on the part of Mr. Oswald?

CURRY. So far as I know there is no indication.

COMMISSION EXHIBIT No. 2144—Continued

Q. Are you satisfied that you've got him traced directly from the scene of the shooting to his arrest?

CURRY. Yes. You mean from the scene of the Presidential assassination?

Q. Yes.

CURRY. No, we haven't got all--

Q. How much time is involved in this--how big a lapse of time?

CURRY. Roughly 45 minutes, I believe.

Q. You still don't know--he doesn't have a car? -- too far to walk?

CURRY. I understand that he does not have a car.

Q. Do you have anything other than circumstantial evidence to rely on?

CURRY. Well, we have some physical evidence.

Q. Can you tell us anything about that physical evidence?

CURRY. No, sir. I don't think I should discuss that.

COMMISSION EXHIBIT No. 2144—Continued

Q. Do you know whether any of the witnesses who have appeared here this morning have given any information that would contribute to the case?

CURRY. I don't know that.

Q. Do you feel that this case is proceeding as effectively as you would like it to proceed, or are some doubts beginning to grow as to whether this in fact is the man?

CURRY. No doubts are beginning to grow, but it is a very difficult investigation for the very fact that you see here--it's surrounded by literally hundreds of newspeople and there are so many witnesses and people that we need to talk to. It is a very difficult investigation, but I am not beginning to have any doubts.

Q. Are the resources being applied to this investigation adequate in your opinion?

CURRY. Yes.

Q. Would you describe them for us?

CURRY. We're just using all means possible in scientific investigations. Of course, these are interrogations and scientific--other scientific means outside of physical evidence, and any other means that we have.

COMMISSION EXHIBIT No. 2144—Continued

Q. In addition to the Dallas Police Department who else is directly aiding in the investigation?

CURRY. There has been an FBI--members of the FBI have been present throughout this, members of the Secret Service and members of the State Police, that is, Rangers have been here; Sheriff Decker has helped us in interviewing many of the witnesses. So we have, but in all of the interrogations there have been an FBI agent present and also a Secret Service agent present.

Q. Who is in direct command of this investigation?

CURRY. This investigation is being conducted by Capt. J. W. Fritz actually; Deputy Chief Stevenson in charge of Criminal Investigation Division; Captain Fritz in charge of the Homicide Bureau.

Q. Is he coordinating the other agencies which are involved in this investigation?

CURRY. Yes.

Q. Will we be able to talk to Captain Fritz sometime this afternoon, Chief Curry?

CURRY. I don't know. That will be up to him.

COMMISSION EXHIBIT No. 2144—Continued

- 10 -

Q. You say you have something in the way of physical evidence. Do these refer to anything else beside witnesses?

CURRY. Yes, but I can't discuss these things with you.

Q. Will these be in the form of writings or indications that he had planned this?

CURRY. I couldn't go into it any further. I could say this: No, at present, we don't have anything to indicate that he had planned this in writing or anything, no.

Q. Have you located the source of the rifle?

CURRY. No, we're still working on that.

Q. Have you had a report as to whether this was the rifle that killed President Kennedy?

CURRY. We don't have a report.

Q. Do you expect that any time soon?

CURRY. We expect it soon, but I don't know just when.

Q. Thank you, Chief.

COMMENTATOR. This was Chief Jesse Curry of the Dallas Police Department. This is Bob Clark, ABC, at Dallas Police Headquarters.

COMMISSION EXHIBIT No. 2144—Continued

WFAA-TV reel PKT 21
Saturday, November 23, 1963

PRESS INTERVIEW WITH POLICE CHIEF JESSE CURRY
DALLAS POLICE AND COURTS BUILDING

CURRY. The FBI has just informed us that they have the order letter for the rifle that we have sent to the laboratory. They have that order letter that they received from a mail-order house in Chicago. This order letter has been to the laboratory in Washington, D.C., and compared with known handwriting of our suspect, Oswald, and the handwriting is the same on the order letter as Oswald's handwriting. The return address on this order letter was to the post-office box in Dallas, Texas, of our suspect, Oswald, and it was returned under another name. But it has definitely been established by the FBI that the handwriting is the handwriting of Oswald.

Q. Was it a recent purchase?

CURRY. This purchase was made on March the 20th of this year.

Q. Of this year?

CURRY. This year.

Q. This in March?

Q. And that is definitely the same gun?

Q. What about the ballistics test, Chief?

CURRY. The ballistics test--we haven't had a final report, but it is--I understand will be favorable.

Q. Is this the development you referred to today as making this case ironclad in your opinion?

CURRY. This was not what I had reference to earlier.

COMMISSION EXHIBIT No. 2145

Q. Will you give us an indication of what that is? Were you referring to the photograph earlier?

CURRY. No.

Q. Where did these photographs come from, Chief?

CURRY. The photographs were found in his--out at Irving, where he had been staying and where his wife had been staying.

Q. These are the photographs of the revolver and the rifle?

CURRY. There is a photograph of him with a revolver on his hip and holding a rifle in his hand.

Q. Does this rifle look like the one that you have, that you think is the murder weapon, sir?

CURRY. It does.

Q. Does it have a telescopic sight?

CURRY. It does.

Q. How is he taking this information as it builds up?

CURRY. I don't know.

Q. Is he aware of the situation--showing any awareness?

CURRY. I don't believe he knows all this, as yet. I think the Captain is talking to him about it at the present time.

Q. Chief, has the order for this gun been connected definitely with the--that is, the order for the rifle been connected with the rifle which you found?

CURRY. It has.

Q. Chief, just a moment ago he came out into the interrogation room, bitterly complaining about being deprived of his citizenship rights because he can't take a shower. Do you have any comment on that?

COMMISSION EXHIBIT No. 2145—Continued

CURRY. I didn't know he had asked to take a shower. We have a shower up there where he could take a shower if he wants one.

Q. Chief, back to the photograph: did he have in his hand a copy of <u>The Worker</u>, a communist publication, with the headline "Be Militant" or it?

CURRY. It seems there are two papers there: on one of them you can see the words <u>The Militant</u>; on the other you can see <u>The Worker</u>.

Q. Is this the weekly <u>Worker</u> from New York?

CURRY. I don't know.

Q. What was the name under which he ordered the gun?

Q. Chief, was the post-office box rented by Oswald?

CURRY. The name--the return--the name on the return address was A. Hidell. A. Hidell.

Q. Are you going to confront him with this evidence now?

Q. How do you spell Hidell?

CURRY. H-I-D-E-double L.

Q. Is that the name under which the post-office box was rented?

CURRY. I don't know that.

Q. Chief, do you feel pretty certain that this is the rifle that killed the President?

CURRY. Yes.

Q. Will you confront him with this evidence now, Chief?

CURRY. That I don't know.

Q. Are you on the way in to show him this evidence now?

CURRY. I'm not.

COMMISSION EXHIBIT No. 2145—Continued

Q. Has he been shown it?

CURRY. Captain Fritz is with him now. He will be shown this evidence by Captain Fritz.

Q. Do you consider the case shut tight now, Chief?

CURRY. We will continue to work on it and try to get every shred of evidence that's possible.

Q. How many photos, Chief, were involved?

CURRY. I do not know.

Q. How was the rifle described?

Q. Can you give us something about the facts you found this morning--the new facts you mentioned this morning?

CURRY. No, sir.

Q. Not at all?

CURRY. No, sir.

Q. How was the rifle described on the order to the mail-order house?

CURRY. That I do not know.

Q. When was the call--?

Q. Did you say you have the order?

CURRY. I said the FBI had the order.

Q. Oh, I see.

Q. Did they get this through a tip? Do you know how it was developed, this evidence?

CURRY. I don't know how the FBI got their information. We received some information ourselves.

Q. As a tip?

CURRY. Yes.

Q. Then that's definitely the same gun which had been sent to Washington?

CURRY. Yes.

Q. Can you tell us what the--?

CURRY. Now, now, let me say this: I can't say for sure on that.

Q. On what? What's that, Chief?

CURRY. He asked if this was the gun that we sent to Washington, the gun that was ordered. I can't say definitely on that; I don't know.

Q. It's the same type of gun?

CURRY. Yes.

Q. The same type of gun?

CURRY. Yes.

Q. Is the serial number the same, Chief?

CURRY. That I don't know.

Q. How much did he pay for the gun, Chief?

Q. But you say ballistic tests are encouraging so far?

CURRY. I believe the gun was supposed to cost $12.78, I believe. I believe it was advertised in some magazine for that.

Q. What was the name of the mail-order house?

Q. Chief, did you say the ballistic tests so far are encouraging?

CURRY. I don't know the name of the mail-order house.

Q. The ballistic tests are encouraging?

CURRY. Ballistic tests are encouraging.

6

Q. Do you have the advertisement out of the magazine which advertises this?

CURRY. No, I don't, Johnny.

Q. Had Oswald ever used the alias Hidell before?

CURRY. I do not know.

CURRY. That's all I have to tell you, gentlemen.

REPORTERS. Thank you very much.

COMMISSION EXHIBIT No. 2145—Continued

WFAA-TV reel PKT 12
Saturday p.m., November 23, 1963

INTERVIEW OF POLICE CHIEF JESSE CURRY
BY PRESS, DALLAS POLICE AND COURTS BUILDING

Q. -- under certain circumstances, what will be done?

CURRY. What will be done?

Q. Yes, sir. What will be done with Oswald?

CURRY. Well, he's been charged and he'll be transferred to the county jail and await, wait for grand jury action on him.

Q. When will he be transferred to the county jail?

CURRY. That I don't know. As soon as we get through talking to him, prob--, maybe sometime this after--

Q. Has he made any admission this morning in your further questioning of him about the killing of President Kennedy?

CURRY. I have not talked to him and I don't think anyone else has.

Q. What are you wating for now, Chief, in terms of further interrogations?

CURRY. Well, we just want to talk to him some more.

COMMISSION EXHIBIT No. 2146

Q. When will you do that?

CURRY. I imagine in a few minutes.

Q. This will be before he's transferred to the county jail?

CURRY. Oh, yes. Yes.

Q. Do you expect that he will be brought down this corridor, Chief?

CURRY. Yes.

Q. Have you heard any more about how he got from downtown to the Oak Cliff section?

CURRY. Not that I know of.

Q. Just so far what evidence has been uncovered, Chief?

CURRY. I wouldn't want to elaborate on all the evidence that has been uncovered.

Q. What about his background?

CURRY. Well, he has a background, of course. It's generally known now he defected to Russia in 1959 and married a Russian girl and then last August, I understand, he went to the American Consul and asked to be brought back to the United States.

COMMISSION EXHIBIT No. 2146—Continued

Q. How would you describe his mood during the questioning?

CURRY. Very arrogant. Has been all along.

Q. What does he still say, Chief?

CURRY. He just denies everything.

Q. Does he say anything else?

CURRY. Not too much. I don't know. I haven't personally been interrogating him.

Q. Has he admitted that he was in the building at the time the shots were fired?

CURRY. Yes. Well, we know he couldn't deny that. We have witnesses that--

Q. -- ?

CURRY. I think he denies everything.

Q. Chief Curry, how long has he been in Dallas?

CURRY. I think approximately two months.

Q. He is an employee of a book binding firm which operated--

CURRY. I understand it's the Texas Book Depository.

COMMISSION EXHIBIT No. 2146—Continued

- 4 -

Q. Is there any doubt in your mind, Chief, that Oswald is the man who killed the President?

CURRY. I think this is the man who killed the President.

Q. You're going to bring him down -- for interrogation in just a few minutes?

COMMENTATOR. That was Dallas Police Chief Jesse Curry. This corridor is packed with some 50 reporters and photographers. We expect in a very few moments that Oswald, the 24-year-old ex-Marine accused of killing President Kennedy, will be brought through this door just behind the Chief, down this corridor into the Homicide Bureau, then taken on downstairs to the lower floor to the jail.

Q. Chief, could you tell us what you might have found in his rooming house in the way of literature or any papers connecting him-- ?

CURRY. We found a great, great amount of Communist literature, Communist books; I couldn't tell you just what all it was, but it was a large box, probably a box that, probably 2 by 2 --

Q. Two feet by two feet?

COMMISSION EXHIBIT No. 2146—Continued

- 5 -

CURRY. Yes, or 2 by 3 feet and probably a foot and a half tall. I'd say it was two-thirds full of different types of books and materials.

Q. Chief, we understand you've had the results of the paraffin tests which were made to determine whether Oswald had fired a weapon. Can you tell us what those tests showed?

CURRY. I understand that it was positive.

Q. What did the tests find?

Q. What does that mean?

CURRY. It only means that he fired a gun.

Q. This doesn't-- ?

Q. Chief, were the powder burns or powder marks on his cheek or on his shoulder?

CURRY. I don't know that. I don't know that.

Q. What do you know about on his hands?

Q. That he fired a gun, Chief, not the rifle or the pistol?

CURRY. That's right. We just say a gun.

Q. Chief, will you give us some details as to what form the literature was in and what kind of literature it was specifically-- where was it found--what did it say?

COMMISSION EXHIBIT No. 2146—Continued

CURRY. I haven't examined all of it. I just understand it was Communist literature.

Q. Was it in English? Eh, in English?

CURRY. Yes, I think it was in English.

Q. Chief, is there any plan for a reenactment of the crime--to take him to the scene or to do anything in that respect?

CURRY. No.

Q. Is there any evidence that anyone else may have been linked with Oswald to this shooting?

CURRY. At this time, we don't believe so. We are talking to a man that works in the same building that we have in our subversive files and we are talking to him but he denies any knowledge of it.

Q. How old is this man, Chief?

CURRY. I don't know.

Q. Has he been associated with Oswald in the past?

CURRY. We don't know that. We know that he works at the same place.

COMMISSION EXHIBIT No. 2146—Continued

Q. How long has he worked there?

CURRY. I don't know how long the other man has worked there.

Q. What time is established-- how Oswald got to the other side of town--is there anything that can be come up about--did he get over by a bus, by a car, did he have to walk?

CURRY. I don't know. We have heard that he was picked up by a Negro in a car.

Q. That is not confirmed?

CURRY. No, it is not confirmed, as far as I know.

Q. Are you looking for the Negro?

CURRY. We would like to know about him if this is so; we'd certainly like to find him.

Q. Chief Curry, could you detail for us what led you to Oswald?

CURRY. Not exactly, except in the building, we, when we went to the building why he was observed in the building at the time, but the manager told us that he worked there and the officers passed him on up then because the manager said he is an employee.

COMMISSION EXHIBIT No. 2146—Continued

- 8 -

Q. Is that before the shooting or after?

CURRY. After the shooting.

Q. Do you think that smudged fingerprints that have been found on the rifle which killed the President will be able to establish the identity of the killer?

CURRY. We hope so, but I couldn't say positively at this time that they will be.

Q. Well, will you know -- to convict him?

CURRY. I don't know whether it will be enough to convict him or not, but if we can put his prints on the rifle, why, it'll certainly connect him with the rifle and if we can establish that this is the rifle that killed the President, why --

Q. How many shots had been fired from the rifle?

CURRY. Three.

Q. Have you been able to trace the rifle? Do you know where it was purchased, or -- ?

CURRY. No, we are attempting to do that at this time.

Q. Is there any connection yet between this and the firing at Major General Walker?

COMMISSION EXHIBIT No. 2146—Continued

- 9 -

CURRY. I do not know.

Q. What was the subversive evidence on the other man who works in the building that you have a subversive file on?

CURRY. Just that he attended meetings and was associated with groups that were left-wing groups--

Q. Fair Play for Cuba groups?

CURRY. I don't know whether that was one of them or not.

Q. You have never found a car-- ?

CURRY. No.

Q. He doesn't have any car, as far as you know?

CURRY. No, as far as we know.

Q. Did you say, Chief, that a policeman had seen him in the building-- ?

CURRY. Yes.

Q. After the shot was fired-- ?

CURRY. Yes.

Q. Why didn't he arrest him then?

COMMISSION EXHIBIT No. 2146—Continued

CURRY. Because the manager of the place told us that he was an employee--said, "He's all right; he's an employee."

Q. Did he look suspicious to the policeman at this point?

CURRY. I imagine the policeman was checking everyone he saw as he went into the building

Q. Chief, after this happened, what was done in terms of getting the trail back to Oswald?

CURRY. The next thing we knew is when he turned up as a suspect in the murder of the police officer--and then the connection was made between the two.

Q. Chief, did anyone see him shoot the police officer?

CURRY. Yes.

Q. Who was that?

CURRY. I don't know the names, but--

Q. Male or female?

CURRY. I think there were three witnesses, I understand.

Q. Three witnesses saw him shoot the officer?

Q. Has he made any admissions at all about the shooting of the police officer?

COMMISSION EXHIBIT No. 2146—Continued

CURRY. No. No, he denies everything.

Q. Why do you think the police officer went to him in the street? What was the reason?

CURRY. I think he suspected him because of a description that had been put out on the radio.

Q. On the police radio?

Q. Chief, has anyone come forward saying they had seen a rifle after hearing the first shot, possibly looking toward the window? Has anyone-- ?

CURRY. I read in the paper where someone said it, but we don't have--

Q. You don't have-- ?

CURRY. I don't have it. Unless--

Q. And the police department would like anybody to come forward who did see it?

CURRY. Yes. Yes.

Q. In other words, you're still looking for public help in this case?

CURRY. Absolutely. Absolutely.

COMMISSION EXHIBIT No. 2146—Continued

Q. Chief Curry, when you first heard of the Dallas policeman's death, what then led you to the theatre? What information did you have from there?

CURRY. I understand that someone called up. I think the ticket taker from the theatre called about the suspicious actions of this person.

Q. Chief, when do you expect the rifle to be returned from Washington?

Q. Can you describe briefly what happened inside the theatre?

CURRY. Well, they were searching the theatre and as the officer approached this man, he jumped up and said, "This is it," and drew a gun--attempted to draw a gun. They grappled with him and were able to twist the gun away from him and he was resisting violently. Several officers subdued him. I had two, two officers that had to have treatment for injuries wrestling around over the seats in the theatre and another officer was scratched up but didn't have to have treatment.

Q. Was he-- ?

Q. This man with the subversive background--was there any surveillance?

Q. Was there any-- ?

CURRY. I'm sorry. There's too many talking. I can't understand--

Q. With this man's apparent subversive background, was there any surveillance? Were police, aware of his presence in Dallas?

CURRY. We in the police department here did not know he was in Dallas. I understand the FBI did know that he was in Dallas.

Q. Is it normally the practice for the FBI to inform the police-- ?

CURRY. Yes.

Q. Chief, do you have-- ?

CURRY. We did not have the knowledge.

Q. But you were not informed?

CURRY. We had not been informed of this man.

Q. Chief, do you have any concern for the safety of your prisoner in view of the high feeling among the people of Dallas over the assassination of the President?

CURRY. No, but precautions, necessary precautions will be taken, of course, but I'm not, I don't think that the people will try to take the prisoner away from us.

Q. Do you regard the county jail as a more secure place to house the prisoner? Is that why you're transferring him from the city jail?

CURRY. It is customary after a man is filed on that he be transferred. We only keep him in our jail until he is filed on. After he's been filed on why then he's the sheriff's responsibility.

Q. Will there be extra police at the county jail to assure his-- ?

CURRY. I don't know. Sheriff Decker--

Q. When will he be transferred, Chief?

CURRY. I do not know.

Q. Where is the county jail?

CURRY. At the end, about a block from where the President was killed.

Q. Chief Curry, when will the formal grand jury action be taken in your estimation?

COMMISSION EXHIBIT No. 2146—Continued

CURRY. Mr. Wade told me last night, or told the press last night, probably the middle of next week.

Q. Chief, can you tell us in summary what directly links Oswald to the killing of the President?

CURRY. Well, the fact that he was on the floor where the shots were fired from immediately before the shots were fired; the fact that he was seen carrying a package to the building; the fact that--

Q. When was he carrying that package -- the same day?

CURRY. Yesterday morning.

Q. Do you figure that was a disassembled rifle?

CURRY. I don't think it was disassembled; the package was large enough for a rifle to be intact.

Q. Was it in a box or was it wrapped?

CURRY. Wrapped. Wrapped in a bo--, in a paper.

Q. Have you a witness that places him there after the time of the shooting?

CURRY. My police officer can place him there after the time of the shooting.

COMMISSION EXHIBIT No. 2146—Continued

Q. When do you expect the report-- ?

Q. The officer who wanted to stop him and then was told by the manager that he worked there?

CURRY. Yes.

Q. Chief, what have you heard from the Civil Liberties Union? Have they sent up-- ?

CURRY. They were up here last night.

Q. Chief, will they probably have a lawyer-- ?

CURRY. I don't know. They haven't sent one up here but they wanted to know if he has been warned of his rights, and so forth, and we told them that he had.

Q. But no lawyer has seen Oswald yet?

CURRY. No lawyer has seen Oswald.

Q. Has Oswald made any request for a lawyer?

CURRY. He has, but he didn't say who he wanted or anything, so we couldn't just go out and start calling lawyers for him. That's not our responsibility.

Q. Will the CLU -- him?

CURRY. I don't know.

COMMISSION EXHIBIT No. 2146—Continued

Q. As of now it would be up to Oswald to hire his own lawyer if he wants one?

CURRY. Yes. His mother, I understand, at this time has said that she would get him an attorney this morning.

Q. Has he been arraigned yet for murdering the President?

CURRY. Yes. He was arraigned last night about 1:30.

Q. Chief Curry, -- ?

CURRY. Yes.

Q. Where does his mother live?

CURRY. I don't know.

Q. Is she from Dallas?

CURRY. No, I think she's from Fort Worth.

Q. You've said, of course, Chief, that Oswald hasn't made any admissions. Is he responding to questions? Is he refusing to answer questions at this stage, or-- ?

CURRY. He doesn't answer questions except to say: "That's ridiculous. That's silly. That's -- " and deny any knowledge of anything--

COMMISSION EXHIBIT No. 2146—Continued

Q. Does he say he was anywhere else at the time this was happening?

CURRY. I don't know.

Q. Does he seem confident of himself?

CURRY. He says he was at the building, but he says he was there because he worked there.

Q. Chief Curry, thank you very much.

Q. Does he seem mentally right, Chief?

CURRY. Yes, he's mentally right.

Q. You don't think the man is off his rocker, do you Chief?

CURRY. No, sir. I don't think so.

Q. Chief, thank you Chief Curry.

COMMENTATOR. We've just been talking here at Dallas Police Headquarters with Chief of Police Jesse Curry. In just a few moments we expect Oswald will be brought through this door from his jail cell one floor above, taken through--

COMMISSION EXHIBIT No. 2146—Continued

KRLD-TV reel 15
Sunday, November 24, 1963

PRESS CONFERENCE OF DALLAS POLICE CHIEF
JESSE CURRY, POLICE AND COURTS BUILDING

CURRY. To my knowledge, he was here a couple of hours. How much of the time was spent in interrogation I don't know, because I think he had to wait for some time before they could get around to talking to him.

Q. Is there absolutely no doubt now that nobody else is involved as an accomplice?

CURRY. I would not make that statement.

Q. Do you have any possible-- ?

CURRY. I wouldn't comment on it because I would certainly hate to say we're convinced that nobody else is involved and then have somebody else involved.

Q. Have you talked to anybody besides this fellow Molina who might conceivably have a role-- ?

CURRY. I don't want to comment on that.

Q. Chief, have you interviewed other people whom you regard as subversives?

CURRY. Sir?

Q. Have you been interviewing other people who have previously been involved in subversive activities?

COMMISSION EXHIBIT No. 2147

2

CURRY. We have interviewed actually hundreds of people. I couldn't say just which groups have been interviewed, but we have interviewed many, many people and will interview many, many more before this case --

Q. [Unintelligible.]

CURRY. That I don't know. Does anybody have any idea?

Q. Chief, you say you're going to take him to the county jail in an armored car. Have you ever had to do this with another prisoner, been called upon to do so?

CURRY. Not to my knowledge.

Q. Is it a commercial-type truck, the kind that banks use?

CURRY. Yes, yes.

Q. There was some confusion last night about this business of the FBI. Is it accepted that the FBI did interview him about a week ago, do you know?

CURRY. I do not know. The statement that I made last night-- I do not know. I heard that, see, but I do not know of my knowledge and I retracted any statement that I might have made that would indicate that I thought they had.

Q. The FBI has now admitted that it did talk to Oswald, I heard on the radio.

COMMISSION EXHIBIT No. 2147—Continued

3

CURRY. I don't know. You'd have to talk to the FBI about that.

Q. Did today's threats on the prisoner's life--did they come in right through the police switchboard?

CURRY. Yes.

Q. Do you have any details at all on them?

CURRY. No.

Q. Is there any way we can get some on them, sir?

CURRY. I don't know who took the calls or what was said.

Q. Could you tell us, sir, if you would, just a little bit about this, the possibility that somebody else might be inter--might be involved in this. We've had statements in the last couple of days saying, "This is the man, and nobody else." Now --

CURRY. This is the man, we are sure, that murdered the patrolman and murdered--and assassinated the President. But to say that there was no other person had any knowledge of what this man might do, I wouldn't make that statement, because there is a possibility that there are people who might have known this man's thoughts and what he might, could do, or what he might do.

COMMISSION EXHIBIT No. 2147—Continued

Q. Sir, has there been any further indication that anybody else anywhere along the way might have been an accomplice, in action, getting him the job, assisting him in getting the job, letting him know where the parade, where the motorcade, was-- ?

CURRY. I don't have any knowledge to that effect.

Q. Does he show any signs of breaking--to make a clean breast of this, or to tell the truth about what happened?

CURRY. No, sir; there is no indication that he is close to telling us anything. He--he just--

Q. --

CURRY. I don't know whether he did or not.

Q. How does he shave, Chief? Do you let him have razor blades?

CURRY. No, there's not, no razor blades allowed to prisoners.

Q. Chief, has he ever said anything that would indicate that he might have suicide remotely on his mind?

CURRY. No, he hasn't indicated it.

Q. Has he seen his children?

CURRY. No, we wouldn't, we do not permit children to go into the jail.

COMMISSION EXHIBIT No. 2147—Continued

Q. Chief, there is a rumor his wife is pregnant with another child. Do you know whether that is true or not?

CURRY. No comment.

Q. Thank you very much, Chief.

Q. Chief, when was Molina released? There seems to be some confusion about that.

CURRY. I don't know exactly. It was sometime yesterday afternoon when they finished with him.

Q. About two hours?

CURRY. I think approximately two hours. Now, it might have --

CURRY. Yes, he might have been here longer; I just know that he was here, and I know that he was released. We didn't hold him after talking to him; we released him.

Q. He works in the same place as Oswald?

CURRY. Yes, he does.

Q. Chief, has there been any significant change in his attitude at all since he's been here? Is it pretty much the same right from the beginning?

COMMISSION EXHIBIT No. 2147—Continued

CURRY. I--the only thing I would say is that he's not quite as belligerent or arrogant now as he was when we first brought him in. I think actually that he, in talking with Captain Fritz--Captain Fritz is a skilled interrogator and he's always been able to more or less gain the confidence of the person that he's talking to, that he's going to shoot square with him--he seems to me that He's a little friendlier with Captain Fritz now than he was when we first brought him in.

Q. Any closer to breaking -- ?

CURRY. No, I don't think so. I understand he has admitted being in the book building; that's about all he has admitted.

CURRY. Yes?

Q. I was always puzzled about the fact that he went home to change his clothes. Can you think of any reason why he would have wanted to change his garb?

CURRY. No, I don't know. He--no, he told us that he was going to the picture show, that he was not going back to work that afternoon, but he didn't give us any reasons why he was not going back to work.

Q. Of course, you have examined the clothes that he had left there when he put on the clothes he had when you arrested him. Is there anything significant about the clothes he took off?

CURRY. Nothing visible on the clothes. As to why he would want to change, I would think this; if a man--if a man was aware that someone

might have seen him and had a description of his clothing, he would--it would be . . . pretty common for people that don't want to be apprehended by the police to change their appearance as soon as possible.

Q. Sir, have you located a holster for that pistol?

CURRY. I saw a holster back in the homicide office in a box where we had a great deal of material. I presume--

Q. Where was the holster found?

CURRY. I don't know.

Q. He didn't have a holster on when the policeman--

CURRY. I don't know, but probably at his home because this was--I saw it in a box with a great deal of this material and other evidence that was taken from his home, so I--

Q. Have you traced the pistol, sir?

CURRY. No, sir.

Q. Is it a .38?

CURRY. I believe it is. I'm not positive about that.

Q. Smith and Wesson?

Q. Sir, some reports suggest that he didn't actually change, he just grabbed a jacket--that's according to his landlady--just grabbed a jacket and ran out.

CURRY. I think he told--I think he told some of the officers that he changed his pants but not his shirt.

Q. Sir, could you tell us whether or not there is a possibility of other people being involved?

CURRY. You're not going to press it because I've already said I'm not making no more comments.

Q. I'll ask one more question to clear one thing which has cropped up recently which would be an indication along those lines, you know.

CURRY. I'll only say this again: we're open-minded regarding this issue, and we will continue to exhaust every effort to explore any possibility that there might have been someone that even was friendly with him that might have known that he even had an idea of trying to harm--

Q. I was going to ask if he was ever heard by any of his acquaintances to make any utterances against the President or the Governor of Texas.

CURRY. Not to my knowledge. I don't know this.

Q. Did he have a wide circle of acquaintances? Or was he a man with very few friends?

COMMISSION EXHIBIT No. 2147—Continued

CURRY. From what we've been able to determine, he wasn't a very friendly person.

Q. Has he said why he had two homes, why he had a furnished room and also a home with his wife?

CURRY. I don't know that.

Q. Do you know anything about a letter that he may have written to Governor Connally when he was Secretary of the Navy?

CURRY. Well, I've heard that he did, but to my knowledge I don't.

Q. He hasn't been questioned about that either. Do you sense that Connally may have been the target and not the President?

CURRY. I don't know that.

Q. Sir, how does he--

Q. He hasn't even been questioned about that--

CURRY. I said I didn't know. You see, they've--they've questioned him for many hours and I have not been present during those times, and I have not sat down with the Captain to say, "Tell me everything that you've asked this man."

Q. How does he converse with his wife, Chief? Does she--does he speak Russian?

CURRY. Yes.

COMMISSION EXHIBIT No. 2147—Continued

Q. He does speak Russian.

CURRY. I understand that he speaks Russian.

Q. Has he seen her to talk to?

CURRY. Yes.

Q. And do they converse in Russian or in English?

CURRY. I don't know that.

Q. Was somebody present when they spoke together?

CURRY. No.

Q. Chief, where is the rifle now?

CURRY. It's in the FBI office, here in Dallas. It will be returned to us today.

Q. Have you gotten an FBI report?

CURRY. Not an official report.

Q. When do you expect that?

CURRY. Probably some time today but I don't know. I couldn't--I couldn't reveal in detail what it says anyway.

Q. So far as--in that--in that point that was left open after your disclosure about the mail order of tying this rifle specifically through

that order to the mail order house last March, that blank has not been filled in yet--

CURRY. The FBI has been doing all this work out of Chicago, and also all the laboratory work, which has been very important to us. It's been very helpful to us and essential to our case, of course. Now, just how far the FBI has been able to tie this gun in with the particular mail order house, to say that this is the weapon that was shipped to this man, I don't know, because, and I don't even know whether or not it is in the report, but I'm sure that the FBI is exhausting every effort to establish this for us.

Q. Chief, could you tell us any more about the snapshots that were found in his Irving, Texas, home showing him holding a gun that looks like the rifle which was used in the assassination?

CURRY. No, sir. I've told you all I could about it last night.

Q. Do you feel that there should be legislation, national legislation to stop the selling of guns by mail order--

CURRY. I don't wish to comment on it at this time.

Q. You don't know where those pictures were made, do you?

CURRY. We haven't established that yet.

Q. Do they show any printer's mark?

Q. His wife, was she in the picture?

CURRY. No, she wasn't in the picture.

CURRY. I don't know about all of the pictures; I've just--actually, I've just looked at one print.

Q. Did it have a date on the back of it, Chief?

CURRY. Sir?

Q. Did it have a date on the back of it as some commercial films do?

CURRY. No, I didn't see it. In fact, I didn't see the one with the gun. I--I looked at a 8 by 10 blow-up.

Q. Oh.

CURRY. But we--

Q. Was there one showing him with the rifle, and does that show him with the pistol also?

CURRY. Yes.

Q. And the cartridge belt?

CURRY. Well, I--I didn't notice the cartridge belt and the holster.

Q. And the holster?

CURRY. Yes.

Q. Does he have any kind of uniform on, or anything that--

CURRY. No.

COMMISSION EXHIBIT No. 2147—Continued

CURRY. No.

Q. That would appear like a uniform?

CURRY. No, if I recall, he was just dressed in black.

Q Black?

Q. Black trousers?

CURRY. Black trousers and a shirt.

Q. T-shirt?

CURRY. I don't recall what kind of, what type shirt he had on.

Q. Any hat?

CURRY No, he was bareheaded.

Q. Does the background look like anything that might--

CURRY. We think it might have been, might have been, but--I mean, there's no--no way of knowing this is true, but we just--we think it might have been in New Orleans. This we will attempt to find out about.

Q. [Unintelligible] shot there?

CURRY. No, sir.

Q. Could a negative be--

CURRY. I don't know.

COMMISSION EXHIBIT No. 2147—Continued

Q. Do you have the negative?

CURRY. What I saw was an 8 by 10 blow-up. Now, I think they've got the negatives in the homicide office but I haven't examined those.

Q. Do you think we'll ever be able to see those before the evidence is presented to the grand jury?

CURRY. I don't know. I--

Q. What is the FBI office view on the rifle?

CURRY. Well, you see there was an FBI agent took the weapon from us so that we--see, we have to establish this continuous chain of possession, so in order not to have too many people involved in it we turned this weapon over to an FBI agent here in Dallas. He flew this to Washington and stayed with the evidence while they were examining the evidence, and then when they finished their examination he brought it back to Dallas and he will bring it back to us and return it to us. That way we will only have this--we'll have to establish that we gave him the evidence and he can testify he gave it back to us.

Q. Never out of his sight?

CURRY. Never out of his sight.

Q. When do you expect to get it back?

CURRY. Well, I say never out of his sight, and right now it's in the vault, but I mean he can testify that it was in his possession during all this time.

Q. When do you expect to get it back?

CURRY. Sometime this morning. I understand it was pretty late when he got in last night and when he gets up and gets down to the office he'll bring it to us.

Q. Chief, is there a serial number on it?

CURRY. I believe so.

Q. Will it establish absolutely that--

CURRY. I believe so; that's what we're hoping, but this I haven't found for sure yet.

Q. Sir, there's a report that with the photograph which you have of the man with the gun and the pistol, that there was also some literature of some sort--something like a newspaper--

CURRY. It looked like two small newspapers folded up; one of them said The Worker, and the other one--I don't know whether the other was a headline on there or whether that was the name of the paper--said, The Militant.

Q. Chief, did you say--

CURRY. The Militant.

Q. Chief, did you say he was holding--a social worker party, a Trotsky-ite party.

Q. And you also said that he was at "present arms." Well, could you describe the picture in detail--what he looked--was he holding at "present arms" with the paper this --

CURRY. Well, the paper he was holding in his hand, up like this, I believe, I believe it was his left hand, and the gun like this, across his upper body, holding the paper just like this with his hand.

Q. So he was holding the stock of the rifle with one hand and the paper up like that.

Q. Holding the rifle in his right hand and the paper in his left hand --

Q. Chief, why don't you show us the picture?

Q. How long do you expect the drive to take from here to the courthouse?

CURRY. How long do we what?

Q. Expect the trip to take from here to the courthouse.

CURRY. Oh, probably ten minutes.

Q. Do you have the line of the route to the prison lined with policemen or anything like that?

COMMISSION EXHIBIT No. 2147—Continued

Q. Any preliminary precautions?

Q. Will you drive over the President's route? To Elm Street? Will you go down there?

CURRY. I don't--I don't know which way we'll go.

Q. Is it about a mile, Chief?

CURRY. It's about that.

Q. Chief, will we be able to--

Q. Is Oswald right-handed?

CURRY. I don't know. I haven't seen him write. I mean, I haven't seen him do anything that would indicate whether he was right or left.

COMMISSION EXHIBIT No. 2147—Continued

— Commission Exhibit No. 2148

KRLD-TV reel 66 and reel 28
Sunday, 1:30 p.m., November 24, 1963

Assembly Room, Basement, Dallas Police and Courts Building

CURRY INTERVIEW ON ONWALD'S DEATH

CURRY. My statement will be very brief. Oswald expired at 1:07 p.m.

Q. He died?

CURRY. He died. At 1:07 p.m. We have arrested the man. The man will be charged with murder.

Q. Who is he?

CURRY. The man--the suspect's name is Jack Rubenstein, I believe. He goes by the name of Jack Ruby. That's all I have to say.

Q. Chief, does this man have a criminal record in this state?

CURRY. I have no other statements to make at this time.

Q. Chief, could you repeat that once more--just what you told us--the statement. We missed it back here. A little bit louder.

CURRY. I only said that Oswald expired at 1:07 p.m. The man who shot him has been arrested and will be charged with murder.

Q. Who is he? What's his name? That's all we need, Chief.

CURRY. The man's name is Jack Ruby. He goes by the name of Jack Ruby. He's a local Dallas man. His real name is Rubenstein.

COMMISSION EXHIBIT NO. 2148

Commission Exhibit No. 2149

KRLD-TV reel 39
Sunday a.m., November 24, 1963

PRESS CONFERENCE WITH CHIEF JESSE CURRY
DALLAS POLICE DEPARTMENT

CURRY. . . . felt yesterday morning that we were capable of presenting our case to the court and had ample evidence for a conviction. However in any criminal case it's impossible to get too much evidence and we continue to search for every bit of evidence that might be available to us regardless of where it is. Yesterday we were able to obtain, as I said, additional evidence which has been very valuable to us.

Q. What do you consider the high points?

CURRY. Well, of course, the--, I don't know what you mean by high points, but we have been able to do this. We have been able to place this man in the building, on the floor at the time the assassination occurred. We have been able to establish the fact that he was at the window that the shots were fired from. We have been able to establish the fact that he did order a weapon that is similar and we feel is the weapon that was used. We have been able to, through the FBI laboratory, to establish the fact that we do have the murder weapon. Their reports have been able to tell us that this is the gun that fired the bullets that killed the President and wounded the Governor.

COMMISSION EXHIBIT NO. 2149

Q. This is a firm ballistics conclusion, is this right, Chief?

CURRY. I do not have the official report. I have been notified that the ballistic reports were very favorable for us.

Q. How much importance do you attach to this picture?

CURRY. Well, it's important to us. Whether or not we will be able to introduce it as evidence will be left up to the attorney and the judge, of course, but it establishes beyond a reasonable doubt in our mind that here is our man with our guns.

Q. Chief Curry, do you have an eyewitness who saw someone shoot the President?

CURRY. No, sir; we do not.

Q. Do you have one who, someone who perhaps saw a gun out of the top window?

CURRY. I have heard that someone did but we have not talked to anyone to my knowledge who saw the barrel of the rifle sticking out the window.

Q. Can you tell us anything about--yesterday you told us that there was a very significant new development in the case. Today you alluded to it again. You said this development was not either the FBI order letter or the photograph of Oswald. Can you tell us anything more about this significant development?

COMMISSION EXHIBIT No. 2149—Continued

CURRY. No, sir; I have told you all I can. We don't want to jeopardize our case.

Q. Can you tell me, sir, whether that development is physical evidence or whether it is testimony from a witness?

CURRY. It was physical.

Q. Thank you very much, Chief.

CURRY. Yes, sir.

NELSON BENTON. That was Chief Jesse Curry of the Dallas Police Department who says that the case is moving along excellently. He also disclosed, of course, in that interview that he has fairly firm information from the examination of the weapon, the rifle, the 6.5 mm foreign-make rifle, that it was indeed the rifle that was used to assassinate President John F. Kennedy. This is Nelson Benton at the Dallas Police Department.

COMMISSION EXHIBIT No. 2149—Continued

— Commission Exhibit No. 2150

KRLD-TV reel 44
Saturday night, November 23, 1963

POLICE CHIEF JESSE CURRY ON TRANSFER OF OSWALD
POLICE AND COURTS BUILDING

CURRY. -- that is, if we plan to transfer this man not tonight, if you men would be here by no later than 10 o'clock in the morning why it will, that will be early enough.

Q. Are you through with him for the night, sir?

CURRY. Captain Fritz says he is finished with him unless possibly some witness might show up that we needed to bring him out for a show-up, but I think, I don't believe there will be any more questioning tonight.

Q. He won't be coming this way?

CURRY. No.

Q. Will he be taken to the county jail?

CURRY. He will be taken to the county jail. He would be turned over to the sheriff.

Q. Tonight or tomorrow?

CURRY. Tomorrow.

Q. Will it be after 10 o'clock?

CURRY. Well, I wouldn't be any later than ten.

Q. Thank you very much, Chief. --

COMMISSION EXHIBIT No. 2150

- 2 -

CURRY. We have one more thing here. We have filed on him for assault to murder --

Q. Assault to what?

CURRY. Assault to murder against Governor John B. Connally. That charge has been filed.

Q. Can you read that charge, sir?

Q. Did he admit owning the rifle?

CURRY. Sir?

Q. Did he admit owning the rifle?

CURRY. He will not admit ever owning a rifle, no sir.

Q. Well, what did he say when you showed him the picture?

CURRY. I wasn't there. It was Captain Fritz but he didn't get much out of him at all.

Q. Since this is probably the termination of your day with Oswald, could you sum up what progress was made today toward a confession, if any?

CURRY. I don't think we've made any progress toward a confession.

Q. You don't think so?

COMMISSION EXHIBIT No. 2150—Continued

CURRY. No.

Q. In building the case? In building your case?

CURRY. I think our case was in good shape this morning and it is much stronger tonight. We will continue to work on every possible shred of evidence that comes to our attention.

Q. Why are you so pessimistic about a confession?

CURRY. Well, you know we've been in the business a good while and, [laughter by group] and sometimes you can sort of draw your own conclusions after talking to a man over a period of time. Of course he might have a change of heart but I'd be rather surprised if he did.

Q. Chief, do you consider the FBI letter and the photograph a real block buster in the investigation?

CURRY. I would say that that was a very helpful link in our chain of evidence, yes.

Q. Chief, is that the warrant you have?

CURRY. This is the warrant of arrest, yes.

Q. Will you hold it up? Thank you. What court would have jurisdiction over this?

COMMISSION EXHIBIT No. 2150—Continued

CURRY. It was filed in the same court, Justice Court Precinct No. 2. The same as the other cases.

Q. When will he be arraigned on the -- ?

Q. On the powder burns, have you anything from the FBI on that yet?

CURRY. No, I haven't had that report yet.

Q. Chief, would you say basically . . . [several talking at once, unintelligible]

CURRY. Basically, yes.

Q. When will the arraignment be on this?

CURRY. I don't know.

Q. Today?

CURRY. No, I don't think so.

Q. Would you give us a typical reaction of Oswald when you showed him, for instance, the picture?

CURRY. I was not present so I couldn't give you that.

Q. Could you tell us why his mother and his wife were here today and what they did?

COMMISSION EXHIBIT No. 2150—Continued

CURRY. They visited with him. I understand that he asked them to attempt to get his attorney, John Abt, out of New York, and I think that is what they were doing.

Q. Has anyone heard anything from Abt?

CURRY. Well, it's hearsay with me and I don't know who said this but somewhere back in the office someone said that they understood John Abt did not want to handle the case. Now that's hearsay as far as I'm concerned.

Q. Do you think we'll have the final ballistics tomorrow?

CURRY. I think so.

Q. What do you think the results will be?

CURRY. I think they'll be good.

Q. Did you get a report through telephone today?

CURRY. I have had some information but not a formal report.

Q. And the information was -- positive?

CURRY. The information was very pleasing to us.

Q. Chief, could I see the warrant again, please, sir?

CURRY. Yes, sir.

Q. Was he confronted today with all the facts that you told us?

CURRY. Yes.

Q. And even the one you didn't tell us about?

CURRY. Yes.

Q. Will we have an opportunity to see the transparencies that showed him with the guns?

CURRY. I don't think so. These might be -- we might have kept these as evidence and it might, Mike tells us, not to be able to introduce them if they have been published in the paper.

Q. Were these clearly identifiable in the photo?

CURRY. They are clearly identifiable.

Q. And so is he?

CURRY. Yes. Sir?

Q. Did he say where they came from?

- 7 -

CURRY. They came from where his wife stays, I believe, out in Irving.

Q. Chief, will you transfer him under heavy guard?

CURRY. I'll leave that up to Sheriff Decker. That's his responsibility.

Q. The sheriff takes custody of him here?

CURRY. Yes. That's all I have, gentlemen, thank you.

[chorus of thank-you's from the group]

COMMENTATOR. Chief Jesse Curry of the Dallas Police Department seems to feel like he's pretty optimistic about the case. He smiled through most of that interview discussing primarily the warrant charging Oswald with assaulting with intent to murder Governor Connally of Texas. Nevertheless when he got into discussion of the evidence, the new evidence that they seem to have against Oswald, he was all smiles. He seems very optimistic about this. This is Nelson Benton at the Dallas Police Department.

COMMISSION EXHIBIT No. 2150—Continued

WRR reel 14
Friday night late, November 22, 1963

POLICE CHIEF JESSE CURRY'S INSTRUCTIONS TO NEWSMEN RE OSWALD'S APPEARANCE IN ASSEMBLY ROOM, DALLAS CITY JAIL

CURRY. I won't try to name them all now.

VOICE. Take

CURRY. --anything goes wrong with his being down there. If there's a rush up here he's immediately going out and that's it. Now, do we understand each other?

REPORTERS. Right. Yes. Right.

COMMISSION EXHIBIT No. 2151

Commission Exhibit No. 2152

WFAA-TV Audio reel 2 at 268
Saturday, November 23, 1963

POLICE CHIEF JESSE CURRY TALKING TO REPORTERS
POLICE AND COURTS BUILDING

Q. Any late developments?

CURRY. Sir?

Q. Any late developments other than the ones previously announced?

CURRY. No, sir.

Q. Do you know if he will be transferred today to the county -- ?

CURRY. I don't believe he will. I was talking to Fritz and Fritz said he didn't believe he would be through with him today. He needs to talk to him and we can't just talk to him constantly; we have to let him rest, you know. We can't just continuously talk to him. He's had a chance to call for his attorneys and he's visited with his mother and his sister [sic] and his brother and they told his brother to go up and visit him if he wanted to.

Q. Has he named any attorneys?

CURRY. He--I understand now that he is trying to contact Attorney Abt, I believe, A-B-T, I believe, out of New York, I think.

Q. New York? What is this attorney's affiliation at present? Do you know that, sir?

CURRY. What is that attorney -- ?

Q. What his affiliation is. Does he have anything to do with the Civil Liberties Union, or anything of that nature?

COMMISSION EXHIBIT No. 2152

2

CURRY. I don't know. I think so, but I wouldn't want to say because I just don't know positively. I understand that he has--it's my understanding that this attorney, Abt, has been involved in some of the defense of some communists.

Q. Sir, naturally you will probably in the investigation be attempting to let the public know as much as you can and still not attempt to prejudice any future jury that's going to be trying this case.

CURRY. That's true.

Q. What are some of the problems that you have had to run into in doing this? Were there many?

CURRY. You just can't tell everything you know, that's all.

Q. Right.

Q. Chief, is he becoming more cooperative? He was a little arrogant, I understand, during the earlier questioning.

CURRY. I think he was a little more--I say a little friendlier with Fritz during the interrogation this morning, I believe. He told Fritz he'd had a good night's sleep and was well rested.

Q. Is he eating well? Is his appetite good?

CURRY. I don't know. I didn't hear him say. He said he had a good night's sleep.

Q. One last question. Would you care to make any comment on just how far the interrogation has progressed? How much good it has done, in your opinion?

CURRY. We are sure of our case; I can tell you that.

COMMISSION EXHIBIT No. 2152—Continued

Q. He has yet admitted nothing?

CURRY. No, he has not, but we are sure of our case.

COMMENTATOR. Thank you, Chief, very much.

COMMISSION EXHIBIT No. 2152—Continued

WFAA-TV reel PKT 25
KRLD-TV reel 20
Saturday, November 23, 1963

PRESS INTERVIEW OF CAPT. J. WILL FRITZ
IN DALLAS POLICE AND COURTS BUILDING

This is Captain Fritz, head of the Homicide squad who has been conducting the investigation and interrogation. Captain, can you give us a resume of what you now know concerning the assassination of the President and Mr. Oswald's role in it?

FRITZ. There is only one thing that I can tell you without going into the evidence before first talking to the District Attorney. I can tell you that this case is cinched--that this man killed the President. There's no question in my mind about it.

Q. Well, what is the basis for that statement?

FRITZ. No, sir. I don't want to go into the basis. In fact, I don't want to get into the evidence. I just want to tell you that we are convinced beyond any doubt that he did the killing.

Q. Was it spur-of-the-moment or a well-planned long-thought-out plot?

FRITZ. That, I'd rather not discuss that, if you don't mind, please, thank you.

COMMISSION EXHIBIT No. 2153

\- 2 -

Q. Will you be moving him today, Captain?

Q. Is he going to remain here?

FRITZ. He'll be here today, yes, sir.

COMMISSION EXHIBIT No. 2153—Continued

—Commission Exhibit No. 2154

WFAA-TV reel PKT 17
KRLD-TV reels 19 and 25
Sunday, November 24, 1963

PRESS INTERVIEW WITH CAPT. J. WILL FRITZ
IN DALLAS POLICE AND COURTS BUILDING

Q. Captain, is there any doubt in your mind that Oswald was the man who killed President Kennedy?

FRITZ. No, sir, there is no doubt in my mind about Oswald being the man. Of course, we'll continue to investigate and gather more and more evidence, but there is no question about it.

Q. Is the case closed or not, then, Captain?

FRITZ. The case is cleared, but we'll be anxious to find out more about it--all we can find out.

Q. Captain, was anyone else connected with Oswald in the matter?

FRITZ. Well, now, not that I know of.

Q. Did Jack Ruby say how he got into the basement here today?

FRITZ. He didn't tell us that.

Q. Did he say when or why, Captain?

COMMISSION EXHIBIT No. 2154

- 2 -

FRITZ. Some of those things I can't answer for you. And he, of course, has talked to his attorney, and those are certain things he don't want to tell me.

Q. -- why?

FRITZ. He did tell me that he had built up a grief--

Q. He said he had been grieving over the President?

FRITZ. He said he had built up a grief. Those are his words, "built up a grief."

Q. Has he been calm and rational?

FRITZ. He seemed rational; he seems very rational.

Q. Did he sign anything at all?

FRITZ. He didn't deny the shooting.

Q. Captain, what excuse -- letting him get that close -- ?

FRITZ. What excuse did he use?

Q. No, what excuse do you-all have, you know, that he got that close?

COMMISSION EXHIBIT No. 2154—Continued

- 3 -

FRITZ. I don't have an excuse.

Q. For what reason-- ? How could it happen--

Q. Captain, are you going to interrogate him more this afternoon or are you done for the day?

FRITZ. I'm not sure about this afternoon.

Q. Has he asked to see a lawyer?

COMMISSION EXHIBIT No. 2154—Continued

— Commission Exhibit No. 2155 —

WFAA-TV reel PKT 21
Saturday, p.m., November 23, 1963

INTERVIEW WITH CAPT. J. WILL FRITZ
IN DALLAS POLICE AND COURTS BUILDING

Q. Does he admit disliking anybody in particular?

FRITZ. He talked a little better than one. Well, I guess I've gone into likes and dislikes for the present. He said he thought that everyone was entitled to like or dislike anyone he wanted to, but he wouldn't--

Q. What's the latest word on Rodriguez Molina?

FRITZ. I haven't talked to him; someone else is talking to him.

Q. Is he still being held?

FRITZ. I'm not sure about that. I don't know.

Q. Where does his wife live?

Q. Ask him about his news with the gun.

Q. Ask him if he had any word to give us one way or the other.

Q. You say he was more cooperative today, a little more informative? Where does his-- ? Did he admit anything?

Q. Did he admit-- ?

Q. Where does his wife live, Captain?

COMMISSION EXHIBIT No. 2155

- 2 -

FRITZ. Where does she live? In Irving.

Q. Do you have an address?

FRITZ. I have it, but I don't have it here with me.

Q. Captain, do you expect a confession?

FRITZ. No, sir; not right now.

Q. Have you got this fellow tied to the murder weapon--the rifle?

FRITZ. Well, we're, we'd like to have him tied to it better than we have, but we're still in pretty good shape.

Q. Captain, how well do you-- ?

FRITZ. Well, I can't go into that because that is very important to the evidence and the District Attorney should pass on that.

Q. Were there any-- ?

FRITZ. I wouldn't want to talk about the prints, and--

Q. Is it hoped that the-- ?

FRITZ. Get ready for court.

Q. Has it been established how he left, what route he took after he left the building?

COMMISSION EXHIBIT No. 2155—Continued

- 3 -

FRITZ. Yes.

Q. How did he actually get back in Oak Cliff?

FRITZ. He left the building and started toward his home by bus.

Q. By bus?

Q. By bus? He caught a bus to go home?

FRITZ. He left the bus along the way and then changed to a cab and rode the cab part of the way and then walked on along the way home.

Q. Why did he say he did this?

FRITZ. He said the bus was traveling too slow.

Q. Which home was this now, the-- ?

Q. Captain, we can't hear you.

Q. Captain--

FRITZ. Yes?

Q. Captain, is it hoped that his wife and his mother may persuade him to confess, is that why they're talking to him?

COMMISSION EXHIBIT No. 2155—Continued

- 4 -

FRITZ. No, sir. We just let them visit because they wanted to, because they're relatives and they might want to talk to him about his attorney.

Q. Did he say why-- ?

FRITZ. Sir?

Q. Did he say why he left his place of work?

Q. Did he say why he went to the movie?

FRITZ. He did, he did give one kind of excuse about leaving work. He said he didn't believe that anyone was going to work that afternoon anyway, so he just left.

Q. You'd call him cooperative, wouldn't you?

[Laughter by group]

Q. In other words,

Q. Where is he now?

FRITZ. He's in jail.

Q. Did he get back to his room over on Beckley and then leave it and then encounter the officer?

FRITZ. That's right. He changed clothes. He went to his room, changed his clothing, then started to the picture show and encountered the officer on the way to the picture show.

COMMISSION EXHIBIT No. 2155—Continued

- 5 -

Q. Did he have the bus transfer in his pocket?

FRITZ. Yes, he did. He had it.

Q. Did he get that from the bus driver?

FRITZ. Yes, sir.

Q. Captain, do you feel any closer to a conf____ ?

Q. The jail? Did you talk to the taxi driver who-- ?

FRITZ. I didn't but some other officer did.

Q. I'll still never get over his--

Q. Captain, do you feel any closer to a confession today than you did last night?

FRITZ. I can't tell about that. That would be a guess, of course.

Q. Wasn't there, didn't he, somebody else beside the taxi, aren't you looking for a driver of another car--

Q. That was an untrue story?

Q. Was that an untrue story?

Q. Do we know where the gun came from--the rifle?

COMMISSION EXHIBIT No. 2155—Continued

- 6 -

Q. Tell me, how far back have you been able to trace it, sir?

FRITZ. I wouldn't want to, to--

Q. Was it bought in town, for instance?

FRITZ. I wouldn't want to talk about that.

Q. What about the bus driver?

Q. Did you talk to him, do you know who he was? The bus driver?

FRITZ. Yes, sir; we know the bus driver.

COMMISSION EXHIBIT No. 2155—Continued

WFAA-TV reel PKT 16
Friday night, November 22, 1963

INTERROGATION OF CAPT. J. WILL FRITZ
BY NEWSMEN, THIRD FLOOR CORRIDOR,
DALLAS POLICE AND COURTS BUILDING

Q. Is there any statement yet from-- ?

FRITZ. Yes, sir, I think so, but it looks like we'll be working next week and for a long time--

Q. Will we get another chance to see him tonight?

FRITZ. I doubt if he'll be back down tonight. I doubt that.

Q. Do you think he'll be back down tomorrow, sir?

FRITZ. I don't know. It's hard to say.

COMMENTATOR. That's it. That was Capt. Will Fritz of the Dallas Police Department.

COMMISSION EXHIBIT No. 2156

KRLD reel 10
Saturday, November 23, 1963

INTERVIEW WITH OFFICER BENTLEY

BENTLEY. His left hand reached for the pistol with his right hand and as he reached for his pistol I grabbed him along with two or three other officers. He fought with us like a wild man and we finally subdued him and took him on out and put him in the police car and brought him into the Homicide Bureau.

Q. Who did he aim the gun at?

BENTLEY. The gun wasn't necessarily aimed, it was started, he started to pull it up to aim it and Officer McDonald had a hold of his, of the gun, I had a hold of his right arm, we got a thumb or something in between the hammer and the firing pin so that it mashed the firing, it just snapped slightly and kept it from going off.

Q. It didn't misfire. In other words you prevented it from firing?

BENTLEY. Yes, my hand was across to prevent it from firing.

Q. But there was a bullet in the chamber?

BENTLEY. Definitely so, it had been hit with the firing pin but not enough to go off.

Q. Did he say what was reported about he got him a president?

COMMISSION EXHIBIT No. 2157

- 2 -

BENTLEY. No, sir, I didn't hear that.

Q. What did he say to you after he was arrested?

BENTLEY. He just said, "This is it. It's all over with now."

Q. Anything else?

BENTLEY. That's all.

Q. Did he give any indication that he thought you were looking for him in connection --

BENTLEY. No.

Q. With the President's assassination?

BENTLEY. No.

Q. Did you say you put your thumb or your finger on him?

BENTLEY. Don't know. It was in the scuffle there. We don't know if it was my thumb, finger or hand. I got a bruised hand from it. I don't know if it was the thumb or the finger.

Q. Did you have proof this gun had been used before?

BENTLEY. I don't know. I didn't look at it enough to say for sure.

COMMISSION EXHIBIT No. 2157—Continued

- 3 -

Q. This was a darkened theatre, was it not, sir?

BENTLEY. No, we had the lights on.

Q. You had the lights on?

BENTLEY. Lights were on.

Q. What kind of attitude would you say he had, an arrogant one -- ?

BENTLEY. Very belligerent, arrogant attitude throughout the whole thing.

Q. Did he mention Russia, communism or anything to you?

BENTLEY. No, he did not.

Q. Did he mention the President -- ?

BENTLEY. No, he did not.

Q. [Unintelligible]

BENTLEY. That's right.

Q. Did he ever talk in a foreign language?

BENTLEY. No, he did not.

Q. Do you think he had any accomplices?

COMMISSION EXHIBIT No. 2157—Continued

BENTLEY. I don't know, I didn't see any others at all.

Q. Mr. Bentley, are you familiar with the subject?

BENTLEY. No, I had never seen him before at all.

Q. Mr. Bentley, what is your first name again, please?

BENTLEY. Paul, Paul Bentley.

COMMENTATOR. Was captured yesterday in a Dallas theatre. This is Detective Paul Bentley who was among the officers who arrested Oswald yesterday near a theatre in a suburban section of Dallas. He just described his injuries. He was an eyewitness to the capture of the man charged with the murder of the President of the United States. This is Nelson Benton at Dallas Police Headquarters.

COMMISSION EXHIBIT No. 2157—Continued

WFAA-TV reel PKT 30
November 24, 1963

INTERVIEW WITH JOY DALE BY WFAA-TV

Q. Will you give your name, please?

DALE. Joy Dale.

Q. Joy, what do you do?

DALE. I dance at the Carousel.

Q. Did you say dance? What kind of dance? What do you mean?

DALE. I work with fans in the exotic dancing.

Q. You are an exotic dancer at the Carousel owned and operated by Jack Ruby?

DALE. That's right.

Q. How long have you been working for Jack Ruby?

DALE. About two or three months.

Q. Are you a Dallas girl?

DALE. Yes, I am.

Q. What, what do you think of Jack?

DALE. I think he is a very swell person.

COMMISSION EXHIBIT No. 2158

- 2 -

Q. Did he, did you start dancing, did you start your career at the Carousel Club under the tutelage of Jack Ruby?

DALE. No, I didn't.

Q. Did you dance somewhere else and then move here?

DALE. Yes, I did.

Q. You say Jack is a wonderful person. What do you mean, he is a wonderful person?

DALE. I know him as a friend, and as a boss also. And I've know the many people that he has given a helping hand that needed it, and it's--

Q. As an example--

DALE. Well, I have a friend out here that came to Dallas, unemployed, know--not knowing anyone. He had met Jack once. Jack gave him a place to stay until he found him a job, gave him money to live off of until he went to work, until he could move out. Another girl that works in the club now as a waitress--she was in Florida. He sent her money to come back with her children and gave her money to live on until she was back up on her feet and able to work.

COMMISSION EXHIBIT No. 2158—Continued

- 3 -

Q. Has Jack helped you in any particular way?

DALE. No, but he has been a very good friend.

Q. What kind of a man was he to work for? Was he--was he an emotional man? Did he have fits of temper? Did he often blow up about nothing, or was he the level-headed type.

DALE. Jack was a very emotional person, as people know. All people that know him know him as an emotional person. He--he'd blow off easily, but he usually had a reason behind it--he had good reason. He usually would stop and think about it. But if you don't yell back at Jack, he'll never yell at you.

Q. Someone said earlier that Jack was the kind of person if he liked you he liked you all the way, and if he did not like you he did not like you all the way. Do you think that's true?

DALE. Yes, I believe that's true.

Q. Have you seen any evidence of this? Have you seen whom Jack did not like and the way he reacted?

DALE. Yes, I have.

Q. Will you tell us about it?

COMMISSION EXHIBIT No. 2158—Continued

DALE. Well, -- said something that maybe Jack didn't approve of, that Jack would say so.

Q. Straightforward?

DALE. Straightforward. And Jack is the type of person if he likes you there is not anything he won't do to help you in any way--money, or just by being a clown-- in a lot of ways. It's hard to just sit here and say.

Q. Do you like Jack Ruby?

DALE. Yes, I like Jack Ruby.

Q. You said earlier, I believe, that one of the performers there in the Carousel recognized Oswald in the audience. Is this possible?

DALE. I would say that this is very hard to do because of the lighting in the club that burns down. And when you are on the stage, which I am seven nights a week, the light--it's right in your eyes. Myself, I wear glasses and I can't see very well without them and so I say this: you can't see beyond the people sitting right around the front of the stage, even with perfect eyesight.

COMMISSION EXHIBIT No. 2158—Continued

Q. I--then I take it that you are saying that it is a possibility but it would be--it is an improbability that you could recognize anyone in the audience.

DALE. He would have to be sitting right on the runway to recognize him.

Q. By runway you mean--

DALE. The edge of the stage.

Q. The edge of the stage. Did you ever see Mr. Oswald at any time in the Carousel?

DALE. No.

Q. You have never heard of Mr. Oswald before?

DALE. No, I have not.

Q. Well, it would be interesting--you are a friend of Jack Ruby. Whenever you--did you hear it on the radio? Television? How did you receive word that Jack Ruby was accused of the slaying today?

DALE. I was over at a friend's house. We were listening to the radio. And when they said that a short, gray-haired man, slightly bald, that he had shot--just shot Oswald, I--that he was a nightclub owner--well, first of all, I said that it's just like Jack.

COMMISSION EXHIBIT No. 2158—Continued

Q. But you didn't believe it?

DALE. No, it's hard to believe, because I talked to Jack Friday afternoon. It was approximately--I'd say it was three o'clock, a little after three, when I went into the Club, because I was dancing and I was giving a girl lessons who was just beginning.

Q. Friday after--that was after the President's--

DALE. Right after the President. I had been to the hospital. My little girl had an appointment there, and I was taking her out to the hospital. Then I came back to the Club, and Jack was there, and he was very upset, and--

Q. Did he say anything? What did he say about--the assassination of Mr. Kennedy? What did he have to say?

DALE. At first, nothing much. But Jack, like I say, he was an emotional man, but I never thought I'd see Jack cry. And tears did come to Jack's eyes. And he said, "It's something just unbelievable! How could a man shoot the President of our country?"

Q. This was Friday, late, around three o'clock?

DALE. This was a little after three o'clock--I'd say 5 or 10 minutes afterward.

Q. Did he close up the Club that night?

DALE. Yes, he did. He said, "The Club won't be open under the circumstances, and I shall close the club tonight and tomorrow night. I don't know how long." But Jack is a person who thinks very highly of the Kennedys, and I myself said Friday, I said, being a mother, I said; "Can you possibly think how this woman feels? She just lost her son, and now she's lost her husband!" And Jack said, "You shouldn't" or something, "He should be killed." That's all. Maybe it wasn't the exact words, but it was very similar.

Q. Now, this was Friday night, and when he announced to you that the Club would be closed because of the assassination of Mr. Kennedy, he said to you--once again, what did he say?

DALE. He--well, when I mentioned Jacqueline Kennedy and her children and how she felt--must feel about her husband, he suggested she--he ought to be killed--he ought to be killed. And--well--I heard other people say this besides Jack. I myself secretly used other words when I heard they killed John Kennedy.

Q. What's going to happen to you now?

DALE. That I don't know.

Q. Thank you very much.

KRLD-TV reel 13
NBC-TV reel 35
Sunday, November 24, 1963

PRESS INTERVIEW WITH SGT. P. T. DEAN
DALLAS POLICE DEPARTMENT, POLICE AND
COURTS BUILDING

Q. -- did you see, did you see that man fire the shot?

DEAN. I didn't see him as he fired it. The moment the shot was fired I turned around. I did see the smoke from the gun. It was an instant. I was looking--

Q. --

DEAN. No, I didn't.

COMMENTATOR. This is Sgt. Patrick Dean of the Dallas Police Department who is standing beside us. Pat, you saw the smoke from the gun?

DEAN. Yes.

Q. And did you see the man?

DEAN. Yes.

Q. What did he look like to you, Pat?

DEAN. Well, he was a man dressed in a suit, good appearance, like one of the pressmen. However, I was at the top of the ramp, Bob, waiting at the armored car which we were supposed to take him to the county jail in.

COMMISSION EXHIBIT No. 2159

- 2 -

Q. Right.

DEAN. Now that's, from that location is when I saw the smoke from the gun. As far as identifying him at that time at that distance, I couldn't.

Q. I know you were--

Q. -- to Oswald?

DEAN. He was taken back into the jail office; an ambulance was called, he is at the hospital now.

Q. Where was he wounded?

Q. Is he at Parkland Hospital?

DEAN. He had a wound in his lower left abdomen.

Q. Was he -- more than one shot?

DEAN. As far as I could tell it was the only one. I think it was only one shot that was fired.

COMMENTATOR. Right. There was only one shot. It was right here, but, Pat, you say it was in his lower left abdomen?

DEAN. Yes, sir.

COMMISSION EXHIBIT No. 2159—Continued

- 3 -

Q. He was unconscious inside?

DEAN. Yes, he was.

Q. Does he look like he's dying?

DEAN. I wouldn't want to say. I--

Q. Did you hear anything he said? Did he say anything? When he clutched himself, did he say anything?

DEAN. Are you talking about Oswald? Or--

Q. Oswald, yes.

DEAN. No, he didn't. He was unconscious.

Q. What about the man? Did he get, did he run at all, or what happened--

DEAN. No, he was immediately subdued by the officers, at the time he fired the shot.

Q. How many shots were fired?

DEAN. Just one shot.

COMMENTATOR. Now then, thus far, Pat, is the man upstairs in a cell?

COMMISSION EXHIBIT No. 2159—Continued

- 4 -

DEAN. Well, as far as I know he's either in the jail or in Captain Fritz' office. He'd probably be in jail.

Q. Do you know this subject? Do you know him? Have you seen him before?

DEAN. Yes, I do.

Q. Is he from Dallas?

DEAN. Yes.

Q. Who is he? Is he a nightclub operator?

DEAN. I couldn't tell you.

Q. I know you can't release the name now, but do you know what kind of business he happens to be in?

DEAN. Bob, I wouldn't want to say.

COMMENTATOR. Right.

Q. Did he have to be disarmed or did he give up?

DEAN. We had to disarm him.

Q. Did he struggle?

DEAN. As much as he could, yes. But he was--

- 5 -

Q. Did he have anything--

Q. The struggle--

DEAN. He was mumbling, I couldn't hear. I couldn't understand what he did say. Now--

Q. Did Oswald-- ?

Q. Was it a pistol that he had? Did he have a pistol?

DEAN. What?

Q. Did he have a pistol?

DEAN. Yes.

Q. Do you know what kind of pistol he was carrying?

DEAN. No, Bob, I never saw the pistol itself. Some other, I think Officer Graves, got the gun immediately after he fired the shot.

Q. Was he in civilian clothes?

DEAN. Yes.

Q. Did he try to get away?

DEAN. No. He was immediately subdued by the officers.

COMMISSION EXHIBIT No. 2159—Continued

- 6 -

COMMENTATOR. He wouldn't have had a chance to get away.

Q. How many shots were fired?

DEAN. One.

COMMENTATOR. One shot.

Q. Did you see-- ?

Q. What was Oswald wearing, do you remember, when he came out?

DEAN. I didn't pay too much attention.

Q. But, did you know the man, did you see the man before?

COMMENTATOR. Yes, he did.

Q. Did you, you saw his face?

DEAN. Yes, sir.

Q. And you knew him?

DEAN. Yes, sir.

COMMENTATOR. Pat, he is a resident of Dallas, is he not?

DEAN. Yes, sir. And that's all I want to say about the man inside.

COMMISSION EXHIBIT No. 2159—Continued

Q. Would you say he was about 3 feet away when the one shot was fired? About 3 feet away? From Oswald? It looked like that to us, was he about 3 feet away when, or how far would you say the shot was fired from?

DEAN. I couldn't tell. I couldn't see Oswald when the shot was fired. I immediately turned. I was waiting at the armored car to ride with the suspect to the county jail. As soon as the shot was fired, I came immediately down the ramp to assist the officers.

Q. Officer, do you know this man personally that's in custody?

DEAN. Yes.

Q. In the line of duty, or in another way?

DEAN. Sir, I wouldn't want to say.

Q. But he is known to you as a police officer?

DEAN. Not--as a police officer?

Q. That is, you as a police officer?

DEAN. I see.

Q. -- know him. Is that correct?

DEAN. Yes.

COMMISSION EXHIBIT No. 2159—Continued

Q. Was he connected in any way with the assassination?

DEAN. I wouldn't, I don't know.

Q. Had you seen him here in the building before the shot was fired?

DEAN. No, sir.

COMMENTATOR. Pat, could you outline briefly some of the security precautions that were taken immediately before this happened?

DEAN. Yes, sir. We thoroughly searched the basement. We had searched even the cars, up on top of the pipes and things that a person might conceal himself. There was about 15 to 20 men that had searched this place prior to, 30 minutes in fact searched it twice--about an hour before and then 30 minutes before.

Q. How many officersdid you have outside, approximately, would you say?

DEAN. About 20.

Q. About 20 uniformed officers?

COMMENTATOR. --outside the building and they're armed with riot guns, pistols, and all kinds of things.

COMMISSION EXHIBIT No. 2159—Continued

- 9 -

DEAN. Yes, sir. Some few of them are.

Q. You were then ready-- ?

Q. You had seen him before, in here?

DEAN. No, sir.

Q. Today?

DEAN. No, sir. Not today.

COMMENTATOR. Is there anything else that you possibly might tell us about him, Pat? I know that at the present time you're, you're bound and can't say very much, but you have said that he is from Dallas and that you do know this, this subject and have seen him before.

DEAN. Yes, sir. I do know him.

COMMENTATOR. He, is there anything that you can say about him further than the fact that he is a resident of Dallas--the man who shot Oswald--to shed some more light on this?

DEAN. Well, Bob, that would be all I want to say, really.

COMMENTATOR. I'm sure that's the case. Now, at present, what in the way of release is going on inside? How soon do you think we're going to be able to know who this man is?

COMMISSION EXHIBIT No. 2159—Continued

- 10 -

DEAN. Well, the information would have to come from Captain Fritz' office.

COMMENTATOR. Captain Fritz came out of this door just a few steps ahead of Oswald--do you know where he is at present?

DEAN. No, sir. I don't.

COMMENTATOR. Capt. Will Fritz is the master interrogator who was carrying on the interrogations yesterday.

Q. -- security precautions had been taken, Were there any threatening phone calls during the night that there might be some effort to take Oswald's life?

DEAN. I couldn't answer that. I don't know.

COMMISSION EXHIBIT No. 2159—Continued

— Commission Exhibit 2160

NBC-TV reel 15
November 22, 1963

PRESS INTERVIEW WITH SGT. GERALD HILL
DALLAS POLICE DEPARTMENT

HILL. The FBI who was in at the arrest with this office.

Q. Sir, did he make any statement? Did he say anything other than "This is it"?

HILL. He did not admit to us while we had him in custody any of the accusations either of shooting the officer or of any other crime that could have been committed. He started demanding that he be allowed to see a lawyer and started talking about his rights--wouldn't even admit that he pulled the trigger on the gun in the theatre. Actually we didn't receive any information as to the actual contents of the crime from him for the entire trip to the station.

Q. What about the matching descriptions, Jerry?

HILL. The description that we had of the suspect in Oak Cliff was similar to the description we had and the man we were looking for as the assassin, but at that time we had not been able to connect the two in any way.

Q. The only--the only discrepancy was two inches in height. Is that correct?

HILL. Approximately two inches in height was the only discrepancy in the description of the man who killed Officer Tippit and the man who shot the President.

Q. What was the description of that man?

HILL. He was described as five six to five eight, slight build, brown hair, having on a jacket and white shirt and dark trousers.

COMMISSION EXHIBIT No. 2160

2

Actually the suspect was about five ten and had discarded the jacket which we found in the Oak Cliff area near a funeral home in the 400 block of East Jefferson, and at the time we arrested the suspect his pistol was again fully loaded and we had a witness that said he saw the suspect stop long enough to reload his pistol after shooting the officer.

Q. What did you find in the building?

Q. Near where the President was shot from?

HILL. In the building on the sixth floor we found an area that, near a window, that had partially been blocked off by boxes of books, and also the three spent shells that had apparently been fired from a rifle. Also we found the remnants of what could have been a meal eaten by the suspect of a chicken dinner. At that time I left the building and later, I understand, in the same general vicinity under some boxes the rifle that was used was found.

Q. The rifle that we saw in the office?

Q. What did the man say when you arrested him?

HILL. The man did not make any definite statement other than demanding to see a lawyer and demanding his rights, and when we arrested him he did not volunteer any information to us at all. The only way we found out what his name was was to remove his billfold and check it ourselves; he wouldn't even tell us what his name was.

Q. What does he--do you believe that he is the same man who killed the police officer?

COMMISSION EXHIBIT No. 2160—Continued

HILL. Having been in it from the very beginning, as far as the officer's death is concerned, I am convinced that he is the man that killed the officer. Now the tie-in on the rest of it will have to be established by somebody else. As to whether the two situations are related, other circumstances that are taking place in another part of the investigation other than what I have been connected with will have to be proved to tie the two together.

Q. Have you -- the information about his background -- has this been released? For public release?

Q. About his past experiences?

HILL. Bill, I don't know too much about his past experiences and the only thing that I could give you would be hearsay, and I would hate to give it in case it was wrong.

Q. Has the suspect admitted shooting the President?

HILL. Not to my knowledge, he hasn't.

Q. What was his name on the billfold?

HILL. What was the name on the billfold?

Q. On the billfold.

HILL. Lee H. Oswald, O-S-W-A-L-D.

Q. At no point did he say anything like "I've got me a President"?

HILL. Not when he was in my custody. I did not hear him make a statement of that type.

Q. Did you hear that statement from anybody?

HILL. I have heard it as a rumor that it was said, but I can't verify it because it was not said in my presence.

COMMISSION EXHIBIT No. 2160—Continued

Q. Are you convinced at this point, sir, that there are three men involved?

HILL. No, sir. I am convinced that the man we have is the man that shot the officer. As to the circumstances that happened prior to the shooting, we can only surmise that the officer stopped a car, on possibly a traffic violation or on information from a citizen, but we can't verify that, and also the only two people that can tell us why the officer stopped him is the officer and the man who shot him.

Q. Jerry, you're an expert --

HILL. I'm not an expert, but I would say the distance was approximately a block. As to--

Q. With a telescopic lens?

HILL. Across the parkway, across the parkway, and he would have had a clear shot, and with a scope it would have probably been real easy.

Q. He was struck from behind, wasn't he?

HILL. I understand that he was, yes, sir. That the shots were fired from behind.

Q. It has been established, hasn't it, Jerry, that the suspect had worked for two and a half months for the book binding company in the building from which the shot was believed to come that killed the President?

HILL. I have been told that this was the case; that he had been there, an employee there, approximately three months.

Q. Where did you get your description of the Presidential assassin?

COMMISSION EXHIBIT No. 2160—Continued

HILL. Sir, it was broadcast on the air. As to what officer actually first received the information as to who the assassin was, I couldn't tell you.

Q. Wasn't there a description called in by some unknown person?

HILL. Suspect now?

Q. As far as the present suspect is concerned?

HILL. The suspect will be interrogated some more. At the same time all the loose ends will be tied together to the best of our ability and the crime lab and other agencies involved that can supply us with additional information on the suspect will all be in operation until we try to tie this thing up in one neat package.

Q. Jerry, do you know if there are any fingerprints on the rifle?

HILL. But, as to the exact time, I don't know.

HILL. Bill, I don't know for sure. I couldn't say one way or the other.

Q. Any idea at all?

Q. Where were the spent bullets in the room?

HILL. [illegible], I did not pick them up.

Q. Does the crime lab . . . idea?

HILL. I have no idea.

COMMISSION EXHIBIT No. 2160—Continued

— Commission Exhibit No. 2161 —

WFAA-TV reel PKT 16
Sunday, November 24, 1963

INTERVIEW WITH JADA (JANET ADAMS CONFORTO)
BY PAUL GOOD, ABC

GOOD. Jada, how long did you know Jack Ruby?

JADA. I knew Jack Ruby for approximately four, five, six months.

GOOD. In what relationship?

JADA. I was employed as the feature at the Carousel Club and I had known Jack before I went to work there, and I had a slight hassle with Jack and I had left, and that was the end of my association with Jack.

GOOD. What kind of a man was he?

JADA. Jack Ruby was a fanatic. He was a very nervous man, a very violent man. He would cause hassles and harrassment, and he was very energetic--

GOOD. Would you say he had a violent streak in him?

JADA. Oh, yeah, very much so. Yes, he would get carried away by something, lose all rational thinking. He would just go off--ZOOM--as if he had to prove something; he had to be somebody.

GOOD. Well, I have heard some stories about him being of a generous type. They tell a story of when a customer of one of his clubs would call for a taxicab Jack would put fifty cents aside in the event the customer left, and when the cab driver would come up and have to go away empty-handed he'd give them the fifty cents. Does this square with his character, as you knew it?

JADA. Oh, yes. Jack was almost a dual nature. He would be very nice and very helpful to me. He would change completely then, and the

COMMISSION EXHIBIT No. 2161

next minute you'd be his worst enemy, and he'd be against you and want everybody to support him against you. He was a very irrational man--very emotional.

GOOD. Did he always carry a gun?

JADA. I don't know. I don't know him that well. But I have seen him with a gun and I presume he carried it every night. It seemed to be a habit of his.

GOOD. What about politics? Did he seem interested in politics, particularly regarding the Kennedys?

JADA. I have heard Jack talk about the Kennedys and I've been trying to think and it's so confusing today, but I believe he disliked Bobby Kennedy.

GOOD. Get no recollection of what he had ever said about the President?

JADA. Yes. He followed that statement up about Bobby with something about Jack Kennedy, but I can't for the minute just form it in my mind.

GOOD. Do you think that Jack Ruby was the type of man that was capable of killing the assassin of President Kennedy out of love for Kennedy, out of political motives?

JADA. I didn't think he loved Kennedy that much. I don't know why he would do it. I'd say he would be perfectly capable of an act like that, very much so.

GOOD. But the reasons for it, those are hard to pin down, as the portrait of Jack Ruby emerges piece by piece.

This is Paul Good, ABC, in Dallas.

COMMISSION EXHIBIT No. 2161—Continued

WFAA-TV PKT 14
Saturday, November 23, 1963

INTERVIEW WITH CAPTAIN GLEN D. KING, DALLAS POLICE DEPARTMENT, BY BOB CLARK, ABC

This is Captain G. D. King, administrative officer of the Dallas Police. Captain Glen King of the Dallas Police force.

Q. -- information a little while ago about the search for additional suspects.

KING. Well, early this morning, members of this Department and the representatives from our district attorney's office, with a search warrant in their possession, went to an address here in Dallas to talk to a person who was associated, where, with the--Oswald--the place where Oswald works. There were met at the door by this person and he asked them to come in, and they went into the house at his--on his invitation. The search warrant was not executed because he did invite them in. They asked permission from him to look around the house; this permission was given. They were not able to find anything there to--that would indicate his association with his--nothing in the house at that time to indicate it, so they asked him to come down to the police station this morning at 11 o'clock for interrogation and he agreed to do so. He did come down this morning at 11. He is at the present time being interrogated, but we do not have anything definite on it, whether there will be any association or not, of course, now we don't know.

Q. Do you regard this man as a suspect in this case at this moment?

COMMISSION EXHIBIT No. 2162

KING. All we regard him as right now is a person to interrogate. Certainly there's not adequate amount of information on him to indicate that he is a suspect. We do have this--the Federal Bureau of Investigation has asked us and we join in with them in requesting that any person who was in the vicinity of the assassination yesterday, who was taking pictures, bring these pictures to the police department here. Anyone who has any information concerning this certainly should contact the police department immediately. But particularly anyone, and this is logical, I think, that since the President's motorcade was going through, someone in that area might have had cameras and might have been taking pictures. We don't know of anyone, but if there are such persons we certainly would urge that they bring their film to the police department.

Q. Do you know, Captain, whether Oswald continued to maintain his innocence during the hour he was questioned here this morning?

KING. I do not know. I haven't talked to them about his questioning this morning.

Q. Is this--is going to this home and bringing this man or asking him to come in for interrogation--does this indicate that Oswald has said something that would lead you to believe other people were associated with him in this alleged--?

KING. Not necessarily, no.

Q. Did the witnesses say-- that Officer Tippit--?

Q. Did they identify this man?

KING. This I do not know.

Q. -- Fair Play for Cuba?

KING. This I do not know.

Q. What's the name of the man involved?

KING. I don't want to identify him, no, because there's not, there's not an adequate amount of evidence of any involvement on his part to warrant identification of him.

Q. Is this person referred to earlier as having a subversive type record who lived--who worked at the same place?

KING. Yes.

Q. Is he a colored man, sir?

KING. No.

Q. What is the present plan now insofar as the prime suspect is concerned?

KING. Actually, we will continue the--the investigation and have something to--on--to find answers to all of the questions on it. The trend the investigation will take or the route it will follow, of course, will be dictated by what happens.

Q. Well, what do you do with Mr. Oswald as of right now--what is, what is the next--?

KING. I understand that he has been returned to the jail cell.

Q. Do you know when he will be transferred to the county jail?

KING. No, sir, we do not.

Q. Will he be interrogated here again this afternoon?

KING. We do not know.

Q. Could we ask you, sir, what do you know about the report that the FBI knew that Oswald was priority one?

4

KING. I know nothing about that.

Q. Sir, the person--that you know of, did he in any way, did he show any indication that he knew that the--?

KING. Not to our knowledge, no, not to our knowledge. I'm not--I'm not sure what pictures you're talking about.

Q. [Unintelligible.]

KING. Not to our knowledge, he did not, no.

Q. Captain King, are you--?

COMMENTATOR. This is Captain Glen King of the Dallas Police force

Q. --who is listed on the Dallas Police Department's subversive list?

KING. I don't think that it's gone to quite this extent yet. I don't think that we are at the present time interrogating all persons who might be on a subversive list, no.

Q. Did you take --?

KING. If there is any indication of a necessity for it, certainly we're not going to pass up any--anybody.

Q. Did you give special consideration to the persons on your subversive list before the President came to town, know where they were, what they were doing?

KING. Yes.

Q. Then if the FBI had known about him ahead of time and had informed your office, you would have checked up on Oswald as well?

KING. I'd rather not speculate on what might have happened if something else had happened.

COMMISSION EXHIBIT No. 2162—Continued

5

Q. We've been given information earlier today that the FBI did know he was here and had interviewed him during the last couple or three weeks.

KING. On this I have no answer.

Q. Captain King, is there any question from the police questioning of Oswald so far that he is mentally competent to stand trial?

KING. He seems to be, certainly.

Q. Would you regard him as a deranged individual in any way?

KING. He doesn't seem to be, no.

Q. What about a lie-detector test?

KING. I do not know.

Q. Thank you, Captain.

Q. Captain King, thank you very much.

COMMENTATOR. That was Captain Glen King of the Dallas Police force. This is Bob Clark, ABC, at Dallas Police headquarters.

. . . Oswald was questioned about an hour ago. We don't know who those witnesses are. We do know that one man, named Joe Rodriguez Molina, was questioned by police earlier this morning, who went to his home with a search warrant. He has been at police headquarters. We are uncertain here whether he is still in the room undergoing questioning. Molina has been identified by Dallas Police as a man--he is listed in Dallas police records as a man who is known to have associated with subversives. He worked in the same building where Oswald worked--in the building where the shots were fired that killed President Kennedy. Police emphasize that he is not regarded as a suspect; they are simply

COMMISSION EXHIBIT No. 2162—Continued

checking him for any possible connection with the case because of his record as one who had associated with subversives. As Oswald himself came out of the room where he had been questioned about an hour ago, he leaned into ABC microphones and said he would like to contact a Mr. Abt of New York City to serve as his attorney. We are not certain who Mr. Abt is. We do know, however, that a Mr. John Abt was the official lawyer for the Communist Party and for Communist officials appearing before Congressional committees in the 1950's. Again I emphasize we are not certain whether this is the man Oswald wants to contact to serve as his attorney. Oswald himself, as far as we know, is at this moment in his jail cell in the Dallas city jail one floor above us. He will be transferred later, we expect sometime later today, to the Dallas county jail.

COMMISSION EXHIBIT No. 2162—Continued

WFAA-TV reel PKT 16
Sunday, November 24, 1963

INTERVIEW OF DETECTIVE JAMES R. LEAVELLE, DALLAS POLICE DEPARTMENT, BY BILL LORD, WFAA-TV

LORD. This is Detective Jim Leavelle, who was this morning handcuffed to Oswald and was bringing him out to the car to be transferred to the county jail. Could you tell us what happened?

LEAVELLE. We were proceeding with the prisoner, as scheduled, from the jail office out to the ramp where the automobile was waiting. And as we reached the area where the car was parked, the man from the crowd emerged and there was a hundred or more newspapermen and cameramen in the area and it was almost a solid wall of flesh in front of us and to our left composed of the news media. When the--when we came through the door with Oswald they began taking their pictures, and in the ensuing time that they were snapping pictures and talking I saw this man come from the crowd, and at the time he emerged from this crowd of people he was not more than six or seven feet from me. And I dare say that had I known that he was going to be there, the swiftness with which it happened, I doubt if anyone could have prevented it.

LORD. Did you see the gun in his hand as he came--

LEAVELLE. I saw the gun in his hand as he emerged from the crowd. But being such a short distance from me, I had no time to say anything. I did jerk Oswald to try to protect him behind me.

LORD. You were handcuffed to him?

LEAVELLE. I was handcuffed to him and also had ahold of the waistband of his trousers. I tried to jerk him behind me, but he had--

COMMISSION EXHIBIT No. 2163

and I reached up and caught ahold of Jack Ruby's shoulder, left shoulder, and shoved back on it, at the same time pulling on Oswald, but he had the--had this .38 snub-nosed pistol and he--all he had to do was pull the trigger--it was a double-action gun--and therefore it only took--the whole episode only took a matter of a second to take place.

LORD. Now, when Oswald fell to the ground, was he unconscious at that point?

LEAVELLE. I would say if he was not, he was near, nearly so. Just as soon as the--my partner on the other side, Mr. Graves, grabbed Jack's hand with the gun in such a manner that he couldn't fire it any more.

LORD. Did he try to fire it?

LEAVELLE. Yes, he was still, with his left hand--he had the gun in his right hand and he was trying to pull it around, and I could tell that he was still trying to snap the pistol. But Mr. Graves had it in such a manner that he couldn't snap it, couldn't fire it any further--any more.

LORD. Did you lend aid to the victim on the ground?

LEAVELLE. Yes, I immediately picked him up then, with another officer--I don't remember who that was--and carried him back inside the jail office to get him away from the area. And I talked, I tried to talk, to him and ask him if he could hear me and if he understood. He never did answer me and his eyes were partially closed. However, I know he never regained consciousness.

LORD. How has this affected morale, the spirit of the police force?

COMMISSION EXHIBIT No. 2163—Continued

LEAVELLE. Well, I think that I can probably speak for all the officers here. I heard many of them comment on it, and I think that they all feel very deeply about it. They regret the incident happening; they regret the thing--the shooting--that occurred of the President on Friday; and certainly this hasn't helped their feelings any at all. The--Mr. Ruby didn't--didn't better our cause any by shooting Oswald.

LORD. Did you recognize him when he came through?

LEAVELLE. Yes. I have known Jack Ruby for a number of years and I recognized him just as soon as he emerged from the crowd.

LORD. But if, even if you knew he was coming, you say you didn't have the time to react quickly?

LEAVELLE. He was so close from the human wall of flesh and of reporters there that it would have been impossible to have stopped him.

LORD. Thank you very much.

The story of what happened when Lee Harvey Oswald was killed this morning. This is Bill Lord, reporting from the Dallas police station.

COMMISSION EXHIBIT No. 2163—Continued

—Commission Exhibit No. 2164

WFAA-TV reel PKT 21
Saturday, November 23, 1963

INTERVIEW WITH PATROLMAN M. N. MCDONALD
BY ROGER SHARP, WFAA-TV, IN DALLAS

Q. Patrolman McDonald, in your experiences with suspects and in the capture of such individuals, did you find anything unique or strange or different about Lee Harvey Oswald?

MCDONALD: Well, not anything you can put your finger on, but he acted just like anybody else would if he were carrying a pistol, because he reached for it immediately as soon as I grabbed ahold of him and my experiences with suspects of this nature, they're all pretty calm unless they have recently or within a few minutes have committed some sort of crime. But he had time enough between the time he had, is suspected of killing of J. D. Tippit to control his nature and he was quite calm and cool.

Q. Did you realize at the time that you may be capturing the man who quite possibly could be charged and perhaps convicted of assassinating the President?

MCDONALD: Well, I had no link in that at all because I didn't know. I was just looking for this suspect that we had a meager description of, that had shot and killed Officer J. D. Tippit. And, I didn't have any association with the shooting of the President at all with this particular suspect.

COMMISSION EXHIBIT No. 2164

- 2 -

Q. How do you feel now that Oswald has been formally charged with the assassination of the President?

MCDONALD: Well, I feel relieved quite a bit because the whole nation has recorded this shock and I'm glad that we caught him here in Dallas instead of waiting around later on.

Q. Dallas has every reason to be proud of its police department today. We have been talking with Detective Paul Bentley and Patrolman M. D. McDonald, two of the men who played a key role in the capture of Lee Harvey Oswald, the man who Dallas police now say they believe is the man who murdered President John Kennedy.

This is Roger Sharp reporting from the studios of WFAA-TV in Dallas.

COMMISSION EXHIBIT No. 2164—Continued

— Commission Exhibit No. 2165

WFAA-TV reel PKT 25
Saturday afternoon, November 23, 1963

INTERVIEW WITH LOUIS NICHOLS,
PRESIDENT OF DALLAS BAR ASSOCIATION

COMMENTATOR. --President of the Dallas Bar Association. He has been talking to Mr. Oswald and he will make a statement for you if he desires.

Q. Could we get your initials first, please?

Q. What is your name, sir?

NICHOLS. My name is H. Louis Nichols--L-O-U-I-S N-I-C-H-O-L-S.

Q. Nichols?

NICHOLS. N-I-C-H-O-L-S. I am the President of the Dallas Bar Association. The organized bar here in Dallas. We had been advised that statements have been made that Mr. Oswald was unable to get any Dallas lawyer who would make any inquiry about representation or that he was unable to get any representation here in Dallas. When I heard about that this afternoon, I decided I should come down and make inquiry as to whether or not he was represented by counsel, whether or not he desired to be represented by counsel, and whether or not he would ask the Dallas Bar Association to furnish representation to him. I have just visited with him in his cell and he advises that his first

COMMISSION EXHIBIT No. 2165

- 2 -

preference is that he be represented by a lawyer in New York, whose name I believe is John Abt, A-B-T. He then stated that if he could not be represented by that individual he would like to have a lawyer who was a member of the American Civil Liberties Union represent him. He says that if he was unable to get anyone from that organization, why then he might call upon the local Bar Association to represent him. I asked him whether or not at this time he was asking the Dallas Bar Association to do anything toward representing him and he advised that he was not, that he did not desire that we take any steps toward obtaining representation for him, and that if he was unable to obtain the other representation he might at a later time ask us to do so, and did ask that I would check back with him at a later time to see whether or not there would be any necessity or desirability that we attempt to furnish representation for him. Having contacted him and satisfied myself that he was not being deprived of representation by an attorney and having satisfied myself that he did not desire to be represented by a Dallas attorney, I then left, and that's the situation as it exists right now.

Q. May I have your name, sir.

NICHOLS. My name is H. Louis Nichols--L-O-U-I-S N-I-C-H-O-L-S.

COMMISSION EXHIBIT No. 2165—Continued

- 3 -

Q. Did he seem in possession of all of his faculties?

[Several people talking at once.]

Q. Did he deny the shooting to you?

NICHOLS. He didn't discuss the details of it. I did not ask him anything. He appeared to me to be perfectly rational and I could observe no abnormalities about him at all in the short time that I visited with him.

Q. Do you know anything about John Abt?

NICHOLS. I don't know anything about him.

Q. --

NICHOLS. No, I'm not.

Q. --

NICHOLS. He didn't say.

Q. --

NICHOLS. He didn't give any reason and I didn't ask him.

Q. Who's going to try to get Abt?

NICHOLS. I don't know.

COMMISSION EXHIBIT No. 2165—Continued

- 4 -

Q. --

NICHOLS. About three minutes.

Q. --

NICHOLS. He said he had talked to members of his family this afternoon, and they would endeavor to get in touch with Mr. Abt.

Q. Did he say why the Civil Liberties was his second choice?

NICHOLS. He said he was a member of that organization and would like to have a lawyer who was a member of that organization represent him.

Q. Does he personally know Abt?

NICHOLS. I don't know.

Q. How would you describe his mood?

Q. Did he appear to be calm?

NICHOLS. Well, he appeared to be calm and --

Q. Was he defiant?

NICHOLS. I didn't understand you.

COMMISSION EXHIBIT No. 2165—Continued

Q. Was he defiant?

NICHOLS. Defiant? He did not appear to be defiant. He discussed the matter with me in a very rational way and very calm way, and we discussed the matter and I am satisfied myself that he knew what he was talking about and didn't desire my services or the services of any member of the Dallas Bar Association.

Q. Did he fully understand the charges against him?

NICHOLS. I don't know.

Q. You didn't discuss it with him?

NICHOLS. I did not discuss the charges with him.

Q. As a lawyer, do you feel that he does not have--

NICHOLS. I do not believe so since he is not asking for a lawyer to represent him at this time.

Q. Do you think it's possible to hear the charges against him at this time?

NICHOLS. Probably. In Dallas it is.

Q. This question has been asked. May I ask it again, Is it possible for this man to get impartial treatment?

COMMISSION EXHIBIT No. 2165—Continued

NICHOLS. Well, it is my opinion it is.

Q. Do you think he can get a fair trial in Dallas?

NICHOLS. I think he can get a fair trial in Dallas.

Q. Do I understand, sir, that you are the boss in getting another--. -- only if it is not to have the Bar Association-- in other words get for him a Dallas attorney.

NICHOLS. Well, I have no control over any other attorney. I have no control over any attorney except myself. It is the feeling of the Dallas Bar Association that an indigent defendant should be represented and one of the programs of the Association is to furnish lawyers to represent defendants in criminal cases who are unable to provide their own attorneys.

Q. Have you had any calls from anyone in your organization about handling this case?

NICHOLS. I have had some inquiry about whether or not there were any Dallas lawyers representing this man and I made inquiry and determined that apparently there are none at this time. He hasn't requested any representative.

Q. Does the Dallas Bar Association--

COMMISSION EXHIBIT No. 2165—Continued

- 7 -

NICHOLS. It's a voluntary bar association. The State Bar of Texas is the integrated bar; the Dallas Bar Association is a voluntary association.

Q. Does the representation of indigent people include Communists? Has a Communist ever been so represented in Dallas?

NICHOLS. I don't know.

Q. --

NICHOLS. I did not. I merely asked him whether or not he desired to have an attorney appointed by the Association to assist him and he said, no.

Q. Were these calls from people in the attorney profession, or were they citizens?

NICHOLS. They were other lawyers that I am acquainted with.

Q. They were anxious to-- ?

NICHOLS. No, sir, they made inquiry as to whether or not the Dallas Bar Association was doing anything to see whether or not this man could obtain local representation and I decided I'd find out.

Q. Were these local members involved-- ?

COMMISSION EXHIBIT No. 2165—Continued

- 8 -

NICHOLS. I have not talked to any attorneys at all about it.

Q. Would you be willing to represent him?

NICHOLS. I do not practice criminal law and I've never tried a criminal case so I don't know, the answer to that.

Q. Thank you, Mr. Nichols.

COMMISSION EXHIBIT No. 2165—Continued

KRLD-TV reel 9
NBC-TV reel 17
KLIF reel 8 Item 5, reel 10 Item 2
November 23, 1963 12:10 a.m.

OSWALD'S APPEARANCE IN ASSEMBLY ROOM

OSWALD. Well, I was questioned by a Judge [Johnston]. However, I protested at that time that I was not allowed legal representation during that very short and sweet hearing. I really don't know what the situation is about. Nobody has told me anything except that I am accused of, of, murdering a policeman. I know nothing more than that. I do request someone to come forward to give me legal assistance.

Q. Did you kill the President?

OSWALD. No. I have not been charged with that. In fact nobody has said that to me yet. The first thing I heard about it was when the newspaper reporters in the hall asked me that question.

Q. You have been charged --

Q. Nobody said what?

OSWALD. Sir?

Q. You have been charged --

Q. Nobody said what?

Q. What happened to your eye?

COMMISSION EXHIBIT No. 2166

Q. When were you in Russia?

Q. Mr. Oswald, how did you hurt your eye?

OSWALD. A policeman hit me.

REPORTER. Can somebody give us a fill in from up front?

COMMENTATOR. That was Oswald, Lee Oswald, who was charged with the murder of the President of the United States, although he said he did not know it. He's being taken back upstairs, he's being taken back upstairs for further investigation, as Henry Wade pointed out earlier.

COMMISSION EXHIBIT No. 2166—Continued

Commission Exhibit No. 2167

WFAA-TV reel PKT 12
Saturday morning, November 23, 1963

INTERVIEW OF DEPUTY POLICE CHIEF M. W. STEVENSON
BY BOB CLARK, ABC, DALLAS

This is Bob Clark, ABC, at Dallas Police Headquarters. Deputy Chief M. W. Stevenson has been on duty here all night helping to direct this investigation.

Q: Chief, can you tell us something about how Oswald spent the night here in his cell?

STEVENSON: As you know, shortly before midnight last night charges of murder in connection with the death of the President was filed. He was then arraigned and was placed in his cell and to my knowledge he has had a restful night and we have had no trouble in the jail. We have had a security guard on him through the night.

Q: There will presumably be further questioning of Oswald this morning?

STEVENSON: Of course as to what our further actions or investigations will be at this time would be purely speculation. I don't know at what time we will question him or what part of our further investigations we will take up. That will be governed by the circumstances as they come up in the investigation.

COMMISSION EXHIBIT No. 2167

- 2 -

Q: Are there any other suspects in this case besides Oswald?

STEVENSON: To my knowledge, at the present time, no.

Q: We understand the murder weapon, the rifle, was found in the building where the shots were fired and sent to the FBI headquarters.

STEVENSON: That's right.

Q: Could you tell us whether there were any fingerprints found on that rifle?

STEVENSON: To my knowledge, I don't know.

Q: How about the empties?

Q: How about the empty shells that were found on the floor -- were they also turned over to the FBI?

STEVENSON: I believe they were.

Q: There is no question at this point that this was the murder weapon?

STEVENSON: Well, I wouldn't say that because we are not through with our tests and our investigation. We're satisfied in our own

COMMISSION EXHIBIT No. 2167—Continued

mind that it was, but to say definitely we must complete our investigation and our tests.

Q: Where is Oswald at this moment?

STEVENSON: He is in the cell on the fourth floor of the city jail.

Q: Has he had breakfast?

STEVENSON: I believe he has. I believe they feed up there at about 8.

Q: Can you tell us what activities are going on at the moment as far as investigation of the case goes?

STEVENSON: No, sir, I cannot. I wouldn't be in a position to divulge information on that, on investigations we have underway until we have completed them.

Q: Could you say whether any new evidence has been uncovered -- any evidence in addition to the murder weapon and the --

STEVENSON: Not since we stopped last night when the case was filed. No additional evidence has come up to my knowledge since that time.

Q: Chief, thank you very much.

COMMISSION EXHIBIT No. 2167—Continued

— Commission Exhibit No. 2168

WBAP Audio reel 12 "A"
NBC-TV reels 23, 35
WFAA-TV reels PKT 27, 16
WFAA-TV reel PKF 1
KRLD-TV reel 17
Sunday P.M., November 24, 1963

PRESS CONFERENCE WITH DISTRICT ATTORNEY HENRY WADE
DALLAS POLICE AND COURTS BUILDING

WADE. The purpose of this news conference is to detail some of the evidence against Oswald for the assassination of the President. This evidence was gathered by--largely by--the Dallas police who did an excellent job on this with the help of some of the Federal agencies, and I am going through the evidence piece by piece for you. Number one, some of this you will already know, some of it you won't, I don't think. As all of you do know, first, there is--we have a number of witnesses that saw the person with the gun on the sixth floor of the Book Store Building. The window--detailing the window where he was looking out--inside this window the police found a row of books, cases, boxes hiding someone sitting in the window from people on the same floor looking in. On the window was some boxes where--in the little circle around the window by the book cases--some boxes where apparently the person was sitting, because he was seen from that particular window.

On this box that the defendant was sitting on, his palmprint was found and was identified as his. The three ejected shells were found right by the box. The shells were of an odd caliber of the type and later determined, the gun, that was found on the floor. The gun was hidden on this same floor behind some boxes, some book cases. It, as I think you know, has been identified as having been purchased last March by the, Oswald, from a mail-order house by a--through an--

COMMISSION EXHIBIT No. 2168

assumed name, named Hidell, mailed to a post-office box here in Dallas. On his person was a pocket book. In his pocket book was identification card with the same name and post-office box on it. Pictures were found of the defendant with this gun and a pistol on his--in his holster.

Immediately that morning--it was unusual, but that morning--a neighbor brought the, Oswald from Irving, Texas. He usually brought him on Monday morning, I think, but this day he went home one day early on Thursday night and came back to--with this fellow--and when he came back he had a package under his arm that he said was window curtains, I believe, or window shades. The wife had said he had the gun the night before; it was missing that morning after he left. He got out around 8 o'clock and went to the building behind some cars and went to work.

A police officer, immediately after the assassination, ran in the building and saw this man in a corner and started to arrest him, but the manager of the building said that he was an employee and was all right. Every other employee was located but this defendant, of the company. A description and name of him went out by police to look for him.

The next we hear of him is on a bus, where he got on a bus at Lamar Street; told the bus driver the President had been shot. The President [he] told a lady who--all this was verified by statements--told a lady on the bus that the President had been shot. He said, how'd he know. He said that a man back there had told him. He went back to talk to him. The defendant said, "Yes, he's been shot," and laughed very loud.

Q. This was to a lady?

WADE. A lady.

He then--the bus--he asked the bus driver to stop, got off at a stop, and caught a taxicab driver.

Q. Where?

WADE. In Oak Cliff--I don't have the exact place--and went to his home in Oak Cliff, changed his clothes hurriedly, and left.

As he left, three witnesses saw a police officer, Officer Tippit, motion to him or say something to him. He walked up to the car, Officer Tippit stepped out of the car, and started around it. He shot him three times and killed him.

Q. Was this in front of the boarding house or near it?

WADE. No. It's not in front of the boarding house.

Q. How near is it?

WADE. I don't have the exact--. It's more than a block. It's a block or two.

Q. Was he on foot when Tippit saw him?

WADE. Yes, he was on foot, and apparently headed to the Texas Theatre. He then walked across a vacant lot. Witnesses saw him eject the shells from the revolver and place--reload the gun. Someone saw him go in the Texas Theatre. A search was made of that later by a number of police officers. At the time, an officer of the Dallas police spotted him and asked him to come out. He struck at the officer, put the gun against his head, and snapped it, but did not--the bullet did not go off. We have the snapped bullet there. Officers, officers subdued him at that time.

Q. Was that an attempted suicide, sir?

Q. Against his head or the officer's?

WADE. Against the officer's head.

Q. Which officer?

Q. Do you know why the gun didn't go off?

WADE. McDonald was his name.

Q. Do you know his first name?

WADE. It snapped; it was a misfire. Then officers subdued him--some six officers subdued him there in the Theatre, and he was brought to the police station here.

Q. Mr. Wade, why didn't the gun fire?

WADE. It missed the firing pin on the pull, the shell didn't explode. It hit it, but it didn't explode. It didn't fire the shell.

Q. There was one officer who said that he pulled the trigger, but he managed to put his thumb in the--in the part before the firing pin. It didn't strike the bullet, or really explode it out.

WADE. I don't know that. I know he did snap the gun, is all I know about it.

Q. We can say that it was a misfire?

WADE. It didn't fire.

Q. What other evidence is there?

Q. Let's get the story again.

COMMISSION EXHIBIT No. 2168—Continued

WADE. Let's see. The--his fingerprints were found on the gun. Have I said that?

Q. Which gun?

WADE. On the rifle.

Q. You didn't say that.

Q. What about the paraffin tests?

WADE. Yes, I've gone into that. The paraffin tests showed he had recently fired a gun. It was on both hands.

Q. On both hands?

WADE. Both hands.

Q. Recently fired a rifle?

Q. A gun?

WADE. A gun.

Q. The rifle fingerprints were his? Were Oswald's?

Q. Were there any fingerprints-- ?

WADE. Yes, sir. Palmprints rather than fingerprints.

Q. Were there palmprints on the gun?

Q. Were there any fingerprints at the window?

WADE. Yes, on--

Q. On the rifle?

WADE. Yes, sir.

Q. Where are--on the gun?

WADE. Under, on part of the metal, under the gun.

Q. Did he still ever say anything about it? Admit anything at all?

COMMISSION EXHIBIT No. 2168—Continued

WADE. He never did admit, admit any of the killings. Now I didn't--you ask me this--I didn't do any interrogation of him.

Q. I thought maybe you'd listed that as part of the evidence.

WADE. No, it is not listed here.

Q. Did he display any animosity towards the President? Any conversation with any officers?

WADE. He was bitter toward all of the officers that examined him, is what I've been told.

Q. Will you continue, sir, and we'll question you later.

Q. Let's finish this--

WADE. We, have, that's about all.

Q. How about ballistics tests?

Q. Ballistics test, Mr. Wade?

WADE. Well, I've said this was the gun that--

Q. Killed the President?

WADE. Yes.

Q. Does the FBI report elaborate-- ?

Q. Did the ballistics-- ?

WADE. I won't go-- I'm not at liberty to go into the FBI report.

Q. Did you say the gun was mailed to a post office box in Dallas in March?

WADE. March of this year.

Q. Was he living in Dallas then?

WADE. Yes. I presume he was. He got it here.

Q. I see.

Q. Previously he lived in New Orleans?

Q. He said he'd only been here two months, Mr. Wade--

WADE. He came to Fort Worth sometime in the fall of '62. And then moved here awhile and apparently went to New Orleans for a while and came back. Now when the period of that is, I'm not sure.

Q. Mr. Wade, what was the evidence that we were told was startling evidence that could not be told to the press Saturday morning? They said it came in Saturday morning and that it could not be revealed. It was--

WADE. I don't know. That wasn't me that said that, I don't think.

Q. Have you given us everything that-- ?

WADE. I've given you everything that I--

Q. Do you know whether he's been recognized as a patron of Ruby's nightclub here?

WADE. I don't know that.

Q. Do you know of any connection between Mr. Ruby and-- ?

WADE. I know of none.

Q. Are you investigating reports that he might have been slain because Ruby might have feared he would implicate him in something?

WADE. The police are making an investigation of that murder. I don't know anything about that.

Q. The investigation-- ?

WADE. Although charges have been filed, it will be presented to the grand jury on Rubin immediately within the next week and it'll probably be tried around the middle of January.

Q. Has the District Attorney's office closed its investigation of the assassination of the President?

Q. When did you know that-- ? Before sending the gun to Washington?

WADE. Before.

Q. Before sending the gun to Washington?

WADE. Yes.

Q. Do you think it was unusual for Jack Ruby to be in that crowd?

WADE. I don't pass on that. Unusual to be in that crowd?

Q. There are reports that he had planned to--

WADE. Well, I wasn't, I haven't been here since last night so I don't know anything about it--today's happenings.

Q. Mr. Wade, how do you feel about not being able to try Oswald as the killer of President Kennedy?

WADE. Well, we will try Ruby and ask the death penalty on him, about the same time.

Q. Well, how about-- ?

COMMISSION EXHIBIT No. 2168—Continued

WADE. I don't want to go into why's or wherefore's on anything.

Q. Has your office closed its investigation into the death of President Kennedy?

WADE. No, sir. The investigation will continue on that with the basis, towards, and we have no concrete evidence that anyone assisted him in this. But the investigation I'm sure will go on with reference to any possible accomplice or-- that assisted him in it.

Q. Do you have any suspicion now that there were?

WADE. I have no concrete evidence nor suspicions at present.

Q. Would you be willing to say in view of all this evidence that it is now beyond a reasonable doubt at all that Oswald was the killer of President Kennedy?

WADE. I would say that without any doubt he's the killer-- the law says beyond a reasonable doubt and to a moral certainty which I--there's no question that he was the killer of President Kennedy.

Q. That case is closed in your mind?

WADE. As far as Oswald is concerned, yes.

Q. Mr. Wade, will we be able to have copies of the photographs showing Oswald-- ?

WADE. If you have them, you'll have to get them from the Dallas Police.

COMMISSION EXHIBIT No. 2168—Continued

10

Q. What do you think was the motive of Ruby?

WADE. I don't know. I haven't talked with him.

Q. Mr. Wade, what do you feel is the strongest evidence on that list?

WADE. Well, it's like any case based on a series of circumstances. They all have to fit together. You put a man in the window with a gun. People cannot positively identify him from the ground. He fits their general description. You have his fingerprints there. You have the shells there. You have his gun that he purchased--

Q. What do you think was Oswald's motive?

WADE. Don't--can't answer that.

Q. Did you find any fluctuation in Oswald's bank account or his finances?

WADE. I know of nothing, know nothing about that.

Q. Mr. Wade, his palmprint, was it found on both the gun and the boxes?

WADE. Yes, sir.

Q. On both of them?

WADE. Both of them.

Q. The rifle and the box-- ?

Q. Mr. Wade, was-- ?

WADE. They were found by the Dallas police.

Q. How do you explain-- ?

COMMISSION EXHIBIT No. 2168—Continued

11

WADE. They were co-workers that left him there around 12 o'clock to go to eat lunch. I didn't mention that witnesses put him on the fourth floor at 12 o'clock and shortly thereafter.

Q. Fourth floor?

WADE. I mean the sixth floor.

Q. Where the box is?

WADE. Where the box is.

Q. What did you say the ballistics -- I missed the part about the ballistics test.

WADE. This was the gun. The bullet from this gun killed the President.

Q. Was that from the FBI, sir?

WADE. I can't go into anything from the FBI. I'm not at liberty to.

Q. -- the story that Oswald and Ruby were previously acquainted?

WADE. I think I heard it on radio, or something, but I don't know anything about it.

Q. Will we have a chance to talk to Ruby?

WADE. I have not talked with--no, sir, I have not talked with either one of them.

Q. But will we get a chance to talk to him, or something?

WADE. I don't know anything about that. This was entirely about going over the evidence that I thought some of you would want.

COMMISSION EXHIBIT No. 2168—Continued

Q. Did you know Ruby before?

WADE. No, sir. Saw him in this very same room Friday night when we had the defendant up here.

Q. Were you at the steak party for the Texas Bar Association in the Adolphus Hotel? Were you there?

WADE. No, sir, I wasn't there. As a matter of fact, some of, oh, excuse me. If some of you will recall, he asked a question from out here in the audience or answered a question. He was standing right back here and I didn't know who he was. I thought he was a member of the press. And he told me as we walked out of here that he was a nightclub operator.

Q. What question did he ask?

WADE. What?

Q. What question did he ask?

WADE. I don't remember, but he --

Q. He answered one question.

WADE. Maybe it was an answer, but he said something. I don't--

Q. You remember it was Friday night when I asked you to do an interview with me on the phone. You had another call and Ruby was hanging around in the background. You were on the phone, and I said, and then you had to go away and I asked Ruby, because he seemed to me like a detective, he seemed to be all over this place-- I said could you see if you could get him on the phone and he-- he went around and he got you and brought you to my telephone.

COMMISSION EXHIBIT No. 2168—Continued

WADE. It might have been where he told me who he was-- I didn't know who he was either, when he, I think someone here answered that question in that he answered a question. Somebody asked something and he answered it back there. I don't know what it was. I think it was some question about a street or an address or a name, or something.

Q. He looked to be like your good friend, I don't know.

Q. Do you feel that list is complete? Anything is withheld by Government agencies, Federal Bureau of-- ?

WADE. This is all that I know of.

Q. That's all you know?

WADE. Yes.

Q. In arguing this case, what would you use as a theory as to his motive?

WADE. Well, of course, that has to develop. You have to develop that from all of the evidence and I can't go into motive. It depends on what you get in evidence. If you get everything that's been written in the papers in evidence, you could put a pretty good motive there, but I don't--a lot of that I don't think would be admissible.

Q. What can you tell us-- ?

WADE. And you gotta base your motive on what you have before the jury.

Q. What can you tell us so far about your investigation of Jack Ruby?

COMMISSION EXHIBIT No. 2168—Continued

WADE. I haven't had anything to do with it. I was, I haven't, no, I know nothing about it.

Q. Will you be involved?

WADE. I will try him, prosecute him.

Q. Is the Justice Department heading up that investigation?

WADE. As far as I know the Dallas police is.

Q. How would you evaluate the work of the Dallas police in investigating the death of the President?

WADE. I think the Dallas police did an excellent job on this and before midnight on when he was killed had the man in custody and had sufficient evidence what I think to convict him.

Q. Mr. Wade, could you identify the gun positively as the one that was purchased--and the gun which-- ?

WADE. It can be positively identified.

Q. -- serial number?

WADE. Serial number.

Q. -- by serial number?

WADE. Serial numbers--and both that and on the scope too.

Q. Oh, he bought the scope off?

WADE. No, the scope was on the gun but, of course, a different person makes it, a different company makes the scope.

Q. When he bought the gun, did he buy the gun with the scope? A unit?

WADE. The scope was on it when he purchased it.

COMMISSION EXHIBIT No. 2168—Continued

Q. Do you know what kind of gun it was?

WADE. I don't have the exact--it was a foreign made gun of 6--6.5 millimeters, and I understand is a used gun of Italian make, probably.

Q. You say that-- ?

WADE. It was mounted as I understand it when it came.

Q. Do you see that the easy availability of guns such as this requires new and more stringent laws?

WADE. That is an old question that's been off-- It's obvious if you didn't have any guns you probably wouldn't have any murderers with guns, but it's nearly impossible to keep a person who wants to kill from finding a gun somewhere.

Q. Do you know Oswald's activities nine or ten days ago?

WADE. I never heard of him until he was arrested and brought in here.

Q. Mr. Wade, the State Department put out some information in Washington that related the importance of telling this evidence to the American people to a situation that's developing in Russia, as a Russian Marxist mentioned in relation to Oswald's background. Can you tell us anything in your evidence that relates to a Marxist background?

WADE. No, sir, I can't. There's some things found on him like newspapers and things--didn't necessarily connect him with

COMMISSION EXHIBIT No. 2168—Continued

the organization, like the Communist Daily Worker, or something. I don't think you can necessarily say he was--the fact he read it doesn't necessarily mean that he's, you couldn't prove that he belonged to it. I've read quite a bit about this subject. I know what you're talking about, but I've read interviews from reporters from over in Russia all on this subject but apparently they know quite a bit more about it than I do.

Q. Was there material found here?

WADE. There's no material that said he belonged to any group other than this Fair Play for Cuba, that I know of--

Q. Nothing found in his room--?

WADE. There's lots of material dealing with that movement thing.

Q. Henry, were you ever able to ascertain whether he went to Washington and took part in the House Un-American Activities Committee riot?

WADE. I know nothing about that. I don't think he told anybody he was and I don't know of any, not to my knowledge. I assume someone has been trying to check that but I don't know anything on that subject.

Q. Did Ruby do that? Were you answering about Ruby or Oswald?

WADE. This was about Oswald, wasn't it? I don't know of anything on either one of them upstairs, for that matter. I believe that's about it.

COMMISSION EXHIBIT No. 2168—Continued

Q. Thank you, Henry.

Q. Mr. Wade, I'd like to ask you one more question. Why did you call us tonight and why did you go over this evidence?

WADE. Well, there's a lot of reasons. Probably the main one--I received a call from Paris, France, and Stockholm, Sweden, and nearly every foreign country asking me about this evidence and I thought from those newsmen in those countries--

Q. Did Robert Kennedy or anyone from his office-- ?

WADE. I have heard nothing from any of the -- from Washington or any of the officials in this country on this matter. But I decided, that I heard, I've had, a number of newsmen call me from all over the world wanting to know why and it wasn't, and I thought in my own mind--decided that it's a good idea. So, --

Q. Are you aware that the Justice Department before you made this announcement and before you came into the building tonight had said that new evidence, the evidence would all be released and given to newsmen--

WADE. No, sir, I'm not familiar with that other than as I walked out of the door one of the--one of your men--I think, called me and told me that there was something on that--that they were considering that, but I was already up and was coming out to see you. It had nothing to do with me getting this ready.

COMMISSION EXHIBIT No. 2168—Continued

Q. Is there any doubt in your mind that if Oswald was tried that you would have, have him convicted by a jury? With the evidence you have.

WADE. I don't think there's any doubt in my mind that we would have convicted him, but, of course, you never know what. We've had lots of people we thought that somebody might hang the jury or something, but there's no question in my--

Q. As far as you are concerned, the evidence you gave us, you could have convicted him?

WADE. I've sent people to the electric chair on less.

Q. This was more than enough then?

WADE. Yes.

Q. Will you seek the death penalty for Ruby?

WADE. Yes.

Q. Even if he pleads guilty?

WADE. Yes.

Q. Is it an automatic death penalty?

Q. Does the FBI have additional evidence?

WADE. I don't know. I don't know. I'm not--I don't know what they have.

Q. Sir, do you know when you'll present the Ruby case to the grand jury?

WADE. Within a week, I said. I might say on this that, you asked about the penalty on this. This latter case was an assassination of a man under arrest, handcuffed. That to me is a very aggravated case and warrants the death penalty.

Q. Are you investigating the possibility-- ?

WADE. A second assassination doesn't help a first one.

Q. Do you have a signed statement from Mr. Ruby?

WADE. I haven't seen it, but I think they have.

Q. Are you investigating the possibility that Ruby might have killed Oswald because he feared Oswald might implicate him in some plot?

WADE. I'm not investigating anything. I'll try whatever, I'll try the case.

Q. Concerning the Oswald evidence, Mr. Wade, is there any one single portion of that that you consider most important?

WADE. Well, the gun being his and the gun that killed him and his fingerprints on it and his fingerprints by the window make out a pretty good case. His flight also is important. It is like one of these things -- you can't just go and say this one thing will convict him. On any case based on circumstantial evidence it has to--all the circumstances have to point to the guilt and exclude every other reasonable hypotheses which we, I think, all of them will.

Q. The combination of those fills the bill?

WADE. Yes, sir.

Q. Will he be before the J.P. tomorrow?

WADE. I think he's already been before the J.P., hasn't he? I think he was taken before the J.P. The J.P. was here today, I know. He called me. If they have an examining trial in which they may convict, that I don't know when that will be or whether it has been set yet.

Q. When will you be prepared to go before the grand jury?

WADE. Well, we're prepared to go now and--but it will probably be Wednesday before we can, I mean. We'd sort of set up to have the other one Tuesday afternoon or Wednesday and so we will run this one in its place.

Reporters. Thank you very much, Mr. Wade.

COMMISSION EXHIBIT No. 2168—Continued

KRLD-TV reel 23
NBC-TV reel 43
KLIF Audio reel 8
WRR Audio reel 14
WFAA-TV reel PKT 27

Saturday, November 23, 1963 — 12:30 a.m.

PRESS CONFERENCE OF DISTRICT ATTORNEY WADE IN ASSEMBLY ROOM, DALLAS POLICE AND COURTS BUILDING

WADE. He's been formally charged in Precinct 2 of Dallas County Judge David Johnston. He's been taken before the judge and advised of his rights. He's been charged with both killing Officer Tippit and John F. Kennedy--

Q. Can you tell any of the evidence against him so far, sir?

WADE. No. We are still working on the evidence. This has been a joint effort by the Secret Service, the Federal Bureau of Investigation, the Dallas Police Department, the Dallas Sheriff's office, my office, and Capt. Will Fritz has been in charge of it.

Q. What does he tell you about the killing of the President? Does he volunteer anything or what has he got to-- ?

WADE. He denies it.

Q. -- was he charged with the President's killing?

COMMISSION EXHIBIT No. 2169

- 2 -

WADE. 11:26 he was -- 11:26 he was charged on the latter charge.

Q. -- good case -- with the murder of President Kennedy? On the basis--

WADE. Evidence gathered by the four agencies mentioned.

Q. Do you have a good case?

WADE. I figure we have sufficient evidence to convict him.

Q. Are there other people involved?

Q. -- this was an organized plot or was it just one man?

WADE. There is no one else but him.

WADE. -- he has been charged in the Supreme Court with murder with malice. The charge carries the death penalty, which my office will ask in both cases.

Q. Is there a similar Federal charge?

WADE. I don't know of any.

Q. -- ?

COMMISSION EXHIBIT No. 2169—Continued

- 3 -

WADE. Well, there is a lot of the physical evidence that was gathered, including the gun, that is on its way by Air Force jet to the FBI crime lab in Washington. It will be back here tomorrow. There are some other things that's going to delay this for probably the middle of next week before it's presented to the grand jury.

Q. -- witnesses to use against him in the killing of President Kennedy?

WADE. We have approximately 15 witnesses.

Q. Who identified him as the killer of the President?

WADE. I didn't say that.

Q. What did they do?

WADE. That have evidence that indicates his guilt.

Q. --the President or the police officer, District Attorney Wade? -- evidence from the fifteen -- ? The police officer or the President's killing?

WADE. Both.

Q. Do you have anything to indicate why the man killed the President, if he so did? -- motive ?

WADE. Well, he was a member of the movement--the Free Cuba movement--

COMMISSION EXHIBIT No. 2169—Continued

Q. What's the make of the rifle, sir?

WADE. It's a Mauser, I believe.

Q. Does the suspect deny the -- ?

WADE. Yes, he denies them both.

Q. Are you through questioning him?

WADE. No, we have further questioning to do now. We will probably let him sleep -- and -- talk to him in the morning.

Q. What about motive, Mr. Wade?

WADE. Sir?

Q. Motive.

Q. What was his politics?

WADE. He didn't give any motive since he denies them both.

Q. Does he have a lawyer?

WADE. His, I don't know whether he has or not. His mother has been here and his brother has been here all afternoon.

Q. Does he appear sane to you?

WADE. Yes, he does.

Q. Is he a member of any Communist-front organization?

COMMISSION EXHIBIT No. 2169—Continued

WADE. That I can't tell you at the present time.

A. Any organizations that he belongs to that you know of?

WADE. Well, the only one I mentioned was the Free Cuba movement or whatever that--

Q. Fair--fair --

WADE. Fair Play for Cuba, I believe was it.

Q. Why do you think he would want to kill the President?

WADE. The only thing I do is take the evidence, present it to a jury, and I don't pass on why he did it or anything else. We, we're just interested in proving that he did it, which I think we have.

Q. Did he struggle on arrest?

WADE. There was a struggle at the time of the arrest. There was a struggle in the Texas Theature when a Dallas police officer was arresting him, and the pistol was snapped at another police officer's head and didn't fire. At that time a scuffle ensued inside of the Texas Theatre where he was arrested by six officers.

COMMISSION EXHIBIT No. 2169—Continued

Q. Sir, has that pistol been previously discharged?

WADE. Yes. Twice.

Q. Has he told anybody why he killed the President?

WADE. He hasn't admitted killing the President to anyone.

Q. If he's been formally charged with killing the President, how is it he says there is no connection to it?

WADE. I just don't know what he says. He says he didn't do it.

Q. Do you know his place of birth?

WADE. I do not.

Q. Age, and so forth, and other specifications on the man?

Q. What is his correct age, please?

WADE. Twenty-four, I believe.

Q. Full name?

WADE. His full name is Lee Harvey Oswald, O-S-W-A-L-D.

Q. Has he been in trouble before in Fort Worth or Dallas?

WADE. I think he has been in Dallas only two months.

COMMISSION EXHIBIT No. 2169—Continued

Q. Where does he come from? From where?

WADE. New Orleans.

Q. What is his mother's name?

WADE. I do not have that with me.

Q. Was he in Russia? Henry, was he in Russia?

Q. -- and no longer has citizenship to the United States. Is this correct, sir?

WADE. I can't verify it or deny that.

Q. Mr. Wade, where will he be held? Where will he spend the night?

WADE. He will spend the night in the Dallas city jail, upstairs.

Q. Do you intend to move him, Henry?

WADE. He will be moved probably the first of the week.

Q. Are you planning to charge anyone else in this at all at this moment?

WADE. As of the moment, we do not.

Q. Are you looking for any other suspects at all now that you've got-- ?

COMMISSION EXHIBIT No. 2169—Continued

WADE. Well, we're always looking for other suspects, but we have none at present.

Q. Henry, do you think this is part of the Communist conspiracy?

WADE. I can't say that.

Q. Well, do you have any reason to believe that it might be?

WADE. No, I don't have any reason to believe either way on it.

Q. Was there any good prints on the rifle?

Q. Has he said under questioning--

WADE. What?

Q. Has he said under questioning that he is either a Communist or a Communist sympathizer?

WADE. I don't know whether he has or not. I do not know the answer to that question.

Q. Does he have a wife living in Dallas?

WADE. Yes, in--

Q. Is she Russian?

COMMISSION EXHIBIT No. 2169—Continued

WADE. I haven't talked with her. She's been up here though, tod-- tonight.

Q. What time will you begin in the morning with him?

WADE. Seven or eight o'clock I would say, roughly.

Q. Do you have some prints on him?

WADE. They are on their way to Washington at present.

Q. Who? Which?

Q. What's on the way to Washington?

WADE. The gun. The rifle.

Q. Both guns?

WADE. Both guns.

Q. Can you say whether you have a witness who says he saw the man pull the trigger?

WADE. No, I cannot.

Q. What was the result of the paraffin test?

WADE. I am not going into the evidence here.

Q. Henry, what did he say his reason was for carrying a pistol?

COMMISSION EXHIBIT No. 2169—Continued

WADE. I don't think he gave any reason.

Q. Where are you going to move him to on Monday?

WADE. Down to the county jail.

Q. How much longer do you plan to question him tonight?

WADE. No longer, I don't think.

Q. What was his line of work?

WADE. -- the leg work for the Texas Depository Books.

Q. Is that a State institution?

WADE. No, sir. It's a company that sells books--sells books to public schools, as I understand it.

Q. Mr. Wade, you said that he did not know that he was charged with the murder of the President. Has he been officially advised that he is charged with that now?

WADE. I do not know. He has just been charged. I know he has been advised of the other and taken before the magistrate.

Q. Is the magistrate in this building?

WADE. He was in this building.

Q. In the same room where the suspect was interrogated?

WADE. Yes, sir.

Q. Who was the magistrate?

WADE. David Johnston.

Q. Is he a J.P.?

WADE. J.P., Precinct 2, Dallas County, Texas.

Q. Did he answer that question whether the man had been advised that he's been charged? The man said here that he didn't know he had been, Dave, how about that?

JOHNSTON. He has not been advised that the charge of the murder of the President, because he is on capital offense on the other.

Q. He has not been advised?

JOHNSTON. He has not been advised.

Q. He has been charged?

JOHNSTON. He has not been arraigned on the second charge.

Q. No, but has he been charged?

JOHNSTON. Yes, he is formally charged.

Q. When will the arraignment be for the President?

WADE. I imagine in -- tonight sometime.

Q. He has NOT been arraigned on the assassination?

WADE. No.

Q. He will be arraigned sometime this evening?

WADE. Probably.

Q. When will he be arraigned?

WADE. Shortly.

Q. Where will that arraignment take place, sir?

WADE. Here, right here at the City Hall.

Q. Will Justice of the Peace Johnston do that?

WADE. I don't know, actually know, for sure when. He has already been arraigned and held without bond on another murder charge.

Q. Mr. Wade, what was his address here in Dallas?

WADE. I don't have them -- he had two.

Q. Was Officer Tippit struck by two or three shots?

WADE. I'm not sure about that, three, I believe, but I don't know. Somebody here says three.

COMMISSION EXHIBIT No. 2169—Continued

Q. Has he some fingerprints-- ?

WADE. I don't know that. I'm sure someone does, but I don't.

Q. When will he be arraigned? Tomorrow?

WADE. I believe he, tonight or first thing in the morning.

Q. Mr. Wade, do you have anything else on his background--education, his family life or anything like that?

Q. The Russian trip--is it exact he went to Russia?

WADE. He did spend some time in Russia.

Q. Do you know when, sir?

WADE. I do not.

Q. Was he a talkative suspect, or did he just clam up? Did he talk at all?

WADE. I think he talked quite a bit.

Q. Did he make any conflicting statements?

WADE. He, he denied the, both murders all the way, though.

Q. Did ~~he admit possession~~ of the gun?

COMMISSION EXHIBIT No. 2169—Continued

WADE. Denied both of them.

Q. Any complicity-- ?

WADE. Had one on him when he was arrested.

WADE. He denied possession and ownership of both guns.

Q. Did his fingerprints match the fingerprints on the gun or the rifle?

WADE. That's part of the evidence that we'll later determine a little more definite on. The gun has just been sent to Washington.

Q. Is he a former Marine?

WADE. Sir?

Q. Is he a former Marine?

WADE. I don't know the answer to that.

Q. Mr. Wade, was he well-known to the Dallas police up to this time, as a--because of his Communist background?

WADE. I don't think so.

Q. Was there any reaction to the death of the President from this man--at all?

WADE. I don't know the answer to that because I was out at Parkland Hospital until about 5:30 and the reason for a lot of this I don't know.

Q. Sir, did he express any regret?

WADE. He denied it.

Q. Do you have any evidence that he is a Communist?

Q. -- the President's death?

WADE. No, sir.

Q. Do you have any evidence that anyone is behind him--an organization or group?

WADE. No, sir.

Q. Did anyone contact you on his behalf?

Q. -- knows whether this rifle was definitely the murder weapon, or is that something-- ?

WADE. That has not been determined as yet.

Q. Have there been ballistic tests made locally on the gun?

WADE. No, sir.

Q. Has anyone contacted you on his behalf?

- 16 -

WADE. No, sir.

Q. He has no counsel at the present time?

WADE. I don't know if he -- someone has talked to the police about it, but I don't, not to me in person.

Q. Mr. Wade, did his brother or mother enlighten you on any of his background?

WADE. I didn't talk with either one of them.

Q. Did Chief Curry, by chance, talk to either one of them?

WADE. You will have to ask him.

WADE. Is that about all?

Q. Did you find his fingerprints on the snub-nosed revolver that killed the police officer, sir?

WADE. That's sent to Washington for that examination.

Q. That was also sent along with the rifle?

WADE. Yes, sir.

Q. In other words, material evidence doesn't deal with weapons at all?

COMMISSION EXHIBIT No. 2169—Continued

- 17 -

WADE. Sir?

Q. Material evidence doesn't have anything to do with weapons -- with the -- the gun?

WADE. Yes, that is material evidence. That is material evidence, the gun.

Q. Do you have the results of the paraffin tests?

WADE. No, sir. I don't have them in front of me.

Q. Do you know what they are?

WADE. I know a little about it, but I don't want to go into the evidence.

Q. Sir, can you confirm the report that his wife said he had in his possession as recently as last night, or some recent time, the gun such as the one that was found in the building?

WADE. Yes, she did.

Q. She did?

WADE. She did, but--

Q. She did what? She did what?

WADE. She said that he had a gun of this kind in his possession.

COMMISSION EXHIBIT No. 2169—Continued

Q. Rifle? A rifle?

Q. Last night?

WADE. Last night. It's that -- the reason I answer that question--the wife in Texas can't testify against her husband, as you may or may not know.

Q. Did she say anything about his, you know, talking about this assassinating the President, at any time?

WADE. I haven't talked with her.

Q. Who is the name of the interpreter who was with his wife, sir?

WADE. I don't know.

Q. -- assassination?

Q. And he flatly denies everything?

WADE. Denies it all.

Q. Denies he was in the building?

WADE. Yes, that day.

Q. He does work there.

WADE. He works there.

Q. What did he say he did today?

WADE. I don't remember. He has no--

Q. Does he have a police record?

WADE. I don't know. You can find that out from Captain Fritz.

Q. That's a good job, Henry.

Q. He has no, he has no alibi that will-- ?

WADE. I don't think he has any, but I'm not sure of that--

Q. Was that one of his children that the wife brought with them? The infant couldn't have been only a couple months old.

WADE. He does. His wife had a baby about 2 months ago, so that must have been the wife.

Q. Are they separated or are they together? Do you know?

WADE. That I don't know.

Q. Mr. Wade, was he under any kind of Federal surveillance because of his background prior to today, today's events?

WADE. None that I know of. We didn't have any knowledge--

Q. His movements weren't accountable to anyone as far as you know?

WADE. We didn't have any information on him. When I say we, being the Dallas police or the Dallas sheriff's office.

Q. What leads you to say he was a very intelligent man?

WADE. He answered the questions very easily.

Q. What kind of-- ? A very intelligent man.

WADE. Well, I don't, I don't mean by that a Ph.D., but I mean he can carry on a conversation with you and tell while you're getting ready to ask him by the time you've asked it.

Q. What about this Free Cuba thing? Has this been known to operate in Cuba? I mean, is this the first time you-all have heard of it, or is there a known group in-- ?

WADE. I think the name of this, this Fair Play for Cuba, isn't it? There seems to be two different organizations.

Q. Yeah. Fair Play for Cuba, Fair Play for Cuba.

Q. Is this something that has been known to exist in Dallas, this Fair Play thing?

COMMISSION EXHIBIT No. 2169—Continued

WADE. I didn't know of it. I don't think they--

Q. -- Texas Theatre?

WADE. Yes.

Q. You wouldn't know the name of the movie showing there, would you?

REPORTERS. "WAR IS HELL."

WADE. I heard it on--. I'm ready to get away.

Q. I believe that's it, unless Captain Fritz--

Q. Can we talk to Captain Fritz?

WADE. Certainly.

Q. Can we talk to Captain Fritz?

Q. What about the charge against Lee Oswald?

Q. But you have charged him with the assassination of the President?

WADE. Yes, sir.

Q. And what's the next step?

WADE. Gather a little more evidence and present it to a grand jury.

COMMISSION EXHIBIT No. 2169—Continued

Q. Do you think you've got a good case against him?

WADE. I think we have sufficient evidence.

Q. Sufficient evidence to convince--to convict him of the assassination of the President?

WADE. Definitely. Definitely.

Q. Was there any indication that this was an organized plot against him or was it just one man after the President?

WADE. We don't know that answer. He's the only one we have.

Q. -- any emotion over the death of the President as far as-- ?

WADE. What's that?

Q. He has shown little or no emotion over the death of the President?

WADE. He shows no emotion over anything that we can tell.

Q. How was he captured? Can you tell us that?

WADE. He was captured in the Texas Theatre.

Q. How did that go?

WADE. One of the officers was trying to arrest him and he snapped a gun at him and some of the other officers got him between the seats--six officers.

Q. Did he put up a fight?

Q. -- ?

WADE. I do not know.

Q. Did he put up a big fight?

Q. -- ?

WADE. I don't know of any.

Q. Was there a very big fight -- ?

WADE. Quite a big fight.

Q. You talked to his wife--is that correct--today and--what did she say to you about the gun?

WADE. She talked to someone else. I haven't talked with her.

Q. And what did she say about the gun?

WADE. She said the gun, he had a gun, a gun of this kind in his possession last night.

- 24 -

Q. Where was the gun?

Q. At any time was he asked was he sorry that President Kennedy had been killed?

WADE. I do not know what all he was asked.

Q. -- political sentiments regarding the President's -- ?

WADE. No, we actually were working entirely on the murder.

Q. Does he have a Communist record?

WADE. -- the assassination.

Q. Does he have a Communist record?

WADE. I don't know.

Q. What about this Free, rather, the Fair Play for Cuba Committee? Was he associated with-- ?

WADE. The first time I'd ever heard of that organization, but you can draw your own--

Q. Does he give any indication of breaking down?

WADE. No, not particularly.

Q. Are you willing to say whether you think this man was inspired as a Communist or whether he is simply a nut or a middleman?

COMMISSION EXHIBIT No. 2169—Continued

- 25 -

WADE. I'll put it this way: I don't think he's a nut.

Q. Do you think he is sane?

WADE. Yes, I think he's sane; don't think he's a nut.

Q. -- ?

WADE. That's you talking. I haven't said that.

Q. Does he understand the charges against him?

WADE. Yes.

COMMISSION EXHIBIT No. 2169—Continued

KRLD-TV reel 20
Saturday morning, November 23, 1963

PRESS INTERVIEW WITH DISTRICT ATTORNEY HENRY M. WADE
DALLAS POLICE AND COURTS BUILDING

" -- President of the United States -- just as --

Q: Was that the case, do you think?

WADE: No, this is a fiction. That the grand jury --

Q: The grand jury --

WADE: I refuse to go into any of the evidence here on anything, any type of evidence they got. I won't go into it for reasons -- we don't want to have all that run before -- we can't get jurors.

Q: Mr. Wade, you're the District Attorney. Do you agree with Captain Fritz, head of Homicide Squad, that this is a cinched case against Lee Oswald?

WADE: There's no cinched cases. I think it's a good case.

Q: Thank you very much, sir.

Q: What sort of man is he, how would you describe Oswald?

WADE: I, -- see, the reason I say there is no cinched cases on that thing -- you got to get all twelve jurors to agree, one that he

COMMISSION EXHIBIT No. 2170

is guilty, and all twelve have to say the death penalty too, you know. All it takes is one to hang a jury.

Q: But what sort of man would you say that he is?

WADE: I, I couldn't say. I can't describe him. (I'll get out here, out of your way.) I can't describe him any other than -- the murderer of the President, is about all the way I put on it, but I don't know anything about the accused -- his psychological background or anything.

Q: Mr. Wade, is this the first time the Dallas Transit Company has ever been used for a getaway car?

COMMISSION EXHIBIT No. 2170—Continued

NBC-TV reel 17
Friday, November 22, 1963

PRESS INTERVIEW WITH DISTRICT ATTORNEY HENRY WADE
DALLAS POLICE AND COURTS BUILDING

Q. -- Federal charge?

WADE. I don't know of any.

Q. -- Attorney General?

WADE. No.

Q. What's the next -- ?

WADE. There are some other things that's going to delay this for, probably the middle of next week before it is presented to the grand jury.

Q. Mr. District Attorney, do you have any witnesses to use against him in the killing of President Kennedy?

WADE. We have approximately 15 witnesses.

Q. Who identify him as the killer of the President?

WADE. I didn't say that.

Q. What do they do?

WADE. That have evidence that indicates his guilt.

COMMISSION EXHIBIT No. 2171

WFAA-TV reel PKT 25
Saturday, November 23, 1963

INTERVIEW WITH DISTRICT ATTORNEY HENRY M. WADE BY
THE PRESS, DALLAS POLICE AND COURTS BUILDING

WADE. Well, since I've been District Attorney I've tried 24 death-penalty cases, in which we asked for death penalty.

Q. And how many death verdicts did you get?

WADE. Twenty-three.

Q. Are you going to try this personally?

WADE. Yes, sir. Yes, sir.

Q. And what was your decision in that, sir? Why did you make that decision?

WADE. This is a proper case for the death penalty.

Q. Beg pardon?

WADE. This is a proper case for the death penalty. Is that what--?

Q. Why did you decide to try this personally, yourself?

WADE. Well, I generally try the major cases, and I believe this will be classed as a major case.

Q. Did he -- it's going to be -- I would imagine, yes, it would.

Q. Mr. Wade, are you elected or appointed?

WADE. I'm elected, every four years. I'm starting my fifth term. I'm in my first year of my fifth term, serving the four-year term.

Q. Mr. Wade, do you expect to call Mrs. Kennedy or Governor Connally, if he's able, in this trial as witnesses?

WADE. We will not, unless it's absolutely necessary, and at this point I don't think it'll be necessary.

COMMISSION EXHIBIT No. 2172

Q. How soon could we expect a trial?

WADE. I'd say around the middle of January.

Q. May I recap a few high points of the things you've said with you, Mr. Wade? First of all, has the investigation in your opinion advanced materially today?

WADE. I'm not familiar with all of the advancing. It's mostly routine today, interviewing witnesses at the scene, and I haven't--I don't know everything that's been done, but I think it's progressing satisfactorily.

Q. Now the pace in the questioning of Oswald seems to have dropped off sharply in comparison to last night. Is there any particular reason for that?

WADE. None that I know of.

Q. You talked to Oswald for about how long?

WADE. Practically none, personally.

Q. Have you observed him for a number of hours?

WADE. I've seen him a time or two but I didn't get--the interrogation started before I got down here and I left them with him.

Q. Well, from what you've seen, how do you sum him up as a man, based on your experience with criminal types?

WADE. Well, I think he's a man that planned this murder weeks or months ago and has laid his plans carefully and carried them out, and has planned at that time what he's going to tell the police that are questioning him at present.

COMMISSION EXHIBIT No. 2172—Continued

Q. Within these plans, do you have any inkling as to the why, the reason for it?

WADE. No, very little.

Q. It is commonly supposed because of his affection for Castro's Cuba and communism that he was led to engineer this plot.

WADE. I can't say whether that was it. It's apparently on its face that contributed some, quite a bit to it.

Q. Do you characterize Oswald as superior in intelligence?

WADE. I'd say above average.

Q. What about any other personality traits that you can detect in him? Because as you know anybody who would attempt something so heinous and complex as this must present an interesting personality to the world.

WADE. I'm sure it does, but I know--I don't know--I know very little about personality, psychology, and the like; I'm not an authority by any means on that.

Q. Has he ever expressed any hatred, ill-will, toward President Kennedy or, for that matter, any regret over his death?

WADE. He has expressed no regret that I know of. I don't know about the other.

Q. Now his wife and his mother and his brother are talking to him, I believe, right now up on the fourth floor. Is there any hope that they might convince him to confess?

WADE. I don't know. I understand they want him to.

Q. Have they expressed that wish to the police officials?

COMMISSION EXHIBIT No. 2172—Continued

WADE. That I don't know. His brother indicated that to me, that he thought he ought to tell the truth about it.

Q. Are the two brothers close, do you know?

WADE. I doubt it. Robert hasn't seen him since November a year ago, and they've been living right here within --

Q. This man, it seems, wasn't close to anybody. Have you discovered any close friends in Dallas?

WADE. No, sir.

Q. This in itself suggests a certain type of personality that perhaps is inward, can do without people, can be perhaps dedicated?

WADE. Not mixing with other people very much.

Q. It's rumored that perhaps this case would be tried by a military court because of course President Kennedy is our Commander-in-Chief.

WADE. I don't know anything about that. We have him charged in the State court and he's a State prisoner at present.

Q. And you will conduct the trial?

WADE. Yes, sir, I plan to.

Q. And you will ask the capital verdict?

WADE. We'll ask the death penalty.

Q. In how many cases of this type have you been involved, that is, when the death penalty is involved?

WADE. Since I've been District Attorney we've asked--I've asked the death penalty in 24 cases.

Q. How many times have you obtained it?

COMMISSION EXHIBIT No. 2172—Continued

WADE. Twenty-three.

COMMENTATOR. Thank you, Mr. District Attorney.

That was District Attorney Wade. We now return to the studios of WFAA.

COMMISSION EXHIBIT No. 2172—Continued

WFAA-TV reel PKT 11
Friday night, November 22, 1963

PRESS INTERVIEW WITH DISTRICT ATTORNEY WADE,
CAPTAIN FRITZ, AND POLICE CHIEF CURRY IN CORRIDOR
ON THIRD FLOOR OF DALLAS POLICE HEADQUARTERS

WADE: There is still some -- immediately to the grand jury as soon as some of the evidence is examined. It will be examined today, tonight, and tomorrow. He has been filed before--filed in Judge David Johnston's, Justice of the Peace Precinct 2 of Dallas, then held without bond on this case and the other case too. It will probably be the middle of next week before it goes to the grand jury because of some more evidence that has to be examined by the laboratory.

Q. Has he engaged a lawyer, sir?

Q. Mr. Wade, could you elaborate on the physical evidence?

WADE: Well, we've gone into some other things that were gathered. The gun is one of them.

Q. Could you tell us if he has engaged a lawyer?

FRITZ: We don't know. His people have been here but we don't know of any particular individual.

Q. Mr. Wade, you say the gun. Has it specifically been connected with him? That is the murder weapon? It is his weapon, sir?

Q. Are you going to bring him out?

COMMISSION EXHIBIT No. 2173

WADE: I --

Q. Can we get in a room where we can get a picture of him?

Q. Can we get a press conference where he can stand against the wall and we can talk to him --?

WADE: I don't know where he is.

Q. Huh?

Q. Mr. Wade? Mr. Wade?

WADE: Yes, sir.

Q. Do you expect a confession from this man?

WADE: No.

Q. Would you say it's a strong case for conviction?

WADE: I think it's a case for --

Q. What is the evidence that links him with the gun?

WADE: I don't care to go into the evidence now--any of the details.

Q. Mr. Wade, please --

WADE: It'll be in the Dallas County Grand Jury.

COMMISSION EXHIBIT No. 2173—Continued

Q. -- ?

Q. Henry! Mr. Wade!

FRITZ: We can go down there.

WADE: We're going to get in a larger room here. That's what we are talking about here.

Q. We want the assembly room!

WADE: Is that all right? Let's go down there.

WADE: Let's go down there where the --

Q. Will the prisoner be brought out -- ?

COMMENTATOR: He'll be taken down to the basement assembly room where he will confront the assembly of press gathered here in the police station.

. . . .

COMMENTATOR. Capt. Will Fritz, the chief interrogator of Lee Oswald here at the Dallas County Police Station. It is now 10 minutes past twelve Central Standard Time in Dallas, as Lee Oswald is being taken from this third floor where he has been for the past several hours down to the assembly room. There the police chief, Chief Curry, along with District Attorney -- excuse me, with the District Attorney and the Police Chief, -- along with the suspect will meet the press.

COMMISSION EXHIBIT No. 2173—Continued

KRLD Audio reels 2"B" and 3"A" Item 19
Friday, November 22, 1963

KRLD NEWS REPORT

A Dallas police inspector named J. H. Sawyer said the police found the remains of fried chicken and paper on the fifth floor indicating he said that apparently the person had been there for quite a while waiting for this moment in history.

COMMISSION EXHIBIT No. 2174

THIRD FLOOR PLAN
DALLAS POLICE DEPARTMENT
DALLAS, TEXAS

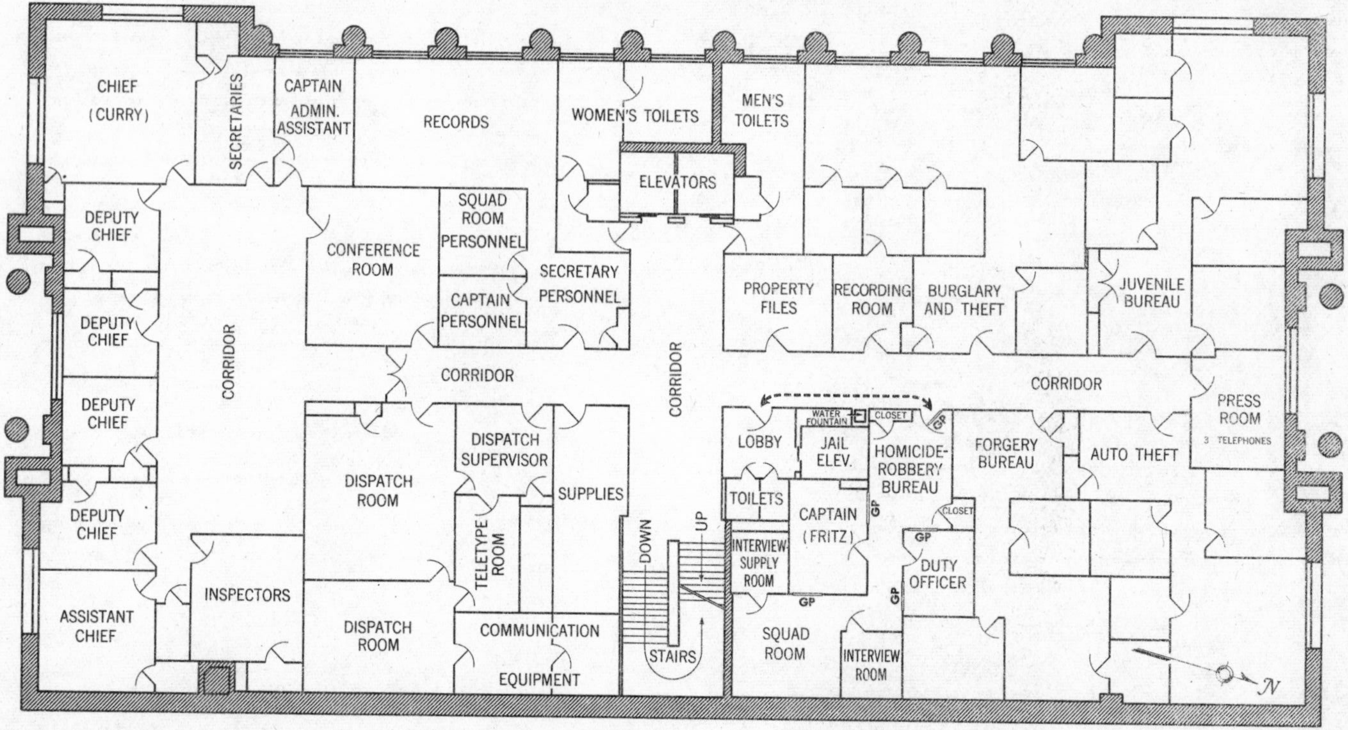

APPROX. 23 FT. — Oswald's route between Homicide-Robbery Bureau and jail elevator lobby

GP — Glass panel in upper part of wall and door

0 5 10 15 20 25 30 35 40 45 50
Scale In Feet

PKA - 6

:00

TOM PERRYMAN

Was at home when President was shot. Arrived at station in about ten minutes. Everyone had gone out in mobile units, and the networks and literally hundreds of stations were clamouring for feeds. He and everyone who could be found - even weatherman Dale Milford - were feeding stations. Coffee and sandwiches were brought in. Left station about 2:30 A. M. Returned about 9:00 A. M. Saturday to resume constant feeds.

4:25

Saturday at the county jail for Oswald's transfer. Was interviewed by Radio Free Berlin. Oswald was not transferred as planned.

6:00

Went to county jail with recorder again Sunday morning to await Oswald's transfer.

7:10

Reporters at jail get news that Oswald has been shot. Crowd applauds.

8:30

Dashes to City Hall.

9:30

Reporters interviewing reporters in the hallway.

11:00

Hid a telephone behind a desk so he could keep a direct line open to NBC. Interviewed Tony Zoppi for a description of Jack Ruby - very fine interview.

12:35

Curry announces Oswald's death.

ENDS ABOUT 13:30

BOB THORNTON

Went to Ft. Worth in Mobile Unit to cover President's speech outside Texas Hotel. Crowd in rain.

17:20

Connally appears.

17:50

President appears to screams of delight from teenagers. Makes brief speech.

19:00

Returns to Dallas to WFAA newsroom.

25

COMMISSION EXHIBIT No. 2176

JAIL OFFICE AND IMMEDIATE VICINITY

BASEMENT, DALLAS POLICE DEPARTMENT

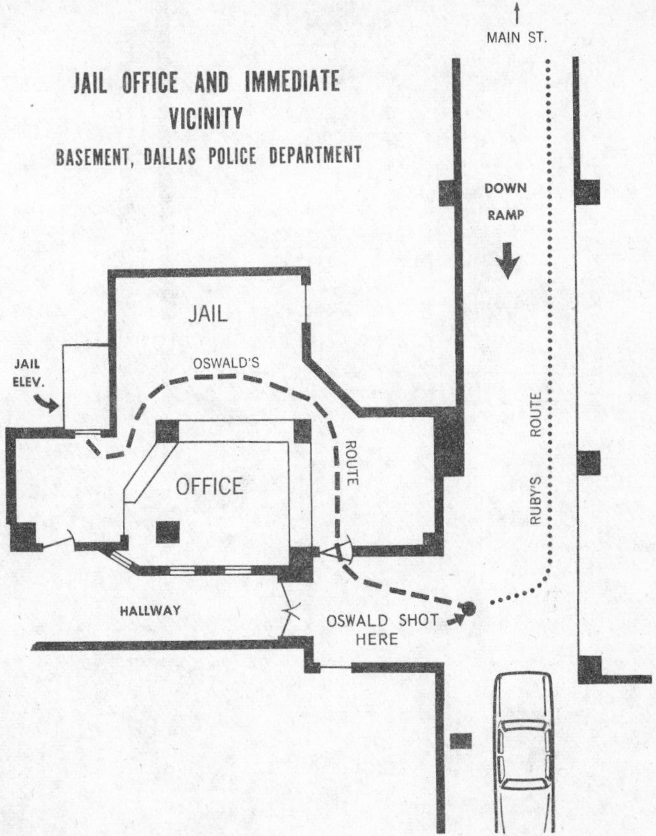

COMMISSION EXHIBIT No. 2177

Marked Map Discovered Among Oswald's Effects

By WARREN BOSWORTH, Staff Writer

A Dallas city map with X marks and a line similar to the trajectory of the bullets which killed President Kennedy was found in Lee Harvey Oswald's apartment Dist. Atty. Henry Wade confirmed Monday.

He also said that Oswald's fingerprints were found on the foreign-made rifle used in the assassination.

Meanwhile, the Police Department said Monday that it intends to make the department file on the Oswald case public unless federal authorities object.

"Unless we are specifically instructed otherwise from Washington, we believe it can and should become public information," the statement signed by Chief Jesse Curry said. "At this time we cannot designate when the release will be made."

The district attorney, in discussing the map found in Oswald's apartment, said Xs marked various downtown intersections. A line was drawn from the intersection of Houston and Elm streets tracing a rough trajectory similar to that of the gunfire which took the President's life.

Oswald's fingerprints also were found on two cases of books which the assassin used to prop the rifle on when he fired the deadly blast into the motorcade below.

The district attorney's disclosures came during a tense press conference late Sunday night at police headquarters.

Mr. Wade called the press conference after Russia's Tass News Agency and Radio Moscow turned the President's murder into an international incident, declaring Oswald was framed for the assassination.

Mr. Wade denied emphatically that the 24-year-old avowed Marxist was framed for the murder.

"There is no doubt in my mind that Oswald was the man who assassinated Presdient Kennedy," he said.

All evidence compiled by Homicide Capt. Will Fritz and his investigators points directly to Oswald, Mr. Wade said.

The district attorney said there were 10 major points uncovered in the exhaustive around-the-clock investigation that proved beyond a doubt that Oswald was the killer.

THEY WERE:

1. Eyewitnesses saw a man fitting Oswald's description in the window of the Texas Schoolbook Depository building from which the fatal shots were fired.
2. Oswald's fingerprints were found on the book cartons.
3. Oswald had ordered a foreign-made rifle under an assumed name from a Chicago firearms company. The weapon was found near the window minutes after the shooting.
4. Police obtained a photograph of Oswald holding a rifle which appeared to be the same weapon as used in the assassination. The photograph also revealed the man was armed with a pistol, presumably used in the slaying of Officer J. D. Tippit.
5. Oswald was the only employe in the School Book Depository Building unaccounted for at the time of the slaying.
6. Oswald caught a bus only blocks from the shooting scene a few minutes after the President was gunned down, saying to the driver, "The President has been shot." He then broke into laughter, the driver told investigators.
7. Oswald later emerged from the bus, hailed a taxicab and went to the Oak Cliff rooming house where he had rented

See OSWALD'S on Page 35

THE DALLAS TIMES HERALD
City News
Monday, Nov. 25, 1963 A—31

Commission Exhibit No. 2178

COMMISSION EXHIBIT No. 2178

BASEMENT

DALLAS POLICE DEPARTMENT, DALLAS, TEXAS

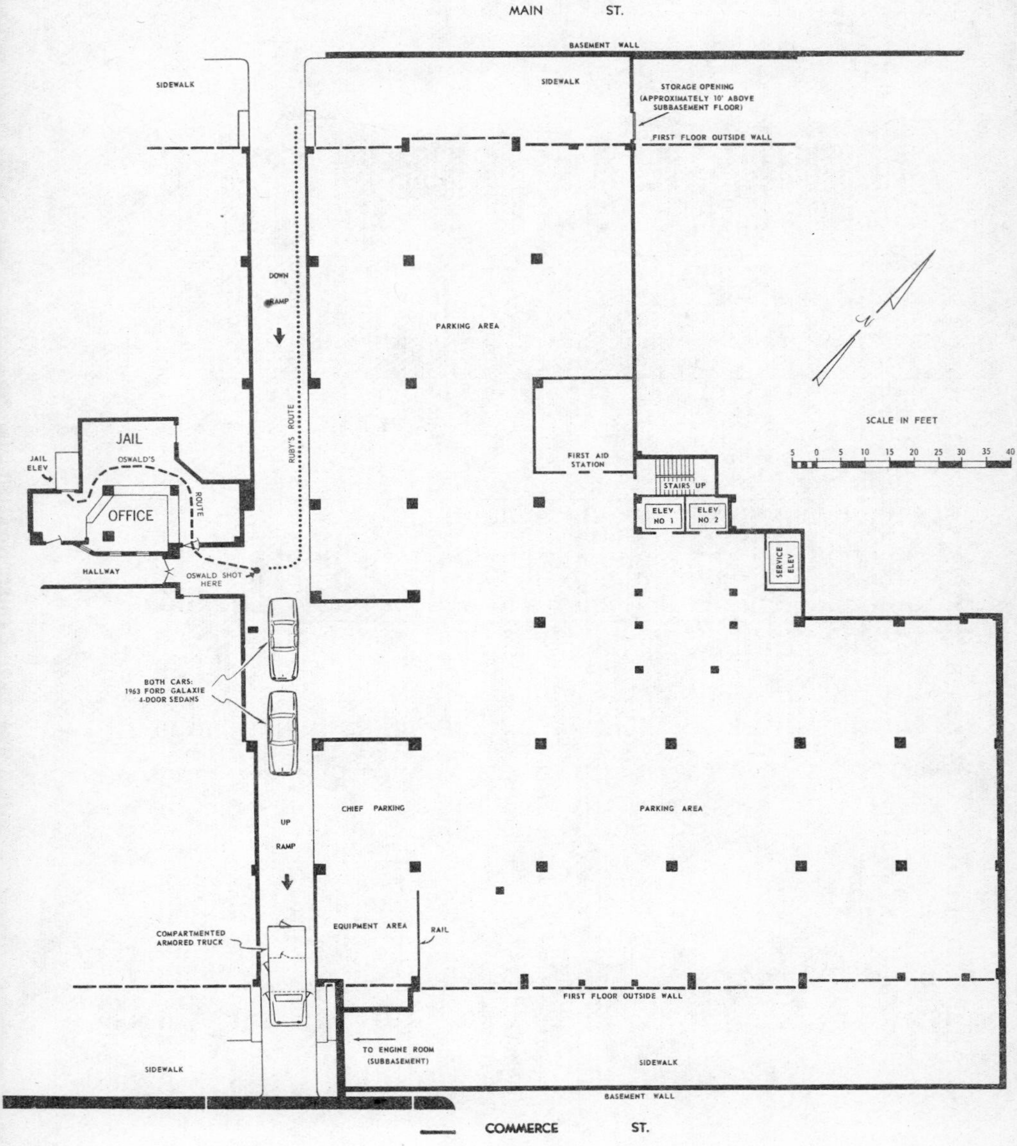

Commission Exhibit No. 2179

THE WASHINGTON POST Tuesday, Nov. 26, 1963 A7

Dallas Prosecutor Discusses State's Case Against Oswald

...ed with Gov't issue M84 2½x crosshair scope, mount and cheekpiece $134.95

6.5 ITALIAN CARBINE

Late military issue. Only 40" overall. Weighs 7 lbs. Shows only slight use. test-fired and head spaced. ready for shooting. Turned-down bolt. 6-shot. clip fed. rear sight. thumb safety.

C20-1196 .... $12.78

C20-750. Carbine with brand new 4X Scope -¾" dia. illustrated $19.95

E20-751. 6.5mm Italian military ammo. 108 rds. 6-shot clip free. $7.50

United Press International

Reproduction of a part of an advertisement for Klein's Sporting Goods, Chicago mail order house, featuring an Italian-made 6.5 Carcano rifle. Authorities have said that the late Lee Harvey Oswald, prime suspect in the slaying of President Kennedy, had ordered the weapon used in the President's murder from this firm.

Dodd to Push Harder for Gun Controls

Sen. Thomas J. Dodd (D-Conn.) yesterday served notice he will press harder than ever for action on legislation strengthening the Federal Firearms Act in the wake of the assassination of the President and two other slayings in Dallas.

"It points up tragically the need to make it more difficult to purchase handguns or rifles, particularly by persons with a police record," said Dodd.

Dodd's bill, introduced Aug. 2, followed his investigation of juvenile delinquency and was aimed particularly at sales of firearms to juveniles.

But had it been on the books, Dodd told The Post yesterday, it would have made it far "tougher" for Lee Harvey Oswald to have purchased by mail order the imported rifle he acquired for $12.78.

The tragic round of events in Dallas meanwhile brought influential new support to the measure. "You keep after that ... bill, I'm with you," Sen... Majority Leader Mike ... told the ... Democratic ... yester-

Old, Reputable Firm Sold Murder Weapon

Chicago Tribune Press Service

CHICAGO, Nov. 25 — The Klein Sporting Goods Inc., from which Lee Harvey Oswald bought the mail order gun used to kill President Kennedy, is a large and reputable firm in business since 1885.

It operates seven retail stores in the Chicago area, in addition to a mail order plant on Chicago's west side. Two stores are large downtown area establishments.

The Company sells a complete line of sporting goods and also publishes books on sports. Milton P. Klein, president of the Company, noted that the percentage of the firm's business in selling guns is small in relation to its overall sales. He said the sale of fishing tackle is the largest part of Klein business and that bowling equipment sales also are large.

Thousands of mail order companies sell hunting rifles of the type Oswald purchased, apparently under an assumed name. Such guns also can be purchased over the counter in many sporting goods stores.

Klein said his company maintains records required in gun sales.

Chicago police superintendent Orlando W. Wilson said today he would like to see a tightening up of laws pertaining to the sale and possession of guns.

"Hand guns in particular need tighter control than we have," he said. "There are too many of them floating around Chicago. I don't think we can do much in the case of sporting guns."

Lt. Vincent Burke of the police youth division, which most frequently handles crimes committed with guns, expressed belief Chicago has adequate weapons ordinances.

He pointed out that purchasers of both pistols and rifles in Chicago must have permits but that one need only go outside city limits, or order by mail, to obtain such weapons practically without interference.

Illinois State law requires that sellers of concealable weapons must register them to show the name of the purchaser, date of purchase, serial number and purpose, but imposes no restrictions on rifles. Lt. Burke said that some states prohibit the purchase of guns by mail, but that Illinois is not one of them.

NEW YORK, Nov. 25 (AP) The following is a statement and news conference by District Attorney Henry Wade of Dallas County late yesterday concerning the evidence against Lee Harvey Oswald, accused assassin of President Kennedy. It was recorded on tape by WNBC-TV.

Wade: The purpose of this news conference is to detail some of the evidence against Oswald for the assassination of the President. This evidence was gathered by—largely by—the Dallas police, who did an excellent job on this, with the help of some of the Federal agents. And I am going through the evidence piece by piece for you. No. 1 (some of this you already know; some of it you won't; I don't think that all of you do know.) First, there was a number of witnesses that saw the person with the gun on the sixth floor of the bookstore building, the window—detailing the window—where he was looking out. Inside this window the police found a row of books, cases, boxes hiding someone sitting in the window, from people on the same floor looking in. On the window were some boxes where, in the little circle around the window, by the bookcases, some boxes where, apparently, the person was sitting, because he was seen from that particular window.

On this box that the defendant was sitting on, his palm print was found and was identified as his. The three ejected shells were found right by the box. The shells were of an odd caliber of the type and as later determined, the gun, that was found on the floor.

The gun was hidden on this same floor behind some boxes and bookcases. It, as I think you know, has been identified as having been purchased last March by Oswald, from a mail order house, through an assumed name named Hidell, mailed to a post office box here in Dallas. On his person was a pocketbook. In his pocketbook was an identification card with the same name as the post office box on it.

Pictures were found of the defendant with this gun and a pistol on his—in his holster.

Immediately that morning—it was unusual, but that morning—a neighbor brought Oswald from Irving, Texas. He usually brought him on Monday morning, I think, but this day he went home one day earlier on Thursday night, and came back to—with this fellow—and when he came back he had a package under his arm that he said was window curtains, I believe, or window shades. The wife had said he had the gun the night before, and it was missing that morning after he left. He got out around 8 o'clock and went to the building behind some cars and went to work.

A police officer, immediately after the assassination, ran in the building and saw this man in a corner and tried to arrest him; but the manager of the building said he was an employe and it was all right. Every other employe was located but this defendant of the company. A description and name of him went out by police to look for him.

The next we hear of him is on a bus where he got on a bus at Lamar street, told the bus driver the President had been shot, the President. (He) told the lady—all this was verified by statements—told the lady on the bus that the President had been shot. He said, how did he know. He said a man back there told him. The defendant said, Yes, He's been shot, and laughed very loud.

Q: This was to a lady?

A: A lady. He then—the bus, he asked the bus driver to stop, got off at a stop, caught a taxicab driver, Darryl Click—I don't have his exact place—and went to his home in Oak Cliff, changed his clothes hurriedly, and left.

As he left, three witnesses saw a police officer—Officer Tippitt—motion to him or say something to him. He walked up to the car. Officer Tippitt stepped out of the car and started around it. He shot him three times and killed him.

Q: Was this in front of the boarding house?

A: No, it's not in front of the boarding house.

Q: Where was it?

A: I don't have it exact. It's more than a block. It's a block or two.

Q. Was he on foot when Tippitt saw him?

A: Yes, he was on foot. And apparently headed for the Texas Theater. He then walked across a vacant lot. Witnesses saw him eject the shells from a revolver and place—reload—the gun. Someone saw him go in the Texas Theater. A search was made of that later by a number of police officers. At the time, an officer of the Dallas police spotted him and asked him to come out. He struck at the officer, put the gun against his head and snapped it, but did not—the bullet did not—go off. We have the snapped bullet there. Officers—officers apprehended him at that time.

Q: Was that an attempted suicide, sir?

A: Against the officer's head.

Q: Do you know why the gun . . .

Q: Which officer?

A: Macdonald was his name.

Q: Why didn't it go off?

A: It snapped. It was a misfire. Then officers subdued him—some six officers—subdued him there in the theater, and he was borught to the police station here.

Q: Mr. Wade, why didn't the gun fire?

A: It misfired, being on the—the shell didn't explode. We have where it hit it, but it didn't explode. It didn't fire the shell.

Q: There was one officer who said that he pulled the trigger, but he managed to put his thumb in the part berofe the firing pin. It didn't . . .

A: Well . . .

Q: ". . . strike the—the bullet didn't explode. Is that . . .

A: I don't know whether it's that or not. I know he didn't snap the gun is all I know about it.

Q: You would say it was a misfire?

A: It didn't fire.

Q: Let's get the story again.

Q: What other evidence is there?

A: Let's see . . . His fingerprints were found on the gun, have I said that?

Q: Which gun?

A: On the rifle.

Q: You didn't say that.

Q: What about the paraffin tests?

A: Yes, I've got paraffin tests that showed he had recently fired a gun—it was on both hands.

Q: On both hands?

A: Both hands.

Q: Recently fired a rifle.

Q: A gun?

A: A gun.

Q: The rifle fingerprints were his, were Oswald's?

A: Yes.

Q: Were there any fingerprints . . .

A: Palm prints rather than fingerprints.

Q: Were there any fingerprints at the window?

Q: Palm prints on the what?

A: Yes, on . . .

Q: On the rifle?

A: Yes, sir.

Q: Where are they on the rifle?

A: Under—on part of the metal—under the gun.

Q: Did he still . . . ever say anything about it, admit anything at all?

A: He never did admit any of the killing. I didn't—you ask me this—I didn't do any of the interrogation.

Q: You have not listed it then as part of the evidence?

A: No, it's not listed.

Q: Did he display any animosity towards the President, in any conversation with any officers?

A: He was bitter toward all of the officers that examined him is what I've been told.

Q: Do you think he deserved . . .

Q: Let's finish the . . .

A: We have—that's about all.

Q: How about ballistics tests?

Q: Ballistic test was made?

A: Well, I said this was the gun that . . .

Q: Killed the President?

A: Yes.

Q: You talked with the FBI this morning. Did you leave the rest with the FBI?

A: I won't go—I'm not at liberty—to go into the FBI report.

Q: Did you say the gun was mailed to a post office box in Dallas in March?

A: March of this year.

Q: Was he living in Dallas then?

A: Yes. I presume he was. He got it here.

Q: I see.

Q: Previously he lived in New Orleans?

Q: He said he'd only been here two months.

Q: Mr. Wade . . .

A: He came to Fort Worth sometime in the fall of '62. And then moved here a while, and apparently went to New Orleans for a while and came back. And when the period to that is, I'm not sure.

Q: Mr. Wade, what was the evidence that we were told was startling evidence that could not be told to the press . . .

Q: Saturday morning. They said it came in Saturday morning, and it could not be revealed. It was . . .

A: I don't know. That wasn't me that said that, I don't think.

Q: Have you given us everything?

A: I've given you everything that I . . .

Q: Do you know that he has been recognized as a patron of Ruby's night club here?

A: I don't know that.

Q: Do you know of any connection between Mr. Ruby and the . . . the assassin?

A: I know of none.

Q: Are you investigating reports that he may have been slain because Ruby might have feared he would have been implicated in something?

A: The police are making investigation of that murder. I don't know anything about that. The investigation and charges have been filed. It will be presented to the grand jury on Ruby, immediately within the next week; and it'll probably be tried around the middle of January.

Q: Did the District Attorney's office follow the police investigation of the assassination of the President, before sending again to Washington?

A: Before.

Q: Do you think it was unusual for Jack Ruby to be in that crowd?

A: I won't pass on that—unusual to be in that crowd?

Q: There are reports that he had planned to.

A: I haven't been here since last night, so I don't know anything about it.

Q: Mr. Wade, how do you feel about not being able to try Oswald as the killer of the President?

A: Well, we will try Ruby and ask the death penalty on him, about the same time.

Q: Well, how about Oswald?

A: I don't want to go into the whys or wherefores on anything.

Q: Has your office closed the investigation into the death of President Kennedy?

A: No, sir. The investigation will continue on that, with the basis, of course, that we have no concrete evidence that anyone assisted him in this. The investigation, I'm sure, will go on with reference to any possible accomplice or person that assisted him in it.

Q: Do you have any suspicions now that there were?

A: I have no concrete evidence or suspicions at present.

Q: Thank you.

Q: Would you be willing to say, in view of all this evidence, that it is now beyond a reasonable doubt at all that Oswald was the killer of President Kennedy?

A: I would say that without any doubt he is the killer—the law says beyond a reasonable doubt, to a moral certainty, which I have—there is no question that he was the killer of President Kennedy.

Q: That case is closed in your mind?

A: As far as Oswald's concerned.

DALLAS TIMES HERALD NOV 24, 1963 A-3

★ OSWALD LINKED WITH RIFLE

Continued From Page 1

sniper assassination of President Kennedy and the fatal shooting in Oak Cliff minutes later of a Dallas policeman, 39-year-old J.D. Tippit.

Capt. Fritz said Oswald still denies everything, "but he is responding better to questioning." He said the investigation concerning the assault on Gov. John Connally would be turned over to Capt. O.A. Jones for preparation of charges and added, "It's ready to be filed now."

Gov. Connally was wounded in the shooting just before 12:30 p.m. Friday in which President Kennedy was slain by one or more rifle shots fired from a sixth-story window at the corner of Elm and Houston streets. His condition Saturday was reported satisfactory.

CAUGHT IN THEATRE

Oswald was arrested an hour later after a wild scuffle with police in an Oak Cliff theater. Officer Tippit already had been shot to death at 10th and Patton streets in Oak Cliff.

City detectives, Secret Service, Federal Bureau of Investigation, sheriff's deputies and a representative of Dist. Atty. Henry Wade were all involved in the lengthy interrogations of Oswald.

In late afternoon Saturday, anticipating Oswald's rumored transfer fro mthe city jail to county jail, hundreds of Dallasites lined the west side of Houston street near the driveway to the Dallas County Jail. On the opposite side of Houston street at least 50 TV cameras moved into range.

Dallas Transit Co. reported that traffic in the area—and nearby, where the President was shot—was so heavy that buses were running up to 35 minutes behind schedule.

SPECULATION SWIRLS

Speculations swirled around Oswald's background, and especially his alleged pro-Russian and pro-Castro feelings.

said ¼ -.. ¼ ⅛..⅛..⅛..⅛⅛

Capt. Fritz. said Oswald has said he is pro-Castro and is a member of the American Civil Liberties Union.

A foreign-made rifle, some shells and a pistol were all sent to Washington Friday night for fingerprint checking. The rifle and shells were found in the sixth-floor room from where the deadly shots were fired as the presidential motorcade moved toward Stemmons Freeway just after Friday noon. The pistol was taken from Oswald when he was arrested in the theater.

Police Chief Jesse Curry said Lt. Carl Day of the Police Department's identification bureau believed that partial palm prints found on a packing box at the sixth floor window were definitely Oswald's.

Police also learned that a 19-year-old Dallas man who drove Oswald to work from his home in Irving Friday morning noticed he was carrying a long object wrapped in brown paper. It was the approximate length of a rifle and the man said Oswald told him it was window shades.

MANY QUESTIONED

Many witnesses were being questioned by Capt. Fritz and others throughout Saturday. Among them were believed to be the driver of a bus which Oswald rode one block from the shooting scene, and a cab driver who may have taken Oswald to an address on Beckley where he had a room.

Police theorize Oswald then changed clothes, went outside and shortly encountered Officer Tippit.

Oswald was an employe of Texas Book Depository, occupant of the seven-story building at Elm and Houston from where the shots were fired.

Another employe of the firm was interviewed at length Saturday after appearing voluntarily. Capt. W.P. Gannaway of the Police Department's Special Services Bureau said this man's name has been in the subversive files of the department since 1955. He was not jailed and police said he was not arrested.

Chief Curry said Oswald had lived in Dallas about two months.

QUIZZED EARLIER

A controversy almost blossomed Saturday when The Times Herald learned that the FBI interrogated Oswald and his Russian-born wife less than two weeks ago. Police Chief Curry said, regardless, Oswald had never been recorded by the Dallas police as either a subversive or a criminal. Later, Chief Curry called a press conference to emphasize there were no differences between his department and the FBI.

Capt. Fritz said that Oswald, during interrogations and in front of the press as well, had asked for a lawyer. On one of the prisoner's many trips through the halls he halted suddenly before a TV reporter, leaned toward the microphone and said in a low voice, "I want to talk to Mr. Abt."

United Press International, in a dispatch out of New York, identified the man as John J. Abt, and said: "During the 1940's and 1950's his name was almost synonymous with the legal defense of the Communist party in the United States."

LETTER REVEALED

In the fast-moving developments, Oswald's service record as a Marine aroused added in[terest.]

A 1961 letter from the Pent[agon] personnel files shed a new [light] on the Dallas crimes.

Dated Jan. 30, 1961, it was [writ]ten in longhand from Min[sk,] the Soviet Union, and was [signed] by Lee Harvey Oswald. It [was] addressed to then Secreta[ry of] the Navy John Connally [and] asked a reversal of Oswald['s un]desirable discharge from th[e Ma]rine Corps.

The letter raised the qu[estion] of whether the primary tar[get of] Friday's tragedy was Gov. [Con]nally or President Kennedy.

In part, the letter stated [" I] shall employ all means to [right] this gross mistake or injusti[ce to] a bona-fide U.S. citizen and [ex-]serviceman."

Commission Exhibit No. 2181

UNITED STATES DEPARTMENT OF JUSTICE

FEDERAL BUREAU OF INVESTIGATION

In Reply, Please Refer to File No.

Dallas, Texas
August 6, 1964

JACK L. RUBY;
LEE HARVEY OSWALD

By letter dated July 23, 1964, the President's Commission on the Assassination of President Kennedy requested investigation relative to six enumerated points. Item 1 concerns whether Captain Glen King, Dallas, Texas, Police Department, Dallas, Texas, obtained authority of Deputy Chief Ray Lunday or Deputy Chief George L. Lumpkin to permit newsmen in the third floor corridor of the Police and Courts Building on November 22, 1963. Item 2 concerns a telephone call by Lieutenant T. L. Baker, Dallas Police Department, on November 24, 1963, to the basement jail office.

Attached hereto are reports of interviews with Deputy Chiefs Lunday and Lumpkin with respect to Item 1, and with Lieutenant Baker regarding Item 2.

FD-302 (Rev. 3-3-58)

FEDERAL BUREAU OF INVESTIGATION

Date 8/4/64

1

RAY LUNDAY, Deputy Chief of Police, Dallas Police Department, advised that Captain GLEN KING of the Dallas Police Department never consulted him for permission for television cameramen or other news media to enter the third floor corridor of the Police and Courts Building, Dallas, Texas, on November 22, 1963.

Deputy Chief LUNDAY stated that the administrative offices in which LUNDAY's office is situated are located at the end of the third floor corridor. On the afternoon of November 22, 1963, LUNDAY related that Captain GLEN KING came to him and asked if it would be all right for the television cameramen to run cables from their truck to their large cameras in the corridor bringing such cables through the window of his office running them across out through his door to his office and into the hallway. LUNDAY stated this was the only conversation he had with KING and this was not for permission to permit the television and news media on the third floor corridor, but merely for the purpose of running the cables through his office. LUNDAY stated as far as he knew KING did not have to have the permission of anyone to permit news media representatives on the third floor corridor of the Police and Courts Building. He stated that as far as he knew KING acted on his own in permitting the news media representatives on the third floor corridor of the Police and Courts Building.

Deputy Chief LUNDAY stated he was not aware of any loose press cards or badges that might have been found lying in the basement of the Police and Courts Building, Dallas, Texas, on November 24, 1963.

on 7/31/64 at Dallas, Texas File # DL 44-1639

by Special Agent VINCENT E. DRAIN:vm Date dictated 8/3/64

This document contains neither recommendations nor conclusions of the FBI. It is the property of the FBI and is loaned to your agency; it and its contents are not to be distributed outside your agency.

2

FEDERAL BUREAU OF INVESTIGATION

Date 8/4/64

1

Deputy Chief of Police GEORGE L. LUMPKIN, Dallas Police Department, Dallas, Texas, advised he was never consulted by Captain GLEN KING concerning television cameramen at the Police and Courts Building, Dallas, Texas, on November 22, 1963. He stated that KING asked him no questions concerning whether the television or press men could enter the third floor corridor of this building. LUMPKIN related that as a matter of fact KING, as far as he knew, was operating on his own and was directly responsible to Chief of Police JESSE E. CURRY since KING more or less handled the press relations for the Chief of Police. LUMPKIN stated that as far as he knew Captain KING dealt solely with the television and press people and he never heard of KING soliciting permission for these people to enter the third floor corridor of the Police and Courts Building.

Deputy Chief LUMPKIN stated he was not aware of any loose press cards or badges that might have been found lying in the basement of the Police and Courts Building, Dallas, Texas, on November 24, 1963.

on 7/31/64 at Dallas, Texas File # DL 44-1639

by Special Agent VINCENT E. DRAIN:vm Date dictated 8/3/64

This document contains neither recommendations nor conclusions of the FBI. It is the property of the FBI and is loaned to your agency; it and its contents are not to be distributed outside your agency.

3

COMMISSION EXHIBIT No. 2182—Continued

FEDERAL BUREAU OF INVESTIGATION

Date 8/4/64

1

Lieutenant T. L. BAKER, Homicide Bureau, Dallas Police Department, stated he was one of the detectives in Captain WILL FRITZ' office on the third floor of the Police and Courts Building, Dallas Police Department, on November 24, 1963. Lieutenant BAKER stated that at approximately 11:15 a.m., November 24, 1963, he telephoned to the basement jail office and talked with Lieutenant WOODROW WIGGINS in the basement jail office to make sure that all security measures were in effect. He stated he asked WIGGINS if everything was all set and WIGGINS replied that it was and he relayed this information to Captain WILL FRITZ. He stated this was as near to actually what was said as he could remember. He stated he reported to Captain FRITZ that "Everything is all set." He stated that his call to Lieutenant WIGGINS took approximately 30 seconds and that he immediately reported the results of this conversation with Lieutenant WIGGINS to Captain FRITZ. Lieutenant BAKER advised he was not aware of any similar telephone calls that were made to the basement immediately before the transfer party left FRITZ' office on Sunday morning, November 24, 1963.

Lieutenant BAKER stated he was not aware of any loose press cards or badges that might have been found lying in the basement of the Police and Courts Building, Dallas, Texas, on November 24, 1963.

on 7/31/64 at Dallas, Texas File # DL 44-1639

by Special Agent VINCENT E. DRAIN:vm Date dictated 8/3/64

This document contains neither recommendations nor conclusions of the FBI. It is the property of the FBI and is loaned to your agency; it and its contents are not to be distributed outside your agency.

4

COMMISSION EXHIBIT No. 2182—Continued

Commission Exhibit No. 2183

news from the American Bar Association — Committee on Public Relations

Headquarters
American Bar Center
1155 East Sixtieth St.
Chicago, Illinois 60637

Telephone
(312) 493-0533

John Shaw Field
Chairman

Don Hyndman
Director of Public Relations

For Release at 4 p.m. Saturday, December 7, 1963

AMERICAN BAR STATEMENT "DEPLORES" PROPOSALS TO TELEVISE RUBY TRIAL

Chicago -- The Board of Governors of the American Bar Association released the following statement through ABA headquarters in Chicago:

The American Bar Association deplores proposals that the trial of Jack Ruby be televised. The related events already have reflected discredit upon certain aspects of criminal justice in this country.

The shocking assassination of President Kennedy and its aftermath have received unprecedented coverage in the news media of the world. The broadcast media and the press performed a worthy public service in bringing to the public, fully and promptly, the essential facts of that tragic and portentous event. In addition to the deep human interest and distress, there was an urgent public concern in knowing that the law enforcement authorities were discharging their duty with all the promptness, thoroughness and faithfulness that the situation demanded. The public certainly was entitled to know the facts about the arrest of Oswald and also to know that the evidence was deemed sufficient to charge him with the crime.

But what occurred in Dallas went far beyond the requirements of this legitimate public interest. It struck at the heart of our fundamental rule of law with its guarantees of a fair trial for everyone, however heinous the crime

involved. The widespread publicizing of Oswald's alleged guilt, involving statements by officials and public disclosures of the details of "evidence," would have made it extremely difficult to impanel an unprejudiced jury and afford the accused a fair trial. It conceivably could have prevented any lawful trial of Oswald due to the difficulty of finding jurors who had not been prejudiced by these public statements.

Official laxity resulting in excessive and prejudicial publicity reached its climax in the pre-announced removal of Oswald from the city jail and the spectacle of his murder--literally in the arms of police officers and before the eyes of the television audience. This act, in addition to its utter lawlessness, has now forever precluded the determination by judicial process of Oswald's guilt or innocence and perhaps the resolution of important related questions of background and associations.

The American Bar Association commends the appointment of a Presidential Commission to investigate and report publicly on the assassination. But this cannot be and is not intended as an adequate substitute for a fair judicial trial of Oswald.

The American Bar Association also commends the Dallas Bar Association for its solicitude for a fair trial for Oswald and for its prompt tender of legal assistance to him.

Although the excesses in the Oswald case were doubtless influenced by the extreme emotional stress surrounding the assassination of President Kennedy, it must be acknowledged that excessive and prejudicial publicity with respect to criminal cases is not unusual in America. The Judiciary and the Bar have long

- 3 -

been disturbed by a tendency of some law enforcement authorities as well as some defense counsel to try their cases outside the courtroom. Responsible elements in the news media also have recognized that the media have sometimes contributed to such violations of fair trial by sensational and prejudicial stories and pictures relating to accused persons.

The American Bar Association does not suggest the imposition of involuntary restrictions on freedom in news presentation, but recent events have dramatically emphasized the urgent need for voluntary restraints on the part of law enforcement officers, members of the bar, and the news media alike.

The trial of Jack Ruby may afford a partial opportunity to repair some of the damage to the image of criminal justice in America. The judicial process must not be further impaired by additional sensationalism, which would inevitably result if television of the trial were permitted. Such a use of television also would violate Canon 35 of the Canons of Judicial Ethics of the American Bar Association, which provides in part as follows:

> "...The broadcasting or televising of court proceedings detract from the essential dignity of the proceedings, distract participants and witnesses in giving testimony, and create misconceptions with respect thereto in the minds of the public and should not be permitted."

Canon 35 recently has undergone the most careful study and re-examination, and was reaffirmed by the House of Delegates of the American Bar Association in February, 1963.

The American Bar Association believes that the paramount interest in the trial of Ruby is a fair trial, conducted with the full dignity of the law. It urges that the public authorities, defense counsel and the news media join in reaffirming by example what is meant in America by justice under law.

COMMISSION EXHIBIT No. 2183—Continued

The New York Times - November 28, 1963 - Page L - 23

San Francisco Bar Decries News Media in Dallas Case

Special to The New York Times

SAN FRANCISCO, Nov. 27—The Bar Association of San Francisco called today for a greater degree of self-control by the news media. It said, "We believe that television, radio and the press must bear a portion of the responsibility which falls primarily on the Dallas law-enforcement officials."

"Both press media and law-enforcement officials must seek to protect the rights of accused persons against the damage to them, and consequently to our system of justice, which can came from revealing information concerning the accused at times when the revelation might inflame the public," said a letter signed by Ben. K. Lerer, president of the association.

The letter suggested that a joint committee of news media representatives and law-enforcement officers be set up to work out rules governing such highly publicized criminal arrests as that of Lee H. Oswald, accused assassin of President Kennedy.

COMMISSION EXHIBIT No. 2184

Press Intelligence, Inc.
WASHINGTON 1, D. C.

BALTIMORE, MD.
SUN
m. 188,156
e. 212,245
S. 321,686

Front Page / Edit Page / Other Page 9

Date: FEB 27 1964

Commission Exhibit No. 2185

Press Should Share Blame In Oswald Death, Says Editor

Evanston, Ill., Feb. 26 (AP)—A Dallas newspaper editor said today the press should accept part of the blame for the death of Lee Harvey Oswald, accused of assassinating President Kennedy.

Felix R. McKnight declared pressure by newsmen, some of whom "implied that the police were physically beating a confession out of Lee Oswald" forced the Dallas police chief to "display the prisoner."

Oswald was slain by Jack Ruby in view of TV and still cameras as police were transferring Oswald to another jail.

The press corps, McKnight added, again is swarming on Dallas "in the same disorderly array" for Ruby's trial on a charge of murdering Oswald.

Addressed Students

McKnight, executive editor and vice president of the Dallas *Times-Herald* addressed the students of Medill School of Journalism of Northwestern University. He is one of ten news executives appearing in a series of lectures sponsored by the Robert R. McCormick Charitable Trust.

The editor critized segments of the press for blaming Dallas for the killing of President Kennedy.

"The sting of slanted reporting still is felt in Dallas," he said. "The Dallas resident wonders about the integrity of the entire communications field.

"The rape of Dallas has come from a backdrop supplied by a radical few. Dallas, a city of 1,000,000, is the reluctant owner of a typical minority of fewer than 500 that has, admittedly, produced the embers of small-time bigotry and political hatred."

Extremist Leadership Denied

He denied that extremists are in positions of leadership in Dallas.

He added that the charges against Dallas are getting renewed life from the news media which quote Ruby's lawyer, Melvin Belli, whom McKnight termed "a courtroom exhibitionist." Belli contends Ruby cannot get a fair trial in Dallas.

McKnight described Dallas as "a city of extreme tolerance, a city that meticulously integrated every facet of its life without a single incident or arrest."

Commission Exhibit No. 2185

OFFICE OF THE DIRECTOR

UNITED STATES DEPARTMENT OF JUSTICE
FEDERAL BUREAU OF INVESTIGATION
WASHINGTON, D.C. 20535

August 26, 1964

BY COURIER SERVICE

Honorable J. Lee Rankin
General Counsel
The President's Commission
200 Maryland Avenue, N. E.
Washington, D. C.

Dear Mr. Rankin:

Reference is made to your letters dated July 7 and July 8, 1964, dealing with Joe R. Molina, formerly an employee of the Texas School Book Depository, Dallas, Texas.

In response to the requests in letters of reference there are enclosed two copies each of a report concerning Joe Rodriguez Molina dated August 20, 1964, at Dallas, Texas, and a memorandum of evaluation of same date relating to the sources concealed in the report. There are also enclosed two copies of a memorandum captioned "American GI Forum" dated August 25, 1964.

With specific reference to question number one in your July 7, 1964, letter, we have been advised by the Department of Justice that a review of the files of that Department has disclosed no information concerning Joe Rodriguez Molina. In addition, we have been advised by Mr. Sidney B. Rawitz, Deputy Associate Commissioner for Security, Immigration and Naturalization Service, that a search of the records at the Central Office, Immigration and Naturalization Service, failed to disclose any information in the files of that agency identifiable with Joe Rodriguez Molina. We would further advise that Joe Rodriguez Molina was never the subject of an investigation by this Bureau prior to November 22, 1963, and that at no time has this Bureau furnished any information to the Dallas Police Department concerning any alleged subversive activities by Molina.

Commission Exhibit No. 2186

The enclosed material and the information set forth herein conclude our inquiry into the matters outlined in your letters of reference.

Upon detachment from the classified enclosures, this letter may be regarded as unclassified.

Sincerely yours,

J. Edgar Hoover

Enclosures (6)

COMMISSION EXHIBIT No. 2186—Continued

CITY OF DALLAS
TEXAS
POLICE DEPARTMENT

August 25, 1964
A-2

Mr. J. Lee Rankin
General Counsel
President's Commission on the
Assassination of President Kennedy
200 Maryland Avenue, N.E.
Washington, D. C. 20002

Dear Mr. Rankin:

I am enclosing my affadavit to answer specifically the question which arose with reference to my testimony on page 175 of my deposition.

With reference to the second letter, I am enclosing a copy of the jail card on Lee Harvey Oswald, indicating the times and dates of visitors and telephone calls which he made. I am also enclosing copies of all of the telephone sheets kept on prisoner's phone calls for the dates of November 22, 23 and 24, 1963. You will note one entry on these sheets involving Lee Harvey Oswald. I am also enclosing affadavits from all of the jail personnel involved in handling this prisoner in these matters.

Referring to the Visitor's Permits on page 393 of the Police Report, I refer you to the affadavit of Officer J. R. Stacy; also, to the reports of Detectives Rose, Stovall and Adamcik on page 170 of the Police Report and Detective M. G. Hall on page 207 of the Police Report. It is apparent that Mrs. Marina Oswald and her mother-in-law both visited Lee Harvey Oswald on the one visitor's card.

The arrest sheet on page 70 of the Police Report was made at the time the prisoner was booked and indicates the time of the arrest - in this case 1:40 p.m. on November 22, 1963. But, the time indicated on this arrest sheet is not necessarily the time the prisoner is placed in jail. In this instance, Lee Harvey Oswald was booked but was retained in the custody of the Homicide Bureau for questioning. The enclosed copy of the jail card indicates that he was actually placed in the custody of the jail officers at 12:23 a.m., November 23, 1963. This time should not be confused with the times of three telephone calls which he made from the jail and which are noted on the bottom of the jail card. The jail card is made on the fourth floor of the jail at the time the prisoner is searched and assigned a cell. The card then goes with the prisoner to the fifth floor and is filed in alphabetical order. This is so that the jail crew on the fifth floor has a record of the prisoners in their custody. In

COMMISSION EXHIBIT No. 2187

Mr. J. Lee Rankin
August 25, 1964
Page 2

the left-hand margin of the jail card, you will note two entries preceded by the letter "V". This indicates a visitor and may be checked against the visitor's cards.

I hope this material will be of help in clarifying questions the commission may have in connection with phone calls and visitors of Lee Harvey Oswald.

Yours very truly,

J. E. Curry
J. E. CURRY
Chief of Police

JEC:cp

COMMISSION EXHIBIT No. 2187—Continued

CELL No.			
First Name	Middle Name	Last Name	
LEE	HARVEY	OSWALD	
Address 1026 No BECKLEY			
Age 24	Race W	Sex M	
E-2	Charge INV. MURDER		
Remarks V 11-23 · 1 1/2 pm V 11-23 · 3 2/3	Charge Changed to		
	Released by [crossed out]		
	TRAN TO CO 11-24/1120am		

TELEPHONE RECORD

TIME: 12 23 A CONTACT ____ YES ____ NO ✓

DATE: 11-23-63 INITIAL GRH

11-23-63 1 40PM Jes Ewing (5th Fl J)

Form No. CPS-272

11-23-63 4 2/3 pm 11-23-63 8PM

COMMISSION EXHIBIT No. 2187—Continued

Platoon 3Rd. PRISONERS TELEPHONE CONTACT FORM Date 11-22-63

Prisoner's Name	Cell	Contact Yes	Contact No	Officer's Name
James Reed	B-13	✓		Haliegman
Teddy Watson	A-4	✓		Reed
Chas. H. Elkes	A-8	✓		Haliegman
Jack Allard	A-6	✓		GRH
Lewis Johnson	B-5	✓		GRH
Curlee Jones	B-2	✓		GRH
James Hunter	B-2	✓		GRH
Antonio Garcia	A-3	✓		GRH
James Allbrook	A-7	✓		GRH
T. W. Rogers	A-5	✓		GRH
Walter Goodman	A-13	✓		GRH
Paul Harris	A-13	✓		GRH
Leroy Ervins	E-4	✓		[illegible]
Edward G. Robinson	E-6	✓		Robinson
Lee H. Oswald	F2	✓		Bellingfield

Form No. 1588 (Revised)
Memorandum Report
(7-1-60)

UNITED STATES SECRET SERVICE
TREASURY DEPARTMENT

ORIGIN Field	OFFICE Dallas, Texas	FILE NO. CO-2-34,030
TYPE OF CASE Assassination of President Kennedy	STATUS Continued	TITLE OR CAPTION Elm Street
INVESTIGATION MADE AT Dallas, Texas	PERIOD COVERED 7-8/9-64	
INVESTIGATION MADE BY SA John Joe Howlett		

DETAILS

SYNOPSIS

History of Elm Street and the formation of the Triple Underpass.

DETAILS OF INVESTIGATION

Investigation was requested by Inspector Kelley on July 8, 1964.

Other Investigations

Investigation revealed that there is no single document that can certify the name of the curved street in front of the Texas Schoolbook Depository Building to be Elm Street. Therefore, five documents are included, four of which are certified copies, that show the history and formation of the Triple Underpass and the three streets leading to it from Houston Street, Dallas.

A certified copy of the map of Dallas, as filed with the Clerk of the Dallas County Court in April 1855, is attached. This map shows the streets of Dallas as they were originally laid out. It will be noticed that there were two streets west of Houston, being Broadway and Water Streets. These streets were later closed when the triple underpass was built.

Certified copies of the resolutions adopted June 6, 1934 and June 13, 1934 by the Dallas City Council, setting forth the need for purchase of land to extend Elm Street, Main Street, and Commerce Street, are included. These two resolutions are only part of the resolutions and pertain to the north half of the block bounded by Elm Street to the north, Houston Street to the east, Main Street to the south, and Broadway Street to the west, known as City Block, figure 2 over 11. The other resolutions pertaining to the south half of block, figure 2, over 11, block 1, over 12, block 11, over 3, and block 10, over 4, are similar in wording.

ION	COPIES	REPORT MADE BY	DATE
Chief	Orig & 2 cc	SPECIAL AGENT	7-9-64
Dallas	2 cc	APPROVED Forrest V. Sorrels SPECIAL AGENT IN CHARGE	DATE 7-9-64

U. S. SECRET SERVICE

(CONTINUE ON PLAIN PAPER) U. S. GOVERNMENT PRINTING OFFICE 16—61500-1

COMMISSION EXHIBIT No. 2188

2.
CO-2-34,030

A copy of the City of Dallas plat book page showing blocks 1 to 13 is included. This page shows original blocks dotted in and the present condition drawn. This drawing also shows Broadway and Water Streets being closed in vicinity of the Triple Underpass.

No document could be found giving an official name to the curved streets just west of Houston Street between Elm Street and Commerce Street. Other than the above resolutions which say that Elm Street, Main Street, and Commerce Street, were to be extended to and under a triple underpass known as the Commerce-Main-Elm-Street Underpass.

A letter is included with the original of this report from Mr. Harold G. Shank, City Secretary of the City of Dallas, certifying that there has not been a name change for the street known as Elm Street, in Dallas.

DISPOSITION

This phase of the investigation is considered closed.

ATTACHMENTS

Map of the town of Dallas, April 1855 (Certified copy)
Certified copy of Resolution adopted by Dallas City Council June 6, 1934
Certified copy of Resolution adopted by Dallas City Council June 13, 1934
Copy of City of Dallas plat book, page showing blocks 1 to 13
Certification letter from Mr. Harold G. Shank, City Secretary of the City of Dallas, Texas

JJH:vd

COMMISSION EXHIBIT No. 2188—Continued

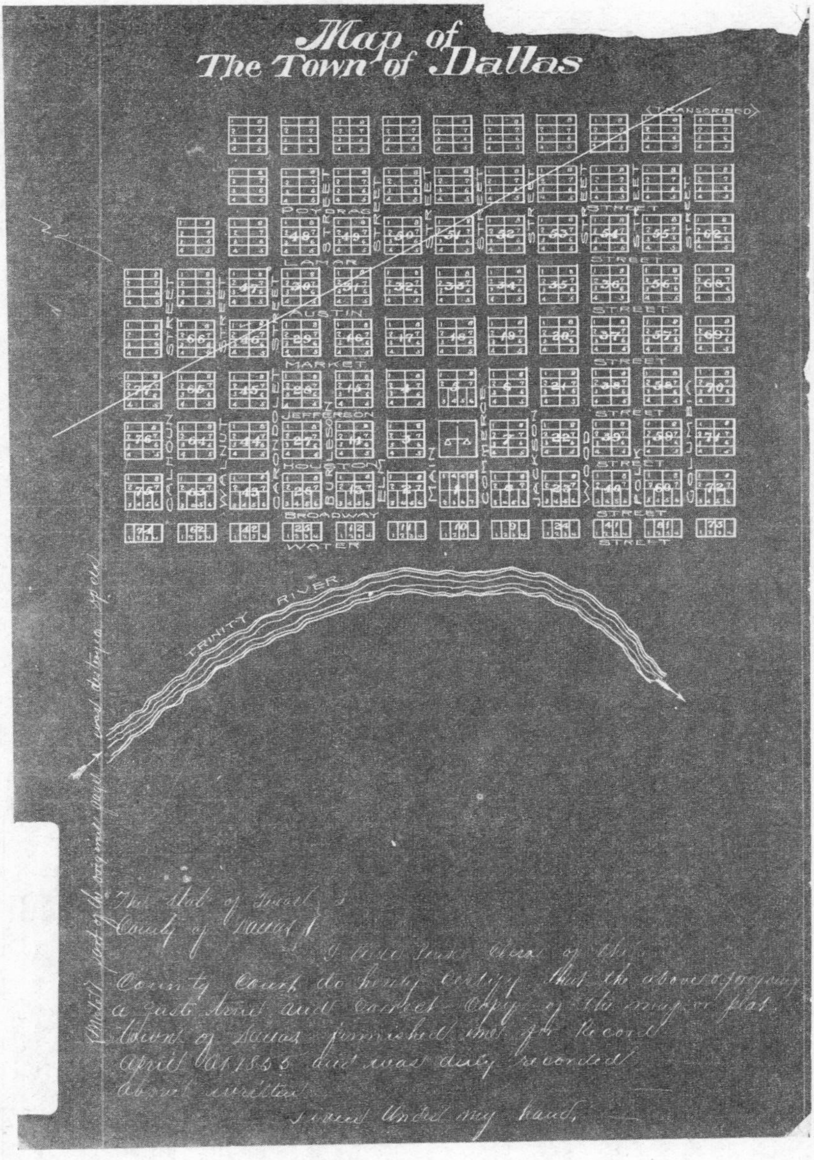

COMMISSION EXHIBIT No. 2188-A

THE STATE OF TEXAS } I, TOM E. ELLIS, County Clerk in and for said
COUNTY OF DALLAS, } County and state, do hereby certify that the
above and foregoing is a true and correct copy of Map of the Town of Dallas

as the same appears on file and/or of record in my office in Vol. D
Page 698 of Map Records of Dallas County, Texas.
WITNESS my hand and seal of office Dallas, Texas, this 9th
day of July 19 64.
TOM E. ELLIS, County Clerk Dallas County, Texas
By Dana Courier Deputy

COMMISSION EXHIBIT No. 2188-A—Continued

A RESOLUTION DETERMINING THE NECESSITY FOR THE ACQUISITION OF THE PROPERTY DESCRIBED HEREIN, WHICH APPROPRIATION IS MADE NECESSARY FOR A PUBLIC IMPROVEMENT IN THE CITY OF DALLAS, KNOWN AS THE TRIPLE UNDERPASS, COMMERCE, MAIN AND ELM STREETS, AND AUTHORIZING THE DIRECTOR OF PUBLIC WORKS, OR ANY OTHER PERSON, TO MAKE AN OFFER OF THE SUM OF MONEY STATED HEREIN, REPRESENTING THE AMOUNT OF DAMAGES LEGALLY ALLOWABLE AT LAW BECAUSE OF SAID APPROPRIATION.

WHEREAS, the governing body has heretofore determined and does at this time determine that the appropriation of the hereinafter described property belonging to the hereinafter named property owner is necessary to carry out a public improvement known as the triple underpass, at Commerce, Main and Elm Streets, and the appropriation of said property is required for the public purpose of creating a thoroughfare in the prolongation of Commerce, Main and Elm Streets, under the tracks of the Union Terminal Railway Company; and,

WHEREAS, it becomes necessary in the acquisition of said property, or as a prerequisite to condemnation, to make a bona fide offer of a sum of money representing, in the opinion of the governing body, the sum of money legally allowable to said property owner growing out of the appropriation of said property; Now, Therefore,

BE IT RESOLVED BY THE CITY COUNCIL OF THE CITY OF DALLAS:

Section 1. That it is hereby determined to be necessary to acquire and appropriate under the exercise of the right of eminent domain the hereinafter described property to be devoted to a public improvement in the City of Dallas known as the Commerce, Main and Elm Streets Underpass in the prolongation of said streets under the tracks of the Union Terminal Railway Company, and others, said property, when acquired, to be used for highway, streets and parkway appurtenant to and incident to highway and street purposes, said property being described as follows:

Being all that lot, tract or parcel of land, being situated in the City and County of Dallas, Texas, and being the north one-half of Lots 1 and 2, Block 2/11, official City numbers; and,

Beginning at the intersection of the south line of Elm Street with the west line of Houston Street;

Thence westerly with the south line of Elm Street a distance of 100 feet;

Thence southerly 100 feet from and parallel with the west line of Houston Street a distance of 50 feet;

Thence easterly 50 feet from and parallel with the south line of Elm Street a distance of 100 feet to the west line of Houston Street;

Thence northerly with the said west line of Houston Street a distance of 50 feet to the place of Beginning.

Section 2. That said property is now owned by A. T. Walraven, and if it should be found that any other persons own or claim any interest therein, either by leasehold or otherwise, then this determination as to appropriation and the acts authorized to be performed herein shall apply as well to said interest owners whether named herein or not.

Section 3. That the Director of Public Works, his assistants, or John M. Young, is hereby authorized to transmit to said property owner the offer to pay the sum of money mentioned herein, which said sum represents in the opinion of the Council the compensation legally allowable at law, growing out of and accruing to said property owner by reason of the appropriation of said property above described.

Section 4. That the sum of money authorized herein to be paid to or offered said property owner is $15,000.00.

Section 5. The said Director of Public Works, his assistants, or John M. Young, is hereby required to report back to the governing body of the City of Dallas what action, if any, was taken by the property owner, that is to say, whether said offer was accepted or rejected.

Section 6. The sums of money authorized herein shall be paid out of Overhead Crossing & Underpass Fund No. 176.

Section 7. This resolution shall take effect from and after its passage as in the charter in such cases made and provided.

It was moved and seconded that resolution be adopted.

ROLL CALL ON MOTION:
Aye - Burroughs, Hexter, Moore, Morrell, Painter - 5
Nay - Camp, Webb, Thompson - - 3
Absent - Turner - - 1.
Carried - - - - Resolution adopted.

COMMISSION EXHIBIT No. 2188-B

STATE OF TEXAS
COUNTY OF DALLAS
CITY OF DALLAS

I, Harold G. Shank, City Secretary of the City of Dallas, Texas do hereby certify that the above and foregoing is a true and correct copy of Resolution (~~passed~~-adopted) by the City Council of the City of Dallas, Texas June 6, 1934

WITNESS MY HAND AND THE SEAL OF THE CITY OF DALLAS, TEXAS, This the 9 day of July A.D. 1964

Harold G Shank
City Secretary of the
City of Dallas, Texas

COMMISSION EXHIBIT No. 2188-B—Continued

A RESOLUTION DETERMINING UPON THE NECESSITY FOR THE CONDEMNATION OF LAND NECESSARY FOR THE COMMERCE, MAIN AND ELM STREETS UNDERPASS IN THE CITY OF DALLAS, AND AUTHORIZING THE INSTITUTION OF NECESSARY CONDEMNATION PROCEEDINGS.

WHEREAS, for the purpose of constructing and extending public thoroughfares in the City of Dallas, to-wit, Commerce, Main and Elm Streets, and to provide adequate outlets for traffic in the area adjacent to the present dead end existing on said streets where the Union Terminal Railway tracks are maintained, it is deemed necessary that the City of Dallas acquire the hereinafter described property belonging to the hereinafter named owners and to exercise the right of eminent domain appropriating and acquiring said property for the purposes herein stated; and,

WHEREAS, the Union Terminal Company, a corporation, is the owner of the hereinafter described property, and it appears after persistent and bona fide efforts on the part of the agents and representatives of the City of Dallas that said named persons cannot agree with the City of Dallas and have been unable to agree with the City of Dallas upon the amount to be paid as compensation or damages for the said land being sought for the purposes herein mentioned; Now, Therefore,

BE IT RESOLVED BY THE CITY COUNCIL OF THE CITY OF DALLAS:

Section 1. That a necessity exists for the appropriation by the City of Dallas, under its power of eminent domain, to acquire and appropriate the hereinafter described property belonging to the hereinafter named owners for the purpose of extending Commerce, Main and Elm Streets and the construction of a triple underpass under the tracks of the Union Terminal Company in the prolongation of said Commerce, Main and Elm Streets so as to furnish adequate access to the area known as the lower down town section of the City of Dallas, and it is hereby determined by the City of Dallas to take said property under and by virtue of the power of eminent domain.

Section 2. That the purpose for which said property shall be taken is for the construction of a triple underpass known as the Commerce-Main-Elm-Street underpass at and under the tracks of the Union Terminal Company so as to provide necessary and needed public thoroughfares in the City of Dallas, and more particularly to provide adequate outlets for traffic in the down town section of the City of Dallas.

Section 3. That said property necessary for the purposes herein stated and to be acquired by eminent domain is owned by the Union Terminal Company, a corporation, and said property of said Union Terminal Company desired to be acquired under the right of eminent domain is described as follows:

Situated in the City and County of Dallas, State of Texas, being Lots 3 and 4 and south one-half of lots 1 and 2, Block 2/11, official city numbers;
BEGINNING at the intersection of the south line of Elm Street with the east line of Broadway Street;
THENCE southerly with the east line of Broadway Street a distance of 100 feet;
THENCE easterly 100 feet from and parallel with the south line of Elm Street a distance of 200 feet to the west line of Houston Street;
THENCE northerly with the west line of Houston Street a distance of 50 feet;
THENCE westerly 50 feet from and parallel with the south line of Elm Street a distance of 100 feet;
THENCE northerly 100 feet from and parallel with the west line of Houston Street a distance of 50 feet to the south line of Elm Street;
THENCE westerly with the south line of Elm Street a distance of 100 feet to the place of beginning.

Section 4. That the City Attorney's Department is hereby instructed to cause a statement to be made in writing describing said property and giving the names of the owners thereof and their residence, if known, and the purpose for which said property is to be taken under the right of eminent domain, and to file such statement with the Judge of the County Court of Dallas County, at Law, No. 2, or the judge of any court having jurisdiction by law to act in condemnation proceedings, and the commissioners shall thereupon be appointed as provided by the general laws in such matters for the purpose of condemning said land for the right of way herein declared to be necessary for the purpose above stated, and the City Attorney's Department is authorized to add the names of such other persons claiming interest in said land as may be necessary for the purpose of acquiring said right of way and placing title in the City of Dallas for the purpose herein stated.

Section 5. It is hereby determined that the City of Dallas has been unable to agree with said property owners as to the amount of compensation legally allowable at law and that the offers heretofore made and authorized by the governing body have been rejected and denied, and, therefore, the City of Dallas is forced to exercise the right of eminent domain in order to carry out a public improvement, to-wit, Commerce, Main and Elm Streets Underpass.

Section 6. That this resolution shall take effect from and after its passage as in the Charter in such cases is made and provided.

It was moved and seconded that resolution be adopted.

ROLL CALL ON MOTION:
Aye - Burroughs, Camp, Hexter, Moore, Norrell, Painter, Turner - 7
Nay - - 0
Carr ied - - - - Resolution adopted.

COMMISSION EXHIBIT No. 2188-C

STATE OF TEXAS
COUNTY OF DALLAS
CITY OF DALLAS

I, Harold G. Shank, City Secretary of the City of Dallas, Texas do hereby certify that the above and foregoing is a true and correct copy of Resolution (~~passed~~-adopted) by the City Council of the City of Dallas, Texas June 13 1934

WITNESS MY HAND AND THE SEAL OF THE CITY OF DALLAS, TEXAS, This the 9 day of July A.D. 1964.

Harold G. Shank
City Secretary of the
City of Dallas, Texas

COMMISSION EXHIBIT No. 2188-C—Continued

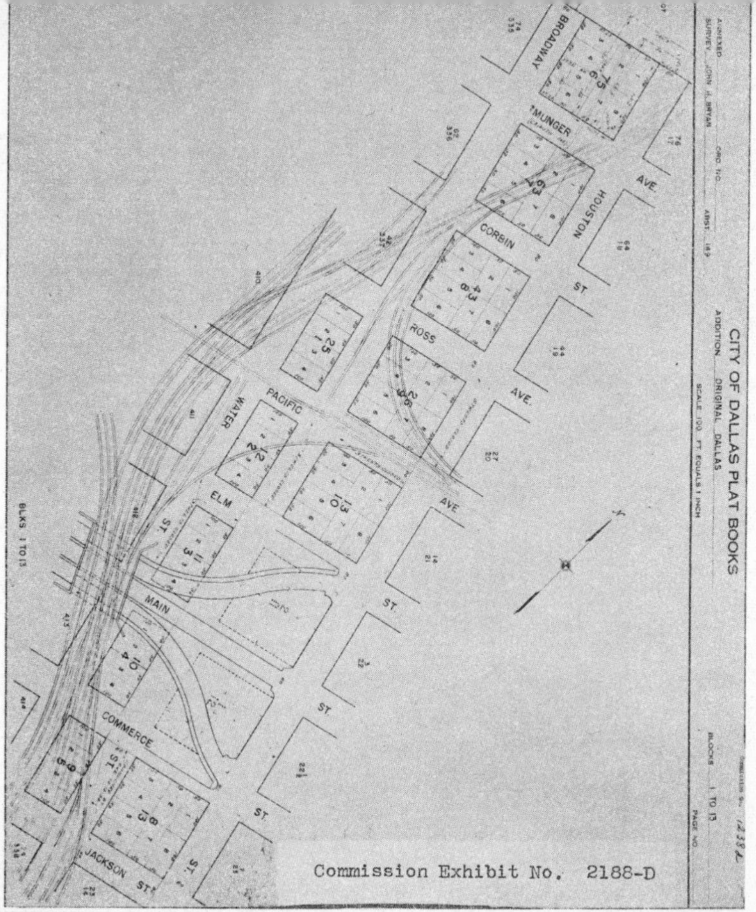

COMMISSION EXHIBIT No. 2188-D

CITY OF DALLAS
TEXAS
HAROLD G. SHANK
CITY SECRETARY

STATE OF TEXAS:
COUNTY OF DALLAS:
CITY OF DALLAS:

I, Harold G. Shank, City Secretary of the City of Dallas, Texas, do hereby certify that a search of this office reveals no change in street name of the street named Elm Street, in the City of Dallas, Texas.

WITNESS MY HAND AND THE SEAL OF THE CITY OF DALLAS, TEXAS, This the 9th day of July A.D. 1964.

Harold G. Shank
Harold G. Shank
City Secretary of the
City of Dallas, Texas

COMMISSION EXHIBIT No. 2188-E

Form No. 1588 (Revised)
Memorandum Report
(7-1-60)

UNITED STATES SECRET SERVICE
TREASURY DEPARTMENT

ORIGIN Field	OFFICE Dallas	FILE NO. CO-2-34,030
TYPE OF CASE: Protective Research	STATUS: Continued	TITLE OR CAPTION: Assassination of President Kennedy, Dallas, Texas [redacted]
INVESTIGATION MADE AT: Dallas & Fort Worth, Texas	PERIOD COVERED: November 26 - December 11, 1963	— Commission Exhibit No. 2189
INVESTIGATION MADE BY: Special Agents Charles Kunkel, Maurice Miller, William N. Carter & Arthur W. Blake		

DETAILS

SYNOPSIS

During the above-indicated period, inquiries were made in Dallas and Fort Worth, Texas, to establish a chronology of residences and places of employment for Lee Harvey Oswald from the time he returned to Fort Worth from the Soviet Union until November 22, 1963.

DETAILS OF INVESTIGATION

This report will be divided into two sections, the first section covering residences of Oswald and the second section covering employments. These inquiries were made between November 26 and December 11, 1963.

Residences

June 10, 1962 to August 8, 1962

Robert L. Oswald, brother of the subject, furnished the information that it was June 10, 1962, to the best of his memory, that he drove to Love Field, Dallas, Texas, to meet Mr. and Mrs. Lee Harvey Oswald and their daughter on their arrival by plane from New York City. Several days prior to that time, Robert Oswald had been contacted by some welfare agency in New York City, and had been advised that Lee Oswald and family were in New York City, having just arrived from overseas, and were in need of funds to continue their journey to Fort Worth. Robert Oswald stated that he immediately sent $200 to his brother, Lee Oswald, in care of a New York City welfare agency for use as plane fare for the Lee Oswald family to travel to Fort Worth.

On the arrival of the Lee Oswald family in Dallas, Robert Oswald took them to his home at 7313 Davenport Street, Fort Worth, Texas, where the Lee Oswald family lived for about two months. Lee Oswald was not employed during this

DISTRIBUTION	COPIES	REPORT MADE BY	DATE
Chief	Orig. & 2	Arthur W. Blake (signature), SPECIAL AGENT	12-12-63
Dallas	2	APPROVED: (signature), SPECIAL AGENT IN CHARGE	12-12-63
-1-		641	

(CONTINUE ON PLAIN PAPER) U. S. GOVERNMENT PRINTING OFFICE 16—61806-1

CO-2-34,030
Page 2

time, and Robert Oswald furnished shelter and food for the subject and his family. This information was furnished by Robert L. Oswald during a personal interview on November 27, 1963.

August 8, 1962 (Approximately) to August 17, 1962

When the Lee Oswald family moved from the Robert Oswald home at 7313 Davenport Street, Fort Worth, Texas, they moved into an apartment at the Rotary Apartment Building, 1501 7th Street, Fort Worth, Texas, where Lee's mother, Mrs. Marguerite Oswald was living. There are some discrepancies in the information available as to the date that this move took place. Robert Oswald claims that Lee and family lived with him for about two months upon their return to Fort Worth from the Soviet Union, which would make the date of the move sometime in early August 1962. Marguerite Oswald, mother, stated when interviewed on November 27, 1963, that she thought the date of the move would have been early in July 1962, since her birthday is July 17 and it is her recollection that Lee was living with her on her birthday.

Mr. James Young, Trust Department-Rental Division, Fort Worth National Bank, Fort Worth, Texas, furnished the information that his records show that Marguerite Oswald first rented Apartment 110 at the Rotary Apartments on August 8, 1962, and that at some subsequent date she moved to Apartment 301 at the same address and lived there continuously until November 1, 1962. It would therefore appear that Lee Oswald could not have moved there before August 8, 1962. This apartment building is located on the southwest corner of Summit and W. 7th Street, Fort Worth, Texas, and on December 3, 1963, the present manager Mrs. Christine Yarbaro, 802 Summit, Fort Worth, was interviewed. She advised that she has acted as manager only since October 9, 1963, and has no records or knowledge concerning the dates that the Oswalds may have lived in the building.

Telephone Number ED 5-0755, found on a slip of paper in Oswald's possessions, was found to be listed to a pay station located in the lobby at 1501 W. 7th Street, Fort Worth.

On November 1, 1962, Marguerite Oswald filed a change of address card from 808 Summit, Apartment 301, to 3833 Westcliff Road, Fort Worth, Texas, and a copy of this change of address card was obtained and is attached. 808 Summit is around the corner from 1501 W. 7th Street, Fort Worth, and is another apartment in the same building. On August 17, 1962, Lee Harvey Oswald filed a change of address card from 7313 Davenport Street, Fort Worth, Texas, to 2703 Mercedes Avenue, Fort Worth, Texas. A copy of this change of address card was obtained and is attached.

August 17, 1962 to October 7, 1962

As noted above, Oswald filed a change of address to 2703 Mercedes Avenue, Fort Worth, Texas, on August 17, 1962. His mother Marguerite Oswald furnished the information that he made this move to be within walking distance of his employment which was at the Louv-R-Pak Division of Leslie Welding, Inc., 200 N. Vacek Street, Fort Worth, Texas.

641

The Mercedes Street address is a duplex located at the southwest corner of Carol and Mercedes Streets in Fort Worth, and the property is owned by Mr. C. A. Riggs of Orbit Industries, Fort Worth. Mr. Riggs was interviewed at his office and furnished the following information. These duplexes are furnished and rent for $59.50 per month. For these reasons he experiences a high rate of turnover and he does not maintain any record of the names of tenants. His records indicate only the income which he receives from each rental unit. Mr. Riggs is unable to determine the date, but he did recall that Lee Oswald had contacted him by telephone inquiring about the unit at 2703 Mercedes Street. A "For Rent" sign had been exhibited in front of the building giving Mr. Riggs' name and telephone number. Arrangements were made for Oswald to view the dwelling. Mr. Riggs met Lee and Marina Oswald who had a child and they rented the duplex known as 2703 Mercedes, paying $59.50 in cash for one month's rent. It is Mr. Riggs' recollection that he issued Lee Oswald a receipt, handwritten on the back of a blank check. Mr. Riggs never observed the Oswalds with an automobile but occasionally observed Lee walking back and forth to work at a welding company on Vacek Street in Fort Worth. Mr. Riggs stated he did not obtain an application and no contract was made at the time the duplex was rented and he is unable to furnish any other background information except that he understood from one of the Oswalds, Lee or Marina, that they had purchased a television set from Montgomery-Ward Co. in September 1962. He believes Marina had a child while residing here and he collected rent in cash from her on one or two occasions. He seldom saw Lee Oswald at the house, but when he did, Lee was preoccupied in reading and Mr. Riggs does not recall that he ever spoke. Mr. Riggs also recalled the Postal Inspection Service making some inquiries regarding subversive literature while the Oswalds were occupants of 2703 Mercedes.

On October 12, 1962, Lee Oswald filed a change of address with the Post Office from 2703 Mercedes to Box 2915, Dallas, Texas.

<u>Credit Bureau, Fort Worth, Texas</u>. Mrs. Grace Scruggs, Assistant Manager, Retail Merchants Credit Association, Fort Worth, Texas, was interviewed December 3, 1963, and she advised that the FBI contacted her office on February 27, 1961, February 7, 1963, and November 23, 1963, regarding Lee Harvey Oswald. This is the only record concerning Oswald which she has been able to find in her office. She was Questioned regarding the television set Mr. Riggs claimed was purchased by the Oswalds at Montgomery-Ward Co. She stated Mr. E. L. Carter, Credit Manager of Montgomery-Ward Co., had called on her since the assassination of the President to inquire about Oswald's credit. During this conversation he stated his office had been unable to locate a credit file on Lee Oswald.

On December 4, 1963, Mr. Carter was contacted by telephone and he advised he has now located an application for credit and had furnished the information to the FBI. The application shows that on September 22, 1962, Lee Oswald, residing at 2703 Mercedes, Fort Worth, Texas, applied for credit in connection with the purchase of a television set. He listed employment as Leslie Welding Company, White Settlement Road,

641

COMMISSION EXHIBIT No. 2189—Continued

Fort Worth, and claimed to have been employed as a welder there under Supervisor Tom Yates at $250 per month for a period of four months. He listed prior employment as U. S. Marine Corps, El Tore, California, and said he had been so occupied for a period of four years. He listed his wife's name as Marina, stated he had no previous charge account at Montgomery-Ward Company and no credit or personal references. His brother Robert Oswald co-signed the application. The application shows that on an unknown date Oswald's address was changed to P. O. Box 2915, Dallas, and in October 1962, the account was closed and a refund voucher issued. Mr. Carter stated this indicates the television set was returned to Montgomery-Ward Company but the files reflecting this information have not yet been located.

Records at the Southwestern Bell Telephone Company, Fort Worth, disclosed that there is no record that Lee or Marina Oswald ever had telephone service in Fort Worth, Texas.

<u>October 7, 1962 to October 19, 1962</u>

As noted above, Lee Oswald filed a change of address on October 12, 1962, from 2703 Mercedes Street, Fort Worth, Texas, to P. O. Box 2915, Dallas, Texas.

Mrs. Marina Oswald had furnished the information that Lee Oswald had stayed at the YMCA in Dallas during this period. Mr. Russell Urquhart, Executive Secretary, YMCA, 605 N. Ervay Street, Dallas, was interviewed and he advised that he was not able to furnish the exact dates of Oswald's residence there, since the FBI had taken all of his records that would show this information. He did verify that Oswald had stayed there sometime during October 1962, and his recollection was that the dates were October 15 through 19, 1962.

Inquiry with the FBI, Dallas, disclosed that records in their possession show that Oswald was registered at the Ervay Street YMCA from October 15 through 19, 1962.

Oswald's last two paychecks from the Leslie Welding Company, Fort Worth, are dated October 6 and October 13, 1963, and were mailed to him in care of Post Office Box 2915, Dallas. Under Oswald's endorsement on the back of these two checks, appears the address 3519 Fairmount Street. These checks bear bank stamp dates October 16 and October 22, 1962, respectively, and they were cashed at the Mercantile National Bank of Dallas.

On December 1, 1963, inquiry was made at 3519 Fairmount Street, Dallas, and a Mrs. Gates, the present manager, was interviewed. She advised that she had just recently assumed the manager's position and she had no knowledge of the tenants residing there prior to the time she became manager. She furnished the name of Mrs. Elizabeth Randal, 3211 Beverly Drive, Dallas, who had been the building manager in October 1962. Mrs. Randal was then interviewed and she stated that Oswald's name was not familiar to her, and that if he had stayed in the building, he apparently stayed in an apartment with some other

641

COMMISSION EXHIBIT No. 2189—Continued

registered tenant. Mrs. Randal telephoned the owner of the apartment building, Mrs. Edith Burdick, 3929 Normandy Road, Dallas, and Mrs. Burdick advised that she had never heard the name Lee Harvey Oswald as a tenant, and her records did not show his name as having occupied an apartment at 3519 Fairmount Street.

On December 10, 1963, Mrs. Burdick was interviewed at her home, 3929 Normandy Road, Dallas, and her records were examined. These records showed that a Gary Taylor occupied Apartment 18 and later Apartment 12, at the Fairmount Street address, and he was living there during October 1962. Mrs. Burdick's records indicated that Gary Taylor and a Mr. O. A. Hess had both occupied Apartment 12 during October 1962. Therefore, Mr. Hess was located and interviewed at his present address, 2129 Tucker Street, Apartment A, Dallas, and he advised that he and his wife had occupied Apartment 12 at 3519 Fairmount Street from sometime in June 1962 until October 1, 1962, at which time they moved to their present residence. Mr. Hess continued that he did not know Gary Taylor, that he had never heard his name before, but he did state that he knew someone else was moving into Apartment 12 as soon as he moved out.

It was determined that Gary Edward Taylor is presently living at 4115 Falls Drive, in the Oak Cliff Section of Dallas. Taylor is described as a white, male, 6'2", 195 lbs., brown hair, hazel eyes, medium complexion, and he was born December 24, 1939, at Wichita, Kansas. Taylor's name and the Fairmount Street address were found listed in a book among Oswald's possessions.

Taylor was interviewed at his home on the evening of December 10, 1963, by Special Agents Blake and Miller and at that time he furnished the following information: He was married to a daughter of George deMohrenschildt, and late in September or early October 1962, the de Mohrenschildts attended a concert of Van Cliburn in Fort Worth. The deMohrenschildts invited Taylor and his wife to meet them at the Oswald home on Mercedes Street in Fort Worth after the concert. That was the first time Taylor had met the Oswalds. During the conversations, Lee Oswald mentioned that he was moving to Dallas and it was suggested by the deMohrenschildts that Marina Oswald and her child could stay with the Taylors until the Oswalds found an apartment, and the Taylors agreed. Mr. Taylor advised that it was probably that same evening that he drove the Oswalds to Dallas. Lee Oswald was left at the YMCA on Ervay Street, and Marina Oswald and her child stayed at the Taylor home for about two weeks, at which time she went to the home of Mrs. Elena Hall in Fort Worth. Sometime later, and Mr. Taylor was not certain of the date, he drove Lee Oswald to Mrs. Hall's home in Fort Worth and picked up Marina Oswald, her child, and their belongings and moved them to an apartment near Zangs Boulevard and Davis Street in Dallas. This is the apartment at 604 Elsbeth Street.

It is Taylor's recollection that during the time Marina Oswald lived at the Hall residence in Fort Worth, Lee Oswald continued to live at the YMCA on Ervay Street in Dallas, and that he lived there until the time they moved to the apartment on Elsbeth Street.

641

Taylor stated that he saw the Oswalds on several occasions after they moved to Dallas, and the last time was in late Spring or early Summer, 1963, when he stopped in at their apartment and talked briefly with Marina. Lee was not at home.

Taylor also stated that during the time Marina Oswald lived at Mrs. Hall's residence in Fort Worth, he drove Lee Oswald over there to visit Marina on one occasion. He added that he had never driven Lee Oswald anywhere outside of Dallas on any other occasion than those mentioned. He also said that Oswald did not know how to drive an automobile. Taylor is presently employed at the Sellers Recording Studio, 2102 Jackson Street, Dallas. A signed statement was taken from Taylor on December 11, 1963.

Mrs. Elena Hall, 4760 Trail Lake Drive (Telephone WA 6-3741), Fort Worth, Texas, was interviewed by Special Agent Miller. Mrs. Hall stated that she had met the Oswalds through a mutual friend, George Bouhe, a retired accountant. Both Bouhe and Mrs. Hall speak Russian.

Mrs. Hall continued that Mrs. Oswald moved in with her sometime between October 1 and October 15, 1963. Shortly thereafter, Mrs. Hall was involved in an automobile accident and was hospitalized for a period of time. On October 31, 1962, Mrs. Hall left for a trip to New York State, and Mrs. Oswald was staying at the Hall home at that time. When Mrs. Hall returned from her trip, about November 15, 1963, she found that Mrs. Oswald had moved out, and she subsequently learned that the Oswalds were living in an apartment at 604 Elsbeth Street, Dallas.

A signed statement was taken from Mrs. Hall by Special Agent Miller on December 3, 1963.

Mrs. Hall and her husband John R. Hall now operate the Crown and Bridge Prosthesis, 1313 E. Seminary Drive, Fort Worth, Texas.

Mrs. Marina Oswald was interviewed on December 11, 1963, by SA Gopadze and she was specifically asked about her residence at the Taylor apartment at 3519 Fairmount Street, Dallas. She recalled that she had lived with the Taylors at that address for a short period of time, probably less than a week, in October 1962. Mrs. Oswald stated that it was also her recollection that during the period from the time they left Mercedes Street, Fort Worth, until they moved into 604 Elsbeth Street, Dallas, her husband was staying at the YMCA in Dallas.

<u>November 2, 1962 to March 2, 1963</u>

604 Elsbeth Street, Apartment 2, Dallas, Texas. On December 1, 1963, Special Agent Blake and Carter interviewed the managers of this building, Mr. and Mrs. Mahlon F. Tobias, Sr., at 602 Elsbeth Street, Apartment 7, Dallas, and they furnished the following information:

641

On November 3, 1962, Lee Oswald paid a $5 deposit on Apartment 2, but he did not return to occupy the apartment until about a week later. Several days after they moved in, Lee received a telephone call from a man named George, later identified as George Bouhe, and he carried on the entire conversation in a foreign language.

Oswald paid his rent promptly each month and he always paid in cash. The apartment rented for $68 per month. Mrs. Tobias stated that Oswald's Russian wife frequently visited her apartment during the day when Oswald was away at work, that she appeared to be lonely but did not have much to say.

Mrs. Oswald told Mrs. Tobias that her husband did not want her to tell people that they spoke Russian, because if anyone found out, some men would be around to see them. The Tobias received several complaints from other tenants that Oswald was beating his wife, and that they were very noisy. Mrs. Tobias described Oswald as odd, stating that he never spoke to any of the other tenants, and would not even return a greeting. The Oswalds did not have a telephone in the apartment, and they used the telephone in the Tobias apartment for all their calls. They did not make any long distance calls from the Tobias telephone.

Mrs. Tobias recalled only a few visitors having been at the Oswald apartment. On one occasion a woman described as white, 35 years, 5'3", 140 lbs., dark brown hair, olive complexion, came to the building and told Mrs. Tobias that the Oswalds had called her because they did not have any money for the baby. This woman stated that she was Russian and that she worked in downtown Dallas. She was later identified as Lydia Dymitruk who now lives at 3542½ Kent Street, Fort Worth, Texas.

About a month after the Oswalds moved in, Mrs. Tobias noticed an automobile in the driveway and it appeared that someone was moving out, so Mrs. Tobias went outside to determine who was moving. She described the automobile as a cream-colored convertible, of a late model. The man who was loading this automobile was described as white, 6' tall, 180 to 190 lbs., 45 years or older, brown hair, and neatly dressed in a brown suit. This man told Mrs. Tobias that Mrs. Oswald was moving out, and Mrs. Tobias noticed that a baby bed and some baby clothes were already loaded in the car. This man was later identified by Mrs. Oswald as George de Mohrenschildt. Mrs. Oswald also stated that she was moving out at that time since she had argued with her husband, and she moved in with a friend, Mrs. Anna Meller, 5930½ La Vista, Dallas, telephone TA 3-2219. After staying with Mrs. Meller for about a week, Mrs. Oswald moved back with her husband in the Elsbeth Street apartment.

It was Mrs. Tobias' recollection that the Oswalds had moved out of that apartment on Elsbeth Street sometime around the first few days of March 1963.

641

COMMISSION EXHIBIT No. 2189—Continued

March 2, 1963 to April 12, 1963

214 W. Neely Street, upstairs, Dallas. On March 2, 1963, Lee Oswald paid $60.00 for a month's rent on this apartment. It is not known exactly what date he moved in, but probably on that same date. Mr. M. W. George, 6769 Inverness Lane, Dallas, the owner of the property, was personally interviewed and he furnished for examination his rent receipts. Mr. George continued that Oswald had called him by telephone in response to a sign placed in front of the rental property. Mr. George met Oswald at the apartment at which time Oswald agreed to rent the apartment and paid $60.00 in cash. On April 3, 1963, Oswald paid another $60.00 cash for rent to Mr. George. This payment would have paid for the rental of the property through May 2, 1963. Mr. George recalled that several days after the rent was due on May 2, 1963, he went to the apartment to collect the rent, and found it vacated. He had no idea, therefore, when the Oswalds moved out, and had no other contact with them.

Mr. George furnished the information that a George B. Gray had lived in the downstairs apartment at 212 W. Neely Street, Dallas, during the entire time that the Oswalds lived upstairs. The Gray family has now moved and Mr. George does not know where they moved to.

It was determined that the photograph of Oswald found in his effects and showing him holding a rifle, was taken in the backyard at the Neely Street address. On November 29, 1963, accompanied by Captain Will Fritz and Detective B. G. Brown, Police Photographer, Dallas Police, SAIC Sorrels and SA Blake went to that address and took photographs of the backyard area.

April 12, 1963 to May 9, 1963

757 French Street, New Orleans, Louisiana. Oswald was fired from his job in Dallas, Texas, on April 6, 1963, and on April 12, 1963, he made a claim for unemployment benefits at the Texas Employment Commission, 2206 Main Street, Dallas 1, Texas. A copy of that claim has been obtained and is attached to this report. On April 29, 1963, Oswald made a claim for unemployment insurance through the Louisiana Employment Security Office, New Orleans. Therefore, he apparently moved from Dallas to New Orleans sometime between April 12 and April 29, 1963.

SA Vial, New Orleans, in his report dated December 3, 1963, furnished the information that during the first few days Oswald was in New Orleans, he lived with relatives at 757 French Street, New Orleans. Mrs. Charles Murrett, sister of Lee Oswald's mother, was interviewed at 757 French Street, New Orleans, on November 23, 1963, and she furnished the information that probably sometime in May 1963, Oswald came to stay at her home for a few days stating that he was in town looking for a job. Several days later Oswald advised that he had found a job and shortly thereafter, Mrs. Oswald and her child arrived in New Orleans with Mrs. Ruth Paine of Irving, Texas. The same day they arrived, Lee Oswald left the residence of Mrs. Murrett, stating that he had found an apartment for his family at 4907 Magazine Street, New Orleans. Mrs. Murrett stated that she had never seen any of the Oswald family since that day.

641

COMMISSION EXHIBIT No. 2189—Continued

May 9, 1963 to September 26, 1963

4907 Magazine Street, New Orleans, Louisiana. Mr. and Mrs. Jesse James Garner, 4911 Magazine Street, New Orleans, furnished the information that Oswald had rented the apartment from them on May 9, 1963, and that he had moved in either that date or the following date. His wife and child moved in with him within the next two days, having been brought to New Orleans by Mrs. Ruth Paine of Irving, Texas.

Records at the New Orleans Public Service Co., Inc., show that Oswald made application for gas and electric service at 4907 Magazine Street, May 9, 1963, and paid a $5 deposit. The records also show that this service was discontinued on October 7, 1963, when the caretaker of the building telephoned to notify that the apartment had been vacated. Copies of these records were obtained and are attached to this report.

Oswald last paid his rent on August 9 for the month ending September 9, 1963. During September 1963, Oswald advised Mrs. Garner that his wife was going to Texas to have her baby.

Mrs. Garner stated that on September 22, 1963, Mrs. Oswald and her child departed by station wagon with the same woman who had first brought them to New Orleans. It has been established that this was Mrs. Ruth Paine of Irving, Texas. Oswald was seen once in the neighborhood after his wife had left, and on September 24 or 25, 1963, Mr. Garner entered their apartment and found it vacated.

When Mrs. Ruth Paine drove Marina Oswald and her child back to Irving, Texas, Mrs. Oswald moved in with Mrs. Paine and continued to reside with her until the day of the assassination. During the time Oswald lived in New Orelans, he received mail at P. O. Box 30061.

September 26, 1963 to October 3, 1963

The newspaper Excelsior of Mexico City stated in a newspaper account dated November 24, 1963, that Lee Harvey Oswald had entered Mexico at Nuevo Laredo on September 26, 1963, and that he returned to the United States by the same route on October 3, 1963. Two newspaper accounts of this trip are attached to this report. This information has been verified by Customs Bureau.

October 3, 1963 to October 4, 1963

Information was received that Oswald had stayed at the YMCA, 605 N. Ervay Street, Dallas, on the night of October 3, 1963. This information was verified by Mr. Russell Urquhart, Executive Secretary of that YMCA on December 3, 1963.

October 4, 1963 to October 6, 1963

It is believed that Oswald spent this time with his wife and child at the home of Mrs. Ruth Paine, 2515 W. 5th Street, Irving, Texas. Mrs. Paine

has stated that she recalls Oswald being at her home for several days and stating that he had been in Houston, Texas, seeking employment and that he had returned to Dallas several days prior to his arrival at the Paine home.

October 7, 1963 to October 14, 1963

On this date, Oswald rented a room from Mrs. Mary Esther Bledsoe, at 621 N. Marsalis Street, Dallas (Telephone WH 2-1985), and paid $7 for a week's rent. He told Mrs. Bledsoe that he was married, that his wife lived in Irving, Texas. Oswald made several telephone calls as soon as he moved in. On the following day, Oswald was neatly dressed and he told Mrs. Bledsoe that he was looking for a job. He spent much of his time hanging around the house, and when Mrs. Bledsoe complained that he was disturbing her privacy, he promised not to disturb her again. On Friday of that week, October 11, 1963, Oswald stayed in the house all day. On Saturday, October 12, Oswald took a bag and prepared to leave, asking Mrs. Bledsoe to clean his room, and telling her that he would be back. At that time, she told him that she did not want to rent the room to him any longer. On Monday, October 14, 1963, Oswald returned and moved all of his belongings out of the room. Mrs. Bledsoe added that Oswald did not make any long distance telephone calls from her home during the time he lived there, and left nothing in the room which has since been rented to a woman. He did not receive any mail or visitors, and Mrs. Bledsoe does not think that he worked at all during that week.

On November 22, 1963, Mrs. Bledsoe had gone downtown in Dallas to see the President, and after the parade passed her location, she walked to Elm Street and boarded a bus near the Athletic Club to return home. Somewhere along the route, probably about Elm & Murphy Streets, Oswald got on the bus, and took a seat near the rear of the bus. After riding only a few blocks Oswald got off the bus and that is the last time that Mrs. Bledsoe saw him. She feels that he undoubtedly saw her and recognized her, and that is the reason he left the bus so soon after getting on. It is Mrs. Bledsoe's recollection that Oswald was wearing an old brown shirt, with holes in the elbows of the sleeves, and possibly with the shirttail hanging out.

October 14, 1963 to November 22, 1963

1026 N. Beckley, Dallas, Texas. On October 14, 1963, Oswald using the name O. H. Lee, rented a room for $8.00 a week from Mr. and Mrs. A. C. Johnson, owners of the property at that address. The Johnsons have room for 18 tenants at their home, but the room they rented to the man they knew as Lee was not usually rented out. They save that room for the use of their grandchildren when they come for a visit. The room is quite small, about 12 feet by 5 feet, and is located just off the dining room. Mrs. Johnson stated that they decided to rent the room to "Lee" since he had stopped a few days earlier and inquired about a room and was told there were no vacancies. When he came back the second time, Mrs. Johnson decided to give him the small room.

Several days later when a larger room was vacated, Mrs. Johnson told "Lee" that he could move, but he stated that he was satisfied with the small room and he remained there.

Mr. and Mrs. Johnson and their housekeeper, Mrs. Earlene Roberts, all described "Lee" as a very quiet person. He had no visitors, received no mail, and spent most of his free time, when not working, in his room. He usually made one or two telephone calls on returning from work each evening and always spoke a foreign language. Mrs. Roberts stated that "Lee" did not receive any telephone calls.

Mrs. Johnson and Mrs. Roberts both advised that "Lee" never spoke to any of the other tenants at this house, even though he might sit in the living room with them watching television.

During the time "Lee" lived there, he usually did not spend his week-ends there. On one occasion, probably the week-end of November 16 - 17, 1963, he did spend the week-end at 1026 N. Beckley, and it is Mrs. Johnson's recollection that he was away from the house only a few minutes at a time over the whole week-end. Mrs. Johnson also added that "Lee" did not use his room on the night of November 21, 1963, the night before the assassination.

Mrs. Roberts stated that in the early afternoon of November 22, 1963, she was sitting in the living room at her home watching television and the news about the attack on the President. At about 1:00 P.M. the man she knew as Lee came in the front door and appeared to be in a hurry. Mrs. Roberts made some remark to him but he did not reply. He went directly to his room and returned a moment later. He had put on dark-colored jacket and was zipping up the front of the jacket as he walked out the front door. Again, he did not speak to Mrs. Roberts. Several minutes later, Mrs. Roberts looked out the front window and saw "Lee" standing by the bus stop on Beckley Street, and she did not see him again.

About 30 minutes later three Dallas policemen came to the house looking for Lee Harvey Oswald. Since Mrs. Roberts did not know that was "Lee's" true name there was some discussion about the various tenants who might fit the description the police had.

After a few minutes, Oswald's picture was shown on television and at that time Mrs. Johnson and Mrs. Roberts informed the police officers that was the man they knew as O. H. Lee, and they directed the officers to "Lee's" room. While the Dallas Police Officers were searching the room, two FBI agents arrived and assisted in the search. These officers removed all of Oswald's belongings from the room and made a complete search.

A signed statement was taken from Mrs. Roberts covering her knowledge of the events of November 22, 1963, and that statement is attached to this report.

641

COMMISSION EXHIBIT No. 2189—Continued

November 21, 1963

Lee Harvey Oswald spent the night of November 21, 1963, at the home of Mrs. Ruth Paine, 2515 W. 5th Street, Irving, Texas, where Oswald's wife and children had been living. Oswald rode there after work at the depository with Buell Wesley Frazier, another employee at the depository, who also lives in Irving.

November 22, 1963

On the morning of November 22, 1963, Oswald rode from Irving to his job at the depository with Frazier. Oswald remained at the Texas School Book Depository, 411 Elm Street, Dallas, until a few minutes after the assassination, which took place at about 12:30 P.M. Oswald was taken into custody by Officers of the Dallas Police Department at the Texas Theatre, 231 W. Jefferson Street, Dallas, at about 2:00 P.M.

Oswald was in custody at the Dallas City Jail from that time until the morning of November 24, 1963, at which time he was shot to death in the basement of the Dallas Police Building.

Employment

It appears that Oswald was unemployed from the time of his return to Fort Worth about June 10, 1962, until July 17, 1962. During that time he was living with his brother Robert Oswald, who furnished support for Lee Oswald and family.

July 17, 1962 - October 8, 1962

Louv-R-Pak Division, Leslie Welding Company, Inc., 200 North Vacek Street, Fort Worth, Texas. On July 13, 1963, Oswald filled out an application for employment with this firm and he went to work as a sheet-metal worker on July 17, 1963. A copy of the application for employment was obtained and shows the following information: Age, 22; born October 18, 1939; Social Security Number 433-54-3937; residence, 1501 7th Street; 5'9", 150 lbs.; dependents, wife and one child, age 5 months; claimed 2½ years experience as a sheet metal worker; and service in the United States Marine Corps from 1956 to 1962, having been honorably discharged with no disability. He further stated on the application that he had attended the R. Glen West Grammar School in Fort Worth, Texas, and Jackson Senior High School, New Orleans, from 1953 to 1956. He listed as references Peter P. Gregory, Continental Life Building, occupation Consultant, oil engineering, and Robert Oswald, Acme Brick Company, Junior Executive.

Payroll information record shows the additional information that Oswald began work at this job on July 17, 1962, at the rate of $1.25 per hour, and he was classed as a sheet metal helper. A copy of his Form W-4, Employee's With-Holding Exemption Certificate, was obtained and is attached.

641

COMMISSION EXHIBIT No. 2189—Continued

A copy of the Termination of Employment Record was also obtained and is attached. This form shows that Oswald terminated on October 8, 1962, for the reason that he had accepted a better paying position, and that he would be eligible for rehire. Also obtained was a copy of a letter in Oswald's handwriting, undated and advising that he wished to terminate his employment. He requested that his check be forwarded to him to Box 2915, Dallas, Texas.

Through the Internal Revenue Service, Intelligence Division, Dallas, Texas, copies of thirteen payroll checks issued to Lee Harvey Oswald were obtained. These checks are dated from July 21, 1962 to October 13, 1962, and cover Oswald's entire period of employment. These checks show that Oswald's take home pay was in the range of $45 to $55 per week.

On November 27, 1963, Mr. H. L. Conway, manager of the Louv-R-Pak Division, Leslie Welding Co., Inc., was interviewed at his office, 200 N. Vacek Street, Fort Worth, Texas. Mr. Conway advised that Oswald's duties were mainly layout work in the assembly and production of various sheet metal items, and further that Oswald was one of the best employees he had ever employed in that particular type of work.

October 12, 1962 - April 6, 1963

Jaggers - Chiles - Stovall, 522 Browder Street, Dallas, Texas. On October 12, 1962, Oswald completed an employee identification questionnaire at this firm showing the same information as given on the employment application he made at the Leslie Welding Company.

On December 6, 1963, Mr. R. L. Stovall, co-owner of this firm was personally interviewed and he furnished the following information: Oswald was referred to this firm by the Texas Employment Service and actually started work on October 12, 1962. Oswald worked as a trainee making photographic prints of advertising material. He did not adapt himself to this type of work and did not seem to grasp his duties. His resignation was requested the last week of March 1963, and his employment was terminated April 6, 1963.

Copies of twenty-six payroll checks issued to Oswald during this period of employment were obtained and are attached. These copies and copies of other records were obtained through the Internal Revenue Service, Intelligence Division, Dallas, Texas. The checks show that Oswald's take home pay varied from $49 to $74 per week at that time.

- - - - -

On April 12, 1963, Oswald filed a claim for Unemployment Compensation with the Texas Employment Commission, 2206 Main Street, Dallas, Texas, furnishing the information that he was residing at 214 W. Neely Street, Dallas, and that he had been laid off from his employment at Jaggers-Chiles-Stovall for lack of work. There is no indication of the disposition of this claim.

On April 29, 1963, Oswald filed a claim for unemployment insurance with the Employment Security Agency, New Orleans, Louisiana, furnishing his address as 757 French Street, New Orleans. At the same time he completed an application for employment, stating that he had experience as a shipping clerk and as a photographer.

The record further shows that Oswald's claim was active from April 29, 1963, to June 25, 1963, at which time it became inactive. The claim was active again from July 22, 1963, until October 16, 1963, at which time it again became inactive. During the time that the claim was active, Oswald claimed no earnings and he received unemployment benefits for those periods which totaled 12 weeks. It appears from the record that he received his last benefits for the week ending September 27, 1963, but the claim did not become inactive until October 16, 1963.

May 10, 1963 to July 19, 1963

William B. Reily Co., Inc., 640 Magazine Street, New Orleans, Louisiana. On May 9, 1963, Oswald completed an application for employment with this company, furnishing the following information: That he resided at 757 French Street, New Orleans, and had lived there for the past three years; born October 18, 1939, 5'9", 150 lbs., and in excellent health. He further stated that he had attended Beauregard Junior High School, and Warren Eastern Senior High School from where he graduated in 1959. He stated that he was married and had one child, 15 months of age.

He listed as references, John Murrett, 757 French Street, New Orleans; Sgt. Robert Hidell, on active duty with the U. S. Marine Corps; and Lieutenant J. Evans, active Duty U. S. Marine Corps. He also stated that he had made application for this job as a result of a newspaper ad he had seen. He was accepted for employment and went to work on May 10, 1963, at the rate of $1.50 per hours.

Copies of his Application for Employment; Form W-4, Employee's Withholding Exemption Certificate; and Safety Instructions to Employees, signed on May 21, 1963, were obtained and are attached.

Oswald's job with this firm was as maintenance man, and he was principally engaged in oiling and maintaining various machinery. The firm handles a brand of coffee known as "Luzianne Coffee." He earned a total of $548.41 during the period of this employment which was terminated on July 19, 1963.

- - - - -

From July 19, 1963 to October 16, 1963, Oswald was apparently unemployed. As noted above, he was receiving unemployment benefit payments from July 22, 1963, through September 27, 1963, and as far as is known, this was his only source of income during that period.

Oswald's wife and child returned to Irving, Texas, from New Orleans on about September 24, 1963, and Oswald made his trip to Mexico City at about the same time.

October 16, 1963 to November 22, 1963

Texas School Book Depository, 411 Elm Street, Dallas, Texas. On October 16, 1963, Oswald went to work as an order filler for this firm at the rate of $1.25 per hour. He had obtained this job through the efforts of Mrs. Ruth Paine, 2515 W. 5th Street, Irving, Texas, with whom Oswald's wife and child had been living since about September 24, 1963. Mrs. Paine had a neighbor whose brother, Buell Wesley Frazier, who was employed by this firm and Frazier had stated that he thought there might be a vacancy.

Oswald was interviewed for the job by Mr. Roy S. Truly, Superintendent of Operations, on October 15, 1963. He was hired and went to work on the following day, October 16, 1963. A copy of his W-4 Form, Employee's Withholding Exemption Certificate executed on October 16, 1963, was obtained and is attached. All other employee records with regard to Oswald have been taken by the FBI.

Mr. Truly stated that Oswald appeared to be a quiet type person, followed directions properly, and did his work in a satisfactory manner. He worked from 8:00 A.M. to 4:45 P.M. five days a week, and had never missed a day's work. This firm is engaged in the warehousing of school books for numerous publishers, and it was Oswald's job to fill orders for books by locating the necessary books for each order wherever they might be stored on the various floors and bring them to the first floor shipping room where they were packed and wrapped for shipping.

Oswald worked at his normal duties for this firm on the morning of November 22, 1963, but failed to return to work after the lunch hour. Since the assassination took place at about 12:30 P.M. on that date and Oswald could not be located when the employees were being accounted for, he became a suspect and was subsequently apprehended.

ATTACHMENTS

Copy, change of address form for Marguerite Oswald, dated 11-1-62
Copy, change of address form for Lee H. Oswald, dated 8-17-62
Copy of statement made by Mrs. Elena A. Hall, 4760 Trail Lake Drive, Fort Worth, Texas
Copy, Character-Financial Report of Retail Credit Company, New Orleans, La., dated 5-29-63
Copy service order #21575, New Orleans Public Service Co., dated 5-9-63
Copy, Remove Order, New Orleans Public Service Company, dated 10-7-63
Two Newspaper articles concerning Oswald's visit to Mexico.

Statement of Earlene Roberts taken December 5, 1963
Copy of Employment Application at Leslie Welding Co., Fort Worth; Copy of W-4 executed by Oswald 7-17-62; copy of payroll information record; Copy of Termination of employment record; Copy of Oswald's letter of resignation, undated; Copies of thirteen payroll checks issued to Oswald by Leslie Welding Company.
Copy of Employee Identification Questionnaire dated 10-12-62 for Jaggers-Chiles-Stovall, Inc., Dallas
Copies of 26 payroll checks issued to Oswald by Jaggers-Chiles-Stovall, Dallas
Copy of Claim and correspondence, Texas Employment Commission. Claim dated 4-12-63
Copy of Application for Employment made by Oswald 5-9-63 at the William B. Reily Co., New Orleans
Copy of Employee's Withholding Certificate (W-4) dated 5-10-63
Copy of Safety Instructions to Employees dated 5-21-63
Copy Form B-11, Texas Employment Commission, dated 5-10-63
Copies of 7 documents from the Louisiana Department of Employment Security
Copy of Employee's Withholding Exemption Certificate dated 10-16-63
Statement of Gary E. Taylor taken December 11, 1963.

AWB:amr

City of Dallas
State of Texas

I, Gary E. Taylor, wish to make the following statement to Special Agents Arthur W. Blake and Maurice A. Miller, U.S. Secret Service.

During September, 1962, I met Lee H. Oswald through my father-in-law, George deMohrenschildt, at 2703 Mercedes, Ft. Worth, Tex. During this first visit the Oswalds stated their intention of moving to Dallas and my in-laws, the deMohrenschildts, suggested that Marina stay with my wife and I until the Oswalds found a place to live. I believe it was the same evening that I drove the Oswalds to Dallas. I let Lee out at the YMCA on Ervay Street and Marina accompanied my wife and I to our residence, an apartment at 3519 Fairmount. I believe Marina Oswald and her child stayed with me and my family for about two weeks and then she went to live with Mrs. Elena Hall in Ft. Worth, Texas. I don't recall how long Marina stayed with Mrs. Hall, but during this period of approximately four to five weeks, October 7 to early November, 1962, Lee Oswald was staying at the Ervay Street YMCA in Dallas. I have seen the Oswalds occasionally since they moved to Dallas, and the last time was some-time in late spring or early summer, 1963, when I stopped at their apartment near Zang's Blvd. and Davis Street in the Oak Cliff area of Dallas. I visited Marina in the absence of Lee.

I drove Lee Oswald to Ft. Worth on one occasion to visit Marina at Mrs. Hall's, but I have not driven him anywhere else other than the occasions I have mentioned, and never anywhere outside Dallas.

I have read the foregoing statement of one page and it has been read to me. I have had an opportunity to make corrections. All the information contained herein is true.

Gary E. Taylor

WITNESS:

Maurice A. Miller
Maurice A. Miller
Special Agent, U.S. Secret Service

641

SUBSCRIBED & SWORN TO BEFORE ME
DECEMBER 11, 1963:

Arthur W. Blake
Arthur W. Blake
Special Agent, U.S. Secret Service

COMMISSION EXHIBIT No. 2189—Continued

NAME: Oswald Marguerite — PRINT OR TYPE—LAST NAME FIRST — EFFECTIVE DATE: 11/1/62

OLD ADDRESS: HOUSE NO. AND STREET, APT. NO., OR BOX OR R. D. NO. (In care of): 808 Summit Apt 301
CITY, ZONE, AND STATE: Ft Worth Tex

NEW ADDRESS: HOUSE NO. AND STREET, APT. NO., OR BOX OR R. D. NO. (In care of): 3833 Westcliff Rd -S-
CITY, ZONE, AND STATE: Ft Worth Texas

641

SIGN HERE: (If signed as agent, include title) Marguerite C Oswald

COMPLETE OTHER SIDE

GPO

COMMISSION EXHIBIT No. 2189—Continued

CHANGE OF ADDRESS ORDER
MAIL OR DELIVER — POST OFFICE OF OLD ADDRESS

This order provides for forwarding of first-class mail, and all parcels of obvious value, unless you or the sender direct otherwise.

CHECK IF:
FORWARDING POSTAGE IS GUARANTEED FOR
☒ NEWSPAPERS & MAGAZINES
CHANGE FOR
☐ ENTIRE FAMILY OR FIRM ☐ INDIVIDUAL SIGNER ONLY
CHANGE IS
☒ PERMANENT (Expires after 2 years—not renewable) ☐ TEMPORARY UNTIL (Give date)

Orders to forward general delivery mail (at delivery offices) expire in 30 days unless renewed.

ENDORSEMENT OF CLERK OR CARRIER: 225 — DATE ENTERED: 11-2-62

POD Form 3575, Aug. 1960

AFFIX STAMP HERE WHEN MAILED

Postmaster

Ft Worth Tex
(City and State)

641

COMPLETE OTHER SIDE

COMMISSION EXHIBIT No. 2189—Continued

NAME — PRINT OR TYPE—LAST NAME FIRST: OSWALd, LEE H. | EFFECTIVE DATE: 7-17-62

OLD ADDRESS — HOUSE NO. AND STREET, APT. NO.; OR BOX OR R. D. NO. (In care of): 7313 DAVANPORT ST.

CITY, ZONE, AND STATE: FORT WORTh, TEXAS

NEW ADDRESS — HOUSE NO. AND STREET, APT. NO.; OR BOX OR R. D. NO. (In care of): 2703 Mercedes AV.

CITY, ZONE, AND STATE: FORT WORTh, TEXAS

SIGN HERE — (If signed as agent, include title): Lee H. Oswald

COMPLETE OTHER SIDE

GPO c55—16—73917—3

COMMISSION EXHIBIT No. 2189—Continued

CHANGE OF ADDRESS ORDER

MAIL OR DELIVER TO POST OFFICE OF OLD ADDRESS

THIS ORDER PROVIDES FOR THE FORWARDING OF FIRST-CLASS MAIL. IT ALSO PROVIDES FOR THE FORWARDING OF ALL PARCELS OF OBVIOUS VALUE, UNLESS YOU OR THE SENDER DIRECT OTHERWISE.

CHECK IF

FORWARDING POSTAGE IS GUARANTEED FOR

[✓] NEWSPAPERS AND MAGAZINES

CHANGE FOR

[✓] ENTIRE FAMILY OR FIRM [ ] INDIVIDUAL SIGNER ONLY

CHANGE IS

[✓] PERMANENT [ ] TEMPORARY UNTIL (GIVE DATE)

AFFIX STAMP HERE WHEN MAILED

Postmaster

(City and State)

ENDORSEMENT OF CLERK OR CARRIER | DATE ENTERED 8/18/62

POD FORM 3575, July 1961

COMPLETE OTHER SIDE

COMMISSION EXHIBIT No. 2189—Continued

Ft. Worth, Tex.

I, Mrs John R. Hall, hereby make the following statement to Maurice G. Miller, Special Agent, U. S. Secret Service, regarding my association with Lee Harvey Oswald and his wife, Marina.

I am 37 years of age, married to John R. Hall, and presently reside with him at 4760 Trail Lake Dr., Ft. Worth, Tex. My husband and I now operate the Crown and Bridge Prosthesis, 1313 E. Seminary Dr., Ft. Worth, but I worked as a dental technician at Patterson Porcelain Lab. 2920 W. 6th, Ft. Worth, about four years – from November 1959 to May 1963.

I was born in Teheran, Iran, of Russian parents. My father, Ivan Alkhazoff, died in 1949, and my mother, Marguerite Elistratova, died in Teheran in February 1963. I moved to the United States in

E. A. H.

2.

E. A. H.

September 1957 to attend the Kepel School of Dental Technology, 120 Columbus Ave., New York City. At that time it was my intention to return to Teheran, but I met John Hall while in school and we married in 1959. We divorced in February 1962 and remarried November 17, 1962.

I speak fluent Russian, Iranian, French, Turkish and Armenian, and am acquainted with most of the persons in the Dallas-Ft. Worth area who speak these languages.

One morning in June 1962 one of these friends, George Bouhe, a retired accountant, resides 4740 Homer St., Dallas, Tex., came to my residence at 4760 Trail Lake Dr. Ft. Worth, and introduced me to Lee Harvey Oswald (whose name I knew from newspaper articles in connection with his defection to the Soviet Union) and Lee's wife, Marina. Mr. Bouhe told me Marina needed help in

E. A. Hall.

E. A. H. 3

connection with a missing upper central tooth. He told me he could give me $50.00 or $75.00 for the necessary work. I knew this work would cost $200-$300 and indicated I might make some arrangements through Charity organizations. Mr. Bouhe, Russian born, Marina and I conversed about nothing in particular while Lee sat and listened. I learned the Oswalds were staying at 2703 Mercedes, a duplex located near Montgomery Ward in Ft. Worth. As they got ready to leave my house after their 30 or so minute visit, Mr. Bouhe gave me some money and asked me without Marina's knowledge to buy some things for Marina and her child. It was obvious the Oswalds were destitute.
The following week I stopped at 2703 Mercedes and took Marina to Montgomery Ward. There I bought her some clothes and shoes.
I continued to stop and visit with

E. A. H.

641

COMMISSION EXHIBIT No. 2189—Continued

E. A. H. 4

Marina about once each week to see how she and the child were doing. Only occasionally did I see Lee and on these few dates he was un-communicative. He was working at a welding shop near Montgomery at the time. During these visits with Marina, she told me of beatings she and the child received from Lee.
Around October, 1962, Lee left his job at the Welding Co and stated his intention of moving to Dallas because of better job opportunities. I was concerned for Marina & the child's welfare and suggested that Marina & the child live with me until Lee got established in Dallas.
Between the 1st & 15th of October, 1962, I went and got Marina & the child and their things and they moved into my house. Lee moved to the YMCA in Dallas.
I was seriously injured in an automobile

E. A. H.

641

COMMISSION EXHIBIT No. 2189—Continued

5

E. A. H.

accident in Ft. Worth in October. I went to St Josephs Hospital and Marina & the child continued to stay at my home. I left the hospital for home ten days after admission and Marina & the child were at my house. I left Ft Worth 10-31-62, to visit friends in Garden City, N.Y., and when I returned to my home November 15, 1962, Marina and the child were gone. I learned through some Russian friends in Dallas that Marina & the child were staying with Lee in an apartment at 604 Elsbeck.
I visited the Oswalds twice after that - once on Christmas & then at Easter time when I took gifts to the child.
I do not know that Lee ever spent the night at my home. He could have stayed there without my knowledge while I was in the hospital or in New York.
I never discussed politics with Lee because

E. A. H.

641

COMMISSION EXHIBIT No. 2189—Continued

6

E. A. H.

I knew from books I had seen in his possession, many from the Ft. Worth Library, that he had Marxist leanings. While Marina was staying with me she asked that I make arrangements to have her child baptized; that Lee was against it, but this was a good opportunity to do it because he was in Dallas and would have no knowledge of it. I took Marina & the child to the Eastern Greek Orthodox Church in Dallas. I stood for the child and she was baptized in October, 1962, by Father Dimitri, 4203 Newton, Dallas.

I have read this statement of six pages and have had an opportunities to make corrections, all the information contaiend is true.

Elena A. Hall.
Mrs. John R. Hall.

Witness: Maurice A. Miller

641

COMMISSION EXHIBIT No. 2189—Continued

CHARACTER—FINANCE REPORT

New Orleans, La.

Acct. No. 6605 ns

5-16-63 16

OSWALD, LEE HARVEY
New Orleans, La. 757 French St.
Maintenance-Standard Coffee Co

Transaction: –
Amount $ –
Mo. Notes $ –

IDENTITY:	1. How long known to you and informants?	1. You – Informants 10yrs-2
	2. How long has applicant resided at present residence address?	2wks-Prev U.S. Marines intv Aunt
	3. About what is his age? (If around 21 verify if possible.)	23
	4. Is he married? Number of dependents including wife?	4. Yes Number of Dependents?
	5. Show racial descent.	5. AS
BUSINESS:	6. Show name of present employer.	6. Standard
	7. In what line of business is applicant engaged?	7. Coffee Business
	8. What position does he hold?	8. Maintenance Man
	9. How long with present employer?	9. one week*prev U.S. Marines
STABILITY:	10. Is he employed FULL TIME? (If not, show how many days per week he works, etc.)	10. Yes
	11. Are prospects for continued permanent employment good?	11. Yes
	12. Is he steady, progressive and does he live within his income?	12. Yes
FINANCES:	13. Estimate applicant's net worth.	13. 2,500(Est)
	14. Of what does worth consist principally?	14. Personal affects and Saving
	15. Does he own or rent his home?	15. rent
	16. What is applicant's ANNUAL EARNED	16. 3,500(Est)
	17. Estimate added ANNUAL income ...	17. None Source
	18. If wife employed, by whom? ...	18.
	19. Do you learn of any ... judgments, failures, garnishments, bankr... (If so, which, give details.)	19. No
CHARACTER—HOME SURROUNDINGS:	20. Are home surro...	20. Yes
	21. In what typ... (Show middle class, wealthy ...)	21. middle class
	22. Any critici... character ...	22. No
	23. Do you ...	23. No
	24. Do you ... doing business with applicant?	24. No

REMARKS: 25. BUSINESS: Cover ... and present business connections, ... reputation ... for future and general stability.
26. FINANCES: Comment on present and past financial standing, record for living ... illness or physical impairments that might affect his earning capacity.
27. CHARACTER-HOME SURROUNDINGS: Comment on character, habits, ... morals ... associates. Give type of neighborhood, stability and class of residents in the section.

1. Lee Harvey Oswald is employed as a maintenance man for the Standard Coffee Company, and has been so engaged in this occupation for the past one week, and enjoys a favorable business reputation. Previous to this, he was in the U.S. Marines for some three years. He enjoys a favorable business reputation, and his prospects for the future appear to be favorable.

FINANCES: His present and past financial standing is good, and he is regarded as an individual who lives within his means. Learned of no illiness or physical impairments that might affect his earning capacity.

CHARACTER-HOME SURROUNDINGS: His character, habits, and Morals are good, and he is known to keep good associates, and well regarded. He resides with his wife, and child. They live in a middle class residential section with frame homes that are well kept, and living conditions are adequate. Stability and class of residencts in this section is good.

RCD lcc

641

May 2, 1964

RETAIL CREDIT COMPANY
Form 1310—10-52

Signature of person making report ________ CHARACTER—FINANCIAL

COMMISSION EXHIBIT No. 2189—Continued

SERVICE ORDER No. 21575

ELECTRIC X RATE R6 POWER RATE GAS X RATE R6 3

NAME LEE H. OSWALD PHONE NO 1B

NEW ADDRESS 4907 MAGAZINE ST. APT. LOWER CENTER ZONE

ACCOUNT NUMBER 18-353-6480-68

MOVED FROM

DEPOSIT DATE 5-9-63 AMT. 5 DEPOSIT DATE NO. AMT. 5

LAST ADDRESS 757 FRENCH ST.

METER IN OK

EXECUTE SET 5-10AM

SPECIAL INSTRUCTIONS: Light Pilot

EMP. (?) ISRAEL Co 3800 MAGAZINE

ISSUED BY DATE 5-9-63

641

METER DEPT. DATE METER DEPT. DATE
FIELD ORDER NO. TIME FIELD ORDER NO. TIME

COMMISSION EXHIBIT No. 2189—Continued

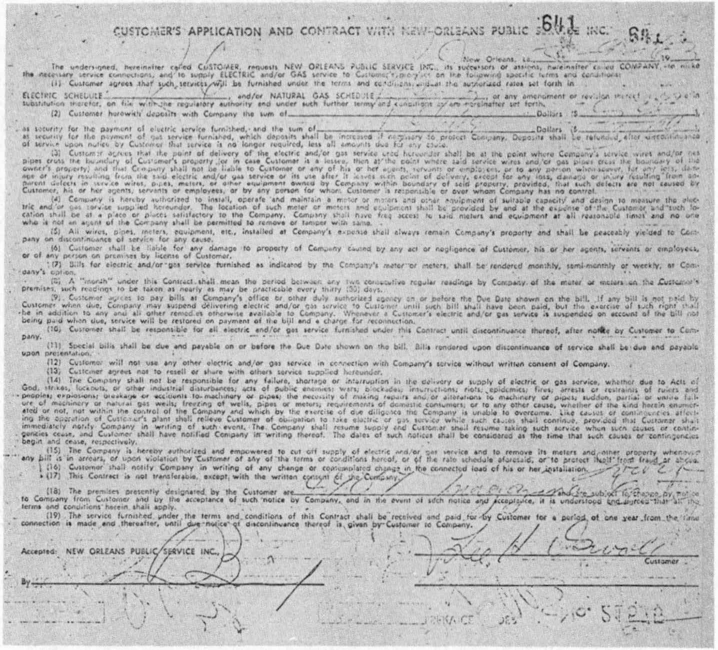

641

CUSTOMER'S APPLICATION AND CONTRACT WITH NEW ORLEANS PUBLIC SERVICE INC.

New Orleans, La., ____________ 19____

The undersigned, hereinafter called CUSTOMER, requests NEW ORLEANS PUBLIC SERVICE INC., its successors or assigns, hereinafter called COMPANY, to make the necessary service connections, and to supply ELECTRIC and/or GAS service to Customer's premises on the following specific terms and conditions:

(1) Customer agrees that such services will be furnished under the terms and conditions and at the authorized rates set forth in ELECTRIC SCHEDULE ____________, and/or NATURAL GAS SCHEDULE ____________, or any amendment or revision thereof or in substitution therefor, on file with the regulatory authority and under such further terms and conditions as are hereinafter set forth.

(2) Customer herewith deposits with Company the sum of ____________ Dollars ($____________), as security for the payment of electric service furnished, and the sum of ____________ Dollars ($____________), as security for the payment of gas service furnished, which deposits shall be increased if necessary to protect Company. Deposits shall be refunded after discontinuance of service upon notice by Customer that service is no longer required, less all amounts due for any cause.

(3) Customer agrees that the point of delivery of the electric and/or gas service used hereunder shall be at the point where Company's service wires and/or gas pipes cross the boundary of Customer's property (or in case Customer is a lessee, then at the point where said service wires and/or gas pipes cross the boundary of the owner's property) and that Company shall not be liable to Customer or any of his or her agents, servants or employees, or to any person whomsoever, for any loss, damage or injury resulting from the said electric and/or gas service or its use after it leaves such point of delivery, except for any loss, damage or injury resulting from apparent defects in service wires, pipes, meters, or other equipment owned by Company within boundary of said property, provided, that such defects are not caused by Customer, his or her agents, servants or employees, or by any person for whom Customer is responsible or over whom Company has no control.

(4) Company is hereby authorized to install, operate and maintain a meter or meters and other equipment of suitable capacity and design to measure the electric and/or gas service supplied hereunder. The location of such meter or meters and equipment shall be provided by and at the expense of the Customer and such location shall be at a place or places satisfactory to the Company. Company shall have free access to said meters and equipment at all reasonable times and no one who is not an agent of the Company shall be permitted to remove or tamper with same.

(5) All wires, pipes, meters, equipment, etc., installed at Company's expense shall always remain Company's property and shall be peaceably yielded to Company on discontinuance of service for any cause.

(6) Customer shall be liable for any damage to property of Company caused by any act or negligence of Customer, his or her agents, servants or employees, or of any person on premises by license of Customer.

(7) Bills for electric and/or gas service furnished as indicated by the Company's meter or meters, shall be rendered monthly, semi-monthly or weekly, at Company's option.

(8) A "month" under this Contract shall mean the period between any two consecutive regular readings by Company of the meter or meters on the Customer's premises, such readings to be taken as nearly as may be practicable every thirty (30) days.

(9) Customer agrees to pay bills at Company's office or other duly authorized agency on or before the Due Date shown on the bill. If any bill is not paid by Customer when due, Company may suspend delivering electric and/or gas service to Customer until such bill shall have been paid, but the exercise of such right shall be in addition to any and all other remedies otherwise available to Company. Whenever a Customer's electric and/or gas service is suspended on account of the bill not being paid when due, service will be restored on payment of the bill and a charge for reconnection.

(10) Customer shall be responsible for all electric and/or gas service furnished under this Contract until discontinuance thereof, after notice by Customer to Company.

(11) Special bills shall be due and payable on or before the Due Date shown on the bill. Bills rendered upon discontinuance of service shall be due and payable upon presentation.

(12) Customer will not use any other electric and/or gas service in connection with Company's service without written consent of Company.

(13) Customer agrees not to resell or share with others service supplied hereunder.

(14) The Company shall not be responsible for any failure, shortage or interruption in the delivery or supply of electric or gas service, whether due to Acts of God, strikes, lockouts, or other industrial disturbances; acts of public enemies; wars; blockades; insurrections; riots; epidemics; fires; arrests or restraints of rulers and peoples; explosions; breakage or accidents to machinery or pipes; the necessity of making repairs and/or alterations to machinery or pipes; sudden, partial or entire failure of machinery or natural gas wells; freezing of wells, pipes or meters; requirements of domestic consumers; or to any other cause, whether of the kind herein enumerated or not, not within the control of the Company and which by the exercise of due diligence the Company is unable to overcome. Like causes or contingencies affecting the operation of Customer's plant shall relieve Customer of obligation to take electric or gas service while such causes shall continue, provided that Customer shall immediately notify Company in writing of such event. The Company shall resume supply and Customer shall resume taking such service when such causes or contingencies cease, and Customer shall have notified Company in writing thereof. The dates of such notices shall be considered as the time that such causes or contingencies begin and cease, respectively.

(15) The Company is hereby authorized and empowered to cut off supply of electric and/or gas service and to remove its meters and other property whenever any bill is in arrears, or upon violation by Customer of any of the terms or conditions hereof, or of the rate schedule aforesaid, or to protect itself from fraud or abuse.

(16) Customer shall notify Company in writing of any change or contemplated change in the connected load of his or her installation.

(17) This Contract is not transferable, except with the written consent of the Company.

(18) The premises presently designated by the Customer are 4907 Magazine and are subject to change by notice to Company from Customer and by the acceptance of such notice by Company, and in the event of such notice and acceptance, it is understood and agreed that all the terms and conditions herein shall apply.

(19) The service furnished under the terms and conditions of this Contract shall be received and paid for by Customer for a period of one year from the time connection is made and thereafter, until due notice of discontinuance thereof is given by Customer to Company.

Accepted: NEW ORLEANS PUBLIC SERVICE INC.,

By ____________

Lee H. Oswald
Customer

Commission Exhibit No. 2189—Continued

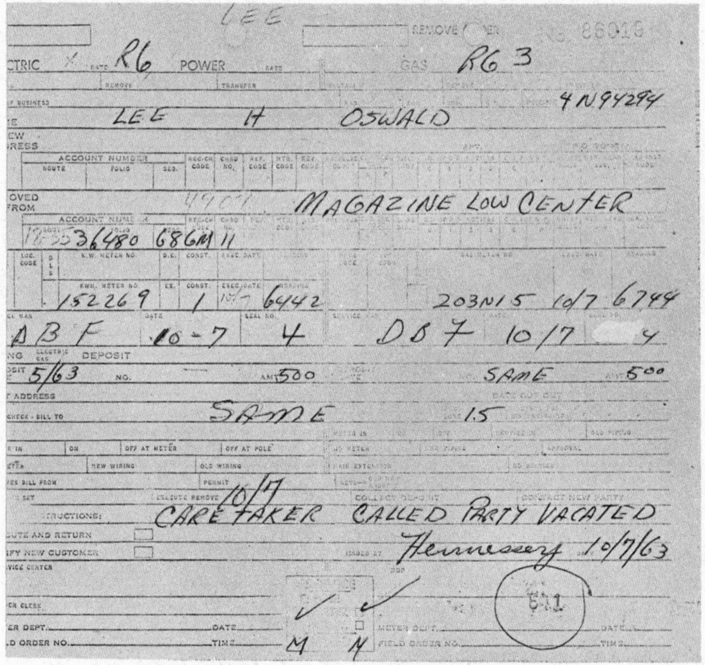

LEE

ELECTRIC X RATE R6 POWER RATE GAS R6 3

4N94294

NAME LEE H OSWALD

NEW ADDRESS

ACCOUNT NUMBER

MOVED FROM 4907 MAGAZINE LOW CENTER

ACCOUNT NUMBER 36480 686M 11

KWH. METER NO. 152269 CONST. 1 EXEC. DATE 10/7 READING 6442

203N15 10/7 6744

ABF 10-7 4 DO7 10/17 4

ELECTRIC GAS DEPOSIT

DEPOSIT 5/63 NO. AMT. 500 SAME AMT. 500

SAME 15

INSTRUCTIONS: 10/7 CARETAKER CALLED PARTY VACATED

ROUTE AND RETURN

NOTIFY NEW CUSTOMER

SERVICE CENTER

ISSUED BY Hennessey 10/7/63

METER DEPT. DATE

FIELD ORDER NO. TIME M M

Commission Exhibit No. 2189—Continued

Paper Says Oswald Sought Cuba Visa

MEXICO CITY (AP)—The newspaper Excelsior said Sunday night it had evidence that Lee Harvey Oswald, accused assassin of President Kennedy, visited the Soviet and Cuban consuls here in September and tried to get a visa.

The newspaper did not disclose the source of its story, but said that it was from "a high official source." It said it corroborated the report and found that Oswald was in Mexico from Sept. 26 to Oct. 3. Oswald was shot to death earlier Sunday in Dallas.

Excelsior said the story of Oswald's visit would be published in its Monday editions.

The newspaper said Oswald crossed the border at Nuevo Laredo Sept. 26, met with Cuban Consul Eusebio Azcue the next day and requester a visa so he could travel to the Soviet Union via Cuba.

Excelsior said the consul told Oswald his request would have to be submitted to the Cuban Foreign Ministry for clearance, a procedure usually taking about three weeks.

At that, the story said, Oswald's temper flared and he left the Cuban consul's office, slamming the door.

On Sept. 28, the newspaper said, Oswald visited the Soviet Consul in Mexico with the same request. The newspaper said he said he was "a militant Communist, married with a Soviet citizen," and a resident of Russia for three years.

According to Excelsior, Oswald told the Russian consul that his marriage to a Soviet girl could be ascertained by calling her long distance in New Orleans, where she was waiting for him.

The consul was not identified.

Again Oswald was told that some time would have to elapse until his visa request could be cleared by the Soviet Foreign Ministry, probably as much as three or four months.

Oswald had a bitter argument with the consul, the newspaper said.

841

The newspaper said that "investigations made in Mexico seem to point out that during his stay here, Oswald had no other interviews with high officials of the Cuban or Russian embassies."

Irish Honor Unit To Attend Rites

DUBLIN (UPI)—An honor guard of Ireland's elite officer cadet corps flew to the United States Sunday in a unique gesture of reverence for President Kennedy.

The handpicked unit of 24 young potential officers will take part in the funeral ceremonies in Washington.

Leading the Irish delegation to the Kennedy funeral was 81-year-old President Eamon de Valera.

The decision to send an Irish honor guard came after a personal request from Mrs. Jacqueline Kennedy was relayed Saturday night by U.S. Ambassador Matthew McCloskey to Premier Sean F. Lemass.

It was regarded here as a heart-warming tribute by the Kennedy family to the ancestral home of the slain President.

Oswald Was After Russ Visa

By DAVE WEBER
Special to The News

MEXICO CITY — Consular offices of the Soviet Union and Cuba admitted Monday that Lee Harvey Oswald requested rapid clearance here in late September for a trip to Russia via Havana.

Cuban Consul Eusebio Azcue said Oswald made the request for a transit visa to Russia at his office on Sept. 27 and left angrily after being informed that his request would have to go through normal channels.

Two days later, Oswald attempted to get direct clearance to Russia at the Soviet consul's office here. Again, he was told that it would take 10 to 12 days for clearance. A spokesman for the Soviet Consul said Oswald stormed from the office and slammed the door.

Oswald first crossed the Texas-Mexico border on Sept. 26 by car at Laredo, after obtaining a tourist permit from the Mexican consulate in New Orleans. He returned to the United States by the same route Oct. 3. 841

The U.S. Ambassador to Mexico, Thomas C. Mann, declined comment on Oswald's entry into Mexico, saying "We cannot disclose confidential matters."

COMMISSION EXHIBIT No. 2189—Continued

I, Earlene Roberts, after being duly sworn, do depose and state:

I live at 1026 Beckly, Dallas, Texas, where I serve as housekeeper for a rooming house owned by Mr. & Mrs. A. C. Johnson.

On Friday, November 22, 1963, at approximately 1:00 pm I was sitting in the living room watching television about the President's assassination when a man I knew as O. H. Lee but who has since been identified as Lee Harvey Oswald, came into the front door and went to his room. Oswald did not have a jacket when he came in the house and I don't recall what type of clothing he was wearing.

Oswald went to his room and was only there a very few minutes before coming out. I noticed he had a jacket he was putting on.
641 I recall the jacket was a dark color and it was the type that zips up the front. He was zipping the jacket up as he left.

Oswald went out the front door. A moment later I looked out the window. I saw Lee Oswald standing on the curb at the bus stop just to the right, and on the same side of the street as our house. I just glanced out the window that once. I don't know how long Lee Oswald stood at the curb nor did I see which direction he went when he left there.

About thirty minutes later three Dallas policemen came to the house looking for Lee Harvey Oswald. We didn't know who Lee Harvey Oswald was until sometime later his picture was flashed on television. I then let the Dallas policemen in the room occupied by Lee Oswald. While the Dallas police were searching the room two FBI agents came in.

The police and FBI agents took everything in the room that belonged
641 to Lee Oswald and also took our pillow case and two towels and wash cloths.

page 3

I have made this statement, consisting of three pages, to Special Agents William N. Carter and Arthur W. Blake of the U.S. Secret Service. I have read this statement over and I find it to be true to the best of my knowledge.

Earlene Roberts

Subscribed and sworn to before me this 5 day of December 1963. (Auth Title 5, Sec 93, USC)

William N. Carter, Special Agent
U.S. Secret Service

Arthur W. Blake

641

Commission Exhibit No. 2189—Continued

PAYROLL INFORMATION RECORD

PLANT: FT. WORTH DATE OF EMPLOYMENT: 7-17-62 RATE: $1.25 hr.

NAME: LEE HARVEY OSWALD S.S. NO.: 433-54-3937 DEPENDENTS: 3

ADDRESS: 1501 WEST 7TH. CITY: FT. WORTH STATE: TEXAS

JOB DESCRIPTION: SHEET METAL HELPER TEMPORARY: ☐ PERMANENT: ☒

ATTACHED TO THIS FORM ARE:

Employee's Withholding Exemption Certificate; FEDERAL (FORM W4)
" " " " GEORGIA
Any other forms which may be required for payroll calc

APPROVED BY: Tommy

FORM W-4 (Rev. June 1958)
U. S. Treasury Department
Internal Revenue Service

EMPLOYEE'S WITHHOLDING EXEMPTION CERTIFICATE

Print full name LEE HARVEY OSWALD Social Security No. 435-54-3937

Print home address 1501 WEST 7th ST. City FORT WORTH Zone TEXAS

EMPLOYEE: File this form with your employer. Otherwise, he must withhold U. S. income tax from your wages without exemption.

EMPLOYER: Keep this certificate with your records. If the employee is believed to have claimed too many exemptions, the District Director should be so advised.

HOW TO CLAIM YOUR WITHHOLDING EXEMPTIONS

1. If SINGLE, and you claim an exemption, write the figure "1" ....
2. If MARRIED, one exemption each for husband and wife if not claimed on another certificate.
   (a) If you claim both of these exemptions, write the figure "2"
   (b) If you claim one of these exemptions, write the figure "1" 2
   (c) If you claim neither of these exemptions, write "0"
3. Exemptions for age and blindness (applicable only to you and your wife but not to dependents):
   (a) If you or your wife will be 65 years of age or older at the end of the year, and you claim this exemption, write "1"; if both will be 65 or older, and you claim both of these exemptions, write "2" ....
   (b) If you or your wife are blind, and you claim this exemption, write the figure "1"; if both are blind, and you claim both of these exemptions, write the figure "2" ....
4. If you claim exemptions for one or more dependents, write the number of such exemptions. (Do not claim exemption for a dependent unless you are qualified under instruction 4 on other side.) 1
5. Add the number of exemptions which you have claimed above and write the total 3
6. Additional withholding per pay period under agreement with employer. See Instruction 1 .... $

I CERTIFY that the number of withholding exemptions claimed on this certificate does not exceed the number to which I am entitled.

(Date) July 17, 1962 (Signed) Lee H Oswald

Commission Exhibit No. 2189—Continued

INSTRUCTIONS:

(1) All forms MUST be TYPEWRITTEN except for signature.
(2) Forms must be completed before the employee starts work.
(3) Forms on all new employees must be sent to the Franklin Park plant with the time cards covering the week in which the employee is hired.
(4) All spaces and lines of this form MUST be filled in.
(5) Use LEGAL NAMES only. DO NOT use nicknames or abbreviations.

TERMINATION OF EMPLOYMENT RECORD

PLANT: FT. WORTH DATE HIRED: 7-17-62 DATE TERMINATED: 10-8-62

NAME: LEE OSWALD S.S.NO. 433-54-3937 WOULD YOU REHIRE? YES

ADDRESS: 1501 WEST 7TH. CITY: FT. WORTH STATE: TEXAS

REASON FOR TERMINATION: ACCEPTED BETTER PAYING POSITION.

APPROVED BY: H. L. Conway

NOTE:
This report must be TYPEWRITTEN:

COMMISSION EXHIBIT No. 2189—Continued

Leslie Welding Co.
210 N. EAST Peach St.
Fort Worth, Texas
% Tom Yates-Foreman

Dear Sir;

This is to explain that I have moved permanently to Dallas, Texas, where I have found other employment.

I ask that my check for work preformed during the week Oct. 1-8 be forwarded to me now, and the other check coming to me from my first week of work be forwarded as soon as possible.

I futher request that my name be withdrawn from those whom you presently employ.

Very respectfully,
Lee H. Oswald

LEE H OSWALD
BOX 2915
Dallas,
Texas

COMMISSION EXHIBIT No. 2189—Continued

APPLICATION FOR EMPLOYMENT

Date JULY 13, 1962

me (Last Name First) Oswald Age 22 Born: Mo. Oct Day 18 Year 1939

ldress 1501 7th ST. Telephone PE-23245 Soc. Sec. No. 433 54 3937

ow long have you lived at this address? Birthplace? NEW ORLEANS Citizen? ✓ yes

ale ✓ Female Weight 150 Height 5 9 Any serious illness? none

ngle Married ✓ Other No. Children 1 Ages 5 months

ther Dependents wife Explain

hat kind of work are you applying for? sheet metal

hat special qualifications do you have? 2½ years Experiance

hat office machines can you operate? none

ho referred you to us? TEXAS STATE EM.

o you have any relatives working for this Company? NO

MILITARY SERVICE RECORD

ave you served in the Armed Forces? yes From 1956 To 1962

ranch of Service U SMC Duties SHEET METAL & mich.

ank or rating at time of enlistment PRV. Rating at time of discharge SGT

ype of discharge HONOURABLE Any disability? NO

EDUCATION

SCHOOL	DATE FROM	DATE TO	NAME OF SCHOOL	CITY	COURSE	DID YOU GRADUATE
GRAMMAR	1950	1953	RiGlea west	F. W.	GEN	
HIGH	1953	1956	JACKSON SHS	NEW ORLEANS	GEN	
COLLEGE						
OTHER						

EXPERIENCE (ENTER LAST JOB FIRST)

NAME AND ADDRESS OF COMPANY	DATE FROM	DATE TO	LIST YOUR DUTIES	STARTING SALARY	FINAL SALARY	REASON FOR LEAVING
Active DUTY USMC			michinist AND SHEET METAL worker			

REFERENCES (NOT RELATIVES)

NAME	ADDRESS	OCCUPATION
PETER P GREGORY	CONTIN. LIFE Bldg.	CONSULTANT Oil ENGN
ROBERT OSWALD	ACME BRICK CO.	JUN. EX.

TOPS FORM 3286 LITHO IN U. S. A.

COMMISSION EXHIBIT No. 2189—Continued

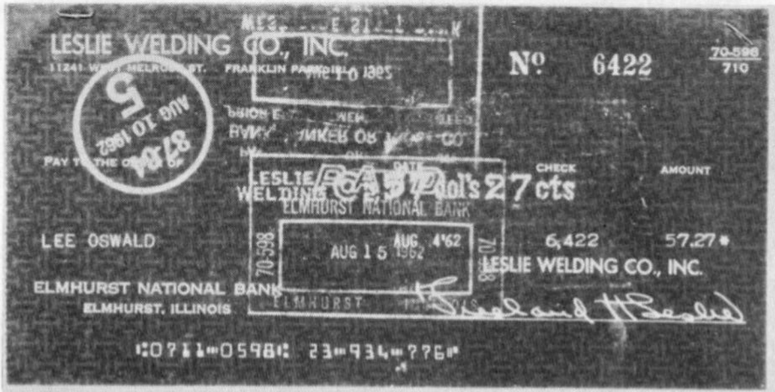
LESLIE WELDING CO., INC.
11241 WEST MELROSE ST. FRANKLIN PARK, ILL.
Nº 6422
70-598
710
PAY TO THE ORDER OF
DATE
CHECK
AMOUNT
LESLIE WELDING
dol's 27 cts
LEE OSWALD
6,422
57.27
ELMHURST NATIONAL BANK
AUG 15 1962
LESLIE WELDING CO., INC.
ELMHURST NATIONAL BANK
ELMHURST, ILLINOIS
AUG 10 1962

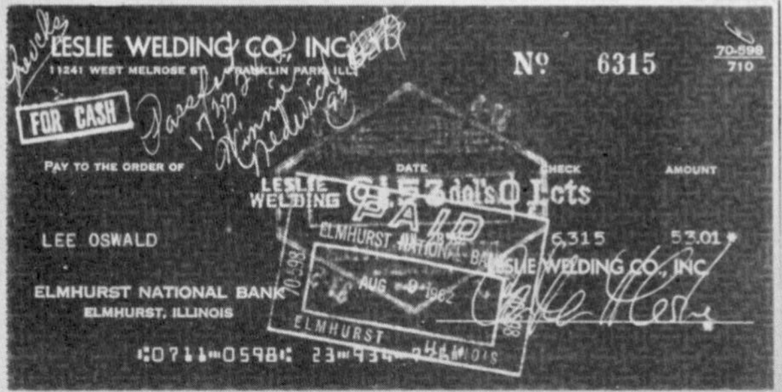
LESLIE WELDING CO., INC.
11241 WEST MELROSE ST. FRANKLIN PARK, ILL.
Nº 6315
70-598
710
FOR CASH
PAY TO THE ORDER OF
DATE
CHECK
AMOUNT
LESLIE WELDING
dol's 01 cts
PAID
ELMHURST NATIONAL BANK
LEE OSWALD
6,315
53.01
LESLIE WELDING CO., INC.
ELMHURST NATIONAL BANK
ELMHURST, ILLINOIS

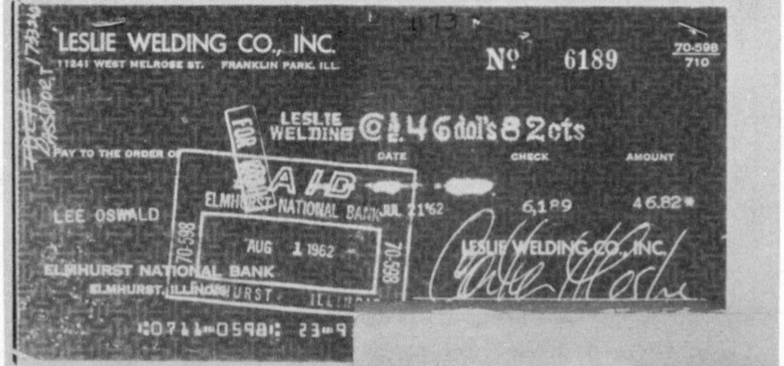
LESLIE WELDING CO., INC.
11241 WEST MELROSE ST. FRANKLIN PARK, ILL.
Nº 6189
70-598
710
LESLIE WELDING
46 dol's 82 cts
PAY TO THE ORDER OF
DATE
CHECK
AMOUNT
PAID
ELMHURST NATIONAL BANK
JUL 21'62
LEE OSWALD
6,189
46.82
AUG 1 1962
LESLIE WELDING CO., INC.
ELMHURST NATIONAL BANK
ELMHURST, ILLINOIS

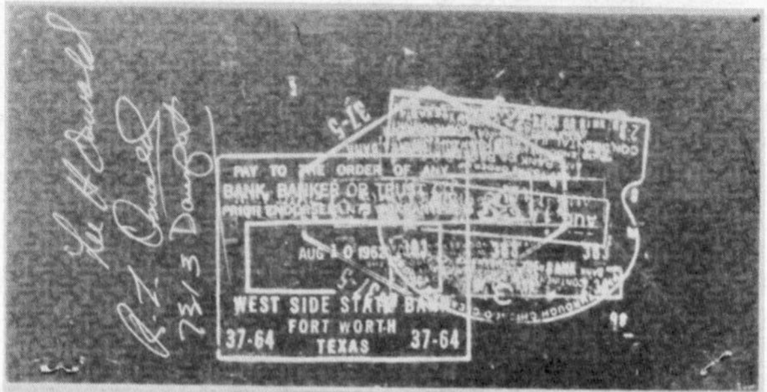
PAY TO THE ORDER OF ANY
BANK, BANKER OR TRUST CO.
WEST SIDE STATE BANK
FORT WORTH
TEXAS
37-64
37-64

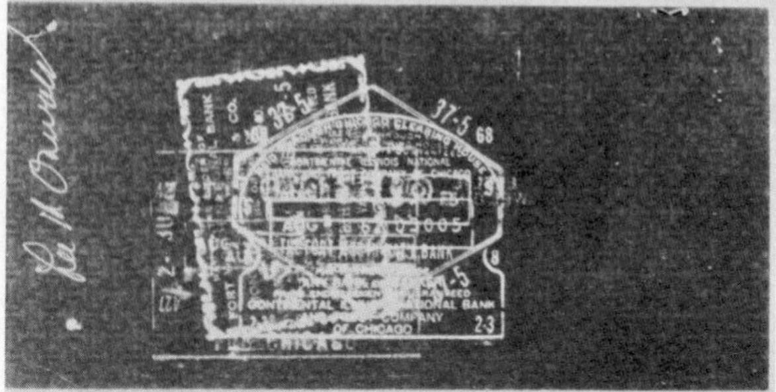
37-5 68
CONTINENTAL ILLINOIS NATIONAL BANK
AND TRUST COMPANY
OF CHICAGO
2-3

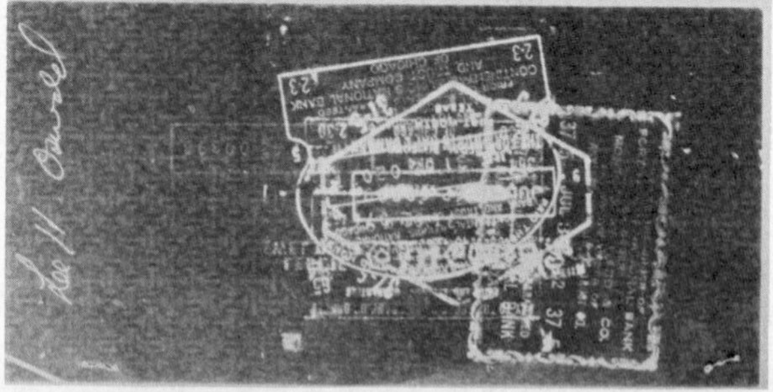
CONTINENTAL ILLINOIS NATIONAL BANK
AND TRUST COMPANY
OF CHICAGO
2-3
37

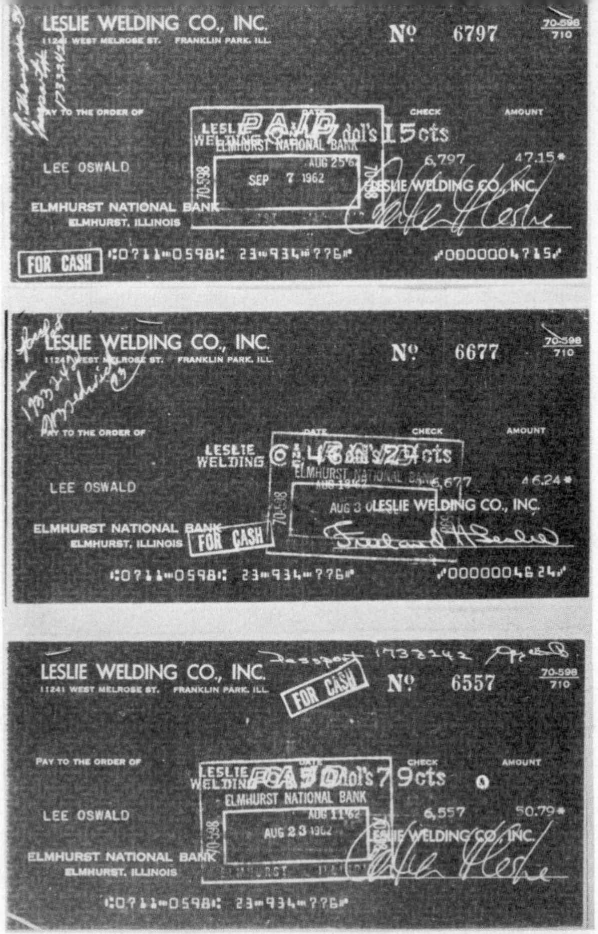

COMMISSION EXHIBIT No. 2189—Continued

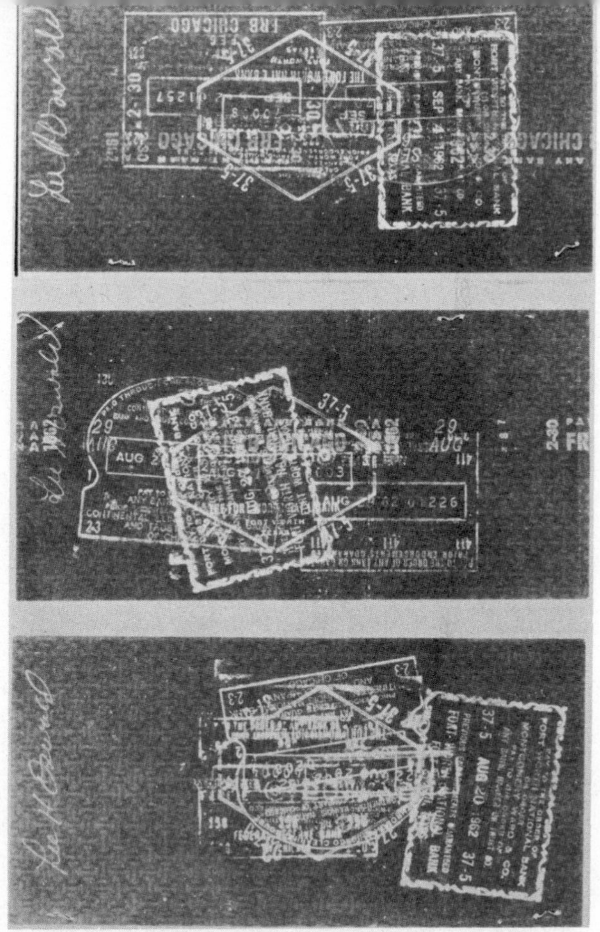

COMMISSION EXHIBIT No. 2189—Continued

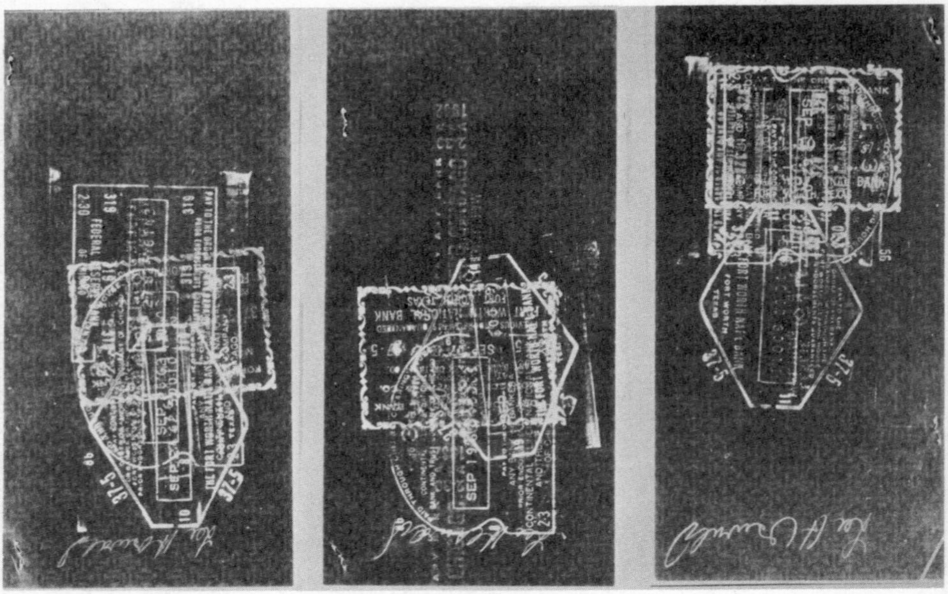

LESLIE WELDING CO., INC.
11341 WEST MELROSE ST. FRANKLIN PARK, ILL.
Nº 7192
70-598
710
FOR CASH
PAY TO THE ORDER OF
LEE OSWALD
CHECK
AMOUNT
7,192
46.24*
LESLIE WELDING CO., INC.
ELMHURST NATIONAL BANK
ELMHURST, ILLINOIS
⑆0711⑉0598⑆ 23⑉934⑉776⑈

LESLIE WELDING CO., INC.
11341 WEST MELROSE ST. FRANKLIN PARK, ILL.
Nº 7067
70-598
710
PAY TO THE ORDER OF
LEE OSWALD
CHECK
AMOUNT
7,067
46.24*
LESLIE WELDING CO., INC.
ELMHURST NATIONAL BANK
ELMHURST, ILLINOIS
⑆0711⑉0598⑆ 23⑉934⑉776⑈ ⑈0000004624⑈

LESLIE WELDING CO., INC.
11341 WEST MELROSE ST. FRANKLIN PARK, ILL.
Nº 6952
70-598
710
PAY TO THE ORDER OF
LEE OSWALD
CHECK
AMOUNT
6,952
47.96*
LESLIE WELDING CO., INC.
ELMHURST NATIONAL BANK
ELMHURST, ILLINOIS
⑆0711⑉0598⑆ 23⑉934⑉776⑈

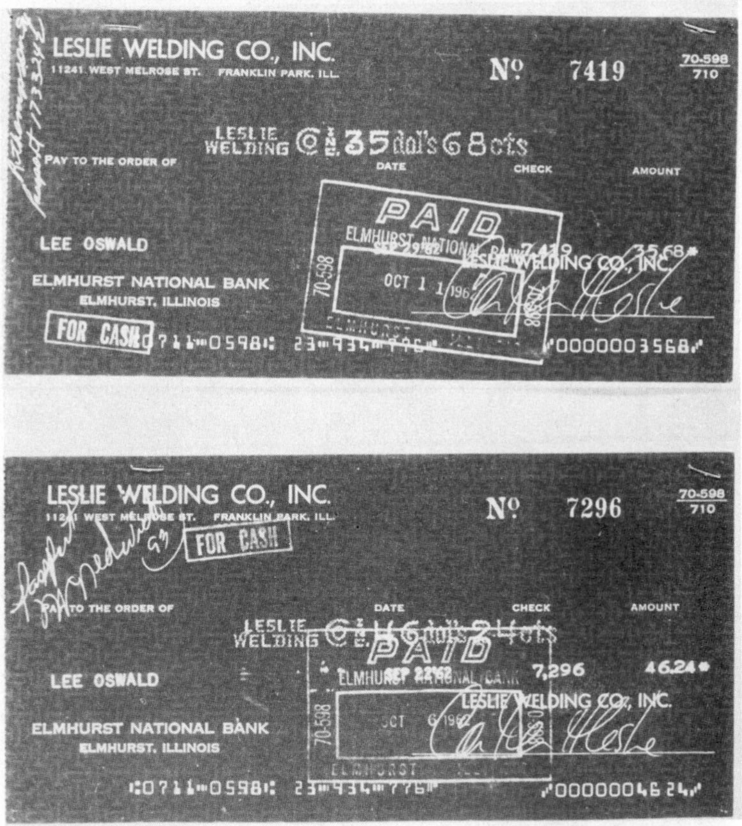

Commission Exhibit No. 2189—Continued

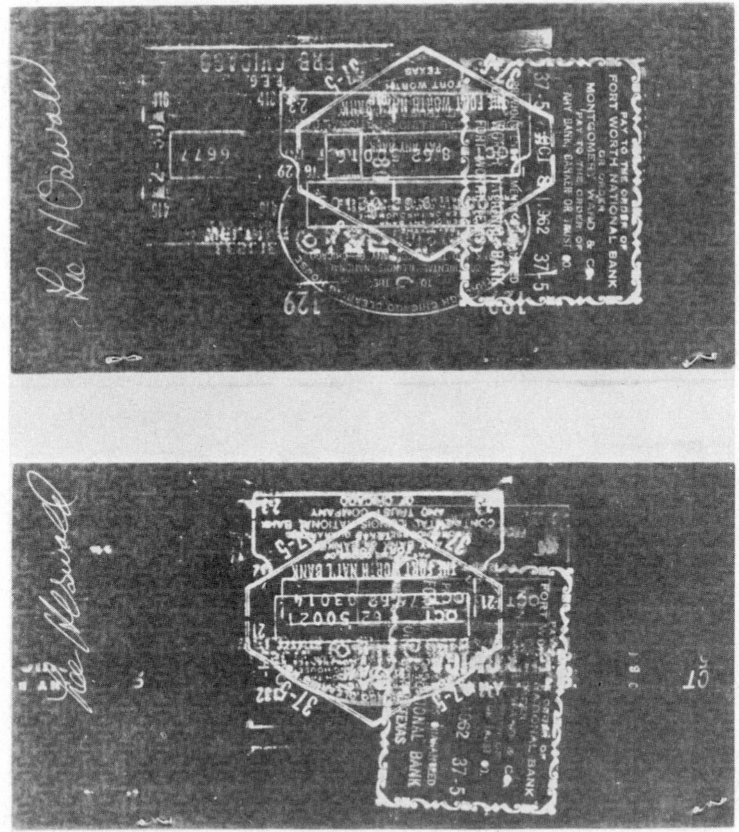

Commission Exhibit No. 2189—Continued

COMMISSION EXHIBIT No. 2189—Continued

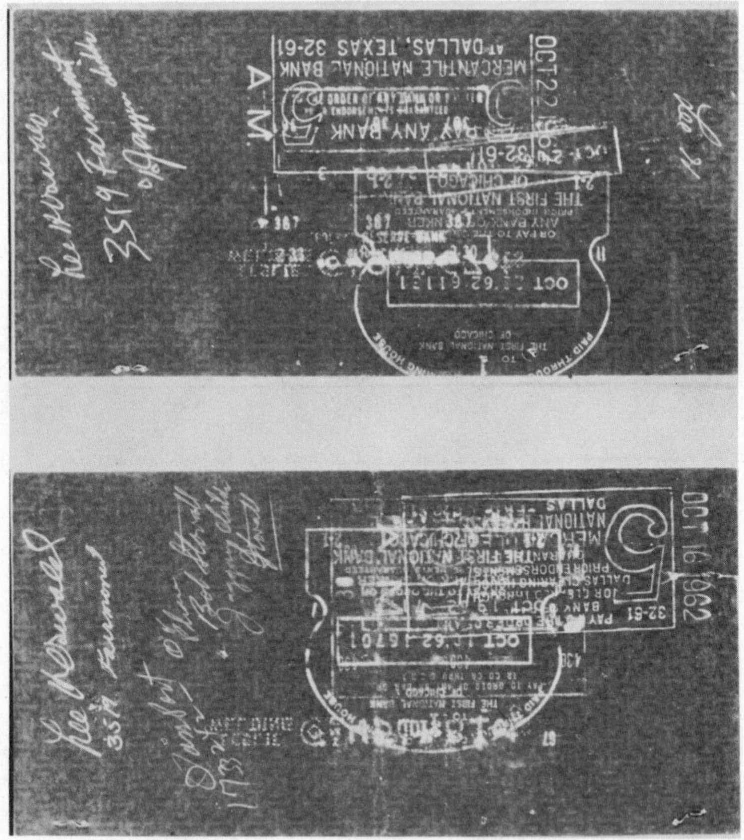

COMMISSION EXHIBIT No. 2189—Continued

Terminated 4-6-63

EMPLOYEE IDENTIFICATION/QUESTIONNAIRE

DATE EMPLOYED Oct 12, [illegible]

LEE HARVEY OSWALD NAME IN FULL (First, Middle, Last)		SOCIAL SECURITY NO. 433-54-3739
602 ELSBETH ST 3519 FAIRMOUNT PRESENT ADDRESS		PHONE NO. LA 10692
PO BOX 2915 PERMANENT HOME ADDRESS	DATE OF BIRTH Oct 18, 1939	RACE w
SAME	HEIGHT 5' 9" / WEIGHT 150	NO. OF DEPENDENTS 3
☐ SINGLE ☑ MARRIED ☐ FEMALE ☑ MALE		
WIFE OR HUSBAND'S FULL NAME MARINA N OSWALD wife		
IN CASE OF ACCIDENT NOTIFY— wife	PHONE NO. LA-10692	

DO YOU HAVE ANY OF THE FOLLOWING AILMENTS? NO

☐ Tuberculosis ☐ Back injury ☐ High Blood Pressure ☐ Heart Disease ☐ Kidney trouble ☐ Illness due to chemicals.

HAVE YOU EVER BEEN CHARGED WITH OR CONVICTED OF A FELONY? ☐ Yes ☑ No

Signed Lee H Oswald

JAGGERS CHILES STOVAL INC

DALLAS TEXAS

641

Commission Exhibit No. 2189—Continued

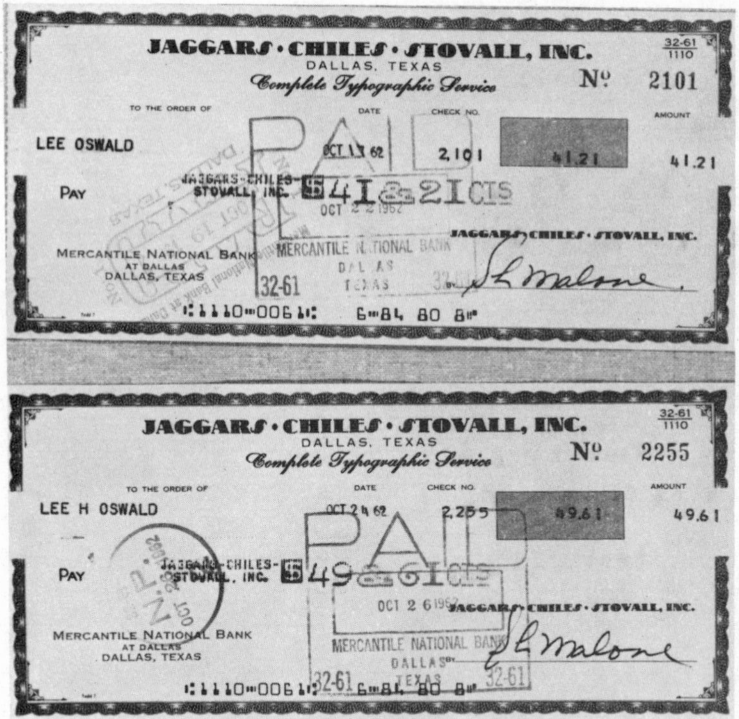

Commission Exhibit No. 2189—Continued

Commission Exhibit No. 2189—Continued

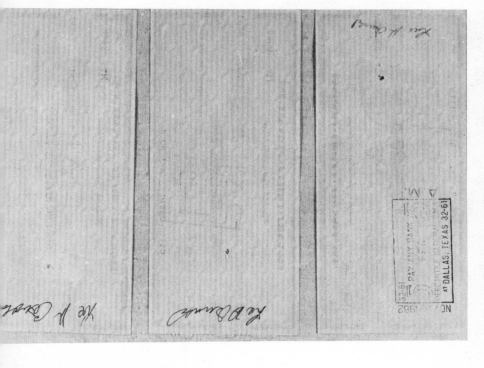

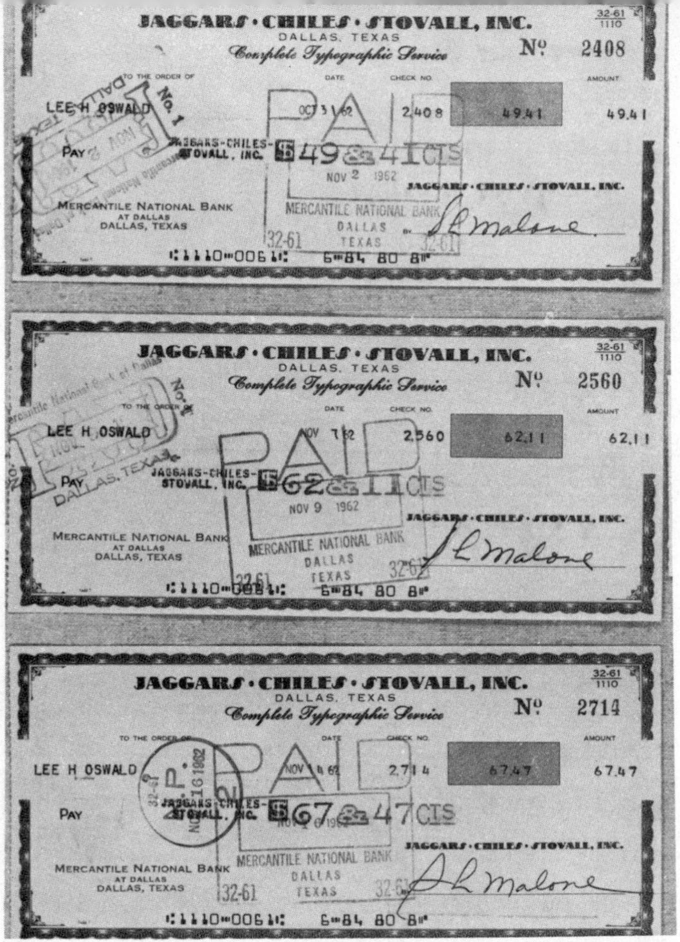

Commission Exhibit No. 2189—Continued

Commission Exhibit No. 2189—Continued

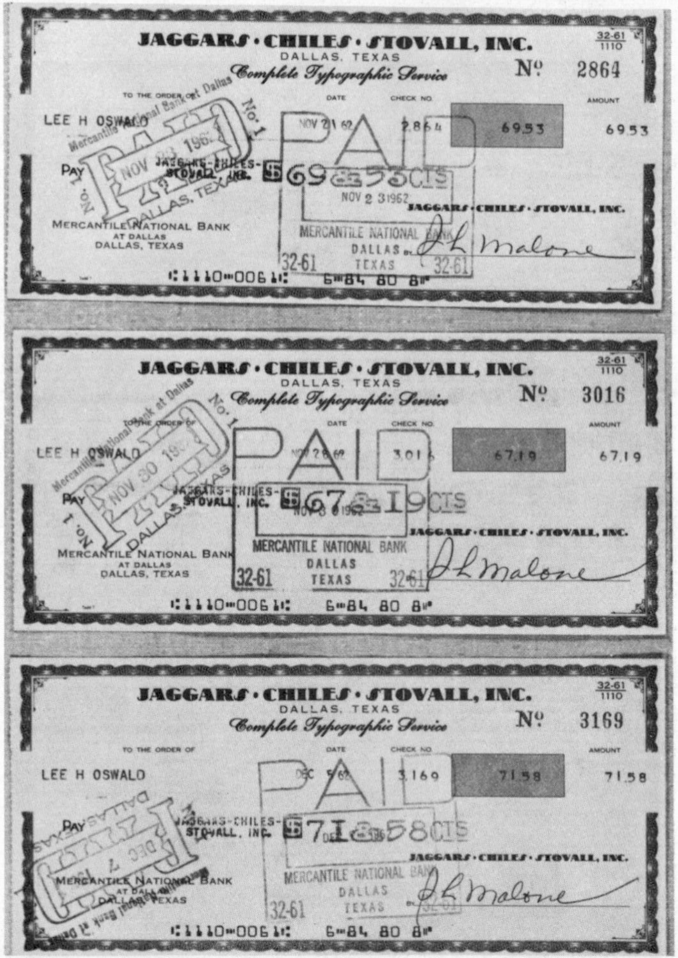

JAGGARS · CHILES · STOVALL, INC.
DALLAS, TEXAS
Complete Typographic Service
No. 2864
32-61 / 1110
TO THE ORDER OF LEE H OSWALD
DATE NOV 21 62 · CHECK NO. 2864 · AMOUNT 69.53
PAY $69.53 CTS
MERCANTILE NATIONAL BANK AT DALLAS, DALLAS, TEXAS
JAGGARS-CHILES-STOVALL, INC.
By J L Malone
⑆1110⑆0061⑆ 6⑈84 80 8⑈

JAGGARS · CHILES · STOVALL, INC.
DALLAS, TEXAS
Complete Typographic Service
No. 3016
32-61 / 1110
TO THE ORDER OF LEE H OSWALD
DATE NOV 28 62 · CHECK NO. 3016 · AMOUNT 67.19
PAY $67.19 CTS
MERCANTILE NATIONAL BANK AT DALLAS, DALLAS, TEXAS
JAGGARS-CHILES-STOVALL, INC.
By J L Malone
⑆1110⑆0061⑆ 6⑈84 80 8⑈

JAGGARS · CHILES · STOVALL, INC.
DALLAS, TEXAS
Complete Typographic Service
No. 3169
32-61 / 1110
TO THE ORDER OF LEE H OSWALD
DATE DEC 5 62 · CHECK NO. 3169 · AMOUNT 71.58
PAY $71.58 CTS
MERCANTILE NATIONAL BANK AT DALLAS, DALLAS, TEXAS
JAGGARS-CHILES-STOVALL, INC.
By J L Malone
⑆1110⑆0061⑆ 6⑈84 80 8⑈

Commission Exhibit No. 2189—Continued

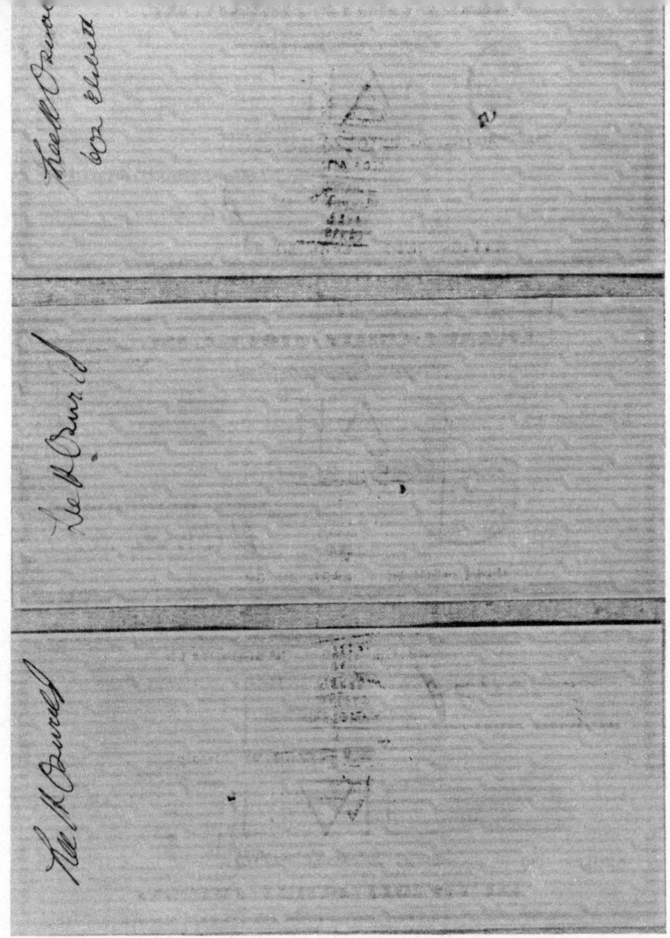

Commission Exhibit No. 2189—Continued

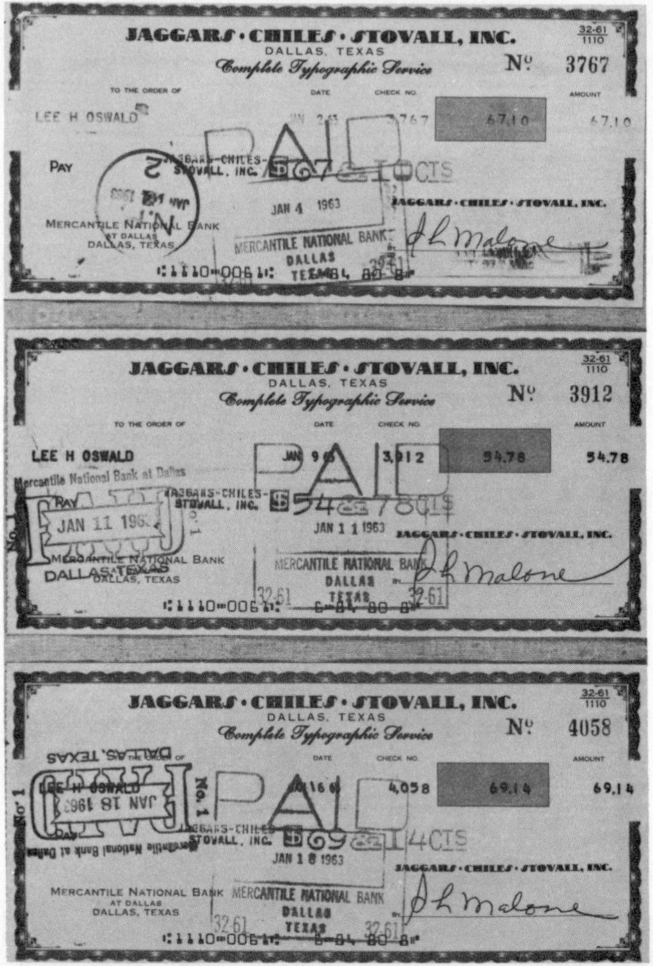
JAGGARS • CHILES • STOVALL, INC.
DALLAS, TEXAS
Complete Typographic Service
No. 3767
32-61 / 1110
TO THE ORDER OF
DATE
CHECK NO.
AMOUNT
LEE H OSWALD
67.10
PAY
MERCANTILE NATIONAL BANK
AT DALLAS
DALLAS, TEXAS
JAN 4 1963
MERCANTILE NATIONAL BANK
DALLAS
JAGGARS • CHILES • STOVALL, INC.
JAGGARS • CHILES • STOVALL, INC.
DALLAS, TEXAS
Complete Typographic Service
No. 3912
32-61 / 1110
LEE H OSWALD
54.78
JAN 11 1963
MERCANTILE NATIONAL BANK
DALLAS
TEXAS
JAGGARS • CHILES • STOVALL, INC.
JAGGARS • CHILES • STOVALL, INC.
DALLAS, TEXAS
Complete Typographic Service
No. 4058
32-61 / 1110
DALLAS, TEXAS
JAN 18 1963
69.14
JAN 18 1963
MERCANTILE NATIONAL BANK
AT DALLAS
DALLAS, TEXAS
MERCANTILE NATIONAL BANK
DALLAS
TEXAS
JAGGARS • CHILES • STOVALL, INC.

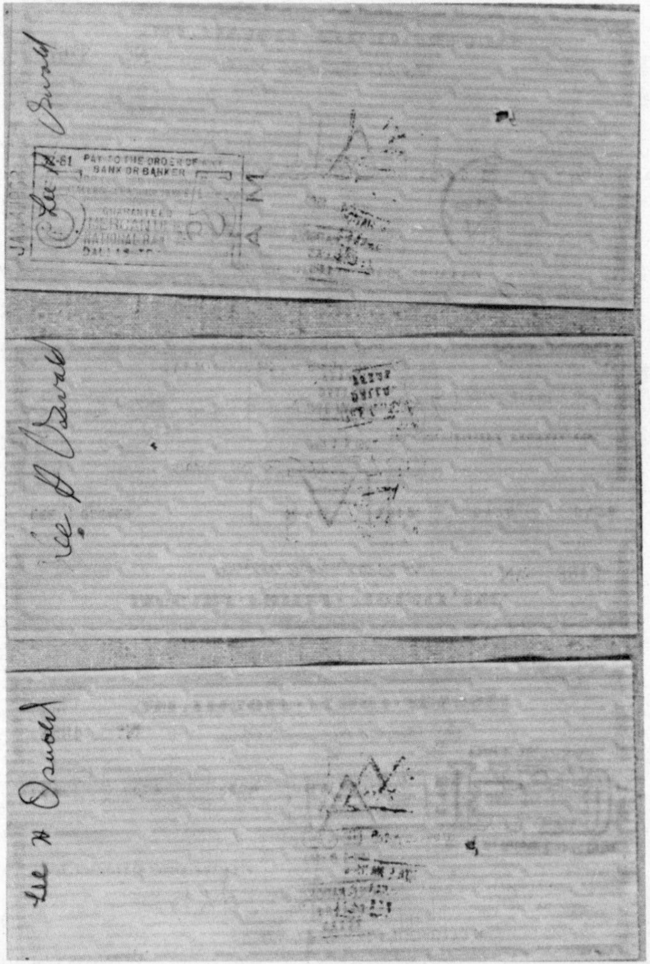
PAY TO THE ORDER OF
BANK OR BANKER

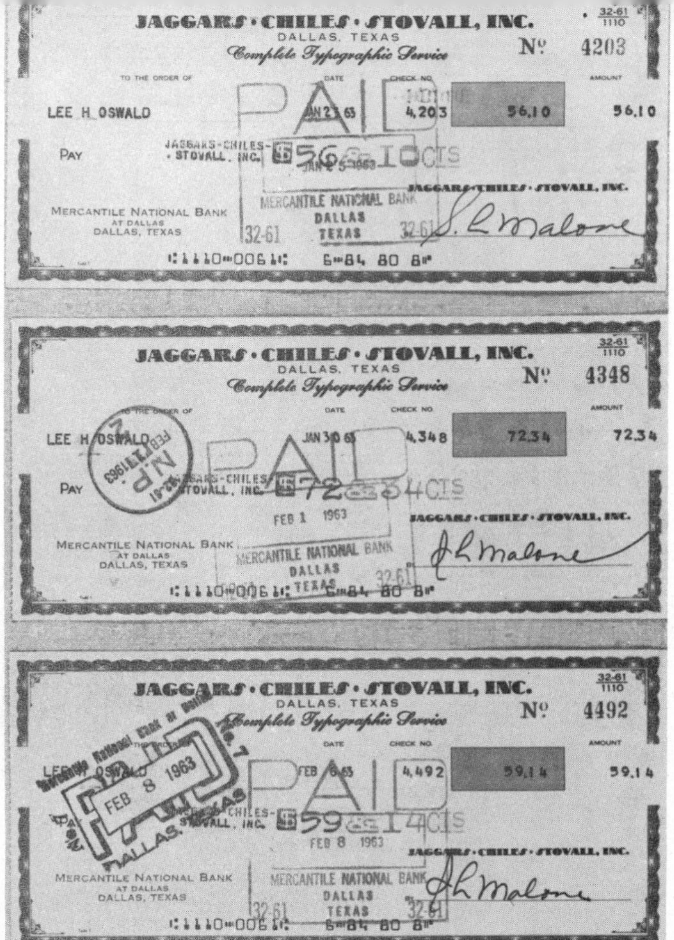

JAGGARS · CHILES · STOVALL, INC.
DALLAS, TEXAS
Complete Typographic Service
Nº 4203 32-61/1110
TO THE ORDER OF LEE H OSWALD
DATE JAN 23 63 CHECK NO. 4,203 56.10 AMOUNT 56.10
PAY JAGGARS-CHILES-STOVALL, INC. $56 10 CTS
MERCANTILE NATIONAL BANK AT DALLAS DALLAS, TEXAS
JAGGARS-CHILES-STOVALL, INC.
S. L. Malone
PAID JAN 25 1963 MERCANTILE NATIONAL BANK DALLAS TEXAS 32-61

JAGGARS · CHILES · STOVALL, INC.
DALLAS, TEXAS
Complete Typographic Service
Nº 4348 32-61/1110
TO THE ORDER OF LEE H OSWALD
DATE JAN 30 63 CHECK NO. 4,348 72.34 AMOUNT 72.34
PAY JAGGARS-CHILES-STOVALL, INC. $72 34 CTS
MERCANTILE NATIONAL BANK AT DALLAS DALLAS, TEXAS
JAGGARS-CHILES-STOVALL, INC.
J. L. Malone
N.P. FEB 1 1963 32-61
PAID FEB 1 1963 MERCANTILE NATIONAL BANK DALLAS TEXAS 32-61

JAGGARS · CHILES · STOVALL, INC.
DALLAS, TEXAS
Complete Typographic Service
Nº 4492 32-61/1110
TO THE ORDER OF LEE H OSWALD
DATE FEB 6 63 CHECK NO. 4,492 59.14 AMOUNT 59.14
PAY JAGGARS-CHILES-STOVALL, INC. $59 14 CTS
MERCANTILE NATIONAL BANK AT DALLAS DALLAS, TEXAS
JAGGARS-CHILES-STOVALL, INC.
J. L. Malone
PAID FEB 8 1963 DALLAS, TEXAS
PAID FEB 8 1963 MERCANTILE NATIONAL BANK DALLAS TEXAS 32-61

Commission Exhibit No. 2189—Continued

Lee H Oswald
PAY TO THE ORDER OF Mercantile National Bank at Dallas M-3703 DALLAS, TEXAS M-3703 FOR DEPOSIT ONLY MART LIQUOR STORE
00000-
JAN 25 1963 PAY ANY BANK P.E.G. MERCANTILE NATIONAL BANK AT DALLAS, TEXAS 32-61 A.M.

Lee H Oswald

Lee H Oswald

Commission Exhibit No. 2189—Continued

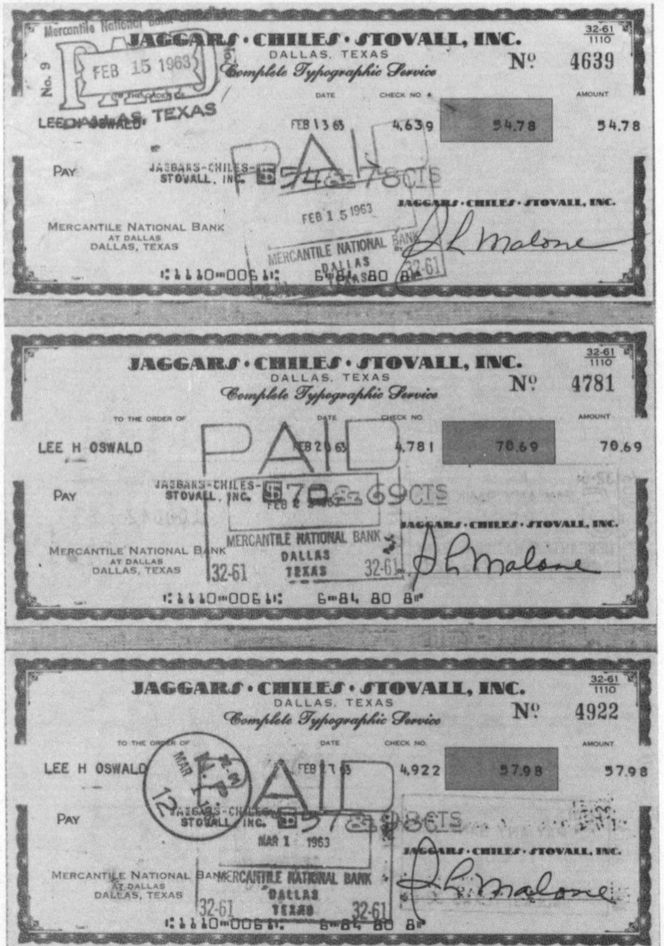

COMMISSION EXHIBIT No. 2189—Continued

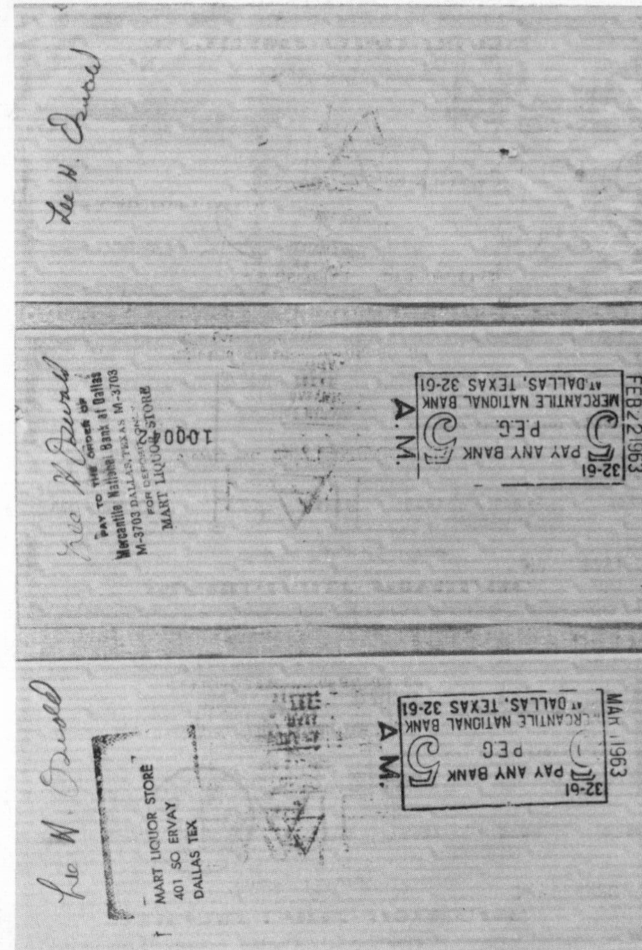

COMMISSION EXHIBIT No. 2189—Continued

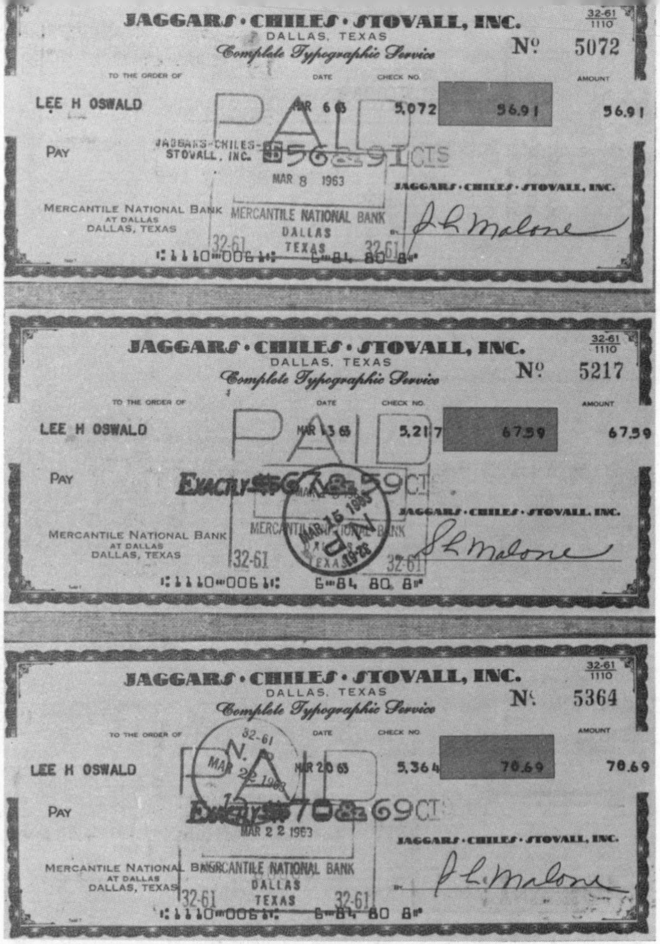

JAGGARS · CHILES · STOVALL, INC.
DALLAS, TEXAS
Complete Typographic Service
32-61
1110
No. 5072
TO THE ORDER OF | DATE | CHECK NO. | AMOUNT
LEE H OSWALD | MAR 6 63 | 5,072 | 56.91 | 56.91
PAY JAGGARS-CHILES-STOVALL, INC. $56 & 91 CTS
PAID MAR 8 1963 MERCANTILE NATIONAL BANK DALLAS TEXAS 32-61
MERCANTILE NATIONAL BANK AT DALLAS DALLAS, TEXAS
JAGGARS · CHILES · STOVALL, INC.
By J L Malone

JAGGARS · CHILES · STOVALL, INC.
DALLAS, TEXAS
Complete Typographic Service
32-61
1110
No. 5217
TO THE ORDER OF | DATE | CHECK NO. | AMOUNT
LEE H OSWALD | MAR 13 63 | 5,217 | 67.59 | 67.59
PAY EXACTLY $67 & 59 CTS
PAID MAR 15 1963 32-61
MERCANTILE NATIONAL BANK AT DALLAS DALLAS, TEXAS
JAGGARS · CHILES · STOVALL, INC.
By J L Malone

JAGGARS · CHILES · STOVALL, INC.
DALLAS, TEXAS
Complete Typographic Service
32-61
1110
No. 5364
TO THE ORDER OF | DATE | CHECK NO. | AMOUNT
LEE H OSWALD | MAR 20 63 | 5,364 | 70.69 | 70.69
PAY EXACTLY $70 & 69 CTS
PAID MAR 22 1963 MERCANTILE NATIONAL BANK DALLAS TEXAS 32-61
MERCANTILE NATIONAL BANK AT DALLAS DALLAS, TEXAS
JAGGARS · CHILES · STOVALL, INC.
By J L Malone

COMMISSION EXHIBIT No. 2189—Continued

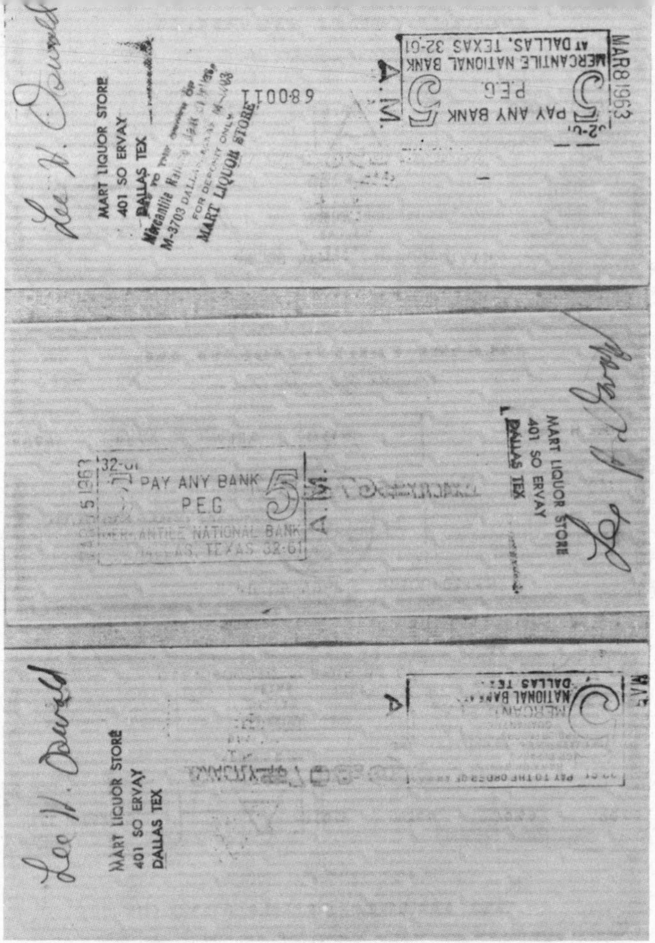

Lee H. Oswald
MART LIQUOR STORE
401 SO ERVAY
DALLAS TEX
MART LIQUOR STORE
FOR DEPOSIT ONLY
M-3703
MAR 8 1963
PAY ANY BANK
P.E.G.
MERCANTILE NATIONAL BANK AT DALLAS, TEXAS 32-61
A.M.

MART LIQUOR STORE
401 SO ERVAY
DALLAS TEX
PAY ANY BANK
P.E.G
MERCANTILE NATIONAL BANK
DALLAS, TEXAS 32-61
A.M.

Lee H. Oswald
MART LIQUOR STORE
401 SO ERVAY
DALLAS TEX
MERCANTILE NATIONAL BANK DALLAS TEX

COMMISSION EXHIBIT No. 2189—Continued

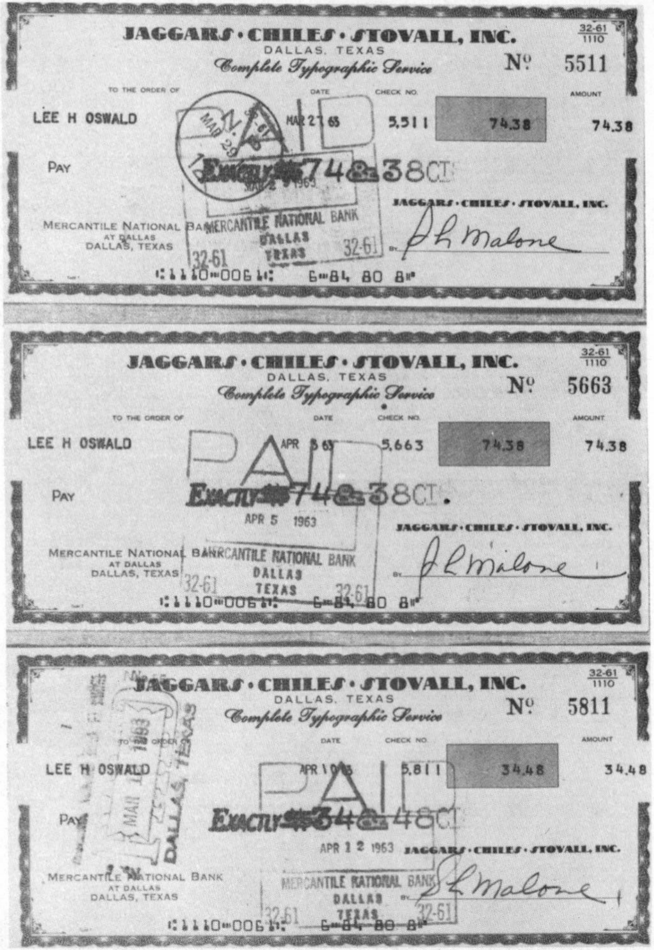

COMMISSION EXHIBIT No. 2180—Continued

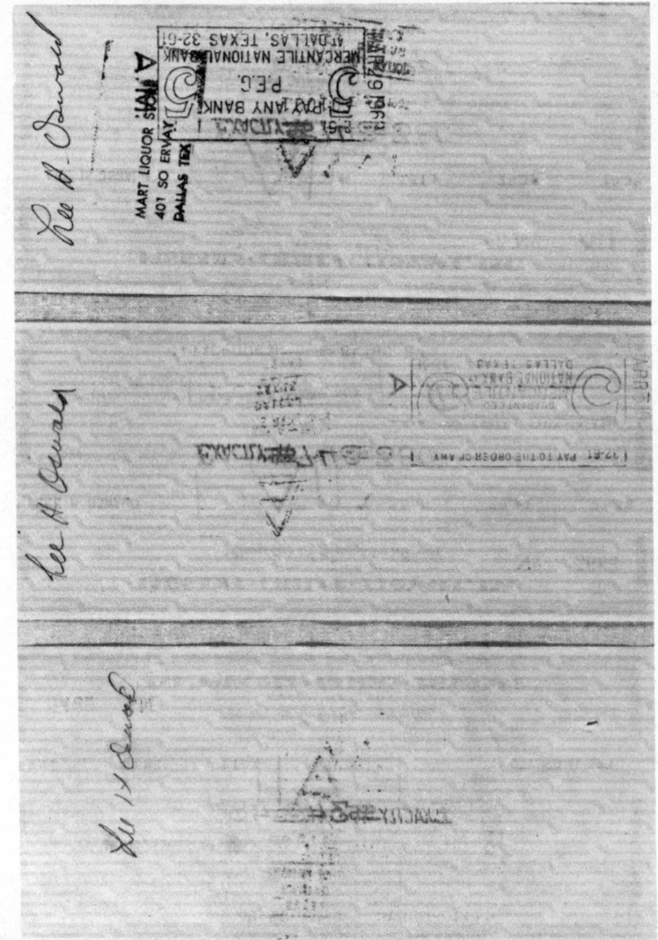

COMMISSION EXHIBIT No. 2180—Continued

NAME LEE H. OSWALD
FIRST MID LAST

ADDRESS 214 N. NEELY
NUMBER STREET OR R.F.D.

DALLAS 8, TEXAS
CITY

2. S.S. NO. 433-54-3937

17. CLAIM DATE 4-12-63 18. ☐ INV. ✓

19. DATE FILED IF OTHER THAN CLAIM DATE

20. ☑ UI ☐ UCFE ☐ UCX

21. OFFICE NO. 0931

DO NOT WRITE IN THIS BOX

4. SEX: ☑ MALE ☐ FEMALE 5. AGE 23

6. NAME OF MY LAST EMPLOYER JAGGER-CHILES-STOVAL

7. THE LOCATION OF THIS JOB WAS ✓

STREET OR RFD 522 BROWDER

CITY STATE DALLAS 1, TEXAS

8. MY OCCUPATION WAS PHOTOGRAPHER

9. DATE MY LAST WORK BEGAN 10-12-62

10. THE LAST DAY I WORKED 4-5-63

11. I WAS SEPARATED FROM MY LAST WORK BECAUSE I was laid off by John Graves, head of Photography & Art Dept. due to lack of work

12. EXCEPT FOR ANY STATEMENT SET FORTH IN THE SPACE FOR "EXCEPTIONS" IMMEDIATELY FOLLOWING THESE STATEMENTS, I CERTIFY THAT:

(1) I am able to work; (2) I am ready, willing and available for work; (3) I am not self-employed; (4) I am not farming; (5) I am not attending school; (6) I am not receiving any wages in lieu of notice, vacation pay, Workmen's Compensation, Old Age Benefits (Social Security) or Railroad Retirement Benefits; (7) I am not receiving veteran's education and training allowance or education assistance under the War Orphans Education Assistance Act; (8) I have not worked for the Federal Government as a civilian or performed any active military service during the last eighteen months.

EXCEPTIONS TO STATEMENTS (1) THROUGH (8) ABOVE:

NOTICE TO EMPLOYER

See reverse side for circumstances which may affect claimant's rights to unemployment benefits and information about the charging of benefit wages to taxable employers.

YOUR NOTIFICATION MUST BE MAILED TO: →

TEXAS EMPLOYMENT COMMISSION
2206 MAIN STREET
CENTRAL CLAIMS OFFICE
DALLAS 1, TEXAS

BE SURE TO SHOW CLAIMANT'S SOCIAL SECURITY NUMBER IN CORRESPONDENCE ABOUT THIS CLAIM

SEE REVERSE SIDE FOR SUMMARIES OF STATUTORY PROVISIONS

INITIAL CLAIM FOR BENEFITS
TEXAS EMPLOYMENT COMMISSION

Form B-3 (163)

641

COMMISSION EXHIBIT No. 2189—Continued

TEXAS EMPLOYMENT COMMISSION
AUSTIN, TEXAS

EMPLOYMENT SERVICE
EMPLOYMENT INSURANCE
FARM LABOR SERVICE

May 6, 1963

Jaggars
Chiles - Stovall, Inc.
7522 Browder Street
Dallas, Texas

Gentlemen:

Claimant: 433-54-3937
Lee H. Oswald
757 France St.
New Orleans, La.

This claimant filed a claim for unemployment insurance through the Employment Security Agency of Louisiana, on 4-29, 1963, and stated that he had last worked for you. This notice is to inform you of the claim.

If you have knowledge of any facts that may adversely affect this claimant's right to unemployment insurance, please notify the Commission of such facts promptly. On the back of this form there is a brief description of circumstances which might have such adverse effect.

If you are taxable under the Texas Unemployment Compensation Act, please likewise notify the Commission promptly of any facts that may affect a charge to your experience-rating tax account. The charge is limited by law and cannot be more than the total amount of taxable wages you paid this claimant during the first 4 of the last 5 completed calendar quarters immediately preceding the date (shown in the first paragraph above) of this claim. Your own payroll records will give you these wage figures. If this claimant is found to be entitled to benefits, this charge will be made at the time he is given his first benefit check. The law permits noncharging only under the circumstances described on the back of this form.

IMPORTANT If you do not, within 10 days from the date of this letter, mail or deliver to the Commission the notification described in the paragraphs immediately above, you will be deemed to have waived all your rights in connection with this claim, except with respect to clerical or machine errors as to amount of wages.

YOUR NOTIFICATION MUST BE MAILED TO THE TEXAS EMPLOYMENT COMMISSION, INTERSTATE UNIT, AUSTIN 1, TEXAS.

Be sure to show claimant's Social Security number in correspondence about this claim.

TEXAS EMPLOYMENT COMMISSION

Interstate Unit

641

COMMISSION EXHIBIT No. 2189—Continued

TEXAS EMPLOYMENT COMMISSION

May 6, 1963

EMPLOYERS PROTEST TO INITIAL CLAIM FOR BENEFITS

Gentlemen:

If you have basis for protest to the claimant's rights to receive unemployment insurance or, if a Texas employer, you are protesting a chargeback to your tax account as a result of this claim, please furnish the following information:

433-54-3937
Lee H. Oswald
757 Franco St.
New Orleans, La.

Date Employed ______ Date Separated ______

Occupation ______ Wage Rate ______

Reason for Separation: ☐ Quit ☐ Discharged ☐ Other

Name of Firm ______

Employer Representative ______ Title ______
Signature

B-72 (163)

Perm

Please print or type

APPLICATION FOR EMPLOYMENT Date May 9, 1963

Company Wm. B. Reily & Co. Inc. Location 640 Magazine St

LEE HARVEY OSWALD 433-54-3937
Name in full: Social Security Number

5/15 757 French St. HU 84326
Present address: number, street, city and state. Telephone number HU 843—

How long have you lived there? 3 1/2 mths.

same
Permanent or last address, Street

same
City State

How long lived there?
Address at which you lived longest in last 5 years:

Street

City State

How long lived there?

Do you live with parents? ___ Board ___ Rent ___

Own home?

List under Employment Record on next page all additional addresses at which you lived in the past 5 years with street addresses and how long at each.

Have you taken recent physical examination? yes

For what purpose?

Did you pass? yes

Time lost through accident or illness in past two years

What is present condition of your health? Good

Are you willing to take physical examination? yes

Age 23 Date of Birth Oct. 18, 39 Sex: ☑ Male ☐ Fem

Physical Qualities:

Height 5 9 Weight 150 Health Excel

Marital Status: ☐ Single ☑ Married ☐ Divorced ☐ Widow ☐ Separated ☐ Engaged

Number of Children 1 15 months

How long married? 26 m. Separated? no Other dependents none

Education: Completed High school

Weekly income from last job

Minimum living expenses

Previous Occupation, name exact duties Active Duty U.S.M.C.

Does applicant have any other income, personally or from spouse? no

If so, what amount

Number of jobs held in last five years

Length of time since last employed

Physical deformity or impairment — Hernia none

Speech No Right eye No Left eye No Hearing No

Feet & Legs No Back No Hands & Arms No

Any other defect none

Grammar school — Name Beauregard J.H.S. Grade Finished ___ Age at end ___

High school — Name Warren Easton S.H.S. Year graduated N/A

Name of college — Course ___ Year graduated ___ Degree ___

Name of night school — Course taken ___

Special Study Courses —

EMPLOYMENT RECORD

(Print or type clearly)

Show every job you have had in the past 5 years starting with the present or last job. Give exact dates as shown in the example. Where the employer has more than one branch or plants in more than one place, show where you worked and under whom. When the employer has gone out of business, give the name and present address of the former owner or manager and the names and addresses of three persons who can confirm your employment. Use more than one line for each job if necessary and complete on separate page if you haven't space enough below. No application will be considered without full information on the applicant's employment. Account for all of the last 5 years.

From EXAMPLE 1-30-56	To 1/15/61	NAME OF EMPLOYER (SHOW PRESENT POSITION FIRST)	STREET ADDRESS	CITY & STATE	NAME OF FOREMAN OR SUPERVISOR	NATURE OF WORK	WEEKLY EARNINGS	REASON FOR LEAVING OR WANTING TO LEAVE
1957	1963	U S M C						
—	1953	(Present Job - If Any) School						
		(Last Job)						
		(Next Preceding)						
		(Next Preceding)						
		(Next Preceding)						

Are you employed at present: no May we write your present employer now: ______ Were you in the Armed Services yes What type of discharge have you ____ Show your discharge to your supervisor: ______ What is your draft status Inactive Reserves

PERSONAL CHARACTER REFERENCE: NAME	OCCUPATION	STREET NO. OR BOX AND TOWN AND TELEPHONE
1 John Murret	[illegible]	757 French St. NO 84326
2. [illegible]	[illegible]	[illegible]
3 Lieut J. Evans	Active Duty	U.S. M.C.

Have you ever been employed by us before? ______ In what capacity? ______

Name relatives in our employ, if any none

Name personal acquaintances in our employ no

IN WHAT WAY WERE YOU FIRST INTERESTED IN WORK WITH US?

[illegible] Ad in paper

In making this application to the Company, I unders[illegible] am at liberty to investigate it [illegible] its record in any manner I see fit. The informatio[illegible]ven above is for the purpose of [illegible]bling the Company to investigate me and my record [illegible] manner it sees fit.

It is agreed that any proposition made me is predicated upon the truthfulness of the state[illegible] made above.

I authorize the investigation of my application and authorize each of my former employers [illegible] character references to render full report to the Company, its employees and its investiga[illegible] on my character, personal habits, ability, and any and all other information requested.

I hereby specifically relieve and release the Company, its employees, its investigators, my [illegible]ner employers, their employees, and my character references from any and all liability for [illegible] of any nature whatsoever, happening or arising in any manner, on account of the [illegible]ishing of this information. Further, if the Company refuses or accepts my application, I do [illegible] relieve all parties of any responsibility and specifically waive all my rights to any and damages suffered. I extend this release to former employers I may have neglected to name [illegible] application and to anyone who shall report to the Company with reference to this applica[illegible]

It is further understood that either party, upon completing his investigation, is at liberty to withdraw and to cancel these negotiations without obligation to the other. Because the information customarily received in investigations is confidential, it is understood that neither party is obligated to give any reason for its withdrawal.

Lee H Oswald
(signature of Applicant)

Group Number VA

Accepted By Al Alvarado

Starting Date 5-10-63 Starting Salary $ 1.50 per hr

COMMISSION EXHIBIT No. 2189—Continued

Extra

FORM W-4 (Rev. July 1961)
U. S. Treasury Department
Internal Revenue Service

EMPLOYEE'S WITHHOLDING EXEMPTION CERTIFICATE

Print full name .... LEE H. OSWALD .... Social Security Account Number 433-54-3937

Print home address .... 757 French St. .... City .... New Orleans .... Zone .... State .... LA

EMPLOYEE: File this form with your employer. Otherwise, he must withhold U. S. income tax from your wages without exemption.

EMPLOYER: Keep this certificate with your records. If the employee is believed to have claimed too many exemptions, the District Director should be so advised.

HOW TO CLAIM YOUR WITHHOLDING EXEMPTIONS

1. If SINGLE, and you claim an exemption, write the figure "1" ....
2. If MARRIED, one exemption each is allowable for husband and wife if not claimed on another certificate.
   (a) If you claim both of these exemptions, write the figure "2"
   (b) If you claim one of these exemptions, write the figure "1" 2
   (c) If you claim neither of these exemptions, write "0"
3. Exemptions for age and blindness (applicable only to you and your wife but not to dependents):
   (a) If you or your wife will be 65 years of age or older at the end of the year, and you claim this exemption, write "1"; if both will be 65 or older, and you claim both of these exemptions, write "2" ....
   (b) If you or your wife are blind, and you claim this exemption, write the figure "1"; if both are blind, and you claim both of these exemptions, write the figure "2"
4. If you claim exemptions for one or more dependents, write the number of such exemptions. (Do not claim exemption for a dependent unless you are qualified under instruction 4 on other side.) 1
5. Add the number of exemptions which you have claimed above and write the total 3
6. Additional withholding per pay period under agreement with employer. See Instruction 1 .... $........

I CERTIFY that the number of withholding exemptions claimed on this certificate does not exceed the number to which I am entitled.

(Date) .... May 10, ... 1963 .... (Signed) .... Lee H. Oswald

---

Oswald .... Lee .... H.
(LAST NAME) (FIRST NAME) (MIDDLE NAME)

SAFETY INSTRUCTIONS TO EMPLOYEES

1. Report at once to your supervisor all injuries no matter how slight.
2. Be thoughtful and orderly in your conduct. Many injuries are the result of "horseplay" and fooling.
3. Always use the safety devices which are provided by the company for your protection.
4. Report to your supervisor any conditions or practices which appear to be unsafe.
5. Employees should, at all times, do everything possible to avoid getting hurt, and avoid injuring any other employee.
6. Be safety conscious and give your supervisor any suggestions you have for improving safety measures or devices.

I have (read) — (had explained to me) and will observe the SAFETY INSTRUCTIONS set forth above.

Signature .... Lee H Oswald .... Date .... May 21, 63

I have reviewed these instructions with the employee and outlined the safe practices to be followed on the work assigned

Supervisor .... Department ....

The best safety device is a CAREFUL WORKER

L.P. 542

641

Commission Exhibit No. 2189—Continued

B C D E F G H I J 1 2 3 4 5 6 7 8 9

1. PRINT LAST NAME	FIRST	MIDDLE	4. SOC. SEC. NO.
Oswald,	Lee	Harry	433-54-3937

2. NUMBER AND STREET ADDRESS, R.D. OR P. O. BOX NO.	5. TELEPHONE NO.
757 French Street	Hu 8-4326

3. CITY	POSTAL ZONE	STATE
New Orleans, La.		

6. DATE OF BIRTH	7.	8. HEIGHT	9. WEIGHT
10 18 39 (Mo. Day Year)	☒ MARRIED ☐ SINGLE ☐ WIDOWED	5 9 (Ft. In.)	145 (Pounds)

10. IF VETERAN, ENTER YOUR LAST MILITARY SERVICE

ENTRY ON ACTIVE SERVICE	RELEASE FROM ACTIVE SERVICE	SERIAL NO.
Mo. Day Year	Mo. Day Year	

11. IF UNION MEMBER, GIVE NUMBER, NAME AND AFFILIATION OF LOCAL

12. CIRCLE HIGHEST YEAR OF EDUCATION COMPLETED AND GIVE DEGREES RECEIVED

GRADE SCHOOL	HIGH SCHOOL	COLLEGE	DEGREES
1 2 3 4 5 6 7 8	1 2 (3) 4	1 2 3 4 5 6 7	

NAME OF SCHOOL AND LIST COURSES OF TRAINING (INCLUDING MILITARY) WHICH PREPARED YOU FOR WORK. GIVE LENGTH AND DATES ENDED.

Additional Application Card—LSES 512 7-61 22-11

DO NOT WRITE BELOW THIS LINE

TITLES	CODES
Shipping Clerk	1-34.14
Photographer, Commercial	0-56.11

SKILLS, KNOWLEDGE, ABILITIES	DATES
	4.26.63
	4.29.63

GATB B-1002	TEST RESULTS					DATE
G	1 2 3 4 5 6 7 8 9 10					
V	11 12 13 14 15 16 17 18					
N	19 20 21 22					
S						
P	B-215	233	257	277	291	
Q		299	307	309	319	321
K		329	332	334		
F						
M						

641

COMMISSION EXHIBIT No. 2189—Continued

IMPORTANT CIVILIAN AND MILITARY EXPERIENCE

DESCRIBE YOUR LONGEST AND MOST IMPORTANT JOBS. BEGIN WITH YOUR MOST RECENT JOB

13. NAME EMPLOYER OR BRANCH OF MILITARY SERVICE	NAME JOB AND DESCRIBE EXACTLY WHAT YOU DID AND HOW YOU DID IT
Lov-R-Pak Co. ADDRESS 201 N. E. Vacek St. Ft. Worth, Texas. EMPLOYER'S BUSINESS Ventilator Co. YRS. or MOS. ON JOB 3 DATE LEFT Oct. 1962 PAY $1.25 hr.	Shipping Clerk-As clerk in stock and mailing department. ~~Filling out bills of Lathe~~ Receiving of goods ect.
14. NAME EMPLOYER OR BRANCH OF MILITARY SERVICE ADDRESS EMPLOYER'S BUSINESS YRS. or MOS. ON JOB DATE LEFT PAY	NAME JOB AND DESCRIBE EXACTLY WHAT YOU DID AND HOW YOU DID IT
15. NAME EMPLOYER OR BRANCH OF MILITARY SERVICE ADDRESS EMPLOYER'S BUSINESS YRS. or MOS. ON JOB DATE LEFT PAY	NAME JOB AND DESCRIBE EXACTLY WHAT YOU DID AND HOW YOU DID IT
16. NAME EMPLOYER OR BRANCH OF MILITARY SERVICE ADDRESS EMPLOYER'S BUSINESS YRS. or MOS. ON JOB DATE LEFT PAY	NAME JOB AND DESCRIBE EXACTLY WHAT YOU DID AND HOW YOU DID IT

17. COMMENTS

COMMISSION EXHIBIT No. 2189—Continued

3937

1. NAME: (Print) Lee (First) H. (Middle) Oswald (Last)

Name worked under (if different) Same

2. LOCAL MAILING ADDRESS: P.O. Box 30061 (No.) (St. or Rural Route)
N.O. (City) (Zone No.) La. (State)

3. ☒ Male ☐ Female No. of dependents —

4. DATE OF BIRTH: 10-18-39

5. SSA No. 433 54 3937

☒ UI ☐ UCFE ☐ UCX ☐ New ☒ Additional

6. Liable State Texas

7. Actual date claim taken 4-29-63

8. Backdating requested to — Explain in item 24

9. Date of last claim (any type) against above liable State 4-12-63

10. Local office at (Number and Street) Dallas (City) Texas (State)

11. Main occupation Photographer 0-56.11 Other occupation Shipping Clerk 1-34.44

(Give JOB TITLE and, if known, the code number as shown on your identification card)

12. WORK RECORD: Show the information requested below for all of your employers, including any periods of self-employment, government and military service, during the past 24 months.

EMPLOYER NAME (Name of Company)	EMPLOYER ADDRESS (Show number, street, city, and State)		DATES WORKED From	Through
LAST EMPLOYER regardless of state: Jaggars-Chiles-Stovall, Inc.	Address where work performed	522 Browder St.	10-12-62	4-6-63
	Address where payroll records are kept	Dallas, Texas	Reason for Separation: Lack of work ☒ Other* ☐	
NEXT TO LAST EMPLOYER: Wage credits are due	Address where work performed			
	Address where payroll records are kept		Reason for Separation: Lack of work ☐ Other* ☐	
NEXT EMPLOYER: for ... not on ...	Address where work performed			
	Address where payroll records are kept		Reason for Separation: Lack of work ☐ Other* ☐	
NEXT EMPLOYER: ... information see ...	Address where work performed			
	Address where payroll records are kept		Reason for Separation: Lack of work ☐ Other* ☐	

REMARKS

EMPLOYER NAME (Name of Company)	EMPLOYER ADDRESS (Show number, street, city, and State)		DATES WORKED From	Through
LAST EMPLOYER regardless of state: Wm. B. Reily	Address where work performed	Same	5-10-63	7-19-63
	Address where payroll records are kept	640 Magazine N.O. La.	Reason for Separation: Lack of work ☐ Other* ☐ 641	
NEXT TO LAST EMPLOYER	Address where			

WBA 33 MBA 369 BYE 4/64 Claimant's signature Lee H. Oswald

Code assignment

Date claim filed	Week ending date	Earnings	Remarks	Claim taker's initials
		Texas	LCES 407 to E. S. (Claim Active) IV 4-29-63	
4-29-63		IB1	IBID	HS
4-29	5-6-63		IB, 4	
5-7	5-6	—	IB, IB, O	
5-15	5-13	—		6-25-63
7-22-63		IB1 —	LCES 407 to E. S. (Claim Active) 7-22-63	
7-30	7-29	—	IB, IB, O	
8-6	8-5			
	8-12	—		
	8-19	—		
8-27	8-26	—		
	9-2	—		
9-10	9-9	—		
9-17	9-16	—		
9-24	9-23			
			OCT 1 6 ...	
			LCES 417 to E. S. (Claim Inactive)	

641

IB-1A, p. 2

COMMISSION EXHIBIT No. 2189—Continued

COMMISSION EXHIBIT No. 2189—Continued

DESCRIBE YOUR LONGEST AND MOST IMPORTANT JOBS. BEGIN WITH YOUR MOST RECENT JOB.

13. NAME EMPLOYER OR BRANCH OF MILITARY SERVICE
Jaggars-Chiles-Stoval Typo.
ADDRESS
522 Browder, Dallas, Texas.
EMPLOYER'S BUSINESS
Typography
YRS. or MOS. ON JOB 5 | DATE LEFT April 10 | PAY $1.35 hr.

NAME JOB AND DESCRIBE EXACTLY WHAT YOU DID AND HOW YOU DID IT
Comm. Photographer
Developing and taking of film negatives, printing photos from them enlarging photo's etc.

14. NAME EMPLOYER OR BRANCH OF MILITARY SERVICE
Lov-R-Pak Co.
ADDRESS 201 N. E, Vacek, St. Ft. Worth, Tex.
EMPLOYER'S BUSINESS
Ventilator Co.
YRS. or MOS. ON JOB 3 | DATE LEFT Oct. '62 | PAY $1.25 hr.

NAME JOB AND DESCRIBE EXACTLY WHAT YOU DID AND HOW YOU DID IT
Shipping Clerk-As clerk in stock and mailing department-filling out bills of lading-receiving of goods, etc.

15. NAME EMPLOYER OR BRANCH OF MILITARY SERVICE
U. S. M. Ca.
ADDRESS
California
EMPLOYER'S BUSINESS
YRS. or MOS. ON JOB 3 | DATE LEFT | PAY

NAME JOB AND DESCRIBE EXACTLY WHAT YOU DID AND HOW YOU DID IT
Radar Operator-Attended electronic radar operators school-says not qualified for civilian job.

16. NAME EMPLOYER OR BRANCH OF MILITARY SERVICE
ADDRESS
EMPLOYER'S BUSINESS
YRS. or MOS. ON JOB | DATE LEFT | PAY

NAME JOB AND DESCRIBE EXACTLY WHAT YOU DID AND HOW YOU DID IT

17. SUMMARY OF OTHER WORK EXPERIENCE (GIVE JOB TITLE, DURATION AND DATE ENDED)

DO NOT WRITE BELOW THIS LINE

SPECIAL INFORMATION
U. S. Citizen- No car.

Has one child- 14 mos. daughter
Returned to N. O. La. 2-25-63 having been born here. Lived here 14 yrs.

EMPLOYMENT COUNSELING STATEMENT

LEISURE TIME ACTIVITIES

COMMENTS Will travel on limited basis. Will relocate
Min. $1.25 hr. Neat-Suit Tie, Polite.

INTERVIEWER J. Rachal

841

CALLED	REFERRED	EMPLOYER OR AGENCY	JOB TITLE OR PURPOSE	DUR.	PAY	RESULT	REMARKS
5-28-63	NF	Commerce Pictures	Developer	P	WD		Br 2.59

A B C D E F G H I J 1 2 3 4 5 6 7 8 9

1. PRINT LAST NAME Oswald | FIRST Lee | MIDDLE Harry
4. SOC. SEC. NO. 433-54-3937
2. NUMBER AND STREET ADDRESS, R.D. OR P. O. BOX NO. 757 French Street
5. TELEPHONE NO. Hu 8-4326
3. CITY New Orleans, La. | POSTAL ZONE | STATE
6. DATE OF BIRTH 10 18 39 (Mo. Day Year)
7. [X] MARRIED [ ] SINGLE [ ] WIDOWED
8. HEIGHT 5 Ft. 9 In.
9. WEIGHT 145 Pounds
10. IF VETERAN, ENTER YOUR LAST MILITARY SERVICE
ENTRY ON ACTIVE SERVICE 7 23 59 (Mo. Day Year) | RELEASE FROM ACTIVE SERVICE 7 22 62 (Mo. Day Year) | SERIAL NO. 1653230
11. IF UNION MEMBER, GIVE NUMBER, NAME AND AFFILIATION OF LOCAL
12. CIRCLE HIGHEST YEAR OF EDUCATION COMPLETED AND GIVE DEGREES RECEIVED
GRADE SCHOOL 1 2 3 4 5 6 7 8 | HIGH SCHOOL 1959 1 2 3 (4) | COLLEGE 1 2 3 4 5 6 7 | DEGREES
NAME OF SCHOOL AND LIST COURSES OF TRAINING (INCLUDING MILITARY) WHICH PREPARED YOU FOR WORK. GIVE LENGTH AND DATES ENDED.
Arlington Heights H. S. (Mech. Drawing)
Ft. Worth, Texas (Art)
Completed High School while in service (M.E.C.)

APPLICATION CARD LSES-511

DO NOT WRITE BELOW THIS LINE

TITLES	CODES
Dark Room Man (Any Ind)	5-86.
Photographer (Commercial)	0-56.

SKILLS, KNOWLEDGE, ABILITIES
Types, little Add. Mach. 101
Photo Enlarger-Large still modification Camera

DATES 4-26 4-29-6

GATB B-1002	TEST RESULTS	DATE
G	1 2 3 4 5 6 7 8 9 10	
V	11 12 13 14 15 16 17 18	
N	19 20 21 22	
S		
P	B-215 233 257 277 291	
Q	299 307 309 319 321	
K	329 332 334	
F		
M		

641

COMMISSION EXHIBIT No. 2189—Continued

COMMISSION EXHIBIT No. 2189—Continued

DO NOT WRITE BELOW THIS LINE

CALLED	REFERRED	EMPLOYER OR AGENCY	JOB TITLE	DUR.	PAY	RESULT	REMARKS
	4-26	Geo Reggel Studio	Comm Photog	P	WD	OR	-V

A B C D E F G H I J 1 2 3 4 5 6 7 8 9

1. PRINT LAST NAME / FIRST / MIDDLE: Oswald LEE Harvey
4. SOC. SEC. NO.: 433-54-3937
2. NUMBER AND STREET ADDRESS, R.D. OR P. O. BOX NO.: P.O. Box 30061
5. TELEPHONE NO.: HU-84323
3. CITY / POSTAL ZONE / STATE: NEW ORLEANS LA.
6. DATE OF BIRTH: 10 18 39 (Mo. Day Year)
7. MARRIED / SINGLE / WIDOWED: [x] MARRIED
8. HEIGHT: 5 9 (Ft. In.)
9. WEIGHT: 145 (Pounds)
10. IF VETERAN, ENTER YOUR LAST MILITARY SERVICE — ENTRY ON ACTIVE SERVICE: 7 23 59 (Mo. Day Year); RELEASE FROM ACTIVE SERVICE: 7 23 12 (?) (Mo. Day Year); SERIAL NO.: 1653230
11. IF UNION MEMBER, GIVE NUMBER, NAME AND AFFILIATION OF LOCAL: N/A
12. CIRCLE HIGHEST YEAR OF EDUCATION COMPLETED AND GIVE DEGREES RECEIVED — GRADE SCHOOL 1 2 3 4 5 6 7 8; HIGH SCHOOL 1 2 (3) 4; COLLEGE 1 2 3 4 5 6 7; DEGREES
NAME OF SCHOOL AND LIST COURSES OF TRAINING (INCLUDING MILITARY) WHICH PREPARED YOU FOR WORK. GIVE LENGTH AND DATES ENDED.
Arlington Heights H.S. Mech Drawing (ART) Ft Worth, Tex
completed High school while in service (M.C.)

APPLICATION CARD LSES-511 (Rev. 10-62)

DO NOT WRITE BELOW THIS LINE

TITLES	CODES
PHOTOGRAPHER COMMERCIAL	0-56
SHIPPING CLERK II (Clerical)	1-34
DARKROOM MAN (any ind.)	5-96

SKILLS, KNOWLEDGE, ABILITIES	DATES
types, lit. Add Mach	4-26
Photo. Enlarger, Large still	4-29-6
Camera	7-27

GATB B-1002	TEST RESULTS	DATE
G	1 2 3 4 5 6 7 8 9 10	
V	11 12 13 14 15 16 17 18	
N	19 20 21 22 23 24 25 26	
S	27 28 29 30 31 32 33 34	
P	35 All None	
Q		
K		
F		
M		

Form IB-10
Rev. 1-60
Louisiana 19

Budget Bureau No. 44-R1004.1

INTERSTATE CLAIM SUPPLEMENT

COMPLETE BOTH COPIES AND RETURN THEM ON YOUR NEXT VISIT
(USE BACK OF SHEET IF YOU NEED MORE SPACE FOR ANY ANSWER)

433 54 3937 (S. S. A. No.)

Name: LEE HARVEY OSWALD Liable State TEXAS.

1. Why did you come to this area? I was born and raised here in N.O.
2. When did you get here? April 12 3. How long do you expect to stay here? PERMANENTLY.
4. What kind of work are you seeking? PHOTOGRAPHIC At what wage? $ 1.35 HR.
5. What kind of work do you usually do? PHOTOGRAPHER
6. List any other kinds of work you can do. SHIPPING CLERK
7. Do you expect to return to your last job? ☐ Yes ☑ No
   If "Yes", when? ____ If not, why not? ____
8. Do you have a definite prospect for work with any other employer? ☐ Yes ☑ No
   If "Yes", date: ____ Employer's Name ____
9. Have you ever been employed in this area? ☐ Yes ☑ No
10. Are you working for anyone at the present time? ☐ Yes ☑ No
11. Are you self-employed or in business of any kind? ☐ Yes ☑ No
12. Are you or any member of your household engaged in, or planning, a farming activity? ☐ Yes ☑ No
13. Is there any reason why you cannot accept a permanent full-time job at once, here or elsewhere (such as physical, health, home responsibilities, care of children, aged persons, or sickness in your family, receipt of a pension or social security)? ☐ Yes ☑ No
14. Do you expect to obtain work through a union? ☐ Yes ☑ No
    If "Yes", in what union, local and city, are you in good standing? ____
15. Do you attend, or plan to attend school? ☐ Yes ☑ No
16. Do you receive or have you applied for a pension or Social Security? ☐ Yes ☑ No
    If "Yes", from what source ____
17. What means of transportation do you have to get to work? PUBLIC TRANSPORTATION
18. To be answered by women only:
    (a) Are you pregnant? ☐ Yes ☐ No
    (b) If you have minor children, give their ages: ____

I certify that the above answers are true and correct to the best of my knowledge.

Date: april 26, 1963. Lee H Oswald (Claimant's Signature)

Form IB-10
Rev. 7-62
Louisiana

INTERSTATE CLAIM SUPPLEMENT

Budget Bureau No. 44-R-1064

Liable St TEXAS

Name (Print) LEE H. OSWALD Age 23 Soc. Sec. Account No. 433-54-3937

1. Do you have definite prospects of work with: • If 'Yes' give date you will start to work and employer's name
   a. Your Last Employer? ☐ •Yes ☑ No
   b. With another employer? ☐ •Yes ☑ No
2. Do you expect to get work through a Union? ☐ •Yes ☑ No — If 'Yes', give Local Union number, name of Union and city.
   a. If 'Yes', are you registered with the Local of your Union here? ☐ Yes ☑ No
3. Name the occupations in which you have had experience. (List the kind of work you usually do first)
   PHOTOGRAPHER, CLERK SHIPPING
   a. What kind of work do you plan to look for? PHOTO
   b. What is the lowest rate of pay you will accept now? $1.40 c. What was your wage on your last job? $1.45
4. a. How far do you live from where you might find work? 2 MILES b. How will you travel to and from work? PUBLIC TRANS.
5. Do you usually live here? ☑ Yes ☐ •No • If 'No', a. When did you get here?
   b. How long will you stay?
   c. Why did you decide to come here?
6. Have you ever been employed in this area? ☑ •Yes ☐ No • If 'Yes', give date you last worked here and employer's name.
   JULY 19th '63, WM B. REILY CO. NEW ORLEANS
7. Do you
   a. Work for anyone now? ☐ •Yes ☑ No • If 'Yes', explain your activity, what hours of the day and how many hours a day you spend at it. (If you plan to attend school, give name of school and expected starting date).
   b. Farm, live on a farm, work on a farm, or own, rent or control any farm land or livestock? ☐ •Yes ☑ No
   c. Spend any time as self-employed or in business of any kind? ☐ •Yes ☑ No
   d. Attend school or plan to attend school? ☐ •Yes ☑ No
8. Can you accept a permanent full-time job at once? ☑ Yes ☐ •No • If 'No', state the reason you cannot accept work now.
9. Are you claiming, receiving, or have you applied for: • If 'Yes', describe: showing date of application, amounts, source and other details.
   a. Sick or disability benefits? ☐ •Yes ☑ No
   b. Workmen's Compensation ☐ •Yes ☑ No
   c. A pension? ☐ •Yes ☑ No
   d. Social Security ☐ •Yes ☑ No
10. TO BE ANSWERED BY WOMEN ONLY
   a. Are you pregnant? ☐ •Yes ☐ No • If 'Yes', expected date of birth
   b. Do you have minor children? ☐ •Yes ☐ No • If 'Yes', give their ages ______ Who will care for them if you find work?

I certify that the foregoing answers are true and correct to the best of my knowledge.

Date 7-29-63 Write Your Name Here X Lee H. Oswald

CLAIMANT—DO NOT WRITE BELOW THIS LINE

DIVISION OF EMPLOYMENT SECURITY
630 CAMP STREET
NEW ORLEANS 12, LOUISIANA

A Reason or IB-9 Code C-2

641

COMMISSION EXHIBIT No. 2189—Continued

CLAIMANT—DO NOT WRITE ON THIS SIDE

11. FACT FINDING REPORT (Use in lieu of IB-11 when entries on the other side raise a potential issue).

I certify that the above is true and correct to the best of my knowledge.

Claimant's Signature

12. EXAMINER'S STATEMENT (Describe local labor market conditions relating to the claimant's occupation and wage demand. Comment on all entries on the other side of this form which affect claimant's reemployment or require clarification. Also evaluate statement in item 11, if any.)

Claimant has not had steady employment over past 2 years. His requests are reasonable

B Hunley
Local Office Representative

641

COMMISSION EXHIBIT No. 2189—Continued

Form IB-14
Rev. 1-61
LOUISIANA—19

INTERSTATE REQUEST FOR RECONSIDERATION OF MONETARY DETERMINATION

Budget Bureau No. 44-R1004.1

1. NAME (Print) LEE (First) H. (Middle) OSWALD (Last)
3. SSA No. 433 54 3937

2. LOCAL MAILING ADDRESS 757 French St. (No.) (St. or Rural Route)
New Orleans (City) (Zone No.) La (State)

☑ UI ☐ UCFE ☐ UCX

4. Liable State Texas

5. Monetary determination date 4-16-63

6. I request reconsideration for the following reasons:

☐ Employment in my base period as noted below was omitted or incorrectly stated on my determination:

a. Employer Name Jaggars-Chiles-Stovall Inc. Nature of business Printing Co.
Address where work performed 522 Browder St. No. of employees 0200
Address where records kept Dallas, Texas
I worked from Oct 12-62 through April 6-63 in 19 weeks for $ 1697.⁸⁰
Qtr. Wages: 19 62 1st. Q $ 727.⁸⁰, 19 63 2nd Q $ 970.⁰⁰, 19__ 3rd Q $ —, 19__ 4th Q $ —

b. Employer Name ______ Nature of business ______
Address where work performed ______ No. of employees ______
Address where records kept ______
I worked from ______ through ______ in ______ weeks for $ ______
Qtr. Wages: 19__ 1st. Q $______, 19__ 2nd Q $______, 19__ 3rd Q $______, 19__ 4th Q $______

c. Enter below any other information which may apply (a) other names under which worked; (b) other social security account numbers used; (c) badge or clock number; (d) the employer's plant number; (e) name of the department; (f) occupation.
(B) claimant's employer reported under wrong SS# which is 433-54-3739

☐ WBA and MBA incorrect because ______

☐ Other ______

7. The above facts are true to the best of my knowledge and belief ______ (Claimant's Signature)

8. Documents Attached ☑ Yes ☐ No Title and Date of Documents attached W-2 form

9. Request filed If in person, enter date filed 4-29-63
If by mail, enter postmark date ______ and receipt date ______

10. Use L.O. stamp or enter L.O. address and No.
DIVISION OF EMPLOYMENT SECURITY
630 CAMP STREET
NEW ORLEANS 12, LOUISIANA

Itinerant Point Location ______

11. I certify that I have verified the claimant's social security number.
[signature] (Claims Examiner's Signature)

Distribution: Original and one to liable interstate unit; copy to claimant; copy for agent state local office.

641

A C 5

Local Office Representative: Add comments, circle A or C, if C add number showing interview interval, and state reasons for code assignment; include statement reclaimant's prospects for employment in the light of local labor market condition; date and sign.

Unfavorable because of short work history. We have nothing to offer

5-6-63 (Date) C Brown (Local Office Representative)

amp or write in local office address. If ierant point, show address.

-10, p. 2

641

FORM W-4 (Rev. July 1961)
U. S. Treasury Department
Internal Revenue Service

EMPLOYEE'S WITHHOLDING EXEMPTION CERTIFICATE

Print full name LEE HARVEY OSWALD Social Security Account Number 433-54-3937

Print home address 2515 WEST 5th ST City IRVING Zone ...... State TEXAS

EMPLOYEE:
File this form with your employer. Otherwise, he must withhold U. S. income tax from your wages without exemption.

EMPLOYER:
Keep this certificate with your records. If the employee is believed to have claimed too many exemptions, the District Director should be so advised.

HOW TO CLAIM YOUR WITHHOLDING EXEMPTIONS

1. If SINGLE, and you claim an exemption, write the figure "1" ....
2. If MARRIED, one exemption each is allowable for husband and wife if not claimed on another certificate.
   (a) If you claim both of these exemptions, write the figure "2"
   (b) If you claim one of these exemptions, write the figure "1"
   (c) If you claim neither of these exemptions, write "0" 2
3. Exemptions for age and blindness (applicable only to you and your wife but not to dependents):
   (a) If you or your wife will be 65 years of age or older at the end of the year, and you claim this exemption, write "1"; if both will be 65 or older, and you claim both of these exemptions, write "2" ....
   (b) If you or your wife are blind, and you claim this exemption, write the figure "1"; if both are blind, and you claim both of these exemptions, write the figure "2" ....
4. If you claim exemptions for one or more dependents, write the number of such exemptions. (Do not claim exemption for a dependent unless you are qualified under instruction 4 on other side.) 2
5. Add the number of exemptions which you have claimed above and write the total 4
6. Additional withholding per pay period under agreement with employer. *See* Instruction 1 .... $........ V

I CERTIFY that the number of withholding exemptions claimed on this certificate does not exceed the number to which I am entitled.

(Date) Oct 16, 1963 o43—16—73008—2 (Signed) Lee H. Oswald

COMMISSION EXHIBIT No. 2189—Continued

Form B-11 (1-62)

TEXAS EMPLOYMENT COMMISSION — AUSTIN
BENEFIT CLAIM DETERMINATION
(SUFFICIENT WAGES)

The wages listed below were reported for you by covered employers as wages received by you during your "Base Period" from 1-01-42 to 12-31-62. They are sufficient, provided you are eligible and not disqualified, to authorize weekly benefit payments of $ during your "Benefit Year", which is the one-year period ending . The total maximum you can be paid during the benefit year is $ 369.00 SEE REVERSE SIDE FOR APPEAL RIGHTS AND EXPLANATION OF THIS DETERMINATION.

CLAIMANT'S NAME AND ADDRESS	Social Security Account Number	CLAIM DATE	CONTROL DATE	Local Office	DATE MAILED
L H OSWALD 757 FRANCE STREET NEW ORLEANS LOUISIANA	3 433-54-3937	04-29-63	00-07-63	9019	5-04-63

EMPLOYER NO.	EMPLOYER'S NAME	QTR.-YR.	PAGE	REPORTED WAGES
194,107	LOUV-R-PAK DIV	3-62	002	$ 540.34
194,107	LOUV-R-PAK DIV	4-62	002	96.15
005,914	JAGGARS AND CHILES	4-62	004	727.81
			641	
			727 81	1,364.31

RIGHT TO REDETERMINATION

You may request an administrative redetermination of your claim (or file an appeal) within twelve (12) days from the date this determination is mailed, if you think it is incorrect. The "Date Mailed" is shown on the reverse side. You may request such a redetermination by completing a written redetermination request at your local Commission Office, or by writing to the Insurance Department, Texas Employment Commission, Austin 1, Texas. If you request a redetermination, you should continue to file claims if you are still unemployed. Ask your local Commission Office about your appeal rights.

WHENEVER YOU WRITE TO THE COMMISSION, BE SURE TO GIVE YOUR SOCIAL SECURITY ACCOUNT NUMBER.

EXPLANATION OF DETERMINATION: As shown on the reverse side of this form, a weekly benefit payment amount and a maximum total amount, based upon the wages listed, have been computed for you. These weekly payments may be made only, if you are unemployed, file a claim, are eligible, and are not disqualified with respect to any particular benefit period of 7 days. If you are found to be ineligible or disqualified at the present time, you will be notified of such fact and its effect upon your benefit rights.

PENALTIES: The Texas Unemployment Compensation Act provides fine and imprisonment for knowingly making a false statement or representation or failing to disclose a material fact either (1) to obtain or increase benefits, or (2) to prevent or reduce the payment of benefits.

TERMS: "Benefit Year" is the one-year period beginning with the date of an individual's valid initial claim.
"Base Period" is the first four out of the last five completed calendar quarters immediately preceding the date of an individual's initial claim.

DETERMINE YOUR BASE PERIOD IN THIS MANNER:

If you claim insurance between:	Your base period is the preceding:
January 1 and March 31	October 1 through September 30
April 1 and June 30	January 1 through December 31
July 1 and September 30	April 1 through March 31
October 1 and December 31	July 1 through June 30

COMMISSION EXHIBIT No. 2189—Continued

E
842.9
.A54
v.24

ARNULFO L. OLIVEIRA
MEMORIAL LIBRARY
1825 May St. Ft. Brown
Brownsville, Texas 78520